ARCHITECTURAL GEOMETRY

First Edition

Authors
Helmut Pottman
Andreas Asperl
Michael Hofer
Axel Kilian

Editor
Daril Bentley

Formatters
Elisabeth Kasiz-Hitz and Eva Reimer

Bentley Institute Press
Exton, Pennsylvania USA

Architectural Geometry

First Edition

ISBN Number: 978-1-934493-04-5

Library of Congress Control Number: 2007935192

Published by:

Bentley Institute Press
Bentley Systems, Incorporated
685 Stockton Drive
Exton, PA 19341
www.bentley.com

Bentley Institute Press

www.bentley.com/books

Printed in the U.S.A.

Preface

Geometry lies at the core of the architectural design process. It is omnipresent, from initial form-finding stages to actual construction. It also underlies the main communication medium; namely, graphical representations obtained by precise geometric rules. Whereas the variety of shapes that could be treated by traditional geometric methods has been rather limited, modern computing technologies have led to a real geometry revolution.

These days we are facing dramatic changes, the tools at our disposal becoming seemingly unlimited. However, the increase in possibilities did not go along with an increase in the depth of geometry education. In fact, the opposite is true. Thus, it is the most important task of this book to close the gap between the technical possibilities and an effective working knowledge of the new methods of geometric design.

Modern architecture takes advantage of the greatly increasing design possibilities, yet architects are not just a new group of CAD users. Scale and construction technologies pose new challenges to engineering and design. We are convinced that such challenges can be met more effectively with a solid understanding of geometry.

Geometric computing is a broad area with many branches. An interdisciplinary field such as architecture benefits from such variety. We have tried to provide views into this larger scientific context. In fact, we believe that a new research area—which might be termed *architectural geometry*—is currently evolving and we hope that our book will help to promote its future development.

To advance this emerging field, a close cooperation between geometers and architects is of highest importance. This book may be seen as an example. The stimulating cooperation of three geometers and an architect (Axel Kilian) developed the book's geometric content, the discussion of its marriage with modern architecture, and the presentation of both. Moreover, it led to the identification of challenging research problems—some of which are described in the later chapters of the book.

Intended Use

Our book has been written as a textbook for students of architecture or industrial design. It comprises material for a basic course in geometry at the undergraduate level. Roughly starting with parts of Chapter 11, there is plenty of material for a more advanced geometry course at the undergraduate or graduate level. This finally leads us to the cutting edge of research in architectural geometry, which starts to appear in

Chapter 15 and leads to a presentation of our own most recent research on discrete freeform structures in the final chapter.

Traditionally, the constructive geometry curriculum has been largely based on descriptive geometry. Computers are now changing geometry education in many ways. This book may also provide a path to constructive geometry education in the digital era beyond the specific application toward architecture.

This book is also intended as a geometry consultant for architects, construction engineers, and industrial designers. Hopefully, scientists interested in geometry processing with applications in architecture and art may benefit from it and derive some inspiration. There is a lot of room for exciting research in architectural geometry. We hope that this book stimulates research in this challenging and largely unexplored direction.

Prerequisites

Our target audience is generally not well trained mathematically, and we therefore only assume some basic high school knowledge of mathematics and geometry. In later chapters, knowledge of basic linear algebra and calculus is of great advantage, but not absolutely necessary. We have collected some high school geometry in Appendix A: Geometry Primer, but are aware of the fact that it is both incomplete and a very subjective collection of some essential background material.

Throughout the text, some math is collected whose reading is recommended but may not be necessary to further proceed with the study of the book. Sections marked by an asterix * are more advanced and may be skipped in a first reading.

Features

This book is intended to fill a gap in the geometry literature. Geometry books written for architecture mainly discuss elementary material or classical descriptive geometry. We explain concepts of descriptive geometry only very briefly. Instead, we focus on efficient CAD construction methods and use CAD to support geometry teaching and understanding.

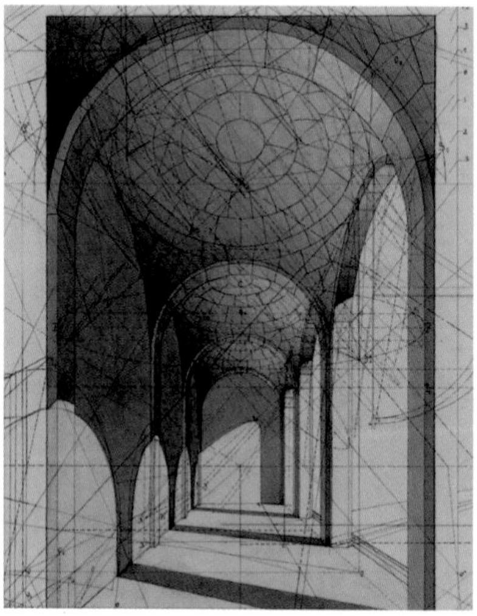

Most books about the geometric aspects of CAD require a reasonably high level of math knowledge, which most students of architecture will not have. Therefore, we have tried to explain new geometries available in CAD systems (such as freeform curves and surfaces) without much math. We explain the material via geometric considerations and support those with numerous figures.

Wherever possible, we replace the use of calculus with *discrete models* and then obtain properties of smooth analogues by a limiting process. For example, when studying curves we first investigate the geometry of polygons. The transition to curves is performed by a refinement process that generates in the limit a smooth curve. This is not a new approach, but it receives increasing interest due to the fact that many computations are actually based on discrete representations.

Fortunately, the math used in the limiting process can be omitted without a significant loss of insight. As pointed out by the modern field of *discrete differential geometry*, this approach can actually be beneficial in showing which elementary geometric facts serve as kernels of certain geometric results about curves or surfaces. Calculus may hide such an insight.

There are many threads from basics to research. An example is depicted in the following figure: polyhedra and polyhedral surfaces (Chapter 3) → subdivision curves (Chapter 8) → subdivision surfaces and meshes (Chapter 11) → planar quad strips as models of developable surfaces (Chapter 15) → discrete freeform structures (Chapter 19).

Discrete concepts appear frequently in this book because they are easier to grasp than methods from mathematical analysis. They are even more powerful than mathematical methods, especially in view of applications in architecture. This illustration shows an example of a thread of discrete ideas from basics to research.

Chapter 3

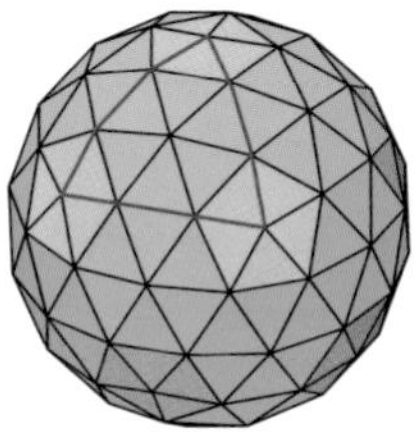

Chapter 8

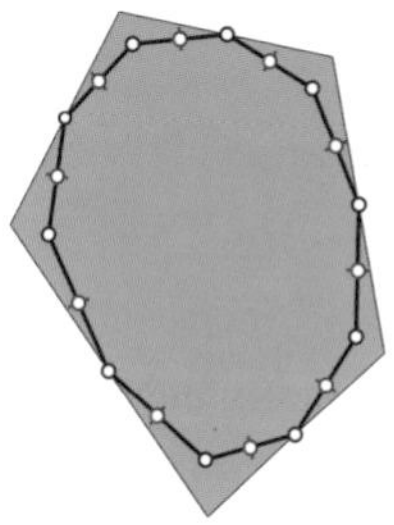

Chapter 11

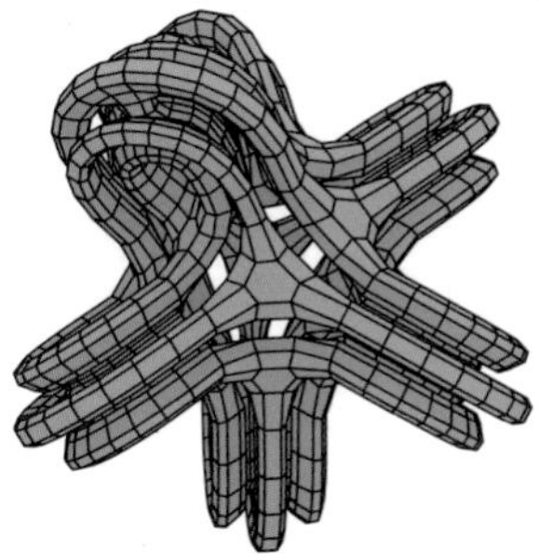

Chapter 15

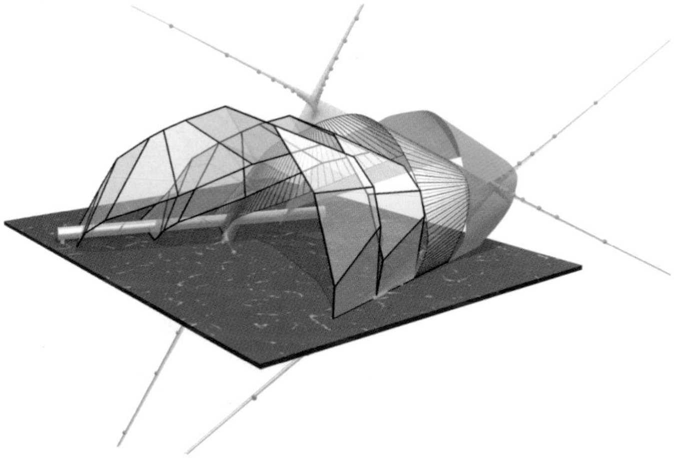

Chapter 19

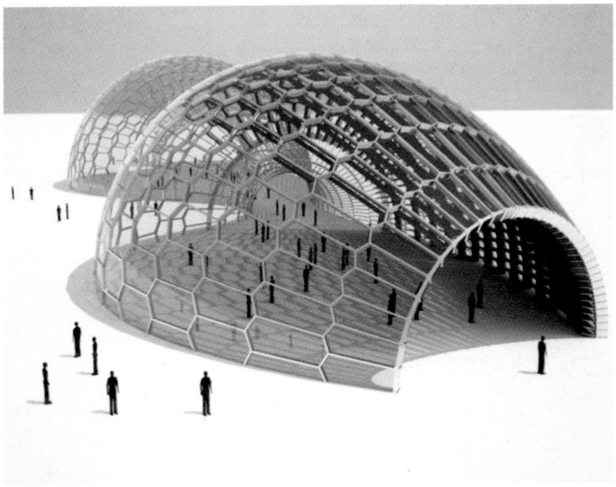

Of course, our presentation of geometry is accompanied by examples of built architecture, architectural projects, and artwork. However, the selections are for purposes of example, are very subjective, and are not the main intent of the book. We even included some interesting and hopefully inspiring geometric insights that may not yet have been used in architecture but may carry some potential of being useful in the future.

Teaching Support and Feedback

A web site located at *www.architecturalgeometry.at* will serve as a discussion forum for anyone interested in architectural geometry. Your feedback will help us tailor our work even more toward the actual needs in geometry teaching and architectural design. The web page currently contains some teaching material, exercises and solutions to lab sessions, and results of student projects.We hope that this material will see a significant growth in the near future.

Acknowledgments

This book is the result of a large effort by many people to whom we would like to express our deepest gratitude. Scott Lofgren and Jeff Kelly of Bentley have supported us in the best possible way during the entire process, and our lecturer Daril Bentley did a great job in smoothing our texts.

We are very grateful for Bentley's financial support, which has been used as an additional motivation for the students involved in the design of figures. In fact, the work on the figures has been the most time-consuming part of the entire project.

The research performed in connection with the book has been supported by grants S9201 and P19214-N18 from the Austrian Science Fund FWF. We would like to thank the members of the research group Geometric Modeling and Industrial Geometry at the Vienna University of Technology, who have helped in proofreading: Simon Flöry, Martin Peternell, Niloy Mitra, and Peter Paukowitsch.

Special thanks go to the many people who helped us with the figures: Miriam Zotter, Christian Leeb, Markus Forstner, Heinz Schmiedhofer, Benjamin Schneider, Boris Odehnal, Philip Grohs, and Michael Wischounig. Martin Reis did a great job of finalizing the figures, achieving color harmony and helping in the layout process. We enjoyed working with our graphical designers Elisabeth Kaziz-Hitz and Eva Riemer and admire the result of their work.

Many friends from the scientific community have provided results of their work to illustrate the state of the art in geometric computing and we want to thank them for their help. We are very grateful to Georg Franck for his continuing support of geometry in the architectural curriculum at the Vienna University of Technology and Johannes Wallner, whose deep geometric insight and unbelievable working speed provided great help in the critical final phase of this project.

Last but not least, our sincerest thanks belong to our families—who supported us with their love and understanding throughout the entire book project. Our families know best how much time it took us to write and illustrate this book on architectural geometry.

Content

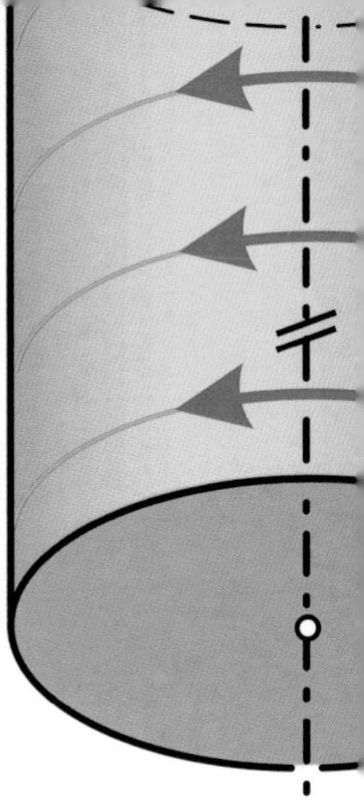

Chapter 1
Creating a Digital 3D Model

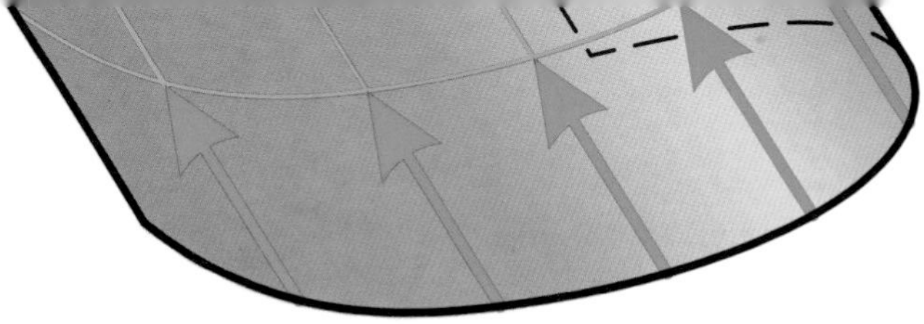

Modeling the Winton Guest House

We have all seen digital architectural models of great complexity in various forms of visualization. But how do we get started? How do we communicate our ideas with the help of a computer? What are the geometric fundamentals that enable us to create digital three-dimensional (3D) models? Many tools and procedures are provided to us by modern computer-aided design (CAD) systems for creating such models. To efficiently employ the existing software—and to go beyond—a good knowledge of geometry is essential.

It goes without saying that the architect's design work starts before geometric modeling. According to Frank O. Gehry, his inspiration for the Winton guest house in Wayzata, Minnesota, came from the still-life paintings by Giorgio Morandi. When asked to build a guest house for a client in the 1980s, he set a counterpoint to the main house—designed by Philip Johnson in 1952.

Gehry conceived the guest house as a large outdoor sculpture in which each room would constitute its own mini-building (Figure 1.1). Based on sketches, scaled physical 3D models and plan drawings were created manually. In this chapter we learn how to create a digital 3D model of this structure.

Fig. 1.1
The Winton guest house by Frank O. Gehry. Sketches (top), scaled physical models (bottom left), photo of the building (bottom right).

Cartesian coordinates. Geometric objects can be described as a collection of points that delineate the shape of the object. To describe the position of a point p in 3D space, we use an ordered triplet of numbers called *coordinates.* These coordinates are measured with respect to a chosen *coordinate system*. A *Cartesian coordinate system* (Figure 1.2) is given by three mutually perpendicular oriented axes called the x-, y-, and z-axis.

The three axes are labeled x, y, and z and pass through a common point o called the *origin*. On each coordinate axis we use the same unit length. With respect to a chosen system, a point p in 3D space has the three Cartesian coordinates (x_p,y_p,z_p). They are called the *x-coordinate* x_p, *y-coordinate* y_p, and *z-coordinate* z_p. The positive coordinates always lie on the ray starting at the origin and pointing in axis direction.

To get from the origin o with coordinates (0,0,0) to a point p with coordinates (x_p,y_p,z_p) there are six different *coordinate paths*—all of which lie on a *coordinate cuboid* of length x_p, width y_p, and height z_p. The eight vertices of the coordinate cuboid have respectively the coordinates (0,0,0), $(x_p,0,0)$, $(0,y_p,0)$, $(0,0,z_p)$, $(x_p,y_p,0)$, $(x_p,0,z_p)$, $(0,y_p,z_p)$,and (x_p,y_p,z_p). Each pair of coordinate axes spans a plane called a *coordinate plane*. We have the *xy-plane*, the *yz-plane*, and the *zx-plane*. Note that in each coordinate plane we have a 2D Cartesian coordinate system given by the two coordinate axes that span the respective plane.

Right- and left-handed coordinate system. Let us use a Cartesian coordinate system (Figure 1.3). When we look along negative z-direction into the xy-plane, a counter-clockwise turn of 90 degrees aligns the x-axis with the y-axis. Such a *right-handed* Cartesian coordinate system can easily be visualized with the first three fingers of the right hand.

Starting with the right hand as a fist, we open the thumb in the direction of the x-axis and the forefinger in direction of the y-axis. Then we can open the middle finger such that it points in the direction of the z-axis of a right-handed Cartesian coordinate

Fig. 1.2
A Cartesian coordinate system with the three coordinates (x_p,y_p,z_p) of a point p in 3D space. A coordinate path that connects the origin o to the point p lies on a coordinate cuboid with length x_p, width y_p, and height z_p.

Fig. 1.3
Right-handed Cartesian coordinate system.

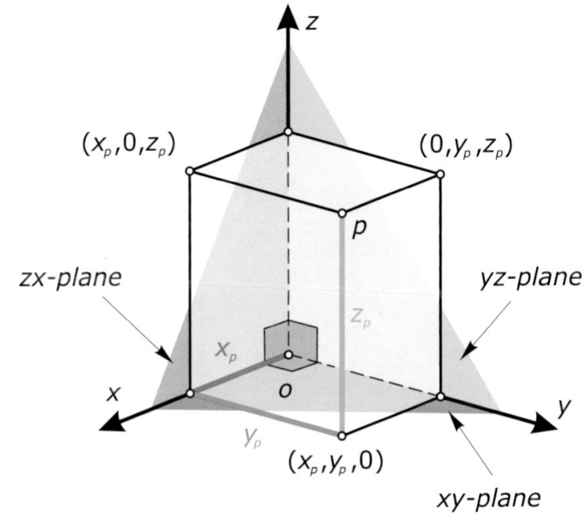

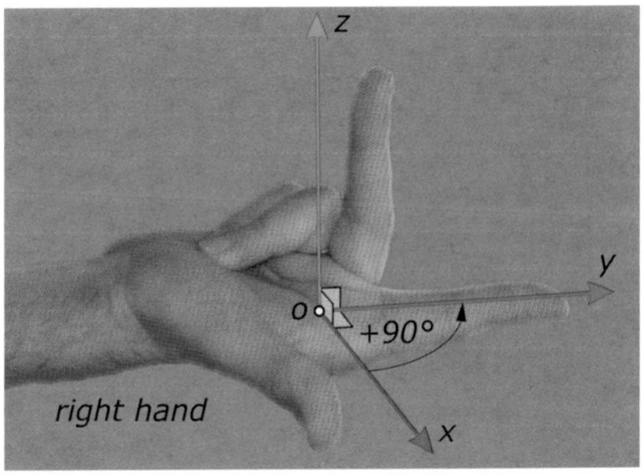

system. If we change the direction of the z-axis, we get a *left-handed* Cartesian coordinate system that can be modeled using the thumb, forefinger and middle finger of the left hand. Thus there are two possible orientations of a 3D Cartesian coordinate system.

Throughout this book we will use a right-handed coordinate system because this is common practice in geometry. For data exchange between different CAD systems, it is important that the handedness of the coordinate system be the same. Otherwise, all objects will be mirrored about the xy-plane.

Cuboids. A *cuboid* generalizes the shape of a *cube*. Whereas a cube has six congruent square faces, a cuboid consists of three pairs of congruent rectangles that are mutually orthogonal to one another. The geometric entities of a cuboid are its 8 vertices, 12 edges, and 6 planar faces. Let us create the fireplace alcove of the Winton guest house. The alcove consists of two cuboids.

For modeling purposes, we choose the xy-plane as a horizontal plane—with the z-axis pointing upward. We place the first cuboid such that one of its corners is aligned with the coordinate planes. This corner coincides with the origin of the Cartesian coordinate system (Figure 1.4, left). We pick the origin as one corner and define the length and width of the base rectangle in the direction of the x- and y-axes. Finally, we input the height h_1 of the first cuboid. To obtain a cube, we would choose length equal to width equal to height.

One CAD design principle is that digitally we always work at full scale. Thus, we use the actual measurements of the cuboid. The second cuboid we will construct is the chimney, which we will place on top of the first cuboid. We draw the square base onto the top face of the first cuboid by entering the coordinates of three of its vertices: p_2, p_3, and p_4 (Figure 1.4, right). Then we define the height h_2 of the chimney and we obtain the second cuboid.

Fig. 1.4
Modeling two cuboids that appear in the fireplace alcove of the Winton guest house.
(left) The bottom part is almost a cube, (right) and the chimney is a cuboid with a square base. The square is defined by three vertices p_2, p_3, and p_4.

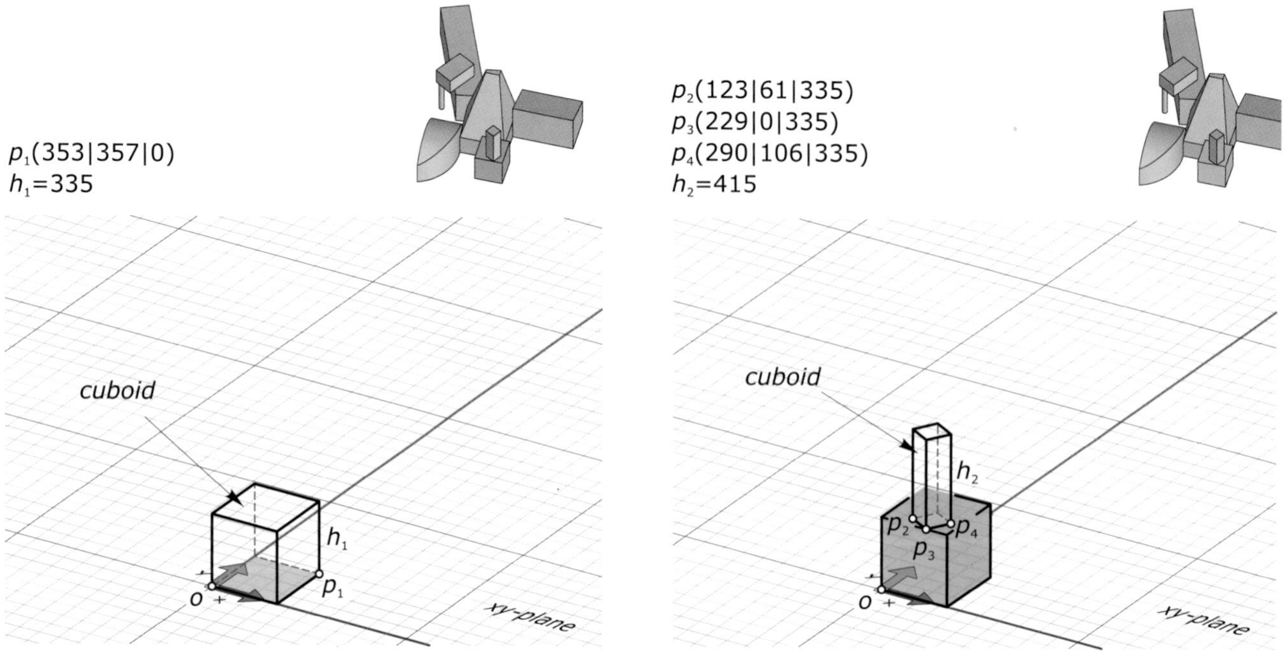

Surface and solid models. A geometric model with the same boundary surface can be either a surface (skin-like) model or a solid (volumetric) model, as shown in Figure 1.5 for a cuboid. To understand the difference between a surface and a solid model, we draw a comparison to the arts and to fashion design. In the arts, a sculptor starts with a block of stone or wood (a solid model) and removes material to obtain the desired sculpture. On the contrary, a fashion designer uses pieces of fabric (a surface model) to form a garment.

We are currently working on an abstract geometric level, creating only the base shapes while neglecting wall and slab thicknesses and openings such as windows and doors. In Chapter 4, we will encounter a first set of tools that allows us to further modify our geometric models. For the moment, we will continue to work solely with the basic geometric shapes associated for the most part with solid models.

Extrusion. The bottom part of the living room of the Winton guest house is not a cuboid. However, it still has vertical walls—even though the base is no longer a rectangle. With the Parallel Extrusion tool we create a *prism* by extruding a polygon to a desired height (see Chapter 3). Whereas a polygon is a closed object, a *polyline* is "open" in the sense that two endpoints are connected by a sequence of straight line segments. Parallel extrusion of a polyline P derives a *prism surface* (Figure 1.6, left).

Fig. 1.5
Surface and solid models illustrated by means of a cuboid with a part cut away.

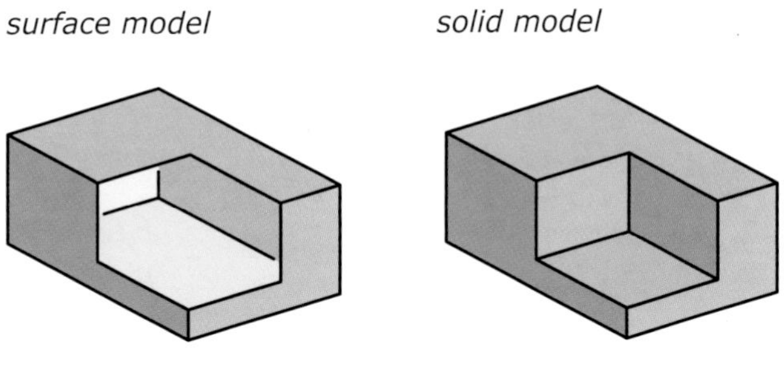

Fig. 1.6
(left) Parallel extrusion of a polygon generates a prism.
(right) Central extrusion of a polygon generates a pyramid.

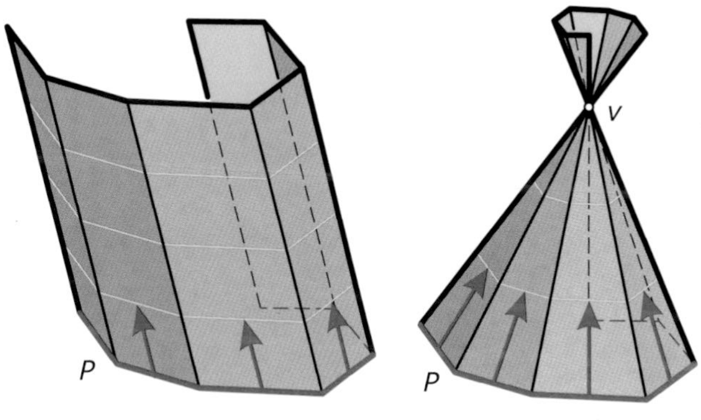

A related tool is Central Extrusion. Thereby, the polygon P is extruded toward a single point v in space and we generate a *pyramid* (see Chapter 3). If we use a polyline, we generate a *pyramid surface* (Figure 1.6, right). To create the bottom part of the living room of the Winton guest house as a prism, we draw the base quadrangle in the xy-plane via the four vertices p_5, p_6, p_7, and p_8 and then extrude it to the desired height h_3 in the z-direction (Figure 1.7).

Global and local coordinate systems. So far we have worked in a *global* (*world, absolute*) coordinate system. This global system is usually a right-handed Cartesian coordinate system. For geometric design, it is often desirable to employ *local* (*user-defined, auxiliary, relative*) coordinate systems to simplify modeling tasks. If we enter local coordinates in a CAD system, they are automatically transformed into global coordinates.

Fig. 1.7
The bottom part of the living room in the Winton guest house is a prism generated with the parallel extrusion tool.

Fig. 1.8a
The four planar quadrangles of the living room roof are constructed using local coordinate systems (visually represented as "lcs"). We show the construction for one of the four roof planes.

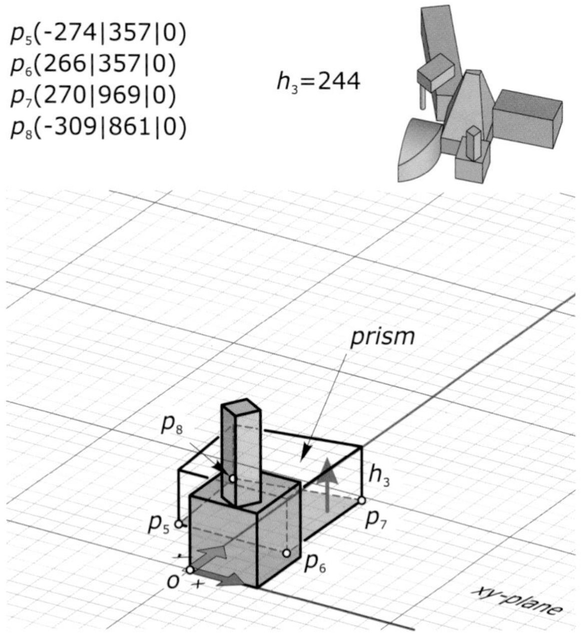

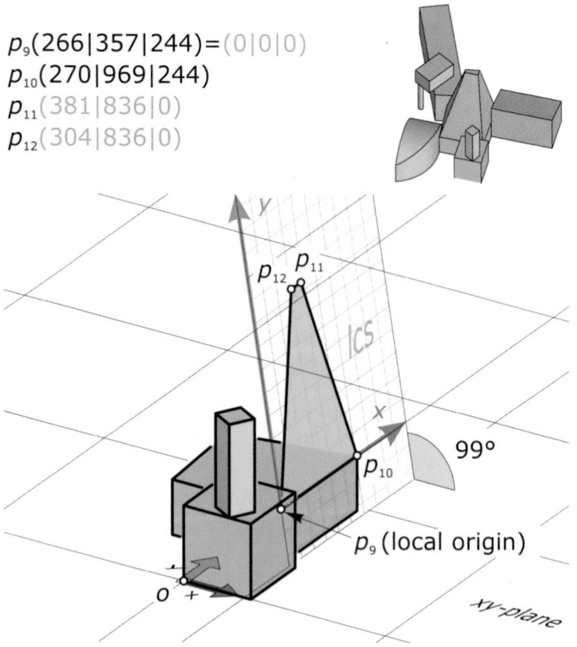

The top part of the living room in the Winton guest house is not a truncated pyramid (discussed in Chapter 3). Thus, the Central Extrusion tool is inappropriate because we require a different modeling approach. Each of the four sides of the roof is a planar quadrangle that can be drawn using a local coordinate system (LCS; sometimes represented visually as *lcs*), as shown in Figure 1.8. Together, the four quadrangles form a surface model of the living room's roof.

The first bedroom of the Winton guest house has a prismatic shape that we generate by parallel extrusion. For this purpose we define a local Cartesian coordinate system using one wall of the living room as the local *xy*-plane (Figure 1.9). Then we draw the base polygon in that local *xy*-plane and extrude it in the local *z*-direction to generate the desired prism.

Fig. 1.8b
We show the construction for another one of the four roof planes. The other two are modeled analogously. Local coordinates are given in a different color and are always measured with respect to the shown local system.

Fig. 1.9
A local coordinate system with origin p_{17} (x-axis is parallel to p_6p_7, y-axis is vertical) is used to generate the first bedroom via parallel extrusion.

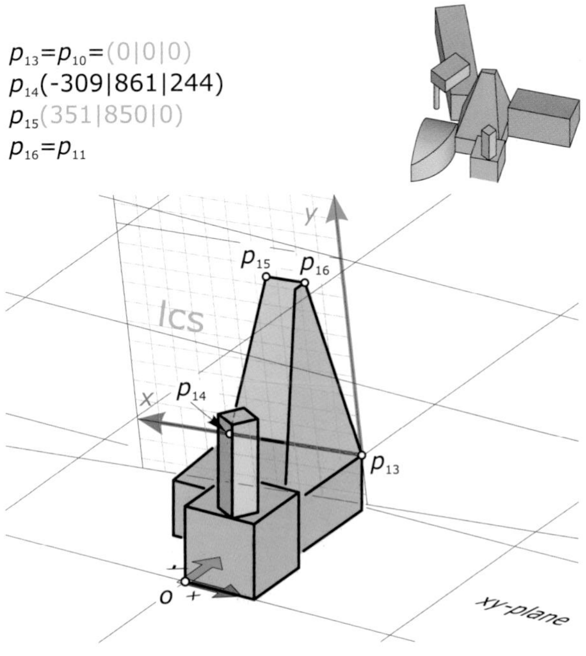

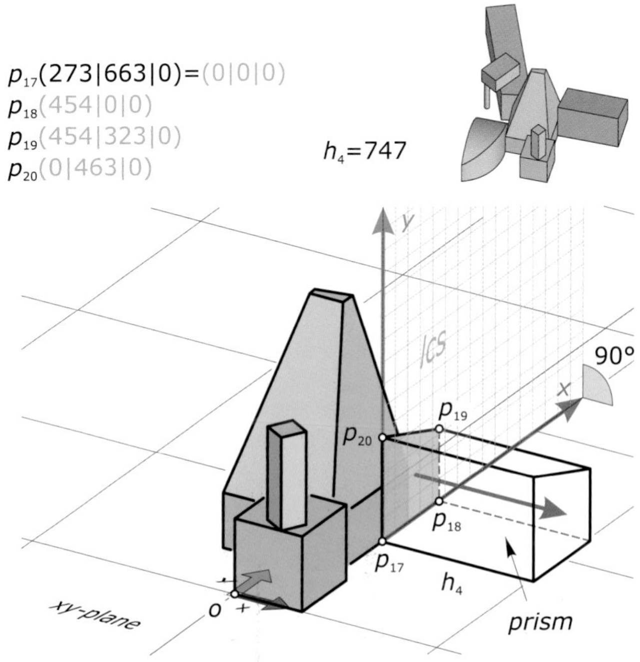

Polar coordinates. In addition to planar Cartesian coordinates, there is another useful way of defining planar coordinates. *Polar coordinates* (r,φ) of a point p measure the radial distance r of the point p to the origin o, and the angle $0 \leq \varphi < 360°$ to the *polar axis* (Figure 1.10, left). The polar axis is usually chosen as the positive ray of the x-axis. Whereas planar Cartesian coordinates measure the distance to two orthogonal axes, polar coordinates measure the radial distance r to the origin and the angle between the ray op and the polar axis.

Polar coordinates are very useful, especially for local operations when designing with a CAD system. The Cartesian coordinates of the points of a circle with the center at the origin and radius r are $(r \cdot \cos\varphi, r \cdot \sin\varphi)$. As shown in Figure 1.10 (right), we use this fact to convert from polar coordinates (r,φ) to Cartesian coordinates (x,y) by

$$x = r \cdot \cos\varphi,$$

$$y = r \cdot \sin\varphi.$$

The kitchen and the garage of the Winton guest house together form another prism. We know the degree of an angle formed between a wall of the living room and a wall of the kitchen. We also know the length of the building. Thus, the base polygon is best drawn using local polar coordinates (Figure 1.11). We employ this local polar coordinate system in the global xy-plane. The local polar axis points in the direction of one of the living room edges. By parallel extrusion of the base polygon in the global z-direction to the desired height, we obtain another prism.

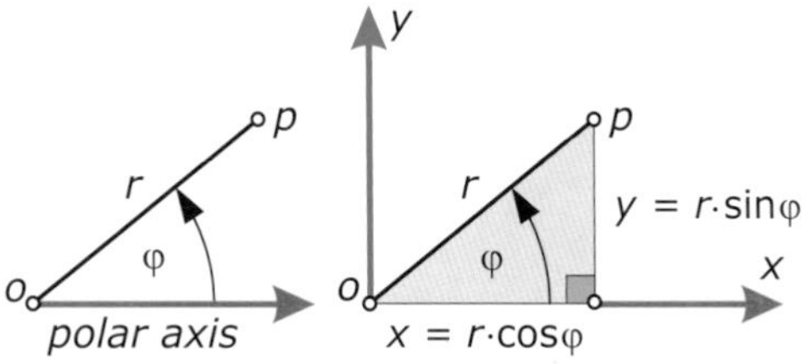

Fig. 1.10
Planar polar coordinates and their conversion to planar Cartesian coordinates.

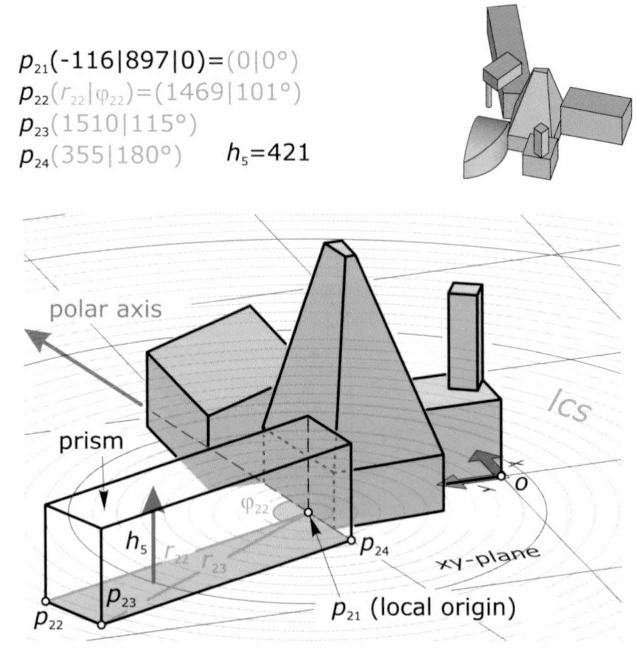

Fig. 1.11
The base polygon $P = (p_{21}, p_{22}, p_{23}, p_{34})$ of the kitchen and garage is drawn using local polar coordinates. Parallel extrusion of P in the z-direction to a height h_5 generates the prism.

Cylindrical coordinates. Related to planar polar coordinates are the spatial *cylindrical coordinates* (r, φ, z). They are simply polar coordinates in the xy-plane augmented with the z-coordinate (Figure 1.12). Thus, the difference between this system and a 3D Cartesian coordinate system is that we replace the Cartesian x- and y-coordinates with the polar r- and φ-coordinates. The conversion of cylindrical coordinates into Cartesian coordinates follows from the previously cited conversion of polar coordinates and is given by

$$x = r \cdot \cos\varphi,$$

$$y = r \cdot \sin\varphi,$$

$$z = z.$$

Using cylindrical coordinates, we can easily specify positions on rotational cylinders.

Rotational cylinder. A *rotational cylinder* is the set of all points in 3D space that are equidistant from a straight line (called its *axis*). A rotational cylinder can be generated by extruding a circle c that lies in a plane P (Figure 1.13, left). Thereby, the extrusion direction is orthogonal to P. All straight lines lying on a rotational cylinder are called *generators*. An alternative generation of a rotational cylinder is by rotating a straight line g around an axis A parallel to g (Figure 1.13, right).

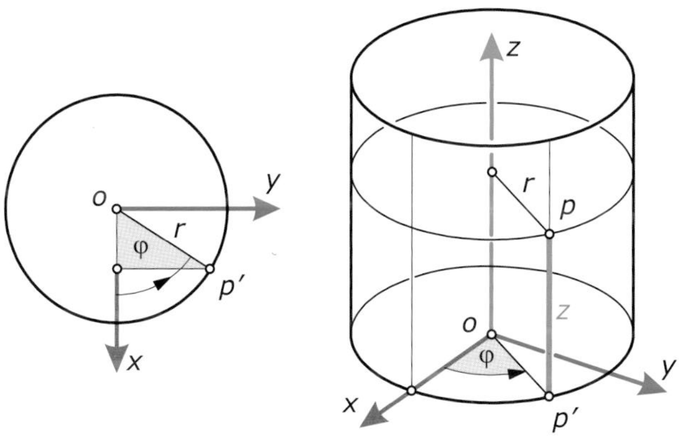

Fig. 1.12
Cylindrical coordinates (r, φ, z) are polar coordinates (r, φ) augmented with the Cartesian z-coordinate.

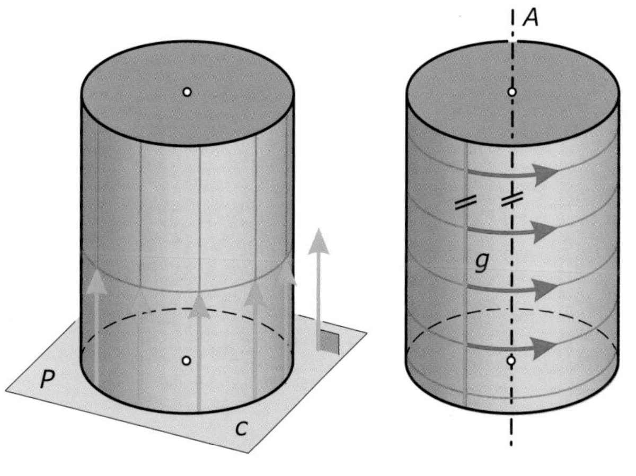

Fig. 1.13
(left) A rotational cylinder can be generated by extrusion of a circle c lying in a plane P.
(right) The extrusion direction is orthogonal to P. An alternative generation is performed by rotating a straight line g around an axis A parallel to g.

Rotational cylinders are fundamental shapes contained in CAD systems. They are usually defined by a base circle and a height. In the Winton guest house, a rotational cylinder appears as a column that supports the loft above the kitchen (Figure 1.14). We use the global Cartesian coordinates of the base circle's center p_{25} to correctly position the cylinder.

Snapping. *Snapping* is one of the convenient CAD modeling techniques. Whenever we work with a CAD system, it is not enough to roughly click with our input device (e.g., a mouse) on the point we intend. Instead, it is essential to tell the CAD system to *snap* to the specific point. This technique makes our constructions accurate. A variety of snap functions is usually provided. Available choices for points include snapping to endpoints, midpoints, intersection points, arbitrary curve points, and centers of various shapes.

Of course, there are also snap functions associated with other geometric entities such as lines, circles, and so forth. Let us use a snap function to position the loft (a cuboid) so that it rests on top of the kitchen and is supported by the cylindrical column (Figure 1.15). We will use a local coordinate system whose origin is at the center p_{26} of the top circle c of the rotational cylinder. We snap the center with the applicable tool and make it the origin of a local xy-plane that contains the circle c.

The angle between the directions of the global and local x-axis is indicated on the floor plan. Now we can draw the base polygon of the cuboid (Figure 1.15) and then enter its height. An advanced form of snapping is to store the association created by this modeling step. This preserves the relationships among the various parts if we later modify, for example, their size or position (see the section on feature-based modeling in Chapter 4).

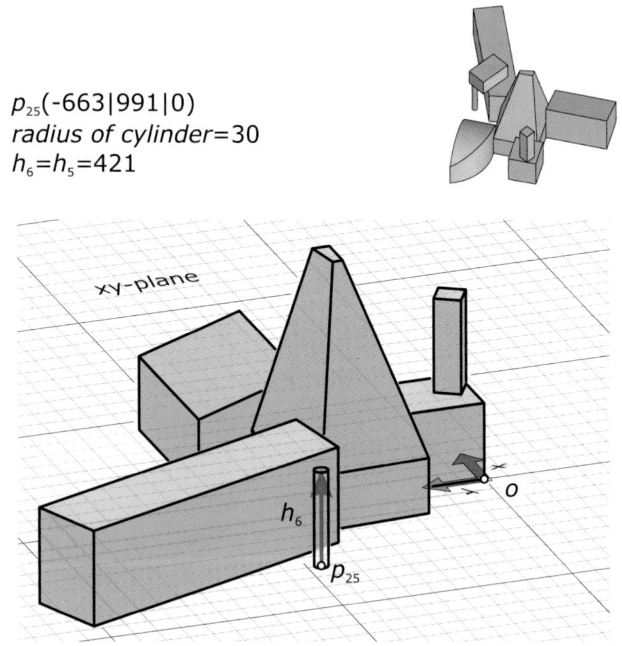

Fig. 1.14
A rotational cylinder is used as a column to support the loft above the kitchen.

Handles. Geometric objects in a CAD system usually have some associated *handles*. These allow easy and straightforward basic object manipulation. Using handles together with snapping, we can drag and drop geometry and perform some simple readjustments of the design. Handles are usually those special points that help define the shape under consideration.

Typical handles of a cuboid are its corners and the centroid. If we click on one of the corners, we can modify the size of the cuboid interactively. By clicking on the centroid, we can move the entire cuboid to a different position in space. Typical handles of a rotational cylinder are two points that define the axis and another point that defines the radius.

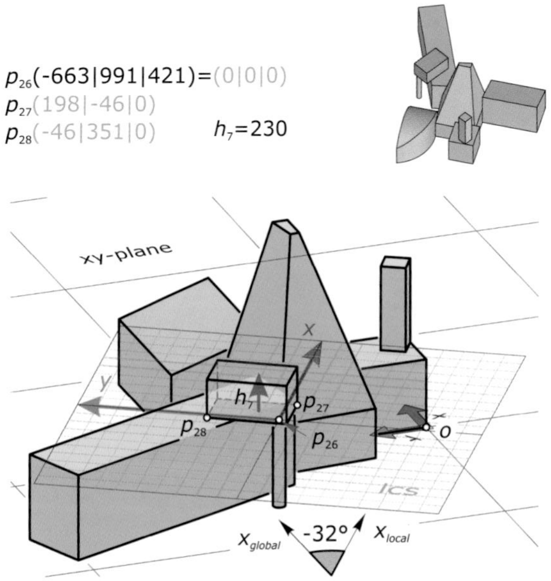

Fig. 1.15
We use the Snap to Center tool to position the origin p_{26} of a local coordinate system at the center of the top circle of the rotational cylinder. The angle between the global x-axis and the local x-axis is −32 degrees. With the help of this local system, we can generate the cuboid that represents the loft above the kitchen.

Modeling the second bedroom. Now we will model the curvilinear second bedroom of the Winton guest house (Figure 1.16). A geometric analysis reveals that two different rotational cylinders are involved. Part of the first cylinder is a vertical wall, and part of the second is the roof. We generate the second bedroom as the intersection of two solids. In the *xy*-plane, we draw the base shape of the first solid and extrude it to a certain height.

Then we use a vertical local coordinate system with the local *xy*-plane positioned in the back wall of the bedroom. The local origin is the point p_{29}. The local *x*-axis points in negative global *y*-direction and the local *y*-axis is parallel to the global *z*-axis. In the local *xy*-plane, we draw the base shape of the second solid—which we then extrude in the local *z*-direction.

The intersection of the solids (see Chapter 4, on Boolean operations) gives us the desired geometric model of the second bedroom. Thus, we created all of the basic shapes of the Winton guest house above ground.

Fig. 1.16
We generate the second bedroom using parallel extrusion twice and intersection of the resulting solids.
The base shape of the first solid has vertices p_{29}, p_{30}, p_{32}, *and* p_{33}. Thereby, the circular arc starting at p_{30} and ending at p_{32} has center p_{31} and radius *r*. We extrude to a height of 500 units.

The base shape of the second solid has vertices p_{29}, p_{30}, p_{34}, p_{35}, *and* p_{36}, and the last three vertices form a circular arc. We extrude in the local z-direction to a height of 400 units. Intersection of both solids yields a solid model of the curvilinear second bedroom.

Fig. 1.17
We use a different layer to model the windows and doors of the Winton guest house.

p_{29}(-660|542|0)=(0|0|0)
p_{30}(-660|-232|0)=(774|0|0)
p_{31} ... circular arc center
p_{32}=p_5
p_{33}(-284|501|0)
p_{34}(774|266|0)
p_{35}(387|457|0)
p_{36}(0|266|0)

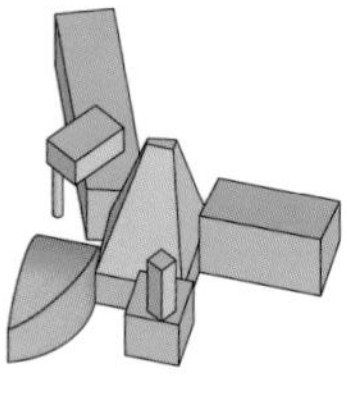

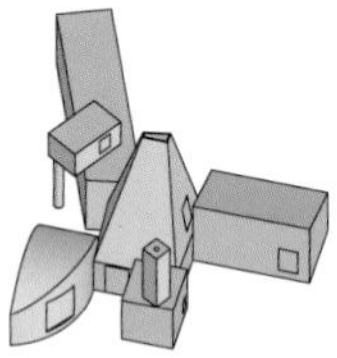

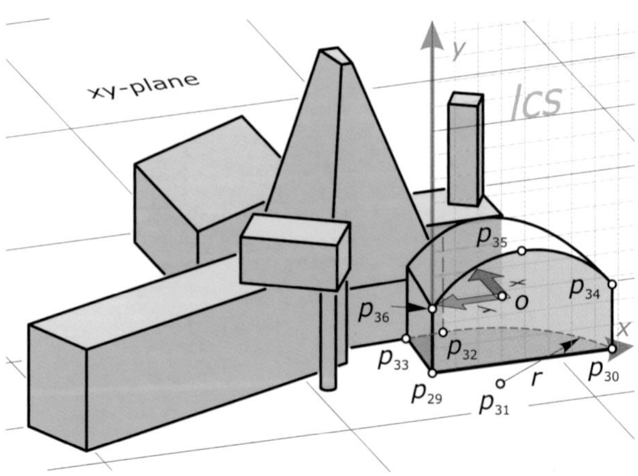

Winton guest house with window layer

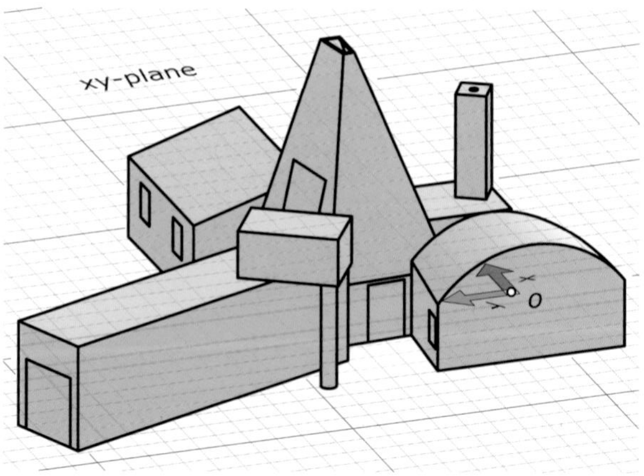

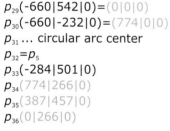

Layers. Layers are a further fundamental CAD technique we employ. A single sheet of paper can be seen as a single layer to work on. By overlaying sheets of transparent paper, we create several layers—each layer carrying different information. In a CAD system, each layer is a 3D copy of space lying at the exact same position in the global coordinate system.

Each layer can carry different parts of a design and we can easily turn them on and off. This allows us to display only the currently relevant information. The user simply has to place each piece of geometry on the applicable layer. If we were to continue to model the Winton guest house, we might (for example) save a copy of the base shapes on one layer. Then we might model the windows and doors and place them on a separate layer (Figure 1.17).

The pipe system and electricity installations might be placed on a further layer. If the 3D CAD model is used for maintenance, a layered structure also simplifies facility management after the building has been erected.

Color, texture, and material. In the initial design stages, we often work with a *wireframe* representation of a geometric shape. It simply shows us some straight lines or curves of the shape (Figure 1.18, left). Thereby, we see through the object like an X-ray machine and need mental spatial visualization abilities to create a more complete image in our mind. A *hidden line rendering* gives us an improved impression by removing the hidden parts of the object and only showing those vertices, edges, and faces of the objects in the scene that are visible from the current point of view (Figure 1.18, middle).

An alternative is to draw visible lines as solid lines, draw hidden lines as dashed lines, and color the visible faces (Figure 1.18, right). To better distinguish the various shapes we assign different colors to them. To make them look more realistic, we want to apply digital plaster or paint or say that we have a brick wall here and a concrete wall there. This can be achieved by applying textures or correspondingly applicable defining materials (Figure 1.19). The creation of a realistic or artistic image is often referred to as *rendering*.

In this book, in regard to rendering we discuss only geometric issues. Rendering methods are developed in the field of computer graphics. To produce a good rendering, we require knowledge about color, texture, material, lighting, and several other factors. Light sources are necessary because without light a rendered image would be black. In Chapter 2 you will learn the geometric background of various lighting models.

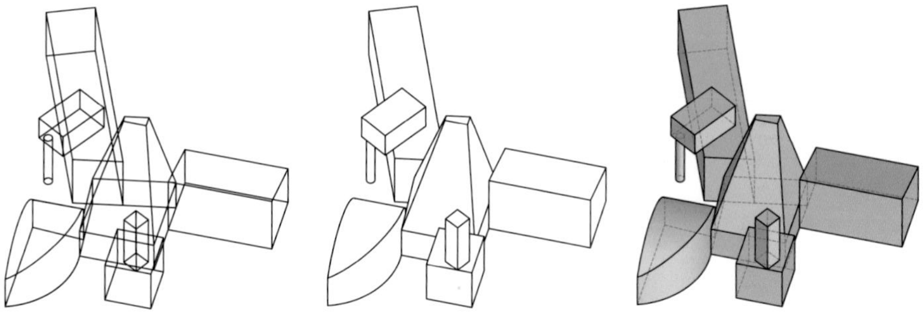

Fig. 1.18
(left) Different representations of the same geometric shape: wireframe,
(middle) hidden line rendering,
(right) and visible lines solid, hidden lines dashed, and visible faces colored.

Fig. 1.19
A rendering of the Winton guest house.

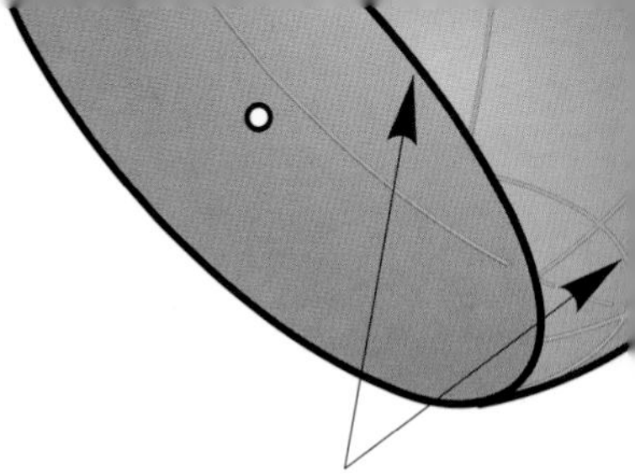

Spheres, Spherical Coordinates and Extrusion Surfaces

Sphere. A *sphere* with *center c* and *radius r* is the set of all points in 3D space that are at a distance *r* from the center *c* (Figure 1.20). A *ball* with *center c* and *radius r* is the set of all points in 3D space that have a distance less than or equal to *r* from the center *c*. What is the difference between a sphere and a ball? A sphere is the bounding surface of a *ball*.

Whereas a sphere is a *surface model* a ball is a *solid model* (as stated previously). If the radius equals $r = 1$, we speak of a *unit sphere* or of a *unit ball*. Every planar curve on a sphere is a circle. We speak of a *great circle* if the center of the circle coincides with the center of the sphere, and of a *small circle* otherwise (Figure 1.20).

Fig. 1.20
A sphere is the bounding surface of a ball and is defined by center *c* and radius *r*. All planar curves on a sphere are circles. Those with center *c* are great circles. All others are small circles.

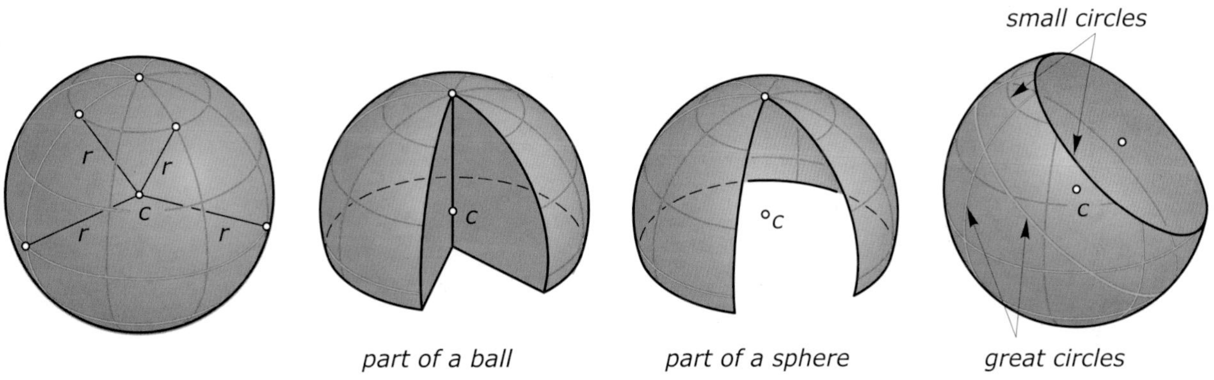

Spherical coordinates. In addition to Cartesian and cylindrical coordinates, *spherical coordinates* (r, φ, θ) are another possibility in describing 3D space (Figure 1.21). They consist of one positive number r and two angles φ and θ. Spherical coordinates are defined as follows. We fix a plane P (think of the xy-plane of a Cartesian coordinate system). Then we choose an origin o in P and a ray in the direction of the x-axis.

The first spherical coordinate r is a positive real number that gives the distance of the point p to the origin o. The second spherical coordinate is an oriented angle φ ($-180° < \varphi \leq 180°$) that is measured between the x-axis and a horizontal ray through the origin and the point p'. The point p' is obtained by orthogonal projection of p into the plane P. The third spherical coordinate is the oriented angle θ ($-90° < \varphi \leq 90°$) measured between the rays op' and op.

To convert spherical coordinates (r, φ, θ) into Cartesian coordinates (x,y,z), we proceed as in the case of polar coordinates. The length of the straight line segment op is r. Using trigonometry, we find the lengths of the straight line segments op' and pp' to be $r \cdot \cos\theta$ and $z = r \cdot \sin\theta$. Again using trigonometry, we also derive the x- and y-coordinates:

$$x = r \cdot \cos\varphi \cdot \cos\theta,$$

$$y = r \cdot \sin\varphi \cdot \cos\theta,$$

$$z = r \cdot \sin\theta.$$

Spherical coordinates defined in such a way correspond to geographic coordinates.

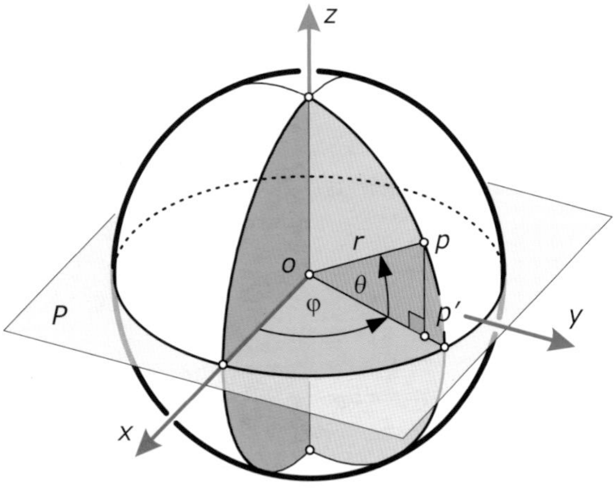

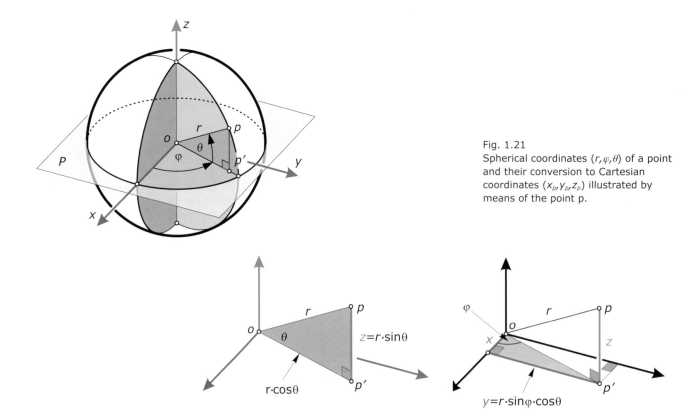

Fig. 1.21
Spherical coordinates (r,φ,θ) of a point and their conversion to Cartesian coordinates (x_p, y_p, z_p) illustrated by means of the point p.

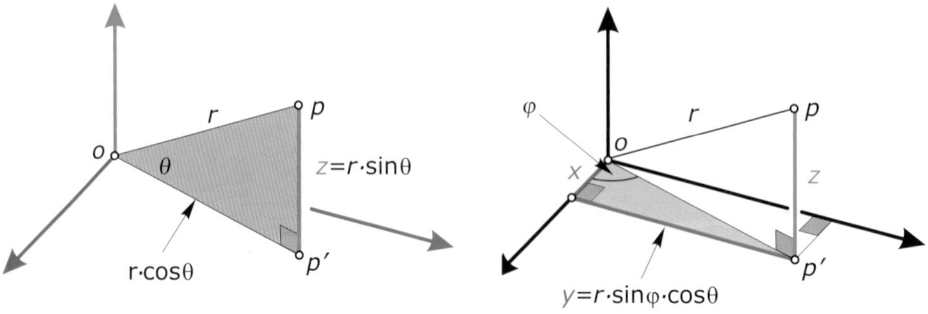

Geographic coordinate system. The surface of our planet Earth is roughly a sphere with a radius $r = 6370$ km. To describe a global position p on our planet, geographic coordinates can be used (Figure 1.22). These are a special case of spherical coordinates for which r is fixed and only *longitude* φ and *latitude* θ vary. Latitude is the angle between the *equator* plane and the ray op, and longitude is the angle between the plane of the *prime meridian* passing through Greenwich (UK) and the plane of the meridian through p.

To completely define the position p on the surface of the earth, we need a third coordinate called *elevation*. Elevation is measured as the vertical signed distance of p to a reference surface, usually at mean sea level. Using the Global Positioning System of satellites it is possible to determine longitude, latitude, and elevation of a given geographic position with high accuracy.

The geographic coordinates of Wayzata, Minnesota—where the Winton guest house is located—are N44°58', W93°30'. The N stands for north of the equator and the W stands for west of Greenwich. The elevation of Wayzata is 287 m above sea level.

Extrusion revisited: cylinder and cone surfaces. Parallel extrusion of a smooth curve generates a *cylinder surface* (Figure 1.23, left). Central extrusion of a smooth curve generates a *cone surface* (Figure 1.23, right). Both surface classes carry straight lines called *generators*. For a cylinder surface, these lines are all parallel. For a cone surface, they all pass through a common point v (the *apex*). We already encountered the rotational cylinders as a special case of cylinder surfaces. *Rotational cones* are generated by central extrusion of a circle toward a point on the axis of the circle.

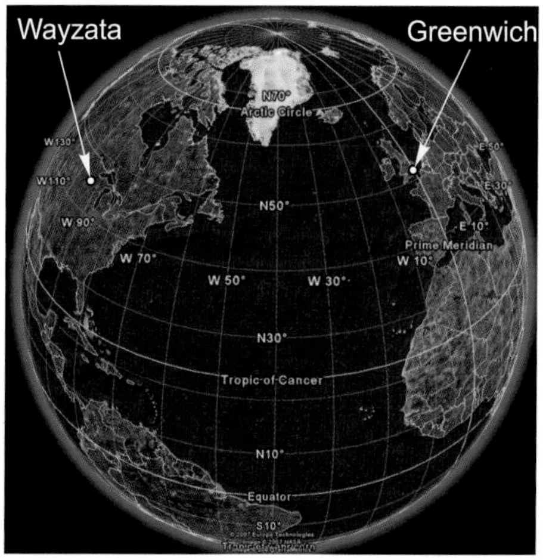

Fig. 1.22
Geographic coordinates of the Winton guest house.

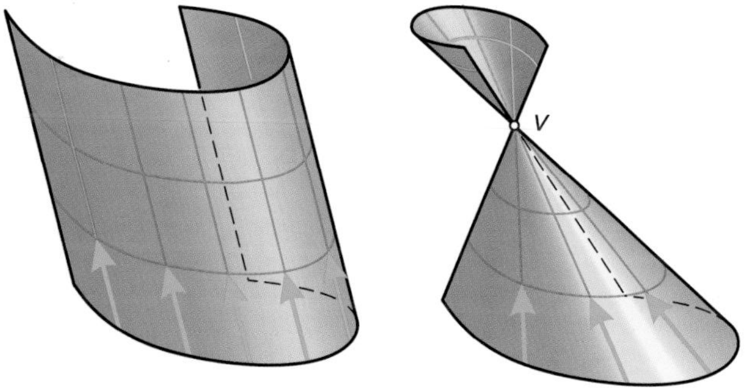

Fig. 1.23
(left) Cylinder surface generated by parallel extrusion.
(right) Cone surface generated by central extrusion.

The *axis* of a circle is the line through the center of the circle orthogonal to the plane that contains the circle. A rotational cone can also be generated by revolving a line g around an intersecting axis A (Figure 1.24, left). This intersection point is the apex of the cone. If g is parallel to A, we have a rotational cylinder. If g is not orthogonal to A, the rotational cone is actually a *double cone*—which consists of two parts: an upper and a lower cone (with the same axis, connected at their common apex). Usually when we speak of a cone we refer to only one part of a double cone.

Often a double cone is additionally bounded by a circle in a plane orthogonal to the axis. Such a rotational cone is defined by center m and radius r of the base circle and its height h, which is the distance of m to the apex v (Figure 1.24, right). Note that we can generate solid or surface models of cones and cylinders. Figures 25 and 26 illustrate cones and cylinders in architecture.

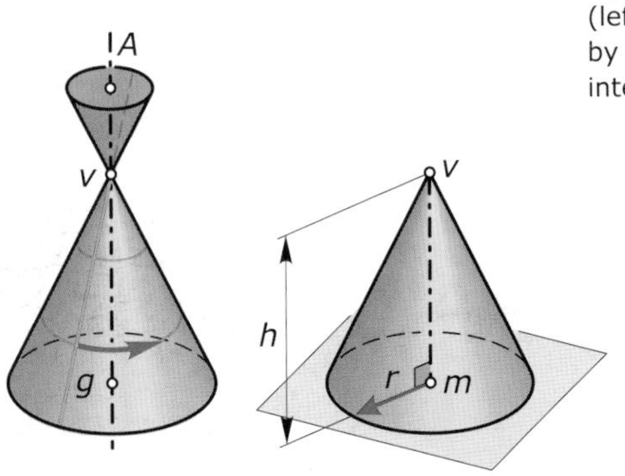

Fig. 1.24
(left) A rotational cone is obtained by revolving a line g around an intersecting axis *A*.

(right) We define a rotational cone by the center *m* and radius *r* of the base circle and the height *h.*

Fig. 1.25
A tilted rotational cone in the *Tacoma Museum of Glass* (1998-2002) by Arthur Erickson.

Outlook. Cones have a natural connection to pyramids. By refining the base polygon of a pyramid, we obtain a smooth curve (and the refined surface is a cone surface). Pyramids are explored in Chapter 3, and the connection between discrete and smooth surfaces is a topic in Chapter 11. Planar sections of rotational cones lead to the *conic sections*; namely, ellipse, parabola, and hyperbola.

These curves have been used in design since ancient times and are still of great importance. We will encounter them again in Chapters 6, 7, and 8. Cone and cylinder surfaces are two of the three basic types of *developable surfaces*, examined in Chapter 15. As we progress from chapter to chapter, we will be able to create more complicated geometric models and employ them for architectural purposes.

Fig. 1.26
The *IKMZ* (1998–2004) in Cottbus by Herzog & de Meuron has the shape of a general cylinder.

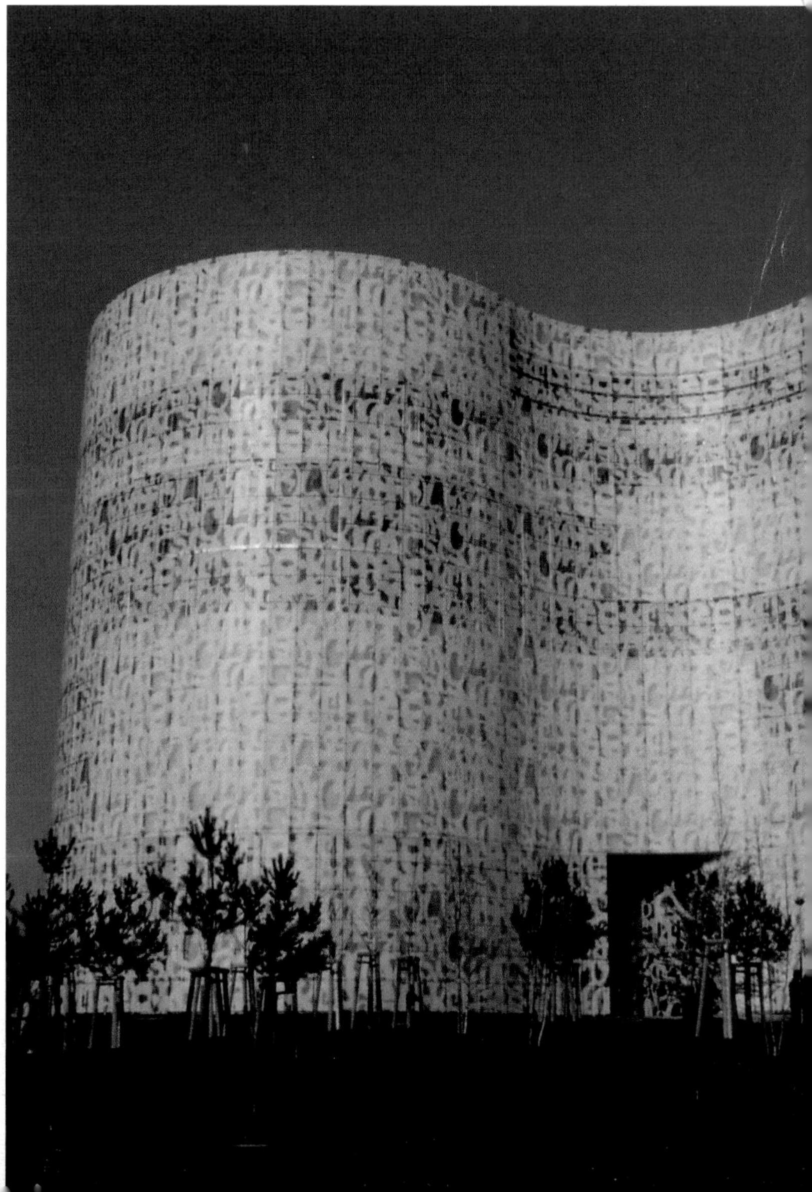

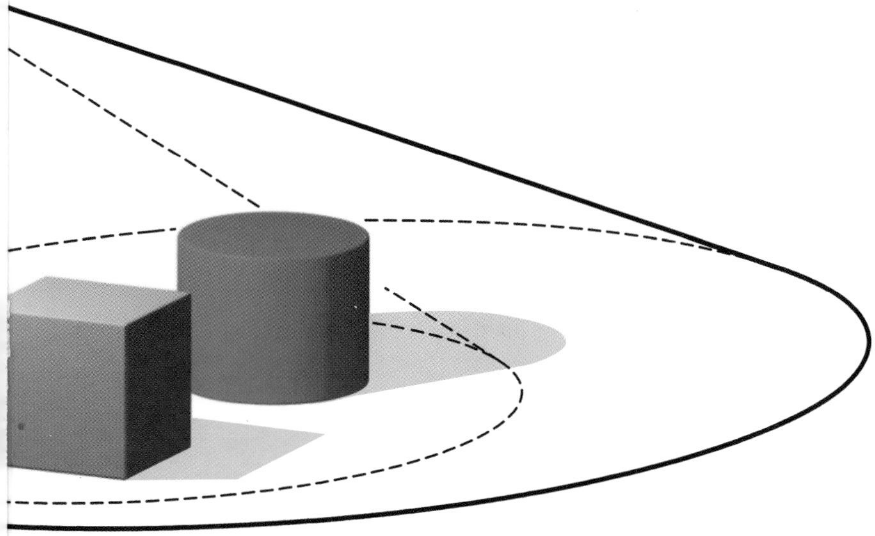

Chapter 2
Projections

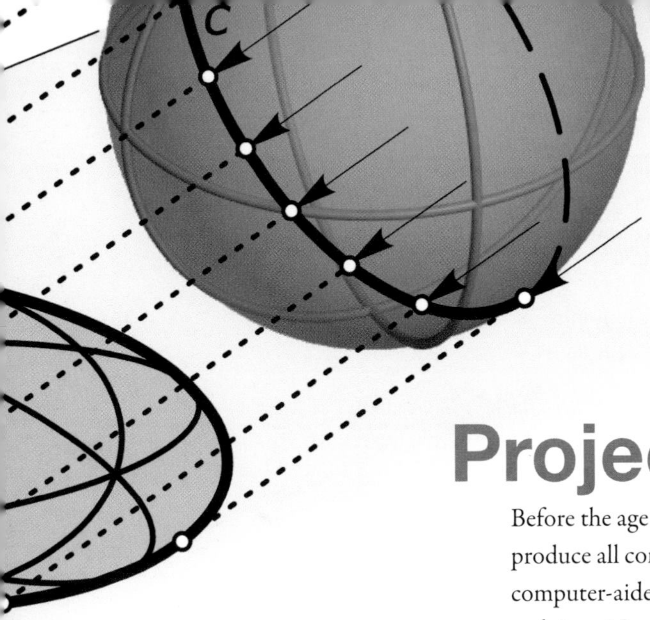

Projections

Before the age of computer graphics, good knowledge of projections was needed to produce all constructions by hand in a reasonable amount of time (Figure 2.1). Today, computer-aided design (CAD) systems compute all types of classical projections in real time. However, some theoretical background is still necessary to make best use of the available parameters for visualizing geometry. This includes basic descriptive geometry for correctly sketching 3D objects and constructing perspective views.

Fig. 2.1
A woodcarving by Albrecht Dürer (1471–1528) shows a device that helped artists produce realistic drawings. Using a quadrilateral grid (right) to capture a figure as seen by the artist was a widespread device for generating perspective views. To the right you notice the woman as seen by the artist.

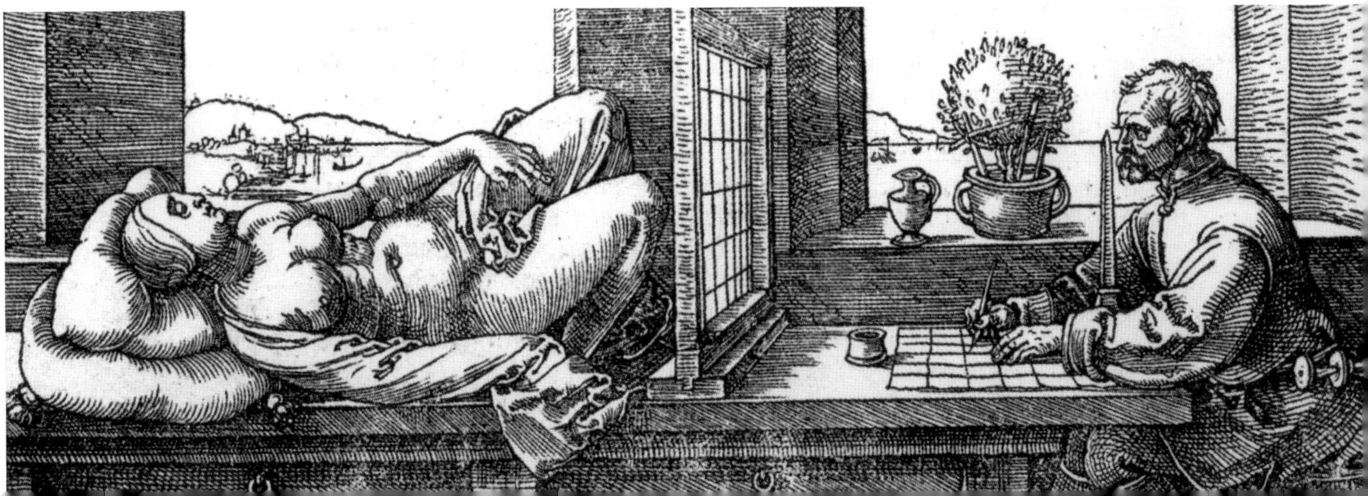

Geometric models of light and shadow are actually special cases of projections. Such insights lead us to a deeper understanding of how light and shadow influence the appearance of architectural scenes (Figure 2.2). The study of various rendering processes and methods (such as flat shading, Gouraud shading, and Phong shading, as well as ray tracing and more recent methods such as radiosity) enables us to improve our visualization skills.

We finish this chapter with more sophisticated projections. Artistic usage of nonlinear projections for presentation of architectural projects brings us in contact with the modern arts.

Projections. For many years, the design of 3D objects has been done by drawing on a 2D sheet of paper. General views have been used to visualize the objects, and with the help of special views details such as dimensions can be transmitted properly from designer to manufacturer.

Thus, extensive use of different projections and a good knowledge of the principles of projections have been necessary for every design process. *Descriptive geometry*, which studies the properties of projections, has become the language of designers and engineers.

Today, the design of 3D objects is for the most part done using an applicable CAD system. Nevertheless, the ability to generate a correct sketch of a geometric model or a spatial situation on a sheet of paper is often helpful and necessary. Basic knowledge of the fundamentals of projections enables us to sketch correctly and thus to communicate our geometric ideas.

A very intuitive approach to projections is to look at shadows generated by sunrays or light emerging from a single point source (Figure 2.3). Through every point q of an object there exists a projection ray l_q. The intersection of this ray with the *projection plane* P is called the projection of the point q. In the case of parallel rays (i.e., a geometric model of sunlight) we have *parallel projection*.

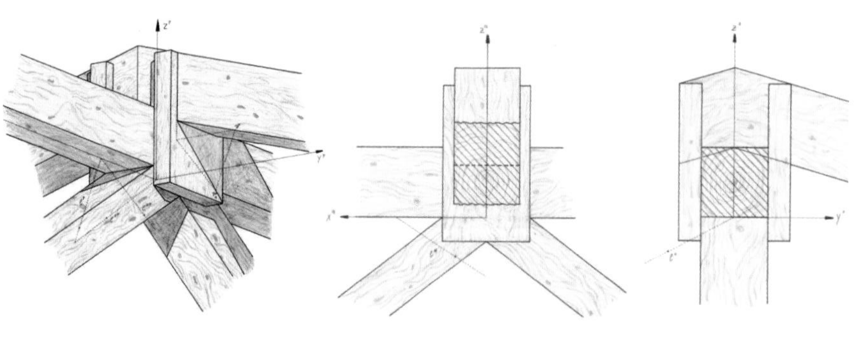

Fig. 2.2
(a) An auxiliary view of a space frame structure is used to illustrate the spatial situation, whereas special orthographic drawings show the dimensions of the frame structure.

(b) Today, CAD software allows for an even more realistic visualization.

The intersection point q^p is called the parallel projection of the point q (the superscript p indicating parallel projection). Otherwise, when all rays are emanating from a fixed point e we obtain *central projection*—which refers to the geometric model of illumination with a punctual light source or taking a photo with a camera.

Before studying projections in more detail, note that from the geometrical point of view the term *projection* always means the spatial process of depicting objects. Nevertheless, the term *projection* is also commonly used to refer to the images (views) generated by the projection. A careful distinction tends to result in complicated formulations. Thus, for the sake of readability we use *projection* for both situations: the spatial process and the planar outcome.

Parallel Projection. Obeying the properties of shadows generated by sunlight, we easily derive the following important properties of parallel projection (Figure 2.4).

(a) In general, the parallel projection of a spatial line a is a line a^p. In the special case, when a line c is parallel to the projection rays the parallel projection degenerates to a point c^p.

(b) The parallel projections a^p, b^p of parallel lines a, b (not parallel to the projection rays) are parallel.

(c) The ratio of distances is preserved under parallel projection. This means that if a point f divides the spatial line de in a certain ratio the point f^p divides the projected line d^pe^p in the same ratio. For example, the midpoint m of a line is projected into the midpoint m^p.

(d) Parallel line segments of equal length in space are projected onto parallel line segments of equal length in the plane.

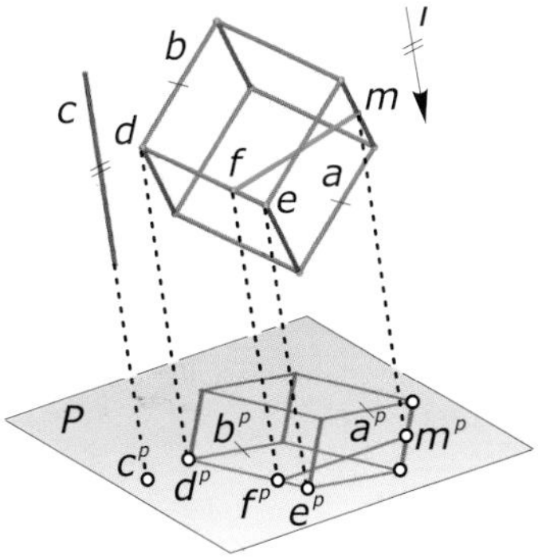

Fig. 2.4
Essential properties of parallel projection.

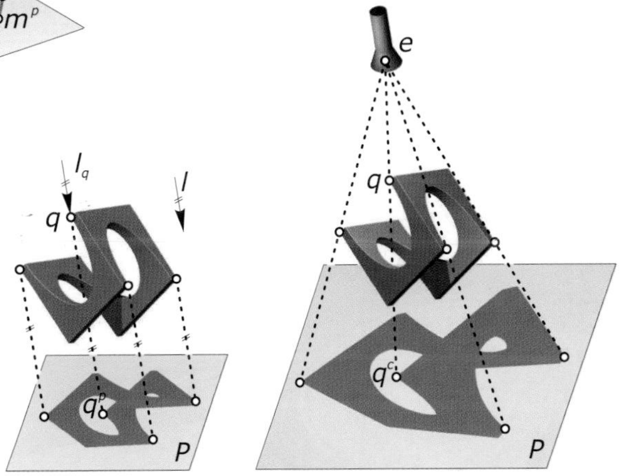

Fig. 2.3
The intersection of a light ray through a point q with the projection plane P is called the projection of the point q.
(a) Using parallel rays, we obtain the parallel projection q^p.
(b) A projection with rays emanating from a single point e is called a central projection. Here, the superscript c denotes central projection.

Most of the illustrations in this book, made by hand or with the usage of a CAD software, are *parallel views* of spatial situations. They have been generated obeying the essential rules cited previously. The use of appropriate parallel views to illustrate spatial situations has the main advantage that the parallelism of lines is preserved in contradiction to perspective views.

In fact, most perspective views look more natural. However, the loss of parallelism can be a great disadvantage when visualizing geometric properties (Figure 2.5). Thus, modeling and design of an object should be done in parallel views, whereas photorealistic rendering is best performed in perspective views. We will study perspective views in the section about central projection.

Fig. 2.5
In general, parallel views illustrate geometric properties much better than perspective views (Taipeitower (1999–2004) in Taipei by C. Y. Lee). Note that the large distance at which the left-hand photo was taken simulates a parallel projection.

As we have seen, the parallel projection of parallel lines generates parallel lines. However, two parallel lines in a single parallel view can originate from skewed (not parallel and not intersecting) lines in 3D space (Figure 2.6). This property is sometimes used by artists to produce apparently impossible views.

In most cases the parallel projection $a^p b^p$ of a line ab is longer or shorter than the spatial length of ab. The ratio $d = \text{dist}(a^p,b^p) : \text{dist}(a,b)$ of the two distances $\text{dist}(a^p,b^p)$ and $\text{dist}(a,b)$ is called the *distortion factor* of the line ab. This distortion factor also tells us whether the parallel projection of a line is longer or shorter than the spatial line.

If we consider shadows generated by sunlight, we see that the distortion factor can assume every positive value. The higher the sun stands above the horizon (at noon) the shorter the shadow will be. Otherwise, sunrays in the late afternoon (when the sun is near the horizon) cast very long shadows (Figure 2.7).

The distortion factor of lines also causes distortions of angles and areas. Thus, in general parallel projection does not preserve angles and areas. Only parts of objects that lie in planes parallel to the projection plane retain their real shape.

Fig. 2.6
Two skew lines in 3D space generating parallel-looking lines in the projection plane. This was used by M. C. Escher to generate images of seemingly impossible objects.

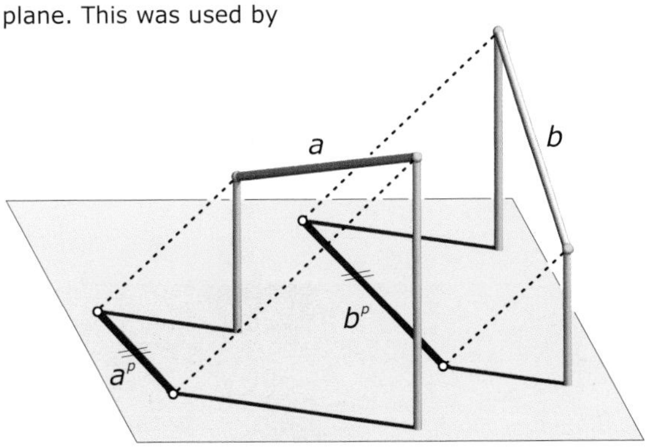

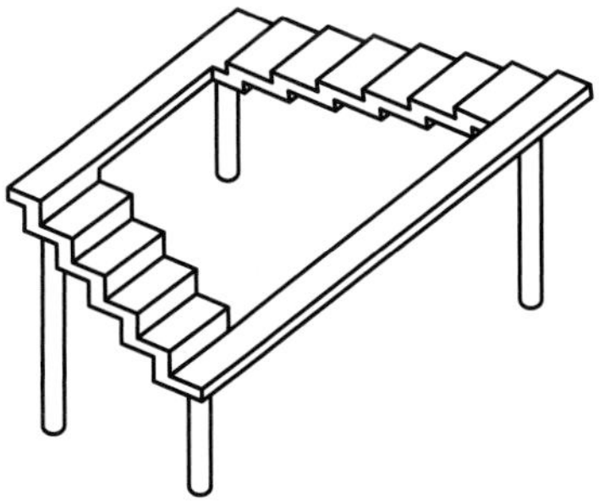

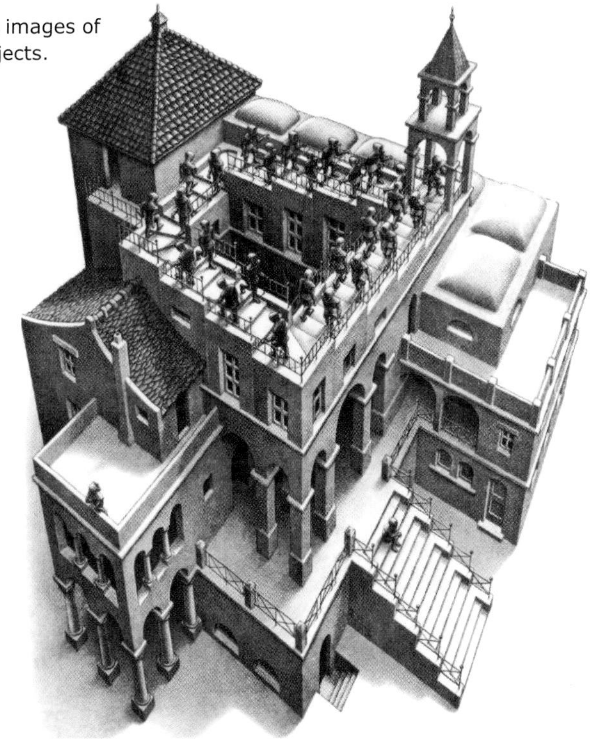

Fig. 2.7
Depending on the location of the sun, an object casts different shadows. Generally, angles are not preserved by parallel projection—with the exception of shapes lying in planes parallel to the projection plane.

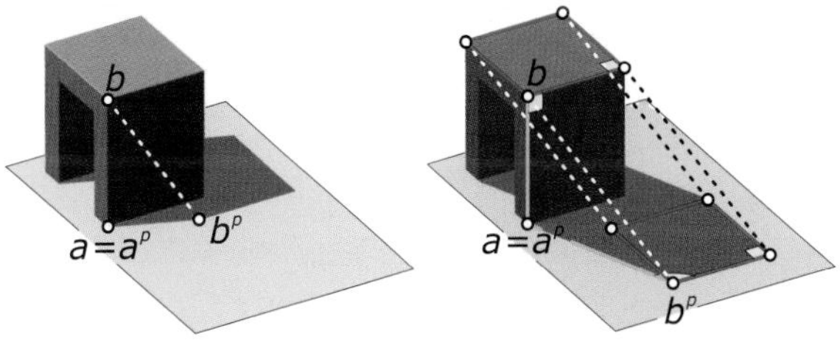

As a consequence, the parallel projection of a circle in an arbitrary plane is not a circle because different diameters are projected with different distortion factors (Figure 2.8). Without a proof, we state that generally the parallel projections of circles and spheres are ellipses (see Chapters 6, 7, and 8). Therefore, views based on general parallel projections often appear to be unnatural. This is because the observer wants to recognize the image of a sphere as a circle.

Axonometric views (also referred to as *auxiliary views*) are based on parallel projections and were used extensively before the age of CAD systems. With this relatively simple technique, meaningful visualizations of 3D objects and spatial situations can be produced by hand (Figure 2.9).

These techniques are helpful in creating freehand sketches, in visualizing design ideas, and in generating extraordinary views of 3D objects for presentational purposes. Later in this chapter we will briefly explore basic construction methods involved in creating such views.

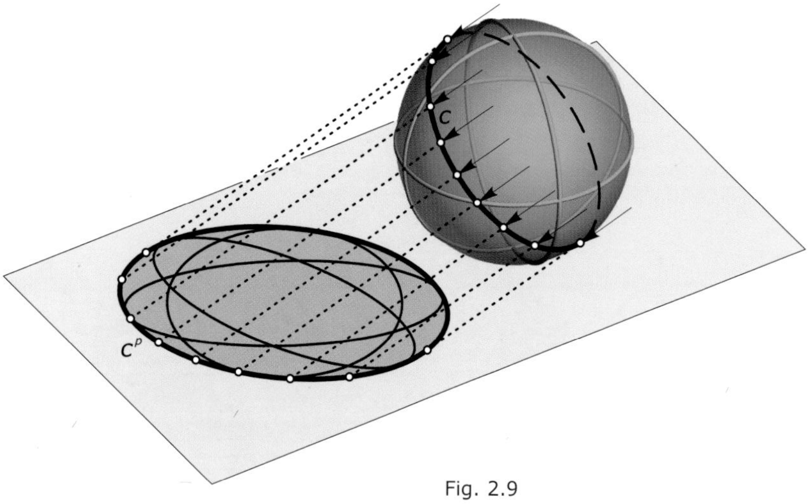

Fig. 2.8
In general, parallel projection of circles and spheres yields ellipses.

Fig. 2.9
Axonometric views based on parallel projection can be sketched easily by hand. They are sometimes used for presentational purposes.

Local TV station (1968–1972) in Salzburg by G. Peichl (left). Moller house (1927–1928) in Vienna by A. Loos (right).

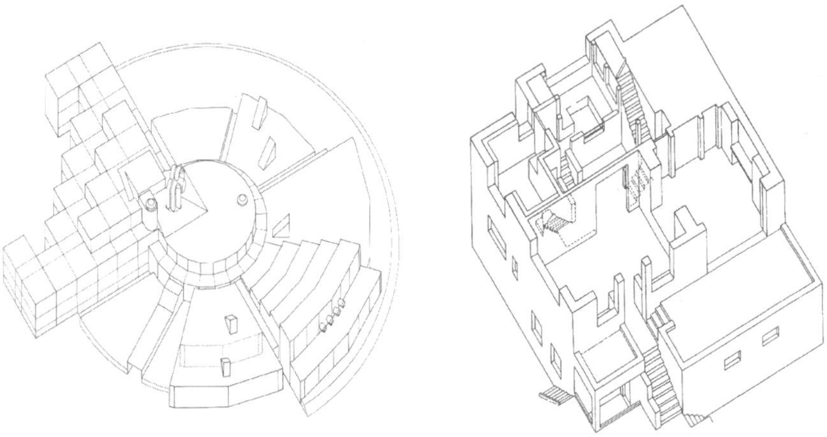

Normal Projection: A parallel projection whose projection rays are perpendicular to the projection plane is called a *normal projection* (Figure 2.10). Normal projections are special cases of parallel projections and thus inherit all properties of parallel projections. In addition, the normal projection of a sphere is always a circle.

All projection rays touch the sphere along a circle c, which lies in a plane perpendicular to the direction of the projection. Thus, the circle c lies parallel to the projection plane. It is depicted as a circle c^p, which has the same radius as the sphere. This is one reason views based on normal projections look more realistic than views based on general parallel projections.

Auxiliary views based on parallel projections are a good means of illustrating spatial situations or of visualizing design ideas. However, to communicate dimensions of objects we use normal projection and orthographic views.

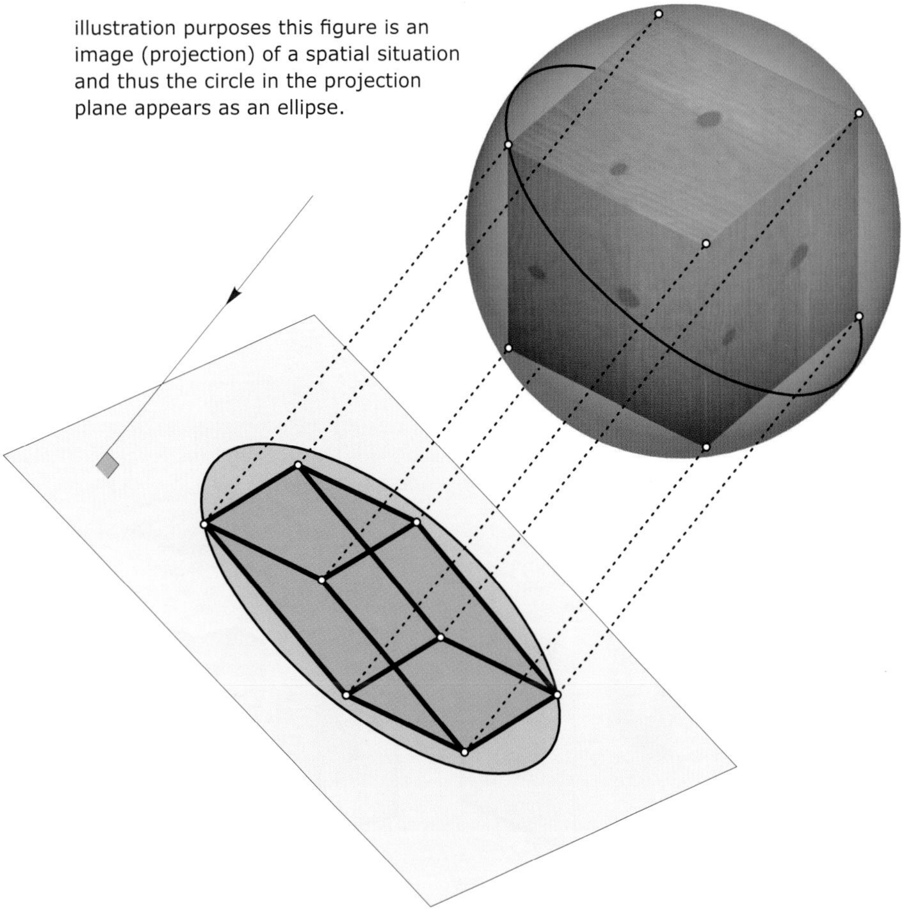

Fig. 2.10
The projection rays of a normal projection are perpendicular to the projection plane. Compared to parallel projection, the normal projection of a sphere is a circle. Note that for illustration purposes this figure is an image (projection) of a spatial situation and thus the circle in the projection plane appears as an ellipse.

All lines and objects in planes perpendicular to the projection rays lie parallel to the projection plane. Therefore, the normal projection of these lines and objects shows their original dimensions. Given a 3D Cartesian coordinate system with a vertical z-axis we recognize three normal projections that are linked to it in a very natural way (Figure 2.11).

- The vertical normal projection with projection rays r_1 in direction opposite that of the z-axis shows the *top view* of the object.
- The horizontal normal projections with projection rays r_2 and r_3 show respectively the *front view* and the (right hand) *side view* of the object.

If we additionally consider the normal projections along the coordinate axis, we have three more main views of the object. These projections (Figure 2.12) show the *bottom view* (projection ray $-r_1$), the *rear view* ($-r_2$), and the *left side view* ($-r_3$). Technical drawings usually include only the top, front, and side views because together they are considered sufficient to completely describe an object's shape.

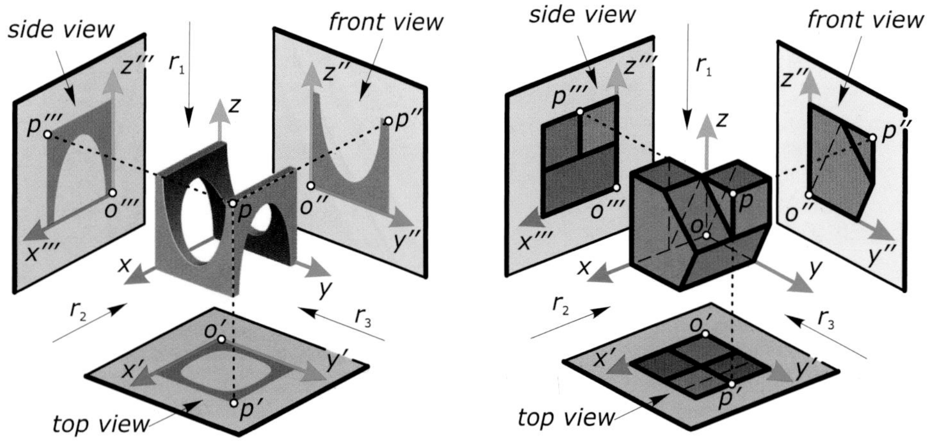

Fig. 2.11
Three normal projections are linked to every Cartesian coordinate frame.

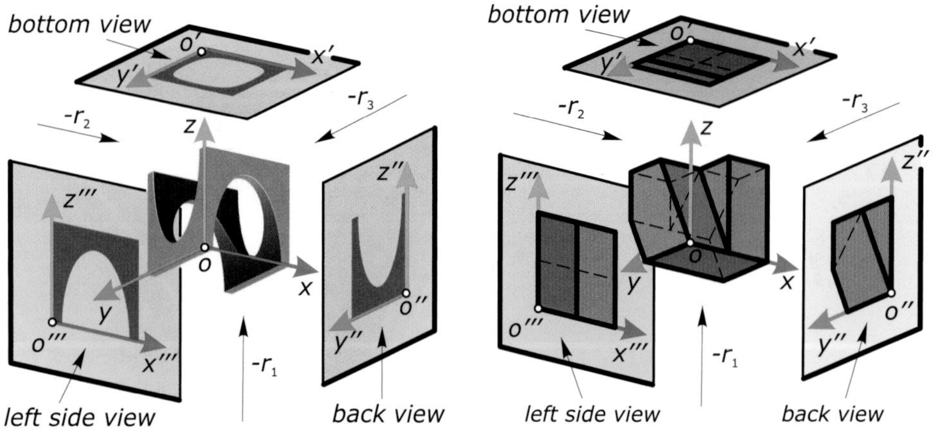

Fig. 2.12
Three additional main views of an object.

In technical drawings, often the main views are positioned so that the relative position of the views allows for a transfer of information between the views. Depending on the "historical evolution of Descriptive Geometry", there are two commonly used positioning schemes.

- The front view is located directly above the top view, and the right side view is directly to the left of the front view (Figure 2.13, bottom). This scheme (influenced by Figure 2.11) is familiar in Europe.
- The use of a type of "projection cuboid" (Figure 2.13, top), which contains the object, suggests locating the top view directly over the front view and the right side view directly to the right side of the front view.

Fig. 2.13
Two different positioning schemes for the main views are commonly used.

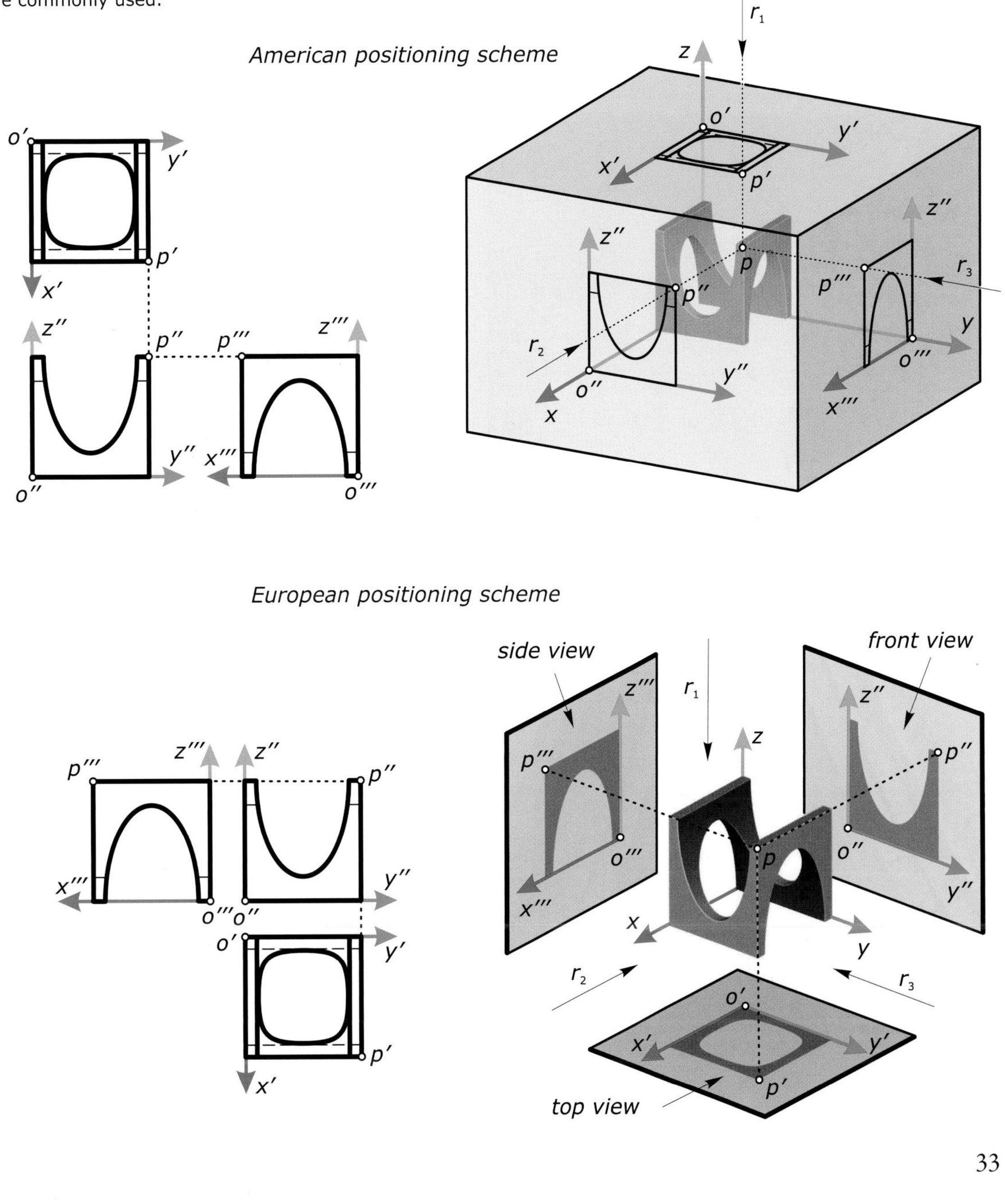

Most CAD systems allow the user to arrange the main views arbitrarily. Nevertheless, when distributing official blueprints one has to follow the standard arrangement of main views.

Remember that the primary purpose of these multiview drawings is to obtain views of an object on which actual measurements can be shown. Therefore, it is important to fit the coordinate frame to the object such that the major parts of the object are positioned parallel to the coordinate planes.

In recent high-profile projects involving more free-form geometries, this blueprint-based approach has begun to change in favor of digital-model–based formats. Here, digital files containing geometry information for fabrication of parts are directly sent to manufacturers or transferred directly to sites via laser positioning devices.

One such example is the Stata Center (at MIT), designed by Frank Gehry (Figure 2.14). It was one of the first cases in which the 3D model served as the legal basis for all contractors regarding proof of measurements.

Fig. 2.14
Stata Center of MIT
(1999–2003) in Cambridge by F. Gehry.

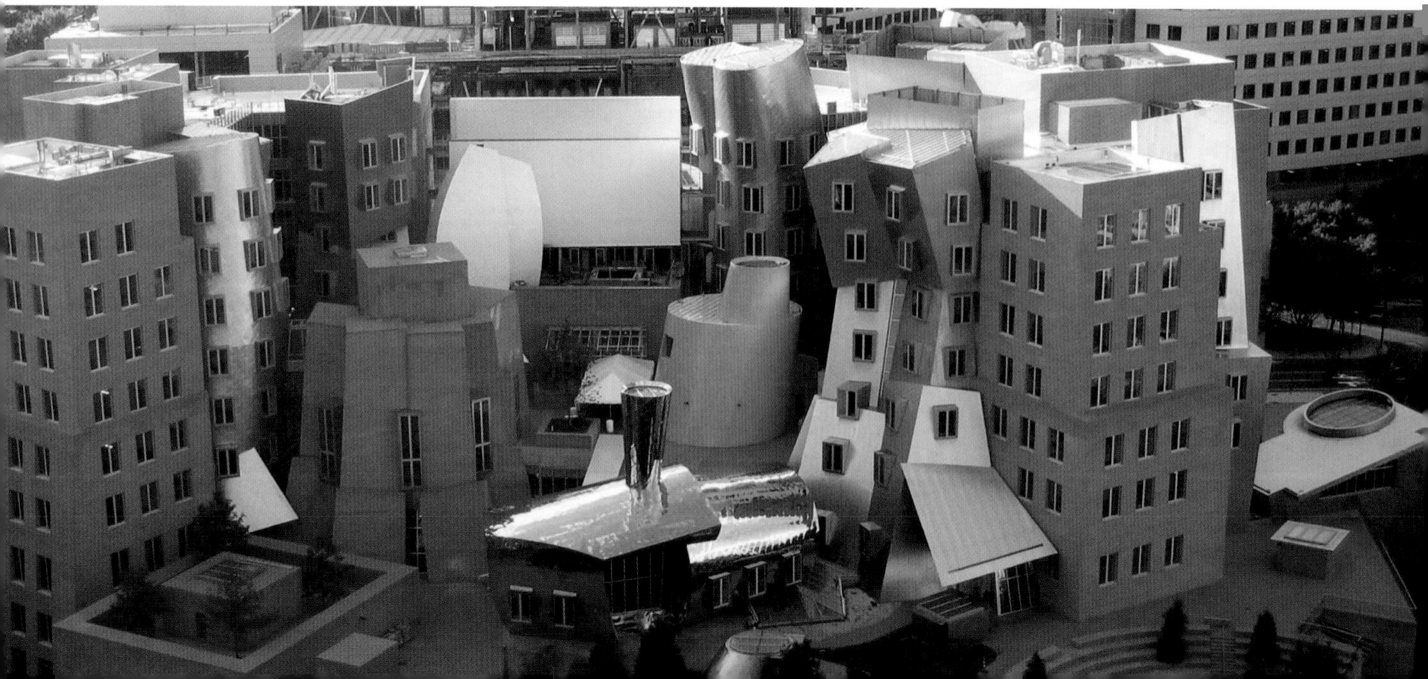

Perspective Projection

So far we have dealt with parallel and normal projections as effective tools for visualization of design ideas, assessment of the geometric properties of objects, and communication of spatial dimensions. To produce natural-looking images, perspective projection is necessary.

The first approaches to central perspective were made in the fifteenth century, when Italian architects and artists such as Filippo Brunellesci, Leon Battista Alberti, and Piero della Francesca tried to develop some basic rules and methods for the generation of realistic-looking images.

The old masters sometimes used a wooden frame and a stretched thread (Figure 2.1) to produce perspective drawings. The thread realized the projection ray, whereas the wooden frame served as projection plane. The transfer of points from the projection plane onto a sheet of paper was done by means of a thread grid.

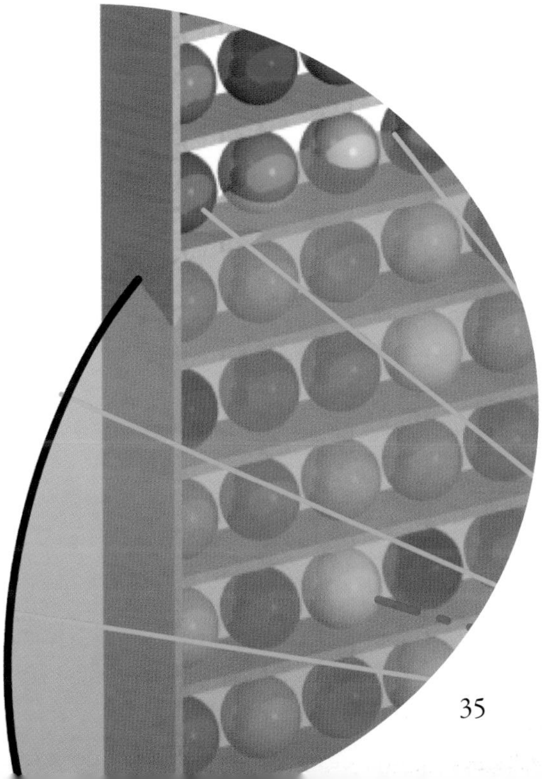

By abstracting this very practicable idea, we deduce a very simple method of generating perspective views. In Figure 2.15 we substitute for the wooden frame a vertical projection plane *P* and for the stretched thread a projection ray *r* through a fixed eye point *e*. Points *p* of the object are projected into the projection plane *P* by intersecting the projection ray *r* with the plane *P*. Note that the perspective views of points *p* are usually labeled with p^c, where the *c* refers to central projection.

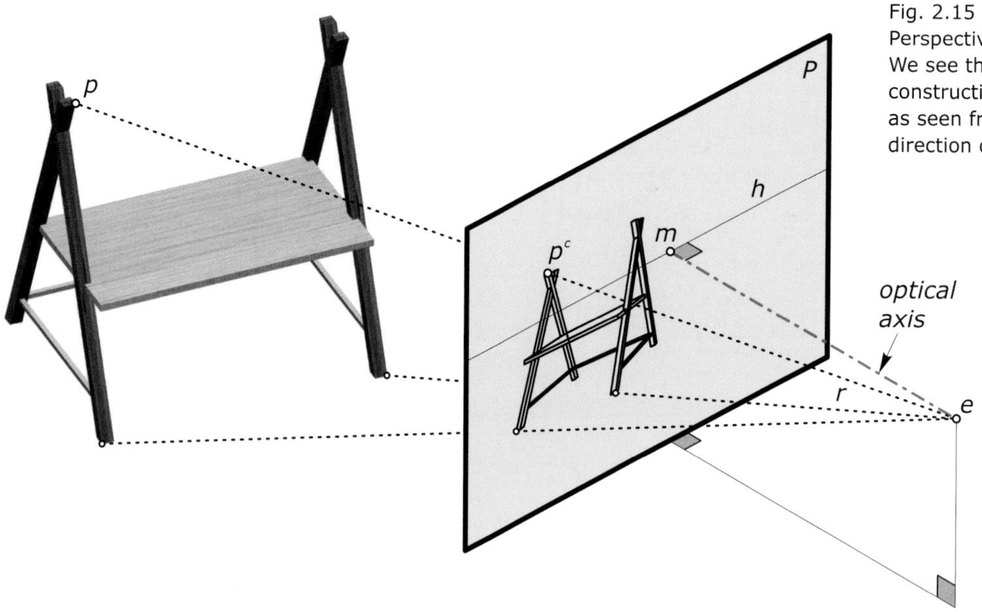

Fig. 2.15
Perspective projection of a table. We see the 3D situation during the construction (top). The final image as seen from position e looking in direction of the optical axis (bottom).

There is one projection ray through the eye point *e*, which is perpendicular to the projection plane. This ray specifies the *optical axis* of the perspective projection and intersects the projection plane *P* in the *principal point m*. A horizontal plane through the eye point *e* intersects the projection plane *P* along a line *h*.

Now we position the observer's eye in the eye point *e* and let him or her look in the direction of the optical axis. Then the perspective drawing gives the same impression as in reality (Figure 2.15, bottom). The horizontal line *h* would then be the horizon—the border between "the horizontal earth" and the sky. Thus, *h* is called the *horizon line.*

The same situation appears when we photograph a scene in reality (Figure 2.16). The camera is located at point *e*, and the camera's *optical axis* is orientated toward the principal point *m*. Therefore, we often refer to the eye point *e* as *camera position* and to the principal point *m* as *camera target*.

After taking the picture, the principal point *m* becomes the midpoint of the produced image. In Figure 2.16, we can recognize another well-known effect of perspective images: perspective views of parallel and horizontal lines apparently intersect at the horizon line.

Fig. 2.16
3D situations and 2D results when photographing a house.

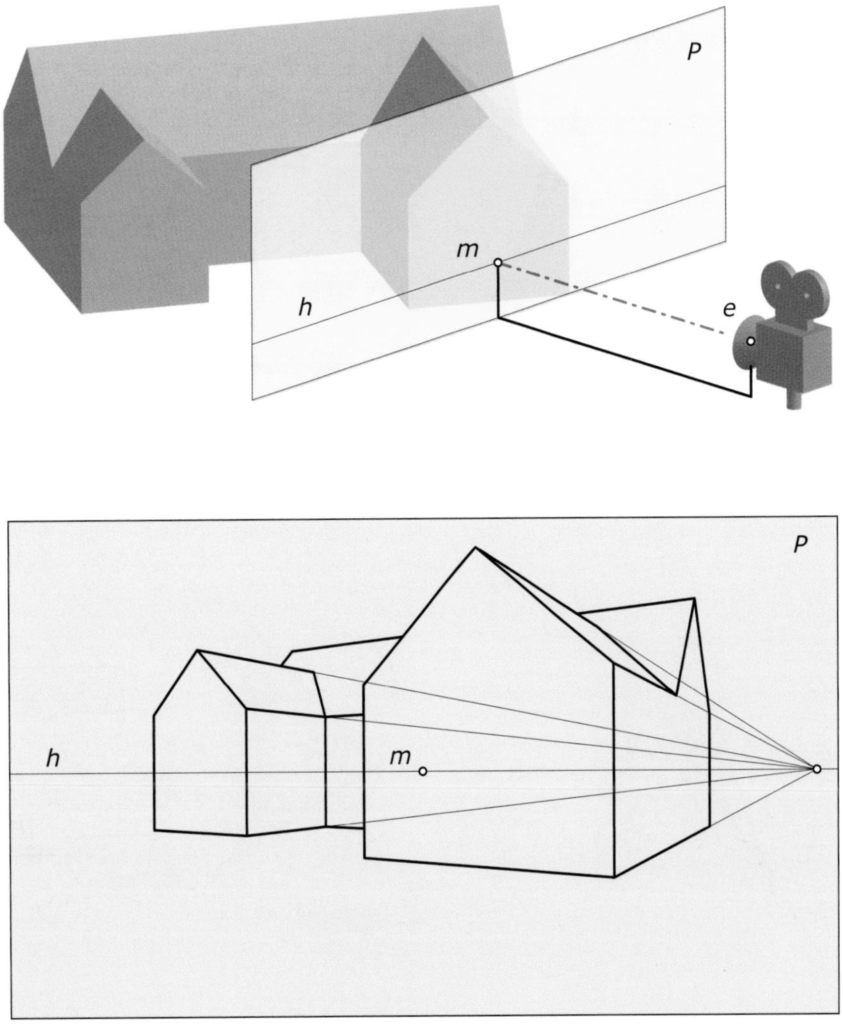

Figure 2.17 illustrates the proof of this fact. To obtain the projection l^c of an arbitrary straight line l, we have to intersect plane E (which contains eye point e and the line l) with the projection plane P (Figure 2.17, left). Now we take two arbitrary parallel and horizontal lines l_1 and l_2 (Figure 2.17, middle).

To construct their perspective views l_1^c and l_2^c, we connect both lines with the eye point and get two planes E_1 and E_2. The intersection line l_v of these planes contains the eye point e and is parallel to l_1 and l_2. The intersection point v_l of l_v with the projection plane P lies on the horizon line h. It is called the vanishing point v_l of all lines parallel to l_v.

These points are crucial when sketching perspective views by hand. Generally, the perspective views of arbitrary parallel lines k_1 and k_2 intersect each other in the vanishing point v_k of the lines k_1 and k_2. The vanishing point v_k is the intersection point of k_v with the projection plane, where k_v is the straight line through the eye point e parallel to k_1 and k_2. Thus, we see that contrary to parallel projection perspective projection generally does not preserve parallelism and ratios.

Fig. 2.17
Construction of vanishing points.

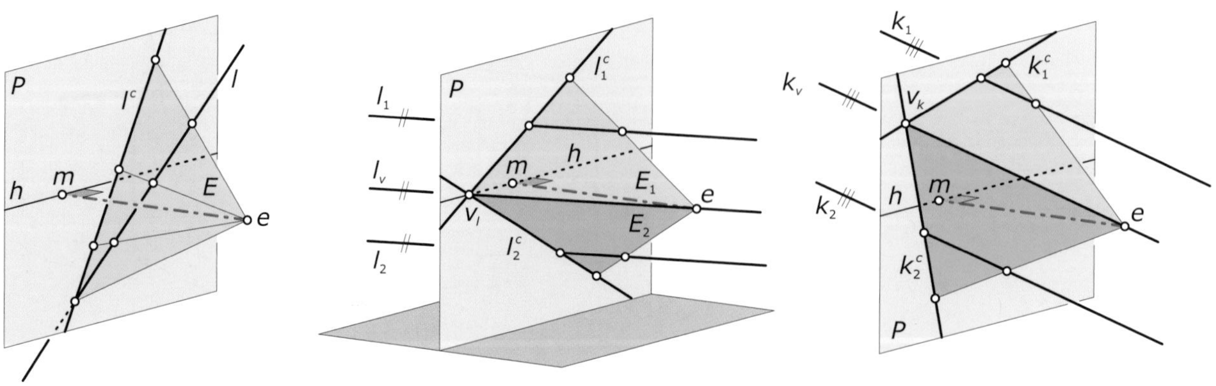

The distance between the eye point *e* and the principal point *m* on the horizon line controls the distance between the eye point and the projection plane. We call it the *distance* of the perspective view. Changing the distance only causes a magnification or shrinkage of the perspective image. It does not affect the image's impression (Figure 2.18, top row). Otherwise, moving the camera along the optical axis can cause dramatic changes of the image (Figure 2.18, bottom row).

Fig. 2.18
Perspective views of a model showing the "Endless Staircase" (1991, Ludwigshafen) of Max Bill.
With fixed eye point and changing distance (top row).
With moving eye point and fixed projection plane (bottom row).

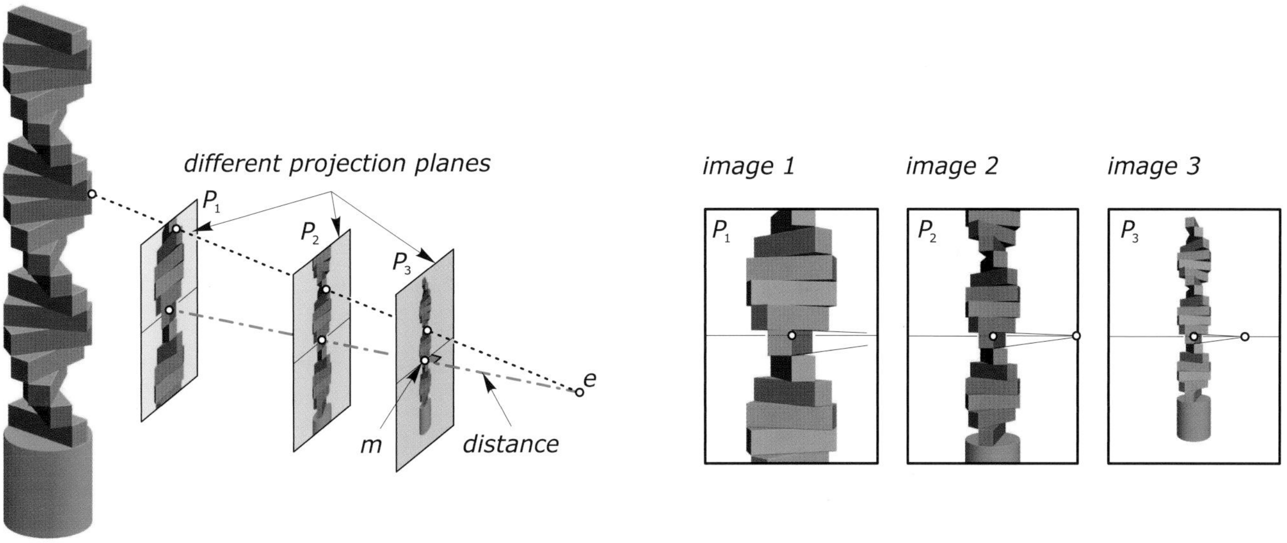

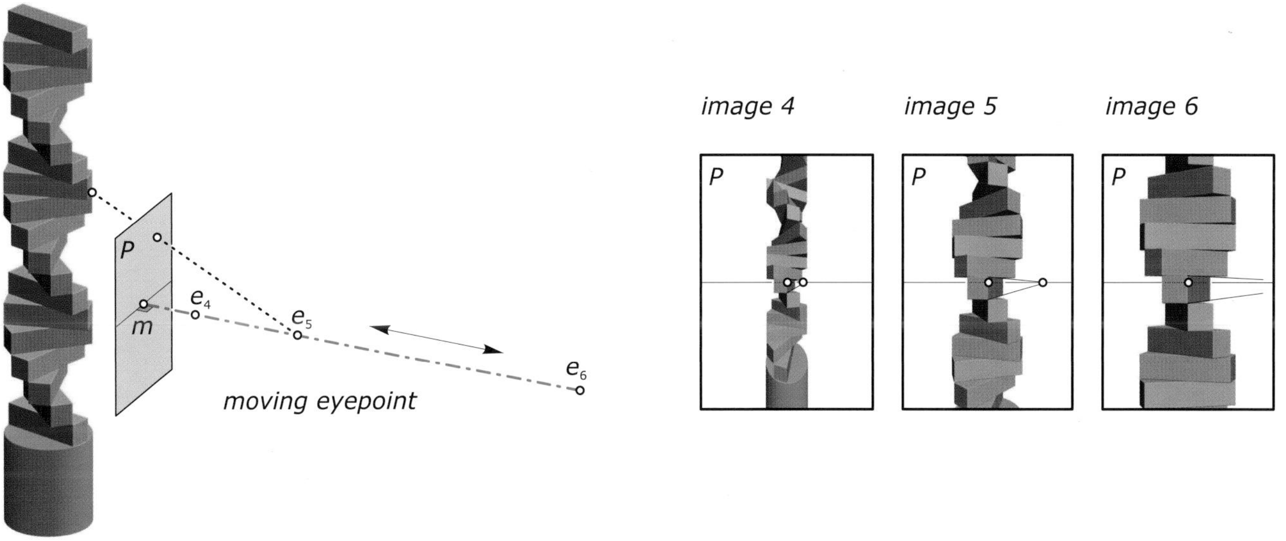

Example:

Constructing a perspective view of a house by hand. To generate perspective images by hand, we arrange top and front views of the spatial situation as shown in Figure 19. We construct the top and front views of a point p^c by intersecting the projection ray *ep* with the projection plane *P*. To generate the true image of the objects lying in *P*, we transfer the points obeying the horizontal distance d_h and the vertical distance d_v of p^c to the principal point *m*.

The horizontal distance d_h is seen in the top view as the distance between *m*' and $p^{c\prime}$, whereas the vertical distance d_v can be found in the front view as the distance of $p^{c\prime\prime}$ from the horizon line *h*. Thus, the perspective view of all object points can be found and the perspective view of the object can be generated.

European positioning scheme

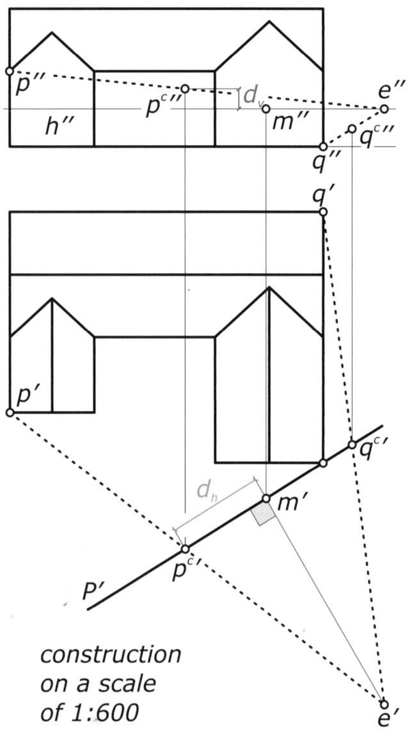

American positioning scheme

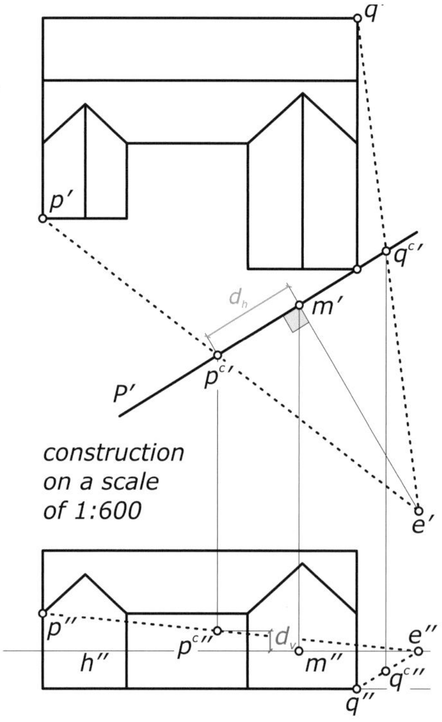

Fig. 2.19
Constructing a perspective view of a simple house model.
The construction is performed in two different positioning schemes on a scale of 1:600 (top).
The result is sketched on a scale of 1:300 (bottom).

result on a scale of 1:300

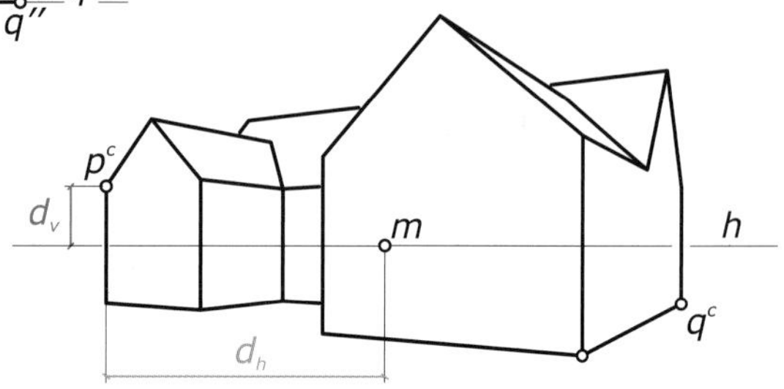

Example:

Creation of perspective views using vanishing points. A pointwise construction can be improved by using vanishing points (Figure 2.20). We find top and front views of the vanishing point v_l of an arbitrary straight line l as the intersection point of l_v with the projection plane P, where l_v is a straight line through eye point e parallel to l. The perspective view of v_l is then constructed by transferring the distances d_v and d_h as described previously.

Using vanishing points improves the accuracy of the construction and decreases the amount of construction lines. For example, to find the perspective view of the points q and r lying on a y-parallel line through an already constructed point p, we use the vanishing point v_y and have only to determine the horizontal distances d_h. This can be done involving just the top view. Analogously, we construct the perspective views of points lying on x-parallel edges using the vanishing point v_x.

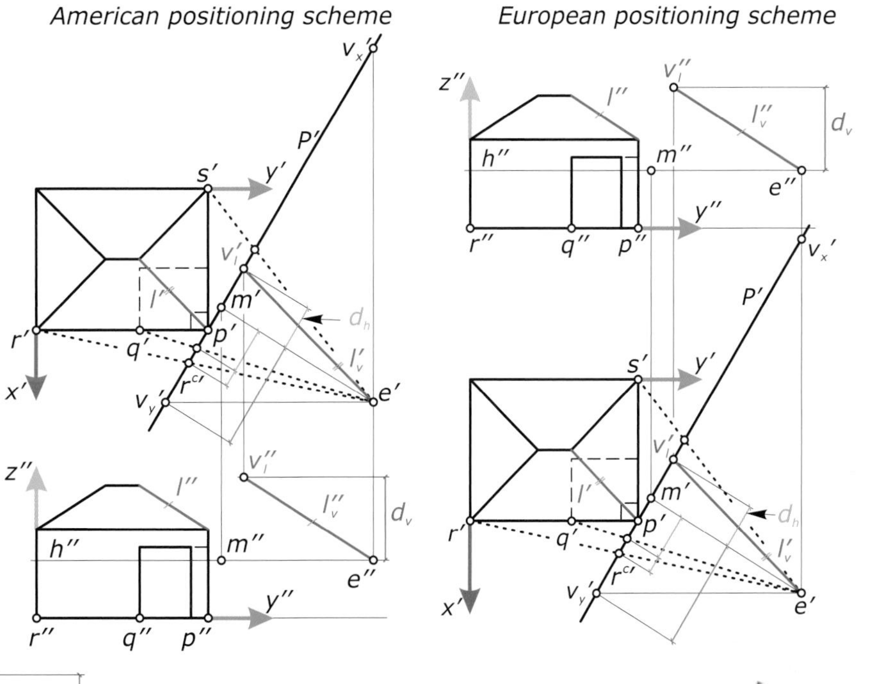

Fig. 2.20
Construction of a perspective view with the help of vanishing points. The construction is performed in two different positioning schemes (top).

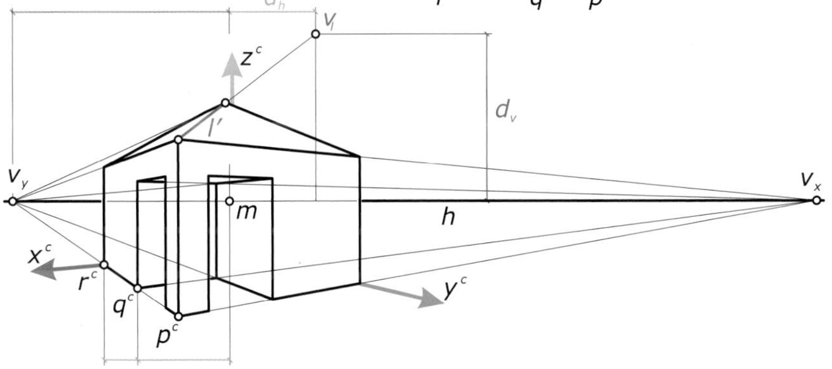

Note that these construction techniques are best suited to projecting objects with only planar faces. Application of these methods for the generation of perspective views of cylinders, spheres, or objects with nonplanar faces is much more complicated and time consuming.

The latter has been a main topic of traditional descriptive geometry and we will not describe it here. However, it is very helpful to be able to sketch the perspective image of simple objects with planar faces (as described previously). Understanding the basics of perspective projections also improves our ability to find appropriate perspective views when using a CAD system.

Fig. 2.21
Different heights of camera position and camera target generate aberrant z lines.

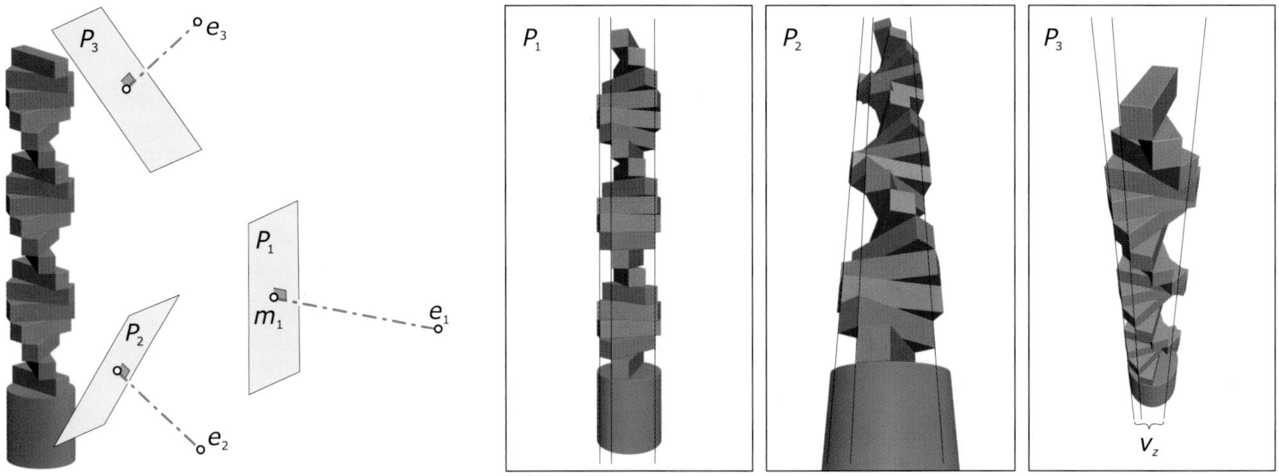

Fig. 2.22
The visual cone and the visual pyramid limit the area depicted.

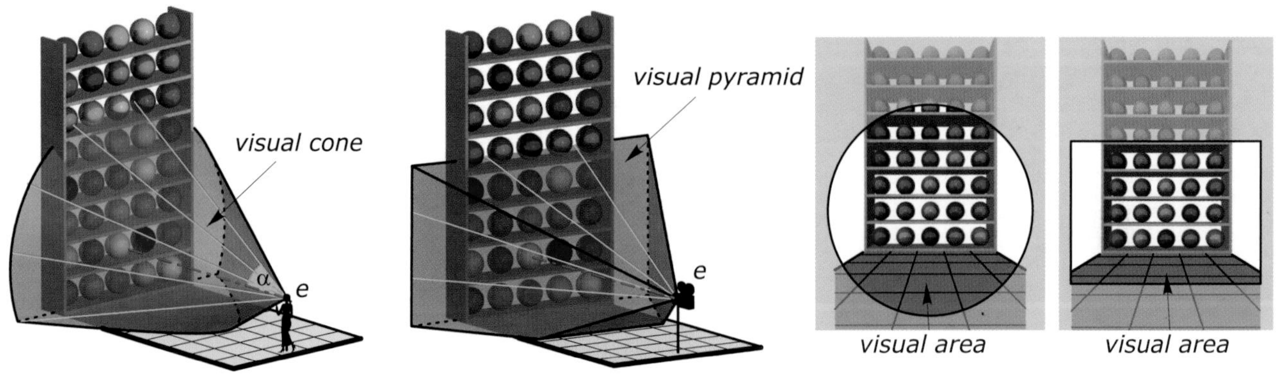

Hints for creating realistic images. Perspective views are practical for presentational purposes because they simulate the one-eyed vision of the modeled scene. To obtain realistic images, the following tips can be useful (Figures 2.21 and 2.22).

- Recall that the camera position is the location where the observer's eyes are. We represent it by a single eye point whose position should be between 1.5 and 2 m above the flat terrain.
- Selecting a horizontal optical axis e_1m_1 leads to perspective images, where z-parallel lines appear as vertical parallel lines. Thus, camera position and camera target should have the same z-coordinate.
- If the camera target is higher than the camera position, the direction of the optical axis e_2m_2 points upward. The vanishing point v_z is lying above the horizon line. Thus, we have convergent z lines.
- A camera position e_3, which is higher than the camera target, also results in convergent z lines wherein the vanishing point v_z is positioned below the horizon line.
- The visual area, which normally can be absorbed by a human's eye without moving the head, is limited approximately to a *visual cone* wherein the angle α of the cone to its axis is about 30 degrees (Figure 2.22). When we use a CAD system or a camera to generate perspective views, this visual cone is replaced by a *visual pyramid*. Most CAD systems provide tools for manipulating this visual cone to adjust the perspective view. As shown in Figure 2.23, the angle α should not exceed 30 degrees in order to obtain realistic renderings.

Fig. 2.23
Renderings of a scene with different visual pyramids: an angle α of less than 30 degrees generates realistic pictures, whereas images with larger angles lack realism. Otherwise, this effect can be used for artistic purposes.

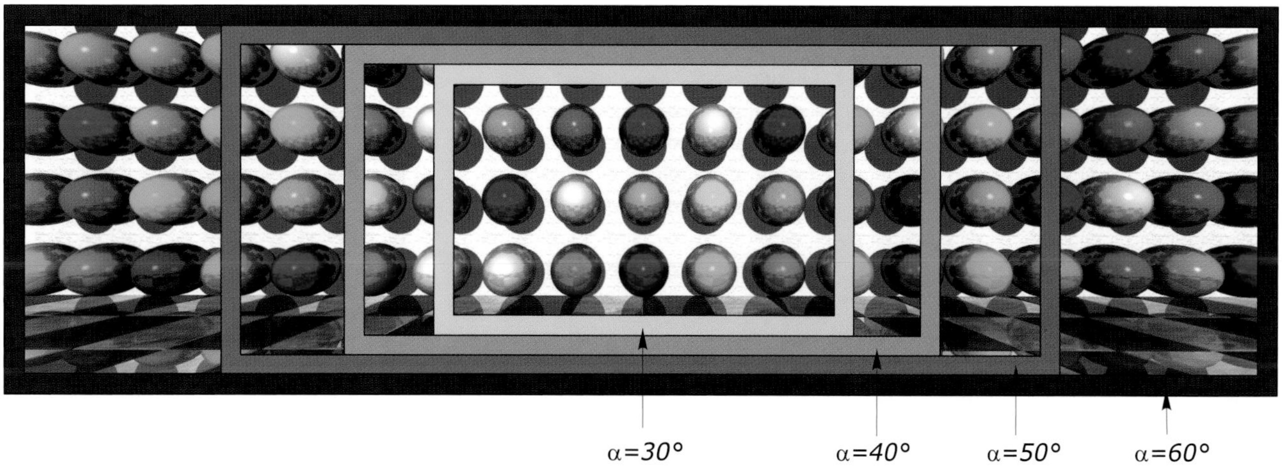

Generation of optical illusions. So far we have dealt with perspective projection as a means of generating views that represent the surrounding 3D space in a realistic way. However, taking advantage of the properties of perspective projection, one can also deceive the observer's senses.

Those deceiving aspects have also been applied successfully to the generation of optical illusions, as illustrated in Figure 2.24. The underlying geometric idea is the knowledge that all points lying on the same projection ray *r* have the same perspective image.

History: During the last centuries this possibility was extensively used by architects and painters to simulate 3D objects on flat walls or domes. An impressive example can be seen in the Church of St. Ignazio, Rome. There, over the years 1684 and 1685 Andrea Pozzo succeeded in painting a flat ceiling that as appears to be a perfect 3D dome (Figure 2.24).

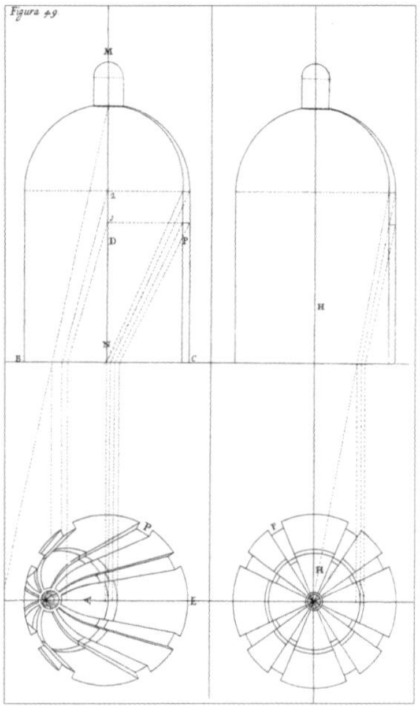

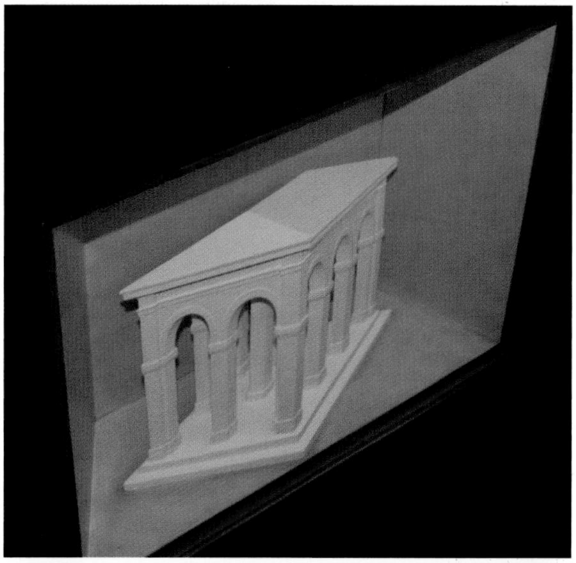

Fig. 2.24
Artistic use of perspective projection can be found in architecture, stage architecture, and street graffiti. The ceiling of the church of St. Ignazio in Rome by Andrea Pozzo (1621–1685) features a fake cupola painted on a flat ceiling (left).
In stage architecture, perspective is used to fake larger stage settings on small stages. Two views of such a model are shown here (top).
The artist Julian Beever uses properties of perspective projection in a creative way in street painting (bottom). (Pavement art copyright Julian Beever).

Let us take a cube and a polyhedron (polyhedra are discussed in Chapter 3) such that each pair of corresponding vertices of these two shapes is located on the same projection ray. In Figure 2.25 (left) we illustrate this by means of rays passing through the vertices p_1, p_2, and p_3 of the polyhedron and vertices q_1, q_2, and q_3 of the cube. Then both 3D objects possess exactly the same perspective image.

For psychological reasons, humans naturally recognize regular objects (such as a cube) instead of irregular ones. Therefore, a person looking from point e orthogonally to the projection plane P would assume to see a cube (when looking at the polyhedron). Note that the images $p_1^c p_2^c$ and $q_1^c q_2^c$ of the corresponding lines $p_1 p_2$ and $q_1 q_2$ of the two objects pass through the vanishing point v_x, whereas the images of $p_2 p_3$ and $q_2 q_3$ pass through v_y.

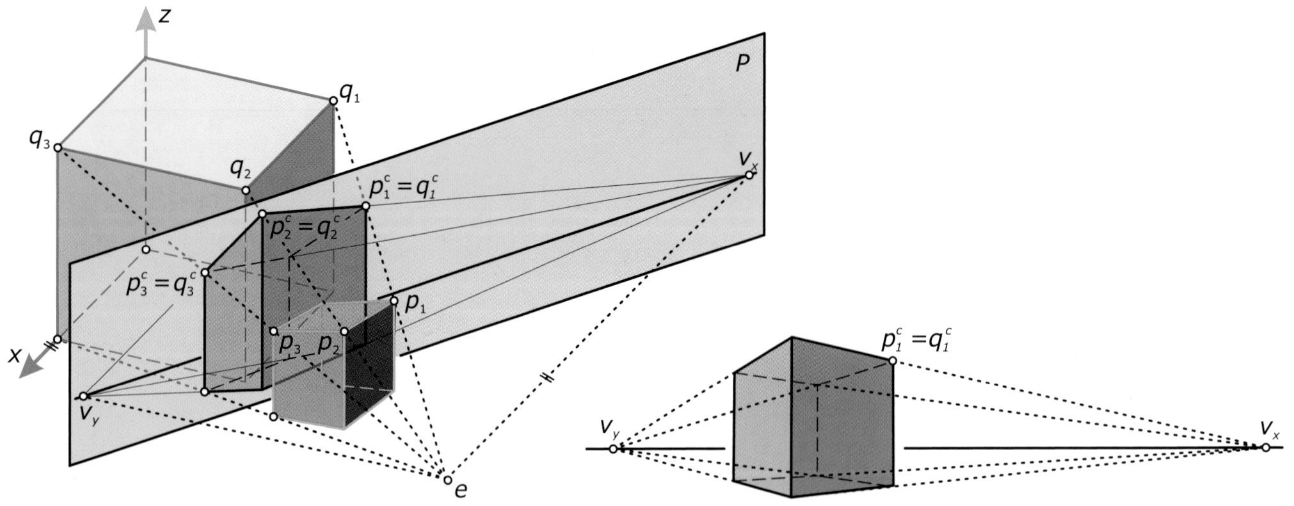

Fig. 2.25
How to deceive human vision. An observer in point e looking at the polyhedron would think he or she is seeing a cube (left).

The polyhedron as seen by the observer (middle).
The geometry behind Julian Beever's street paintings (right).

In Figure 2.25 (right) we have two different projection planes: a vertical plane P (which contains a picture of the final scene) and a horizontal plane P_1 (which serves as a drawing board). Every point r on a projection ray ep has the same image $r^c = p^c$ in the vertical projection plane P. Thus, the intersection point p_1 of the ray ep with the horizontal drawing board P_1 generates the same image p^c as the point p on a real object.

From the geometric point of view, to reproduce such street paintings we only have to project all points of the desired final scene in P into another projection plane P_1. Then, after removing the vertical plane P an observer positioned at point e would believe he or she is seeing the original scene while looking at a distorted image (blue lines) on the pavement.

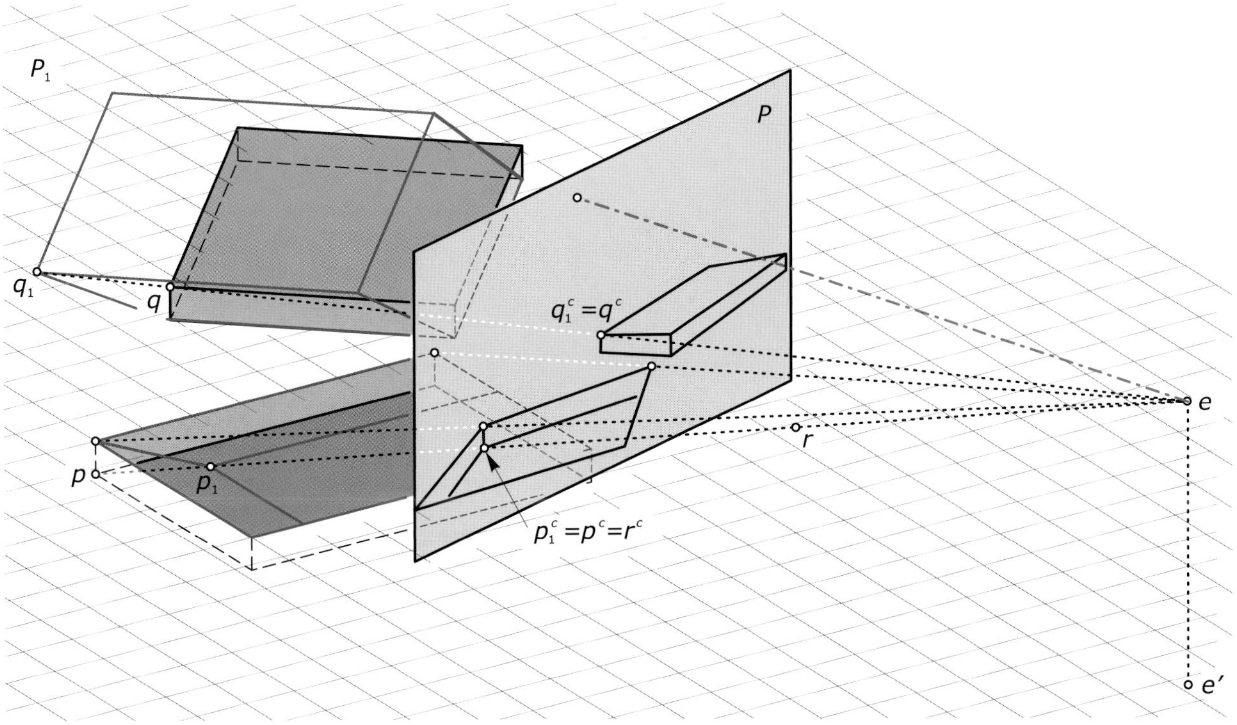

Fig. 2.26
Lighting with distant light, point light, or spotlight casts sharp shadows.

distant light *point light* *spot light*

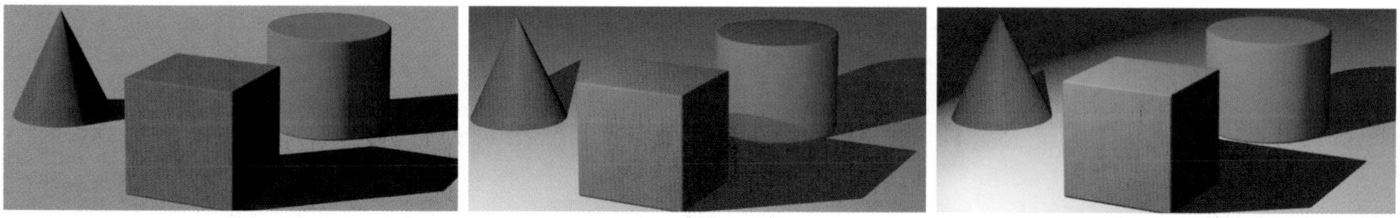

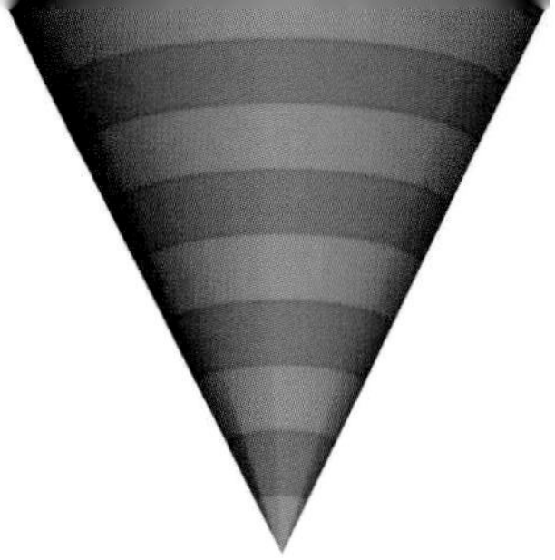

Light, Shadow, and Rendering.

A proper application of perspective projection is one key for presenting architecture and design in a realistically looking way. But without appropriate lighting our modeled objects would appear "flat" instead of spatial. To get the best visualization results, we now deal with various light sources and rendering methods.

Light sources. From the geometric point of view, we have lighting with *distant light* and *point light* as companion pieces to parallel projection and perspective projection. These lighting methods have the same properties as their corresponding projections.

In addition to these geometric properties, we have to obey the principle that distant light is considered of constant luminance, whereas point light is fading (Figure 2.26). The farther away the point light is the less light is received by the object. Rendering software normally assume that light is fading reciprocally to the squared distance.

Lighting with a *spotlight* is a special form of lighting with a point light. Contrary to point light, only a limited area within a cone is lighted. Therefore, this light type is very useful for lighting specific areas of an object. In addition, a second coaxial cone is available. This cone controls the width of the falloff zone from the illuminated cone to the spotlight edge (Figure 2.27). Within this area, the spotlight slowly fades away to no light.

Fig. 2.27
Spotlight.

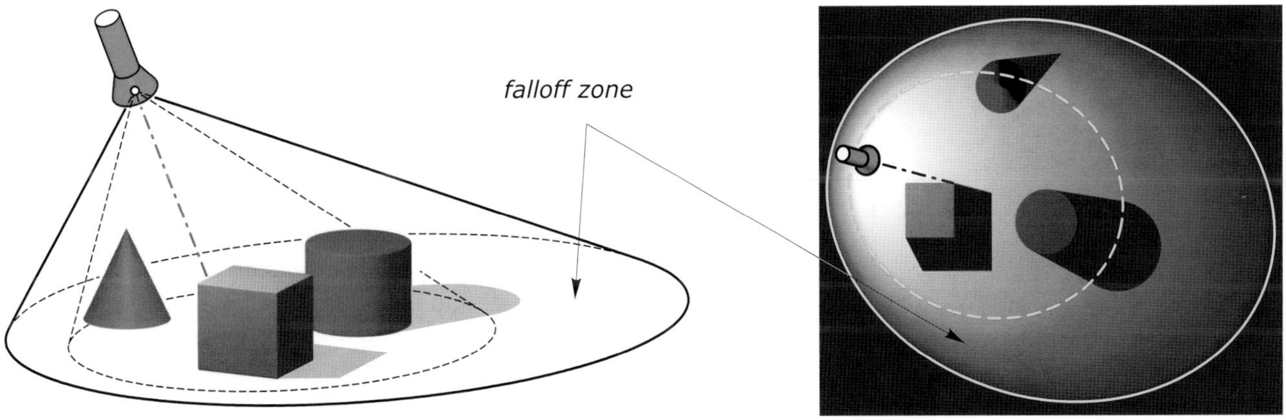

Boundaries of shadows—cast by a single distant light, a point light or a spotlight—are very sharp and therefore not too realistic. To obtain a smooth transition between illuminated and shadowed areas, we can bring into play a bunch of point lights or spotlights and position them within a small area.

These lights cast realistic-looking shadows, but with the disadvantage of increasing computing time. Therefore, rendering software provides more sophisticated lighting methods such as those provided by *linear* and *area lights.* Linear light can be considered a set of point lights positioned along a line. Such point lights send out light equally in all directions (Figure 2.28).

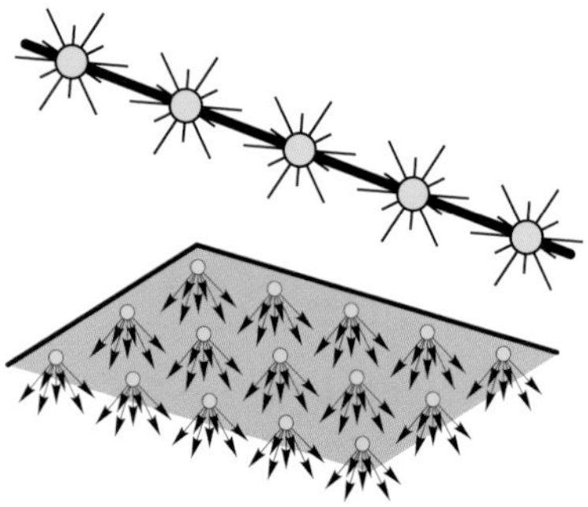

Fig. 2.28
Linear and area lights can be considered sets of point lights located on a line or within a polygon.

By placing light sources within a flat polygon, we obtain an area light. These light sources send out light rays with the same luminance. Point and area lights are great for indoor lighting, when fluorescent lamps or flat light panels are used (Figure 2.29).

Two other important lights provided by most rendering systems are *ambient light* and *flash light*. Ambient light controls the brightness of the entire scene, whereas flash light is a special point light located at the camera's position. Changing the luminance of the flash light brightens all faces seen from the camera position. Note that ambient light and flash light do not cast visible shadows. Their only purpose is to regulate the brightness of the scene.

area light

Fig. 2.29
Linear and area lights are largely used for the rendering of indoor scenes (images courtesy of Benjamin Schneider, Georg Wieshofer, Gerhard Schmid).

Rendering methods. To achieve high-quality images, we additionally assign textures and materials to our objects. To ensure realistic-looking textures, there are various *lighting models* that try to describe the interaction between surfaces and lights. Lighting models combine numerous factors that specify the color of an object.

For best simulation of the behavior of light, physical effects such as reflection, transparency, or even refraction are also integrated into the mathematical description of lighting models. These mathematical models are designed to produce a good approximation of real-world lighting in a feasible computing time. A deeper exploration of these methods is far beyond the scope of this book. Therefore, we only deal with some basic aspects. We distinguish between *local* and *global lighting models* (Figure 2.30).

- Local lighting models include only the interaction of the light source with the object. They are rough but good approximations of real-world lighting and are therefore used for fast rendering methods such as *flat* or *Phong shading* (explained in material following).
- Global lighting models are more accurate approximations of reality. They take into consideration physical properties and the interaction between light and objects as well as the interaction between objects. Therefore, these models also allow the representation of mirror and refraction effects. They integrate all objects of a modeled scene to calculate the color of every object point. Typical rendering methods based on global lighting models are *ray tracing* and *radiosity*. Because of the complexity of the underlying mathematical models, these rendering methods are more time consuming than local lighting models.

To understand the various rendering methods, we consider the local interaction between the light and a single face of an object (Figure 2.31). We study the reflection of a single ray r at a plane P. Let n be a line perpendicular to the plane P. The physical law of reflection says that the incoming light ray r_i, the outgoing light ray r_o, and n are lying in a plane.

Fig. 2.30
Local lighting models (such as Phong shading) versus global lighting models, such as ray tracing.

Fig. 2.31
The wave angle determines the interaction between light and an object's face.

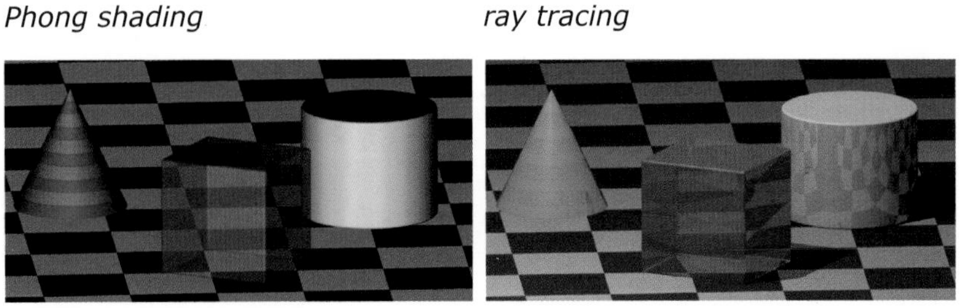

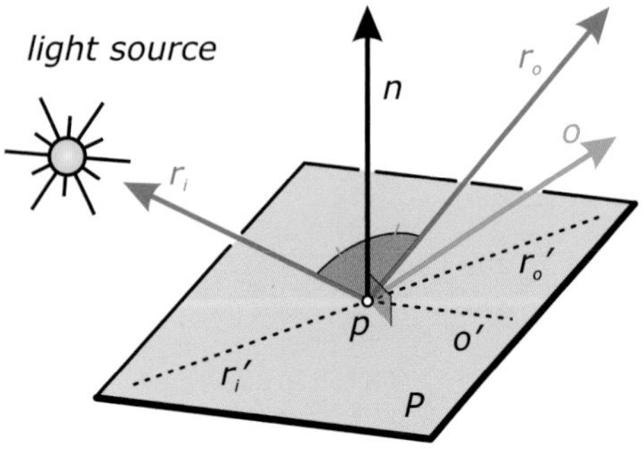

In addition, the angle between r_i and n is equal to the angle n and r_o. Let o be a ray pointing toward the observer's eye or the camera position. Then, the angle between r_o and o defines the intensity of the light reflected in the direction of the camera. If o and r_o coincide, a maximum of light is reflected toward the observer. Obeying this principle and other specifications of the attached material, a specific color is calculated. This color is then associated with point p.

To simplify the calculation process, we assume that all 3D objects are represented as polyhedral models with planar faces (Figure 2.32). As we have seen, the position of the normal n is crucial to the appearance of the plane P. Therefore, in a first step the normal of every planar facet is calculated.

By means of Figure 2.33, we recognize that at different points of the same facet the angle between the incoming ray and the normal can change its magnitude, although the normals are parallel in all of these points. As a consequence, every point of this facet reflects the light ray in another direction. This means that every point appears to have another color.

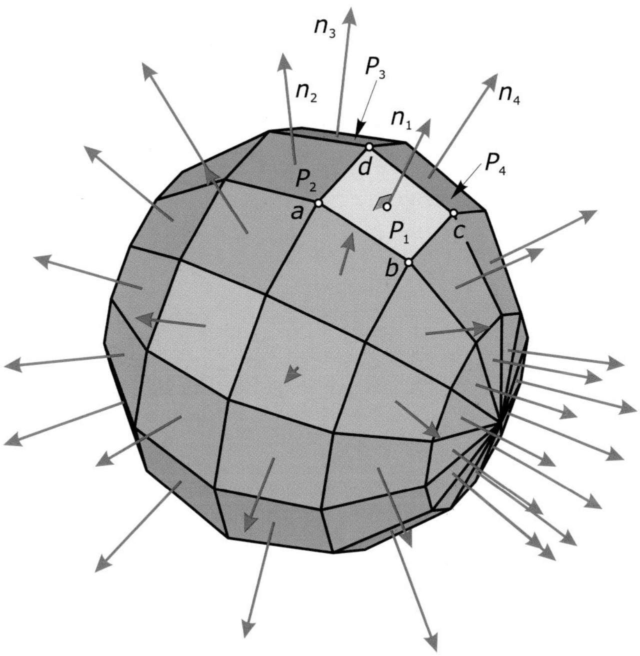

Fig. 2.32
Polyhedral model of a sphere and the normals of the polygons.

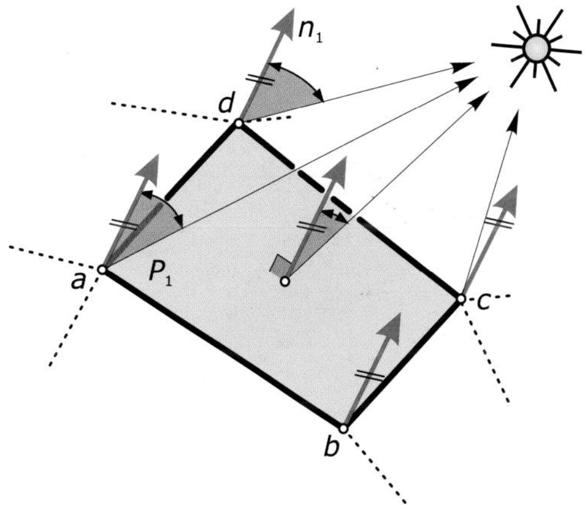

Fig. 2.33
When applying point light, we have different angles in each point of a plane.

Computing the color of each point (pixel) in the entire scene is very complex and time consuming. Thus, various simplifications are made to obtain good results in a reasonable amount of time. Depending on the type of simplification, we distinguish among the following rendering methods.

- *Flat shading*: Only one color is assigned to all points of the same polygon. This algorithm is very fast, but the quality of the image is poor. The boundaries of the polygons are clearly visible.
- *Gouraud shading* (Figure 2.34): The luminance is calculated in the vertices of the polygon to associate specific colors with these points. With the help of a linear interpolation process (see Geometry Primer), the color of every point (pixel) of the facet is approximated. First, the color is linearly interpolated along the edges. Thus, for example, the color changes from blue to green along the edge *da* and from blue to red along the other edge *db*. Then, using a linear interpolation along a scan line *ef* we obtain the color for point *p*. This algorithm is more time consuming than flat shading, but the quality increases enormously. In addition, we need to calculate the normal in a vertex of a facet. To explain the calculation procedure, let's take another look at Figure 2.34. In vertex *d*, four facets with different normals meet. To obtain a smooth transition between these facets we take the mean vector $n = 1/4(n_1 + n_2 + n_3 + n_4)$ of all adjacent facets.

Fig. 2.34
Gouraud shading: knowing the luminance of the vertices, the color of each point is calculated via linear interpolation. Phong shading: starting with the normals of the vertices, first the normal at a point *p* is calculated using the same linear interpolation process. Then the color of the point *p* is evaluated.

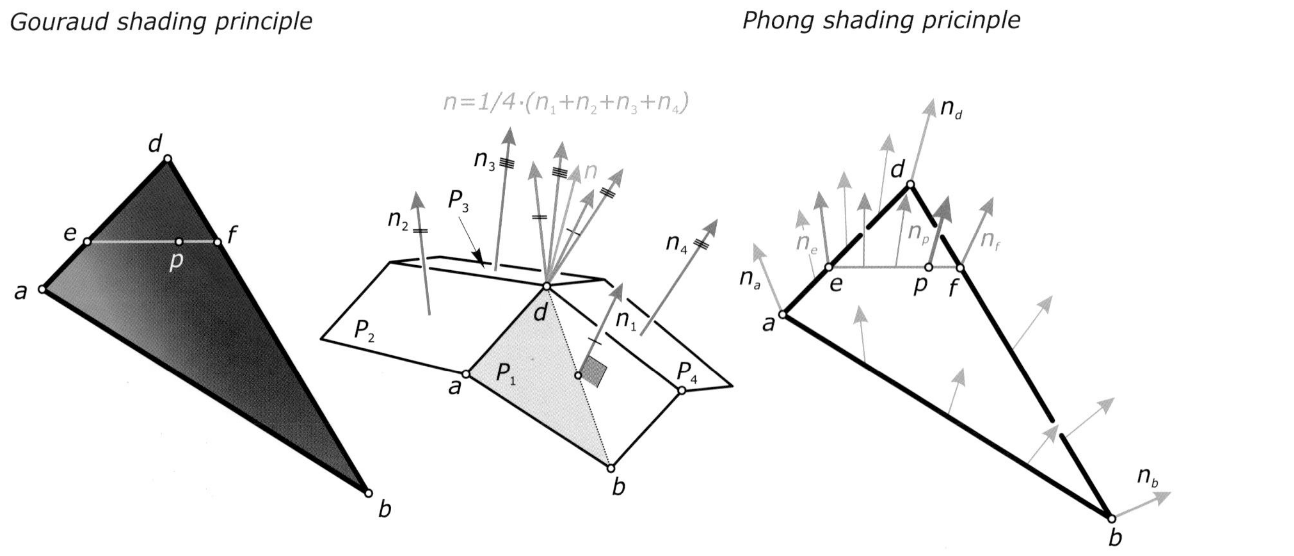

- *Phong shading*: This method applies a linear interpolation to the vertices' normals. This interpolation process is the same as that applied to Gouraud shading, with the difference that we obtain an interpolated normal vector n_p in point p. With the help of n_p the point's color is finally evaluated. This algorithm demands more computer power but produces results with better quality. Especially when using glossy materials, Phong shading should be applied to obtain the best results in a reasonable length of time.

Using a simple geometric object, the differences and limits of these local rendering methods are illustrated in Figure 2.35. These methods are acceptable approximations of reality, but not with regard to physical effects such as reflection or refraction. To achieve photorealistic renderings, we have to use global methods such as ray tracing and radiosity.

Ray tracing is based on the scanning of the pixels of the screen. Rays emitted from the eye point are sent through every pixel of the screen. Then each ray r is tracked back through the entire scene until it has reached a light source. During its way through the scene the ray is reflected or refracted at all intersection points with objects and thereby split into different parts (Figure 2.36).

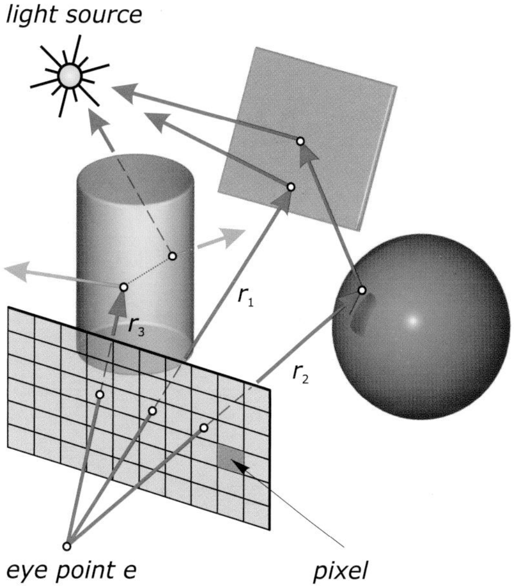

Fig. 2.36
Ray tracing: a ray r is tracked back from the eye to the light source.

Fig. 2.35
The image quality depends on the rendering method. Whereas flat shading is a very fast algorithm with poor quality, Gouraud shading and Phong shading yield good quality at the expense of increasing rendering time.

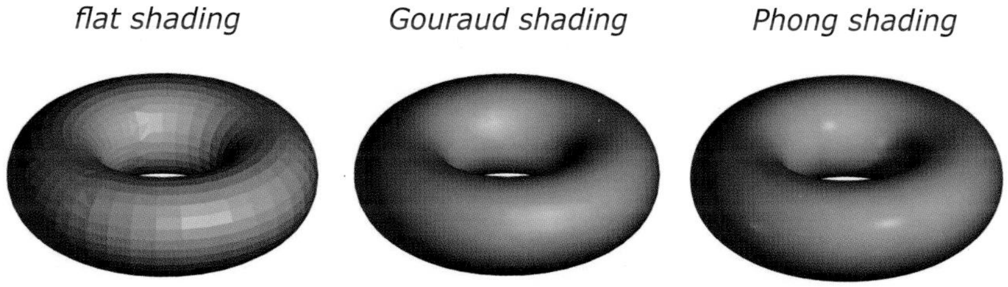

These new arising rays are handled like the original rays. They are in turn also tracked back to the light sources and can again split into further rays when striking an object. Thus, scenes with an extensive amount of objects generate an immense number of rays coming from multiple reflections. The ray tracing method is more time consuming but supplies rather good-looking images.

Radiosity is an even more complicated rendering method, with the disadvantage of enormously increasing computation time. It employs sophisticated mathematical methods. Especially when we use this method for indoor renderings, we are also able to visualize diffuse reflections. This leads to impressive images (Figure 2.37).

So far we have learned only the basics about lighting models and rendering methods. Further important facts for sophisticated renderings can be found in specialized literature on rendering techniques.

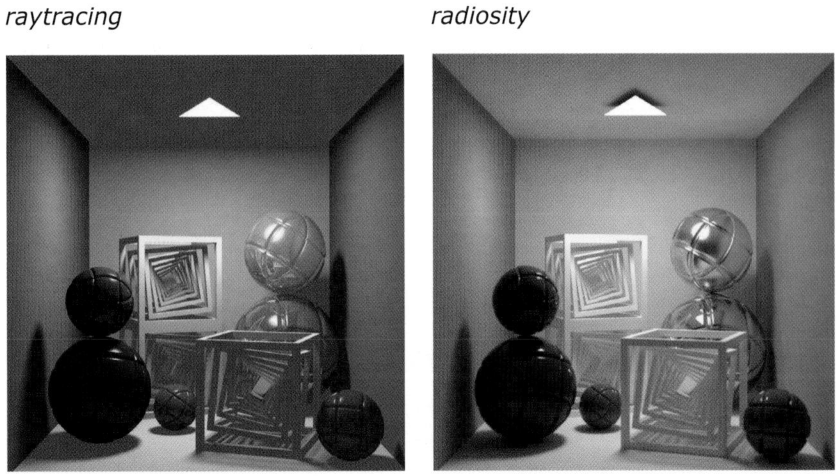

Fig. 2.37
The same scene rendered with ray tracing and radiosity. Using only a single area light illustrates the differences between these two rendering methods. Radiosity even calculates the diffuse light reflections of all objects. (Images courtesy of Alexander Wilkie and Andrea Weidlich.)

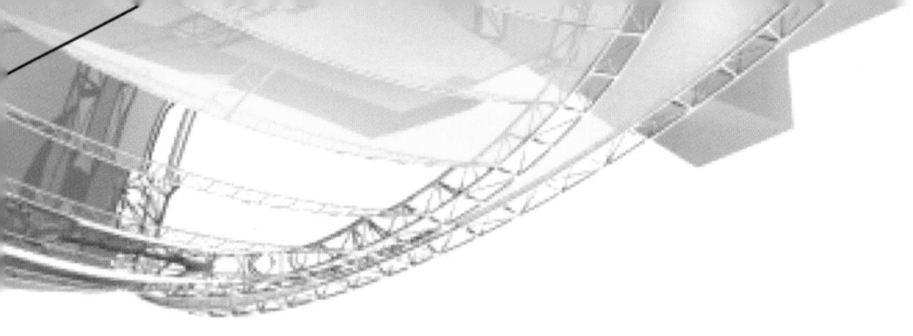

Orthogonal and Oblique Axonometric Projections

The ability to create freehand sketches is an important skill of designers and architects. Many design concepts and ideas are difficult to express verbally. Quickly created sketches can be a powerful aid in communicating design ideas. The few properties of parallel projection mentioned previously enable us to correctly sketch auxiliary views of objects.

Given the distortion factors d_x, d_y, and d_z respectively of the three axes x, y, and z of a Cartesian coordinate system, we can draw the images x^p, y^p, z^p of the coordinate axes arbitrarily (Figure 2.38). With these specifications, we can draw the parallel projection of the unit points $u_x(1,0,0)$, $u_y(0,1,0)$, and $u_z(0,0,1)$. By drawing lines parallel to the

Fig. 2.38
Drawing of an auxiliary view of a point $q(0.5|2|2)$.

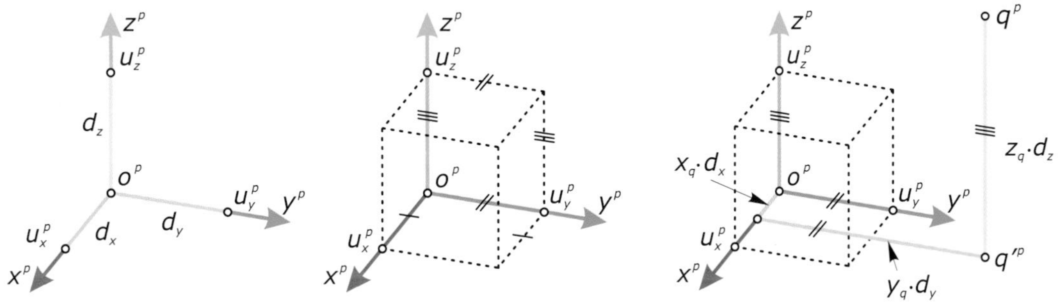

Fig. 2.39
An appropriate choice of distortion factors and the images x^p, y^p, and z^p of the coordinate axes produces more realistic sketches.

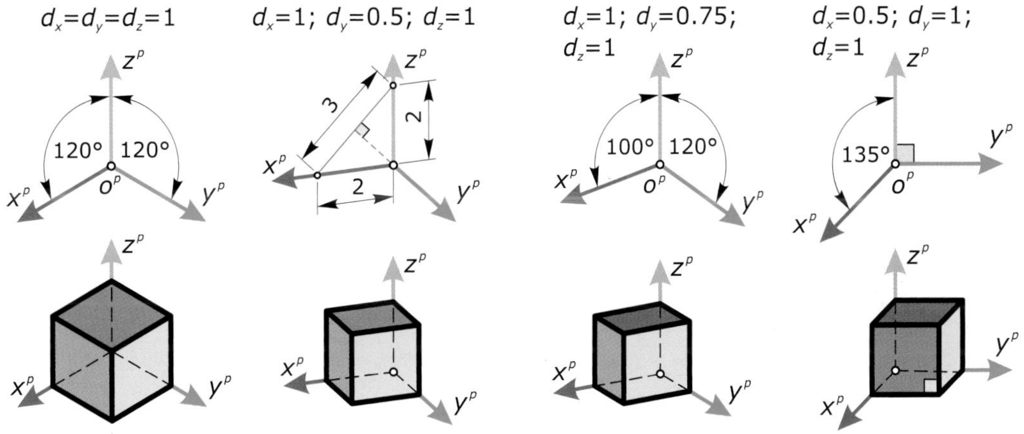

coordinate axes through the unit points, we obtain the parallel projection of a cube with edge length 1. This *unit cube* can be a quick visual help in determining whether the chosen specifications will generate a convenient view.

The parallel projection of an arbitrary point q with coordinates x_q, y_q, and z_q is then determined as shown in Figure 2.38. The coordinates of q are multiplied with the corresponding distortion factor and all necessary construction lines are parallel to the axes.

Example:

Parallel projection of a canopy. Given are top and front views of a simplified canopy, the parallel projections of the coordinate frame, and the distortion factors (Figure 2.40a). We start with sketching the octagon in the xy-plane, obeying the distortion factors and the parallelism of the lines. Then we draw the vertical columns (Figure 2.40b). Connecting the images of the endpoints of these columns with point v, we obtain the parallel projection of the canopy (Figure 2.40c).

Now we are going to construct an additional quadratic pyramid with the base polygon *a, b, c* and *d,* which intersects the existing canopy (Figure 2.40d). We choose an appropriate height (15 units) and sketch the image w^p of the pyramid's apex. The intersection lines of the canopy's faces and the pyramid can now be constructed directly in the picture.

The lines aw and $1v$ lie in the same plane. Therefore, we obtain the intersection point e immediately. The pyramid's face abw intersects the vertical plane through the edge $2v$ in the line f. Thus, we obtain the point g—the intersection point of the line $2v$ with the pyramid. The remaining intersection points and lines can be constructed analogously, or as an alternative, we take advantage of the symmetry of the object (Figure 2.40e).

Fig. 2.40
Sketching of a simplified model of a canopy.
(a) Given are top view and front view of the canopy, coordinate frame, and distortion factors.
(b) Construction of the octagon and the vertical columns.
(c) Sketching of the canopy.
(d) Construction of the intersection of the canopy with a quadratic pyramid.
(e) Finishing the sketch.

(a)

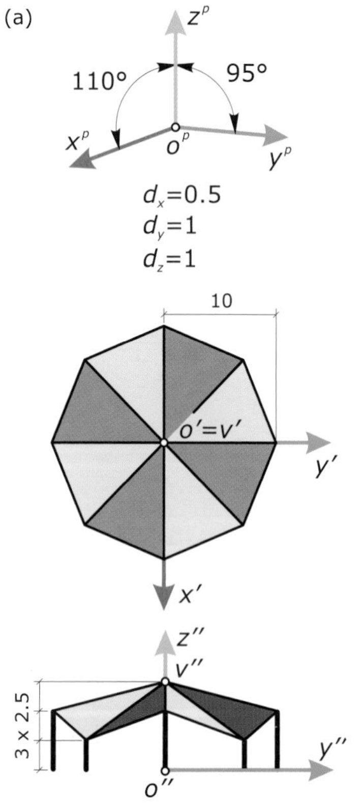

(b)

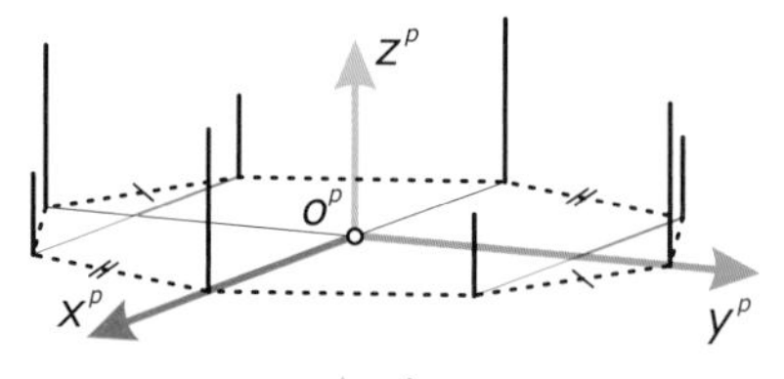

(c)

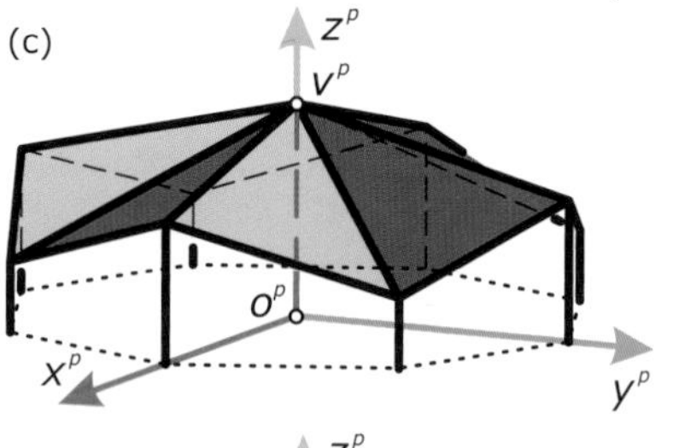

(d)

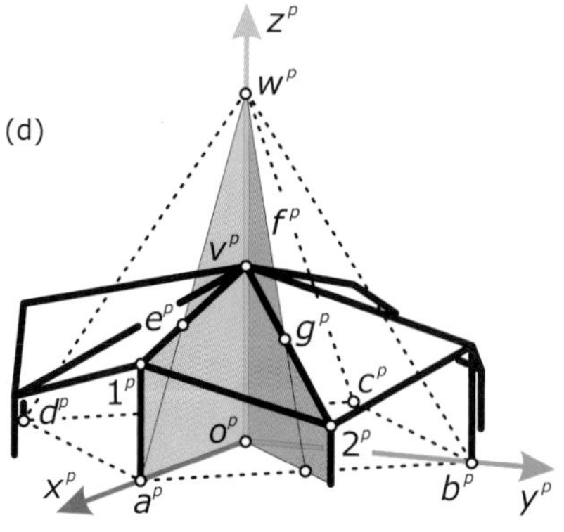

(e)

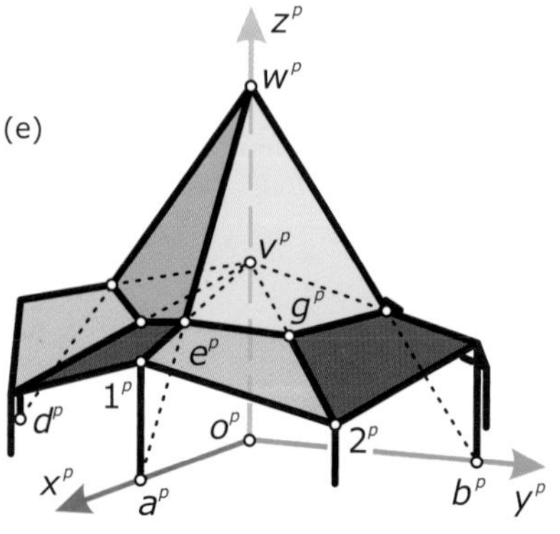

Assuming that we can select arbitrary distortion factors and views of x, y, and z, this construction ensures the correct sketching of every point q of the 3D space. Note that we are completely free in our choice of the distortion factors and the drawings of x^p, y^p, and z^p.

Nevertheless, if we use improper values the drawing will be geometrically correct but practically unusable. Some proper assumptions for values of the distortion factors d_x, d_y, and d_z and the parallel projections x^p, y^p, and z^p are shown in Figure 2.39.

Visibility of objects. In most cases, we sketch our design ideas and objects so that we are looking onto them from above (i.e., from the upper side of the xy-plane). But sometimes it can be necessary to create sketches that show the bottom of the objects. Thus, we have to provide a view of the bottom side of the xy-plane.

The choice of the mutual position of the parallel projections x^p, y^p, and z^p of the axes x, y, and z already determines from which side the object is seen. This is the case because we always assume a right-hand orientation of the coordinate frame. We recognize that by looking at the upper side of the xy-plane, the 90-degree rotation of the x-axis into the y-axis is always seen in counterclockwise direction (Figure 2.41a,b). Otherwise, when looking at the bottom side of the xy-plane, this rotation appears as a clockwise rotation (Figure 2.41c).

In this way, we obtain an easy rule that helps us determine the correct view. If the "shorter" rotation (rotation angle smaller than 180 degrees) of the x^p-axis into the y^p-axis is counterclockwise (this rotation is called mathematically positive), a view from above is given. In the case of a clockwise rotation, a view from below is determined. Therefore, by looking at the sketches of the coordinate axes we can easily find out which view is given. Figure 2.42 illustrates this rule with examples.

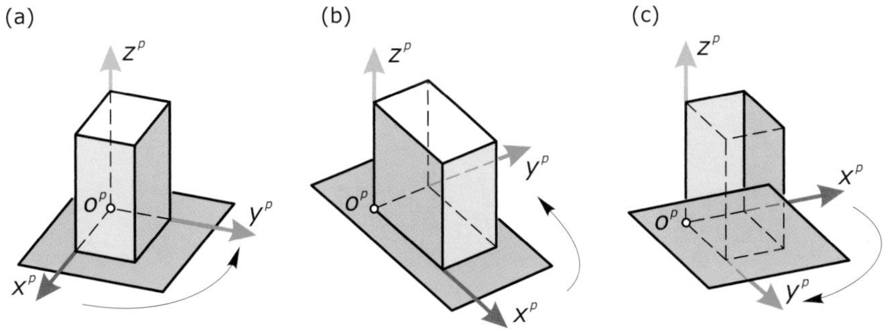

Fig. 2.41
The mutual position of x^p, y^p, and z^p determines if the object is seen from above (a,b) or from below (c).

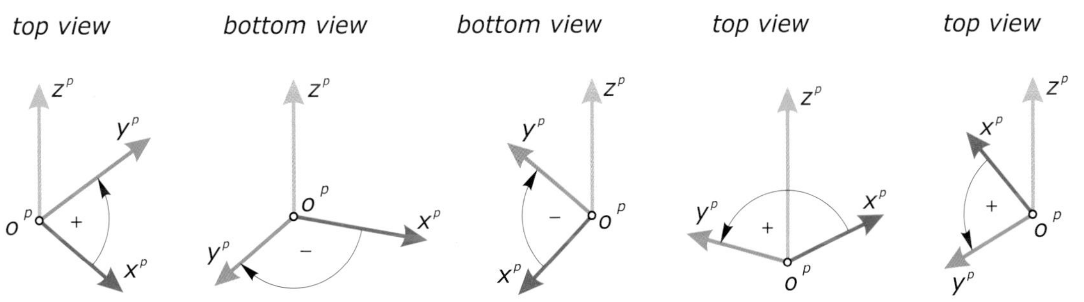

Fig. 2.42
Views and corresponding coordinate frames.

Construction of shadows. Sometimes hand-constructed axonometric views seem to lack spatial expression. The remedy is to add shadows. Thus, when using an appropriate distant light (which casts striking shadows) we can enhance the image with little effort. To construct geometrically correct shadows, we have to know some basic terms and rules (Figure 2.43).

We distinguish between object faces that are turned toward the light source and those turned away from the light source. The boundary between these two types of faces is called the *shading* or *the shade line*. Points on the shading are candidates for casting the *shadow lines* of the object. The shadow lines are the border between the *cast shadows* and the illuminated areas.

To construct the shadow lines, we intersect light rays passing through the shading with planes and surfaces that contain cast shadows. Note that all faces turned away from the light source are unlit and form the so-called *attached shadow*, sometimes also referred to as the *shade*. The spatial impression may be improved even further by coloring the shade brighter than the cast shadows.

In the case of distant light, we find the cast shadow p^s of a point p in the horizontal plane P as the intersection point of the light ray l_p and its top view l'_p (Figure 2.43, bottom right). Given the fact that all light rays are parallel, we easily find the cast shadows of all object points contained in the shading.

Recall the properties of parallel projection introduced at the beginning of the chapter. Using them improves the construction of the shadow lines. Thus, a line segment pq parallel to P casts a shadow p^sq^s of equal length parallel to pq.

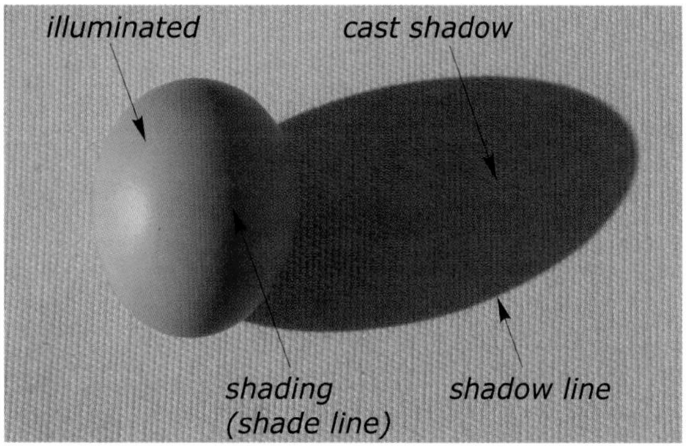

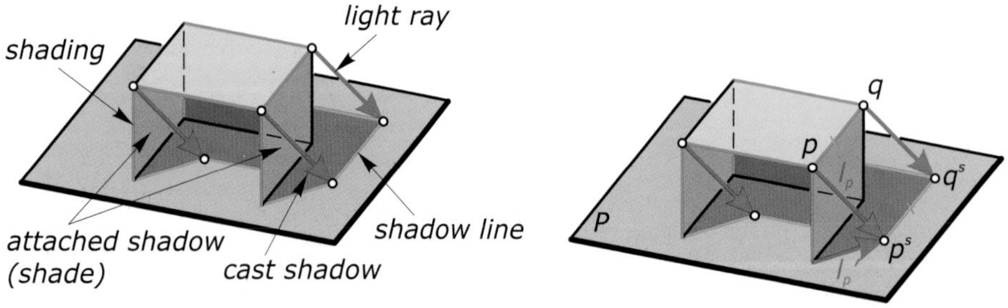

Fig. 2.43
Some terminology and basic rules for constructing geometrically correct shadows.

Sectional views. Occasionally, important parts of internal structures are not visible in the principal views. In this case, *sectional views* can be used to expose those internal details. Figure 2.45 shows an object intersected by *cutting planes* in perspective and sectional view. Hatching represents those parts of the object where the cutting plane passes through solid material.

We recognize that sectional views do not contain hidden lines, but they include all lines that are directly visible. Thus, sectional views are often easier to understand and help to clarify orthographic views that would be difficult to understand because of an excessive amount of hidden lines. In addition to standard top, front, and side orthographic views, sectional views are helpful in visualizing the dimensions of an object.

Example:

Constructing shadows by hand. Given are the axonometric view of a simple geometric model and the direction of the light rays. We sketch all existing shadows visible in this view (Figure 2.44). Regarding the direction of the given light ray, we find the faces of the cuboid with attached shadows and the shading of the entire object (marked in green). Analogous to Figure 2.43, we construct the projection of the shading and thus the cast shadows in the horizontal plane *P*.

Then we continue with the cast shadow of the vertical edge *e* into the inclined plane *E*. We construct the intersection point *1* of the vertical line *e* with the plane *E*. The cast shadow of *e* is defined by the points 1 and 2 and ends in the cast shadow p^s of *p*. Finally, the cast shadow of the horizontal line *pq* in the plane *E* can be found by back-projecting the point $d^s_{1,2}$, which is the cast shadow of the points d_1 and d_2. Note also that point 3, the intersection point of *pq* with *E*, could be used to construct the cast shadow of *pq* in *E*.

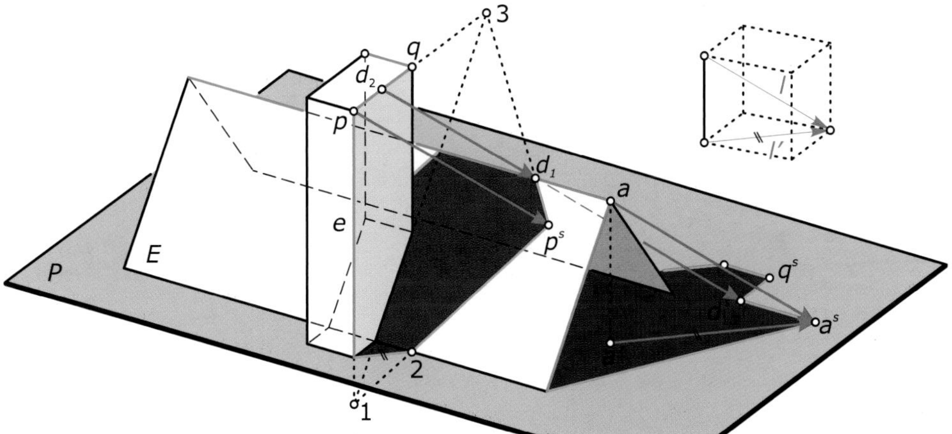

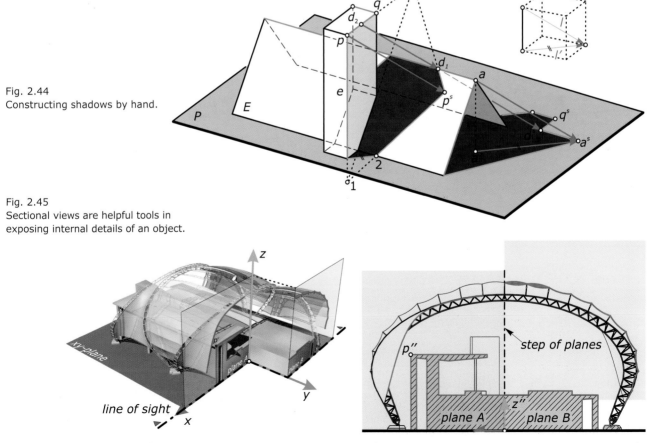

Fig. 2.44
Constructing shadows by hand.

Fig. 2.45
Sectional views are helpful tools in exposing internal details of an object.

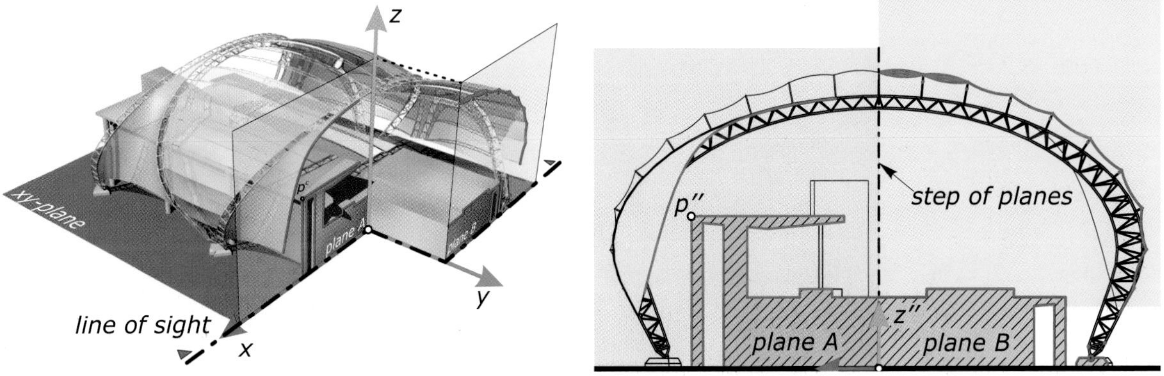

Sketching images of curves and circles. Sketching straight lines and objects with only planar faces is easily done obeying the few simple rules stated previously. To sketch curves, we draw the projections of a sufficient number of curve points and tangents (tangents are explained in Chapter 7). We join the projected curve points to a smooth curve. Thereby, we respect tangency of the image curve to the projected tangents (Figure 2.46).

Sketching spheres. Sketching spheres is generally trickier than sketching circles: In 3D space, all projection rays that touch a sphere form a cylinder (Figure 2.8). This cylinder touches the sphere along a great circle c. The image c^p of c is the image of the sphere.

In the case of a normal projection, the situation is simple (Figure 2.10). The circle c lies in a plane parallel to the projection plane and hence its image is also a circle. Thus, the image of a sphere under normal projection is a circle. In the case of an oblique projection, the situation is more difficult (Figure 2.8). In general, c is not lying in a plane parallel to the projection plane and thus the image c^p of the sphere is an ellipse.

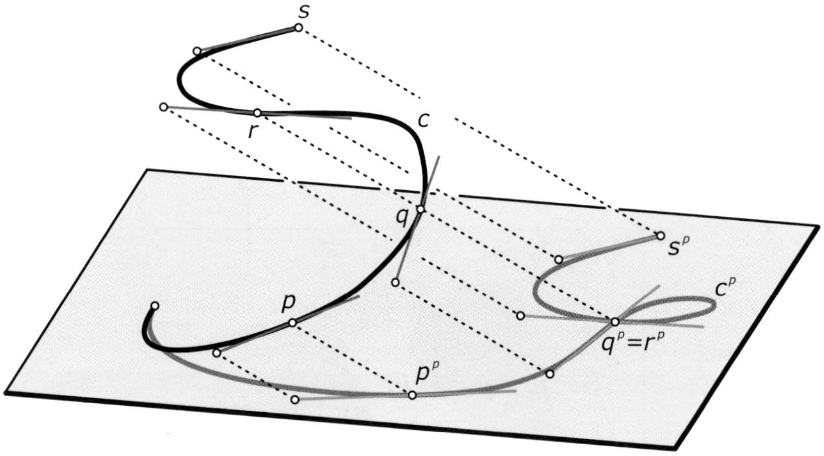

Fig. 2.46
The projections of curve tangents touch the projected curve.

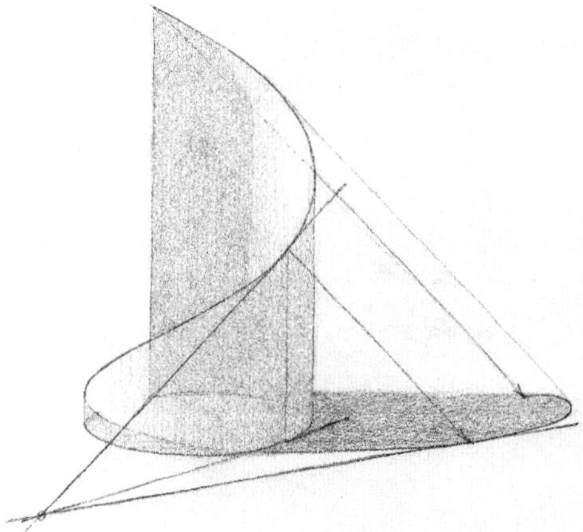

Example:

Sketching of a cubical clock. The parallel projection of the coordinate system is given as shown in Figure 2.47 (top). For simplification, all distortion factors are taken equal to 1. We create the projection of the clock's housing—which has the form of a truncated cube (see Chapter 3)—as described in the example "canopy" (Figure 2.40).

The vertices of the circumscribed octagon lie on the edges of the cube. They can be found exactly by calculating their distances from the vertices of the cube (Figure 2.47, bottom right). The sides of this octagon touch the projection of the circle at the midpoints. Thus, we have eight points and tangents—which is sufficient to sketch the smooth curve c^p. We mention here without a proof that the parallel projection of a circle c is an ellipse c^p.

Fig. 2.47 Sketching of an axonometric view of a circle.

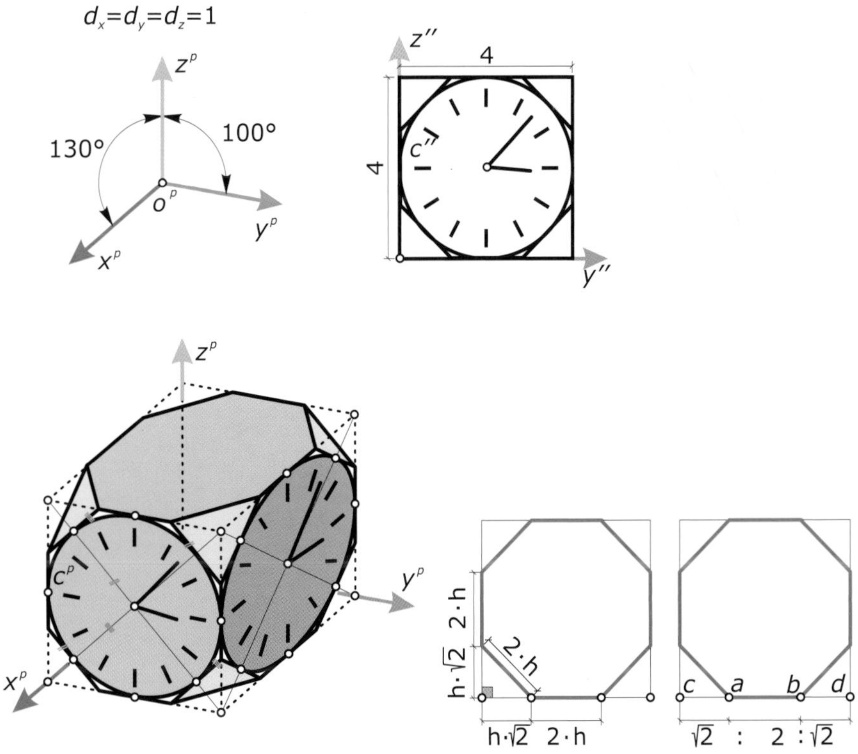

Note that in general the images of the points where the circle touches the octagon are not the vertices of c^p. As we can see, the ratio dist(a,b) : dist$(c,d) = 2 : 2 + \sqrt{2} \approx 4{:}9.666...$ which is approximately 4:10. This property can be used when producing a freehand sketch of a circle. We divide the sides of a circumscribed square with the ratio 3:4:3 to get a rather good approximation of the points *a* and *b* (Figure 2.48). Using lines parallel to the diagonals of the square, we can easily sketch the circumscribed octagon and the ellipse c^p.

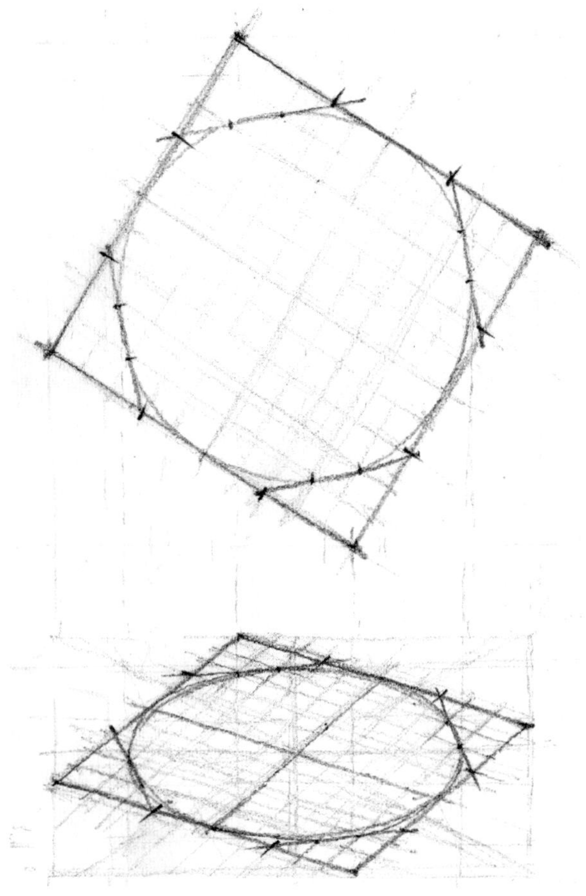

Fig. 2.48 Freehand sketch of a circle using two circumscribed squares.

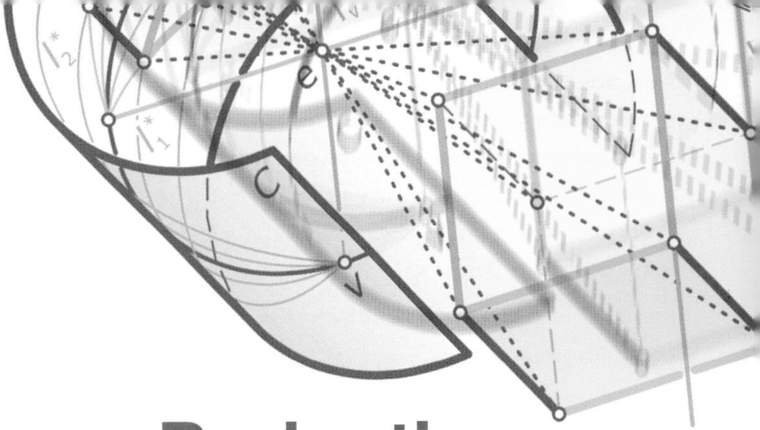

Nonlinear Projections

Parallel and perspective projections are good tools for producing photorealistic images. Both projections are based on the fact that generally straight lines in space appear as straight lines in the image. We call them *linear projections*. By generalizing the concept of projections, we will derive some interesting new knowledge that can be used for design purposes.

Recall the introduction of perspective projection (Figure 2.15). We used a projection plane P and an eye point e. To construct the projection of a point p we constructed the intersection point of the ray $r = ep$ with the projection plane P. Let us now exchange the plane P by a projection cylinder C with vertical generators (Figure 2.49).

The image p^* of a point p is generated exactly the same way as described previously. In addition, the projection of a line l is created with the same instruction: we connect the line l with the eye point e to get a plane E, which has to be intersected with the projection cylinder C. Thus, we recognize that the images of vertical lines are straight lines, whereas the images l^* of arbitrary lines l are curves. This type of projection does not preserve linearity. We call it a *nonlinear projection*.

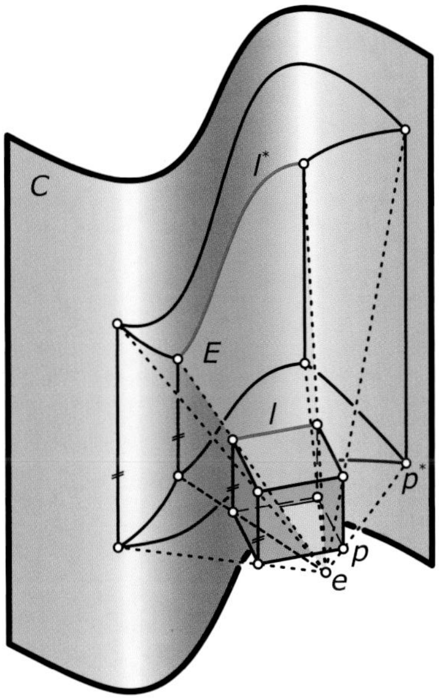

Fig. 2.49
Projection of a cube onto a cylinder.

Nonlinear projections arise from perspective projection by exchanging the projection plane with a cylinder or a sphere. In the following we examine the projection of spatial points and curves onto a spatial projection surface. Subsequently, the chapter discusses the more difficult task of deriving a planar image.

Actually, the usage of a spherical projection surface seems to be an obvious idea because the human eyeball is more a sphere than a simple plane. One might also use more complex projection surfaces to obtain even more fancy-looking images on nonplanar surfaces.

Cylindrical projection. Let C be a rotational cylinder with z-parallel axis (Figure 2.50). Then the images of vertical straight lines in space are the vertical generators of C. All lines lying in the horizontal plane through the eye point e are projected into the horizon h, which is a horizontal circle. All other straight lines, with the exception of the projection rays and the lines parallel to the generators of the cylinder, have ellipses as images.

In contradiction to perspective projection, the images of parallel lines l_1 and l_2 meet in two vanishing points v, w assuming that e lies within the projection cylinder. These vanishing points can be found as intersection points of the line l_v with C (compare this fact with the construction of vanishing points in perspective projection).

Note that the assumption that e lies within the cylinder C is an essential one. Otherwise, there would be many points in space that could not be depicted by this projection. A further remarkable fact is that in general the images c^* of circles c are not conics. They are the intersection curves of cones with the projection cylinder (see Chapter 7).

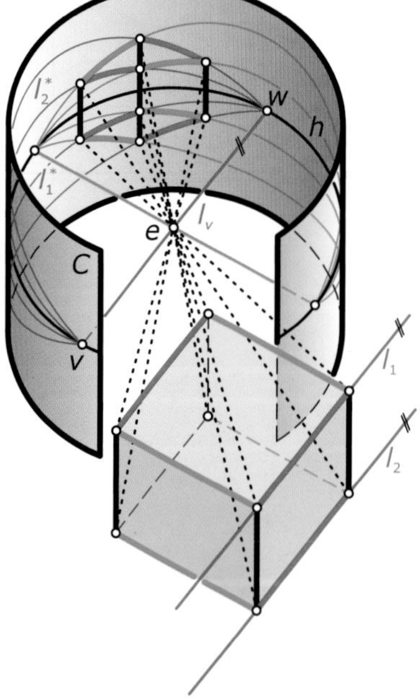

Fig. 2.50
Cylindrical projection of a cube.

Spherical projection. Now we exchange the projection plane P with a projection sphere S (Figure 2.51). We position the eye point e within the sphere to obtain images of all spatial points. The images of all straight lines, except the projection rays through e, are circles. Again, the images of parallel lines intersect each other in two vanishing points.

The images of circles are even more complicated curves. They are obtained as the intersection curves of a cone with apex e and the sphere S (see Chapter 7). If we move the eye point into the centre of the sphere, we have a special case. The vanishing points v and w are antipodal points of the sphere and the image of a circle whose axis passes through e is again a circle.

Creating a planar image. So far we have not dealt with the problem of how to transfer the 3D image, which lies on a curved projection surface, onto a flat sheet of paper. Projection cylinders can easily be unfolded, but during this process the curved images l^* of 3D straight lines l are distorted once more to l^{*d} (Figure 2.52). This unfolding procedure is a more complex type of nonlinear mapping, which is examined in detail in Chapter 15.

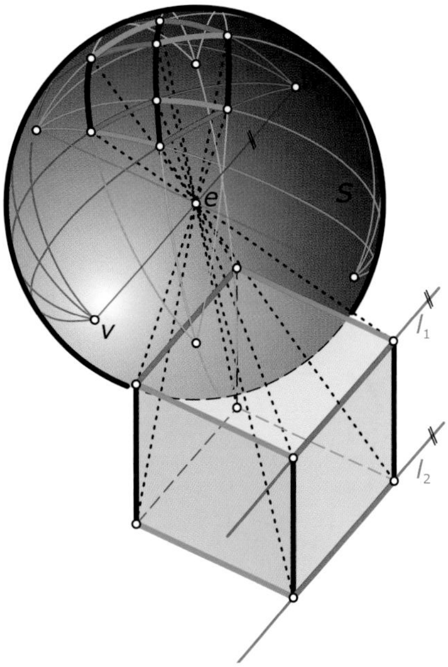

Fig. 2.51
A spherical projection with the eye point at the center of the projection sphere.

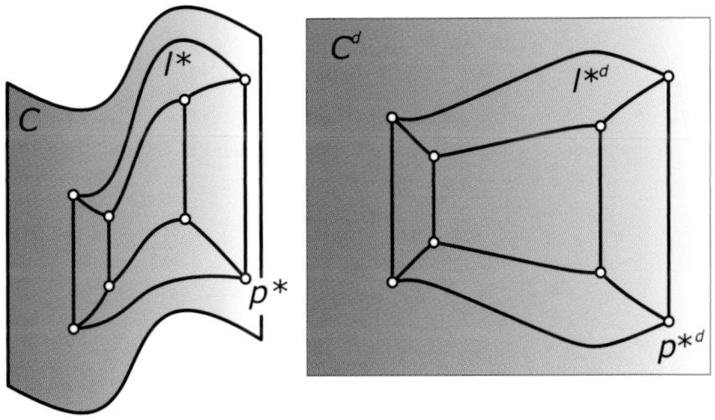

Fig. 2.52
A projection cylinder is unfolded into a plane.

It is impossible to unfold a sphere. Thus, we introduce another nonlinear projection—the *stereographic projection* (Figure 2.53). It projects the points of a sphere into a plane P. We select the projection center p (the new eye point) on the sphere (e.g., at the North Pole). The projection plane P has to be orthogonal to the line cp, where c is the center of the sphere.

Without a proof we state that circles, which lie on the sphere, are projected into circles or straight lines. Thus, a combination of a spherical projection and a stereographic projection depicts spatial straight lines as straight lines or circles—which makes it a perfect tool for generating interesting images.

Note that the stereographic projection is also used to map the earth's surface onto a plane because it additionally preserves the magnitude of angles.

Nonlinear projections can also be used to enlarge the vision cone. When we have to project objects that are outside the vision cone or the vision pyramid, nonlinear projections can be used to improve the visual impression. Moreover, nonlinear projections are appropriate tools for approximating panoramic (fish-eye) views. They have also been used by artists in paintings (Figure 2.54).

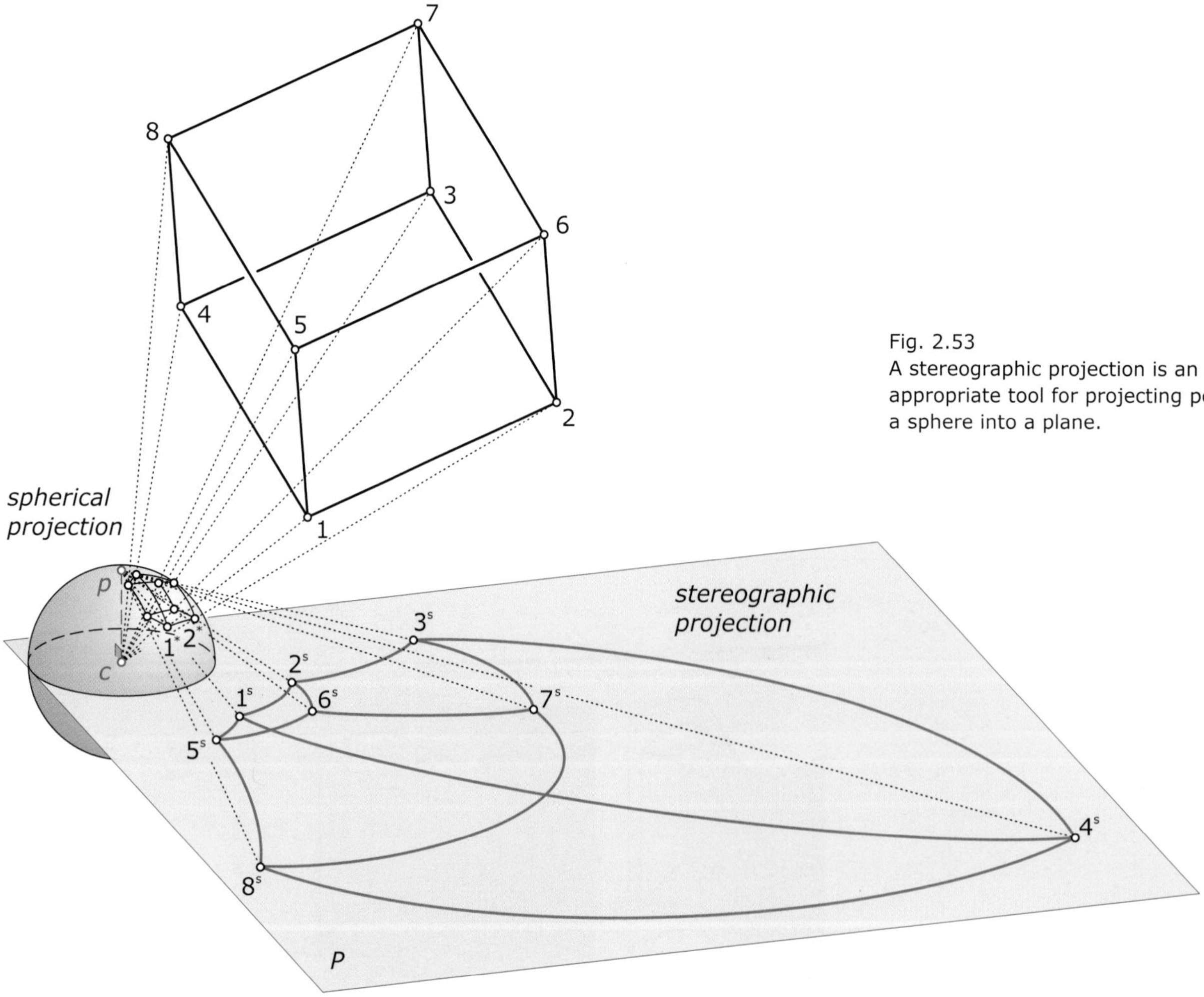

Fig. 2.53
A stereographic projection is an appropriate tool for projecting points of a sphere into a plane.

Fig. 2.54
(a) Pieter Neffs the Younger used a nonlinear projection to enlarge the vision cone in his 1746 painting "The Interior of the Cathedral in Antwerpen" (courtesy of Residenzgalerie Salzburg).
(b) A fish-eye photo and a modification (courtesy of Georg Glaeser).

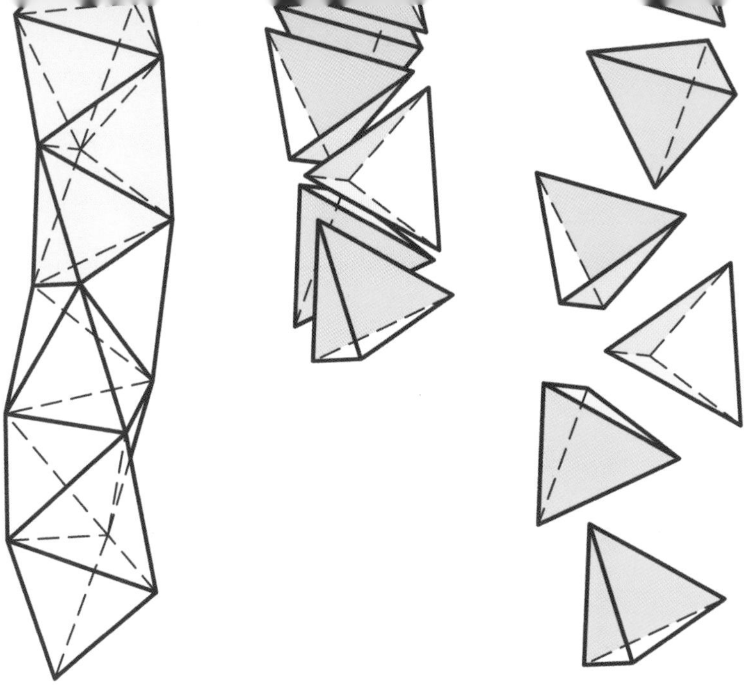

Chapter 3
Polyhedra and Polyhedral Surfaces

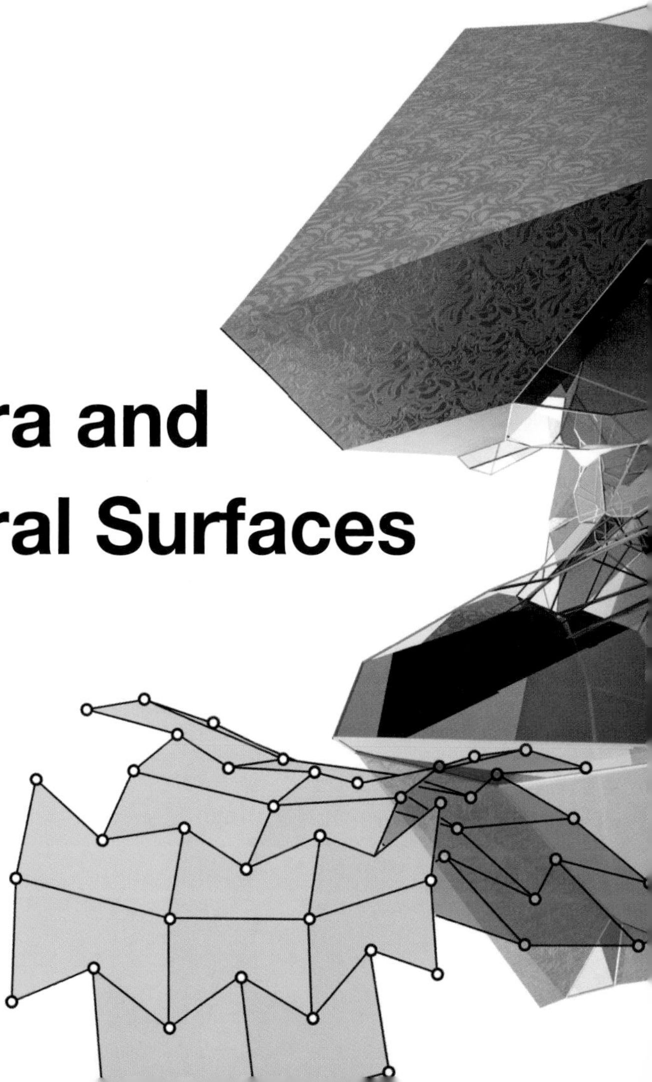

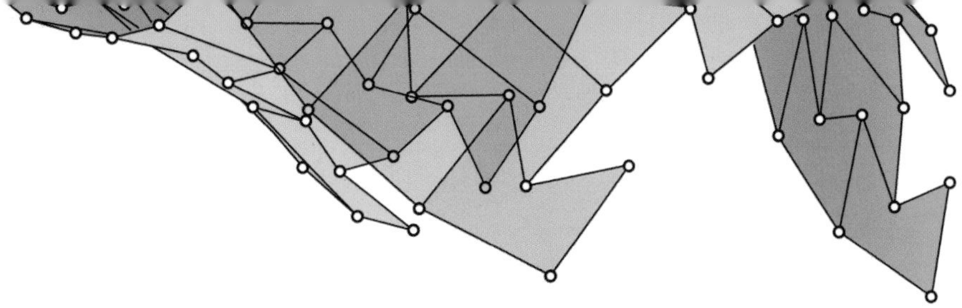

Polyhedra and Polyhedral Surfaces

Polyhedra and polyhedral surfaces are shapes bounded by planar faces. They are fundamental to many modeling purposes and are often found in architecture (Figure 3.1). Actually, most architecture features polyhedral surfaces because planar parts are easier to build than curved ones. We start our discussion with classical polyhedra such as pyramids and prisms that can be generated by extrusion of a polygon. To better understand why only a certain limited number of polyhedra can be realized with congruent regular faces, we study Platonic and Archimedean solids and some of their properties. Several of the Archimedean solids can be generated by appropriately cutting off vertex pyramids of Platonic solids. One of the Platonic solids, the icosahedron, is also the polyhedron from which geodesic spheres are usually deduced.

Parts of geodesic spheres are well known in architecture as geodesic domes. Geodesic spheres derived from an icosahedron consist of triangular faces only. Polyhedral surfaces are of great recent interest in architecture for the realization of freeform shapes (e.g., as steel-and-glass structures with planar glass panels.)

Fig. 3.1
Polyhedra and polyhedral surfaces in architecture.
(Left) The Seattle Public Library (1998-2004) by Rem Koolhaas and Joshua Ramus.
(Right) Part of the glass roof of the Dubai Festival Centre (2003-2007) by Jerde and HOK (image courtesy of Waagner-Biro Stahlbau AG).

Polyhedra and Polyhedral Surfaces. A *polyhedron* is a 3D shape that consists of planar *faces,* straight *edges* and *vertices*. Each edge is shared by exactly two faces and at each vertex at least three edges and three faces meet (Figure 3.2, left). The bounded volume enclosed by the polyhedron is sometimes considered part of the polyhedron. A *polyhedral surface* is a union of finitely many planar polygons (again called *faces*) that need not enclose a volume (Figure 3.2, right). A polyhedral surface can have *boundary vertices* on *boundary edges.* The latter only belong to one single face.

Before studying polyhedra in more detail, we note that the term *polyhedron* is commonly used for solid and surface models of objects bounded by planar faces. A careful distinction tends to result in complicated formulations which we want to avoid. The same holds for the term *polygon* which we use for polygons and polylines.

Fig. 3.2
The geometric entities of a
(a) polyhedron and a
(b) polyhedral surface are its faces, edges, and vertices.

(c) The *Spittelau Apartment Houses* (2004-2005) in Vienna by Zaha Hadid.
(d) The Booster Pump Station East (2003-2005) in Amsterdam East by Bekkering and Adams.

(a)

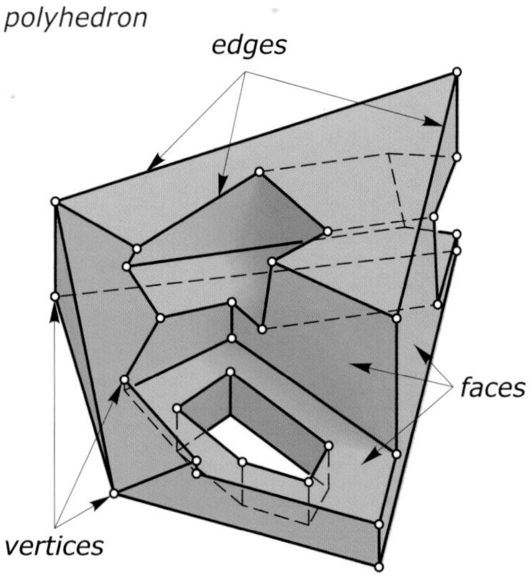

(b)

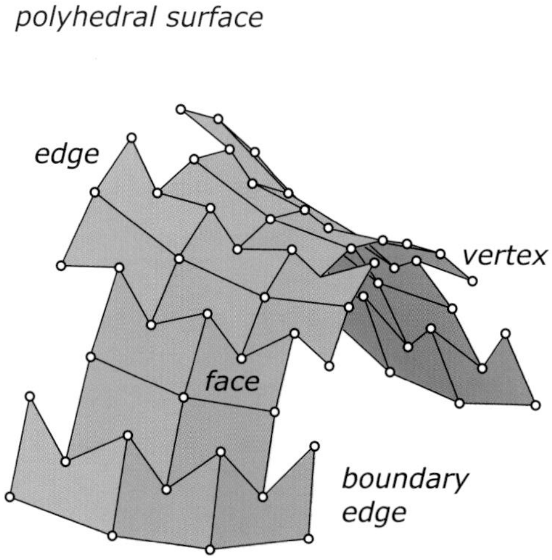

(c)

(d)

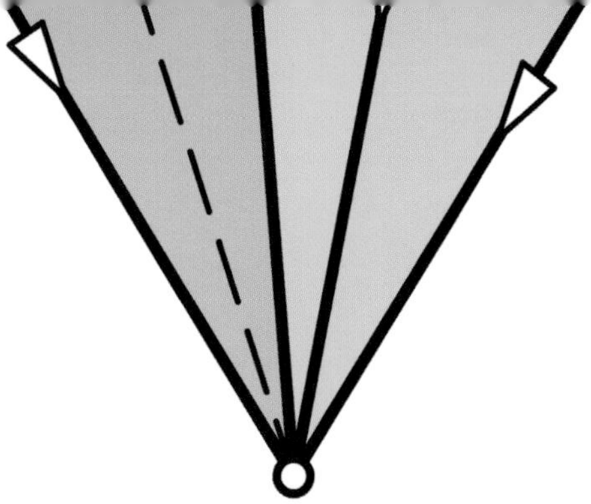

Pyramids and Prisms

Pyramids. One prominent type of polyhedron used in architecture is the *pyramid*. The base of an Egyptian pyramid is usually a square, and its other four faces are triangles. A general pyramid consists of a base polygon B in a plane P that is connected by triangular faces to the apex v not lying in P (Figure 3.3). Thus, the *mantle* M of a pyramid is a polyhedral surface with triangular faces. We obtain a *pyramidal frustum* by cutting the pyramid with a plane E parallel to P. The pillar of an *obelisk* is one example of a pyramidal frustum (Figure 3.3).

Fig. 3.3
A pyramid consists of a base polygon B that is connected by triangular faces to the apex v. If we cut the pyramid with a plane E parallel to the base plane P we get a pyramidal frustum. If we put a pyramid on top of a pyramidal frustum we have an obelisk.

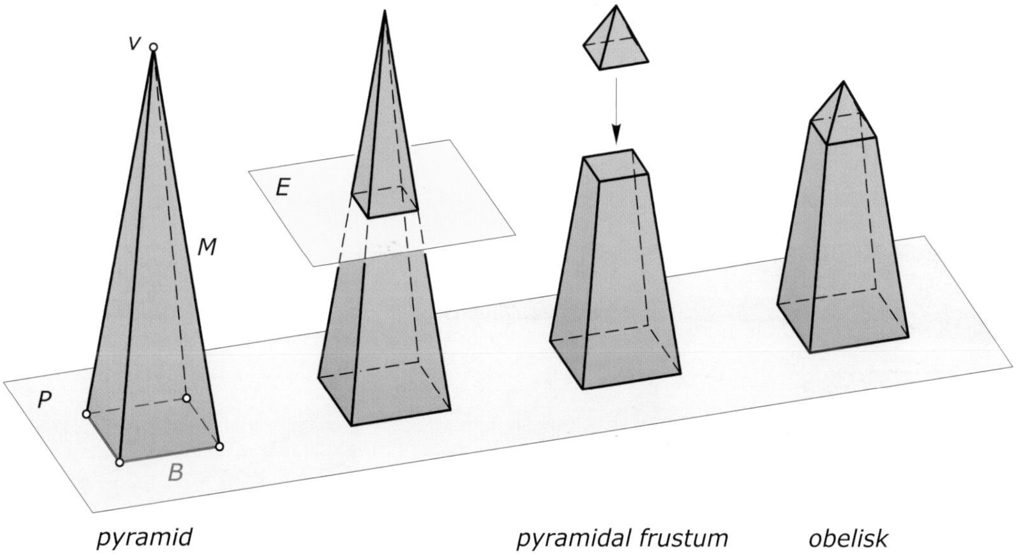

Prisms. A *prism* is a polyhedron whose bottom and top face are translated copies of each other in parallel planes (Figure 3.4). The vertices of the bottom and the top face are connected by parallel straight line segments. Thus the side faces of a prism are parallelograms and the mantle formed by them is a polyhedral surface. If the top face is obtained by a translation orthogonal to the plane containing the bottom face we have the special case of a *right prism* (all side faces are rectangles). A special right prism is the cuboid previously encountered in Chapter 1.

Example:

Modeling pyramids and prisms using extrusion. Special pyramids and prisms are often included as basic shapes in CAD systems. To model a pyramid or prism with a general base polygon B, we use the extrusion command (Figure 3.4). We draw the polygon B in a plane P (e.g., the xy-plane) and extrude it. A *parallel extrusion* takes the profile polygon B and extrudes it along parallel straight lines. If the extrusion direction is orthogonal to the reference plane we generate a right prism. Otherwise (if the extrusion direction is not parallel to the reference plane) we generate a prism. A *central extrusion* takes the profile polygon B in P and extrudes it along the connecting lines with a chosen extrusion center v (Figure 3.4). Thus a central extrusion generates a pyramid or pyramidal frustum whose shape depends on B and on the position of the apex v. Examples of pyramids and prisms in architecture are shown in Figures 3.5 and 3.6.

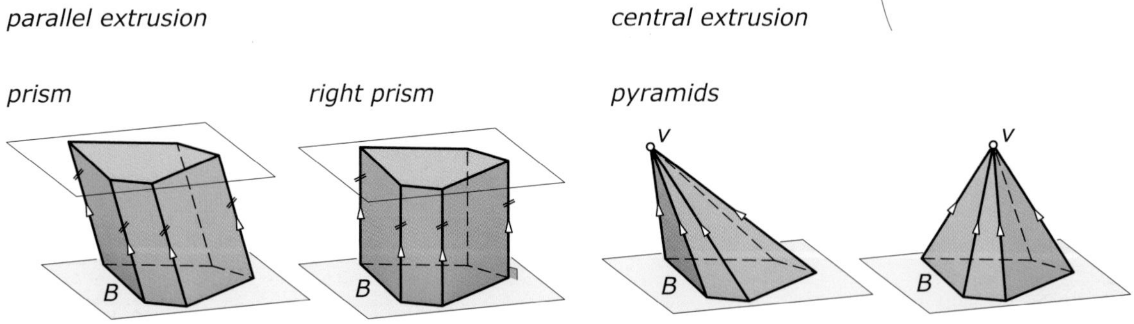

Fig. 3.4
Prisms and pyramids can be generated by parallel and central extrusion of a planar polygon.

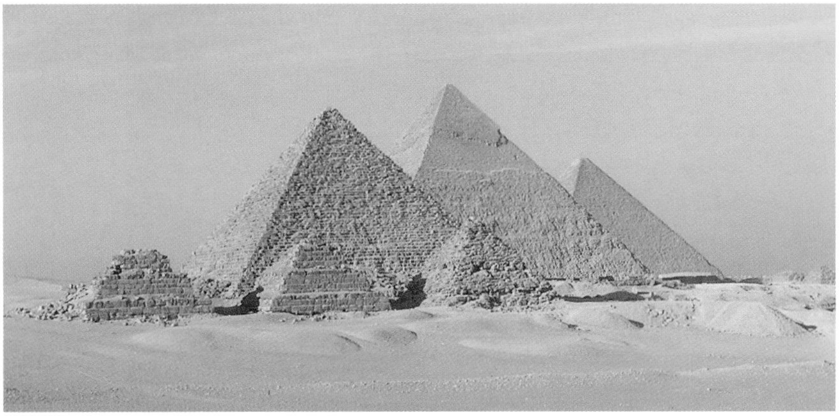

Fig. 3.5
Pyramids in architecture:
(a) The ancient Egyptian pyramids of Giza (around 2500 B.C.).
(b) The main pyramid in front of the Louvre (1989) in Paris by I.M. Pei. Its base square has a side length of 35 meters and it reaches a height of 20.6 meters.
(c) The Transamerica pyramid (1969-72) in San Franciso by William Pereira is a four-sided slim pyramid with a height of 260 meters. It has two wings on opposing sides containing an elevator shaft and a staircase.
(d) The Taipei 101 (1999-2004) in Taipei by C. Y. Lee. The 508 meters high building features upside down pyramidal frustums.

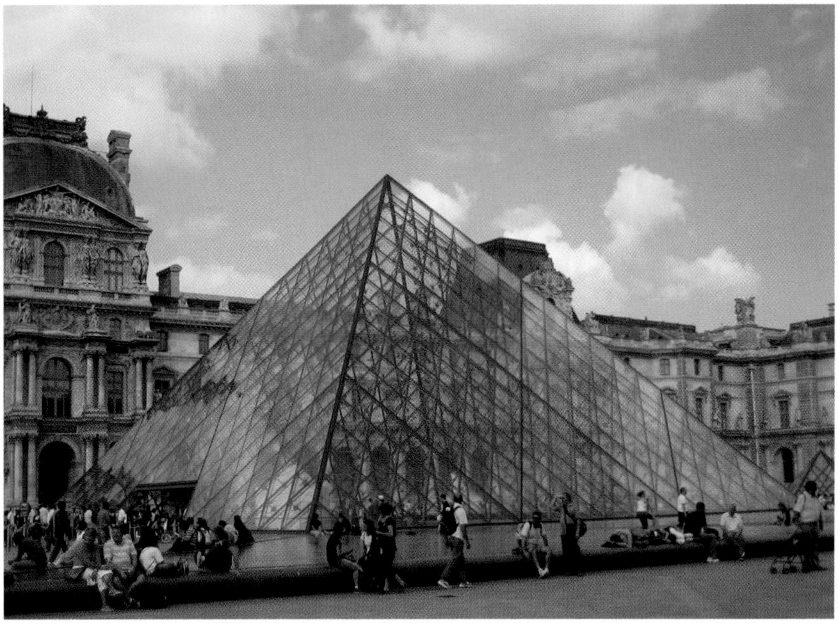

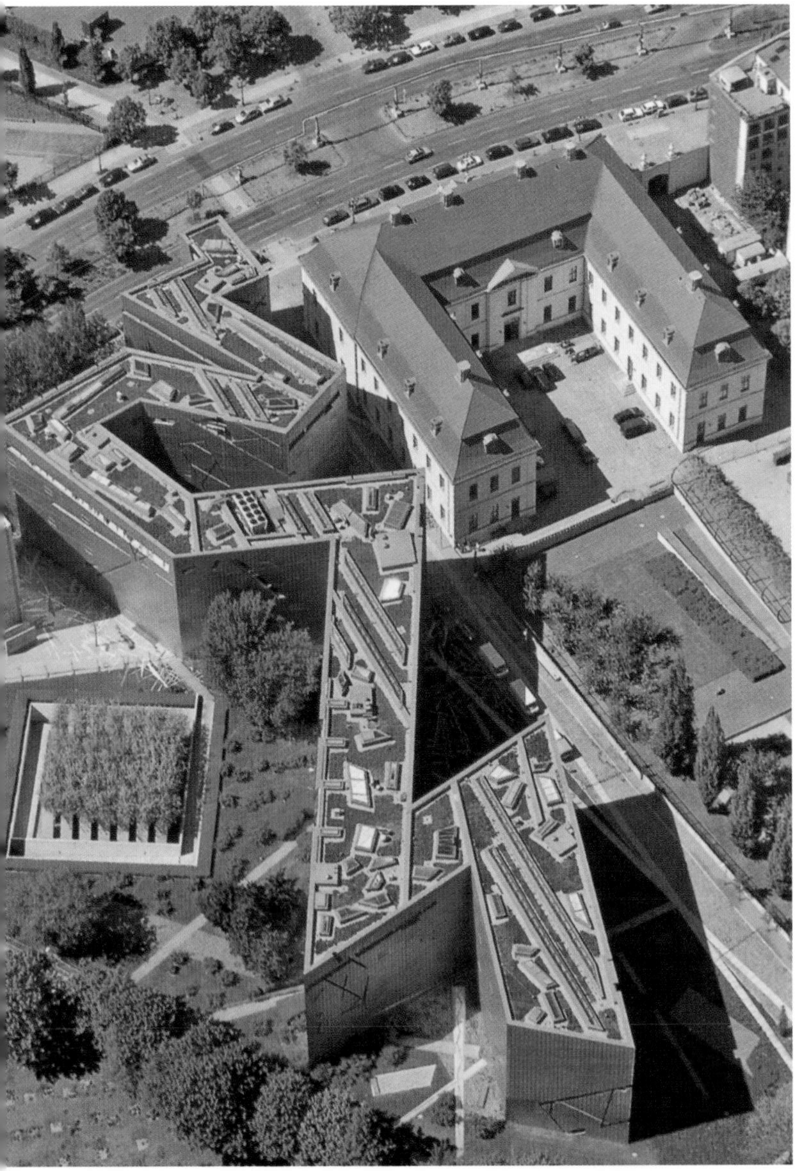

Fig. 3.6
Prisms in architecture:
(a) Castel del Monte in Bari by the Holy Roman Emperor Frederick II (around 1240).
(b) The Jewish Museum Berlin (1998-2001) by Daniel Libeskind.

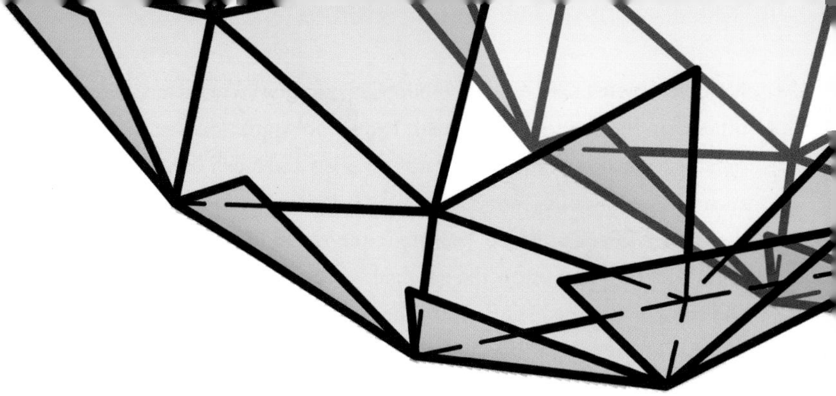

Platonic Solids

A cube is a special case of a cuboid whose faces are congruent squares. Geometrically a cube is a polyhedron with 6 square faces, 12 edges and 8 vertices. In each vertex of the cube three squares meet. All dihedral angles (i.e., the angles between faces that meet in a common edge) are equal to 90 degrees. A cube has several symmetries that can be used to reflect and rotate it (see Chapter 6) so that it is always transformed onto itself. A cube also has the property to be a convex polyhedron.

Math:

Convex sets. A set is convex if it contains with any pair of its points also the straight line segment connecting them (Figure 3.7). A polygon or a polyhedron is convex if it is the boundary of a convex set.

A *regular polygon* has its vertices equally spaced on a circle such that the non-overlapping edges are of equal length. Examples of regular polygons are the equilateral triangle, the square, and the regular pentagon. All regular polygons are convex. Pyramids and prisms whose base is a regular polygon are convex polyhedra. If the base polygon is non-convex the pyramid or prism is a non-convex polyhedron.

Fig. 3.7
Convex and non-convex domains in 2D and 3D.

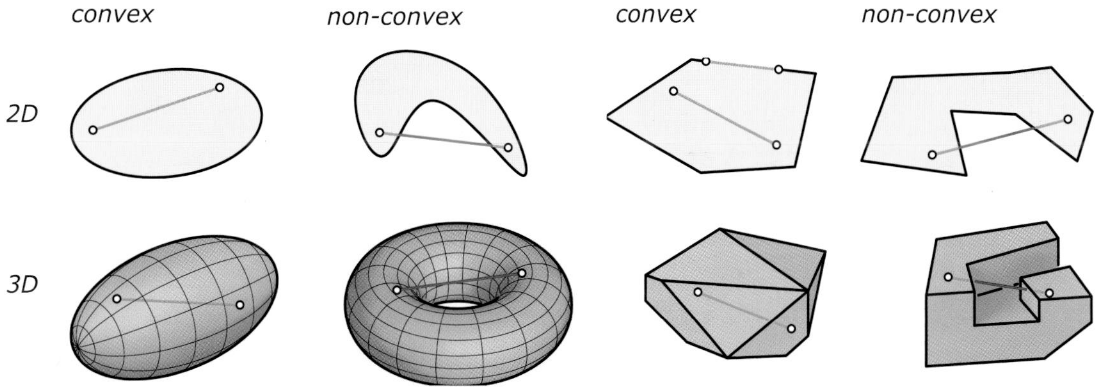

Now we devote ourselves to the following question: Are there any convex polyhedra other than the cube with congruent regular polygonal faces such that the same number of faces meet at each vertex? The answer is yes and it can be shown that there are five such polyhedral solids. They are called the *Platonic solids* (Figure 3.8), named after the ancient Greek philosopher Plato (circa 428–348 BC). The five Platonic solids are known as the tetrahedron, the hexahedron (cube), the octahedron, the dodecahedron, and the icosahedron. The prefix in the Greek name of a Platonic solid tells us the number of faces that make up the polyhedron: *tettares* means four, *hex* six, *okto* eight, *dodeka* twelve, and *eikosi* twenty. Because other polyhedra with the same number of faces commonly carry the same name, the Platonic solids are often distinguished by adding the word *regular* to the name. In this section a „tetrahedron" always means a *regular tetrahedron* and the same applies to the other Platonic solids. Let us begin with the construction of paper models of the Platonic solids.

Paper models of the Platonic solids. We can construct paper models of the Platonic solids by first arranging their faces in a plane as shown in Figure 3.8. These „unfolded" polyhedra are cut out of paper or cardboard and then folded and glued together along the edges. For a tetrahedron, we need four equilateral triangles, for a cube, six squares, for an octahedron, eight equilateral triangles, for a dodecahedron, twelve regular pentagons, and for an icosahedron, twenty equilateral triangles. Of course, there are different possibilities in arranging the faces of each Platonic solid on a cut-out sheet.

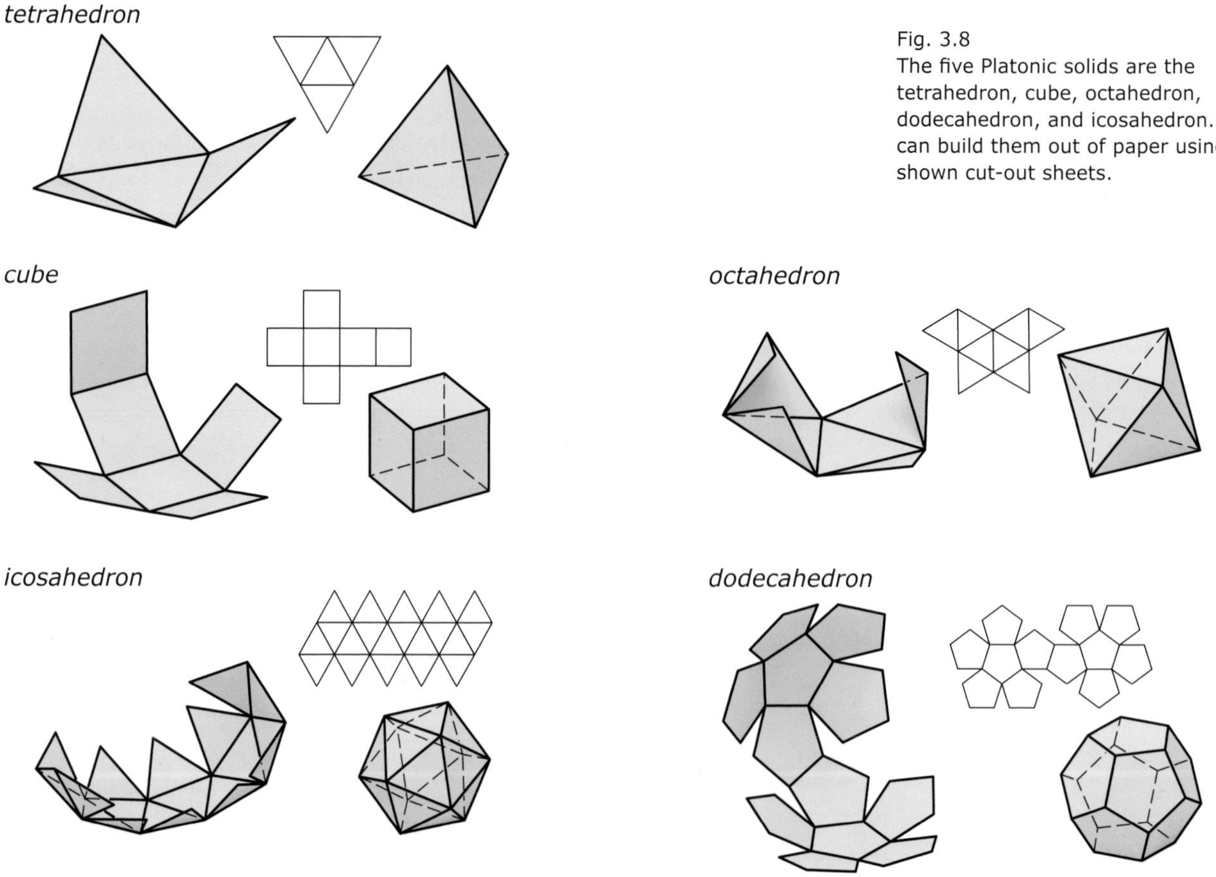

Fig. 3.8
The five Platonic solids are the tetrahedron, cube, octahedron, dodecahedron, and icosahedron. We can build them out of paper using the shown cut-out sheets.

How to find the five Platonic solids? A convex polyhedron is a Platonic solid if the following criteria hold.

- All faces are congruent regular polygons.
- At each vertex, the same number of faces meet.

Three is the minimum number of polygons (and edges) that have to meet in a vertex v of a polyhedron. All faces and edges that meet in v form the *vertex pyramid*. Note that by vertex pyramid we mean the mantle of a pyramid and this pyramid may have a non-planar base polygon (Figure 3.9). A polyhedron vertex is convex if the sum of angles between consecutive edges is less than 360 degrees. This is clearly the case for the cube (Figure 3.10) because we get $3 \cdot 90 = 270$ degrees for the three squares joining in each vertex. If we put together four squares the angle is $4 \cdot 90 = 360$ degrees and all four squares are contained in a plane. Therefore, we do not get a spatial polyhedron. Five or more squares will not work either. Thus, the cube is the only Platonic solid made up of squares. Let us now use equilateral triangles instead of squares.

- Three equilateral triangles meeting in a vertex are allowed ($3 \cdot 60 = 180$ degrees). We get the tetrahedron by adding a fourth equilateral triangle as a pyramid base (Figure 3.10). The resulting polyhedron has four faces, four vertices, and six edges. It fulfils the previously cited criteria and is thus a Platonic solid.
- Four equilateral triangles meeting in a corner are also allowed ($4 \cdot 60 = 240$ degrees). We obtain the octahedron simply by gluing together two such vertex pyramids along their base squares (Fig 10). Again both criteria cited previously are fulfilled and we have derived another Platonic solid. It has 8 faces, 6 vertices, and 12 edges.

Fig. 3.9
The vertex pyramid of the polyhedron vertex v is formed by all edges and faces joining in v. We also show the unfolded vertex pyramids.

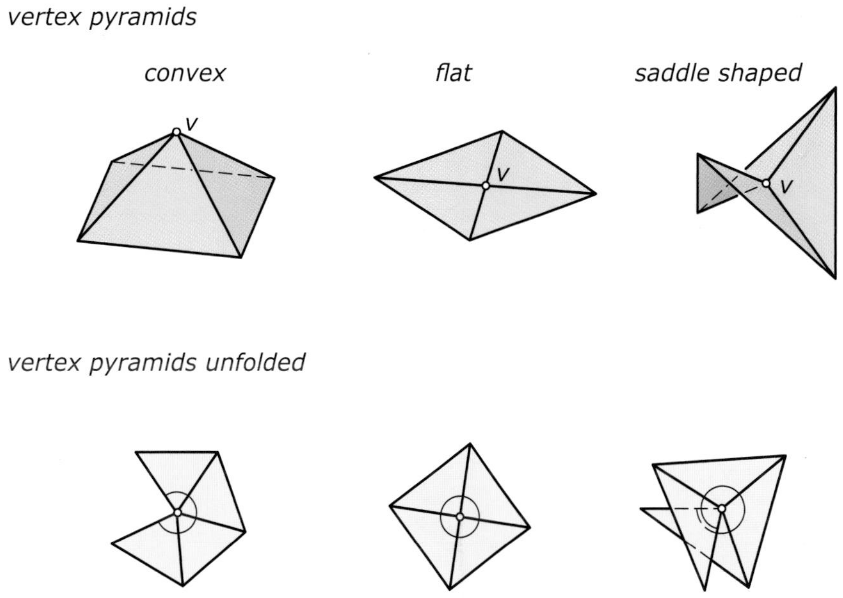

- Five equilateral triangles meeting in a corner are the most we can achieve (5·60 = 300 degrees). But now we are not allowed to simply glue two such vertex pyramids along their pentagonal bases. The criterion would not be fulfilled for the base vertices. It turns out that we have to connect two such pyramids with a band of 10 additional equilateral triangles (Figure 3.10) to obtain an icosahedron. Now both criteria hold again and we have found a fourth Platonic solid. It has 20 faces, 12 vertices, and 30 edges. Note that actually all vertex pyramids of the icosahedron are formed by five equilateral triangles and are congruent.

Six equilateral triangles meeting in a vertex form a planar object (6·60 = 360 degrees), and more than six cannot form a convex vertex anymore. Thus, we have derived all Platonic solids whose faces are made up of equilateral triangles or squares.

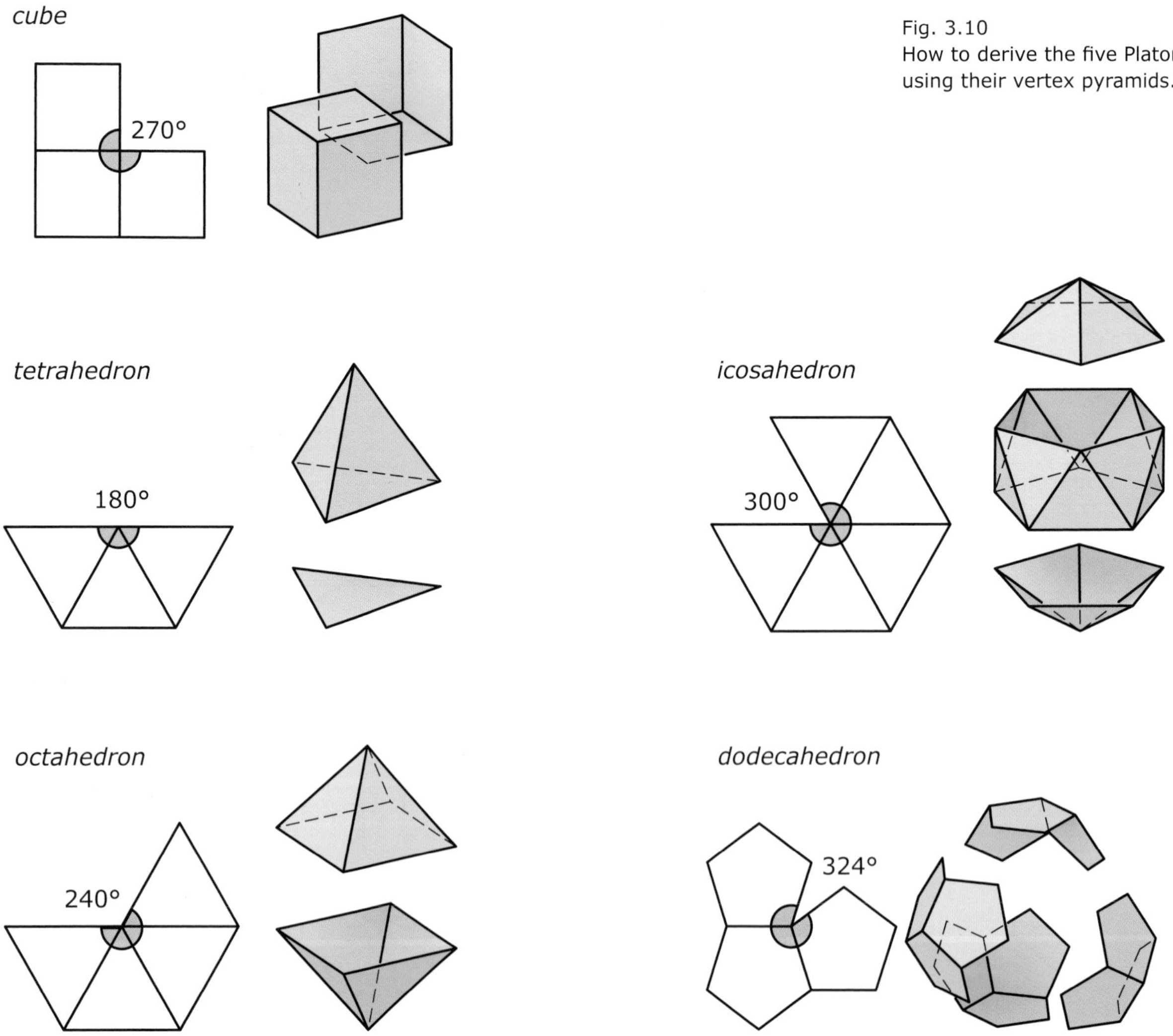

Fig. 3.10
How to derive the five Platonic solids using their vertex pyramids.

The next regular planar polygon is the regular pentagon with five edges and an inner angle of 108 degrees. Because $3 \cdot 108 = 324 < 360$ degrees we can form a convex corner out of three congruent pentagons. Then the dodecahedron is obtained by connecting four such caps consisting of three congruent pentagons (Figure 3.10). Both criteria are fulfilled and we have derived the fifth Platonic solid. It has 12 faces, 20 vertices, and 30 edges. If we put four pentagons together, we have $4 \cdot 108 = 432 > 360$ degrees which no longer yields a convex corner.

Are there Platonic solids with regular polygonal faces other than triangles, squares, or pentagons? The answer is no. The following explains why this is the case. For a regular hexagon the face angle is 120 degrees and thus three hexagons meeting in a corner are already planar ($3 \cdot 120 = 360$). Since the face angles of the regular 7-gon, 8-gon, and so on are becoming larger and larger we can no longer form convex vertex pyramids anymore.

History:

Platonic solids in higher dimensions. The mathematician Schläfli proved in 1852 that there are six polyhedra that fulfill the properties of the Platonic solids in 4D space. In spaces of dimension $n = 5$ and higher there are always only three such polyhedra. The three Platonic solids that exist in any dimension are the *hypercube* (n-dimensional cube), the *simplex* (n-dimensional tetrahedron), and the *cross polytope* (n-dimensional octahedron). In dimension 3 we additionally have the dodecahedron and the icosahedron. In dimension 4 there are the *24-cell*, the *120-cell*, and the *600-cell*. We are all used to seeing 2D images of 3D objects. Similarly we can create 3D images of 4D objects. Such a 3D image of a 600-cell is shown in Figure 3.11.

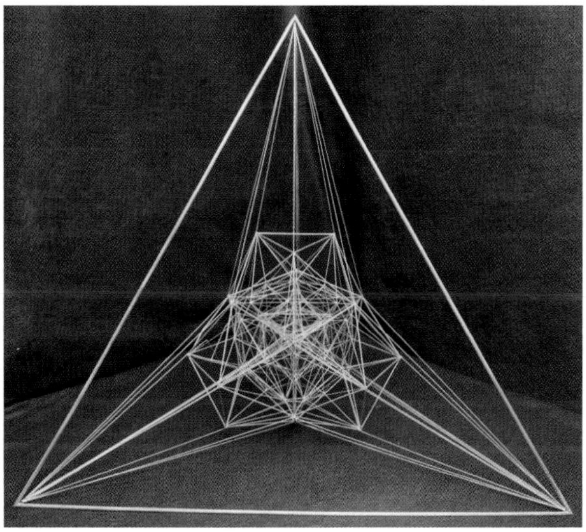

Fig. 3.11
Photo of a 3D image of the 600-cell at TU Vienna.

Convex polyhedra whose faces are equilateral triangles. Note that there are actually eight different convex polyhedra consisting of equilateral triangles. Three of them are the Platonic solids tetrahedron, octahedron, and icosahedron. The other five are no longer as regular and have 6, 10, 12, 14, and 16 equilateral triangular faces (Figure 3.12). They are obtained as follows. Gluing together two tetrahedra gives the first new object. Gluing together two pentagonal pyramids generates the second one.

Splitting a tetrahedron into two wedges and stitching them together with a band of eight equilateral triangles yields the third one. Attaching three square pyramids to the side faces of a triangular prism generates the fourth. Finally, by attaching two square pyramids to a band of eight equilateral triangles we obtain the fifth one. Note that all faces that are glued together are then removed from the generated polyhedron.

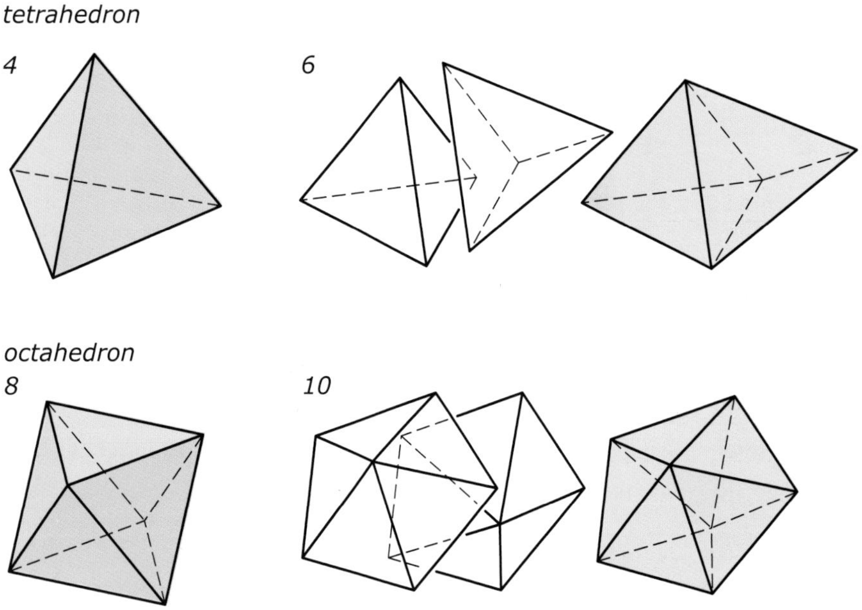

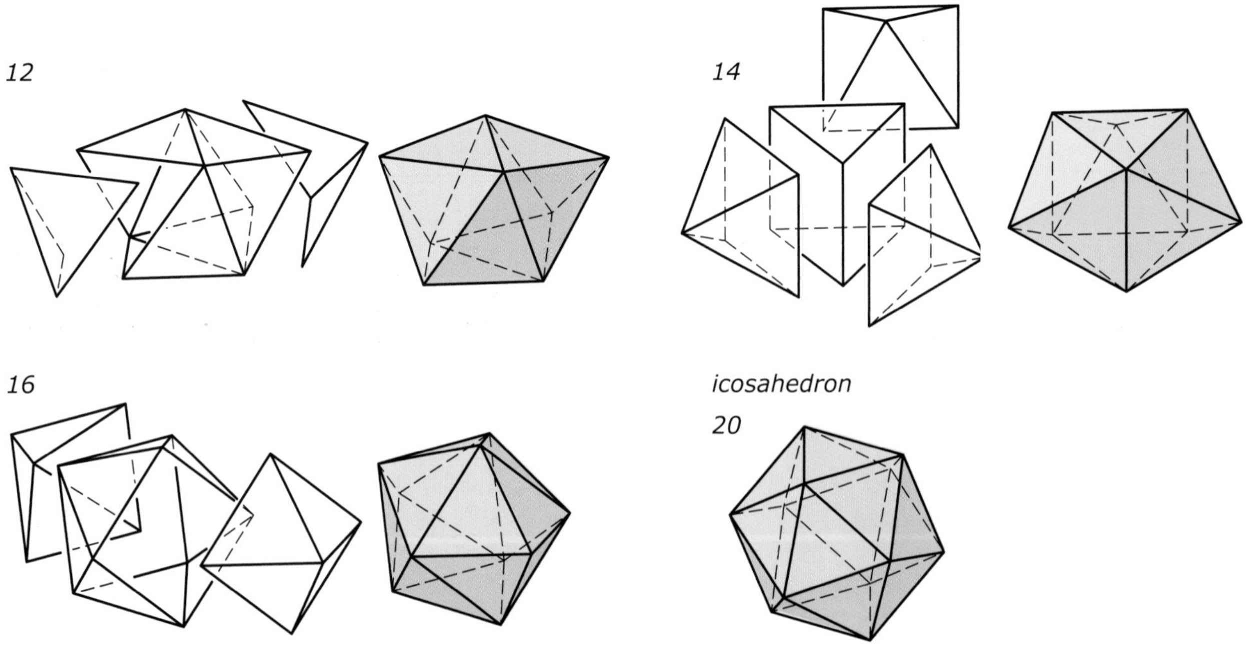

Fig. 3.12
The eight different convex polyhedra that are made up of equilateral triangles. Only three of them are Platonic solids.

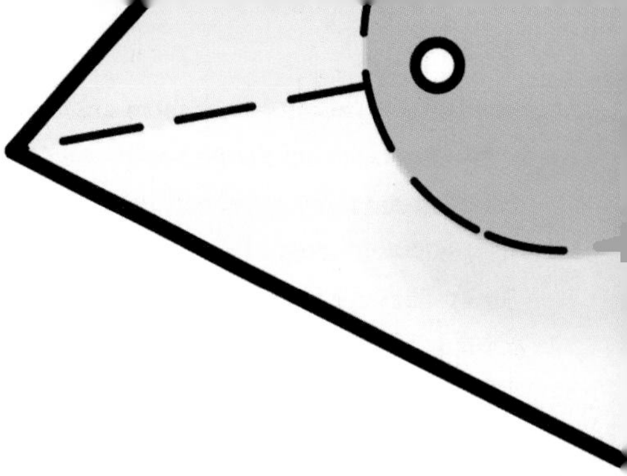

Properties of Platonic Solids

The faces of a Platonic solid are congruent equilateral triangles (tetrahedron, octahedron, icosahedron), or congruent squares (cube), or congruent regular pentagons (dodecahedron). Table 3.1 summarizes the number of faces (f), the number of vertices (v), and the number of edges (e) that form each Platonic solid.

Table 3.1 Number of Faces, Vertices, and Edges Associated with Platonic Solids

Platonic Solid	f	v	e
Tetrahedron	4	4	6
Cube	6	8	12
Octahedron	8	6	12
Dodecahedron	12	20	30
Icosahedron	20	12	30

The Euler formula. It is easy to verify that for the five Platonic solids the number of vertices v minus the number of edges e plus the number of faces f is always equal to 2:

$$v - e + f = 2.$$

This polyhedral formula, derived by the mathematician Leonhard Euler (1707-1783), actually holds for all polyhedra without holes. We verify it for the pyramid with a square base: $v - e + f = 5 - 8 + 5 = 2$. In Chapter 14 we will learn more about the Euler formula and other so-called *topological properties* of geometric shapes.

Fig. 3.13
Platonic solids and their duals. The tetrahedron is self-dual. The cube and the octahedron are duals of each other. The same holds for the icosahedron and the dodecahedron.

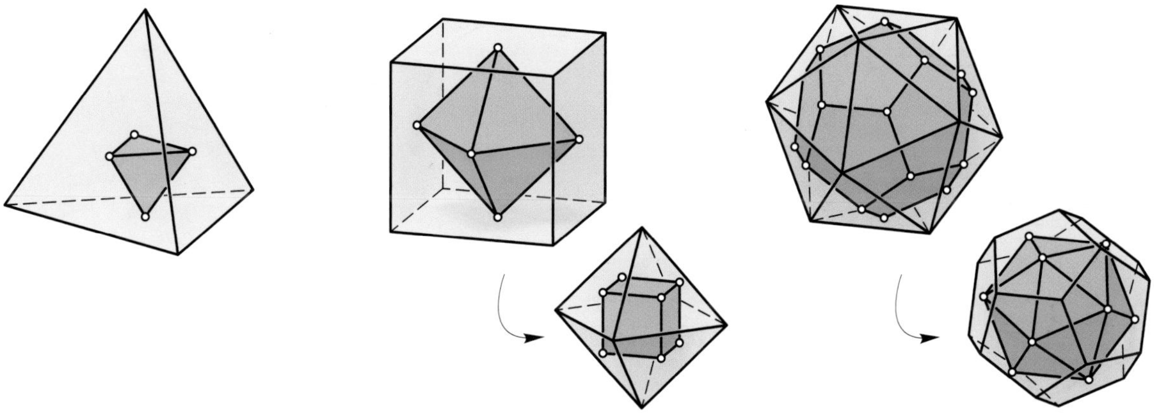

Platonic solids and their duals. The face midpoints of each Platonic solid are the vertices of another Platonic solid, called the solid's *dual* (Figure 3.13). Let us first derive the dual of a tetrahedron. Each of the four vertex pyramids consists of three equilateral triangles. Because of the symmetry of the tetrahedron the three face midpoints of each vertex pyramid form another equilateral triangle. Thus, we again obtain a convex polyhedron consisting of four equilateral triangles. Thus the dual of a tetrahedron is again a (smaller) tetrahedron contained in the original one.

Let us now derive the dual of a cube. For each vertex pyramid of the cube (consisting of three congruent squares) we connect the face midpoints by an equilateral triangle. Thus each vertex of the cube gives rise to an equilateral triangle (a face of the dual polyhedron), and each face of the cube yields a vertex of the dual (which is the face midpoint of the square). Hence the dual of a cube consists of eight equilateral triangles that form an octahedron. Obviously the number of vertices of a Platonic solid corresponds to the number of faces of the dual and vice versa. The number of edges is the same for a Platonic solid and its dual (see Table 3.1). Note that the dodecahedron and the icosahedron are duals of each other.

Spheres associated with Platonic solids. There are three spheres with the same center naturally associated with each Platonic solid (Figure 3.14). One sphere contains all vertices (the *circumsphere*), the second touches all faces in their face-midpoints (the *insphere*), and the third touches the edges at their edge-midpoints.

Symmetry properties. The vertex pyramids of a single Platonic solid are congruent with one another. By construction, all faces are congruent regular polygons and thus all edges have the same length. This means that if we want to construct a Platonic solid we have the following advantages.

- We only need one type of face.
- All edges have the same length.
- The dihedral angles between neighbouring faces are equal.
- All vertex pyramids are congruent.

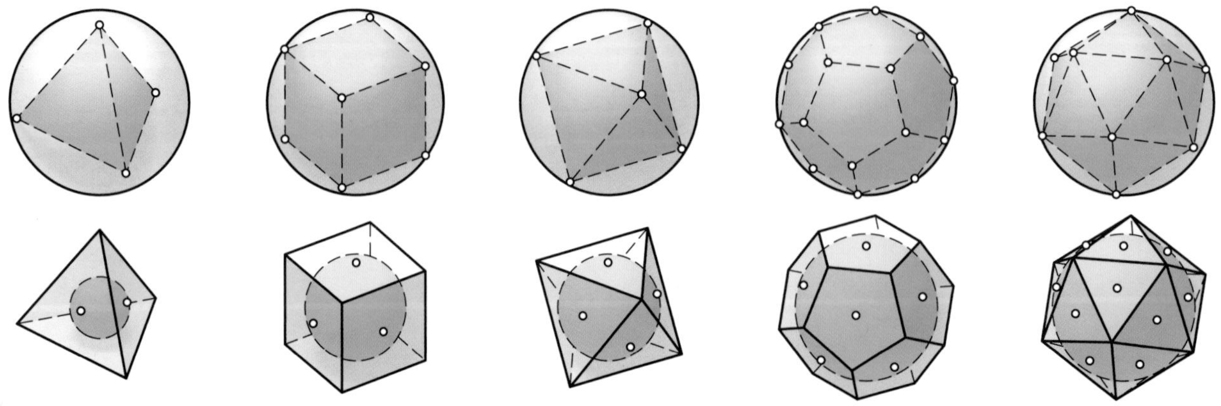

Fig. 3.14
Each Platonic solid has three associated spheres with the same center. Here we show the circumspheres and the inspheres.

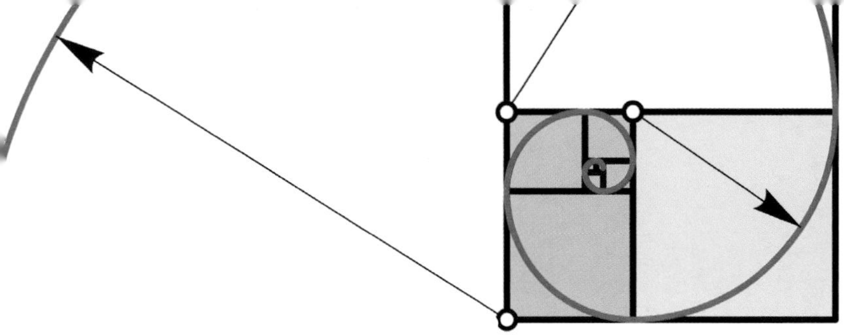

The Golden Section

The golden section. The *golden section* (also known as *golden ratio* or *divine proportion*) is the number

$$\varphi = (1+\sqrt{5})/2 \approx 1.618033989...$$

We obtain the exact golden section if we divide a line segment into two parts (a larger one of length c, and a smaller one of length d) so that the following holds (Figure 3.15): the ratio of c and d is the same as the ratio of $c + d$ and c. Stated another way, "larger to smaller as total to larger." Formally, we write

$$c : d = (c + d) : c.$$

If we use a new variable $\varphi := c/d$ we have $\varphi = 1 + 1/\varphi$ which leads to the quadratic equation $\varphi^2 - \varphi - 1 = 0$. The positive solution $(1+\sqrt{5})/2$ is the golden section. Interestingly, the golden section can be approximated by the ratio of two successive numbers in the so-called *Fibonacci series* of numbers 1, 1, 2, 3, 5, 8, 13, 21, 34, … . Although 3:2 = 1.5 is a rough approximation of φ, 5 : 3 = 1.666... is already a little bit better. Continuing in the same fashion we obtain better approximations. For example, the value 13:8 = 1.625 already approximates the golden ratio within 1% accuracy.

The golden rectangle. The dimensions of a golden rectangle are always in the golden ratio $\varphi : 1$. To construct a golden rectangle, we start with a square of side length c. As shown in Figure 3.15 we obtain a larger *golden rectangle* with dimensions $(c + d) : c$ and a smaller one with dimensions $c : d$.

The Fibonacci spiral. Let us continue the above construction as follows. We divide the smaller rectangle into a square of side length d and another golden rectangle of dimensions $d : (c - d)$. If we continue in the same fashion the result is a whirling square diagram. By connecting opposite corners of the squares with quarter circles we obtain the *Fibonacci spiral* (Figure 3.15).

History:

The golden section in art and architecture. In art the golden section has been found in numerous ancient Greek sculptures—including those by Phidias (fifth century BC) whose name motivated the choice of φ as the symbol for the golden section. The golden section also appears in paintings ranging from Leonardo da Vinci's *Mona Lisa* (1503) to Mondrian's *Composition with Red, Yellow, and Blue* (1921).

In architecture it is argued that the golden section was used in the *Cheops pyramid* (around 2590-2470 B.C.), in the *Parthenon* temple (447-432 B.C.) in Athens, in the *Pantheon* (118-125) in Rome, in various triumphal arches, or in the facade of the *Notre Dame* cathedral (1163-1345) in Paris. In the twentieth century, Le Corbusier developed the golden-section-based modular system for architectural proportions and applied it in his famous building *Unité d'Habitation* (1952) in Marseille (Figure 3.16).

Fig. 3.15
The golden section, the golden rectangle, and the golden spiral.

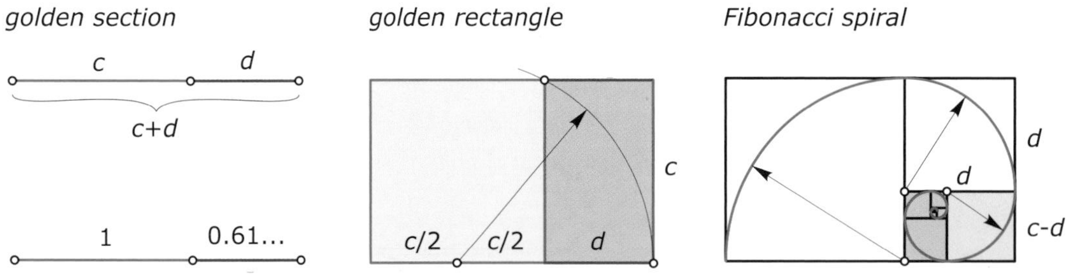

Fig. 3.16
Unité d'Habitation (1952) by Le Corbusier.

Modeling the Platonic solids. CAD software often provides Platonic solids as fundamental shapes. If this is not the case all five Platonic solids can also be modeled in the following way. The most difficult part here is the construction of an icosahedron and its dual, the dodecahedron—which exhibits a beautiful relation to the golden ratio.

- To model a cube, we can use parallel extrusion of a square with edge length *s* in a direction orthogonal to its supporting plane to a height *s*.
- To model a tetrahedron, we cut it out of a cube as shown in Figure 3.17. The planar cuts generate a polyhedron whose six edges are diagonals of the cubes faces which are congruent squares. Thus, the new edges are of equal length. The four faces of the new polyhedron are congruent equilateral triangles. Hence the polyhedron is a tetrahedron.
- To model an octahedron (Figure 3.17), we select its six vertices as unit points on the axes of a Cartesian system: (1,0,0), (0,1,0), (–1,0,0), (0,–1,0), (0,0,1), (0,0,–1). Alternatively we could also model it as the dual of a cube.

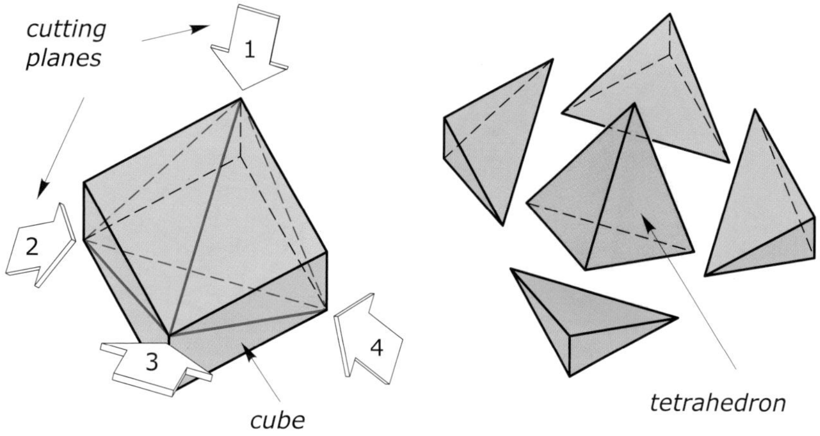

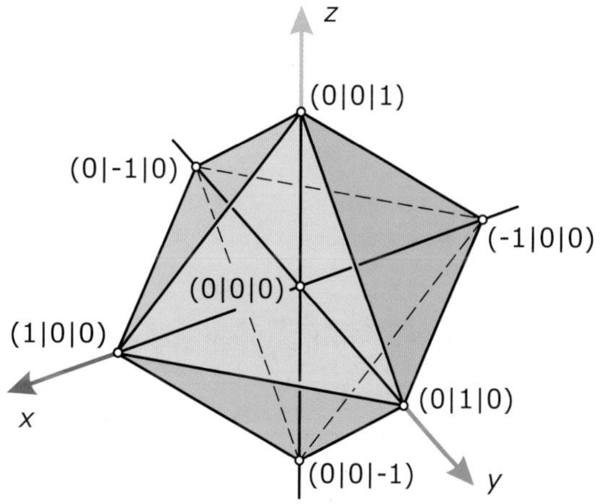

Fig. 3.17
(a) Modeling a tetrahedron by cutting it out of a cube.
(b) Modeling an octahedron by choosing its six vertices as the unit points on the axes of a Cartesian system: (1,0,0), (0,1,0), (-1,0,0), (0,-1,0), (0,0,1), (0,0,-1).

- To model an icosahedron we use three congruent golden rectangles which we position mutually orthogonal with coinciding centers in the origin as shown in Figure 3.18. The twelve vertices of the three golden rectangles have Cartesian coordinates $(\pm\varphi,\pm1,0)$, $(0, \pm\varphi,\pm1)$, $(\pm1,0, \pm\varphi)$ and are the vertices of an icosahedron of edge length $s = 2$.
- We model a dodecahedron as the dual of an icosahedron (Figure 3.18). The twenty face midpoints of the icosahedron are the vertices of the dodecahedron.

The cube is the most widely used Platonic solid in architecture. One unorthodox use is illustrated in Figure 3.19a. The tetrahedron also finds its way into architecture (Figure 3.19b). In material following we will learn how geodesic spheres can be derived from an icosahedron.

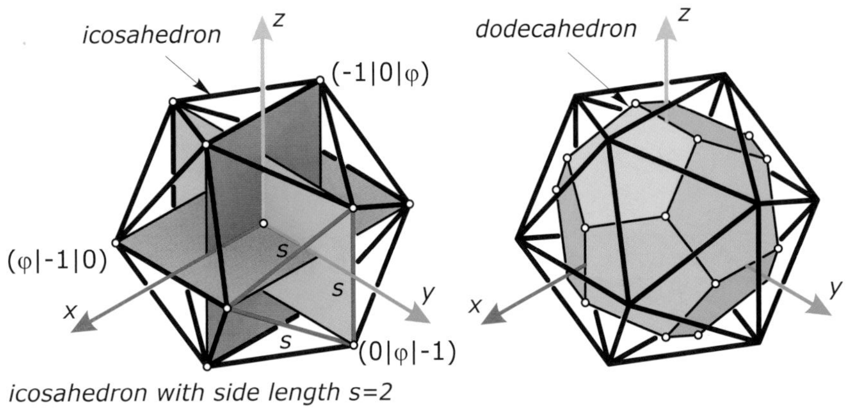

Fig. 3.18
(Left) Modeling an icosahedron of edge length $s = 2$: The vertices of three congruent golden rectangles of width 2 and length 2φ define the twelve vertices of an icosahedron.
(Right) Modeling a dodecahedron as the dual of an icosahedron.

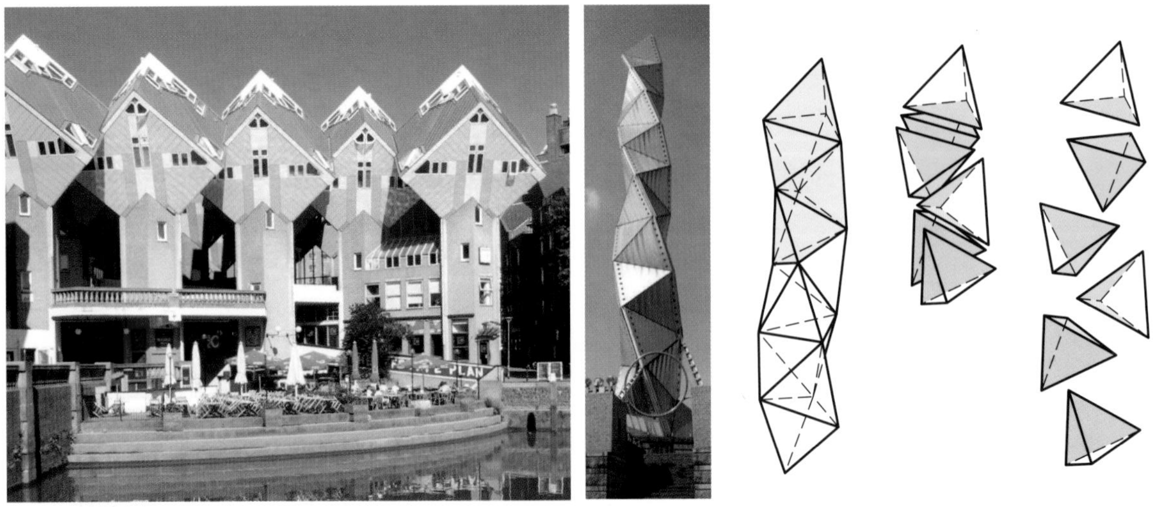

Fig. 3.19
(a) The *Cube Houses* (1984) in Rotterdam by Piet Blom feature cubes with one vertical diagonal resting on prisms with a hexagonal base polygon.
(b) The *Art Tower* (1990) in Mito by Arata Isozaki can be modeled as a stack of tetrahedra.

Archimedean Solids

Archimedean solids are convex polyhedra that are consisting of two or more types of regular polygons so that all vertex pyramids are congruent. These special polyhedra were known to the ancient Greek genius Archimedes more than 2000 years ago. As in the case of Platonic solids, all edge lenghts are equal in an Archimedean solid. Thus, the real difference is that more than one type of planar face appears. Each face still has to be a regular polygon but not all of them have to be congruent.

Corner cutting of Platonic solids. By cutting off the vertices of a Platonic solid we can generate some of the Archimedean solids. For a better understanding of possible cuts we first discuss corner cutting (along straight lines) for regular polygons. For each regular polygon we can perform two different corner cuts so that we again obtain a regular polygon (Figure 3.20):

- Type 1: Cuts that generate a regular polygon with the same number of edges.
- Type 2: Cuts that generate a regular polygon with twice as many edges.

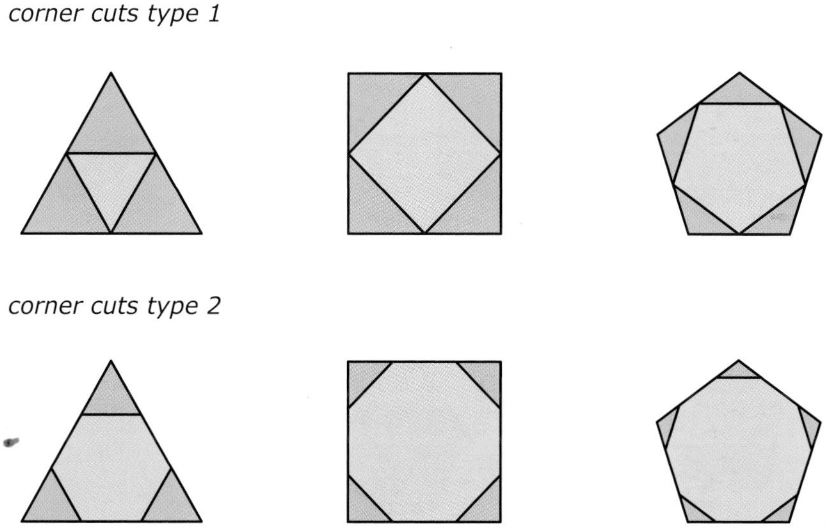

Fig. 3.20
The two types of corner cuts of regular polygons that generate another regular polygon. We illustrate the cuts for the equilateral triangle, the square, and the regular pentagon.

The first type of cut passes through the edge midpoints, and the second type of cut has to be performed in such a way that the generated polygon with twice as many edges is again regular. We can perform these two types of corner cuts for a Platonic solid in an analogous way and thus generate Archimedean solids. In we do so we cut off parts of the vertex pyramids.

Corner cuts of type 1. Let us start with cuts through the edge midpoints (Figure 3.21).

- For a tetrahedron we chop off four smaller regular tetrahedra and what remains is an octahedron, Thus, we again have a Platonic solid and not a new type of polyhedron.
- For a cube, we obtain the so-called *cuboctahedron* consisting of six congruent squares (which remain from the six faces of the cube) and eight congruent triangles (which remain from the eight corners of the cube).
- If we cut off the corners of an octahedron, we obtain a polyhedron whose faces are eight congruent equilateral triangles (one for each of the octagon faces) and six congruent squares (one replacing each corner of the octahedron). This is again a cuboctahedron. Indeed, by corner cutting through the edge midpoints dual Platonic solids generate the same polyhedron. This also holds for the dodecahedron and its dual, the icosahedron.
- With planar cuts through the edge midpoints of a dodecahedron we obtain a polyhedron whose faces are 12 congruent regular pentagons (one for each of the twelve faces of the dodecahedron) and 20 congruent equilateral triangles (one for each of the 20 vertices of the dodecahedron). The derived polyhedron is known as the *icosidodecahedron*. Its name reveals the fact that it can also be generated from an icosahedron via corner cutting through the edge midpoints (Figure 3,21).

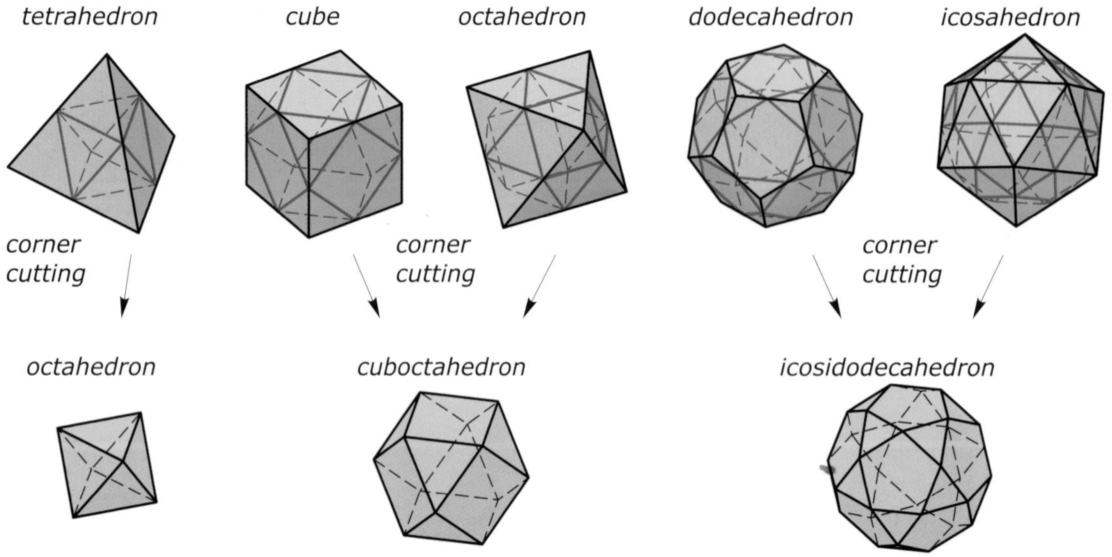

Fig. 3.21
New polyhedra generated by corner cutting of Platonic solids with cuts through the edge midpoints.

Corner cuts of type 2. With corner cuts of the second type we can generate one further Archimedean solid for each of the five Platonic solids (Figure 3.22). Figure 3.20 indicates by means of a single face how we have to perform the necessary cuts that chop off parts of the vertex pyramids of each Platonic solid. Archimedean solids generated by truncation are called *truncated tetrahedron*, *truncated cube*, *truncated octahedron*, *truncated dodecahedron*, and *truncated icosahedron*.

The truncated icosahedron is very likely the most recognized Archimedean solid because it is represented in the classic shape of a *soccer ball* (Figure 3.22). The same polyhedron was also named a *buckyball* by chemists, because it resembles the shape of the geodesic spheres of Buckminister Fuller which we study in the next section. It can be generated from the icosahedron by corner cutting so that we chop off 1/3 of each edge on both edge ends. We generate for each of the 12 vertices a regular pentagon, and for each of the 20 triangles of the icosahedron a regular hexagon. Corner cutting is a fundamental idea in generating new shapes from existing ones. We encounter this idea again in future chapters including Chapter 8 (on freeform curves) and Chapter 11 (on freeform surfaces).

In total, there are 13 different Archimedean solids (Figure 3.22) other than certain prisms and anti-prisms (discussed in material following). Three of the Archimedean solids even consist of three different types of regular polygonal faces.

Fig. 3.22
From the 13 Archimedean solids the seven named in this figure can be generated from Platonic solids via corner cutting. The classic soccer ball is one of them.

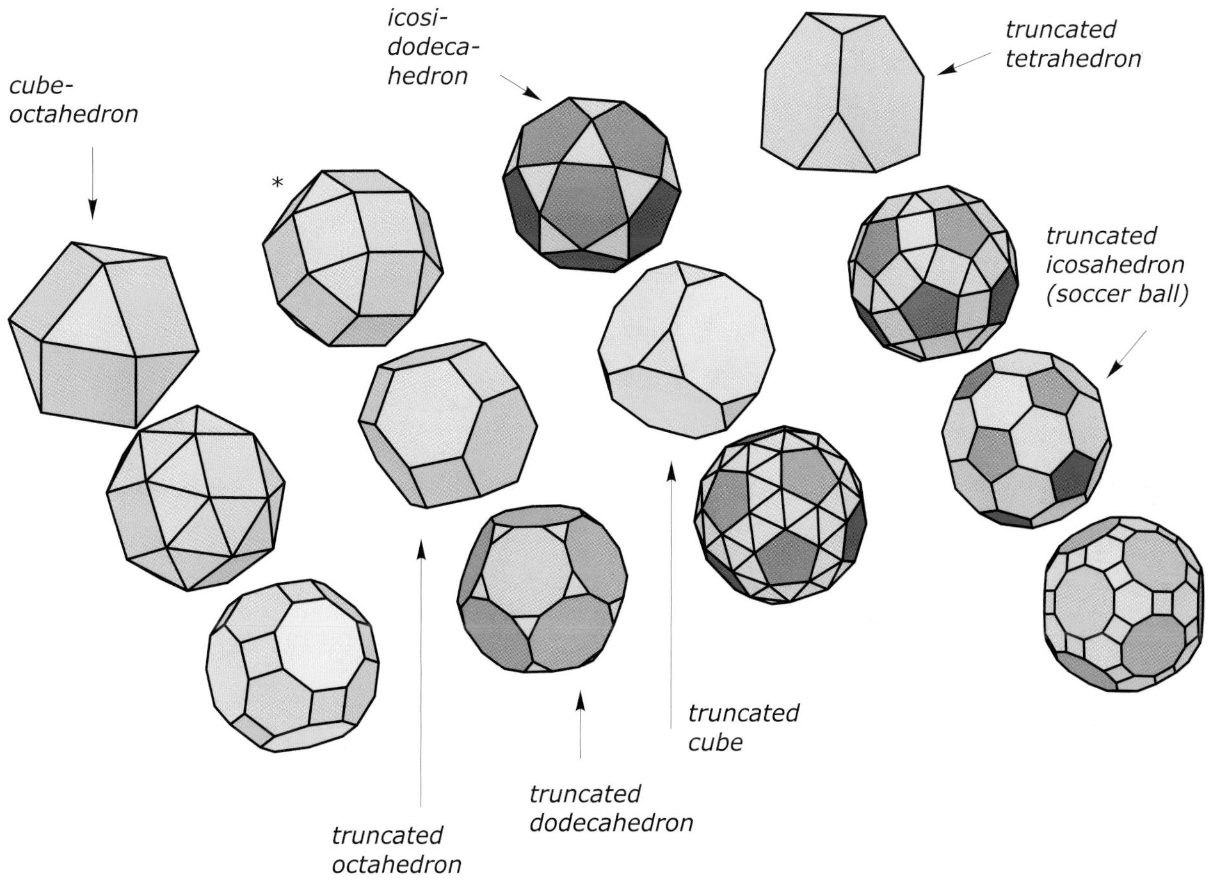

Remark. Note that the classical definiton of an Archimedean solid is also fulfilled by a 14th polyhedron. It was found 2000 years after Archimedes by J. C. P. Miller and V. G. Ashkinuze. This polyhedron is obtained by cutting a rhombicuboctahedron (the polyhedron marked by an * in Figure 3.22) in half, rotating one part by 45 degrees, and then gluing the two parts together.

Some Archimedean solids inherently closely resemble the shape of a sphere, with the further advantage that they can be made of struts of equal length. From Platonic solids we derive polyhedra that resemble the shape of a sphere even better. These are the geodesic spheres and spherical caps of them are called geodesic domes.

Example:

Prisms and anti-prisms that are Archimedean solids. A prism whose top and bottom faces are congruent regular polygons and whose side faces are squares is an Archimedean solid (Figure 3.23, top). Recall that for an Archimedean solid all edge lengths have to be equal. An *anti-prism* has congruent regular polygons as bottom and top faces. The top face is a rotated and translated copy of the bottom face and both are connected by a strip of triangles. If we use equilateral triangles we obtain polyhedra that fulfill the properties of an Archimedean solid (Figure 3.23, bottom).

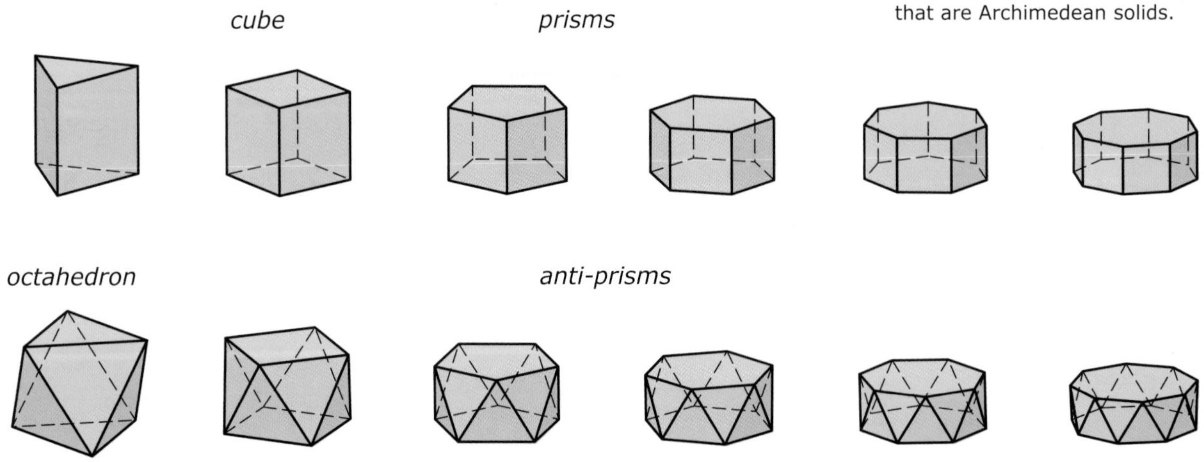

Fig. 3.23
Examples of prisms and anti-prisms that are Archimedean solids.

Geodesic Spheres

A *geodesic sphere* is a polyhedron with an almost spherical structure. The name is derived from the fact that

- all vertices lie on a common sphere *S* and
- certain sequences of vertices are arranged on great circles of *S*.

The great circles of a sphere are the shortest paths that connect two distinct points on a sphere. These shortest paths on a surface are called *geodesics*, and thus the polyhedra we study in this section are called geodesic spheres. All faces of a geodesic sphere are triangles. However, not all of them are congruent. Geodesic domes are those parts of geodesic spheres (Figure 3.24) that are actually used in architecture (Figure 3.25). Built domes range from sizes covering almost a full geodesic sphere to only half a geodesic sphere. The latter are called hemispherical domes.

History:

In 1954 R. Buckminster Fuller first displayed a geodesic dome at the Milan Triennale—an international exhibition dedicated to present innovative developments in architecture, design, crafts, and city planning. The 42-foot paperboard geodesic dome of Fuller gained worldwide attention and Fuller won the Gran Premio. Buckminster Fuller built several domes including a large one in Montreal (Figure 3.25) to house the U.S. Pavilion at Expo 1967. Fuller also proposed enclosing midtown Manhattan with a 2-mile-wide dome.

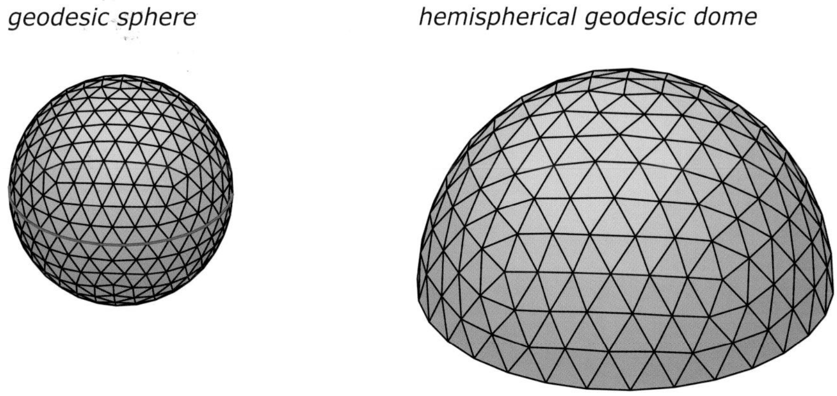

Fig. 3.24
A geodesic sphere and a hemispherical geodesic dome.

(a)

Used by permission from Disney Enterprises, Inc.

(b)

Fig. 3.25
(a) The *Geodesic Dome* (1967) in Montreal by Buckminster Fuller comprises three-quarters of a geodesic sphere. The outer-hull is made out of triangles and is linked to the inner hull consisting of hexagons.
(b) The *Spaceship Earth* geodesic dome (1982) in Orlando is almost a full geodesic sphere.
(c) The *Desert Dome* (1999-2002) in Omaha is hemispherical.

(c)

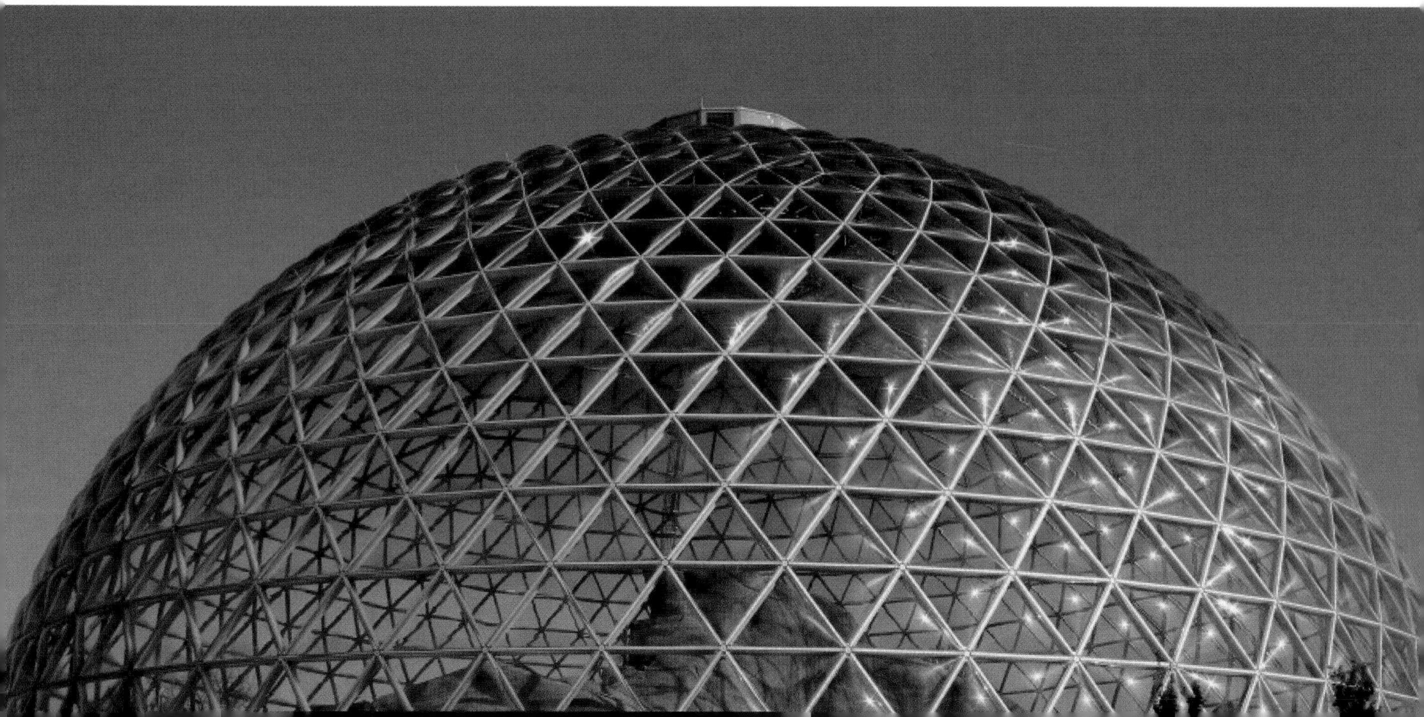

Starting with Platonic solids we derive different forms of geodesic spheres by applying the following iterative process: we subdivide each face into a regular pattern of triangles and project the new vertices onto the circumsphere of the Platonic solid. From our considerations on Platonic solids it is evident that geodesic domes cannot be built with all triangular faces being congruent. However, we try to obtain only a small number of different faces.

Geodesic domes derived from an icosahedron: Alternative 1. Because the icosahedron closely approximates its circumsphere it is often used as a starting point for deriving geodesic spheres. We start by subdividing the triangular faces into smaller triangles (Figure 3.26b). An equilateral triangle can be split into four smaller equilateral triangles by adding the edge midpoints as new vertices. Then three new edges parallel to the original edges are inserted.

We do this subdivision for each of the 20 congruent faces of the icosahedron to obtain a total of 80 = 20·4 triangles. Now we project the newly inserted 30 vertices (the midpoints of the 30 edges of the icosahedron) radially from the center of the icosahedron onto its circumsphere (Figure 3.27). From the 80 triangles of this geodesic sphere, 20 are still equilateral. The remaining 60 are only isosceles. Thus this geodesic sphere can be made up of two types of triangles (colored differently in Figure 3.28, level 1).

Fig. 3.26
Subdividing a triangle into smaller triangles: By splitting each edge into 2, 3, 4 equal segments we get 4, 9, 16 smaller triangles. In general, splitting each edge into n equal segments yields n^2 smaller triangles.

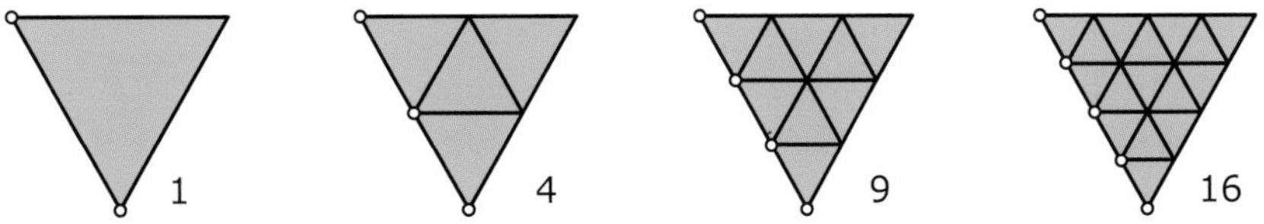

Fig. 3.27
Projecting the edge midpoints of an icosahedron onto its circumsphere results in a geodesic sphere.

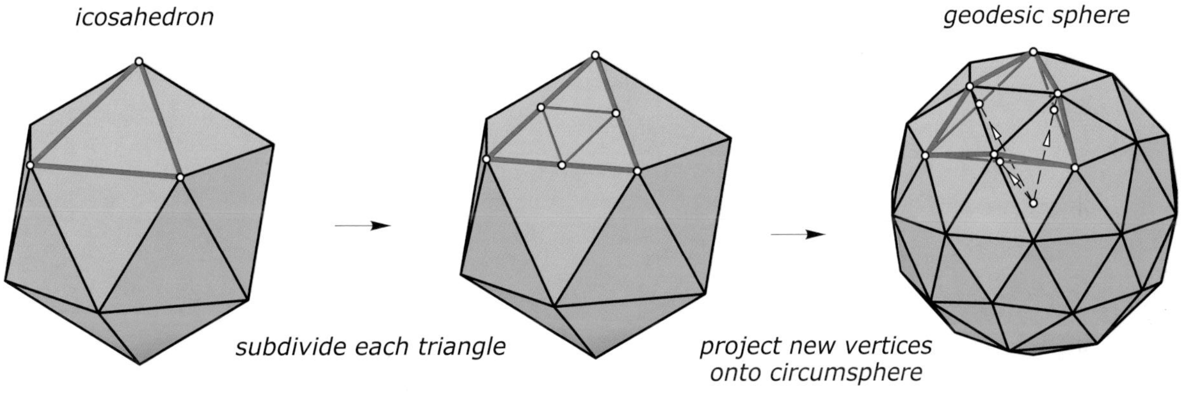

If we want to construct a larger geodesic sphere, it is advantageous to have more triangles. Let us again derive such a geodesic sphere from an icosahedron. We subdivide each edge of the icosahedron into three equal parts and obtain for each triangle nine smaller triangles (instead of four, as previously; Figure 3.26c). Then we project the 80 new vertices (2 on each of the 30 edges of the icosahedron, and one for the midpoint of each of the 20 faces) again radially onto the circumsphere of the icosahedron.

This geodesic sphere has a total of 92 vertices, $20 \cdot 9 = 180$ triangles, and 270 edges (Figure 3.28, level 2). It follows from the construction that all triangles are isosceles. However, there are two different types of triangles: 60 congruent ones that form the vertex pyramids around the 12 original vertices of the icosahedron and 120 congruent ones that form the 20 vertex pyramids around the displaced midpoints of the icosahedron's triangles.

Note that there are only three different edge lengths involved. If we subdivide each triangle of the icosahedron into 16 triangles (Figure 3.26d), and then project all new vertices onto the circumsphere, we obtain a geodesic sphere at level 3 with $20 \cdot 16 = 320$ triangles (Figure 3.28, level 3). If we keep subdividing the triangles of the icosahedron in this fashion, we generate a geodesic sphere at level k with $20 \cdot (k+1)^2$ triangles.

Geodesic domes derived from an icosahedron: Alternative 2. An alternative approach in generating geodesic spheres also starts with an icosahedron. However, it recursively splits each triangle of the geodesic sphere at the previous level into four smaller triangles and then projects the new vertices onto the circumsphere (Figure 3.29). The first subdivision level gives exactly the same geodesic sphere with $20 \cdot 4 = 80$ triangles as before. But the second and third level already produce geodesic spheres with $20 \cdot 16 = 320$, and $20 \cdot 64 = 1280$ triangles respectively. Thus, by the second subdivision approach a geodesic sphere of level k has $20 \cdot 4^k$ triangles. At level 1, both alternative constructions return the same geodesic sphere. However, at higher levels we obtain geometrically different results because the order in which we perform the subdivision and projection steps is different.

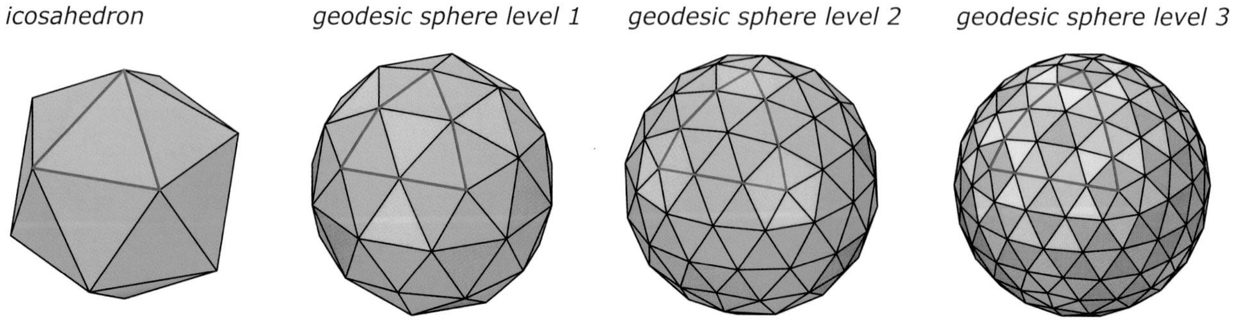

Fig. 3.28
Geodesic spheres generated by subdividing the triangles of an icosahedron and projecting the new vertices:
(a) At level 1 we have 80 triangles of two types (20 equilateral, 60 isosceles in different colors).
(b) At level 2 we have 180 isosceles triangles of two types marked with different colors.
(c) At level 3 we have 320 triangles of five different types. Only 20 of them are equilateral, all others are isosceles.

Figure 3.30 shows a circular section and the different results obtained by changing the order in which subdivision and projection are performed starting with a single edge. Thus, although the number of triangles of a geodesic sphere at level 2, 3, 4, ... with the second approach is the same as the number of triangles of a geodesic sphere at level 3, 7, 15, ... generated with the first approach, the geometry of the resulting objects is slightly different. By varying the generation process (subdivision and projection) we can obtain even other variants of geodesic spheres.

Remark. Note that a geodesic sphere still contains the 12 vertices of the icosahedron from which it is constructed. These 12 vertex pyramids consist of only 5 triangles. All other vertex pyramids of a geodesic sphere consist of 6 triangles which yields a natural relation to hexagons that can be formed around those vertices. Recent projects (such as "Eden" by Grimshaw and partners) are revisiting large spherical roofs using a hexagonal pattern (see Chapter 11 for details).

Fig. 3.29
Geodesic spheres generated with the second subdivision alternative. In each step the triangles of the previous step are split into four smaller triangles and the new vertices are projected again radially onto the circumsphere of the icosahedron.

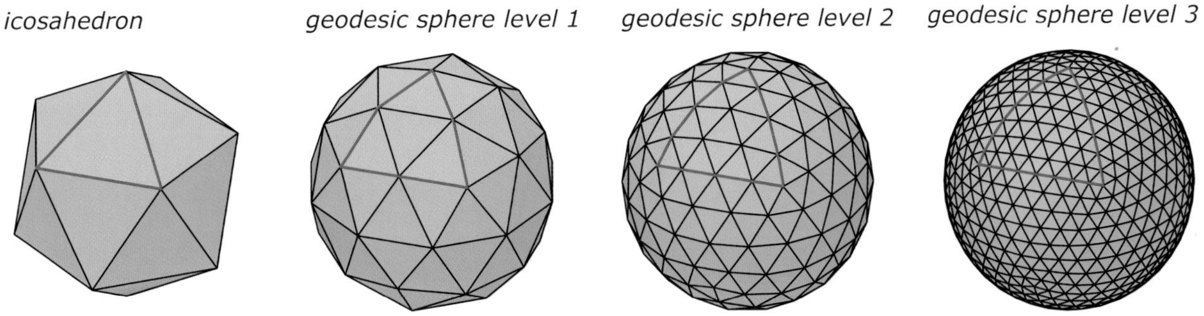

Fig. 3.30
The order of subdivision and projection steps matters. This is illustrated at hand of a circular section.

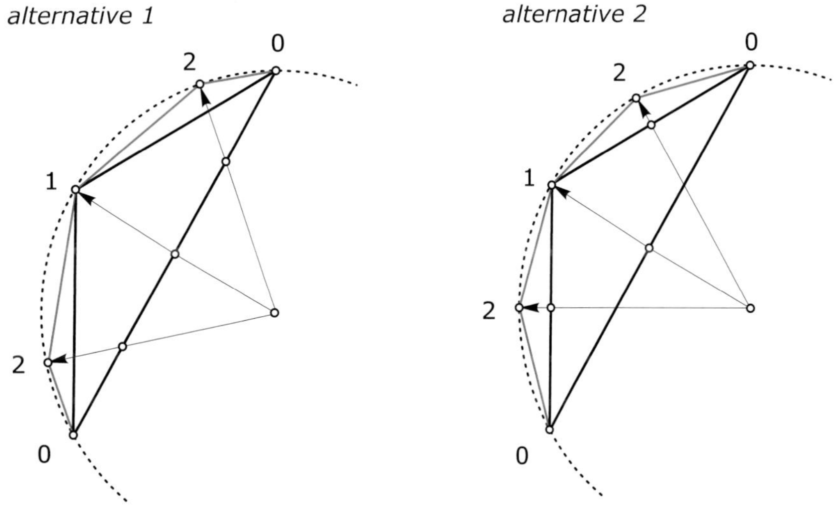

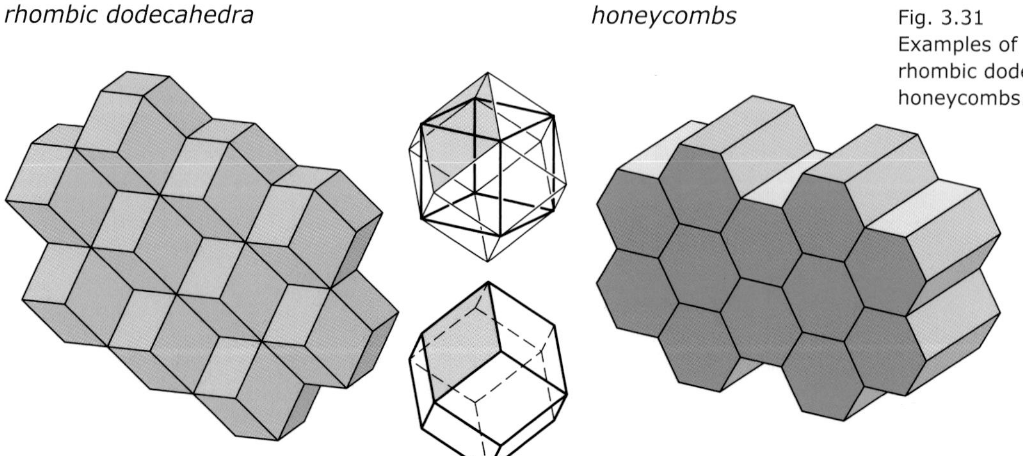

Fig. 3.31
Examples of space filling polyhedra: rhombic dodecahedra and honeycombs.

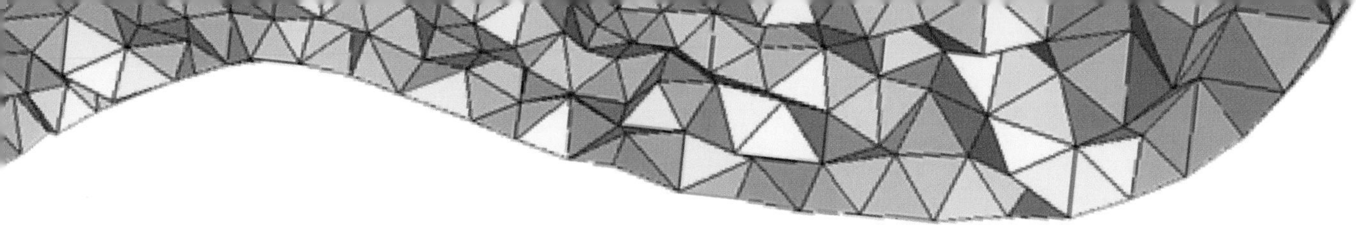

Space Filling Polyhedra

Obviously the cube is a space-filling polyhedron. This means that we can stack congruent cubes and completely fill 3D space with them. Actually, the cube is the only Platonic solid that has this property. Nevertheless, there are other polyhedra that have the space-filling property. One example is the following: If we add square pyramids of height $s/2$ to each face of a cube with edge length s, we obtain a so-called *rhombic dodecahedron* (Figure 3.31a). All faces of a rhombic dodecahedron are congruent rhombi which are non-regular polygons of equal edge length in the form of a sheared square.

Let's examine why the rhombic dodecahedron is also a space-filling polyhedron. We take a cube and attach six congruent cubes to its faces. Replacing these six cubes by rhombic dodecahedrae, the initial cube is completely filled by six congruent pyramidal parts of the adjacent rhombic dodecahedrae. Thus, if we replace in a space-filling assembly of cubes every second cube (in a 3D checkerboard manner) with a rhombic dodecahedron, we find a space-filling by dodecahedra. Space-filling polyhedra appear in nature (e.g. as regular six-sided prisms that form the building blocks of honeycombs, Figure 3.31b).

It is of course possible to fill space with non-congruent polyhedra, although it becomes much more complicated to do this in a meaningful way. For practical applications we sometimes want to fill a certain volume with polyhedra. For simulation purposes one

Fig. 3.32
Volume filling tetrahedra (image courtesy of Pierre Alliez).

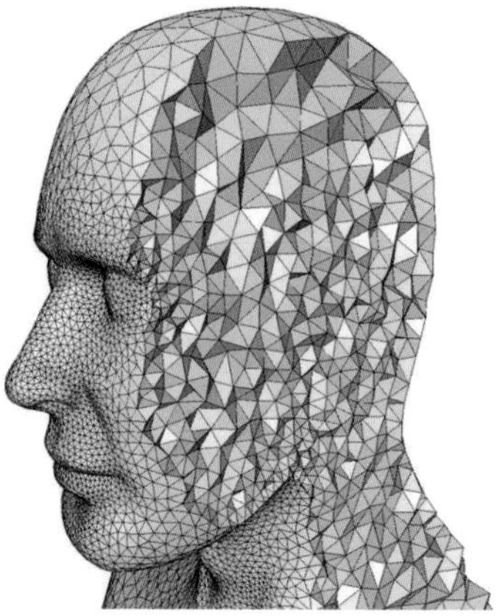

often uses tetrahedra (Figure 3.32). One recent example in architecture that employs space-filling polyhedra of varying shape is the National Swimming Center in Beijing (Figure 3.33). An architectural design that employs polyhedra derived from so-called Voronoi cells (see Chapter 17) is shown in Figure 3.34.

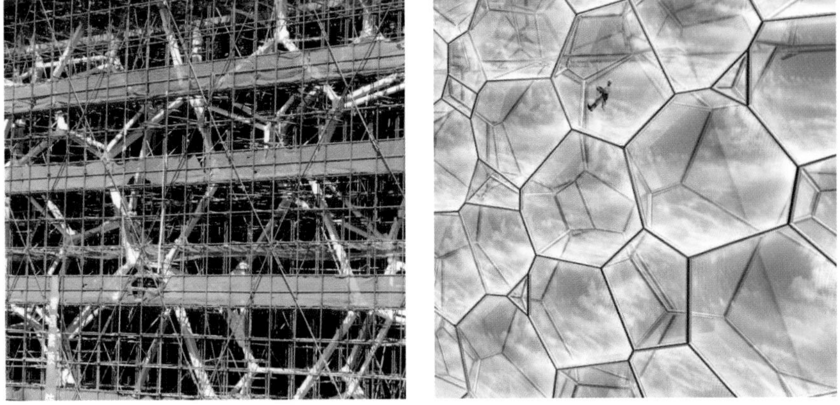

Fig. 3.33
Volume filling polyhedra in architecture: National Swimming Center in Beijing.

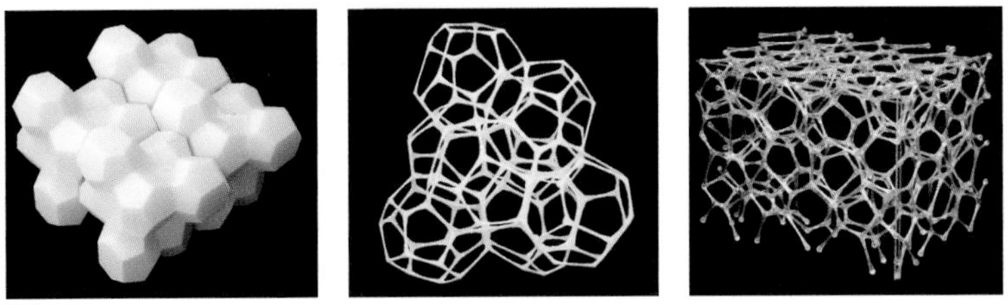

Fig. 3.34
An architectural design based on irregular space filling polyhedra (image courtesy of B. Schneider).

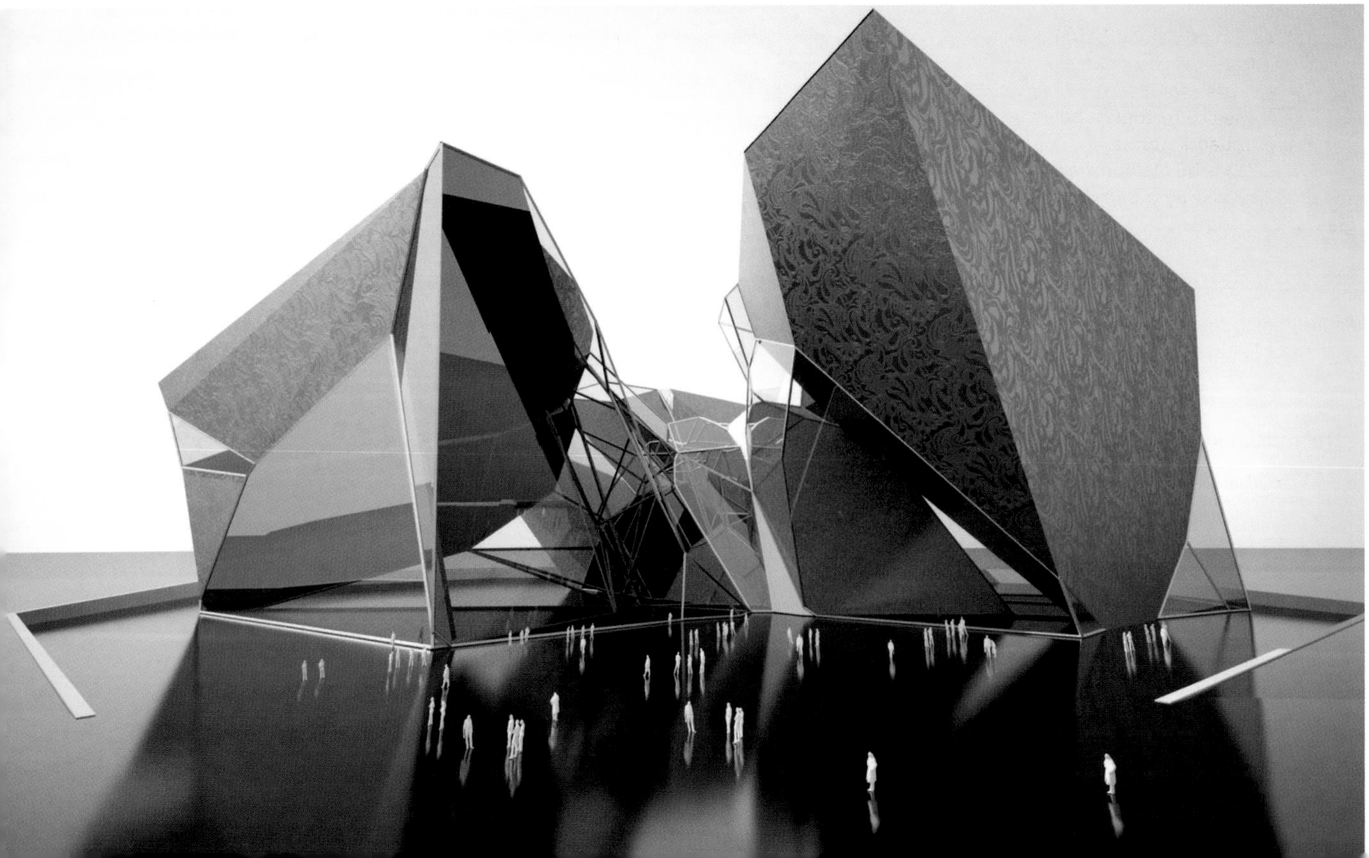

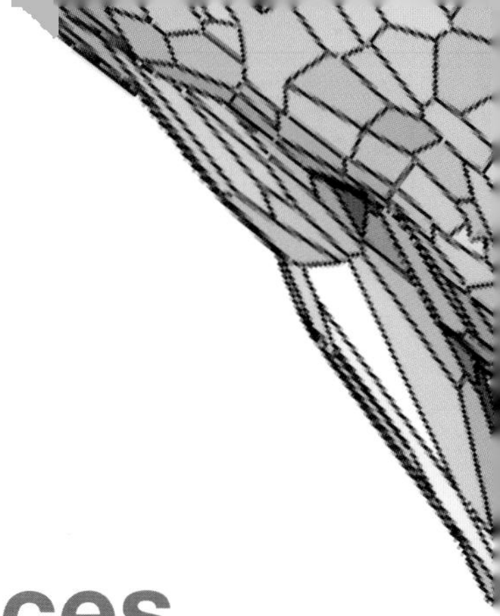

Polyhedral Surfaces

If a smooth surface is approximated by a polyhedral surface we also speak of a *discrete surface*. In architecture discrete surfaces are of special interest in the realization of a design.

Approximation of cylinders and cones by polyhedral surfaces. The first idea is to take a smooth cylinder surface and replace it with a strip model (Figure 3.35a). We can also divide each strip into *planar* quadrilaterals. The same holds for a cone surface. Figure 3.35b shows a strip model and a model with planar quadrilaterals. Note that the quadrilaterals are planar because two opposing edges are lying in the same plane by construction.

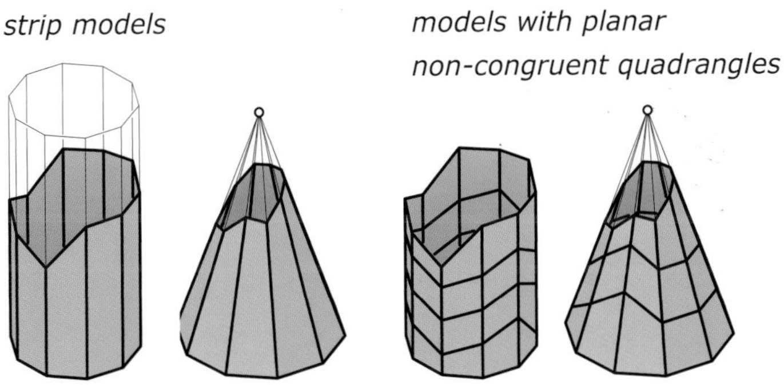

Fig. 3.35
Approximation of cylinders and cones by polyhedral surfaces.
(a) Simple strip models.
(b) The strips are further subdivided into planar quadrilaterals.
(c) Since 1991 the Melbourne Shot Tower is covered by a 84m high conical glass roof designed by Kisho Kurokawa.

Example:

A model of the courtyard roof of the Abbey in Neumunster. The previous idea was used to cover a rectangular area by a curved roof with planar glass panels in an interesting way (Figure 3.36a). The shape of the roof consists of three parts: a cylindrical section in the middle and two congruent conical sections at either side. The circular arc c is the base curve of two adjacent surfaces. Then, a parallel extrusion generates the cylindrical part—and a central extrusion with vertex v generates the conical one. The

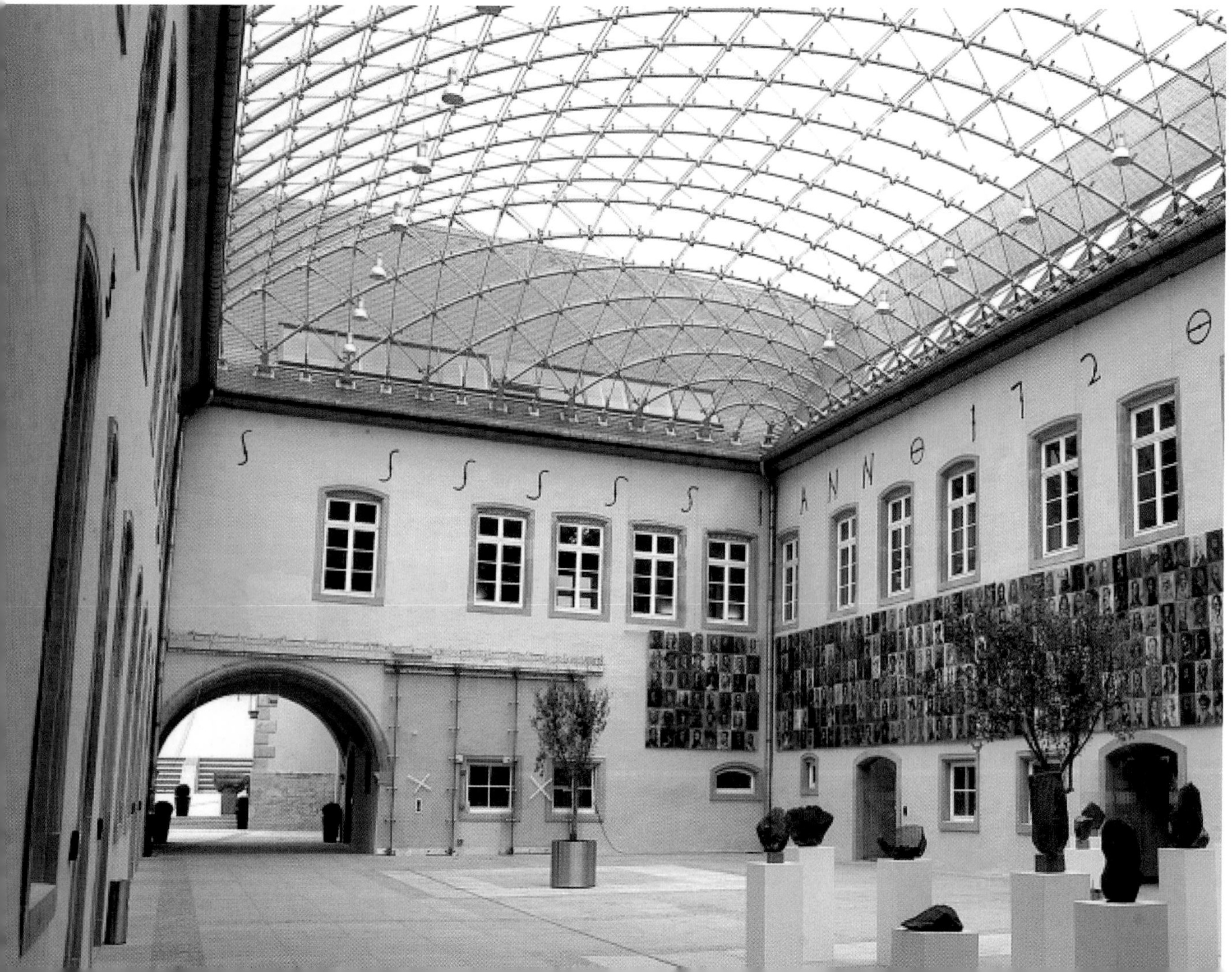

cylinder surface is approximated by congruent planar quadrilaterals using the generators of the cylinder.
If we approximate the conical parts by planar quadrilaterals using the cone generators, the outcome might be undesirable (Figure 3.36b). However, if we use a different decomposition into quadrilaterals, they are no longer planar. Thus, to realize this design with planar glass panels one has to subdivide each nonplanar quadrilateral into two triangles (Figure 3.36c).

Fig. 3.36
(a) The courtyard roof of the Abbey in Neumunster (2003) by Ewart-Haagen & Lorang Architects built by RFR.
(b) A design only using the generators of the cylinder and the cones.
(c) An alternative design that discretizes the conical parts into triangles.

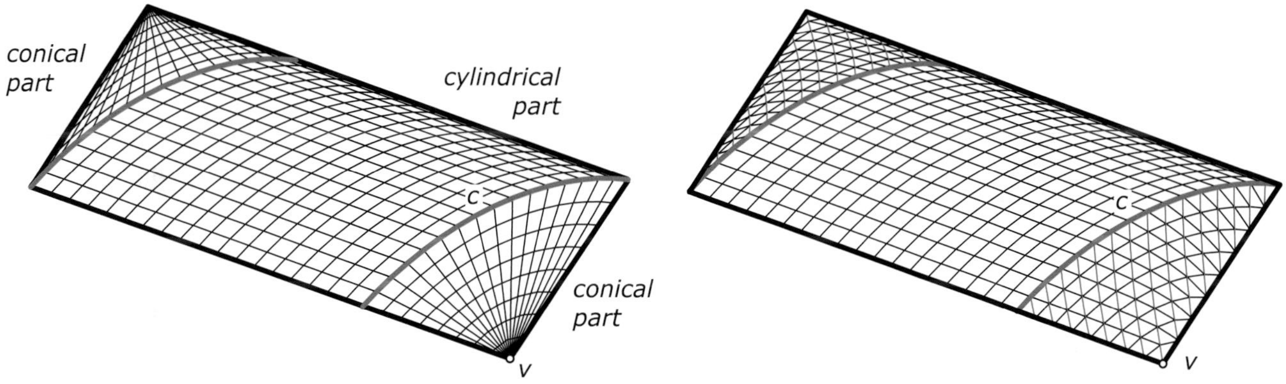

In general, the approximation of a freeform shape by triangles is much simpler than by planar polygons. This fact is intensively used in computer graphics, in which objects are decomposed into triangles (e.g. for rendering purposes, recall Chapter 2). In architecture, freeform-shapes are enjoying increased popularity. For the design of roofs constructed as steel-and-glass structures with planar panels, the simplest polygons are triangles (Figure 3.37).

Fig. 3.37
The *Złote Tarasy* (polish for "Golden Terraces") in Warsaw by Jerde Partnership International opened in 2007. The freeform shape roof is geometrically a polyhedral surface with triangular faces (images courtesy of Waagner-Biro Stahlbau AG).

Whereas three vertices of a triangle in space are always contained in a single plane, this need not be the case for four or more points. The design of polyhedral freeform surfaces with planar faces other than triangles is a difficult task that is a topic of current research. As illustrated in Figure 3.38, computer graphics has already developed algorithms for the approximation of arbitrary shapes by polyhedral surfaces. However, these methods generate a variety of differently shaped planar polygons and thus may not be the best solution for architectural design. Therefore, in Chapter 19 we study a different approach that better meets the needs of architecture.

Fig. 3.38
Shape approximation by polyhedral surfaces applied to Michelangelo's David (image courtesy of Pierre Alliez).

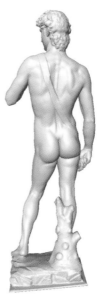

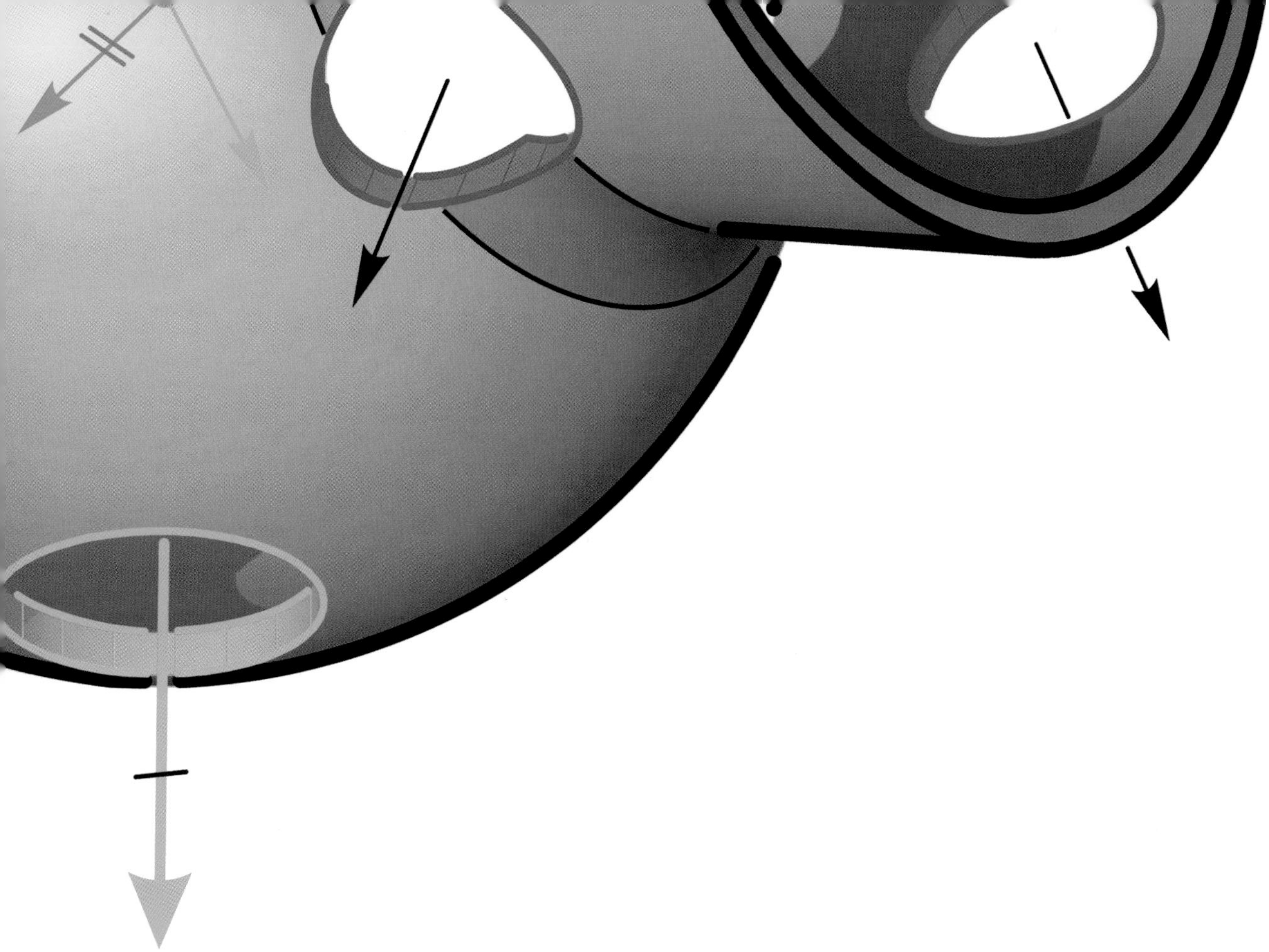

Chapter 4

Boolean Operations

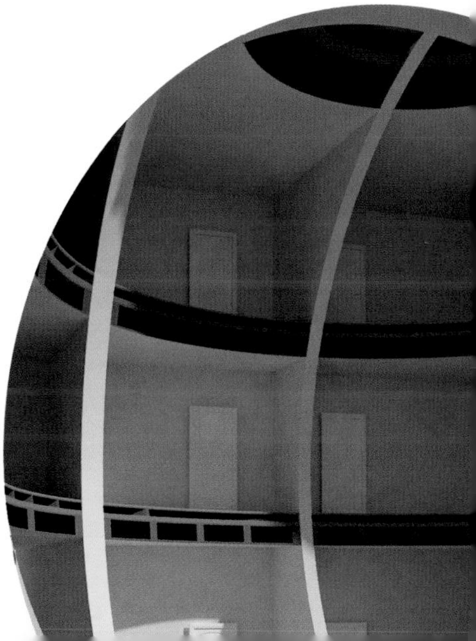

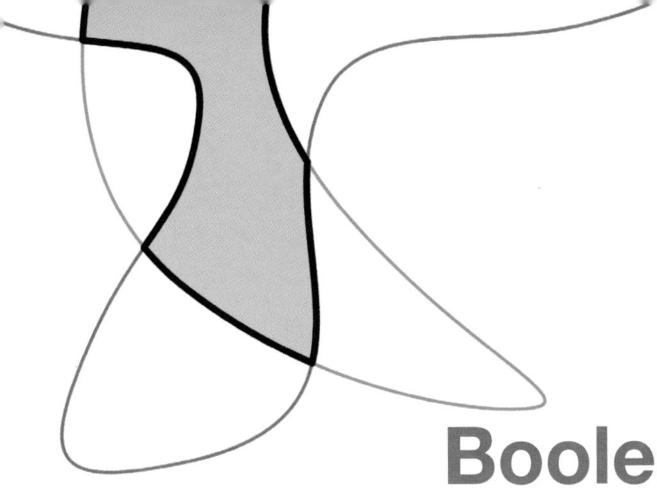

Boolean Operations

So far we have learned a lot about basic objects. Now we will explore how to manipulate these objects to derive more complicated shapes. To modify solids, we use the Boolean operations union (gluing), difference, and intersection. For surface modeling, we need the techniques trimming and splitting to modify our shapes (Figure 4.1).

By combining Boolean operations, a feature-based computer-aided design (CAD) system associates operations such as creating holes, fillets, chamfers (blending), bosses, and pockets to specific edges and faces. When we change the position of the edges or faces, the original relationships are preserved and the feature operation moves along with it. Thus, using feature-based models the designer can test various sizes of details to determine the best solution. One simply adjusts the parameters for the details and regenerates the model. In this way, all relationships such as the relative position of a window or door are preserved.

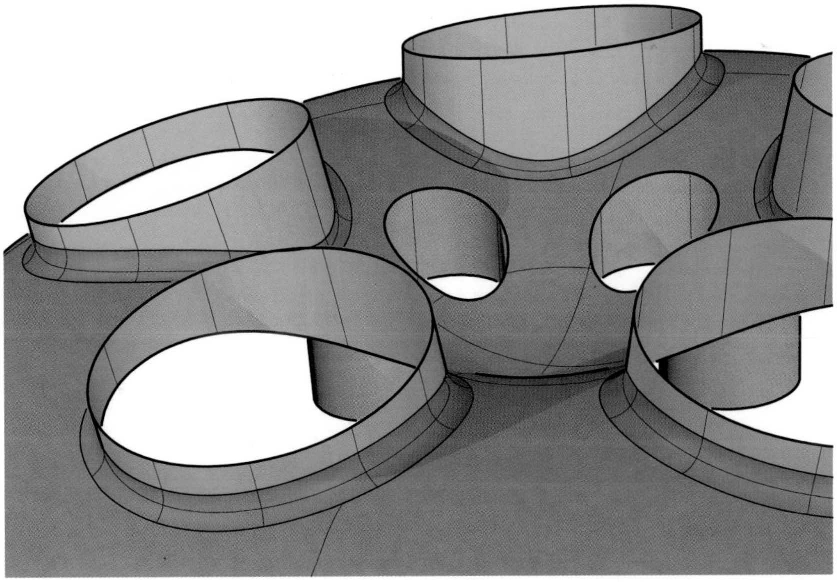

Fig. 4.1
(a) Trimming and splitting techniques are powerful tools for modifying surfaces.

Fig. 4.1
(b) Boolean operations are analogous tools in manipulating solids.

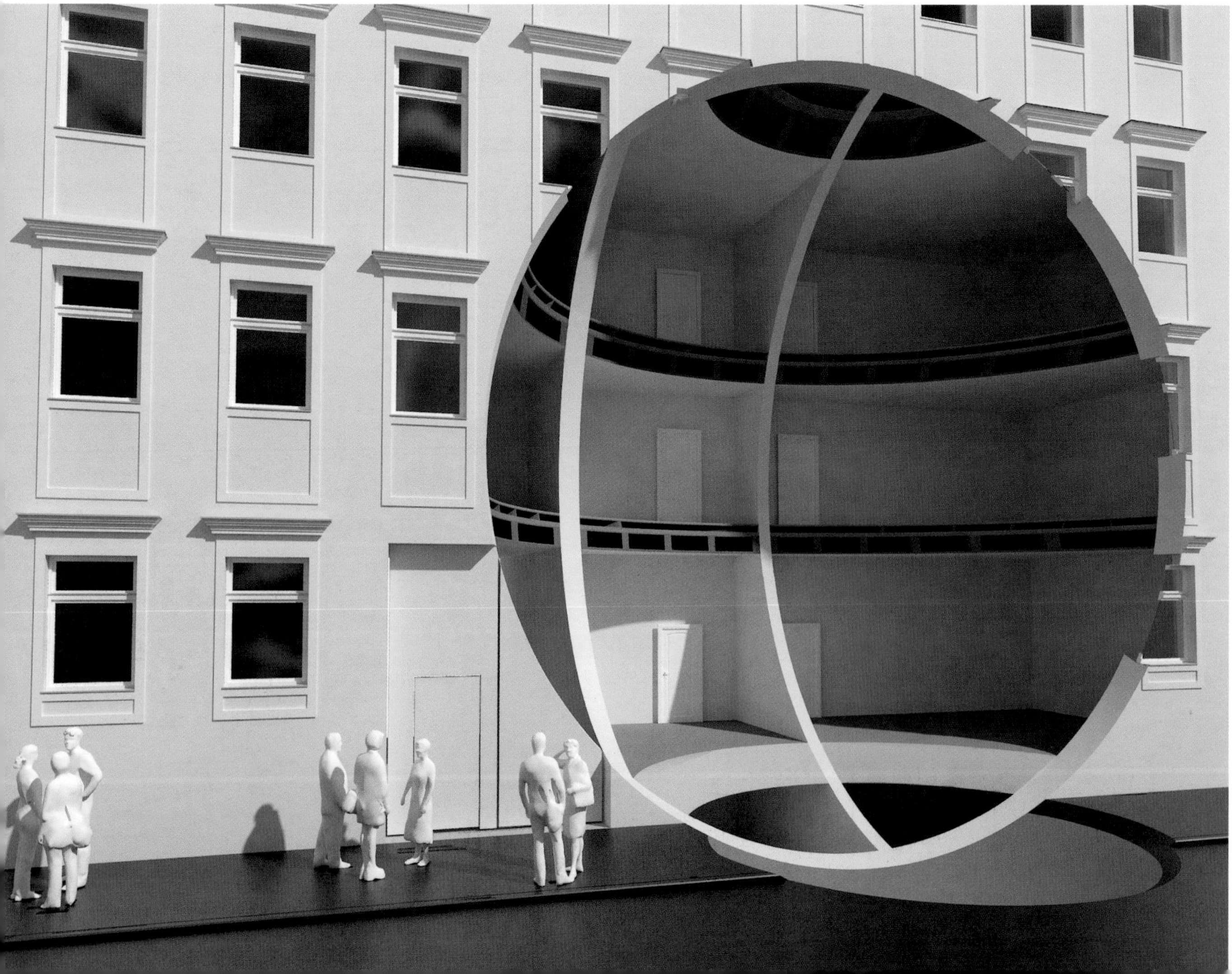

Union, Difference, and Intersection

Let us start with two planar sets. Set A consists of all points inside the red T-shaped boundary, whereas set B includes all points inside the blue moonlike border. Figure 4.2 illustrates (shaded areas) various possibilities of combining both sets.

- The set that contains all points of set *A* and all points of set *B*, but nothing else, is called the *union* of *A* and *B*.
- The *intersection* of *A* and *B* is defined as the set of all points that belong both to *A* and to *B*.
- The *difference* of *A* and *B* contains only those points of *A* that do not lie in *B*. Analogously, the difference of *B* and *A* consists of points of *B* that are not contained in *A*.

Fig. 4.2
The union, intersection, and both differences of two sets *A* and *B*.

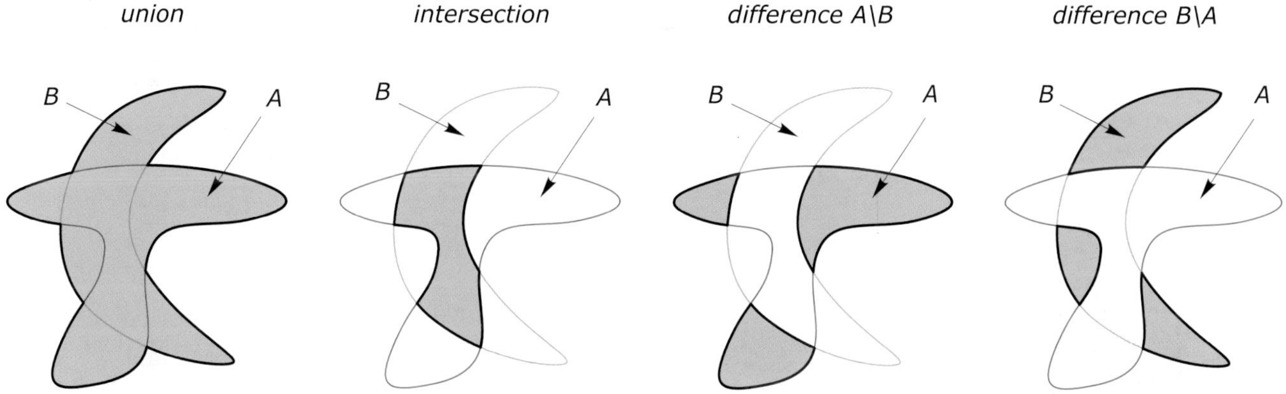

Now we transfer this theoretical concept to solids in 3D space. Figure 4.3 shows various operations that combine two shapes, a cube and a sphere, to produce new shapes:

- The *union* operation combines both objects into one single entity. We can consider the union operation simply as adding or gluing one object to the other. To avoid problems in the subsequent modeling process, the involved objects should have common spatial regions or should at least touch each other.
- The *intersection* operation joins both objects but keeps only those parts that lie in both objects.
- The *difference* operation removes the overlapping portions of the second object from the first object. It is the same effect when countersinking the second object from the first—a typical milling procedure. Bear in mind that the order of selecting the objects radically influences the appearance of the combined shape.

sphere and cube

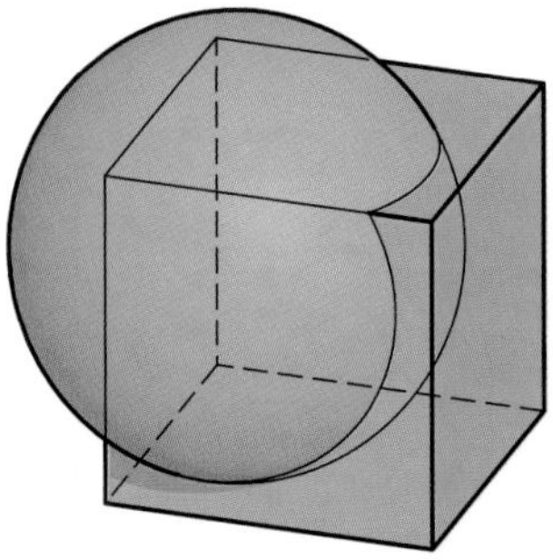

Fig. 4.3
Application of Boolean operations to a cube and a sphere. For a better understanding, the original painting of both objects has been preserved in these pictures.

union *intersection* *difference sphere\cube* *difference cube\sphere*

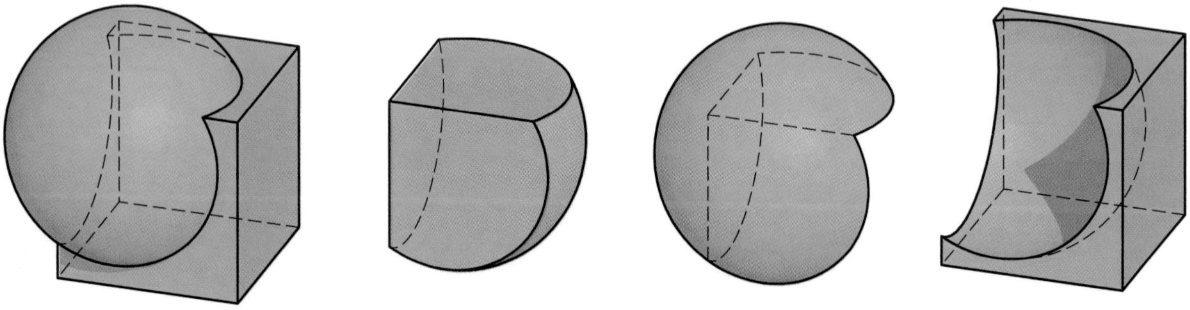

These operations are called *Boolean operations*. They can be performed not only on two objects but on a set of given objects. Skillful usage of Boolean operations gives your modeling a highly productive capability by modifying large amounts of geometry (each must be a solid) with a single operation. Some examples, which demonstrate the power of Boolean operations, are shown in Figures 4.1 and 4.4.

History:

Boolean operations are named after the English mathematician George Boole (1815–1864), who taught at University College Cork. He introduced an algebraic system of logic that has many applications in electronics and in computer hardware and software.

(a)

(b)

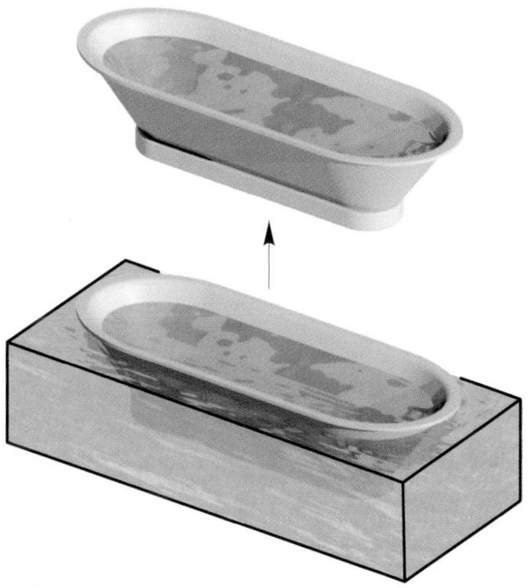

(c)

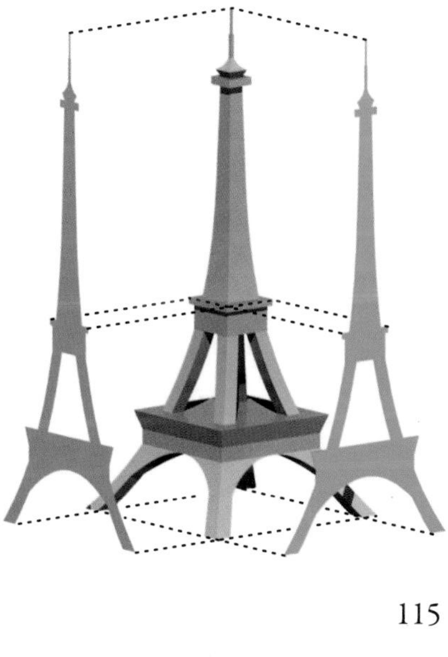

Fig. 4.4
(a) By applying Boolean operations to two bodies of extrusion with profiles consisting of letters, we obtain interesting logos.
(b) To "fill water" into a CAD model of a bathtub or a swimming pool, we can use a fitting block and the Boolean difference operation.
(c) With two congruent bodies of extrusion with appropriate profiles and the Boolean intersection, we easily model a tower.

From the mathematical point of view, Boolean union and intersection are commutative operations. This means that the order in which the objects are fed into the operation does not matter. Nevertheless, in CAD the sequence of selecting the involved objects influences the attributes of the emerging object. The newly created object inherits the attributes of the first selected object.

Sometimes CAD software seems to fail mysteriously in completing Boolean operations. Why does this matter, and how can we avoid such problems? To understand why Boolean operations do not succeed, one has to consider that these operations are multistep processes. They basically combine the following.

- Computing the intersection curves
- Splitting all involved objects along these curves
- Deleting those parts not contained in the solution
- Joining all remaining parts

Boolean operations typically fail because the calculation of the intersection curves creates curves with gaps due to badly modeled objects or inaccuracy of computations. To support your CAD software in performing Boolean operations you should observe the following.

- Try to extend your trimming objects beyond the faces of the modified object.
- Avoid combining objects with co-planar faces.
- Avoid nearly tangent surfaces.

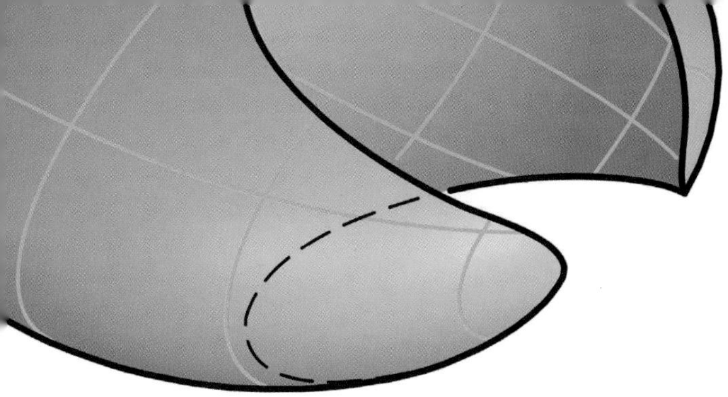

Trim and Split

Boolean operations are powerful tools for the shaping of solids. But when applying these tools on *surfaces* we recognize that the concept of Boolean operations does not always work in the desired way. For example, the Boolean difference of two surfaces would generate an exact copy of the first surface—with only the intersection curve missing. Otherwise, the Boolean intersection of two surfaces would only produce the intersection curve.

When working with solids, there is no doubt which areas are inside and which are outside a CAD model. On the one hand, it is relatively easy to calculate (for example) the Boolean intersection as the set of all parts inside all bodies involved. On the other hand, it is not decidable which are the inner and outer areas of open surfaces. Therefore, Boolean operations do not work when surfaces are involved.

When it comes to modeling with surfaces, we use the techniques of *trimming* and *splitting*. Applying these operations to surfaces, the intersection curves are calculated and the surfaces are divided along these curves. The resulting parts either can be manipulated as independent objects (splitting) or deleted automatically (trimming). These operations are used to trim (cut) one surface with another, or to split one surface along its intersection curve with a second surface. Figure 4.5 shows the splitting of a torus with a cylinder.

Fig. 4.5
By splitting the torus with the cylinder, we obtain four parts (indicated by different colors). Otherwise, if we split the cylinder with the torus we derive four distinct objects. We obtain a cylinder with three holes and three small caplike parts. For reasons of better visualization, these parts are displaced from their original positions.

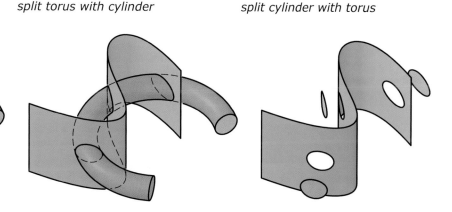

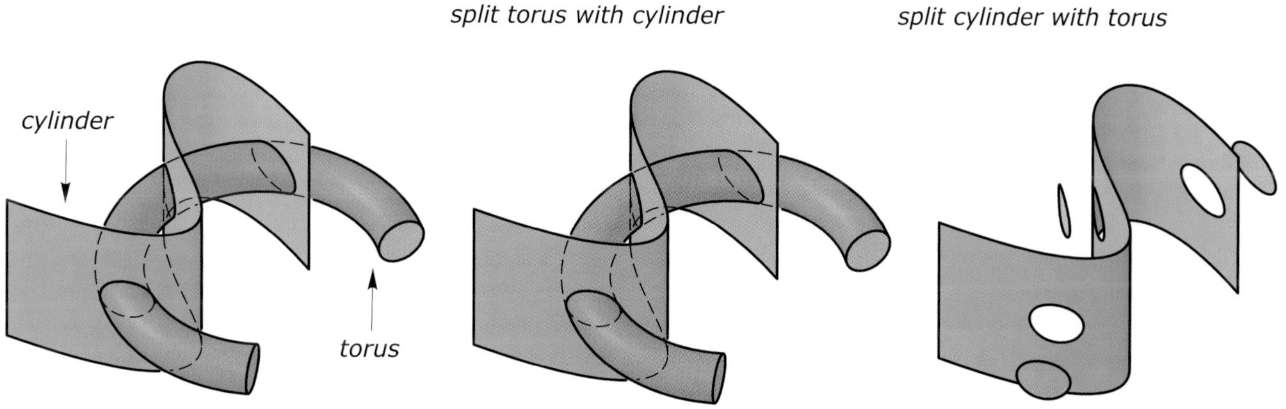

The trim operation demands a user-controlled intervention to define those parts, which have to remain after the trimming process. Figure 4.6 illustrates various results of the trim operation being used on an ellipsoid and a cylinder.

During the trimming process, the intersection curve is being calculated. Thus, it can be used as a new profile for generating new surfaces or solids (see Figure 4.6d).

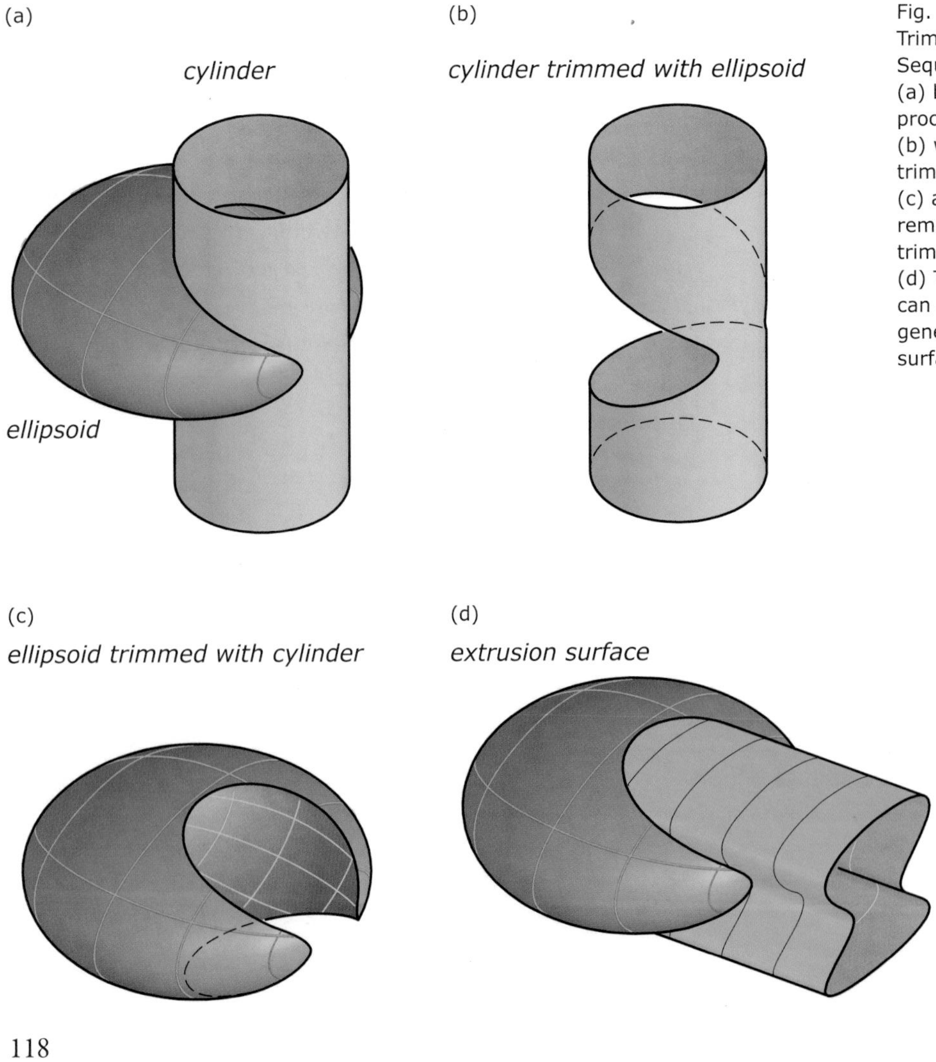

Fig. 4.6
Trimming of a cylinder and an ellipsoid. Sequentially, the pictures show
(a) both objects before the trimming process,
(b) when the ellipsoid has been trimmed away, and
(c) alternatively when the ellipsoid remains while the cylinder has been trimmed away.
(d) The calculated intersection curve can also be used as a profile to generate a consistently connecting surface.

Most CAD systems also provide a special tool for joining ("gluing together") trimmed surfaces with common intersection curves. This *stitching* operation (Figure 4.7) for surfaces is the equivalent of the Boolean union for solids. When surfaces are stitched, CAD software often not only joins the surface patches but tries to uniform the surface normals of the object so that all adjacent surfaces have the same front/back orientation. If your CAD system does not supply this functionality, you should change the surface's front/back orientation manually before stitching them. In the case of assigning "orientated material" to the stitched surfaces, you will see the difference immediately.

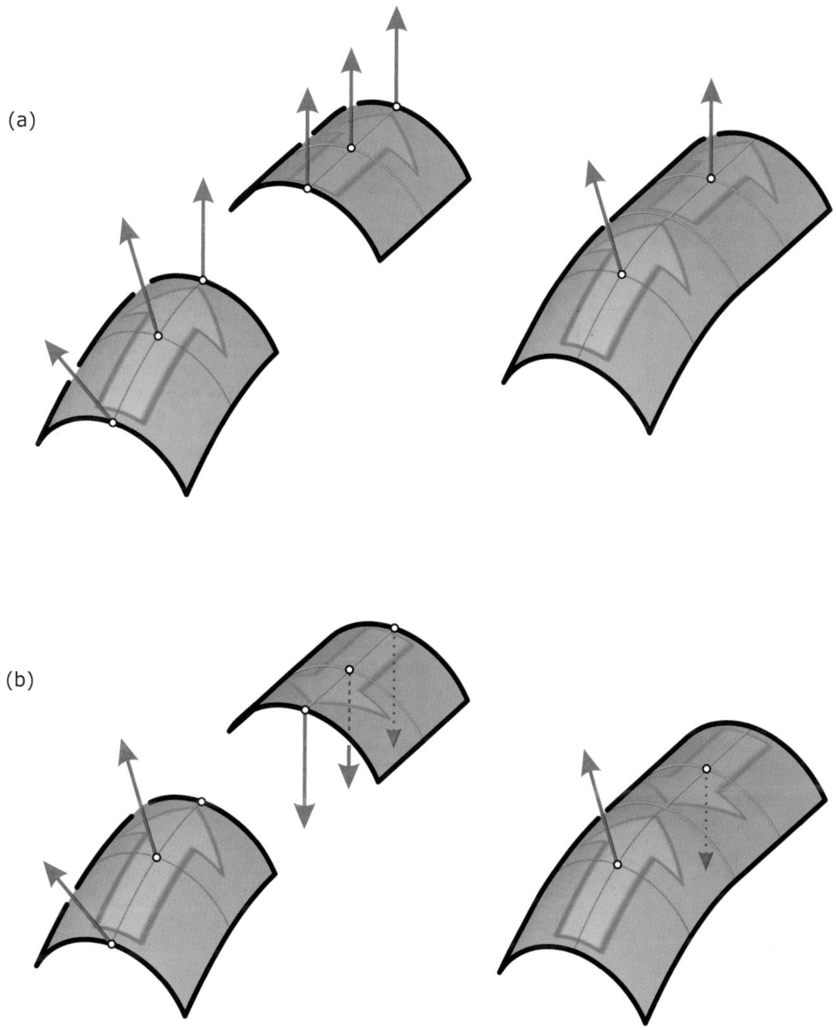

Fig. 4.7
Stitching of two surfaces
(a) with the same front/back orientation generates continuous texturing.
(b) Different orientations of the stitched surfaces result in discontinuities of oriented textures.

Trimming and splitting techniques can also be used to trim solids with surfaces. This can be used to create parts of solids that have freeform surfaces as boundaries. Figure 4.8 shows an application of this technique in modeling a hexagonal prism with a saddle-shaped boundary.

Often, surface and solid objects can be trimmed or split with simple lines or curves. In this case, we can also define the direction of the trimming. These directions depend on the world coordinate system, on a user-specific auxiliary coordinate system, on a reference plane, or on an arbitrary vector. In all of these cases, the CAD software calculates the projection (along the specified direction) of the curve onto the original object.

Depending on the user's selection, it then either punches a hole in the surface or splits the surface along the projected curve. This technique can also be considered a combination of generating a surface of extrusion and trimming or splitting the original object with this surface of extrusion. The profile of this surface of extrusion is the projected curve. The direction of the extrusion is defined by the direction of the projection. Figure 4.9 shows this effect in terms of a hole punched into a paraboloid (see Chapter 9).

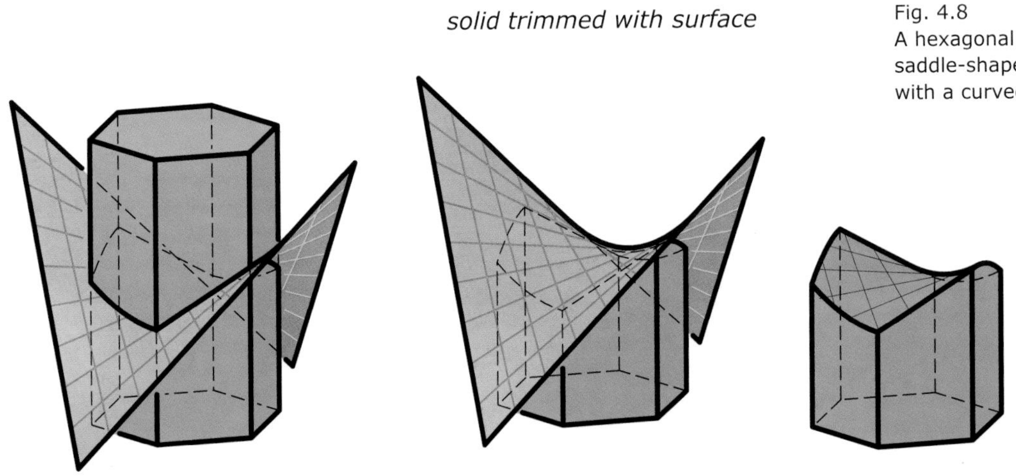

Fig. 4.8
A hexagonal prism is trimmed with a saddle-shaped surface to obtain a solid with a curved boundary.

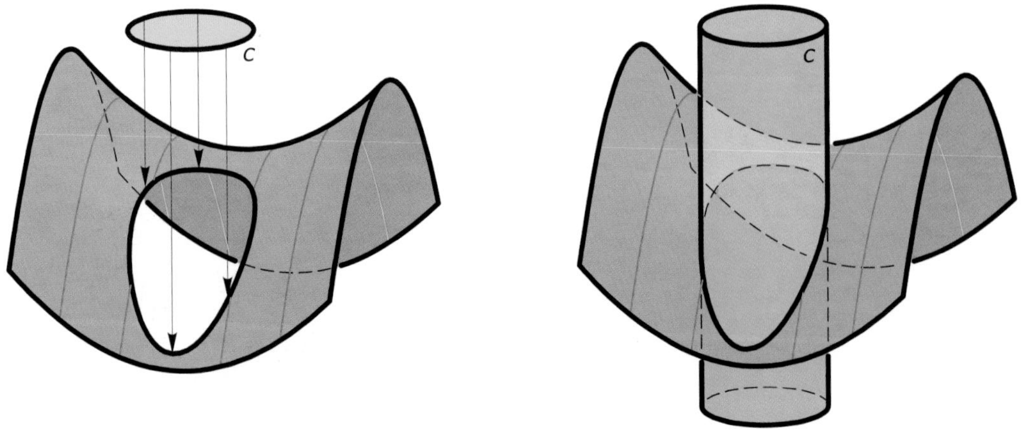

Fig. 4.9
The projection of a circle c onto a paraboloid punches a hole in the surface. This process can also be considered as trimming the paraboloid with a surface of extrusion (with profile c).

***Orthogonal projection onto a surface.** A special case of this technique consists of defining the direction of the projection using the surface's normals. For the following description, we need a rough understanding of surface normals (Figure 4.10). Starting with an ordinary point *p* on a surface *S*, we consider a curve *c* through point *p* lying completely on the surface. We take a neighboring point *q* on the curve *c*. The points *p* and *q* define a straight line *l*. Now we move the point *q* along the curve *c* toward point *p*.

In the limit, when *q* coincides with *p* the straight line *l* becomes the *tangent t* of the curve *c*. This tangent touches the curve *c* and the surface *S* in the point *p*. Now we consider all curves through point *p* that lie completely on the surface *S*. If all curve tangents in *p* define one single plane *P*, we call *P* the *tangent plane* of the surface *S* in *p*. The tangent plane touches the surface *S* in *p*. The *normal n* to the surface *S* at the point *p* is then the straight line orthogonal to the tangent plane *T* through *p*. A more thorough discussion of these terms is found in Chapter 7.

When we punch a hole in the direction of the surface normals, the boundary of the generated hole consists of all surface points whose normals intersect the projected curve. To understand what the CAD system really calculates, one has to consider the intersection of the surface with a special ruled surface (see Chapter 9). The generators of this auxiliary surface are the normals of the surface along the intersection curve.

Fig. 4.10
The tangents of all curves through an ordinary point *p*, which lie completely on the surface *S* form the tangent plane *P*. The tangent plane *P* touches the surface in *p*. It is orthogonal to the surface's normal *n* in point *p*.

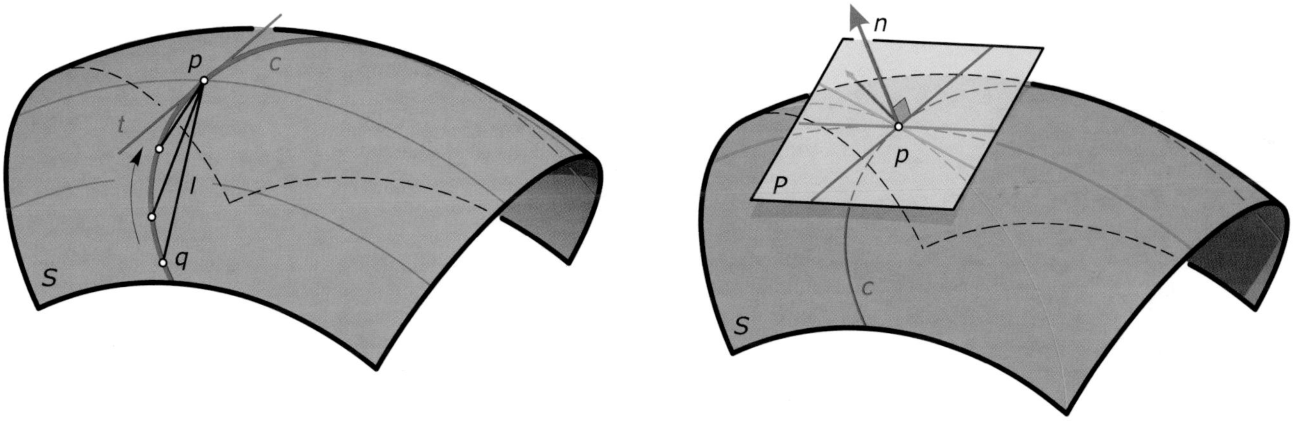

Example:

Punched rotational surfaces (Figure 4.11). All surface normals of rotational surfaces intersect the axis of revolution. Thus, when punching rotational surfaces the involved ruled surface is a special one; namely, a conoid (see Chapter 9). In the case of a sphere, all surface normals run through the center of the sphere. Therefore, the ruled surface is a cone with vertex v in the center of the sphere.

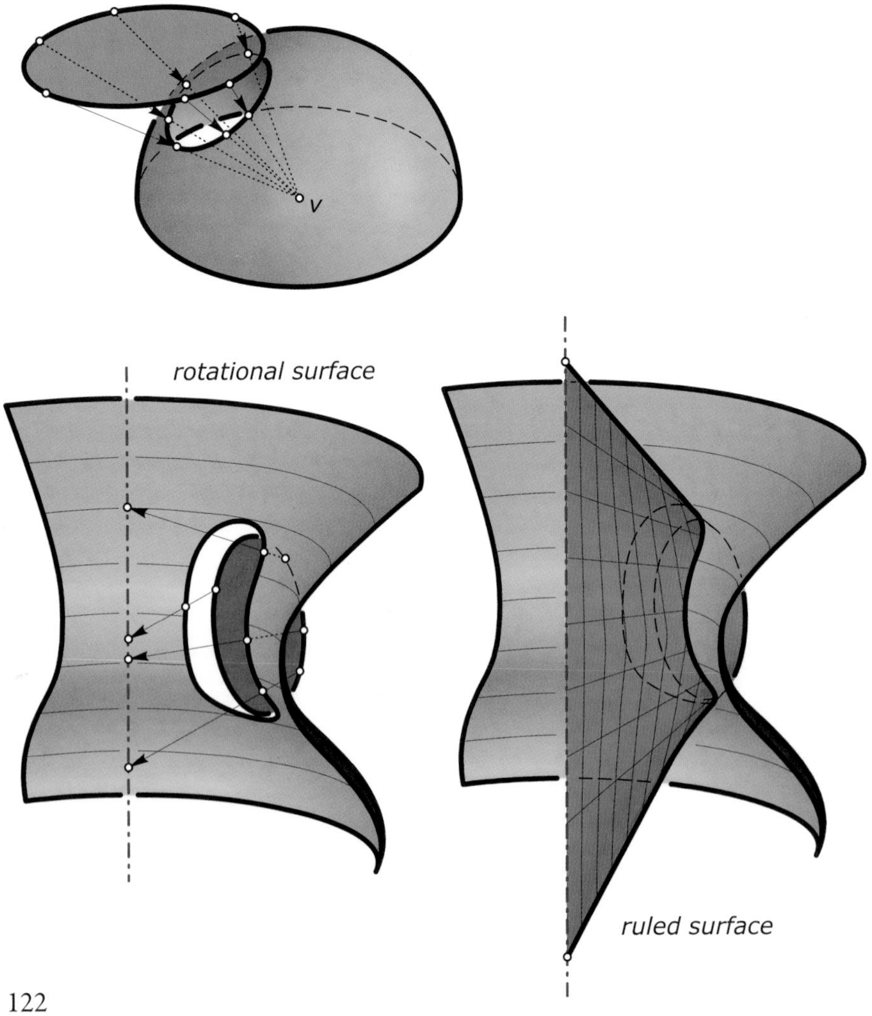

Fig. 4.11
Trimming a rotational surface with a curve c in the direction of the surface normals can be considered trimming of a ruled surface (here a conoid) with the rotational surface. In the special case of a sphere, the involved ruled surface is a cone.

With the exception of these special cases, most of the emerging ruled surfaces have a very complex shape. As a consequence, the generated intersection curves can take on rather unexpected forms.

As previously stated for Boolean operations, one also has to obey some restrictions for these trimming and splitting techniques. They do not work properly when the calculated intersection curves are not closed or when they have gaps. Therefore, understanding how these operations work is of great significance in avoiding undesirable results.

Often, intersection curves of curved surfaces assume complicated forms even when the involved surfaces are simple ones—such as cylinders or cones (Figure 4.12a). However, when we consider the intersection of two half cylinders with the same radius and orthogonally intersecting axis (Figure 4.12b, c) we have a cross-shaped vault with two planar intersection curves.

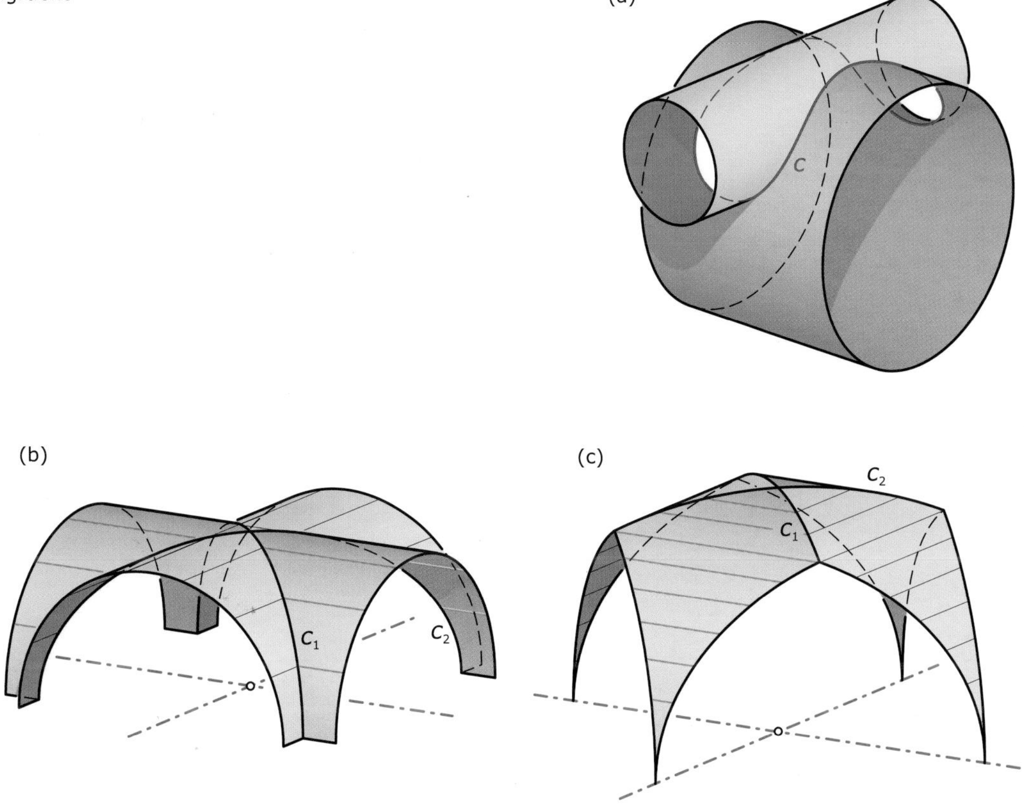

Fig. 4.12
(a) Generally, the intersection curve of two cylinders is a spatial curve *c*. (b, c) By trimming two congruent half cylinders with crossing axes, we obtain a cross-shaped vault with planar intersection curves.

These curves are contained in the two bisecting planes of the cylinder axes. Reflecting one cylinder at such a bisecting plane, we get the other cylinder. Therefore, the intersection curve degenerates into two parts consisting of ellipses. This desired and well-known effect has been intensely used by architects for centuries to build not only interesting but very stable sacral buildings. With the help of cross-shaped vaults, it has been possible to canopy large halls without a great number of columns.

Fig. 4.12
Different forms of vaults have been used in architecture for centuries.
(d) The *Abbey of Fontevrault* founded in 1099 by Robert of Arbrissel (image courtesy of Luke M. van Grieken).
(e) The *Danish Jewish Museum* (opened 2004) in Copenhagen by Daniel Liebeskind.

(d)

(e)

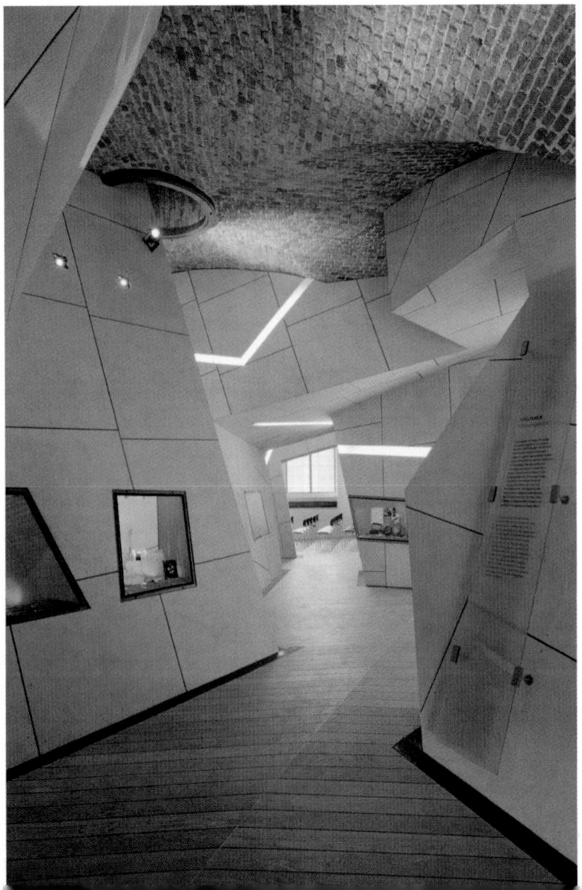

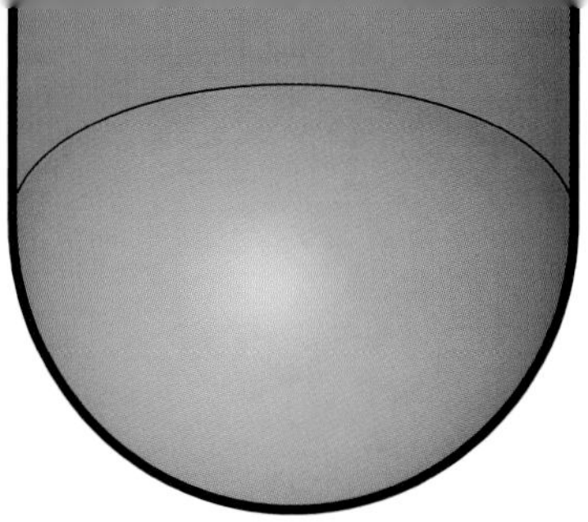

Feature-Based Modeling: An Efficient Approach to Shape Variations

Boolean operations allow us to design new objects out of the given primitives with only a few mouse clicks. The emerging objects are calculated and stored within the CAD system solely as solids consisting of many faces. In parametric systems, the *parents* of the operation are stored and allow one to edit the shapes used in the Boolean operation. In earlier CAD systems, the forms are lost once the operation is applied.

This can become a very expensive problem for the designing architect. To avoid those troubles, modern CAD systems offer a more sophisticated type of Boolean operation. They behave like the normal Boolean operations but store the entire design history together with the model. In combination with parametric solids, we then have the possibility of controlling the dimensions and the relative positions of all participating objects during the entire generation process.

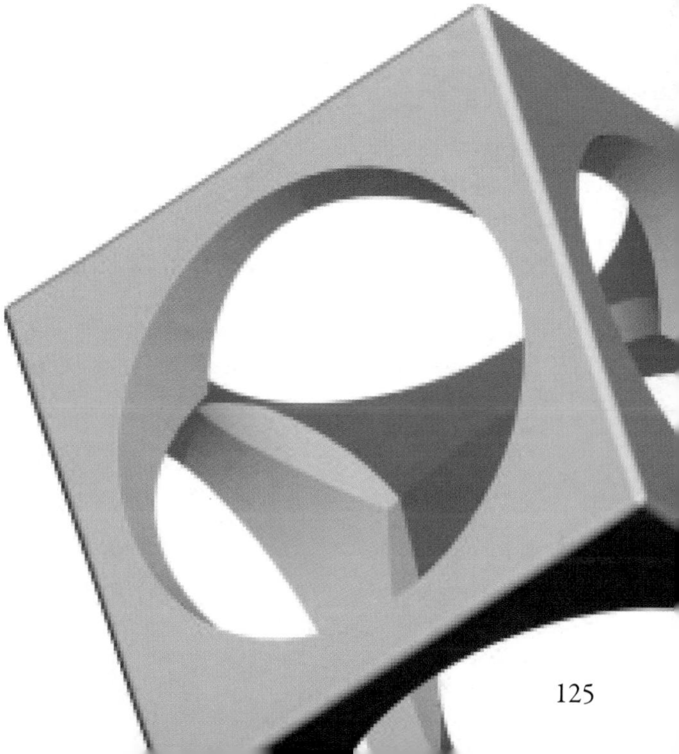

To gain even more flexibility in the design process, a sophisticated CAD system allows also manipulation of the Boolean operations and substitution of profile curves. As a result, one can change the order of the Boolean operations. One also has the possibility of deleting them or of replacing generating curves by new ones even after finishing all of the modeling work.

To illustrate the benefits of this technique, we consider a cubical sculpture with three holes, rounded edges, and a cylindrical socket with vertical axis (Figure 4.13a). We assume that the sculpture was modeled in the following order.

- Positioning of the cube
- Rounding of the edges
- Drilling of the holes
- Positioning of the cylindrical socket and
- Boolean union

Working with ordinary Boolean operations (i.e. not feature based), we would have no difficulty enlarging the diameter of the drilled holes by removing more material. However, reducing the diameter would cause a lot of additional work since we cannot return already removed material. Using a feature-based CAD system we can change the diameter of a drill hole in a Boolean operation at any time.

The software, which has stored not only the parameters of the involved primitives and the design history, recalculates all operations depending on the changed parameter (Figure 4.13b). If we now enlarge the diameter of the cylindrical socket, we recognize a new problem. The height of the cylinder also has to be adjusted to grant a proper compound of the socket with the cube (Figure 4.13c). At this point, we see that adjusting the height is very critical.

If the height is too small, we produce unwanted faces on the top of the cylinder. Otherwise, if the height is too large there would be parts of the cylinder seen inside the drilled holes. Figure 4.13d shows this effect after enlarging the height of the cylinder of the starting object. This happens because the drilling affects only the cube and not the cylinder due to the fact that the union was the last operation. By rearranging the order of the Boolean operation (Boolean union before drilling), we can avoid this problem. Thus, we are able to alter the diameter of the socket without worrying about the correct height (Figure 4.13e).

During the design process, we often position objects and afterward apply Boolean operations. For example, to drill a hole into an object we first place a cylinder in the correct position and then apply the Boolean difference. By combining these two operations to a single "hole tool," modern CAD software helps to accelerate the modeling process. This hole tool is even more efficient when the relative position of the drilling cylinder to the original object or to a user-specific coordinate systems is obeyed and stored automatically. If the CAD system also allows us (by storing the design history) to change the dimensions and relative positions of all participating objects, we get even more flexibility.

This technique is called *feature-based modeling*. The design is executed by means of features, which we can roughly define as component parts of the models. The designer does not only specify the geometry and shape of the model but relevant information about the technological and functional aspects. We can loosely classify the features as follows.

- Body features (basic objects such as cuboids, balls, extrusion solids, freeform solids, and so on)
- Form features (holes, pockets, bosses, and so on)
- Operation features (blends, fillets, chamfers, offsets, and so on)

Fig. 4.13
Feature-based CAD systems do not only support changes of all of the object's dimensions but also a rearrangement of the design history even after finishing the modeling job.

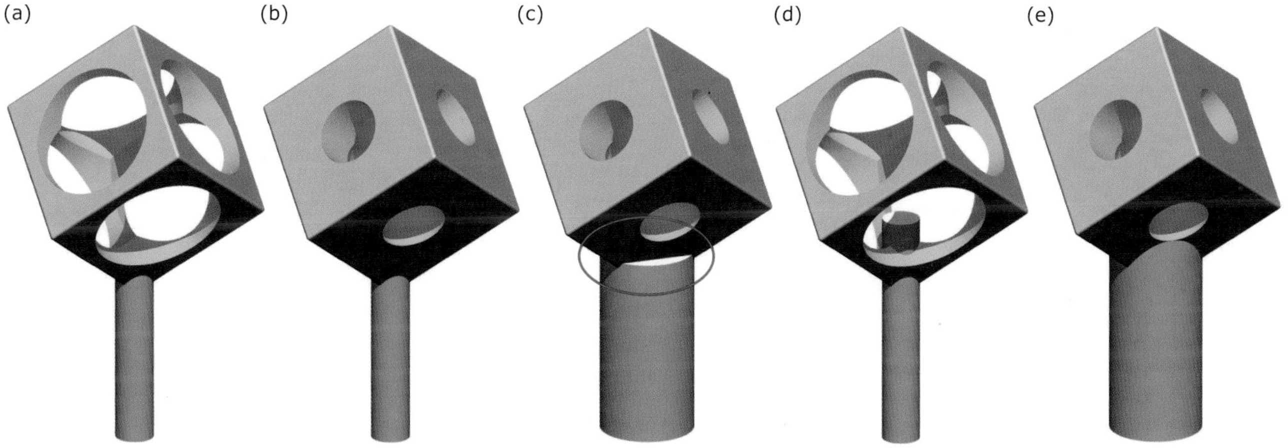

Example:

Hole feature. Assume we have a model consisting of a half sphere and part of a cone (body features) that have been combined via Boolean union. The inner parts have also been modeled as a cone and a sphere, and have been split away using Boolean difference. Finally, the intersection curve has been rounded (operation feature). Now we apply the form feature *hole* to punch the object (Figure 4.14, left).

- The two holes of the half sphere are drilled with respect to different coordinate systems. The drill axis of the blue hole at the top is parallel to the z-axis of the world coordinate system. The drill axis of the green hole is parallel to the y-axis of the user-defined coordinate system, which can be seen in the middle of the sphere.
- The remaining purple holes through the cone and the blending are adjusted with respect to the direction of the surface's normals. To support the designer in adjusting the holes precisely, a user-friendly CAD system calculates the normals (black arrows) of the punched objects in real time and indicates them during the entire modeling process.

Feature-based CAD software stores all geometric and functional information. Thus, after modeling of the entire object the functionality of the holes will be maintained when moving the holes along the surfaces. This means that the relative positions of the drillings with respect to the surfaces or the coordinate systems are recalculated. Figure 4.14 (right) shows this effect.

• The blue hole has been moved along the surface of the half sphere. During this movement, the drilling direction is maintained parallel to the *z*-axis of the world coordinate system.

• The green hole has even been repositioned on the cone. Nevertheless, it keeps the drilling direction parallel to the *y*-axis of the user-defined coordinate system.

• One of the purple holes has also changed its position. This hole keeps the information that the drilling direction is in the direction of the surface normal at the current position.

Fig. 4.14
(a) When applying a hole feature to a model, there are various possibilities for the direction of the drilling (e.g. parallel to the *z*-axis of the world coordinate system or parallel to a surface normal). These directions are indicated during the design process.
(b) Three hole features are moved along the object. Thereby, the information about the drilling direction is preserved.

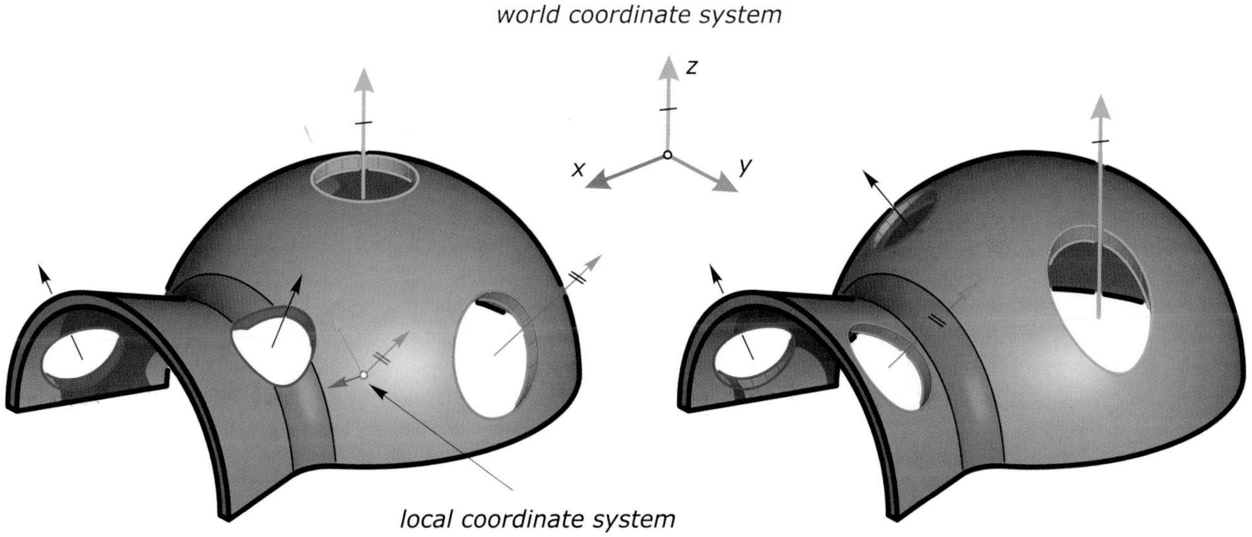

The form feature *hole* can be described as a combination of positioning a cylinder and applying the Boolean difference. If we substitute the Boolean difference by the Boolean union, we obtain the *protrusion* or *boss* feature. It works in a manner similar to that of the *hole* feature, with the difference that it adds material instead of removing it. As we see in Figure 4.15, the protrusion feature also fills the gaps between the attached cylinder and the surface. In addition, boss and protrusion features include automatic blending of the protrusion and the original object.

Another possibility in expanding the functionality of protrusion and hole features is the substitution of the circular profile by more general profiles. In combination with other functional properties, such as drilling or protruding up to the next surface or up to all faces of the modeled work piece, we obtain very powerful tools for designing sophisticated objects.

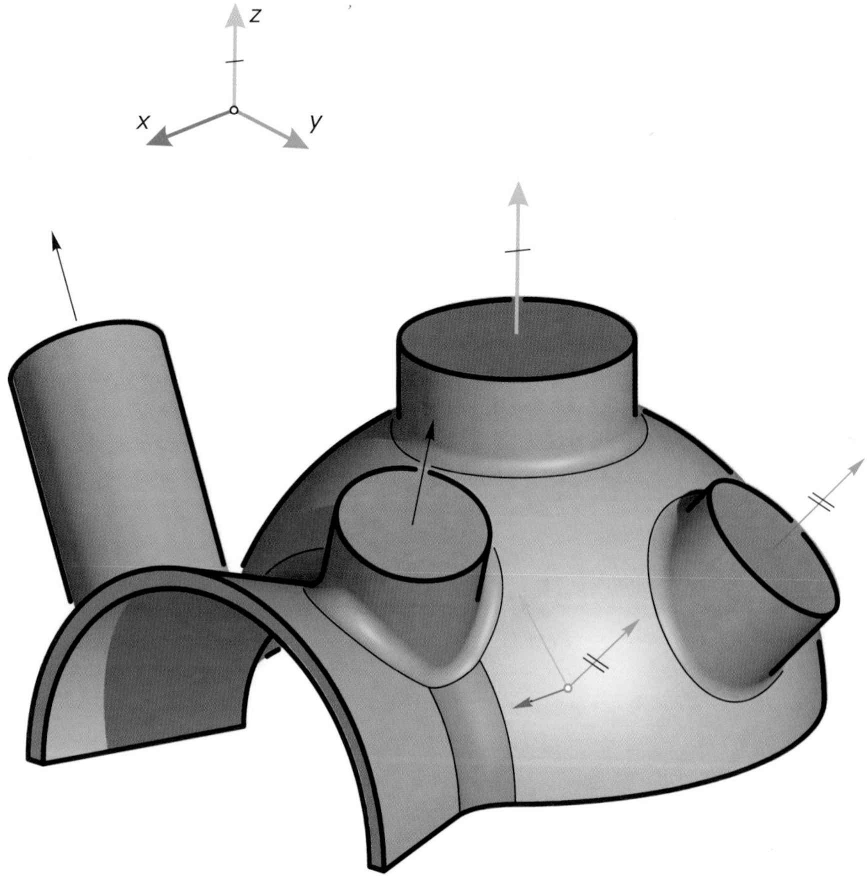

Fig. 4.15
The boss feature combines the positioning of a cylinder with Boolean union. The user-specified directions can depend on local or global coordinate systems or on the surface normals.

Example:

Handrail. As an example of an application, we show these techniques by designing different models of a handrail. After modeling the stairs as bodies of extrusion and the handrail as an extrusion of a circle along a combination of straight lines, both objects are combined via the Boolean union. To construct the vertical bars, we prepare a circle as a profile for the protrusion feature and some lines for easier positioning of the bars (Figure 4.16a, b).

We first apply the protrusion on to the handrail and the stairs with the option of protruding in both directions up to all faces. The vertical bars extend automatically up to the handrail and down to the floor (Figure 4.16c). Otherwise, when we restrict the downward protrusion to the next face we obtain the model shown in Figure 4.16d. By substituting the circular profile (for example) with a hexagonal profile, we obtain another prototype of a vertical bar for which a proper illumination produces sharper borders between light and shadow.

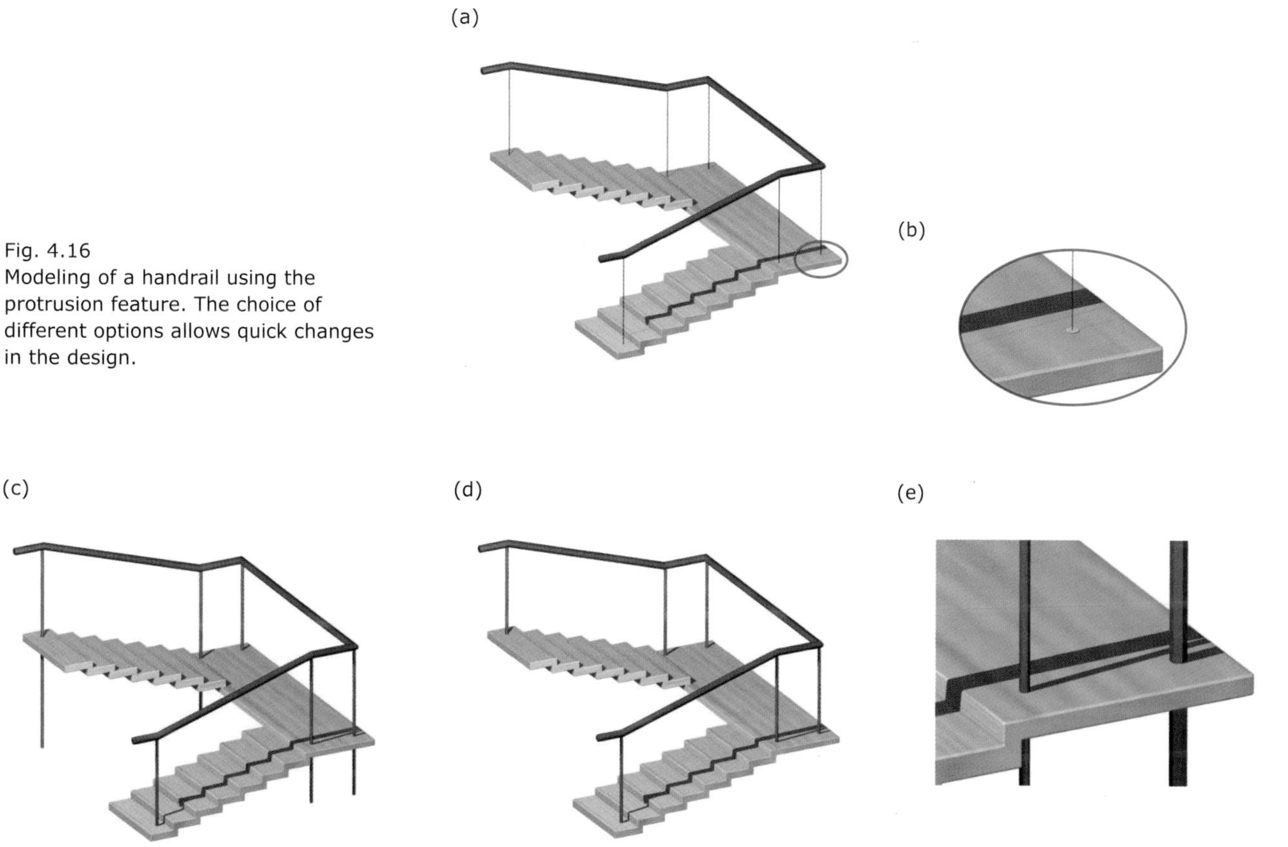

Fig. 4.16
Modeling of a handrail using the protrusion feature. The choice of different options allows quick changes in the design.

Operation features such as blends, chamfers, tapers, and offsets (see Figure 4.17) give the designer a variety of sophisticated tools that accelerate the design process. Depending on the capacity of the CAD software employed, these features are associated with many options.

At this point, we are not able to understand all of the geometric and mathematical background of these techniques. For example, we do not know much about surface normals or which surfaces are generated when we are blending two solids. Thus, sometimes when these techniques do not work it is largely a matter of a geometrically impossible choice of parameters.

Fig. 4.17
By means of a triangular prism as base object, we illustrate the operations taper, chamfer, and blend. The resulting shapes appear in architecture. (a) The *Chamber of Commerce and Industry* (1991–1995) in Dubai by Nikken Sekkei (image courtesy Martin Reis).

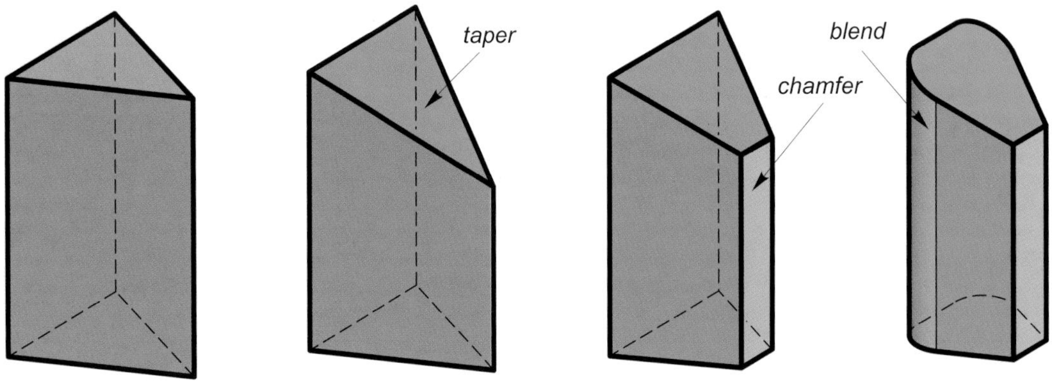

(a)

(b)

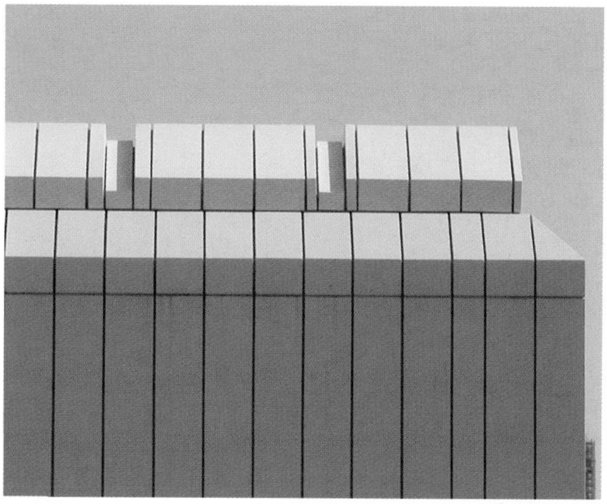

(c)

Fig. 4.17
(b,c) Blends and chamfers applied on built architecture.
(d) The *Gleimstraße Loft* (2003-2004) in Berlin by GRAFT features many blendings.

(d)

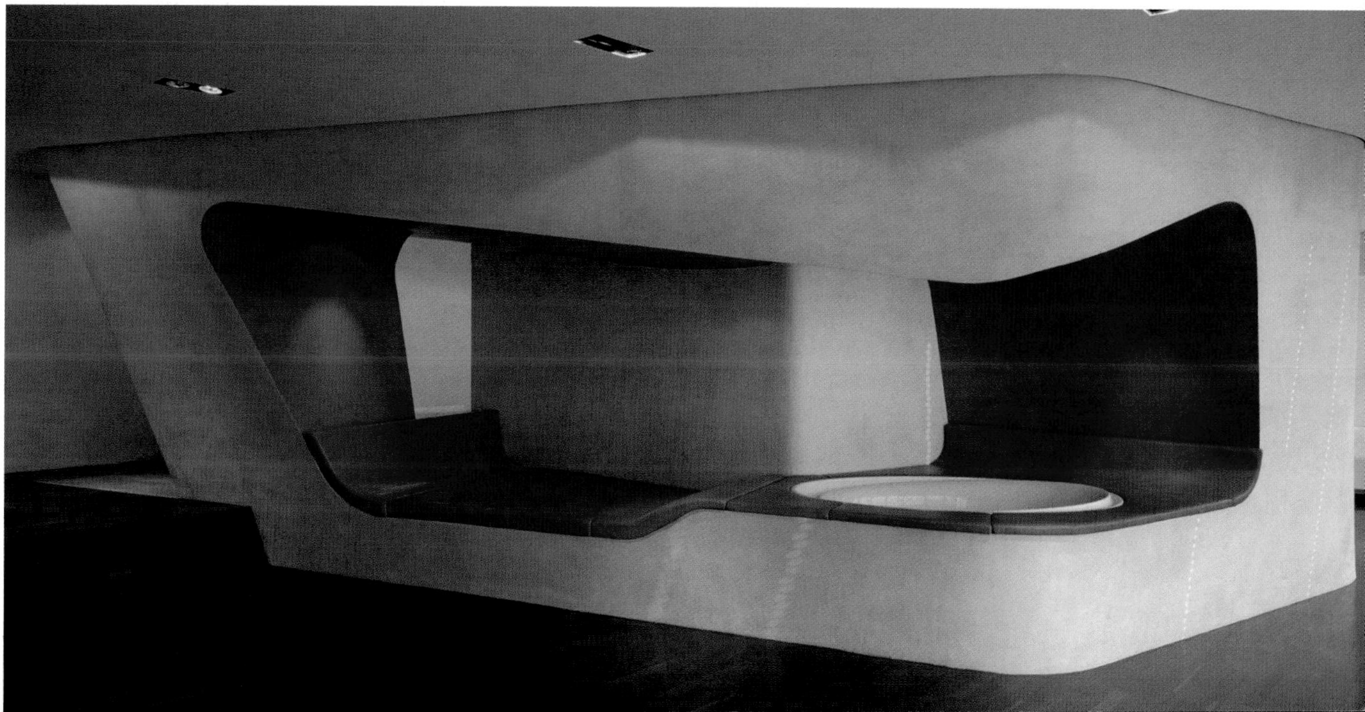

Figure 4.18 illustrates one of these problems when we try to blend a boundary circle c of a cylinder. As long as the radius of the blending is smaller than the radius of the cylinder, there is no problem. The CAD software calculates the parameters and position of a torus tangent to both faces of the cylinder. We can consider this computation as finding a pipe surface (see Chapter 9) when a sphere (radius is equal to the blending radius) is moved along a circle while touching permanently both the top face and the mantle of the cylinder. If the blending radius equals the radius of the cylinder, we obtain a cylinder with a spherical cap. Therefore, selecting an even larger blending radius is impossible.

* **Blending surfaces.** More generally, we can explain the blending of two surfaces in the following way (Figure 4.19a): To manage a smooth transition of two surfaces, we move a sphere with given blending radius along the intersection curve. During the entire motion, this sphere touches both surfaces along the curves c_1 and c_2, and simultaneously generates part of a pipe surface (see Chapter 9).

The path of the center of the sphere can be calculated as the intersection curve of two offset surfaces (see Chapter 10). If there exists any position during the motion at which the moving sphere fails to touch both surfaces, the blending surface cannot be generated. More generally, we can also use a varying blending radius. Geometrically, this can be considered moving a sphere whose radius is changing during the motion (Figure 4.19b).

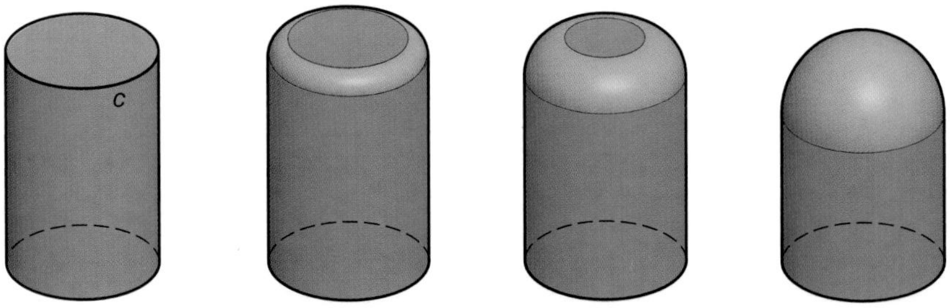

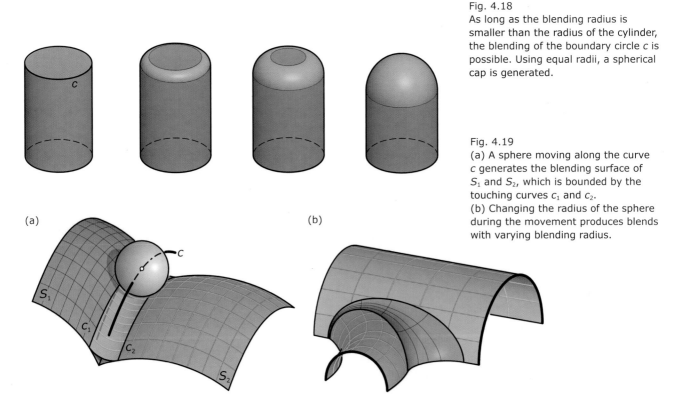

Fig. 4.18
As long as the blending radius is smaller than the radius of the cylinder, the blending of the boundary circle c is possible. Using equal radii, a spherical cap is generated.

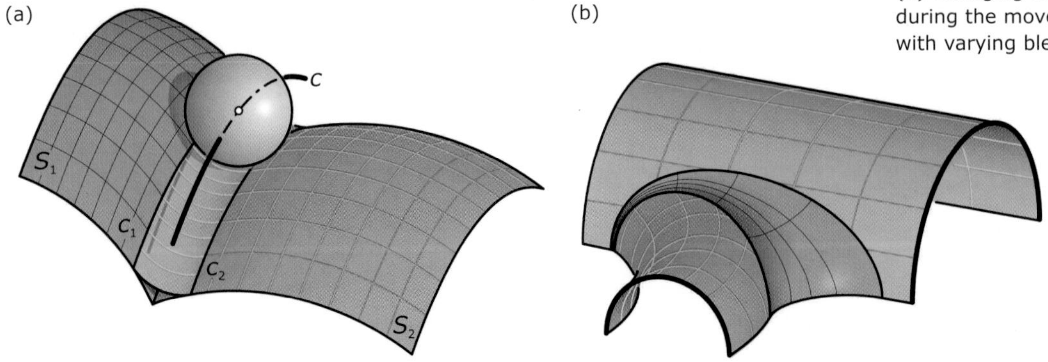

Fig. 4.19
(a) A sphere moving along the curve c generates the blending surface of S_1 and S_2, which is bounded by the touching curves c_1 and c_2.
(b) Changing the radius of the sphere during the movement produces blends with varying blending radius.

To avoid problems and to get a better understanding, we have to learn more about the properties of freeform surfaces (Chapter 11). This will help us select correct parameters when working with sophisticated feature tools. Depending on the design process, there are often alternative ways to get the same model. At first glance, those models seem to be equal. However, from the geometric point of view they are not. By changing parameters of the participating features, we easily see that different geometric approaches result in different models with different properties—which allows dissimilar changes.

Example:
Variations of a simple dome model. We generate a spherical roofing for a prismatic hall. On the one hand, we model it using the Boolean intersection of a prism and a sphere (Figure 4.20a). On the other hand, we create a half sphere by rotating a quarter-circle *c* around the *z* axis. Then we trim away parts using the cutting feature (Figure 4.20b). Thus, we obtain two equal-looking models with different functionality and possibilities for changing the shape. Let us explore some simple shape variations.
We consider only those changes of the objects' parameters that do not disturb the symmetry. By decreasing the diameter of the sphere, we can derive (for example) the object shown in Figure 4.20c. If we reduce the height of the prism, we obtain the one shown in Figure 4.20d. The second model in which we used profiles to generate the object allows more extensive changes by substitution of the profiles. Thus, we can derive Figure 4.20e by replacing the square with a regular octagon. We are even able to obtain a model like that shown in Figure 4.20f (which seems to have nothing in common with the starting object). To obtain this object, we simply substitute the profile of the rotational solid with a curve consisting of a straight line and two circular arcs.

This simple example involves only two basic body features and one form feature. It demonstrates the variety of possibilities when working with feature-based CAD systems. By learning more about curves, surfaces, and shapes (in the following chapters)—and by combining this knowledge with feature-based modeling—we will master the design of complex projects even more efficiently.

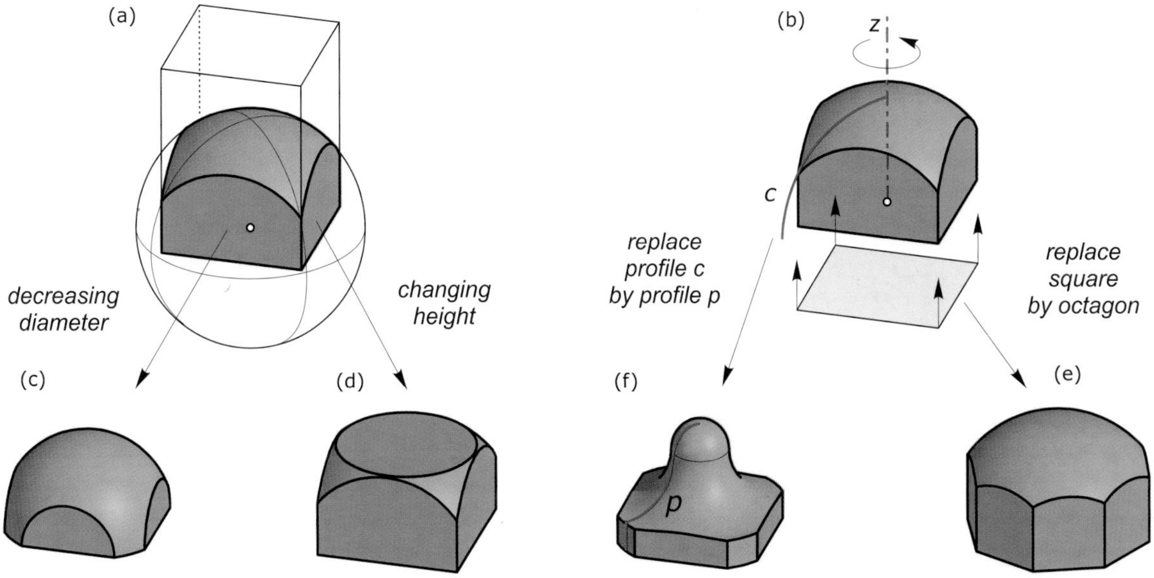

Fig. 4.20
Two equal-looking models with different geometric approaches have different functionality and allow different possibilities of changes to them.

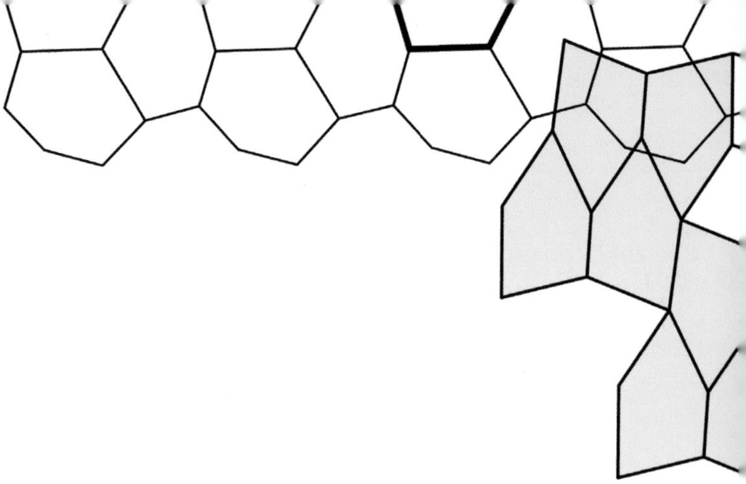

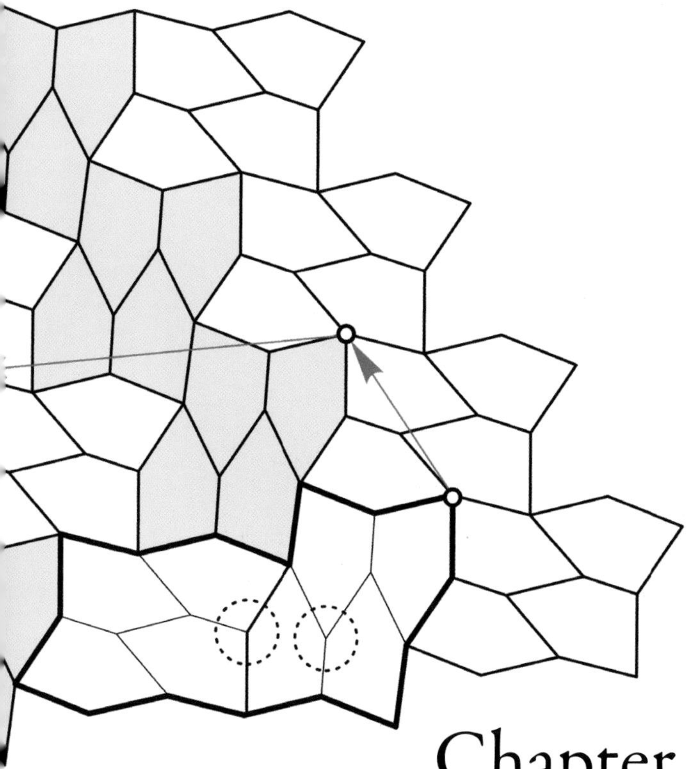

Chapter 5
Planar Transformations

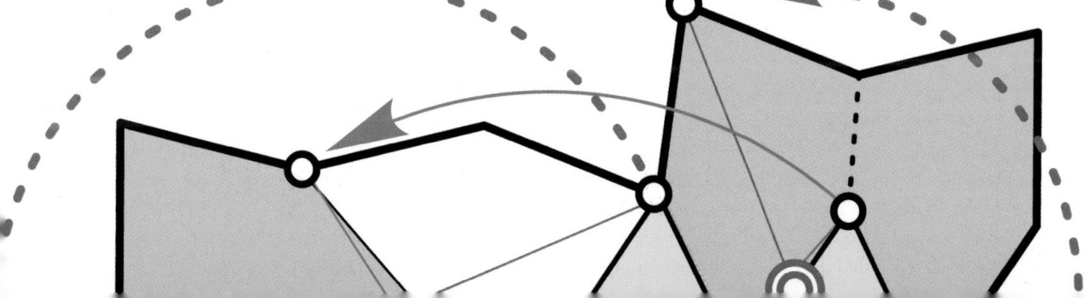

Planar Transformations

Besides Boolean operations and their surface counterparts, transformations are important tools for generating geometric and architectural objects. We first consider linear transformations in the plane ("linear" means they map straight lines onto straight lines). Other properties of those maps are used to classify and discuss linear transformations.

Important basic transformations are congruence transformations (translation, rotation, reflection), which preserve all lengths and angles occurring on an object. Slightly more general are similarity transformations, which still preserve angles but multiply all distances by the same factor. Furthermore, we look at the shear transformation—which preserves the area of the transformed objects. Finally, the scaling transformation provides even more freedom for shape modification (but it is still linear).

The art of M. C. Escher illustrates in a perfect way various types of transformations. He masterly used his knowledge of the properties of planar transformations to generate beautiful, nontrivial tessellations. We study some of his many remarkable sketches to learn about tilings, which can be useful in creating sophisticated facades or surface tilings (Figure 5.1). To round off this chapter, we introduce nonlinear transformations—where straight lines are bent into curves, for example into circles.

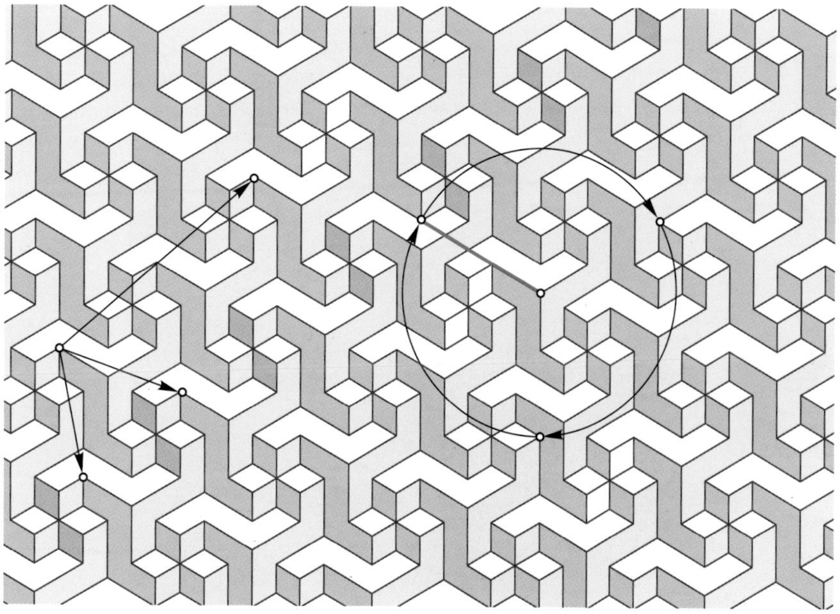

Fig. 5.1
(a) Congruence transformations, like translations and rotations, are the basic instruments for generating tilings.

Fig. 5.1
(b) Various tilings in a building in Uzbekistan (image courtesy Martin Reis).
(c) Hexagonal wall tiles in a station in municipal railway San Francisco.
(d) An irregular tiling of a facade in Melbourne.

(b)

(c)

(d)

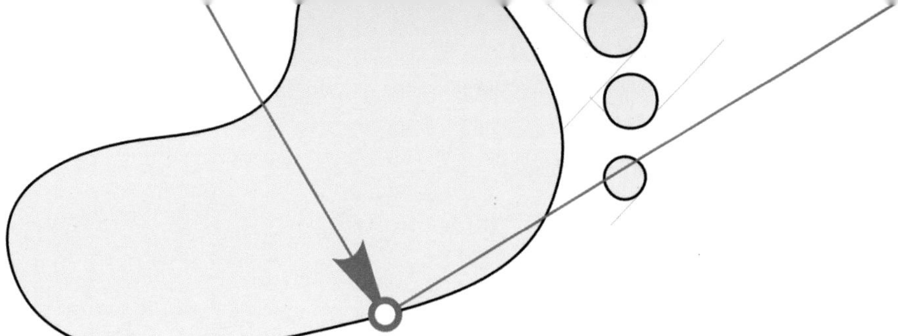

Translation, Rotation, and Reflection in the Plane

Two triangles *abc* and $a_1b_1c_1$ with equal side lengths always have the same angles, and thus have the same shape. We call them *congruent* triangles. Shapes other than triangles need not be congruent even if all side lengths are equal (Figure 5.2).

The triangle *abc* (the *pre-image*) can be mapped into the triangle $a_1b_1c_1$ (the *image*) by applying a *congruence transformation* (Figure 5.3). This congruence transformation does not change the distances between any two points of the triangle. Thus, the congruence transformations are also called *isometries*.

Fig. 5.2
(left) Triangles with equal side lengths are always congruent,
(right) whereas other shapes with equal side lengths need not be congruent.

Fig. 5.3
Two congruent triangles can be mapped into each other either by a direct or an opposite congruence transformation.

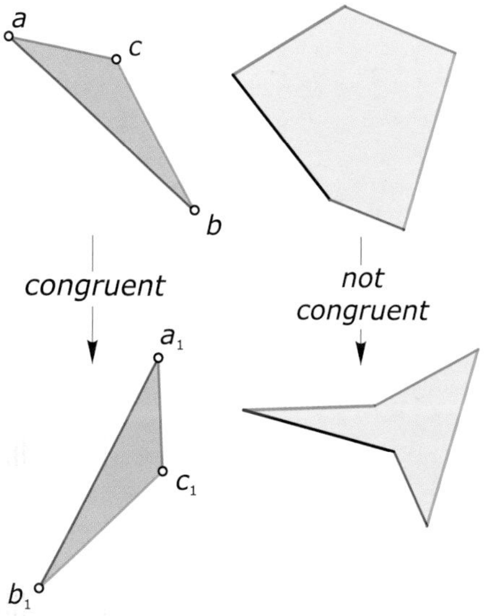

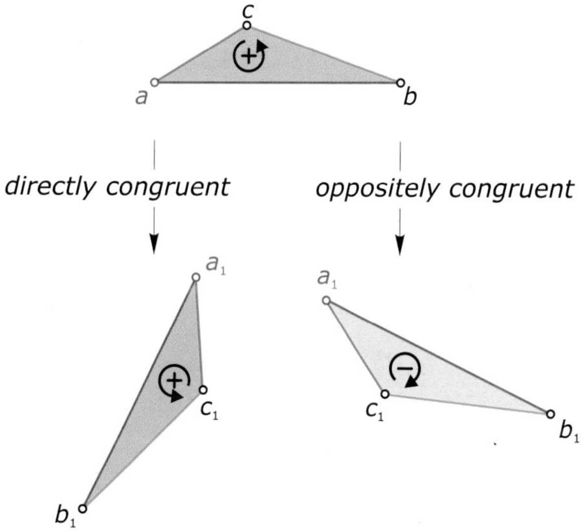

In general, congruence transformations preserve the distances between any two points of all transformed objects. Two figures that can be mapped into each other by applying a congruence transformation are called *congruent*. If we want to construct a triangle $a_1b_1c_1$ that is congruent to a given triangle *abc*, we recognize that there are two possible solutions for this task (Figure 5.3).

- If the circulation sense of the triangles *abc* and $a_1b_1c_1$ agrees (e.g., both clockwise or both counterclockwise), then we have a *direct congruence transformation*.
- If the circulation senses are different, we call this transformation *oppositely congruent*.

Direct congruence transformations of the plane include translation, rotation, and as a special case the identity transformation—whereas reflection and glide reflection are opposite congruent transformations. We will now study some properties and a mathematical description of these planar congruence transformations.

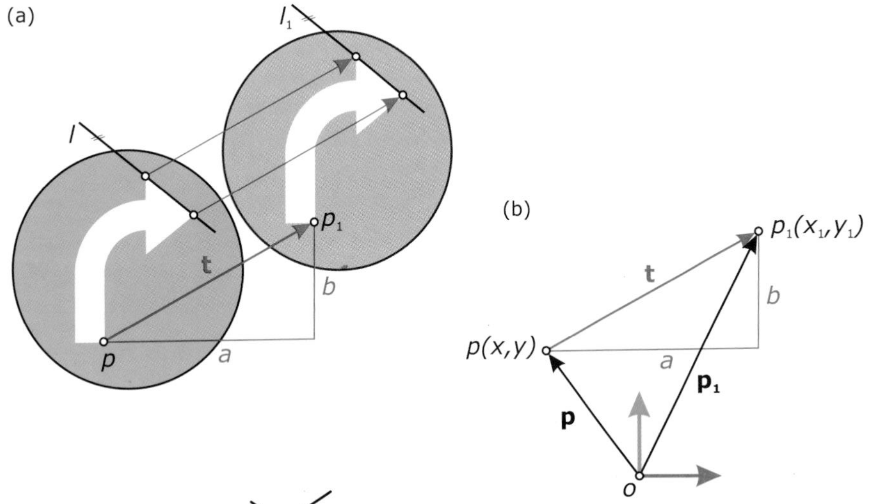

Fig. 5.4
(a) A translation is defined by a translation vector **t**.
(b) The coordinates of the translated point p_1 can be calculated by adding the vectors **p** and **t**.

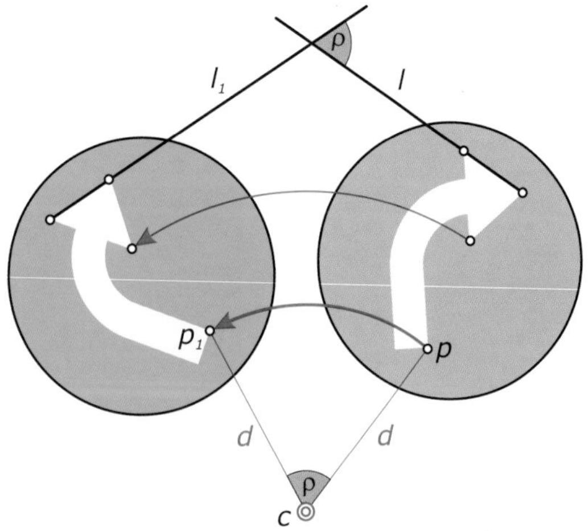

Fig. 5.5
A rotation is defined by the center of rotation and the rotational angle.

Translation. A translation is defined by a *translation vector* **t**, which specifies the *direction* and the *magnitude* of the translation. As we can see in Figure 5.4a, the line l and and its image l_1 are parallel.

To derive a mathematical description, we denote the position vector of every point p with **p**—where the position vector points from the origin o to the point $p(x,y)$ (Figure 5.4b). Let's now consider a translation defined by the vector $\mathbf{t} = (a,b)$, which maps a point p into a point p_1. Then we get the vector $\mathbf{p_1} = (x_1,y_1)$ simply by adding the vector **t** to the vector $\mathbf{p} = (x,y)$. Thus, we calculate the coordinates of the image p_1 via $(x + a, y + b)$ and a translation can be described with

$$x_1 = x + a,$$

$$y_1 = y + b.$$

Rotation. We define a rotation by a fixed point c, the *center of rotation*, and the *rotational angle* ρ. Figure 5.5 illustrates that a point p and its image p_1 have equal distances d to the center of rotation. We can also see that the angle between two corresponding lines l and l_1 is equal to the rotational angle ρ.

Let us now consider Figure 5.6, in which the point $p(x,y)$ is revolved about the origin o into the point $p_1(x_1,y_1)$. We denote the rotational angle with ρ. To calculate the coordinates of p_1 we use the rectangle $oapb$ and its rotated image $oa_1p_1b_1$. The coordinates of $a_1(x \cdot \cos(\rho), x \cdot \sin(\rho))$ and $b_1(-y \cdot \sin(\rho), y \cdot \cos(\rho))$ can be derived with simple trigonometry (see Geometry Primer). The vector $\mathbf{p}_1$ is the sum of the position vectors $\mathbf{a}_1$ and $\mathbf{b}_1$ and thus we obtain the coordinates of the point p_1 as $(x \cdot \cos(\rho) - y \cdot \sin(\rho), x \cdot \sin(\rho) + y \cdot \cos(\rho))$. A rotation with center o and rotational angle ρ is then described with

$$x_1 = x \cdot \cos(\rho) - y \cdot \sin(\rho)$$

$$y_1 = x \cdot \sin(\rho) + y \cdot \cos(\rho)$$

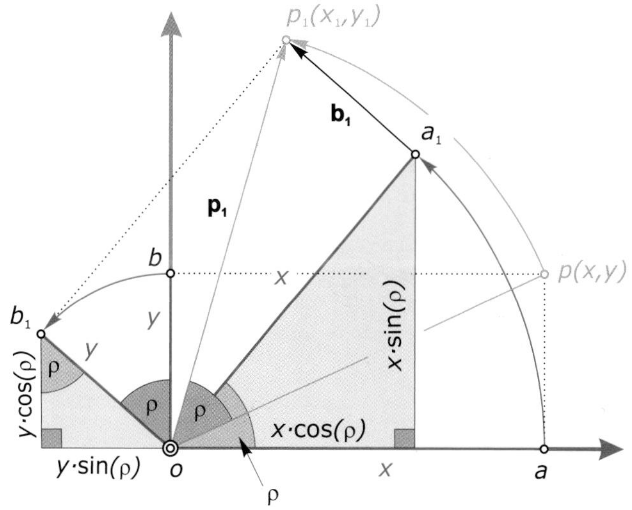

Figure 5.6
Rotation of a point p about the origin.

Reflection. Every time you are looking in a mirror you can see an exact, but reversed, copy of yourself (i.e., a reflection). Thus, we recognize that the reflection about a straight line r, the *reflection line*, does not preserve the orientation. It is an opposite congruent transformation. Figure 5.7 illustrates the reflection of a triangle abc about the reflection line r. We see that two corresponding points b and b_1 have equal distances to the reflection line r. Thus, the reflection line r is the perpendicular bisector of every corresponding pair of points. Moreover, we can recognize that every line and its image l_1 intersect in a point of the reflection line r.

Math:

All transformations we have studied so far are special cases of planar affine transformations. A uniform description is the following

$$x_1 = a \cdot x + b \cdot y + e,$$

$$y_1 = c \cdot x + d \cdot y + f,$$

where a, b, c, d, and e are arbitrary real numbers (such that $a \cdot d - b \cdot c \neq 0$) . Every affine transformation maps straight lines to straight lines, and the ratio of three collinear points is equal to the ratio of the image points (cf. parallel projections, Chapter 2).

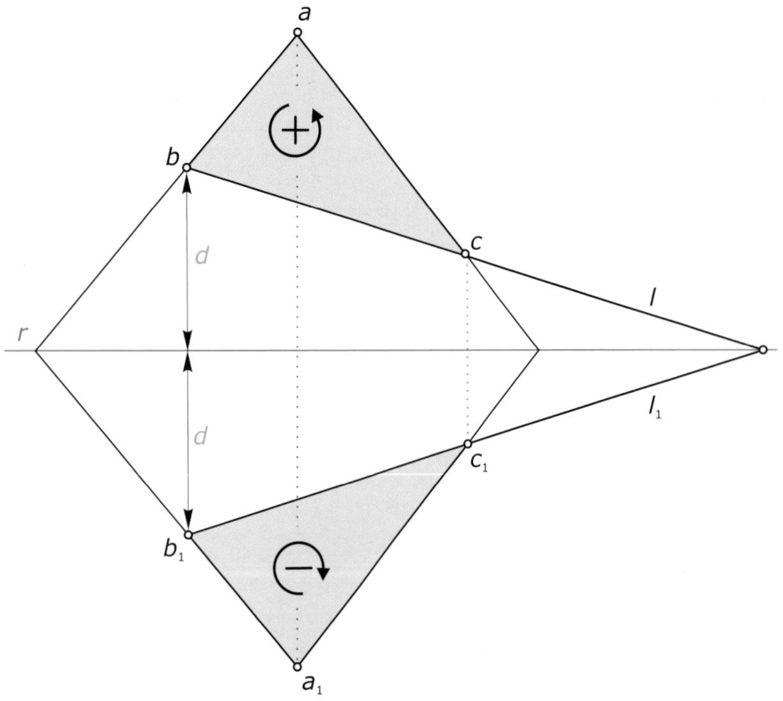

Fig. 5.7
A reflection about a line r does not preserve the orientation.

As a special case, we study the reflection about the coordinate axes (Figure 5.8). If we reflect a point $a(x,y)$ about the x-axis we only have to change the sign of the y-coordinate to obtain the coordinates of a_1. Thus, a reflection about the x-axis is described with

$$x_1 = x,$$

$$y_1 = -y,$$

and analogously we obtain the reflection about the y-axis with

$$x_2 = -x$$

$$y_2 = y.$$

Glide reflection. A glide reflection (Figure 5.9) is a composition of a translation and a reflection in which the translation vector is parallel to the reflection line r. When you walk along a line r, the correspondence between your left footprints and your right footprints approximately is a glide reflection. If we connect corresponding points a and a_2, we see that the midpoints of these lines are positioned at the reflection line.

For a mathematical description, we assume that the reflection line is the x-axis. We then get the coordinates of a point a_2 by adding the translation vector $\mathrm{t} = (t,0)$ to the position vector of $a_1(x,-y)$ and finally

$$x_2 = x + t,$$

$$y_2 = -y.$$

Fig. 5.8
The composition of the reflections about the x-axis and the y-axis is a half turn with center o. It maps, for example, point a to point a_2.

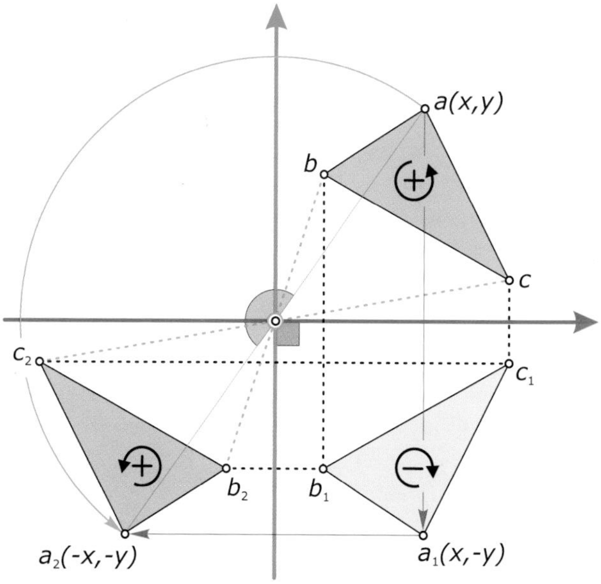

Fig. 5.9
A glide reflection is a composition of a reflection and translation parallel to the reflection line r.

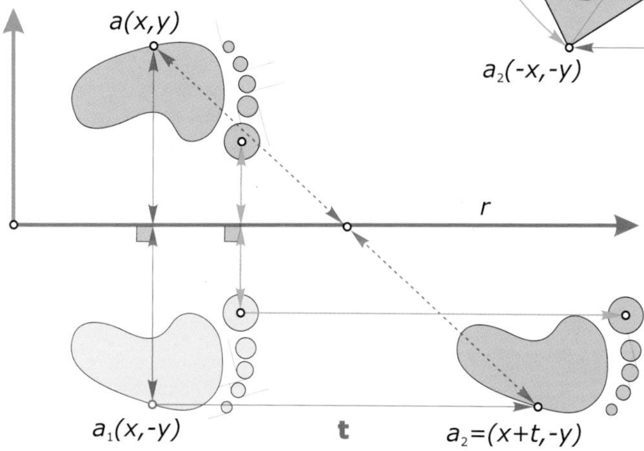

Composition of congruence transformations. In Figure 5.8 the triangle $a_2b_2c_2$ can also be considered the image of the triangle *abc* when applying a single rotation about the origin with a rotational angle of 180 degrees. We recognize that the intersection point of the two reflection lines is the center of the *half turn*. The rotational angle has twice the dimension of the angle between the two reflection lines. This turns out to be a special case of the following theorem which is explained in Figure 5.10:

Every composition of two reflections with intersecting reflection lines is a rotation. The center of the rotation is the intersection point of the two reflection lines. The rotational angle has twice the dimension of the angle formed by the reflection lines.

If the reflection lines are parallel, the composition of the two reflections is a translation. The defining translation vector **t** is orthogonal to the reflection lines and the magnitude is twice the distance *d* of the two reflection lines.

When we are given two direct congruent objects, we can always find a single rotation or translation that transforms the first object into the second one (and vice versa). Figure 5.11 illustrates how the center of rotation *c* can be found as the intersection of two bisectors of corresponding points p,p_1 and q,q_1. If we interpret the two congruent objects as two distinct positions of one object, we have verfied the following important fact about motions.

Given are two distinct positions of a planar, rigid body. Then there always exists a unique rotation or unique translation that transfers one position into the other.

So far we have studied the composition of two reflections, which is always a single rotation or a single translation. In general, we can say that the composition of two opposite congruence transformations or of two direct congruence transformations is always a direct congruence transformation.

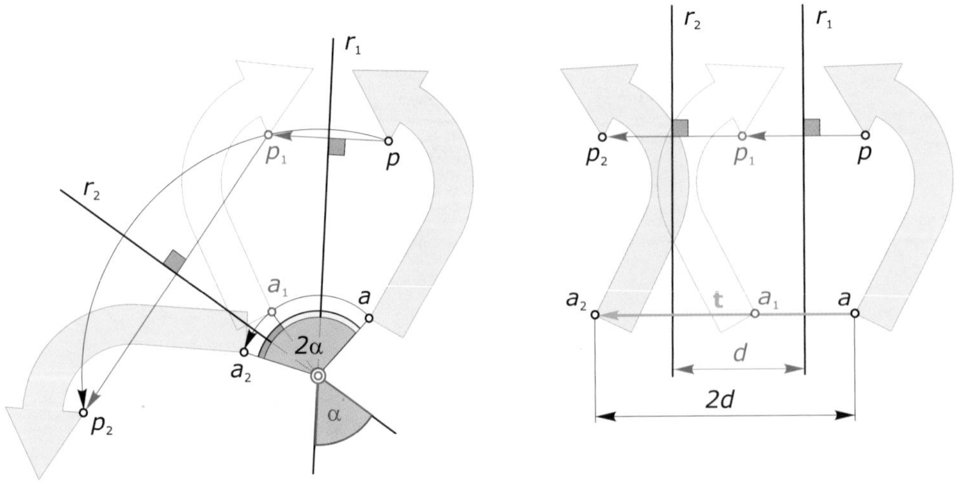

Fig. 5.10
A composition of two reflections is always a single rotation or a translation.

On the contrary, the composition of a direct and an opposite congruence transformation (or vice versa) is always an opposite congruence transformation. In Figure 5.12, two different compositions of congruence transformations are illustrated. We recognize the important fact that the order in which we apply those transformations affects the end position.

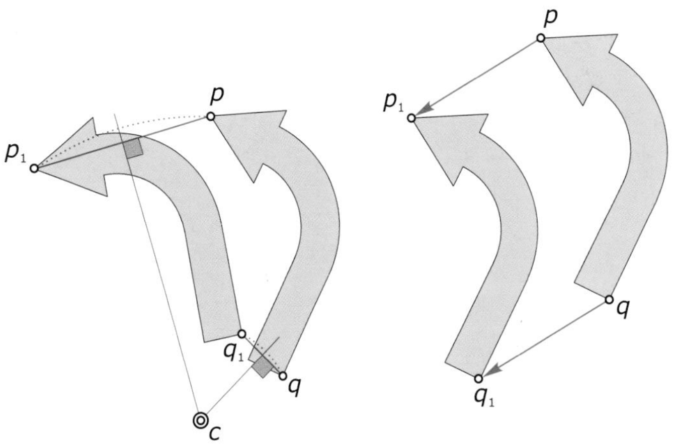

Fig. 5.11
Two directly congruent objects can always be transformed into each other through a single rotation or translation.

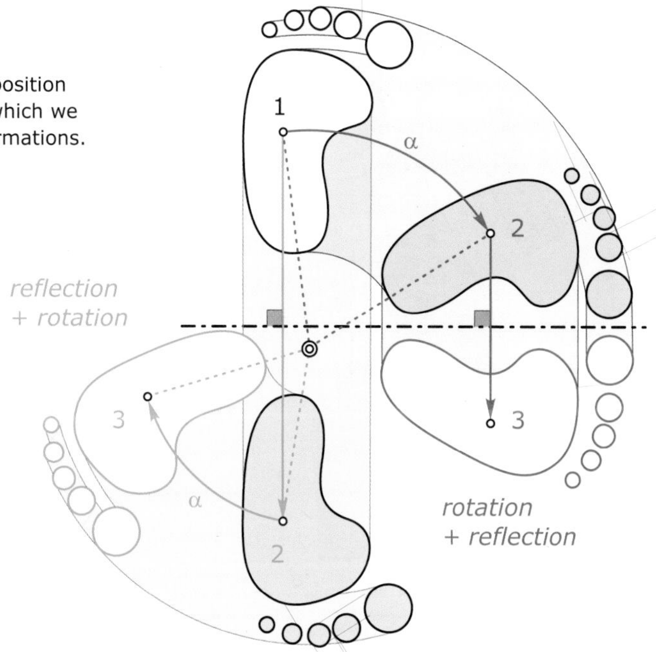

Fig. 5.12
In general, the resulting position depends on the order in which we apply congruence transformations.

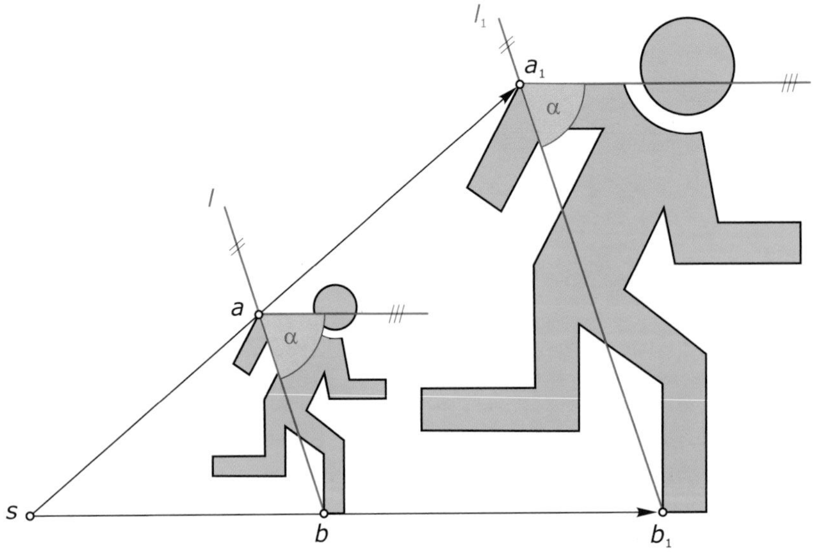

Fig. 5.13
A uniform scaling preserves angles and thus the shape of the object.

Scaling and Shear Transformation

Congruence transformations preserve shape and distances. They are essential tools for moving objects to a different position without changing their shape. When we want to modify planar objects, we need more freedom in changing their shape. Thus, we now study transformations that do not simultaneously preserve shape and distance.

Uniform scaling. A uniform scaling is defined by the *center of scaling s* and a *scaling factor* (Figure 5.13). The center of scaling is the reference point about which an object is scaled, whereas the scaling factor specifies the ratio between corresponding distances a_1b_1 and ab. All rays through corresponding points a and a_1 originate in the center of the scaling, whereas corresponding lines l and l_1 are always parallel. Let f be the scaling factor and o the center of the scaling (Figure 5.14, left). Then the image p_1 of a point $p(x,y)$ is calculated with $(f\cdot x, f\cdot y)$. Therefore, a uniform scaling can be written as

$$x_1 = f\cdot x,$$
$$y_1 = f\cdot y.$$

Fig. 5.14
A uniform scaling is defined by a single scaling factor f. An independent scaling with different scaling factors f_x, f_y changes the shape.

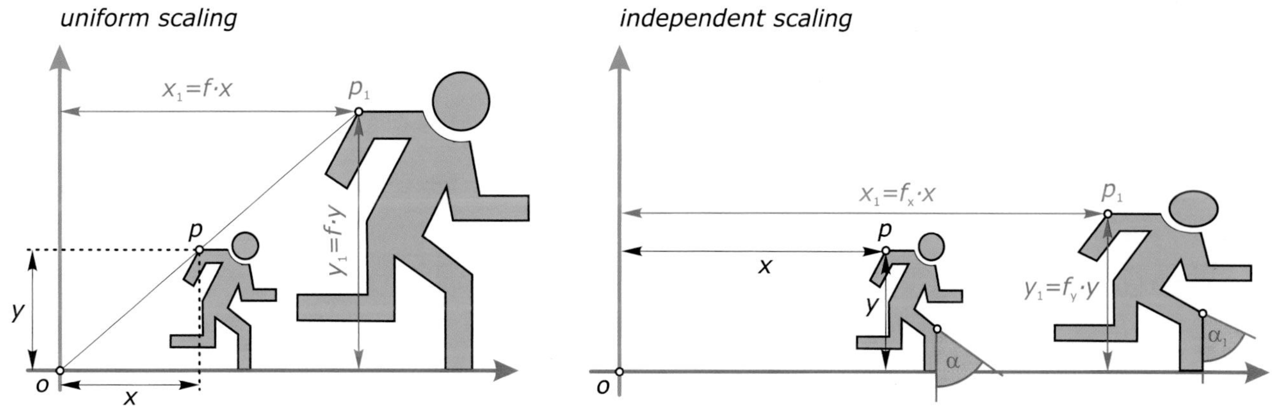

This transformation is also known as a *central dilation*, but in most CAD systems it is referred to as a special type of scaling. Although distances are changing, the angles and the shapes of the objects are preserved when we apply a uniform scaling. A uniform scaling is a special *similarity transformation*. A general similarity transformation is the composition of a uniform scaling and a congruence transformation.

If we employ different scaling factors f_x and f_y for x- and y-coordinates, respectively, we get an independent scaling (Figure 5.14, right). The composition of an independent scaling with translations or rotations is the most general form of all transformations that map straight lines into straight lines and preserve ratios. Note that in the special case of an independent scaling with $f_x \cdot f_y = 1$ the area of the transformed objects is also preserved.

Shear transformation. The shear transformation also preserves the area but changes the shape of the transformed object. A shearing is defined by a fixed line g and an angle α. Corresponding points are connected via lines parallel to the fixed line g. Corresponding lines l and l_1 intersect in a point of the fixed line g. These transformations are primarily used to generate objects with equal area.

To find a mathematical description, we locate the fixed line in the x-axis. From Figure 5.15, we see that the position vector $\mathbf{p}_1$ is the sum of the vectors $\mathbf{p} = (x,y)$ and $\mathbf{v}$, where $\mathbf{v} = (y \cdot \tan(\alpha), 0)$ is parallel to the fixed x-axis. Thus, we obtain

$$x_1 = x + y \cdot \tan(\alpha),$$

$$y_1 = y.$$

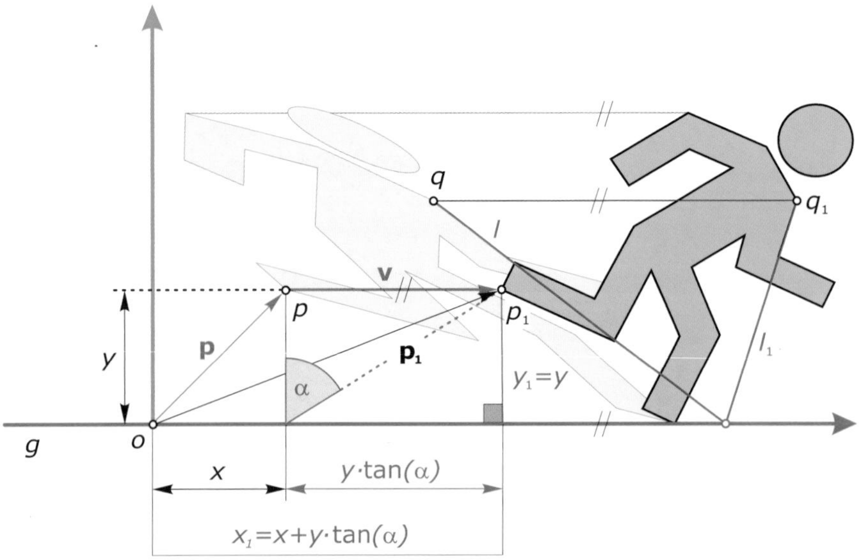

Fig. 5.15
A shear transformation changes the shape but preserves the area of the object. It is a planar affine transformation and thus maps straight lines into straight lines and preserves ratios.

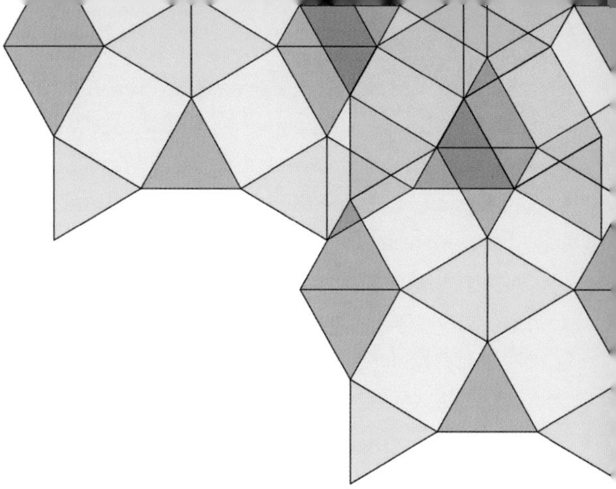

Tilings

So far we have dealt with planar congruence transformations as effective tools for positioning objects in the plane. But they are also very useful in creating regular tessellations and tilings. By means of the beautiful work of M. C. Escher, we study different types of tessellations and we learn some basics of design tiles. In fact, the art of designing tilings and patterns has a long history and is therefore well developed (Figure 5.16).

(a)

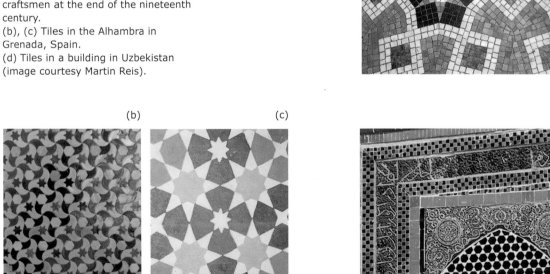

Fig. 5.16
The art of designing tilings is very old and widespread.
(a) Tiles on the floor of the Turkish Baths in Harrogate, laid by Italian craftsmen at the end of the nineteenth century.
(b), (c) Tiles in the Alhambra in Grenada, Spain.
(d) Tiles in a building in Uzbekistan (image courtesy Martin Reis).

(b)

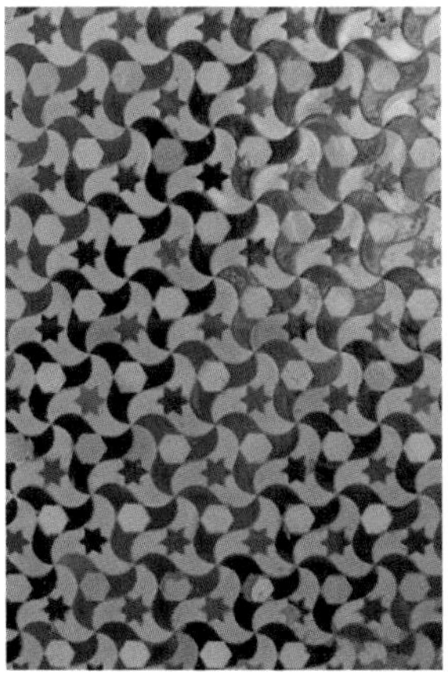

(c)

(d)

Regular and semi-regular tessellations. Informally, a *tessellation* is a way of filling the entire plane with congruent shapes without overlaps or gaps. The term *tiling* is sometimes used to describe a special tessellation of the plane using only planar polygons. Note that the terms *tessellation* and *tiling* are often used interchangeably. There are numerous types of tessellations. For example, any triangle and any arbitrary quadrilateral can be used to tile the plane (Figure 5.17). There are 14 classes of convex pentagonal tilings known and three classes of tilings with irregular hexagonal tiles. Some of these tilings are shown in Figure 5.18.

If we additionally want the tiles to be congruent regular polygons, we have *regular tessellations*. There exist only three regular tessellations due to the fact that the vertex angle of the tiles must be a divisor of 360 degrees. Therefore, we only have regular tessellations with regular triangles, squares, and hexagons (Figure 5.19).

Fig. 5.17
Any triangle or any quadrilateral tiles the plane.

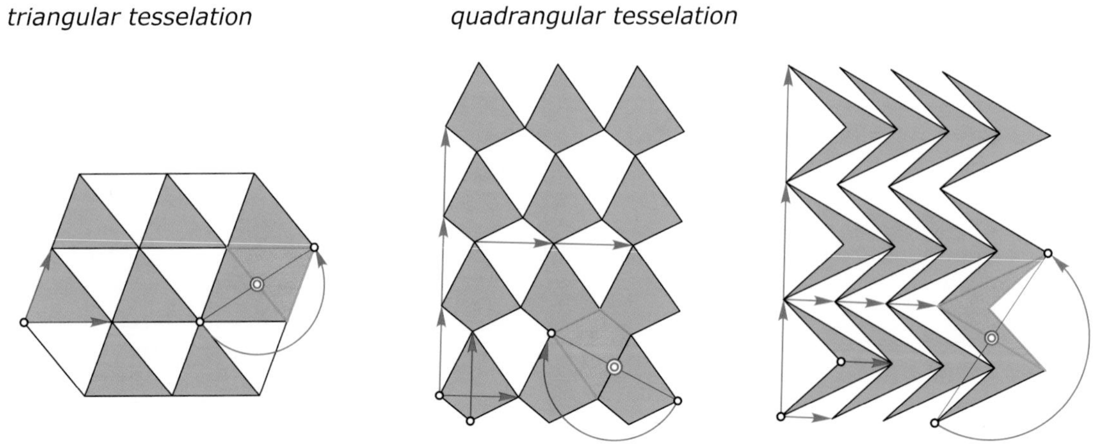

irregular pentagonal tilings

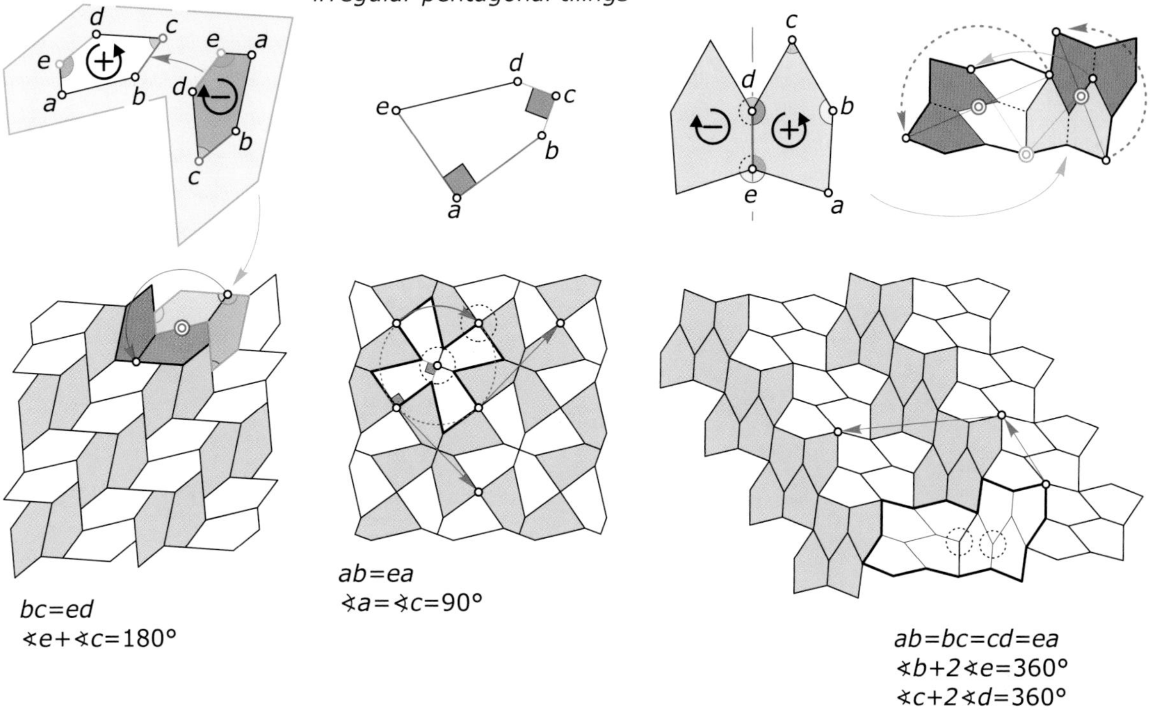

irregular hexagonal tilings

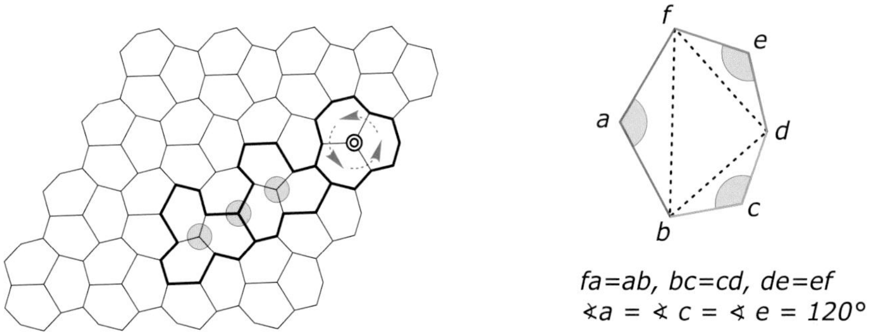

Fig. 5.18
Some examples of tilings with irregular convex pentagonal and hexagonal tiles. The shapes of the tiles are determined by the specified lengths and angles.

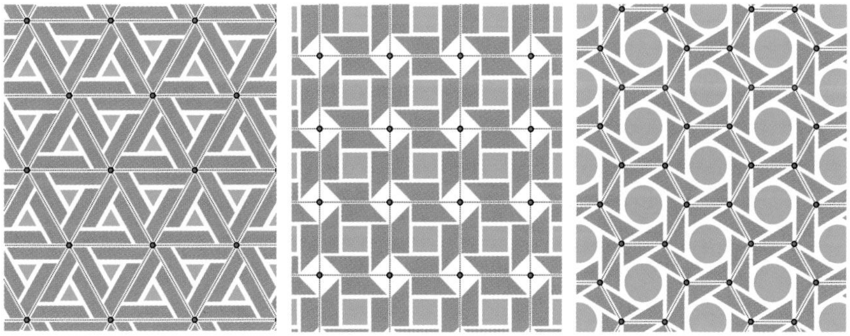

Fig. 5.19
There exist only three regular tessellations with regular triangles, squares, and hexagons.

Considering tessellations that use two or more different regular polygons, we add the rule that every vertex must have exactly the same configuration. This means that in every vertex there has to be the same number and the same sequence of congruent regular polygons. Tessellations that follow these rules are called *semi-regular*.

Recall the section about polyhedra. There we also had five regular Platonic polyhedra and 13 semi-regular Archimedean polyhedra. In the plane we have eight different semi-regular tessellations, which are illustrated in Figure 5.20. To name the various types, we simply write down their vertex configuration. For example, if in each vertex a square, a regular hexagon, and a regular dodecagon meet we write 4,6,12.

Fig. 5.20
The eight semi-regular tessellations are named by their vertex configuration.

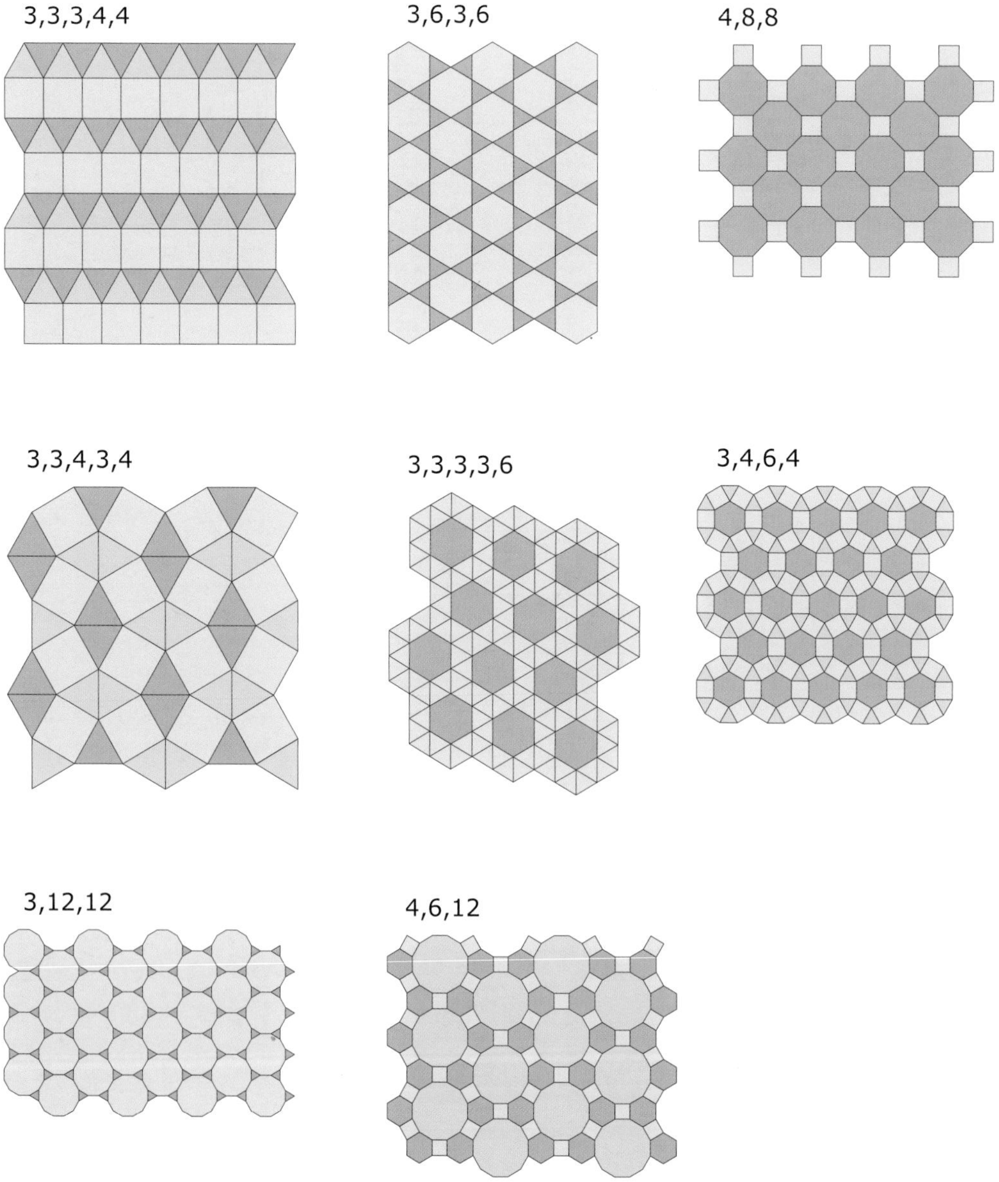

Tesselations and congruence transformations. Figure 5.21 shows a tessellation in which M. C. Escher used a human figure to fill the plane. Additionally the underlying geometric structure in form of a triangular grid is shown. We consider those congruence transformations that do not change the pattern. For example, if we move the pattern by a translation from point *a* to point *b* (or to point *c*), the entire tessellation will be preserved.

The same holds true if we turn the pattern around point *d* with a rotation angle of 120 or 240 degrees. We see that every composition of these translations and rotations will also preserve the entire pattern. Thus, we have an infinite number of possible congruence transformations that do not change the pattern. However, they can all be derived by iteratively combining the two translations and a single rotation.

Translations, rotations, reflections, and glide reflections are the only transformations that can be applied on patterns without changing the pattern. Some patterns remain unchanged only under translations, whereas others allow all types of congruence transformations at the same time. Depending on the number and type of distinct congruence transformations which do not change a pattern, we distinguish among 17 different possibilities (*crystallographic groups*). As an interesting fact, we note that all of these ways to tile the plane appear in M. C. Escher's art.

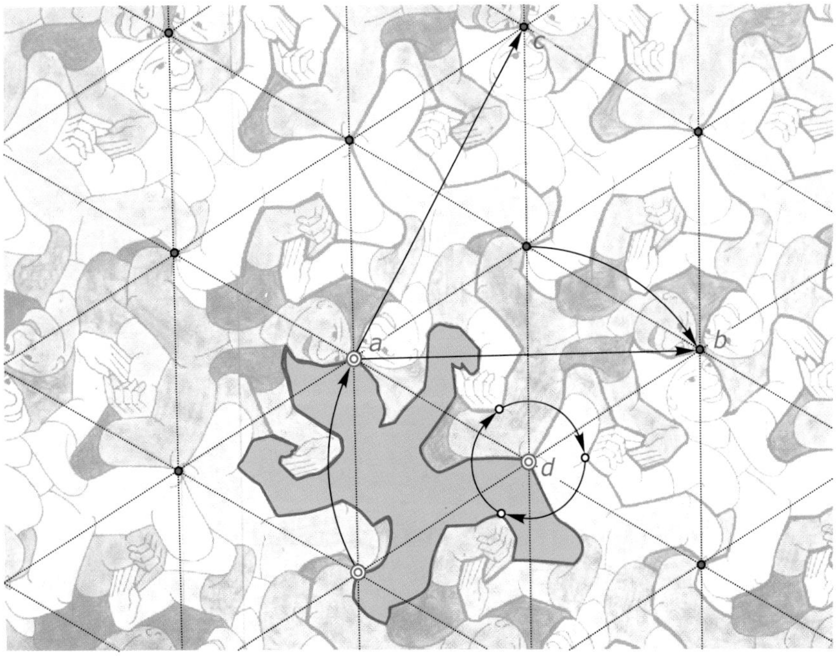

Fig. 5.21
Rotations and translations preserving a tessellation.

How to design nontrivial tiles. More interesting than the theoretical knowledge about different types of crystallographic groups is the practical skill to design tiles. Let's start with the definition of T-curves and C-curves, which are parts of most single tiles.

The congruent curves *ab* and *dc* are parts of the boundary of Escher's flying fish tile (Figure 5.22). The boundary *ab* can be transformed into *dc* via a translation. Thus, we denote these curves as *T-curves* and write T_{ab} and T_{dc}. Note that the rest of the boundary of the flying fish consists of the congruent T-curves T_{ad} and T_{bc}. If we repeatedly apply translations with vectors **u** and **v** we obtain the entire tessellation of the plane. This pattern is only unchanged under translations, and allows no other congruence transformation. Note that in this case the underlying geometric structure is a grid of parallelograms.

If we now consider the boundary of a "three-butterfly" tile (Figure 5.23), we recognize that there are no T-curves that always appear pairwise. But we see that we can half turn the curve C_{ab} around the midpoint m_{ab} of *ab*. We call such a curve C_{ab} a *C-curve* because it is centrally symmetric with respect to the midpoint. Again, all boundaries of this tile are exclusively of one type; namely, C-curves (Figure 5.23).

If we do not obey the coloring of the tiles, we see that the tessellation of the entire plane can be obtained by applying translations along the vectors **u** and **v**. The pattern also allows rotations around the vertices of the triangle *abc* and around the midpoints. Thus, it belongs to a different group compared to the previous pattern.

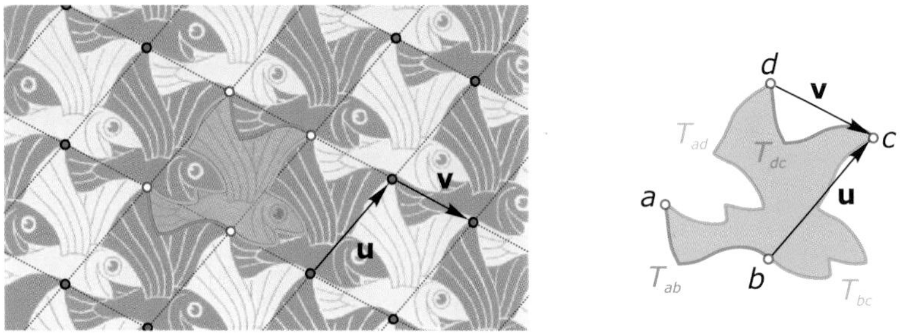

Fig. 5.22
The boundary of Escher's flying fish tiles consists exclusively of T-curves.

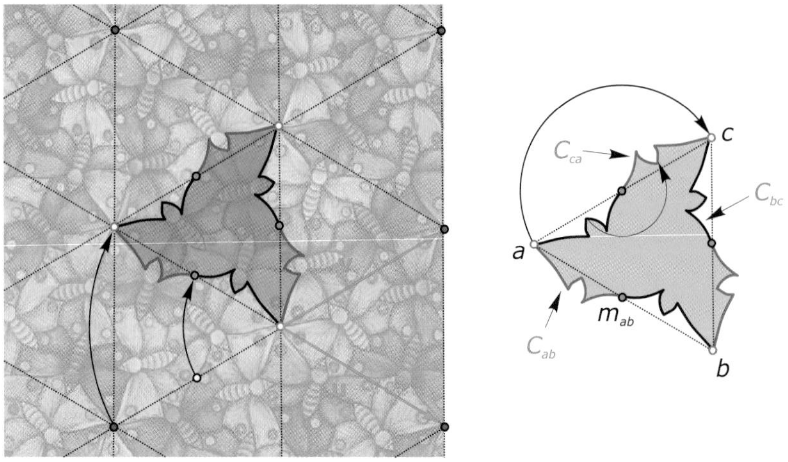

Fig. 5.23
C-lines that are centrally symmetric are boundaries of Escher's butterfly tiles.

The previous tile was constructed with three C-curves that replaced the sides of a triangle. As stated previously, an arbitrary quadrilateral can also be used for tessellation. Thus, we replace the sides of a quadrilateral with C-curves to obtain another type of tile. Escher used this type when designing another fish tile (Figure 5.24a).

Using a regular tessellation with squares, we do not even need T-curves and C-curves to design correct tiles. For example, we can replace two adjacent sides of the square with arbitrary curves. Then we quarter turn them around points *b* and *d,* respectively, and get a tile used by Escher in another drawing of lizards (Figure 5.24b). A similar idea is used in Figure 5.24c, where a tessellation with regular hexagons is used as the base of the pattern. Again, we replace three nonconsecutive sides of the hexagon by arbitrary curves and apply 120-degree rotations about the vertices *a*, *c*, and *e*.

We have seen how to generate some types of tiles using T-curves and C-curves. Altogether, there are 28 different types of tiles. Knowledge of these possibilities could be a good inspiration when planning, for example, a facade.

(a)

(b)

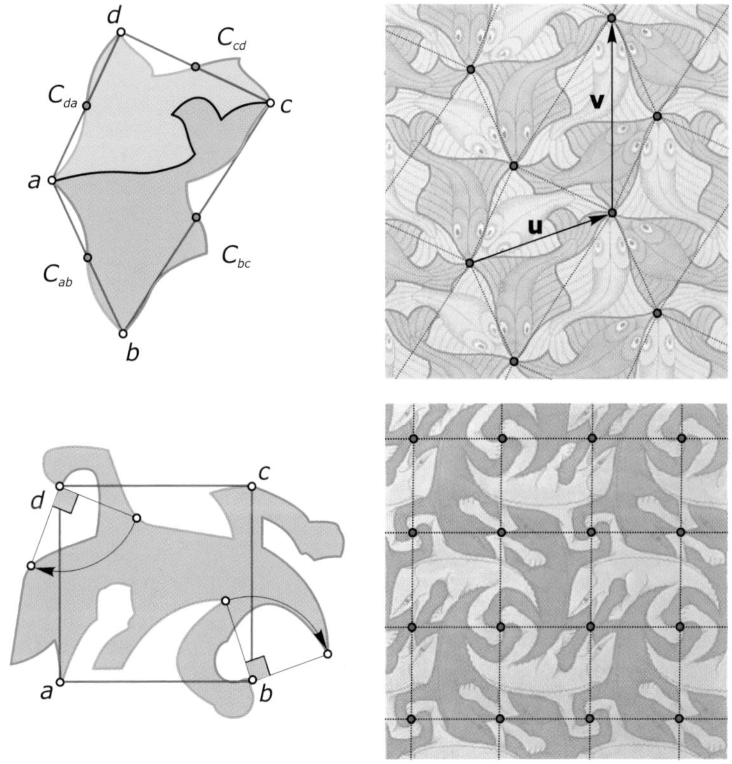

Fig. 5.24
Some further tilings which exhibit more freedom in the design of the tiles.

(c)

Fig. 5.24
Some further tilings which exhibit more freedom in the design of the tiles.

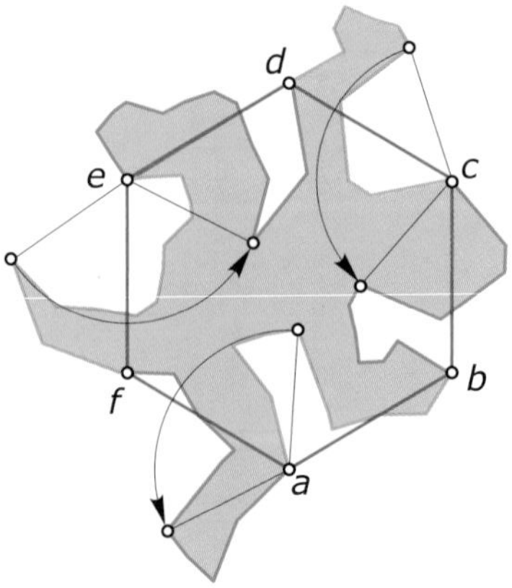

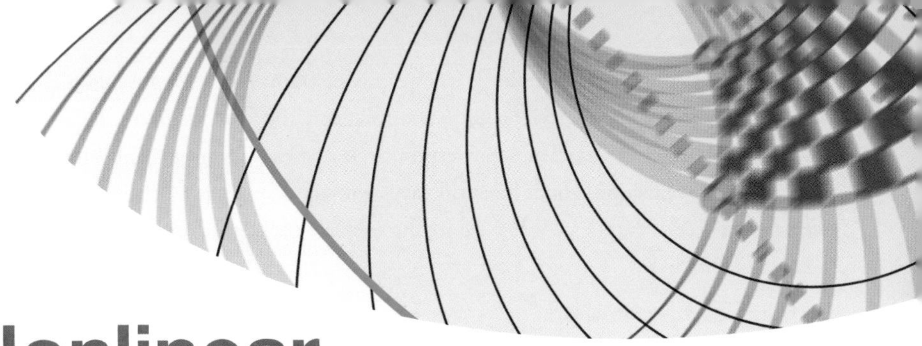

*Nonlinear Transformations in 2D

So far we have only dealt with *linear transformations*—transformations that map straight lines into straight lines. In addition to linear transformations, many interesting *nonlinear transformations* exist. In general, these transformations map straight lines into curves. Thus, they can be useful tools in generating interesting geometry out of simple objects. Moreover, we will find a connection between some nonlinear transformations and the concept of complex numbers. We will also work out some basic aspects of nonlinear transformations that will support us in understanding some of the advanced topics of this book.

Reflection along a circle: inversion. In Figure 5.25a, the point p_1 is generated in the following way. Let c be a circle with center o and the line segments ps and pt tangent to the circle c. Then the point p and the intersection point p_1 of the line op with st are called *inverse points* with respect to the *inversion circle* c. The process that transforms the point p into the point p_1 (or the point p_1 into the point p) is called an *inversion*.

Fig. 5.25
(a) p and p_1 are inverse points with respect to the circle c.
(b) The inverse image of a straight line is a circle passing through o.

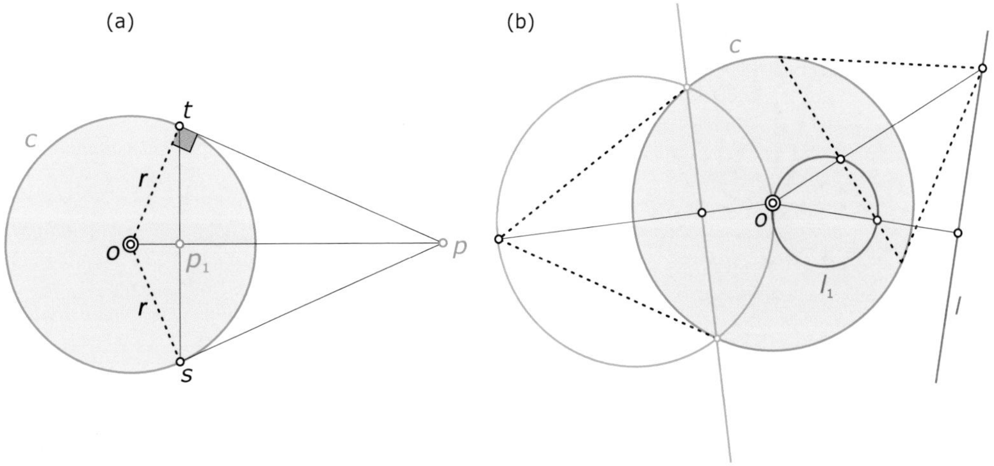

Note that every point on the circle c is its own inverse point. Thus, the inversion circle c is a *fixed curve*. Analogous to reflections about lines, a line l and its inverse image l_1 intersect each other in points of the inversion circle c (if they intersect at all). But in contrast to the reflections about lines, the inverse image of a line is a circle through the inversion center o (Figure 5.25b). We note the similar triangles opt and otp_1 (Figure 5.26), and conclude

$$\text{dist}(op) : r = r : \text{dist}(op_1),$$

and thus we find

$$r^2 = \text{dist}(op) \cdot \text{dist}(op_1),$$

or equivalently

$$\text{dist}(op_1) = r^2/\text{dist}(op).$$

Then let the origin o be the inversion center and let p be the point with coordinates (x,y). Then the coordinates x_1 and y_1 of p_1 can be calculated as

$$x_1 = x \cdot r^2/(x^2 + y^2),$$

$$y_1 = y \cdot r^2/(x^2 + y^2).$$

Figure 5.27 shows how lines, circles, and more general curves are transformed when applying an inversion. If we consider straight lines as circles with infinite radius, we can state that an inversion maps circles to circles. Figure 5.27 illustrates the following properties of an inversion.

- The magnitude of angles is preserved.
- The orientation is reversed.
- The interior of the inversion circle is mapped onto the entire exterior, and vice versa.

These properties are illustrated by means of an inverted H and an inverted checkerboard (Figure 5.28).

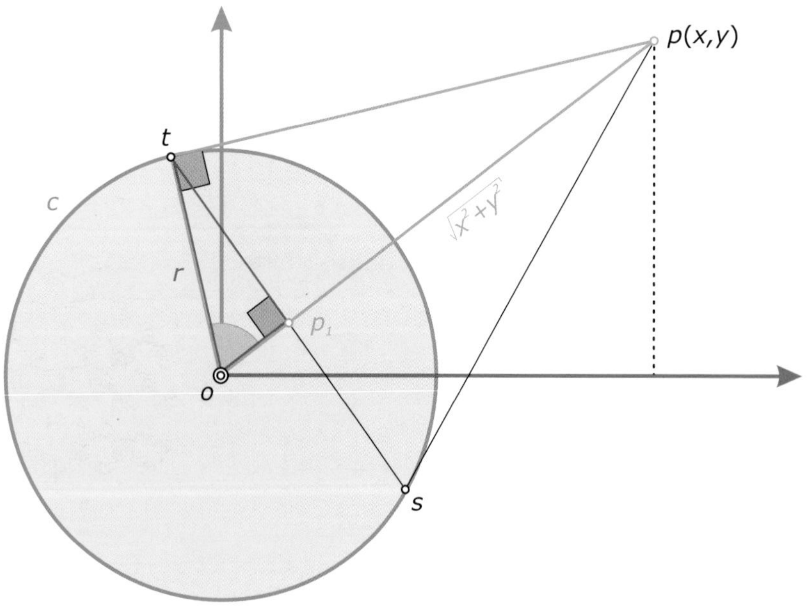

Fig. 5.26
Deriving the mathematical description of an inversion.

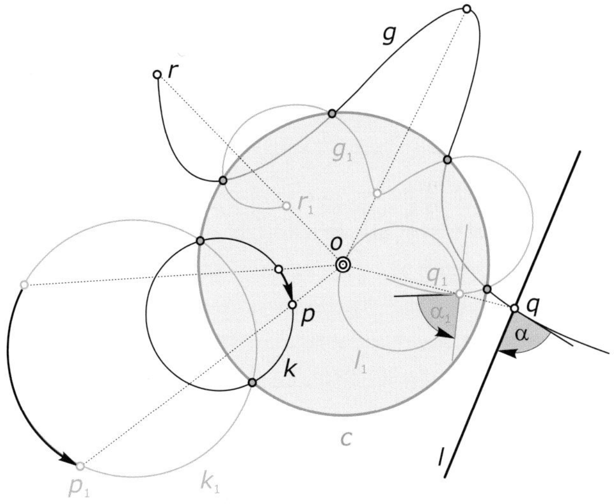

Fig. 5.27
We illustrate inversion at a circle c applied to a straight line l, a circle k, and a general curve g. The figure also illustrates important properties of an inversion including the angle preservation.

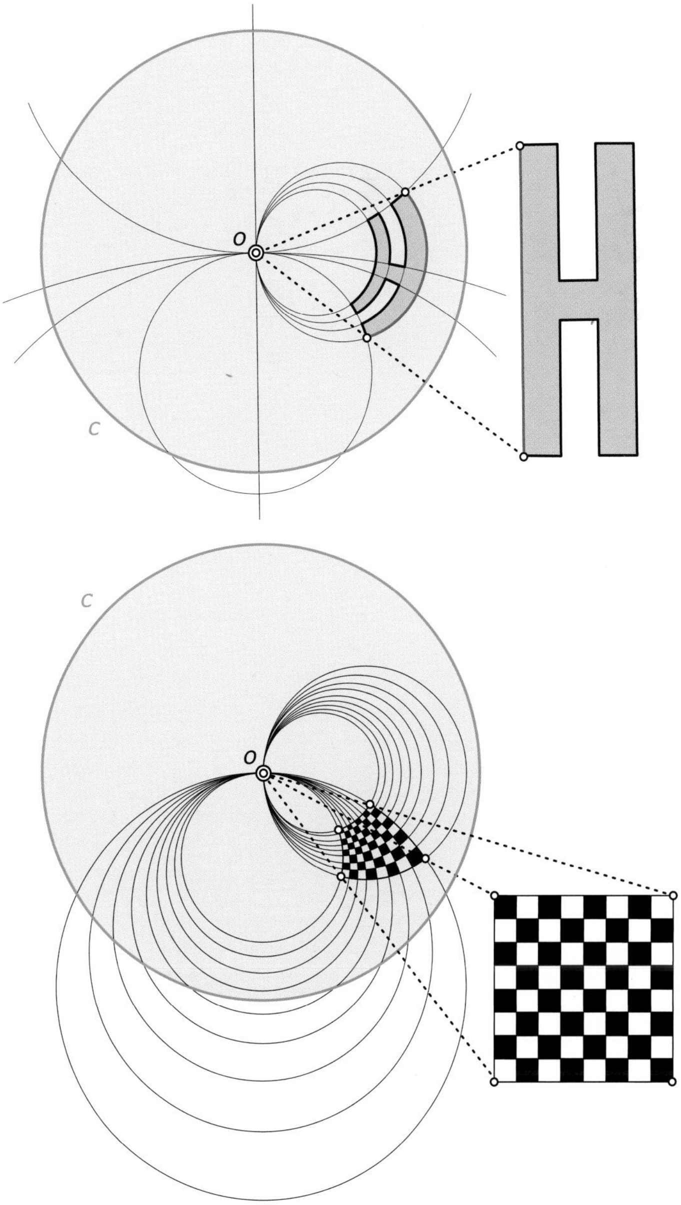

Fig. 5.28
Inversion applied to the letter H and to a checkerboard.

Planar transformations and complex numbers. We will now employ complex numbers as an elegant mathematical approach to an important class of planar transformations. We suggest reading the section on complex numbers in the Geometry Primer first. We start with revisiting congruence transformations, but this time using complex numbers.

In the Gaussian plane, every point $p(x,y)$ can be uniquely described by a single complex number $z = x + iy$. When we reflect the point p over the x-axis we obtain $p_1(x,-y)$, which corresponds to $\bar{z} = x - iy$, the so-called complex conjugate of z. Thus, using complex numbers the reflection over the x-axis can simply be written as $z_1 = \bar{z}$. Figure 5.29 also illustrates that a translation defined by the vector $\mathbf{t} = (a,b)$ can be described as addition of the two complex numbers z and $t = a + ib$.

However, the rotation with rotation center o turns out to be a multiplication of z with a special complex number z_3, where the argument of z_3 specifies the rotation angle and the absolute value of z_3 has to be 1. The multiplication of z with a general complex number z_4 describes a rotation combined with a uniform scaling. The scaling factor is the absolute value of z_4.

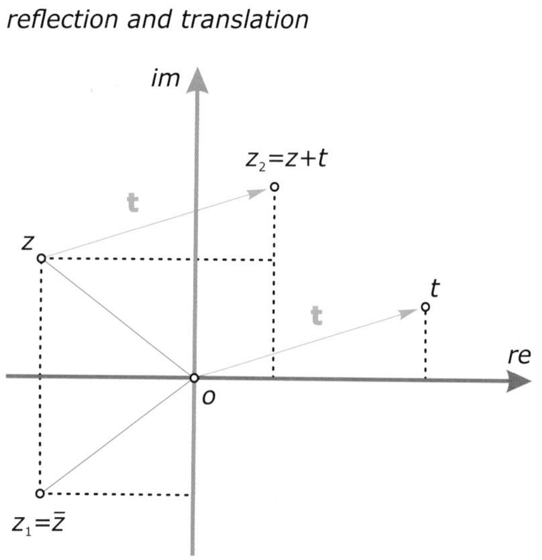

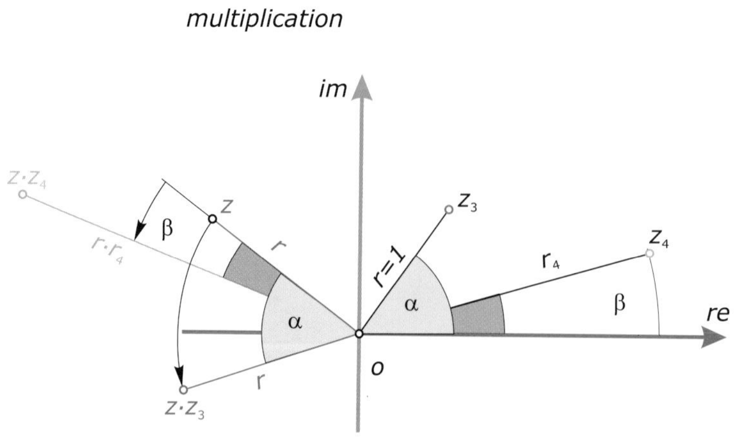

Fig. 5.29
Some congruence transformations in the Gaussian plane.

This connection between complex numbers and planar transformations can even be extended to the inversion (Figure 5.30). So far we did not derive a geometric interpretation for the division of complex numbers. Let us start with the computation of $z_1 = 1/z$.

We multiply

$$z_1 = \frac{1}{z} = \frac{1}{x+iy} \text{ with } 1 = \frac{x-iy}{x-iy}$$

and get

$$z_1 = \frac{1}{x+iy} \cdot \frac{x-iy}{x-iy} = \frac{x-iy}{x^2+y^2}.$$

Because $x - iy = \bar{z}$ is the complex conjugate of z, the transformation of the point p into the point p_1 is a composition of a reflection over the real axis and a uniform scaling with the factor $1/(x^2 + y^2)$. If we then apply another reflection over the real axis, we obtain the point p_2, which is obviously the inverse point of p with respect to the unit circle c_0. Thus, we obtain a description of the inversion with respect to the unit circle with

$$z_2 = \frac{1}{\bar{z}}.$$

The inversion with respect to a circle of radius r centered at o is given by $z_2 = r^2/\bar{z}$.

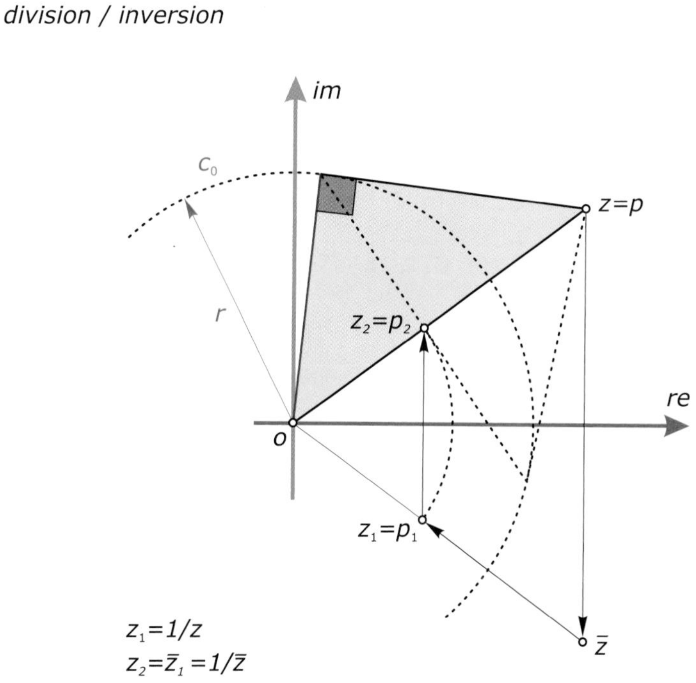

Fig. 5.30. In the Gaussian plane, the inversion can be computed via $z_2 = 1/\bar{z}$.

Möbius transformations. The transformation $z_2 = r^2/\bar{z}$ is a special case of so-called *Möbius transformations*, which are defined by

$$z_1 = \frac{a \cdot \bar{z} + b}{c \cdot \bar{z} + d}$$

or

$$z_1 = \frac{a \cdot z + b}{c \cdot z + d},$$

with a, b, c, and d as arbitrary complex numbers. We do not allow those equations where $a \cdot d = b \cdot c$. This restriction excludes only a few transformations, which are not properly defined. Without a proof, we state that all Möbius transformations map circles into circles (in the sense that lines are circles with infinite radius) and that they preserve angles. Some Möbius transformations are illustrated in Figure 5.31.

For $c = 0$ and $d = 1$, the first formula simplifies to $z_1 = a \cdot z + b$—which describes direct *similarities* (transformations that preserve angles and orientations). We note also that all congruence transformations are included in the set of Möbius transformations.

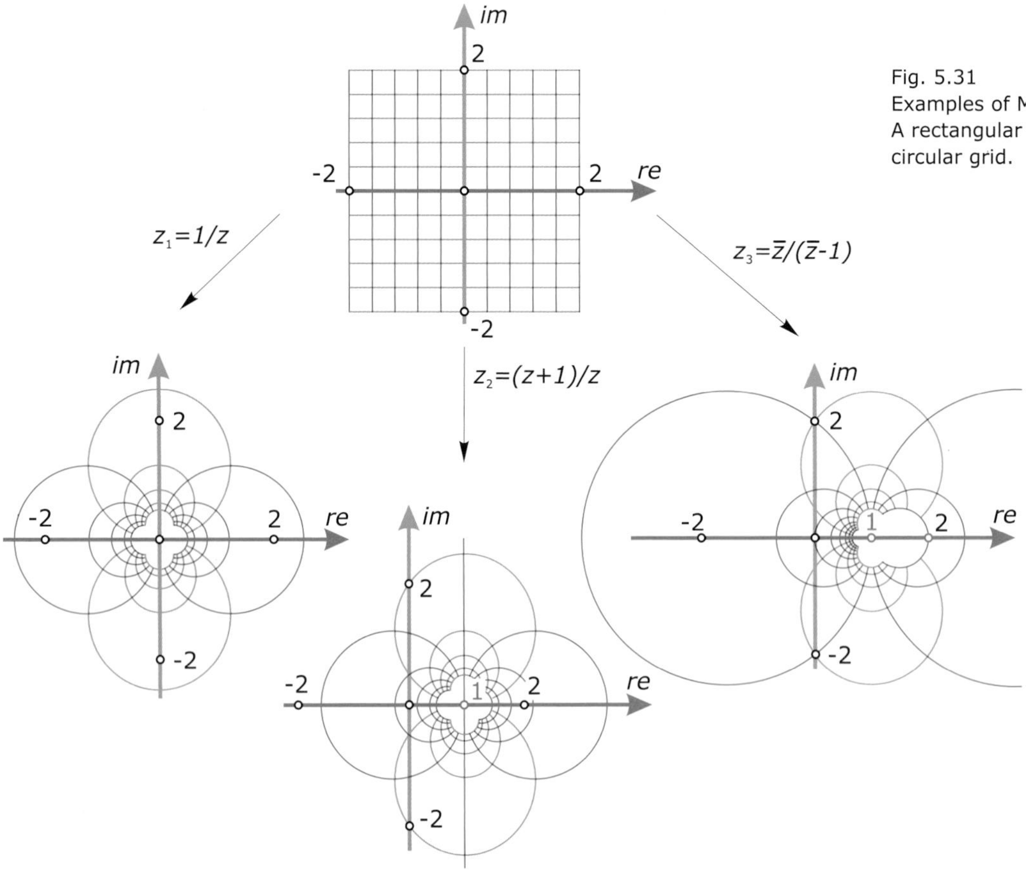

Fig. 5.31
Examples of Möbius transformations. A rectangular grid is mapped onto a circular grid.

Analogous to the fact that all congruence transformations can be generated by applying compositions of reflections about lines, we remark that every Möbius transformation can be generated as a composition of suitable inversions.

Conformal mappings. Figure 5.32 illustrates the following properties of Möbius transformations.

- Circles are mapped onto straight lines or circles.
- The intersection angle of two curves is preserved.

If we waive the circle-preserving property but insist on the preservation of angles, we have the set of *conformal transformations*. Conformal transformations or conformal mappings are extremely important in many areas of mathematics and also play a role in engineering and physics. They can also be very useful in generating patterns by deforming planar objects. This even more general approach to transformations is also based on complex numbers and on the theory of functions of complex variables (which is beyond the scope of this book). Figure 5.33 illustrates images of quadrilateral grids of two "simple" conformal transformations defined by complex functions.

In summary, we can say that complex numbers allow us to derive a uniform description of a wide variety of transformations. They may even be useful instruments for design purposes.

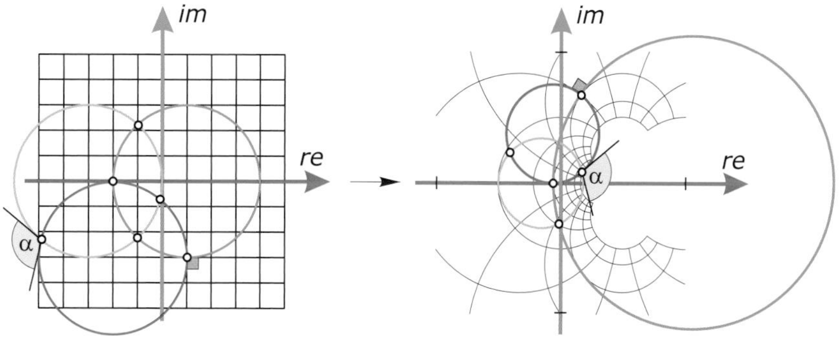

Fig. 5.32
Möbius transformations preserve both circles and angles.

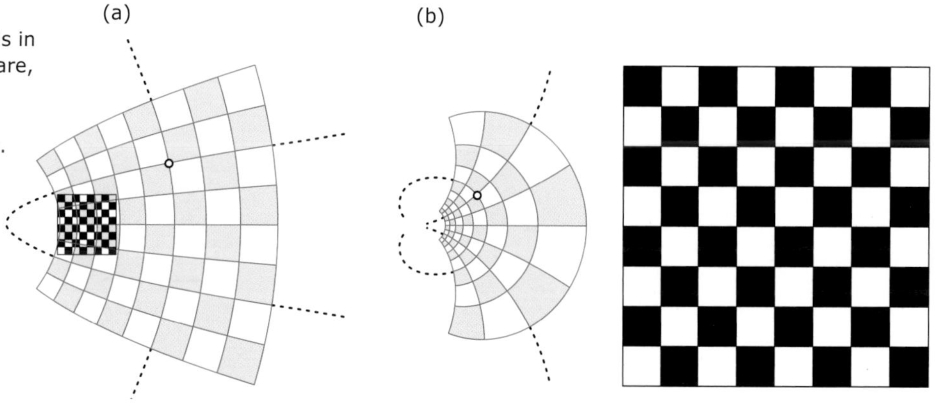

Fig. 5.33
Conformal mappings are useful tools in generating patterns. Straight lines are, for example, mapped into
(a) parabolae ($z_2 = z^2$), or
(b) more general curves ($z_3 = 1/z^2$).

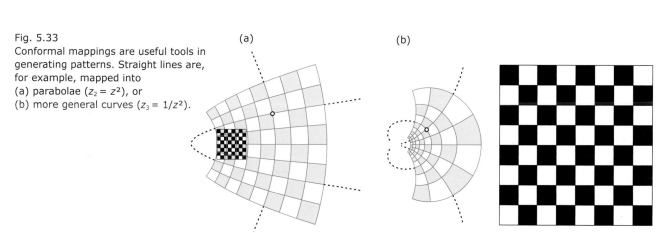

Chapter 6
Spatial Transformations

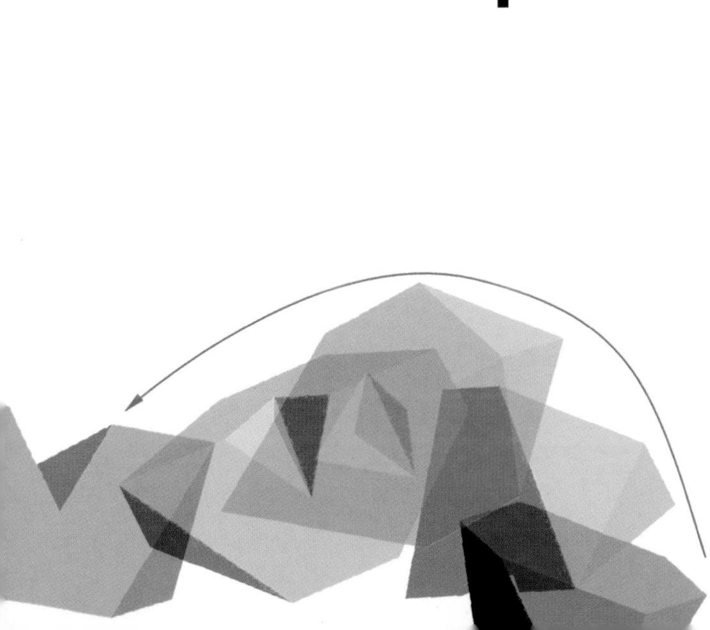

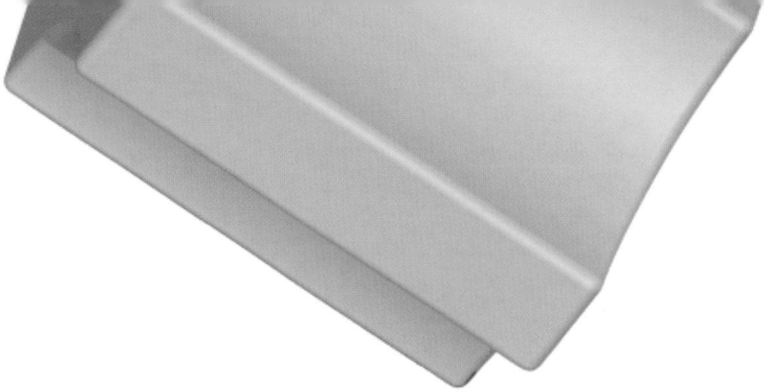

Spatial Transformations

A good understanding of spatial transformations is very useful for positioning three-dimensional objects. We begin by generalizing planar congruence transformations to spatial ones. In three dimensions there are new transformations (such as the helical motion) that have no counterpart in two dimensions. We will show that there always exists a unique helical motion, a rotation, or a translation that maps two positions of a rigid body onto each other—a property very useful in practice.

In addition to the shape- and distance-preserving congruence transformations, there are other transformations useful for deforming objects. We introduce affine transformations to study transformations from a more general point of view. From the mathematical description of these transformations, we can recognize that many of the transformations discussed so far are special cases of affine transformations.

As a practical application of transformations, we introduce the concepts of key frame animation and animation scripts for the production of animated architectural presentations. We include some analytic treatment because this is absolutely necessary in facilitating scripting of smooth motions and animations.

Finally, we discuss projective transformations, which empowers us to gain a deeper insight into perspective projection. This is also the basis of understanding the principles of three-dimensional reconstruction from images and the geometric background of relief perspective (the art of stage architecture).

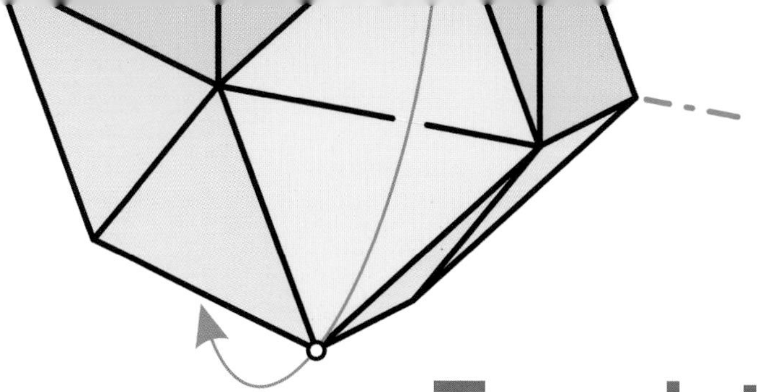

Translation, Rotation, and Reflection in Space

Translation, rotation, and reflection in two dimensions can be generalized to three dimensions. Such transformations have properties similar to those of their two-dimensional counterparts. They are shape- and distance-preserving transformations and are therefore *spatial congruence transformations*. As in two dimensions, we distinguish between direct and opposite congruence transformations (Figure 6.1).

In this sense, every congruence transformation that transforms a right-handed coordinate frame into a right-handed coordinate frame is called direct. An opposite congruence transformation changes the type of the coordinate frame. This means that a right-handed coordinate frame is mapped into a left-handed coordinate frame, and vice versa.

Fig. 6.1
Direct congruence transformations preserve the "handedness" of the coordinate frame, whereas opposite congruence transformations change the type.

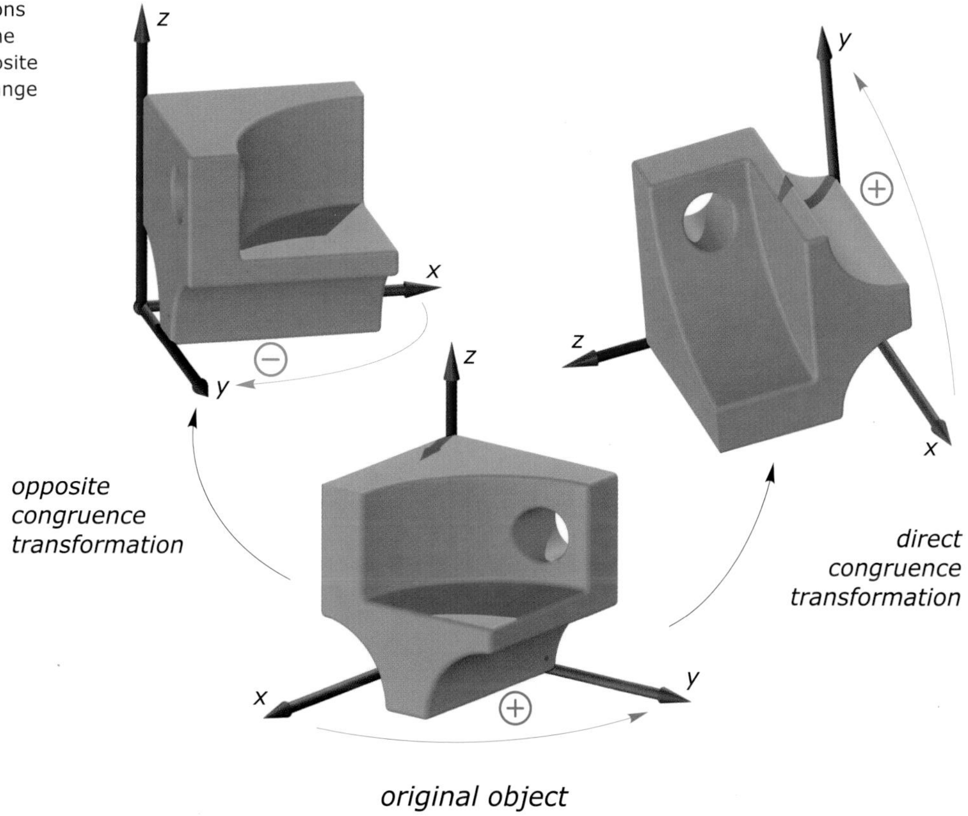

When dealing with direct congruence transformations, we distinguish between the transformation and the associated smooth motion. On the one hand, we have the transformation (sometimes referred to as *discrete motion*)—which describes the relative position of the pre-image and the image of a three-dimensional object. On the other hand, the associated smooth motion (also referred to as *rigid body motion*) describes the process that moves a body from the start position into the end position (Figure 6.2). Let's examine three-dimensional congruence transformations in detail.

Translation. Analogously to the planar case, a spatial translation is defined by a translation vector **t**. This vector specifies the direction and the magnitude of the translation. Translating a point means adding **t** to it. Thus,

$$x_1 = x + a,$$

$$y_1 = y + b,$$

$$z_1 = z + c,$$

describes the translation with translation vector $\mathbf{t} = (a,b,c)$. The point $p_1 = (x_1,y_1,z_1)$ is the image of the point $p = (x,y,z)$. As in the two-dimensional case, a line l and its image l_1 are parallel. In addition, in three dimensions a plane P and its image P_1 are also parallel (Figure 6.3).

Rotation. A planar rotation turns an object around a fixed point. In three dimensions, we rotate about a fixed *rotation axis A* (Figure 6.4). We also have to specify a *rotation angle* ρ, which defines the amount of rotation. During a rotational motion, every point p moves along a circle c_p—which lies in a plane orthogonal to the rotational axis.

Fig. 6.2
(left) A transformation describes the relative position of two different spatial positions of an object,
(right) whereas a motion is the continuous process that transfers the object from the initial position to the end position.

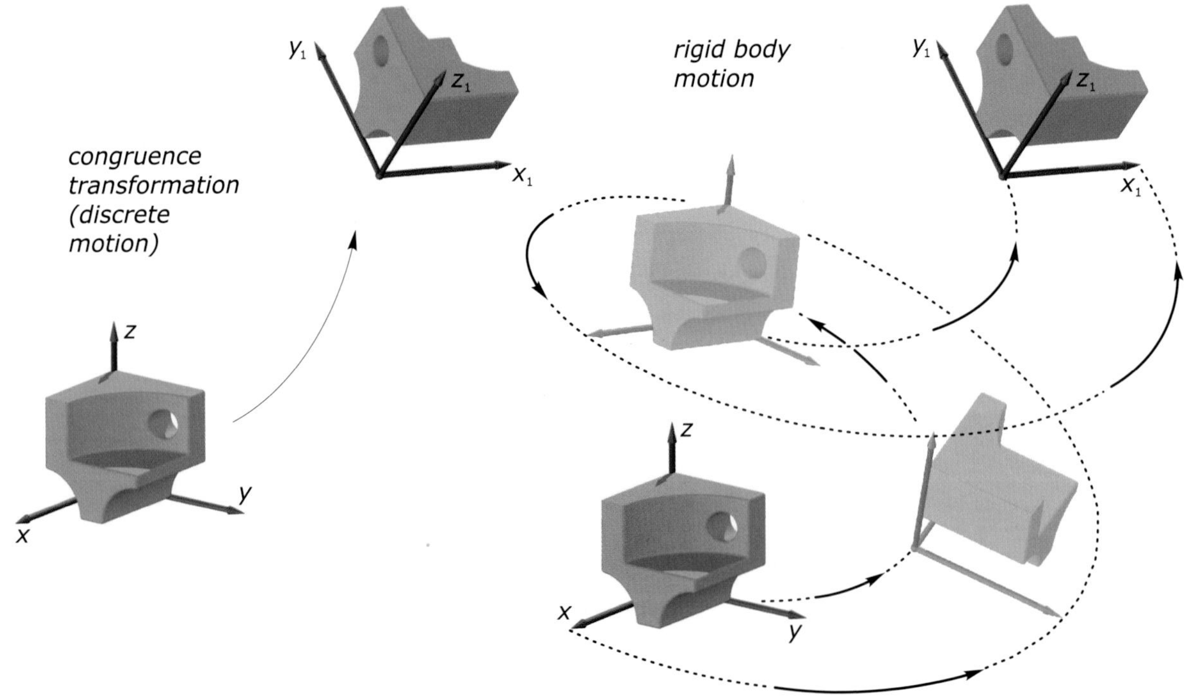

The intersection point of this plane with the rotational axis A is the midpoint m_p of the circular path of the point p. The rotational angle ρ can also be seen as an angle between $m_p p$ and $m_p p_1$. To specify in which direction the rotation has to be applied, we need to have an *orientation* of the axis A and a sign (orientation) of the angle ρ. The planar rotations happening in the normal planes of A must appear with the oriented angle ρ when we look at these planes against the orientation of A (Figure 6.4).

A rotation about the z-axis does not change the z-coordinates. In the top view, this rotation behaves like a planar rotation about the origin. Thus, we have the following mathematical description for a rotation with angle ρ about the z-axis:

$$x_1 = x \cdot \cos\rho - y \cdot \sin\rho,$$
$$y_1 = x \cdot \sin\rho + y \cdot \cos\rho,$$
$$z_1 = z$$

Analogously, a rotation about the x-axis and the y-axis are respectively given by

$$x_1 = x, \qquad\qquad x_1 = x \cdot \cos\rho + z \cdot \sin\rho,$$
$$y_1 = y \cdot \cos\rho - z \cdot \sin\rho, \qquad\qquad y_1 = y,$$
$$z_1 = y \cdot \sin\rho + z \cdot \cos\rho, \qquad\qquad z_1 = -x \cdot \sin\rho + z \cdot \cos\rho.$$

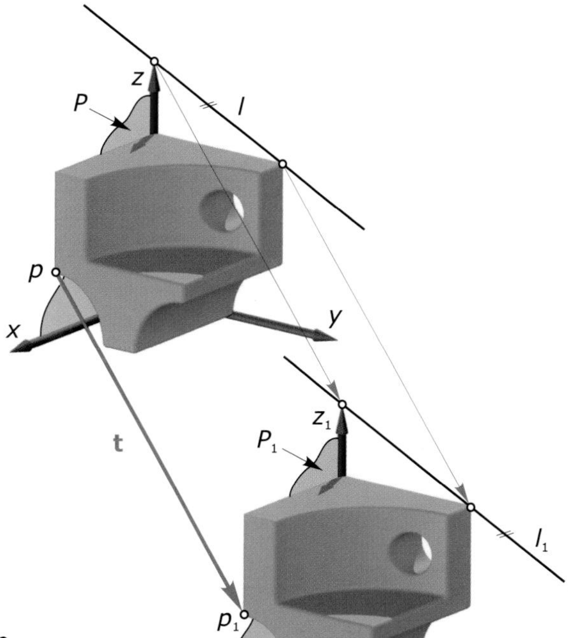

Fig. 6.3
A translation is defined by a translation vector **t**.

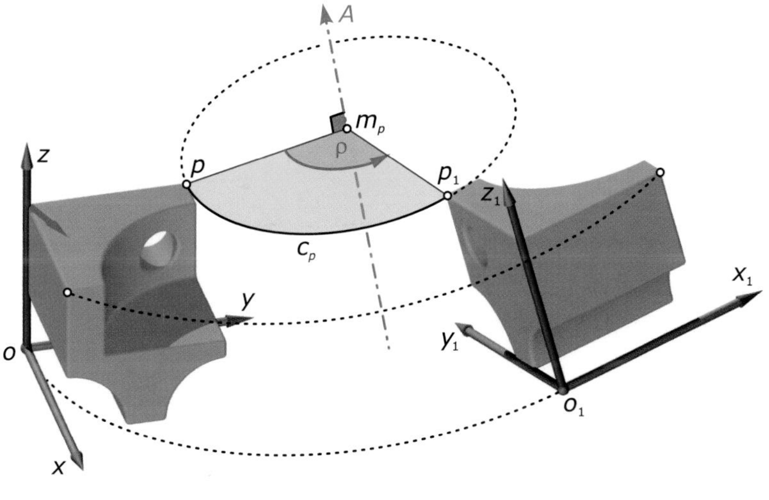

Fig. 6.4
A rotation is defined by an oriented axis A and an oriented angle ρ.

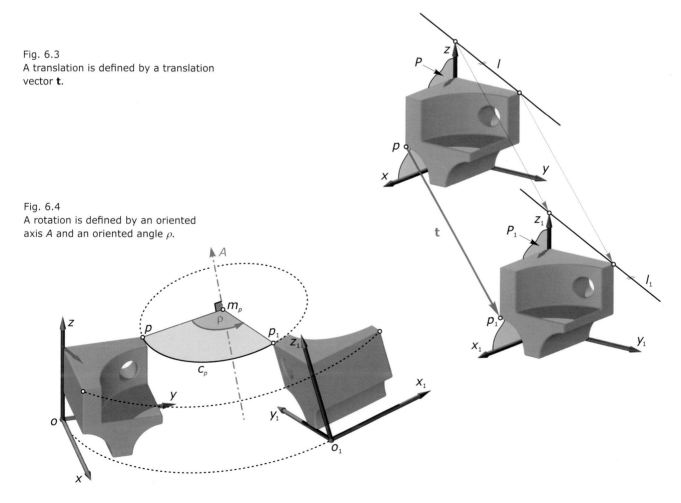

Example:

Reconstruction of an arbitrary rotational axis. Assume that we are given two positions s and s_1 of the same straight line segment. The endpoints in the respective positions are labeled a,b and a_1,b_1 (Figure 6.5). Analogously to the planar case, we can always find a unique rotation (or translation) that transforms s into s_1.

Due to the fact that a and a_1 as well as b and b_1 have equal distances to the rotational axis A, this axis is contained in the bisector planes of the point pairs a,a_1 and b,b_1. Thus, the axis A can be constructed as an intersection line of these bisector planes. The rotational angle ρ can be measured as the angle betweeen the straight lines $m_a a$ and $m_a a_1$.

Reflections. One generalization of a two-dimensional reflection is a three-dimensional *reflection about a straight line* r, called the *reflection line*. Alternatively, we can reflect an object about a *reflection plane* R (Figure 6.6). As in the planar case, every point p and its image p_1 have the same distance to the fixed reflection line or plane—and the connecting line pp_1 is orthogonal to the line r or to the plane R, respectively.

Although both types of reflections have similar properties, there is one essential difference. The reflection about a plane R transforms a right-handed coordinate frame into a left-handed one. Thus, this type of reflection is an opposite congruence transformation. In contrast, the reflection about a line r preserves the handedness of the coordinate system. Therefore, it is a direct congruence transformation. In fact, the reflection about a line r is exactly the same as the rotation about r with a rotational angle of 180 degress (a half turn about the reflection axis).

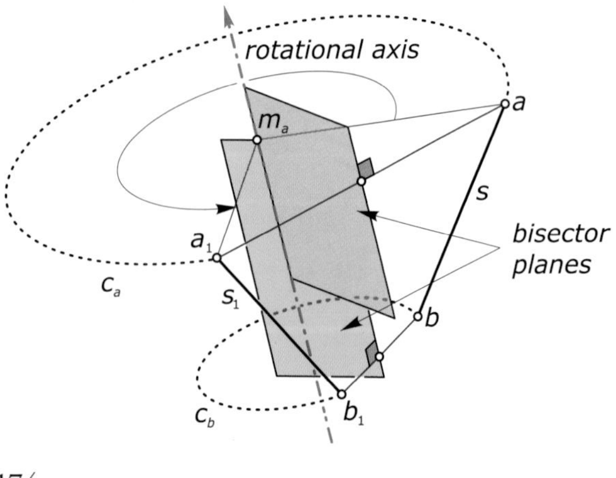

Fig. 6.5
The rotational axis A is the intersection line of two bisector planes.

For a mathematical description, we first consider the reflection about the coordinate planes. Analogously to the planar reflection, we simply have to change the sign of one coordinate. Therefore, we have the following formulas.

Reflection about the

xy-plane:	*yz*-plane:	*zx*-plane:
$x_1 = x,$	$x_1 = -x,$	$x_1 = x,$
$y_1 = y,$	$y_1 = y,$	$y_1 = -y,$
$z_1 = -z.$	$z_1 = z.$	$z_1 = z.$

We derive the formulas for the reflections about the coordinate axes by substituting the rotational angle ρ with 180 degrees in the formulas of the rotations described previously. Obeying the fact that $\sin(180°) = 0$ and $\cos(180°) = -1$, we obtain the following.

Reflection about the

x-axis:	*y*-axis:	*z*-axis:
$x_1 = x,$	$x_1 = -x,$	$x_1 = -x,$
$y_1 = -y,$	$y_1 = y,$	$y_1 = -y,$
$z_1 = -z.$	$z_1 = -z.$	$z_1 = z.$

In the case of a reflection about a coordinate axis, we have to change two signs—whereas a reflection about a coordinate plane changes only one sign. This expresses the fact that a reflection about a coordinate axis can be seen as a composition of two reflections about coordinate planes.

Fig. 6.6
The reflection about a line *r* is a direct congruence transformation, whereas the reflection about a plane *R* is an opposite congruence transformation.

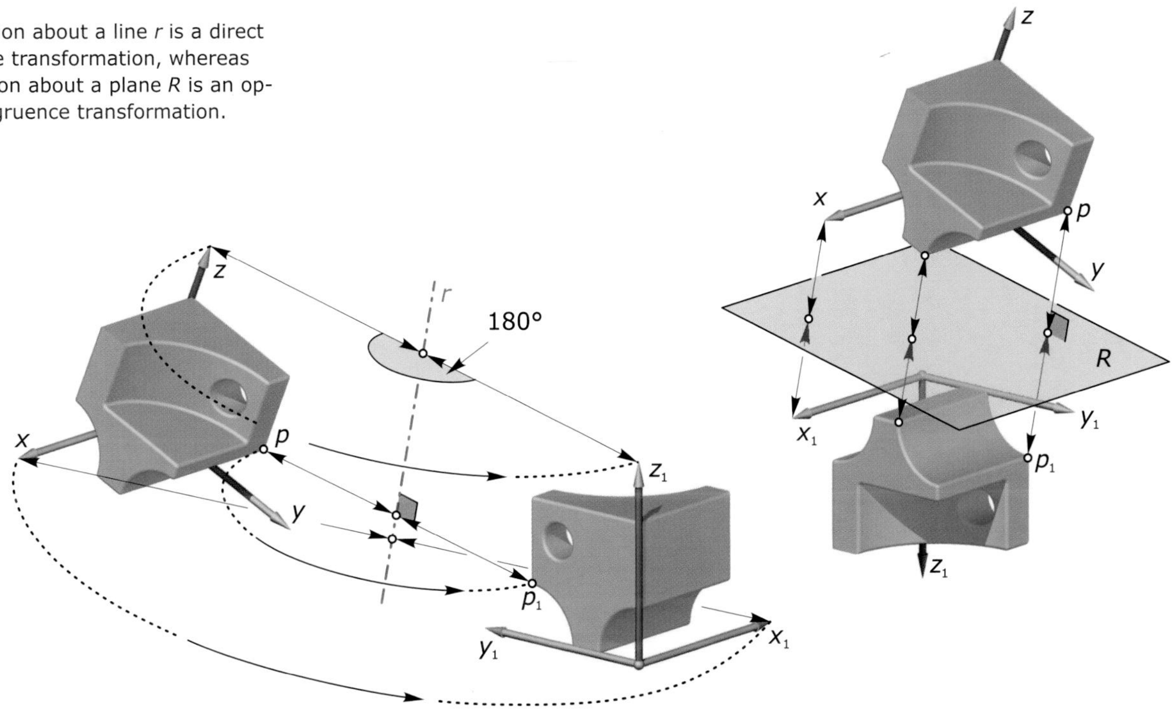

Glide reflection. Again we aim at generalizing the two-dimensional case. The composition of a reflection about a line and a translation parallel to this line is a composition of a half turn and a translation. This is a direct congruence transformation and a special case of a helical motion studied later in this section. Thus, we concentrate on a composition of a reflection about a plane R and a translation with a translation vector $\mathbf{t}$ parallel to R (Figure 6.7).This spatial glide reflection is an opposite congruence transformation with exactly the same properties as the planar glide reflection.

For the mathematical description, we assume that the xy-plane is the reflection plane. Then the translation vector $\mathbf{t}$ has to be parallel to the xy-plane. It follows that the z-coordinate of $\mathbf{t} = (a,b,0)$ has to be zero. We combine the formulas that describe reflections and translations to obtain

$$x_1 = x + a,$$

$$y_1 = y + b,$$

$$z_1 = -z.$$

Spatial congruence transformations are an essential tool when modeling objects. Recognizing spatial symmetries and applying the appropriate transformation accelerates the design process. Figure 6.8 shows by means of interesting architectural designs the application of these transformations.

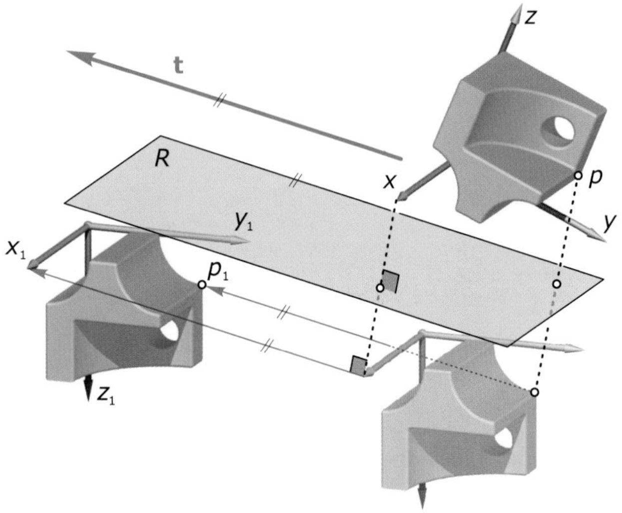

Fig. 6.7
A glide reflection is a composition of a reflection about a plane R and a translation parallel to that plane.

Fig. 6.8
(a) The *railway station Atocha* (opened 1992) in Madrid by José Rafael Moneo consists of many congruent parts. These can be mapped onto each other via a translation.
(b) A translational motion is used in the *Palacio Vistalegre Arena* (2000) in Madrid by Jaime Pérez to open or close part of the roof.
(c) The *Château de Chambord* (1519–1547) has reflective symmetry with respect to a vertical plane.

(a)

(b)

(b)

(c)

Example:

Dodecahedron with rhombic faces. In Chapter 3 we encountered the rhombic dodecahedron, which can be used to tesselate three-dimensional space. To construct a rhombic dodecahedron, we start with a cube and add six congruent pyramids (Figure 6.9a). The height of the pyramids has to be half the edge length of the cube. Thus, two triangular faces of neighboring pyramids have one plane in common.

To simplify the modeling process, we only construct one pyramid. To copy this pyramid to the other five positions, we apply rotations about two symmetry axes A_1 and A_2 of the cube. Finally, we combine all seven objects by applying the Boolean union. Figures 9b-d show a sequence of this modeling process.

Fig. 6.9
(a) A rhombic dodecahedron can be generated by adding congruent pyramids to the six side faces of a cube.
(b,c) Using appropriate rotations simplifies this process.
(d) By applying the Boolean union to the cube and the six pyramids, we obtain the rhombic dodecahedron.

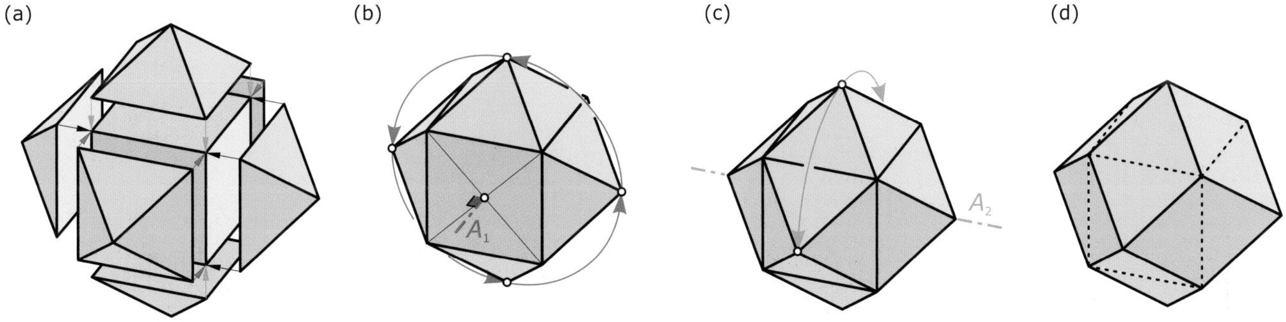

Composition of transformations. As in the two-dimensional case, the composition of two direct or two opposite congruence transformations generates a direct congruence transformation. However, the composition of a direct and an opposite congruence transformation results in an opposite congruence transformation. We illustrate these properties by means of several examples (Figure 6.10).

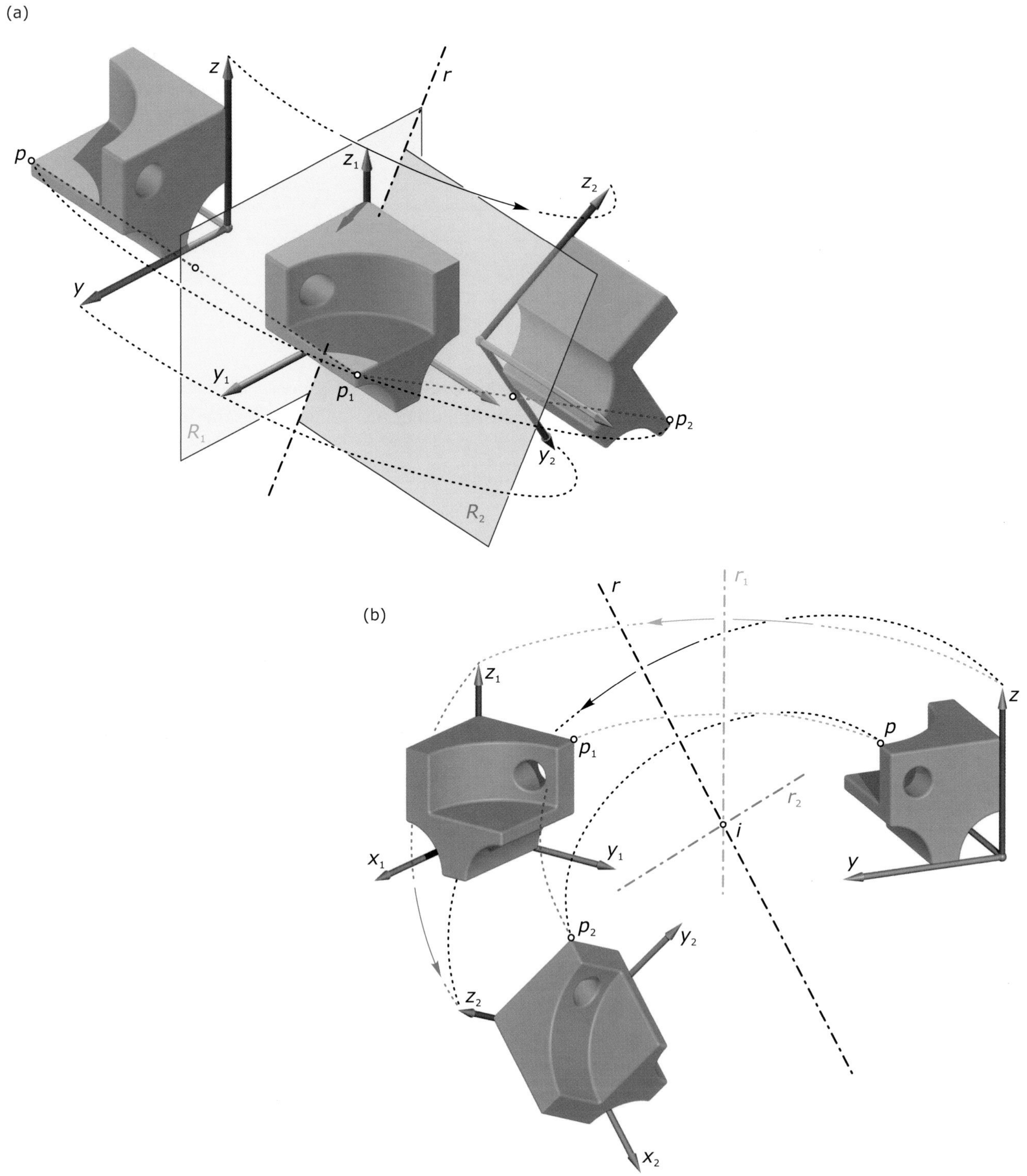

- The composition of two reflections about nonparallel reflection planes R_1 and R_2 is a rotation about an axis r, which is the intersection line of the two reflection planes. Note that the rotation angle is twice the angle between the two planes R_1 and R_2 (see the analogous facts in regard to two dimensions in Chapter 5).
- Two rotations about intersecting axes r_1 and r_2 can be replaced by one single rotation about another axis r. The intersection point i is a fixed point of both rotations. Therefore, it also has to be a fixed point of the composite rotation. This implies that the new rotation axis passes through the point i.
- The composition of a rotation and a reflection about a plane R, where the plane R contains the rotation axis r, generates a reflection about another plane R_1. All points of the rotational axis r remain fixed during either transformation. Thus, the new reflection plane R_1 also contains the rotational axis r.

In the last example, we had a special mutual position between the reflection plane and the rotational axis. Therefore, the composition of the two transformations could be replaced by a single reflection about a plane. In general, one can prove that the composition of a reflection and a rotation is always a single glide reflection or a simple reflection.

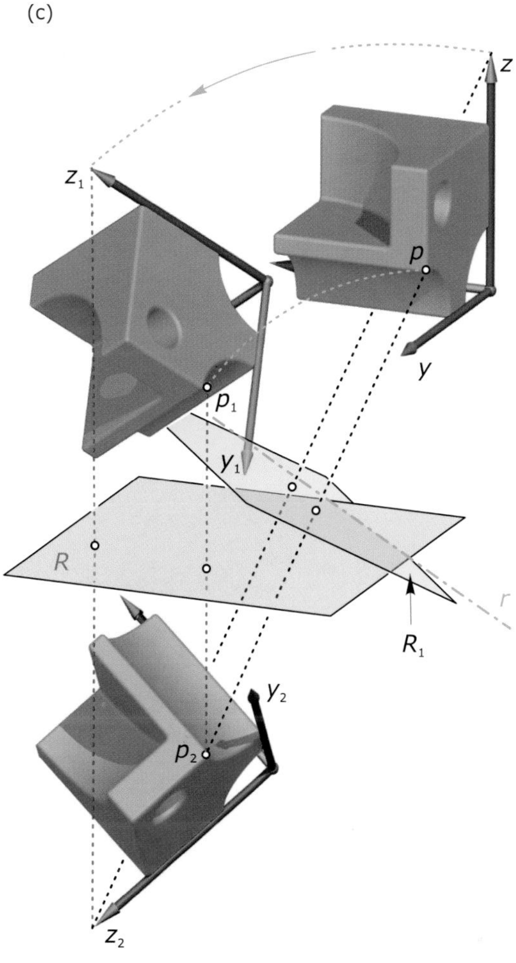

Fig. 6.10
Compositions of direct and opposite congruence transformations.
(a) Two reflections can be replaced by a single rotation.
(b) Two rotations with intersecting axes result in a single rotation.
(c) A rotation and a reflection where the reflection plane R contains the rotation axis r can be replaced by a single reflection.

However, the general case of the second example (the composition of two rotations about skew axes) turns out to be different from a single translation or a single rotation. This is also true for the composition of a translation and a rotation. In fact, there is one more direct congruence transformation in space we have not yet dealt with. Before we study this transformation, we state again the important fact that changing the order of the compositions can affect the end position of the transformed objects in an essential way (Figure 6.11).

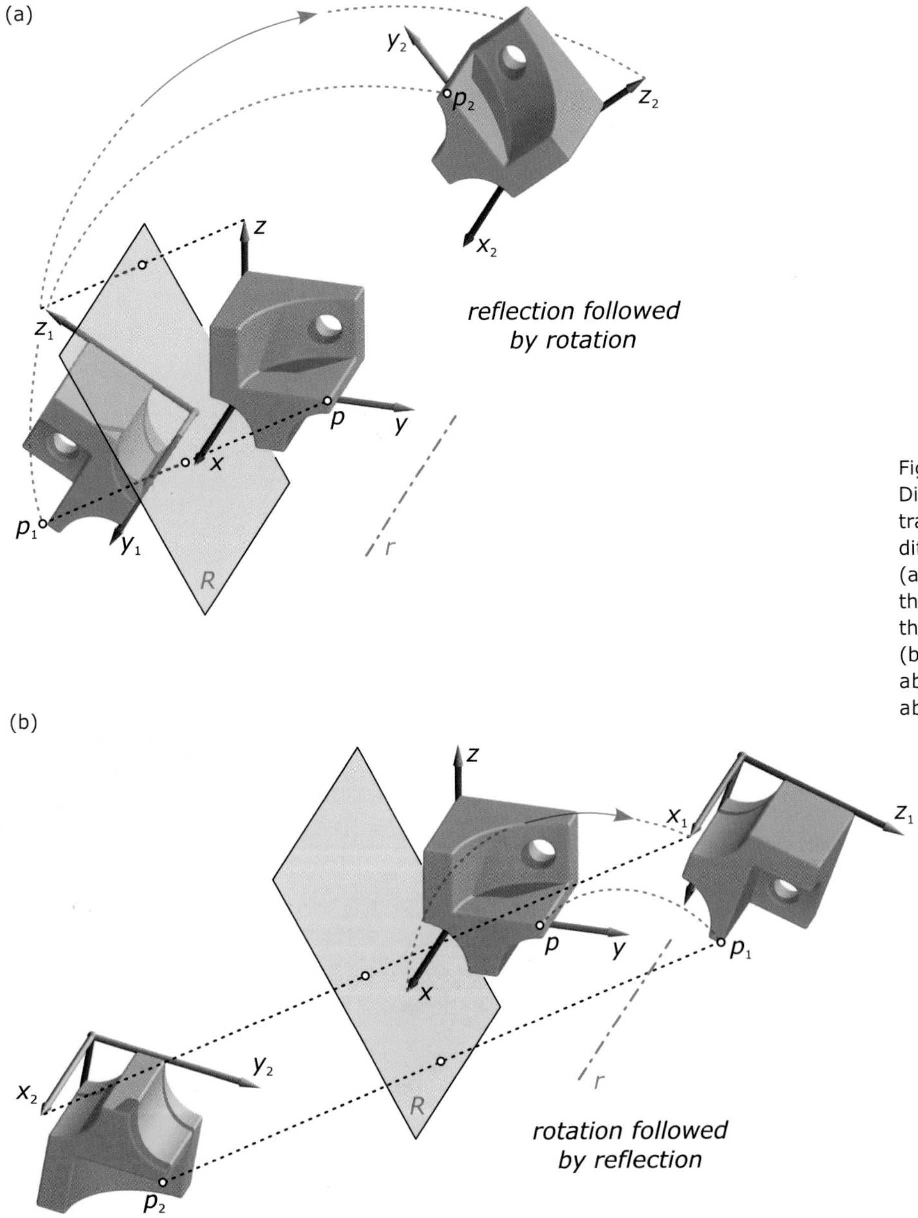

Fig. 6.11
Different orders in which transformations are applied result in different composite transformations.
(a) The object is first reflected about the plane *R*, and then rotated about the straight line *r*.
(b) Here, the object is at first rotated about *r* and afterward reflected about *R*.

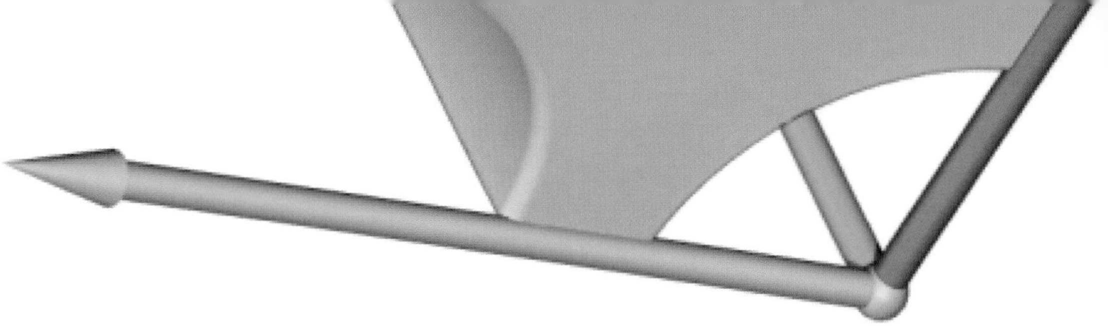

Helical Transformation

The most general opposite congruence transformation is the glide reflection, a combination of a reflection and a special translation. The *helical transformation*, as the direct congruence counterpart to the glide reflection, is the composition of a rotation about the *helical axis A* and a translation parallel to this axis (Figure 6.12). It is the most general direct congruence transformation in space.

In the section about planar transformations, we learned that there is always a unique rotation (or in special cases, a translation) that transfers an object from a given position into another one. If we consider translations and rotations as special cases of helical transformations, we have a similar statement in space that is very important for the study of spatial motions.

Given any two distinct (directly congruent) positions of a rigid body, we can always find a unique helical transformation that transfers one position to the other.

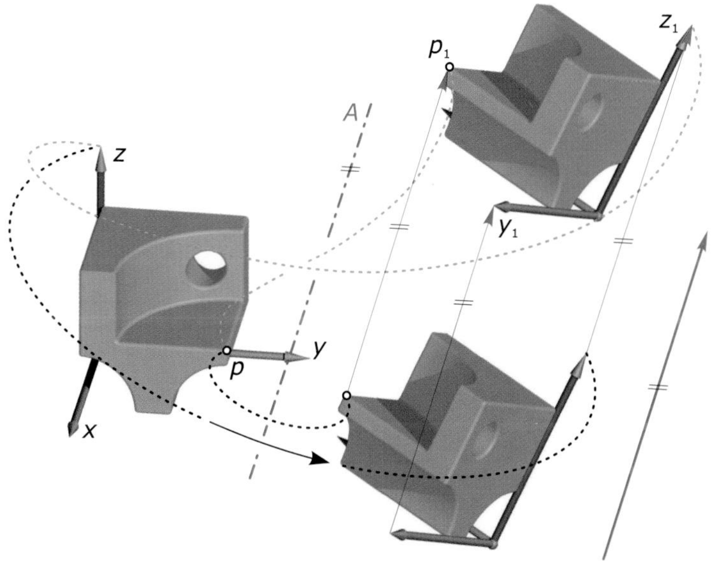

Fig. 6.12
A helical transformation is a composition of a rotation about an axis *A* and a translation parallel to this axis.

To move an object or an auxiliary coordinate system from one position to another, a single helical transformation can be used. Fortunately, most computer-aided design (CAD) systems provide a tool for specifying such a helical transformation. In fact, it is sufficient to define two positions $a_1b_1c_1$ and $a_2b_2c_2$ of a triangle *abc* associated with the object (Figure 6.13a). In practice, we proceed as described in the following example.

Example:

Repositioning of an object. Given is an object in three-dimensional space in arbitrary position (Figure 6.13b). We want to reposition the object such that the object points *a*, *b*, and *c* lie in the plane *P*.

Using a CAD system, we interactively define the point *a* as the origin and the line *ab* as the *x*-axis of an auxiliary coordinate system. By selecting a third point *c* we specify the *xy*-plane and the direction of the *y*-axis. This also defines the *z*-axis of that auxiliary coordinate system. To reposition the object, we specify the new position of that auxiliary coordinate system.

We define the new position *a*' of *a*, a point 1 on the new *x*'-axis, and a point 2 in the plane *P*. This defines the helical transformation that maps the triangle *abc* into the triangle *a*'*b*'*c*'. Depending on the choice of the point 2 (right or left of the *x*'-axis), the object lies above or below the plane *P*.

(a)

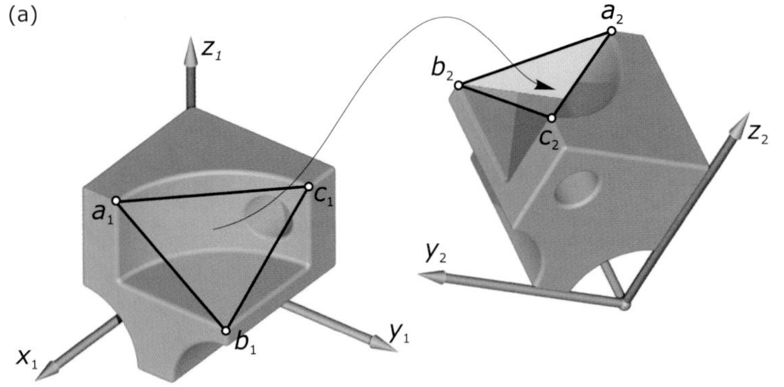

(b)

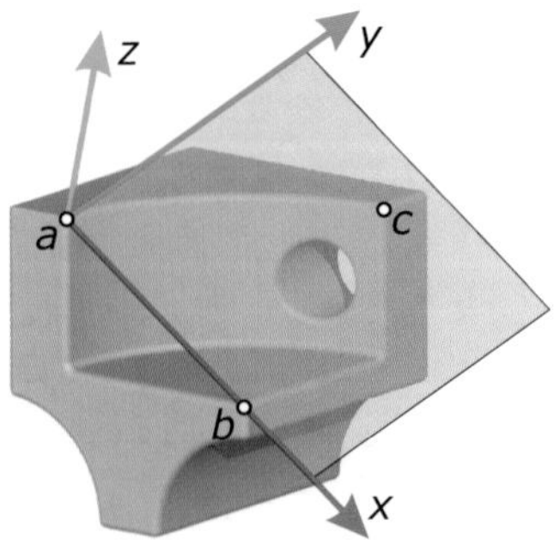

(c)

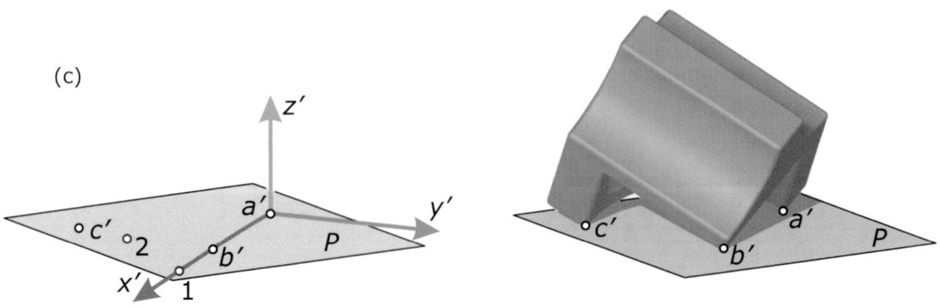

Fig. 6.13
(a) A direct congruence transformation of an object can always be defined by two positions $a_1b_1c_1$ and $a_2b_2c_2$ of a triangle *abc*.
(b) To reposition an object in three dimensions, we use three object points *a*, *b*, and *c* to define an auxiliary coordinate system. The new position of this auxiliary coordinate system is defined by the points *a*′, 1, and 2.

Example:

Reconstruction of the helical axis. We assume to know two positions $a_1b_1c_1$ and $a_2b_2c_2$ of a triangle abc and we want to find out the helical axis, the rotational angle, and the translational vector. A vector $\mathbf{a} = \mathbf{a}_2 - \mathbf{a}_1$ (defined by the two positions a_1 and a_2 of the triangle vertex a) can be considered the sum of the translational vector $\mathbf{t}$ and a vector $\mathbf{r}_a$, where $\mathbf{t}$ is parallel and $\mathbf{r}_a$ is orthogonal to the helical axis (Figure 6.14a).

This holds for all three vectors **a**, **b**, and **c**, which are defined by the two positions of the triangle vertices (Figure 6.14b). Thus, as the simple calculation $\mathbf{a} - \mathbf{b} = \mathbf{r}_a + \mathbf{t} - (\mathbf{r}_b + \mathbf{t}) = \mathbf{r}_a - \mathbf{r}_b$ shows, the difference of each pair of these vectors is a vector orthogonal to **t**.

If we now attach the vectors **a**, **b**, and **c** to the origin o, we can interpret them as position vectors of three points p, q, and r that define a triangle pqr in the plane P (Figure 6.14c). The sides of this triangle define the difference vectors $\mathbf{a} - \mathbf{b}$, $\mathbf{b} - \mathbf{c}$, and $\mathbf{c} - \mathbf{a}$. Thus, all sides of the triangle pqr are orthogonal to the translational vector **t** and therefore the entire plane P is perpendicular to **t**. We find the direction of the helical axis as a normal of the plane P. Moreover, the distance of the origin o from the plane P gives the magnitude of the translational vector.

Using the negative vector $-\mathbf{t}$ we translate the triangle $a_2b_2c_2$ into the intermediate position $a_0b_0c_0$, which can be transferred into the original position via a simple rotation. The axis of this rotation is the helical axis we are looking for. Finally, this axis and the rotational angle can be found by intersecting two bisector planes (refer to the example where we reconstructed the rotational axis). Special cases are the following.

- If the vectors **a**, **b**, and **c** are parallel, they have to be of equal length and therefore the transformation simplifies to a translation with the translational vector $\mathbf{a} = \mathbf{b} = \mathbf{c}$.
- If the plane P contains the origin o, the translational part vanishes and we have a rotation (which we studied in an earlier example).

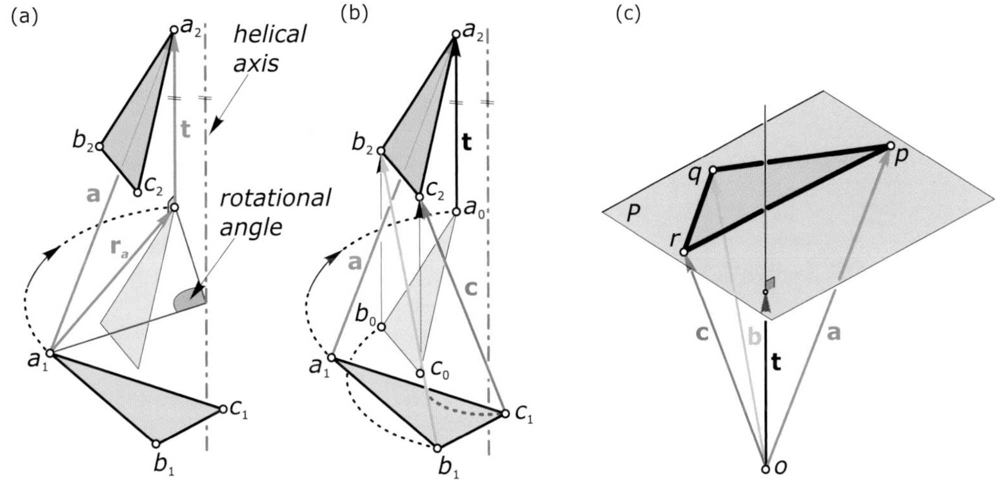

Fig. 6.14
Reconstructing the helical axis of a direct congruence transformation.

Helical motion. The transfer of a rigid body from one position to another can be performed by a helical transformation, which can be embedded into a simple smooth motion called a *helical motion*. The object is continuously rotated about the helical axis and simultaneously translated along the axis such that the length of the translation is proportional to the rotational angle ρ.

Let's examine this in more detail. Assume that a point q is moved into the position q_1 by a rotation about an axis A (rotational angle ρ_1) and a translation parallel to A. The translational distance shall be s_1. We measure s_1 with a sign (positive if the translation happens in direction of the orientation of A and negative otherwise). We can repeat the same helical transformation again and again to obtain points q_2, q_3, and so on. Note that q_2 is obtained from q by helical transformation with rotational angle $\rho_2 = 2{\cdot}\rho_1$ and translational distance $s_2 = 2{\cdot}s_1$.

The nth position q_n is related to q by a rotation with angle $n{\cdot}\rho_1$ and a translation with distance $n{\cdot}s_1$. If we refine this process and regard all intermediate positions we obtain a smooth helical motion (Figure 6.15). Any two positions of a rigid body that undergoes a helical motion are related to each other by a rotation about A and a translation parallel to A. The magnitude of the translation is a multiple $p{\cdot}\rho$ of the rotational angle ρ. The factor p is constant and can be computed from any two positions (e.g., from q and q_1 via $p = s_1/\rho_1$). This constant ratio of the translational distance and rotational angle is called the *helical parameter* or the *pitch*.

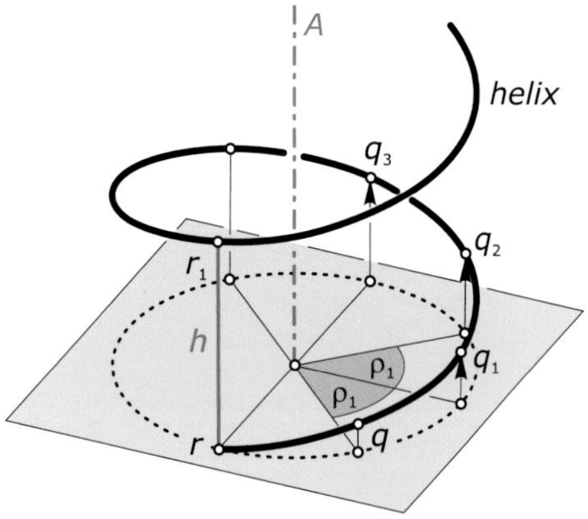

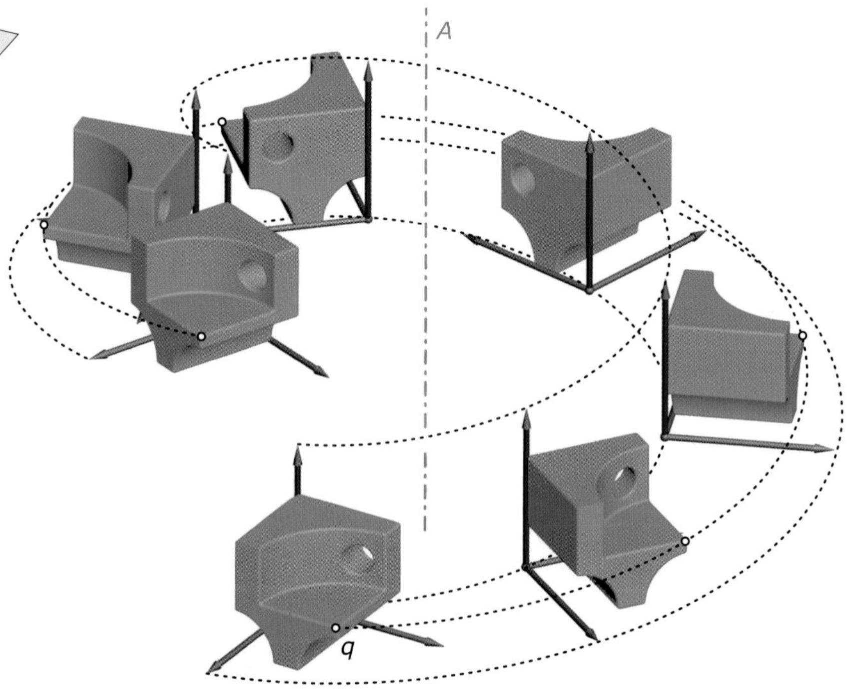

Fig. 6.15
During a helical motion, a point q runs on a helix.

According to our sign conventions, p has a positive sign if a positive rotational angle results in a translation in direction of the orientation of A. Otherwise, p is negative. In the case of a positive pitch ($p > 0$), we speak of a *right-handed helical motion*—whereas a negative pitch ($p < 0$) belongs to a *left-handed helical motion*. For $p = 0$, we obtain the rotational motion—whereas $p = \infty$("infinity") specifies a continuous translation parallel to A, a limit case of a helical motion.

During a helical motion, every point q outside the helical axis runs on a curve called a *helix*. After one full turn, a point r arrives at a position r_1. The corresponding translational distance is called the *height h* of the helix. Thus, the pitch p is connected to the height h via the formula $p = h/(2\pi)$ if we use the arc measurement of angles. The notions of left- and right-handed also apply to helixes. Note that one cannot turn a right-handed helix upside down to obtain a left-handed one (it remains right-handed).

Helixes have a lot of nice properties that make them interesting objects for architecture and design (Figure 6.16). Some of these properties are illustrated in Figure 6.17.

- Every helix lies on the surface of a rotational cylinder F. The axis of this supporting cylinder is the helical axis.
- The angle α between the tangents of all points of the helix and a normal plane of the axis is constant.
- As a consequence, when we cut the supporting cylinder along a straight line (parallel to the axis) and unfold the cylinder into a plane the helix c becomes a straight line c^d in this planar development F^d.
- If we apply to a helix the generating helical motion, it moves in itself (as a whole). This is important for the working effect of screws.

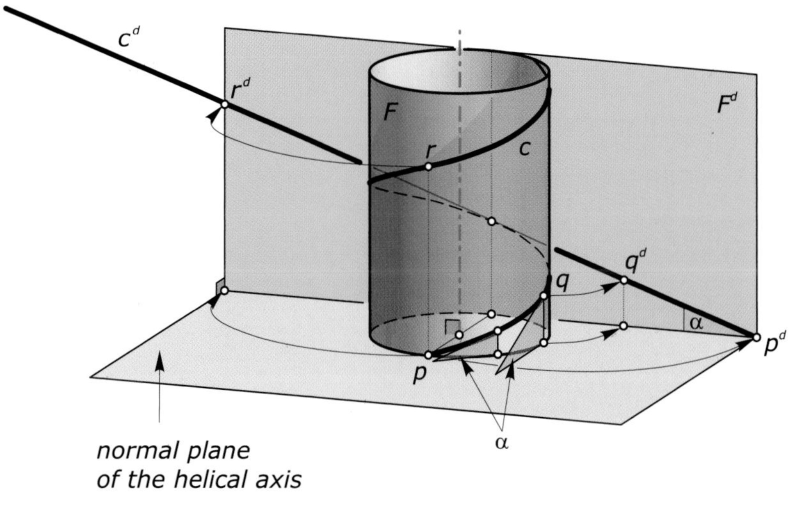

Fig. 6.16
Some remarkable properties of a helix.

Mathematical description. For a mathematical description of the helical transformation, we assume the helical axis to be the z-axis. Then we have to compose the rotation about the z-axis with a translation along the z-axis.

$$x_1 = x \cdot \cos \rho - y \cdot \sin \rho,$$

$$y_1 = x \cdot \sin \rho + y \cdot \cos \rho,$$

$$z_1 = z + p \cdot \rho.$$

Here, ρ and p denote the rotational angle and pitch, respectively. For a fixed value ρ, we obtain the helical transformation (or discrete motion). If ρ takes all values within a specified range, we obtain a continuous helical motion.

(a)

Fig. 6.17
Applications of helixes in architecture and design.
(a) A staircase of *Hartenfels Castle* in Torgau.
(b) A staircase tower of the *Waddesdon Manson* (1874–1889) in Buckinghamshire, England.
(c) A stairway in the *Vatican Museum* in Rome.

(b)

(c)

Fig. 6.18
Three basic scenarios when working with animations:
(a) static camera and moving object,
(b) moving camera and static object,
(c) and moving camera and object.

(a)
moving object, static camera

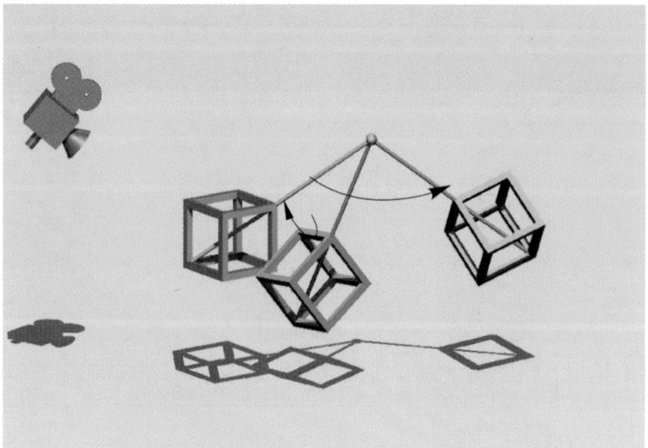

(b)
static object, moving camera

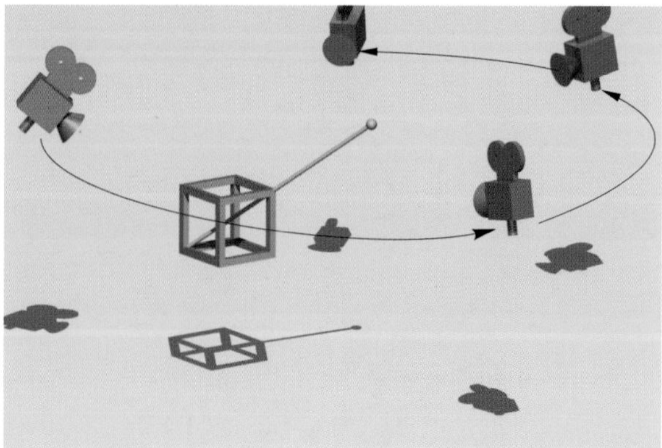

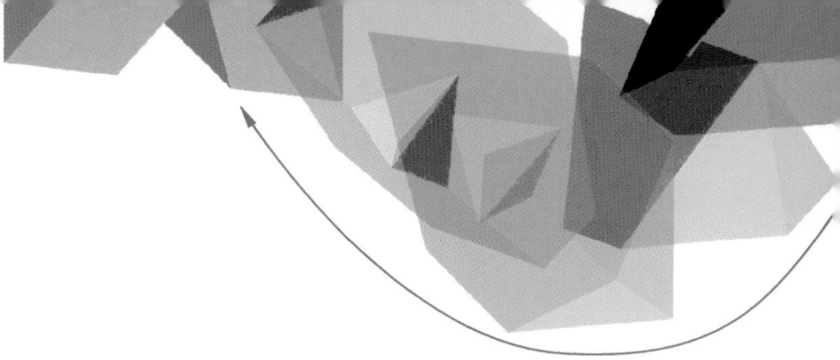

Smooth Motions and Animation

High-quality renderings and professional animations are tools for successfully presenting architectural projects. Moving objects and cameras visualize ideas and intentions of architects better than static images. Having studied the basics of discrete transformations and their associated continuous motions, we are now able to deal with the basic concepts of animation.

To understand the process of creating animations, one only has to put oneself in a director's seat. A director always has to deal with three basic scenarios (Figure 6.18).

- A fixed camera recording moving actors and objects
- A moving camera recording a scene with static elements
- A moving camera recording moving actors and objects

By analogy, we create animations based on similar scenarios. But instead of recording with a real film camera we apply appropriate transformations on our digital models and/or virtual cameras. Then we generate a sequence of slightly different still images to create the illusion of a smooth motion. These still images, which are generated individually by the CAD software, are called *frames*. To create a really convincing illusion of a smooth motion, 30 frames per second should be played.

Most CAD systems provide a lot of sophisticated tools for automating the process of generating a series of still images. Among these tools we will find the following three major basic concepts, which help to describe smooth motions of objects and cameras with little effort.

(c)

moving object, moving camera

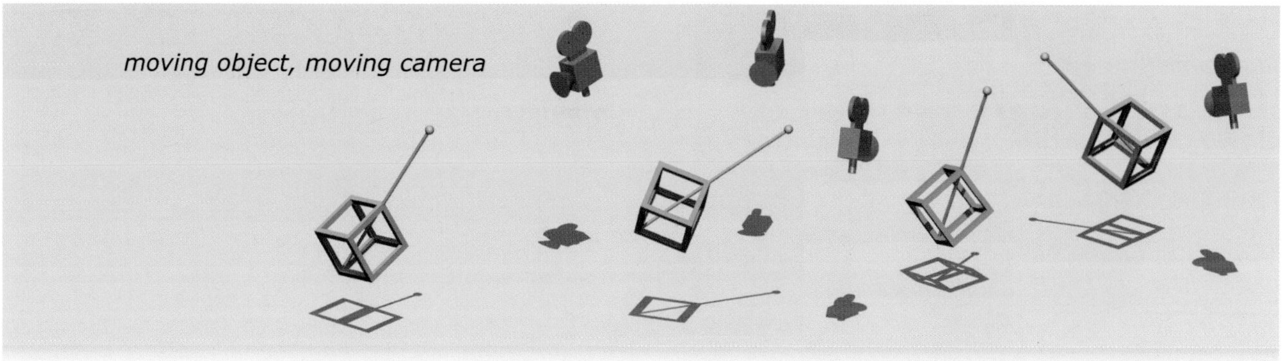

- Defining *key frames*, which specify the positions of objects or parameter values at a given set of time steps. The software then computes intermediate positions between the key frames.
- Defining *paths* on which the objects or cameras are moved.
- Specifying the spatial position and the defining parameters of objects, cameras, and lights with the help of a mathematical description. This is done by *scripting* the entire process to control the parametric motion.

Combining these methods, we can create animated representations of our digital models.

Working with key frames. Using key frames to create animations is really easy. The basic idea is to record different positions of an object (the key frames) and let the software compute positions between these key frames. In Figure 6.19, we illustrate this technique when decomposing F. R. Brüderlin's "ZETA object." For example, we define four positions (key frames) the brown part passes through during its motion.

To simulate a smooth motion, the software has to work out further positions of the object between two consecutive key frames. The calculation of the interpolating objects' positions between two key positions is largely done with the help of quaternions and vector calculus. Quaternions are often used to describe spatial rotations in a compact form. They are a mathematical concept that generalizes complex numbers.

To get best results with the key frame technique, we define the state of our objects especially at critical points. Whereas the software takes control of the overall motion, the user has the power to influence the motion at least at critical positions. In Figure 6.19, the motion of the brown part is composed of an upward translation, followed by an arbitrary motion that turns the object upside down, and finally a downward translation that moves the part again to the base plane. Thus, to obtain the desired composed motion we used key frames at the beginning and end of the translational motions (which are the key positions of the motion).

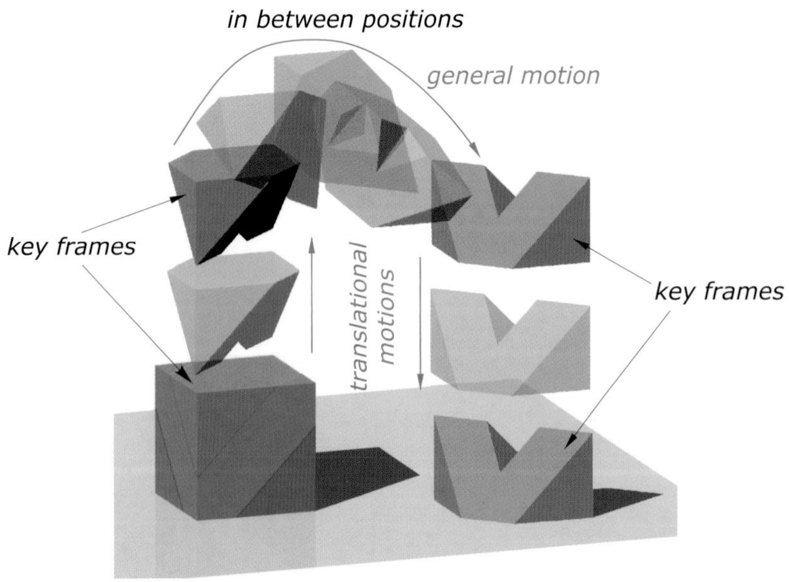

Fig. 6.19
When decomposing the "ZETA object," key frames are used to define the motion of the upper part. Then the software computes further positions by interpolating the key frames' positions.

Summarizing, we can say that working with key frames is a quick and easy way of generating animations. It works pretty well as long as we do not need to have full control over the motion.

Animations with paths. Another simple approach to animation is to define a path along which an object is moved. We only have to generate a curve and attach the object to it. Then this object follows the path and thus simulates a smooth motion (Figure 6.20). Most CAD systems also allow for a definition of the velocity of the motion that steers the object. Thus, we can define at which time instance the object is positioned at which point along the path (Figure 6.21). The object can pause, move backward, or even oscillate.

Prescribing the path of a single point p of the moving body is not sufficient to determine a smooth motion. To understand this basic fact, let's associate the moving body with a local coordinate system whose origin is the point p. Clearly, the position of the origin does not fully describe the position of the coordinate system.

Fig. 6.20
Moving the second part of the ZETA object along a path.

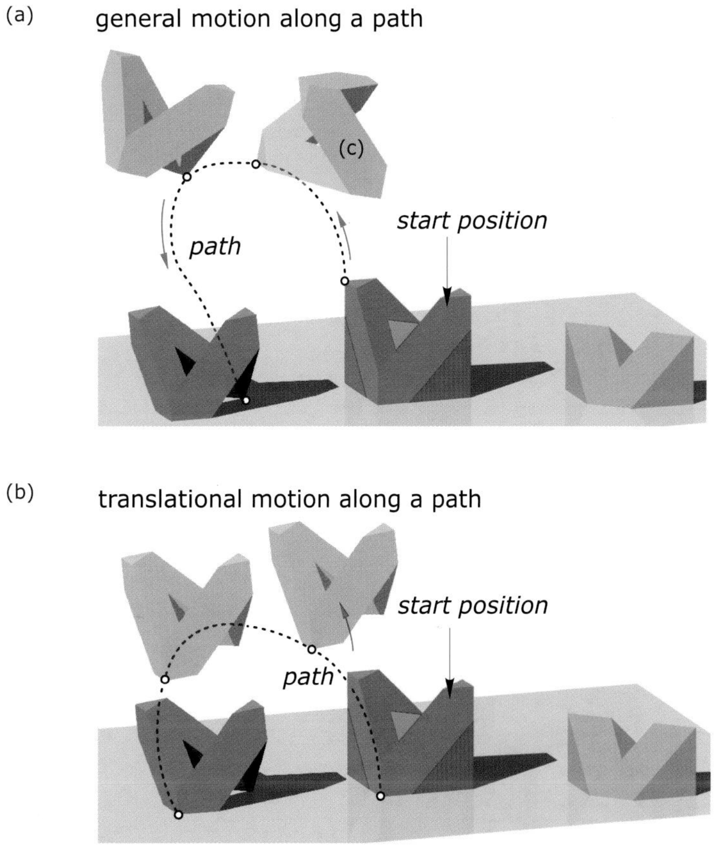

Fig. 6.21
With the help of a velocity diagram or a path-time diagram, we can define the velocity of an object during the motion.

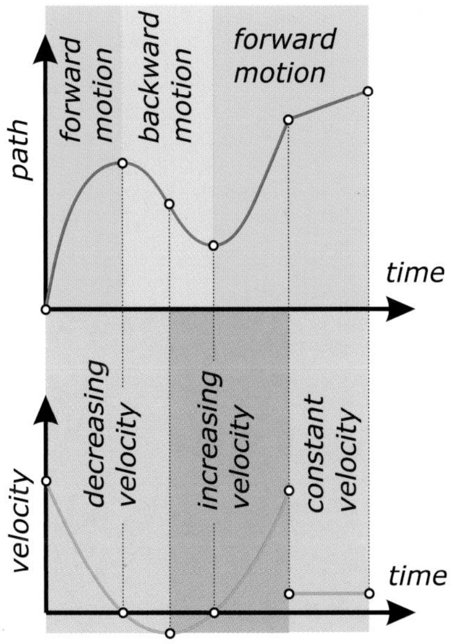

We also need to know the directions of the axes (often referred to as the *orientation* of the moving body). Hence, during a motion along a path the object might be automatically rotated as the curve changes directions (Figure 6.20a)—or only shifted along the path without a rotation (Figure 6.20b). In the second case, we have a pure translational motion along a path.

Animation scripts. Working with key frames and paths affords us easy and rapid methods of producing animations. But these techniques do not allow us to take control over every detail of a motion. Therefore, the generation of complex animations requires more sophisticated methods that let us specify the position (of a reference point) and the orientation of the objects as a function of time. The range of the involved motions is largely restricted to small local areas. Thus, we define the position of these objects with respect to local coordinate systems associated with the moving parts (Figure 6.22).

We control the behavior and motion of each moving part by scripting it with equations. Using built-in variables and mathematical functions, the CAD software assists the definition of these equations.

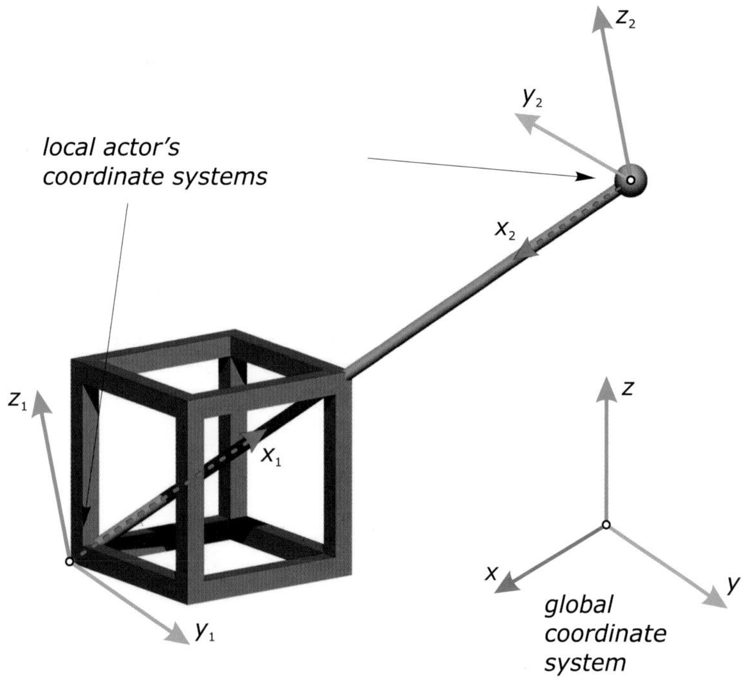

Fig. 6.22
A parametric motion is defined relative to the axes of a local coordinate system associated with the moving object.

Example:

Motion of an advertising cube. An advertising cube performs a full rotation about a horizontal axis within 12 seconds while it is simultanously rotated about its own spatial diagonal ag with double velocity (Figure 6.23). To generate an appropriate animation, we define two local coordinate systems linked to the rotating bar and the cube.

Then we define the rotation of the bar by scripting it in terms of the number of frames. Using a frame rate of 30 frames per second means that the bar has to rotate one degree per frame to finish one complete rotation within 12 seconds $(12 \cdot 30 = 360)$.

We attach the cube to the bar. Therefore, the cube is also rotated about the horizontal axis of the bar. To specify the rotation of the cube about one of its spatial diagonals, we script this motion with double velocity (two degrees per frame).

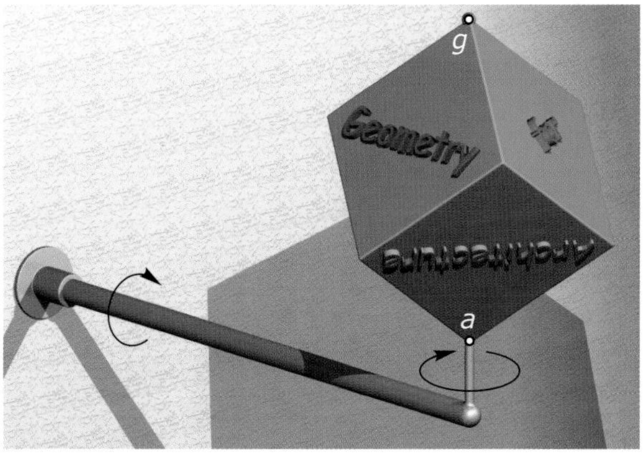

Fig. 6.23
An advertising cube rotates twice about its own spatial diagonal while it is rotated once about a horizontal bar.

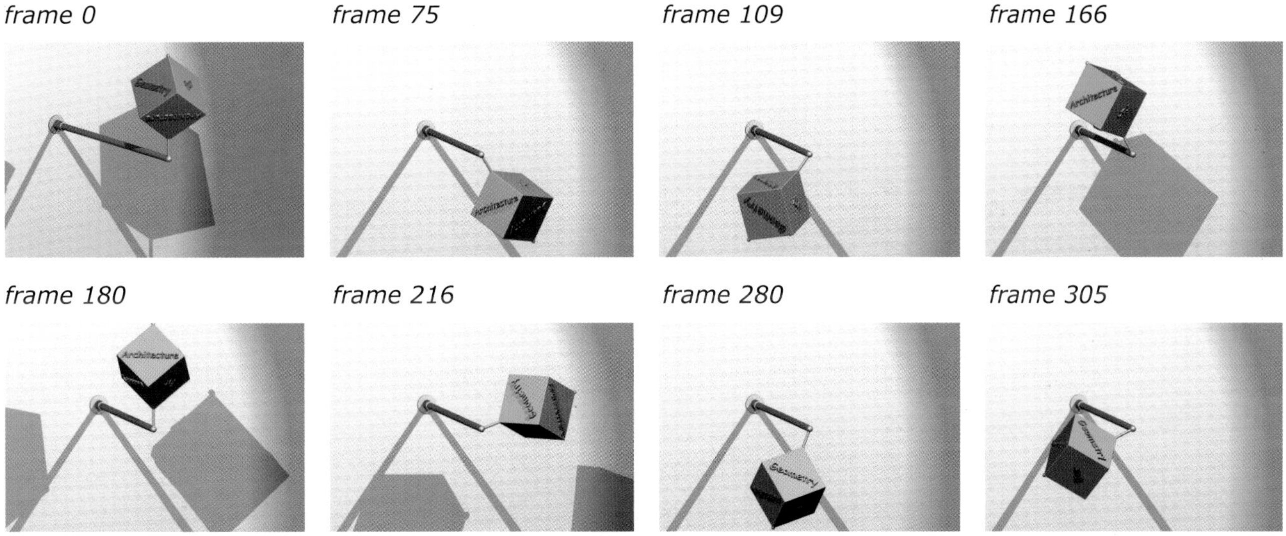

In an animation of a more complex assembly, each moving part would be assigned an equation describing its motion. Cameras that record the virtual scene are also treated as moving parts. They can be animated with the methods described previously to generate instructive walkthroughs or fly-arounds to communicate the overall design. Thus, animations allow a complete exploration of the entire design space—with precise camera movement and lens adjustments.

Using appropriate local coordinate systems and the mathematical description of spatial transformations derived previously, we are able to generate instructive animations. The previously described basic techniques are appropriate tools to visualize smooth motions. To generate more sophisticated animations that include the deformation of objects, specific animation software has to be used. The CAD models are imported into this software, and techniques such as morphing and warping are applied to the objects. In this way, we obtain animations that (for example) illustrate the deformation of a house (Figure 6.24).

At the end of this subsection, we emphasize that an accurate lighting is a very important aspect of each design scene. Lighting effects contribute a lot to the atmosphere and emotional response effected by a scene. Thus, we recognize that lighting is an essential factor in producing meaningful animations with aesthetic and visual quality.

Fig. 6.24
Specific animation software provides tools for generating animations where objects are deformed. Here we show four scenes from the animation *Plumber* by Red Rover Studios.

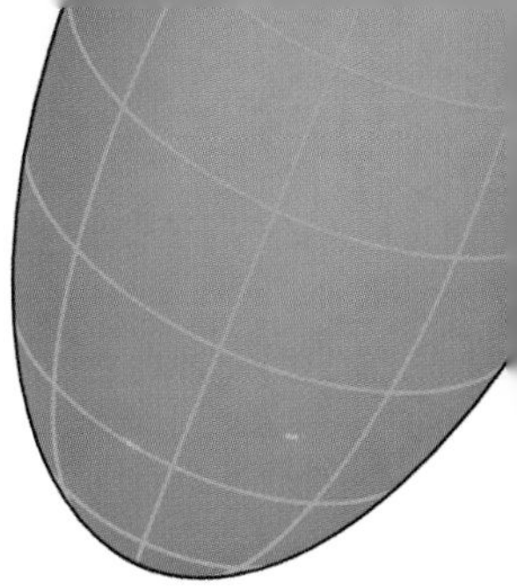

Affine Transformations

We learned in Chapter 5 (on planar transformations) that there are interesting transformations other than the shape- and distance-preserving congruence transformations. To study some of these transformations, we introduce a more general mathematical approach to linear transformations. All spatial transformations we have studied so far can be derived from the following general type.

$$x_1 = a{\cdot}x + b{\cdot}y + c{\cdot}z + u,$$

$$y_1 = d{\cdot}x + e{\cdot}y + f{\cdot}z + v, \quad \text{(A)}$$

$$z_1 = g{\cdot}x + h{\cdot}y + i{\cdot}z + w.$$

The parameters $a, b, \ldots i$ define the deformation, whereas the parameters u, v, and w determine the translation vector $\mathbf{t} = (u,v,w)$. All of these parameters are given (real) numbers. A transformation of type (A) is called an *affine transformation*. As illustrated in Figure 6.25, affine transformations have the following properties.

- Straight lines are mapped into straight lines.
- Planes are mapped into planes.
- Parallel lines (planes) are transformed into parallel lines (planes).
- The ratio of the lengths of two line segments on parallel lines is preserved during the transformation.

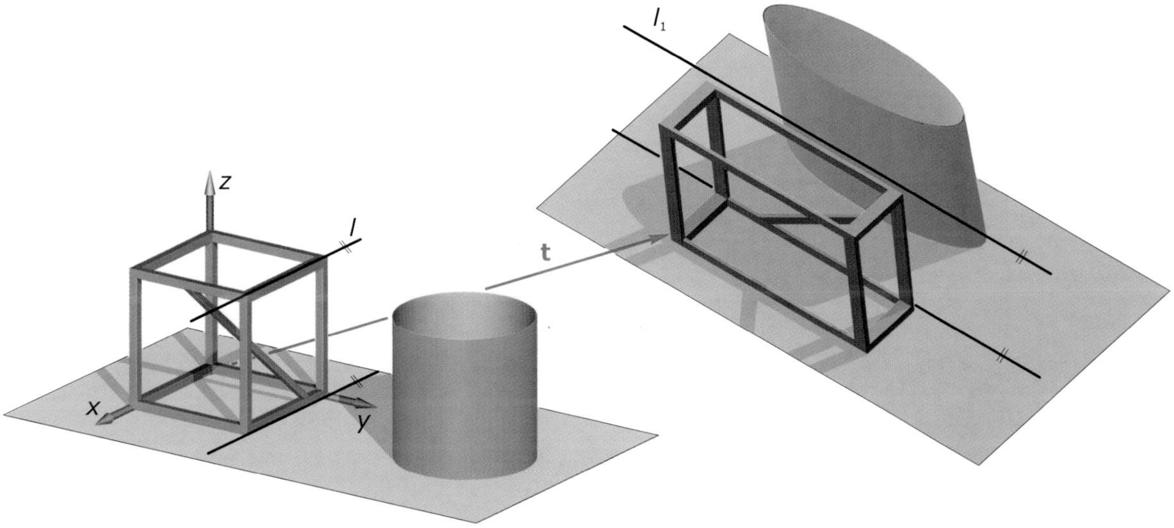

Fig. 6.25
A general affine transformation applied to a cube and a rotational cylinder.

These properties (apart from those about planes) remind us of a parallel projection. Indeed, parallel projection is also a special case of an affine transformation—where three-dimensional space is mapped into a plane. Replacing the last equation in (A) with $z_1 = 0$ ($g = h = i = w = 0$) leads to a general description of a parallel projection into the *xy*-plane.

Let's now consider some special choices for the values of the parameters to deduce new spatial transformations. To simplify our considerations, we assume that there is no translational part [i.e., the translation vector is given by $\mathbf{t} = (0,0,0)$].

Scaling. As a generalization of the planar uniform scaling, we obtain the *spatial uniform scaling*. It is defined by the *center of scaling* b [we select b at the origin (0,0,0)] and a single *scaling factor* (Figure 6.26). The uniform scaling has the same properties as the two-dimensional analogon. If we use different scaling factors for each coordinate, we obtain an *independent scaling* that can be described by

$$x_1 = a \cdot x,$$

$$y_1 = e \cdot y,$$

$$z_1 = i \cdot z.$$

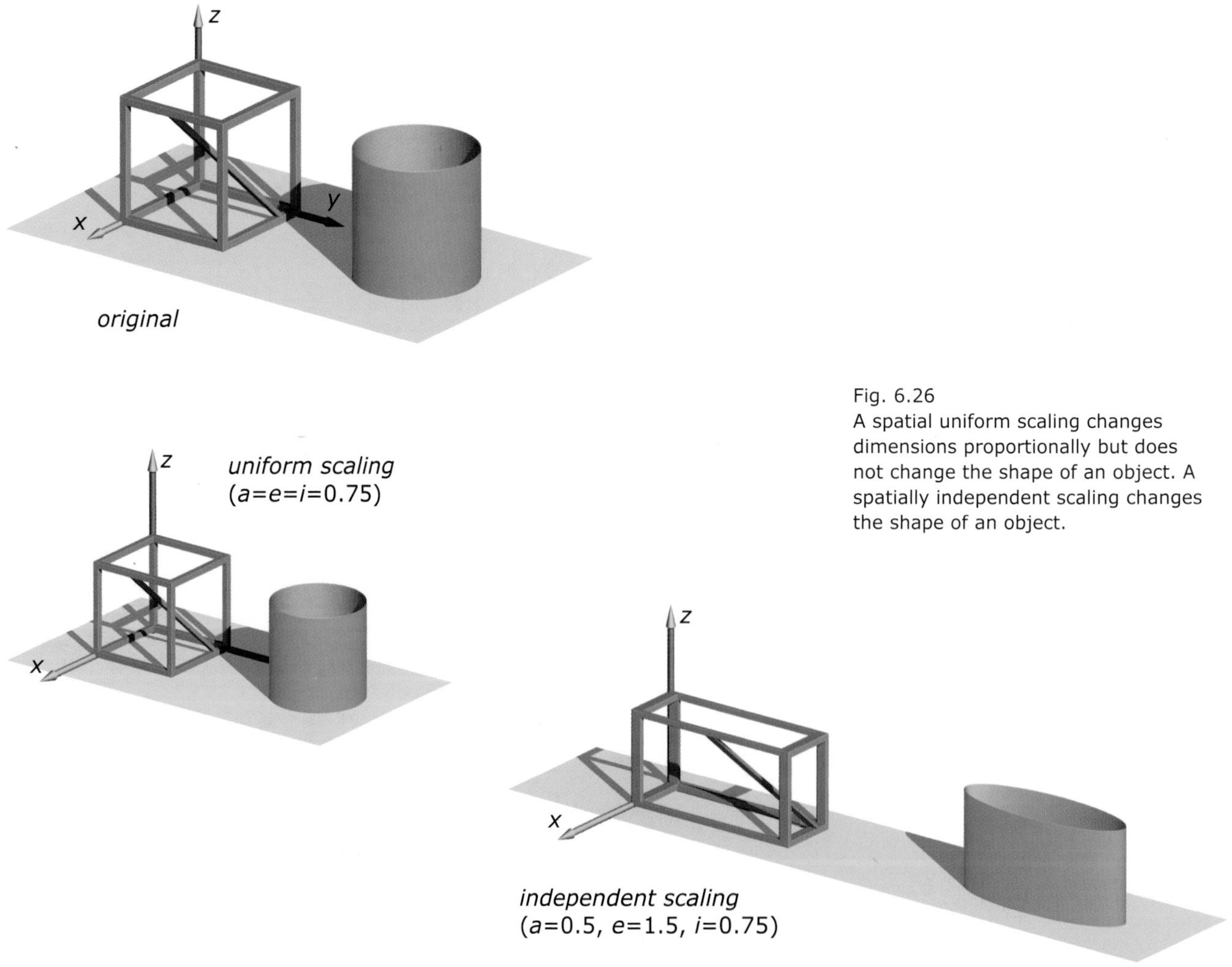

Fig. 6.26
A spatial uniform scaling changes dimensions proportionally but does not change the shape of an object. A spatially independent scaling changes the shape of an object.

Independent scaling is often used to deform objects along coordinate axes. Applying an independent scaling to a sphere, we obtain an ellipsoid for which most circles on the sphere are transformed into ellipses (Figure 6.27). If we only want to stretch a model of a tower without changing the base, we apply an independent scaling ($a = e = 1, i = 1.5$).

(a)

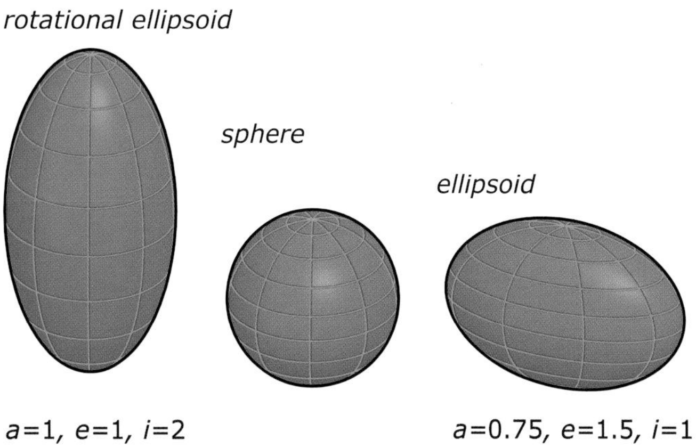

Fig. 6.27
Applications of independent scaling.
(a) A sphere is transformed into ellipsoids.
(b) A tower is stretched.
(c) The *Chrysler building* (1928–1930) in New York by William Van Alen.
(d) The *Pagoda of Kew Gardens* (1757–1762) in London by William Chambers.

(b)

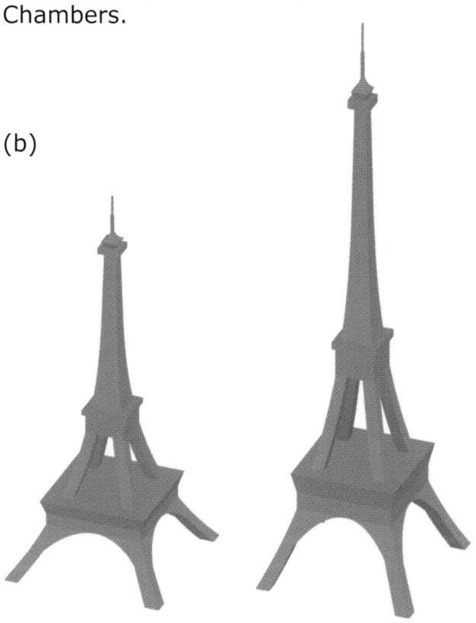

(c)

(d)

Shear transformation. Now we study transformations of the type

$$x_1 = x + c \cdot z,$$

$$y_1 = y + f \cdot z,$$

$$z_1 = z,$$

to obtain a spatial shear transformation. We see that the xy-plane ($z = 0$) is a fixed plane P, whereas a point $p(0,0,1)$ is mapped into the point $p_1(c,f,1)$. The fixed plane P and one pair of corresponding points p, p_1 define this transformation (Figure 6.28). The third equation shows that the z-coordinates of points are not changed by the shear transformation. Thus, corresponding points lie on lines parallel to the fixed plane. In analogy to the planar case, corresponding lines and planes intersect each other in the fixed plane. An application of the shear transformation is illustrated in Figure 6.29.

Fig. 6.28
Spatial shear transformation.

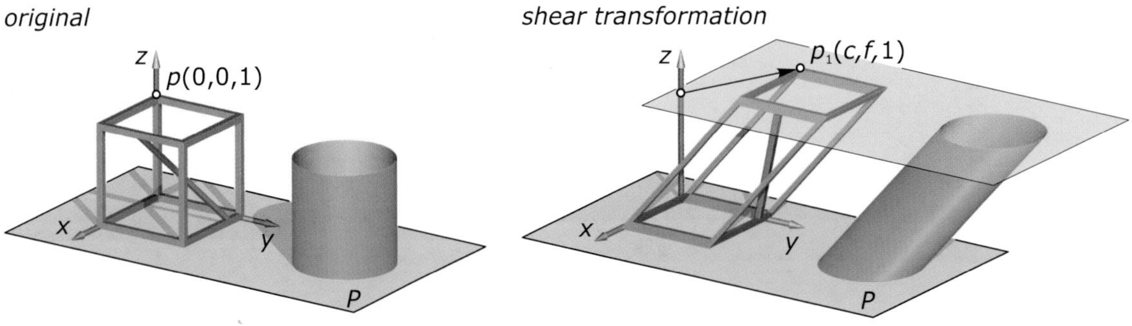

Fig. 6.29
Application of the spatial shear transformation. The *Puerta de Europa* (opened 1996) in Madrid by Pedro Senteri Cardillo and Johnson/Burgee.

Spiral transformation. We now generalize the helical transformation by combining a rotation about an axis A with a special scaling whose center lies on the axis A. To simplify the mathematical description, we assume the scaling center to be the origin and the z-axis to be the axis A. Then, the spiral transformation possesses the following description:

$$x_1 = k(\rho)\cdot x\cdot \cos\rho - k(\rho)\cdot y\cdot \sin\rho,$$

$$y_1 = k(\rho)\cdot x\cdot \sin\rho + k(\rho)\cdot y\cdot \cos\rho,$$

$$z_1 = k(\rho)\cdot z.$$

with $k(\rho) = e^{p\rho}$.

If ρ takes all values within a specified range we have the description of a smooth spiral "motion" that scales and rotates an object at the same time (Figure 6.30). A spiral curve generated by a spiral motion lies on a cone of revolution, intersects the rulings of the cone under a constant angle, and moves (as a whole) in itself under the generating spiral motion. This is a type of generalization of a helix, which intersects the rulings of a rotational cylinder under a constant angle and is transformed in itself under the generating helical motion.

Fig. 6.30
(a) The trajectory of a point p during a continuous spiral motion is a spiral curve c. It lies on a cone of revolution and intersects the rulings of the cone under a constant angle. The normal projection c' into the base plane P is a logarithmic spiral curve, which intersects the lines through the spiral center under a constant angle.
(b) During a spiral "motion," an object is rotated and scaled at the same time.

(a)

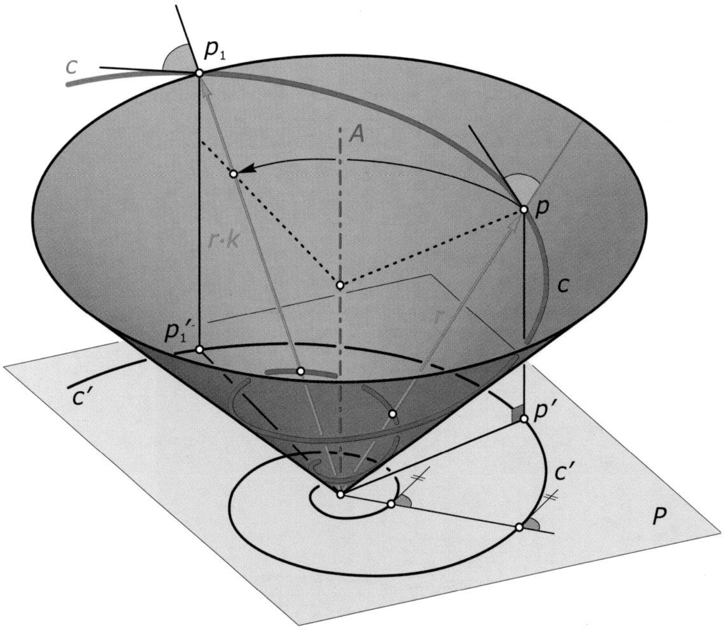

(b)

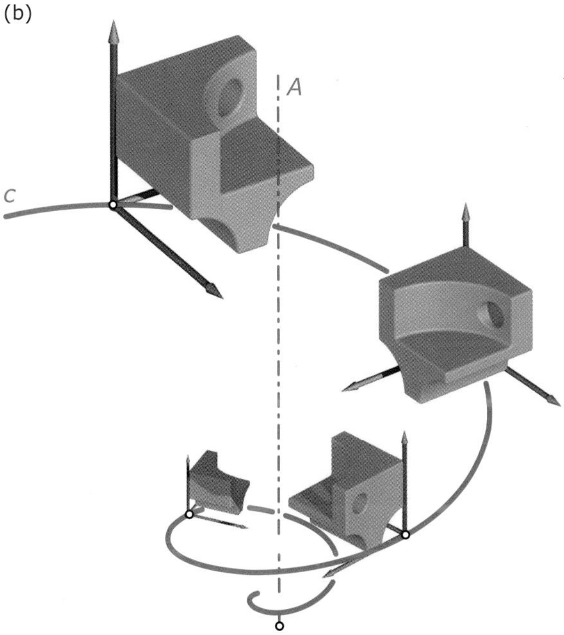

The spiral transformation has the following important meaning in geometry: One can always find a unique spiral transformation that transfers a spatial object into a *directly similar* one. Some natural growth processes are based on the exponential rule. Thus, it is not surprising that spirals also appear in nature. For example, the shells of certain mussels or snails are good approximations of spiral surfaces [i.e., surfaces generated by a profile curve undergoing a spiral motion (Figure 6.31)].

(a)

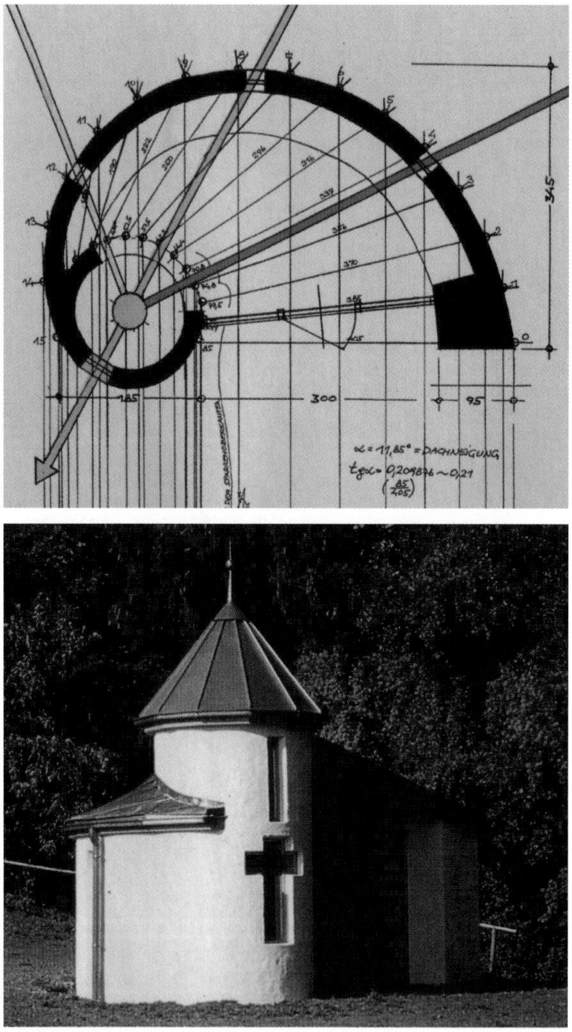

(c)

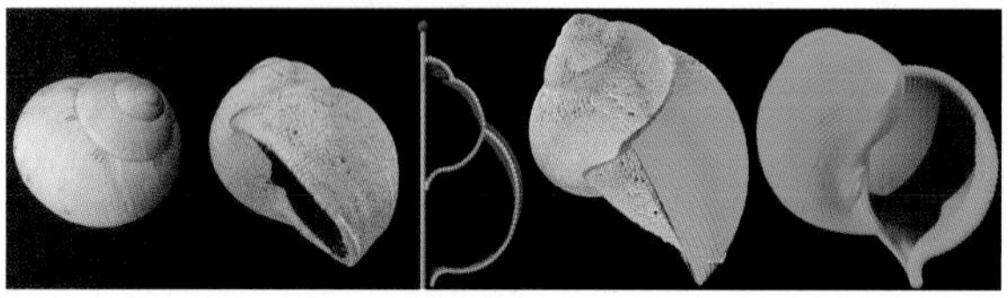

Fig. 6.31
Spirals in architecture and nature.
(a) A church in Texing, Austria.
(b) A temple in Independence, Missouri, USA.
(c) The shell of a helix pomata, three-dimensional data points of its surface obtained with a laser scanner (Chapter 17), and a CAD model.
(d) A nautilus shell.

(b)

(d)

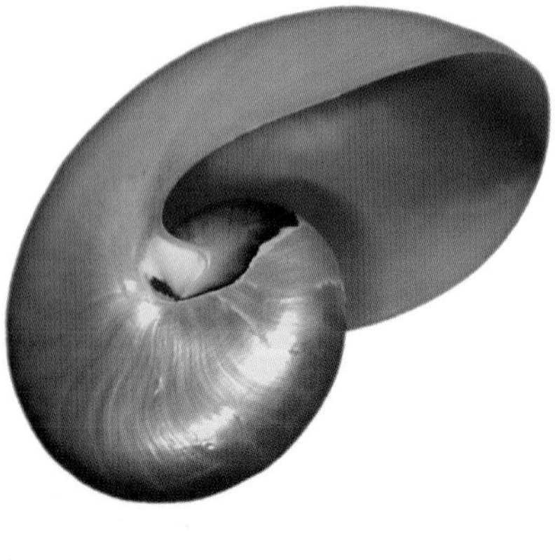

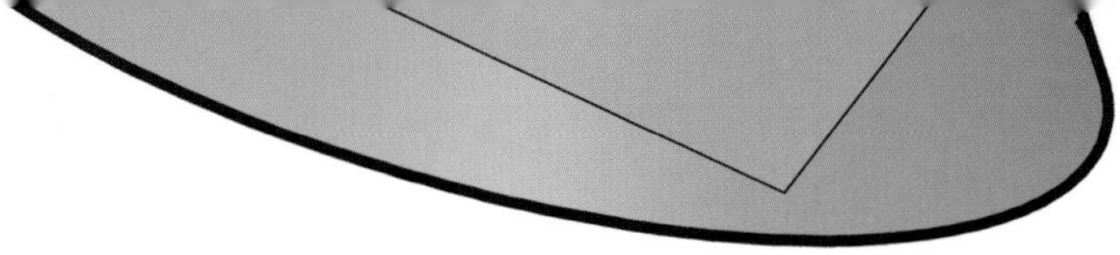

*Projective Transformations

Affine transformations constitute the class of *linear transformations* (i.e., line-preserving) that maps parallel lines into parallel lines. If we compare affine transformations with parallel projection (Chapter 2), we will immediately see their similar properties. In fact, a parallel projection is also captured by equations of type (A) and thus it is a (degenerate) affine transformation.

Degenerate here means that a parallel projection maps three-dimensional space to a two-dimensional plane, whereas nondegenerate affine transformations map spatial objects into spatial objects. Also note that a parallel projection maps certain lines (namely, projection rays) into points, whereas general affine transformations always map straight lines into straight lines.

Projective transformations are related to perspective projection just as affine transformations are related to parallel projection. The perspective projection maps three-dimensional space into a two-dimensional plane. Most straight lines are mapped to straight lines, an exception being projection rays (which are mapped into points).

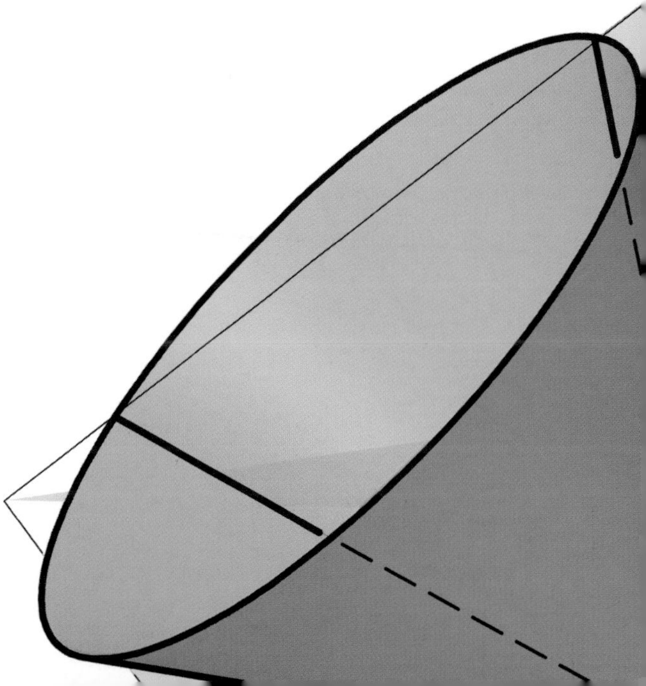

General projective transformations map three-dimensional space into three-dimensional space such that any straight line is mapped into a straight line. However, we will see that one has to enrich the set of points and lines to make this possible. Thus, projective transformations are the most general type of linear transformations. They give us full control over all possible line-preserving deformations of an object.

General projective transformations do not preserve lengths, angles, parallelism, or ratios. They are the basic building block in a special field of geometry, called *projective geometry*. It allows for a unified approach to various geometric issues (explored later in the book). To get a better overview of the properties of linear transformations, we summarize them in the following table.

	Euclidean	**similarity**	**affine**	**projective**
transformations				
translation	✓	✓	✓	✓
rotation	✓	✓	✓	✓
uniform scaling		✓	✓	✓
scaling			✓	✓
shear			✓	✓
perspective projection				✓
invariants				
length	✓			
angle	✓	✓		
ratio of lengths	✓	✓	✓	
parallelism	✓	✓	✓	

As we saw in Chapter 2, a perspective projection maps parallel lines (which are not parallel to the projection plane) to intersecting lines. Therefore, we introduced the concept of vanishing points. In studying properties of projective transformations and perspective projections, it is important to regard parallelism as a special form of intersection. This can be realized by the concept of *projective extension of three-dimensional space.*

Projective extension of the plane. For a better understanding, we first introduce the projective extension of the plane. We add a *point at infinity* to each line such that parallel lines share the same point at infinity. Thus, any two lines in the plane have one point in common—a proper point if they intersect each other or a point at infinity if they are parallel. Note that every line contains exactly one point at infinity, which can be approached by moving along the line in either direction. All points at infinity form the *line at infinity*. We will see in the following that it makes sense to speak of a line.

Homogeneous coordinates. To describe proper points and points at infinity in a unified way, we introduce homogeneous coordinates (Figure 6.32a). We select a Cartesian x,y-coordinate system in the plane E. The points p of the plane E are represented by Cartesian coordinates $p(x,y)$. We embed this plane E into a three-dimensional space whose points are described by coordinates x_1, x_2, and x_3.The plane E is positioned parallel to the x_1,x_2-plane of the three-dimensional space such that it can be identified by the plane $x_3 = 1$.

Every point $p(x,y)$ of the two-dimensional plane E uniquely defines a line through the origin o of the three-dimensional coordinate system. Every coordinate triple $(s{\cdot}x, s{\cdot}y, s)$ with $s \neq 0$ is a direction vector of this line. Thus, to every point p with two coordinates (x,y) we can assign three coordinates $(s{\cdot}x, s{\cdot}y, s)$ that are only determined up to a constant multiple.

Every triplet $(s{\cdot}x, s{\cdot}y, s)$ where $s \neq 0$ defines exactly the same point as the triplet $(x,y,1)$. We call them *homogeneous Cartesian coordinates* and denote them $p = (s{\cdot}x, s{\cdot}y, s) = (x_1, x_2, x_3)$. To express that only the ratio of homogenous coordinates is important, one often writes them as $(x_1{:}x_2{:}x_3)$. For proper points, the relation between the usual (*inhomogeneous*) coordinates and homogeneous coordinates is given by

$$x = x_1/x_3,\ y = x_2/x_3. \quad \text{(H)}$$

The importance of homogeneous coordinates lies in the fact that they can also represent points at infinity (Figure 6.32b). Connecting a point at infinity (of a straight line l) in E with o yields a line parallel to E (and to l). Thus, the homogeneous coordinates of points at infinity are characterized by $x_3 = 0$. If (a,b) is a direction vector of a straight line l in E, $(a{:}b{:}0)$ are the homogeneous coordinates of its point at infinity.

Obviously, parallel lines have the same direction vector (up to a scalar factor). Thus, parallel lines are assigned equal homogeneous coordinates (up to an unimportant common factor) of its common point at infinity. Connecting a line l in E with o, we obtain a plane. Connecting all points at infinity with o, we obtain the plane $x_3 = 0$—which shows that it makes sense to speak of a line at infinity.

Fig. 6.32
(a) Introduction of homogeneous coordinates in the plane E.
(b) Points at infinity.

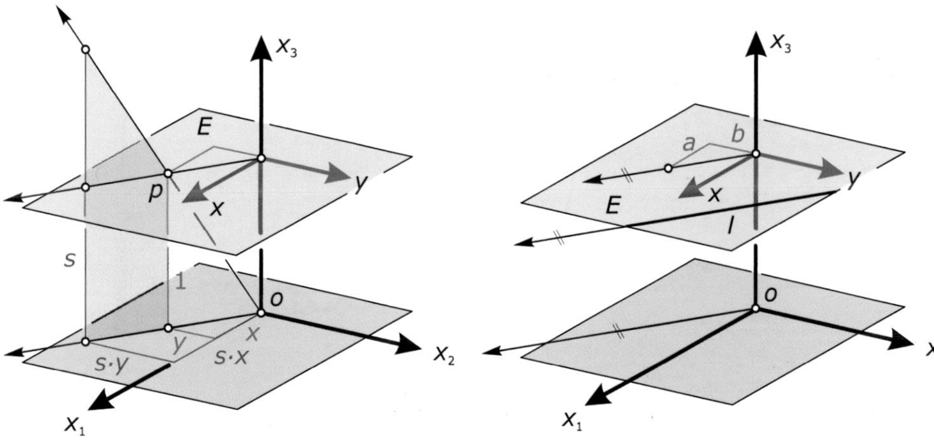

Example:
Homogeneous coordinates of points. The homogeneous coordinates of the proper points $p(-2,3)$ and $q(0,3)$ are $p = (-2:3:1)$ and $q = (0:3:1)$. By equations (H), points r and s with homogeneous coordinates $r = (6:-1:2)$ and $s = (3:2:3)$ have usual coordinates $r\,(3,-0.5)$ and $s(1,2/3)$, respectively. The point $t = (1:1:0)$ is the point at infinity of the line $y = x$ because $(1,1)$ is a direction vector of this line.

Planar projective transformations. In homogeneous Cartesian coordinates, projective transformations can be described as

$$\begin{aligned} x_1' &= a_{11}\cdot x_1 + a_{12}\cdot x_2 + a_{13}\cdot x_3, \\ x_2' &= a_{21}\cdot x_1 + a_{22}\cdot x_2 + a_{23}\cdot x_3, \qquad \text{(P)} \\ x_3' &= a_{31}\cdot x_1 + a_{32}\cdot x_2 + a_{33}\cdot x_3. \end{aligned}$$

Here, $(x_1':x_2':x_3')$ are the coordinates of the transformed point x'. This description includes all linear transformations we studied in Chapter 5 as special cases.

An easy way to understand the effects of a projective transformation is the following. At first, we slightly generalize the concept of a projective transformation by the use of two different planes: a plane P [in which we use coordinates $(x_1:x_2:x_3)$] and a plane P' [in which coordinates $(x_1':x_2':x_3')$ are employed]. Now P is mapped to P' using the transformation equations (P). It turns out that we obtain all projective transformations between two planes (up to a congruence transformation of one plane) by *perspective projection*.

Fig. 6.33
A planar figure and a photo of it are related by a projective transformation. Making just a few measurements on the original object, it is therefore possible to reconstruct the full original from the photo. (Image courtesy of the Institute of Photogrammetry and Remote Sensing, Technical University, Vienna).

We place the two planes in three-dimensional space, select a projection center (eye point) e (not in P and not in P'), and project the points of P onto P'. Thus, *a planar figure and its perspective view are related by a projective transformation*. Moreover, if we append to the projection a motion that brings P' into another position (perhaps even identical to P), the relation between corresponding figures is still a projective transformation. Thus, a planar object and a photo of it are related by a projective transformation.

This fact is used to reconstruct the original undistorted object from a photo of it (Figure 6.33). Using more projective geometry, it is even possible to automatically reconstruct a three-dimensional object from several planar images (Figure 6.34). These techniques also require algorithms for the automatic extraction of corresponding points in the images.

The interpretation of a projective map via the perspective projection of a plane P also shows that the images of the points at infinity in P lie in general on a proper straight line of P'. We have encountered this fact in Chapter 2 in regard to vanishing points. Recall an important example: the images of the points at infinity of a horizontal plane lie on the horizon. It is easy to see that there exists a straight line of P whose image points are points at infinity. Thus, the line-preserving property is only valid without exception if we add the line at infinity.

The previously discussed affine transformations and their special cases are all included in the family of projective transformations. In equations (P) we use as third equation $x_3' = x_3$. We can then divide the first two equations by x_3' (left-hand side) and by x_3 (right-hand side) to obtain

$$x' = a_{11} \cdot x + a_{12} \cdot y + a_{13},$$

$$y' = a_{21} \cdot x + a_{22} \cdot y + a_{23}.$$

This is obviously an affine transformation, and therefore all affine transformations are special projective transformations.

Fig. 6.34
Projective geometry is a key ingredient in state-of-the-art algorithms for the reconstruction of three-dimensional objects from several images of that object. The figure shows the reconstruction of "St. George rotunda". (Courtesy of H. Cornelius, D. Martinec, T. Pajdla.)

Example:

A general projective transformation. Consider the projective transformation

$x'_1 = 1{\cdot}x_1 - 1{\cdot}x_2,$

$x'_2 = -1{\cdot}x_1 + 2{\cdot}x_2, \qquad \text{(E)}$

$x'_3 = -1{\cdot}x_1 + x_3,$

which maps (for example) the points o = (0:0:1) and p = (1:0:1) to the points o' = (0:0:1) and p' = (1:-1:0). Thus, point o is fixed—whereas the proper point p is mapped to a point at infinity. Now consider the circle c, which is centered at o and passes through point p (Figure 6.35). This circle c has in Cartesian coordinates the equation $x^2 + y^2 = 1$. By equation (H), its homogeneous representation is c: $x_1^2 + x_2^2 = x_3^2$. From (E), we compute the relations $x_1 = 2{\cdot}x'_1 + x'_2$, $x_2 = x'_1 + x'_2$, $x_3 = 2{\cdot}x'_1 + x'_2 + x'_3$. Inserting this into the equation of c, we obtain for the image curve c' the equation

$x'^2_1 + x'^2_2 + 2{\cdot}x'_1 x'_2 - x'^2_3 - 4{\cdot}x'_1{\cdot}x'_3 - 2{\cdot}x'_2{\cdot}x'_3 = 0.$

Rewriting c' in inhomogeneous coordinates (dividing the equation by x'^2_3 and using (H)) and omitting the primes, we obtain

$x^2 + y^2 + 2{\cdot}xy - 1 - 4{\cdot}x - 2{\cdot}y = 0.$

This turns out to be a parabola due to the fact that c', the image of the circle c, contains exactly one point at infinity (see the discussion following); namely, $p' = (1{:}-1{:}0)$.

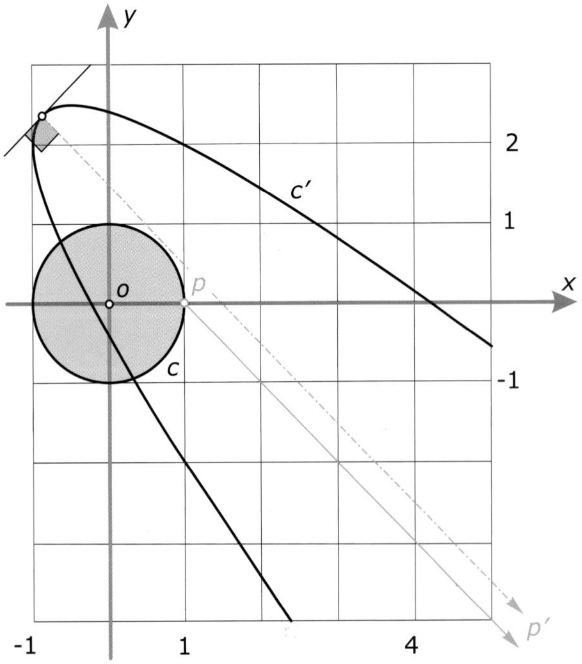

Fig. 6.35
A general projective transformation maps a circle c into a conic c'.

Projective images of circles. The image of a circle c under a projective transformation is always a conic: an ellipse (including the case of a circle), a parabola, or a hyperbola. An equivalent fact is that perspective projection of a circle c always leads to a conic c^c (unless the plane of the circle appears as a straight line).

As shown in Figure 6.36, any perspective projection possesses a plane V whose points have images at infinity. This plane V is parallel to the image plane and passes through the eye point e. It depends on the position of c with respect to this plane V how many points at infinity the image conic c^c has. If c intersects V in zero, one, or two points, the image c^c has zero, one, or two points at infinity. The number of points at infinity determines the type of a conic as follows.

- Conic sections with two points at infinity are hyperbolas. The straight lines connecting the symmetry center with these points at infinity are the *asymptotes*.
- Those conic sections with exactly one point at infinity are parabolas. The point at infinity defines the direction of the parabola's axis.
- Conic sections with only proper points are ellipses.

Figure 6.37 illustrates special points and lines associated with conic sections.

A careful investigation of the previous example also shows that a conic (projectively transformed circle) must be the solution set of a quadratic equation in x and y (a fact addressed again in Chapter 7). Finally, we mention that projective transformations map conics to conics.

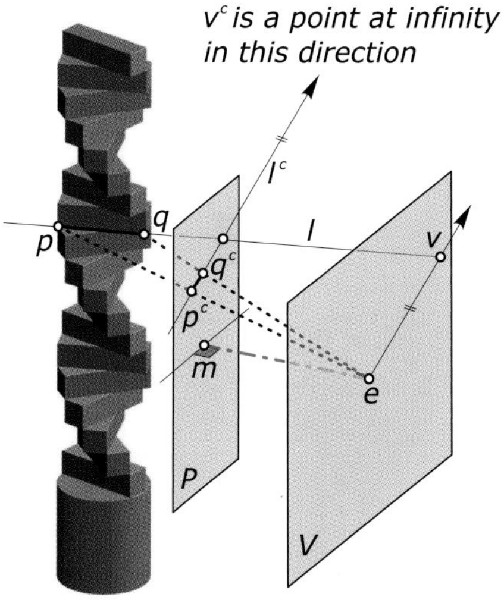

Fig. 6.36
In perspective projection, points in a plane V (parallel to the projection plane P) are mapped to points at infinity.

Fig. 6.37
Important terms concerning the conic sections hyperbola, parabola, and ellipse. The hyperbola and ellipse have a midpoint m, two symmetry axes, two foci f_1 and f_2, and four vertices a, b, c, and d. The hyperbola additionally has two asymptotes u and v. The parabola has only one symmetry axis, one vertex v, and one focus f.

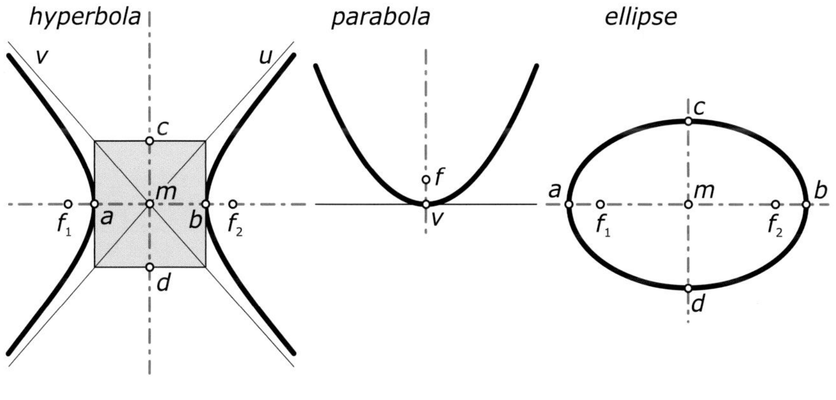

Conic sections. The perspective image of a circle c is the intersection of the image plane with the cone of vision, which connects the eye point with c. This cone is in general an oblique circular cone. It can be shown that all types and shapes of conics are captured if we look just at the planar intersections of a right circular cone.

Intersection of a right circular cone with a plane results in different types of intersection curves, depending on the mutual position of the plane and the cone (Figure 6.38). For all planes that contain the apex of the cone, we have the following three cases.

- Planes H that intersect along two rulings
- Planes P that touch along one ruling
- Planes E that intersect only at the vertex of the cone

According to these cases, we have three different types of nondegenerate intersection curves.

- All planes parallel to a plane H cut the cone along a *hyperbola*.
- All planes parallel to a plane P intersect the cone along a *parabola*.
- All planes parallel to a plane E intersect the cone along an *ellipse*.

We obtain a circle c when the cutting plane is orthogonal to the rotational axis. In this case, the parallel plane through the apex does not contain any rulings. Thus, the circle appears as a special case of the ellipse.

Homogeneous coordinates and projective transformations in three dimensions. It is pretty obvious how to extend our concepts to three dimensions. We use four homogenous coordinates $(x_1{:}x_2{:}x_3{:}x_4)$. For a proper point, they are related to the ordinary coordinates (x,y,z) via

$$x = x_1/x_4,\ y = x_2/x_4,\ z = x_3/x_4.$$

The point at infinity of a line with direction vector (a,b,c) has homogenous coordinates $(a{:}b{:}c{:}0)$. All points at infinity form the *plane at infinity*. A projective

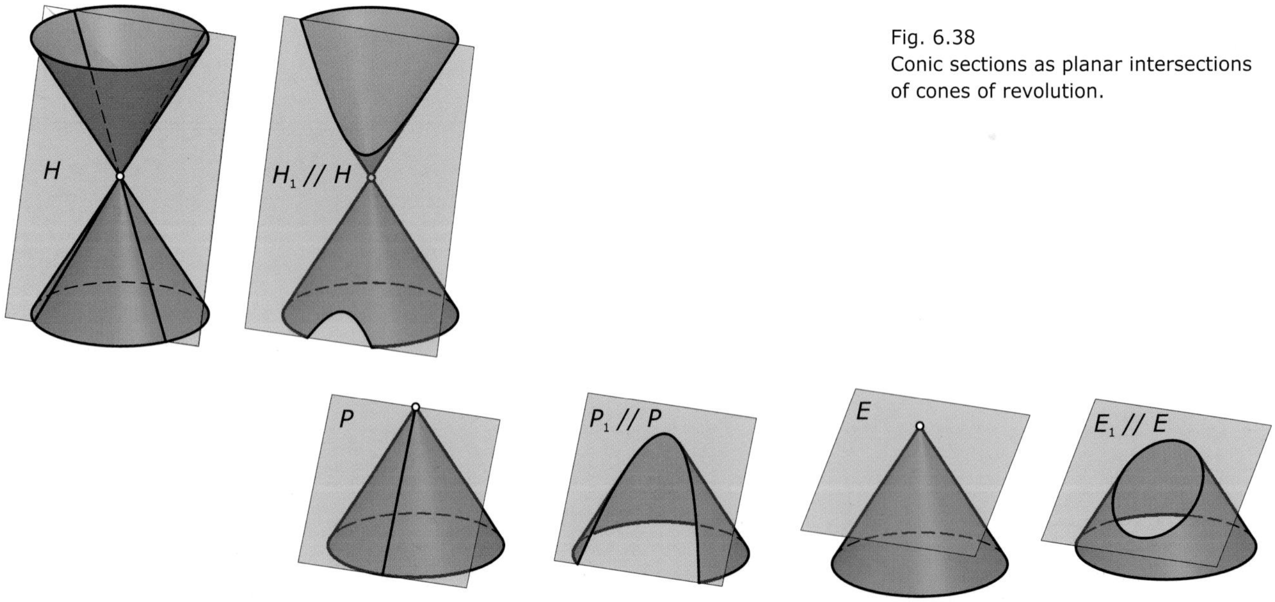

Fig. 6.38
Conic sections as planar intersections of cones of revolution.

transformation has linear equations of the form (P), but now involving all four coordinates. The following are the first and last equation.

$$x_1' = a_{11} \cdot x_1 + a_{12} \cdot x_2 + a_{13} \cdot x_3 + a_{14} \cdot x_4,$$

$$x_4' = a_{41} \cdot x_1 + a_{42} \cdot x_2 + a_{43} \cdot x_3 + a_{44} \cdot x_4.$$

Some projective transformations are degenerate, an example being the perspective projection from three-dimensional space into a two-dimensional plane. If we have no degeneracy, all straight lines are mapped into straight lines, planes are mapped to planes, and conics are mapped to conics. Parallelism is in general not preserved, unless we have an affine transformation ($x_4' = x_4$).

Projective transformations may be useful for slightly breaking the symmetry and regularity of an object, but still keeping its main expression. They are of great importance in getting a more unified view onto geometry. For example, the study of quadric surfaces (Chapter 9) is greatly simplified when one uses projective transformations. They will appear at various places in the subsequent text, including the last chapter (on discrete surfaces)—where they are important both for key aspects of the theory and for design.

Example:

Relief perspective. Stage architecture sometimes uses a technique that maps a large part of space to a much smaller one so that it fits onto the stage but still gives the same impression as the real scene when viewed from an appropriate location (eye point e). The key here is the application of a projective transformation (Figure 6.39). It has a center point e and a fixed plane F.

The center e and all points of F remain fixed under the transformation. In addition, one prescribes the image plane U' of the plane at infinity. It must be parallel to F (because the points at infinity of F are fixed). An important property of the transformation we are looking for is that corresponding points p and p' lie on a line through the center e. It turns out that the prescribed elements e, F, and U and this property uniquely define the transformation.

Figure 6.39 shows how to transform a simple object (using the preservation of straight lines). The designed projective transformation maps the entire half space behind F into the layer between F and U' Stage architecture builds the transformed scene S' instead of the real scene S because it fits better onto the stage. Moreover, when viewed from the area near e it gives the same visual impression as the original larger scene S because corresponding points lie on lines through e.

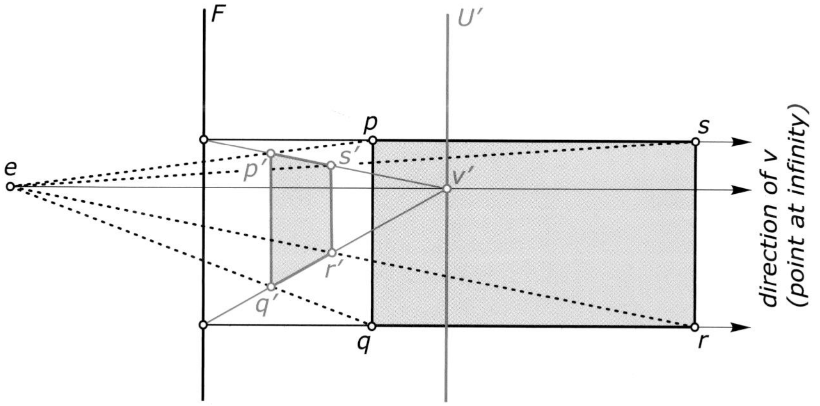

Fig. 6.39
(a) A relief perspective is generated with the help of a projective transformation, which maps the half space behind a fixed plane F into the layer between F and a parallel plane U'. Corresponding points p and p' lie on a line through the center e.

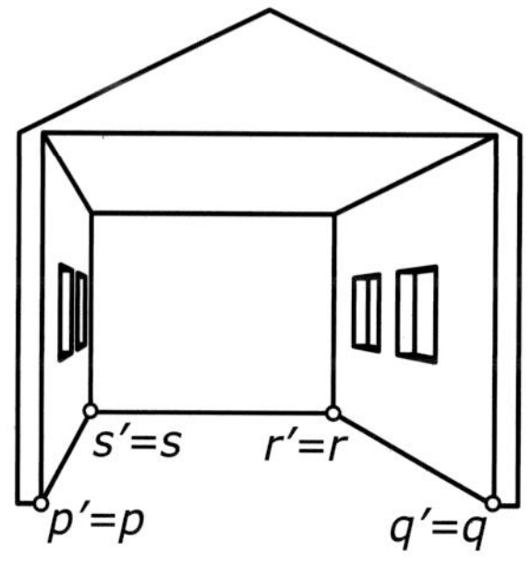

(b) Thus, an observer at e believes he is seeing the real scene S instead of the smaller transformed scene S' (which better fits onto the stage).

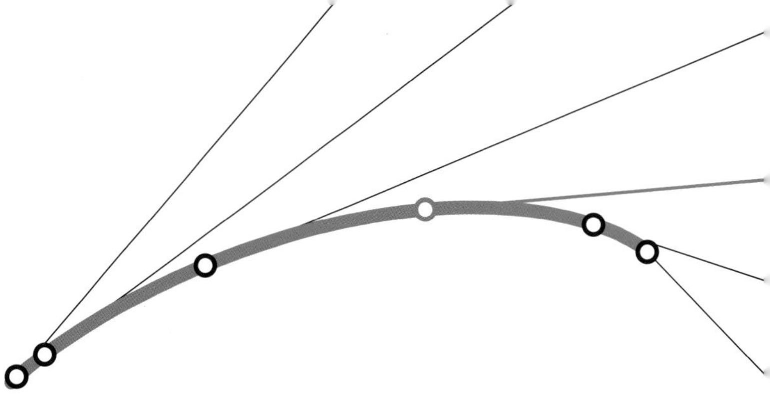

Chapter 7
Curves and Surfaces

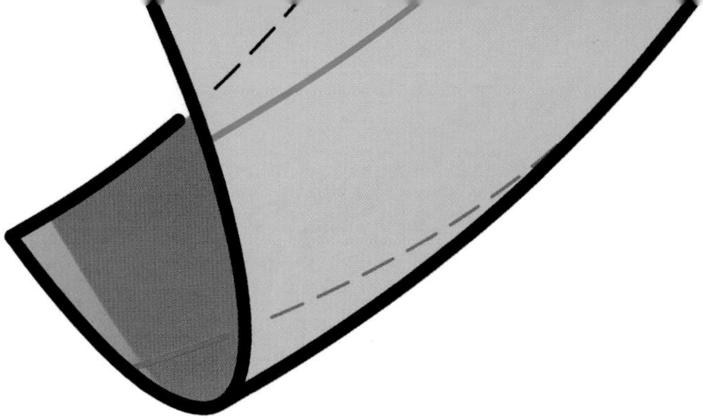

Curves and Surfaces

Curves and surfaces arise in a variety of applications, including art, architecture, and design (Figure 7.1). A good knowledge of the basic concepts in connection with curves and surfaces is essential for understanding the following chapters. Although many concepts apply to both curves and surfaces, curves are easier to study and understand. Therefore, in this chapter we begin with an examination of fundamental curve concepts, including mathematical descriptions of curves.

Fig. 7.1
Curves and surfaces are basic elements in architecture.
(a) *30 Street Mary Axe* (1997–2004) in London by Norman Foster.

(b)

(c)

(d)

We introduce curve *tangents* (Figure 7.2a), the *curvature* of curves, *inflection points* on curves, and so on. Curves may be used as profiles to generate surfaces. In most cases, the shape of the profile curve heavily influences the final shape of the emerging surface. Hence, we study the properties and shapes of some commonly used curves—including the *conic sections*.

The discussion of curves leads to the study of surfaces in a quite natural way. As a generalization of curves, we provide two mathematical approaches to surfaces and study concepts such as *tangent planes* and surface *normals* (Figure 7.2b).

In terms of illuminating surfaces, we are often interested in the border between illuminated and dark areas (i.e., the border between visible and occluded parts of the surface). With the help of tangent planes and normals, we will find these so-called *contour generators* on surfaces. To conclude the chapter, we study intersection curves of pairs of surfaces and illustrate geometric methods of constructing points and tangents of these curves. Furthermore, we deal with interesting phenomena in connection with intersection curves. This knowledge can be useful when designing with surfaces.

Fig. 7.1
Curves and surfaces are basic elements in architecture.
(b) The *Spline Chair* by Unto This Last.
(c) The *Ben Pimlott Building* (2003–2005) in London by Will Alsop.
(d) The *Downland Gridshell* (2000–2002) in Singleton by Edward Cullinan.

Fig. 7.2
Tangents of curves and tangent planes of surfaces are important concepts used to study curves and surfaces.

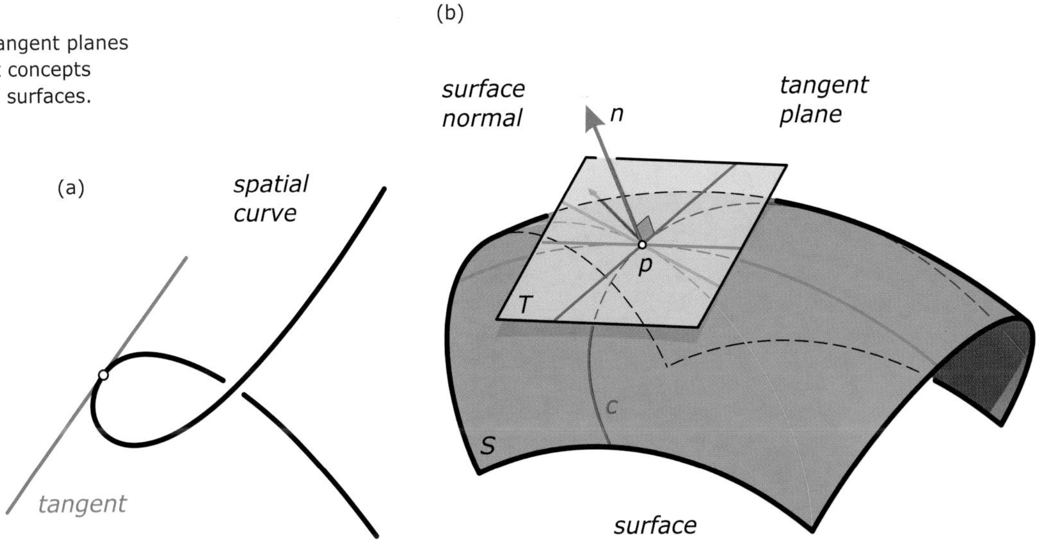

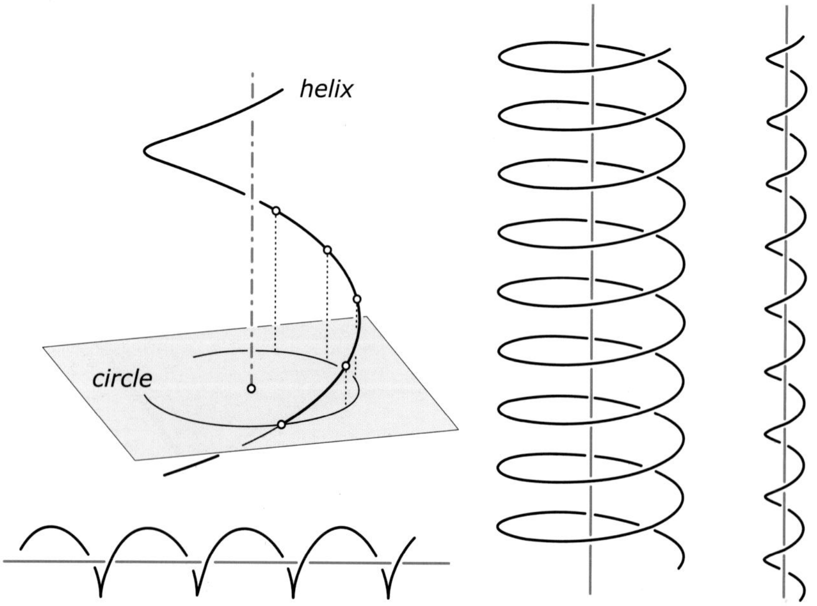

Fig. 7.3
A helix is a true spatial curve. It does not fit into any plane. Here we illustrate several different helixes. In architecture, helixes can be found on cylindrical columns:
(a) helixes on pillars in the *Cathedral* (1173–1195) in Brunswick and
(b) helixes on the two columns in front of the *Karlskirche* (1656–1723) in Vienna by Johann Bernhard Fischer von Erlach.

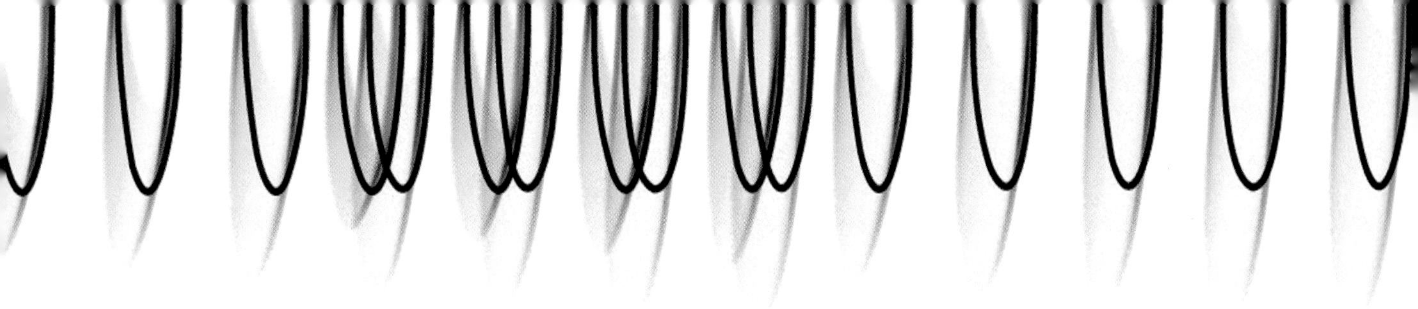

Curves

Previously we have encountered straight lines, circles, helixes, and conic sections as special types of curves. We can think of a curve as a connected one-dimensional series of points. As we know from a hyperbola, these point series can consist of different parts—the *branches* of a curve. All points of a circle or a conic section lie in a plane.

These curves are called *planar curves*, in contrast to *spatial curves* such as helixes (Figure 7.3). In the following we study important concepts for planar and spatial curves. They are largely introduced in an illustrative geometric way, but we also provide the mathematical background. We start with three different mathematical approaches to describing curves.

(a)

(b)

Parametric representation. The coordinates of a point p of a *parametric curve c* are expressed as functions of a variable t. This means that a spatial curve c can be represented by $\mathbf{c}(t) = (x(t), y(t), z(t))$, where t is some parameter assuming all values in an interval I. We could consider a curve as the result of a continuous mapping of an interval I into a plane or three-dimensional space (Figure 7.4). Thereby, every parameter t is mapped to a curve point $p(t)$. Often it is helpful to think about t as time, although t need not be time. The functions $x(t)$, $y(t)$ and $z(t)$ are called the *coordinate functions* and $\mathbf{c}(t)$ is a *parameterization* of c.

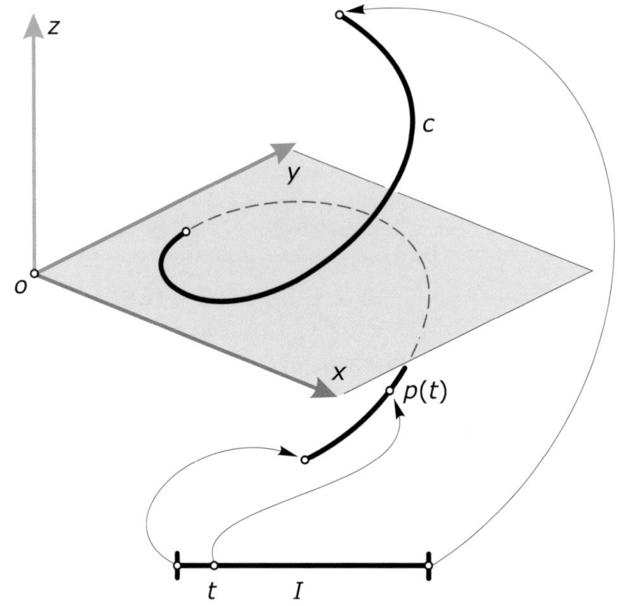

Fig. 7.4
An interval I is mapped to a curve c in three-dimensional space.

Fig. 7.5
The circle as a parametric curve.
(a) A circle in general position.
(b) The unit circle.

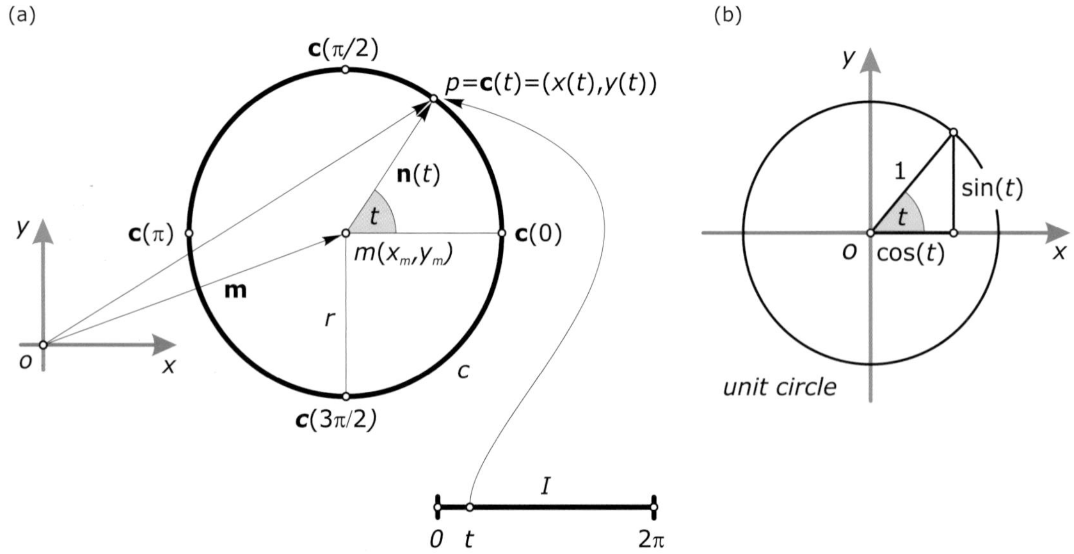

Example:

Circle in parametric representation. Given the center $m(x_m,y_m)$ and the radius r of a circle, we can derive the coordinates of points $p(x,y)$ on the circle by adding the vectors $\mathbf{m} = (x_m,y_m)$ and $\mathbf{n}(t) = (r\cdot\cos(t), r\cdot\sin(t))$, where t is the angle between the horizontal straight line through m and the ray from the center to the circle point p. This angle is measured as an arc length on the unit circle. Thus, the points $p(x,y)$ of the circle are described as

$x(t) = x_m + r\cdot\cos(t), y(t) = y_m + r\cdot\sin(t)$.

Because the position of the circle point $\mathbf{c}(t) = (x(t),y(t))$ depends on a parameter t, we speak of a *parametric representation* of the circle (Figure 7.5). If the parameter t runs in the interval $[0,2\pi]$, we obtain all points of the circle c. By selecting appropriate intervals for the parameter t, we obtain a mathematical description of circular arcs of any opening angle (Figure 7.6).

As we have seen in this example, by restricting the interval of the parameter t we obtain a subset of the curve c (sometimes referred to as a *curve segment*). A parametric curve defined by polynomial functions is called a *polynomial curve*. The highest order of the parameter t in any of the three coordinate functions is called the *degree* of the polynomial curve.

Fig. 7.6
Several circular arcs with varying opening angle.

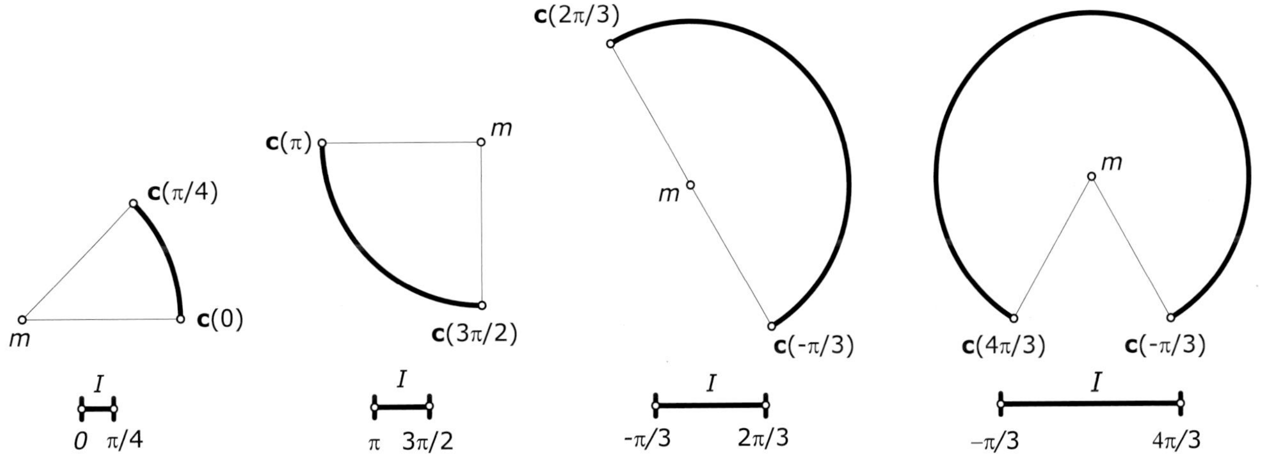

Example:

Parabola and spatial cubic curve. A simple example of a planar polynomial curve is the parabola with a parametric representation $\mathbf{p}(t) = (t, t^2)$. If the parameter t assumes all real numbers, we obtain the entire parabola. Restricting the interval I to $[-3,3]$, we have the curve segment (Figure 7.7a)—which starts in the point $p_0(-3,9)$ and ends in $p_1(3,9)$. The parabola p contains the origin o. It is the curve point to the parameter $t = 0$. The highest exponent with which the parameter t appears is 2. It occurs in the coordinate function $y(t) = t^2$. We therefore say that the parameterization is of degree 2. It can be shown that a polynomial curve of degree 2 is in general a parabola. In special cases, it may degenerate to a straight line segment.

The coordinate functions $x(t) = 12t - 12t^2$, $y(t) = 6t - 6t^2 + 4t^3$, and $z(t) = 12t - 24t^2 + 16t^3$ define a spatial curve c. Using the interval $[0,1]$ for the parameter t, we obtain the curve segment that lies entirely within the cube shown in Figure 7.7b. The highest order (3) of the parameter t can be found in the coordinate functions $y(t)$ and $z(t)$. Thus, we have a polynomial curve of degree 3. All polynomial curves of degree 3 are subsumed under the name *cubic curves*. Another example for a cubic curve is $\mathbf{d}(t) = (t,t^2,t^3)$, which is also illustrated in Figure 7.7c.

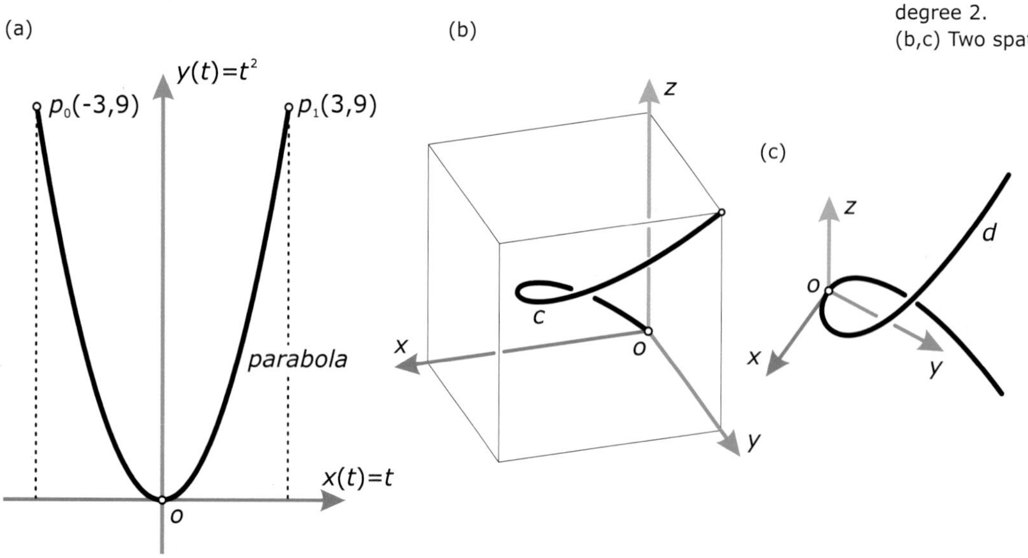

Fig. 7.7
(a) Parabolas are polynomial curves of degree 2.
(b,c) Two spatial cubic curves.

If the coordinate functions of a curve have the form $p(t)/q(t)$, where $p(t)$ and $q(t)$ are polynomial functions, then the curve is called a *rational curve*. We use a common denominator polynomial $q(t)$ for all coordinate functions. Again, we define the degree of this family of curves as the highest order of the variable t occurring in the numerator or the denominator of any coordinate function. Polynomial curves are omnipresent in freeform curve design. Their extension to rational curves is the basic building block of the so-called NURBS freeform design scheme (see Chapter 8).

Explicit representation: graphs. The parabola $\mathbf{c}(t) = (t, t^2)$ studied in the previous example also satisfies the equation $y = x^2$ (Figure 7.9). This parabola may be used to visualize the function $f(x) = x^2$. For each x, we plot the function value $f(x) = x^2$ as a y coordinate. We call a description via $y = f(x)$ an *explicit representation* of a curve. The curve is also referred to as the *graph of the function f*; namely, the collection of all pairs $(x, f(x))$ in the xy-plane. Examples of graphs are shown in Figure 7.10.

Example:
Rational cubic curve.

$$\mathbf{c}(t) = \left(\frac{4t^2 - 1}{3t^2 + 1}, \frac{t(4t^2 - 1)}{3t^2 + 1}\right)$$

is the parametric representation of a planar rational curve of degree 3. Note that the highest order (3) of the parameter t only occurs in the numerator $t(4t^2 - 1)$ of the coordinate function $y(t)$.

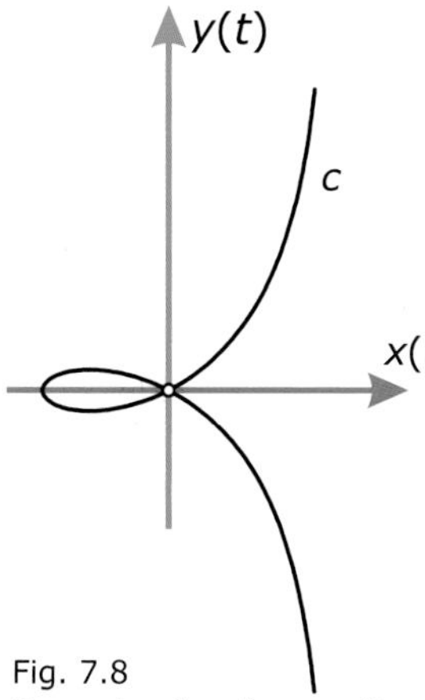

Fig. 7.8
Example of a planar rational curve of degree 3.

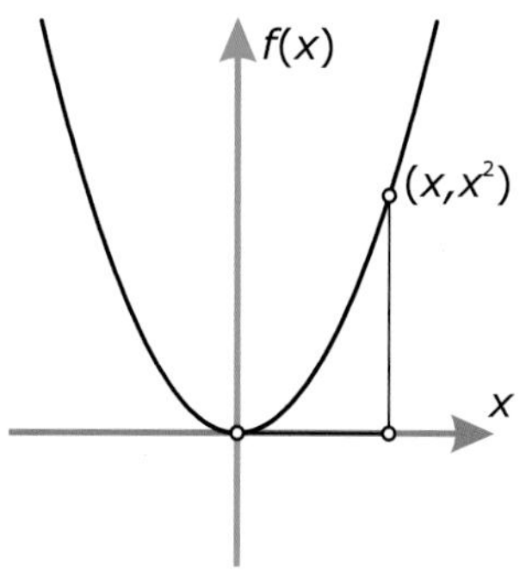

Fig. 7.9
Parabola as a graph of the function $f(x) = x^2$.

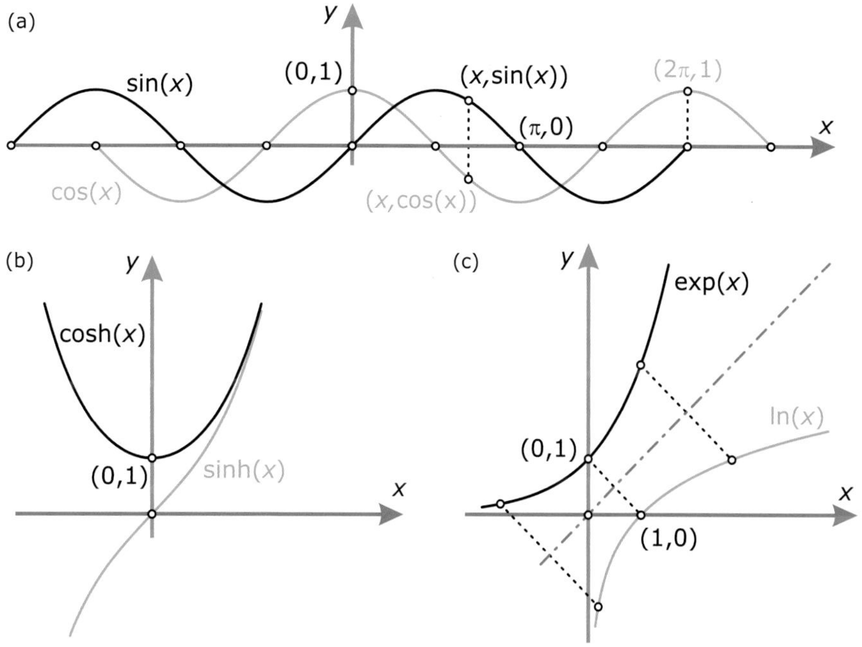

Fig. 7.10
Graphs of
(a) $f(x) = \sin(x)$, $f(x) = \cos(x)$;
(b) $f(x) = \cosh(x)$, $f(x) = \sinh(x)$; for the definition and geometric meaning of these functions see the discussion of the "catenary" in Chapter 18; and
(c) $f(x) = \exp(x)$, $f(x) = \ln(x)$.

Implicit representation. We may write the explicit representation in the form $y - f(x) = 0$. Then, the left-hand side $y - f(x)$ is a special function $F(x,y)$ of two variables—which leads to the following generalization of the explicit representation. If the coordinates (x,y) of points of a planar curve c satisfy an equation of the form $F(x,y) = 0$, we call c an *implicit planar curve* and $F(x,y) = 0$ an *implicit representation* of c.

If F is a polynormal function in the variables x and y, then F is a so-called *algebraic curve*. In general, it will not be possible to rewrite F in the form $y - f(x)$ and thus the implicit representation can capture many more curves than the explicit representation. For additional insight into implicit curves and their generalization to surfaces, see Chapter 12.

Example:

The circle in implicit representation. A circle with center (midpoint) $m(x_m,y_m)$ and radius r is the set of all points $p(x,y)$ in the plane that have equal distance r to the center point m. A mathematical formulation of the previous geometric definition of a circle uses the Euclidean distance between two points (Figure 7.11). From the Pythagorean theorem, we derive the squared distance r^2 between points $p(x,y)$ and $m(x_m,y_m)$ as $r^2 = (x - x_m)^2 + (y - y_m)^2$.

Thus, all points (x,y) that fulfill the equation $F(x,y) = (x - x_m)^2 + (y - y_m)^2 - r^2 = 0$ lie on the circle c.

As with the representation of a circle, some curves can be represented in both implicit and parametric forms. Moreover, if we are given a parametric representation of a curve there are infinitely many other parametric representations of the same curve. If one views the curve parameter t as time, all parametric representations differ in the "timing" (speed profile) used to traverse the curve. The implicit representation is not unique, which will become clearer in Chapter 12.

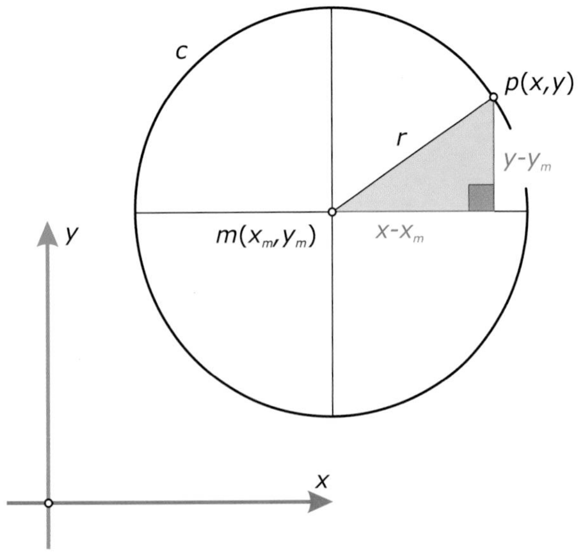

Fig. 7.11
The implicit representation of the circle is based on its definition as a set of all points equidistant from a center point.

The following example derives another parametric representation of a circle from its implicit description. Comparing the result of the last example with the result of the example of a "circle in parametric representation," we recognize that there exist different parametric representations of the same curve.

Example:
Implicit and parametric representation of a circle. Figure 7.12 shows a circle c with center at the origin and radius 1. All points of c satisfy the equation $F(x,y) = x^2 + y^2 - 1 = 0$. Now we try to find a parametric representation of c with the parameter t. Every point $q(t,0)$ of the x axis can be joined with the "south pole" $s(0,-1)$ of the circle c (Figure 7.12a). Each of these straight lines intersects the circle in s and in a further point $p = \mathbf{p}(t) = (x(t), y(t))$. As the point q moves along the x-axis, its corresponding point p moves on the circle. In this way, we capture all points of the circle except the south pole $s(0,-1)$. The latter would belong to the t-value infinity.
The straight line joining the south pole s and the point q on the x-axis has the equation $x = t \cdot y + t$. Plugging this equation into the circle's equation and solving the resulting quadratic equation for y yields two solutions for y. One solution is $y = -1$ because every straight line passes through s, whereas the second solution is $y = (1 - t^2)/(1 + t^2)$.
Plugging this result into $x = t \cdot y + t$ (the equation of the straight line) yields $x = 2t/(1 + t^2)$. Thus, we have derived a *rational* parameterization of the circle c. If t assumes all real numbers, we obtain the entire circle except s— whereas using the parameter interval [0, 1] we obtain only a quarter circle (Figure 7.12b). Note that different parametric representations may lead to a different spacing of curve points (Figures 7.12c and d).

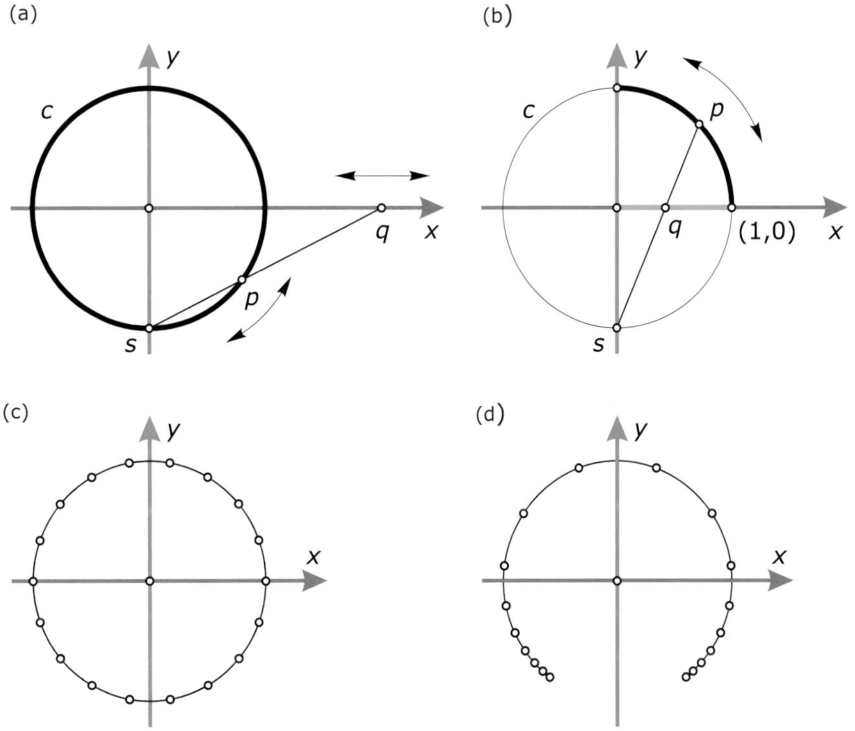

Fig. 7.12
(a,b) Derivation of a rational parametric representation of a circle from its implicit representation.
(c,d) Different parameterizations lead to different spacing of curve points.

To describe spatial curves, a parametric representation is the appropriate approach. This is one of the reasons the most common representation of curves is the parametric representation. A further reason is that drawing a curve based on its parameterization is very simple, whereas the same task is more difficult to achieve with the implicit representation. In the following we derive all concepts about curves exclusively using the parametric representation.

Curve tangent. We can locally approximate a smooth curve c at a point p by a straight line, the curve tangent T. To avoid confusion with the curve parameter t, we denote in this chapter the curve tangent with a capital T. The curve tangent can be found by the following limit process (Figure 7.13a). On the curve c, take any point q that is close to the point p and connect points p and q by a straight line l. This line l is also called a *chord* of c. Then move the point q on the curve c closer and closer to p. In the limit, the point q coincides with p and l assumes a limit position; namely, the *tangent* T of the curve c at p.

We derive a mathematical representation of the curve tangent T as follows. Let $\mathbf{c}(t) = (x(t), y(t), z(t))$ be a parametric representation of the curve c, and $p = \mathbf{c}(t)$ a curve point for some fixed t. A point q (which is close to p) of c is represented by $\mathbf{c}(t + h)$. This implies that the connecting line l of p and q has the vector $\mathbf{c}(t + h) - \mathbf{c}(t)$ as a direction vector. Because this vector would converge to the zero vector if we move q toward p, we use another direction vector of l; namely, $[\mathbf{c}(t + h) - \mathbf{c}(t)]/h$. Moving q to p is achieved by letting h tend to zero. By definition of derivatives, the limit of the direction vector $[\mathbf{c}(t + h) - \mathbf{c}(t)]/h$ of l for $h \to 0$ is the first derivative vector

$$\mathbf{c}'(t) = (x'(t), y'(t), z'(t)).$$

We have just proven that the first derivative vector defines the direction of the curve's tangent. A parametric representation of the curve tangent at point $\mathbf{c}(t)$ can be found with

$$T: \mathbf{x}(u) = \mathbf{c}(t) + u \cdot \mathbf{c}'(t).$$

Here, u is the parameter for describing the points of T. The *normal* of a planar curve is the normal of the tangent in the touching point p (Figure 7.13b). A space curve has a normal plane at each point p. We will later see that there are two special normals in this plane that deserve particular attention.

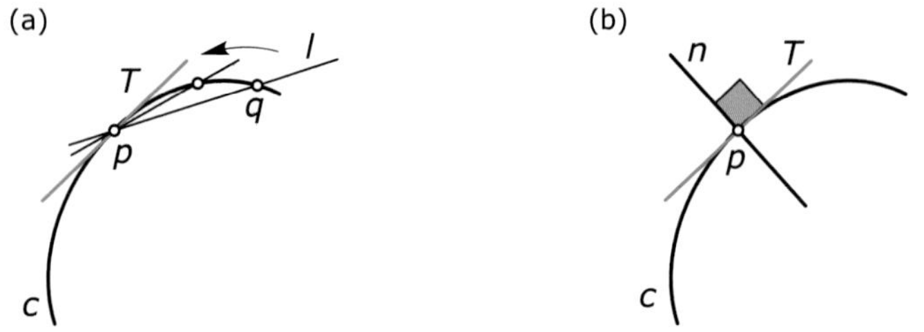

Fig. 7.13
(a) A tangent T touches a curve c. It can be found with the help of a limit process or by calculating the first derivative vector $\mathbf{c}'(t)$.
(b) The normal of a planar curve intersects the curve at a right angle.

Example:

Tangents of a helix. To find the tangents T of the helix $\mathbf{c}(t) = (r \cdot \cos(t), r \cdot \sin(t), p \cdot t)$ (see the section on helical motions in Chapter 6), we calculate the first derivative vector as $\mathbf{c}'(t) = (-r \cdot \sin(t), r \cdot \cos(t), p)$. Note that the angle between the tangents and the z-axis is constant, because the result of the dot product of $\mathbf{c}'(t)$ and $\mathbf{z} = (0,0,1)$ is $p = const.$ This also means that all tangents have a constant inclination angle against the xy-plane.

Points of the curve with a uniquely defined tangent are called *regular points*. All points where the tangent vector $\mathbf{c}'(t)$ is a non-vanishing vector are regular points. Curve points where $\mathbf{c}'(t)$ is the zero vector $\mathbf{o}$ are *singular points*.

Example:

Singular points. Figure 7.15 shows two curves that exhibit singular points. The planar cubic with the parametric representation $\mathbf{c}(t) = (t^2, t^3)$, with t assuming any real number, has the first derivative vector $\mathbf{c}'(t) = (2t, 3t^2)$. With the exception of $t = 0$, this vector is not the zero vector. Thus, the point $p(0,0)$ is a singular point—whereas all other points are regular.

The curve $\mathbf{d}(t) = (\sin^3(t), \cos^3(t))$ is called an *astroid* curve according to its starlike shape. We will encounter this curve again in Chapter 10 (on offsets) and in Chapter 12 (on motions). For t running in the interval $[0, 2\pi)$ we obtain the full closed curve. It possesses four cusps. These singular points are lying in the two symmetry axes of the curve. They are found by solving the equation $\mathbf{d}'(t) = (3 \cdot \sin^2(t) \cdot \cos(t), 3 \cdot \cos^2(t) \cdot \sin(t)) = \mathbf{o}$, whose solutions in $[0, 2\pi)$ are $t = 0$, $t = \pi/2$, $t = \pi$,, $t = 3\pi/2$.

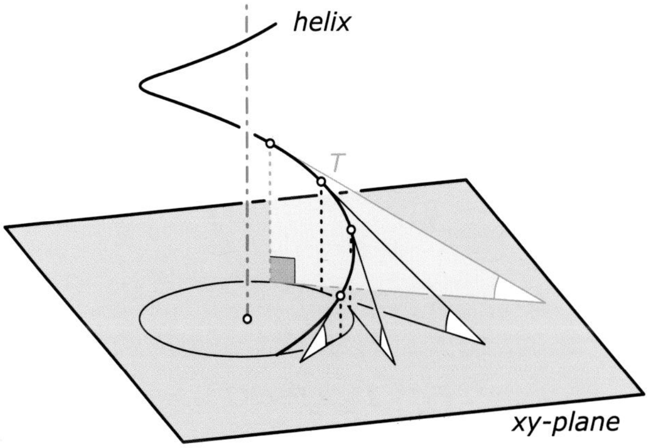

Fig. 7.14
Tangents of a helix.

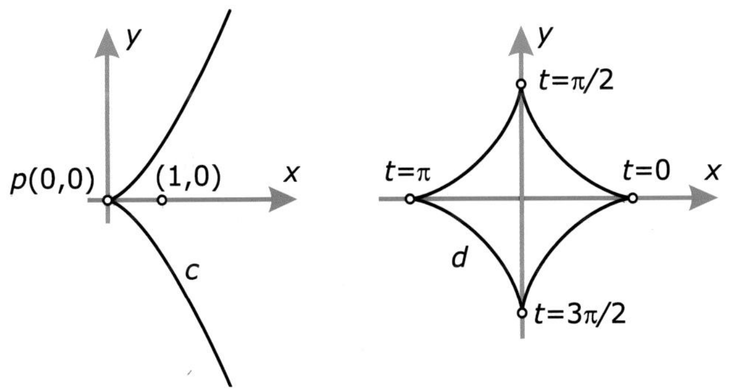

Fig. 7.15
Singular points of curves.

Discrete curves. To understand the geometry of curves without the explicit use of calculus, we take the so-called *discrete* approach (Figure 7.16). Let P_c be a polygon with vertices c_1, c_2, c_3, and so on, and constant edge length L. If we are given a smooth curve c and the length L, we can easily construct this polygon P_c such that its vertices lie on c. The polygon is also called a *discrete curve*. In many practical computations, curves are actually polygons (i.e., discrete curves).

We can also use them for the derivation and visualization of theoretical results on smooth curves. Previously, we have seen that the polygon edges that join consecutive vertices c_1c_2, c_2c_3, and so on become tangents of c if the polygon is refined (i.e., if L tends toward zero). It is actually not necessary that all polygon edges have the same length. We simply need to consider sufficiently uniform refinements toward a smooth curve.

Osculating plane and osculating circle. Let's now go beyond tangents. For this we consider a discrete spatial curve (polygon) P_c (Figure 7.17). Three consecutive vertices of P_c (such as c_1, c_2, and c_3) span a plane O_2. Now we fix c_2, call it p, and refine the polygon P_c by letting the edge length L tend toward zero. Then the limit of the connecting plane O_2 becomes the so-called *osculating plane* O of the smooth curve c at the point p.

By construction, O locally best approximates the given curve and passes through the tangent T of c at p. The mathematical formulation of the limit process shows that the osculating plane at $\mathbf{c}(t)$ is spanned by the first derivative vector $\mathbf{c}'(t)$ and the second derivative vector $\mathbf{c}''(t)$.

Fig. 7.16
A discrete curve is a polygon P_c that approximates a smooth curve. When P_c is refined and in the limit converges to a smooth curve c, the edges of P_c tend toward the tangents of c.

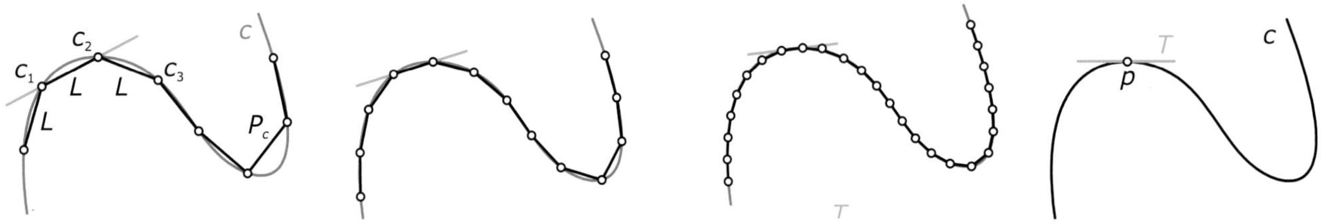

Fig. 7.17
Definition of osculating plane and osculating circle of a space curve with help of an approximation by a polygon P_c.

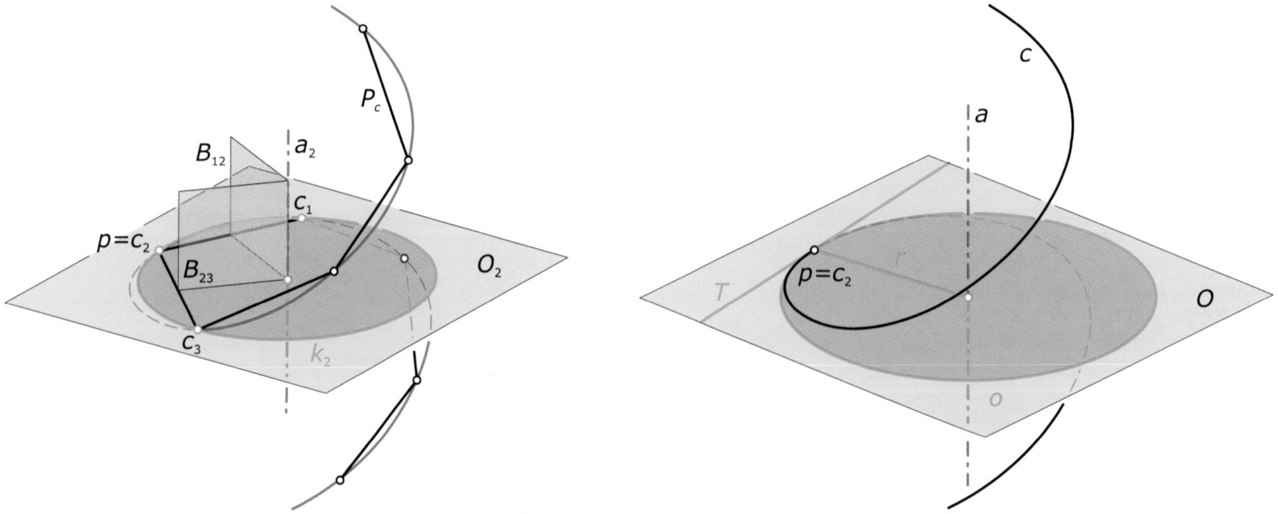

Three consecutive vertices of the polygon P_c possess a circumscribed circle k_2, which lies in the plane O_2. Its rotational axis a_2 is the intersection of the bisecting planes B_{12} of c_1c_2 and B_{23} of c_2c_3. During the refinement process, the points c_1 and c_3 move closer until they coincide with $c_2 = p$. In the limit, the circle k_2 becomes the *osculating circle o* of the curve.

Our derivation shows that the osculating circle lies in the osculating plane (it touches c at p). Its axis a, the limit of a_2, intersects the osculating plane in the center of the osculating circle—which is also denoted as the *curvature center*. If the radius of the osculating circle (also called *curvature radius*) is r, the *curvature k* of the curve c at the point p is defined as the reciprocal value of the radius ($k = 1/r$).

Example:

Computation of the curvature. If α_2 denotes the edge angle at c_2 (Figure 7.18a), trigonometry shows that the radius r_2 of k_2 is given by $r_2 = L/(2 \cdot \sin(\alpha_2/2))$.
R_2 is the discrete curvature radius at c_2. Its reciprocal value $k_2 = 1/r_2$ can be defined as discrete curvature. If we now fix $p = c_2$ and let L tend toward zero, k_2 converges to the osculating circle o of c at point p, r_2 tends to the curvature radius r, and k_2 converges to the curvature k of c at p (Figure 7.18b).

A simpler limit formula for the curvature is obtained as follows. We note that for small angles β (Figure 7.18c), the value β is very close to $\sin \beta$ (precisely, $\beta/(\sin \beta)$ tends toward 1 if β tends toward 0). This shows that the curvature is
$k = \lim(1/r) = \lim(2 \cdot \sin(\alpha/2)/L) = \lim \alpha/L$, for $L \to 0$,
where α denotes the edge angle at p. Thus, curvature measures the local directional change of the tangent. If we are given a parametric representation $\mathbf{c}(t)$ of c, the curvature may be calculated as

$$k = \frac{\|\mathbf{c}'(t) \times \mathbf{c}''(t)\|}{\|\mathbf{c}'(t)\|^3}.$$

For curves $\mathbf{c}(t) = (x(t), y(t))$ in the plane, one can give curvature a sign, and then one uses the formula

$$k = \frac{x'(t)y''(t) - x''(t)y'(t)}{[x'(t)^2 + y'(t)^2]^{3/2}}.$$

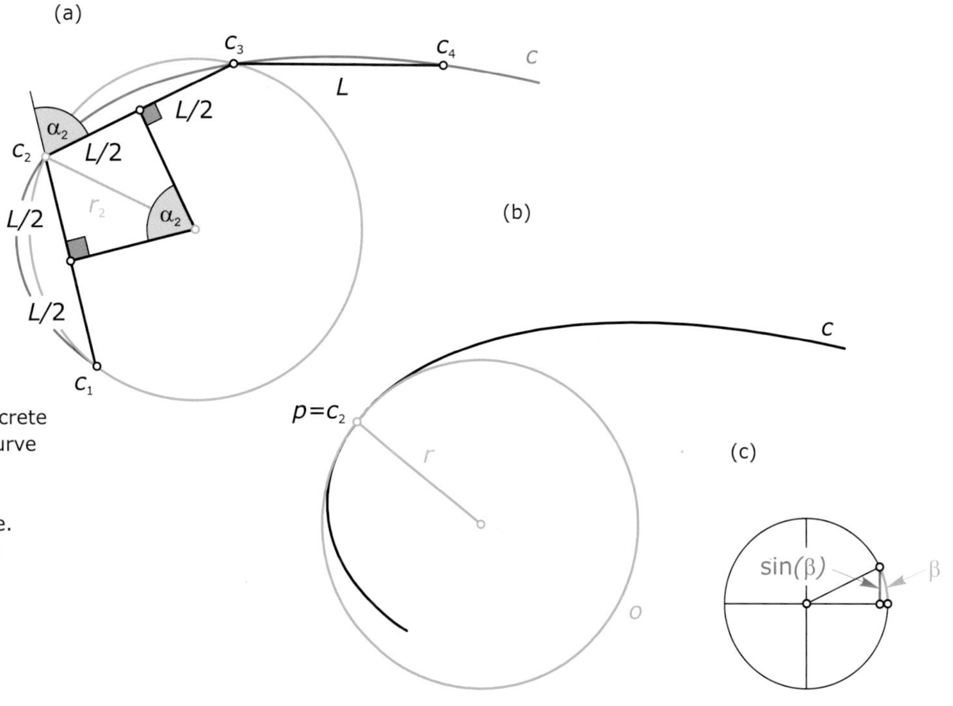

Fig. 7.18
Derivation of a formula for the discrete curvature radius. If the discrete curve is refined to a smooth curve, the discrete curvature radius tends to the radius r of the osculating circle. The reciprocal value $k = 1/r$ is the curvature.

Inflection point and vertex. Osculating circle and curvature are useful tools in studying the properties of curves. In general, a planar curve *c* touches the corresponding osculating circle *o* at point *p* but changes the side of *o* (Figure 7.19a). A point *v* of a curve *c* with a local maximum or minimum of curvature is called a *vertex*. In this case, the osculating circle *o* does not change the side of the curve *c*. In the proximity of a vertex *v*, the curve *c* is very well approximated by the osculating circle *o* (Figure 7.19b). These special points arise, for example, as intersection points of the curve *c* with its symmetry axes.

Other interesting regular curve points are the *inflection points*. At these points, the osculating circle degenerates into a straight line; namely, the tangent *T* of *c*. The curvature in an inflection point *p* is zero and the curve *c* changes the side of the tangent (Figure 7.19c). There may also be points (called *flat points*) with vanishing curvature where the curve does not change the side of the tangent. This happens if the tangent *T* fits even better with the curve. Mathematically, phenomena such as vertices or flat points can only be described and carefully classified with higher-order derivatives (which are beyond the scope of this text).

Evolute. The locus of the centers of all osculating circles of a planar curve *c* is called the *evolute e* of *c*. The evolute of a planar curve can also be generated as envelope of the curve normals. This fact is easily derived from a discrete curve P_c (Figure 7.20, left). We consider the bisector lines b_{12}, b_{23}, and so on of the edges c_1c_2, c_2c_3, and so on.

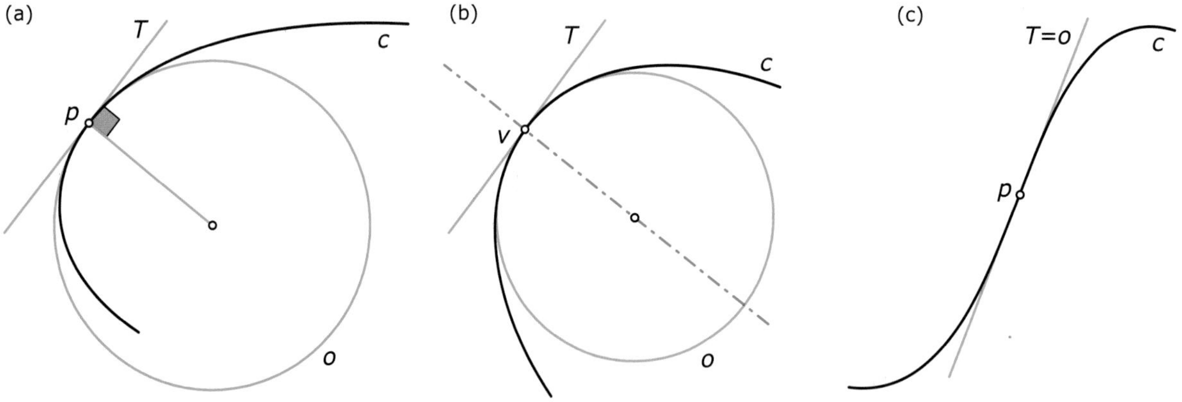

Fig. 7.19
(a) In general, a curve c touches the osculating circle o and changes the side of o.
(b) A vertex v is a point with locally extremal curvature. At a generic vertex, the osculating circle o remains locally on the same side of the curve.
(c) A curve c changes the side of its tangent at inflection points p.

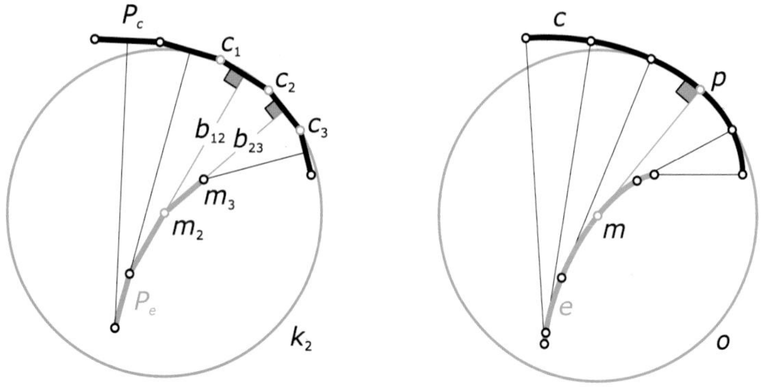

Fig. 7.20
(right) The evolute e of a planar curve c is the set of curvature centers and the envelope of all curve normals.
(left) This is easily derived from a discrete curve.

Consecutive bisectors (such as b_{12} and b_{23}) intersect at the center m_2 of the circle through c_1, c_2, and c_3, which is a discrete version of an osculating circle (see the previous discussion). Hence, all bisectors form the edge lines of the polygon P_e, whose vertices are the discrete curvature centers m_2, m_3, and so on of P_c. If we now refine P_c toward a smooth curve c (Figure 7.20, right), the bisector lines become the normals of c and the polygon P_e converges to the evolute e. Because the bisectors are also the edge lines of P_e, they converge to tangents of e. Hence, the normals of c are the tangents of the evolute e.

It is interesting to note that a vertex of the original curve c induces a cusp at the corresponding evolute e. Figure 7.21 illustrates this remarkable property by means of an ellipse. This figure shows that the evolute e is related to an astroid (see the example "singular points") by an affine transformation. We will again encounter evolutes in Chapter 10 (on offsets) and in the section on curves generated by smooth motions in Chapter 12.

Frenet frame of a space curve. For a planar curve, we have defined curve normals as lines orthogonal to the tangents. In space, there is a plane that intersects the tangent T at the curve point p under a right angle. We call this plane the *normal plane* N of the curve c in the point p. The normal plane N and the osculating plane O intersect along the *principal normal* n of the curve (Figure 7.22). The principal normal intersects the axis a of the osculating circle o at the curvature center m.

The straight line b (through the curve point p) which is normal to O (parallel to the axis a of the osculating circle), intersects the principal normal and the tangent T of the curve at a right angle. We call this straight line the *binormal* b of the curve c.

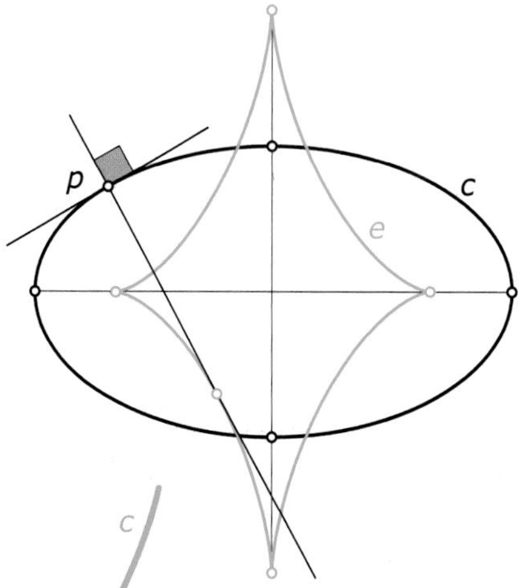

Fig. 7.21
The evolute e of an ellipse c is related to an astroid by an affine transformation. The four cusps of the evolute are the curvature centers of the vertices of the ellipse.

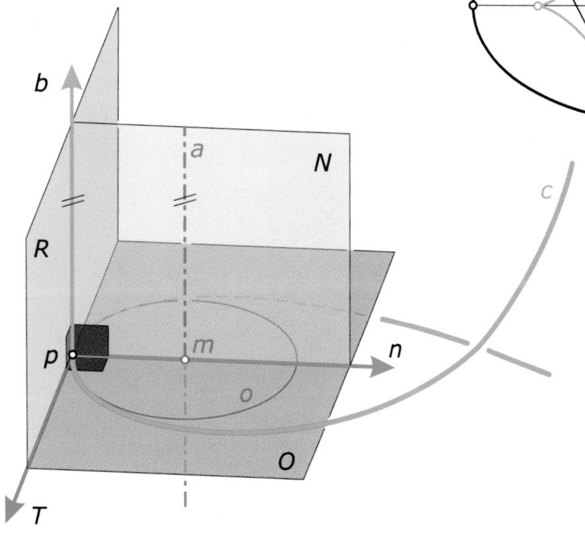

Fig. 7.22
The Frenet frame of a space curve c consists of the tangent T, the principal normal n, and the binormal b. T and n span the osculating plane O.

The tangent T, the principal normal n, and the binormal b define a Cartesian frame at the curve point p. This Cartesian coordinate frame is connected with the space curve in a very natural way. We call it the *Frenet frame* of the curve at the point p. The coordinate planes of the Frenet frame are the osculating plane O $(= Tn)$, the normal plane N $(= nb)$ and the *rectifying plane* R $(= Tb)$.

Example:

Frenet frame and orthogonal projections. To illustrate that curvature is changed under projections, we study the projections parallel to the axes of the Frenet frame (Figure 7.23). We use the cubic space curve $\mathbf{c}(t) = (12t \cdot (1 - t), 2t \cdot (3 - 3t + 2t^2), 4t \cdot (3 - 6t + 4t^2))$, which we introduced in the example "parabola and spatial cubic curve."

The tangent direction at the point $p = \mathbf{c}(1/2) = (3, 2, 2)$ is parallel to the y-axis and the osculating plane is parallel to the xy-plane. Thus, the normal plane and the rectifying plane are parallel to the xz-plane and the yz-plane. The top view (coming from the projection into a plane parallel to the osculating plane) shows the osculating circle o at point p without distortion, whereas the front view and the side view show curves c'' and c''', which possess an inflection point p'' and a cusp p''', respectively.

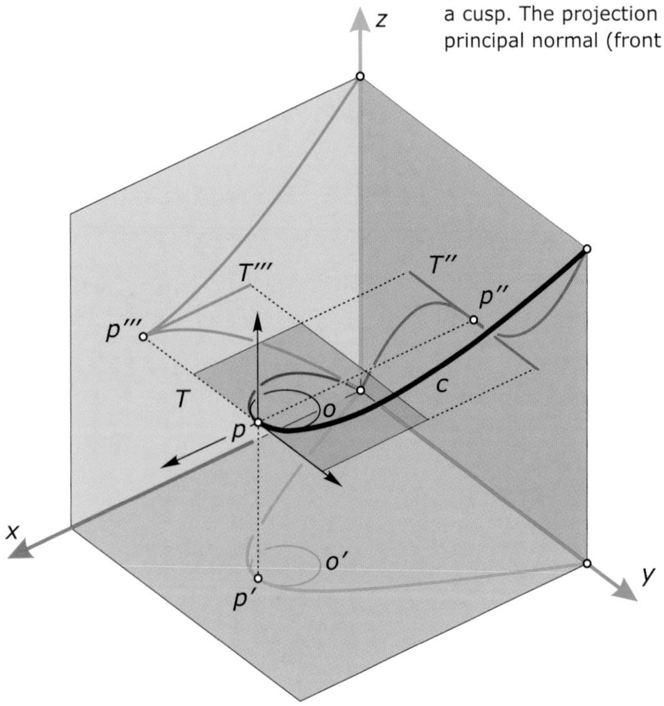

Fig. 7.23
Frenet frame of a cubic c and projections of the curve c into the planes of this frame. The projection parallel to the tangent (side view) has a cusp. The projection parallel to the principal normal (front view) yields an inflection point of the image curve. The local behavior of the projected curve can be understood if we also consider the projection of the osculating circle of the space curve.

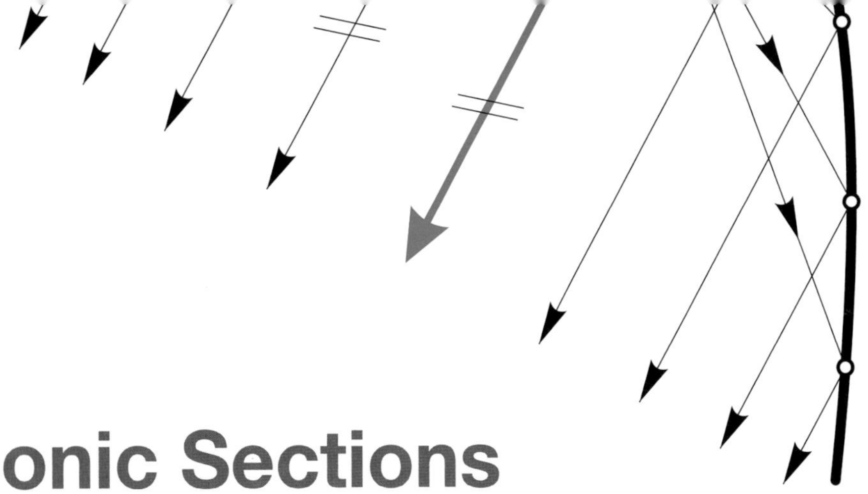

Conic Sections

At the end of the previous chapter we introduced conic sections as planar intersection curves of rotational cones. Now we illustrate principles to generate conic-sections based on the mathematical concepts introduced in this chapter.

Implicit representation. The simplest implicitly defined planar curve is a straight line given by a linear equation $a{\cdot}x + b{\cdot}y + c = 0$. We can define a conic as a curve described by the quadratic equation

$$a{\cdot}x^2 + b{\cdot}x{\cdot}y + c{\cdot}y^2 + d{\cdot}x + e{\cdot}y + f = 0.$$

Different choices of the parameters $a, b, \ldots, f$ lead to different conics. Clearly, a simple multiplication of all parameters by the same factor λ corresponds to a multiplication of the implicit equation by λ and therefore does not change its solution set. Hence, only the ratio $a : b : \ldots : f$ is really important. Depending on the choice of this ratio, we obtain circles, ellipses, parabolas, and hyperbolas (and some degenerate cases such as pairs of straight lines).

Ellipse. A quadratic equation of the form

$$b^2{\cdot}x^2 + a^2{\cdot}y^2 - a^2{\cdot}b^2 = 0$$

describes an ellipse with its center at the origin and the coordinate axes as symmetry axes. The parameters a and b determine the distances of the four vertices from the center (Figure 7.24). The coordinates of the major vertices are $(a,0)$, $(-a,0)$, and those of the minor vertices are $(0,b)$ and $(0,-b)$. Application of the scaling (affine transformation) $(x,y) \rightarrow (x_1,y_1) = (x,y{\cdot}a/b)$ fixes the major vertices and maps the minor vertices to $(0,a)$ and $(0,-a)$.

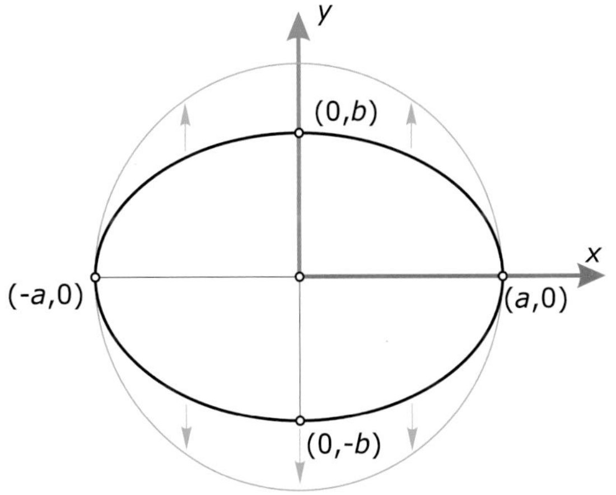

Fig. 7.24
An ellipse has four vertices. It can be transformed into a circle using an applicable scaling.

Insertion of $x = x_1, y = y_1 \cdot b/a$ in the equation of the ellipse results (after division by b^2) in the equation $x_1^2 + y_1^2 - a^2 = 0$, which describes a circle of radius a. Hence, the scaling transforms the ellipse into this circle. There are other scalings that relate an ellipse to circles. For example, the scaling $x_1 = a \cdot x$, $y_1 = b \cdot y$ maps the circle of radius 1 (i.e., $x^2 + y^2 = 1$) into our ellipse.

An ellipse has two foci (also called *focal points*) $f_1(e,0)$ and $f_2(-e,0)$ on the major axis. Their distance e (eccentricity) to the center is computed from a and b by $e^2 = a^2 - b^2$ (Figure 7.25). This shows immediately that the distance of the minor vertices to f_1 and f_2 equals a, which is a special case of the following property.

The sum of distances dist(p,f_1) + dist(p,f_2) of any point p of an ellipse to its two foci is constant (i.e, equal to $2 \cdot a$).

Therefore, an ellipse can be drawn with a string fixed at the foci (Figure 7.25). An analytical proof sets $p(x,y)$, and reduces the condition

$$\text{dist}(p,f_1) + \text{dist}(p,f_2) = \sqrt{(x-e)^2 + y^2} + = \sqrt{(x+e)^2 + y^2} = 2a$$

by simple manipulations to the equation $b^2x^2 + a^2y^2 - a^2b^2 = 0$ of the ellipse. Due to the mechanical interpretation of the string construction, the equal tension forces at p have a resulting force in the bisecting line of pf_1 and pf_2. Thus, the point p can only

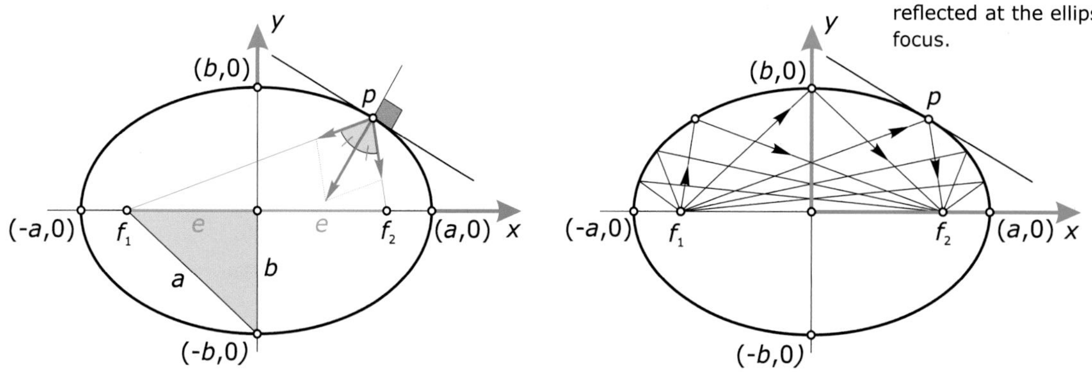

Fig. 7.25
The string construction of an ellipse implies the following property of an ellipse: Rays emitting from a focus are reflected at the ellipse into the other focus.

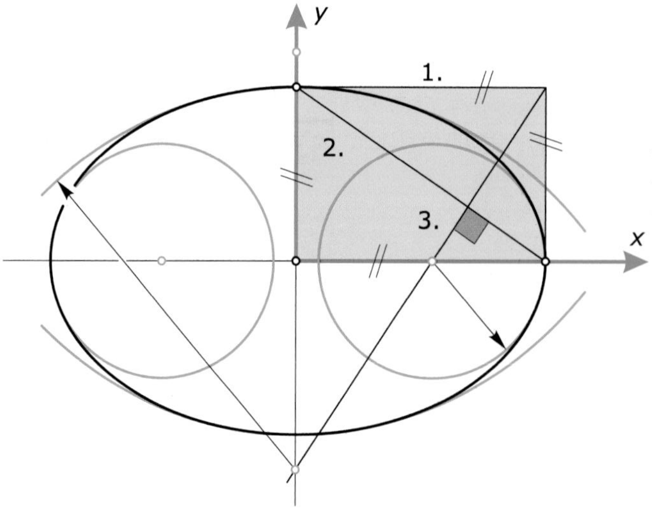

Fig. 7.26
The centers of the osculation circles in the vertices can be found by a simple construction.

move orthogonally to this bisector. In other words, the tangent of the ellipse at p is the outer bisector of pf_1 and pf_2. Hence, a ray emitted from one focus is reflected at the ellipse into the other focus. This property can be applied for illumination or acoustic effects in buildings.

Figure 7.26 shows a simple construction for obtaining the centers of the osculating circles in the vertices. These circles are useful when sketching an ellipse by hand. To find a parametric representation of an ellipse e, we apply the scaling $x_1 = a{\cdot}x, y_1 = b{\cdot}y$ to the unit circle $\mathbf{c}(t) = (\sin(t), \cos(t))$. Thus, we obtain

$$\mathbf{c}_1(t) = (a{\cdot}\sin(t), b{\cdot}\cos(t)).$$

Analogously, we find a rational parametric representation

$$\mathbf{d}_1(t) = (a\cdot\frac{2t}{1+t^2}, b\cdot\frac{1-t^2}{1+t^2}).$$

of an ellipse by applying the same scaling to the rational parameterization of a circle of radius 1. Ellipses arise as planar intersections of rotational cylinders. Thus, they often occur as parts of architectural designs (as illustrated in Figure 7.27).

Fig. 7.27
Ellipses and elliptical arcs are used in architecture and design.
(a) The *Hangar 7* (1999–2003) in Salzburg by Volkmar Burgstaller. The main shape is a tilted ellipsoid with elliptical arcs as support structure.
(b) The *Tycho Brahe Planetarium* (1988–1989) in Copenhagen by Knud Munk.

(a)

(b)

Hyperbola. By replacing a single sign in the implicit representation of an ellipse, we obtain via

$$b^2 \cdot x^2 - a^2 \cdot y^2 - a^2 \cdot b^2 = 0$$

an equation that describes a hyperbola. The center of the hyperbola is the origin o, and the two major vertices are $(a,0)$ and $(-a,0)$. The points $(0,b)$ and $(0,-b)$ do not lie on the hyperbola, but on the axis rectangle, whose diagonals are the so-called asymptotes u and v. A hyperbola consists of two branches, each of which comes arbitrarily close to the asymptotes without touching them. The asymptotes are important in correctly sketching a hyperbola. One can define foci $f_1(e,0)$ and $f_2(-e,0)$, with $e^2 = a^2 + b^2$ (Figure 7.28), and show that the difference of distances $|\operatorname{dist}(p,f_1) - \operatorname{dist}(p,f_2)|$ is constant ($= 2a$) for the points p of the hyperbola.

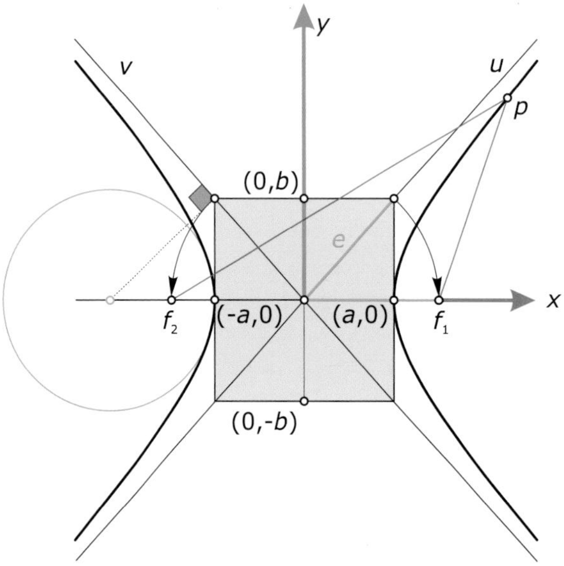

Fig. 7.28
A hyperbola has two vertices and two asymptotes.

Fig. 7.29
Parabolic arcs in architecture.
(a,b) The *Botanical Gardens* (1991–1995) in Graz by Volker Giencke are built using congruent parabolic arcs (images courtesy Walter Obermayer).
(c) Under the *Beach Park Boulevard bridge* in Foster City (image courtesy Peter Kaminski).

(c)

(a)

(b)

Parabola. Parabolas and parabolic arcs are important curves for generating interesting surfaces [see Chapter 9 (on traditional surface classes) and Chapter 11 (on freeform surfaces)]. In addition, because of static properties they can be found in architectural design (Figure 7.29). In an adapted coordinate system, the quadratic equation of a parabola is given by

$$x^2 - 2py = 0.$$

This parabola has its single vertex in the origin. The y-axis is its single symmetry axis and is referred to as the *axis* of the parabola. The *focus* $f = (0,p/2)$ lies on the symmetry axis and the evolute e contains only one cusp. A parabola also has a simple definition with distances (Figure 7.30). We define the *focal line* F: $y = -p/2$. It is normal to the axis and has distance p to the focus f. Thus, for each point q of the parabola the distance dist(q,f) to the focus equals the distance dist(q,F) to the focal line.

To derive an analytical verification, we set $q(x,y)$; rewrite the condition dist(q,f) = dist(q,F) as $\sqrt{x^2 + (y - p/2)^2} = |y + q/2|$; square it; and obtain after some simple manipulations the equation $y^2 - 2px = 0$ of the parabola. Related to the distance property is the following fact: Rays emanating from the focus f are reflected at the parabola into lines parallel to its axis (Figure 7.30).

Note that any two parabolas are similar to each other and that two parabolas with the same parameter p are congruent. In the example "parabola and spatial cubic" at the beginning of this chapter, we introduced a very simple parameterization $\mathbf{c}(t) = (t,t^2)$ of a parabola with $p = 1/2$. A parameterization of the parabola $x^2 - 2py = 0$ is obviously given by $\mathbf{c}(t) = (t,t^2/(2p))$.

Fig. 7.30
A parabola and its special reflection property.

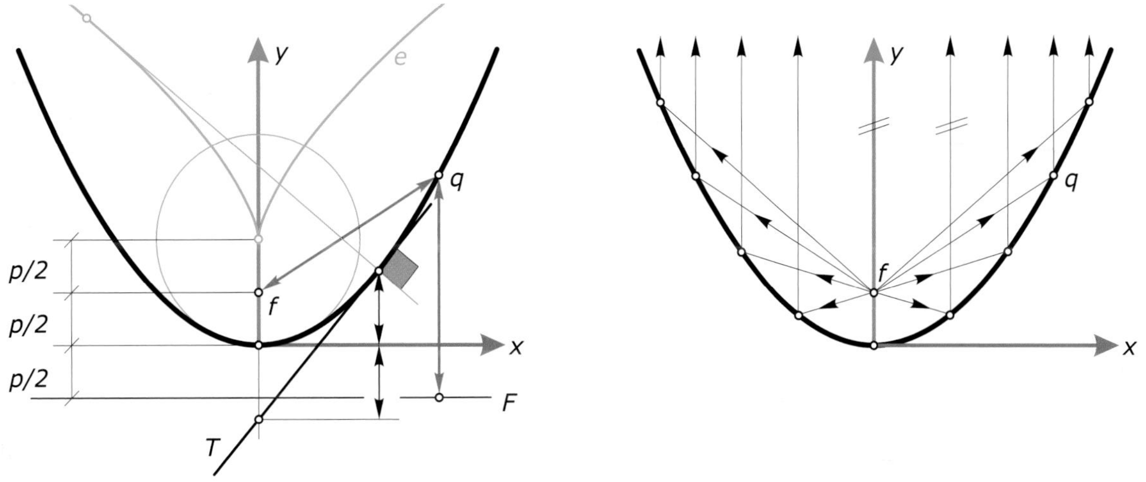

The thread construction of a parabola. Given two contact elements [i.e., points with tangents (b_0, T_0) and (b_2, T_2), as in Figure 7.31], we are looking for a parabolic arc that starts in b_0 with tangent T_0 and ends in b_2 with tangent T_2. By connecting corresponding points on both tangents, we obtain tangents of the parabolic arc we are seeking. How is this correspondence to be defined? Let b_1 be the intersection point of the two tangents T_0 and T_2.

We use linear interpolation to compute points p and q that divide the two line segments $[b_0,b_1]$ and $[b_1,b_2]$ in the same ratio $t : (1 - t)$ (see Figure 7.31). Then the points p and q are corresponding and the line $[p,q]$ is a tangent of the parabola. Moreover, computing the point r that divides $[p,q]$ in the same ratio $t : (1 - t)$, we even find the contact point! By changing the value of t, we generate all points and tangents of the parabola.

Let's cast this construction in terms of the mathematical framework. Starting with the three points b_0, b_1, and b_2 and their coordinate vectors $\mathbf{b}_0$, $\mathbf{b}_1$, and $\mathbf{b}_2$, we first calculate the point $p = \mathbf{p}(t) = (1 - t)\cdot\mathbf{b}_0 + t\cdot\mathbf{b}_1$ and $q = \mathbf{q}(t) = (1 - t)\cdot\mathbf{b}_1 + t\cdot\mathbf{b}_2$ on the line segments $[b_0,b_1]$ and $[b_1,b_2]$. Then the point r at the line segment $[p,q]$ is obtained as $\mathbf{r}(t) = (1 - t)\cdot\mathbf{p}(t) + t\cdot\mathbf{q}(t)$. Now we plug in the previous expressions for $\mathbf{p}(t)$ and $\mathbf{q}(t)$ and obtain $\mathbf{r}(t) = (1 - t)\cdot[(1 - t)\cdot\mathbf{b}_0 + t\cdot\mathbf{b}_1] + t\cdot[(1 - t)\cdot\mathbf{b}_1 + t\cdot\mathbf{b}_2]$. This can be further simplified to the quadratic parametric representation of a parabolic arc

$$\mathbf{r}(t) = (1 - t)^2\cdot\mathbf{b}_0 + 2\cdot t\cdot(1 - t)\cdot\mathbf{b}_1 + t^2\cdot\mathbf{b}_2.$$

By varying the parameter t in the interval $[0,1]$, we compute all points of the parabolic arc. To prove that pq is the tangent at r, we differentiate $\mathbf{r}(t)$ with respect to t and obtain $\mathbf{r}'(t) = 2\cdot[-(1 - t)\mathbf{b}_0 + (1 - 2t)\mathbf{b}_1 + t\mathbf{b}_2] = 2\cdot[(1 - t)(\mathbf{b}_1 - \mathbf{b}_0) + t(\mathbf{b}_2 - \mathbf{b}_1)] = 2\cdot[\mathbf{q}(t) - \mathbf{p}(t)]$. This shows that $\mathbf{q}(t) - \mathbf{p}(t)$ is a direction vector of the tangent and thus the connection of p and q is the tangent at r.

The thread construction of the parabola is a special case of de Casteljau's algorithm for Bezier curves. These are the simplest and most basic freeform curves and are discussed in the next chapter.

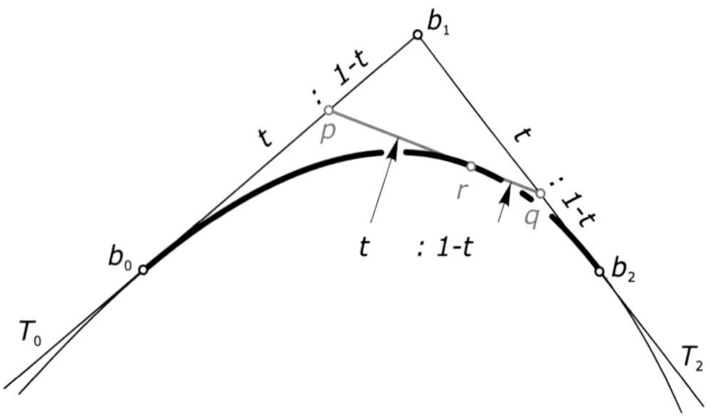

Fig. 7.31
The thread construction of a parabola uses repeated linear interpolation (see Geometry Primer) to generate points and tangents of the parabola defined by two contact elements (b_0, T_0) and (b_2, T_2).

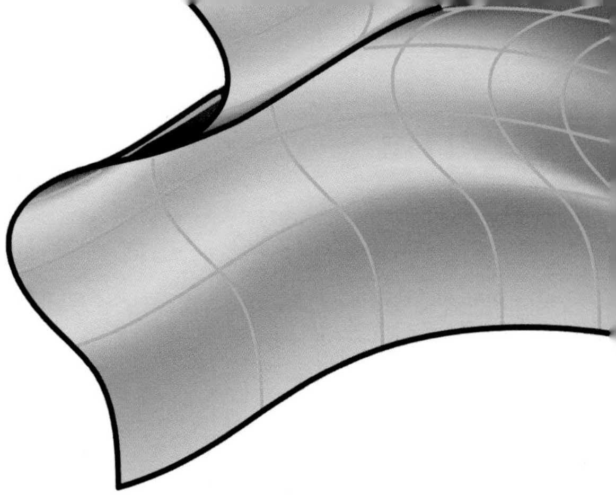

Surfaces

We now generalize the concepts for curves to the study of surfaces. Whereas we have previously viewed curves as a one-dimensional series of points, we now consider surfaces as a type of two-dimensional skin in space. However, this rough representation of surfaces is too inaccurate for studying them in detail. Thus, analogous to the curves we introduce parametric, explicit, and implicit representations of surfaces for mathematically handling surfaces and studying their geometry analytically.

Parametric representation. In contrast with curves, the coordinates of a surface point depend on two different parameters u and v. Thus, a *parametric surface* S can be represented by $\mathbf{p}(u,v) = (x(u,v), y(u,v), z(u,v))$, where the parameters u and v assume all values in a two-dimensional region R (Figure 7.32). Instead of mapping a one-dimensional interval I into space (curve case), we now have a continuous mapping of a two-dimensional region R into space.

Fig. 7.32
The parametric representation describes a mapping from a region R of the (u,v)-parameter plane to a surface patch S in three-dimensional space.

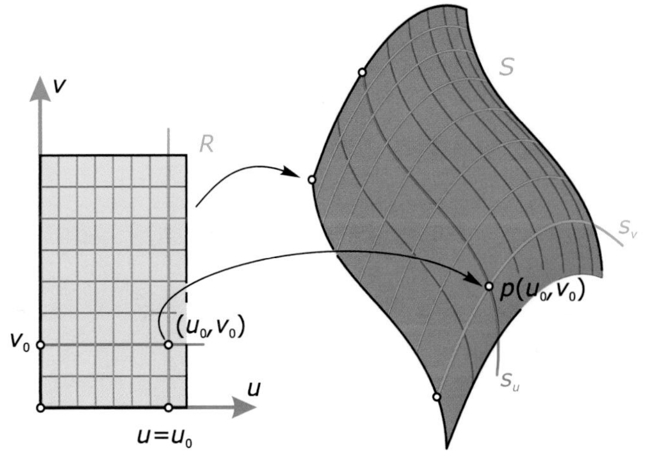

Every pair of parameters u and v that defines a point (u,v) in the region R is mapped to a surface point $p(u,v)$. Analogously with curves, we call the functions $x(u,v)$, $y(u,v)$, and $z(u,v)$ *coordinate functions* and $\mathbf{p}(u,v)$ a *parameterization* of S. When we fix the parameter $u = u_0$, we obtain a *parameter curve* or *v-line* s_v on the surface. The name v-line expresses that v varies (i.e., v is the curve parameter).

On the other hand, a *u-parameter curve* or *u-line* s_u is generated on the surface S when we fix the parameter v. The sketching of parameter lines is often useful in visualizing the spatial structure of a surface. Thus, they can be used as an architectural tool. Figure 7.33 illustrates the benefits of parameter lines.

Fig. 7.33
Parameter lines support the spatial impression of surfaces.
(a) The same surface with and without parameter lines.
(b) The usage of parameter lines in architecture is illustrated by means of the fan vault of the *King's College Chapel* (1446–1515) in Cambridge.

(a)

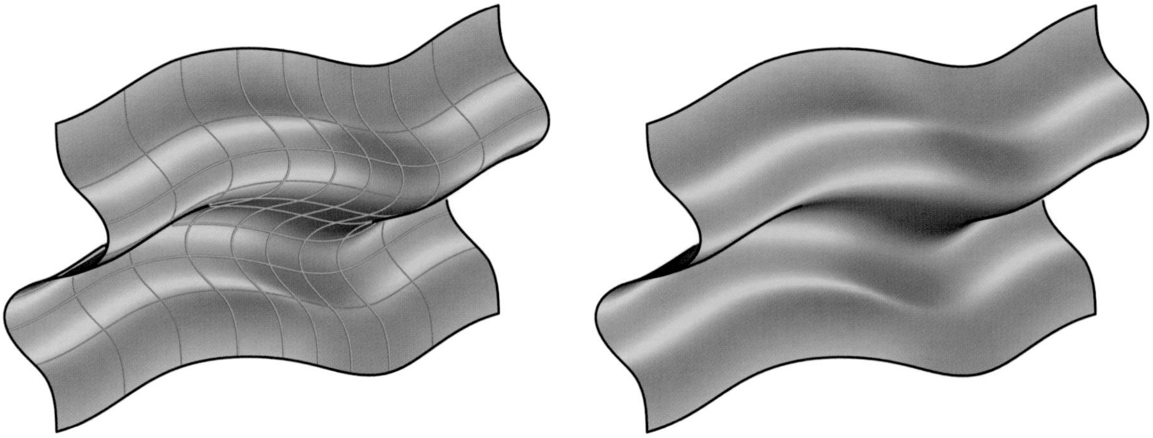

(b)

Example:
Parametric representation of a sphere.
Given are the center $m(0,0,0)$ and the radius r of a sphere. According to Figure 7.34, we derive the coordinates of a sphere point p as
$\mathbf{p}(u,v) = (r \cdot \cos(u) \cdot \cos(v), r \cdot \cos(u) \cdot \sin(v), r \cdot \sin(u))$.

If the parameters u and v assume all values in $[-\pi/2, \pi/2]$ and $(-\pi, \pi]$ respectively, we obtain the entire sphere. Then the v-parameter curves are circles (latitude u = const) in planes parallel to the xy-plane. The u-parameter curves are meridian circles (longitude v = const) running through the north and south poles.

(b)

(a)

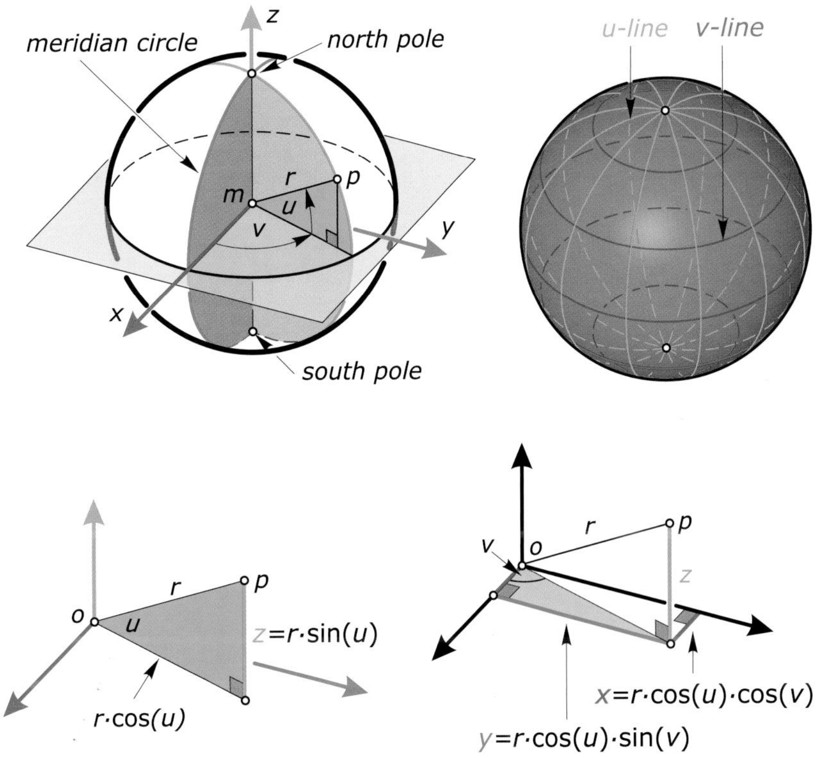

Fig. 7.34
(a) A parametric representation of a sphere can be based on spherical coordinates; namely, the geographic latitude *u* and longitude *v*. The meridian circles run through the north and south poles of the sphere.
(b) The *Rolling Ball* (1992) in Seyring by Richard Künz (image courtesy of E. Mrazek).

Example:

Cylinder. A surface with a parameterization of the form $\mathbf{p}(u,v) = (x(u), y(u), v)$ is a general cylinder, where $c = \mathbf{c}(u) = (x(u), y(u), 0)$ is its base curve in the xy-plane. All u-lines are congruent to c and lie in planes parallel to the xy-plane.

The rulings of the cylinder are the v-lines. They are parallel to the z-axis. Figure 7.35 shows two examples, with $\mathbf{c}(u) = (2{\cdot}\sin(u), 3{\cdot}\cos(u))$—respectively $\mathbf{d}(u) = (2{\cdot}\cos(u) + 2{\cdot}\cos(2{\cdot}u), 2{\cdot}\sin(u) + 2{\cdot}\sin(2{\cdot}u))$—as u-curves in the xy-plane.

Example:

Tangent surface. If $\mathbf{c}(t)$ denotes a parametric representation of a spatial curve c, we have shown that the curve tangent at point $\mathbf{c}(t)$ is described by $\mathbf{c}(t) + u{\cdot}\mathbf{c}'(t)$. If we consider t varying, we obtain the set of all tangents of c. This so-called tangent surface (Figure 7.36) has the parametric representation $\mathbf{p}(u,t) = \mathbf{c}(t) + u{\cdot}\mathbf{c}'(t)$. The u-lines (t = const) are the tangents. Tangent surfaces have important geometric properties (discussed in Chapter 15, on developable surfaces).

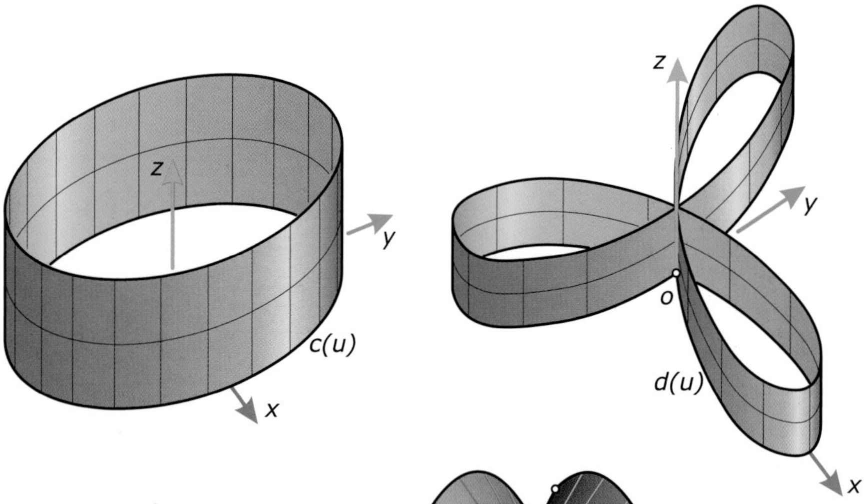

Fig. 7.35
Cylinders with planar u-lines.

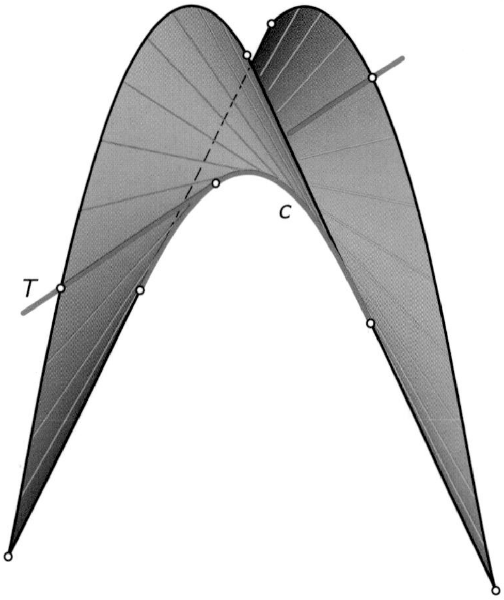

Fig. 7.36
A surface formed by the tangents of a spatial curve.

Explicit and implicit representation. A surface S can also be seen as a set of all points that satisfy a condition of the form $z = f(x,y)$ or $F(x,y,z) = 0$. We call the surface description $z = f(x,y)$ an *explicit representation* and $F(x,y,z) = 0$ an *implicit representation*. The explicit representation $z = f(x,y)$ is mainly used for visualization of a function $f(x,y)$ of two variables. We also call this surface the *graph* of the function $f(x,y)$. Of course, the explicit representation is a special case of an implicit representation.

As an example, we illustrate in Figure 7.37 a hyperbolic paraboloid (see Chapter 9) with the explicit representation $z(x,y) = 2x^2 - 3y^2$ and the "chair" surface with the implicit representation $(x^2 + y^2 + z^2 - ak^2)^2 - b[(z - k)^2 - 2x^2]\cdot[(z + k)^2 - 2y^2] = 0$, where $k = 5$, $a = 0.95$, and $b = 0.8$.

Tangent plane and surface normal. When we replace the parameters u and v in the parametric representation of a surface respectively with arbitrary functions $u(t)$ and $v(t)$, we obtain a curve $\mathbf{c}(t) = (x(t), y(t), z(t))$ on the surface S. Curves on S are also called *surface curves*. We could also say that the surface parameterization maps the curve $(u(t),v(t))$ in the parameter plane to a surface curve. The tangent t_c of such a curve in a point p is called a *surface tangent*.

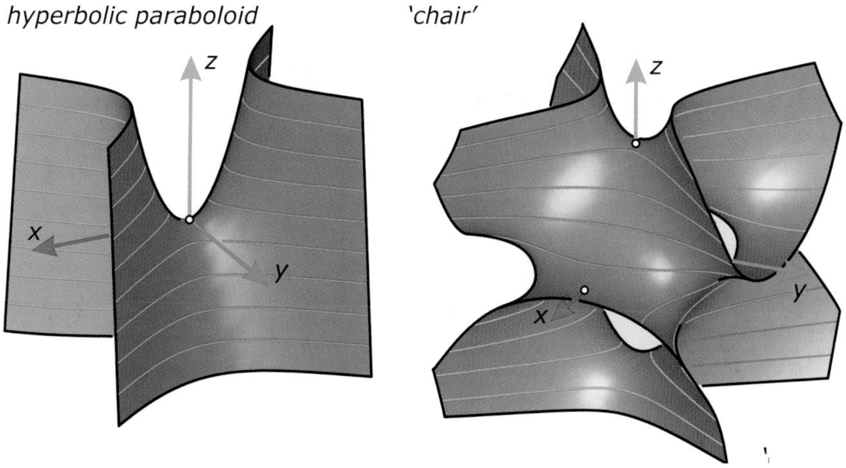

Fig. 7.37
A hyperbolic paraboloid and a "chair" surface serve respectively as examples of surfaces in explicit and implicit representation.

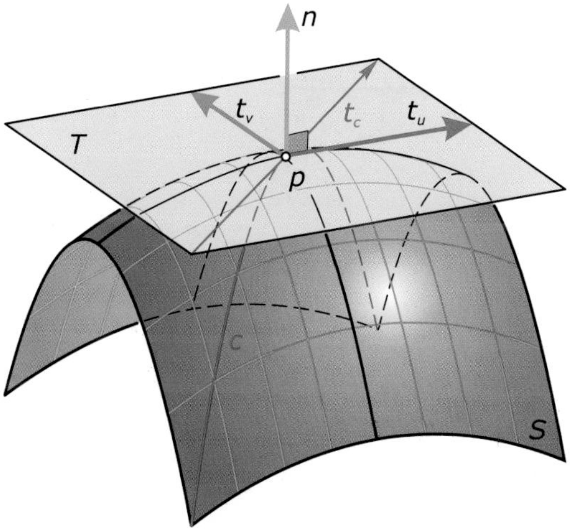

Fig. 7.38
In a regular point p, the tangents of the parameter lines span the tangent plane. Any surface curve passing through p has a tangent in p, which lies in the tangent plane.

In a regular point of the surface, all surface tangents lie in a plane—the *tangent plane* of the surface S in the point p. In this case, the tangents t_u and t_v of the parameter lines define the tangent plane (Figure 7.38). For the reader familiar with basic analysis, we note that the partial derivative vectors of $\mathbf{p}(u,v)$ with respect to u and v are respectively the directions vectors of t_u and t_v. The *surface normal n* is the straight line through p orthogonal to the tangent plane.

Points of a surface, like the apex of a cone, where no unique tangent plane exists are called *singular points*.

Example:

Whitney umbrella. The surface with the parameterization $\mathbf{p}(u,v) = (u, v^2, uv)$ is illustrated in Figure 7.39. Along the y-axis, this surface has a line of self-intersection. At any point on the positive y-axis, we have two different tangent planes. Thus, all points belonging to the surface curve $\mathbf{c}(v) = (0,v^2,0)$ with constant parameter $u = 0$ are singular points. All other points turn out to be regular ones.

Example:

Surface with many singularities. Figure 7.40 shows a remarkable surface with an implicit representation $F(x,y,z) = 0$, where F is a certain polynomial of degree 7. This surface, known as *Labs septic*, carries 99 singular points.

Whitney umbrella

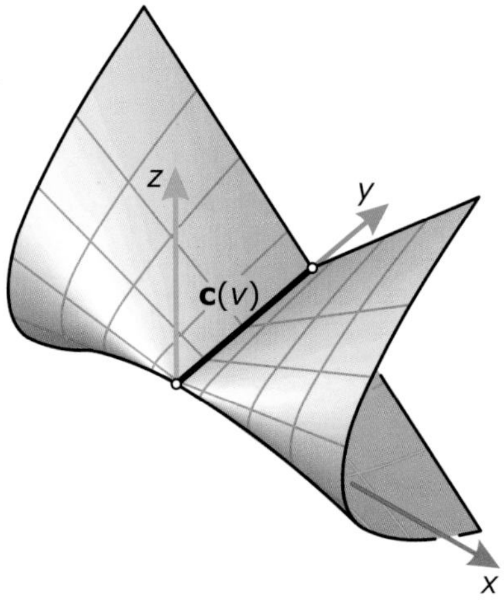

Fig. 7.39
Whitney's umbrella carries a line with singular points.

Fig. 7.40
View of the inner part of the *Labs septic* (image courtesy of Oliver Labs).

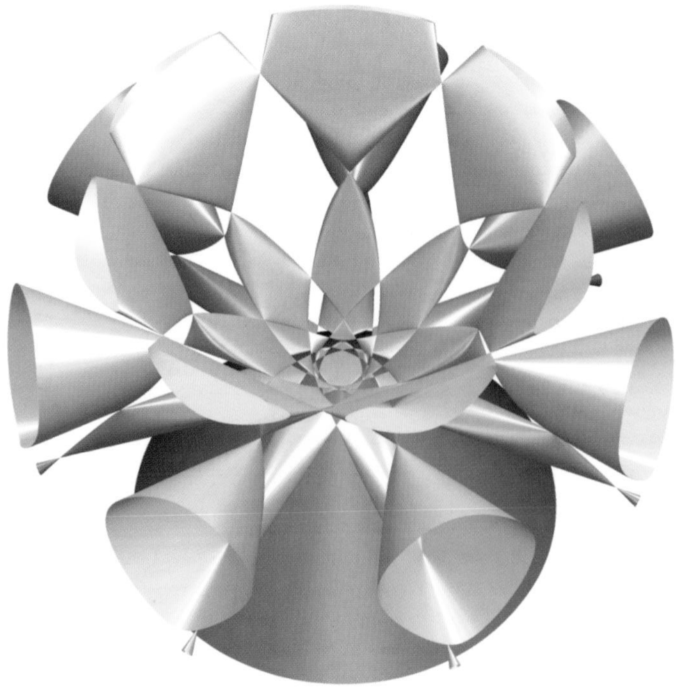

Note that even in the proximity of a surface point the tangent plane can contain more surface points than the touching point p. Figure 7.41 illustrates three different types of the behavior of a tangent plane at a point. According to this, we distinguish among *elliptic*, *hyperbolic*, and *parabolic surface points*. We will study these point types in detail in Chapter 14 (on visualization and analysis of shapes).

Contour and apparent contour. When we sketch a surface S or a CAD program produces an image of it, we need the *contour* of the surface to distinguish between visible and occluded parts of the surface. To obtain the contour, we first define the *contour generator* c^g as a set of all points p on S whose tangent plane T contains the projection ray through p (Figure 7.42).

In the case of a central projection, this implies that T passes through the eye point e. In the case of a parallel projection, T is parallel to the projection rays. In an equivalent formulation, we can say that all projection rays tangent to S form a cone (in the case of a central projection) or a cylinder (in the case of a parallel projection). The contact curve between cone (or cylinder) and S is the contour generator.

The projection of the contour generator c^g is the *apparent contour* c^a. The projection of a point p of c^g yields a point p' of the apparent contour c^a. Because p is on c^g, the image of its tangent plane T is a straight line T'. This line T' is the tangent of the apparent contour c^a in p' (Figure 7.42).

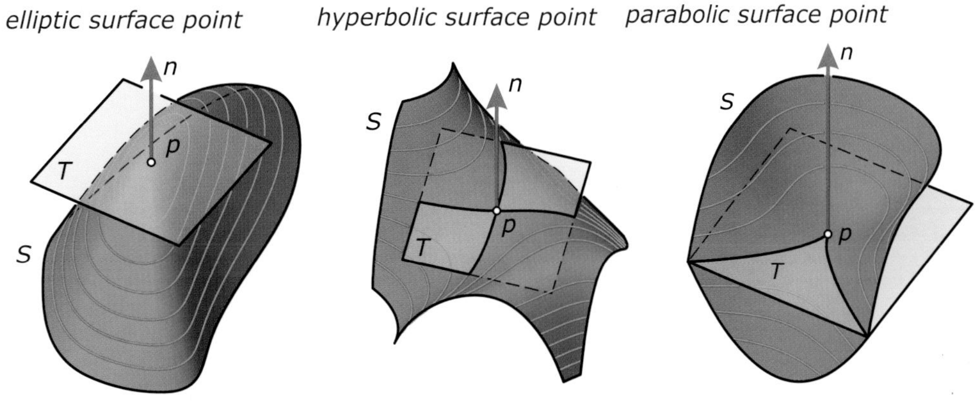

Fig. 7.41
Elliptic, hyperbolic, and parabolic points and the behavior of the tangent plane in these points.

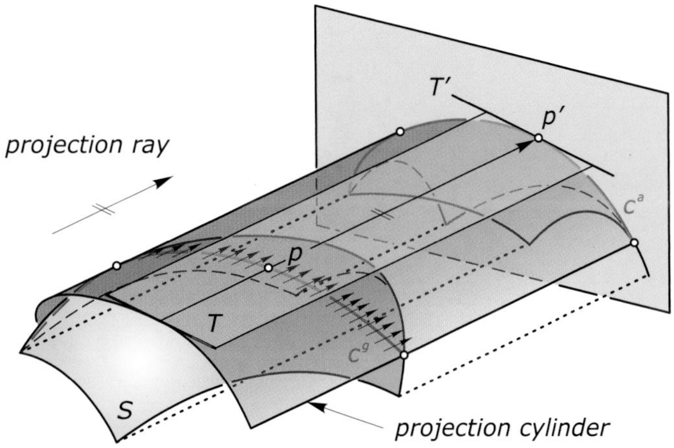

Fig. 7.42
The apparent contour is the projection of the contour generator. The latter is the set of all surface points p where a projection ray touches S.

Figure 7.43 illustrates an interesting property in connection with contours and surface curves. If the curve tangent t_c of a surface curve c is not a projection ray, the image t_c' touches the apparent contour in the point p' (Figure 7.43a). Otherwise, if the tangent t_d of a surface curve d is a projection ray the image d' of the curve d possesses a cusp in the point p' (Figure 7.43b). Because contour generators are already defined via projection rays tangent to the surface, the special event that a projection ray touches the contour generator is not as unlikely. Hence, we quite often find cusps in apparent contours. There, the visibility of the contour may switch (Figure 7.43c).

Fig. 7.43
The behavior of the projections of surface curves.
(a) In general, the projected curve c′ touches the apparent contour c^a.
(b) If a projection ray is tangent to a curve d, the projected curve d′ exhibits a cusp.
(c) Cusps in apparent contours arise from projection rays which are tangent to the contour generator.

(a)

(b)

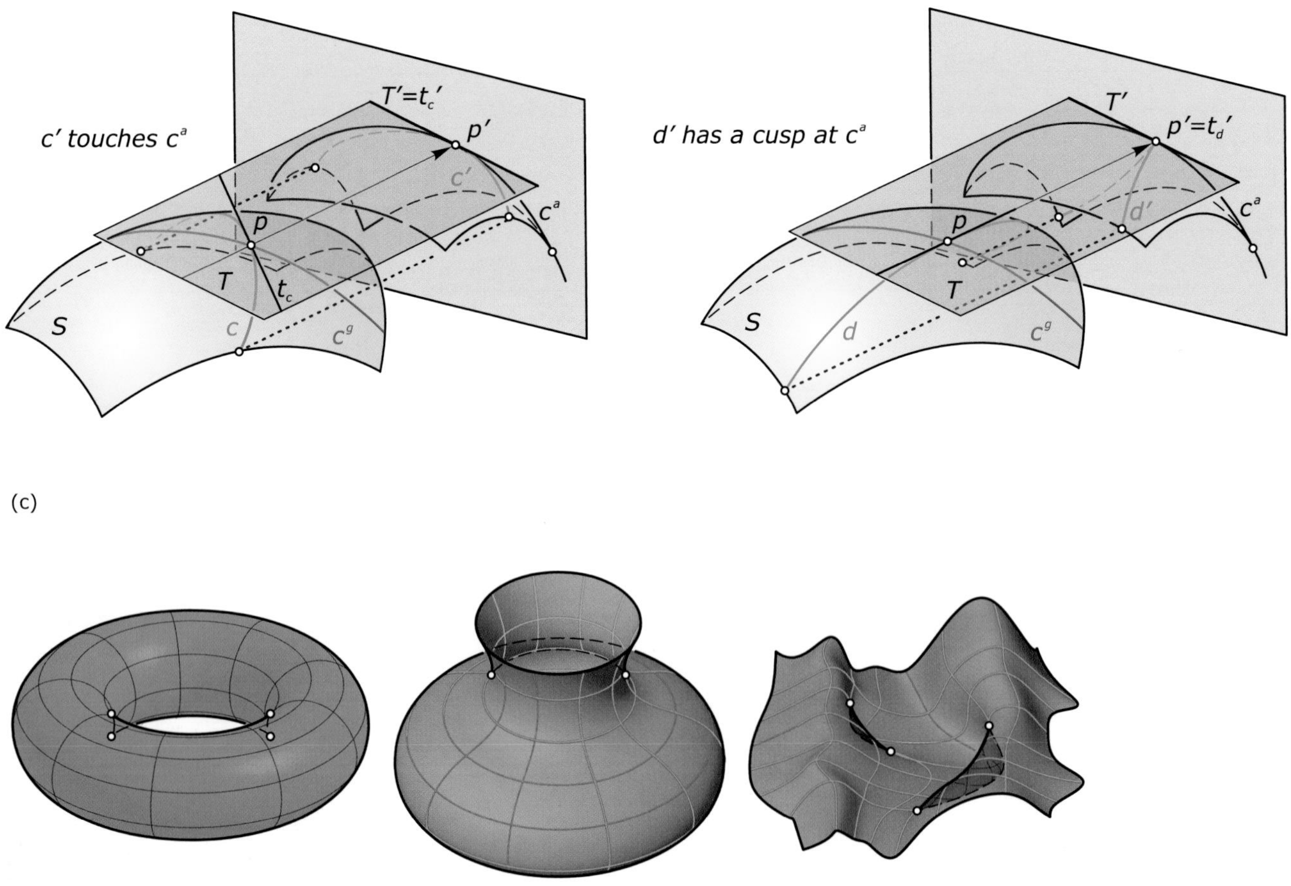

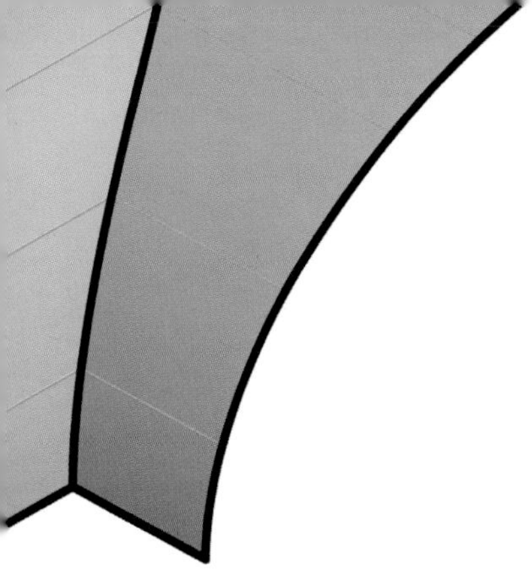

Intersection Curves of Surfaces

In Chapter 4 (on trimming and splitting) we studied intersection curves of two surfaces. We used appropriate CAD tools to generate the intersection curves without any understanding of the process of how to find these curves. With a better understanding of curves and surfaces, in the following we discuss some geometric background of intersection curves. This material shows why a stable implementation of surface/surface intersection is a challenge in the development of any CAD program, and it makes us less critical if this tool sometimes fails. Moreover, it provides some hints for correctly sketching intersection curves by hand.

Constructing points via auxiliary planes. To find points of the intersection curve(s) of two surfaces, we may use a set of auxiliary planes. These auxiliary planes intersect the original surfaces along surface curves c_1 and c_2. The common points of these planar curves are points of the intersection curve c. If we find appropriate auxiliary planes that intersect both surfaces along simple curves c_1 and c_2, we are able to construct points of the intersection curve. Only for very special surfaces can we actually find such auxiliary planes.

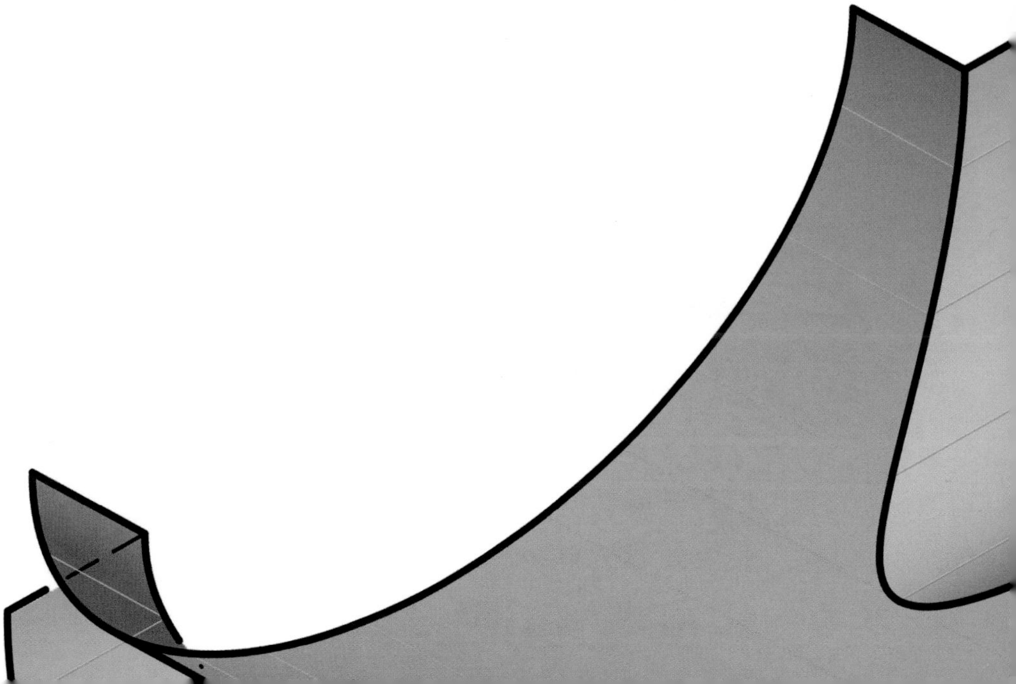

Figure 7.44a illustrates this method for surface/surface intersection in the case of two cylinders. In this case, planes parallel to the generators of both cylinders cut the cylinders along generators. Thus, points of the intersection curve can be found by intersecting straight lines.

The same method can be applied to the construction of the intersection curve of a sphere and a cone. As shown in Figure 7.44b, points of the intersection curve can be found as common points of a pair of straight lines and a circle. We use auxiliary planes through the apex of the cone. In general, these planes intersect the cone along a pair of rulings and the sphere along a circle. As we have seen in both examples, the method of auxiliary planes is an appropriate one when cylinders, cones, or spheres are involved.

Use of auxiliary spheres. Points of the intersection curve of a rotational cylinder and a rotational cone with intersecting axes can also be found with the help of auxiliary spheres. Spheres with center m in the intersection point of the two axes a and b intersect the cylinder and the cone along circles. Their common points belong to the intersection curve c (Figure 7.45).

This method is best used with rotational surfaces (see Chapter 9) with intersecting axes. In Figure 7.46b, we use a projection orthogonal to the plane spanned by the two rotational axes. Then, the images c_1' and c_2' of the circles c_1 and c_2 are straight line segments and the points of the intersection curve c' can be found as common points of c_1' and c_2'.

(a)

(b)

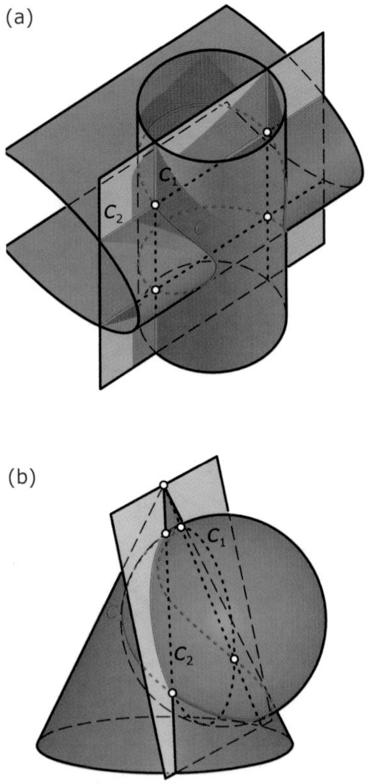

Fig. 7.44
Points of an intersection curve may be constructed with the help of appropriate auxiliary planes.

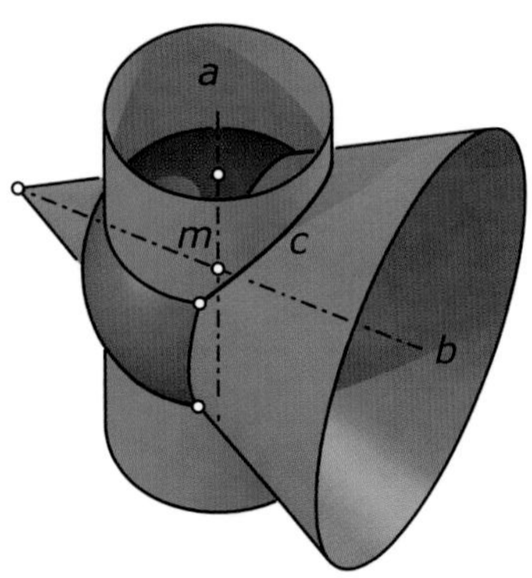

Fig. 7.45
Construction of points of an intersection curve using auxiliary spheres.

(a) (b)

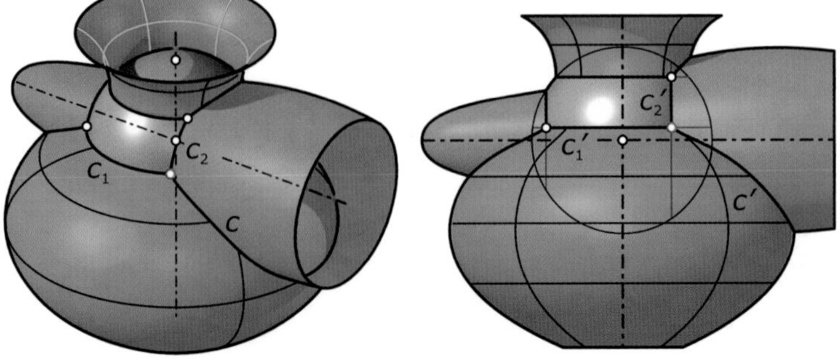

Fig. 7.46
The use of a special projection orthogonal to both axes simplifies the pointwise construction of the intersection curve of two rotational surfaces.

Tangents of intersection curves. When sketching an intersection curve by hand, it is often better to construct a few points plus their tangents instead of generating many points without tangents. The tangents of a surface curve are contained in the respective tangent planes (Figure 7.38). Thus, the tangent t_p in a point p of the intersection curve is the intersection line of the tangent planes T_1 and T_2 of the two surfaces in the point p (Figures 7.47 and 7.48).

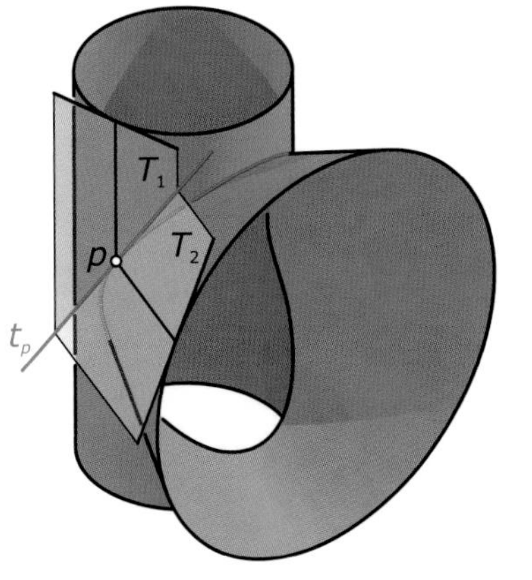

Fig. 7.47
The tangent of the intersection curve is contained in the tangent planes T_1 and T_2 of both surfaces.

Fig. 7.48
In architecture, vaults often feature interesting intersection curves (including parts of conic sections).
(a) Intersection curves in the *barrel vault of the Residenz* (1569–1571) in Munich.
(b) A cross vault in a building entrance (image courtesy of Martin Reis).
(c) Model of a vault.

(c)

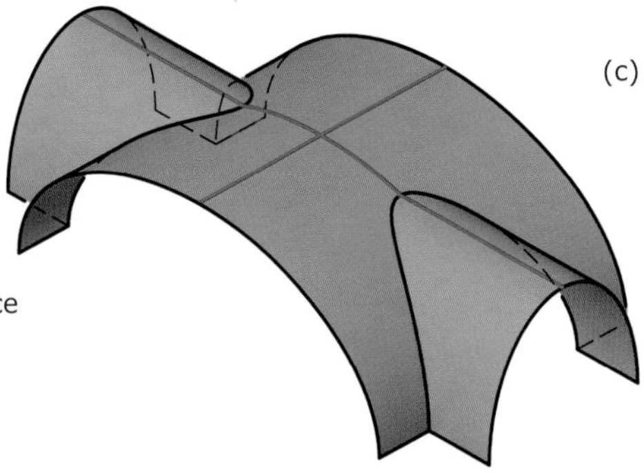

(a)

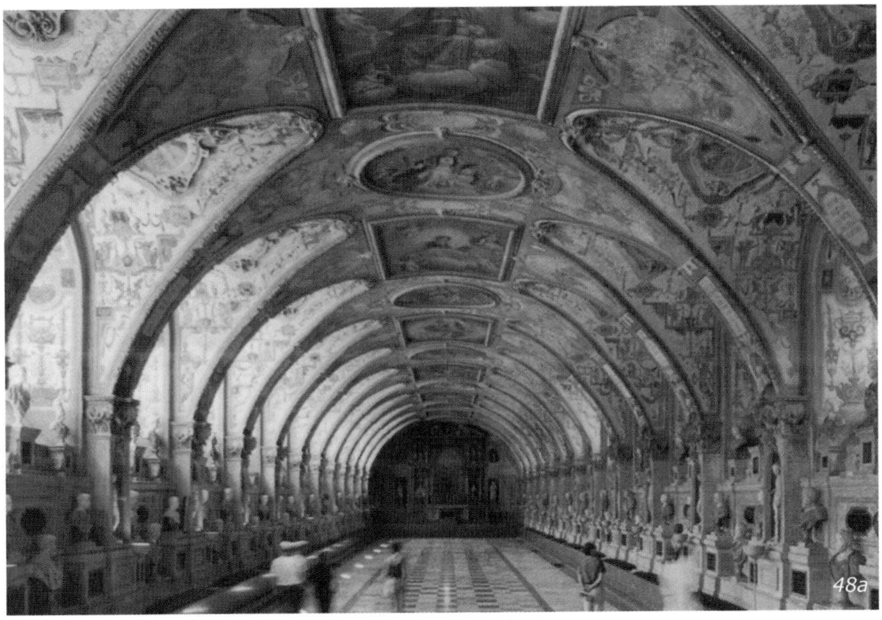

(b)

This construction fails if the given surfaces have the same tangent plane at p. Such points of tangency usually lead to double points of the intersection curve. Figure 7.49 shows an example: the common points of the two ellipses along which the two cylinders intersect are exactly their common points of tangency.

Conic sections as intersection curves. Conic sections as special intersection curves can be found in many applications in the building and constructing industry (Figure 7.48). This principle was extensively used to construct vaults. It can be generalized to the following statement.

If two rotational cylinders or cones possess a common inscribed sphere, their intersection curve decomposes into a pair of conic sections or into a conic section and a single ruling.

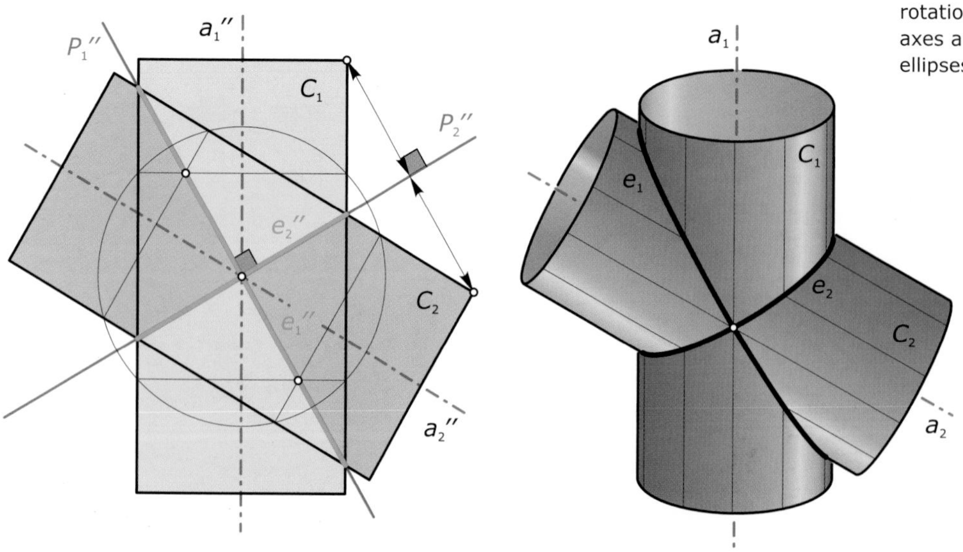

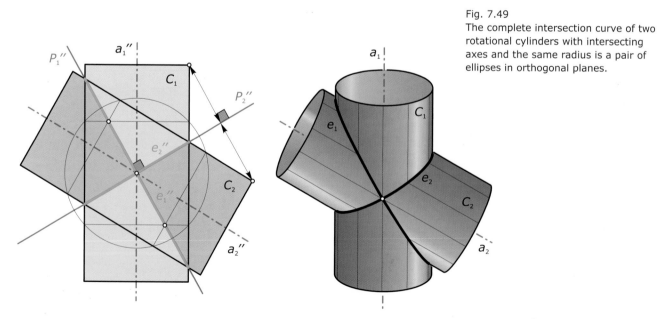

Fig. 7.49
The complete intersection curve of two rotational cylinders with intersecting axes and the same radius is a pair of ellipses in orthogonal planes.

Example:

Rotational cylinders with intersecting axes and equal radius. Given are two rotational cylinders C_1 and C_2 with intersecting axes and equal radius r. We assume the cylinder axes a_1 and a_2 to lie in the yz-plane (Figure 7.49). Using auxiliary spheres for the generation of points of the intersection curve, we recognize that the front view of the intersection curve consists of two straight line segments e_1'' and e_2''. These line segments are parts of the angle bisectors of a_1'' and a_2''. Thus, the intersection curve consists of two planar curves e_1 and e_2.

Due to the fact that planar intersection curves of rotational cylinders are ellipses, the complete intersection curve consists of two ellipses e_1 and e_2 in orthogonal planes P_1 and P_2. These planes are the bisecting planes of the axes a_1 and a_2. Reflecting one cylinder at such a bisecting plane, we obtain the other cylinder. Hence, the intersection curve between a bisecting plane and a cylinder also belongs to the other cylinder and thus to the intersection curve. This argument may also help in understanding intersection curves in other symmetric surface/surface configurations.

Figure 7.50 illustrates planar intersection curves of two rotational cones. We will study an even more general application of this statement in Chapter 9 (on intersection curves of quadrics).

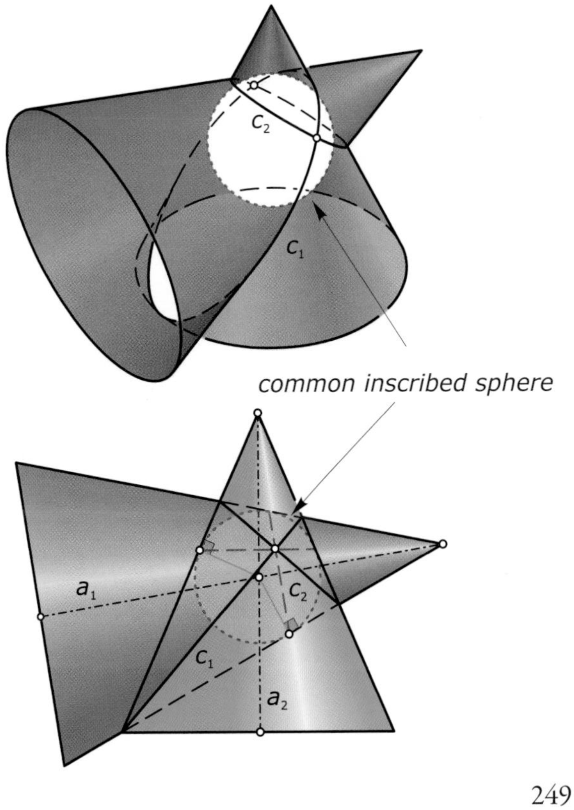

Fig. 7.50
The intersection curve of two rotational cones with a common inscribed sphere decomposes into conic sections.

Space curves as intersection curves of general cylinders. At the beginning of this chapter, we studied the parametric representation of spatial curves. For planar curves, we also introduced explicit and implicit representation. What about implicit representations of spatial curves?

As an example for an explicit representation of a planar curve, we used the parabola c: $y = x^2$—which we derived from the parametric representation $\mathbf{c}(t) = (t, t^2)$. In a similar way, the spatial polynomial cubic curve $\mathbf{d}(t) = (t, t^2, t^3)$ satisfies *two* independent equations $y = x^2$ and $z = x^3$.

These two equations define two cylinders C_1, C_2 with generators parallel to the z-axis and y-axis, respectively. Their base curves in the coordinate planes $z = 0$ and $y = 0$ are the parabola $y = x^2$ and the cubic $z = x^3$, respectively. Thus, the spatial polynomial cubic can be generated as an intersection curve of the two cylinders (Figure 7.51). This example shows that a space curve is defined by at least two implicit equations. However, due to additionally occurring intersection curves we may need even more equations to uniquely define the curve.

This is seen with the same example if we replace the equation $z = x^3$ with the equation $y^3 = z^2$. It is also satisfied by $= (t, t^2, t^3)$ and describes a cylinder C_3 with rulings parallel to the x-axis and a cubic base curve (with a cusp; Figure 7.52) in the yz-plane. Our spatial polynomial cubic is also an intersection curve of the parabolic cylinder C_1 and the cubic cylinder C_3. However, the complete intersection of these two cylinders consists of a second spatial cubic d—which arises from the first spatial cubic by reflection at the yz-plane.

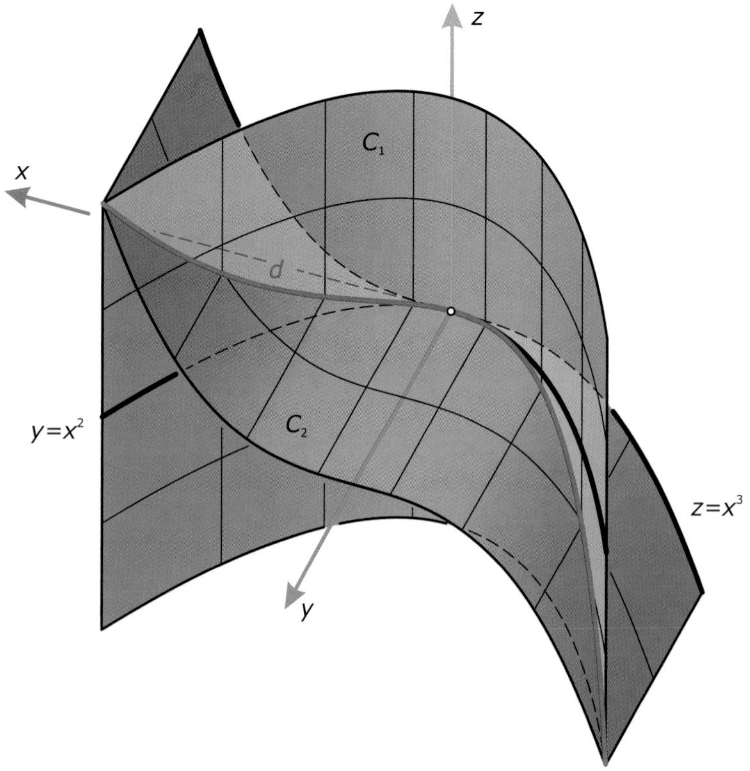

Fig. 7.51
A parametric cubic curve as an intersection curve of two cylinders.

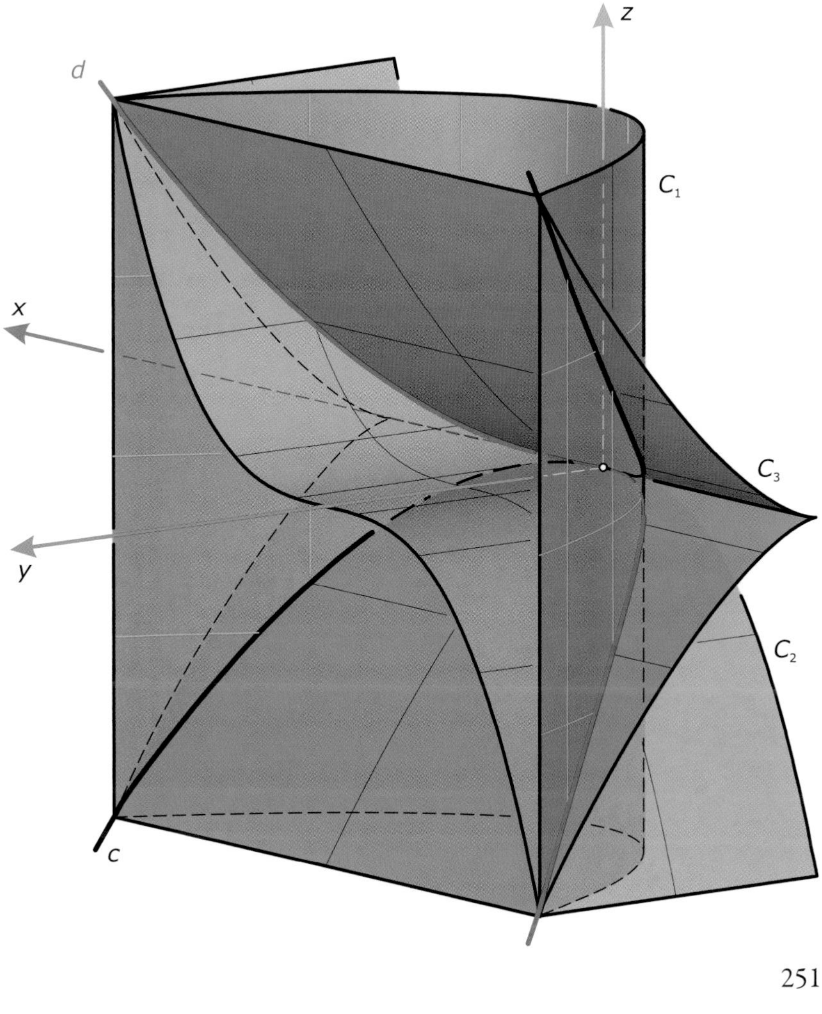

Fig. 7.52
The parametric cubic curve of Figure 7.51 as an intersection curve of a parabolic cylinder and another cubic cylinder. Here, the complete intersection contains a further spatial cubic.

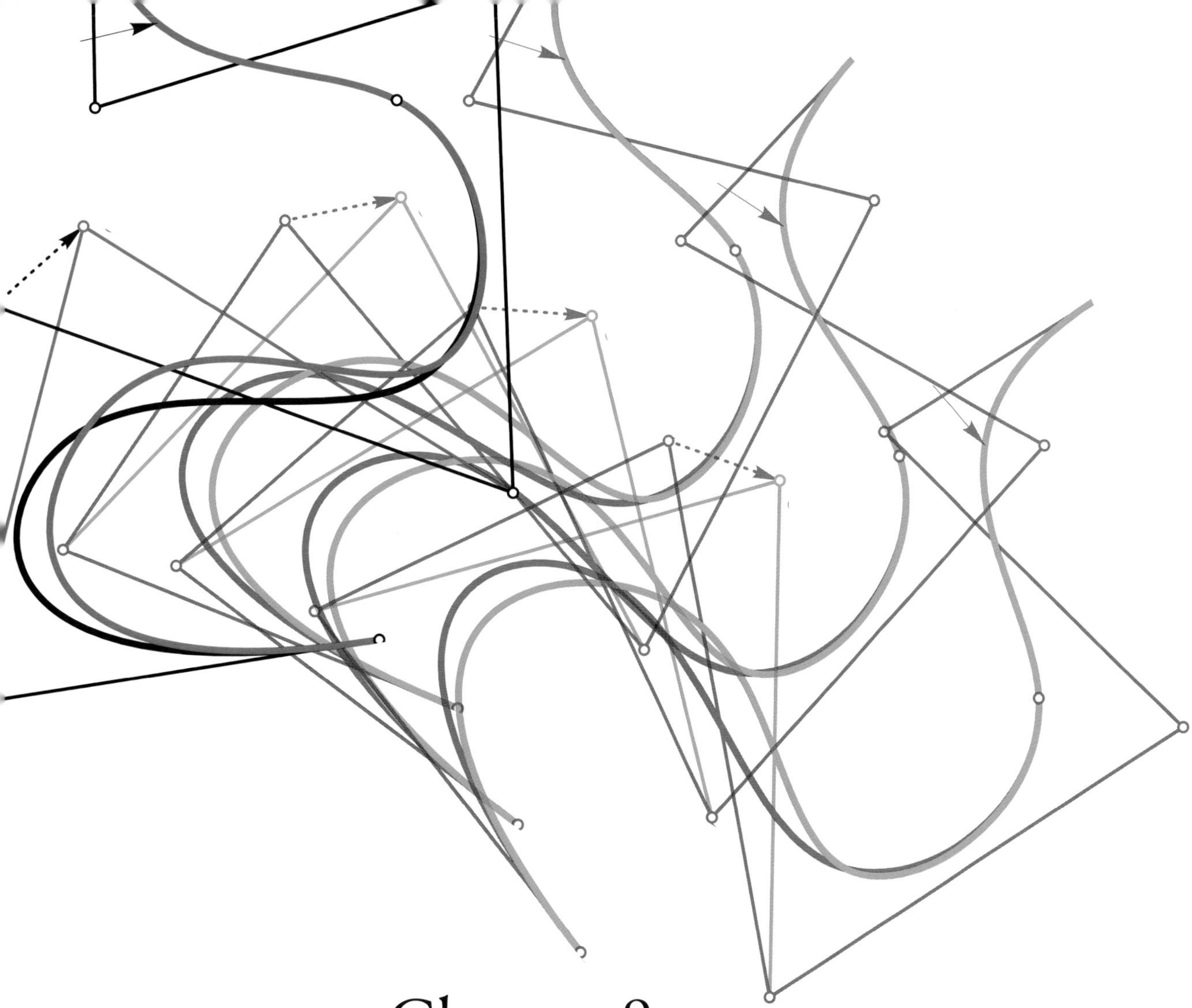

Chapter 8

Freeform Curves

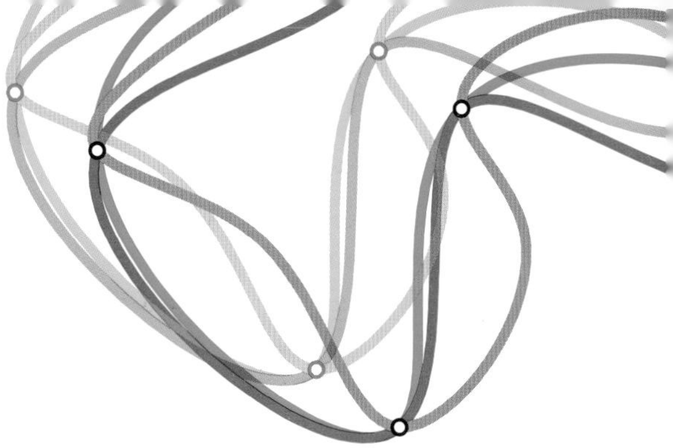

Freeform Curves

Whereas geometric constructions using parts of circles and conic sections have a long history in design, smooth freeform curves that we shape by a small number of control points are recent tools developed from the 1950s on. Basic knowledge of the generation and properties of freeform curves allows the designer to choose the best scheme for the task at hand and to employ it efficiently. Once we master curves, we are able to proceed to freeform surface modeling.

Bézier curves (Figure 8.1a) are among the most widely used freeform curves. We discuss their geometric construction and some of their properties based on the algorithm of de Casteljau. For the design of complex curves, we present the more powerful B-spline curves (Figure 8.1b)—which offer local shape control. B-spline curves can be generated by iteratively refining a given polygon—a process called *curve subdivision*. Nonuniform rational B-spline (NURBS) curves (Figure 8.1c) have further fine-tuning possibilities via weights associated with the control points. They are used to draw the most complex planar and spatial freeform curves, as well as to draw all types of conic sections.

Fig. 8.1
Freeform curves used in design:
(a) Bézier curve,
(b) B-spline curve, and
(c) NURBS curve to the same control polygon.

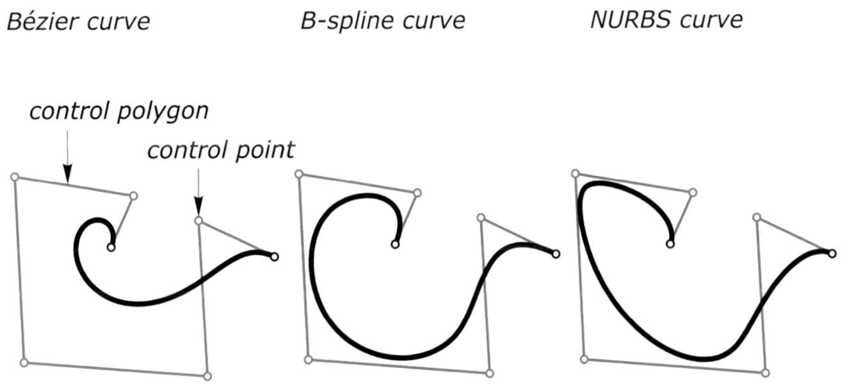

How do we design freeform curves? In freehand drawing, the quality of a curve depends on the skill of the human drawer and possibly on mechanical aids used to guide the hand. We take a pen or pencil and sketch a curve by leading the hand in a smooth way across the paper. For drawing long curves, we have to keep the entire arm moving. However, this makes it more difficult to draw wide-stretching curves. Thus, long before computers were invented designers used mechanical aids to guide their hands. Such aids were called *splines*, which were usually thin bendable rods made out of wood or metal whose shape is controlled via a few points where the rod is fixed (Figure 8.2a).

Freeform curves available in computer-aided design (CAD) software imitate this approach: Bézier, B-spline, and NURBS curves are defined using a small number of *control points* connected to a *control polygon* (Figure 8.2b). From the control points, a smooth curve is derived automatically by a geometric algorithm. The term *control polygon* indicates that we use it to control the shape of the curve. By modifying the control polygon, we change the associated curve (Figure 8.2b).

Note that it is faster to input a few control points and then let an algorithm compute a smooth curve than to draw hundreds or thousands of points by hand. Furthermore, if we later want to change the shape of the curve it is much easier to modify the position of a few control points than to manually reposition hundreds of curve points. There are two slightly different approaches to interactive curve design with control points.

- *Interpolation:* We define ordered points (and possibly tangent directions) and ask for a smooth curve that passes exactly through these points.
- *Approximation:* We define the rough curve shape with a control polygon and ask for a smooth curve that resembles that shape.

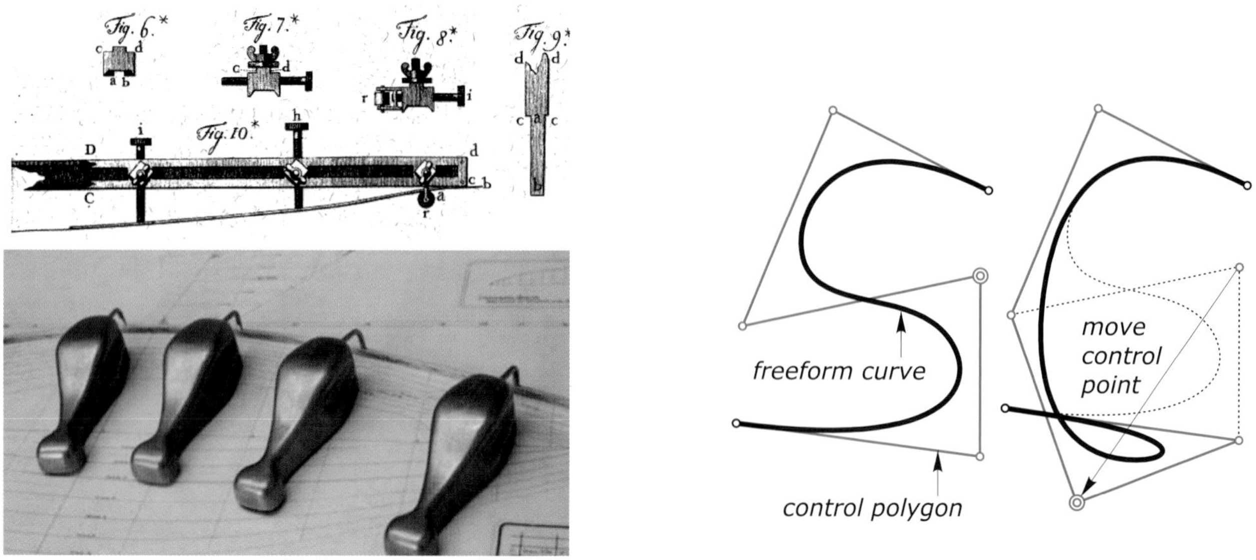

Fig. 8.2
Spline tools used by designers.
(a) Traditional (manual), wherein the weights are used to control the shape of the spline.
(b) Modern (digital), wherein the shape of a freeform curve is controlled using a small number of control points.

Interpolation. The designer defines a few points and an algorithm automatically finds a curve that passes exactly through these points (i.e., it interpolates them). Because there are infinitely many different interpolating curves (Figure 8.3) that pass through the same points, we have to provide additional input. To tell the computer what type of shape we desire, we also specify the curve tangents in the interpolation points. The curve shown in Figure 8.4a has been defined by five interpolation points and five additional points that give the tangent directions (in total, accomplished with 10 mouse clicks). Usually, the order in which these points are chosen is as follows: curve point, direction point, curve point, direction point, and so forth. Note that there are still many possibilities for defining an interpolating curve in this way.

Approximation. Here the designer defines a coarse "angled" control polygon and an algorithm computes a smooth freeform curve that resembles the shape of the control polygon. In Figure 8.4b we show a curve that approximates a control polygon with 10 control points. Note that the first and last control points are interpolated by the curve.

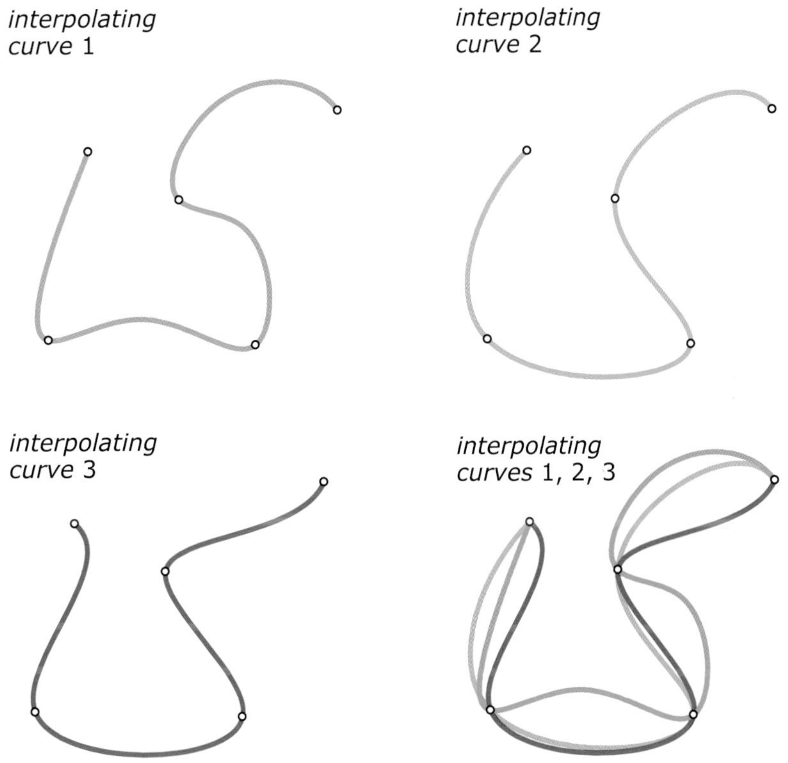

Fig. 8.3
Different freeform curves that interpolate the same five points.

With interpolation and approximation, it is possible to generate similar (or even equal) shapes. Depending on the goal, one or the other approach is favored. Note that simply recording the position of a moving input device (e.g., the mouse) is not recommended for drawing a freeform curve. In Figure 8.4c we show such a "recording" result as a sequence of connected data points. Even if the shape of the curve is similar to the previous two results, the curve is clearly not as smooth.

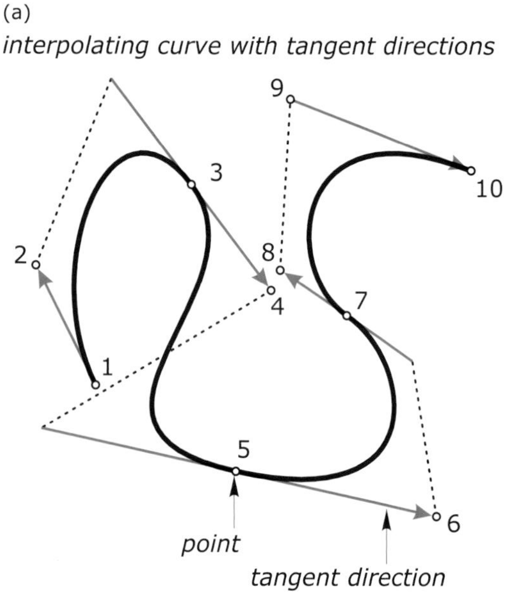

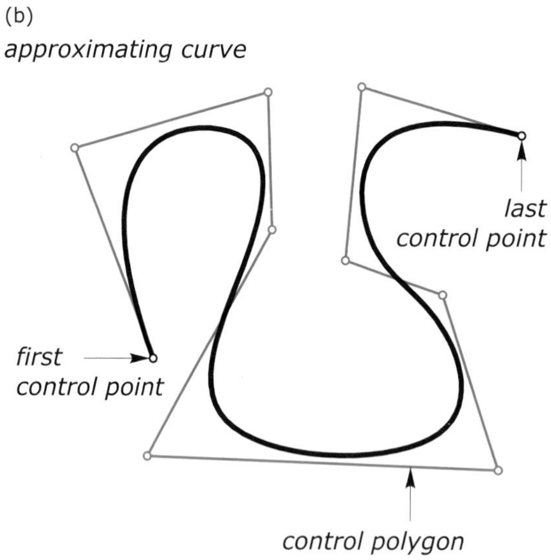

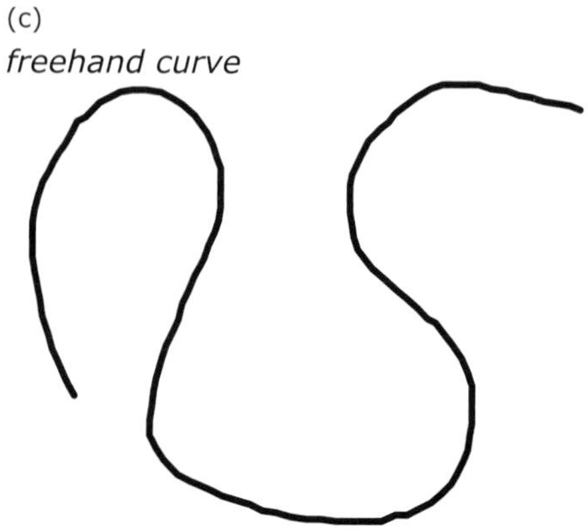

Fig. 8.4
Comparing freeform curves of the same shape designed in three different ways.
(a) The first curve is designed by selecting five points and five tangent directions that are interpolated by the curve.
(b) The second curve approximates a control polygon with 10 control points and renders a similar shape.
(c) The third curve results from recording the position of the computer mouse while we move it. The curve is not smooth and the result is unsatisfactory.

Bézier Curves

As previously stated, Bézier curves are among the most widely used freeform curves They possess an intuitive geometric construction via the *de Casteljau algorithm*, which is based on repeated *linear interpolation*. Linear interpolation is explained in the Geometry Primer. It is the fundamental idea for understanding the generation of the freeform curves discussed in this book. Bézier curves are completely defined by control polygons. In Figure 8.5 we illustrate three different Bézier curves together with their control polygons. In the course of this section, we label control points with the letter b in honor of Pierre Bézier (the inventor of Bézier curves).

History:

Invention of Bézier curves. In the 1950s, the need for more complex curves than parabolas (or the other conic sections circle, ellipse, and hyperbola) arose in the design departments of automotive and airplane industries. In 1959, the Frenchman Paul de Casteljau (working for Citroën) generalized the *thread construction of the parabola* to an algorithm that is today known as the *de Casteljau algorithm*. The idea is the following. Instead of three control points b_0, b_1, and b_2 (as in the case of a parabola), we start with n control points $b_0, b_1, ..., b_n$. Then we run the geometric construction that performs repeated linear interpolation until we end up with a single curve point. By varying the parameter t, we obtain the entire *Bézier curve*, named after their co-creator Pierre Bézier—who invented these curves in 1962 at Renault. He was allowed to publish this "top secret" result earlier than Paul de Casteljau—the reason these curves are today known as *Bézier curves*.

Fig. 8.5
Three different Bézier curves with four, five, and six control points labelled b_0, b_1, b_2, b_3, and so forth.

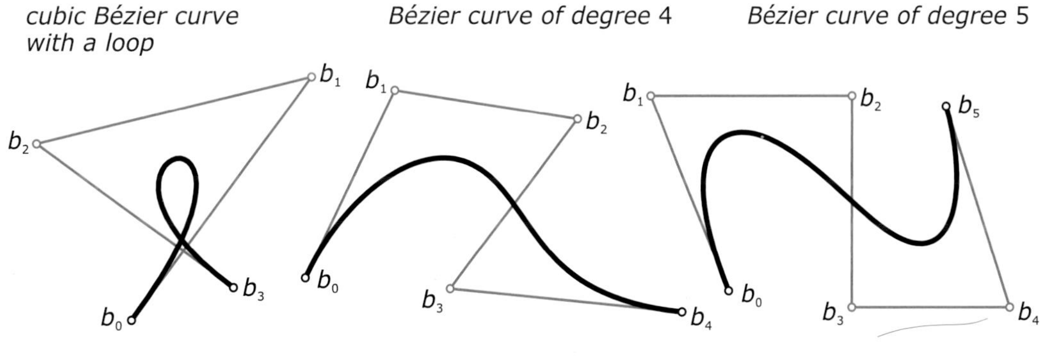

Algorithm of de Casteljau. We illustrate the algorithm of de Casteljau (Figure 8.6) by means of a Bézier curve with four control points b_0, b_1, b_2, and b_3. These four control points can be contained in a plane or can live in 3D space. In the former case, we obtain a *planar* Bézier curve. In the latter case, we obtain a *spatial* Bézier curve. Let t be a parameter in the interval *[0,1]*.

Step 1. In the first step, we perform linear interpolation as follows for pairs of consecutive control points to obtain three new points.

$$b_0^1(t) = (1 - t)\cdot b_0 + t\cdot b_1$$

$$b_1^1(t) = (1 - t)\cdot b_1 + t\cdot b_2$$

$$b_2^1(t) = (1 - t)\cdot b_2 + t\cdot b_3$$

Step 2. We linearly interpolate pairs of consecutive new points (for the same parameter t) as follows to obtain two new points.

$$b_0^2(t) = (1 - t)\cdot b_0^1(t) + t\cdot b_1^1(t)$$

$$b_1^2(t) = (1 - t)\cdot b_1^1(t) + t\cdot b_2^1(t)$$

Step 3. The following final calculation of linear interpolation for the latest two points yields the curve point $b(t)$.

$$b(t) = (1 - t)\cdot b_0^2(t) + t\cdot b_1^2(t).$$

To obtain the complete Bézier curve, we repeat this construction for all t in the interval [0,1]. Because $b(0) = b_0$ and $b(1) = b_3$, a Bézier curve interpolates the first and last control point (Figure 8.6). We rewrite the equation of step 3 as follows such that it only contains the control points b_0, b_1, b_2, and b_3 (and the intermediate points of the construction disappear).

$$b(t) = (1 - t)^3\cdot b_0 + 3\cdot(1 - t)^2\cdot t\cdot b_1 + 3\cdot(1 - t)\cdot t^2\cdot b_2 + t^3\cdot b_3.$$

Note that the degree of the parameter t is at most 3, and thus we speak of a *cubic Bézier curve* or of a *Bézier curve of degree 3*. We see that repeated linear interpolation generates the following cascading scheme of points.

$$\begin{array}{llll} b_0 & & & \\ b_1 & b_0^1(t) & & \\ b_2 & b_1^1(t) & b_0^2(t) & \\ b_3 & b_2^1(t) & b_1^2(t) & b(t) \end{array}$$

Remark. To generate a point on a Bézier curve with n control points, we have to perform $n - 1$ steps of the de Casteljau algorithm.

Tangents of Bézier curves. The algorithm of de Casteljau also constructs the curve tangents (Figure 8.6). In fact, the curve tangent at the point $b(t)$ is given by the line $[b_0^2(t), b_1^2(t)]$. It is of special interest that for $t = 0$ we obtain the curve tangent $[b_0,b_1]$ at the first control point b_0, and similarly for $t = 1$ obtain the curve tangent $[b_2,b_3]$ at the last control point b_3. To convince yourself, just sketch the algorithm of de Casteljau for $t = 0$ and $t = 1$ to see that $[b_0^2(0), b_1^2(0)] = [b_0,b_1]$ and $[b_0^2(1), b_1^2(1)] = [b_2,b_3]$.

Math:

Calculation of the curve tangent. We prove the curve tangent property by a simple calculation. From calculus, we know that the tangent vector of a curve is given by the first derivative vector (Chapter 7). Thus, we compute the first derivative vector of the curve

$$b(t) = (1-t)^3 \cdot b_0 + 3\cdot(1-t)^2 \cdot t \cdot b_1 + 3\cdot(1-t)\cdot t^2 \cdot b_2 + t^3 \cdot b_3$$

as
$$\mathbf{b}(t)' = 3\cdot[-(1-t)^2 \cdot b_0 + (-2\cdot(1-t)\cdot t + (1-t^2))\cdot b_1 + (-t^2 + 2\cdot(1-t)\cdot t)\cdot b_2 + t^2 \cdot b_3].$$

We also compute the vector

$$b_1^2(\mathrm{t}) - b_0^2(\mathrm{t}) = \ldots = 1/3 \cdot \mathbf{b}(t)'.$$

Thus, the line $[b_0^2(t),b_1^2(t)]$ is indeed the curve tangent at the point $b(t)$.

Fig. 8.6
Algorithm of de Casteljau illustrated by means of a planar cubic Bézier curve.

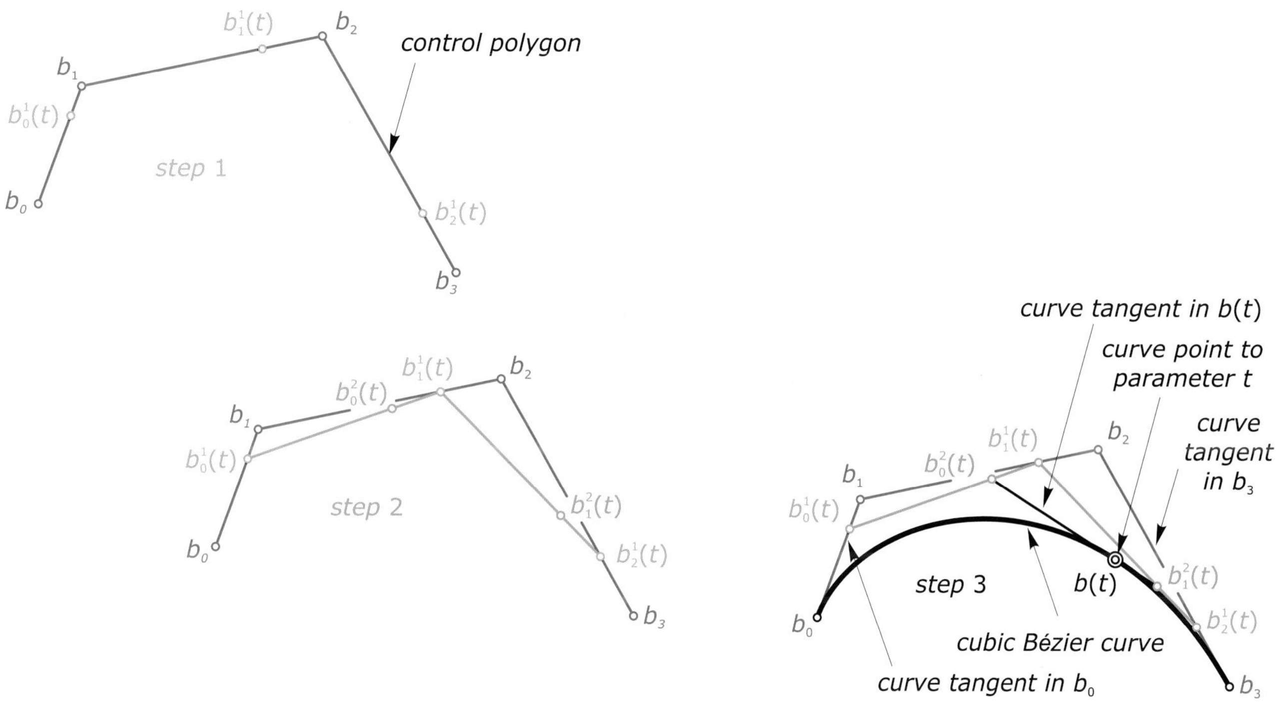

The meaning of the four control points. For a cubic Bézier curve, the meaning of the four control points is straightforward (Figure 8.7). The first and the last control points b_0 and b_3 are simply the two endpoints of the curve. The middle two control points b_1 and b_2 "control" the tangents at the endpoints. Furthermore, for a spatial cubic Bézier curve the first three control points b_0, b_1, and b_2 span the *osculating plane* (see Chapter 7) in the first control point b_0. The last three control points b_1, b_2, and b_3 span the osculating plane in the last control point b_3.

Subdivision of Bézier curves. The algorithm of de Casteljau also "subdivides" a Bézier curve into two Bézier curves with control polygons $c_0, \ldots, c_n$ and $d_0, \ldots, d_n$ (Figure 8.8a). If we repeat the algorithm for the new control polygons and iterate the procedure, we obtain a refined polygon that represents a good approximation of the Bézier curve (Figure 8.8b). This process is also known as *corner cutting*. Corner cutting is one instance of the important idea of generating a smooth shape by refinement of a coarse one. In this chapter we explore the curve subdivision algorithms of Chaikin and Lane-Riesenfeld, and in Chapter 11 we encounter the surface subdivision algorithms of Doo-Sabin, Catmull-Clark and Loop.

Loops and cusps. With cubic Bézier curves, we inherently have the flexibility necessary to design curves that have a single loop or a single cusp. A *loop* is easily achieved by roughly positioning the control points as shown in Figure 8.5 (left). A *cusp* is a curve point where the curve tangent is not well defined (i.e., the first derivative vector vanishes). For a cubic Bézier curve, we know that the first derivative vector $\mathbf{b}(t)'$ at a curve point $b(t)$ vanishes exactly if the vector $b_1^2(t) - b_0^2(t) = 0$ [i.e., if the points $b_1^2(t)$ and $b_0^2(t)$ coincide].

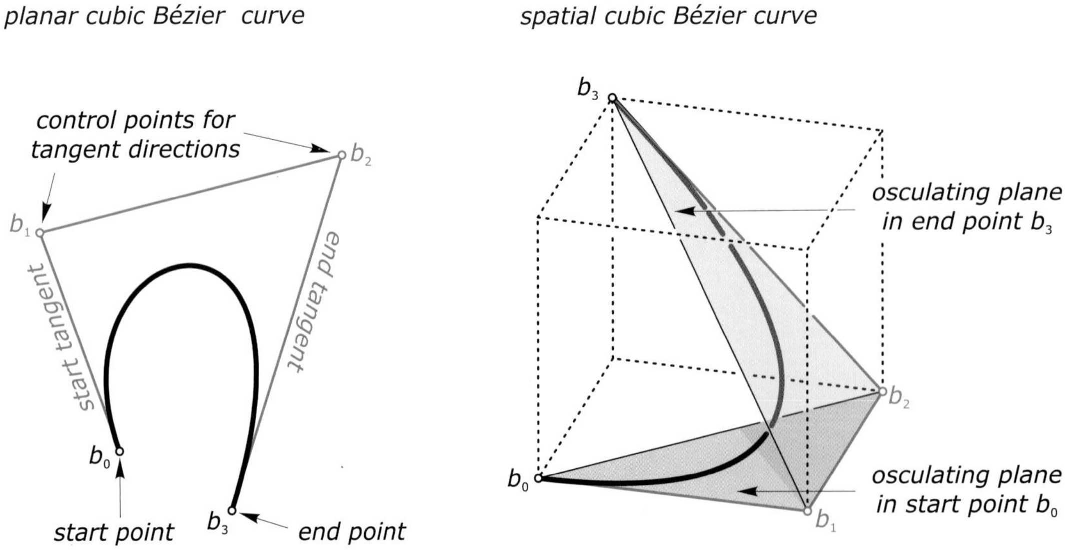

Fig. 8.7
The meaning of the four control points for a cubic Bézier curve. The first and the last control points are the endpoints of the curve. The middle two control points "control" the curve tangents in the endpoints. We also illustrate the osculating planes for a spatial cubic Bézier curve.

At first glance, it seems to be easy to design a cusp. However, if we zoom in we see that we really often have a narrow bump or a small loop and not a real cusp. A simple setup for designing a real cusp is to position the four control points as the corners of a rectangle (Figure 8.9). Then it is guaranteed that the curve point $b(1/2)$ is really a cusp. Bézier curves enjoy several useful properties, among which we discuss the convex *hull property* and the *affine invariance*. In Chapter 3 we learned about the concept of a convex domain. The convex hull is a special convex domain (explained in material following).

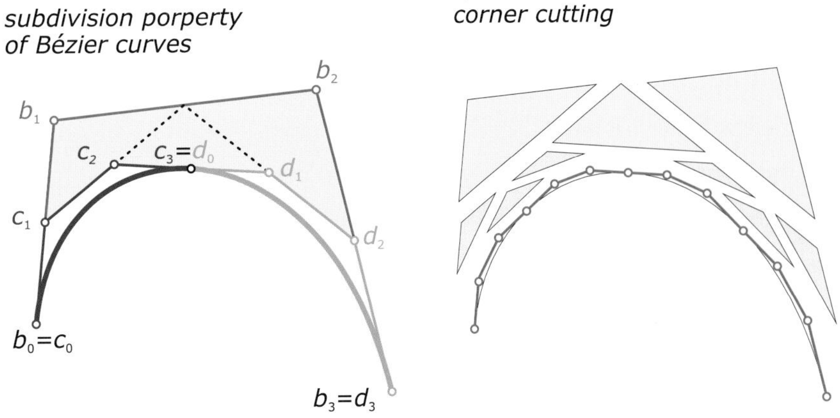

Fig. 8.8
(a) The algorithm of de Casteljau subdivides a cubic Bézier curve with control polygon b_0, ..., b_3 into two Bézier curves with control polygons c_0, c_1, c_2, and c_3 and d_0, d_1, d_2, and d_3, respectively.
(b) After two steps of corner cutting, the refined polygon approximates the Bézier curve fairly well.

Fig. 8.9
To design a planar cubic Bézier curve that contains a cusp is a bit tricky (see zooming in). However, if we select the four control points as corners of a rectangle the curve has a cusp at the curve point $b(1/2)$.

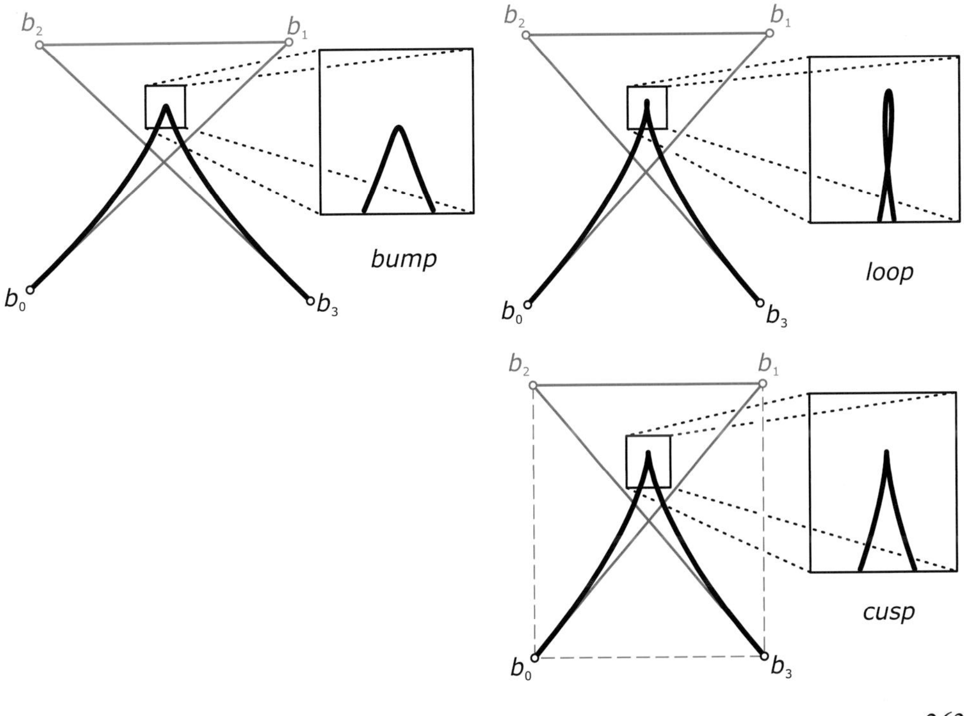

Convex hull property of Bézier curves. Bézier curves enjoy the property that the curve is always completely contained in the *convex hull of its control points* (Figure 8.11). This property follows immediately from the construction via the algorithm of de Casteljau (repeated linear interpolation with a parameter t in $[0,1]$ does not create points outside the convex hull of the control points). The fact that the control polygon defines the area in which the Bézier curve is lying is relevant to the design. A special case of the convex hull property is the so-called *linear precision* of Bézier curves. If the control points of a Bézier curve are contained in a single straight line, the Bézier curve is also contained in the same line.

Math:

Convex hull. The convex hull of a planar point set is obtained intuitively as follows. Think of the points as nails in a piece of wood. Then place a rubber band around all nails and let it loose. The shape of the tight-fitting rubber band shows the convex hull of the point set (Figure 8.10a). The convex hull of a planar point set is a convex polygon, and the convex hull of a spatial point set is a convex polyhedron (Figure 8.10b). It can be shown that the convex hull is the smallest convex domain that encloses a given point set.

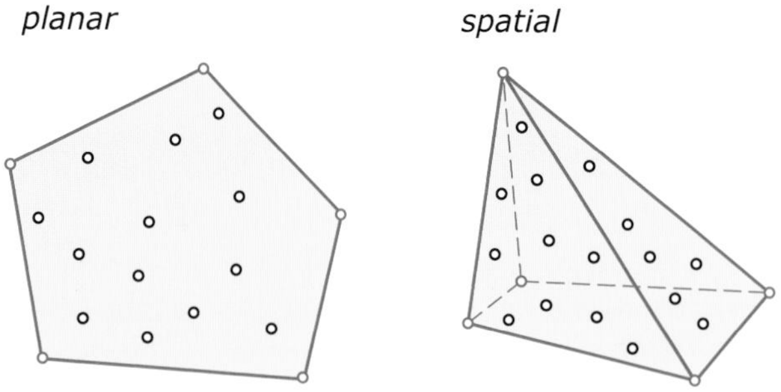

Fig. 8.10
Convex hulls of
(a) planar and
(b) spatial point sets.

Fig. 8.11
Bézier curves are contained in the convex hull of their control polygon. For a spatial curve, the convex hull is a convex polyhedron. One of the examples illustrates a special case, the linear precision: if the control points are collinear, the Bézier curve is also contained in that line.

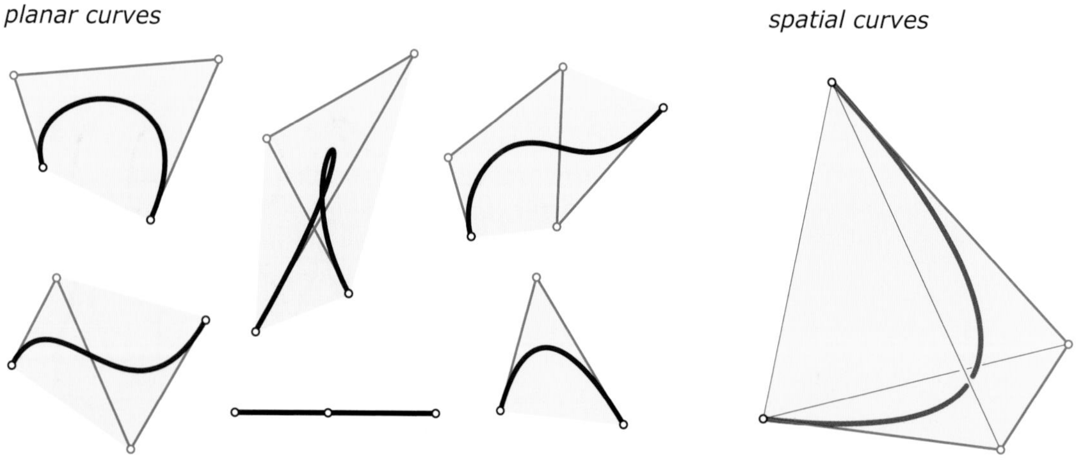

Parabolas are quadratic Bézier curves. Recall the thread construction of the parabola from Chapter 7. It is actually a special case of the algorithm of de Casteljau for three control points. Thus, parabolic arcs are quadratic Bézier curves. It is easy to create simple shapes bounded by quadratic Bézier curves (Figure 8.13a). Quadratic and cubic Bézier curves are commonly used to define TrueType and Postscript fonts (Figure 8.13b), and are standard tools in many software packages.

Math:

Affine invariance. A Bézier curve is affine invariant connected to its control polygon. Examples of affine maps include translations, rotations, similarities, and parallel projections (Chapter 6). Affine invariance of Bézier curves means that the affine image of the Bézier curve coincides with the Bézier curve computed to the affine image of the control polygon (Figure 8.12). Note that central projections are excluded from the set of allowed transformations because they are not affine.

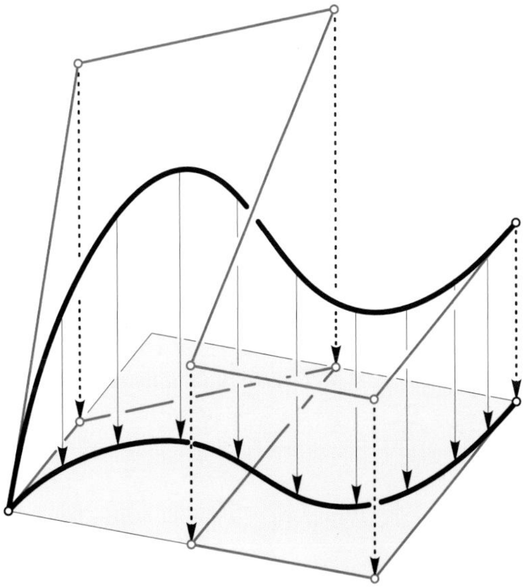

Fig. 8.12
A spatial Bézier curve and its planar parallel projection illustrate the affine invariance property between the curve and its control polygon.

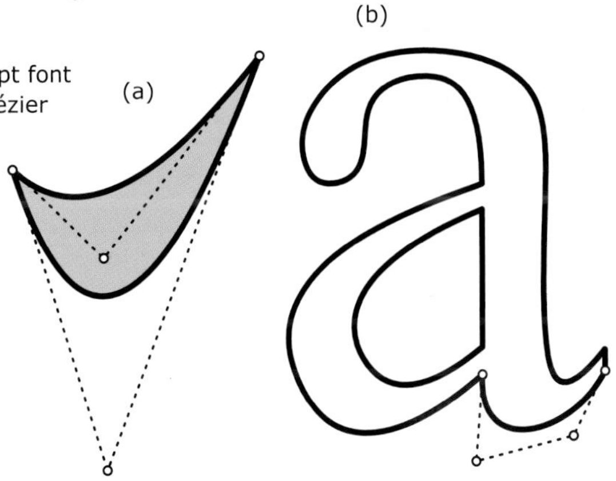

Fig. 8.13
(a) A simple shape bounded by two quadratic Bezier curves.

(b) The letter "a" of a Postscript font is bounded by several cubic Bézier curves.

Example:

Design a parabolic arc with given axis direction and vertex position. To take advantage of the static properties of a parabolic arc, it is important to know its axis and vertex position. In architectural design, we usually want parabolic arcs with vertical axis direction. If we select the three control points b_0, b_1, and b_2 such that they form an isosceles triangle with base b_0, b_2 , the axis of the parabolic arc is given by the line connecting b_1 and the midpoint m of b_0 and b_2 (Figure 8.14a). The vertex of a parabola is the unique parabola point on the axis. Because of the symmetric setup, we find the vertex (using de Casteljau's algorithm) as the curve point to the parameter $t = 1/2$. Note that by the subdivision property of the algorithm of de Casteljau we split (for $t = 1/2$) the larger arc into two parabolic arcs whose common point is the parabola vertex.

From the previous construction, we learn an easy way of designing a parabolic arc with given vertex v and axis A (Figure 8.14b). Select the vertex v as the first control point b_0. Draw a line T through the vertex v that is perpendicular to the axis A. Select an arbitrary point b_1 on T. Then, $T = [b_0, b_1]$ is the vertex tangent. Mirror the point b_0 in b_1 to obtain an auxiliary point p on T. Finally, select the third control point b_2 anywhere on the line through p that is parallel to the axis A. This gives us the parabolic arc with vertex v, axis A, and control polygon $b_0 = v$, b_1, b_2. By mirroring this arc in A, we obtain a symmetric parabolic arc with the same vertex v and the same axis A.

Fig. 8.14
(a) Parabolic arc with vertical axis A as a quadratic Bezier curve with control points b_0, b_1, and b_2. By the subdivision property, the arc is split into two parabolic arcs that meet at the vertex $v = b(1/2)$.
(b) Construction of a parabola with known vertex v and axis A.

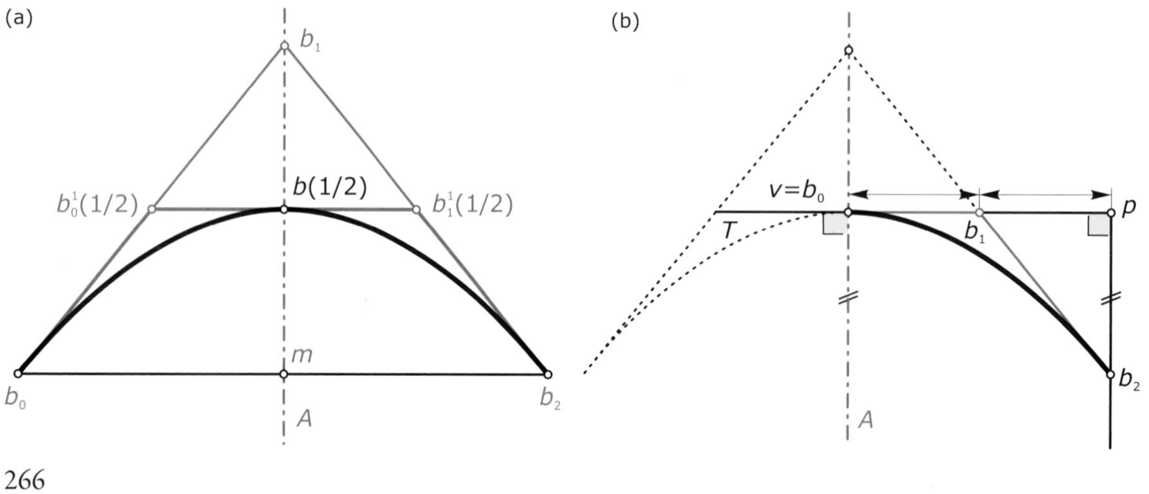

Limitations of Bézier curves. Bézier curves are completely determined by their control points. A Bézier curve with $n + 1$ control points is of degree n (the degree of the polynomials that appear in the mathematical description). This results in the following two major limitations of Bézier curves.

- A Bézier curve with a large number of control points becomes impractical for design. The degree of the curve increases and the curve shape resembles less and less the shape of the control polygon (Figure 8.15a).
- The control points have *global* control on the shape of the curve. This means that if we add a new control point or if we modify the position of one single control point the shape of the entire curve changes. This effect (Figure 8.15b) is unwanted for certain design purposes. If we are satisfied with the shape of the curve in one part, we do not want to change the entire shape by modifying a few control points in a different part of the curve.

Fig. 8.15
(a) A high-degree Bézier curve gets too far away from the control polygon.
(b) Modifying the position of a single control point of a Bézier curve changes the shape of the entire curve.

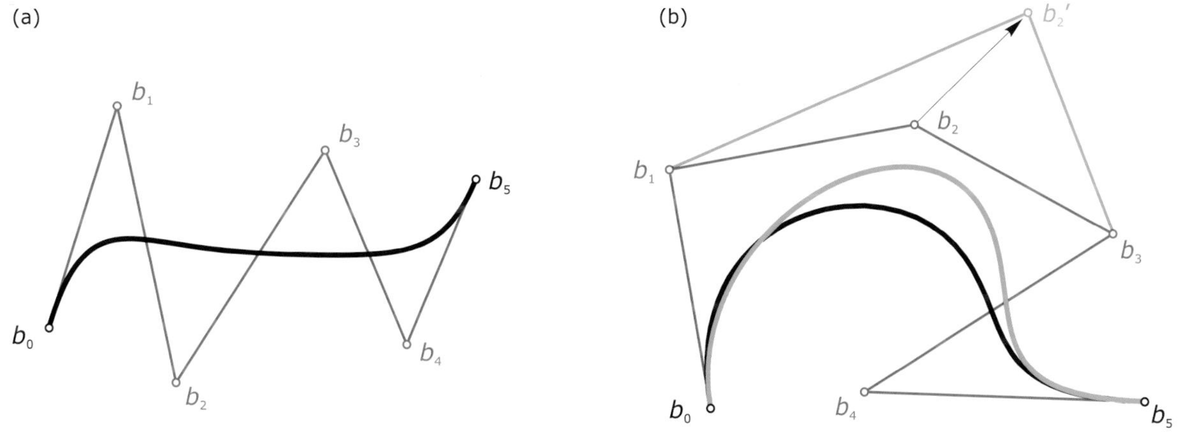

Example:

Piecewise Bézier curves. If we want to design longer freeform curves, we can put together several Bézier curves of low degree (2 or 3). At the connection points, we want the two joining curves to have the same *tangent* (the best we can achieve for quadratic Bézier curves) and the same *curvature* (if we use cubic or higher-degree Bézier curves). For a piecewise quadratic Bézier curve, we can select the first parabolic arc without constraints.

All remaining parabolic arcs have the constraint that we can only select one control point, because for tangent continuity the other two control points are determined by the previous arc (Figure 8.16a). For piecewise cubic Bézier curves, this becomes even more cumbersome. We can still put them together in such a way that each neighboring pair has the same tangent in their connection point (Figure 8.16b). However, how do we select the control points so that the pieces have the same curvature at the connection points? To overcome limitations of Bézier curves and piecewise Bézier curves, scientists invented B-spline curves (examined in the next section).

Fig. 8.16
Piecewise
(a) quadratic and
(b) cubic Bézier curves with continuous tangents. The quadratic and cubic segments are shown in different colors.

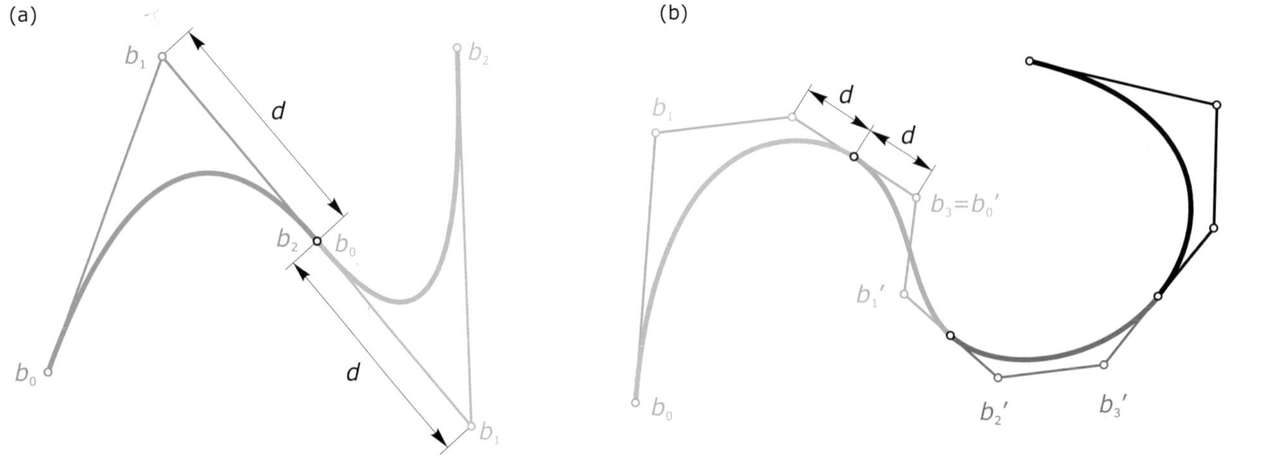

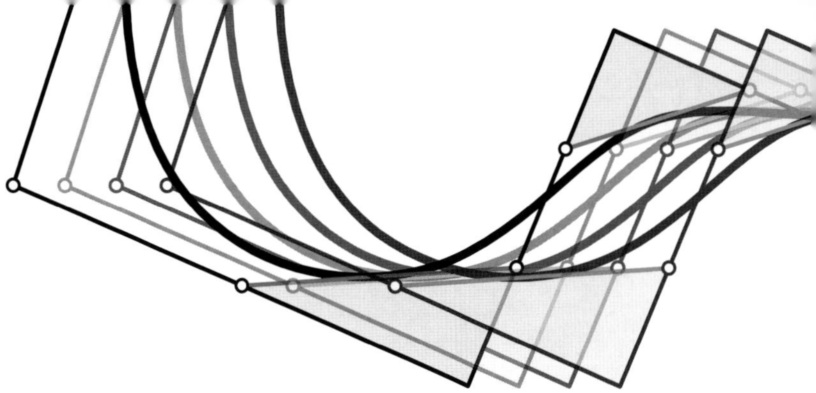

B-Spline Curves

B-spline curves are freeform curves that consist of Bézier curve segments of the same degree and that are knotted together at their endpoints with the highest possible smoothness [i.e., same tangent, same curvature (if possible), and so on]. The fact that the B-spline curve does the concatenation of the Bézier curve segments automatically is remarkable.

Doing the same concatenation by hand is cumbersome (Figure 8.16), prone to error, and makes the later manipulation of the curve more difficult. Another advantage (especially for designing longer B-spline curves) is that they stick to the shape of their control polygon much better than Bézier curves. B-spline curves share the useful properties of Bézier curves, and the latter are actually a special case of B-spline curves.

History:

Spline. The term *spline* comes from a tool used by shipbuilders to draw smooth curves by hand (Figure 8.2). This tool was a thin flexible wooden or metal rod that could be bent to adopt to different shapes of freeform curves as needed by the designer. In geometric modeling, a *spline curve* is a curve that consists of several curve segments that jointly observe continuity.

B-spline. The term *B-spline* was coined by the Romanian mathematician Isaac Schoenberg. The B stands for "basis." We can also use the B as a mnemonic to remember that a *B-spline* curve consists of several *Bézier* curve segments.

Defining a B-spline curve. A *B-spline curve* is defined by

- $m + 1$ control points,
- the degree n, and
- the knot vector.

The *control points* are now labeled $d_0 \dots d_m$ to distinguish them from the Bézier control points. The control points are used to define the overall shape of the curve. The *degree* (denoted by the symbol n) of a B-spline curve is defined as the degree of the Bézier curve segments that together form the entire B-spline curve. Note that for a B-spline curve all Bézier segments have the same degree n (Figure 8.17).
The knot vector collects the "knots" (i.e., parameter values) where the different Bézier curve segments are joined. The standard approach in CAD software is to use uniformly spaced knots. Sometimes B-spline curves with uniform knots are referred to as *uniform* B-spline curves to distinguish them from *nonuniform* curves. Important are the two intuitive design parameters of a B-spline curve: the control points and the curve degree.

Fig. 8.17
A B-spline curve of degree $n = 3$, with $m = 7$ control points $d_0 \dots d_6$. consists of four cubic Bézier curve segments.

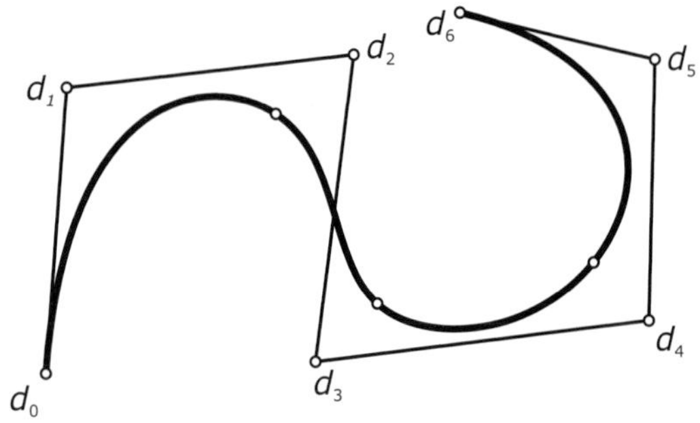

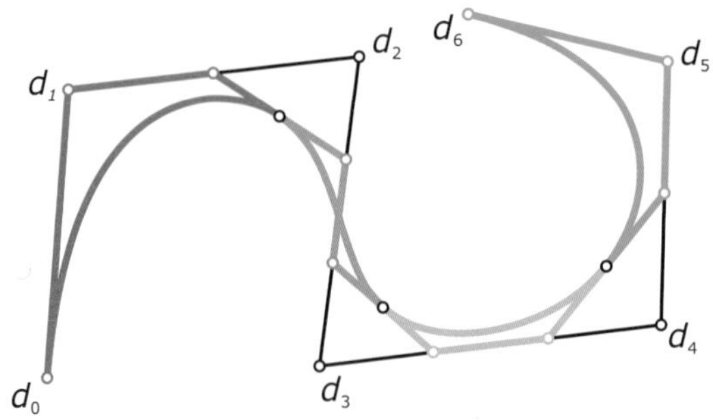

Example:

The influence of the degree on a B-spline curve. Let us fix a control polygon with eight control points and only vary the degree of the corresponding B-spline curve (Figure 8.18).

- *Degree $n = 1$.* A *linear* B-spline curve is simply the control polygon.
- *Degree $n = 2$.* A *quadratic* B-spline curve with eight control points consists of six quadratic Bézier curve segments.
- *Degree $n = 3$.* A *cubic* B-spline curve with eight control points consists of five cubic Bézier curve segments.
- *Maximum degree $n = 7$.* The B-spline curve is a Bézier curve of degree 7. Because one segment is the minimum number achievable, we cannot further increase the degree of the B-spline curve.

In general, a B-spline curve of degree n with $m + 1$ control points $d_0, d_1, \dots d_m$ consists of $m + 1 - n$ Bézier curve segments of degree n. The maximum degree achievable is $n = m$, for which the B-spline curve is actually a Bézier curve to the same control polygon.

Example:

Sketching quadratic spline curves for given control polygons. Given a control polygon, we sketch a quadratic B-spline curve as follows. We simply mark the midpoints on the control polygon (Figure 8.19) and then sketch the quadratic Bézier curve segments (parabolic arcs).

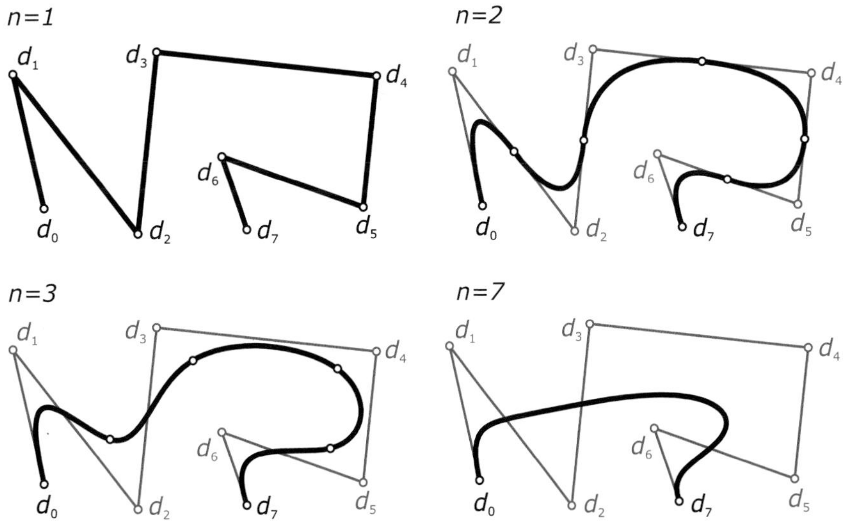

Fig. 8.18
Linear, quadratic, cubic, and maximum-degree seven B-spline curve to the same control polygon with eight control points. Note that the B-spline curve of maximum degree is a Bézier curve.

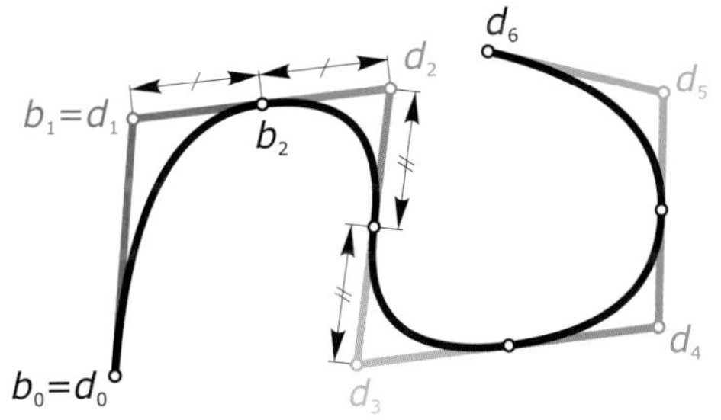

Fig. 8.19
B-spline and Bézier control points of a quadratic B-spline curve.

Local control of B-spline curves. B-spline curves enjoy local control. This means that by changing the position of one single control point the shape of the curve is only modified in a certain limited part of the curve (Figure 8.20). Recall that the shape of a Bézier curve depends on all control points. For a B-spline curve, this is different. Only the curve segments in a certain influence zone around the modified control point are changed. This is why we speak of "local control" of a B-spline curve via its control points.

Open and closed B-spline curves. B-spline curves can be drawn in two different modes: as an *open* curve having two endpoints or as one single smooth *closed* curve (Figure 8.21). An open B-spline curve interpolates the first and last control points. A closed B-spline curve has a closed control polygon that is smoothed as a whole by the curve.

It is important to understand the difference between the open and closed modes of a B-spline curve. If a B-spline curve of a closed control polygon is in open mode, the curve has two endpoints that coincide where the curve has a sharp corner (Figure 8.21). A closed B-spline curve of degree n with $m + 1$ control points always consists of $m + 1$ Bézier curve segments, each of degree n. This is illustrated in Figure 8.22 for linear, quadratic, and cubic B-spline curves to the same control polygon with four control points. The maximum degree is $n = 3$. In general, $n = m$.

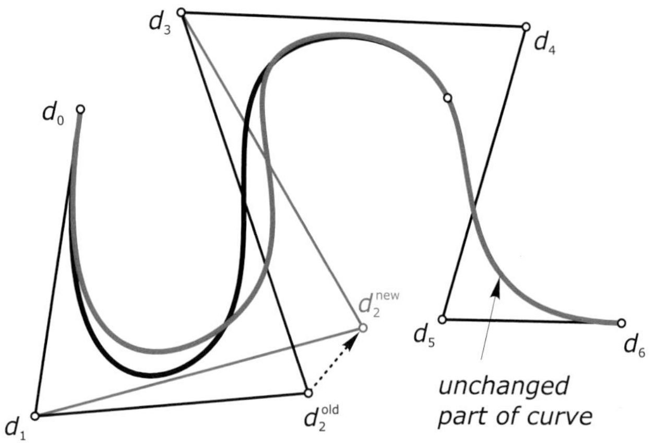

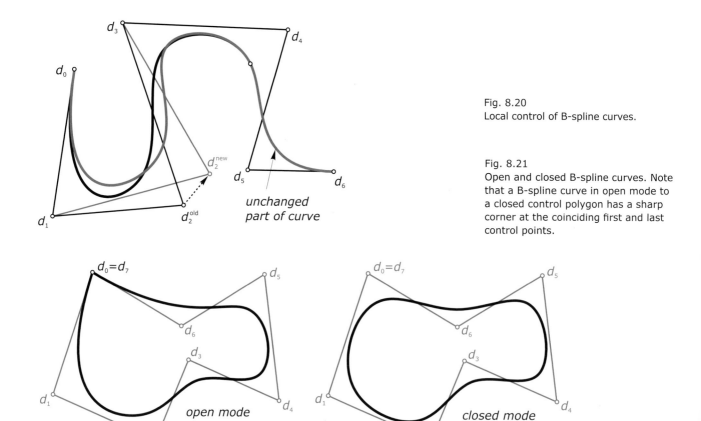

Fig. 8.20
Local control of B-spline curves.

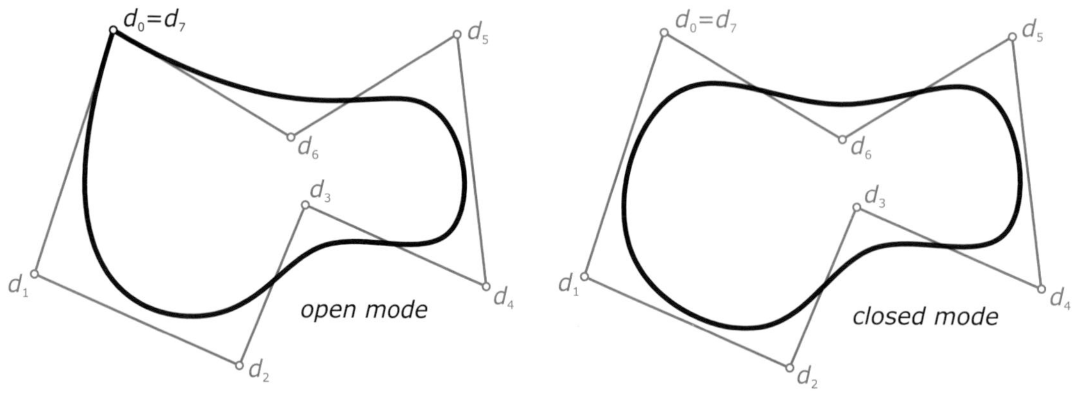

Fig. 8.21
Open and closed B-spline curves. Note that a B-spline curve in open mode to a closed control polygon has a sharp corner at the coinciding first and last control points.

Example:

Bézier control points of cubic B-spline curves. For a *closed* cubic B-spline curve, we first divide all edges of the control polygon into three equal parts. This can be seen as cutting off the corners of the B-spline control polygon. Then, for each cut off corner we insert the midpoint on the connecting line of the two newly inserted points adjacent to that corner (Figure 8.23). Together, the points obtained in these two steps form the set of control points of the Bézier curve segments.

The modifications for an open cubic B-spline curve are as follows. No points are inserted on the first and the last edge of the control polygon. The midpoints are inserted on the second and next-to-last edge, and all other edges are again split into three equal parts (Figure 8.23). All such obtained points together with the first two and last two B-spline control points form the set of Bézier control points of an open cubic B-spline curve.

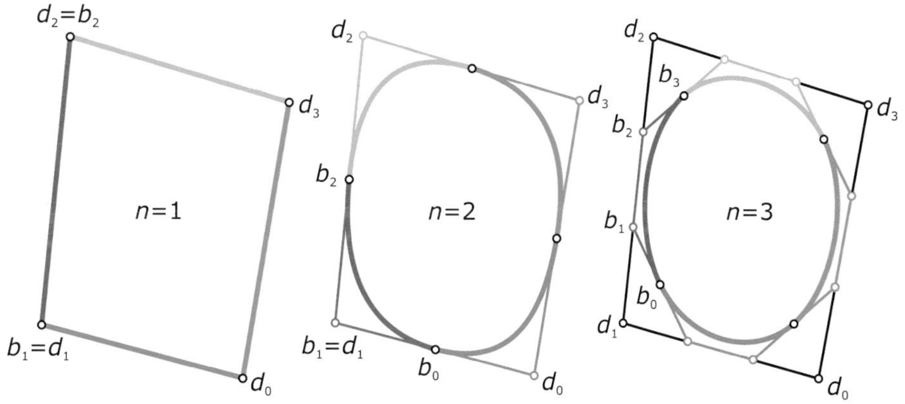

Fig. 8.22
Closed B-spline curves of degrees 1, 2, and 3 to the same control polygon with four control points. The four Bézier curve segments of each B-spline curve are colored differently. Also shown is the Bézier control polygon.

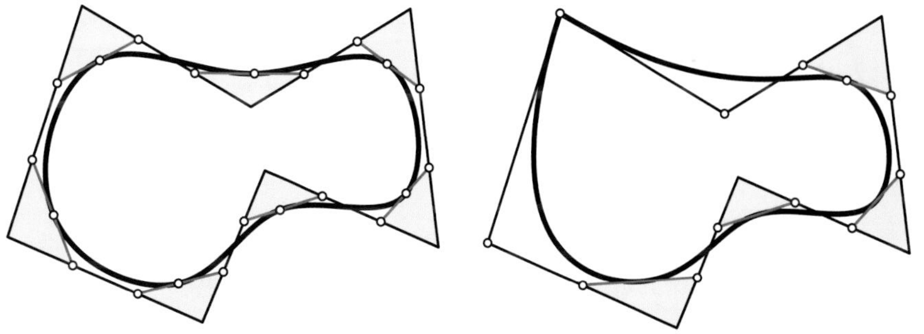

Fig. 8.23
Bézier control points of closed and open cubic B-spline curves.

Why are cubic B-spline curves so popular? If we look at a spline curve put together "manually" from several curve pieces (Figure 8.24), the human eye is able to detect *kinks* (because the curve tangents change abruptly) and *curvature discontinuities* (because the curvature changes abruptly). To obtain spline curves that are pleasant to the human eye, B-spline curves are constructed in such a way that the underlying mathematical principles guarantee that the Bézier curve segments are put together in the smoothest possible way. For cubic B-spline curves, we inherently achieve smooth tangents and smooth curvature at the knot points where the separate curve segments are joined. This is one reason cubic B-spline curves are very popular for design purposes.

Why do we still want more? As we have a deeper understanding of B-spline curves and their use for freeform curve design, a legitimate question is why we still want more. The reason is rather simple. We have a fancy tool for drawing very complicated freeform curves that enjoy many beautiful properties, including local control. However, there is one major drawback.

With B-spline curves, we are not able to represent such simple curves as a circle, an ellipse, or a hyperbola. From the conic sections, only the parabola is a special B-spline curve (actually a Bézier curve). Because the conic sections are often used for design purposes, the material following examines an extension of B-spline curves. These freeform curves are coined NURBS and allow us to draw a circle, an ellipse, and a hyperbola—and of course many other freeform curves.

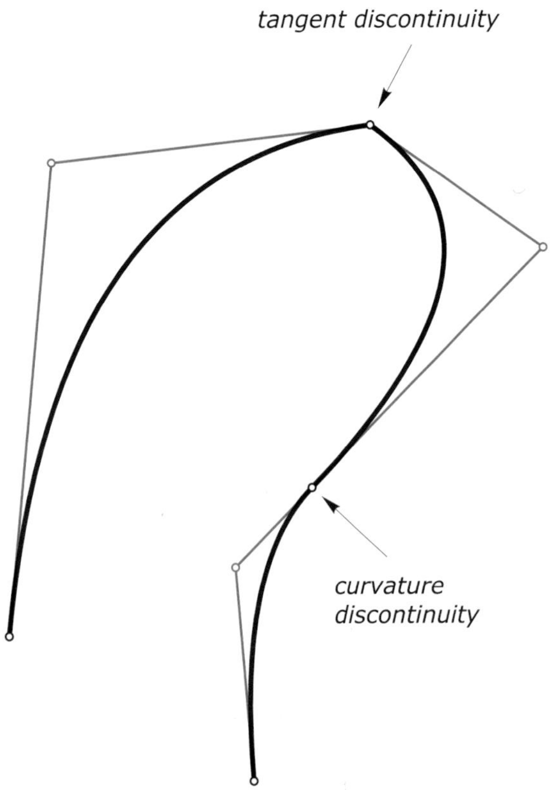

Fig. 8.24
Tangent and curvature discontinuities of handmade spline curves.

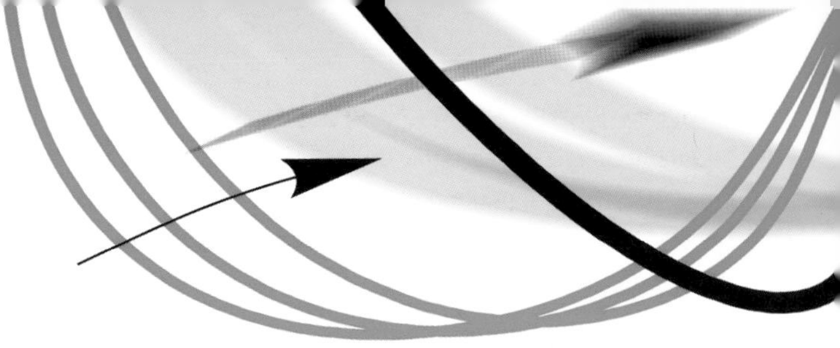

NURBS Curves

As stated previously, the acronym NURBS is an abbreviation of *nonuniform rational B-spline*. We already know that NURBS curves are B-spline curves with a nonuniform knot vector. The NU of NURBS is actually a bit misleading because NURBS curves could also have a uniform knot vector. The term *rational* is the really new thing that comes with NURBS. The term *rational* comes from the mathematical description of these curves (Chapter 7); that is, standard B-spline curves are polynomial—a special case of "rational."

The really new thing about NURBS is that they have an additional shape parameter, the so-called *weights*. These weights are associated with the control points and come into the game by the "rational" property of NURBS. Let's derive a NURBS curve and its weights geometrically. We will see that a NURBS curve living in a space of dimension d is nothing more than the central projection of a regular B-spline curve that lives in a space of dimension $d + 1$.

Geometric derivation of NURBS curves. We start with $m + 1$ control points $d_0, d_1, \ldots, d_m$ that we embed into the plane $z = 1$ (a plane parallel to the xy-plane one unit above) of a 3D Cartesian coordinate system. Then we draw the connecting lines $L_0, L_1, \ldots, L_m$ of the origin to the control points $d_0, d_1, \ldots, d_m$. If we now move the control points d_i on the lines L_i to new positions d_i^*, we generate the control polygon of a spatial B-spline curve c^* (Figure 8.25).

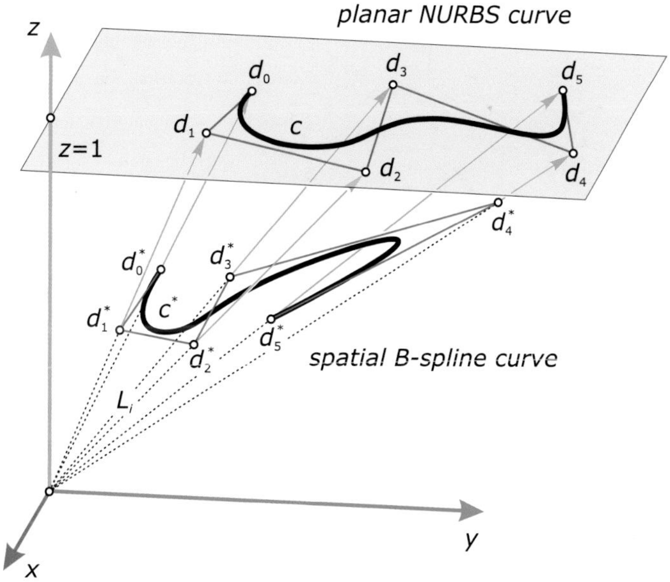

Fig. 8.25
A planar NURBS curve c is obtained as a central projection of a spatial B-spline curve c^*.

Finally, a central projection of the curve c^* onto the plane $z = 1$ (with the origin as projection center) gives a planar NURBS curve c to the control points $d_0, d_1, \ldots, d_m$. Thus, we have a connection between B-spline curves and NURBS curves: a planar NURBS curve is a central projection of a spatial B-spline curve. In addition, a spatial NURBS curve is a central projection of B-spline curve lying in a 4D space.

Weights. Now that we know how to generate NURBS curves, we will discuss the weights. The weights w_i associated with the control points d_i of a planar NURBS curve c are simply the z-coordinates of the control points d_i^* of the associated spatial B-spline curve c^*. This is analogously true for NURBS curves that lie in spaces of higher dimensions. Let's examine the influence of the weights on the curve shape (Figure 8.26). Increasing the weight w_i of a control point d_i drags the curve toward the control point, and decreasing the weight moves the curve away from that control point.

This behavior is intuitive, and thus the weights are a meaningful design parameter. From the geometric derivation, it immediately follows that changing the weight of one control point only has a *local* influence on the shape of the curve (i.e., modifying a weight actually means a displacement of the control point of the corresponding spatial B-spline curve). We also know that displacing a control point of a B-spline curve only has local influence on the overall curve shape.

Remark. Note that we only allow nonnegative weights to avoid points at infinity in the NURBS curve. Such points at infinity would result from the central projection of those curve points of the spatial B-spline curve that are contained in the plane $z = 0$.

B-spline curves are special NURBS curves. A B-spline curve is a special NURBS curve wherein all weights are equal. In the planar case, we have the following geometric interpretation. Equal weights mean that the control points of the associated spatial B-spline curve c^* all have the same constant z-coordinate and are thus lying in a horizontal plane at height $z = w$ (Figure 8.27). Then the central projection of the spatial B-spline curve c^* onto the plane at height $z = 1$ is really a *similarity* (a special affine transformation) between c^* and c.

Fig. 8.26
Weights as shape parameters.

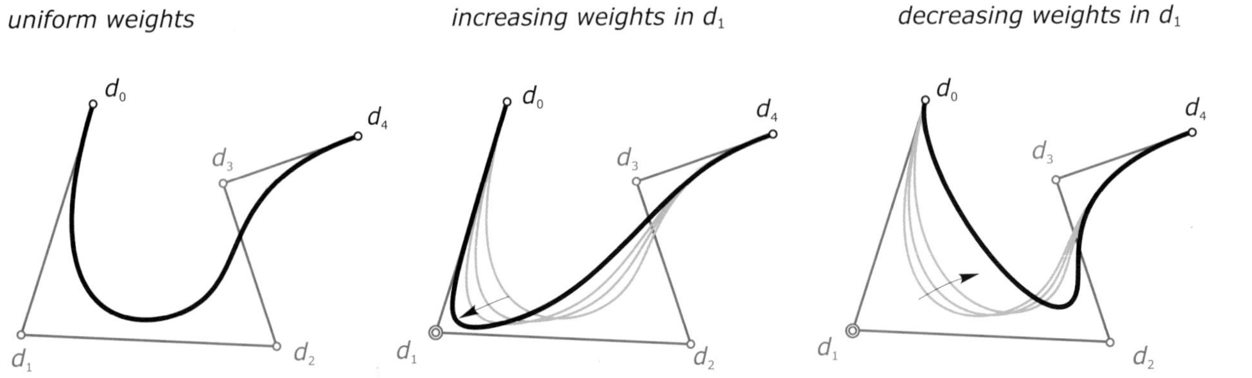

We know that B-spline curves enjoy the property of *affine invariance* (because B-splines curves consist of Bézier curve segments), and thus the curve c is again a B-spline curve. Thus, we have a genuine NURBS curve only if we have at least one weight different from the others.

Design handles. From our derivation it is clear that every Bézier and every B-spline curve is a special NURBS curve. The following table summarizes the design handles we have for Bézier, B-spline, and NURBS curves.

Table 8.1 Design handles for freeform curves.

	control points	degree	weights
Bézier	✓		
B-spline	✓	✓	
NURBS	✓	✓	✓

Table 8.1 should be read in the following way. The symbol ✓ means that this design handle can be set by the user. For a Bézier curve, the user can only modify the control points because the degree follows from the number of control points and the weights are all equal to 1. For a B-spline curve, the user can set the control points and the degree but the weights are all equal to 1. Only for a true NURBS curve can the user employ all three design handles. NURBS curves inherit the useful properties of B-spline curves (such as local control and the convex hull property).

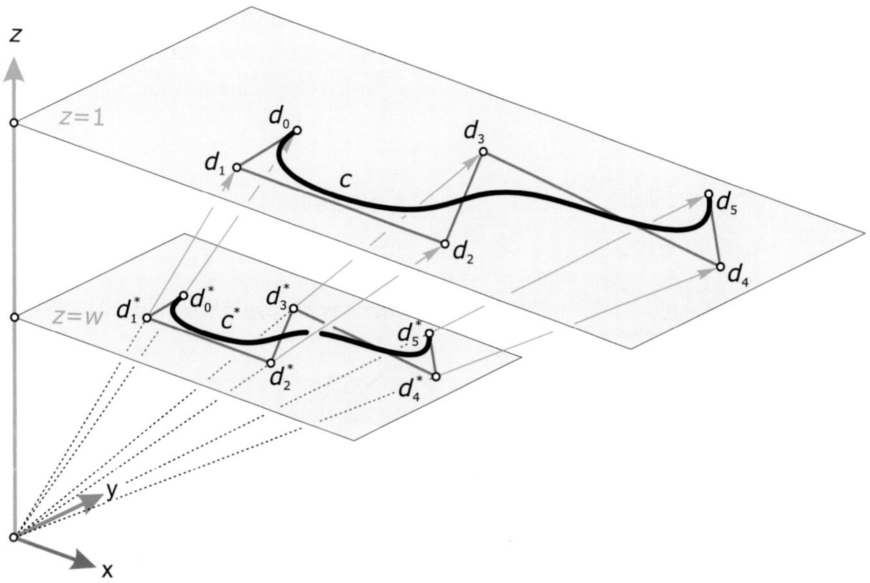

Fig. 8.27
B-spline curves as special NURBS curves with equal weights.

Conic sections as special NURBS curves. For the representation of conic sections as special NURBS curves (Figure 8.28), we use three control points d_0, d_1, and d_2 together with an appropriate choice of weights w_0, w_1, and w_2. We obtain arcs of a parabola, hyperbola, ellipse, and circle according to the following table.

Table 8.2 Choice of weights for the representation of conic sections as special NURBS curves.

	w_0	w_1	w_2
Parabola	1	1	1
Hyperbola	1	> 1	1
Ellipse	1	< 1	1
Circle	1	$\sin(\varphi/2)$	1

Thus, we have reached our goal of one unifying curve scheme that can be used to represent the most complicated freeform curves and the simplest basic curves. It is little wonder NURBS curves quickly became the industrial standard for curve representation in any CAD or design software.

Fig. 8.28
Conic sections as special NURBS curves.

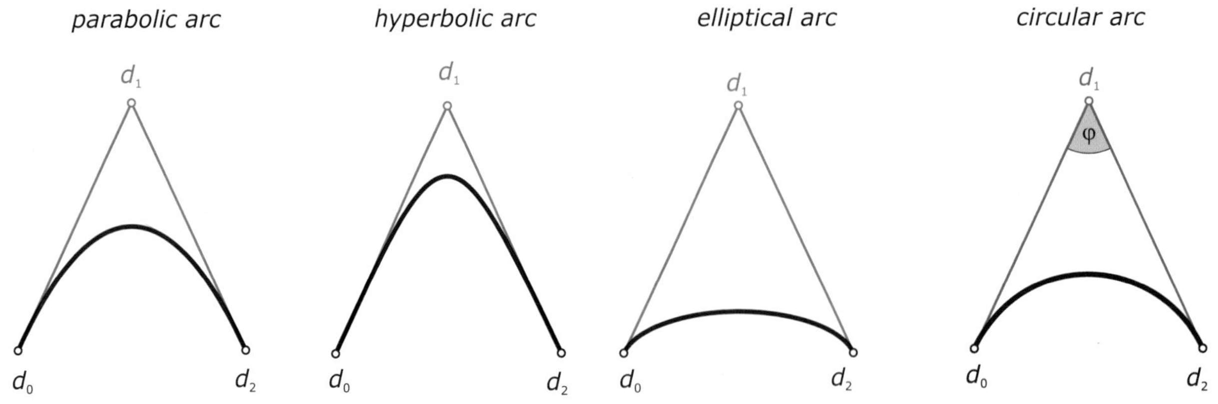

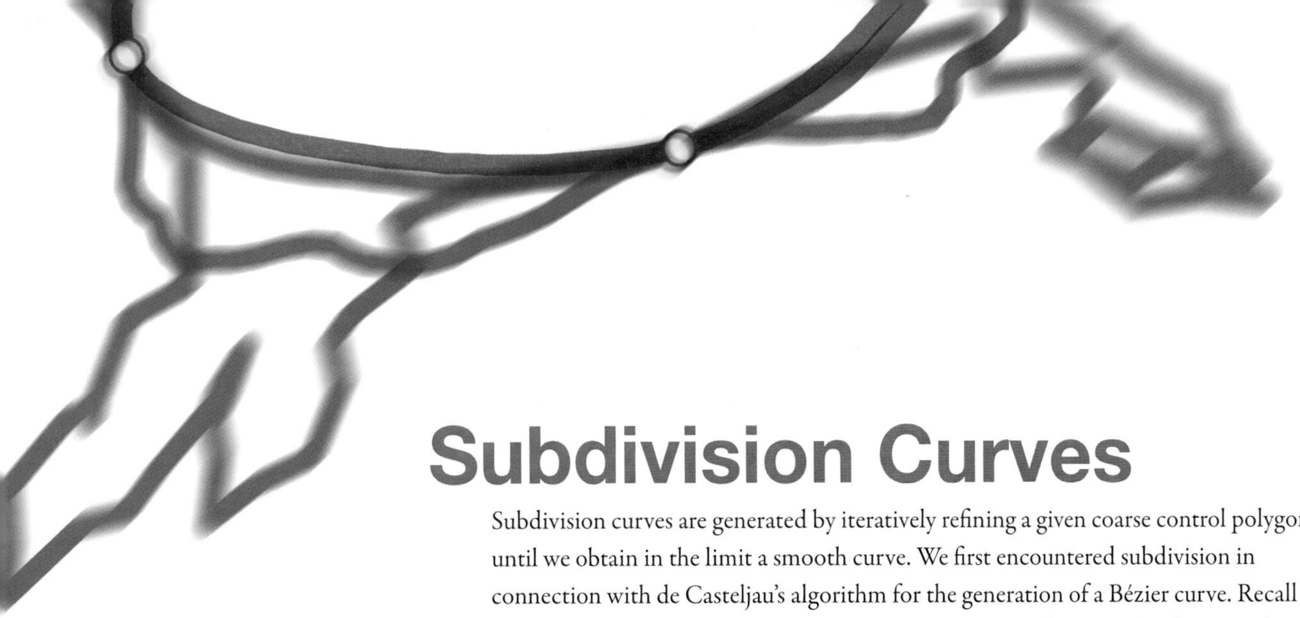

Subdivision Curves

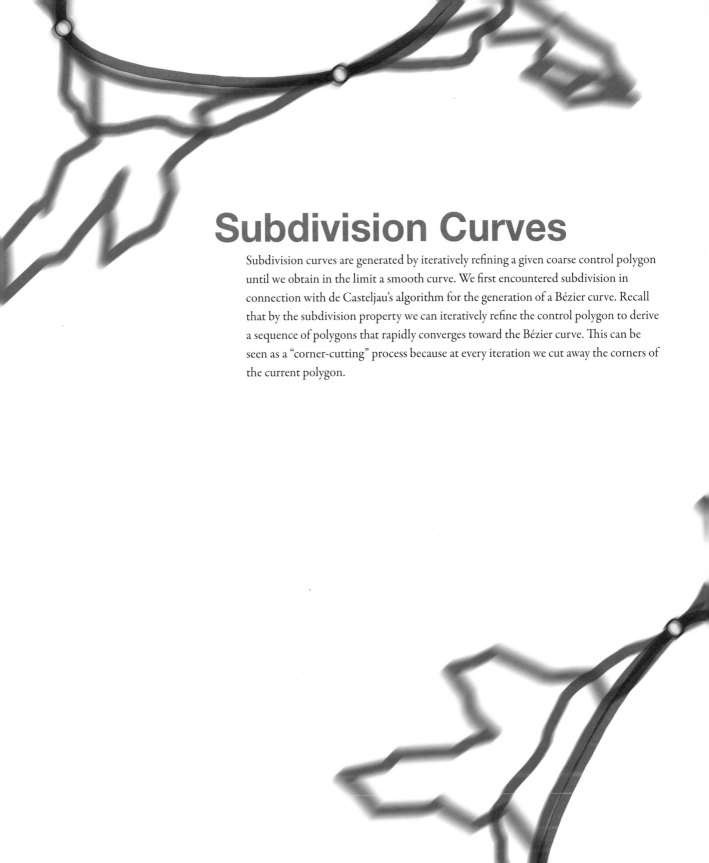

Subdivision curves are generated by iteratively refining a given coarse control polygon until we obtain in the limit a smooth curve. We first encountered subdivision in connection with de Casteljau's algorithm for the generation of a Bézier curve. Recall that by the subdivision property we can iteratively refine the control polygon to derive a sequence of polygons that rapidly converges toward the Bézier curve. This can be seen as a "corner-cutting" process because at every iteration we cut away the corners of the current polygon.

What is a subdivision curve? A subdivision curve is a polygon defined by two entities: the control points and the subdivision (or refinement) level. Thus, if we want to specify exactly what curve we mean we speak of a "subdivision curve at level *k* given by its control points." In this section, we examine approximating and interpolating subdivision algorithms (subdivision surfaces are described in Chapter 11).

We begin with Chaikin's algorithm for the generation of quadratic B-splines. The Lane-Riesenfeld algorithm is a generalization of Chaikin's algorithm that produces in the limit a uniform B-spline curve of degree *n*. Finally, we discuss the four-point scheme (which produces interpolating subdivision curves).

History:

Corner cutting. The idea of using corner cutting to generate smooth curves is actually older than the algorithm of de Casteljau and goes back to G. de Rahm. He introduced in 1947 the first "trisection" subdivision algorithm for curves that performs corner cutting at 1/3 and 2/3. Later, he described a subdivision algorithm that performs corner cutting at 1/4 and 3/4 (Figure 8.29). G. de Rahm found his results before computer graphics was invented. Thus, when G. Chaikin reinvented in 1974 the subdivision algorithm that performs corner cutting at 1/4 and 3/4 for high-speed generation of curves on computer screens (without knowing de Rahms results) the algorithm found widespread acceptance and got stuck with Chaikin's name.

Fig. 8.29
Corner cutting according to de Rahm and Chaikin.

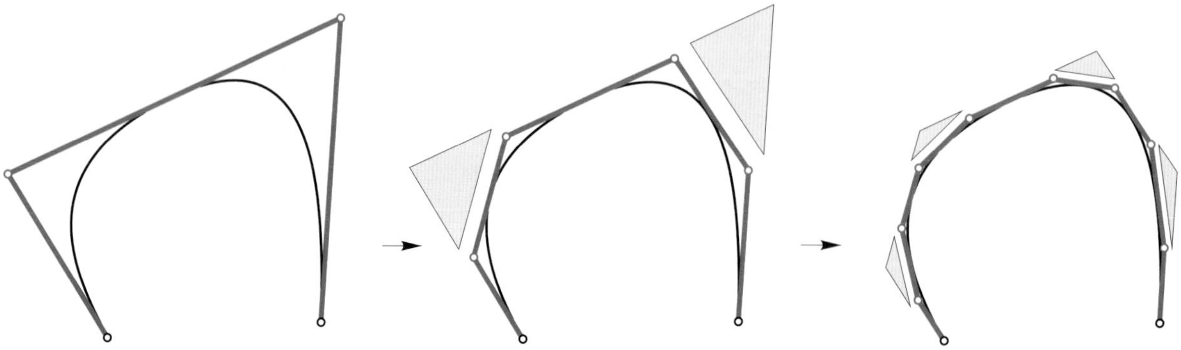

Chaikin's algorithm. Given is a coarse control polygon as shown in Figure 8.29. In every subdivision step, we perform corner cutting. For that purpose, we subdivide the edges of the current control polygon at 1/4 and 3/4 using linear interpolation for parameters $t = 1/4$ and $t = 3/4$. These new points are connected to form a new polygon that already better resembles the shape of the final curve (Figure 8.30).

We iterate the procedure and thereby produce a sequence of polygons that for an infinite number of subdivision steps produces a uniform quadratic B-spline curve with the initial polygon as control polygon. Chaikin's algorithm produces a subdivision curve that approximates the given polygon. For an *open* control polygon, we have to modify Chaikin's algorithm for the first and last polygon edge (Figure 8.30). Instead of subdividing it twice, we subdivide these two edges just once at their midpoints.

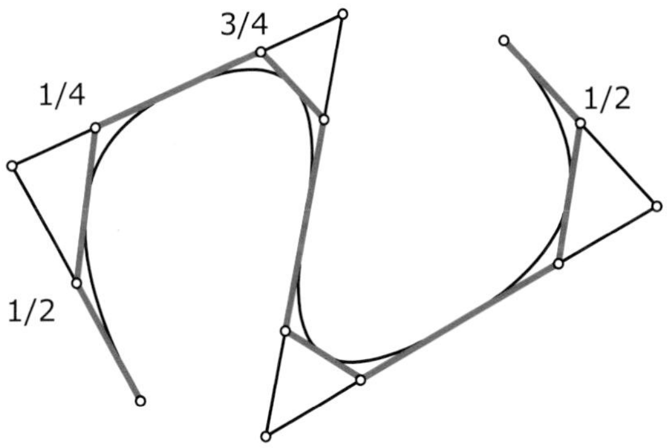

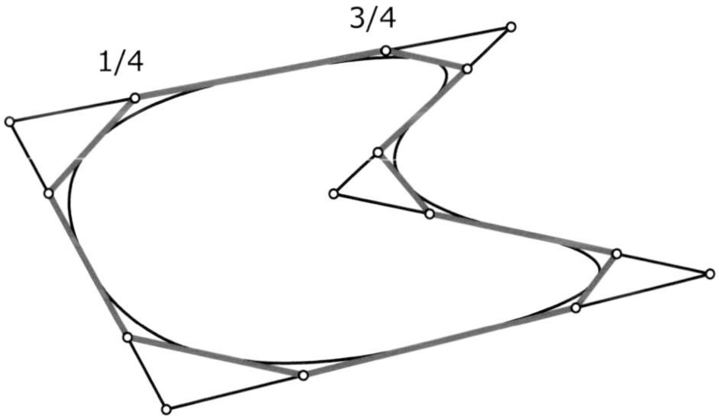

Fig. 8.30
Chaikin's subdivision algorithm for open and closed control polygons

Lane-Riesenfeld algorithm. Chaikin's corner-cutting algorithm can also be seen as a split-and-average procedure (Figure 8.31). In each iteration step, we first split the current polygon by inserting the edge midpoints to obtain a new polygon. Then in the averaging step we compute the midpoints of all edges of the new polygon. Connecting these vertices reveals the polygon for the next subdivision step.

In 1980, Lane and Riesenfeld realized that by generalizing this procedure from "split and 1 × average" to "split and 2 × average" one generates a subdivision curve that in the limit approaches a uniform cubic B-spline curve (Figure 8.32). In general, the subdivision strategy of "split and n × average" produces in the limit a uniform B-spline curve of degree $n + 1$ (a useful result).

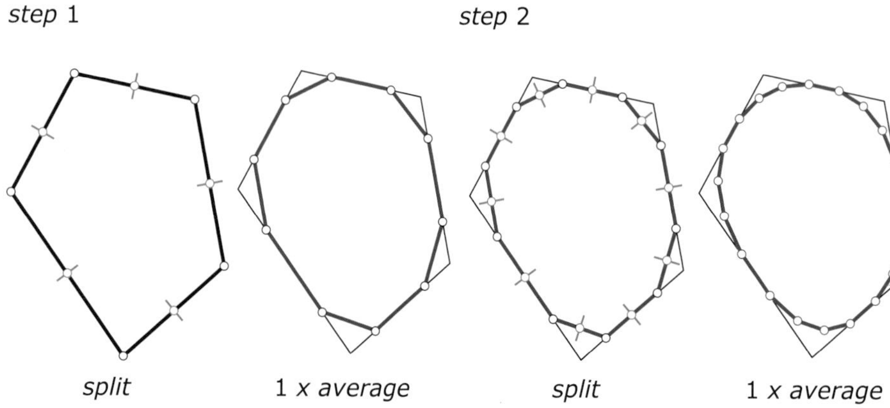

Fig. 8.31
Chaikin's subdivision as "split and 1 × average."

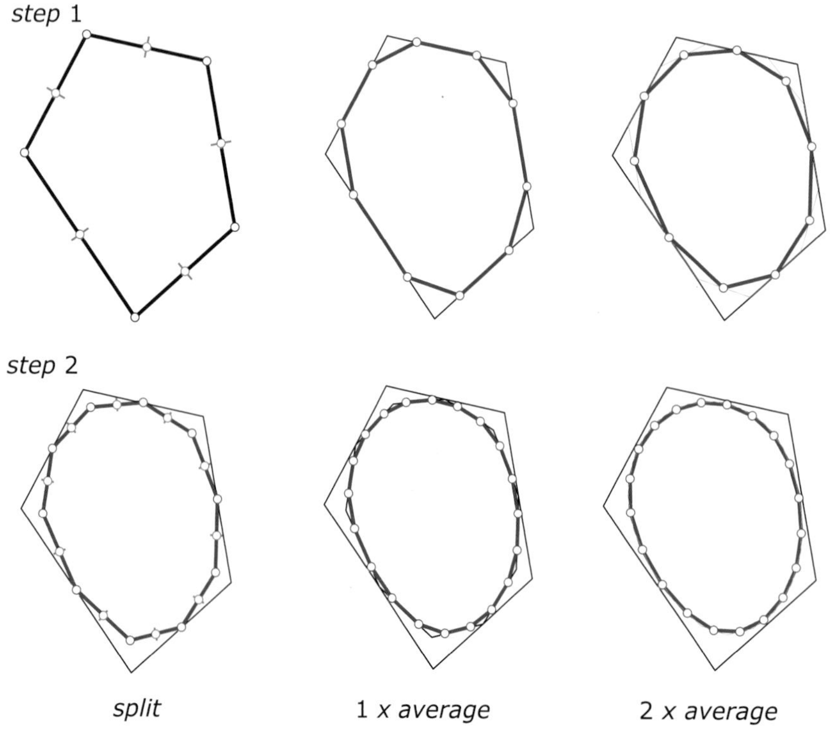

Fig. 8.32
Lane-Riesenfeld's subdivision of "split and 2 × average" produces in the limit a uniform cubic B-spline curve.

The four-point scheme. Given is again a set of points from which we generate a sequence of polygons that in the limit produces a smooth curve. Now the curve is required to *interpolate* the given points. Dubuc (1986) first showed that by computing a new curve point p_i^{new} from *four* old curve points p_{i-1}, p_i, p_{i+1}, and p_{i+2} we can generate a smooth interpolating subdivision curve (Figure 8.33).

Formally, the new point is computed as

$$p_i^{new} = -1/16\,p_{i-1} + 9/16\,p_i + 9/16\,p_{i+1} - 1/16\,p_{i+2}.$$

Note that the coefficients sum to 1 via $(-1 + 9 + 9 - 1)/16 = 1$, an important property for a scheme to be geometrically meaningful. Of course, Dubuc did not simply guess at these coefficients but derived them mathematically using the unique cubic interpolating curve of the four points. One year later, Dyn et al. (1987) generalized the four-point scheme as follows.

$$p_i^{new} = -w \cdot p_{i-1} + (1/2 + w) \cdot p_i + (1/2 + w) \cdot p_{i+1} - w \cdot p_{i+2}.$$

For $w = 1/16$ we have the original four-point scheme. Note that not all values of w will produce a smooth limit curve (Figure 8.34).

Fig. 8.33
The four-point scheme of Dubuc.

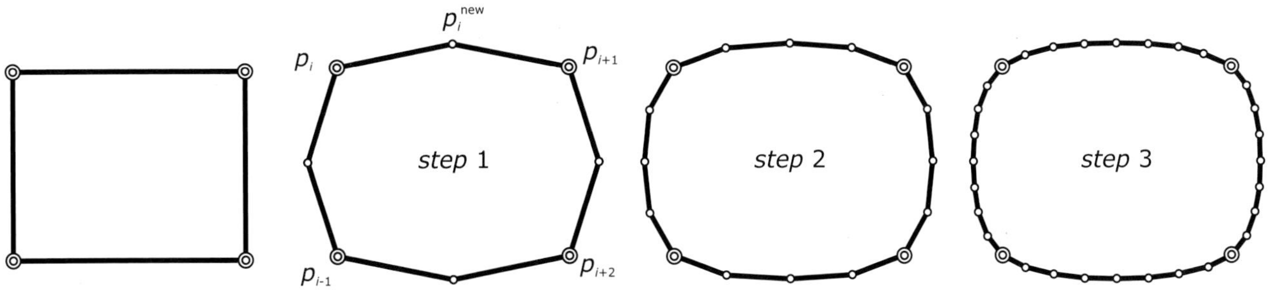

Fig. 8.34
The generalized four-point scheme of Dyn et al. Note that not all values of the weight factor w produce a smooth limit curve.

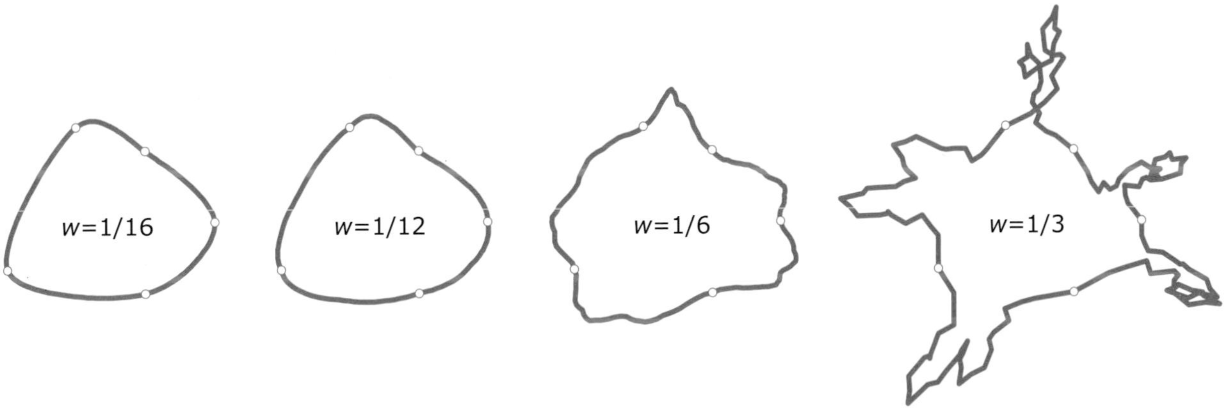

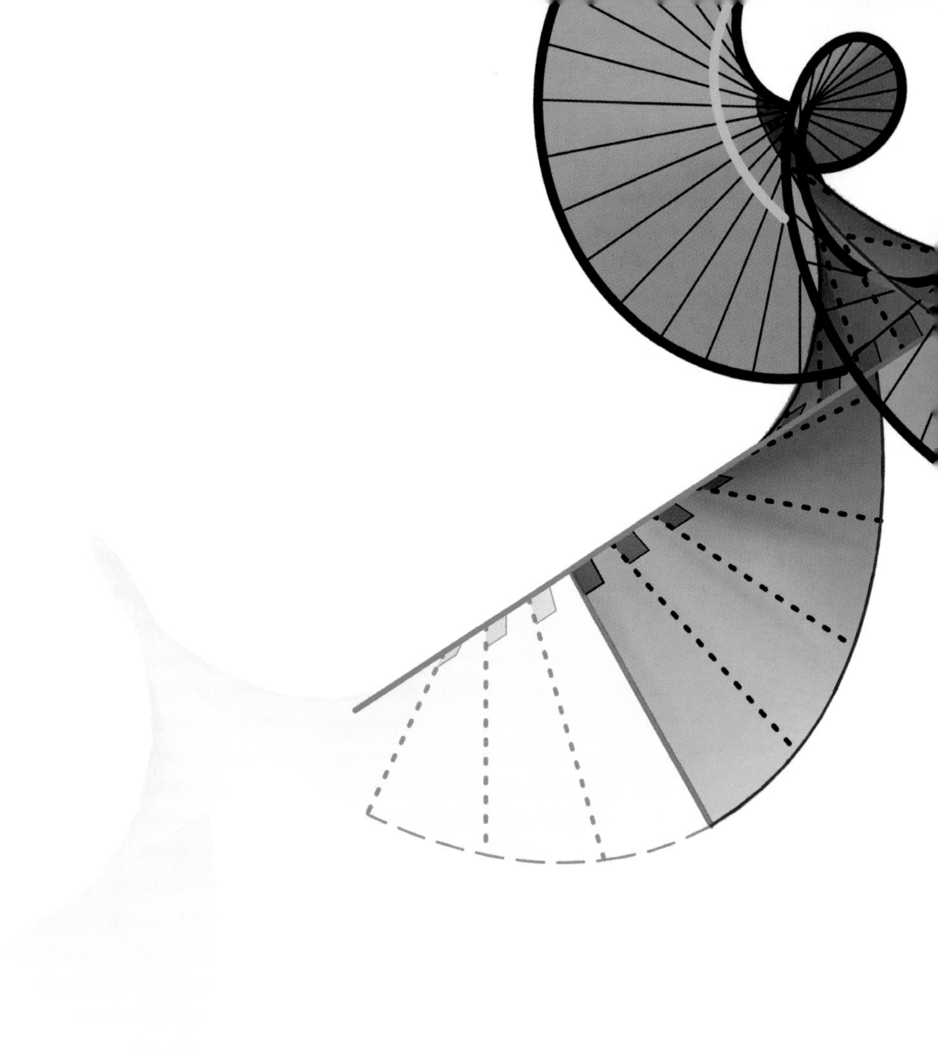

Chapter 9
Traditional Surface Classes

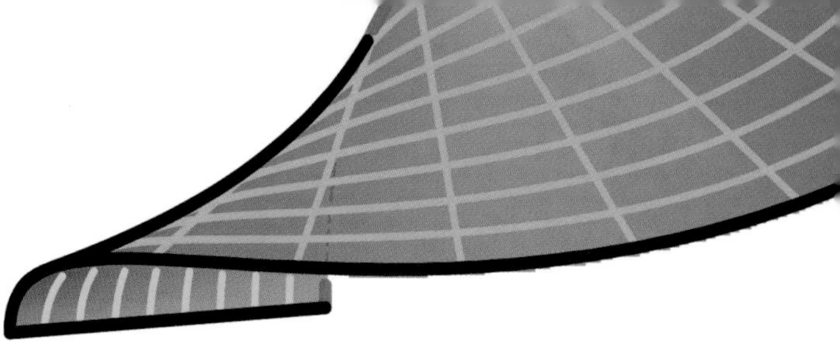

Traditional Surface Classes

Traditional surface classes are largely based on a simple "kinematic" generation. They are swept by a profile curve undergoing a smooth motion. For example, we obtain extrusion surfaces (see Chapter 1) by translating a curve along a straight line, rotational surfaces by rotating a curve (e.g., a B-spline curve) about a straight line, and helical surfaces by applying a smooth helical motion to a curve (see Figure 9.1.).

Translational surfaces are generated by moving a profile curve in an appropriate way along another curve, whereas ruled surfaces can be generated by moving a straight line. Because ruled surfaces carry a family of straight lines, they can be built more easily and can be found in such entities as concrete architecture and timber frame construction. We study various remarkable special cases, including ruled surfaces with two sets of straight lines commonly used as thin shells in architecture.

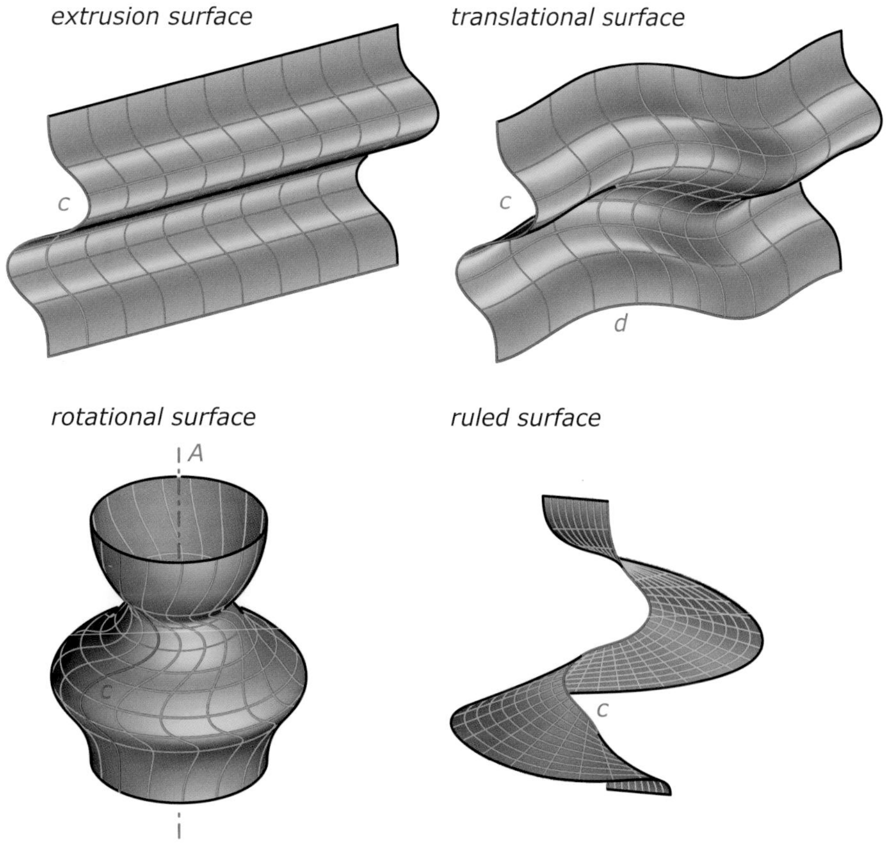

Fig. 9.1
(top left) Translating a curve *c* along a straight line results in an extrusion surface,
(top right) whereas translating this curve along another curve *d* generates a translational surface.
(bottom left) A rotational surface is created by rotating *c* about an axis *A*,
(bottom right) whereas a ruled surface can be generated by moving a straight line.

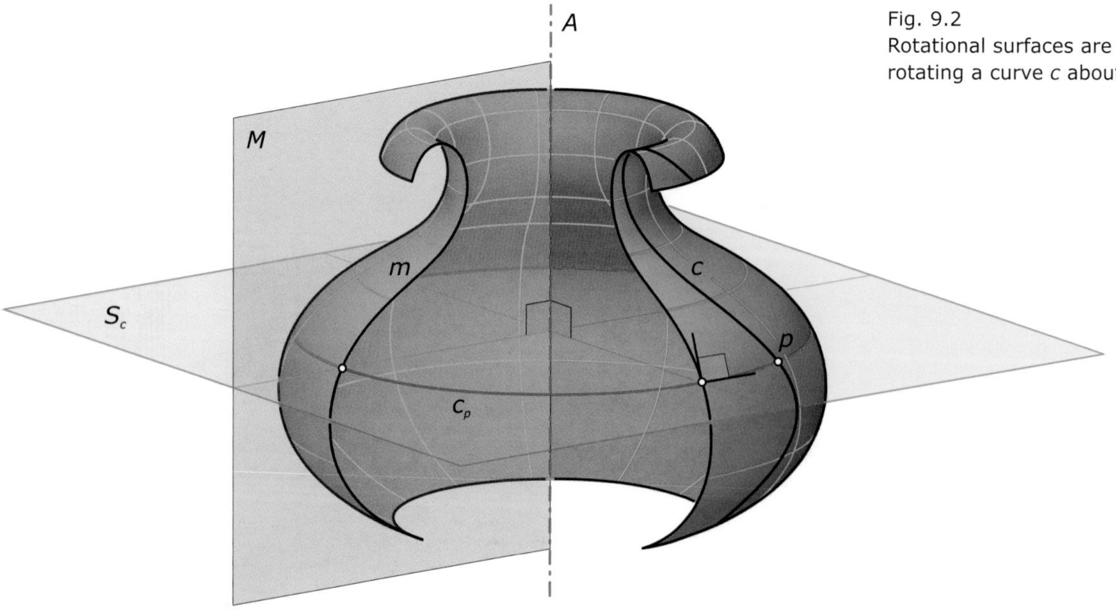

Fig. 9.2
Rotational surfaces are generated by rotating a curve *c* about an axis *A*.

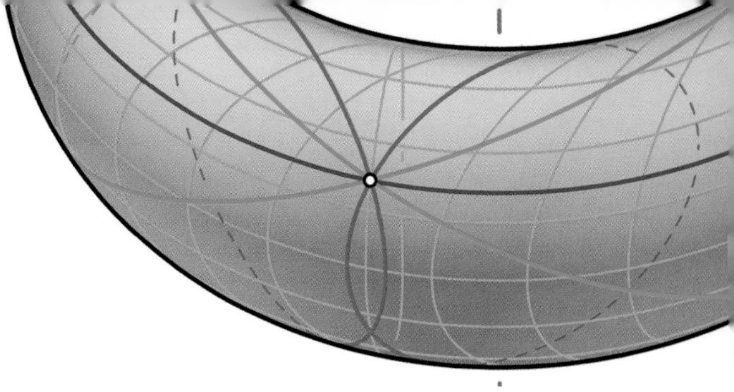

Rotational Surfaces

Rotational surfaces (*surfaces of revolution*) are generated by rotating a (planar or spatial) curve c about an axis A (Figure 9.2). Every point p of the generating curve c describes a circle c_p whose supporting plane S_c lies orthogonally to the axis A. Thus, every rotational surface carries a set of circles in parallel planes—which we call *parallel circles*.

Planes M that contain the axis A of the rotational surface intersect the surface along congruent planar curves m, the *meridian curves*. The supporting planes S_c of the parallel circles c_p and the meridian planes M of the meridian curves m are orthogonal. This implies that the meridian curves and the parallel circles also intersect at right angles. They form a net of orthogonal curves on the surface.

The principle of the generation of rotational surfaces is a very simple one. Thus, they have been used in art, design, and architecture for ages (Figure 9.3).

(a)

Fig. 9.3
Rotational surfaces are found widely in architecture.
(a) The *Church of the Transfiguration of the Savior* (1714) in Kizhi, Russia.

(b)

Fig. 9.3
Rotational surfaces are found widely in architecture.
(b) The *Royal Pavilion* (1815–1823) in Brighton, UK, by John Nash.
(c) *30 St Mary Axe* (1997–2004) in London by Foster + Partners.
(d) The *Torre Agbar* (2000–2005) in Barcelona by Jean Nouvel.

(c)

(d)

The tangent plane T_p at a point p of a rotational surface can be defined by the tangent t_c of the parallel circle c_p and the tangent t_m of the meridian curve m. In every point p, the surface normal n_p has to be orthogonal to the circle tangent t_c. Thus, n_p is contained in the meridian plane M and intersects the axis A (Figure 9.4). The intersection point of the surface normal and the rotational axis A is the center of a sphere that contains the surface point. The sphere and the rotational surface are tangent along a parallel circle.

Meridian curves better indicate the final shape of the rotational surface than arbitrary generating curves. Thus, it is recommended that surfaces of revolution be generated using planar meridian curves rather than arbitrary spatial curves. Meridian curves are symmetric to the rotational axis. Each of the symmetric parts, the *half meridian curves*, or the entire meridian curve can be used to generate the same rotational surface. Using a half meridian, we have to rotate with the full angle of 360 degrees—whereas using the entire meridian curve we have to apply a 180-degree rotation.

If the meridian curves intersect the rotational axis A at an angle different from a right angle, we obtain a singular point on the rotational surface (Figure 9.5). These singular points can become very critical in the subsequent design process. Computer-aided design (CAD) systems may not cope with this problem.

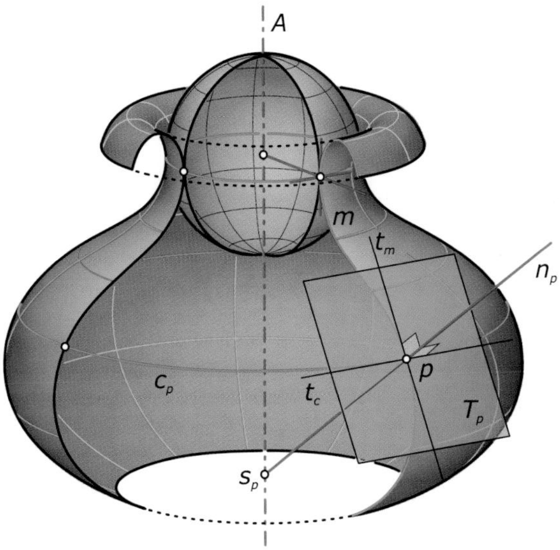

Fig. 9.4
All surface normals of a rotational surface intersect the rotational axis.

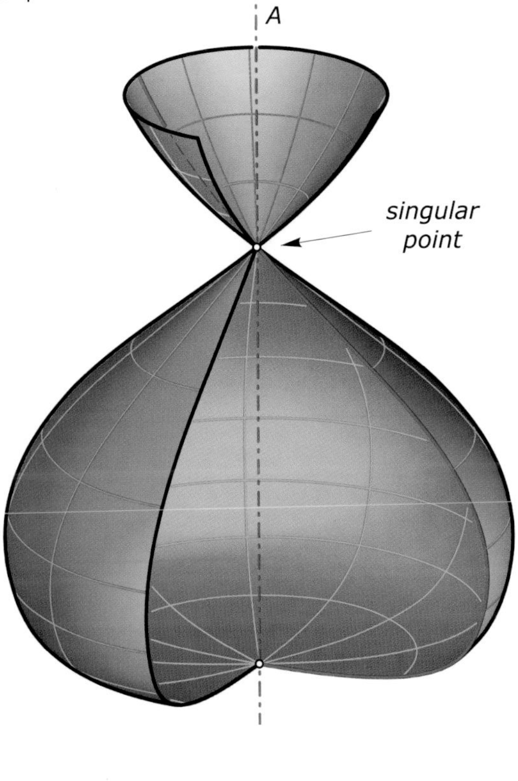

Fig. 9.5
Meridian curves that intersect the rotational axis in an angle different from 90 degrees generate rotational surfaces with singular points.

Mathematical description. To find a parametric representation of a rotational surface, we simply have to apply a continuous rotation about an axis to the generating curve *c*. According to Chapter 6, on spatial transformations, a rotation about the *z*-axis is given by

$$x_1 = x \cdot \cos u - y \cdot \sin u,$$

$$y_1 = x \cdot \sin u + y \cdot \cos u,$$

$$z_1 = z.$$

Substituting *x*, *y*, and *z* with the parametric representation of a spatial curve $\mathbf{c}(v) = (x(v), y(v), z(v))$ we obtain

$$x(u,v) = x(v) \cdot \cos u - y(v) \cdot \sin u,$$

$$y(u,v) = x(v) \cdot \sin u + y(v) \cdot \cos u,$$

$$z(u,v) = z(v).$$

If the rotational angle *u* assumes values in the range $0 \le u \le 2 \cdot \pi$ (using the radian measure), the generating curve completes a full rotation. Using a meridian curve $\mathbf{m}(v) = (x(v), 0, z(v))$ in the *xz*-plane as the generating curve, the parametric representation simplifies to

$$x(u,v) = x(v) \cdot \cos u,$$

$$y(u,v) = x(v) \cdot \sin u,$$

$$z(u,v) = z(v).$$

We call this the *standard representation of a rotational surface.*

Discrete rotational surfaces. Smooth rotational surfaces can be frequently found in modern design. However, they are sometimes not suitable for putting architectural ideas into practice. When constructing actual physical objects, we often need a discrete model that sufficiently approximates the smooth surfaces we have designed with CAD software. Thus, we have to replace smooth surfaces (Figure 9.6a) with appropriate planar faces that can be manufactured in a more convenient way.

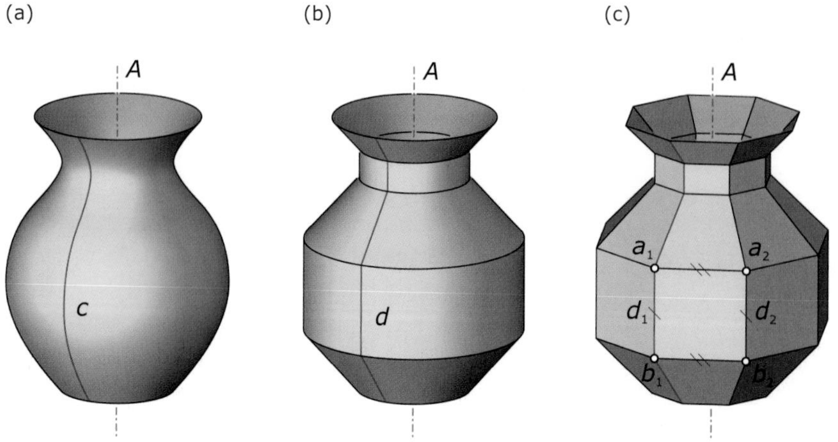

Fig. 9.6
By substituting the meridian curve with a polyline, we obtain a surface formed by conical and cylindrical strips. If we also discretize the rotation, we generate a polyhedral surface (discrete rotational surface).

To generate a discrete rotational surface, we start with a proper polygonal approximation *d* of the generating curve *c*. Using this polyline *d* as the generating curve, we obtain a rotational surface consisting of parts of rotational cylinders and cones (Figure 9.6b). This surface can be used as a suitable replacement for the original surface, whose basic elements can be developed (see Chapter 15) into the plane.

To generate a surface's substitute with planar facets, we rotate the polyline *d* in a discrete way *k* times about the rotational axis *A* with an angle of 360°/*k*. Connecting corresponding points (for example, a_1,a_2 and b_1,b_2) on subsequent positions (d_1,d_2) of the polyline, we obtain planar facets (Figure 9.6c) because all of these connecting lines are parallel.

To summarize the process of discretization, we have to substitute the generating curve with a polyline and then apply a discrete version of the rotational motion onto the polyline. A similar process is used for all surface types generated by moving a profile curve.

Here we have a simple but powerful tool for approximating smooth surfaces by their discrete analogies. However, it should be noted that we will not always achieve planarity of faces in the discrete model. The more we refine the generating polyline and the discrete transformation the better the discrete version will approximate a smooth surface (Figure 9.7).

Special rotational surfaces. Special forms of rotational surfaces are seen widely in architecture and design. Spheres, cylinders, cones, and tori are well-known representatives of this surface class. They are generated by rotating a circle or a straight line about an axis. Depending on the mutual position of the circle or the straight line to the rotational axis, we obtain the following surfaces (Figures 9.8 and 9.9).

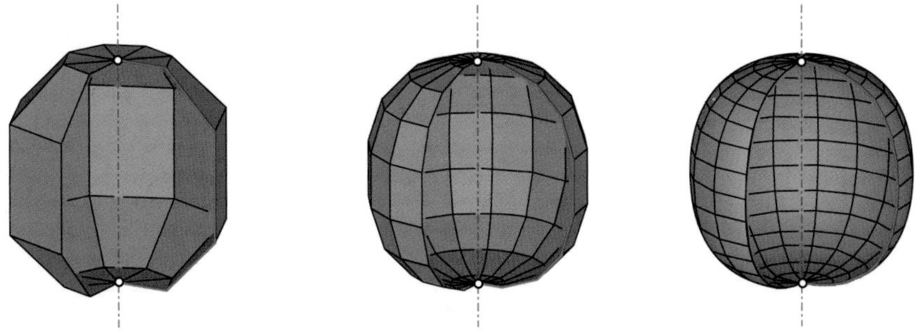

Fig. 9.7
Enlarging the number of vertices in the generating polyline and the number of its positions leads us closer and closer to a smooth surface.

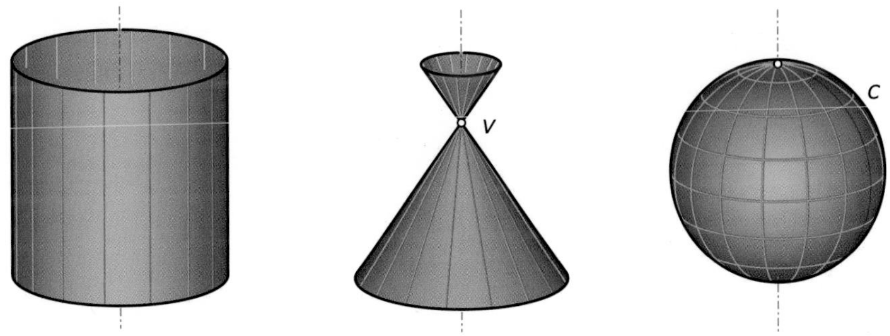

Fig. 9.8
Cylinders, cones, and spheres are special rotational surfaces.

- A cylinder is generated when we rotate a straight line parallel to the axis.
- A straight line that intersects the rotational axis *A* generates a cone when we rotate it about *A*. The intersection point becomes the apex *v* of the cone.
- Rotating a circle *c* about any of its diameters produces a sphere.
- We generate a torus by rotating a circle *c* about an arbitrary line. This straight line has to lie in the supporting plane of the circle *c*. Depending on the number of intersection points of *c* and the rotational axis, we obtain three different types of tori.

Examples where parts of tori were used in architecture are shown in Figures 9.9b and 9.9c.

(a)

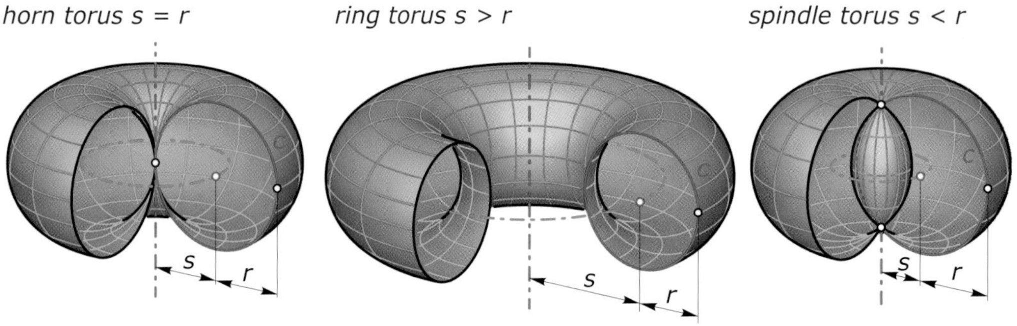

(b)

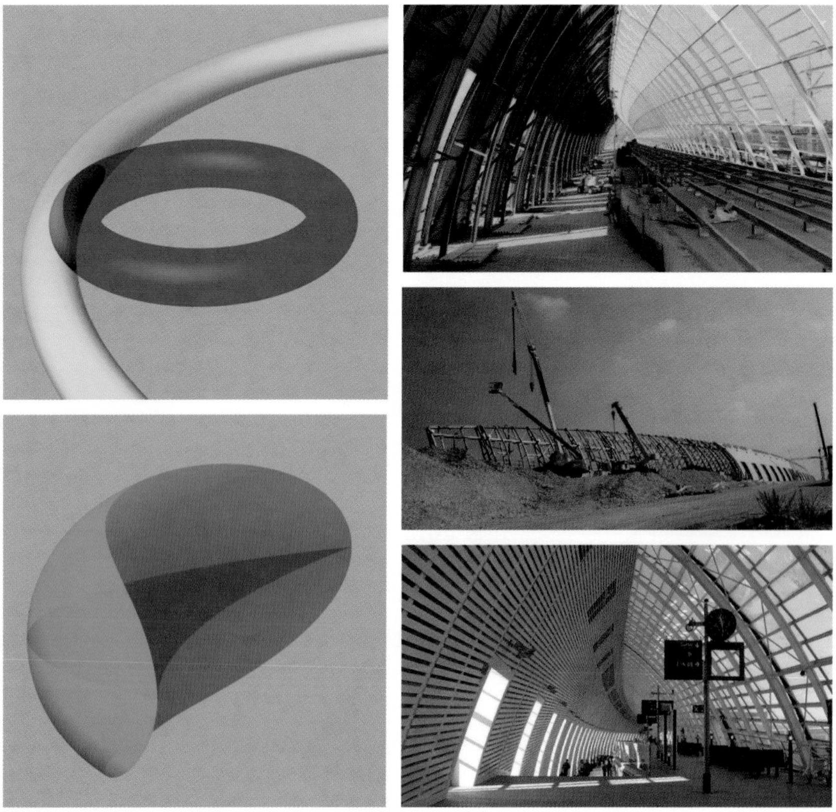

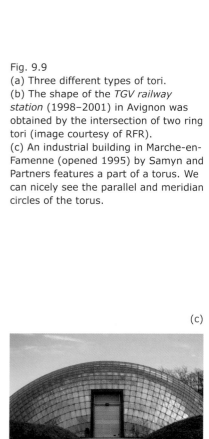

Fig. 9.9
(a) Three different types of tori.
(b) The shape of the *TGV railway station* (1998–2001) in Avignon was obtained by the intersection of two ring tori (image courtesy of RFR).
(c) An industrial building in Marche-en-Famenne (opened 1995) by Samyn and Partners features a part of a torus. We can nicely see the parallel and meridian circles of the torus.

(c)

Example:

Parametric representation of a torus. A circle c in the xz-plane with radius r and center on the x-axis is rotated about the z-axis. During this rotation, the center of c runs on a different circle with radius s. Then the circle c can be parametrized with $c(v) = (s + r \cdot \cos v, 0, r \cdot \sin v)$ and we obtain the parametric representation of the torus as

$x(u,v) = (s + r \cdot \cos v) \cdot \cos u,$
$y(u,v) = (s + r \cdot \cos v) \cdot \sin u,$
$z(u,v) = r \cdot \sin v.$

Thereby, u,v are chosen in $[0,2\pi]$. We are able to distinguish among three different torus types by examining the relative sizes of r and s (Figure 9.9a).

- $s > r$ corresponds to the *ring torus.*
- $s = r$ corresponds to a *horn torus.*
- $s < r$ corresponds to a self-intersecting *spindle torus.*

***Example:**

Villarceau's circles of a torus. Among the three torus types the ring torus has a remarkable property. In addition to the meridian and the parallel circles, a ring torus carries two other families of circles. Each *double tangent plane* (i.e., a plane tangent to the torus at exactly two different points) intersects the surface along two circles. They are named *Villarceau's circles* in honor of their discoverer the French mathematician and engineer Yvon Villarceau (1813–1883). Thus, every point p on a ring torus can have four circles drawn through it (Figure 9.10).

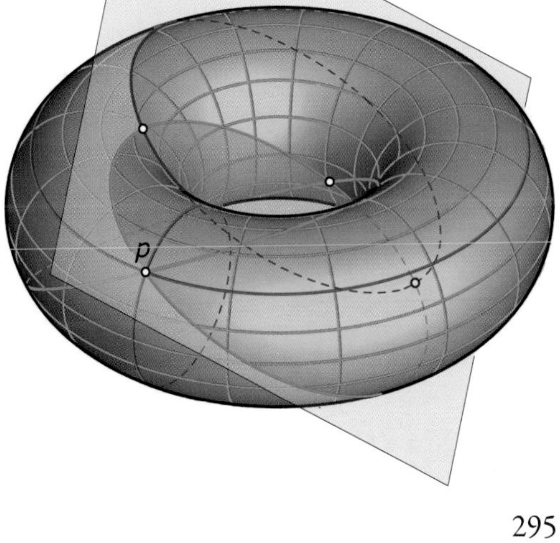

Fig. 9.10
Through every point p of a ring torus there pass four different circles lying on the torus. Two of them are called Villarceau's circles.

In all of the previously cited cases the generating straight line or circle is a meridian curve of the rotational surface. Now we will study rotational surfaces with arbitrary generating circles and straight lines.

We start with a circle *c* whose rotational axis *b* intersects the axis *A* in the point *m*. According to the right-angled triangle with vertices *p*, *m*, and *n*, every point *p* lying on the circle *c* has constant distance $d = \mathrm{dist}(p,m) = \sqrt{r^2 + k^2}$ from the intersection point *m* (Figure 9.11a). Hence, the circle *c* sweeps a segment of a sphere confined by two parallel circles.

Using a circle *c* whose axis is skew to the rotational axis, we obtain rotational surfaces that contain at least three families of circles. We have the congruent family which comes from the generating circle *c* and the family of circles that lie in supporting planes normal to the rotational axis (Figure 9.11b).

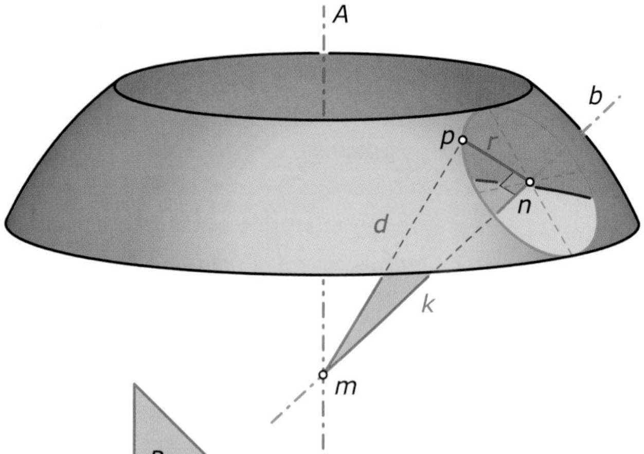

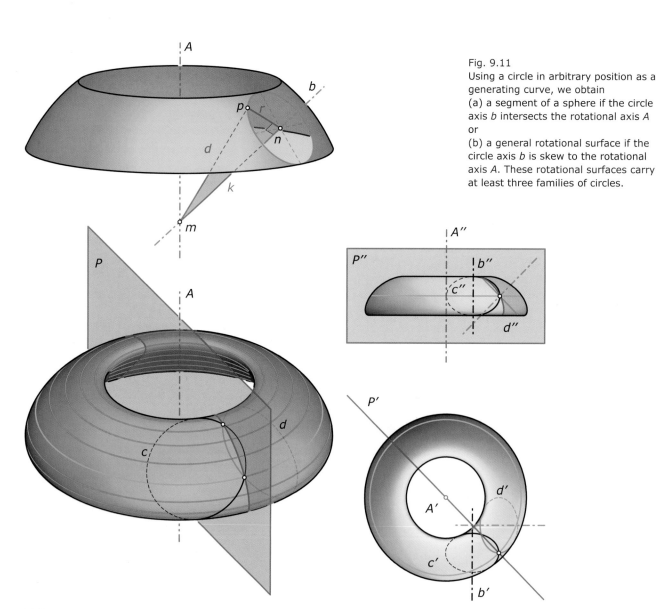

Fig. 9.11
Using a circle in arbitrary position as a generating curve, we obtain
(a) a segment of a sphere if the circle axis *b* intersects the rotational axis *A*
or
(b) a general rotational surface if the circle axis *b* is skew to the rotational axis *A*. These rotational surfaces carry at least three families of circles.

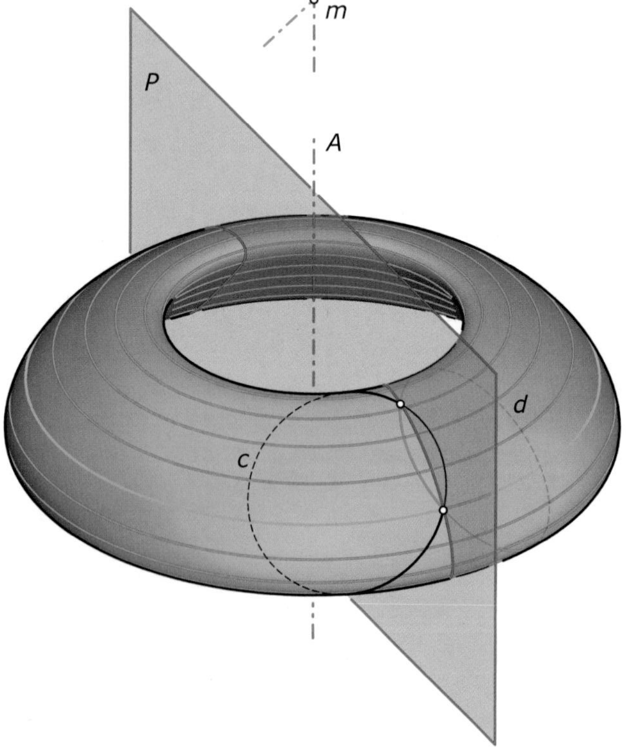

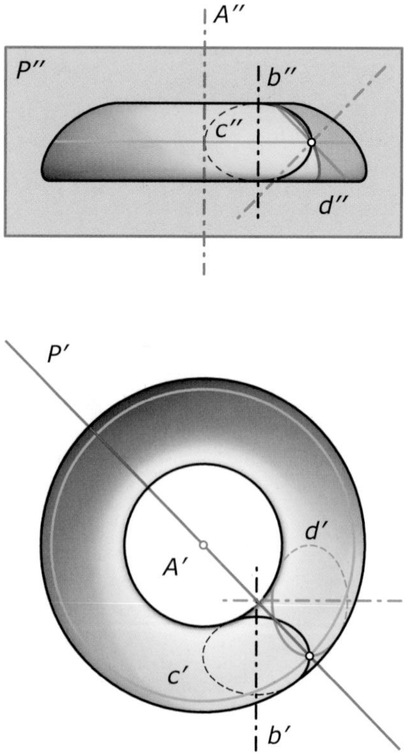

We can also mirror the generating circle *c* about an arbitrary meridian plane *P* to obtain another circle *d*, which also lies on the surface. By rotating *d* we obtain the third family of circles. Many of these surfaces carry two additional systems of circles that are analogues of the Villarceau's circles of the ring torus. They can also be found by intersecting the surfaces with double tangent planes (Figure 9.12).

A generating straight line *g*, skew to the rotational axis *A*, sweeps a rotational surface called a *one-sheet rotational hyperboloid* (Figure 9.13). When we reflect the generator *g* about an arbitrary meridian plane, we obtain another line *h* that is also part of the one-sheet rotational hyperboloid. Thus, the one-sheet rotational hyperboloid contains two sets of lines.

Fig. 9.12
A rotational surface that carries five different systems of circles.

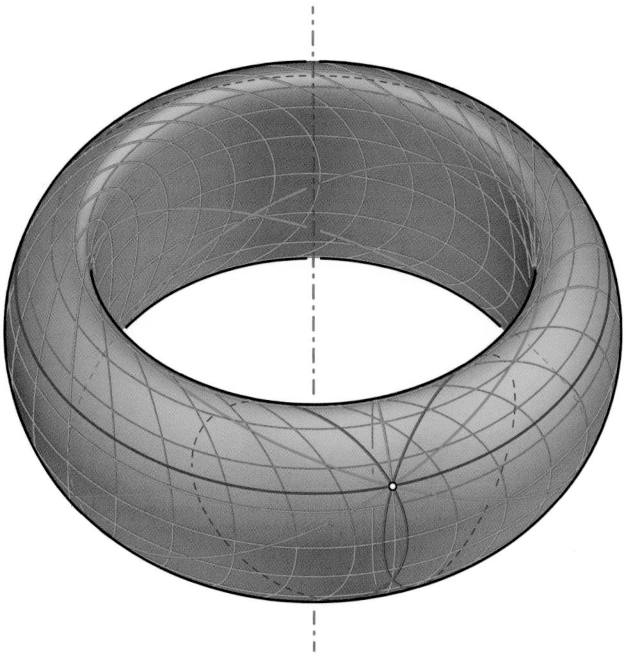

Fig. 9.13
A one-sheet rotational hyperboloid contains two sets of lines. The meridian curves are hyperbolas.

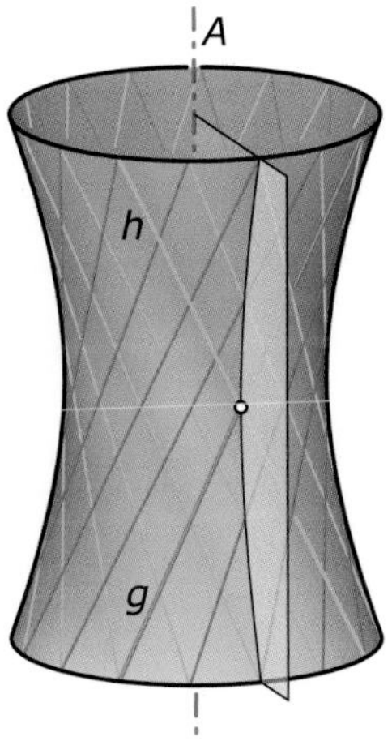

The one-sheet rotational hyperboloid is a special case of the ruled surfaces examined at the end of this section. Without a proof, we note that a one-sheet rotational hyperboloid can also be generated by rotating a hyperbola about its minor axis. Parts of one-sheet rotational hyperboloids are commonly used in architecture and design (Figure 9.14).

(a)

(b)

Fig. 9.14
One-sheet rotational hyperboloids in architecture and design.
(a) The world's first hyperboloid water tower (1896) in Nizhny Novgorod, Russia, by Vladimir Shukhov.
(b) The *Aspire Tower* (2005–2007) in Doha, Qatar, by Hadi Simaan is a 318-meter-high structure (image courtesy of Craig and Steph Tanner).
(c) A cathedral (opened 1970) in Brasilia by Oscar Niemeyer.
(d) The Port Tower in Kobe, Japan.
(e) A structure in the Mediatheque (1998–2001) in Sendai, Japan, by Toyo Ito.

(c)

(d)

(e)

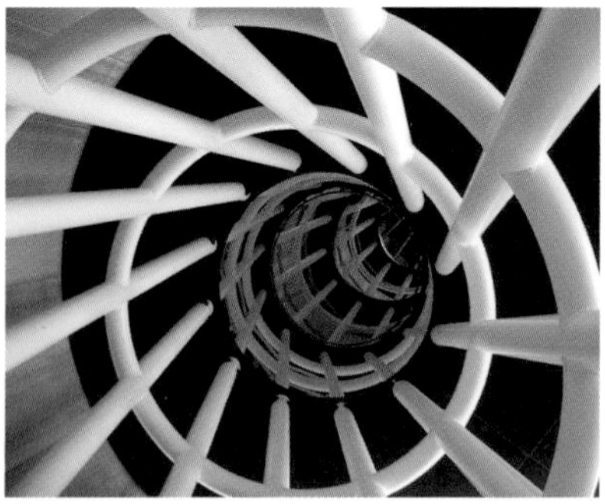

Rotational quadrics. The one-sheet rotational hyperboloid is a rotational surface resulting from a conic section being rotated about one of its axes. We subsume all rotational surfaces generated by rotating a conic section about one of its axes under the term *rotational quadrics* (Figure 9.15).

History:

The interesting fact that rotating a hyperbola or a straight line g skew to the rotational axis generates the same surface was known to Christopher Wren (1632–1723), the famous English architect and mathematician who designed and oversaw the contruction of St. Paul's Cathedral in London.

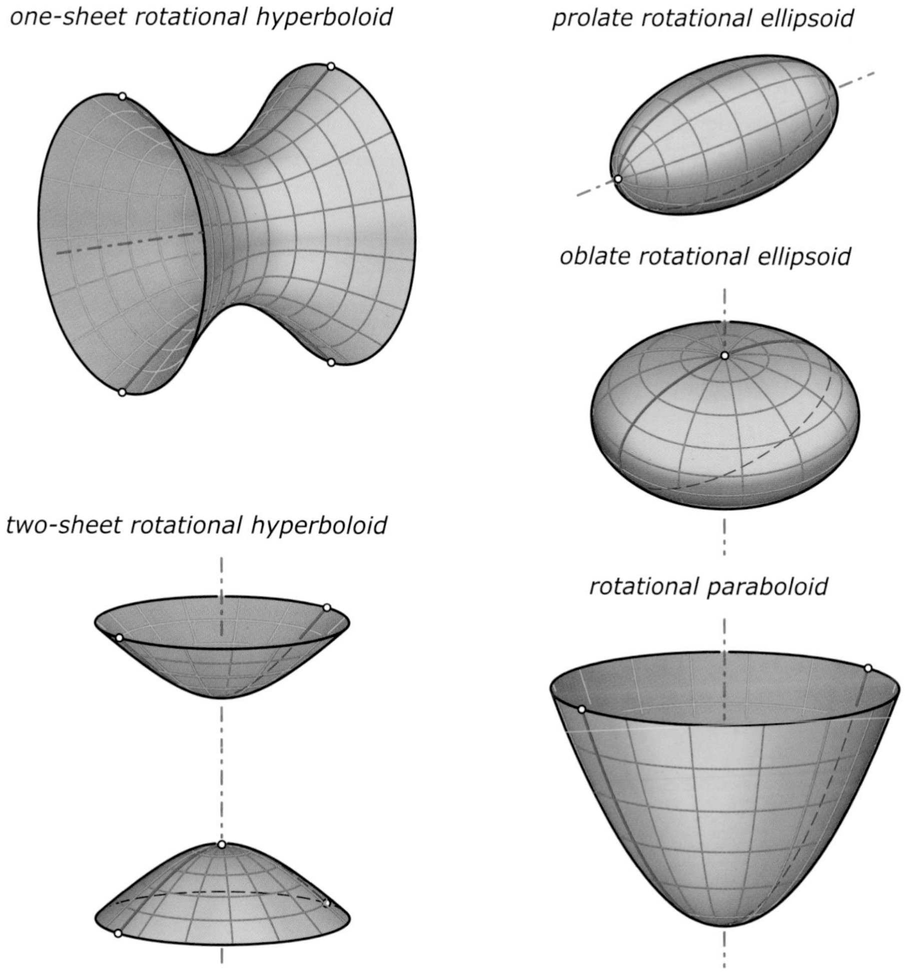

Fig. 9.15
Rotating conic sections about their axes results in rotational quadrics. In addition to the one-sheet rotational hyperboloid, we distinguish among two-sheet rotational hyperboloids, prolate rotational ellipsoids, oblate rotational ellipsoids, and rotational paraboloids.

In addition to the one-sheet rotational hyperboloid, we obtain the *two-sheet rotational hyperboloid* by rotating a hyperbola about its major axis. Note that only the one-sheet hyperboloid contains generating lines. Due to the fact that an ellipse has two different symmetry axes, we find two types of *rotational ellipsoids*: the *oblate rotational ellipsoid* (generated by rotating the ellipse about its minor axis) and the *prolate rotational ellipsoid*.

In the second case we have to rotate the generating meridian ellipse about its major axis. A *rotational paraboloid* arises by rotating a parabola about its axis. Rotational quadrics are useful and important basic elements of many design processes. Thus, we summarize their standard equations in Cartesian coordinates as follows.

- Oblate rotational ellipsoid:
  $x^2/a^2 + y^2/a^2 + z^2/c^2 = 1 \ (a^2 > c^2)$
- Prolate rotational ellipsoid:
  $x^2/a^2 + y^2/a^2 + z^2/c^2 = 1 \ (a^2 < c^2)$
- Two-sheet rotational hyperboloid:
  $x^2/a^2 + y^2/a^2 - z^2/c^2 = -1$
- One-sheet rotational hyperboloid:
  $x^2/a^2 + y^2/a^2 - z^2/c^2 = +1$
- Rotational paraboloid:
  $z = a \cdot (x^2 + y^2)$

Note that the equations of the different types of rotational ellipsoids and hyperboloids only differ in some signs. All rotational quadrics are defined by quadratic functions. Thus, the intersection with an arbitrary plane generally results in a conic section—under the assumption that there exists an intersection curve at all (Figure 9.16).

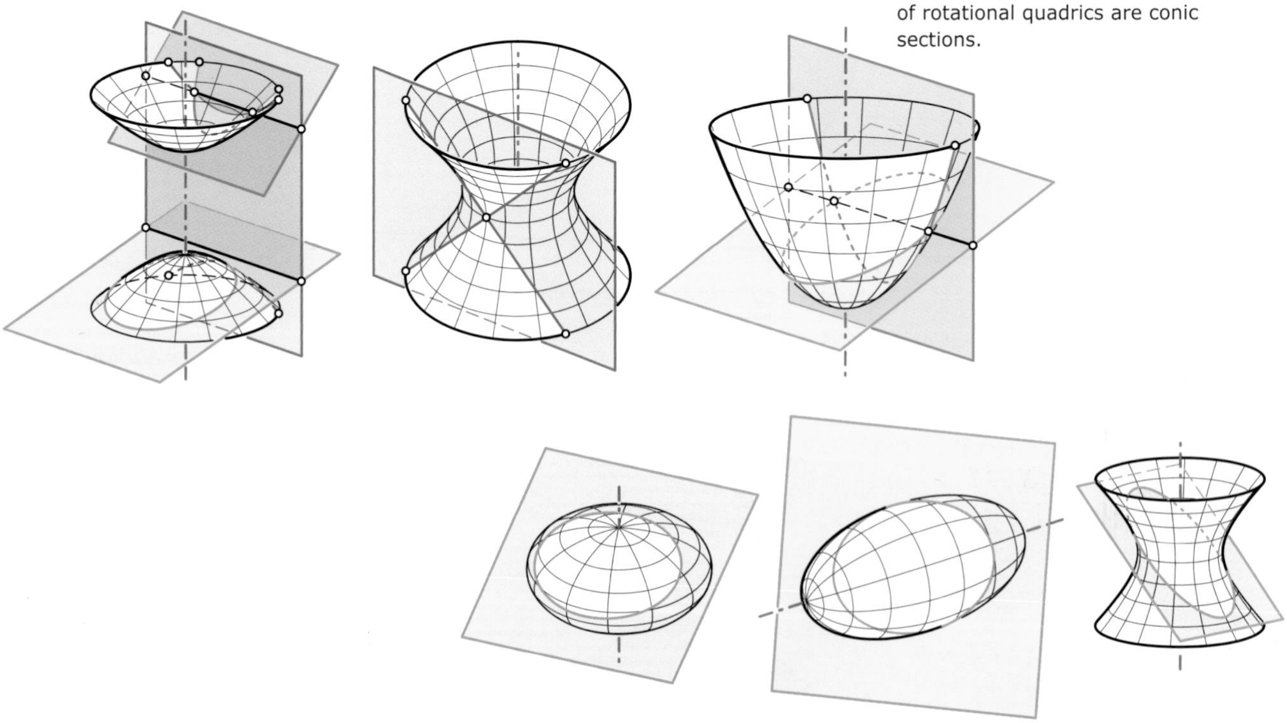

Fig. 9.16
In general, planar intersection curves of rotational quadrics are conic sections.

Both types of ellipsoids are intersected solely along ellipses, whereas paraboloids are intersected along ellipses and parabolas. On the other hand, hyperboloids carry all types of conic sections, ellipses, parabolas, and hyperbolas. Note that the intersection of a rotational one-sheet hyperboloid with a tangent plane is a pair of straight lines, the generating lines.

When we apply independent scalings with fixed coordinate planes to rotational quadrics we obtain more general types of surfaces. They belong to the class of *regular quadrics* (Figure 9.17). In addition to these quadrics (which can be derived from rotational quadrics), we have another type: the hyperbolic paraboloid (examined in the following section on translational surfaces). The type of paraboloid obtained from a rotational paraboloid by an independent scaling (Figure 9.17c) is referred to as *elliptic paraboloid*.

Every quadric type possess at least two planes of symmetry. Hyperboloids and ellipsoids even have three symmetry planes. The intersection point *m* is a symmetry center of the surface and is therefore called the *midpoint*. In addition to noting the large extent of symmetry, when cutting a quadric with parallel planes we obtain similar intersection curves. Thus, we can sweep a quadric with a set of similar conic sections.

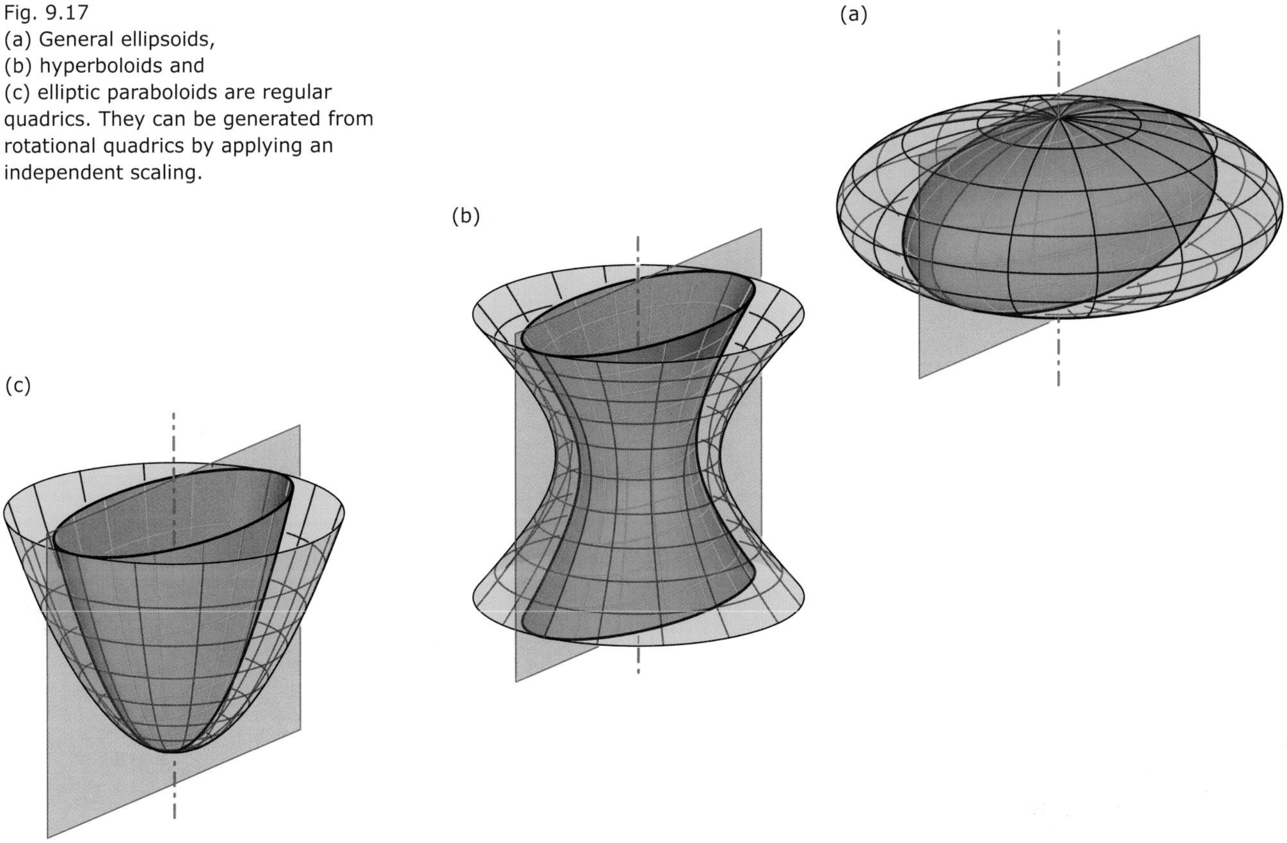

Fig. 9.17
(a) General ellipsoids,
(b) hyperboloids and
(c) elliptic paraboloids are regular quadrics. They can be generated from rotational quadrics by applying an independent scaling.

By reflecting such a set of conics about a symmetry plane of the surface, we can generate a network of similar surface curves (Figure 9.18). Due to the fact that conic sections have traditionally been favored and are well known geometric elements, we find quadrics (and especially rotational quadrics) in architectural design (Figure 9.19).

During independent scaling, the planar surface curves (conics) are mapped into conic sections of the same type—whereas the circles in planes orthogonal to the rotational axis are mapped into ellipses. Thus, all quadrics that can be derived from rotational quadrics carry ellipses. However, they carry many more ellipses than just the images of the parallel circles. Among all of these ellipses we may even find circles. In the following we show how to find these circles.

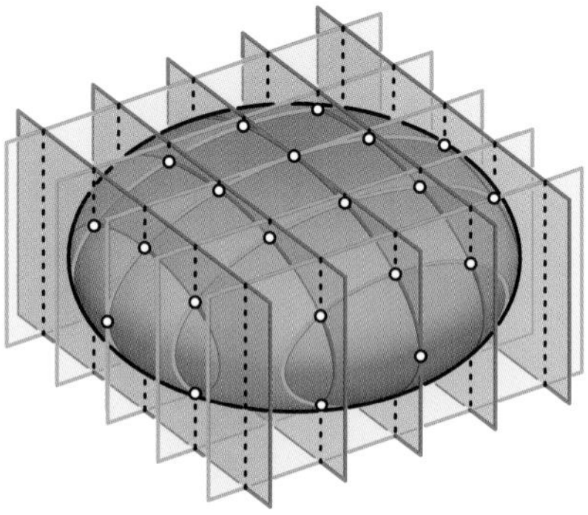

Fig. 9.18
Similar conic sections form a net of surface curves on a quadric.

Fig. 9.19
Parts of ellipsoids in architecture.
(a) The *Reichstag* cupola (opened 1999) in Berlin by Norman Foster has the shape of half a rotational ellipsoid (images courtesy of Waagner-Biro Stahlbau AG).

(b) The *Cornell Medical College* (opened 2004) in Qatar by Arata Isozaki, Perkins & Will.

(a)

(b)

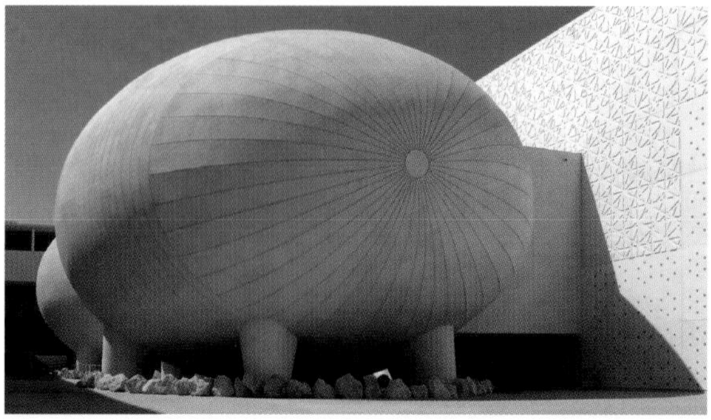

(a)

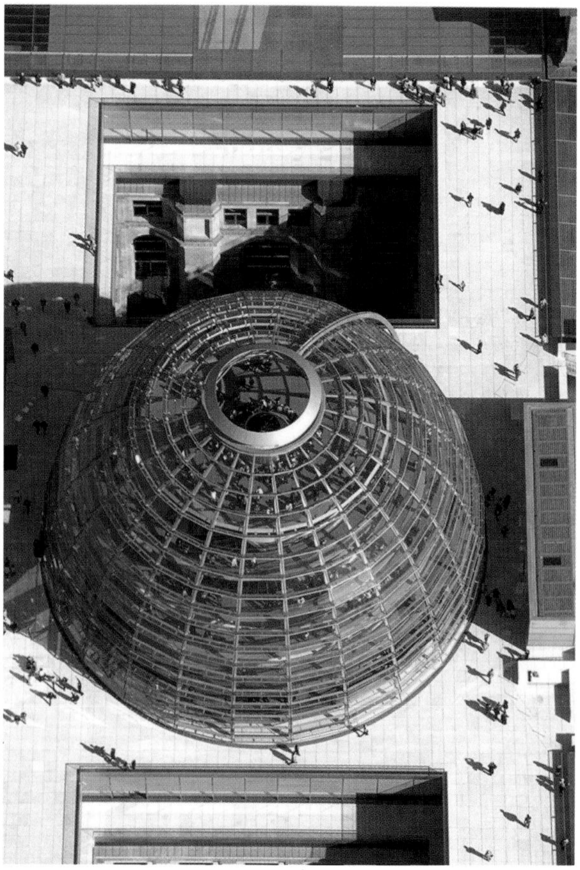

Intersection curves of quadrics. In Chapter 7 we studied the basics of intersection curves. As a special phenomenon, we learned about double points—which appear when a surface S_1 touches a surface S_2 in a point p. Figure 9.20 illustrates this fact again by means of two rotational quadrics. The oblate rotational ellipsoid E touches the one-sheet rotational hyperboloid H in two points p_1 and p_2. As we can see in Figure 9.20, the intersection curve consists of two distinct planar curves. Because they are surface curves of the ellipsoid E, these curves are ellipses.

For design purposes, it can be advantageous to find planar intersection curves. The transition from one surface to the other can then be realized more effectively. As a generalization of the example in Figure 9.20, we can use the following criterion to produce planar intersection curves when designing with quadrics.

If two quadrics touch each other in two points, the complete intersection curve consists of two planar curves (in general, conic sections).

Cylinders and cones can be considered special (nonregular) quadrics, and therefore the statement also holds for cones and cylinders. An application of this geometric fact is illustrated in Figure 9.21 by means of the intersection curve of an elliptic paraboloid and a rotational cone. If we apply the result of this application to the intersection of a quadric and a sphere, we obtain a pair of planar intersection curves. Because they have to lie on the sphere, they must be circles. This is the general idea of the method for finding circles on quadrics.

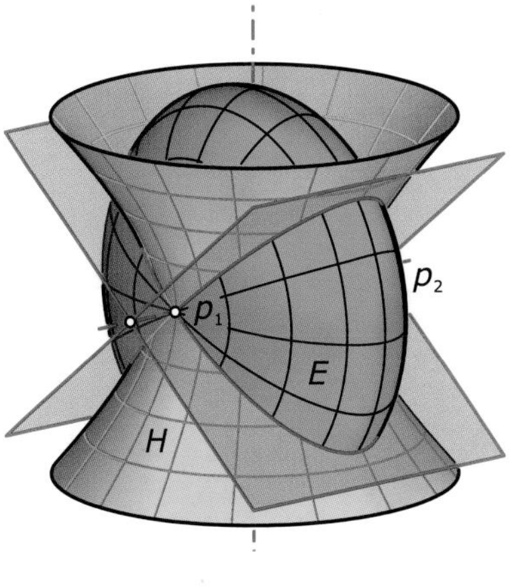

Fig. 9.20
Two rotational quadrics with planar intersection curves.

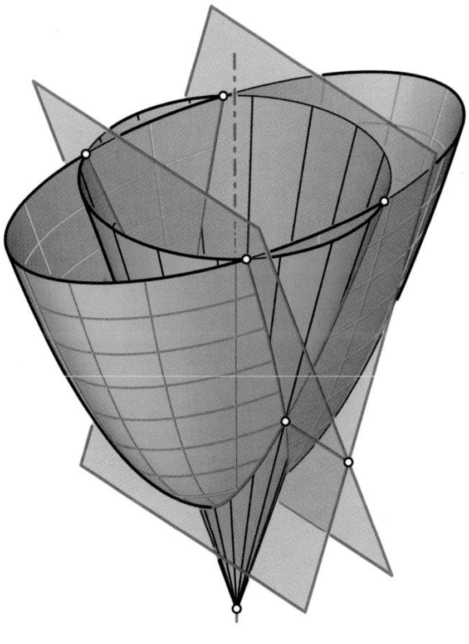

Fig. 9.21
A rotational cone touching an elliptic paraboloid in two points intersects the paraboloid along two planar curves.

For an ellipsoid, this can easily be done by intersecting it with a sphere centered in the midpoint of the ellipsoid and touching it in two points (Figure 9.22). These points of tangency are vertices of the ellipsoid (they lie in two symmetry planes). The intersection curve consists of two circles c_1 and c_2 in planes P_1 and P_2, respectively.

Any intersection curve of the ellipsoid with a plane parallel to P_1 (or P_2) is similar to c_1 (or c_2) and is thus also a circle. Hence, a general ellipsoid carries two families of circles—whereas a rotational ellipsoid contains only the system of parallel circles. In a similar way, we find circles on general hyperboloids and elliptic paraboloids (Figure 9.23).

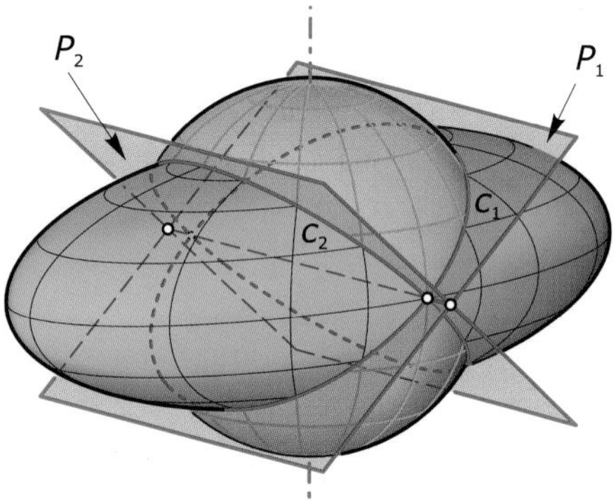

Fig. 9.22
A sphere and a concentric ellipsoid that touch each other in two points have two circles in common.

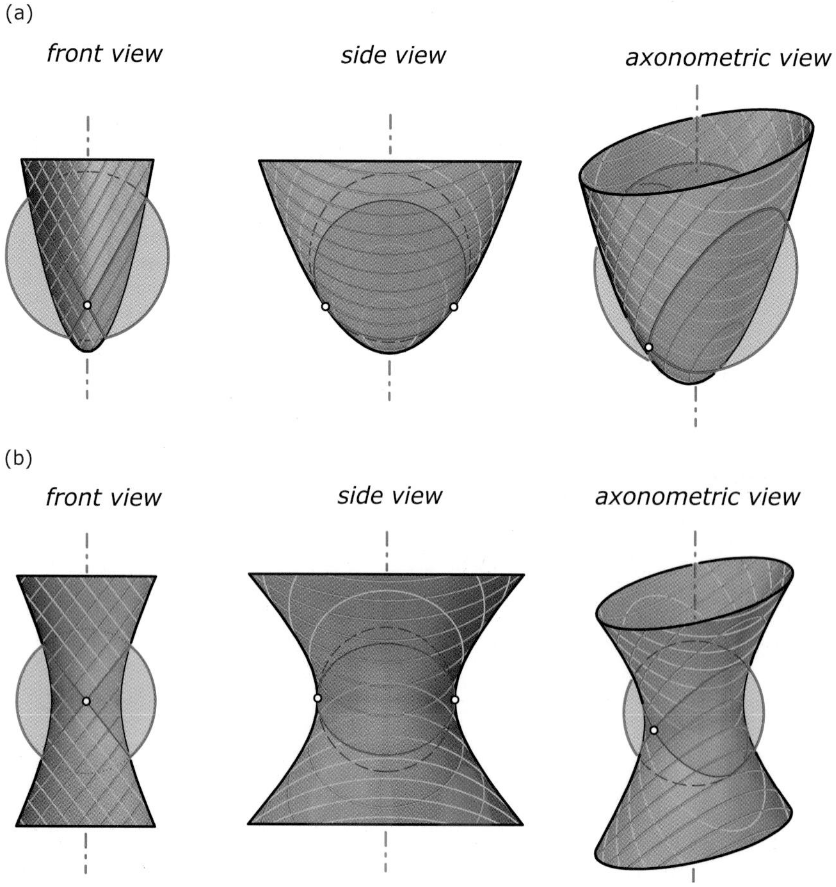

Fig. 9.23
Quadrics carrying two sets of circles.
(a) Elliptic paraboloid.
(b) One-sheet hyperboloid.

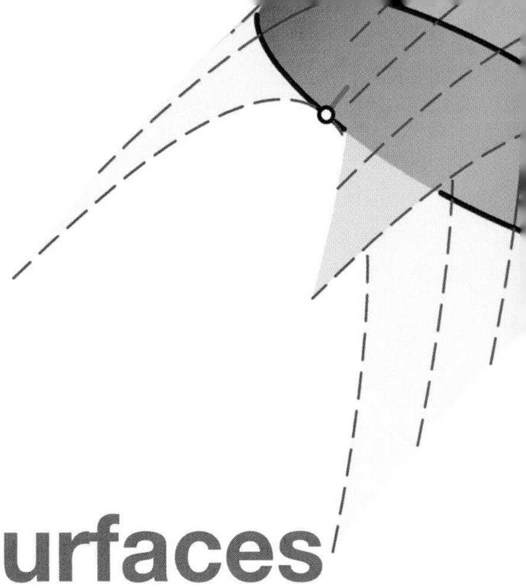

Translational Surfaces

Assume two curves k and l intersecting in a single point, the origin o. Translating the profile curve k along the path curve l, we generate a *translational surface* (Figure 9.24a). Thus, a translational surface contains a set of curves k_p that are congruent with the profile curve k. Each of the profile curves k_p intersects the path curve l in a point p.

We obtain a common point x of the surface curve k_p by translating a point q of the profile curve k with the vector $\mathbf{p}$. This point x of the curve k_p can also be obtained by adding the vector $\mathbf{q}$ to the point p of the path curve l. When we add the vector $\mathbf{q}$ to all points of the path curve l, we obtain the surface curve l_q—which is congruent with the path curve l (Figure 9.24b). Thus, we see that we can change the roles of profile and path curves to generate the same translational surface.

As another consequence, to obtain an arbitrary point x on the translational surface we simply have to add two position vectors $\mathbf{p}$ and $\mathbf{q}$ which are defined by the points of the generating curves k and l. In mathematical notation, the curves k and l can be captured by parametric representations $\mathbf{k}(u)$ and $\mathbf{l}(v)$ with parameters u and v. Thus, we are able to express each point x of a translational surface as

$$\mathbf{x}(u,v) = \mathbf{k}(u) + \mathbf{l}(v). \qquad \text{(T)}$$

Fig. 9.24
(a) Translating a profile curve k along another (path) curve l, we obtain a translational surface.
(b) Translating the path curve along the profile curve generates the same translational surface.

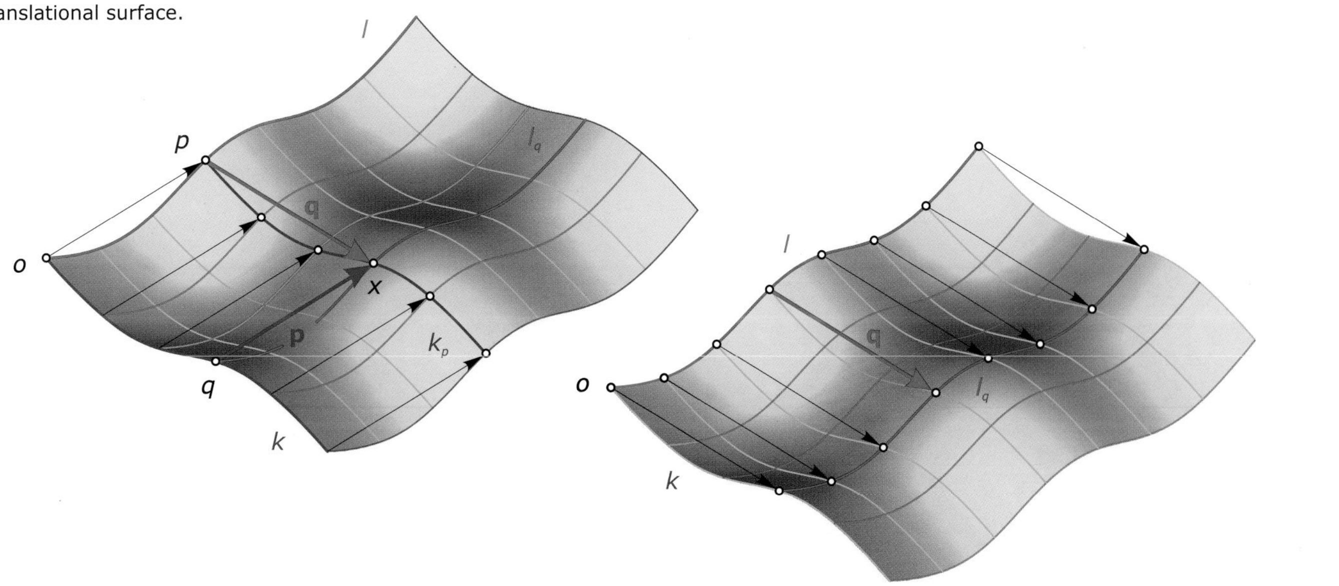

Further, the tangent plane at a point x is spanned by the respective tangents t_k and t_l of the two generating curves. Along a parameter curve $k(u) = k_x$, the tangents of the other family of parameter lines are parallel. They build a cylinder with profile curve k_x. This cylinder is tangent to the translational surface along the curve k_x (see Figure 9.25). Due to the fact that the generating curves can change their roles, the same is true for the parameter curve l_x.

The straightforward generation of translational surfaces by simply translating a curve along another curve, and the fact that they carry two sets of congruent parameter curves, predestine them for design and building processes. Thus, we find many interesting examples of built objects that contain translational surfaces (Figure 9.26).

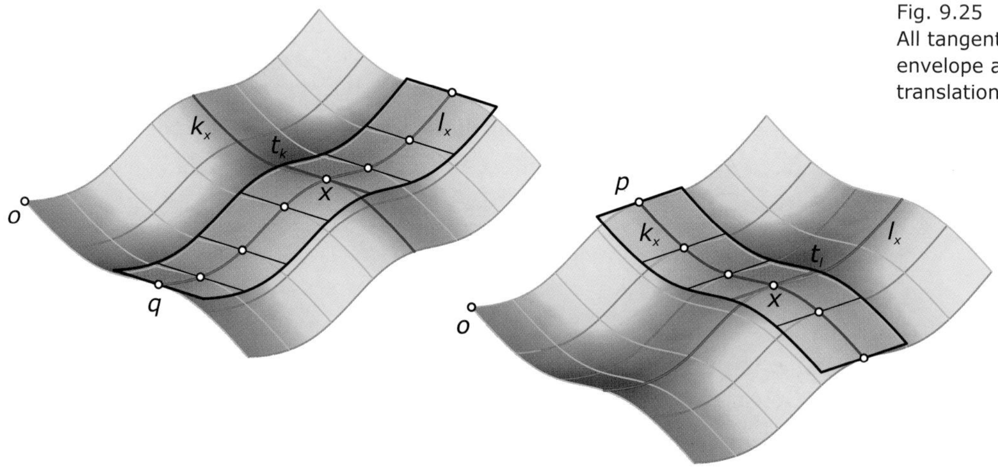

Fig. 9.25
All tangents along a generating curve envelope a cylinder tangent to the translational surface.

Fig. 9.26
Translational surfaces are commonly used elements in architectural design.
(a) The *Eso Hotel* (1998-2002) atop Cerro Paranal by Auer+Weber.

(b) The *Japanese Pavilion* at Expo 2000 in Germany by Shigeru Ban and Frei Otto.

(a)

(b)

Instead of smooth curves, we could also use polylines as generating curves. In analogy to the discrete rotational surfaces, we obtain discrete translational surfaces with planar faces (parallelograms) that are a suitable basis for steel/glass construction (Figure 9.27).

Special translational surfaces. Simple representatives of the class of translational surfaces are the cylinders. For these, one of the generating curves is a straight line (see Figure 9.1). Planar curves that lie in orthogonal planes are frequently used for the generation of translational surfaces. They offer a wide range of interesting possibilities while being easy to handle.

(a)

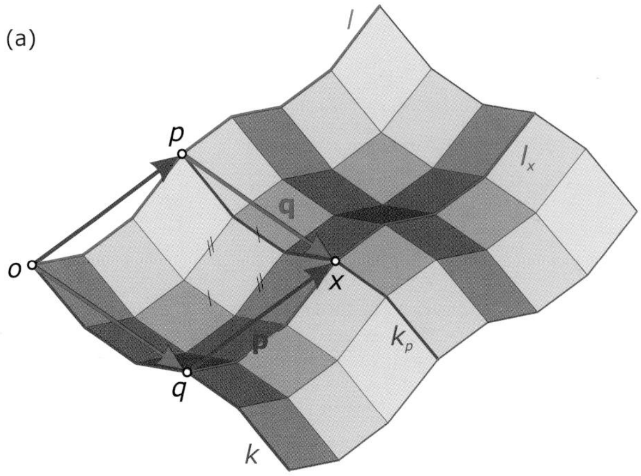

(b)

Fig. 9.27
(a) Approximation of a translational surface using polylines as generating curves.
(b) The Glass dome of the *Hippo House* (1996) at the Berlin Zoo by J. Gribl (image courtesy of Schlaich Bergermann & Partners).

Example:

A rotational paraboloid generated as translational surface. In the section on rotational surfaces, we derived the equation of a rotational paraboloid as $z = a \cdot (x^2 + y^2)$. The surface is generated by rotating the parabola $z = a \cdot x^2$ about the z-axis of the coordinate system. Now we introduce parameters $u = x$ and $v = y$ and obtain the parametric representation of the paraboloid as

$(x,y,z) = (u,v,a \cdot u^2 + a \cdot v^2) = (u,0,a \cdot u^2) + (0,v,a \cdot v^2)$.

This is precisely an instance of Equation (T), showing that the surface is generated by translating the parabola $\mathbf{k}(u) = (u,0,a \cdot u^2)$ of the xz-plane along the parabola $\mathbf{l}(v) = (0,v,a \cdot v^2)$ of the yz-plane. Thus, a rotational paraboloid can also be generated as a translational surface for which we use congruent parabolas in orthogonal planes as generating curves (Figure 9.28). Note that all of these parabolas are opened to the same side.

Elliptic paraboloids. As we have seen, rotational paraboloids are special translational surfaces. The application of an independent scaling on a rotational paraboloid results in an *elliptic paraboloid*. The two congruent profile parabolas in orthogonal planes are mapped into two parabolas with parallel axes that are no longer congruent. However, they can be used to generate the scaled rotational paraboloid by translating one parabola along the other.

The parabolas are open to the same side, and their supporting planes are orthogonal. As an interesting property, we note that all non-singular planar intersection curves are parabolas or ellipses. Moreover, the entire surface only contains elliptical points. Therefore, this paraboloid is called an *elliptic* paraboloid. It possesses two symmetry planes that intersect in the axis of the elliptic paraboloid.

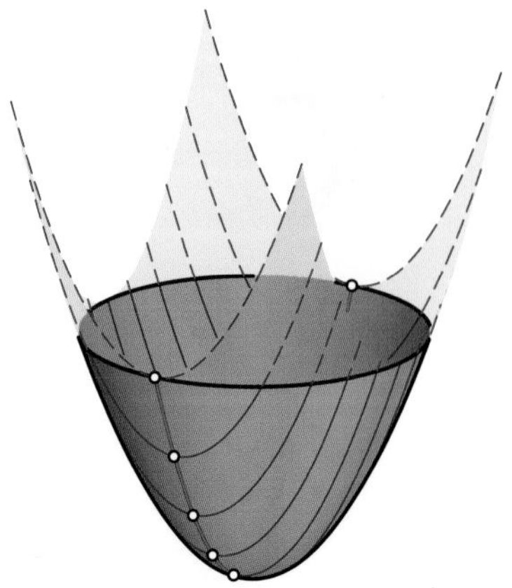

Fig. 9.28
The generation of a rotational paraboloid as a translational surface.

The direction of this axis is parallel to the supporting planes of the generating parabolas, and the intersection point of the axis with the surface is called the *vertex v* (Figure 9.29). The tangent plane in the vertex is orthogonal to the axis. Therefore, the axis is the surface normal in the vertex.

The intersection curve of an elliptic paraboloid and a plane is a parabola if the plane is parallel to the axis of the paraboloid. Otherwise, a planar intersection curve is an ellipse—provided the plane intersects the surface at all (Figure 9.30).

Hyperbolic paraboloid. If we reflect one of the generating parabolas about its vertex tangent, we obtain another type of translational surface that also carries two sets of congruent parabolas (Figure 9.31). This surface is called a *hyperbolic paraboloid*. Just as a remark we mention that both types of paraboloids belong to the class of quadrics we encountered in the section on rotational surfaces. Whereas the elliptic paraboloid can be generated from a rotational paraboloid by applying an independent scaling, this is not true for the hyperbolic paraboloid.

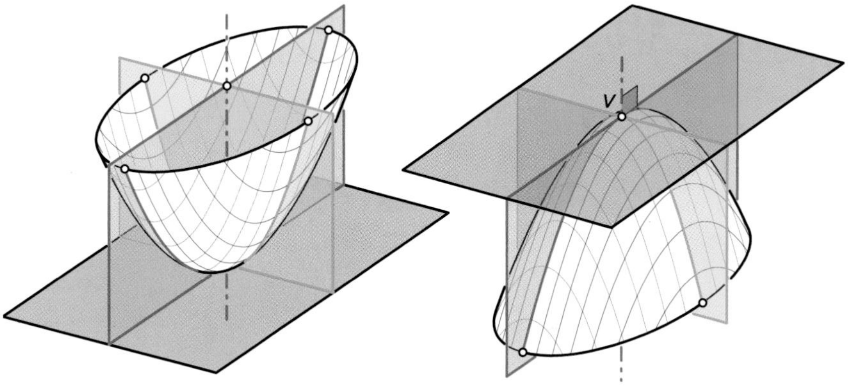

Fig. 9.29
An elliptic paraboloid is generated by translating a parabola along another parabola. Both generating parabolas have to be open to the same side and must have parallel axes. The axis of an elliptic paraboloid is the intersection of the two symmetry planes.

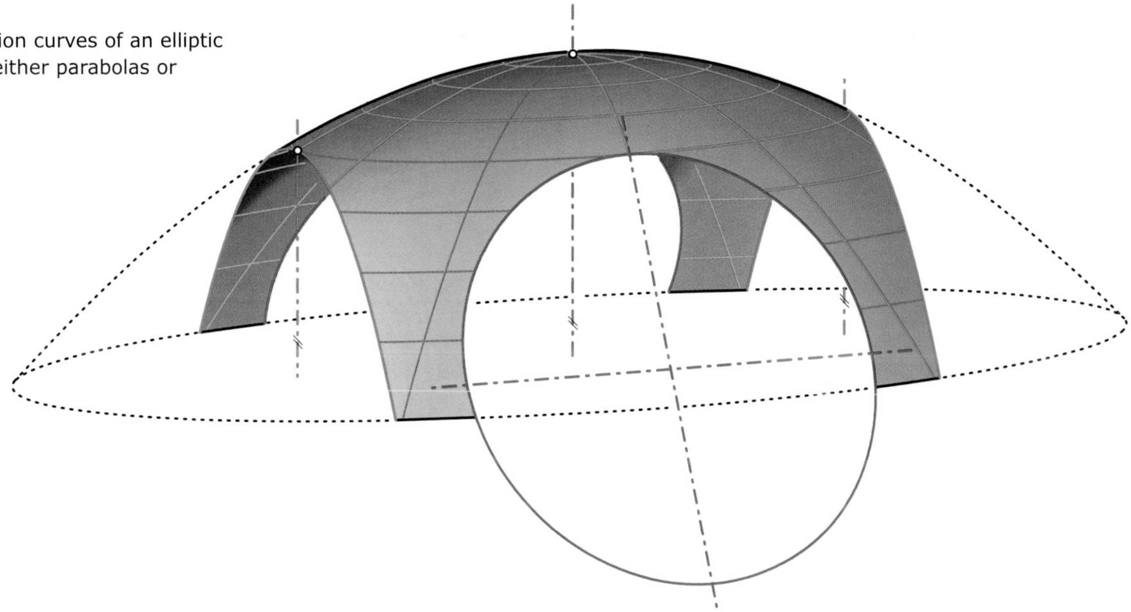

Fig. 9.30
Planar intersection curves of an elliptic paraboloid are either parabolas or ellipses.

A hyperbolic paraboloid carries exclusively hyperbolic points. In other words, every part of this surface is saddle shaped. Analogously to the elliptic case, the intersection line of the two symmetry planes is the axis of the hyperbolic paraboloid (Figure 9.31). The vertex is the intersection point of the axis with the surface, and the tangent plane in the vertex is orthogonal to the axis. Studying the planar intersection curves, we have to distinguish among three different cases (Figure 9.32).

- In analogy to the elliptic paraboloid, planes parallel to the axis intersect the surface along parabolas.
- Tangent planes cut out two lines.
- All other planes intersect along hyperbolas.

The fact that every tangent plane intersects the surface along a pair of different lines implies that the hyperbolic paraboloid carries two sets of lines. Thus, the hyperbolic paraboloid is another example of a ruled surface. As a translational surface with simple profile curves (which can also be generated by moving a straight line), the hyperbolic paraboloid has always been an important basic shape for architectural design. Due to the fact that this surface is often used, the name of the hyperbolic paraboloid is sometimes shortened to *HP surface*.

Although it is possible to generate paraboloids with an arbitrary axis, we suggest using only paraboloids with vertical axes—to take advantage of the positive static properties of this assembly.

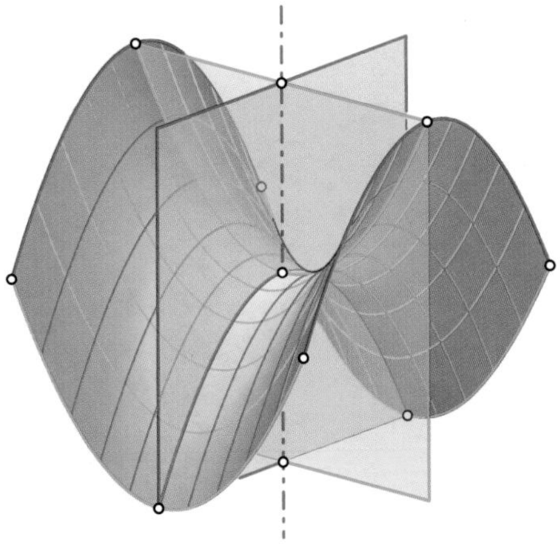

Fig. 9.31
A hyperbolic paraboloid is generated by translating a parabola along another parabola. Both generating parabolas have to be open to different sides. The axis of a hyperbolic paraboloid is the intersection line of the two symmetry planes.

Fig. 9.32
Hyperbolic paraboloids are intersected by planes along parabolas, hyperbolas, or a pair of lines. There are no ellipses on a hyperbolic paraboloid.

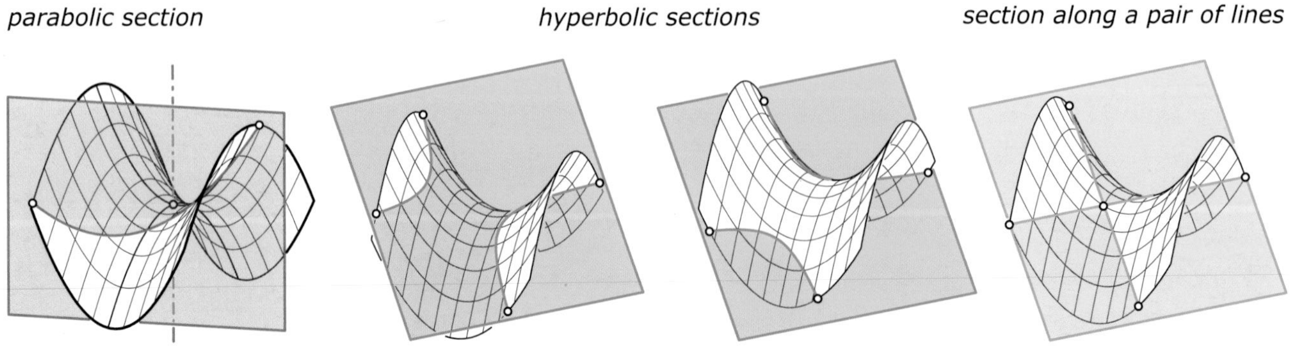

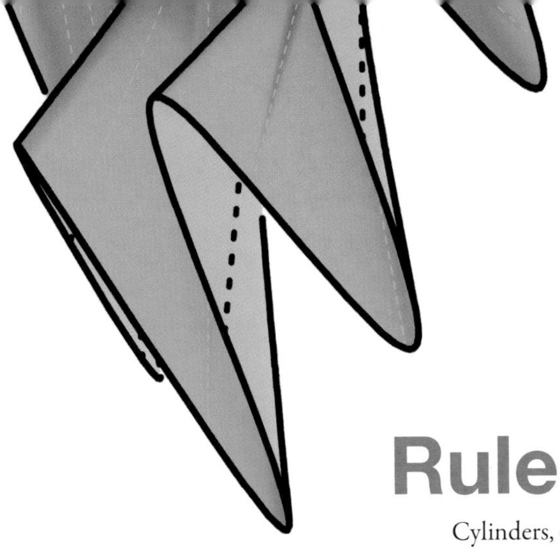

Ruled Surfaces

Cylinders, cones, one-sheet hyperboloids, and hyperbolic paraboloids are surfaces that carry families of straight lines. Thus, they could also be generated by moving a straight line.

In the following we study the class of all surfaces generated by a moving straight line. These surfaces are called *ruled surfaces*. By definition, they contain a continuous family of straight lines called *generators* or *rulings* (Figure 9.33). We will study several possibilities for defining the motion of a line generating a ruled surface.

Each of these approaches has advantages, but some of them will restrict the diversity of ruled surface types. Note that from the geometric point of view ruled surfaces always extend to infinity because the generating straight lines extend to infinity. For practical reasons, we use in this section straight line segments that generate only finite parts of ruled surfaces.

Fig. 9.33
Ruled surfaces in architecture.
(a) The *New State Gallery* (1977–1983) in Stuttgart by James Stirling.
(b) The *Planai* skiterminal (2006) by Hofrichter-Ritter (image courtesy of Hofrichter-Ritter Architekten).

(a)

(b)

Ruled surfaces by moving a straight line along a directrix curve. We start with a curve c_1, called directrix curve, and move one point of a straight line (segment) g along this curve. A single point does not yet define the position of a straight line. We also need to prescribe its direction. The direction varies continuously when moving along c_1 (Figure 9.34).

Assume that $\mathbf{c}(u)$ is a parametric representation of the directrix curve c_1 and $\mathbf{d}(u)$ describes the continuously changing direction vector of the moving straight line segment. Then we calculate the position of an arbitrary point x of the generated ruled surface by adding the vectors $\mathbf{c}(u)$ and $v \cdot \mathbf{d}(u)$. Thus, we obtain a parametric representation of ruled surfaces with

$$\mathbf{x}(u,v) = \mathbf{c}(u) + v \cdot \mathbf{d}(u).$$

As a special case, we obtain cylinders when using a constant direction $\mathbf{d}$.

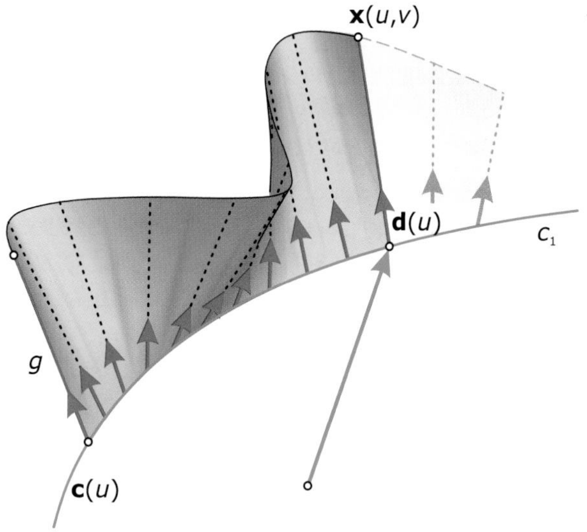

Fig. 9.34
Moving a point of a straight line segment along a curve c_1 and changing its direction simultaneously, we generate a ruled surface.

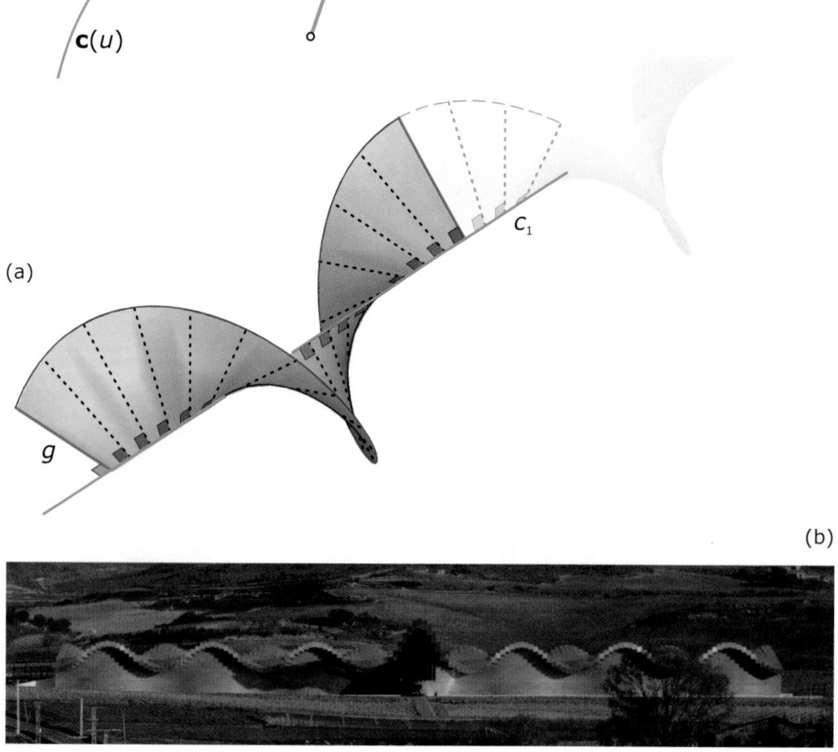

Fig. 9.35
(a) Conoids can be generated by moving a straight line segment along a linear directrix c_1.
(b) The *Ysios Winery* (1998–2001) in Laguardia, Spain, by Santiago Calatrava.
(c) The *Japanese Art and Technology Center* (opened 1995) in Kraków, Poland, by Arata Isozaki.

(c)

Example:

Conoid. We use a straight line as directrix c_1 and a generator g, which intersects c_1 at a right angle. Allowing only rotations about the directrix, we generate a special type of *conoid* (Figure 9.35). Note that we will study a more general approach to conoids at the end of this section. Using the z-axis as directrix c_1, its parametric representation may be chosen as $\mathbf{c}(u) = (0,0,u)$. Because the generators g shall be orthogonal to z, their direction vectors $\mathbf{d}(u)$ have a vanishing z-coordinate. We write them as $\mathbf{d}(u) = (\cos(f(u)), \sin(g(u)), 0)$. Here, $f(u)$ and $g(u)$ are functions of the parameter value (height) u along the directrix. Thus, a parametric representation of the generated ruled surfaces is given by

$x(u,v) = v \cdot \cos(f(u))$,

$y(u,v) = v \cdot \sin(g(u))$,

$z(u,v) = u$.

Figure 9.36 illustrates some of these surfaces. For constant functions $f(u)$ and $g(u)$, we obtain a parameterization of a plane—whereas for identical linear functions $f(u) = g(u) = a \cdot u + b$ common helicoids are generated. We will encounter this special case of a conoid again in the section on helical surfaces.

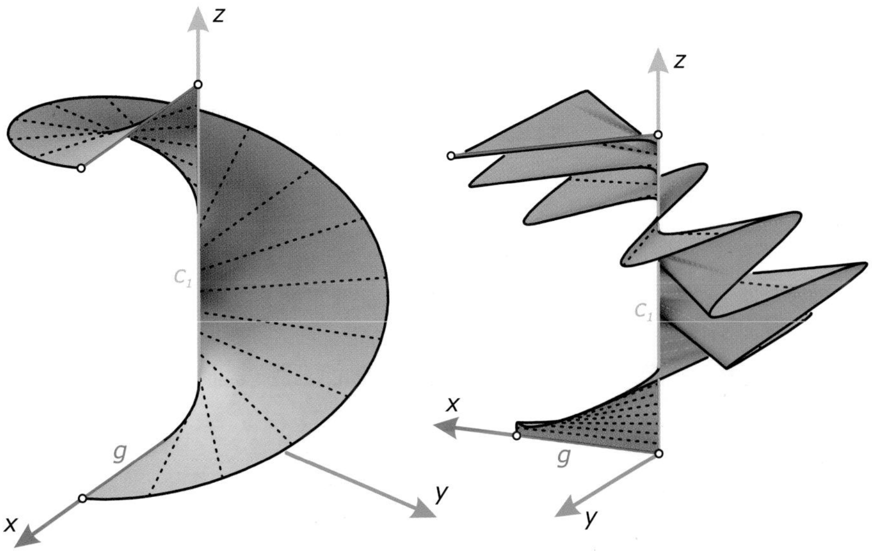

Fig. 9.36
The functions $f(u)$ and $g(u)$ control the variation of the generator's direction and thus determine the final shape of the conoid.
(a) $f(u) = g(u) = u$.
(b) $f(u) = u$, $g(u) = u^2$

Example:

Möbius strip. As a generalization of the previous example, we use a circle c_1 as directrix curve. Now we move a line segment g such that one of its points runs along c_1, whereas g is continuously rotated about c_1 and thus remains orthogonal to c_1. When the line segment arrives again at the starting position, it shall have made one half turn. Thus, the end position of the ruling g coincides with its starting position.

To obtain a parametric representation, we adapt the coordinate frame to the Möbius strip as shown in Figure 9.37. Then the directrix circle c_1 can be described by $\mathbf{c}(u) = (r\cdot\cos(u),\ r\cdot\sin(u),\ 0)$. The generator's rotation in the normal planes of the circle proceeds with the rotational angle $u/2$. Thus, we obtain with $\mathbf{d}(u) = (\cos(u/2)\cdot\cos(u),\ \cos(u/2)\cdot\sin(u),\ \sin(u/2))$ a parametric representation of a Möbius strip:

$x(u,v) = r\cdot\cos(u) + v\cdot\cos(u/2)\cdot\cos(u)$,
$y(u,v) = r\cdot\sin(u) + v\cdot\cos(u/2)\cdot\sin(u)$,
$z(u,v) = v\cdot\sin(u/2)$.

Similar to the example "conoid," we can replace the term $u/2$ with an arbitrary function $f(u)$. Figure 9.38 illustrates the influence of various functions $f(u)$ on the final shape of the ruled surface.

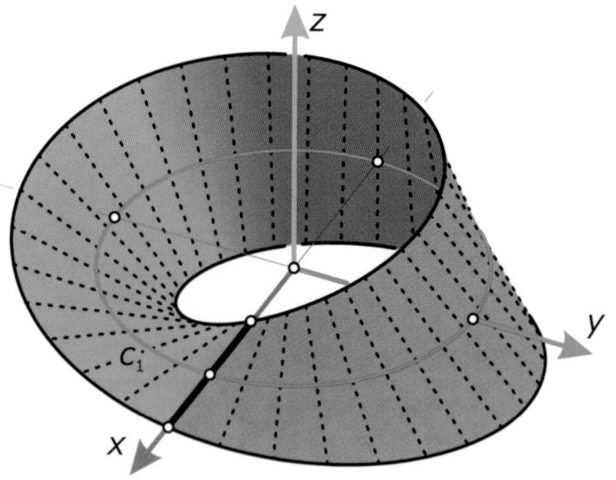

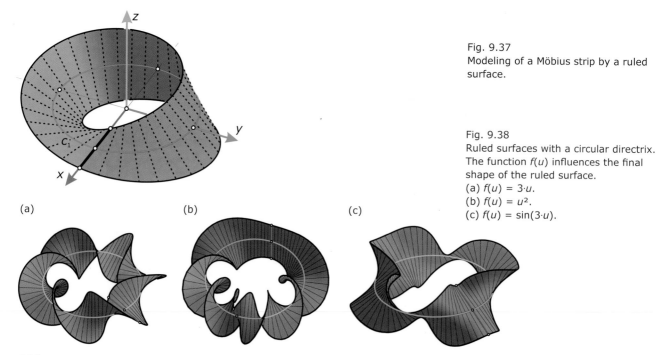

Fig. 9.37
Modeling of a Möbius strip by a ruled surface.

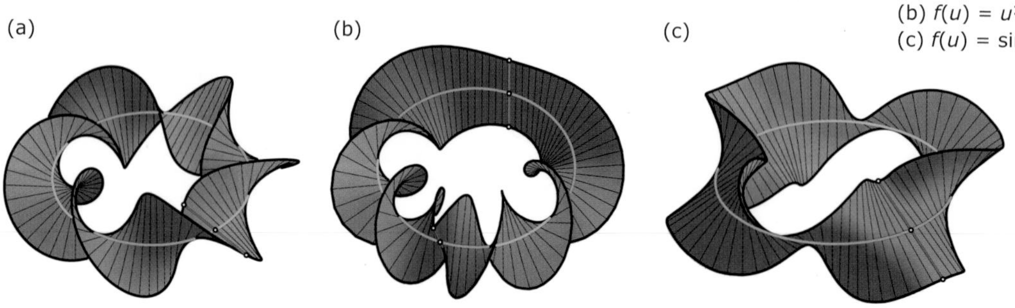

Fig. 9.38
Ruled surfaces with a circular directrix. The function $f(u)$ influences the final shape of the ruled surface.
(a) $f(u) = 3\cdot u$.
(b) $f(u) = u^2$.
(c) $f(u) = \sin(3\cdot u)$.

Ruled surfaces by connecting corresponding points of two generating curves. Let's start with a simple case: a one-sheet rotational hyperboloid. In the previous section, we generated a one-sheet rotational hyperboloid by rotating a straight line about an axis. But we can interpret this generation depicted in Figure 9.39 in a second way: the generators can be found by connecting corresponding points on circles c_1 and c_2.

We now generalize this generation process to create ruled surfaces from two arbitrary spatial curves (directrices) $c_1(u)$ and $c_2(u)$. The generators join curve points that correspond to the same parameter value u. Depending on the parameterization of the two curves c_1 and c_2, we can generate different ruled surfaces to the same directrices c_1 and c_2 (Figure 9.40).

Due to the fact that we have nearly full freedom to choose the directrices and their parameterization, this approach opens a wide diversity of possible shapes (Figure 9.41). Special choices of directrices and their parameterization lead to some remarkable ruled surfaces.

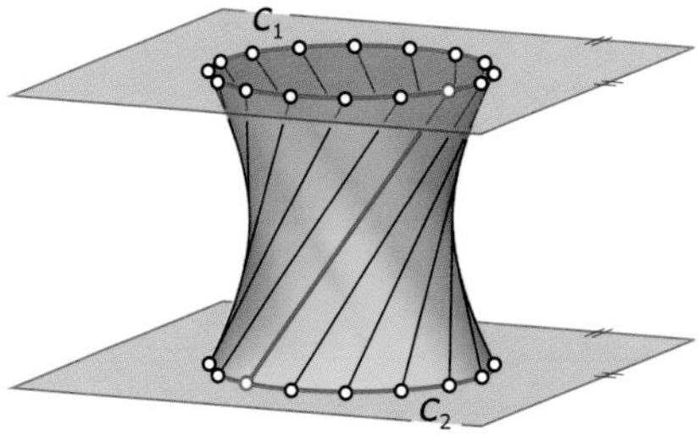

Fig. 9.39
A one-sheet rotational hyperboloid generated by lines connecting points on two circles c_1 and c_2.

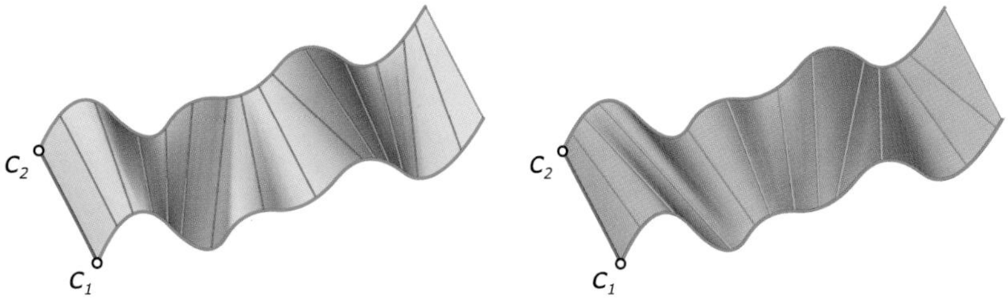

Fig. 9.40
Ruled surfaces can be generated by joining points on two parameterized curves. Different parameterizations of these curves can create different ruled surfaces.

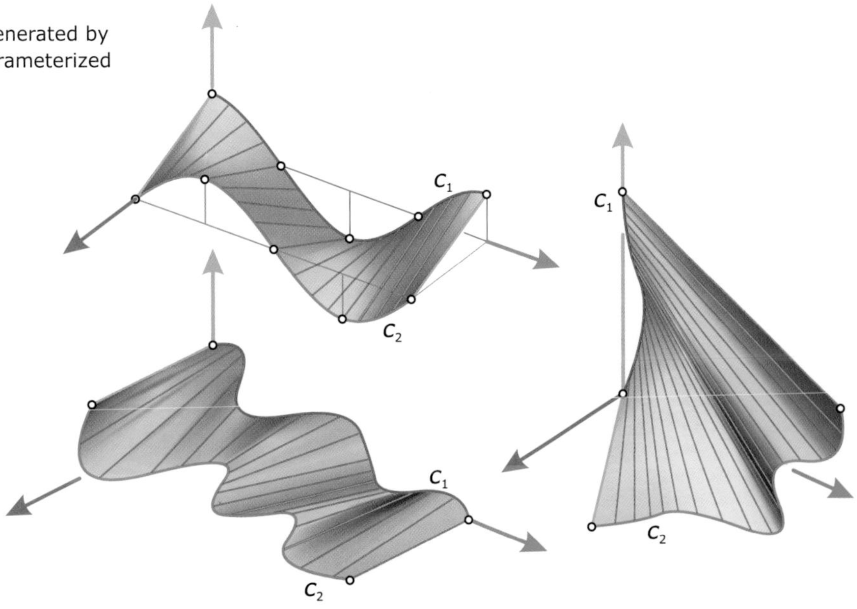

Fig. 9.41
Ruled surfaces can be generated by joining points on two parameterized curves.

HP Surfaces. HP surfaces (hyperbolic paraboloids) are well established in the area of shells. Positive static properties (which are especially good for HP surfaces with vertical axis) allow the construction of shells of large span width with relatively small thickness. They are easy-to-use elements for architectural design and offer many design possibilities (Figure 9.42).

In addition to its generation as a translational surface, an HP surface can be generated as a ruled surface in the following way (Figure 9.43). We start with two skew line segments *ab* and *dc*, and use a linear parameterization to find corresponding points *p* and *q* on *ab* and on *dc*. We then obtain an arbitrary ruling *g* of the HP-surface by connecting the points *p* and *q*.

Manually, this could easily be done by dividing *ab* and *dc* with the same ratio dist(*a*,*p*) : dist(*p*,*b*) = dist(*d*,*q*) : dist(*q*,*c*). To find a parametric representation of the HP surface, we calculate the position vectors of the points *p* and *q* and obtain $\mathbf{p}(u) = \mathbf{a} + u\cdot(\mathbf{b} - \mathbf{a}) = (1 - u)\cdot\mathbf{a} + u\cdot\mathbf{b}$ and $\mathbf{q}(u) = (1 - u)\cdot\mathbf{d} + u\cdot\mathbf{c}$. Then, an arbitrary point *x* on the ruling $g(u)$ that connects the points *p* and *q* can be calculated with

$$\mathbf{x} = (1 - v)\cdot\mathbf{p} + v\cdot\mathbf{q} = (1 - v)\cdot[(1 - u)\cdot\mathbf{a} + u\cdot\mathbf{b}] + v\cdot[(1 - u)\cdot\mathbf{d} + u\cdot\mathbf{c}].$$

Finally, this can be expanded to

$$\mathbf{x}(u,v) = (1 - v)\cdot(1 - u)\cdot\mathbf{a} + (1 - \mathrm{v})\cdot u\cdot\mathbf{b} + v\cdot(1 - u)\cdot\mathbf{d} + v\cdot u\cdot\mathbf{c}.$$

(a)

(b)

Fig. 9.42
HP surfaces in use by architectural design.
(a) The *Pengrowth Saddledome* (opened 1983) in Calgary by Graham McCourt is believed to still be the widest spanning hyperbolic paraboloid concrete shell in the world. The geometric shape is obtained by cutting a hyperbolic paraboloid with a sphere.
(b) Part of a high school sports complex in Houston.

If the parameters v and u take values between 0 and 1, we obtain an HP surface patch confined by the skew quadrilateral *abcd*. Using values greater than 1 or less than 0, we obtain points of the HP surface situated outside this boundary.

The parameterization of an HP surface is linear in both parameters v and u. We can rewrite it as

$$\boldsymbol{x}(u,v) = (1 - u)\cdot[(1 - v)\cdot\mathbf{a} + v\cdot\mathbf{d}] + u\cdot[(1 - v)\cdot\mathbf{b} + v\cdot\mathbf{c}].$$

If we interpret $\mathbf{r}(v) = (1 - v)\cdot\mathbf{a} + v\cdot\mathbf{d}$ and $\mathbf{s}(v) = (1 - v)\cdot\mathbf{b} + v\cdot\mathbf{c}$ as position vectors of points r and s, we recognize that there exists a second familiy of rulings $h(v)$ that can be generated by dividing the line segments *ad* and *bc* with constant ratio (Figure 9.44).

HP surfaces and one-sheet hyperboloids carry two different families g_i and h_i of rulings. All rulings of the same family are mutually skew, whereas an arbitrary ruling of one family intersects all rulings of the other family. Thus, HP surfaces and one-sheet hyperboloids can be interpreted as ruled surfaces in a double sense.

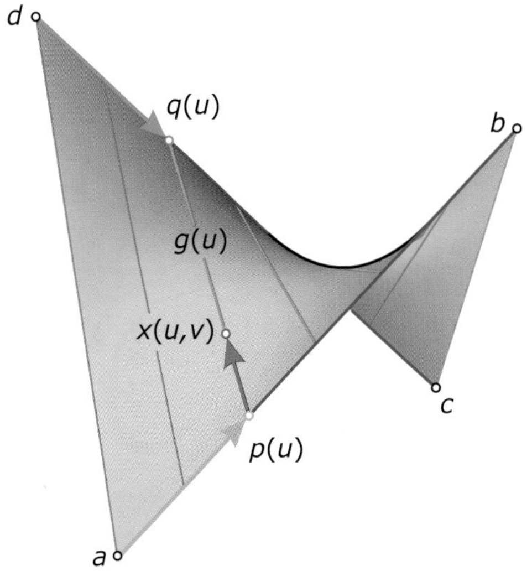

Fig. 9.43
Constructing rulings of an HP surface by connecting linearly parameterized straight line segments.

Fig. 9.44
An HP surface carries two families of generators.
(a) Construction of the second family.
(b) Use in a garden pavilion.

(a)

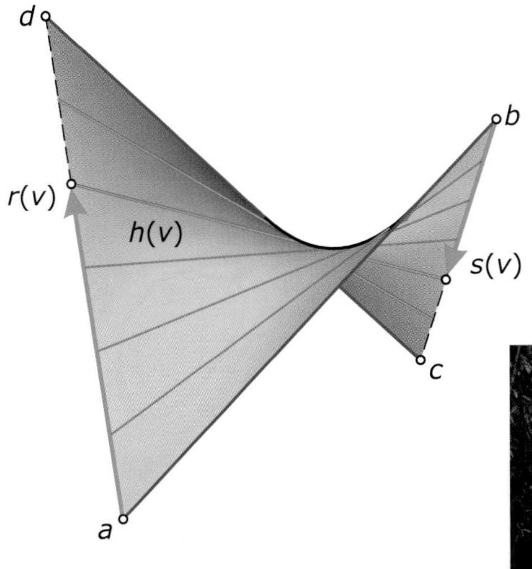

(b)

They are sometimes called *double ruled surfaces*. Through every arbitrary point x of a double ruled surface two different generators g_x and h_x can be drawn. These rulings g_x and h_x define the tangent plane in the point x (Figure 9.45). It can be proved that the HP surfaces and the one-sheet hyperboloids are the only types of double ruled surfaces.

In contrast to the one-sheet hyperboloid, all rulings of an HP surface that belong to the same family are parallel to a *director plane*. To be more precise, every plane D parallel to two different rulings of one family belongs to a set of parallel planes—and each of these planes is called a director plane. An HP surface has two different families of director planes according to the two families of rulings.

There is exactly one tangent plane of an HP surface that is orthogonal to both types of director planes. The corresponding surface point v is the *vertex* of the HP surface, and the surface normal through the vertex v is the axis (Figure 9.46).

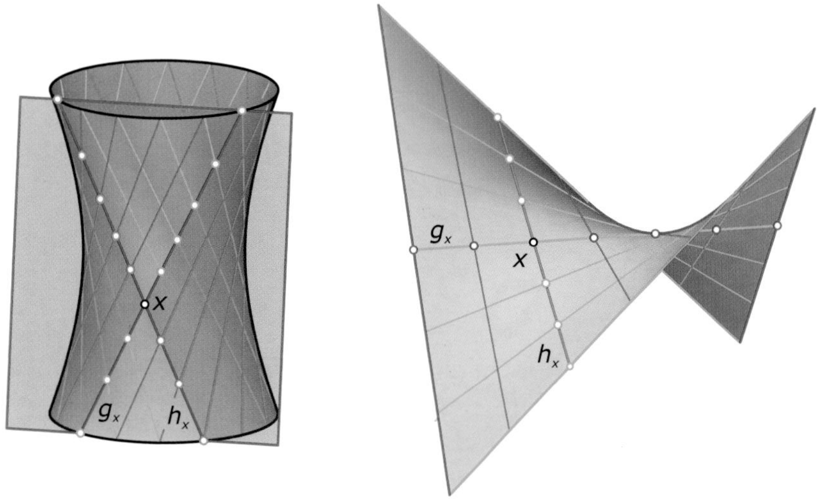

Fig. 9.45
HP surfaces and one-sheet hyperboloids carry two different families of generators.

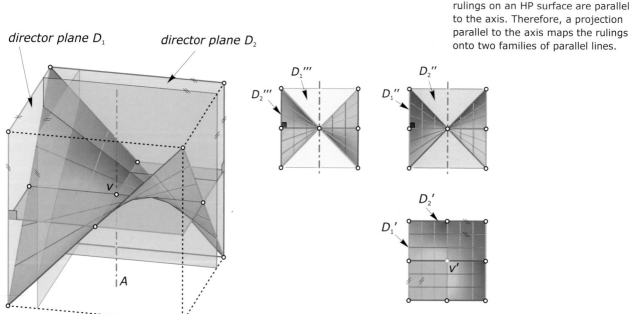

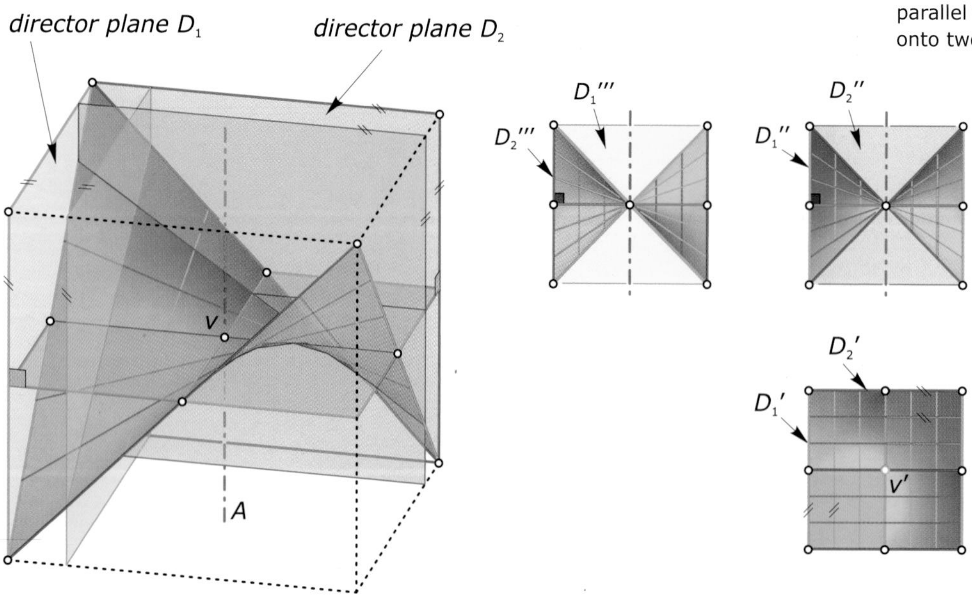

Fig. 9.46
The director planes of both families of rulings on an HP surface are parallel to the axis. Therefore, a projection parallel to the axis maps the rulings onto two families of parallel lines.

Intersections with planes parallel to the axis (but different from director planes) are parabolas. They can be used to generate the HP surface as a translational surface. Figure 9.47 illustrates both generation principles—on the one hand as a ruled surface and on the other as a translational surface.

Conoids. Now we consider a generalization of HP surfaces; namely, ruled surfaces with rulings parallel to a director plane that intersect a single straight line c_1 (Figure 9.48). Parts of these *conoids* are commonly used for the design of shells or shed roofs (Figure 9.35). Although the shape of the second directrix c_2 can be chosen arbitrarily, we have to provide appropriate parameterizations to force all rulings to be parallel to a director plane.

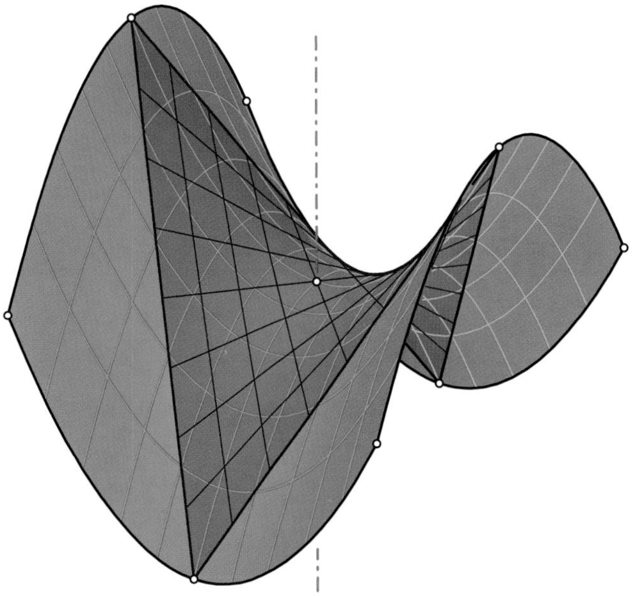

Fig. 9.47
An HP surface can be generated either as a ruled surface or as a translational surface.

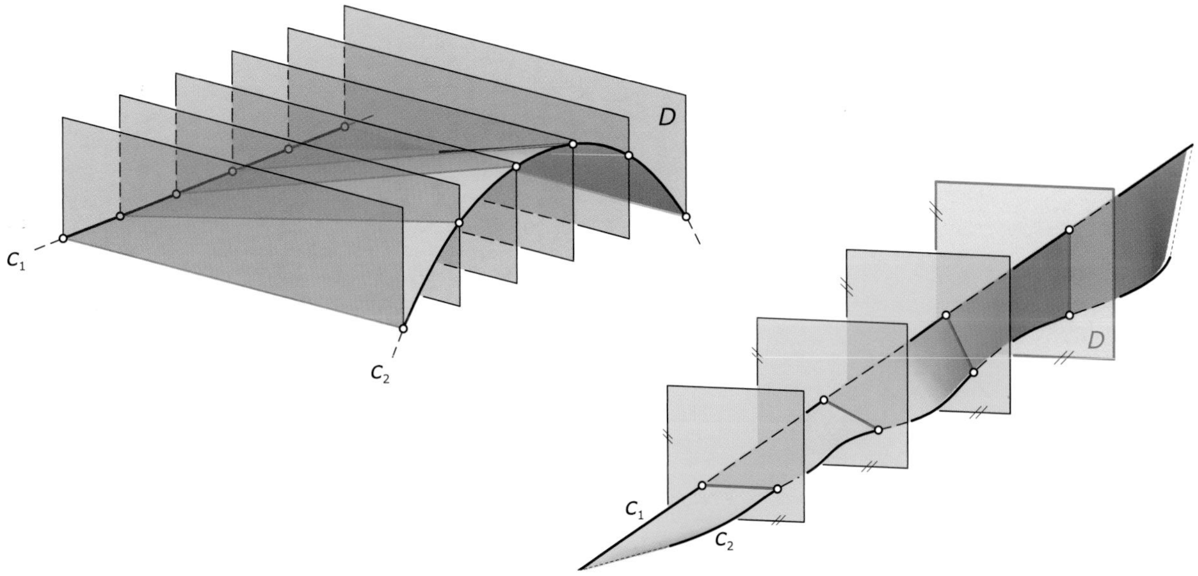

Fig. 9.48
All rulings of a conoid are parallel to the director plane D and intersect a straight line c_1.

Example:

Plücker's conoid. Figure 9.49 shows an example with a horizontal director plane and the z-axis as a directrix. The second directrix c_2 has been chosen as an ellipse, with the major vertex a on the z-axis. In addition, the ellipse is symmetric with respect to the yz-plane and lies on a vertical cylinder of revolution. In Figure 9.49, this *Plücker's conoid* is confined by the intersection curve with a coaxial rotational cylinder. We also mention that every rotational cylinder that contains the z-axis intersects Plücker's conoid along an ellipse.

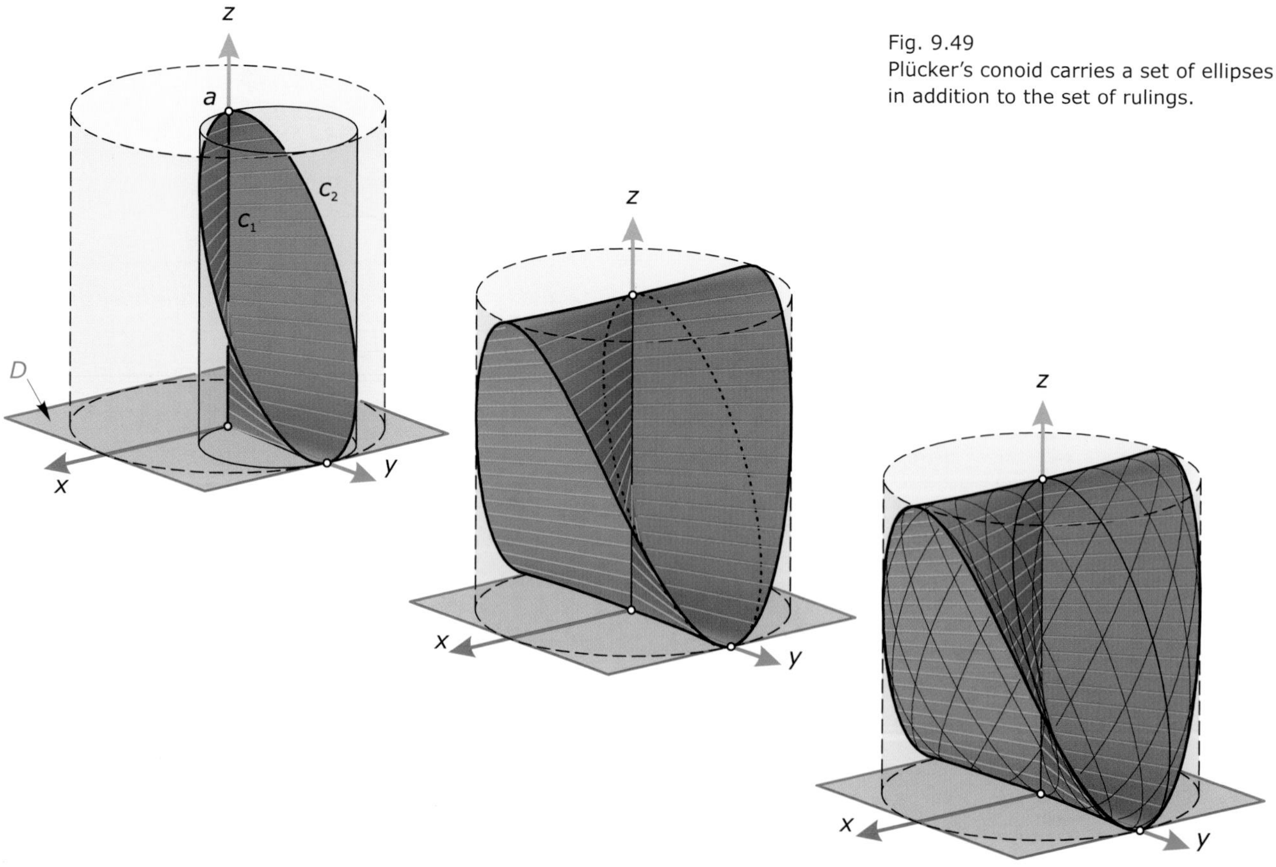

Fig. 9.49
Plücker's conoid carries a set of ellipses in addition to the set of rulings.

Tangent planes of ruled surfaces. The tangent plane in an arbitrary point p of a ruled surface contains the generator g, which runs through p. As illustrated in Figure 9.50, this plane generally is only tangent to the ruled surface in a single point p. If the point p varies along the generator g, the tangent plane rotates about g. We have seen this behavior of a tangent plane on the HP surfaces.

On the other hand, ruled surfaces (such as cylinders and cones) contain rulings where the tangent plane touches the surface along the entire line. Such rulings are called *torsal generators*, to distinguish them from the common case of the *non-torsal generators* (Figure 9.50). All conoids illustrated in Figures 9.49 and 9.51 contain at least one torsal generator. In these cases, the torsal generators are lying in the symmetry planes of the conoids.

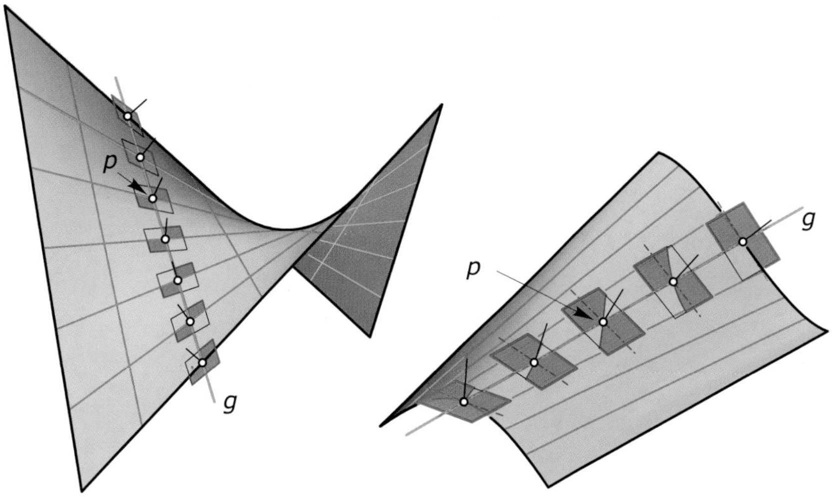

Fig. 9.50
A tangent plane at a point p of a non-torsal generator g only touches the ruled surface in the single point p. Different points of the same generator have different tangent planes.

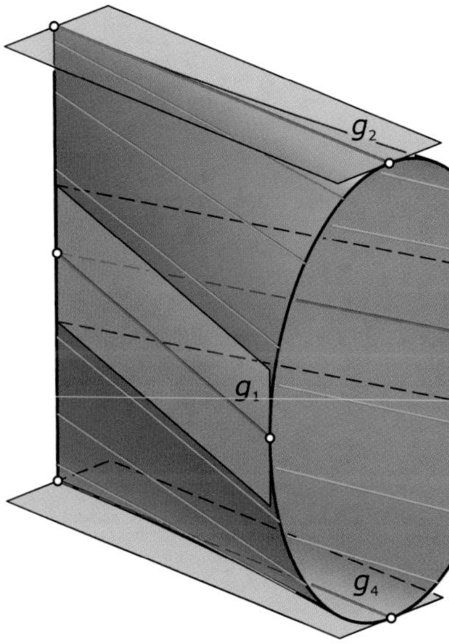

Fig. 9.51
A skew ruled surface with four torsal generators $g_1, \ldots, g_4$.

Ruled surfaces with exclusively torsal generators are called *developable surfaces*, whereas ruled surfaces consisting largely of non-torsal generators are called *skew ruled surfaces* (or *warped ruled surfaces*). Cylinders, cones, and ruled surfaces that consist of tangents of a spatial curve (Figure 9.52) are developable surfaces. We will study this class of surfaces in detail in Chapter 15.

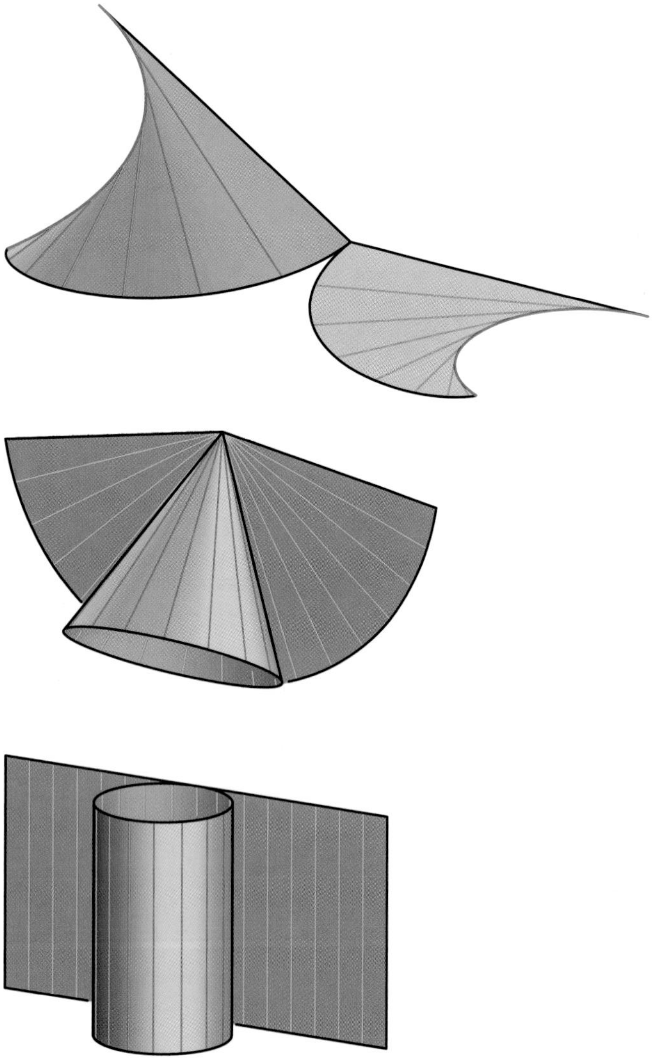

Fig. 9.52
Ruled surfaces that consist of all tangents of a spatial curve are developable surfaces. Together with cylinders and cones, these surfaces have the important property that they can be unfolded into the plane without stretching or tearing.

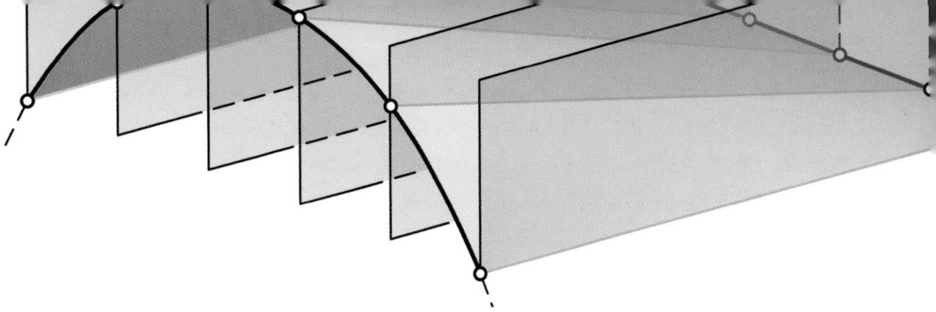

Helical Surfaces

When we apply a smooth helical motion to a spatial curve c, it sweeps a *helical surface* (Figure 9.53). During this motion, every point p of the generating curve c traces a helix h_p. Thus, the net of congruent generator curves c and helixes determines the shape of the helical surface. The tangent plane in an arbitrary surface point q is specified by the tangents t_c and t_h. In analogy to the rotational surfaces, the intersection curve of the helical surface with a plane through the helical axis is called a *meridian m*.

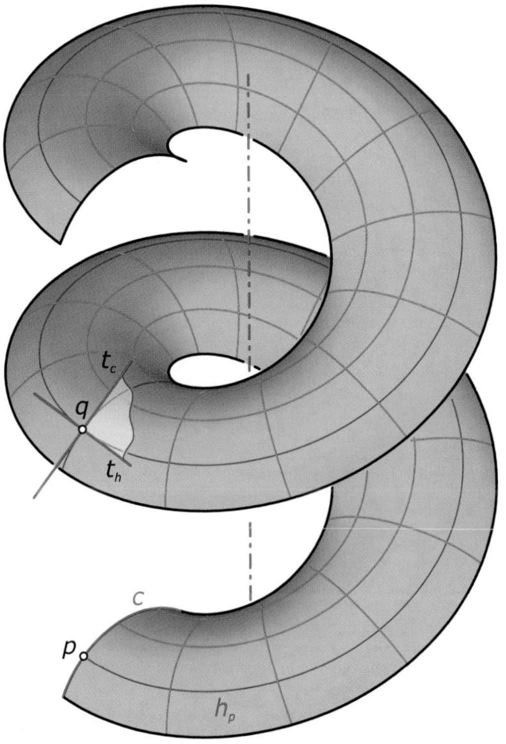

Fig. 9.53
A helical surface is generated by applying a helical motion to a curve c.

Meridians and cross sections orthogonal to the helical axis are often used to characterize the shape of a helical surface (Figure 9.54). It is important to realize that a helical surface is mapped into itself (as a whole) by application of the generating helical motion. Therefore, the surface can also be generated using a meridian curve or a cross section as a generating profile.

Mathematical description. Knowing the parametric representation of the generator $\mathbf{c}(v) = (x(v), y(v), z(v))$, we insert it into the equations for a helical transformation with pitch p,

$$x_1 = x \cdot \cos u - y \cdot \sin u,$$

$$y_1 = x \cdot \sin u + y \cdot \cos u,$$

$$z_1 = z + p \cdot u,$$

to obtain the parametric representation of a helical surface with

$$x(u,v) = x(v) \cdot \cos u - y(v) \cdot \sin u,$$

$$y(u,v) = x(v) \cdot \sin u + y(v) \cdot \cos u,$$

$$z(u,v) = z(v) + p \cdot u.$$

Using a meridian curve $\mathbf{m}(v) = (x(v), 0, z(v))$ in the xz-plane as the generating curve, the parametric representation simplifies to

$$x(u,v) = x(v) \cdot \cos u,$$

$$y(u,v) = x(v) \cdot \sin u,$$

$$z(u,v) = z(v) + p \cdot u.$$

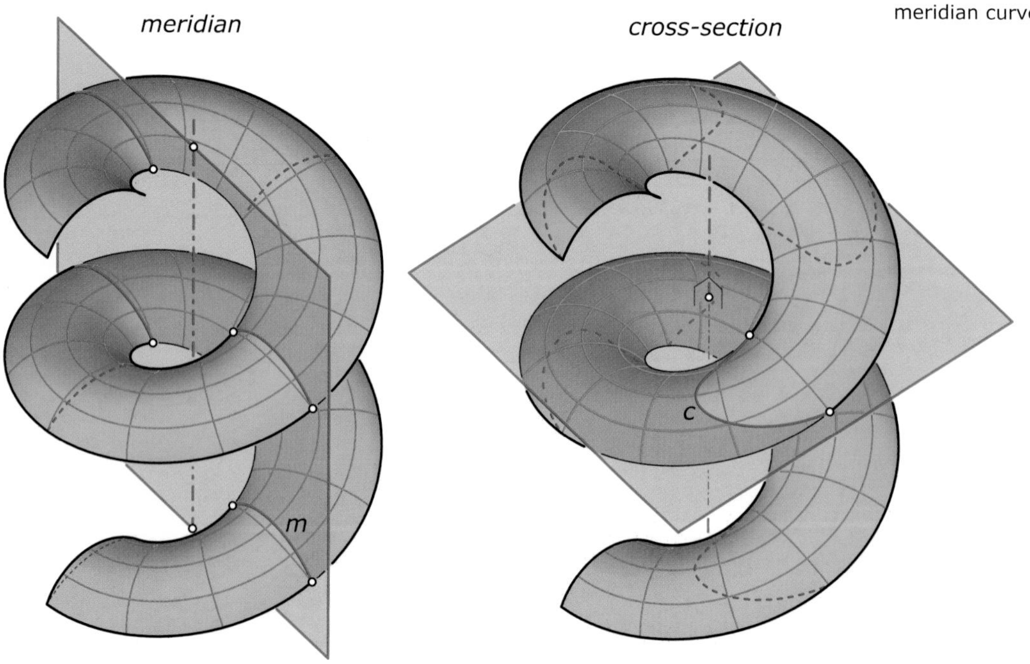

Fig. 9.54
Helical surfaces can also be generated by applying the helical motion to a meridian curve or a cross section.

Special helical surfaces. Among the helical surfaces, those with circles and straight lines as generators are commonly used for modeling purposes. Using circles as meridians or cross sections is useful in generating tubelike screw surfaces, whereas a circle c whose supporting plane is orthogonal to the helix's tangent t_h sweeps a helical pipe (Figure 9.55). The last type of skrew surfaces is representative of the class of pipe surfaces studied at the end of the chapter.

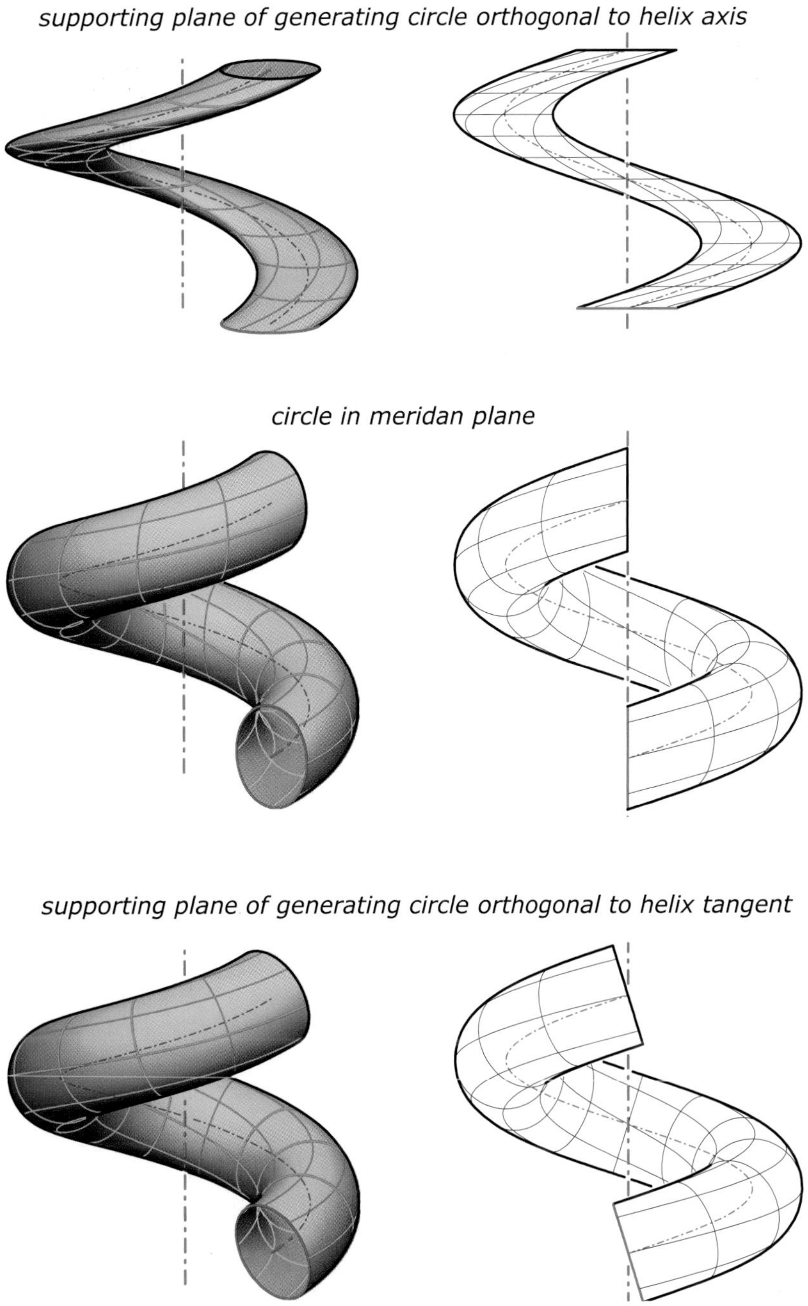

Fig. 9.55
Helical surfaces with circular generators.

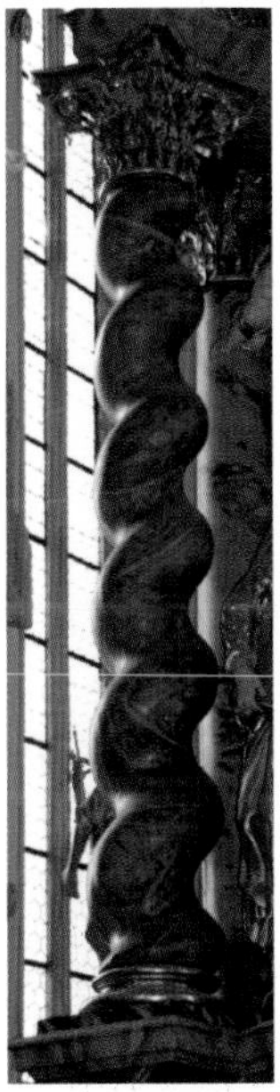

Applying a helical motion to a straight line segment, we obtain helical ruled surfaces. The simplest and at the same time the most important type is the *common* or *right helicoid* (Figure 9.56). It is swept out by a straight line g that orthogonally intersects the axis of the generating helical motion. Therefore, all cross sections are straight lines parallel to a director plane orthogonal to the helical axis.

If we interpret a helix h and the helical axis A as two directrices of a ruled surface, we see that a common helicoid is a special case of a conoid (Figure 9.57). To obtain a parametric representation of a helicoid, we use the parameterization $\mathbf{c}(v) = (v,0,0)$ to describe the generator g and thus we obtain the equations

$$x(u,v) = v\cdot\cos u,$$

$$y(u,v) = v\cdot\sin u,$$

$$z(u,v) = p\cdot u,$$

for the helicoid.

Example:

Intersection of a helicoid and a special cylinder. Given are a helicoid and a rotational cylinder with the helical axis A as a generator (Figure 9.58). We assume the axis b of the cylinder to intersect the x-axis of the coordinate frame in the point $m(r,0,0)$.

Thus, we find the equation of the cylinder with $x^2 - 2\cdot r\cdot x + y^2 = 0$. To calculate the intersection curve of the cylinder and the helicoid, we insert the helicoid's parameterization into the cylinder's equation. We obtain the equation

$v^2\cdot\cos^2 u - 2\cdot r\cdot v\cdot\cos u + v^2\cdot\sin^2 u = 0,$

which we simplify with the steps

$v^2\cdot\cos^2 u + v^2\cdot\sin^2 u - 2\cdot r\cdot v\cdot\cos u = 0,$

$v^2\cdot(\cos^2 u + \sin^2 u) - 2\cdot r\cdot v\cdot\cos u = 0,$

$v^2 - 2\cdot r\cdot v\cdot\cos u = 0,$

to finally find

$v\cdot(v - 2\cdot r\cdot\cos u) = 0.$

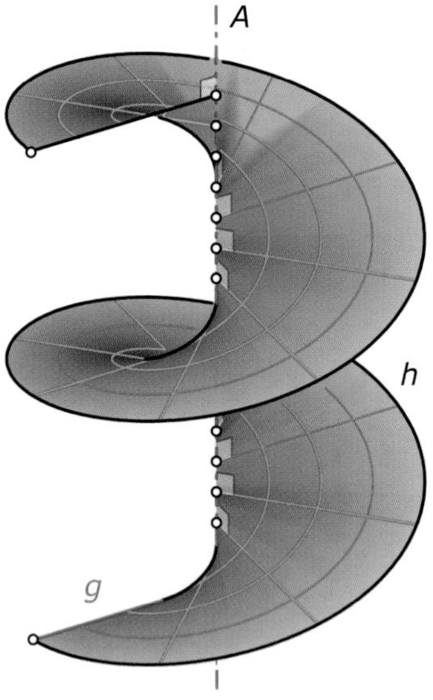

Fig. 9.56
A common helicoid is a helical surface whose generators orthogonally intersect the helical axis.

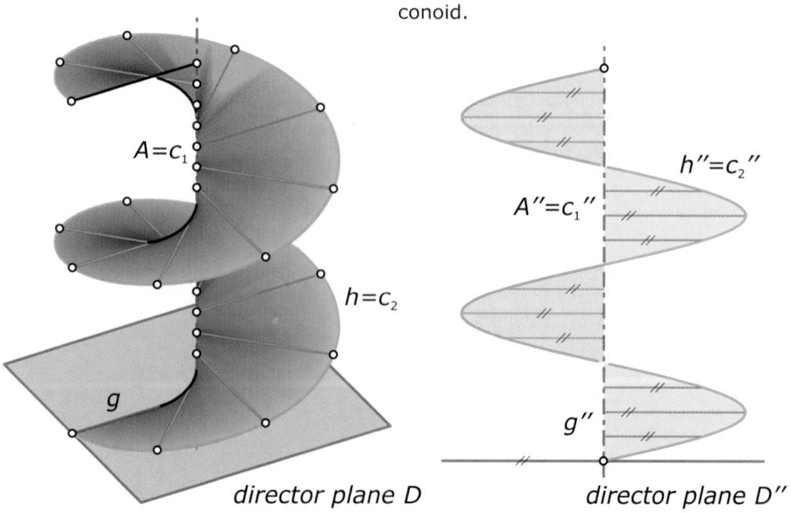

Fig. 9.57
A helicoid can be generated as a conoid.

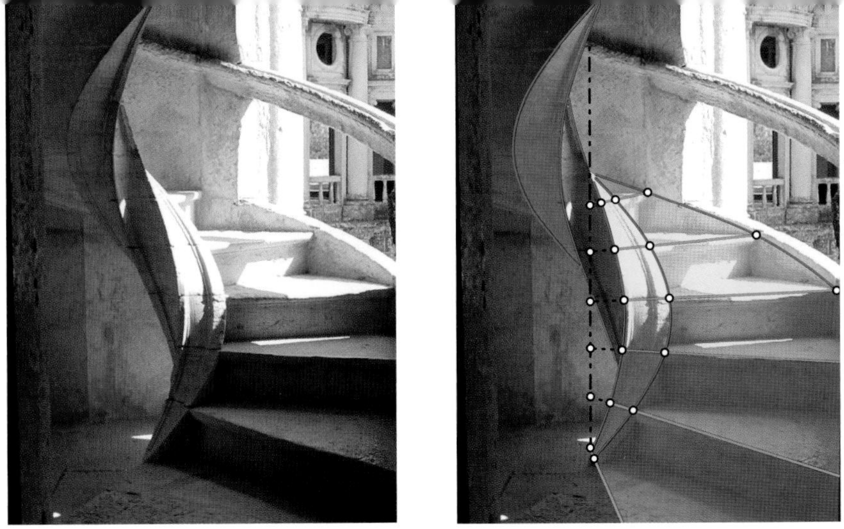

This equation has two different solutions: $v = 0$ (which describes the common z-axis) and $v = 2 \cdot r \cdot \cos u$. We insert the second solution into the parametric representation of the helicoid to obtain a parameterization of the intersection curve I with

$x(u) = 2 \cdot r \cdot \cos u \cdot \cos u,$
$y(u) = 2 \cdot r \cdot \cos u \cdot \sin u,$
$z(u) = p \cdot u.$

Now we apply a translation with translation vector $\mathbf{t} = (-r,0,0)$,

$x(u) = 2 \cdot r \cdot \cos u \cdot \cos u - r,$
$y(u) = 2 \cdot r \cdot \cos u \cdot \sin u,$
$z(u) = p \cdot u,$

and simplify the equations with known formulae for trigonometric functions to

$x(u) = r \cdot \cos(2u),$
$y(u) = r \cdot \sin(2u),$
$z(u) = p \cdot u = (p/2) \cdot 2u.$

This is a parametric representation of a helix i with half the pitch p of the original helical motion. The axes of both helixes are parallel. Thus, in addition to the helical paths every common helicoid contains many more helixes (Figure 9.59). Parts of common helicoids are often used to model spiral staircases or heliclines (Figure 9.60).

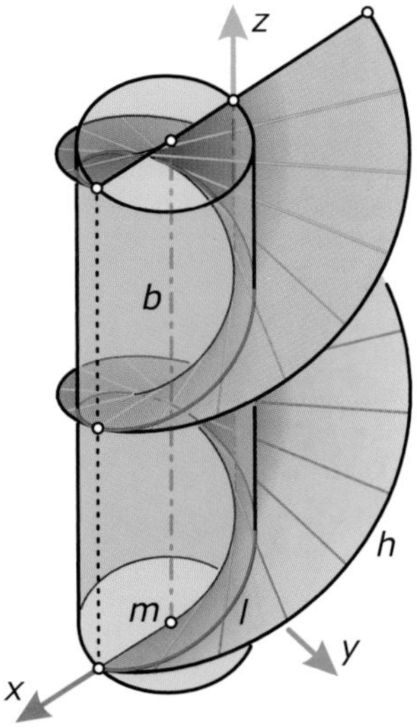

Fig. 9.58
Intersection of a helicoid and a cylinder of revolution through the helical axis.

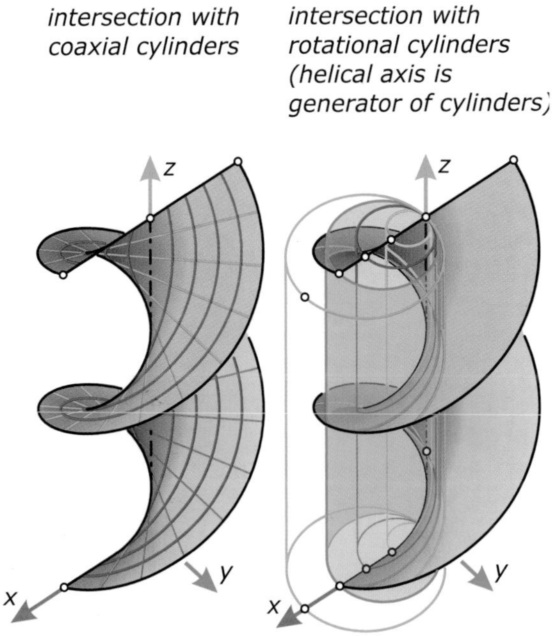

Fig. 9.59
A common helicoid carries different families of helixes.

Fig. 9.60
(top) A common helicoid appears in a "spiral" staircase in Portugal (image courtesy Martin Reis).

Another important case of a ruled helical surface is generated by applying a helical motion to a tangent t_h of a helical path h. This tangent sweeps a *developable ruled surface* (Figure 9.61). The helix h is a singular curve of the surface and creates a sharp edge on it. As is typical of developable ruled surfaces, every tangent plane touches along the entire generator t_h.

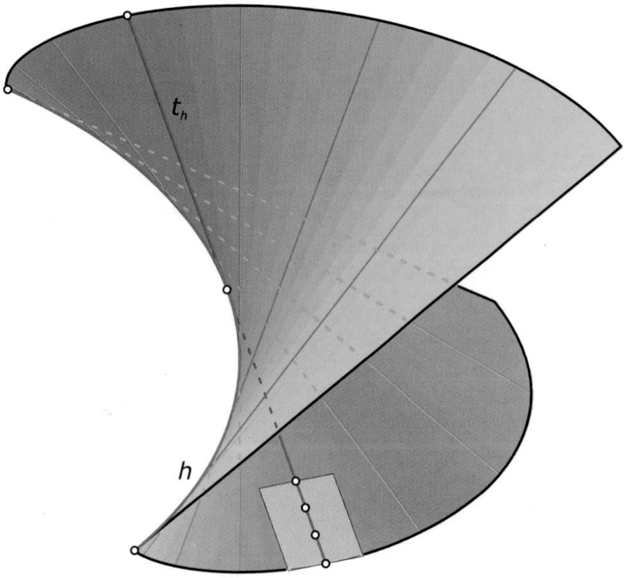

Fig. 9.61
Applying a helical motion to a tangent of a helical path generates a helical surface that is at the same time a developable ruled surface.

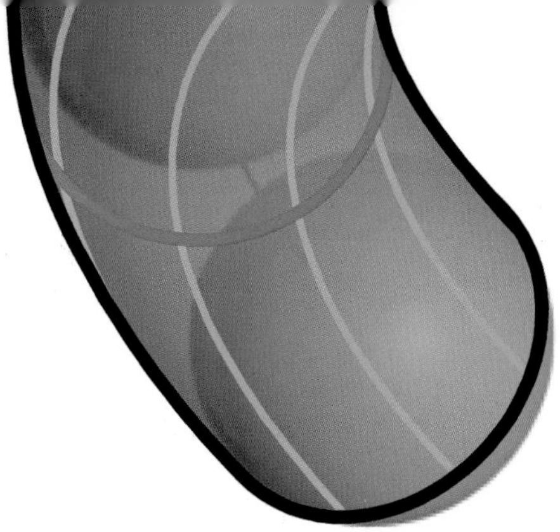

Pipe Surfaces

A *pipe surface* is the envelope of spheres of equal radius r whose centers lie on a curve c, called the *spine curve* or *central curve* c (Figure 9.62). Simple special cases are a rotational cylinder (which arises for a straight line as a spine curve) and the torus, which belongs to a circular spine. The pipe surface is defined by the spine curve and its radius r. It can also be generated as a family of circles of radius r lying in the normal planes of a spatial curve c and having their centers on c.

To actually build curve-like structures in architecture, they need to have a certain thickness. The thickness can be expressed by the radius of a pipe surface. In practice, one uses metal tubes bent into the required form (Figure 9.63). Note that the manufacturing of such bent tubes is challenging.

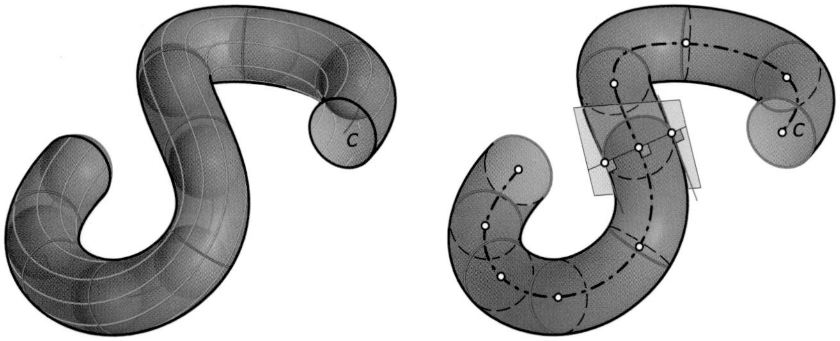

Fig. 9.62
Several pipe surfaces to the same spatial spine curve with two endpoints.

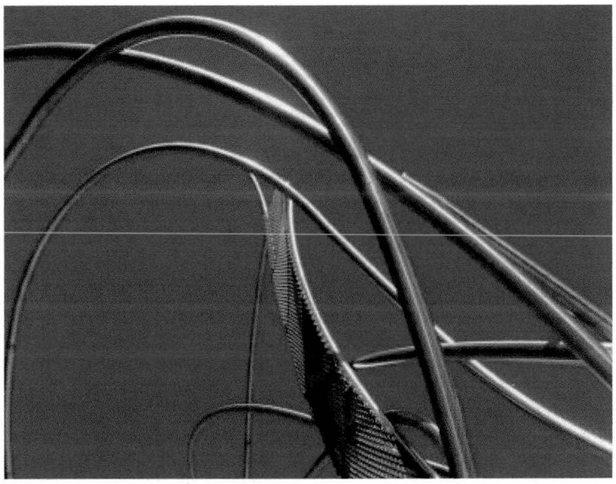

Fig. 9.63
The "Shoal fly-by" public art by SIAL installed at the Melbourne Docklands.

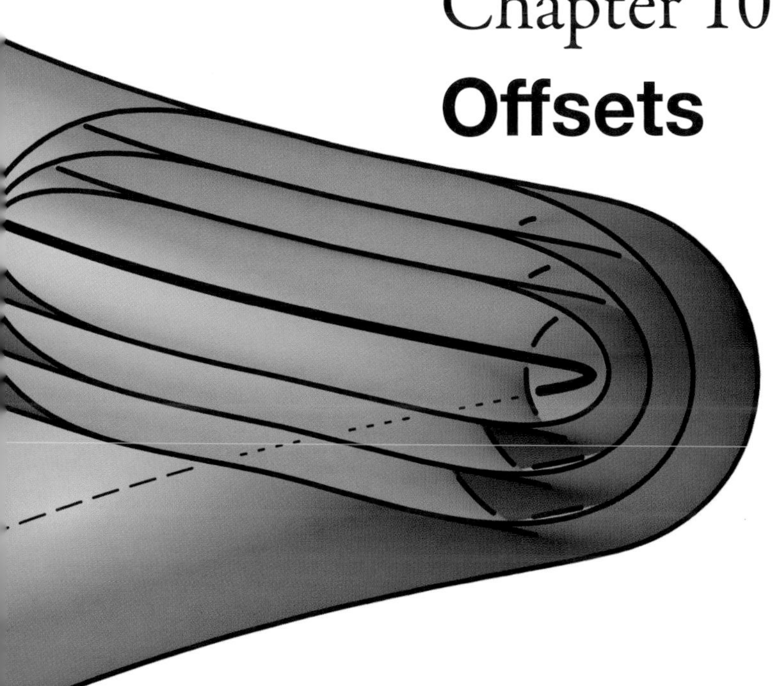

Chapter 10
Offsets

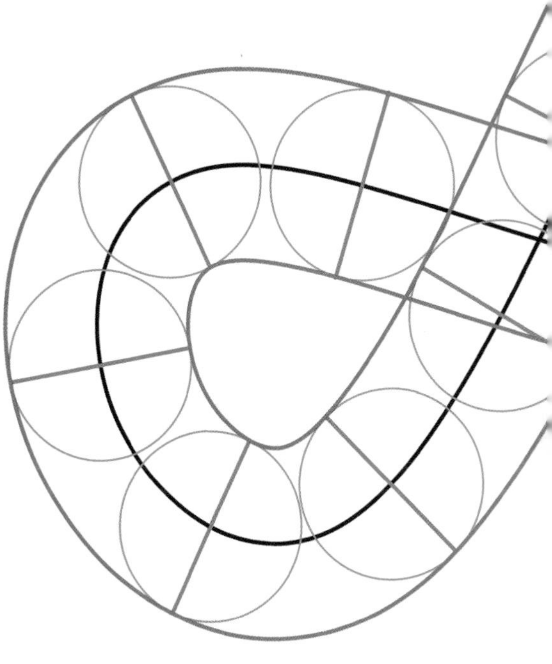

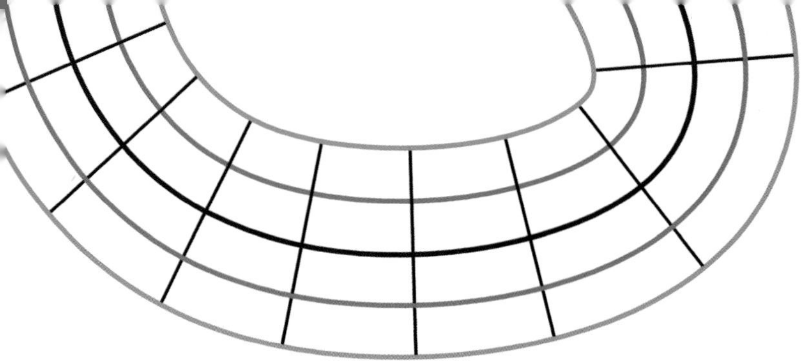

Offsets

In geometric modeling, we often work with surface models to represent geometry. From the geometric point of view, a surface has no thickness. However, in architecture one often builds with shells (Figure 10.1). Thus, we need to give our surface model a certain thickness to make it more realistic. This can be done using the offset operation.

In our following discussion of offsets, we will see that the offset operation may generate self-intersections. It can also result in parts that are closer to the original object than the offset distance. To remove these parts from the offsets, we use the trimming operation. We study offsets for planar curves and for surfaces, in the smooth and discrete settings. The chapter concludes with a discussion of applications of offsets, including rolling ball blends and roof design.

Fig. 10.1
Roof of the conference center in the *DG Bank* (1995–2001) in Berlin by Frank O. Gehry.

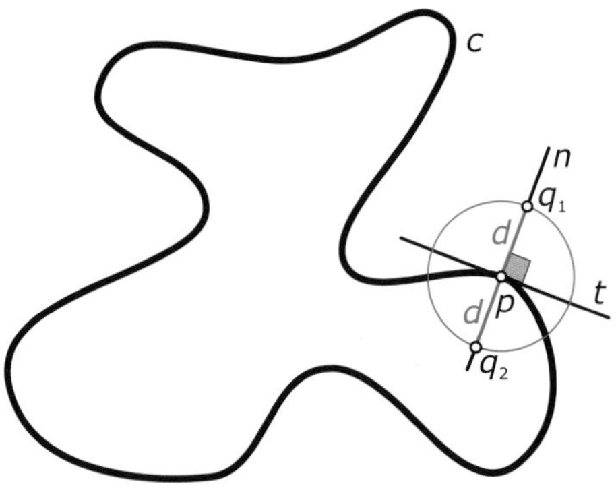

Fig. 10.2
For a smooth planar curve, we have in each curve point a unique tangent and a unique normal. The distance from the curve is measured along the curve normal.

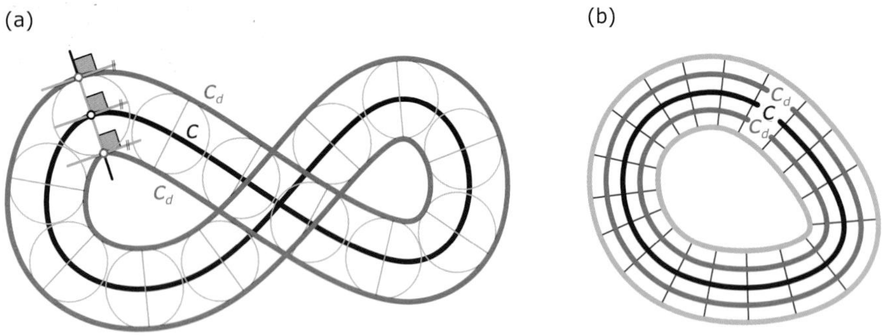

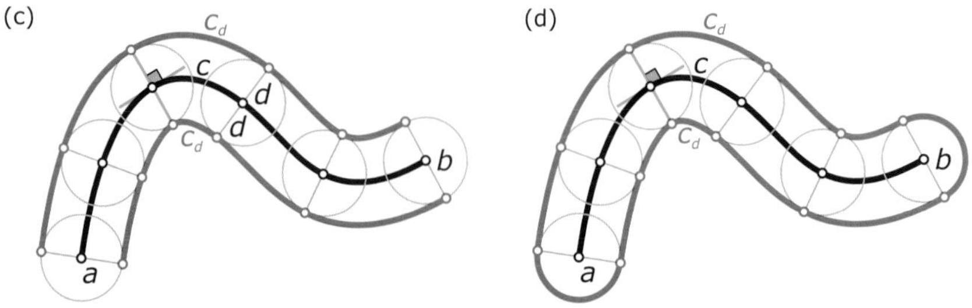

Fig. 10.3
Offsets to smooth planar curves.

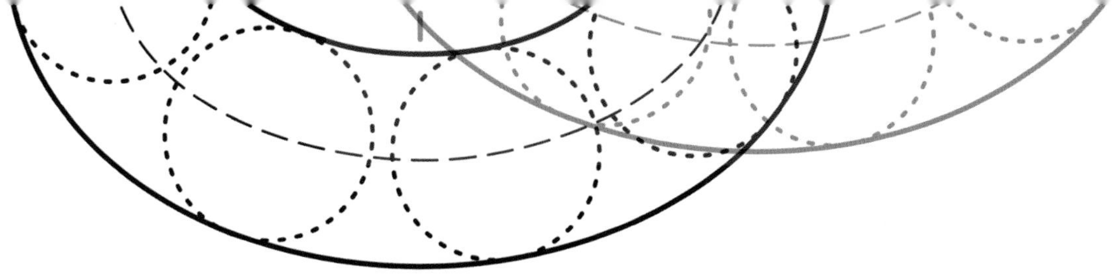

Offset Curves

At each point p of a smooth planar curve c we have a unique curve tangent t and a unique curve normal n (Chapter 7). The normal is orthogonal to the tangent, and is used to measure the distance from the curve. On each curve normal n, there are exactly two points q_1 and q_2 that are at distance d from the curve c. We may find these points by intersecting a circle with center p and radius d with the curve normal n (Figure 10.2).

Offsets of smooth planar curves. For a smooth planar curve c, we define an *offset curve* c_d *at distance d* (for simplicity often just called an *offset*) in the following way. On each curve normal, we mark the two points that are at distance d from the curve c. The set of all of these points forms the offset c_d (Figure 10.3a).

It is easy to show that an offset has the same curve normals as the original curve, and thus the corresponding tangents of c and c_d in corresponding points are parallel. Thus, offset curves are sometimes referred to as *parallel curves*. Figure 10.3 also illustrates that offsets can be obtained as envelopes of circles with radius d centered at the curve c.

By varying the distance d, we can easily generate a family of offset curves. For a closed convex curve, the offsets consist of exactly two branches: one on each side of the original curve c (Figure 10.3b). In the case of an open curve, there exist at least two different possibilities for defining the offset at the endpoints a and b. On the one hand, we may construct two disconnected branches (Figure 10.3c). On the other hand, the offset may be connected—with each of the endpoints contributing a half circle (Figure 10.3d).

Math:

Computing offset curves. Mathematically, we compute an offset curve as follows. Let

$$\mathbf{c}(t) = (x(t), y(t))$$

be a parametric representation of a planar curve. The curve shall be oriented by increasing values of the parameter t. We compute the unit normal vectors $\mathbf{n}(t)$. We obtain these vectors $\mathbf{n}(t)$ by rotating the oriented tangent vectors $\mathbf{c}'(t) = (x'(t), y'(t))$ counterclockwise through 90 degrees. Then we normalize them to unit length by dividing through the length of $\mathbf{c}'(t)$ via

$$\mathbf{n}(t) = \frac{(-y'(t), x'(t))}{\sqrt{x'(t)^2 + y'(t)^2}}$$

The offset $\mathbf{c}_d(t)$ at distance d to $\mathbf{c}(t)$ is obtained as

$$\mathbf{c}_d(t) = \mathbf{c}(t) \pm d \cdot \mathbf{n}(t).$$

Example:

Offsets of a circle and an ellipse. We take a circle with center m and radius r and generate an offset curve at distance d. The offset is of course a pair of circles with the same center m and with radii $r + d$ and $r - d$ (Figure 10.4a). For a circle, all offsets are concentric circles. They all share the same curve normals, and their tangents are parallel at corresponding points. In general, the offset of a planar curve is no longer of the same type.

This is already the case for an ellipse. The offset c_d of an ellipse c is no longer a pair of ellipses. At first glance, this might be surprising. At a small distance d, the offset to an ellipse still looks very much like an ellipse. But we immediately see that the offsets of an ellipse are not ellipses anymore once the inner part starts to have self-intersections (Figure 10.4b).

(a)

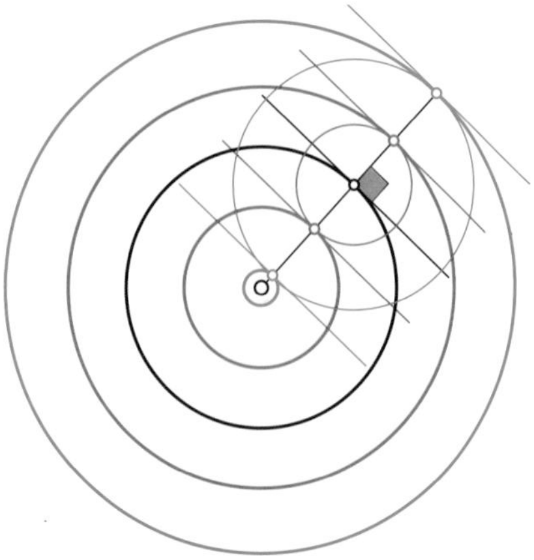

(b)

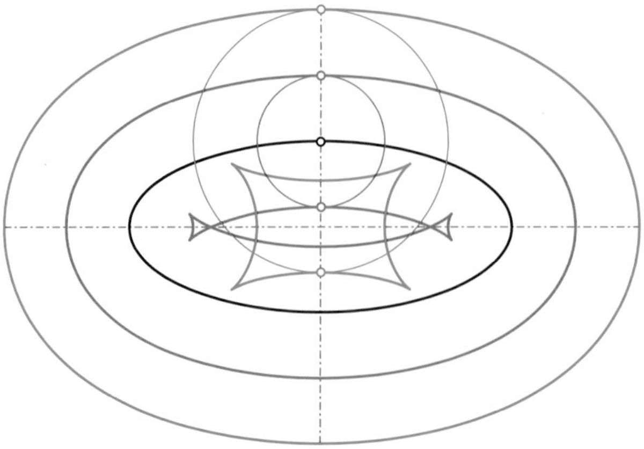

Fig. 10.4
(a) The offsets of a circle are concentric circles.
(b) The offsets of an ellipse are of a more general nature and are no longer ellipses.

Curve, offset, and evolute. Recall from Chapter 7 that the evolute e of a planar curve c is the locus of the centers of all osculating circles. It is also the envelope of all curve normals. Let $k(t)$ be the curvature at a point $\mathbf{c}(t)$, whereby $r(t) = |1/k(t)|$ is the curvature radius. The minimum and maximum curvature radii of a curve are denoted by $r_{min} = |1/k_{min}|$ and $r_{max} = |1/k_{max}|$, respectively. The normals of c and c_d are the tangents of the evolute e. A parametric representation of the evolute can be computed as

$$\mathbf{e}(t) = \mathbf{c}(t) + 1/k(t) \cdot \mathbf{n}(t).$$

One branch of the offset c_d at distance $r_{min} \leq d \leq r_{max}$ has cusps on the evolute e (Figure 10.5a). The cusps are those curve points $c_d(t)$ where $d = r(t)$ [i.e., the constant offset distance d coincides with the varying curvature radius $r(t)$]. At a cusp, the offset curve meets the evolute orthogonally.

Example:

Cusps on an ellipse offset. Note that the inner offset of an ellipse has cusps if the distance d is larger than the minimum curvature radius r_{min} and smaller than the maximum curvature radius r_{max}. For an ellipse, r_{min} and r_{max} are the curvature radii of the major and minor vertices.

Due to its symmetry, the inner offset of an ellipse can have either two or four cusps that lie on the evolute e (Figures 10.5b and 10.5c). We obtain two higher-order cusps for $d = r_{min}$ or $d = r_{max}$ and four cusps for $r_{min} < d < r_{max}$.

Fig. 10.5
(a) One branch of the offset $\mathbf{c}_d(t)$ has cusps on the evolute $\mathbf{e}(t)$ of a planar curve $\mathbf{c}(t)$ if the curvature radius $r(t)$ *of* $\mathbf{c}(t)$ takes on the same value as the constant offset distance d.

(b) The inner offset c_1 of an ellipse at distance $d_1 = r_{min}$ has two higher-order cusps.
(c) The offset c_d at distance $r_{min} < d < r_{max}$ has four cusps that lie on the evolute e of c.

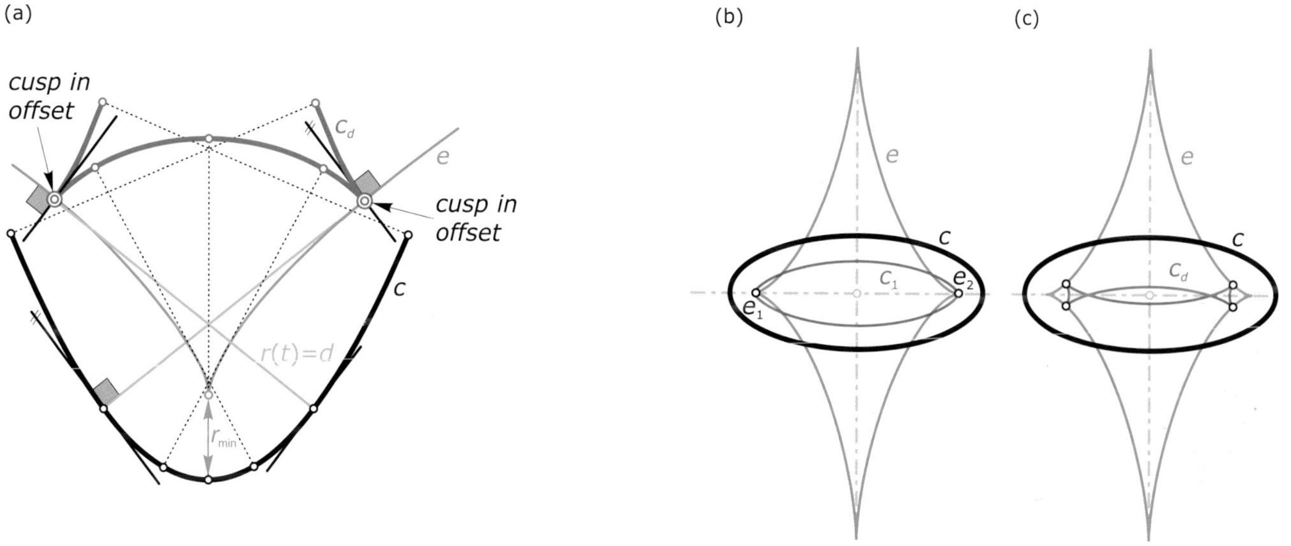

Example:

Silhouette of a torus under normal projection. The offsets of an ellipse appear (for example) as the silhouette of a torus under normal projection. A torus is the envelope surface of a sphere S of constant radius $r = d$ whose center moves along a circle k. The normal projection of the middle circle k of the torus is in general an ellipse k^n. The silhouette of the sphere S under normal projection is a circle of radius d with center on k^n. Thus, the silhouette of a torus under normal projection can be found as the envelope of a family of circles S^n of radius d with centers on k^n. The silhouette is therefore the offset of k^n (Figure 10.6).

Let's examine another geometric interpretation of this simple fact. Along each profile circle c with center m, the torus is also touched by a rotational cylinder C. C has radius d and its axis A is the tangent of the middle circle k in m. The silhouette of C consists of two straight lines parallel to the projection A^n of the axis (which is the tangent of the ellipse k^n). These pairs of straight lines also envelope the silhouette of the torus. Because they are parallel to the tangents of k^n at constant distance d, we see again that the silhouette of a torus can indeed be obtained as the offset of an ellipse k^n at distance d.

The silhouette points are lying on the curve normals of k^n. The outer part of the silhouette is always an oval-shaped curve. The shape of the inner part of the silhouette depends on the inclination angle of the torus axis with respect to the image plane. It can be an oval-shaped curve, a curve with two higher-order cusps, or a curve with four cusps (see also Figures 10.5b and 10.5c).

Fig. 10.6
The offsets of an ellipse appear, for example, as the silhouette of a torus under normal projection.

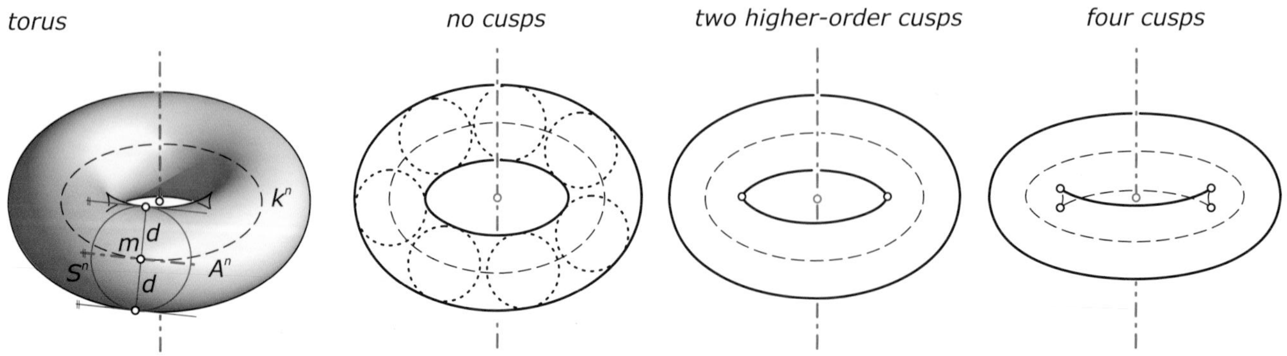

Offsets of planar polygons. Let's take a look at the offsets of planar polygons p. For each edge (i.e., straight line segment) of a polygon, we have a unique normal. However, in each vertex we have an entire fan of normals (Figure 10.7). Thus, one branch of the offset p_d at constant distance d consists of line segments (corresponding to the edges of p) and circular arcs (corresponding to the vertices of p).

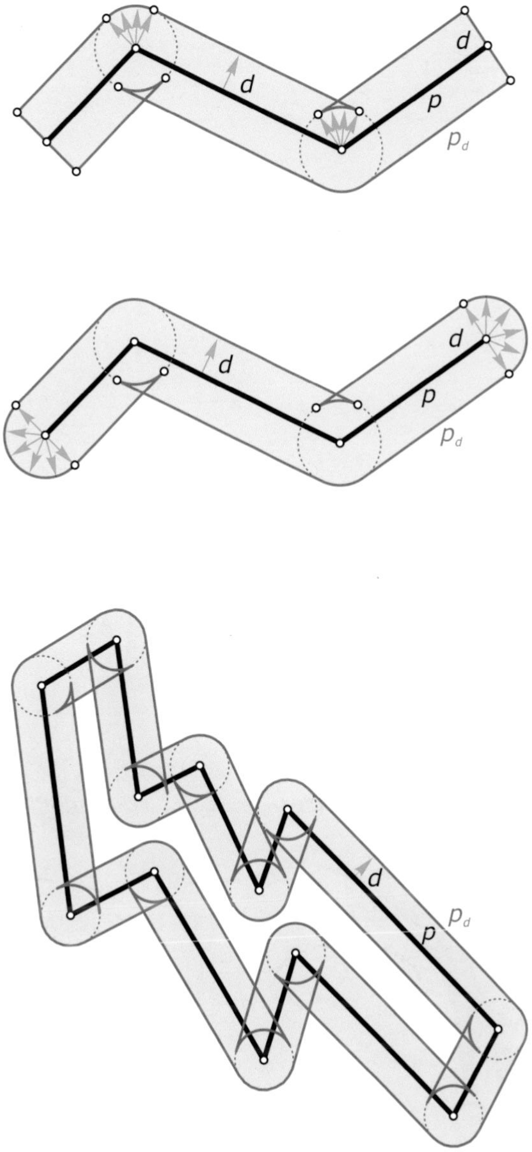

Fig. 10.7
Offsets of planar polygons. For each vertex, the offset is a circular arc.

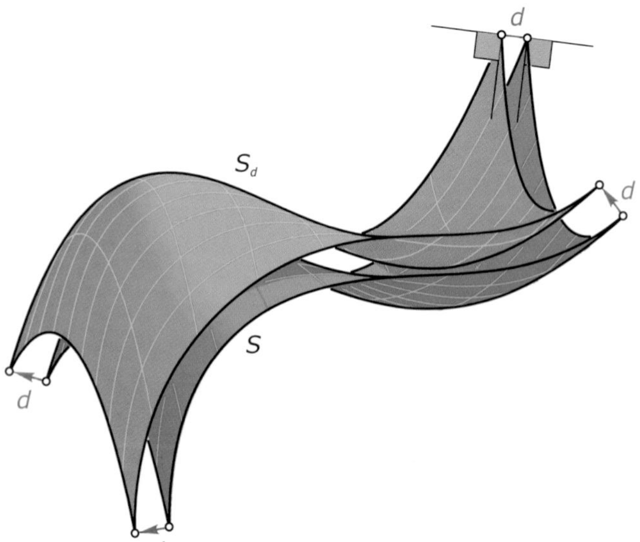

Fig. 10.8
An offset surface S_d of a smooth surface S has the constant distance d to S.

Offset Surfaces

The definition of an offset surface is analogous to the definition of an offset curve. Again, we measure the distance from the surface along the surface normals. For a given smooth surface S, we define an *offset* S_d *at distance* d as follows (Figure 10.8). On each surface normal, we mark the two points that are at a constant distance d from the surface S. The set of all of these points forms the offset surface S_d. It can be shown that the surface S and all of its offset surfaces S_d share their surface normals.

The tangent planes of S and S_d in corresponding points are parallel, and thus offset surfaces are sometimes also called *parallel surfaces*. Analogous to the planar curve case, offsets can be obtained as an envelope of spheres of fixed radius d centered at the base surface S. In the following figures, we only show one part of the offset to make the illustrations more readable.

Math:

Computing an offset surface. Mathematically, we compute an offset surface as follows. Let

$$\mathbf{S}(u,v) = (x(u,v), y(u,v), z(u,v))$$

be a smooth parametric surface in three-dimensional space. We compute the normal vectors $\mathbf{n}(u,v)$ as the cross product of the partial derivative vectors $\mathbf{S}_u(u,v)$ and $\mathbf{S}_v(u,v)$. We normalize them to unit length and orient them so that they all point to the same side of the surface. Then we obtain the offset surfaces $\mathbf{S}_d(u,v)$ at distance d to $\mathbf{S}(u,v)$ as

$$\mathbf{S}_d(u,v) = \mathbf{S}(u,v) \pm d \cdot \mathbf{n}(u,v).$$

Only special surface classes have the property that their offsets are again of the same surface type. These include cylinders and rotational surfaces. For practical purposes, this is a useful property because it allows an easy generation of offsets (as illustrated in the examples following).

Example:

Offsets of spheres and rotational surfaces. Obviously, the offset surfaces of a sphere with center m and radius r at distance d are concentric spheres of radius $r \pm d$ (Figure 10.9a).

Let C be a rotational cylinder with axis A and radius r (Figure 10.9b). The offset consists of two rotational cylinders C_d of radius $r + d$ and $r - d$ with the same axis as C. The surfaces C and C_d share the same surface normals that intersect the rotational axis A orthogonally.

In general, the offsets S_d of rotational surfaces S are again rotational surfaces. A rotational surface is generated by rotating a profile curve c around a coplanar axis A (Chapter 9). The curve normals of the profile curve are also the surface normals of the rotational surface (all normals intersect the rotational axis A). Thus, we obtain the offset S_d in the following way. We first generate a planar offset c_d of the profile curve c. Then we rotate c_d around the axis A to obtain the offset surface S_d as a coaxial rotational surface (Figure 10.9c).

A torus is a special rotational surface enveloped by a sphere whose center moves along a circle. The offsets of the sphere are again spheres, and thus the offsets of a torus are again *tori* with the same axis and the same middle circle (Figure 10.9d). Figure 10.10 illustrates offsets of special surfaces used in architecture.

(a)

concentric spheres

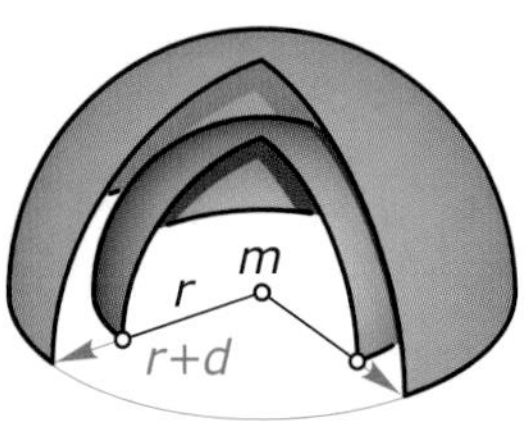

Fig. 10.9
(a) The offset surfaces of a sphere are concentric spheres.
(b) The offsets of rotational cylinders are coaxial rotational cylinders.
(c) The offset surfaces of rotational surfaces are coaxial rotational surfaces.
(d) The offsets of a torus are tori with the same axis and the same middle circle.

(b)

coaxial rotational cylinders

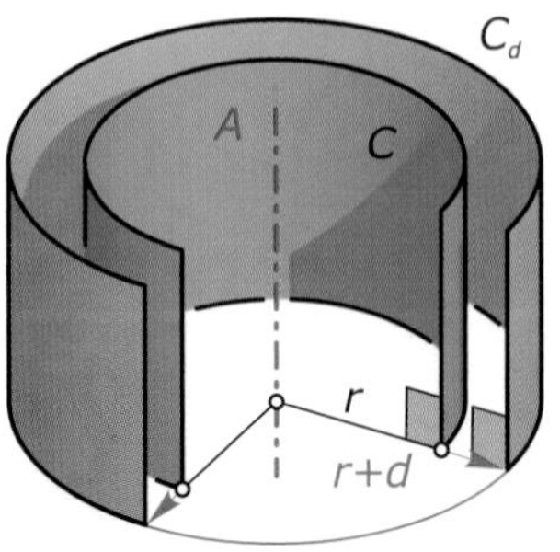

(c)

coaxial rotational surfaces

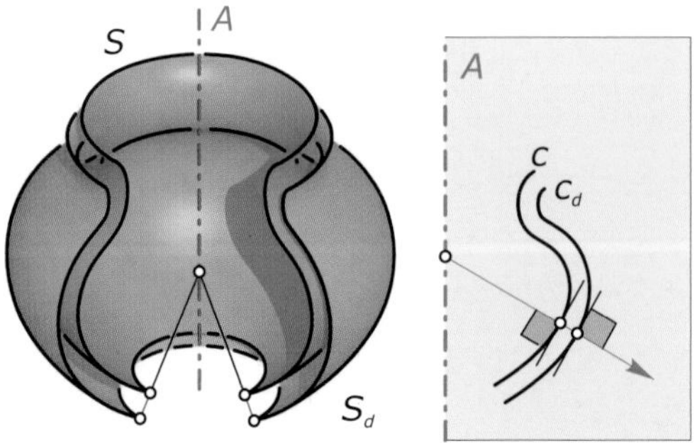

(d)

tori

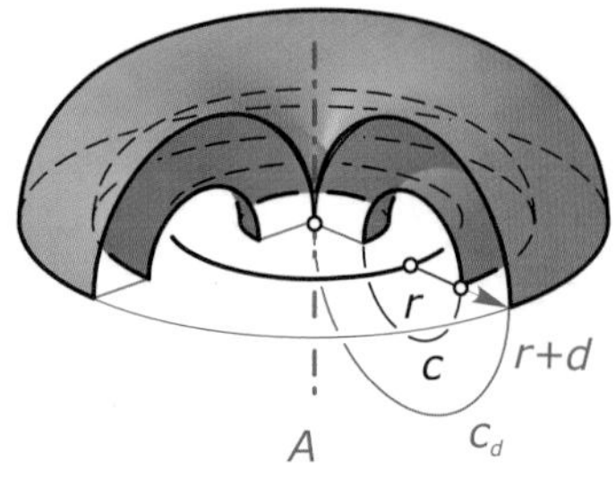

Fig. 10.10
Offsets of special surfaces in architecture.
(a) Parts of concentric spheres appear in the *Jubilee Church* (1996–2003) in Rome by Richard Meier.
(b) The *Imperial War Museum North* (2000–2002) in Manchester, England, by Daniel Liebeskind features offsets of spherical parts.

(a)

(b)

Example:

Offsets of cylinder surfaces. A cylinder surface C can be generated by extruding a smooth planar curve c (lying in a plane P) in a direction orthogonal to P. Now each planar section of C parallel to P is a congruent copy of c. Note that all surface normals of C are parallel to the plane P.

An offset surface C_d of the cylinder C is obtained as follows. We first generate the offset curve c_d of c at distance d in the plane P, and then extrude c_d. Thus, the offset of a cylinder surface is again a cylinder surface. Offsets of cylinders often appear in architecture (Figure 10.11).

Fig. 10.11
(a) The offset of a cylinder surface is again a cylinder surface.
(b) Both vertical parts of a wooden staircase by Sevil Peach are shells generated as offsets of a cylinder surface. The staircase is located in the *Novartis Pharma Headquarters* (2003–2005) by Diener & Diener in Basel, Switzerland.
(c) *Triad* (2000–2002) in Hodaka by Fumihiko Maki.
(d) The *Serpentine Gallery Pavilion* (2003) in London by Oscar Niemeyer.

(a)

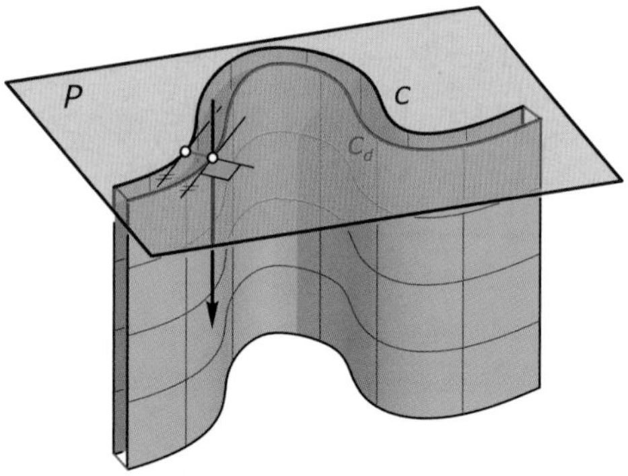

(b)

(c)

(d)

The offset surfaces in the previous examples are all of the same surface type as the base surface to which the offset is computed. This property also holds for pipe surfaces because these surfaces are generated by moving a sphere along a central curve (Figure 10.12). Changing the radius of the moving sphere from r to $r + d$ does not change the type of the surface. Thus, the offsets are again pipe surfaces.

Note that a pipe surface can always be seen as an offset of its central curve. However, not all "simple" surfaces have the property that their offset surfaces are again of the same type. For a cone surface that is not a rotational cone, the offsets are of a more complicated nature (as illustrated in the following example).

Example:

Offsets of cone surfaces. A cone surface C is obtained by connecting a planar curve c with straight lines (called generators) to the apex v. Because C is not smooth at v, the surface has no unique surface normal there. Rather, we can think of a bouquet of surface normals at v. Thus, the offset of v is part of a sphere S (Figure 10.13a). What about the offset of the cone surface itself? The surface normals along a generator g of a cone surface are parallel. Thus, the offset g_d of each generator g is a again a straight line. These straight lines g_d form the offset surface and touch the sphere S along a curve v_d. In general, these straight lines g_d no longer meet in a single point. Thus, the offset is no longer a cone surface. The exception are rotational cones whose offsets are again rotational cones where only the apex has to be treated separately (Figure 10.13b). But even in the general case the surface normals of C_d along g_d are parallel. Thus (see Chapter 9), the offsets of general cone surfaces are *developable surfaces*.

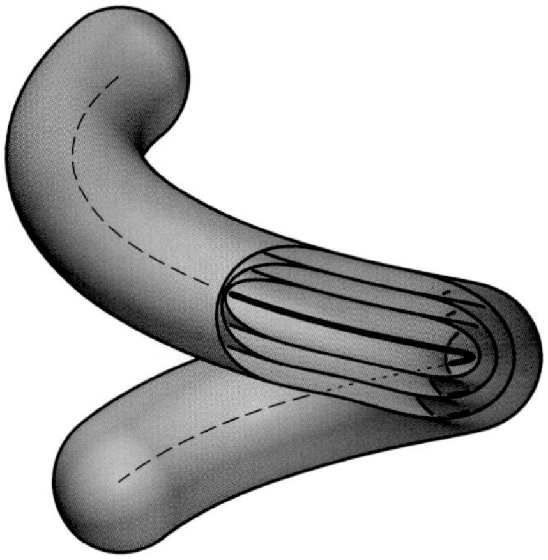

Fig. 10.12
The offsets of a pipe surface are again pipe surfaces.

Fig. 10.13
(a) The offset of a general cone C consists of part of a sphere S and a developable surface C_d.
(b) The offset of a rotational cone is again a rotational cone.

(a)

offset C_d of a general cone C is a developable surface

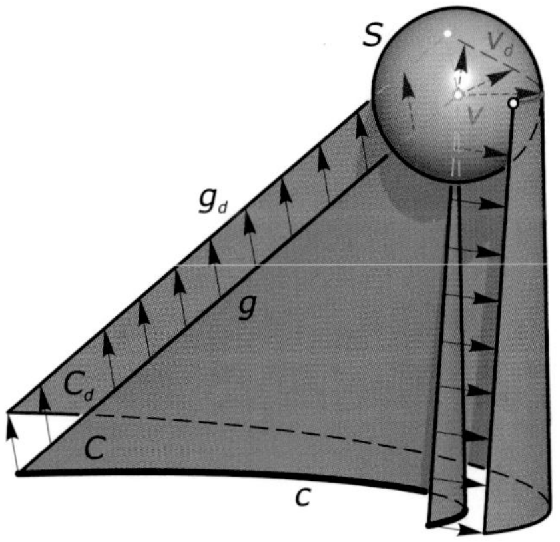

(b)

offset of a rotational cone

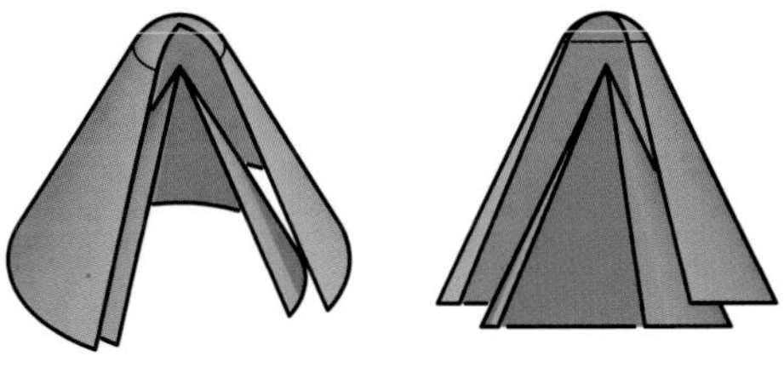

Example:

Offsets of hyperbolic paraboloids. Recall from Chapter 9 that a hyperbolic paraboloid S (HP surface) is a special ruled surface that carries two families of generators. To generate the offset S_d at constant distance d, we study what happens to the generators. When we travel along a generator of an HP surface, the surface normal varies its direction. Thus, the part of S_d resulting from a generator g is actually a spatial curve on S_d and is no longer a straight line (Figure 10.14). This indicates that the offset of an HP surface is no longer an HP surface.

Offsets of polyhedral surfaces. We have considered smooth surfaces as the base objects for offset operations. Let's now examine the offsets of polyhedral surfaces. Recall from Chapter 3 that a polyhedral surface P consists of planar faces, straight edges, and vertices. Each planar face has a unique normal and thus a well-defined offset. However, for an edge and a vertex this is not the case.

Each edge point has a fan of normal lines, and each vertex even has a bouquet of normal lines. Thus, the offset P_d of a polyhedral surface P at constant distance d consists of planar faces, parts of rotational cylinders (corresponding to the edges of P), and parts of spheres (corresponding to the vertices of P). Figure 10.15 illustrates offsets of convex polyhedral surfaces. In Chapter 19, we will again encounter offsets of polyhedral surfaces.

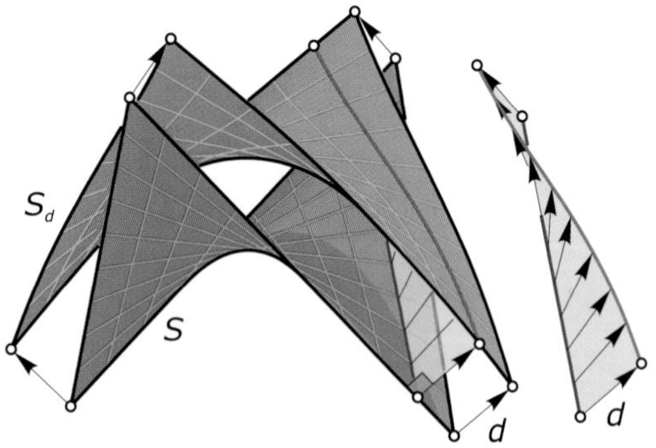

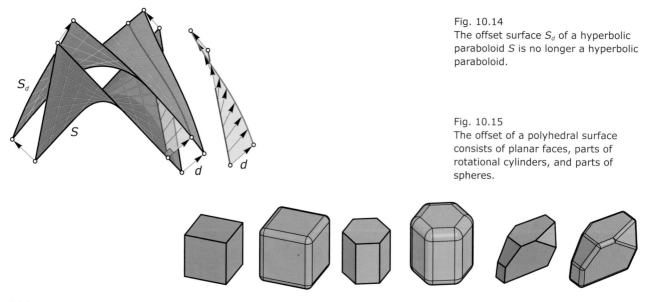

Fig. 10.14
The offset surface S_d of a hyperbolic paraboloid S is no longer a hyperbolic paraboloid.

Fig. 10.15
The offset of a polyhedral surface consists of planar faces, parts of rotational cylinders, and parts of spheres.

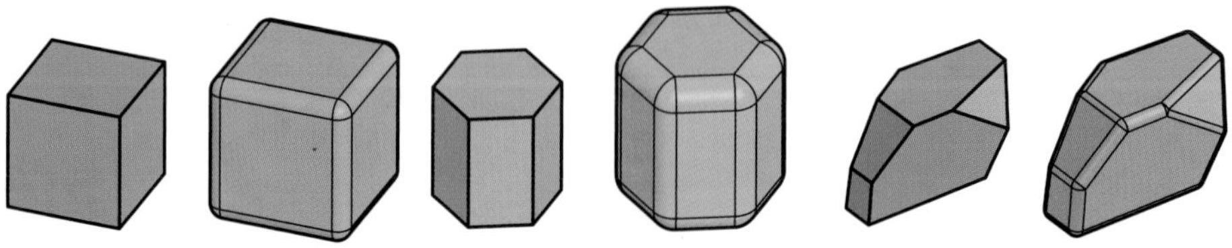

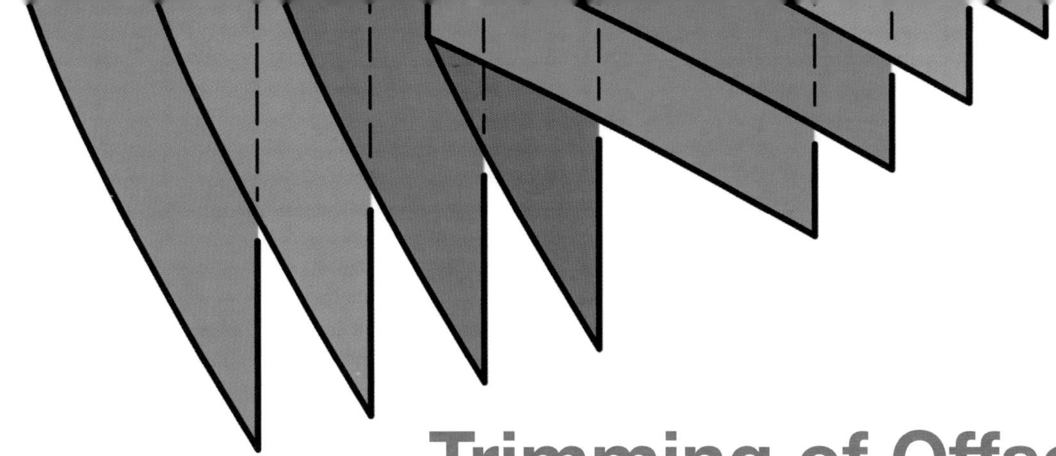

Trimming of Offsets

In some applications, only parts of the offset are useful for the actual purpose. Recall from the example "cusps on an ellipse offset" that the inner offset of an ellipse may have self-intersections. These self-intersections lead to points of the offset closer to the ellipse than the offset distance d. Thus, for practical applications one sometimes needs to remove these parts of the offset curve. The operation that does just that is called *trimming*.

In many computer-aided design (CAD) systems, the offset operation is followed by a trimming operation to automatically remove overlapping parts that are too close to the original curve. Figure 10.16 shows the offset curve to a smooth planar curve before and after trimming. Note that both local and global trimming may be necessary.

By *local trimming* we remove parts of the offset that overlap because the offset curve intersects the evolute of the original curve. *Global trimming* is necessary to remove parts of the initial offset curve that overlap but result from distinct regions of the original curve (Figure 10.16).

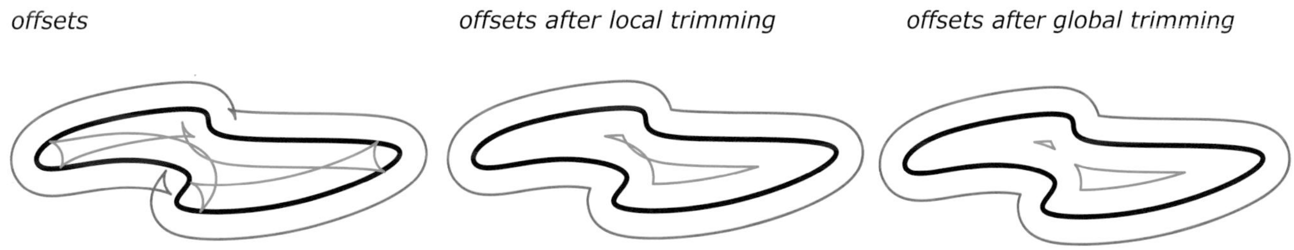

Fig. 10.16
Offset of a smooth planar curve before and after trimming. We illustrate local and global trimming.

Trimming offsets in three dimensions. Trimming offset surfaces is a difficult operation because the offset can be very complex. There might be many overlapping and self-intersection parts in the offset surface. Therefore, local and global trimming might be necessary (Figure 10.17).

Trimming is performed using numerical computations. If a CAD system fails to generate a trimmed offset surface, the operation might just be too complicated for the methods implemented in the system. For special surfaces, we learned that the offset belongs to the same surface class. To avoid unnecessary trimming, we should employ this geometric knowledge. This can be illustrated by means of a cylinder surface with base curve c. Instead of trimming the offset surface, it is much easier to trim the offset curve c_d and then extrude it to obtain the trimmed offset surface (Figure 10.18).

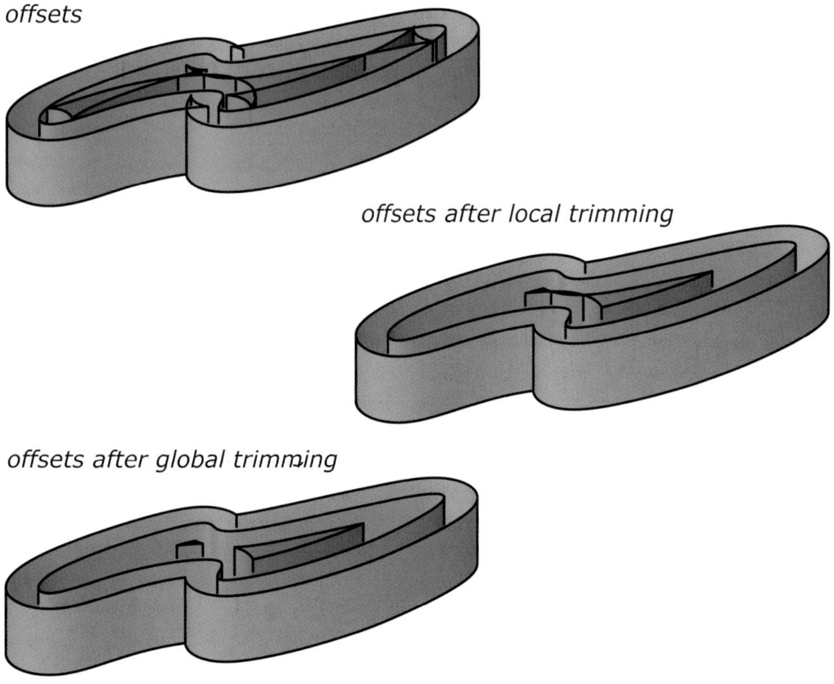

Fig. 10.17
Offset of a smooth surface before and after trimming. We illustrate local and global trimming.

Fig. 10.18
Smart generation of a trimmed offset of a cylinder surface.

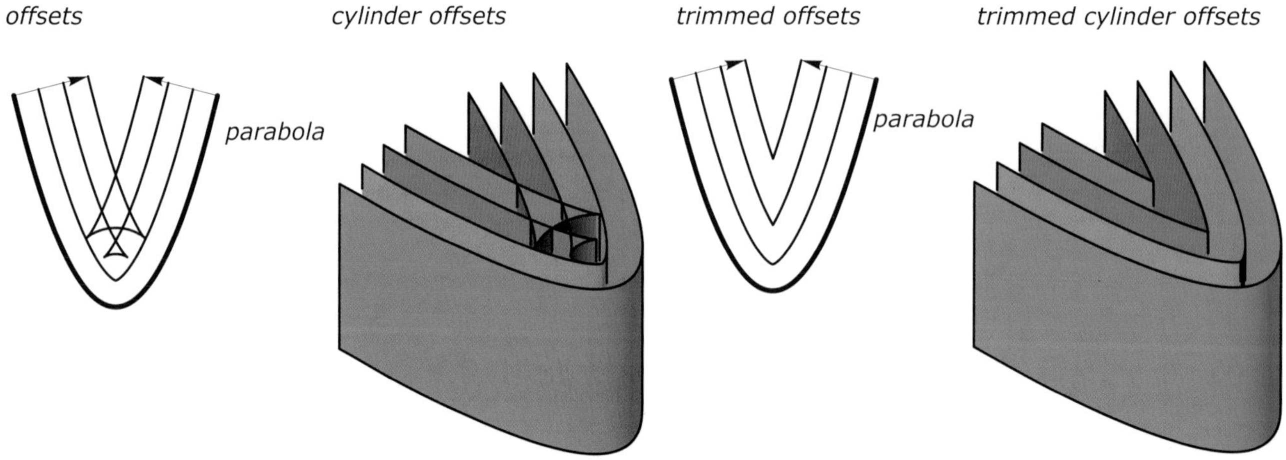

Discrete offsets of planar polygons. Note that some CAD systems provide alternatives for the offset computation of planar polygons. Instead of replacing a vertex of a polygon P with a circular arc, the offset will have a sharp corner. Thus, the offset P_d of a polygon P is again a polygon. However, now some points of P_d might be further away from P than the offset distance d.

We construct this *discrete offset* as follows. Straight lines parallel to the edges of P at a distance d are drawn, and neighboring pairs of straight lines are trimmed at their intersection points (Figure 10.19a). If we refine the polygon P (e.g., using a subdivision algorithm of Chapter 8), we obtain in the limit a smooth curve.

With such a refinement process, the discrete offset converges toward the smooth (trimmed) offset (Figure 10.19b). Note that these different types of offsets can be seen in vector graphics of lines where we can choose between different options of how line corners and endpoints are handled (Figure 10.19c).

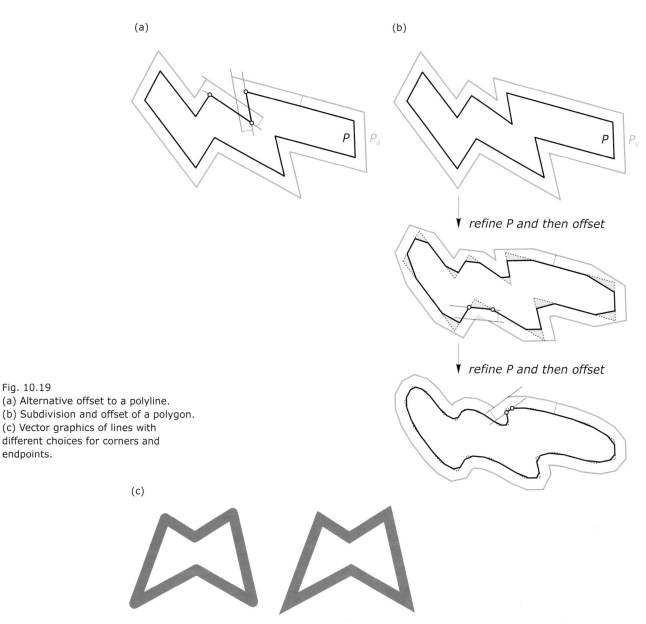

(a)

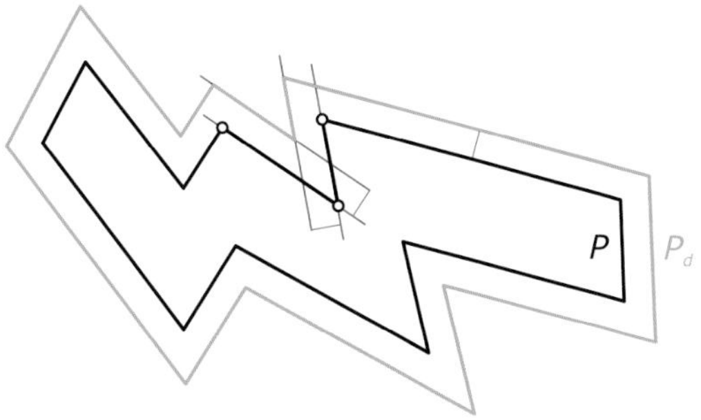

(b)

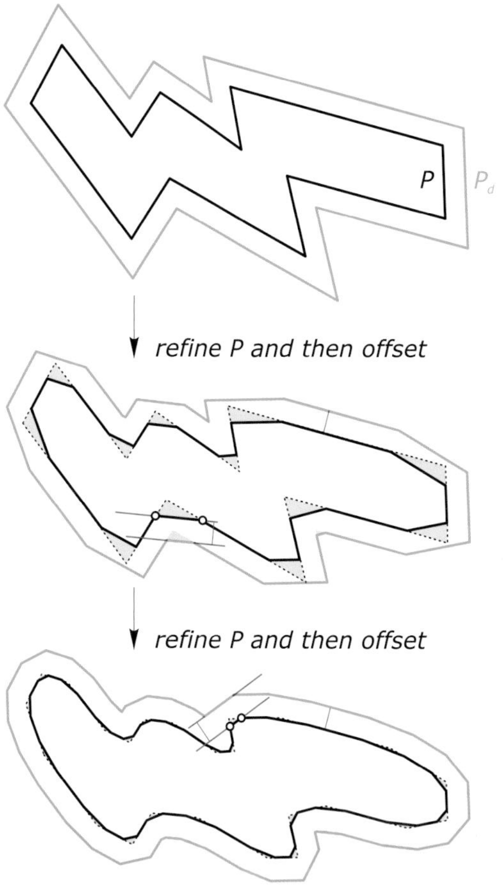

Fig. 10.19
(a) Alternative offset to a polyline.
(b) Subdivision and offset of a polygon.
(c) Vector graphics of lines with different choices for corners and endpoints.

(c)

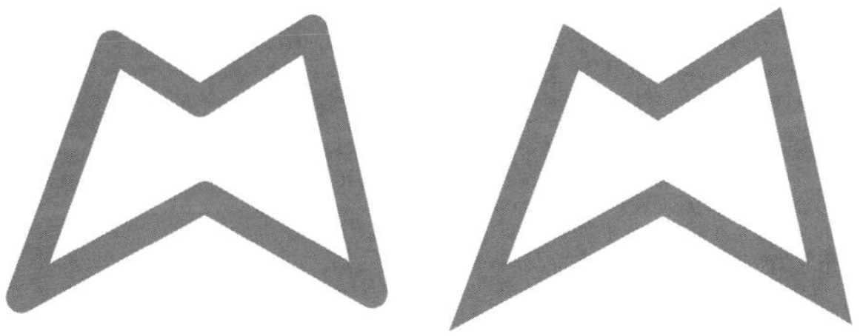

Discrete offsets of polyhedral surfaces. The *discrete face offset* of a polyhedron P is again a polyhedron P_d. We construct a discrete face offset P_d as follows. Offset planes at distance d are computed for each planar face, and neighboring planes are then intersected appropriately (Figure 10.20).

Note that certain points of the offset P_d are actually further away from P than the offset distance d. However, the offset consists again of polyhedra, a property that is sometimes more important than to get the (more complicated) offset at constant distance d. If we need the "true" geometric offset and we are missing such a command, we proceed in the following way. We first generate the polyhedron offset P_d as described previously, and then round the edges and vertices with appropriate tools.

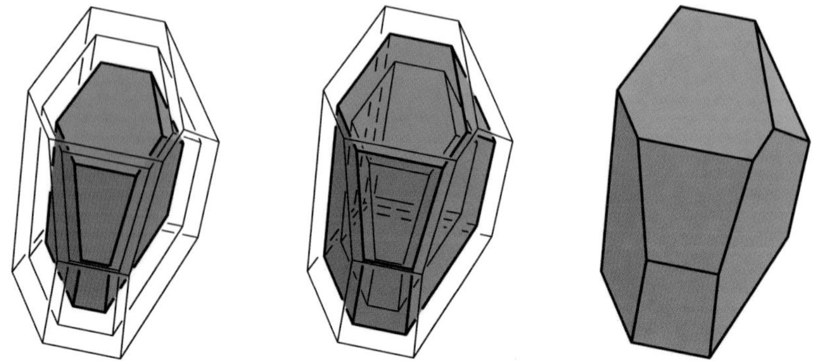

Fig. 10.20
Alternative offset to a polyhedron.

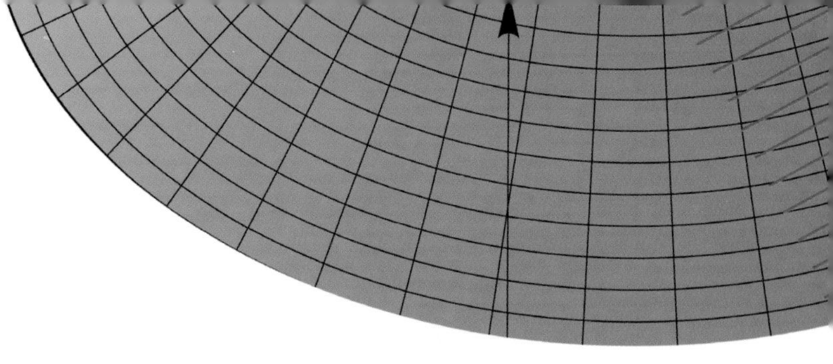

Application of Offsets

Offsets have several useful applications in addition to those mentioned previously. We discuss two of these applications: rolling ball blends and roof design.

Rolling ball blends. In many applications, we want to avoid sharp edges and thus we replace them with rounded edges. If a sharp edge is generated by two intersecting surfaces, one often replaces it with a blending surface (Chapter 4). A common choice for a blending surface is a part of a pipe surface (Chapter 9).

Such a pipe surface is generated by rolling a ball of radius r "along the edge" such that it always touches both surfaces. The central curve c of this pipe surface is generated as the intersection curve of two offsets S_1^r and S_2^r at constant distance r (Figure 10.21a). For the blending, we use the part of the pipe surface shown in Figure 10.21b.

Fig. 10.21
Rolling-ball blend with radius r along a sharp edge.
(a) The central curve c of the pipe surface is found by intersecting offset surfaces S_1^r, S_2^r.
(b) Only a small part of the pipe surface is used for the blending.

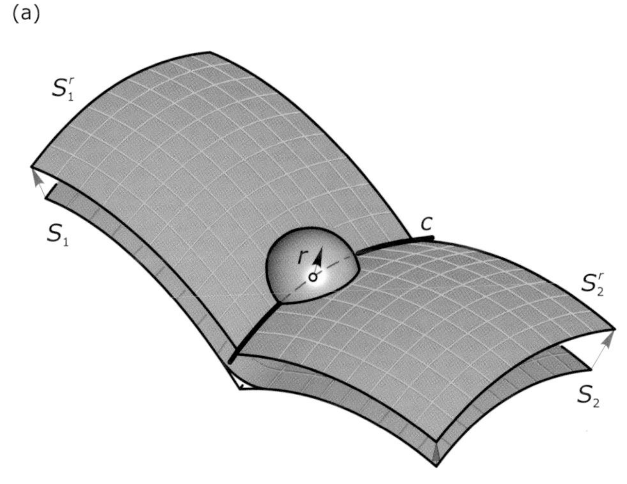

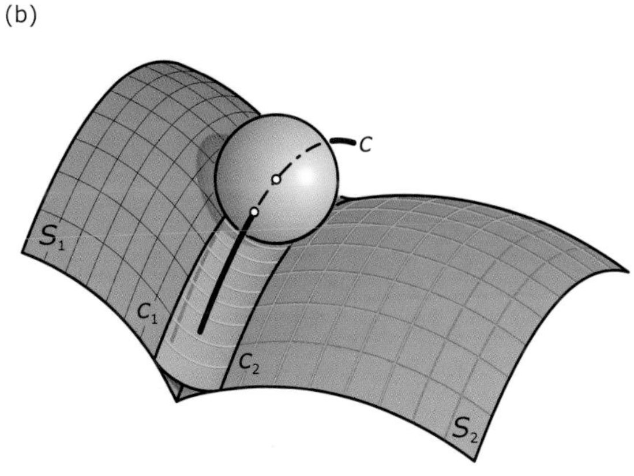

Geometric roof design. The geometric shape of a roof is driven by a combination of drainage constraints, the floor plan, and stylistic considerations. This principle has led to a number of traditional roof forms (Figure 10.22), but can as well be applied to new—possibly less regular—forms of roofs. Here we illustrate how offsets may be employed for geometric roof design. First, however, we need to introduce some special terms commonly used in roof design.

The main purpose of a roof is to protect the bottom part of the building (e.g., from rain and water accumulation). Sloping different roof parts toward the closest edge of the building allows water to run off. Most roofs consist of several planar faces. From a geometric point of view, many roofed buildings resemble a polyhedron. Edges and faces of roofs are named with respect to their function (Figure 10.23).

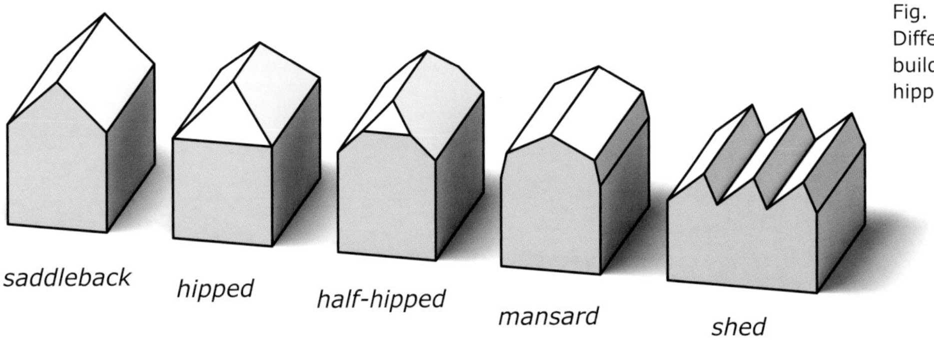

Fig. 10.22
Different roofs to the same base building: saddleback, hipped, half-hipped, mansard, and shed.

Fig. 10.23
The edges and faces of a roof carry special names used in roof design.

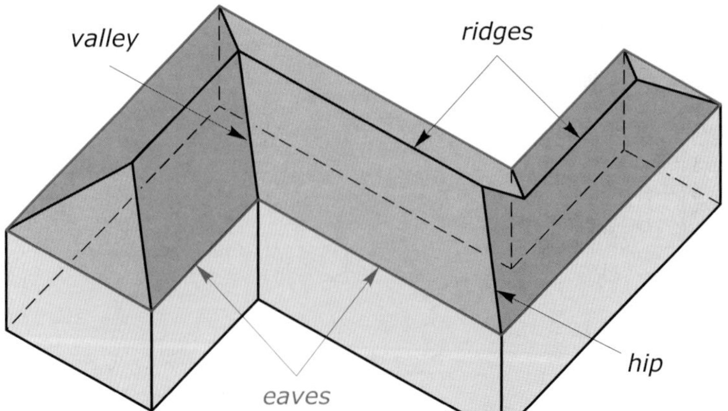

- A *ridge* is the upper (usually horizontal) boundary edge of a non-horizontal roof plane.
- An *eave* is a lower (always horizontal) boundary edge of a non-horizontal roof plane.
- A *hip* is the intersection line of two roof planes in such a way that the hip and the two eaves join in a convex corner.
- A *valley* is the intersection line of two roof planes such that the valley and the two eaves join in a non-convex corner.

The complexity of roof design also depends on the layout of the base building. Figure 10.24 shows a building with about a hundred rooms and many nested roof structures. Special roof design software is available. Nevertheless, a few geometric ideas already allow the design of meaningful roofs. Let's now employ offsets for roof design.

Fig. 10.24
The *Winchester house* in California has about a hundred rooms and many nested roof structures.

Designing roofs of constant slope using offsets. We assume that all roof planes are sloped with the same inclination angle. The main idea is that the offset polygons of the eave polygon (formed by the eaves) are nothing more than the top views of the iso-height contour lines of the roof (Figure 10.25a). The contour lines are generated by intersecting the roof with parallel horizontal planes.

Because we do not have the roof—but want to design it—we work the other way round. We generate the contour lines using the offset operation with appropriate offset distances. From the contour lines, we derive the top views of hips, valleys, and ridges of the roof. Then we complete the roof design by adding the height information.

Let's start with the case that all eaves are at the same height. Using offsets, we find the top views of hips, valleys, and ridges of the roof as follows. We work in the basal plane of the eaves. We generate trimmed offsets P_d at increasing distance d to the eave polygon P until P is completely filled. Thereby, we record events when edges of P_d disappear or coincide. Using the iso-height contour lines of the roof planes, we find the intersection line of two planes and the intersection point of three planes. We use this in the following way.

The lines through corresponding vertices of the family of offset polygons form top views of hips and valleys of the roof (Figure 10.25b). Because all roof planes have the same inclination angle, the top views of hips and valleys are lines of symmetry of neighboring eaves. In addition, top views of ridges are parts of center lines of parallel eaves.

(a)

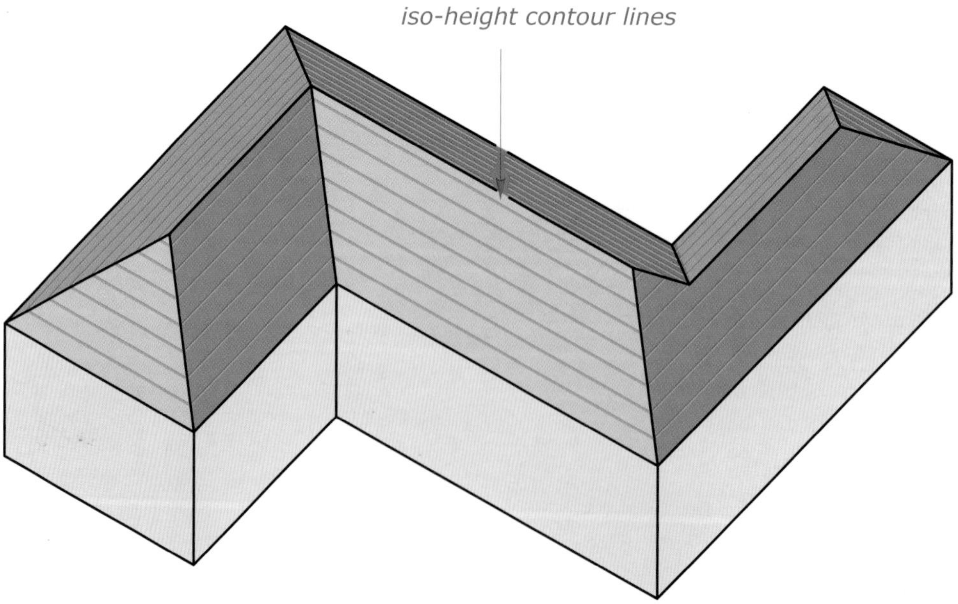

If two edges of the offset polygon coincide, they result from parallel opposite eaves and we have found the top view of a ridge of the roof. If one edge of the offset polygon disappears, this means that its two neighbor edges are now adjacent. Such an event marks a point where three different roof planes meet in a single point. Once we have found the roof layout in the top view, we can construct the roof.

We read off the heights of the relevant points where hips, valleys, and ridges intersect from a simple diagram (Figure 10.25c). Depending on the inclination angle α, an offset distance d corresponds to a certain height h_α in the roof plane. To the same offset distance d, a different inclination angle β yields a different height h_β.

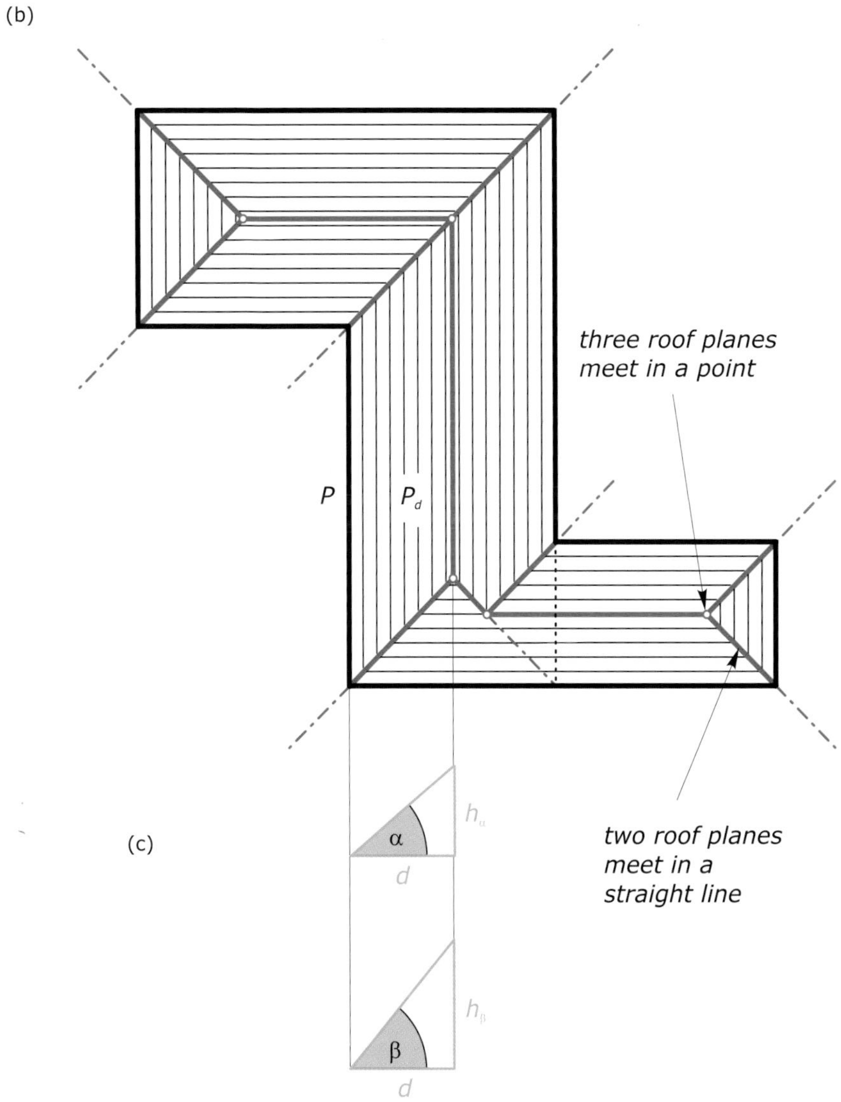

Fig. 10.25
Roof design where all eaves are at the same height and all roof planes are sloped with the same inclination angle.
(a) The iso-height contour lines of a roof.
(b) The top views of the iso-height contour lines of the roof are the offsets P_d of the eave polygon P.
(c) The offset distance d yields for different roof inclination angles α, β different heights h_α, h_β.

Of course, we can also design roofs of constant slope to smooth eave curves. Then the roof will be formed by a developable surface of constant slope (encountered again in Chapter 12 and studied in detail in Chapter 15). Figure 10.26 shows one example where the eave curve is an ellipse. Here, we construct in the top view the iso-height lines of the roof as offsets of the eave ellipse.

We find the top view of the curved ridge as a straight line segment that connects the curvature centers e_1 and e_2. Note that the normals to the offsets intersect the eave ellipse orthogonally. Thus, the water flows down the roof along the generators of the developable surface. Excavation pits can be constructed analogously to roofs. Basically, we just need to mirror a roof at a horizontal plane to obtain an excavation pit.

Fig. 10.26
Roof design to a smooth eave curve.

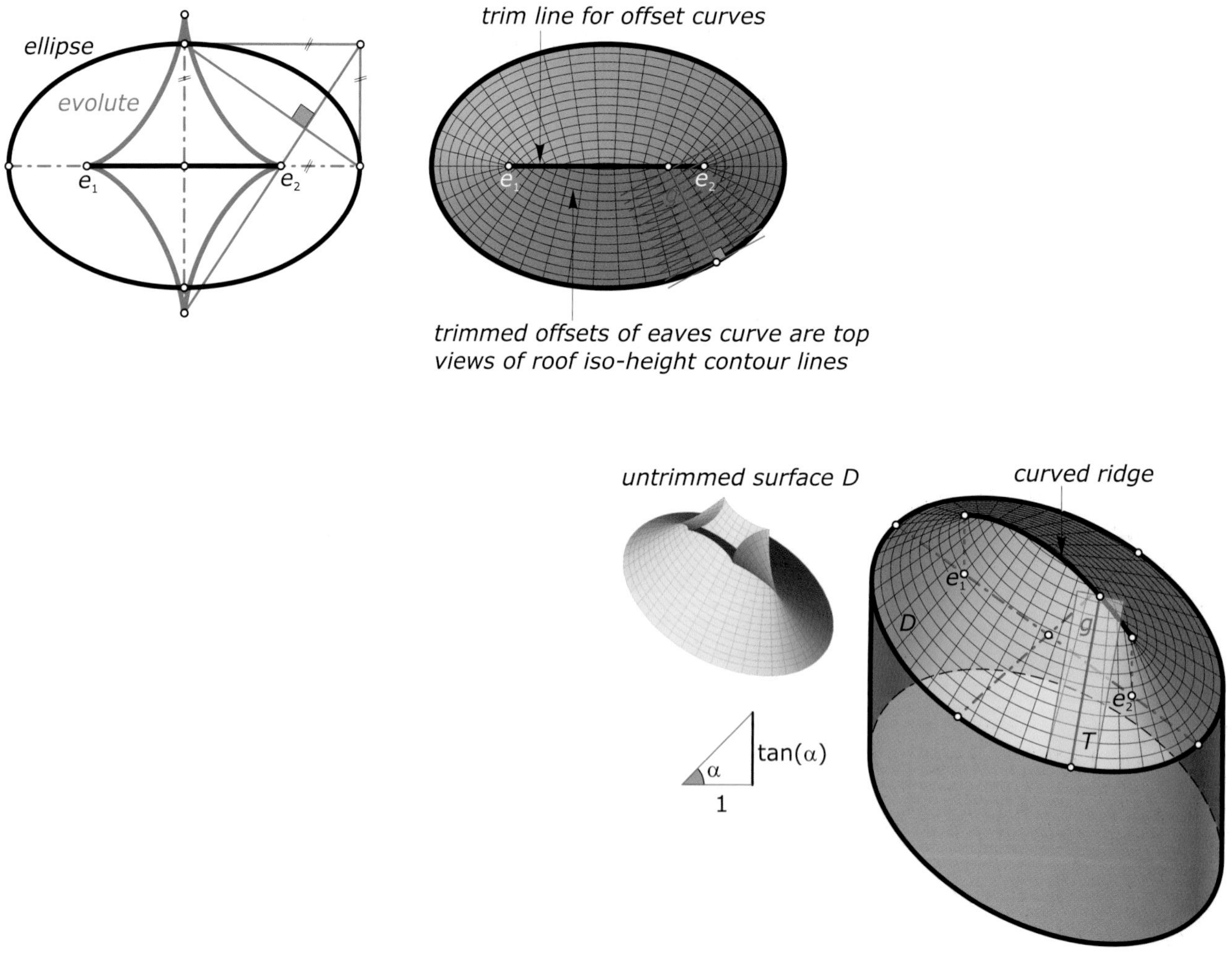

Designing roofs of varying slope. Analogously with the foregoing, we can design roofs where the roof planes have different slopes. Again, we assume that all eaves are at the same height. Otherwise, we work with an auxiliary eave polygon where all eaves are at the same height. For each eave, we know the slope α, β, and γ.

From the diagram shown in Figure 10.27, we read off the distances d_α, d_β, and d_γ corresponding to a constant height h and varying slopes α, β, and γ. In such a way, we can again draw the top views of the contour lines of the roof that we intend to design. However, now these contours are no longer offsets of the eave polygon. The remaining roof design steps are as described previously.

Fig. 10.27
Roof design for roof planes of different slope.

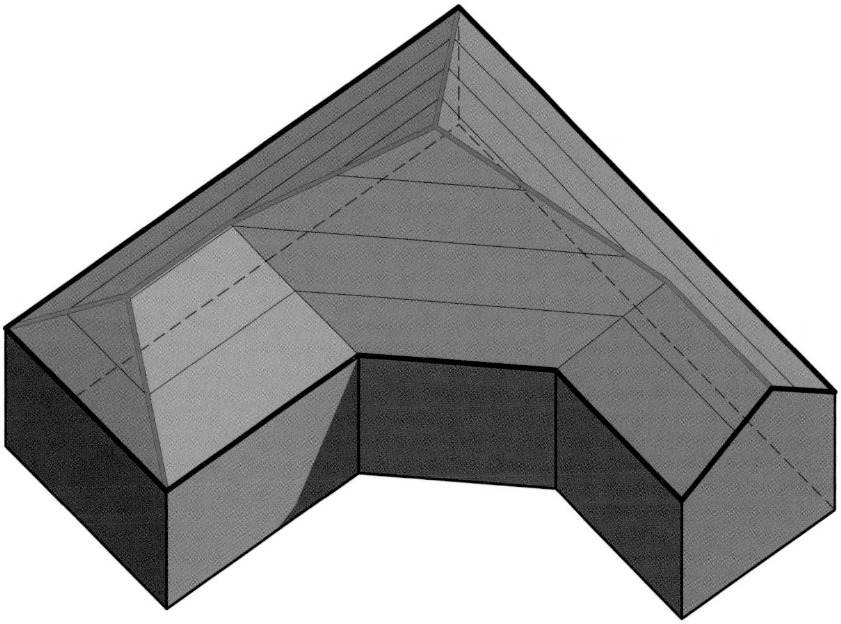

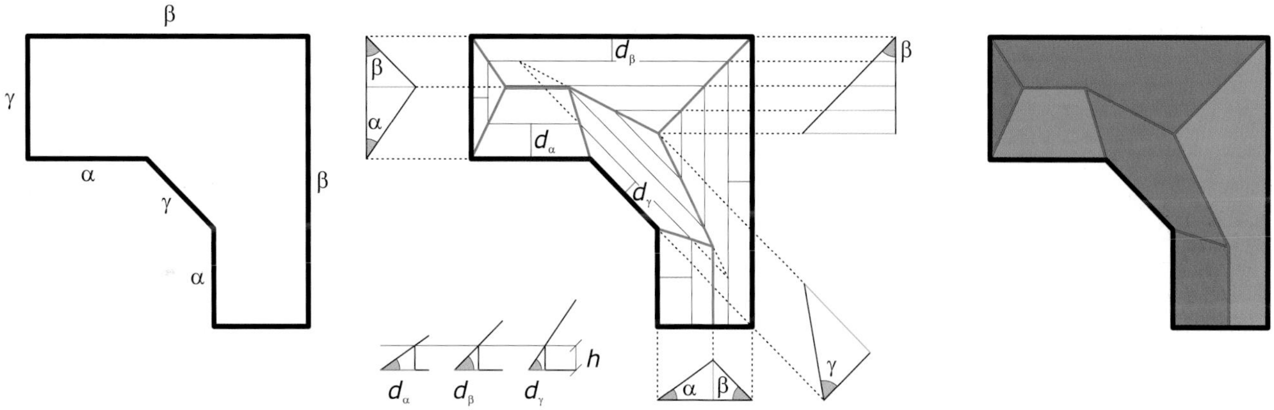

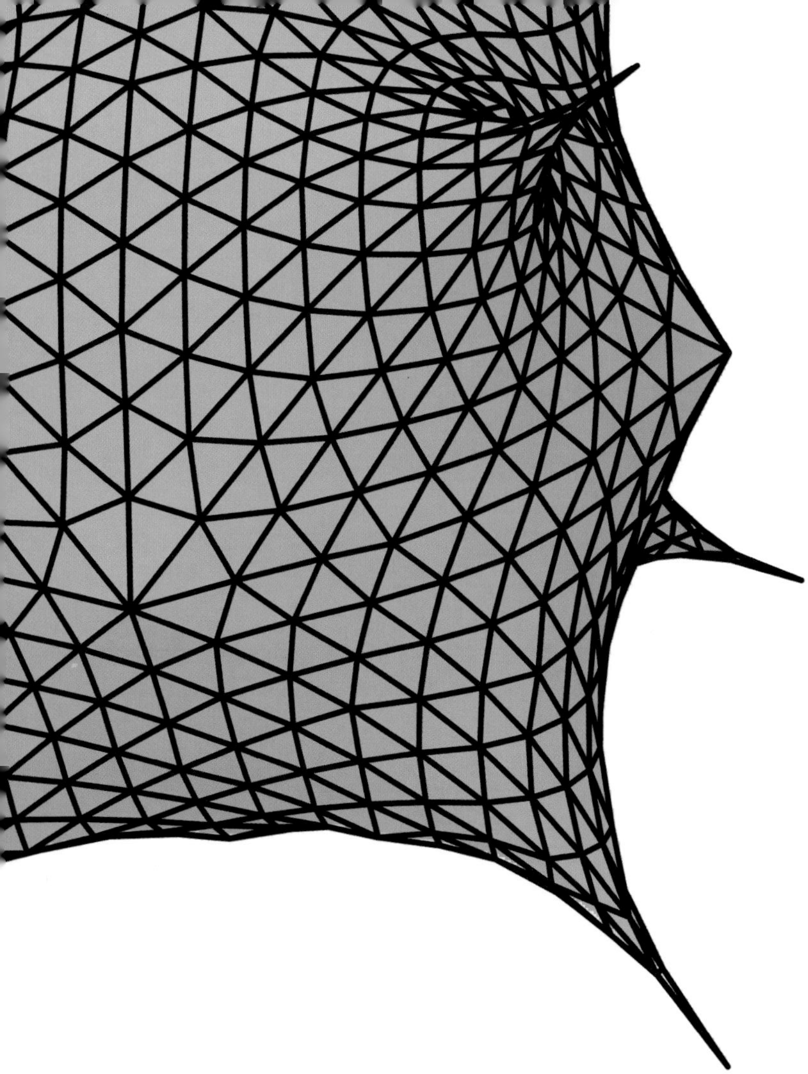

Chapter 11

Freeform Surfaces

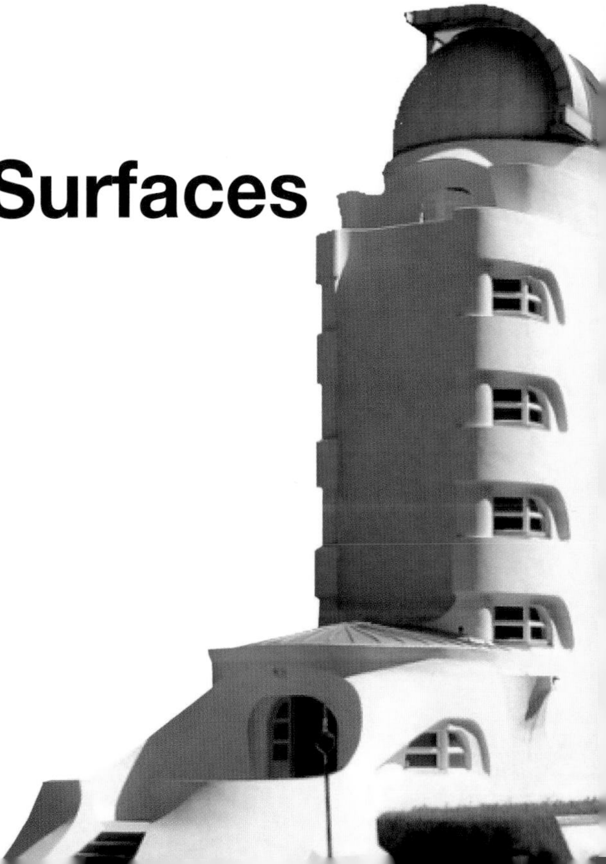

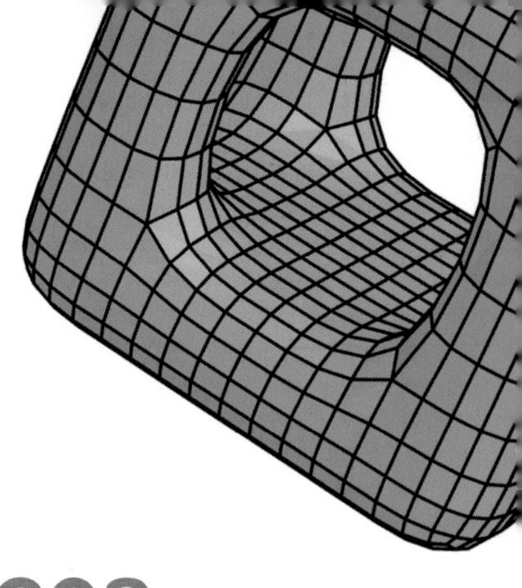

Freeform Surfaces

Sufficient flexibility in the design of 3D shapes is difficult to achieve with classical surfaces such as cylinders, cones, spheres, rotational surfaces, and ruled surfaces. Freeform surfaces offer much more flexibility. In this chapter, we first introduce *Bézier surfaces* and *B-spline surfaces* as natural and easy-to-understand extensions of the corresponding freeform curves.

Whereas the Bézier and B-spline method possesses severe restrictions on topological types, *subdivision surfaces* overcome these limitations in a simple and elegant way (Figure 11.1).Their use is a trend that started in the animation industry. Subdivision surface tools are used in a number of design applications now due to the complex surface modeling necessary for lifelike character animation. Let's go ahead and unpack the secrets of this highlight of modern constructive geometry!

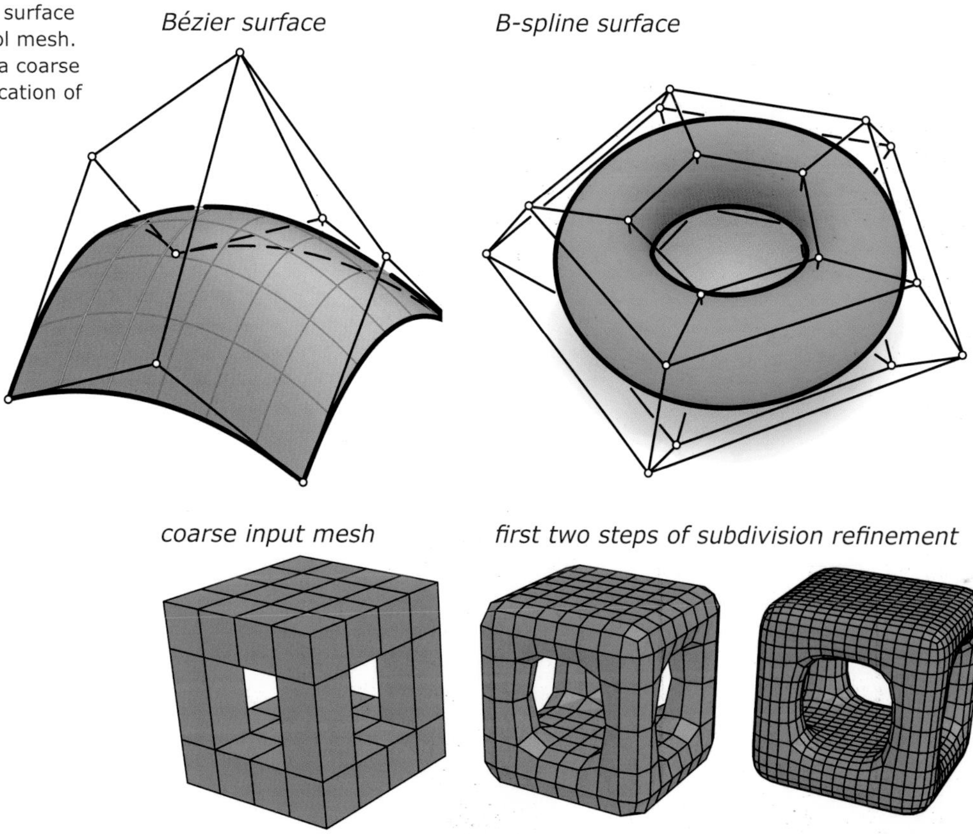

Fig. 11.1
Bézier, B-spline and subdivision surfaces are closely related concepts for freeform surface design. In fact, Bézier and B-spline surfaces are special subdivision surfaces.
(Top) A Bézier and a B-spline surface with the corresponding control mesh.
(Bottom) Subdivision refines a coarse input mesh by repeated application of simple refinement rules.

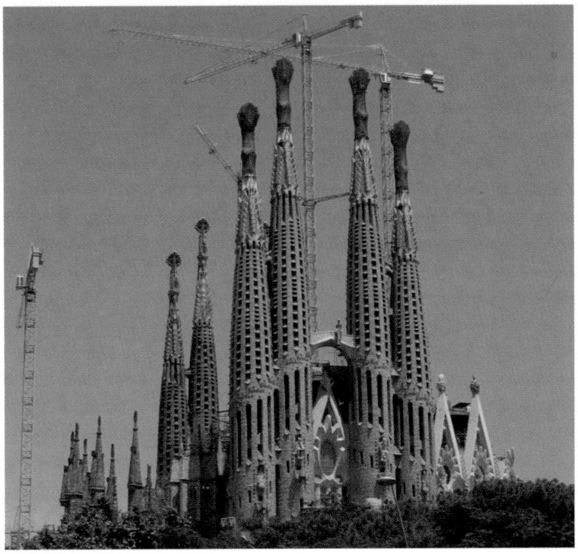

2 (a,b)

3 (a,b)

History of freeform surfaces in architecture. Complex geometries and freeform surfaces appear very early in architecture—dating back at least to the first known dome-like shelters made from wood and willow about 400,000 years ago. Double curved surfaces have existed in domes and sculptural ornaments of buildings through the ages.

It was only in the nineteenth century that architects were granted a significant amount of freedom in their expression of forms and styles with industrialization and improved building materials such as iron, steel, and reinforced concrete (cf. François Coignet, *Béton Aggloméré*, 1855).

Antoni Gaudí (1852–1926) achieved a deep understanding of the statics and shape of freeform surfaces through the development of form-finding techniques and physical models. His *Sagrada Familia* (1882-today) and the *Casa Milà* (1905–1907) are the most prominent examples (Figure 11.2).

Hermann Finsterlin (1887–1973) created hundreds of drawings, watercolors, and physical 3D models of fantastic plastic architecture between 1918 and 1924 (Figure 11.3a). Unfortunately, he could not realize any larger project. In the same period, the rather small but sculpturally impressive *Einstein tower* (1920–1921) was built in Potsdam by Erich Mendelsohn (Figure 11.3b).

Fig. 11.2
History of freeform surfaces in architecture.
(a) The *Casa Milà* (1905-07) and
(b) *La Sagrada Família* (1882-today)
by Antoni Gaudí. The first and second
Goetheanum by Rudolf Steiner.

4 (a)

Reinforced concrete seemed to be a good solution for sculptural forms and wide spans, with a peak of use in the 1960s. Famous examples include *Notre Dame du Haut* (1950–1955) by Le Corbusier and the *TWA Terminal* (1956–1962) of JFK International Airport by Eero Saarinen (Figure 11.4). The limitations of reinforced concrete in terms of weight, cost, and labor were soon realized. Early attempts to reduce weight include the segmentation of the desired surface into structural members and cladding elements.

4 (b)

Fig. 11.3
(a) Unrealized architectural model (1920) by Hermann Finsterlin.
(b)The *Einstein Tower* (1920-21) by Erich Mendelsohn (Image courtesy of Astrophysikalisches Institut Potsdam).

Fig. 11.4
(a) Reinforced concrete has been used to build *Notre Dame du Haut* (1950-55) by Le Corbusier, and
(b) the *TWA Terminal* (1956-62) by Eero Saarinen.

Fig. 11.5
The Sydney Opera House (1957-73) by Jørn Utzen (Image courtesy of Bjarte Sorensen).

A successful example of prefabrication is the spherical shells that form the roof of the *Sydney Opera House* (1957–1973) by Jørn Utzen (Figure 11.5). Projects such as the Sydney opera house made it clear that complex freeform shapes need sophisticated techniques of geometric description and integration of structural and fabrication principles to make them buildable.

One of the first architects to use computer-aided geometric design (CAGD) technologies to build freeform shapes is Frank O. Gehry. He is well known for employing shapes that are approximating developable surfaces (the topic of Chapter 15) in his designs (Figure 11.6a). The Kunsthaus Graz (2002–2003) was designed by Peter Cook and Colin Fournier as a biomorphic freeform shape (Figure 11.6b).

History of freeform surfaces in CAGD. During the 1940s and 1950s, practical needs in the aeronautic and car manufacturing industries initialized the development of mathematical descriptions of freeform geometry. To solve tasks such as "how to store a surface design digitally" or "how to communicate a designed freeform geometry to a numerically controlled milling machine," one needs appropriate mathematical algorithms that can be fed into a computer.

R. Liming and J. Ferguson at Boeing, S. Coons at MIT, M. Sabin at British Aircraft Corporation, P. de Casteljau at Citroën, and P. Bézier at Renault developed solutions to these tasks. In the case of CAGD, the requirements for manufacturing drove the mathematics—and led to the development of mathematics that could describe the types of freeform surfaces seen widely in products today.

Fig. 11.6
(a) The *Guggenheim Museum* (1991-97) in Bilbao by Frank O. Gehry.
(b) The *Kunsthaus Graz* (2002-03) by Peter Cook and Colin Fournier.

(a)

(b)

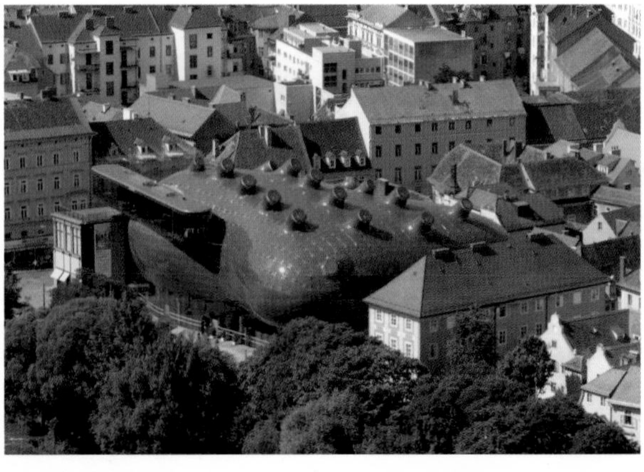

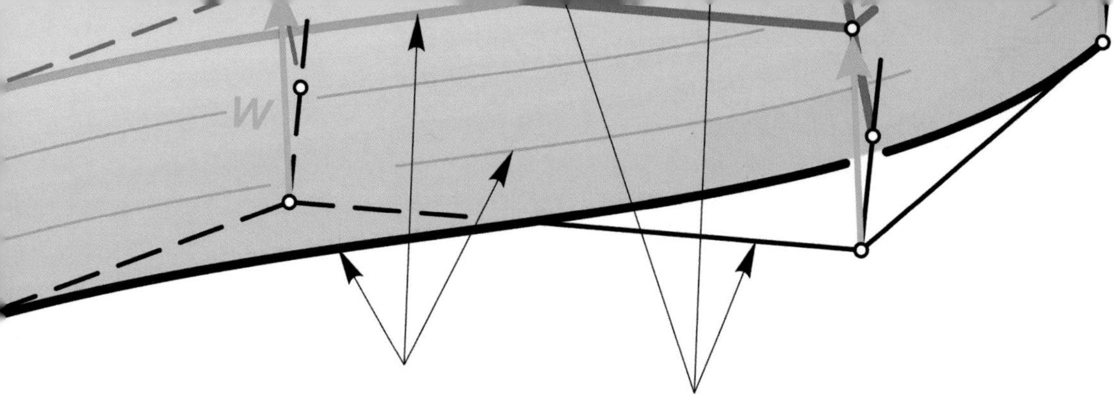

Bézier Surfaces

Translational Bézier surfaces. Let's see how we can create Bézier surfaces from Bézier curves. We start with a simple example (Figure. 11.7) and consider two Bézier curves: one with degree 2 and the other one with degree 3. To become familiar with the double index notation used in the general theory, we denote the three control points of the quadratic Bézier curve b^2 as b_{00}, b_{10}, and b_{20} and the four control points of the cubic curve b^3 as b_{00}, b_{01}, b_{02}, and b_{03}.

Note that the curves have a common endpoint b_{00} and are therefore well suited as profile curves of a *translational surface*. This surface carries a family of quadratic Bézier curves (any of those arises from b^2 by an appropriate translation). The surface also carries a family of cubic curves related to b^3 by translation. It is important to distinguish between the parameters of the two Bézier curves, and thus we denote the parameter on b^2 as u and the parameter along b^3 as v.

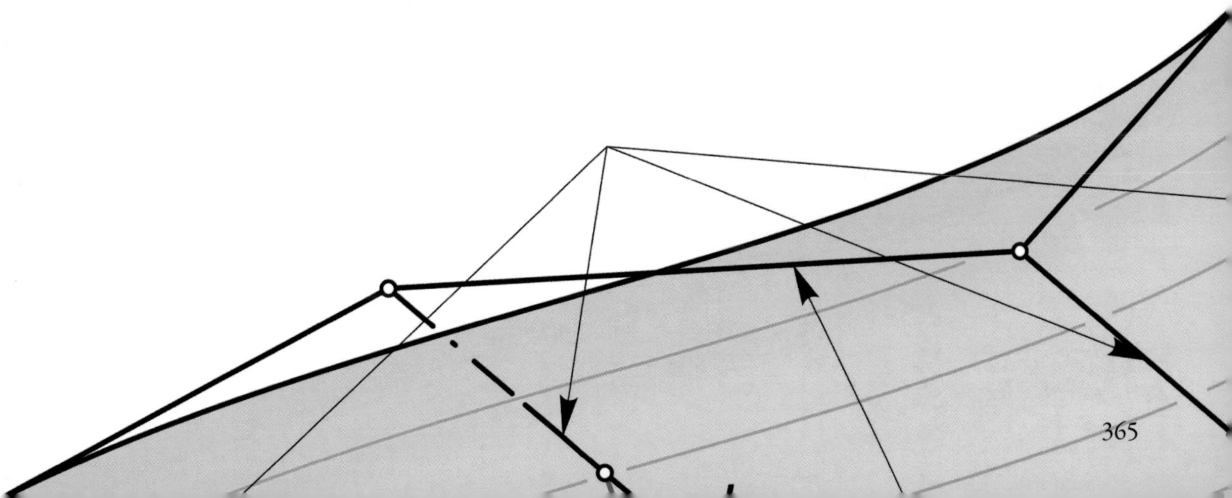

To bring the cubic profile b^3 into a new position, we first compute a point $b^2(u)$ on the quadratic curve—using the algorithm of de Casteljau. We then displace b^3 with the translation, which brings b_{00} to $b^2(u)$. The translation vector is $w = b^2(u) - b_{00}$. The control points of the resulting curve are $b^2(u) = b_{00} + w$, $b_{01} + w$, $b_{02} + w$, and $b_{03} + w$.

There is another way to get these points. We translate the control points of the quadratic curve b^2 in such a way that b_{00} moves to b_{01}. The resulting polygon is called b_{01}, b_{11}, b_{21}. We call such a polygon a *column polygon*, more precisely the one with column index (second index) 1. Likewise, the given control polygon of b^2 is the column polygon with index 0. In the same way, we construct column polygons with indices 2 and 3.

Altogether, we have four column polygons—each with three control points. Now we view each column polygon as a control polygon of a quadratic Bézier curve and compute its point to the same parameter value u. Doing this for all columns, we obtain precisely the control points $b_{00} + w$, $b_{01} + w$, $b_{02} + w$, and $b_{03} + w$ of a cubic Bézier curve lying on the surface.

Fig. 11.7
Translational Bézier surface generated by moving a Bézier curve of degree 3 along a Bézier curve of degree 2. The control points of a position of the cubic Bézier curve, a so-called *v*-curve, can be constructed with the algorithm of de Casteljau: It has to be applied to the 4 column polygons with the same parameter *u*.

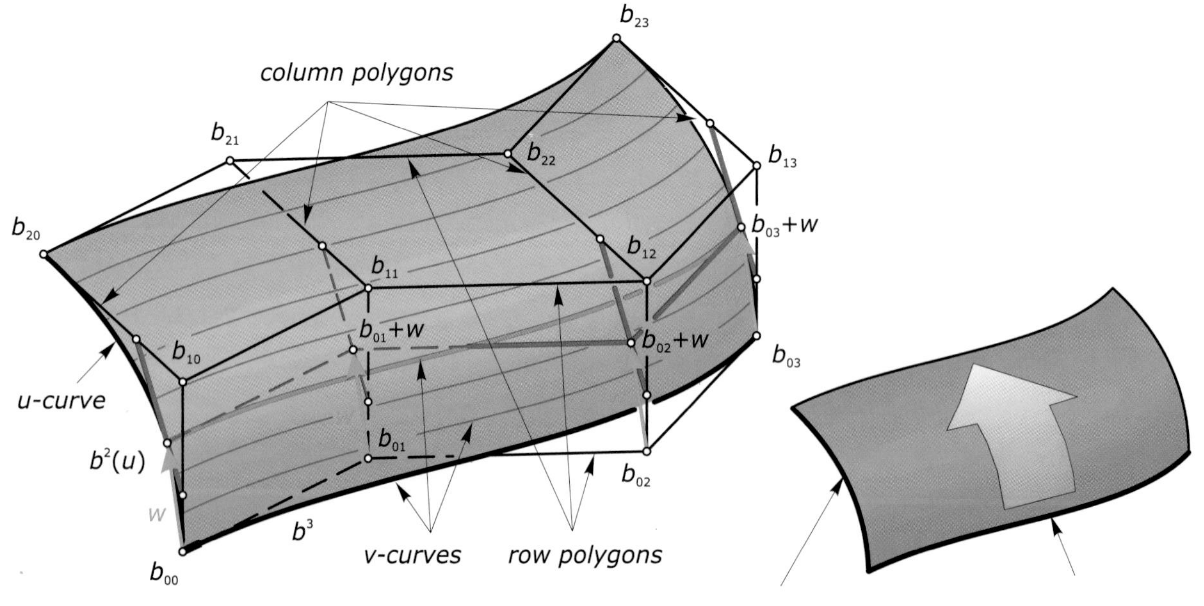

We call such a cubic curve a *v-curve*, because the curve parameter along it is v. The given curve b^3 is also a v-curve; namely, to $u = 0$. Its control polygon is the *row polygon* with row index (first index) 0. The row polygon $b_{20}, \ldots, b_{23}$ with row index 2 also defines a v-curve.

However, the row polygon $b_{10}, \ldots, b_{13}$ does not define a v-curve. The corresponding curve does not lie on the translational surface. Analogously, only two column polygons (namely, those with column index 0 and 3) define Bézier curves that lie on the surface. Column polygons b_{01}, b_{11}, b_{21}, and b_{02}, b_{12}, b_{22} do not define curves on the surface!

So far we have generated the translational surface by moving the cubic curve along the quadratic one. This yielded the family of v-curves. Their control points lie on the four auxiliary quadratic Bézier curves defined by the column polygons.

Analogously, we may move the quadratic curve b^2 along the cubic b^3 (Figure 11.8). A position of such a curve is defined by a point $b^3(v)$ on b^3 and its curve parameter is u. Hence, we call it a *u-curve*. The control points of a u-curve are points on the Bézier curves defined by the row polygons, constructed to the same parameter v.

Fig. 11.8
The translational surface from Fig. 11.7 can also be generated by translation of a Bézier curve of degree 2 along a Bézier curve of degree 3. The control points of a position of the quadratic Bézier curve, a *u*-curve, can be computed with the algorithm of de Casteljau applied to the 3 row polygons with the same parameter *v*.

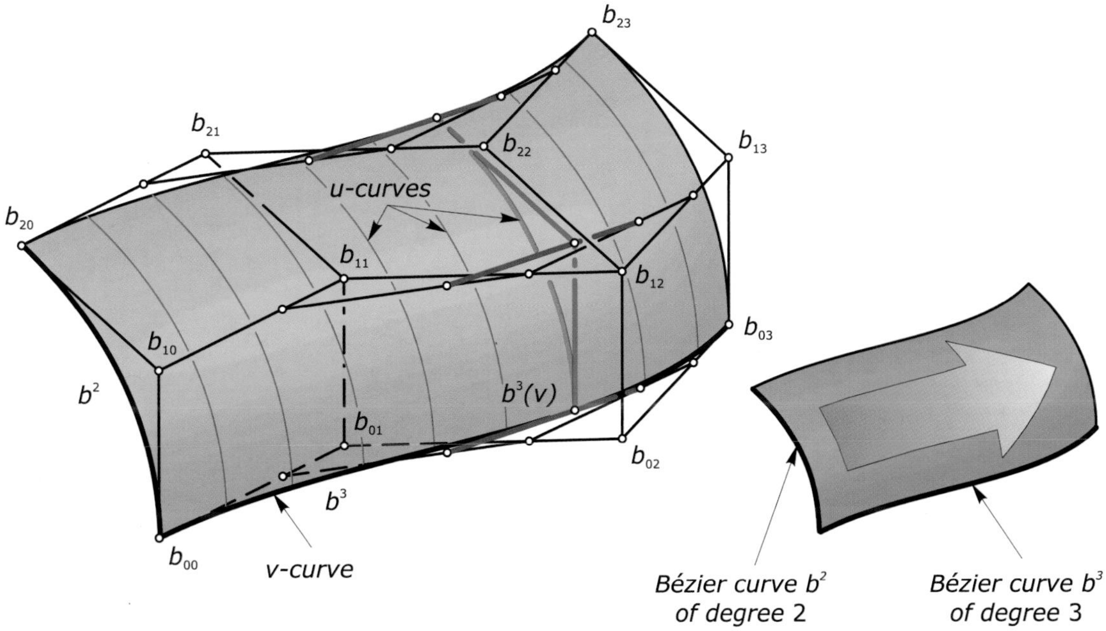

General Bézier surfaces. The extension of translational Bezier surfaces to the general case is straightforward. Input of a Bézier surface is its *control mesh*. It consists of an array of points, visualized as a quadrilateral mesh of row polygons and column polygons.

We use two indices for each control point. The first index attains values $0,1,\ldots,m$ and tells us the row. The second index has values $0,1,\ldots,n$ and defines the column. Thus, altogether we have $(m+1)(n+1)$ control points.

The surface contains two families of Bézier curves: a family of u-curves of degree m and a family of v-curves of degree n. Thus, one speaks of a *Bézier surface of degree* (m,n). Analogous to the case of translational surfaces, *a u-curve is constructed as follows* (see also Figure 11.9).

- Apply the algorithm of de Casteljau to each row polygon using the same parameter value v. This results in $m+1$ points $r_0,\ldots,r_m$.
- The Bézier curve with control points $r_0,\ldots,r_m$ is the desired u-curve.

Analogously, a v-curve is found with help of the column polygons. It is quite simple to see that the families of u-curves and v-curves really lie on the same surface.

In the previous example of a translational Bézier surface, all quadrilaterals in the control mesh are parallelograms and thus are planar. In general, we now do not require planarity of the quads in the control mesh.

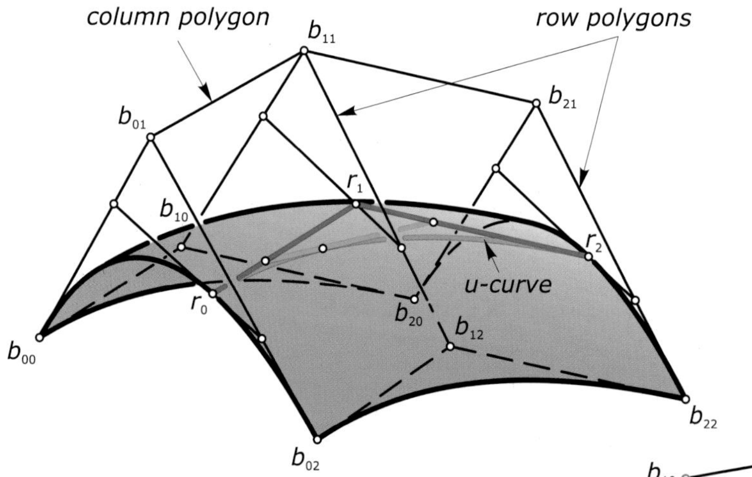

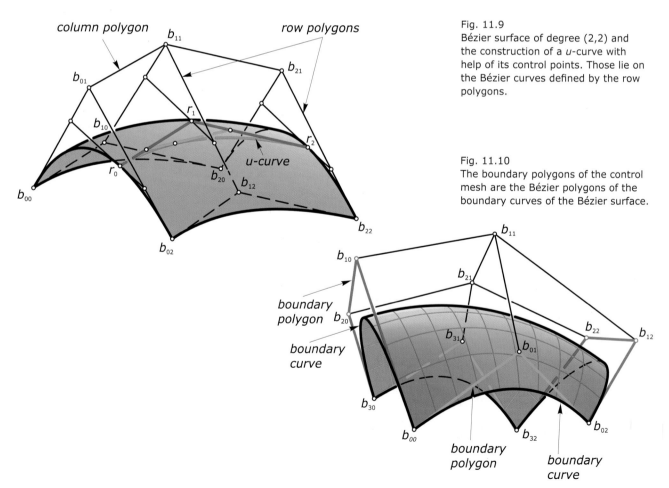

Fig. 11.9
Bézier surface of degree (2,2) and the construction of a u-curve with help of its control points. Those lie on the Bézier curves defined by the row polygons.

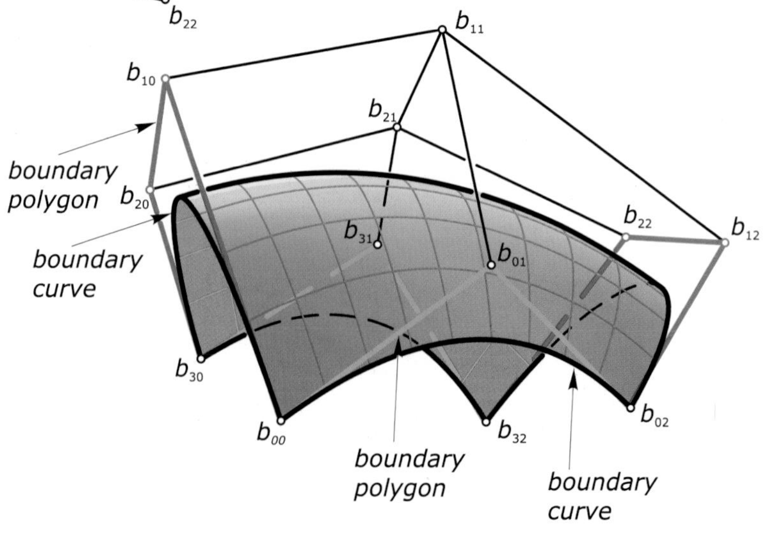

Fig. 11.10
The boundary polygons of the control mesh are the Bézier polygons of the boundary curves of the Bézier surface.

Properties of Bézier surfaces. Each *boundary polygon of the control mesh* defines a Bézier curve that is *a boundary curve of the designed Bézier surface patch* (Figure 11.10). The boundary polygons are the only row and column polygons that define curves on the surface. By the construction explained previously, *the surface lies in the convex hull of the control mesh* (Figure 11.11).

The relationship between control mesh and surface is well suited for design—provided we have sufficiently low-degree m and n. This is due to the fact that we actually apply the Bézier curve construction in u and v direction.

It is worth looking at some Bézier surfaces of low degree in more detail. Their use is appealing in architecture. Moreover, we find interesting relations to surface classes we have studied in previous chapters.

Bézier surfaces of degree (1,1). A Bézier surface patch of degree (1,1) has only one quadrilateral as control mesh (Figure 11.12). The surface contains two families of Bézier curves of degree 1, i.e., straight line segments. Let's construct one of them (e.g., a u-curve). First, we have to compute the points r_0, r_1 on the row polygons to the same parameter value v.

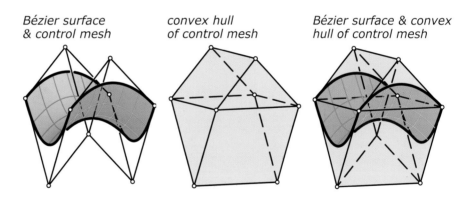

Fig. 11.11
A Bézier surface does not leave the convex hull of its control mesh.

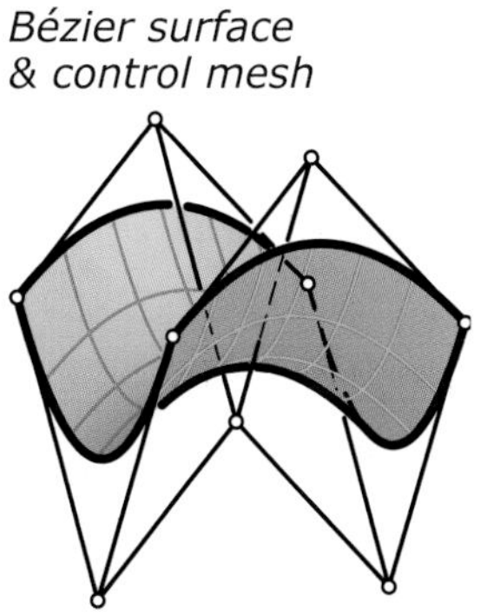

Fig. 11.12
A Bézier surface patch of degree (1,1) is part of a hyperbolic paraboloid. The *u*-curves and *v*-curves are straight line segments.

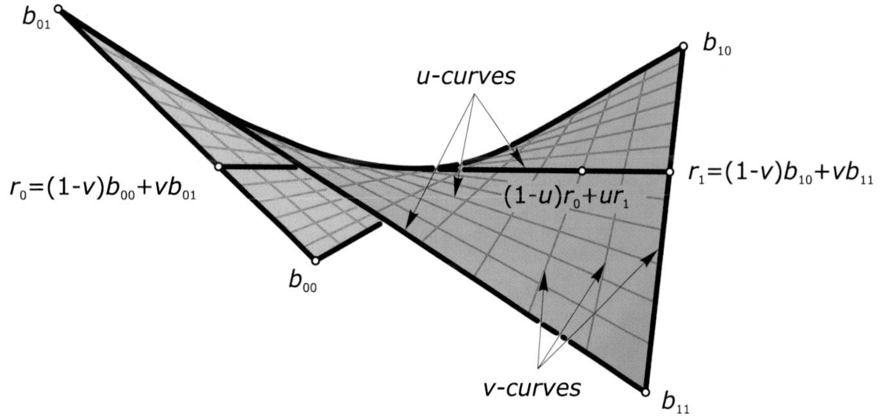

These are points $r_0 = (1 - v)b_{00} + vb_{01}$ and $r_1 = (1 - v)b_{10} + vb_{11}$, which divide opposite boundary segments $b_{00}b_{01}$ and $b_{10}b_{11}$ in the same ratio $(1 - v):v$. The u-curve is the straight line segment r_0r_1. This shows that the surface is (part of) a *hyperbolic paraboloid* (or part of a plane if the control quad is planar). To continue the computation, the line segment r_0r_1 is parameterized by u via $(1 - u)r_0 + ur_1$. Inserting the expressions for r_0, r_1 yields

$$b(u,v) = (1 - u)(1 - v)b_{00} + (1 - u)vb_{01} + u(1 - v)b_{10} + uvb_{11}.$$

If we vary u in the interval $[0,1]$ and v in $[0,1]$, this formula captures all surface points. It is a parameterization of the surface (Chapter 7). As an exercise, you may verify that the v-curves, which are also straight line segments, define the same surface. Evaluating the mathematical representation $b(u,v)$ for arbitrary u and v, not just those in the range between 0 and 1, we obtain the entire hyperbolic paraboloid.

Bézier surfaces that are also ruled surfaces. Consider a Bézier surface of degree $(1,n)$. Its u-curves are Bézier curves of degree 1 and therefore straight line segments. Therefore, this surface is a *ruled surface*—spanning two Bézier curves of degree n (Figure 11.13).

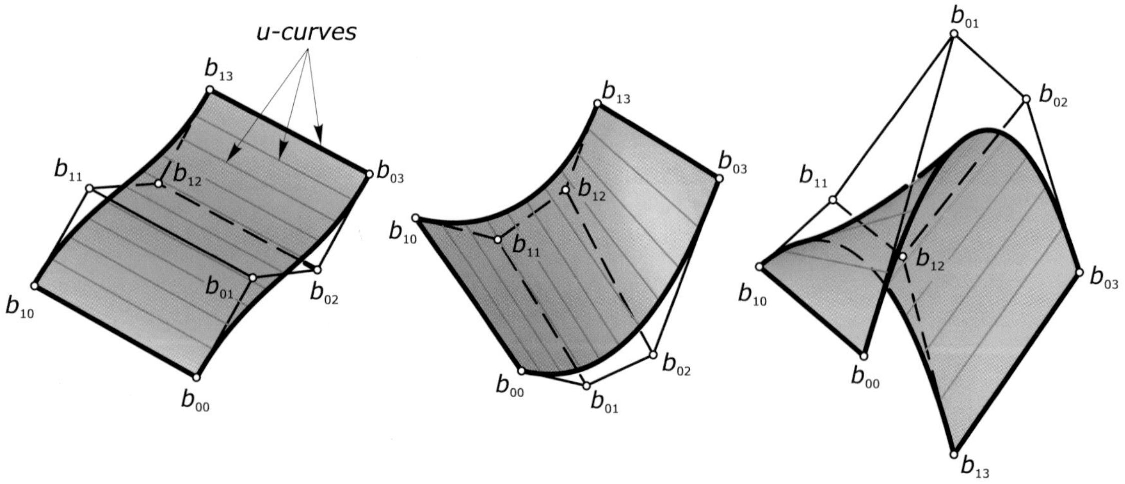

Fig. 11.13
Bézier surfaces where one degree equals 1 are ruled surfaces.

This fact constitutes a very good way of designing ruled surfaces in a CAD environment. Let's add two special cases. If all column segments in the control mesh are parallel (Figure 11.14), we obtain a general *cylinder surface*. Modeling a general cylinder as a Bézier surface of degree $(1,n)$ gives us a lot of freedom in the design of the boundary curves. They need not be congruent.

This is in contrast to the generation of a cylinder by extrusion of a Bézier curve. In addition, control points are allowed to coincide. If all control points of a row fall into the same point $v = b_{00} = \ldots = b_{0n}$, we obtain a *cone surface* patch with vertex v (Figure 11.15).

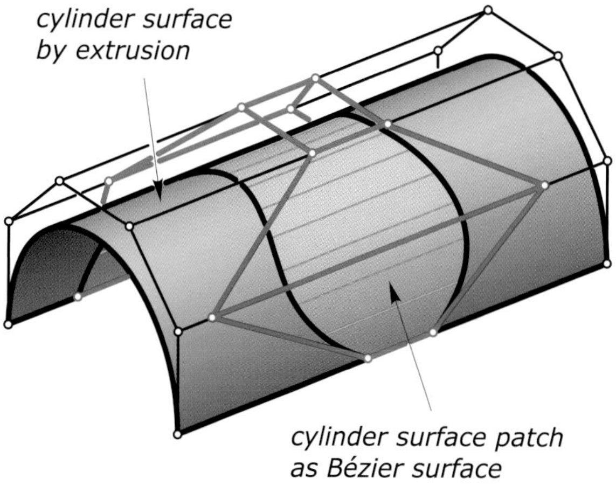

Fig. 11.14
General cylinder surface patches designed as Bézier surfaces with one degree equal to 1. Here we have more degrees of freedom for the design of the boundary curves than the extrusion function would give us.

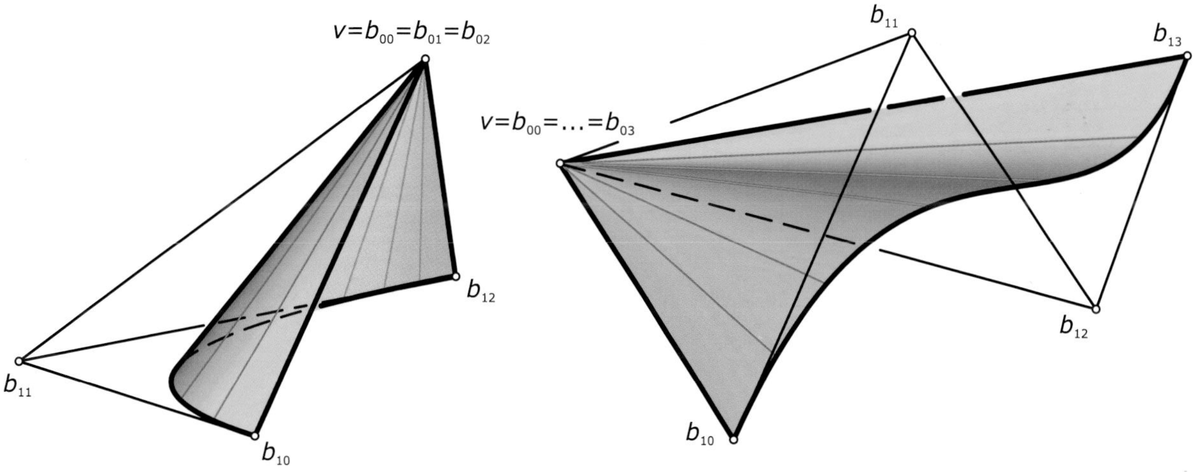

Fig. 11.15
General cone surface patches may also be designed via Bézier surfaces.

Example:

Surfaces from parabolas with vertical axes. Due to their structural efficiency, catenary arcs (refer to chapter 18) and their approximation by parabolic arcs are often used in architecture. To make use of its structural potential, the parabolic arc axis has to be oriented vertically.

As an example for modeling with Bézier surfaces, we show *how to design a Bézier surface from parabolic arcs.* To achieve the desired structural behavior, we define all u-curves of the surface as parabolas with vertical axes. To simplify things, we use a coordinate system with a vertical z axis. How do we place the three control points of a Bézier curve of degree 2 (parabolic arc) so that the curve's axis is vertical? Figure 11.16 shows the solution. We just have to look at the top view in the xy-plane and make sure the top view of the inner control point is the midpoint of the top views of the endpoints. This gives a first simple solution of our surface problem: we use a control grid of a Bézier surface of degree $(2,n)$, whose top view is a rectangular grid (Figure 17.11). For $n=2$ we even obtain a surface whose v-curves are parabolas with vertical axes. In general, this surface is not a paraboloid (which can be obtained if we make sure all quads in the control mesh are parallelograms).

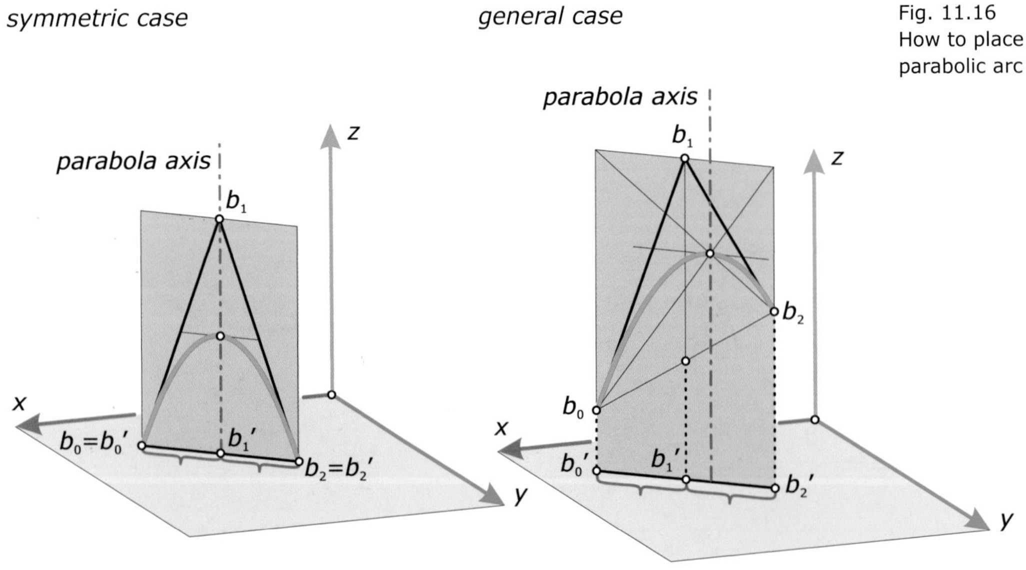

Fig. 11.16
How to place the control points of a parabolic arc with vertical axis.

Fig. 11.17
Surfaces with a family of parabolas with vertical axes may be constructed above a rectangular grid in a horizontal plane. The surfaces on the right hand side have parallelograms as faces of the control mesh; they represent an elliptic or hyperbolic paraboloid, respectively and are special translational Bézier surfaces.

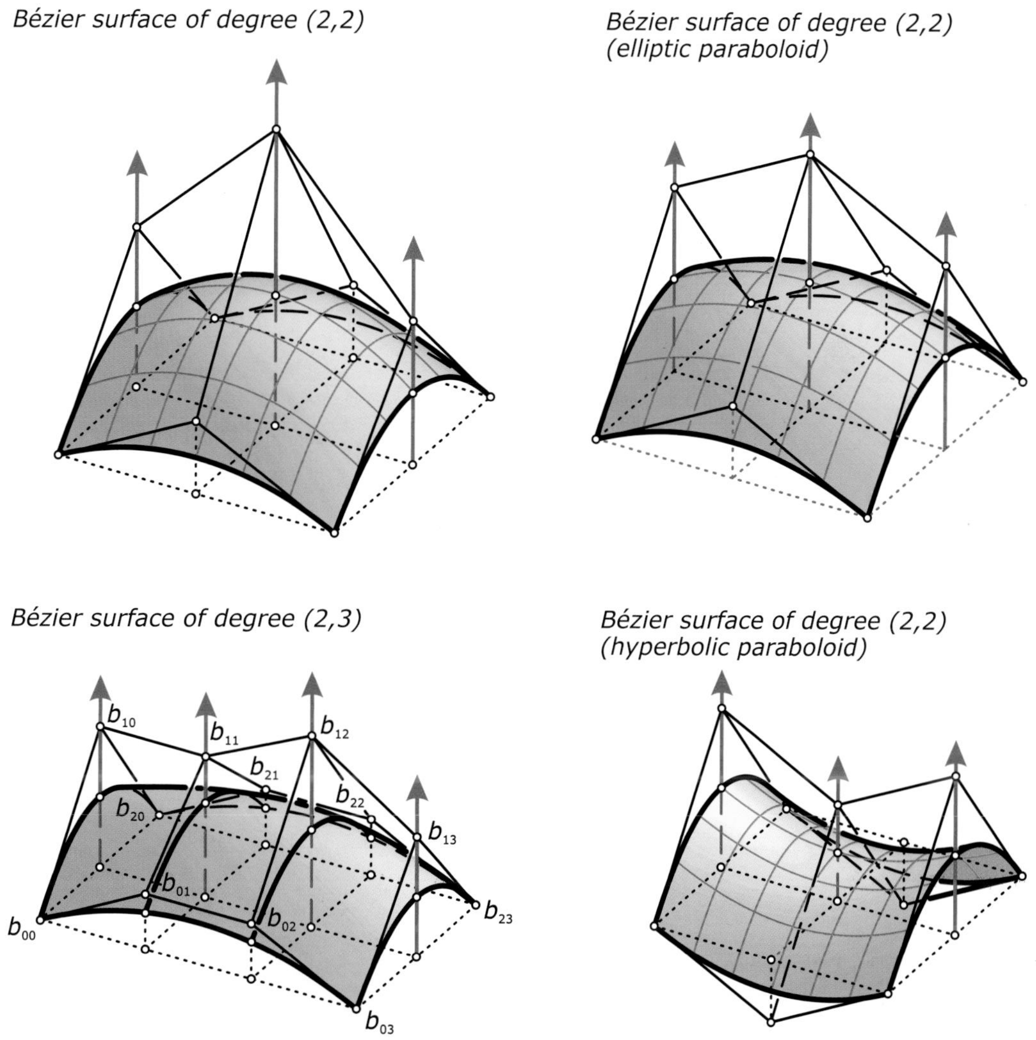

The proof of this construction uses the fact that we can construct the top views of the control points of a *u*-curve directly in the top view by application of the algorithm of de Casteljau (affine invariance of Bézier curves). However, the same proof can be applied to a much more general scenario (Figure 11.18). We just make sure that the top view of our Bézier surface of degree $(2,n)$ has column polygons that satisfy the criterion depicted in Figure 11.16 (three collinear points at equal distance in the top view).
The essence of the proof is already found via $n=1$ and is illustrated in Figure 11.18 (bottom row): for a fixed v, we construct the three control points of a *u*-curve and see that they also satisfy the condition of Figure 11.16 and thus represent a parabola with vertical axis.

Bézier surfaces joined smoothly. Smooth joins between surfaces are much more difficult to achieve than smooth curve joins. There is, however, one construction method for achieving a smooth transition between two Bézier patches that is easy to grasp and quite useful in practice. Figure 11.19 shows a Bézier surface B of degree (3,3) and highlights a boundary polygon and an adjacent polygon of the control mesh.

These two row polygons form a control mesh of a ruled Bézier surface R of degree (1,3). The general construction algorithm for *u*-curves shows that the straight line segments on R are end tangents of the *u*-curves. Hence, R is tangent to B along a boundary curve.

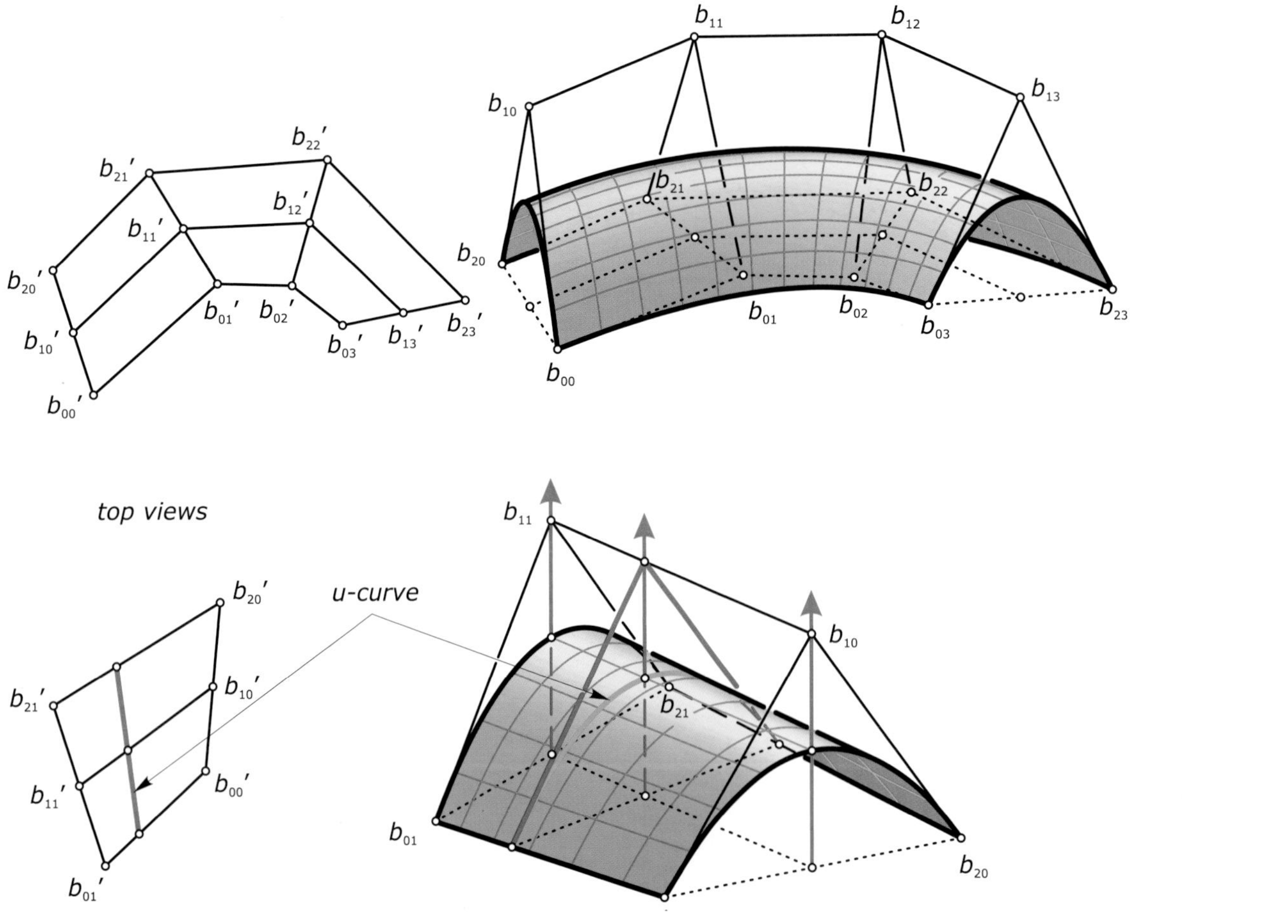

Fig. 11.18
Bézier surfaces formed by a family of parabolas with vertical axes. The restrictions on the top view of the control mesh (left) make sure that any *u*-curve is a parabola with a vertical axis.

Now consider two Bézier surface patches B_1 and B_2 whose control meshes have a common boundary row polygon. This polygon defines a Bézier curve (v-curve) b. The surfaces B_1 and B_2 join along b, but the two surfaces will in general have different tangent planes at points of b. The composite surface possesses a sharp edge along b, which might be undesirable.

To achieve smoothness, we make sure that the tangent ruled surface patches R_1 and R_2 along b lie on the same ruled surface R. Because three v-curves of a Bézier ruled surface R of degree $(1,n)$ possess control points that define the same ratio along the column segments, we obtain the construction via equal ratios depicted in Figure 11.20.

Fig. 11.19
The control mesh of a Bézier surface *B* contains control meshes of ruled surfaces *R,* which are tangent to *B* along its boundary curves.

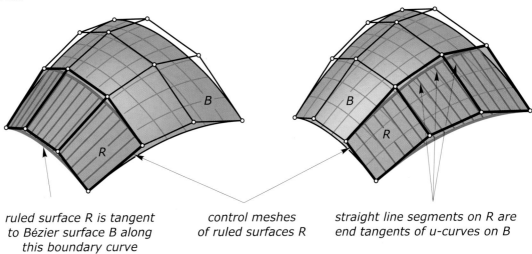

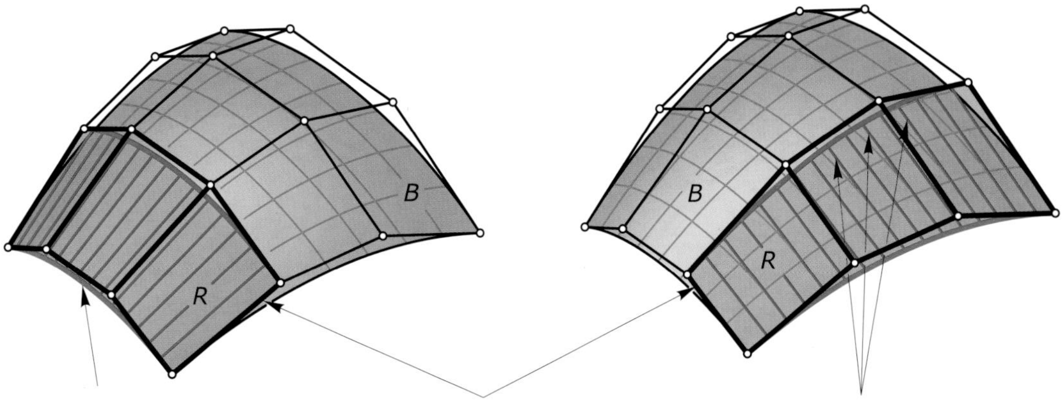

Fig. 11.20
(left) Joining two Bézier patches in a smooth way.

(right) The proof for this construction. Three *v*-curves along the same Bézier ruled surface *R* of degree (1,3) define the same ratio along the column segments.

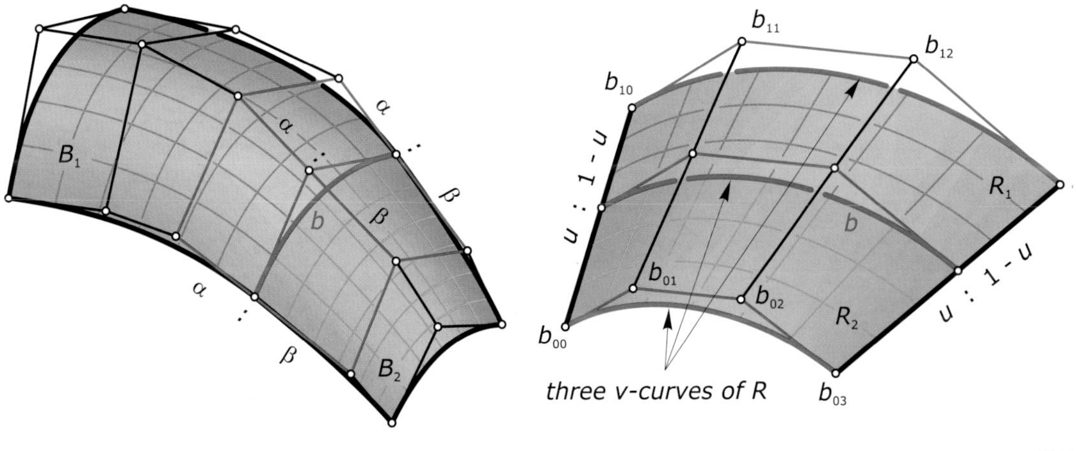

Example:

Smooth Bézier junction between a parabolic cylinder and a plane. As an application of this construction, we discuss the design of a smooth blending surface between a parabolic cylinder C and a plane P (Figure 11.21). As a blending surface, we use a Bézier surface B of degree (2,3) that connects a boundary parabola p_1 of C to a parabola p_2 lying in P.

The first and the last column of the control mesh of B coincide with the control polygons of the two parabolas p_1 and p_2. The second column of the control mesh can be chosen according to the construction via equal ratios (as in Figure 11.20).

The third column just has to lie in the plane P because then the tangent ruled surface is a patch in P and we obtain a smooth join with P. This still gives some choice to the designer in varying the shape of the blending surface. However, this must be done always ensuring a smooth blend between the parabolic cylinder and the plane.

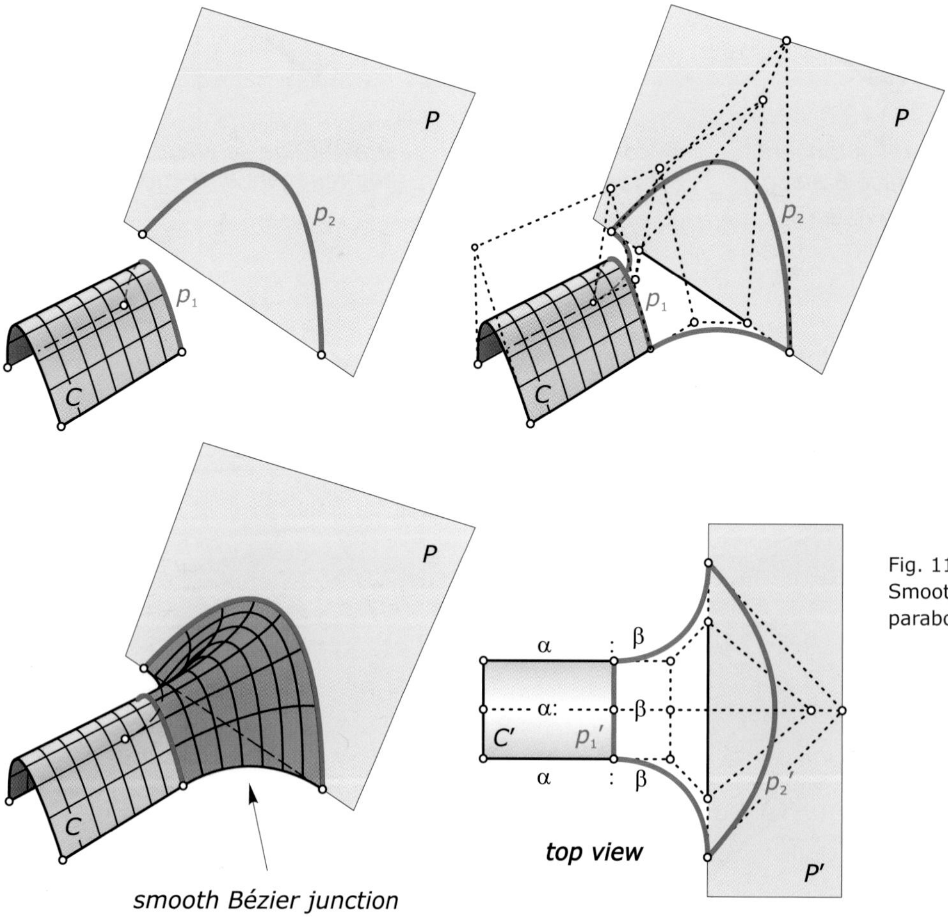

Fig. 11.21
Smooth Bézier junction between a parabolic cylinder and a plane.

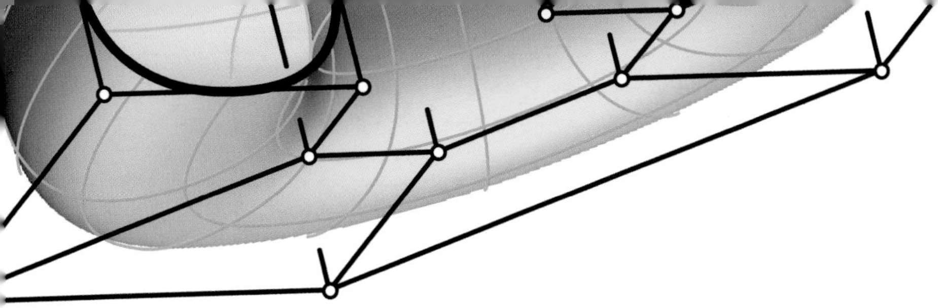

B-Spline Surfaces and NURBS Surfaces

Because Bézier surfaces are just families of Bézier curves, they have the same drawbacks as their curve counterparts: As soon as one degree is too high, they poorly represent the shape of the control mesh. Moreover, changing one control point has a global effect—which makes editing difficult.

To avoid this problem, one can use B-splines for the surface definition. Such a *B-spline surface* is also defined by a quadrilateral control mesh. However, in addition we can choose the degrees for the *u*- and *v*-curves. The implications of the degree on the smoothness of the surface are the same as for curves.

Yet another straightforward extension is the use of *NURBS surfaces*, which have a weight attached to each control point. The effects of changing a weight are the same as for NURBS curves (Figure 11.22).

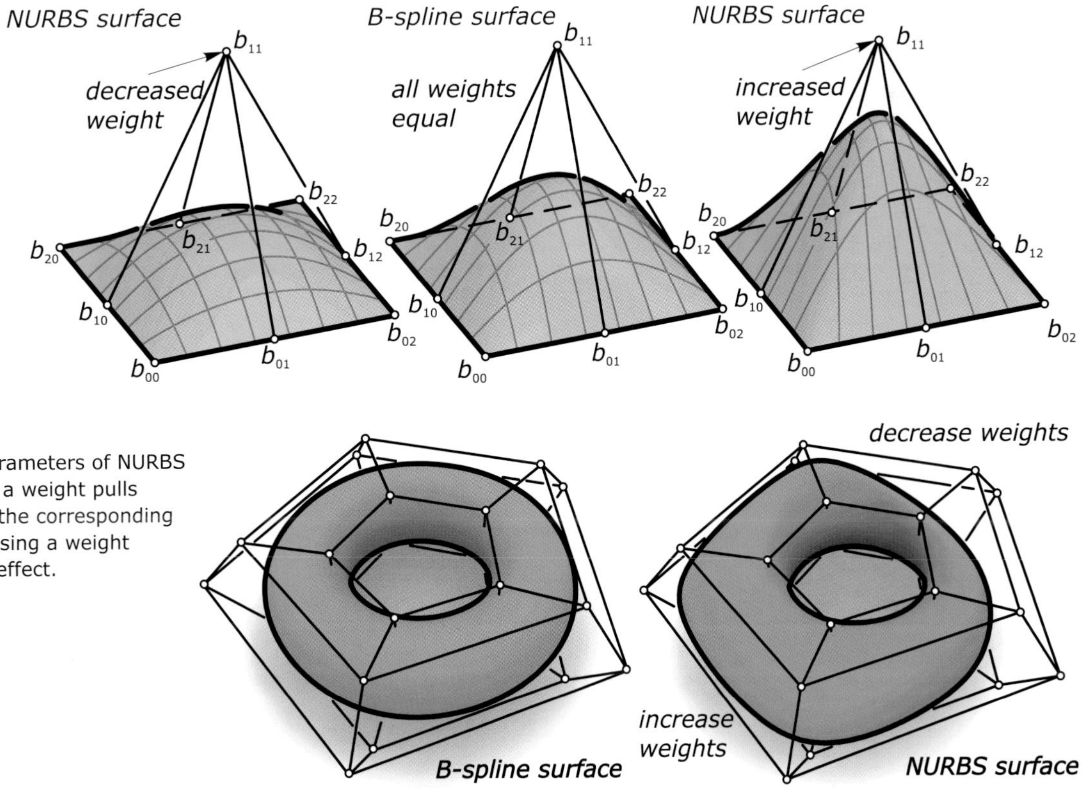

Fig. 11.22
Weights as shape parameters of NURBS surfaces: Increasing a weight pulls the surface towards the corresponding control point, decreasing a weight shows a push-away effect.

Let's examine a few examples, as shown in Figure 11.23. Surface B_1 is of degree (1,3) and has a control mesh of 2 x 6 points. Hence, the *u*-curves are straight lines and the surface is a ruled surface. Surface B_2 is also of degree (1,3), but has 4 x 6 control points. Therefore, the surface is formed by three ruled surfaces that join along sharp edges.

Surface B_3 is of degree (3,3), which implies continuity of curvature (discussed further in Chapter 14). In Chapter 14 we will also point to an important visual effect concerning reflection lines if the surface is polished. Smooth curves generate smooth reflections only if the surface is curvature continuous. At first sight, it is surprising that this does not hold for a surface containing only well-defined tangent planes (no sharp edges).

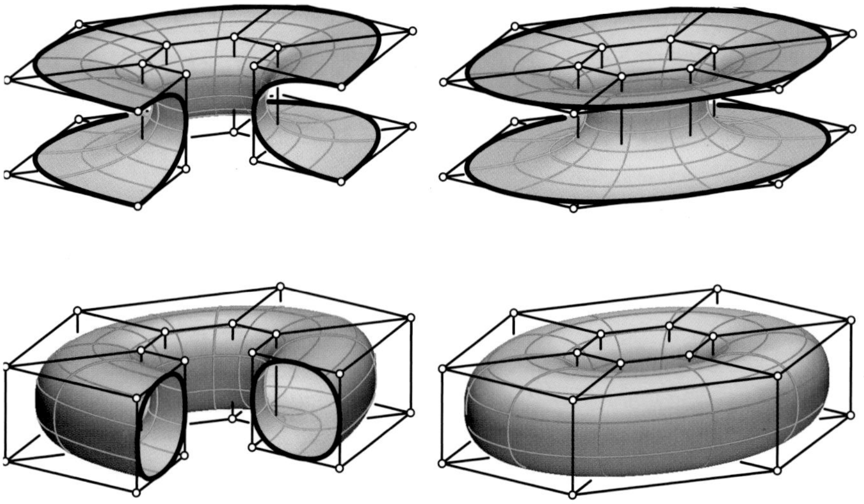

Fig. 11.24
Three different topological types of NURBS surfaces, depending on the chosen mode (open or closed) for *u*- and *v*-curves, respectively.

Fig. 11 .23
Some B-spline surfaces illustrating the influence of the degree.

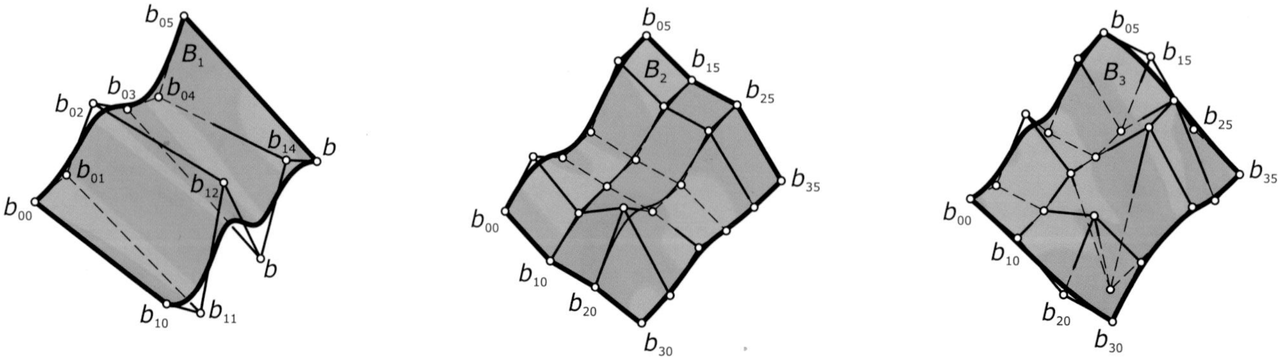

Open and closed mode. B-spline curves and NURBS curves can be constructed in the open or closed mode. In the latter case, the control polygon has to be closed as well. A B-spline surface carries two families of B-spline curves: the *u*-curves and the *v*-curves, which can be in open or closed mode. This yields three quite different ways in which the surface is put together (Figure 11.24).

- Open mode for *u*- and *v*-curves: the surface is a four-sided patch.
- Closed mode in one direction (*u* or *v*), open mode in the other direction: such a surface looks like a deformed piece of a pipe.
- Closed mode in both directions: the surface looks like a deformed torus.

These three types are instances of different topologies. With control meshes in which one or more boundary polygons degenerate to a single point (Figure 11.25), we may model patches with fewer than four curved sides, (as discussed in material following, they are topologically equivalent).

We may also obtain the topology of a sphere (deformed sphere). However, more complex topologies—such as a closed surface, as shown in Figure 11.1 (bottom)—cannot be modeled by a single B-spline surface. Stitching several B-spline patches together to obtain a more complicated surface is difficult and quite far away from being practical. This topological dilemma is resolved by subdivision surfaces. Before discussing them, we address a few other surface types that are very useful in shape modeling.

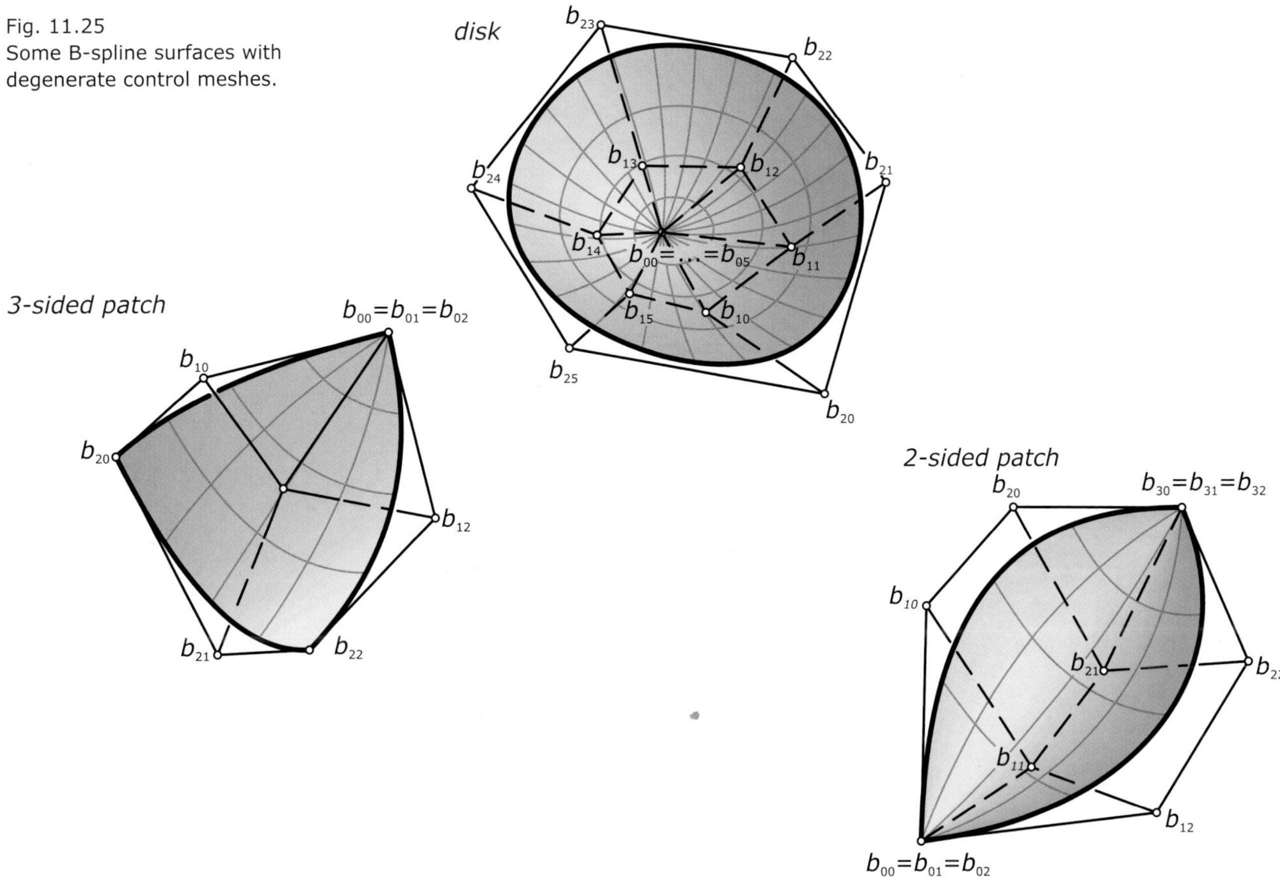

Fig. 11.25
Some B-spline surfaces with degenerate control meshes.

Interpolating spline surfaces. Bézier and B-spline surfaces possess a rich spectrum of possible shapes. They can be interactively designed by editing their control mesh. However, there are other ways of defining and using them. For example, we may require the surface to pass precisely through a given set of points.

This *interpolation* problem in its most general form is difficult to solve. However, the following solution is easy and is implemented in most 3D modelers: Given a set of points, arranged like the control points in a quadrilateral mesh, pass a B-spline surface through it (Figure 11.26).

In our discussion of digital reconstruction in Chapter 17, we will see that we can approximate any given shape or measurement data from a 3D scanner with high accuracy—provided we use a sufficient number of B-spline patches and a good algorithm for computing them.

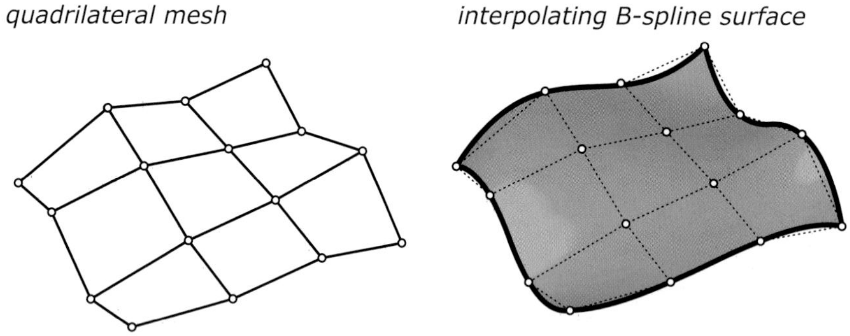

Fig. 11.26
B-spline surfaces may be used to interpolate the vertices of a quadrilateral mesh. The latter is not the B-spline control mesh.

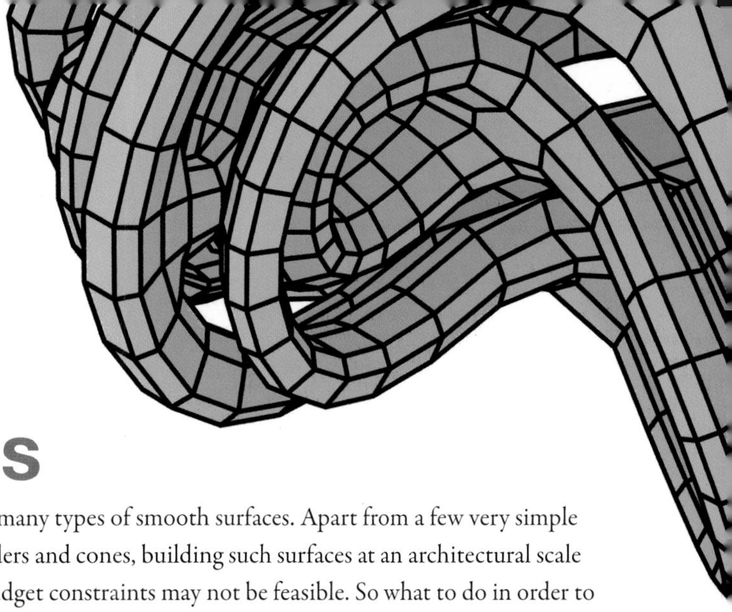

Meshes

We have discussed many types of smooth surfaces. Apart from a few very simple ones, such as cylinders and cones, building such surfaces at an architectural scale within the usual budget constraints may not be feasible. So what to do in order to realize a beautiful design, which includes a nonstandard shape? One answer is to use *meshes*. They come in different types, and some of them are promising candidates for architectural design.

Roughly speaking, a mesh is a collection of points (*vertices*) arranged into basic elements called *faces*. The faces are bounded by polygons. Typically, one type of polygon dominates (e.g., triangle, quadrilateral, or even hexagon). They fit together along common *edges* and roughly describe the shape of a smooth surface (which may, however, have some non-smooth features such as sharp edges or corners).

In fact, almost all seemingly smooth surfaces in animations, games, and the like are actually just smoothly rendered meshes (recall Chapter 2 on rendering) . They are omnipresent in graphics, but are also heavily used for simulations in engineering. Some examples of meshes are shown in Figure 11.27. The use of meshes in architecture enjoys increasing popularity, a few of the many recent projects being displayed in Figure 11.28d–f.

Fig. 11.27
Meshes come in different types: triangle meshes, meshes formed by quadrilaterals or even hexagons. In contrast to triangle meshes, their faces are not necessarily planar, but shall join along common straight edges. The meshes shown here have been designed with software developed by Ergun Akleman.

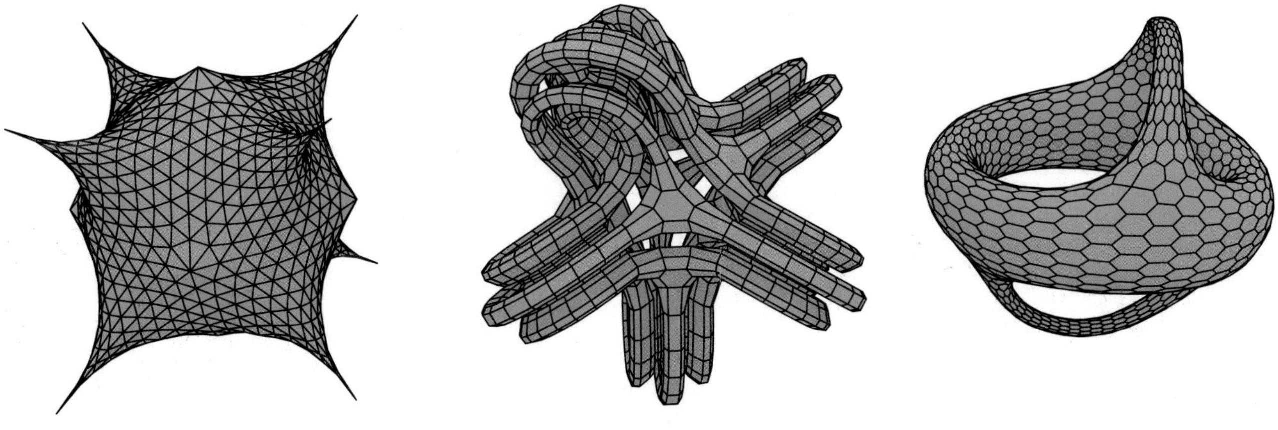

History of meshes in architecture. A milestone for realizing freeform geometric shapes in architecture were the early twentieth-century fabrication methods for glass panels (Irving Colburn, 1905; Emile Fourcault, 1913; Max Bicheroux, 1919). In 1914, the German architect Bruno Taut (1880–1938) used reinforced concrete girders as structural elements for his glass pavillion (Figure 11.28a), with Luxfer glass bricks as glazing elements. Glass, as the epitome of "fluidity and sparkle" and the "highest symbol of purity and death," is the perfect material for Bruno Taut.

The evolution from iron to steel offered new dimensions and possibilities of prefabrication, as well as novel assembling logistics and material compositions for complex geometric lightweight structures. Pioneers are Buckminister Fuller (famous for his geodesic domes), V. G. Suchov, and Frei Otto (known for his suspended structures, Figure 11.28b), and H. Schober and J. Schlaich, with their cable nets and grid shells (Figure 11.28c).

In general, geometric knowledge in combination with new methods of structural computation opens up new approaches to manufacturing and fabrication of freeform surfaces. One example is the *Sage Gateshead* (1994–2004) by Foster and Partners (Figure 11.28d), a building whose roof is geometrically a *quadrilateral mesh*.

Triangular meshes have been used in architecture whenever freeform surfaces cannot be easily planarized in another way. Recent examples include the comparatively small *Mur island* (2003) in Graz by Vito Acconci (Figure 11.28e) and parts of the huge glass roof of the Milan trade fair (2002–2005) by Massimiliano Fuksas (Figure 11.28f).

(b)

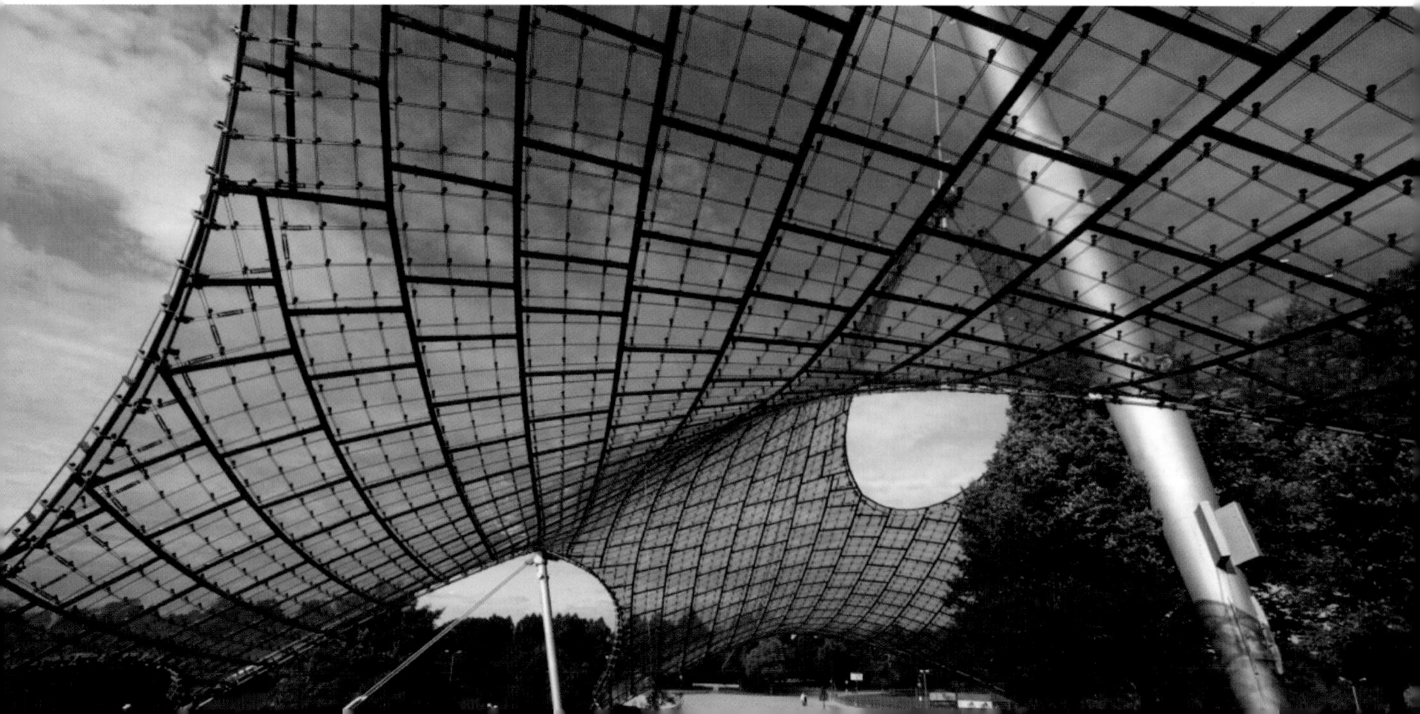

(a)

(c)

(d)

(e)

(f)

Fig. 11.28
(a) The *Glass Pavilion* (1914) by Bruno Taut.
(b) The *Munich Olympia Stadium* (1972) by Frei Otto.
(c) The glass roof of the *Hippo House* (1996) at the Berlin zoo by Schlaich Bergermann und Partner is a quadrilateral mesh with planar faces.
(d) The *Sage Gateshead* (1994-2004) by Foster and Partners has a roof whose geometry is that of a quadrilateral mesh.
(e) The *Mur Island* (2003) by Vito Acconci has a triangle mesh structure.
(f) The roof of the *Trade Fair* (2002-2005) in Milan by Massimiliano Fuksas is a huge half triangle, half quad mesh.

Geometry and connectivity. When dealing with meshes, we should first discuss their *connectivity*—also refered to as their "mesh topology." Roughly speaking, this means that we have to label the vertices of the mesh and know in which way they are joined to form the edges and faces. A more precise description follows.

Meshes with precisely the same connectivity may have very different shapes. We just have to change the coordinates of the vertices (within meaningful limits) and keep all connectivity information (see Figure 11.29).

The larger the number of faces the more freedom we have in our design. However, this may also be a burden and thus we need strategies for the generation of meshes. In our search for such strategies, aesthetics plays a crucial role. Figure 11.30 shows two meshes approximating the same shape, but one is obviously much more balanced than the other.

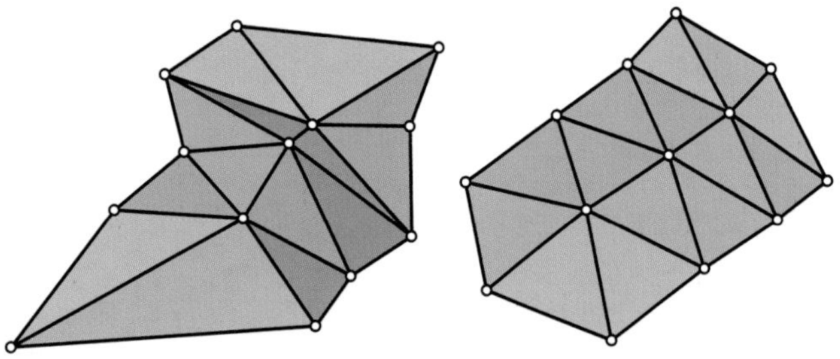

Fig. 11.29
These two triangle meshes have the same connectivity, but represent quite different shapes.

Fig. 11.30
Two triangle meshes may approximate the same shape, but have a very different connectivity. This has an influence on the visual appearance of the mesh.

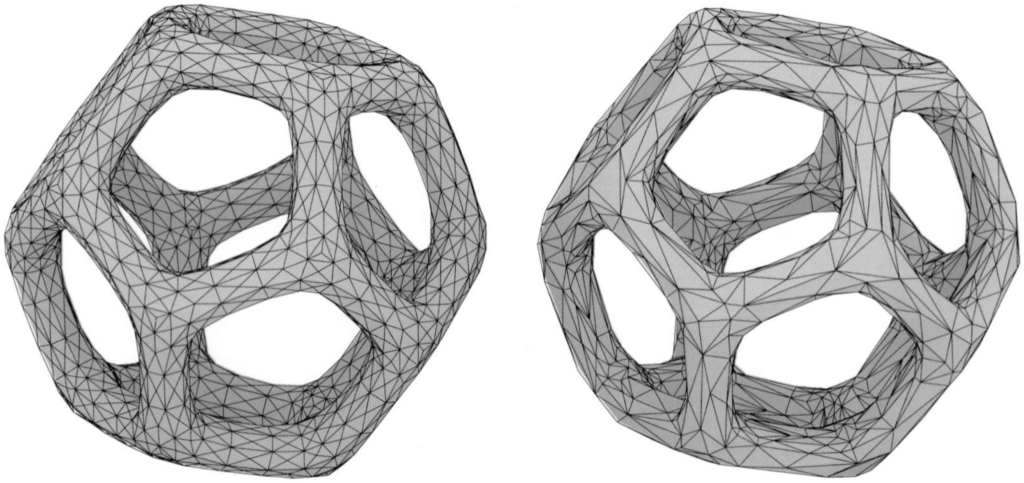

To describe the same geometry with a more balanced mesh, we might have to change the connectivity. Many algorithms in mesh design are basically about a clever interplay of designing/changing connectivity and geometry.

To be more specific about geometry and connectivity, a way is needed for storing the essential information. Among other file formats, the commonly used OBJ format accommodates this approach.

- A list of coordinate triples (x,y,z) is the first part of this format. A list is just an ordered sequence, and the coordinates define the *vertices* of the mesh. The coordinates greatly contribute to the geometry. However, there is more information—given by the order in this list. The coordinate triple (vertex) that comes first may be seen as having label 1, the triple coming next defines the vertex with label 2, and so on. The actual order may not have anything to do with the geometry or connectivity at this moment. The only important insight is that through an ordered list of triples the coordinates of vertices are defined and each vertex is assigned a *label*.
- The next information in such a file are the *face commands*. The face command specifies polygons that represent the faces of the mesh. Let's look at an example (Figure 11.31): (f 1 3 6 4) means that vertices with labels 1, 3, 6, and 4 form a quadrilateral face; (f 2 4 6) defines a triangular face with vertices 2, 4, and 6. Again, more information is contained in the face commands. The order of vertices (such as 1 3 6 4) defines all edges of the face: an edge joining 1 and 3, edge 36, edge 64, and edge 41. We always close a face polygon. Clearly, the same face can be written with the command (f 3 6 4 1). However, (f 4 6 3 1) would make some difference: one assumes here that the underlying surface has an inner and outer side and that the orientation is counterclockwise if we look at the surface from its outer side. Have a look at two faces that join along an edge, such as 46 and 64 in our example. Because of the orientation assumption, we trace the edge in opposite directions for the two faces. For the quad face, we trace it as 64 (go from 6 to 4) and for the triangle we trace it as 46. Just the edges at the boundary of the mesh are traced only once; interior edges are traced twice, in opposite directions. Otherwise, the representation is not consistent.

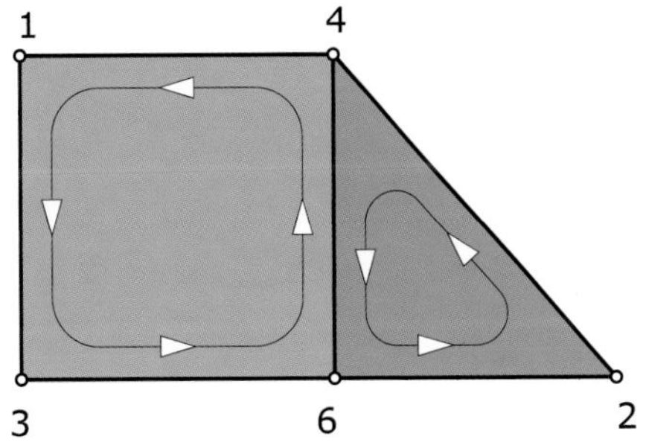

Fig. 11.31
The face information (f 1 3 6 4) and (f 2 4 6) tells us: A quadrilateral face, traced in counter-clockwise order when observing it from the outer side of the surface, has vertices with labels 1,3,6,4. It meets a triangular face with vertex labels 2,4,6 along the common edge with vertices 4 and 6.

This is all we need in order to define both the connectivity and the geometry of the mesh. We will return to this topic in the section on topology in Chapter 14. One useful limitation should be mentioned: It would be an advantage to exclude so-called *T-junctions*, where two faces meet the same edge of another face (see Figure 11.32).

Likewise, we do not want *degenerate triangles* (i.e., triangles whose vertices are all lying on the same straight line, producing T-junctions). Degenerate triangles do not define a face plane and are therefore a potential source of failure in other programs using such a mesh as input.

We have discussed only the basics. Programs may store further information (e.g., surface normal vectors, texture information, material properties, and so on) needed for certain applications, such as rendering.

Meshes are so-called *discrete representations of surfaces*. They generalize the pretty obvious fact that a polygon may be used as a discrete representation of a smooth curve. However, the step from curve to surface is a large one and certainly not easy. Therefore, you cannot expect to easily extract all essential information about the geometry of surfaces (such as curvatures) from meshes.

For curves, this has been very easy. However, for surfaces we will use other tools. In the following you will learn about the most basic types of meshes and which ones have the potential to be visually pleasing.

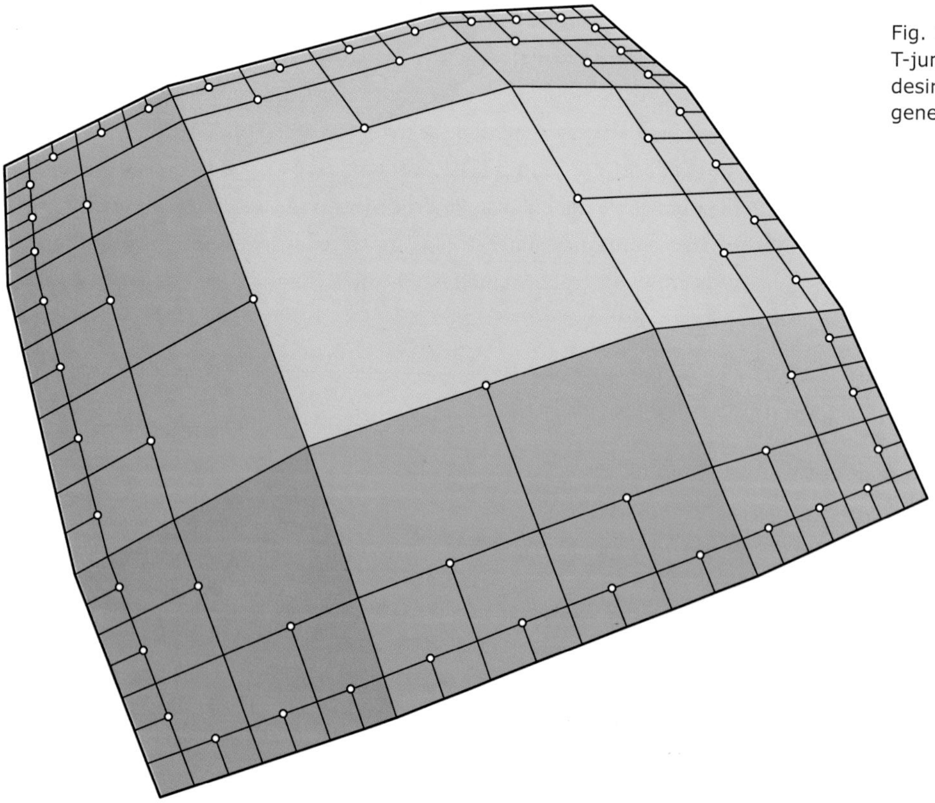

Fig. 11.32
T-junctions in meshes are not desirable, but CAD programs may generate them in large amounts.

Quadrilateral meshes. To obtain nice meshes that represent surfaces, we first consider meshes representing the plane (such as with faces of the same type). The easiest way to tile the plane with quadrilaterals is to use squares (or rectangles) arranged in a regular way. In Figure 11.33, four squares join in a vertex.

A well-formed quadrilateral mesh (also called a quad mesh) will have the same connectivity as this special planar mesh. At an interior vertex (i.e., a vertex that is not at the boundary of the mesh), exactly four faces meet. Of course, four edges meet there too. We speak of a *vertex of valence 4*. In general, the *valence* of an interior vertex is the *number of incoming edges* (the same as the number of faces through that vertex).

In a quad mesh, an interior vertex of valence 4 is called *a regular vertex*. If the valence is different from four, we talk about an *irregular vertex*. Let's have a look at the simplest quad mesh, the cube. Each vertex has valence 3. As a consequence, all vertices are irregular—which might be a surprise at first glance. Note, however, that the cube is not really a satisfying approximation of a smooth surface.

Quad meshes with regular vertices only are shown in Figure 11.34. Do you remember these types from a previous section? Could you imagine a fully regular quad mesh approximating a sphere?

To reduce topological restrictions, one may introduce some non-quadrilateral faces into a quad mesh (which would constitute a *quad-dominant* mesh).

Before moving to other surfaces, understand that the *quadrilaterals in a quad mesh in general are not planar* (although this is certainly a very useful property for applications in architecture). We have already encountered some special surfaces that can be approximated by meshes with planar quads. This interesting topic is explored in detail in Chapter 19.

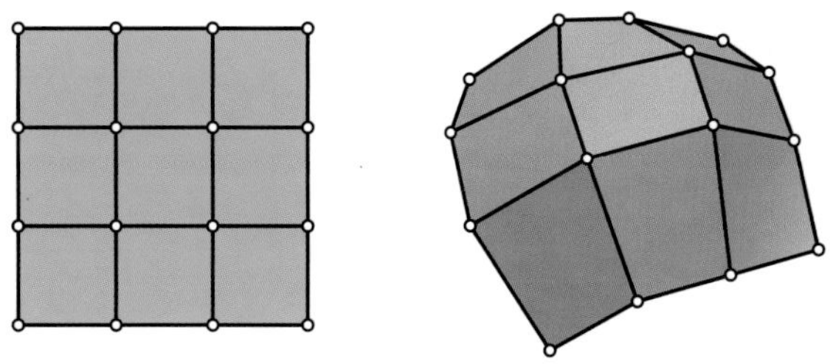

Fig. 11.33
(left) In a regular tiling of the plane with squares, exactly four squares join at a common vertex.
(right) A regular vertex in a quadrilateral mesh has the same property.

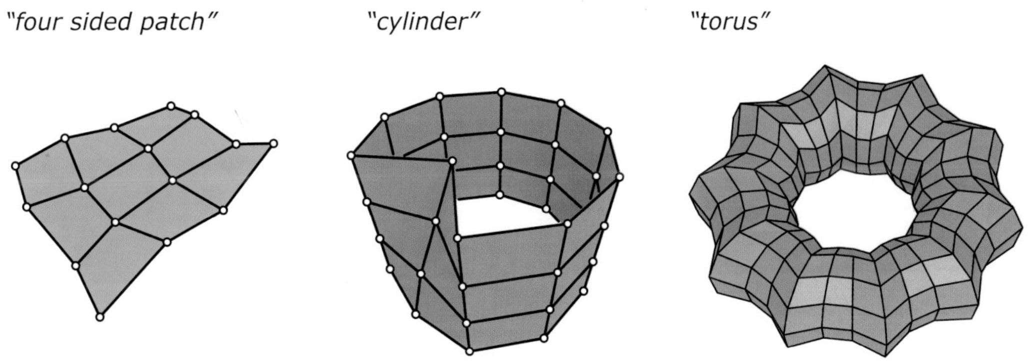

Fig. 11.34
Quad meshes with only regular vertices have limitations concerning their topology; see the section on topology in Chapter 14.

Triangle meshes. A triangle mesh consists exclusively of triangles. In exploring them, we take the previous approach and first have a look at the case of a plane. How do we tile a plane with regular triangles only? This is very simple (Figure 11.35; see also the discussion on planar tilings in Chapter 5).

Obviously, we have to assemble six triangles around a vertex. Note that the same mesh topology is obtained when we split the squares of a square tiling in the plane by one family of parallel diagonals (Figure 11.36).

Conversely, we obtain a tiling via parallelograms by removing a family of parallel lines from a regular triangle mesh in the plane. It is almost needless to say that a regular vertex of a general triangle mesh is an interior vertex of valence 6 (Figure 11.35). The other interior vertices are called irregular.

Triangle meshes are well suited for architecture because their faces are planar. On the other hand, we may roughly need twice as many triangles as quads to represent the same shape (Figure 11.36).

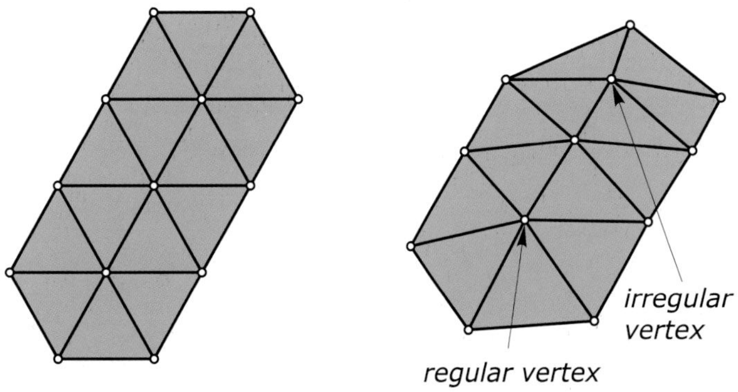

Fig. 11.35
(left) In a tiling of the plane with regular triangles, six faces join at a vertex.
(right) The same is true at a regular vertex of a general triangle mesh.

Fig.11.36
The conversion of a quad mesh into a triangle mesh and vice versa is shown in the plane, but would also work in regular parts of meshes representing surfaces.

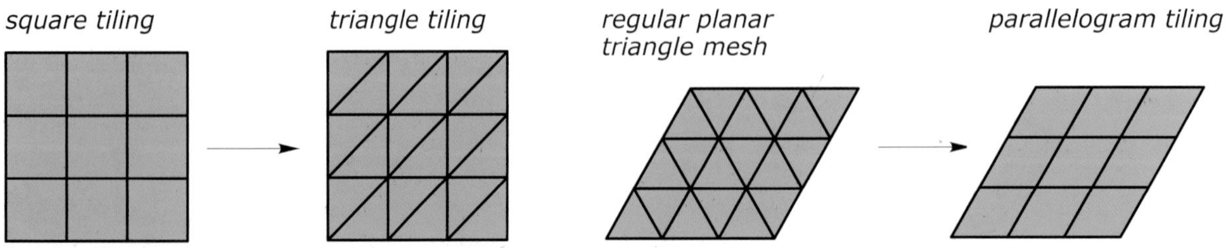

Hexagonal meshes. Can we tile the plane with regular polygons other than squares or triangles? Investigating the edge angles at a vertex of a tiling that consists of regular polygons, one notices that the angles total 360 degrees.

Based on this fact, only one more possibility is left: hexagons (Figure 11.37). Of course, three hexagons of such a honeycomb tiling join at a vertex—which is also considered a regular case for a general hexagonal mesh (Figure 11.38).

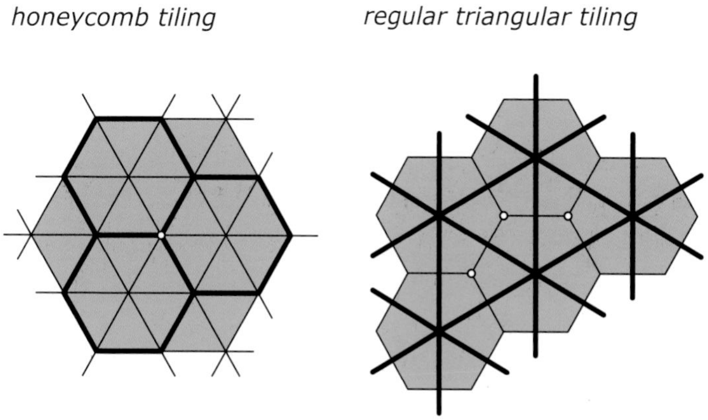

Fig. 11.37
Tilings of the plane with regular hexagons are related to regular triangular tilings very closely; recall the quite analogous duality between Platonic polyhedra.

Fig. 11.38
A hexagonal mesh in architecture (Nicholas Grimshaw, The Eden Project). Note that the hexagonal faces of the mesh cannot be planar regular hexagons. Why is this so?

Mesh refinement. It is sometimes desirable to design a mesh by starting with a coarse mesh and then refining it via an appropriate procedure. Subdivision surfaces (discussed in material following) work in this way. However, before moving to subdivision surfaces let's have a look at some principles of refinement. It is useful to think about refinement as a two-step procedure: change the connectivity (number of vertices and the way they are connected) and then change the geometry (the position of the vertices). At this point, you might want to review the explanation of geodesic spheres in Chapter 3.

Let's first examine triangle meshes. If we insert all edge midpoints and connect them as shown in Figure 11.39, we will end up with a finer triangle mesh that has exactly four times as many faces as the coarse mesh. Each face is split into four new faces. At this point, the geometry is still the same.

But now we are able to change the vertices so that this new mesh follows the design intent. This can represent a lot of work, and therefore the automatic displacement via appropriate algorithms is discussed later in the chapter. Of course, with the increased number of triangles we have more flexibility and a better chance of having the mesh resemble the shape of a smooth surface.

Edge midpoint insertion is not the only means of mesh refinement, but it has the great advantage that it does not introduce new irregular vertices. If we had inserted the barycenter of each triangle and connected it with the vertices (see Figure 11.40), we would immediately destroy the regularity everywhere. Except if the design should exactly look like this, you probably do not want to use such meshes. One can also easily extract quad meshes from a triangle mesh.

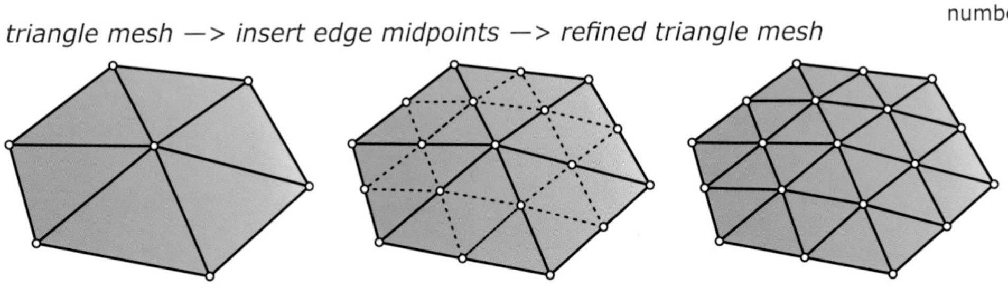

triangle mesh —> insert edge midpoints —> refined triangle mesh

Fig. 11.39
Triangular mesh refinement by edge midpoint insertion quadruples the number of faces.

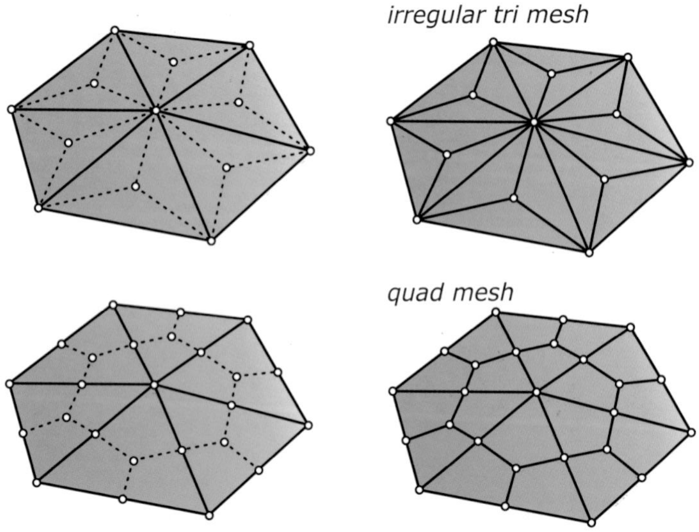

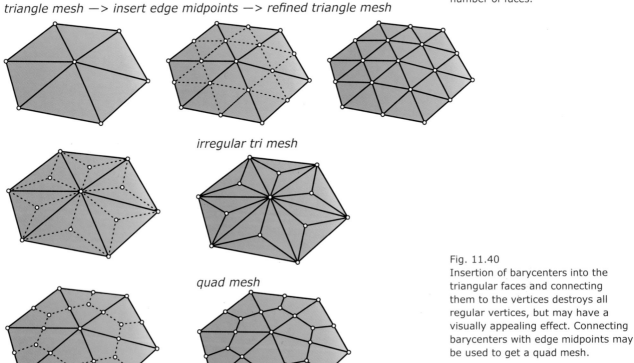

Fig. 11.40
Insertion of barycenters into the triangular faces and connecting them to the vertices destroys all regular vertices, but may have a visually appealing effect. Connecting barycenters with edge midpoints may be used to get a quad mesh.

For quad mesh refinement, we can proceed along the same path. Edge midpoint insertion works very well. As shown in Figure 11.41, we connect the midpoints of opposite edges in a face. These connections join in the barycenter of a face. In this way, we split each face into four subfaces, all of them are lying on the same hyperbolic paraboloid [compare also with our findings on Bézier surfaces of degree (1,1) (Figure 11.12)]. This construction keeps the regularity of vertices and may be the basis for further editing operations on the vertices.

There is yet another quad mesh refinement based on edge midpoints (see Figure 11.42). In this case, we simply connect the edge midpoints of a face to obtain one new quad face. It is an easy exercise to show that this quad is always a parallelogram (the proof is shown in Figure 11.42, bottom row). However, we still have four triangles sitting at the vertices of each old face.

We connect all arising triangles around an old vertex v to form a new poygon. If v is regular, this new face is a quad. Unfortunately, such a quad is in general not planar. Apart from some triangles, which may be left at the boundary, this midpoint insertion scheme roughly doubles the number of faces. If we perform the same construction with a regular square mesh in the plane (see Figure 11.36), the mesh is still regular. We have scaled all faces by a factor of $1/\sqrt{2}$ and have rotated them by 45 degrees.

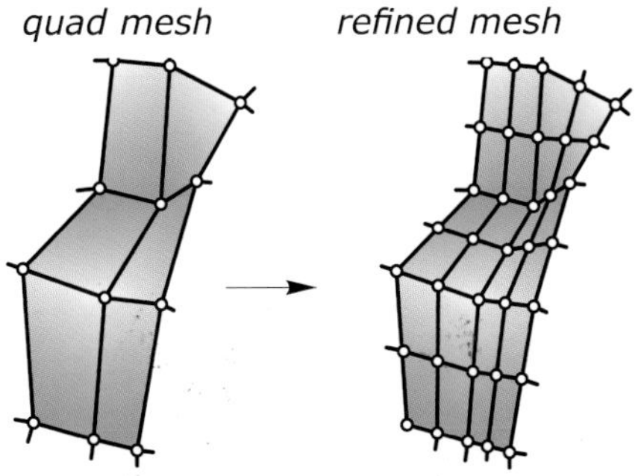

Fig. 11.41
A quad mesh may be refined by insertion of edge midpoints and face barycentres. Note that each skew quad is split into four skew subquads, lying on the same hyperbolic paraboloid.

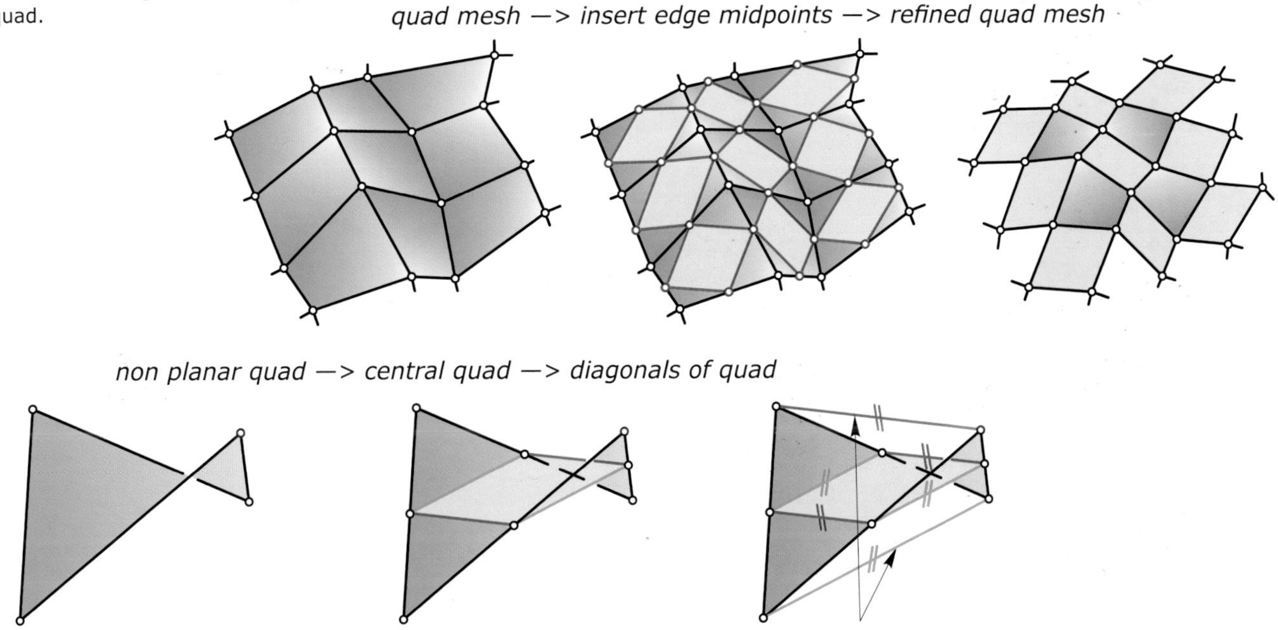

Fig. 11.42
Quad mesh refinement may also be performed via edge midpoint insertion. Note that the central quads arising in each face are always parallelograms, regardless of the planarity of the original face. The top row of the figure gives a geometric explanation: opposite edges of a central quad are parallel to a diagonal of the original quad.

It is further interesting to apply midpoint insertion of the second type twice (Figure 11.43). In fact, applying the rule depicted in Figure 11.42 again and again we will obtain in the limit a smooth surface. This is probably the simplest subdivision algorithm for surface generation and has been studied by J. Peters and U. Reif.

We leave it as an exercise for the reader to think about hexagonal mesh refinement. Hint: try to relate the hexagonal mesh to a triangle mesh!

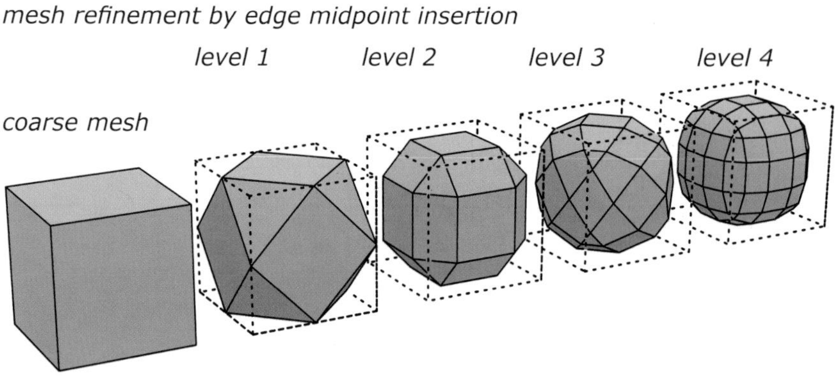

Fig. 11.43
Refinement according to Fig. 42, applied twice, three times, and four times. Continuing this, we get in the limit a smooth surface.

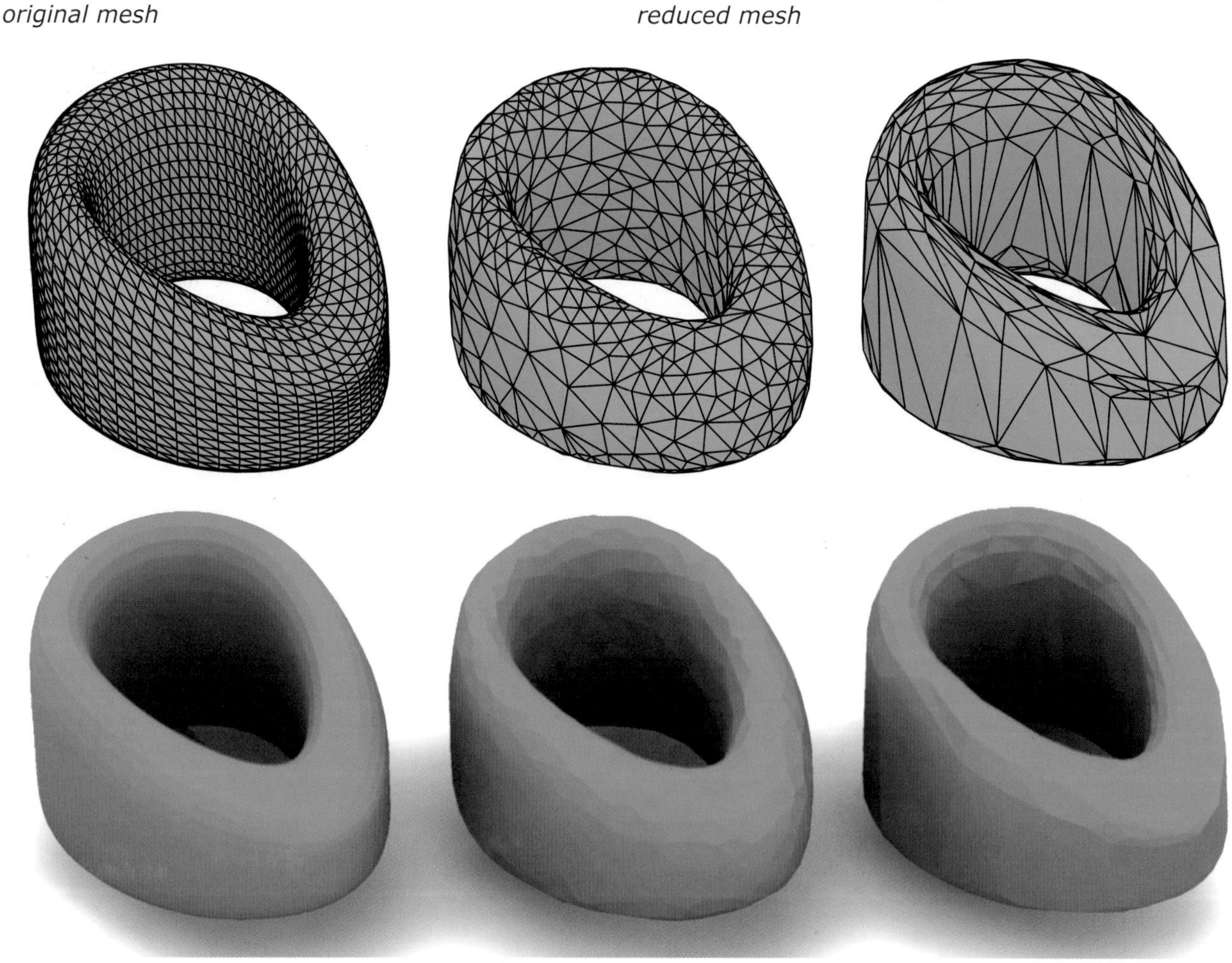

Fig. 11.44
Mesh reduction on a triangular mesh. The reduced meshes may still represent the underlying surface very well so that the differences in the shaded images may hardly be recognized.

Mesh decimation. Although probably not at first intuitive, the reverse of mesh refinement (*mesh decimation*) can be very important as well. For example, a simple mesh decimation process removes "appropriate" vertices (selected by the algorithm according to the local geometry) and connects the remaining ones in a consistent way.

This topic is beyond the scope of this discussion. A more useful aspect is illustrated in Figure 11.44. The figure shows three triangle meshes, one with a significantly larger number of triangles than the other two. However, they are all representing the same underlying shape very well. Such a mesh pattern might not be used in an architectural application, where one actually wants to implement the edges as metal beams.

However, the procedure depicted in Figure 11.44 is an important data reduction step for acceleration of downstream applications such as simulations, fast rendering, and so on. We will encounter this data reduction step again in Chapter 17 in relation to digital reconstruction.

Bad meshes. Whether a mesh is considered a "good" or "bad" one might depend on its purpose. The visual appearance may be one aspect. Too many irregular vertices, distributed in an irregular way, might not look good. But there is something else we need to consider, especially if the mesh is to be used for a simulation (behavior under loads, stresses, stability, and so on) based on the so-called finite element method (FEM).

It can be shown that the numerical algorithms used in FEM do not reach the required precision if a model contains "thin" triangles. In a thin triangle, there is at least one very small angle. In other words, the inscribed circle has a much smaller radius than the circum-circle. CAD software may produce such triangles in large numbers.
An example is shown in Figure 11.45. Another frequent problem for downstream applications are holes in meshes, which, for example, tend to occur near surface/surface intersections.

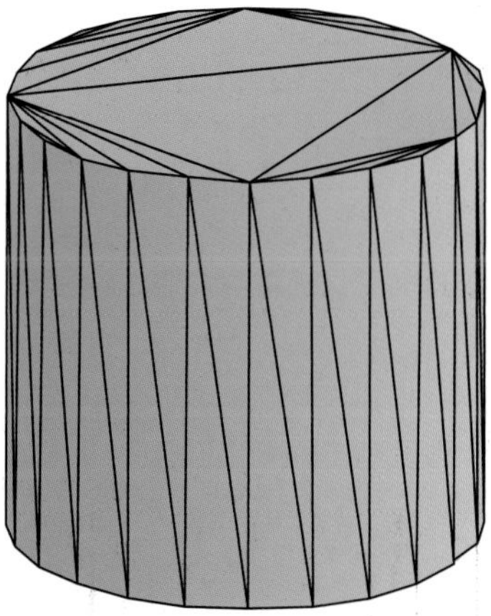

Fig. 11.45
Example of a surface triangulation, generated automatically by certain CAD programs. Note that this mesh has long thin triangles even at places (circular top face), where one does not really need to use them. These long thin triangles are not appreciated by simulation programs since they are a potential source of inaccuracies.

Aesthetics of meshes and relaxation. A more rewarding topic is to think about good ways of enhancing the aesthetic appearance of meshes. Although there exists a subjective aspect when we talk about aesthetics, we can still provide some hints on how to obtain a more balanced node distribution in a mesh.

One basic idea is to adjust all mesh vertices so that the resulting mesh consists of nearly regular faces only. Precisely regular faces (e.g., equilateral triangles) are in general not possible. A related idea is a physical interpretation using a so-called mass-spring simulation system. In such a system one implements the vertices as mass points and the edges as springs. Then, one fixes some points (e.g., all boundary vertices) and lets the other vertices move freely until the entire system achieves an equilibrium .

This technique is called *relaxation*. Very interesting membrane-like shapes may arise in this way. If one wants to remain close to a given design surface, one re-projects the points onto the surface after each relaxation step. As a result of this projection the vertices move on the given surface and achieve an equilibrium position. If we are given a triangle mesh, a simple form of relaxation moves each vertex p toward the barycenter of the (in general, six) vertices joined with p by an edge. This is done again and again until the displacements are fall below a specified cutoff threshold. Relaxation has been used by Chris Williams in the optimization of the triangle mesh for Norman Foster's British Museum project (Figure 11.46).

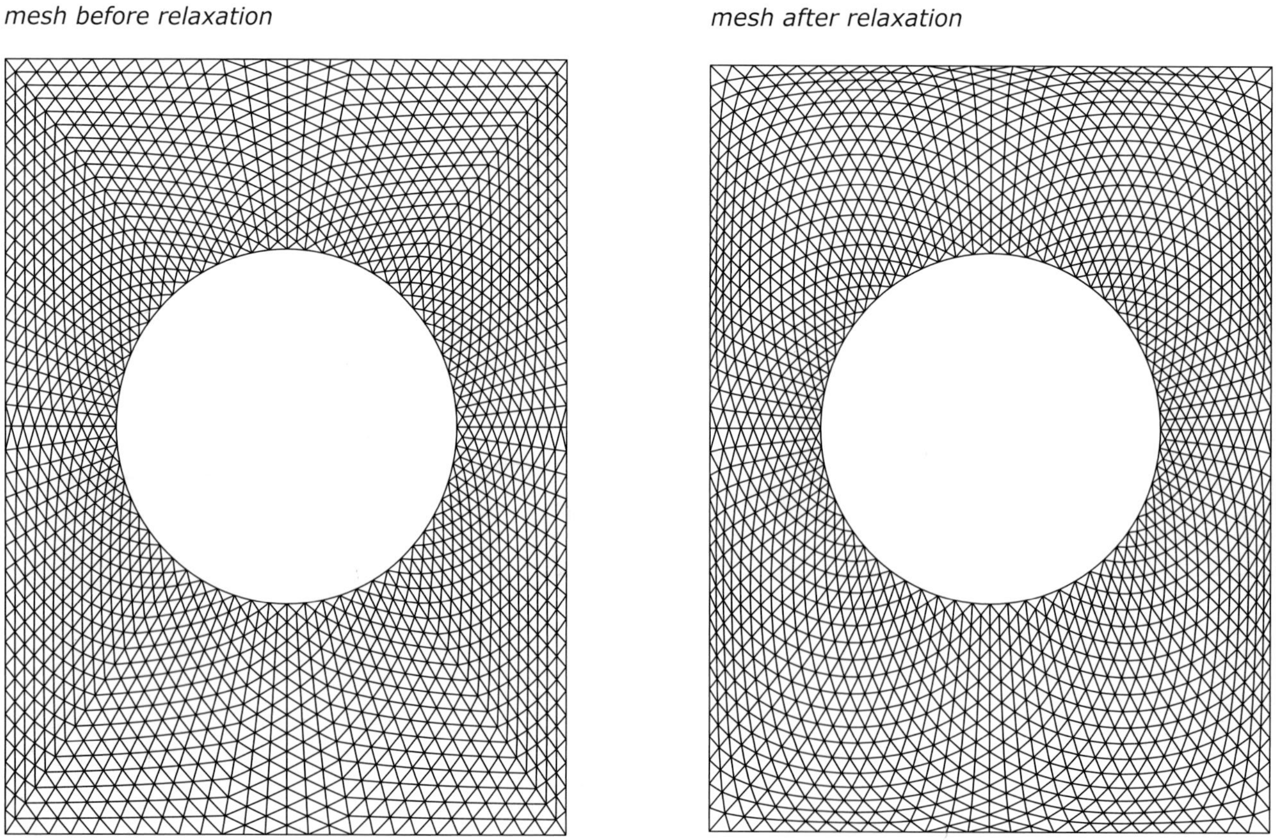

Fig. 11.46
We compare top views of the mesh (left) before and(right) after relaxation and in this way illustrate how much a rather minor displacement of the mesh vertices influences the aesthetic appearance.

Rendering (top) and photo (bottom) of the glass roof of the British Museum. (Figure is courtesy by Chris Williams.)

Fig. 11.47
Subdivision surfaces use a simple refinement rule for meshes and apply it again and again. This leads to a smooth limit surface, but our interest may focus on meshes from appropriate intermediate levels of this refinement process. There is a large variety of different schemes, a few are illustrated here: Doo-Sabin, Catmull-Clark and Loop.

Doo-Sabin subdivision

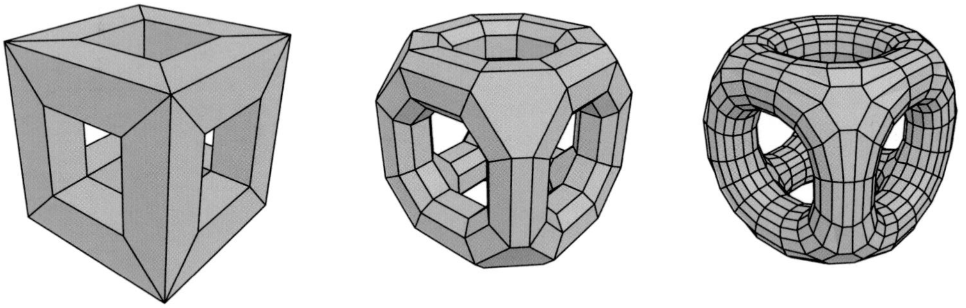

Catmull-Clark subdivision

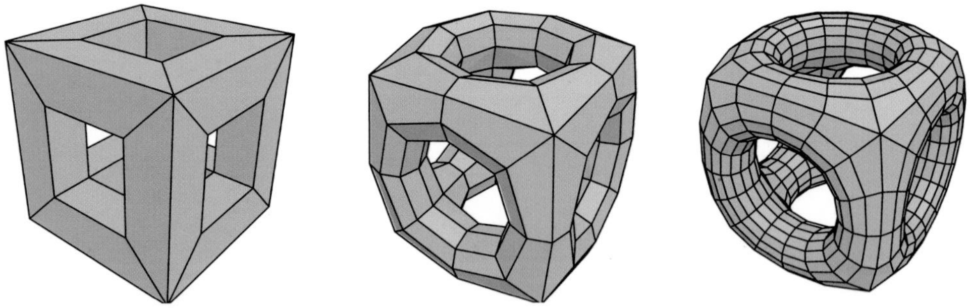

Loop subdivision

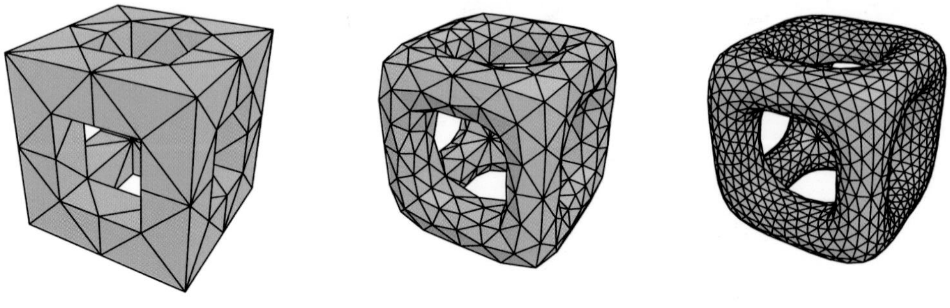

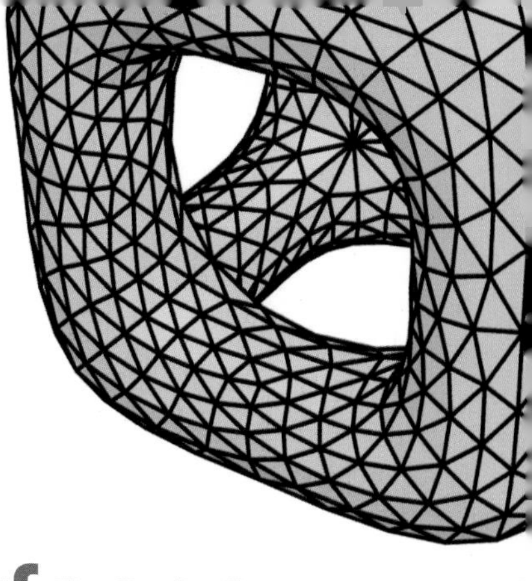

Subdivision Surfaces

Motivation. We have encountered topological restrictions in shape modeling at least twice so far: in our study of B-spline surfaces and in the discussion of quad meshes containing regular vertices only (i.e., vertices of valence 4). There is actually a close relation between these two instances because the control meshes of B-spline surfaces are quad meshes.

If we avoid multiple control points (as in Figure 11.25), the control meshes are regular (Figures 11.24 and 11.34). We will see in the following that a B-spline surface may be viewed as a result of a refinement process, which keeps regularity of quad meshes but refines them to finer and finer levels until in the limit we obtain a smooth surface.

This does not change the topology. Hence, if we want to model surfaces with a more general topology (such as those shown at the bottom of Figure 11.1) we need to use control meshes which have irregular vertices. We also need to know how to refine them (subdivision surfaces do exactly that).

The bottom row of Figure 11.1 also shows some refinement steps. The focus of our interest is not just the smooth limit surface we are getting through repeated refinement. In fact, for applications in architecture one might be much more interested in an intermediate level as appropriate to a particular design (in which the faces are of the desired size only).

Fig. 11.48
Some pioneers of subdivision are M. Sabin, E. Catmull, C. Loop, and T. de Rose. Pixar™ was one of the pioneers using subdivision surfaces for computer animated 3D feature movies.

Tony de Rose

Malcom Sabin

Edwin Catmull

Charles Loop

History of subdivision surfaces. In 1978 two publications appeared which are now regarded as the starting point of research in surface subdivision schemes. Both dealt with refinement rules which in the limit produce B-spline surfaces from a coarse input mesh. One of them, by D. Doo and M. Sabin, deals with surfaces of degree (2,2); the other one, by E. Catmull and J. Clark, with degree (3,3) surfaces.

In 1987, C. Loop developed one of the first subdivision algorithms that works on triangle meshes. For all of these schemes, the subdivision surface at a finer level approximates the subdivison surface at a coarser level. At the same time, an interpolating subdivision scheme (for which the refined surface always passes exactly through the vertices of all previous refinement steps) was published by N. Dyn, J. Gregory, and D. Levin.

Because of smoothness issues at extraordinary vertices, the use of subdivision surfaces in the automotive and aeronautic industries is limited. In the 1990s, Pixar pioneered the use of subdivison surfaces for computer graphics applications. (See Figure 11.48.)

Hence, subdivision must also be seen as *a efficient way of generating visually pleasing meshes*. Fortunately, a number of 3D modeling systems have incorporated this great tool. An exhaustive overview is beyond the scope of this book, but we need to be familiar with the basic properties of a few important subdivision schemes. The "zoo of subdivision schemes" is as crowded as the "zoo of spline types." Figure 11.47 shows a few species.

Quadratic B-spline surfaces via subdivision. Recall Chaikin's subdivision algorithm for the generation of a quadratic B-spline curve (Figure 11.49, top). In this case, we insert on each edge two new points by dividing the edge in the ratios 1:3 and 3:1. Then these new points are connected. This is one refinement step, which is then iterated.

Note that in regard to subdivision we talk about one basic refinement step: how to proceed from the current level to the next finer level. To use the same idea for B-spline surfaces, we have to apply the rule to a regular quad mesh instead of a single control polygon (Figure 11.49, bottom).

As indicated in the discussion of Bézier surfaces, the transfer to surfaces works as follows. First, Chaikin refinement is applied to the column polygons. Second, the new points are connected. Third, we apply it to the already increased number of rows. The role of rows and columns can be swapped. This finally yields a refined quad mesh with roughly four times as many faces as the coarse mesh.

Fig. 11.49
(top) One step of Chaikin's algorithm. (bottom left) Applying this step at first to the column polygons refines the column polygons and introduces new row polygons. (bottom right) Next we apply the same rule to the obtained family of row polygons which also refines these and introduces new column polygons. This has to be seen as a single refinement step of a subdivision algorithm. The refined quad mesh has roughly four times as many faces as the course mesh (the precise number depends on the boundary and vertex valences).

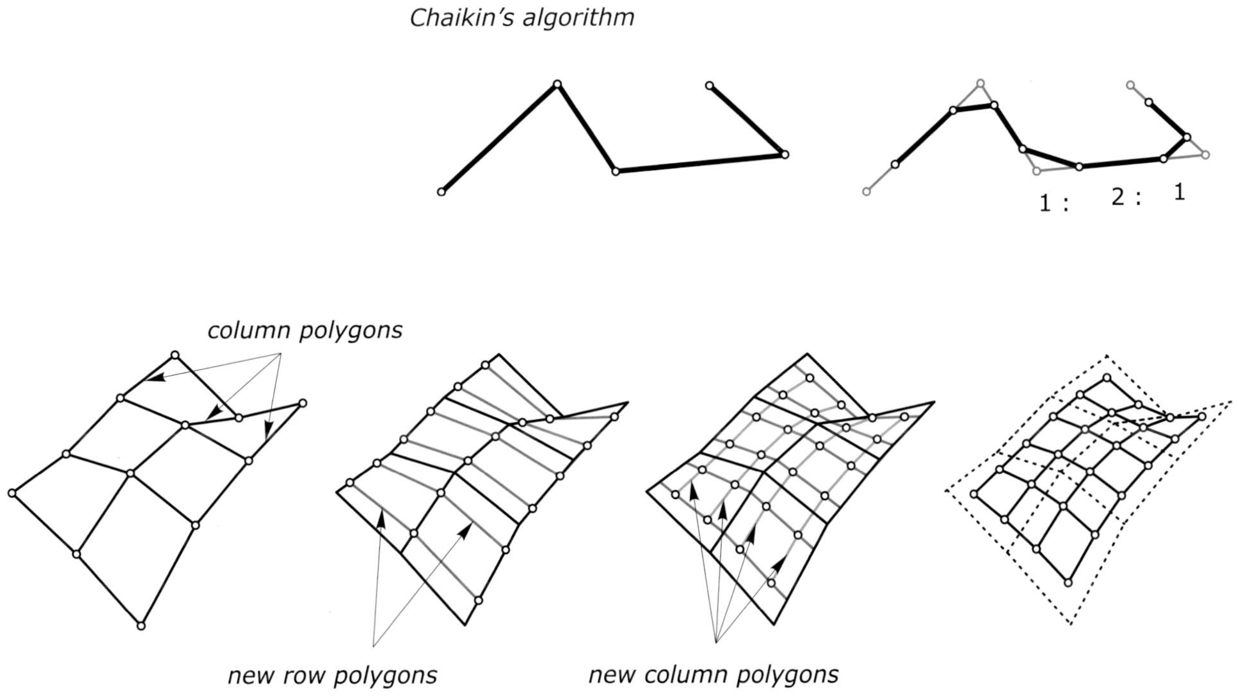

Splitting the transition of a mesh to its next finer level into two steps is awkward. We want to formulate an explanation in a single step, which turns out to be very easy. To understand it, we first look at a single quad with vertices a,b,c,d and see how it is changed (Figure 11.50).

Divide $a\,b$ in the ratio 1:3 and 3:1, respectively. Do the same with $d\,c$ and connect corresponding points. Divide these connections again in the ratios 1:3, 3:1. This is all we have to do. If the quad is skew, it defines a hyperbolic paraboloid [Bézier surface of degree (1,1)]. All lines used in this construction (and of course all involved points) lie on this same hyperbolic paraboloid.

This is very easy to implement, which becomes clear from the following formulae. Let a,b,c,d be the coordinate vectors of the large quad's vertices. Dividing $a\,b$ in the ratio 1:3 yields point $a' = (3/4)a + (1/4)b$. Doing the same with $d\,c$, we obtain $d' = (3/4)d + (1/4)c$. Dividing $a'd'$ in the ratio 1:3 finally yields the new vertex

$$a_1 = (3/4)a' + (1/4)d' = (9/16)a + (3/16)b + (3/16)d + (1/16)c.$$

This means that we only have to multiply the coordinate vectors of the old vertices with coefficients 9/16, 3/16, and 1/16 and add them. Only these coefficients are important, and thus subdivision rules are often graphically depicted by labeling those old vertices with the coefficients needed to obtain a new vertex (see Figure 11.50, right).

To summarize, in each quad we compute with the rule of Figure 11.50 our four new points, which are the vertices of the refined quad mesh. There is one drawback: we can only model special topologies. But there is a surprisingly simple solution to this dilemma; namely; the Doo-Sabin subdivision sceme.

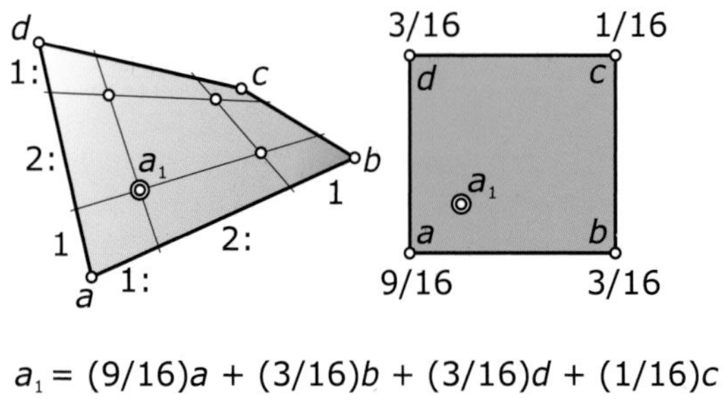

Fig. 11.50
(left) The construction of the new vertices in a quad for one refinement step in a subdivision algorithm for quadratic B-spline surfaces. The computation multiplies the coordinate vectors of the old quad's vertices with certain coefficients and then adds the resulting vectors.
(right) The diagram shows which coefficients are associated with the old vertices to compute the highlighted new vertex a_1.

Fig. 11.51
Doo-Sabin subdivision is an extension of quadratic B-spline subdivision, but also handles the fact that irregular vertices (valence not equal to 4) create extraordinary faces which are not quads. These faces are refined according to the rule in Fig. 11.52

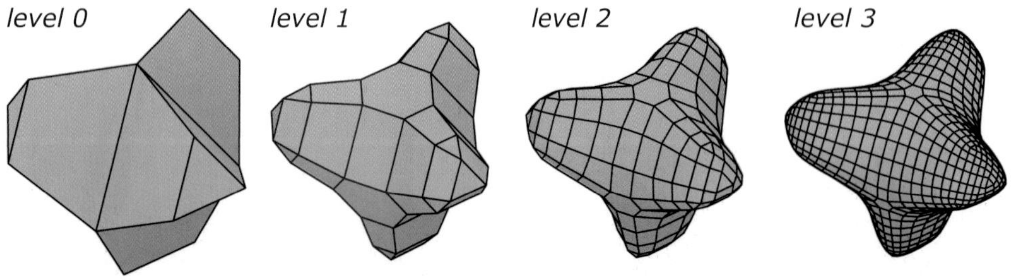

Doo-Sabin subdivision scheme. This scheme does exactly the same for every quad as the procedure previously described. If we assume that there are only quads in our mesh, why don't we just use this rule on any quad mesh? Doo-Sabin does. However, note that a vertex of valence 3 will create a triangle and a vertex of valence 5 will create a pentagonal face in the refined mesh (see Figure 11.51). Therefore, in the next step we need a rule for handling such extraordinary faces.

As in a quad, the rule consists of a multiplication of the vertices' coordinate vectors by coefficients and forming the sum of these vectors. The coefficients are more complicated but for completeness and for the mathematically interested reader the complete calculation is provided in Figure 11.52. If the extraordinary face is a regular planar polygon with K vertices (K-gon) and center m, the refined K-gon is also regular and has the same center. However, it is scaled with the factor 1/2.

Operations that might also be needed for an implementation (but not discussed here) include the proper handling of boundaries and the introduction of features such as creases. So far, we have only discussed a single refinement step. To obtain a *subdivision surface*, one has to apply this subdivision step again and again. It is beyond the scope of this book to provide a proof for the limit being a smooth surface. As a scheme that yields quadratic B-splines for a regular initial mesh, we cannot expect better surface smoothness than we obtain with quadratic B-splines.

The subdivision surface very nicely resembles the shape of the initial mesh. One indicator for this is the following simple fact: When we subdivide a quad Q again and again it remains on the same hyperbolic paraboloid P (or in the same plane P in the case of a planar quad) but shrinks toward the barycenter b of the original quad (Figure 11.53).

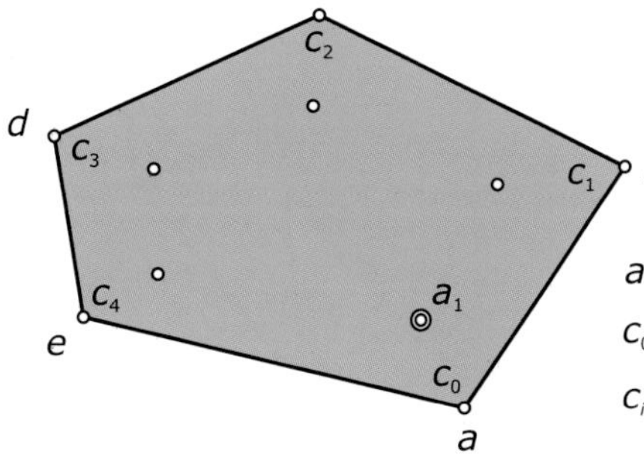

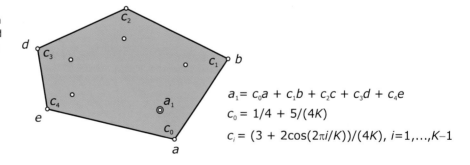

$$a_1 = c_0 a + c_1 b + c_2 c + c_3 d + c_4 e$$
$$c_0 = 1/4 + 5/(4K)$$
$$c_i = (3 + 2\cos(2\pi i/K))/(4K),\ i=1,\ldots,K-1$$

Fig. 11.52
Rule for extraordinary faces in Doo-Sabin subdivision: the diagram shows those coefficients of the vertices which are needed to compute the highlighted vertex of the refined mesh. The figure shows a 5-sided face (K=5), but the formula holds for arbitrary K-sided faces.

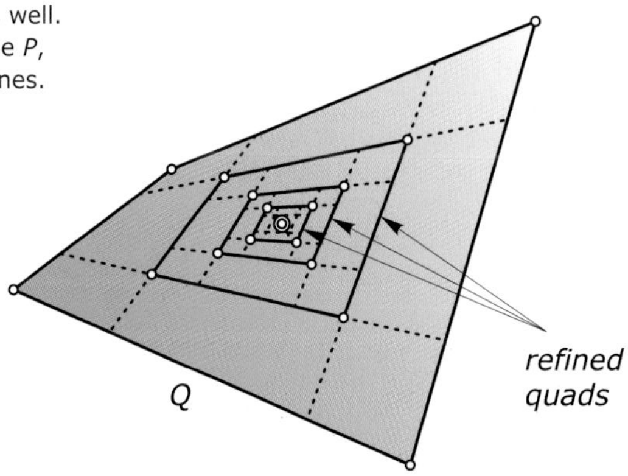

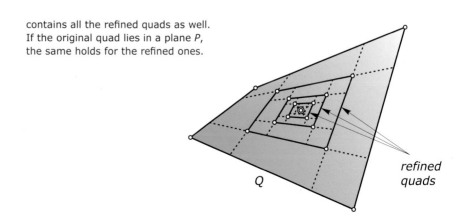

Fig. 11.53
Repeated Doo-Sabin refinement of a quadrilateral Q yields in the limit the barycentre of Q. If Q is skew, it defines a hyperbolic paraboloid P, which contains all the refined quads as well. If the original quad lies in a plane P, the same holds for the refined ones.

Each of these resultant quads lies on one refinement level of the sequence of meshes created in the Doo-Sabin subdivision process. Because the quad's edges converge to tangents of the limit surface, the final surface touches P at the barycenter b (Figure 11.54). This also shows that the initial mesh does not shrink very much during the subdivision process.

From cubic B-splines to Catmull-Clark subdivision. The previously described strategy for obtaining a subdivision scheme for surfaces from a quadratic B-spline curve subdivision rule (Chaikin's algorithm) works for cubic B-splines as well. Generating cubic B-spline curves via subdivision is based on the Lane-Riesenfeld algorithm: insert the edge midpoints of the current polygon and subsequently perform two rounds of averaging (see Figure 11.55).

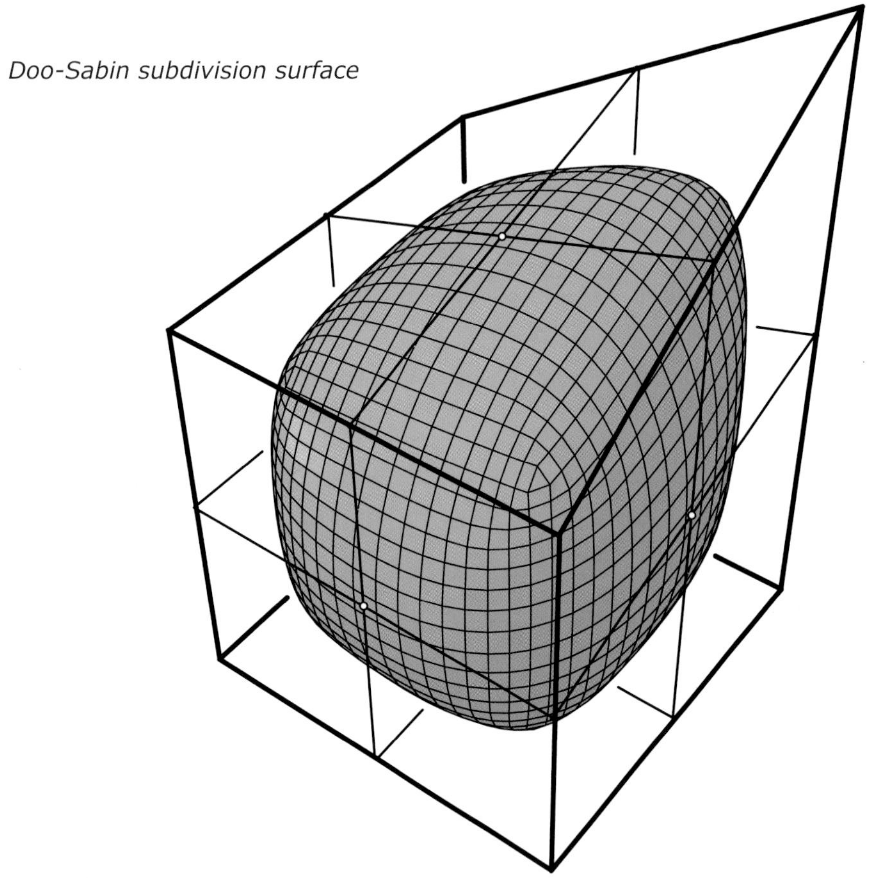

Fig. 11.54
A Doo-Sabin surface passes through the barycenters of the quads in the input mesh and touches there the plane or hyperbolic paraboloid, which is defined by the quad.

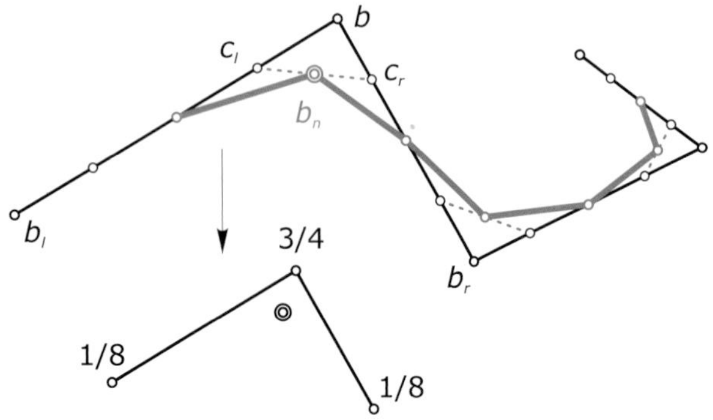

Fig. 11.55
One refinement step of cubic B-spline subdivision according to the Lane-Riesenfeld algorithm requires midpoint insertion and two rounds of averaging (the first round yields exactly the points for the Chaikin rule). The figure also shows the coefficients of the vertices for computing the highlighted point of the refined polygon.

We could say that there are two types of new points: the edge midpoints and points, which are displaced vertices of the coarse polygon. Let's focus on the latter points only and call b_n the new location of b, whose left and right neighbors are denoted b_l and b_r (Figure 11.55). Obviously, b_n is the midpoint of the two Chaikin points $c_l = 1/4\, b_l + 3/4\, b$, $c_r = 3/4\, b + 1/4\, b_r$. Therefore, it has the representation

$$b_n = 1/2\, c_l + 1/2\, c_r = 1/8\, b_l + 3/4\, b + 1/8\, b_r.$$

Let's examine a regular quad mesh (i.e., subdivision for cubic B-spline surfaces). This will lead us to the Catmull-Clark subdivision rules for the regular part of the mesh. To derive the rules, we apply Lane-Riesenfeld subdivision to the columns and then to the rows (or vice versa).

Formulated in a single refinement rule, we will obtain the cases depicted (with coefficients) in Figure 11.56. The coefficients depend on how edge midpoints (depend on two old vertices) and displaced vertices (depend on three old vertices) are combined. Combining the edge midpoints gives the face barycenter, which depends on the four quad vertices.

If an edge midpoint is paired with a displaced vertex, we obtain a new point that may be seen as a displaced edge midpoint of the coarse quad mesh (the computation requires $2 \cdot 3 = 6$ old vertices). The coefficients are the products of $1/2 \cdot 3/4$ and $1/2 \cdot 1/8$ and hence 3/8 and 1/16, respectively. Finally, the combination of two displaced vertex computations (coefficients 3/4 and 1/8) requires $3 \cdot 3 = 9$ points. Their coefficients are $3/4 \cdot 3/4 = 9/16$, $3/4 \cdot 1/8 = 3/32$, and $1/8 \cdot 1/8 = 1/64$, respectively.

Fig. 11.56
Rules for one refinement step in Catmull Clark subdivision (= subdivision rule for cubic B-spline surfaces) in the regular part of the mesh.
(left) There are three cases: face barycentres get inserted, (middle) the midpoint of each edge gets displaced to a new location and (right) each vertex of the coarse mesh is brought into a new position. The figures show the required coefficients for the computation.

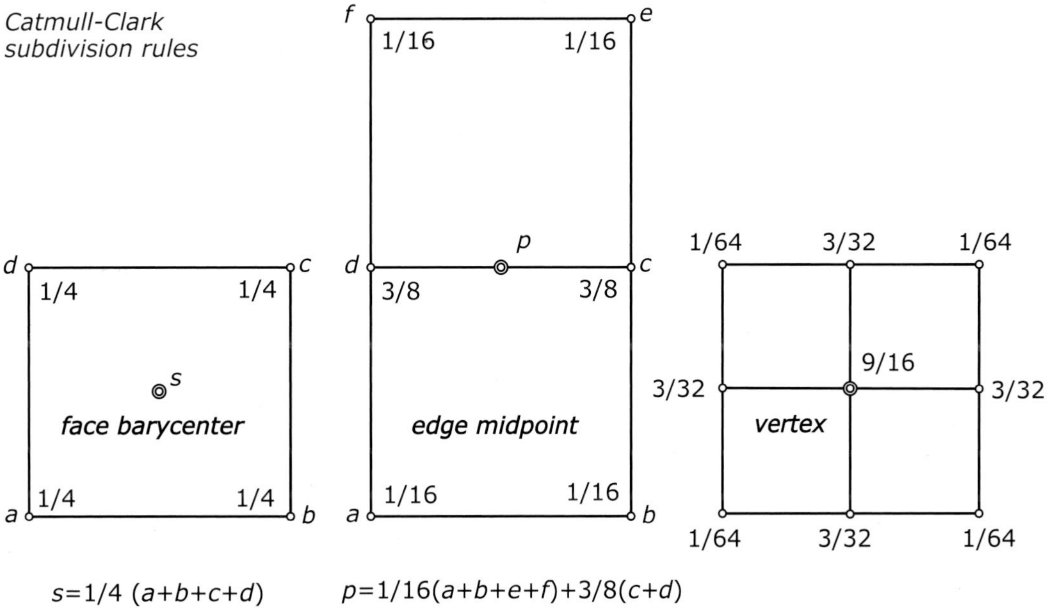

The computation for a displaced vertex is only valid for a regular vertex. For singular vertices (valence K different from 4), the special rule depicted in Figure 11.57 has to be applied.

The smoothness of Catmull-Clark surfaces away from singular vertices is higher than for Doo-Sabin surfaces (reflection lines are also smooth). However, the behavior at the singular vertices is still not as smooth as one might desire for certain applications (such as car body design).

As we have mentioned, however, architecture does not rely as much on surface continuity due to the constraints of building at a large scale. Because more averaging is involved in Catmull-Clark surfaces, they exhibit a stronger smoothing effect and are farther away from the control mesh than Doo-Sabin surfaces (see Figure 11.58).

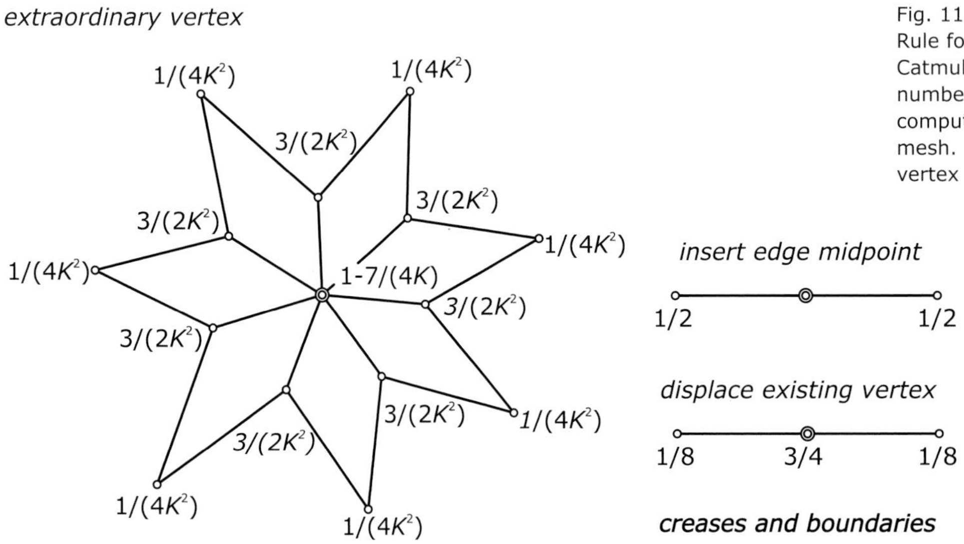

Fig. 11.57
Rule for extraordinary vertices in Catmull-Clark subdivision: the given numbers are the coefficients needed to compute the new vertex of the refined mesh. Here, K is the valence of the vertex (K=7 in the figure).

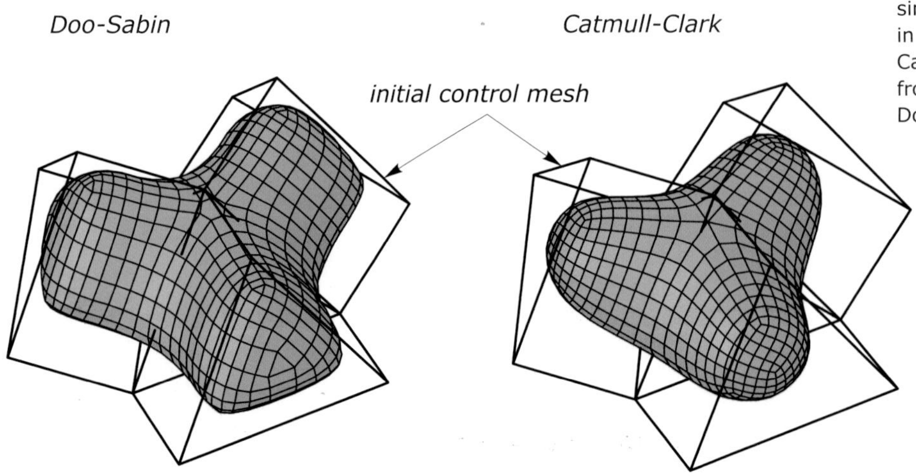

Fig. 11.58
(left) Comparison of Doo-Sabin subdivision and
(right) with Catmull-Clark subdivision. The latter yields the smoother result, since more averaging is involved in each step; because of that, the Catmull-Clark surface is farther away from the initial control mesh than the Doo-Sabin surface.

Skew quad warning. Even if we start with a mesh consisting of planar quads only, subdivision will introduce skew quads. None of the subdivision schemes based on quads and in which refinement is performed with simple linear combination rules (as the schemes previously cited) would preserve planarity of quads.

However, there are "planarization" algorithms that can be combined with subdivision algorithms to maintain planar quadrilateral faces. An example of the action of such an algorithm is shown in Figure 11.59. This interesting topic is investigated in greater detail in Chapter 19.

Fig. 11.59
Standard subdivision algorithms generate lots of non-planar quadrilateral faces even if we start with a mesh that is composed of planar quads only (see Doo-Sabin algorithm, top row). However, one may apply an optimization procedure after each subdivision refinement step, which aims at a minimal displacement of the vertices so that the quads become planar (cf. Chapter 19).

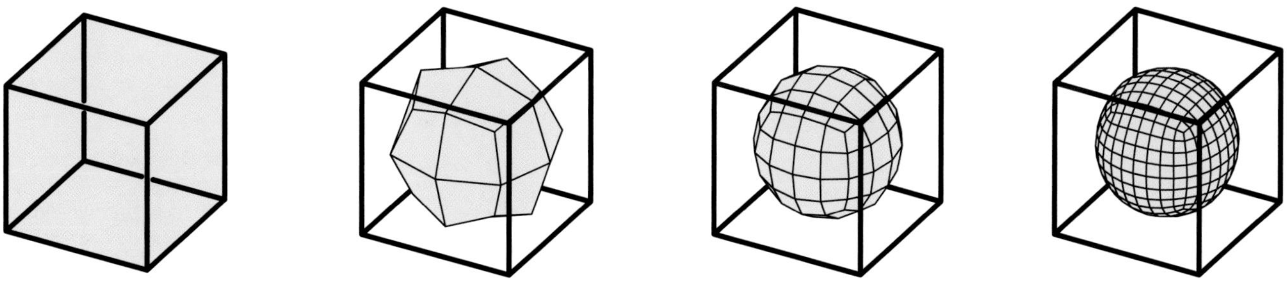

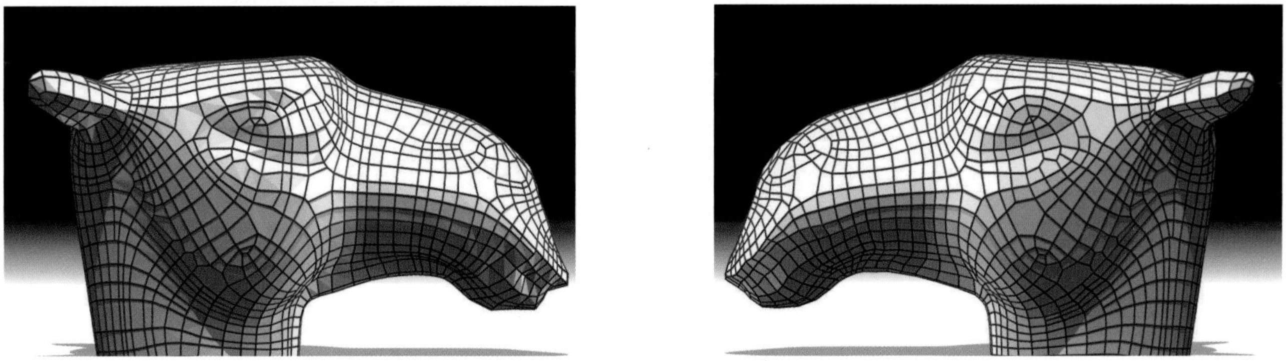

Triangle-based subdivision. Although a triangle mesh representation of a curved surface needs roughly twice as many faces as a quad mesh, it has the great advantage that the faces are always planar. Unfortunately, we cannot just derive triangular subdivision schemes from curve algorithms (as discussed previously).

Thus, we must refrain from any derivation and point directly to one of the most prominent schemes (Loop subdivision). Its rules are illustrated in Figure 11.60, and some results of the algorithm are shown in Figure 11.61. The smoothness obtained with this scheme is the equivalent of that obtained with Catmull-Clark surfaces.

All of the schemes we have presented are based on mesh smoothing. The resulting surfaces do not pass through the vertices of the input mesh. There are various schemes which generate surfaces that pass through the vertices of the input mesh, but we refer the reader to the literature for details on these.

Fig. 11.60
Rules for triangular mesh subdivision according to Loop.

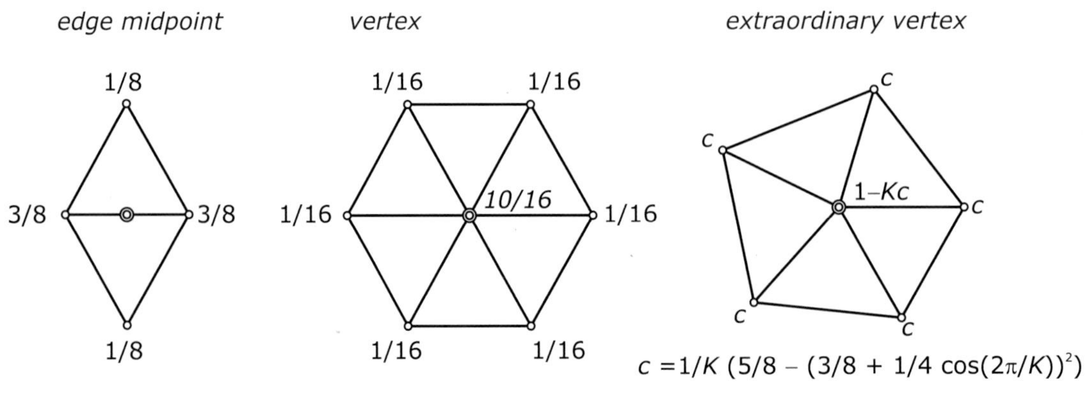

Fig. 11.61
Meshes resulting from Loop's subdivision algorithm.

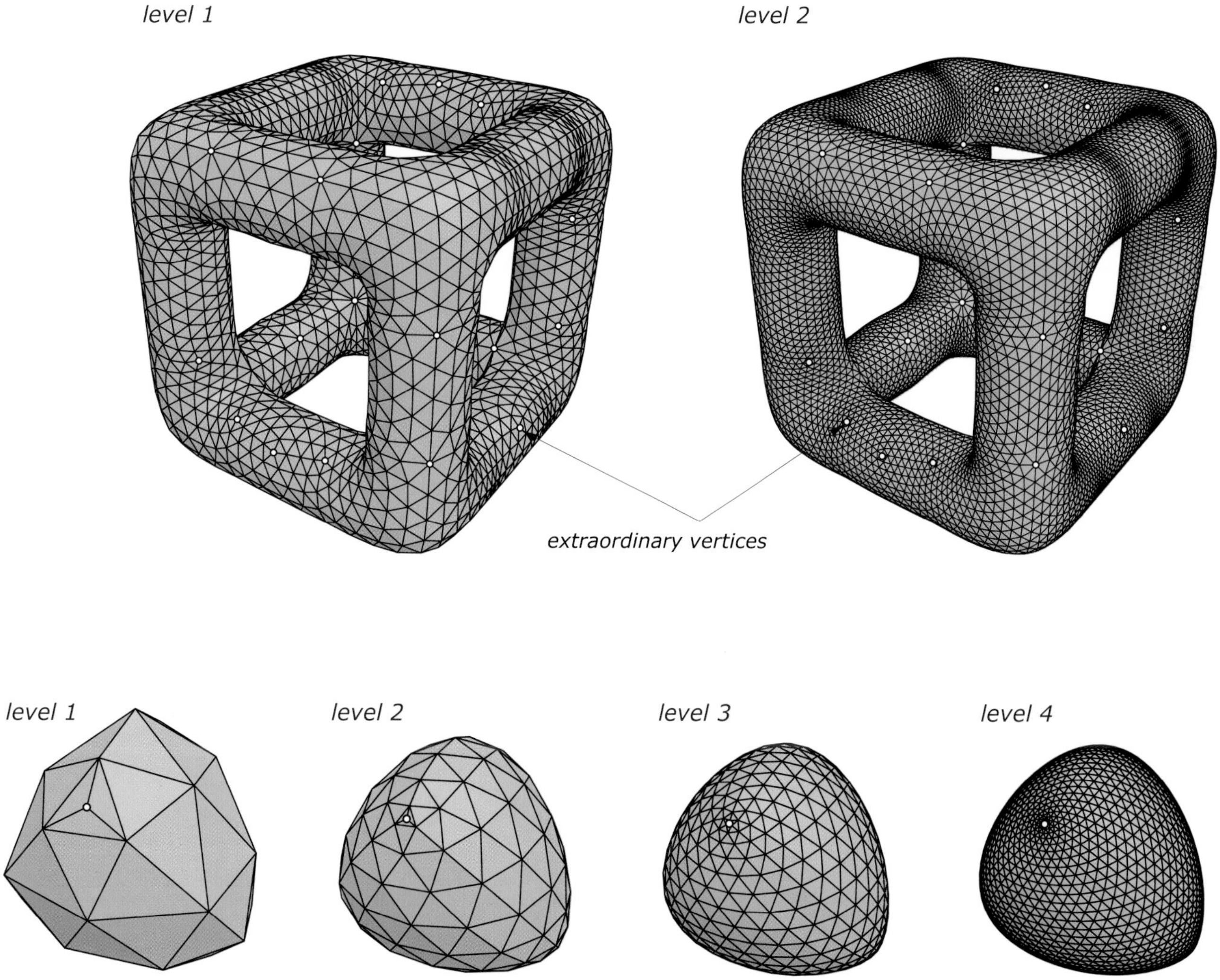

Multi-resolution Modeling. Perhaps you may have the impression that subdivision is a type of machinery activated by an input mesh and run without the designer being able to influence it. This should not to be the case!

We may perform editing operations on any intermediate level of refinement. The resulting limit surface is still smooth: just view the finest mesh on which you made some editing operations as an initial mesh for further subdivision.

It may be advantageous to collect a few basic facts about meshes on different levels of detail. When we start with a coarse mesh and apply subdivision (any refinement rule) on it iteratively we obtain a so-called *coarse-to-fine hierarchy of meshes*. At any level of this hierarchy, we can perform editing operations before proceeding to the next finer level.

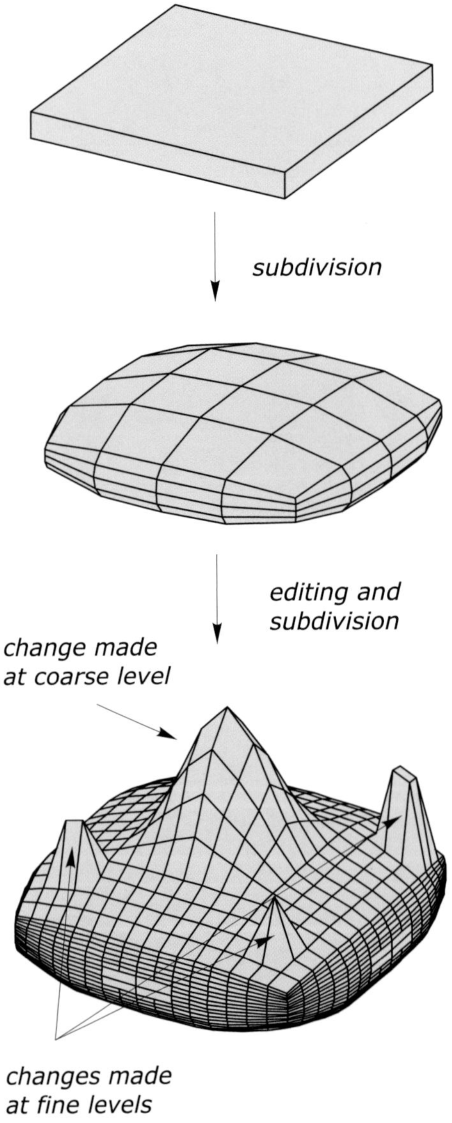

Fig. 11.62
Subdivision algorithms can be combined with editing operations: a change, made at a coarse level, has a broader influence than one made at a fine level. This is the principle of multi-resolution modelling.

Why does this make sense, and why is there a difference at which level we make a change? To resolve this, examine Figure 11.62, in which a change in the initial phase influences a much larger area than a change at finer levels. To prove this claim, think about the neighborhoods needed to compute the new points in a subdivision algorithm (Figures 11.50, 11.52, 11.56 and 11.60).

Thus, basic trends of the surface shape should be integrated right away in the initial control mesh. Large-scale modifications have to be made at early stages of the process, and details can be modeled at finer levels. This technique is called *multi-resolution modeling*, which represents a powerful method of shape modeling. Figure 11.63 shows a model created with this method.

Fig. 11.63
Shape design can be effectively performed with multi-resolution modelling.

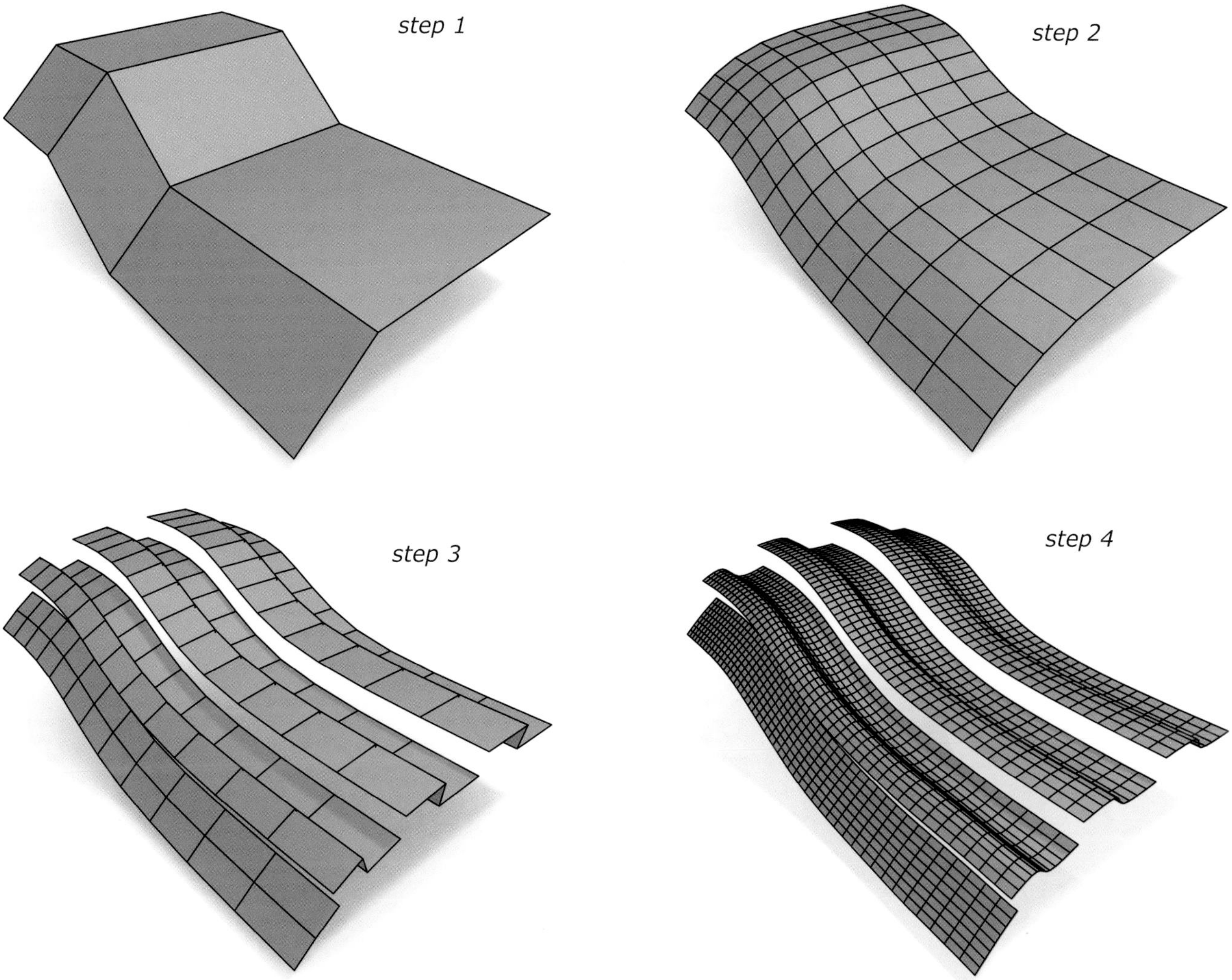

Chapter 12

Motions, Sweeping, and Shape Evolution

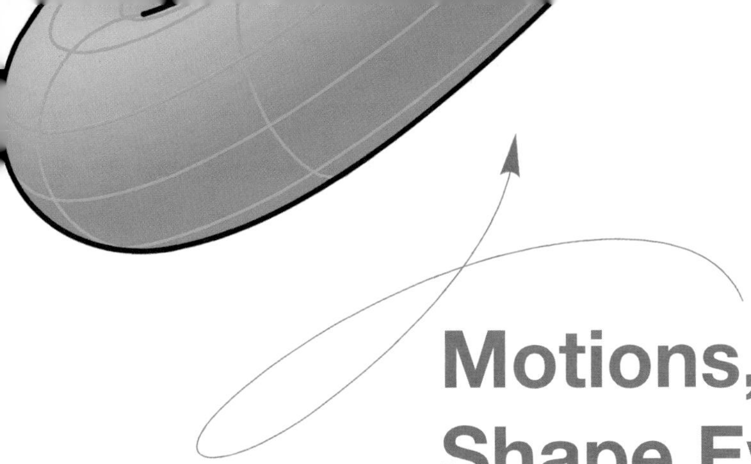

Motions, Sweeping, and Shape Evolution

Several surface classes studied so far can be defined by applying a special motion to a profile curve p (Figure 12.1). If p rotates about an axis, it generates a rotational surface. If p is moved with a continuous helical motion, we obtain a helical surface. Translation of p along another curve yields a translational surface. A pipe surface is generated by a circle p whose center is moved along a curve c and whose plane remains orthogonal to c. Now we will show that there are many more interesting motions that generate surfaces for geometric design. Before we can discuss these surfaces, it is necessary to understand some basics of *kinematic geometry* (geometry of motions).

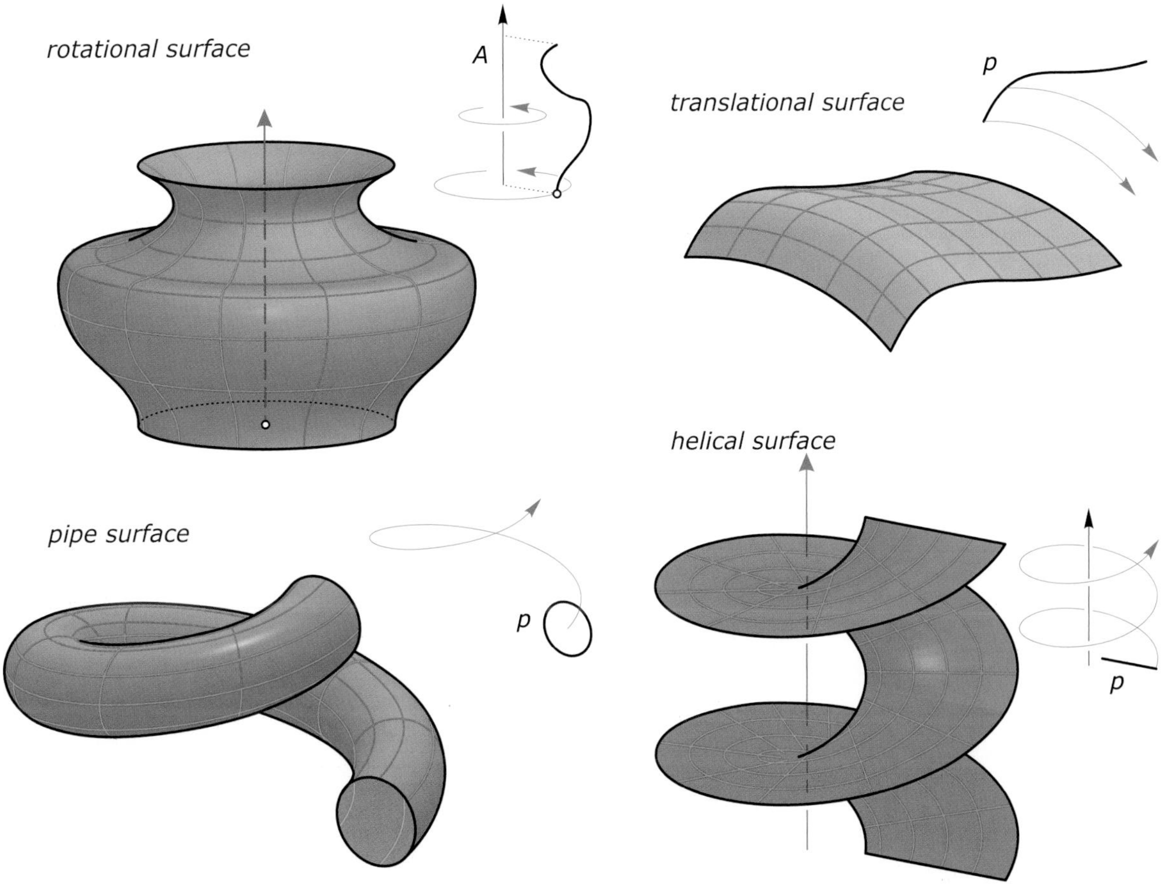

Fig. 12.1
Surfaces generated by applying a continuous motion to a profile curve: rotational surface, helical surface, translational surface and pipe surface.

There are further reasons we should discuss kinematic geometry. Industrial design may require an understanding of kinematics because design and functionality cannot be fully separated. For example, the design of a capsule around a mechanism must not form an obstacle for any moving part of that mechanism. Moreover, contemporary architecture may include flexible elements that can change their shape because there are mechanisms tied to them (Figure 12.2). Designing flexible shapes requires a basic understanding of the geometry of motion.

In this section, we will first study kinematic geometry in the plane and in three dimensions. This will lead us to a number of remarkable surface classes generated by the motion of a profile curve. We will then consider cases in which the profile may change its shape. This motivates us to study curve evolutions. Finally, we will address some related surface generation methods such as skinning and meta-balls.

Fig. 12.2
The *Quadracci Pavilion* (1994–2001), an addition to the Milwaukee Art Museum by Santiago Calatrava. The striking feature of this building is the Brise de Soleil, a sun screen that is raised and lowered throughout the day to provide light and shade to the interior of the museum (images courtesy of Jeff Millies/Hedrich Blessing, Timothy Hursley).

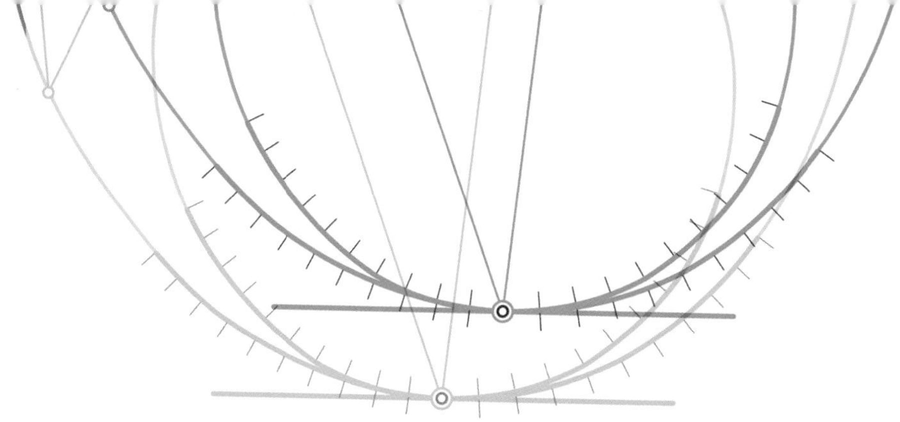

Motions in the Plane

In the following, we consider a planar geometric object M that can move in the plane F in which it is lying. M is considered rigid (i.e., distances between points of M remain unchanged). We call M the *moving system* and F the *fixed system*. Under a *continuous motion*, M assumes time-dependent positions in F. If t denotes time, we call $M(t)$ the position of M in F at time t. We have discussed special continuous motions in earlier sections.

A very simple motion is a continuous rotation about a point p (Figure 12.3). During such a rotation, each point of M moves along a circle with center p. The circle is called the *path* or *trajectory* (the set of positions) of that point. Certainly, the normals of the trajectories (circles) pass through p.

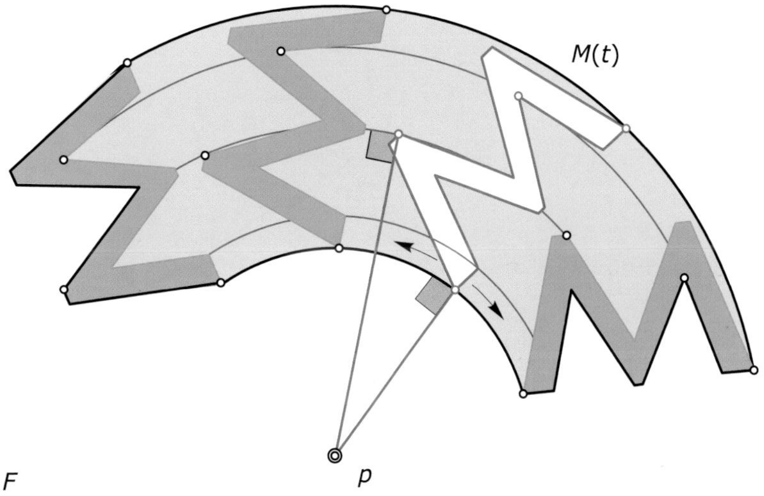

Fig. 12.3
Under a continuous rotation, points of the moving system generate concentric circles as trajectories. The normals of the trajectories pass through the rotational center.

Example:

Four-bar linkage. The kinematics of mechanisms requires the understanding of some of its basic building blocks. One of those is the *four-bar linkage* (Figure 12.4). This is simply a quadrangle *abcd* with rigid edges (bars) and rotational joints at the vertices. We fix the edge with vertices *a* and *b* and call it the fixed system *F*. The two adjacent edges *da* and *cb* perform pure rotations, whereas the motion of the fourth edge *cd* is more complicated.

Of course, point *c* moves on a circle with midpoint *b*. Point *d* runs on a circle with midpoint *a*. This does not mean that the full circles are traced. Depending on the specific geometry, only parts of these two circles may be reached by points *c* and *d*. The picture becomes more complicated if we consider the trajectory of another point *x* on *cd*. Moreover, edge *cd* defines a moving plane *M*, and we may consider the motion of any point of that plane. This is shown in regard to point *y* in Figure 12.4. It depicts the rigid connection with the bar *cd* by a triangle.

This example indicates that general continuous motions may possess rather complicated trajectories of points. However, there is some systematic behavior, and the simplest is the following: *At any time instant* t_0*, the normals to the trajectories pass through a point* $p(t_0)$ *(or they are parallel).* Let's see why this is the case.

At first, we consider two positions $M(t_0)$ and $M(t_1)$ at nearby time instances t_0 and t_1. In Chapter 5, we saw that two directly congruent positions $M(t_0)$ and $M(t_1)$ of a planar figure M can be mapped onto each other by a rotation or a translation (see Figure 12.5). The proof of this result is as follows. To determine a position of a rigid system, it is sufficient to describe the positions of two points (e.g., r and s). Their positions are $r(t_0)$, $r(t_1)$, and $s(t_0)$, $s(t_1)$.

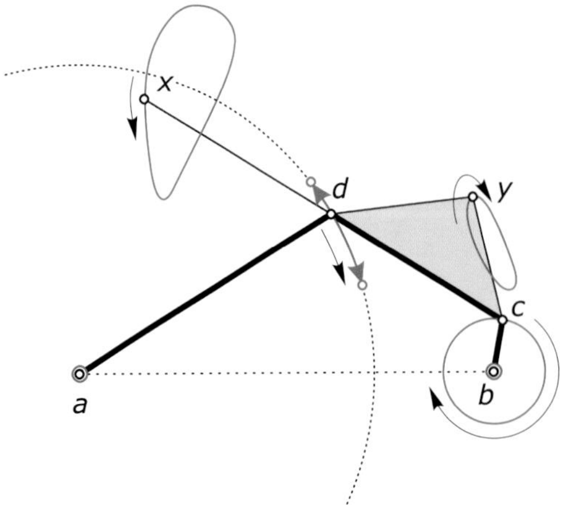

Fig. 12.4
A four-bar linkage: the bar with endpoints *a* and *b* forms the fixed system. We are interested in the motion of the opposite bar *cd*. Its two endpoints move along circles. Any other point *x* of that bar describes a more complicated trajectory, and the same holds for other points *y* of the moving plane defined by *cd*.

The bisecting lines of $r(t_0)r(t_1)$ and $s(t_0)s(t_1)$ either intersect in a point p or are parallel (Figure 12.5). In the first case, p is the center of a rotation—which maps $r(t_0)$ to $r(t_1)$ and $s(t_0)$ to $s(t_1)$, and hence $M(t_0)$ to $M(t_1)$. In the second case, the two line segments $r(t_0)r(t_1)$ and $s(t_0)s(t_1)$ are parallel and of equal length. Because they are nearby positions of a continuous motion, the orientations are the same as well—and therefore $M(t_0)$ and $M(t_1)$ can be mapped onto each other by a translation.

We now consider closer and closer positions (i.e., formally let t_1 tend toward t_0). During this limit process, a connecting line of corresponding points converges to a tangent of a trajectory. Thus, the bisector discussed previously converges to a normal of the trajectory. It is called a *path normal* (Figure 12.6). In the first (general) case, we obtain a limit position $p(t_0)$ for the point p, the so-called *instantaneous pole*.

All path normals of positions at time t_0 run through the pole $p(t_0)$. We can say as well that with respect to path tangents and path normals the moving system behaves at this time instant t_0 like a rotation about $p(t_0)$. We speak of the *instantaneous rotation*. As we have seen in the case of nearby positions, it may happen that the rotation degenerates to a translation. This means that all path tangents (hence, also all path normals) at such a moment t_0 are parallel and we have an *instantaneous translation*.

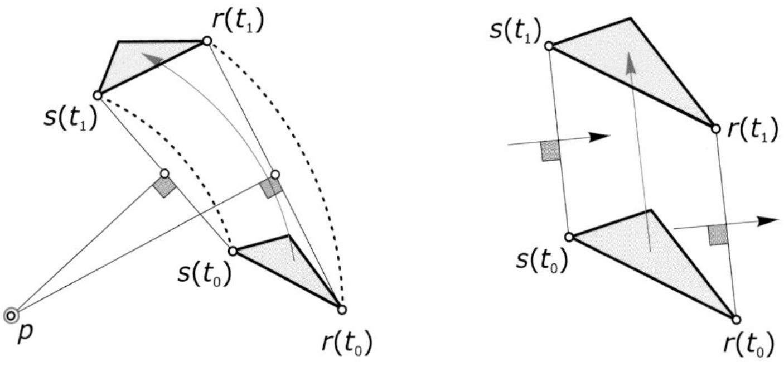

Fig. 12.5
Two directly congruent positions $M(t_0)$ and $M(t_1)$ of a planar figure M can be mapped onto each other by
(left) a rotation or
(right) a translation.

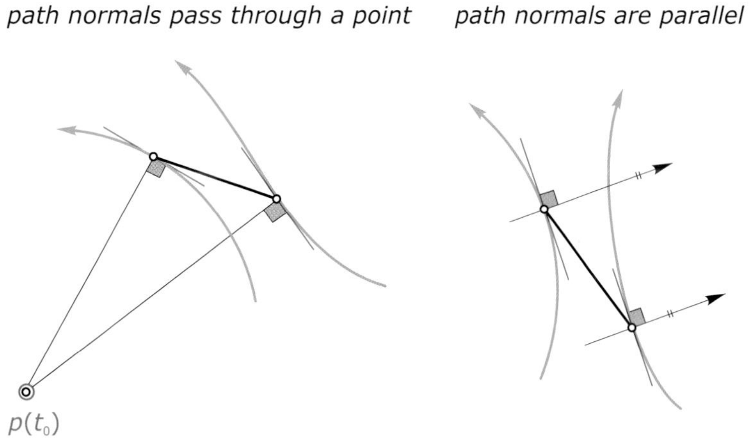

Fig. 12.6
At any time instant t_0 of a continuous motion, the path normals of points of the moving system
(left) pass through a point $p(t_0)$ or
(right) are parallel.

In general, different time instances give rise to different poles. The following also hold (Figure 12.7). The set of poles in the fixed system is a curve p_f, the so-called *fixed polhode*. Because the instantaneous rotation may degenerate to a translation, the pole may lie at infinity and therefore the polhode may have points at infinity. Analogously, we may consider the set of poles as a set of points in the moving system. In this way, we obtain the *moving polhode* p_m (as a part of the moving system).

At any time instant, the current position of the moving polhode is tangent to the fixed polhode at the instantaneous pole. In fact, the motion can be considered a rolling motion of p_m on p_f. "Rolling" means that there is no gliding. In equal time spans, the pole traces parts with equal arc length on moving and fixed polhode (Figure 12.7). We will not investigate this in detail. We look at some simple instructive examples instead.

Just as the position of a figure may be determined by the positions of two of its points we may define a continuous motion by prescribing the trajectories of two points r and s. The simplest choice is discussed in the following example. (See Figure 12.8.)

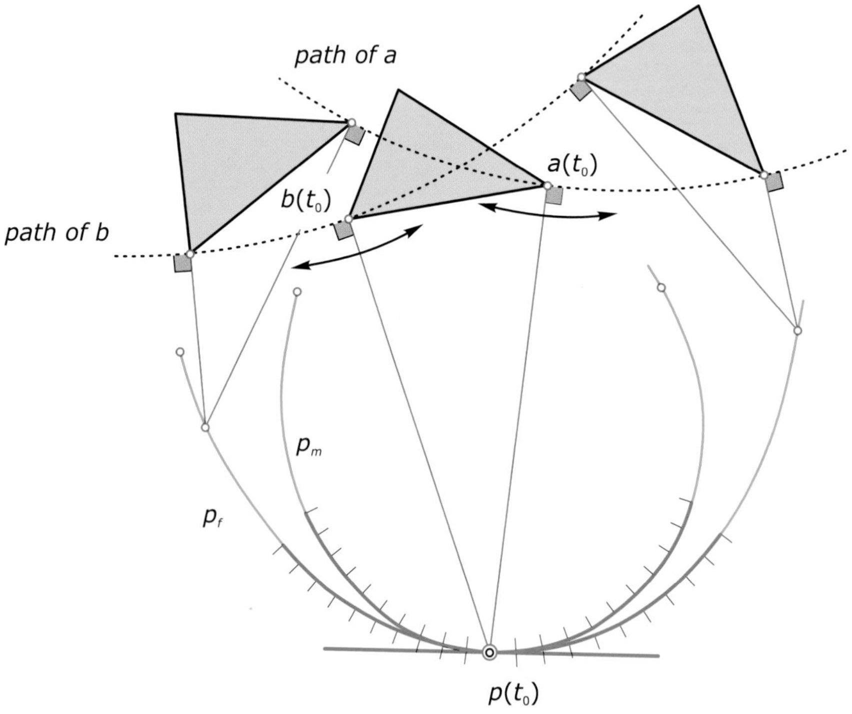

Fig. 12.7
A continuous motion can also be generated by the rolling motion of the moving polhode p_m on the fixed polhode p_f. At any time instance, the point of tangency between the polhodes is the instantaneous pole.

Example:

Cardan motion. This example has been chosen because we will later use it to design some remarkable ruled surfaces. Moreover, it presents a very simple motion whose polhodes can be easily found. We take two points r and s in the moving system and prescribe straight trajectories l_r and l_s (Figure 12.8) for them. For simplicity, we assume that these trajectories are orthogonal.

The intersection point of l_r and l_s is called m. For a position at time t_0, we construct the pole $p(t_0)$ by intersection of the path normals at $r(t_0)$ and $s(t_0)$. Obviously, the distance R between $r(t_0)$ and $s(t_0)$ equals the distance of $p(t_0)$ and m. Hence, the fixed polhode p_f (set of poles in the fixed system) is a circle with center m and radius R. To find the moving polhode, we should try to take the viewpoint of an observer sitting in the moving system.

Such an observer sees that r and s appear from the pole at a right angle. Hence, by the theorem of Thales the moving polhode p_m (set of poles in the moving system) is a circle with diameter line rs and thus radius $R/2$. The motion can also be generated by the rolling motion of the circle p_m in the circle p_f.

All points of p_m, not just r and s, have straight line segments (through m) as trajectories. Rolling means that in equal time spans the pole traces parts with equal arc length on moving and fixed polhodes. Those equal arcs $R{\cdot}\alpha$ = $(R/2){\cdot}2\alpha$ are precisely delineated by the lines through m (Figure 12.9), and therefore points of p_m move along diameter lines of p_f. By an elementary construction of an ellipse, any point x of the straight line rs (x different from r and s) generates an ellipse as a trajectory.

Clearly the midpoint of rs runs on a circle. All other general points x of the moving system have ellipses as paths. This can be proved by passing a diameter line of p_m through x, which brings us back to the special situation we started with (Figure 12.9): two points r', s' run on orthogonal lines and thus a point x on the line $r's'$ generates an ellipse.

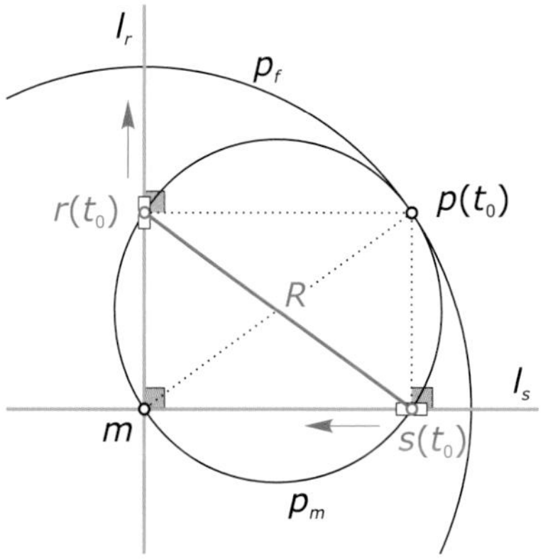

Fig. 12.8
A Cardan motion can be defined via straight trajectories l_r and l_s of two points r and s, respectively. The two points r and s define the moving plane and thus they lie at constant distance R. The motion of the moving plane can be replaced by the rolling motion of a circle of diameter R inside a circle of radius R.

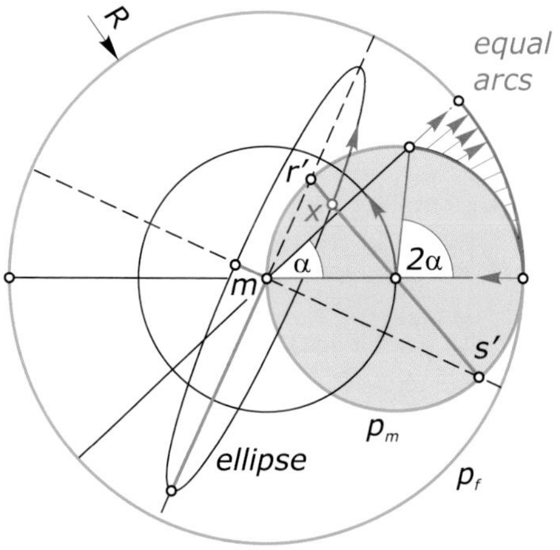

Fig. 12.9
Cardan motion. All points of the moving circle have straight line segments as trajectories. Clearly, the center of the moving circle generates a circle as a path. The trajectories of all other points are ellipses.

Example:

Cusps and loops. Consider the rolling motion of a circle p_m on a straight line p_f (i.e., the motion of a car's wheel; Figure 12.10, bottom). The midpoint m of p_m moves on a line parallel to p_f. Other points x generate *cycloids*. These are periodic curves, one period belonging to a full turn of the moving circle. A point x of the rolling circle generates a trajectory with a *cusp*. Points x_o of the moving system that lie outside p_m have trajectories with *loops*, whereas points x_i inside p_m have paths with two inflection points per period.

These phenomena are much more general. For example, a point x has a cusp in its trajectory at those locations where x is the instantaneous pole (Figure 12.10, top). We have seen this already in the example of the elliptic motion. There, the cusp is a turning point on a straight path. Artists may be inspired by the interesting shapes of curves generated by motions (see Figure 12.11).

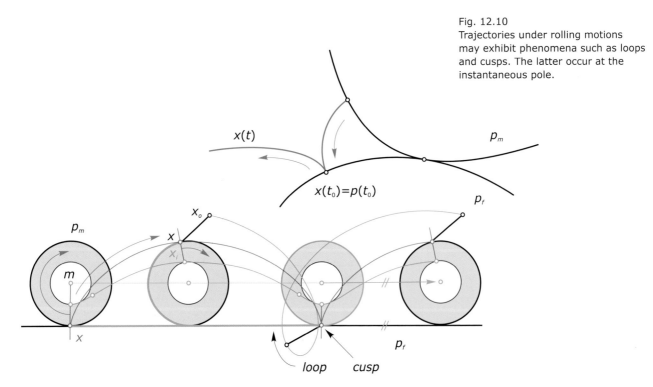

Fig. 12.10
Trajectories under rolling motions may exhibit phenomena such as loops and cusps. The latter occur at the instantaneous pole.

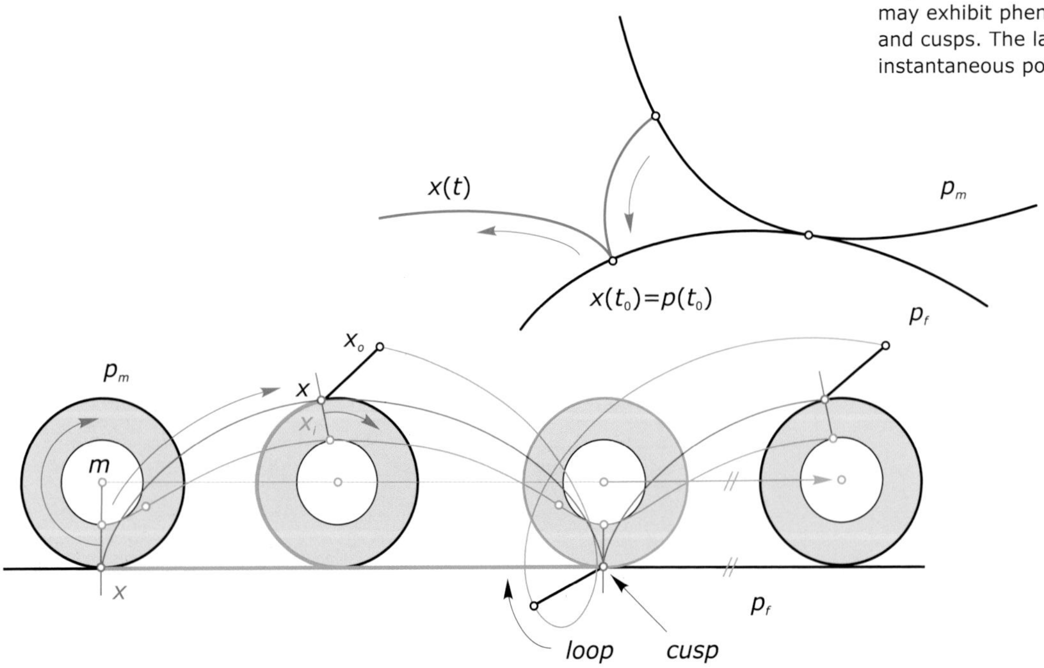

Swept areas and envelopes. The union of all positions of a moving figure M under a continuous motion is called its *swept area*. If the environment in which M is moving contains some (fixed) obstacles, which shall be avoided, the swept area of M is quite useful. An interference free motion of M requires that the swept area of M contain no obstacle. We may also say that the swept area describes the minimal space requirements. We are interested in the boundary of the swept area. It may contain two types of curves (Figure 12.12).

- Parts of trajectories of those points x, which are sharp corners on the boundary of the moving object M
- *Envelopes* of boundary curves b of M

Fig. 12.11
The *Eyebeam Museum of Art and Technology* (project, 2001) by Greg Lynn FORM. In this project, curves with loops and cusps are extensively used.

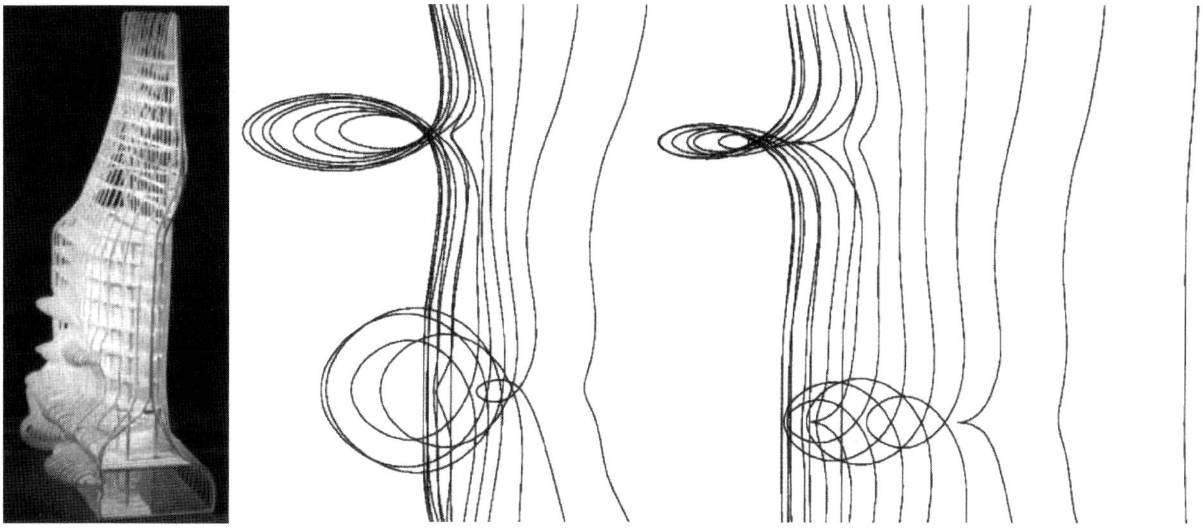

Fig. 12.12
The swept area of a moving object may contain parts of certain trajectories and envelopes at its boundary.

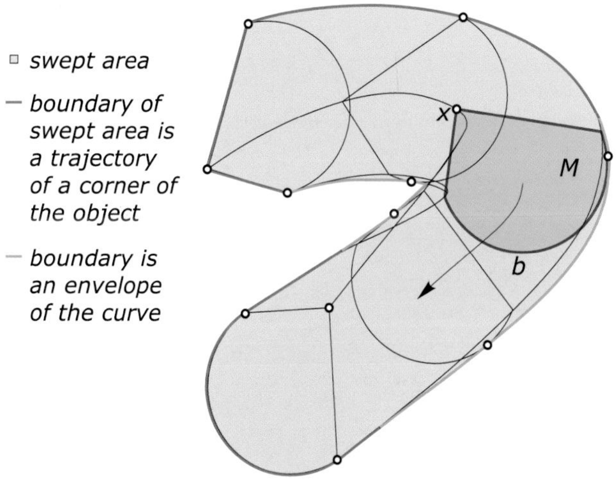

For a better understanding of envelopes, let's look at the envelope of a curve c under a continuous rotation about a point p. The envelope must consist of circular arcs (Figure 12.13). At a contact point $e(t_0)$ between a position $c(t_0)$ of c and the envelope e, the common normal passes through p. This important property is valid for general motions. At any time instant t_0, the contact normals between positions of curves and their envelopes pass through the pole $p(t_0)$. This may result in a simple construction of the contact points. Figure 12.13 illustrates this by means of a straight line segment l whose end points are running on straight lines (Cardan motion).

Example:
Motion of the Frenet frame of a planar curve. We consider a planar curve c and define a motion along it as follows (Figure 12.14). In the moving plane we mark a Cartesian frame. Now we move this frame so that its origin runs on c. The x axis remains tangent to c, and thus the y axis remains normal to c. This means that any position of our frame is a *Frenet frame* of the curve c (recall Chapter 7). Consider such a Frenet frame position at time t with $c(t)$ as the position of the origin. Because c is a trajectory, the curve normal $n(t)$ at $c(t)$ is a path normal and thus $n(t)$ contains the pole $p(t)$. Moreover, the normal $n(t)$ touches the envelope of all normals (the evolute) at the center $e(t)$ of curvature. The contact normal at $e(t)$ also passes through the pole. Therefore, $e(t)$ must be the pole $p(t)$. The *evolute* e is the *fixed polhode* and the y *axis* (curve normal) is the *moving polhode*. Points on the curve normal generate the *offsets* of c. Because the curve normal $n(t)$ contains the pole, the tangents of the offsets are parallel to each other [orthogonal to $n(t)$]. Moreover, their cusps lie on the fixed polhode (i.e., on the evolute; see Figure 12.14).

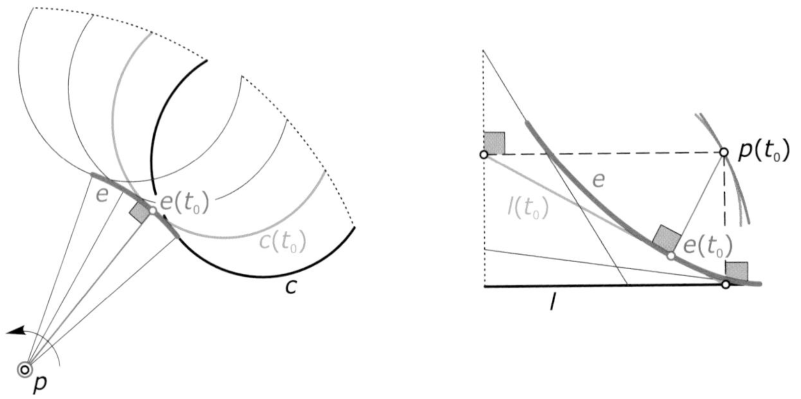

Fig. 12.13
(left) Envelopes under a continuous rotation about a point are circles. (right) Construction of points on the envelope of a moving straight line segment l using the property that the contact normal passes through the instantaneous pole.

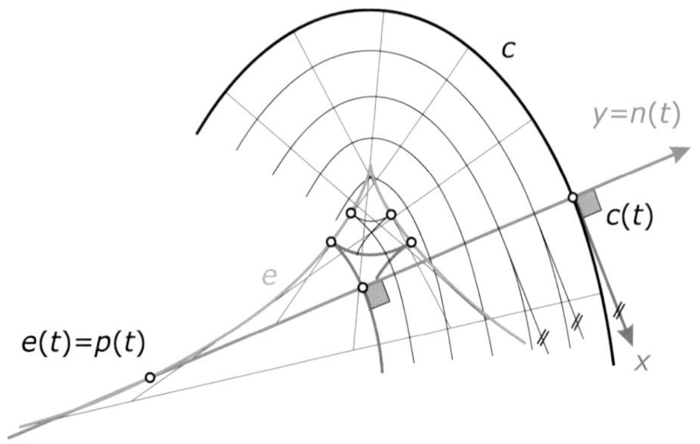

Fig. 12.14
The instantaneous pole of the motion of the Frenet frame along a planar curve c is the center of curvature. During this motion, the curve normal rolls on the evolute of c. Points of the normal have offsets of c as trajectories and thus their cusps lie on c's evolute.

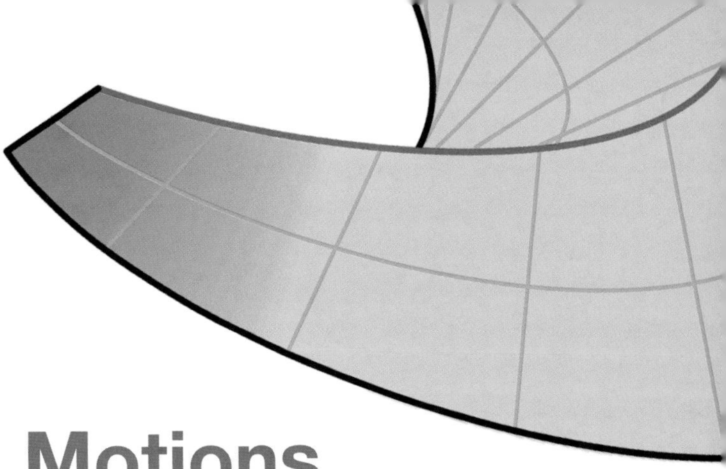

Spatial Motions

Extending planar motions to three dimensions. A motion in a plane F defines a three-dimensional motion in a natural way (Figure 12.15). This is like the motion of a three-dimensional object M with a planar bottom that glides along a table. Points that lie on a normal of F generate congruent trajectories. We may extrude the moving and fixed polhode of the planar motion in a direction normal to F and obtain two cylinder surfaces. During the three-dimensional motion, the moving cylinder rolls along the fixed cylinder. During such a motion, a curved profile in the moving system generates a sweeping surface.

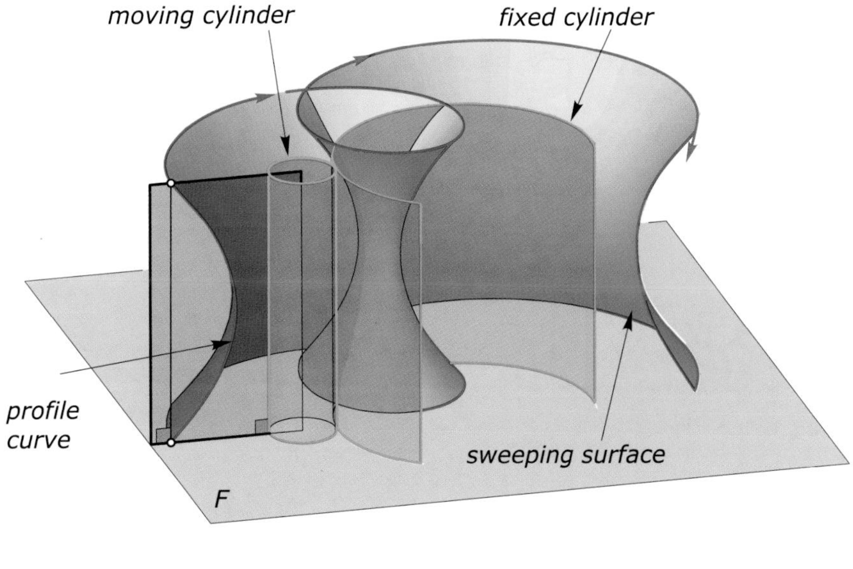

Fig. 12.15
Extending a planar motion to three dimensions. In this case, the two-dimensional motion in F is a rolling motion of two circles. Its extension to three dimensions is a rolling motion of two right circular cylinders. The figure also illustrates a sweeping surface generated by a profile curve in a diameter plane of the moving cylinder.

Example:

A ruled surface with ellipses as cross sections. Figure 12.16 shows a ruled surface generated by a straight profile during the three-dimensional extension of a Cardan motion. The surface carries a family of ellipses that lie in planes parallel to F. All rulings of that surface have a constant inclination angle (slope) against F. An object based on such surfaces is depicted in Figure 12.17.

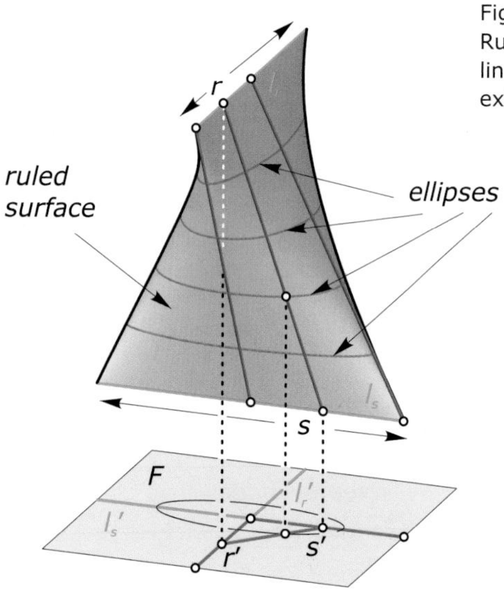

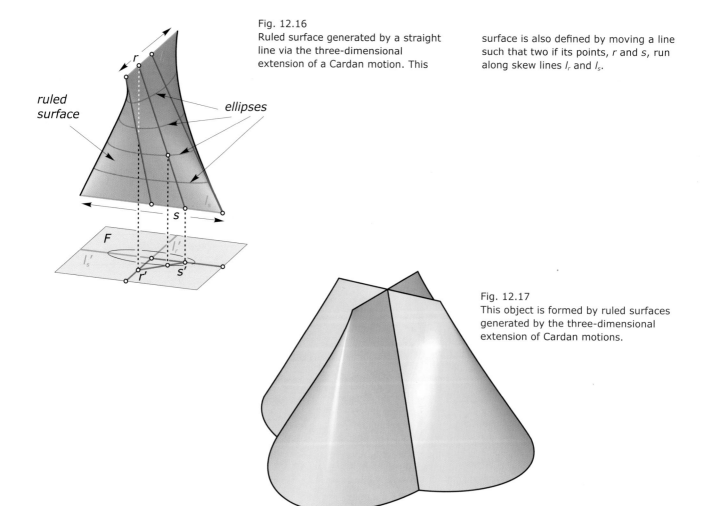

Fig. 12.16
Ruled surface generated by a straight line via the three-dimensional extension of a Cardan motion. This surface is also defined by moving a line such that two if its points, r and s, run along skew lines l_r and l_s.

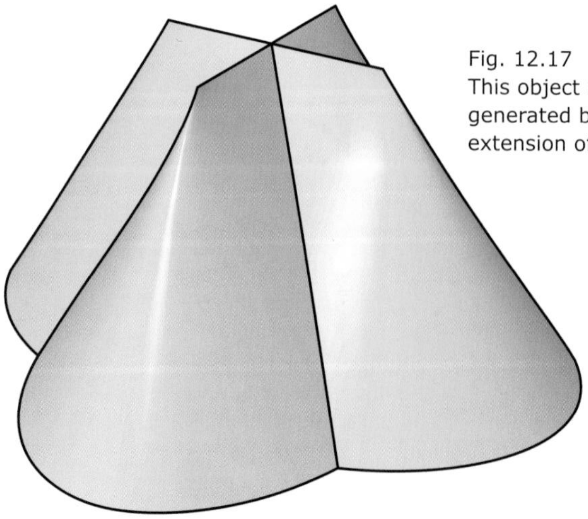

Fig. 12.17
This object is formed by ruled surfaces generated by the three-dimensional extension of Cardan motions.

Sweeping along a planar path and moulding surfaces. We obtain very interesting sweeping surfaces by three-dimensional extension of the Frenet frame motion along a planar curve c. During this motion, a plane N rolls on a cylinder E. N is always normal to c, and E is obtained by extrusion of c's evolute normal to the plane F of c. If we place the profile curve q in N, it generates during the motion a *moulding surface* S (Figure 12.18).

At any time instant, the motion behaves like a rotation about an axis, which is the line of tangency between the position $N(t)$ of N and the cylinder E. Hence, all path tangents of points in $N(t)$ are orthogonal to $N(t)$. Therefore, $N(t)$ intersects the surface S along the profile position $q(t)$ at a right angle. : *The moulding surface* S *intersects a family of planes (namely, the tangent planes of a cylinder* E*) at right angle.*

As the trajectories of points of q (intersections of the surface with planes parallel to the plane F of c) are congruent to offsets of c, they may have cusps. These cusps arise at points of tangency between a profile position $q(t)$ and the cylinder E (Figure 12.19).

Fig. 12.18
A moulding surface is a special sweeping surface, generated by the three-dimensional extension of the Frenet frame motion along a path c in a plane F. The positions $q(t)$ of the moving profile curve lie in the normal planes of c. The intersections of the surface with planes parallel to F are trajectories of the motion and congruent to offsets of c.

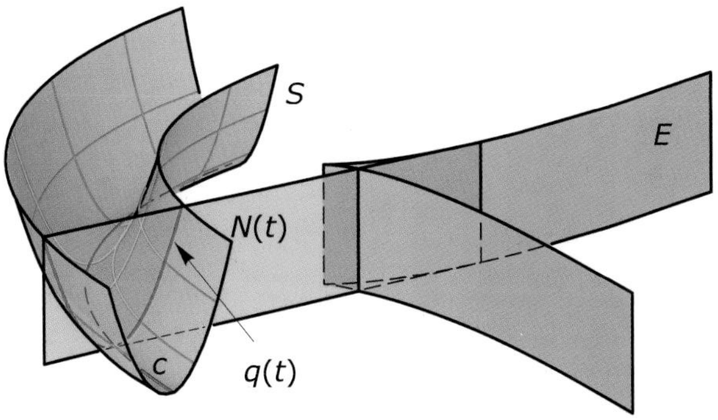

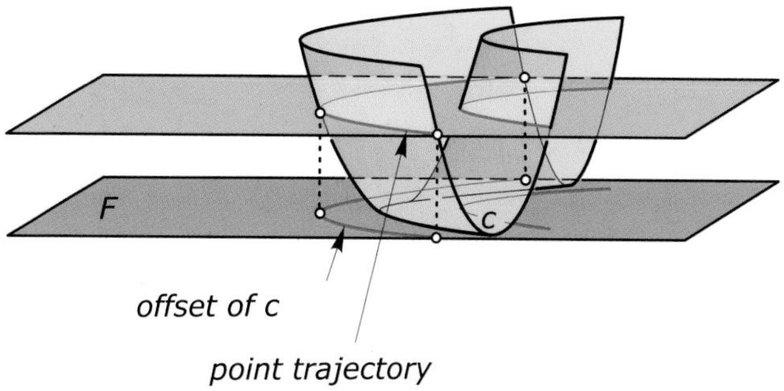

Fig. 12.19
Cusps of trajectories on a moulding surface. These cusps form singular curves on the surface.

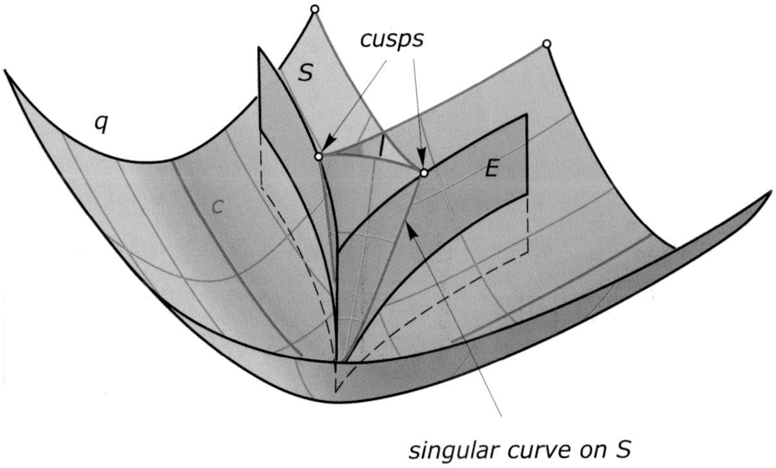

Figure 12.20 shows an example of the use of moulding surfaces in architecture. The availability of congruent profiles is a great advantage in building these surfaces.

It is instructive to look at a *discrete version of moulding surfaces*. We consider a planar polygon P_c [e.g., with edges of equal length and vertices c_1, c_2, c_3, and so on (Figure 12.21)]. Let B_{12} be the bisecting plane of c_1c_2, B_{23} shall denote the bisecting plane of c_2c_3, and so on. These planes pass through the edge midpoints m_{12}, m_{23}, and so on. The plane B_{12} intersects B_{23} in a line a_2, which is the axis of a circle through $c_1c_2c_3$. In the same way, we obtain axes a_3, a_4, and so on. Now we select a polygon q_{12} in the plane B_{12}.

This polygon is copied into the other bisecting planes as follows. Rotate q_{12} about a_2 into B_{23}. Then rotate the resulting polygon q_{23} about a_3 into B_{34}, and so on. We also connect corresponding positions of vertices by straight line segments. The connections between vertices of q_{12} and q_{23} are parallel to $m_{12}m_{23}$, and similarly for higher indices. The result of our construction is a mesh with quadrilateral faces. Each face has two parallel edges, and hence the face is *planar*.

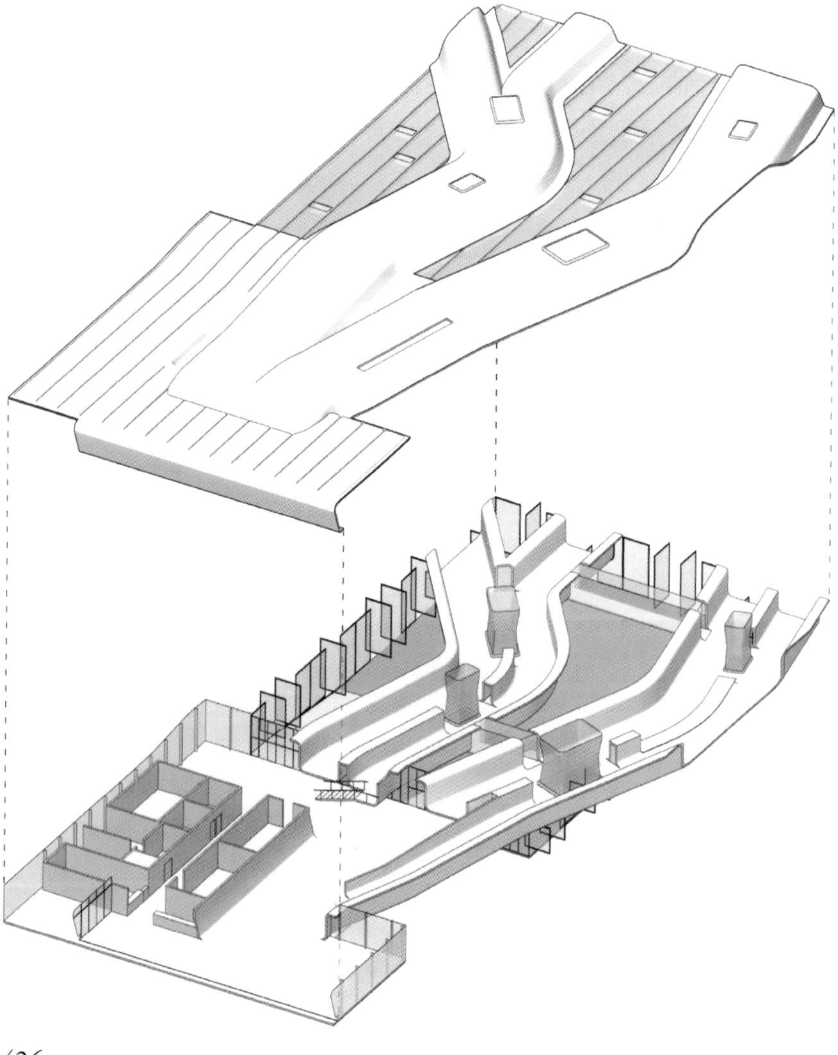

Fig. 12.20
Moulding surfaces in a project design of the *Tomihiro Hoshino Museum* (2001) by Neil M. Denari.

Quadrilateral meshes with planar faces are interesting for architecture, especially for glass structures. This topic is discussed in detail in Chapter 19. Finally, we consider the limit process when the polygon P_c is refined and its edge length tends toward zero. Bisecting planes converge to normal planes; the set of axes $a_2, a_3, \ldots$ converges to the evolute cylinder E; and our quad mesh becomes in the limit a smooth moulding surface. (See Figure 12.22.)

Fig. 12.21
Constructing a discrete version of a moulding surface from a planar polygon yields a quadrilateral mesh with planar faces.

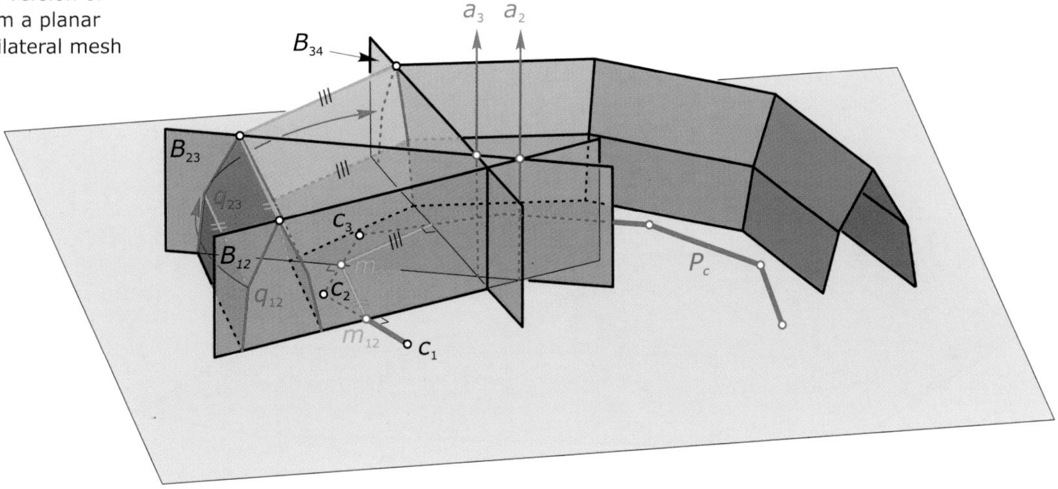

Fig. 12.22
This design is based on a discrete version of a moulding surface (see also Figure 12.21).

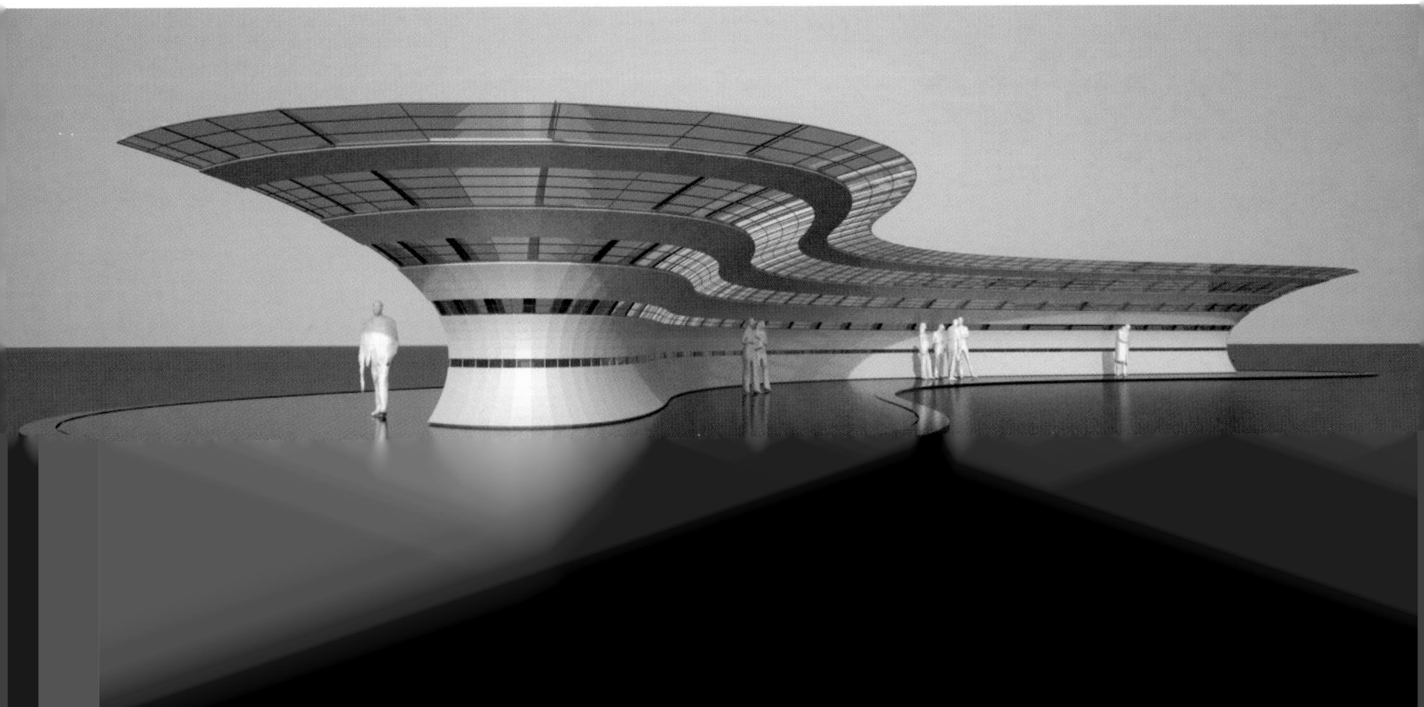

Developable surfaces of constant slope. Even such a simple profile as a straight line q (which is not parallel or normal to the plane F of c) generates a remarkable moulding surface S. Clearly, this surface is a ruled surface—all of whose rulings [positions $q(t)$ of the profile] have a constant inclination angle α against F. Along each ruling $q(t)$, the surface is tangent to a plane with the same inclination angle α (Figure 12.23). This follows from the fact that the surface S intersects the plane $N(t)$ at a right angle. Note that the surface has singularities along a curve s, which lies on the evolute cylinder E. In fact, the surface S is the set of tangents of that curve s. In Chapter 15, we will see that S is a developable surface that can be unfolded into the plane without distortion.

There is another way to obtain these developable surfaces of constant slope. We may move a right circular cone with vertical axis such that its vertex runs along a given curve m and its axis remains vertical. Then, the envelope surface (of all positions of the

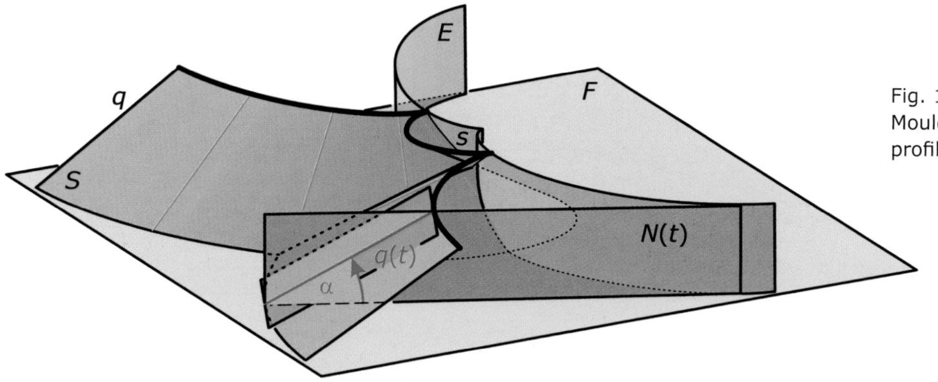

Fig. 12.23
Moulding surfaces with a straight profile are surfaces of constant slope.

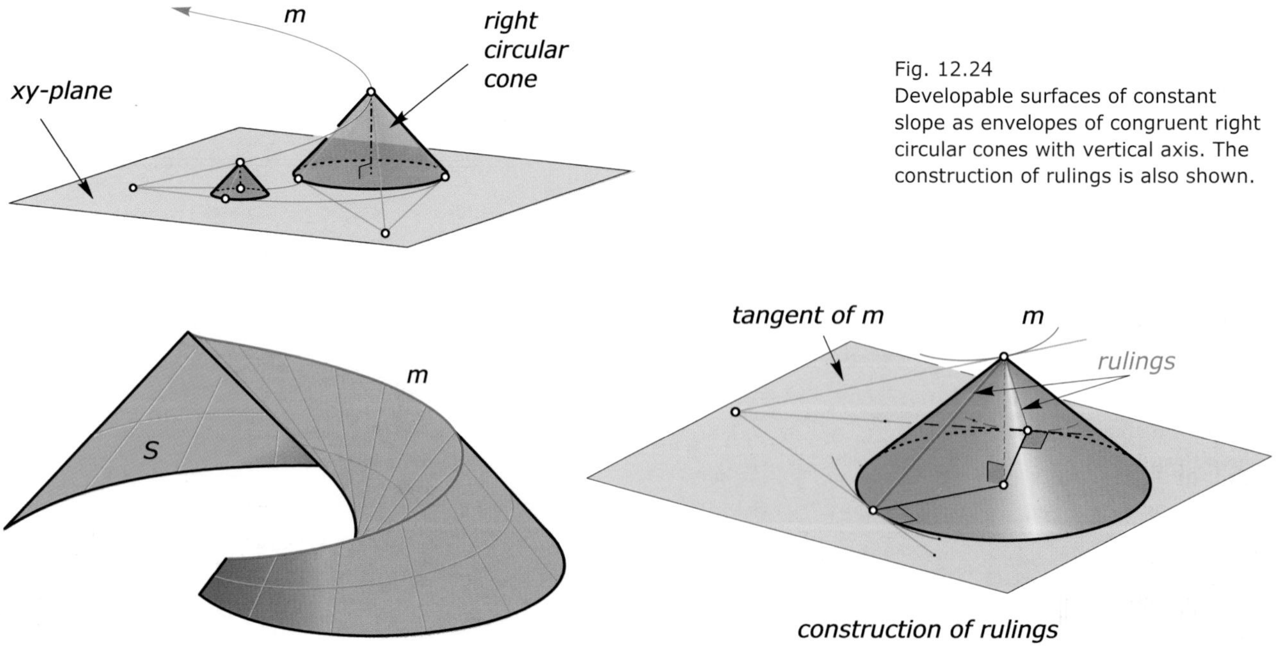

Fig. 12.24
Developable surfaces of constant slope as envelopes of congruent right circular cones with vertical axis. The construction of rulings is also shown.

moving cone) consists of surfaces of constant slope. The construction of the rulings is shown in Figure 12.24. Usually, m is a sharp edge on the resulting envelope. Such objects appear in nature as sand dunes and in architecture as curved roofs of constant inclination angle (Figure 12.25). In civil engineering, surfaces of constant slope are preferred shapes of dams.

General spatial motions. When we turn to general continuous motions in space, we face some difficulties. It is not sufficient to define such a motion via the trajectories of two points r and s. This is because known positions $r(t)$ and $s(t)$ of r and s still leave one degree of freedom; namely, a rotation about the line $r(t)s(t)$. Unfortunately, we cannot prescribe the trajectory of a third point. This would obstruct any motion. Apart from the problem of defining the motion, the instantaneous behavior is more complicated.

Fig. 12.25
Surfaces of constant slope appear for example as shapes of sand dunes or as curved roofs with constant inclination angle (Images on the left courtesy of M. Hofer and M. Reis). *St. Benedict chapel* (1988) in Sumvitg, Switzerland by Peter Zumthor.

Any two positions $M(t_0)$ and $M(t_1)$ of a rigid body M in space can be transformed into each other by a helical motion, a rotation, or a translation (see Chapter 6). Very similar to the discussion of planar motions, we now let t_1 tend toward t_0 and find that *at any time instant a continuous spatial motion has path tangents that are the same as those of a certain helical motion, continuous rotation, or translation*. The helical case is the generic one, and is more complicated as a rotation or a translation. A discussion of the kinematic geometry of motions in space is beyond the scope of this book. We restrict ourselves to discussing a few motions related to the generation of sweeping surfaces. (See Figures 12.26 and 12.27.)

Example:

Superposing uniform rotations. A moving object may be rotating with constant "angular velocity" v_1 about an axis a_1, which itself rotates with angular velocity v_2 about an axis a_2 in the fixed system. Constant angular velocity v means that the rotation angle for a time span T is $v{\cdot}T$ (i.e., in equal time spans the body rotates about the same angle). Figure 12.26 shows surfaces generated by such motions. The two axes are orthogonal and skew. An interesting case is obtained with $v_1{:}v_2 = 1{:}2$ and a straight profile orthogonal to a_1. The resulting ruled surface is one-sided, a Möbius band. Figure 12.27 shows M. C. Escher's version of it (see also the section on topology in Chapter 14).

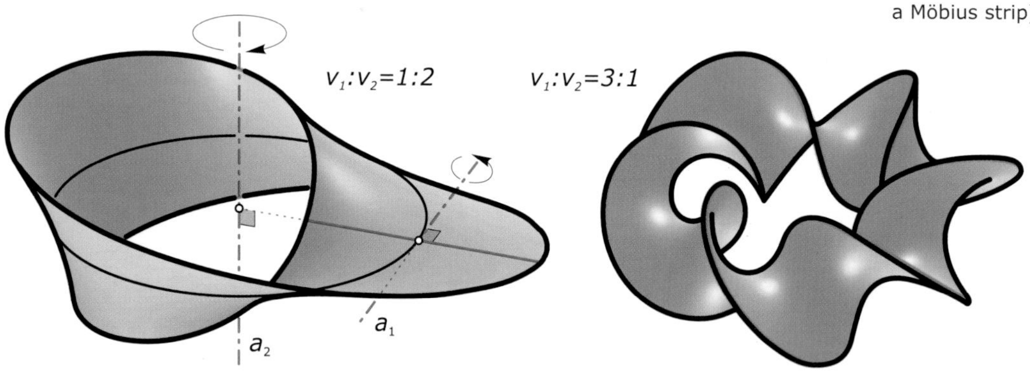

Fig. 12.26
Surfaces generated by motions superimposing two uniform rotations about orthogonal axes. The surface on the left side is a one-sided surface (i.e., a Möbius strip)

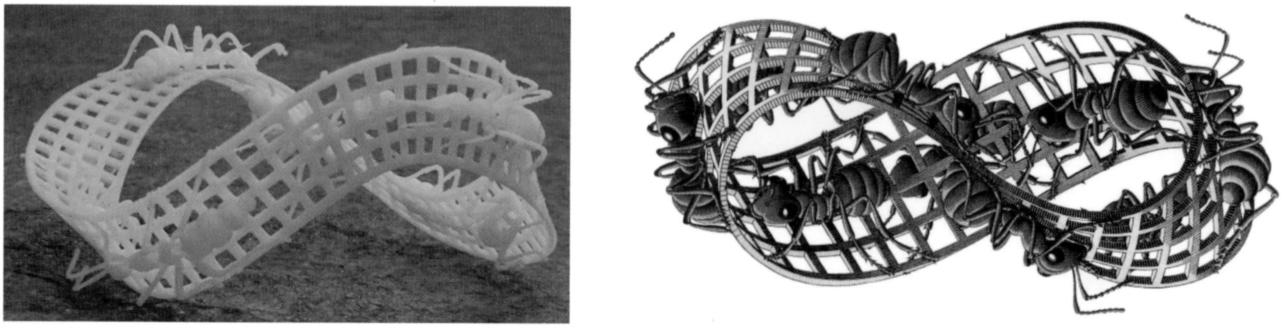

Fig. 12.27
Möbius strip by M. C. Escher (Image of the 3D print courtesy of G. Elber).

Sweeping and Skinning

Sweeping a profile along a curved path. Most modeling systems provide a sweeping tool by which you can select two curves: a *path* c and a *source* q. Assume that q lies in a plane Q. Then, q may be moved such that a prescribed point in its plane Q runs on c—with Q remaining orthogonal to c. Here, we still have some degrees of freedom; namely, a rotation about the tangent of c. A frequently used method of resolving this freedom is to employ the motion of the Frenet frame.

A surface designed in this way is shown in Figure 12.28. This is also a valuable tool in visualizing the variation of the osculating plane. In parts with a high variation of the osculating plane, the motion winds about c quite a lot. For some design applications, this behavior is undesirable.

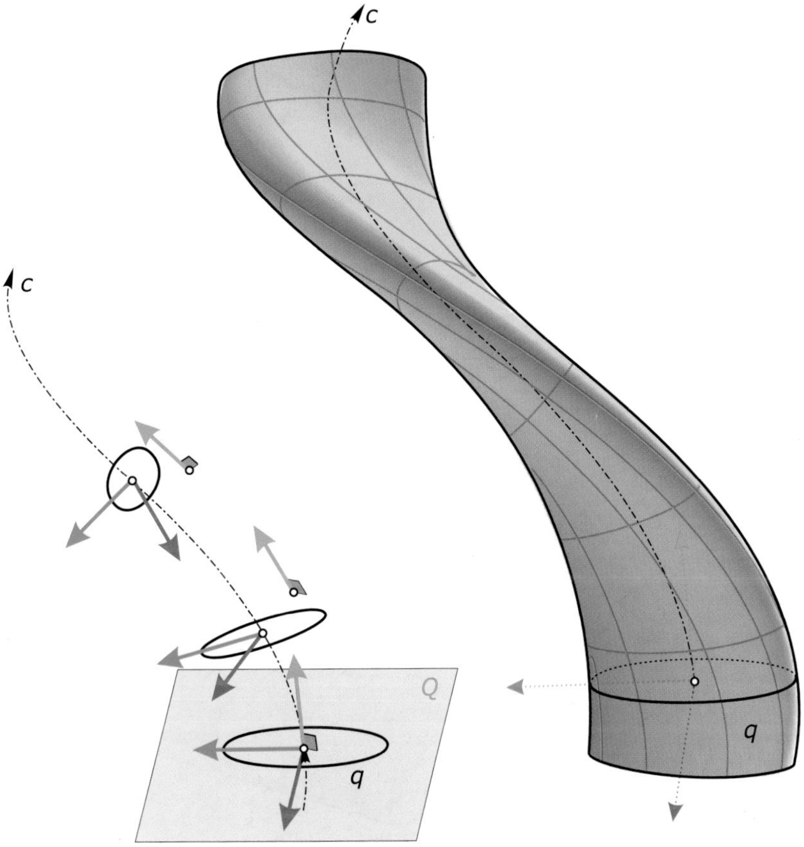

Fig. 12.28
Sweeping surfaces generated by the motion of the Frenet frame along a space curve c. The profile q is placed in the normal plane.

Rotation minimizing frame and quadrilateral meshes with planar faces. There is a motion that minimizes the winding about the path and that is preferred for sweeping surface design. To understand this motion, we take a discrete approach. It is completely analogous to our discussion of discrete moulding surfaces (Figure 12.21). The only difference is that the path c—represented by a polygon P_c with vertices c_1, c_2, c_3, and so on—is not planar. With edge midpoints m_{12}, m_{23},... bisecting planes B_{12}, B_{23}, ... and their intersection lines a_2, a_3,..., the construction proceeds as follows.

Select a polygon q_{12} in the plane B_{12}. Project q_{12} parallel to $m_{12}m_{23}$ into B_{23}. This is the same as rotating q_{12} about a_2 into B_{23}, and thus q_{12} and the resulting polygon q_{23} are congruent. Then project the polygon q_{23} parallel to $m_{23}m_{34}$ into B_{34}, and so on. We also connect corresponding positions of vertices by straight line segments and in this way obtain a *quadrilateral mesh with planar faces* (Figure 12.29). One warning is appropriate: if the polygon P_c is closed, this construction need not close (i.e., when we return with our polygon to B_{12} after traveling through P_c the resulting end position need not be the initial position q_{12}).

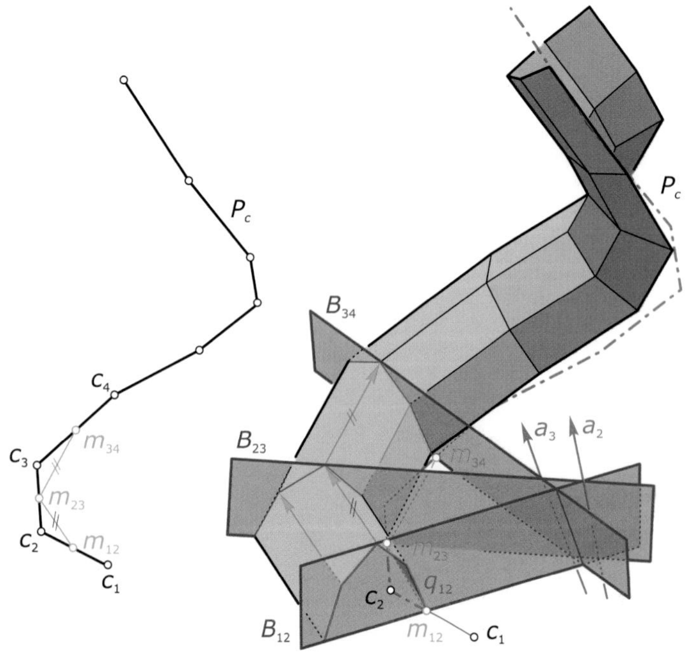

Fig. 12.29
Quadrilateral mesh with planar faces as discrete sweeping surface (generalized moulding surface) generated by a rotation-minimizing frame.

If we refine the polygon P_c by letting its constant edge length tend toward zero such that it converges to a smooth path c, we obtain a smooth generalized moulding surface S (Figure 12.30). The surface carries a family of congruent planar profiles $q(t)$ that lie in the normal planes of c. The surface S intersects these normal planes at a right angle. In fact, S can be generated by the rolling motion of a plane along the envelope surface of all normal planes of c. Another important property is that a straight profile q generates a developable ruled surface (see Chapter 15, on developable surfaces).

Sweeping with several paths and sources. Sweeping tools need not always move a curve like a rigid object. There are advanced options by which the moving profile may change its shape during the "sweep." Hence, one may prescribe more than one path—as well as an initial and a final shape of the source. Typically, we cannot prescribe precisely where these sources will be placed in space. This depends on the chosen part of the modeling menu and on the specific modeling system. Some examples are shown in Figure 12.31.

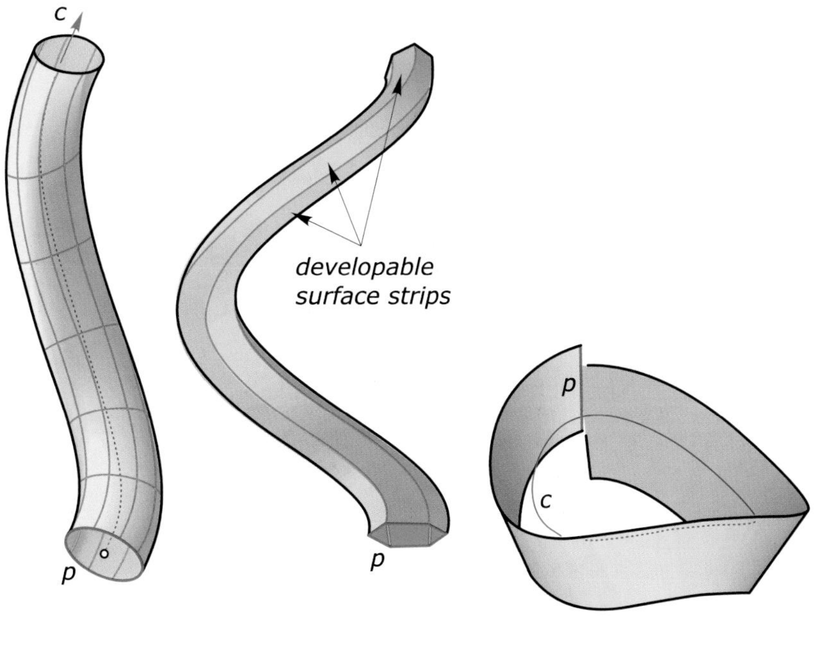

Fig. 12.30
Some sweeping surfaces generated by the motion of the rotation-minimizing frame along a space curve c. A closed curve c need not define a closed surface. A polygon as source q generates a surface composed of developable surface strips (see Chapter 15).

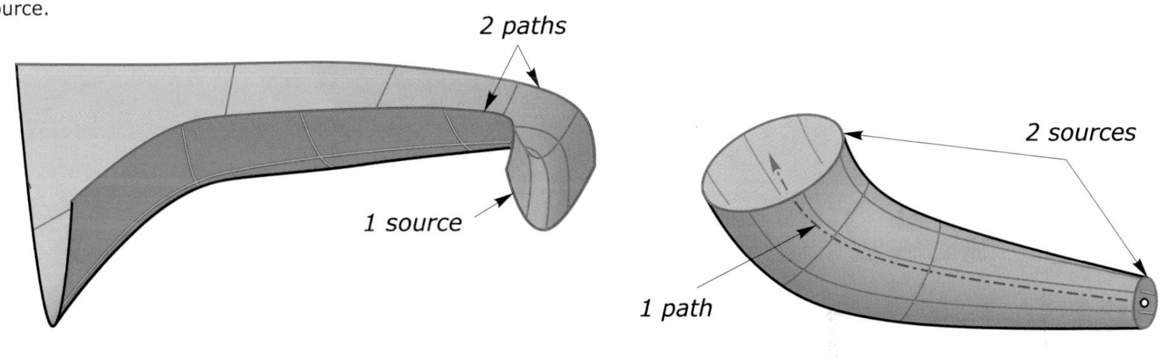

Fig. 12.31
Sweeping surfaces with more than one path and source.

Skinning surfaces. Whereas sweeping often does not allow us to precisely prescribe the location of the sources in space, there is a method for doing so. It is called *skinning*, which wraps a surface (skin) over a given network of curves (Figure 12.32). Because there is an infinite number of surfaces passing through a given curve network, the result of skinning also depends on the specific modeling system and the options we use. Further detail on this is beyond the scope of this book. Suffice it to say that this is a tool you might want to explore. However, if you prefer better shape control it may not be the method of choice.

Fig. 12.32
Skinning surfaces fill the gaps in a network of curves. There is still a lot of freedom in this task, and thus different systems may come up with quite different options and solutions.

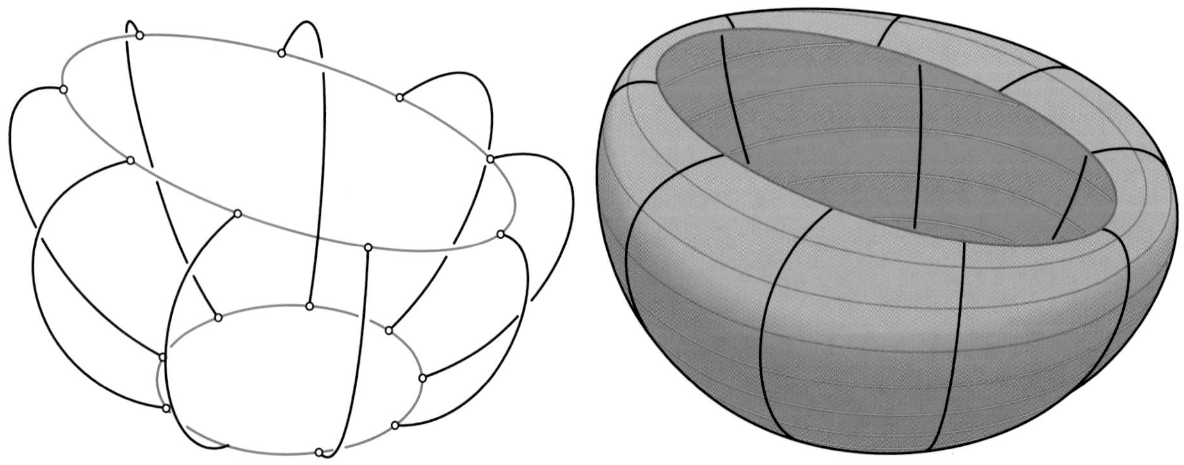

Fig. 12.33
This sculpture (*Wiener Trio* by Philip Johnson) has been modeled with the help of skinning surfaces.

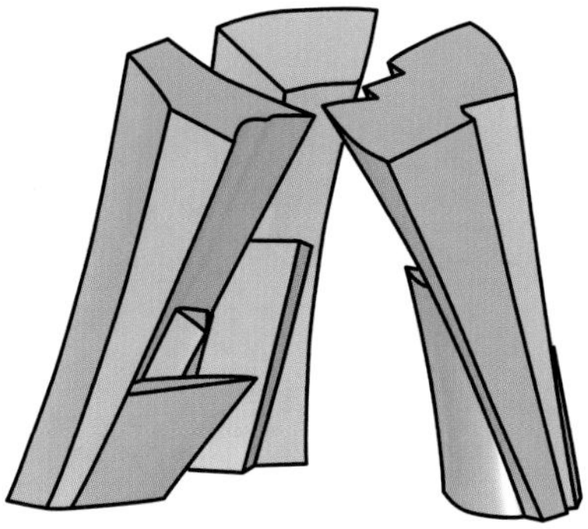

Example:
Skinning surfaces in art and architecture. Figure 12.33 shows a student's project which models the sculpture Wiener Trio by Philip Johnson (1996). An example of a skinning surface, passing through a sequence of ellipses, has been designed by Masaki Endoh and Masahiro Ikeda (Figure 12.34).

Fig. 12.34
The *Natural Ellipse* (2001–2002) in Tokyo by Masaki Endoh and Masahiro Ikeda. The building can be generated as a skinning surface using 24 vertical ellipses.

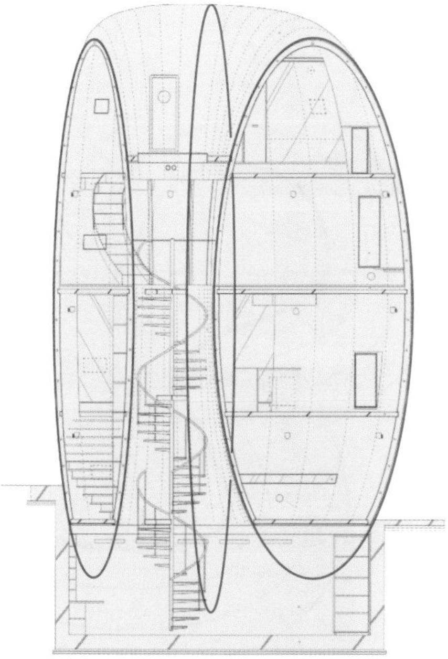

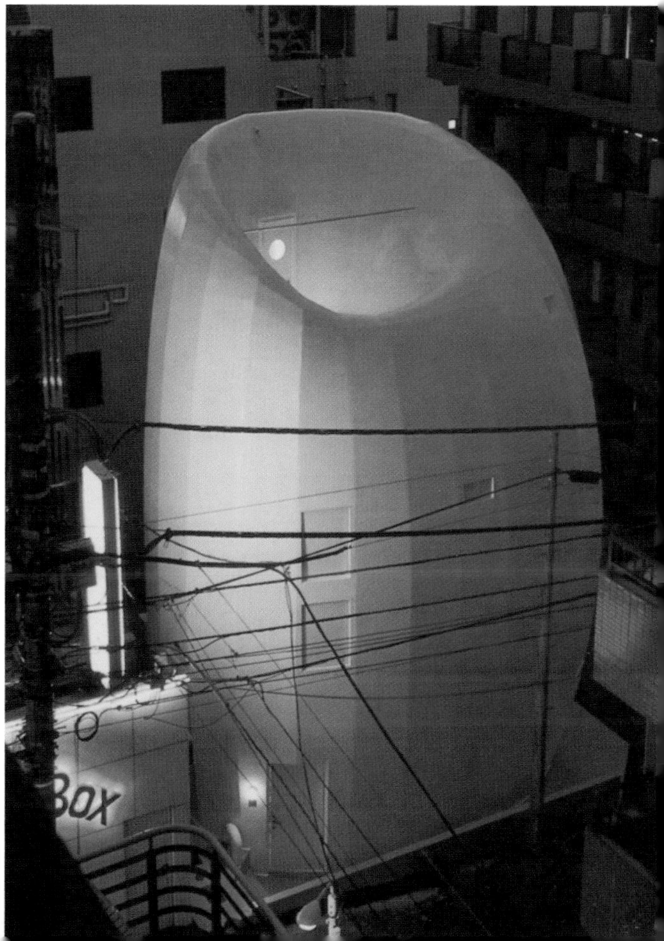

Fig. 12.35
Curve evolution at constant speed produces offsets.

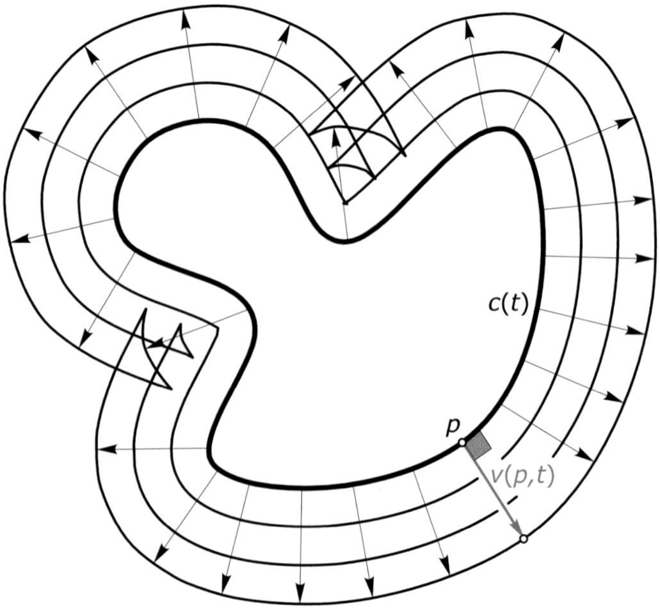

Curve Evolution

To model surfaces with the help of a changing profile, it may be very useful to know methods for the design of changing curves—also called *evolutions of curves* (or *curve flows*). In the following, we point to a few remarkable results on this topic.

We consider a curve c that is changing its shape over time t. Let $c(t)$ be the curve at time t. To describe an evolution, one typically describes the instantaneous velocities at points p of the state $c(t)$ at time t. It is not difficult to see that it is sufficient to consider the component of the local change (velocity vector), which is orthogonal to the current state. Let $v(p,t)$ be this normal component (evolution speed) at a point p of the current state $c(t)$ of the curve. We are now discussing several remarkable examples of curve evolutions.

Constant speed. If $v(p,t)$ is constant over time and positions p, it is pretty obvious that the curve changes into its offsets. Offsets were discussed in Chapter 10. Note that the offsets might be more complicated than the curve we start with (Figure 12.35). There is an implementation of this evolution which avoids the occurrence of self-intersections and thus performs the offset trimming operation discussed in Chapter 10.

Curvature flow. There are evolutions that simplify the shape of the initial curve. Now the starting curve is assumed to be closed. A remarkable and well-studied example is obtained if $v(p,t)$ equals the curvature of the current curve $c(t)$ at p. One can show that this evolution will shrink the curve to a point (Figure 12.36). To visualize in which way the shrinking process takes place, one may at each time rescale the curve. Now the final curve is always a *circle*. Clearly a circle remains a circle under this evolution. This truly remarkable result has applications in image processing, but it may also be useful for design.

A simple polygon evolution. Another astonishing curve simplification flow is obtained in the following discrete version, which operates on polygons and was first described by the French geometer G. Darboux in 1878. One evolution step is defined as follows. Form the polygon of edge midpoints and for the resulting polygon, again compute the polygon of edge midpoints (Figure 12.37).

Rescaling assumed, the final position is always an *affinely regular polygon* (i.e., the affine image of a regular polygon, which is the image of a regular polygon under a parallel projection; see Figure 12.37). Obviously, such a polygon is a fixed shape of the flow. However, the proof of the convergence of any polygon to such a special one is not as simple and is beyond the scope of this text. Figure 12.38 illustrates the smooth version of this flow.

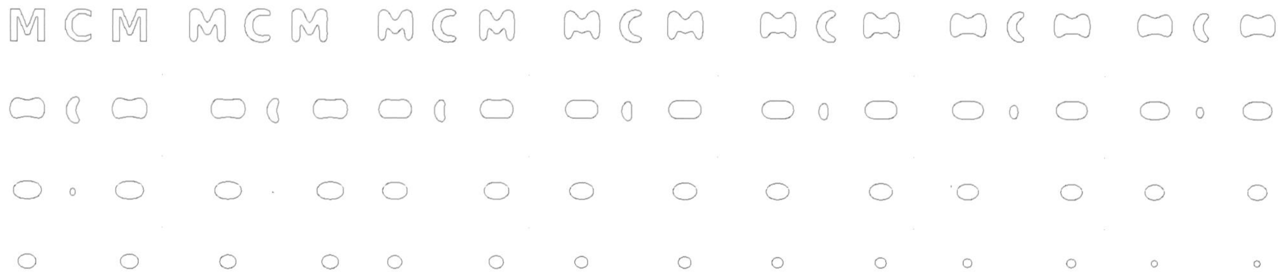

Fig. 12.36
(top) The curve evolution whose speed is given by the curvature at the current position shrinks any closed curve to a point (image courtesy of K. Frick).
(bottom) If we rescale the curve to avoid shrinking, the final position is a circle.

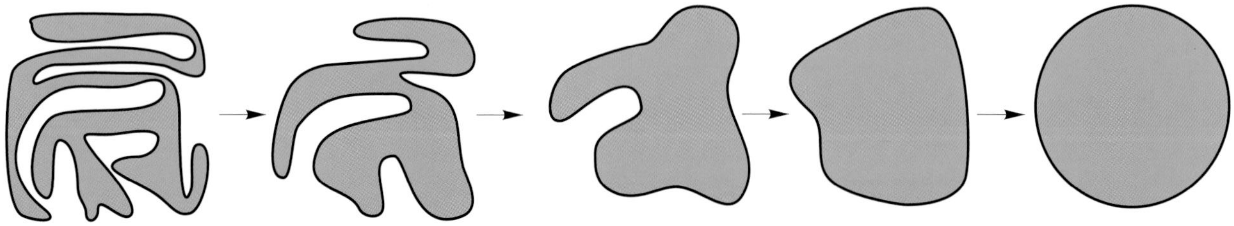

Fig. 12.37
(left) One step of Darboux's polygon evolution forms the polygon of edge midpoints (blue) and does this a second time (black).
(right) If it is rescaled to avoid shrinking, the final shape is an affinely regular polygon. It is the affine image of a regular polygon and hence its vertices lie on an ellipse. The polygon edges and the center of that ellipse form triangles of equal area.

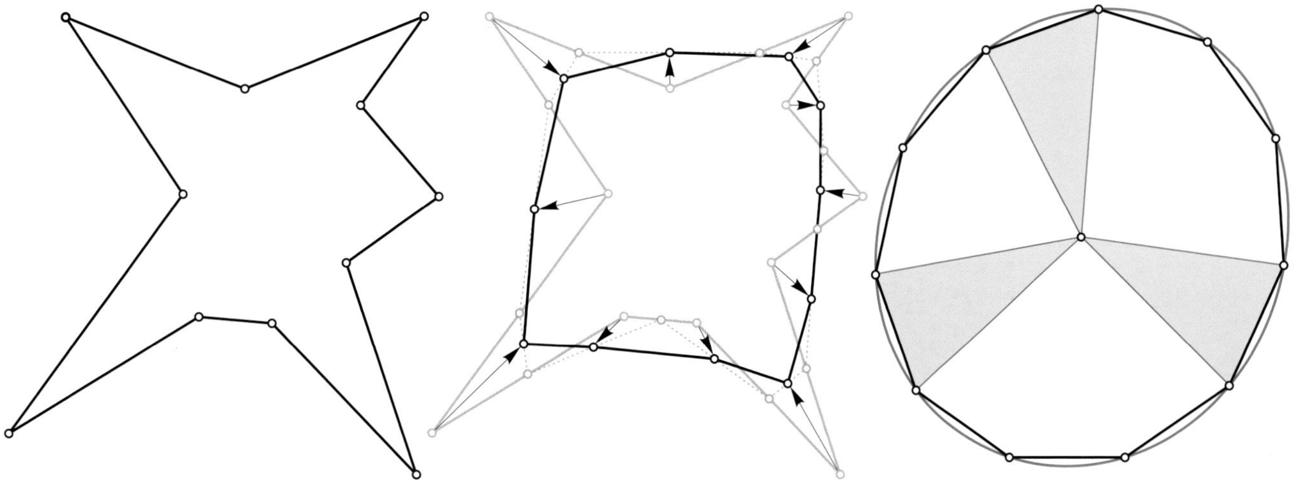

Fig. 12.38
The continuous and rescaled version of Darboux's flow evolves any closed curve (which may even have self-intersections) to an ellipse.

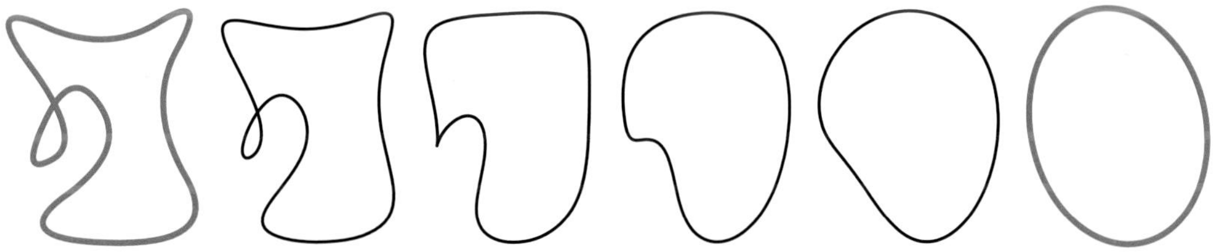

Example:
Surface design via a curve evolution.
A sequence of curves generated by Darboux's evolution forms the basis for the architectural model shown in Figure 12.39. The various evolution states are stacked above one another to form this interesting shape.

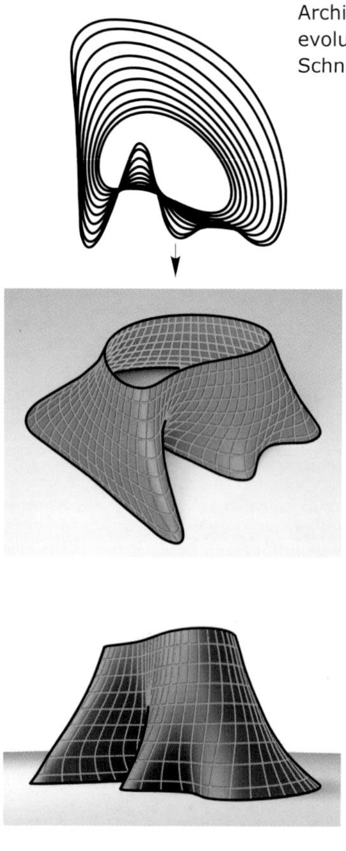

Fig. 12.39
Architectural model based on Darboux's evolution (Images courtesy of B. Schneider).

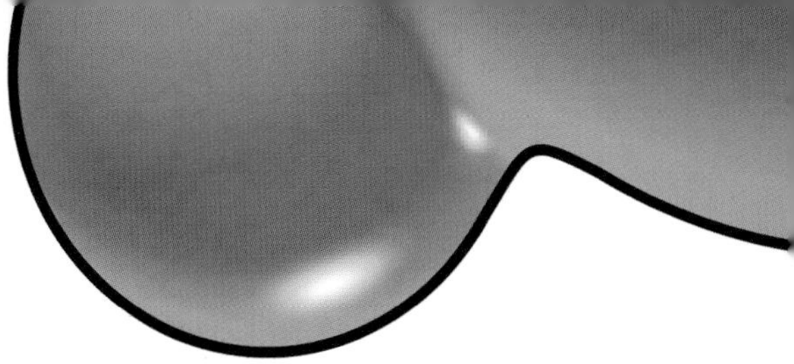

Metaballs and Modeling with Implicit Surfaces

Curves. The understanding of modeling with implicit surfaces becomes easier if we first look at curves. Recall from Chapter 7 that a curve c may be described by a single equation of the form $f(x,y) = 0$. We assume that (x,y) are Cartesian coordinates in the plane. A point of the plane belongs to the curve c if its coordinates (x,y) solve the equation $f(x,y) = 0$. One calls the set of points on c the *zero level set of* f because for all points of c the value of f is 0. The representation of a curve as a level set of a function is also known as *implicit representation*.

We may look at other *level sets of* f (also denoted as *isolines* or *isocurves of* f), which are the loci of points where f has the same value k. Of course, the equation of such a level set is $f(x,y) = k$. Clearly, if we define the new function $g(x,y) = f(x,y) - k$ the k-level set of f appears as the zero-level set of g. This is a simple example for the fact that the representation of a given curve as a level set of a function is not unique. We also see that any implicitly represented curve c: $f(x,y) = 0$ may be embedded into a family of level sets $f(x,y) = k$. By variation of k, we obtain a mathematical description of a *curve evolution*.

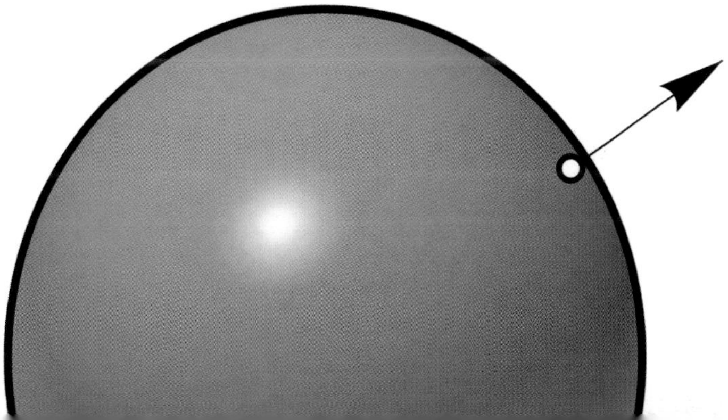

We may visualize a function $f(x,y)$ of two variables by its *graph surface* $(x,y,f(x,y))$. For each point (x,y) in the xy plane, it shows as z coordinate its function value $f(x,y)$. Points with the same function value k lie in the plane $z = k$, and therefore the level set $f(x,y) = k$ is found by intersecting the graph surface with the plane $z = k$ and projecting the intersection into the xy plane (Figure 12.40).

Note that a level set may be composed of several curves. (See Figure 12.41.) Moreover, if the level is changed the number of component curves in the corresponding level set may also change. Figure 12.42 illustrates the situation in which two components merge when the level increases. The border shape between the two types exhibits a double point.

Example:

Isolines for scientific visualization. We are familiar with a number of examples for level sets of functions. In geographic maps, the topography is usually visualized with the help of level sets of the height (i.e., curves of constant height above sea level; Figure 12.41). In weather maps, the visualization is often enhanced by isolines of important measurement data such as temperature or air pressure.

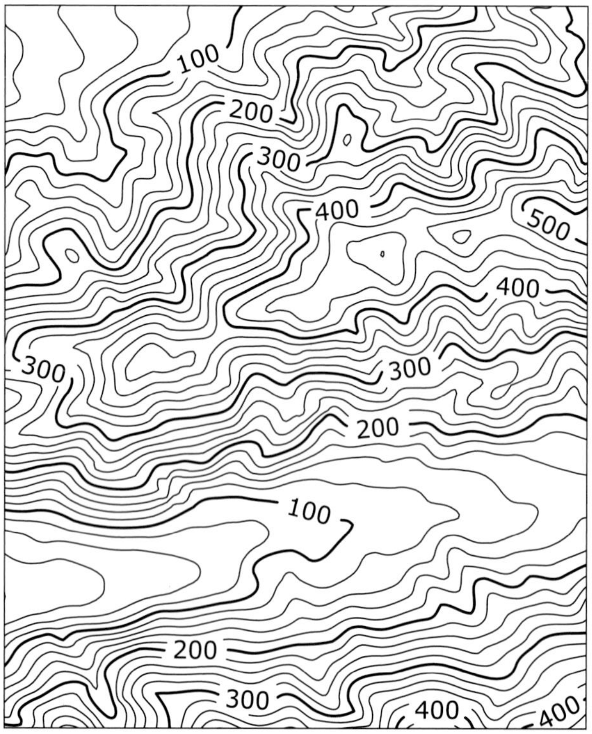

Fig. 12.41
Topographic maps exhibit a very familiar type of level set; namely, curves of constant height above sea level.

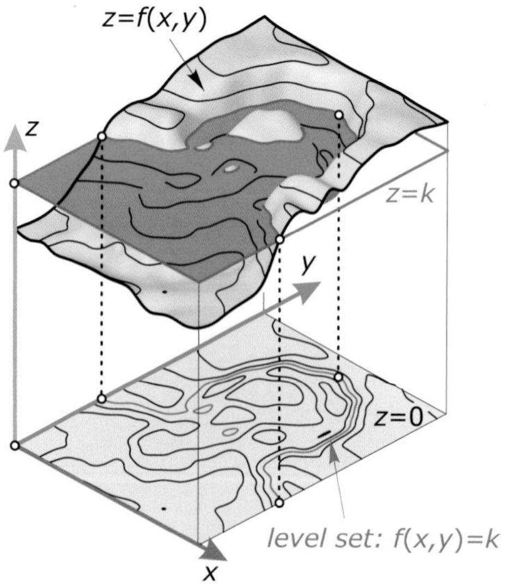

Fig. 12.40
Level sets of a function $f(x,y)$ of two variables are loci of points where f has the same value k [i.e., $f(x,y) = k$]. We may obtain them from the graph surface $z = f(x,y)$ by slicing it with planes $z = k$ and projecting the resulting intersection curves into the xy plane $z = 0$.

Example:

Cassini curves. We consider two points (1,0) and (−1,0) and study those curves (known as *Cassini curves*) for which the product of distances to these two points is constant. The squared distance of point (x,y) to (1,0) is $(x-1)^2+y^2$, and the squared distance to (−1,0) is $(x+1)^2+y^2$. Because the product of distances shall be constant, the product of the squared distances is also constant (e.g., equal to k)—and thus a Cassini curve satisfies the following implicit equation,

$[(x-1)^2+y^2]\cdot[(x+1)^2+y^2]=k,$

In other words, a Cassini curve appears as a level set of the function $f(x,y)=[(x-1)^2+y^2]\cdot[(x+1)^2+y^2]=x^4+y^4+2x^2y^2-2x^2+2y^2+1$ (see Figure 12.42). For levels k less than 1, the complete Cassini curve consists of two ovals. A Cassini curve to a level $k>1$ has only one component. The borderline case of $k=1$ is a figure eight, known as a *lemniscate*, and has a double point at the origin. We see that the shape of a Cassini curve is determined by the two "control points" to which the distances are measured [in our case, the points (1,0) and (−1,0)] and by the level k.

Fig. 12.42
Cassini curves are level sets of a function of two variables, which associates with each point (x,y) the product of its squared distances to the points (1,0) and (-1,0). Curves for which this product k is less than 1 are composed of two ovals. Curves for a product k greater than 1 have only one component. A figure eight shape appears for $k=1$. It is a *lemniscate* and has a double point.

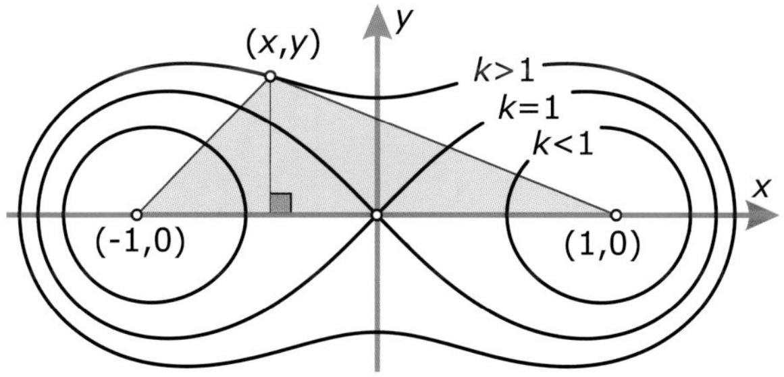

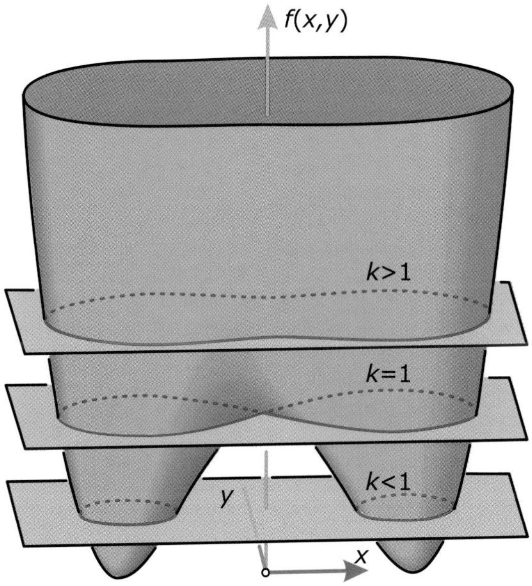

Implicit representation of surfaces. The extension of the implicit representation of curves to surfaces is rather straightforward. A surface is represented as a zero-level set $f(x,y,z) = 0$ of a function of three variables x,y,z. As in the case of curves, the function f is not uniquely determined for a given surface and a given coordinate system. Any implicitly represented surface is embedded into a family of level sets, $f(x,y,z) = k$, and is therefore also a member of a family of surfaces (surface evolution).

If one changes the level, the topological type of the level sets may change. In the case of curves, we have observed this in regard to the number of components. However, for surfaces a topology change may have more fundamental effects on the components as well. For example, a component may obtain a "handle" (or a tunnel). Just think of a sphere-like object turning into a ring shape (Figure 12.43).

Example:

Rotational surfaces with Cassini profiles. Let's rotate a Cassini curve about the bisecting line of its two control points (the y axis of the coordinate system used previously). This may be achieved if we replace the term x^2 in the equation of a Cassini curve with $x^2 + z^2$. The resulting surfaces are the level sets of the function $f(x,y,z) = (x^2 + z^2)^2 + y^4 + 2(x^2 + z^2)y^2 - 2(x^2 + z^2) + 2y^2 + 1$.
The level sets $f(x,y,z) = k$ exhibit a topology change from a sphere-like topology (for $k < 1$) to a ring shape ($k > 1$) (Figure 12.43). Rotating Cassini curves about the x axis yields another change of topology (not shown in Figure 12.43); namely, a change from one to two components. We discuss topology in much more detail in Chapter 14. However, it is important to mention it here because when we model with implicit surfaces such as meta-balls we must be aware of this fundamental effect.

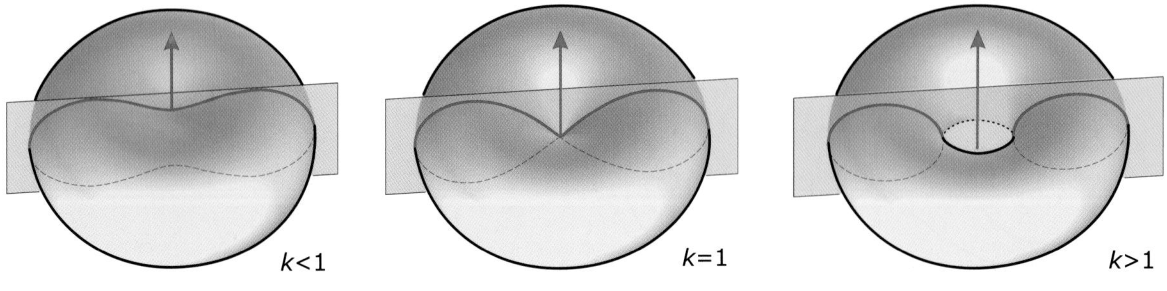

Fig. 12.43
Level sets of the same function may be of different topological type. Here we see how a hole develops and thus a sphere-like object is evolves into a ring shape.

Distance-based functions. In the example of Cassini curves, the function f has been set up via a product of distances to two input points. Combining distances to input shapes (points, lines, simple surfaces) into an implicit surface representation is a frequently used modeling tool. The general procedure is as follows. One sets up *field functions* to the given input shapes, adds these field functions, and then considers the level sets of the resulting function $f(x,y,z)$.

Let's examine this approach for input points only. Each input point $p = (p_1,p_2,p_3)$ (control point of the shape) is associated with a local field function. This is a function $D(r)$ of the distance r to the point and typically decays with increasing r. For example, one may use a decay (as in the Gaussian normal distribution) based on the exponential function $\exp(x) = e^x$:

$$D(r) = a \cdot \exp(-b \cdot r^2).$$

Here, a and $b > 0$ are constant values that are usually set automatically but may be used to fine-tune a shape. Although for large distances r the value of D is small, it is only zero for infinite distance. To have a more local influence of a control point, one often uses alternative functions that have a similar decay behavior but are precisely zero if the distance r exceeds a certain threshold T (Figure 12.44).

Keep in mind that the local field function of point $p = (p_1,p_2,p_3)$ is a function of (x,y,z). For the Gaussian decay model $D(r)$, it reads

$$P(x,y,z) = a \cdot \exp(-b \cdot [(x-p_1)^2 + (y-p_2)^2 + (z-p_3)^2]).$$

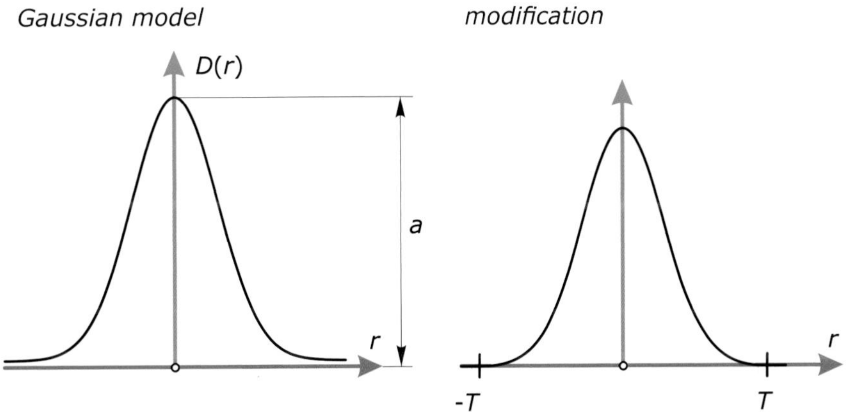

Fig. 12.44
The function $D(r)$, which defines the local field function, usually exhibits a decay as shown in this figure. (left) The Gaussian model and (right) a modification with function value 0 for distances r greater than a threshold T.

Having only one input point is not interesting because the level sets of a single local field function are of course spheres, centered at the corresponding control point p. This is so because the value of the function depends only on the distance to p. However, if we take several control points the situation becomes more interesting. Assume that we have two control points p, q and a local field function P and Q associated with each of them. Then, we consider the sum of these functions $f(x,y,z) = P(x,y,z) + Q(x,y,z)$ and use its level sets for modeling. This is illustrated in Figure 12.45.

Meta-balls. Meta-balls, also known as "blobs" or "soft objects," follow the same principle. Their shape is controlled by input shapes, which are typically simple objects such as points, lines, and simple surfaces. Using the distance to the input shapes, each input shape is associated with a local field function. These local field functions are summed, which yields a function $f(x,y,z)$. Its level sets $f(x,y,z) = k$ are the surfaces one is interested in. An example is shown in Figure 12.46.

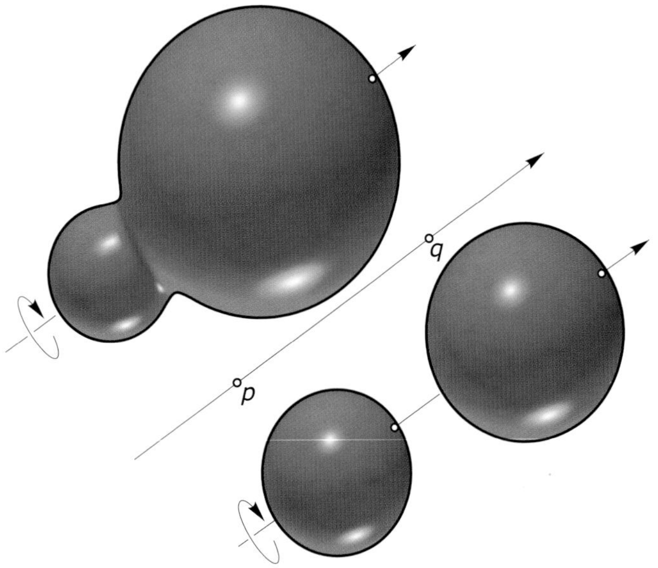

Fig. 12.45
Implicit surfaces modeled with two control points and a Gaussian field function. Depending on the level, we obtain one or two components. Note that these surfaces are rotational surfaces, the axis of rotation being the connecting line of the two control points.

Fig. 12.46
This model has been generated via meta-balls (Image courtesy of B. Schneider).

Fig. 12.47
The *Bubble* (1999) in Frankfurt am Main by ABB Architects with Bernhard Franken.

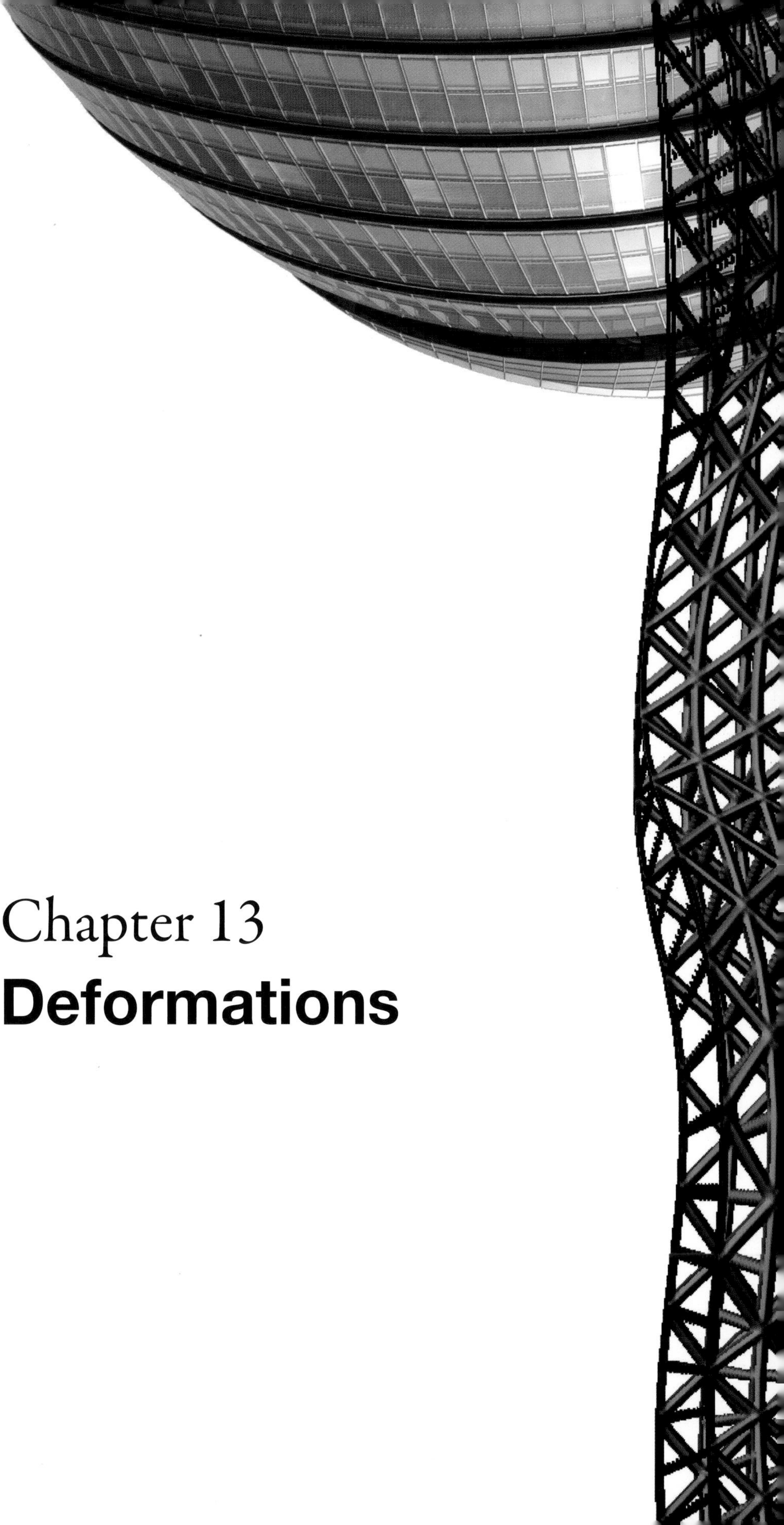

Chapter 13
Deformations

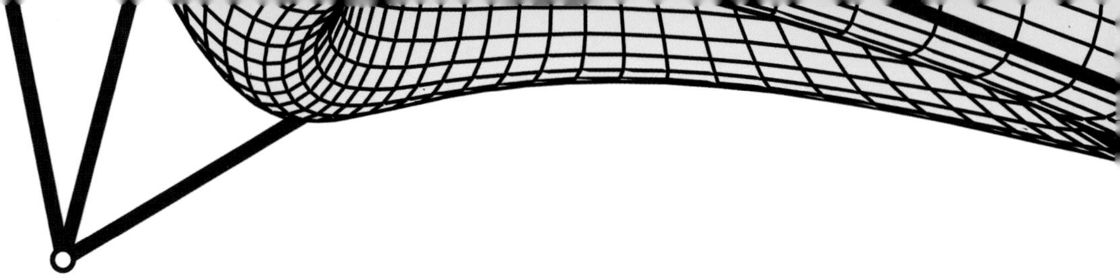

Deformations

Deformations alter the geometry of a shape based on some underlying mathematical principle. Typically, the shape is included in some simple solid and the deformation acts in a more or less intuitive way on that solid and thereby deforms the shape (Figure 13.1). However, the modification of the shape is more general than a deformation performed by an affine or a projective map. It even goes beyond the nonlinear transformations we have already learned about. Deformations can be applied to any shape.

The use of deformations may be seen as a convenient way of performing a change of a design or part of it. Thereby, a valid computer-aided design (CAD) model is mapped to another valid CAD model. Intersections, smooth transitions, blending areas, and so on are automatically transferred to the modified model. Full freedom of shape modification is provided the designer by freeform deformations, which extend freeform curves and surfaces (and like these types of surfaces they can be interactively guided with the aid of control points).

Fig. 13.1
The principle of shape deformations. The shape to be modified is embedded in a simple solid, and typically the solid is then transformed into a new one with the aid of appropriate design handles. This deformation acts on all points of the solid and thus transforms the embedded shape into a new one.

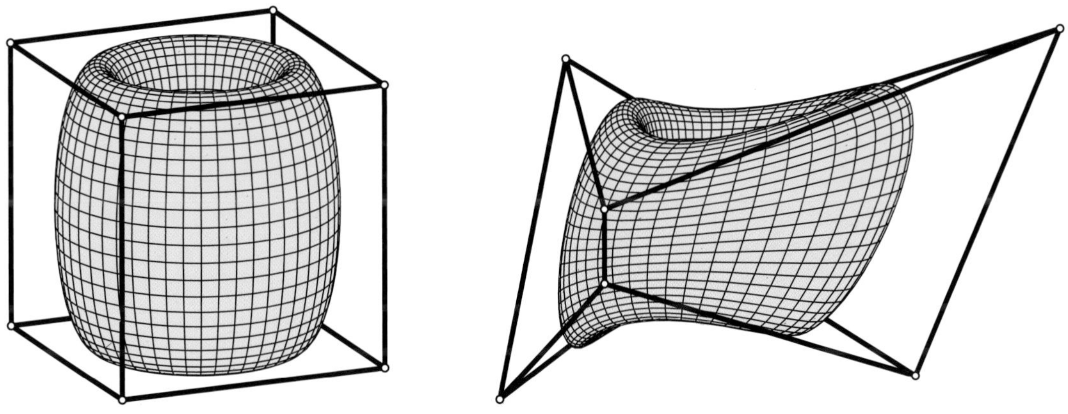

Three-Dimensional Transformations

Continuing the discussion of transformations found in Chapters 5 and 6, we are now investigating the more advanced transformations in three dimensions. To have a solid basis for our study, we first look at the mathematical representation of a transformation in three dimensions.

Math:

Description of transformations in three dimensions. Assume that we are given a Cartesian coordinate system (x,y,z). A transformation maps a point $p = (x,y,z)$ to an image point $p_1 = (x_1,y_1,z_1)$. The analytical representation of the transformation expresses how to compute the coordinates (x_1,y_1,z_1) of p_1 if the coordinates (x,y,z) of p are given :

$$x_1 = f(x,y,z),\ y_1 = g(x,y,z),\ z_1 = h(x,y,z).$$

The functions f, g, and h must be explicitly given in order to compute a specific transformation.

For an affine map the functions f, g, and h are linear. This means that function f is of the form $f = f_0 + f_1x + f_2y + f_3z$ (with given numbers f_0, f_1, f_2, f_3) and analogous expressions hold for g and h (see Chapter 6). Affine maps have some very simple properties. They map straight lines to straight lines and planes to planes, they keep parallelity of lines or planes, and they do not change the ratio of collinear points. There is a more general form of linear transformations in three dimensions in which "linear" means that straight lines are mapped to straight lines and hence planes are mapped to planes (see Chapter 6). These are the projective maps T. Here, the coordinate functions f, g, and h are fractions of linear functions $[f = (f_0 + f_1x + f_2y + f_3z)/D]$ with a common denominator $D = d_0 + d_1x + d_2y + d_3z$—which is the same for all three coordinate functions f, g, and h.

Clearly, if $d_1 = d_2 = d_3 = 0$ $(d_0 \neq 0)$ we have an affine map. Otherwise, the equation $d_0 + d_1x + d_2y + d_3z = 0$ determines a plane V whose points are mapped to points at infinity. Thus, a careful study of projective maps needs a tool for the representation of points at infinity, which is provided by homogeneous coordinates (see Chapter 6).

Mappings different from projective maps and their special cases (such as affine maps) are called *nonlinear transformations.* They have the property that not all straight lines are mapped to straight lines. The study of those nonlinear transformations which are important tools for shape modelling is the content of this chapter.

Slice-based three-dimensional transformations. Many of the simple and frequently used nonlinear transformations operate as follows. One slices the object to be transformed by parallel planes. These slices are then rearranged (displaced, and perhaps also scaled) in a systematic way to a new object (Figure 13.2). For visualization, we may use a simple object such as a box, but we always have to bear in mind that these deformations may be applied to much more general shapes.

In the following, we will study the most common nonlinear transformations (deformations)—many of which are slice based. In several cases, it will be necessary to use a mathematical representation of a simple derivation of important properties. Thus, this chapter may also be seen as an exercise in the use of analytic geometry.

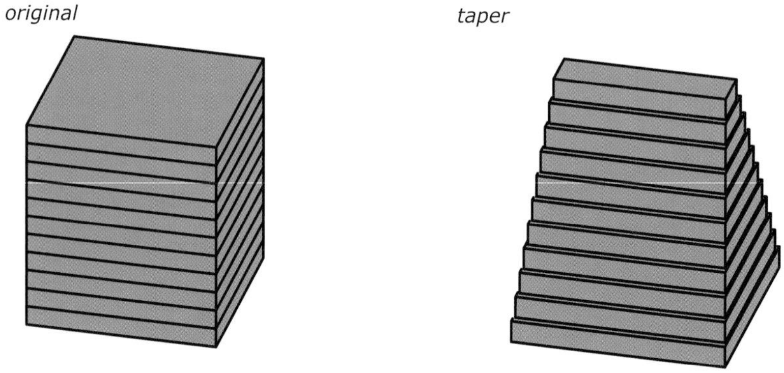

Fig. 13.2
Several frequently used deformation techniques are based on slicing an object with parallel planes and rearranging the slices into a new object.

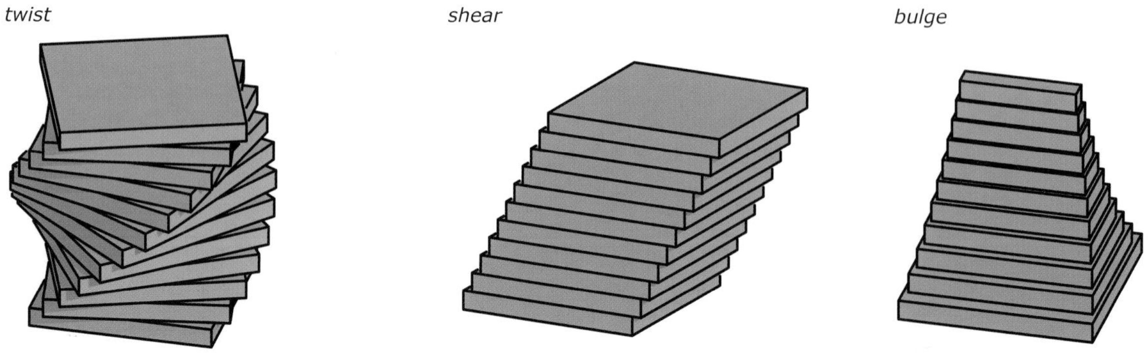

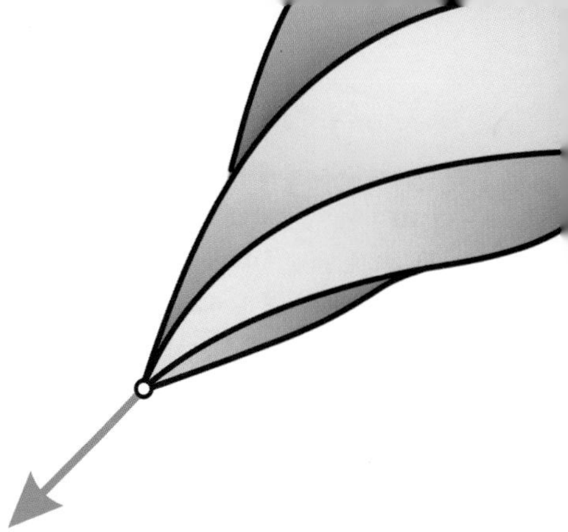

Twisting

To define the twist deformation, we select a fixed bottom plane B and a straight line A (called *twist axis*) orthogonal to the plane B (Figure 13.3). The layers of the object in planes orthogonal to the axis (i.e., parallel to B) are now rotated about A as follows. The bottom plane B remains fixed and the rotational angle $\alpha_{\max}$ of the top plane T is prescribed. We assume that the distance between the bottom and top planes is h, the height of the object to be deformed. The rotational angle $\alpha(z)$ of the slice at height z above B is selected to be

$$\alpha(z) = (z/h)\ \alpha_{\max}.$$

This is a linear variation of the rotational angle with respect to the distance. For the bottom plane B, we have $z = 0$ and thus $\alpha(0) = 0$—which means that the bottom slice remains fixed. As desired, the top plane T ($z = h$) is rotated by the angle $\alpha_{\max}$. The plane at bottom distance $z = h/2$ is rotated by $\alpha_{\max}/2$, and so on.

Fig. 13.3
The twist operation uses an axis A and rotates slices in planes orthogonal to A about A. One fixes a chosen bottom plane B and describes the rotational angle of the upper plane T.

The intermediate slices are rotated automatically, using a linear variation of the rotation angle with respect to the distance from the bottom plane.

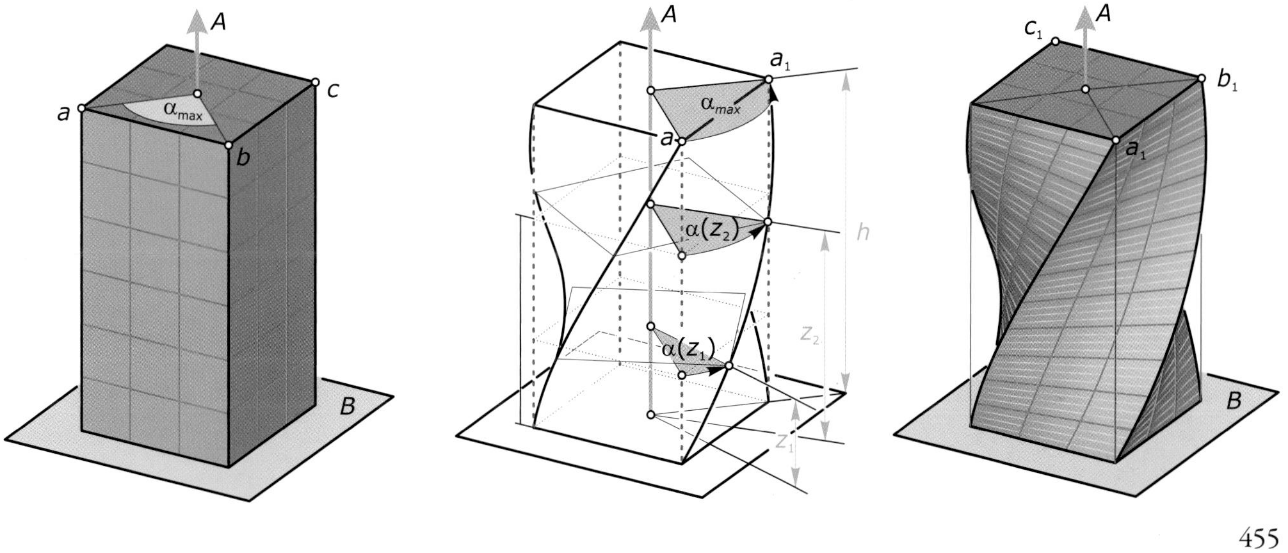

There is an obvious connection with helixes and helical motions (Figure 13.4). Any straight line l parallel to A is mapped to a helix l_1 with axis A. A cylinder surface S with rulings parallel to A is deformed into a helical surface S_1 with axis A. The cross section of S in B serves as a generating curve of the helical surface S_1. This result has some simple and important special cases. A plane P parallel to A is deformed into a helical ruled surface. In particular, the twist operation maps a plane P through A into a helicoid.

Fig. 13.4
The twist operation is closely related to the helical motion. Lines parallel to the twist axis A are mapped to helixes. Cylinder surfaces S with rulings parallel to A are mapped to helical surfaces S_1. In particular, and a plane through A is transformed into a helicoid and a plane parallel to A is mapped to a ruled helical surface.

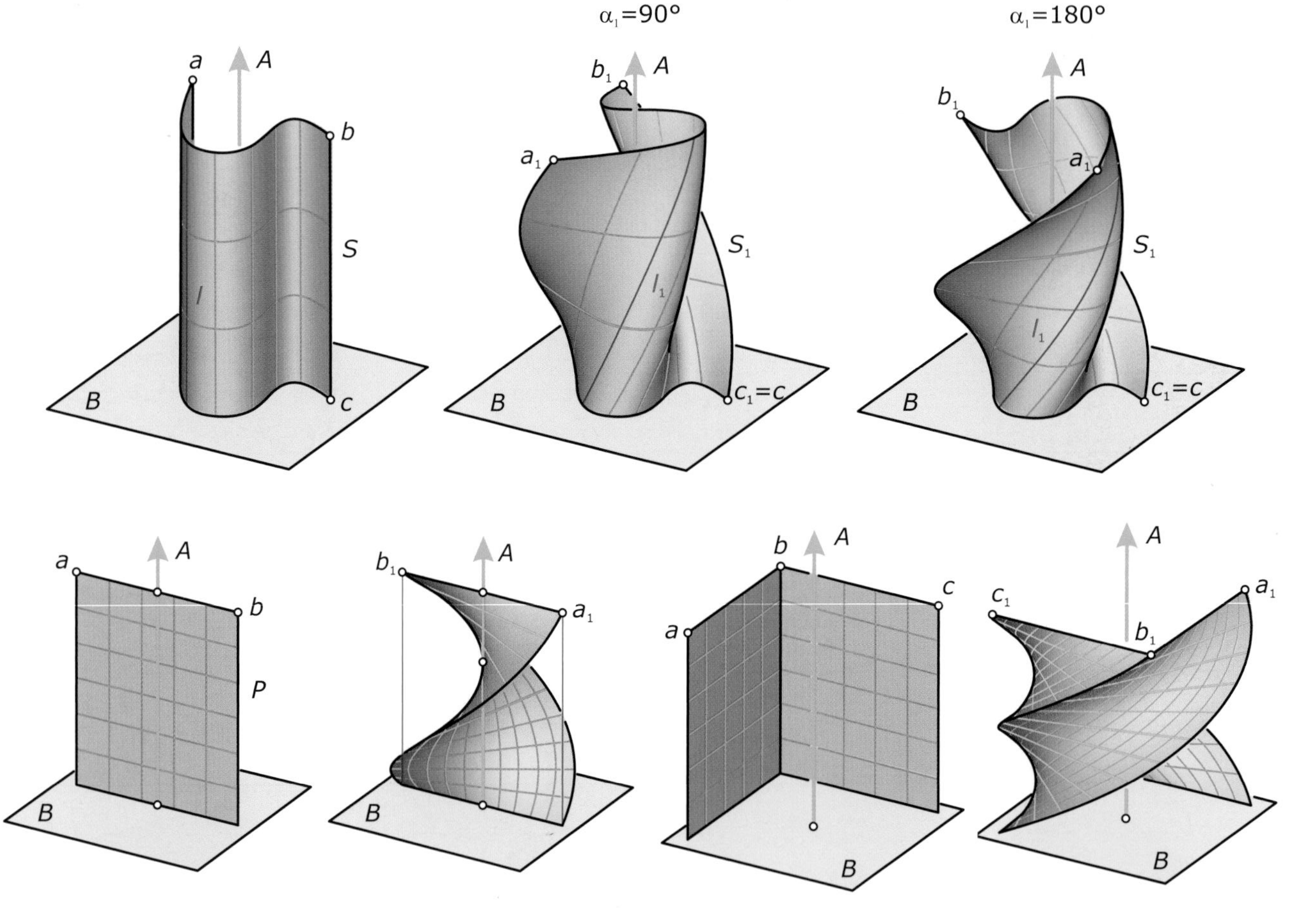

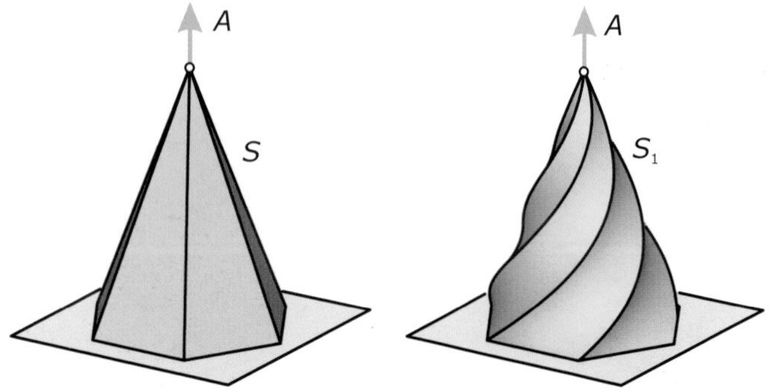

Fig. 13.5
Because the areas of parallel slices and their distance to the bottom are not changed under the twist operation, an object S and its twisted version S_1 enclose the same volume.

Another interesting property of the twist operation is that it *preserves the volume*. By the Cavalieri principle, the volume of an object (solid S) may be obtained by integration of the areas of the slices with respect to the distance z. Because the slices of the original and transformed object are congruent (rotated versions of each other), the areas of the slices agree. Thus, the volume of a solid S and its image S_1 under a twist operation is the same (Figure 13.5). Architecture that can be designed using a twist-like deformation is illustrated in Figure 13.6.

Fig. 13.6
(a) The Turning Torso (2000–2005) in Malmö by Santiago Calatrava.
(b) The Synagogue (2001) in Dresden by Wandel Hoefer Lorch + Hirsch.

(a)

(b)

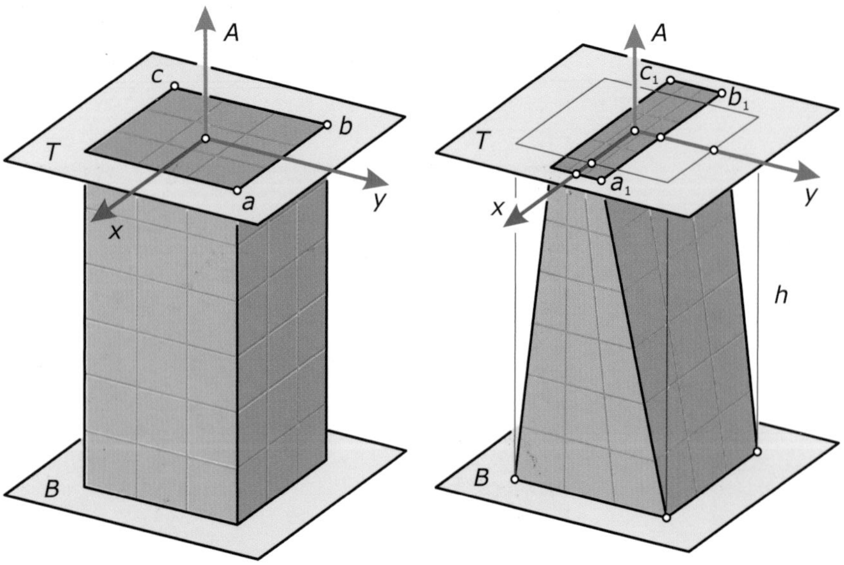

Fig. 13.7
Tapering fixes all points in a plane B and on an axis A, and performs scaling transformations in the planes parallel to B. A further input is the scaling transformation to be applied in the top plane T. The figure shows the image of a quadratic prism. It also shows that straight lines orthogonal or parallel to the taper axis are mapped to straight lines.

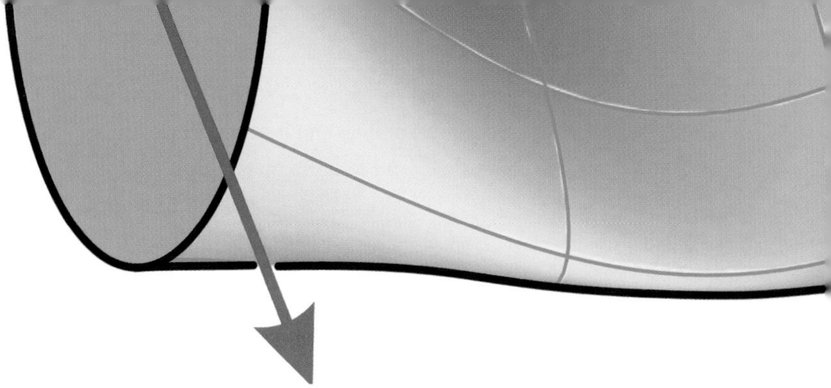

Tapering

We select a reference plane B (say, the bottom plane) and an orthogonal axis A. All points of B and all points of A remain fixed under tapering. One then changes the object by scaling the slices in planes orthogonal to A (i.e., parallel to B). Quite similar to twisting, a further input for the scaling is its action in the top plane T. This requires us to specify two orthogonal scaling directions plus corresponding scaling factors (Figure 13.7). From this input, the scaling factors used for the layers between bottom and top plane are determined automatically.

Math:

To describe the tapering deformation in a precise way, we use a mathematical description and select an adapted Cartesian coordinate system in which A is the z axis and B is the xy-plane. Furthermore, we assume that the scaling directions are parallel to the x- and y-axes, respectively. Hence, in the top plane T [which has the equation $z = h$ (h being the distance between B and T)] the scaling is of the form $x_1 = v{\cdot}x, y_1 = w{\cdot}y$.

Here, we have denoted the user-specified scaling factors in the x and y directions by v and w, respectively. Because the bottom plane remains fixed, we may say it is scaled with factor 1 in both directions. One then uses a linear variation of the scaling factors between bottom and top planes. This means that the scaling factor $v(z)$ for the x direction in height z is equal to

$$v(z) = 1 + z{\cdot}(v - 1)/h.$$

As desired, $v(0) = 1$ and $v(h) = v$. Replacing v with w, we obtain the scaling factor in the y direction. In the plane at height z, the scaling is $x_1 = v(z){\cdot}x, y_1 = w(z){\cdot}y$. Inserting the expressions for the scaling factors, we arrive at the following analytical representation of the tapering operation.

$$x_1 = x + x{\cdot}z{\cdot}(v - 1)/h,$$
$$y_1 = y + y{\cdot}z{\cdot}(w - 1)/h,$$
$$z_1 = z$$

Because we see on the right-hand side terms $x{\cdot}z$ and $y{\cdot}z$, respectively, tapering is not a linear transformation. It is a special quadratic transformation.

The reader is encouraged to discuss the images of planes in a similar way. It is helpful if one views a plane as a set of straight lines and bases the discussion on the images of straight lines (see also Figures 13.7 and 13.8).

Math:

A general straight line l is mapped to a parabola l_1. As an example, take the straight line with the parameterization $x = t, y = t, z = t$. Inserting this into the tapering equations, we obtain the curve parameterization

$$x' = t + t^2\cdot(v - 1)/h, y' = t + t^2\cdot(w - 1)/h, z' = t.$$

Because this parameterization is quadratic in t, the curve is a parabola (recall Chapter 8). More generally, inserting a linear parameterization of a straight line we obtain in general a quadratic parameterization of the image curve and hence a parabola.

Exceptions arise if for all points of a straight line the coordinates x and y are constant (i.e., the line is parallel to the taper axis A) or if z is constant (i.e., the line is orthogonal to the taper axis A). In both of these cases, the terms $x\cdot z$ and $y\cdot z$ only contribute linear terms in t for the image curve. Thus, the image l_1 of a line l that is parallel or orthogonal to the taper axis A is a straight line (see Figure 13.7).

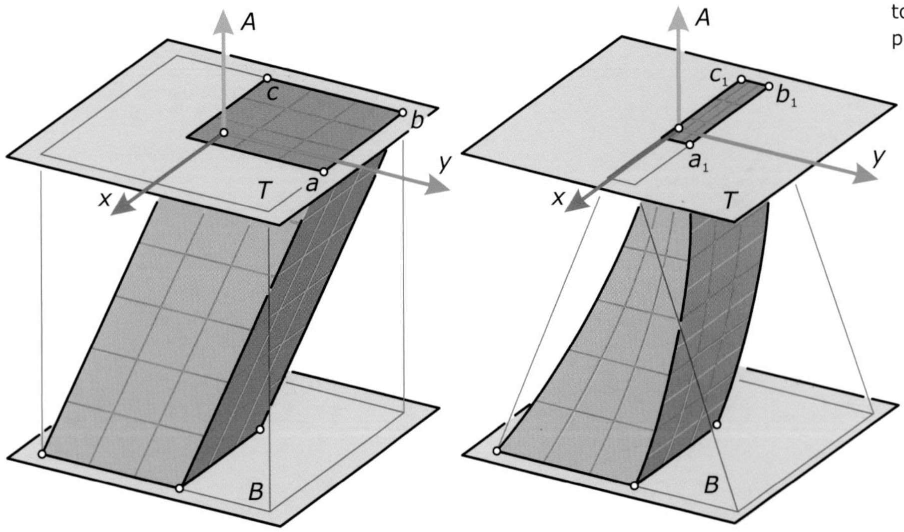

Fig. 13.8
From Figure 13.7 one may erroneously conclude that tapering is a linear transformation. However, this is not the case. Straight lines that are not parallel or normal to the taper axis are mapped to parabolas and only very special planes remain planar.

There are various pretty obvious extensions of tapering, which are illustrated in Figure 13.9. They are actually combinations of the basic tapering operation explained previously. We may classify them by scaling functions v and w, which use different linear functions in certain height intervals. In slices where one switches from one linear function to another, additional edges are created. Figure 13.9b illustrates the scaling function v as a function of the height z for a specific example.

Fig. 13.9
(a) Combinations of the basic tapering operation may be used to obtain effects such as those depicted in this illustration. CAD systems may provide user-friendly ways of handling this type of generalized tapering.

(b) A result of generalized tapering and the corresponding scaling factors v, depending on the height z. We see that $v(z)$ is a piecewise linear function, and therefore the tapered object has edges at those heights where $v(z)$ has corner points.

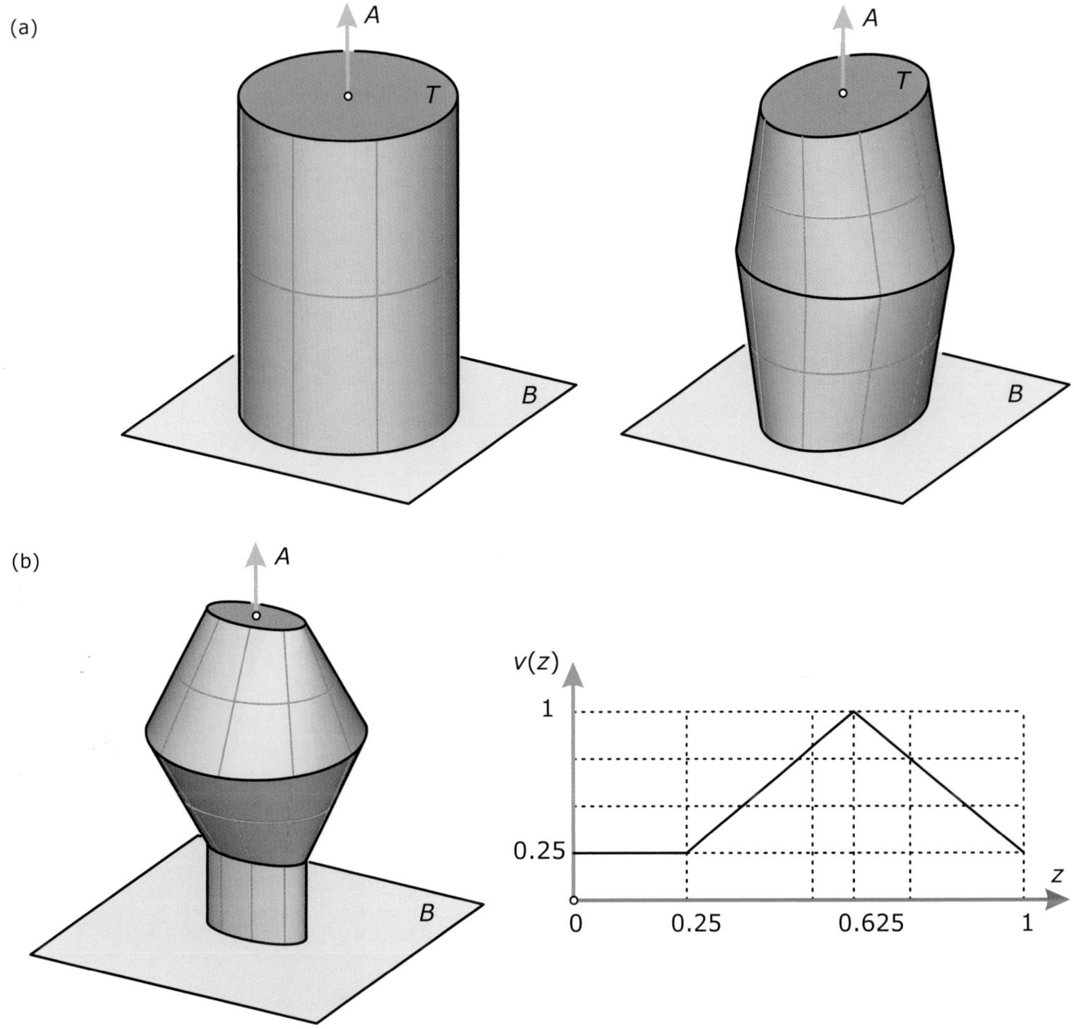

Bulge. If one wants to have thickening or thinning effects without loss of smoothness, one can use a deformation technique sometimes called *bulge*. It works like tapering, but uses smooth scaling functions $v(z)$ and $w(z)$. In the basic type of bulging, quadratic scaling functions are applied. Because a quadratic function is determined if we know its values at three points, one can provide the scaling factors for three heights. Figure 13.10 shows an example in which top and bottom slice remain fixed [i.e., $v(0) = v(h) = 1$, $w(0) = w(h) = 1$)], whereas the middle slice $z = h/2$ is scaled with prescribed factors.

As an exercise, the reader may verify with the mathematical approach provided for tapering that bulge with quadratic scaling functions is a cubic transformation. A straight line parameterized linearly with respect to a parameter t is mapped to a curve with a cubic parameterization in t (contains terms with t, t^2, and t^3). Recall that we have encountered such curves as Bézier curves of degree 3.

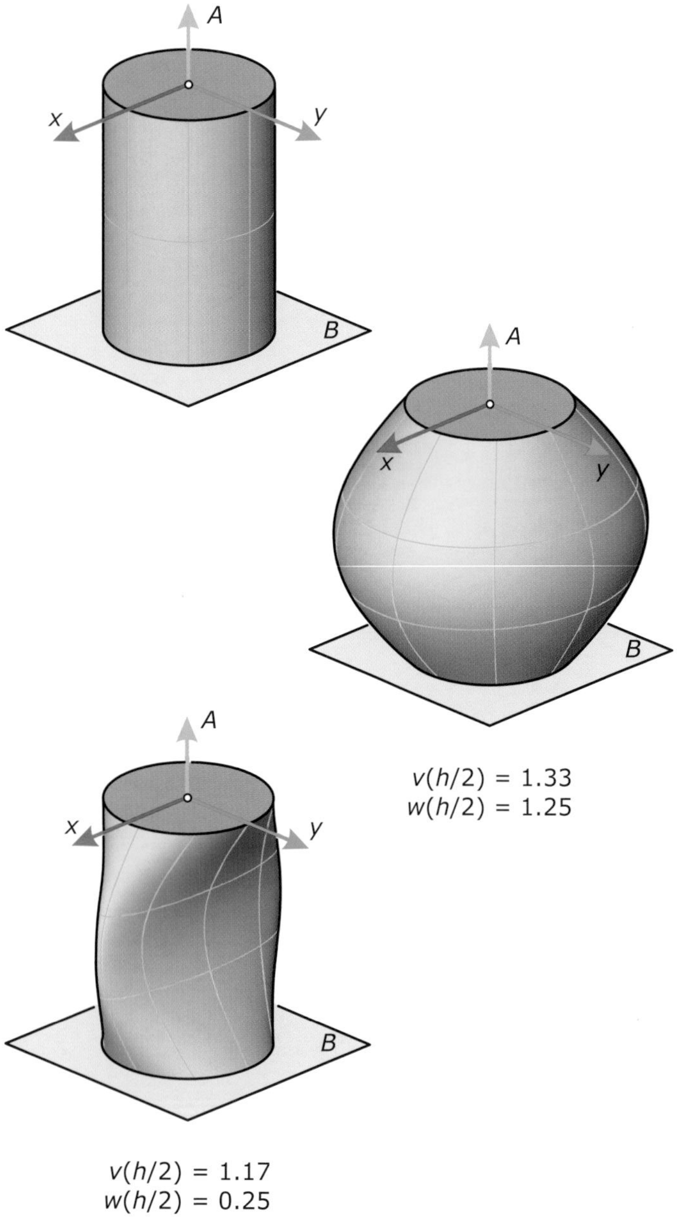

Fig. 13.10
(a) The bulge deformation is based on smooth scaling functions v and w. In this example, the bottom and top slice remain unchanged and the middle slice is scaled with prescribed factors.
(b) The building Le Bureau in Vienna (2004–2005) by Françoise-Hélène Jourda features a bulge.

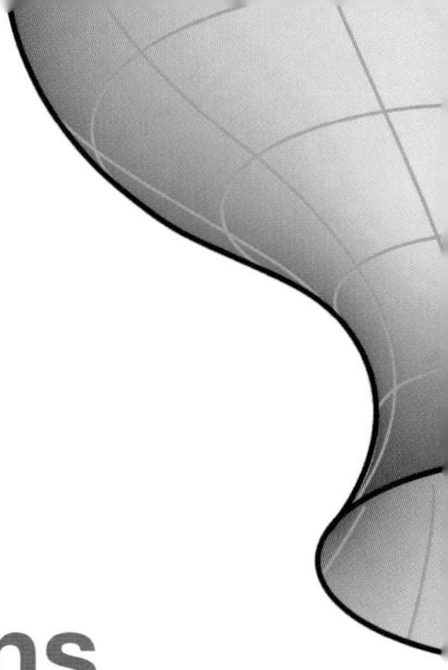

Shear Deformations

Shear deformations are yet another technique of the same family of methods, where slices with parallel planes are transformed within these planes. Twisting rotates the slices. Tapering and bulging scale the slices. Shear deformations apply translations to the slices (Figure 13.11). Because a translation is determined if we know the image point of a single point, one prescribes the image A_1 of the axis A.

The axis is selected orthogonal to a bottom plane B, which remains fixed. Note the following difference to the previously discussed techniques: A shear deformation does not fix the axis but changes it. Moreover, the shear deformation is determined uniquely by the change of the axis.

Fig. 13.11.
A shear deformation applies translations to the slices with parallel planes. These translations are defined by the user-specified image curve A_1 of the axis A.

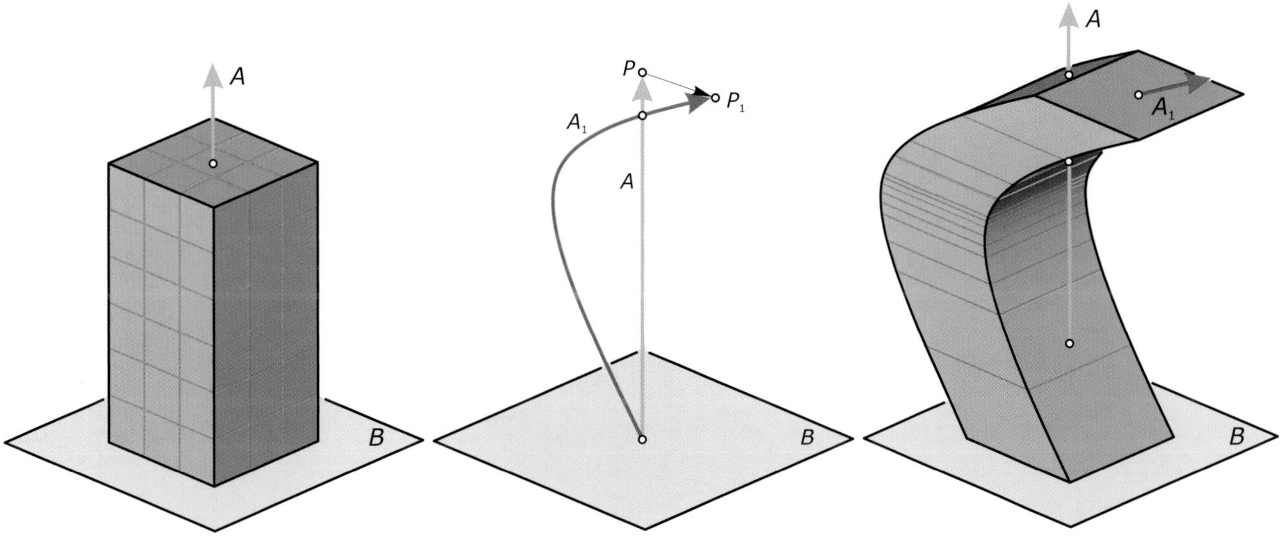

Math:

For a mathematical representation of shear transformations, we use a Cartesian coordinate system in which the *xy*-plane is the bottom plane *B* and where the *z*-axis is the axis *A*. It is natural to use the height *z* as a parameter for the representation of the image curve A_1 of the axis. Hence, we let A_1 be given in the form $(a(z),b(z),z)$.

Functions $a(z)$ and $b(z)$ provide a parameter representation of the top view of A_1. In each height *z*, the translation to be applied to the corresponding slice has the vector $(a(z),b(z),0)$. Because the bottom plane $z = 0$ shall remain fixed, we have $a(0) = b(0) = 0$. We obtain the following representation of a shear deformation.

$$x_1 = x + a(z), y_1 = y + b(z), z_1 = z$$

In the simplest case, we use linear functions $a(z) = c \cdot z$ and $b(z) = d \cdot z$—which implies that the image of the axis *A* is a straight line (through the origin). Then, the representation of the shear transformation is linear in *x,y,z* and is therefore an affine map (recall Chapter 6; see also Figure 13.12). Insertion of quadratic functions $a(z) = c_1 \cdot z + c_2 \cdot z^2$ and $b(z) = d_1 \cdot z + d_2 \cdot z^2$ gives a parabola A_1 as image of the axis *A*. Because the representation of the shear transformation is now quadratic in *z* (linear in *x* and *y*), general straight lines are mapped to parabolas (Figure 13.13). However, straight lines normal to the axis (i.e., in a slicing plane) have constant

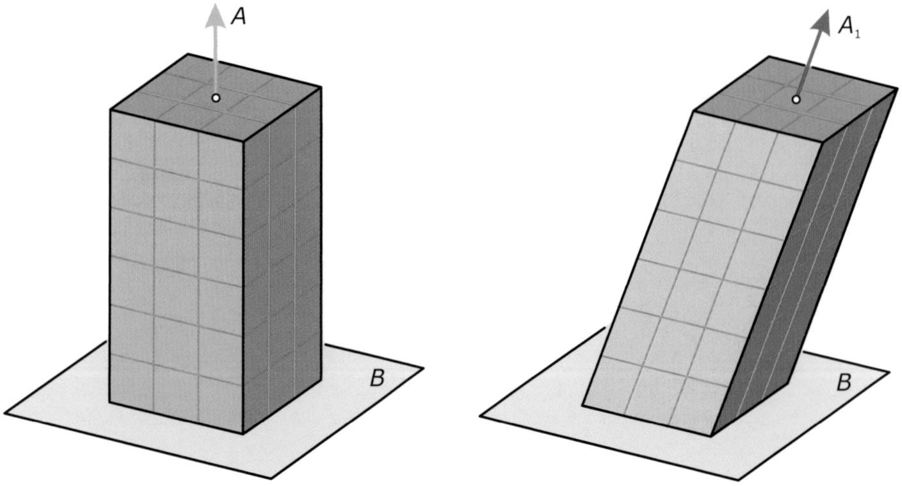

Figure 13.12
A shear deformation for which the image A_1 of the axis *A* is a straight line is an affine map. Thus, in this case straight lines are mapped to straight lines and planes are mapped to planes.

z and are thus mapped to straight lines. This follows also from the fact that in the slicing planes a shear transformation is a translation. A slicing plane remains fixed as a whole (shear performs a translation inside this plane). All other planes P carry only one family of parallel straight lines in slicing planes which remain straight. Any other line in P is mapped to a parabola and thus the image surface P_1 of a general plane P is a parabolic cylinder.

Modeling systems may provide a variety of options for the construction of A_1 and thus for the types of arising shear transformations. Having discussed the simplest cases, it should be easy to understand the others.

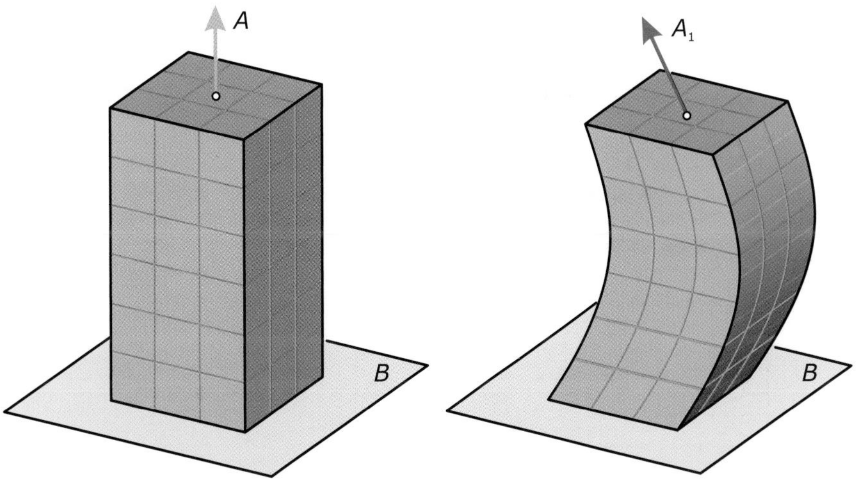

Fig. 13.13
A shear deformation with a parabola A_1 as image of the axis A maps straight lines to parabolas. An obvious exception is given by straight lines in slicing planes (orthogonal to the axis), which remain straight lines. All planes different from slicing planes are therefore mapped to parabolic cylinders.

Shear transformations leave the shape and thus also the area of the slices unchanged. They also preserve the height z of each slice. By Cavalieri's principle, shear transformations are therefore *volume preserving*. The volume of a solid S and its image S_1 are the same (Figure 13.14a). Architecture that may be the result of a shear-like deformation is illustrated in Figure 13.14b.

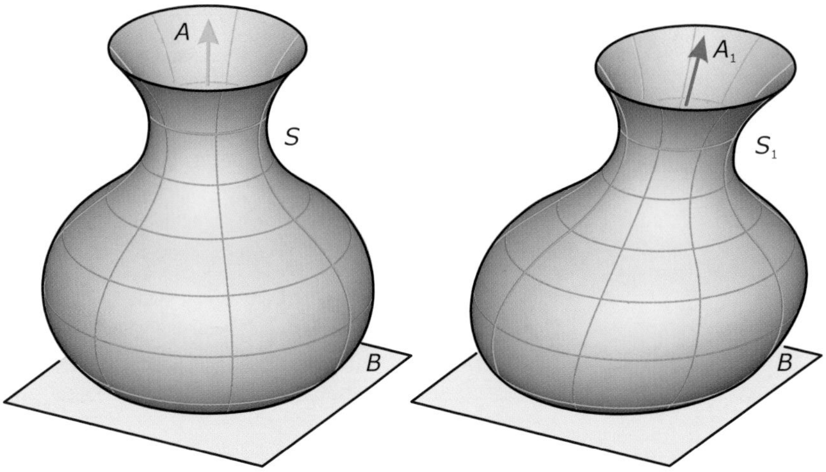

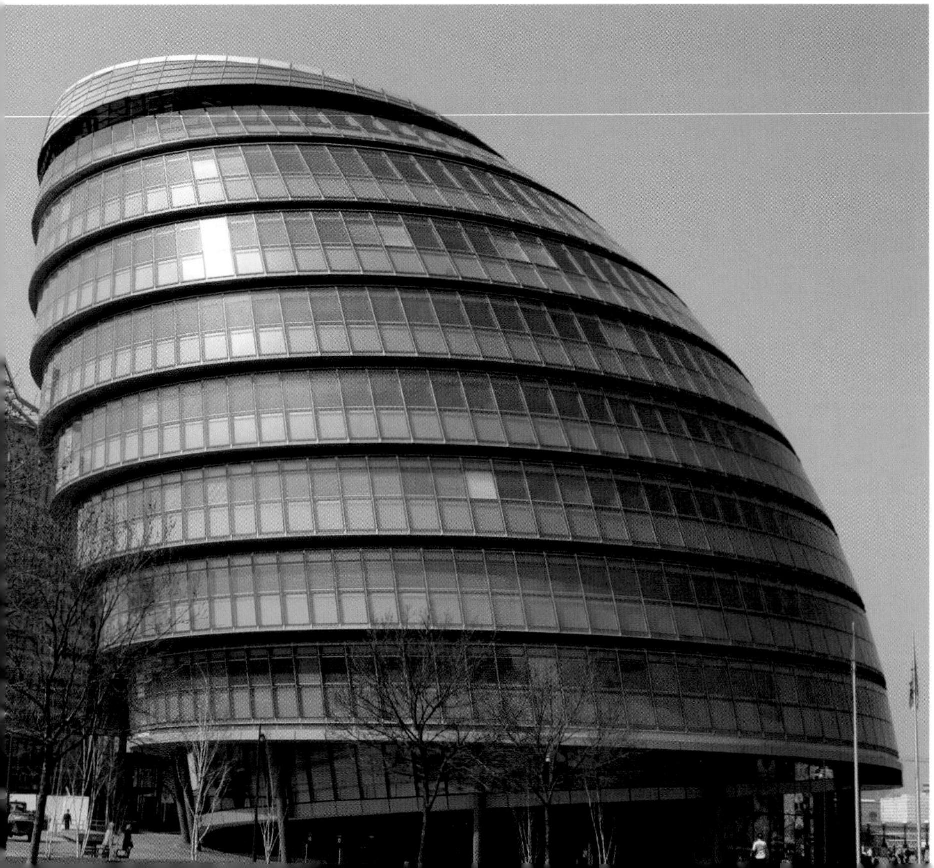

Fig. 13.14
(a) A shear deformation does not change the volume of a solid. These two vases hold the same amount of water.
(b) City Hall (1998–2002) in London by Norman Foster.

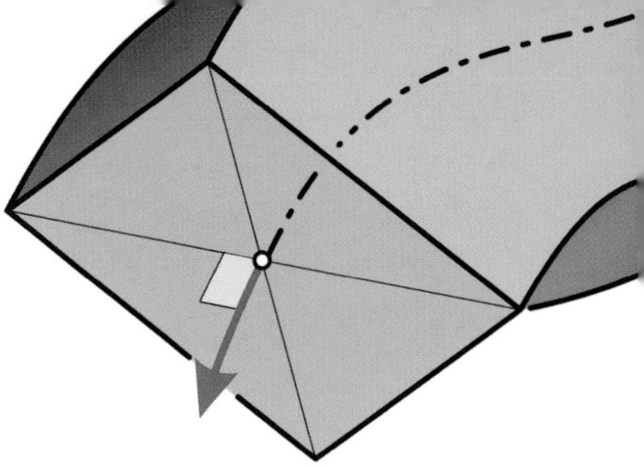

Bending

Some systems may contain the nonlinear shear deformations discussed previously as versions of bending (Parallel option in the menu). In the following we examine bending deformations that also change the orientation of the slices. In an elementary *radial bending* operation, the axis A is mapped to a circle A_1 and the slices are rearranged in planes normal to the circle (see Figure 13.15).

There is some freedom in this construction, even if the circle A_1 is already determined. First, we can select the length of the arc that appears as an image of the axis segment between bottom and top slice. Typically, one selects the axis segment and corresponding circle segment of equal length. Moreover, we have some freedom in the arrangement of the planes because of a possible rotation of each slice about the point on A_1.

Figure 13.15 shows the most common solution to this problem. If A is the z-axis and A_1 lies in the yz-plane, one maps x-parallel lines to x-parallel lines. Thus, radial bending is just a spatial extension of a planar bending deformation in the yz-plane with the aid of x-parallel lines. This is very similar to the extension of a planar motion into a three-dimensional motion, which we have discussed in Chapter 12.

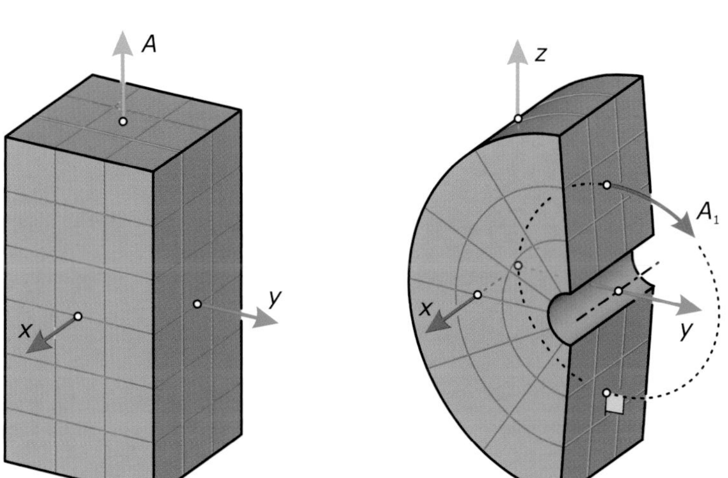

Fig. 13.15
A simple radial bending operation maps the axis A to a circle A_1 and rearranges the slices in planes orthogonal to A_1.

There are also modeling options that change A to a more general curve (e.g., a Bézier curve) and rearrange the slices in planes normal to A_1. The arising freedom of a rotation about A_1 may be resolved as in our discussion of the rotation-minimizing frame (Chapter 12). An example is shown in Figure 13.16.

Fig. 13.16
Bending transformations may map the axis A to a Bézier curve A_1. The slices are automatically rearranged in planes orthogonal to A_1.

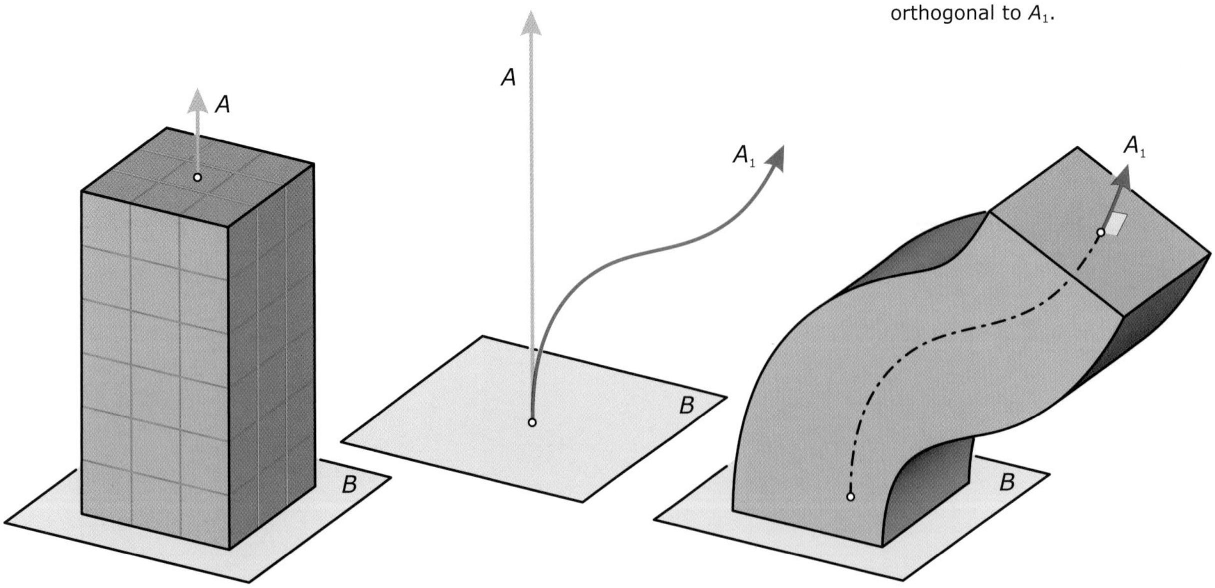

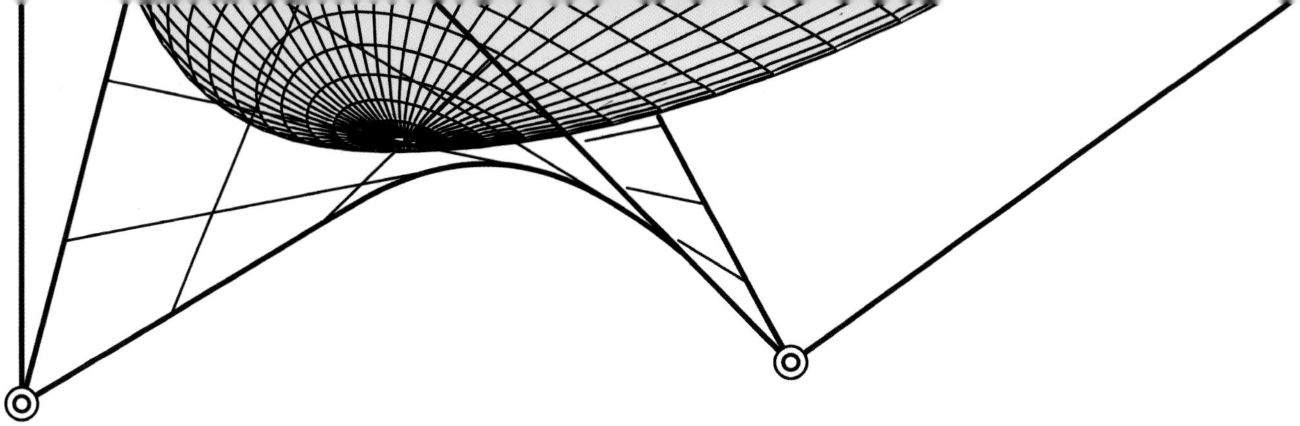

Freeform Deformations

Planar Bézier deformations of degree (1,1). As a preparation for the understanding of Bézier freeform deformations, we consider a Bézier surface patch of degree (1,1) but select its four control points in the same plane (Figure 13.17). The mathematical representation of the patch is given by

$$b(u,v) = (1-u)(1-v)b_{00} + (1-u)vb_{01} + u(1-v)b_{10} + uvb_{11}.$$

Here, b_{00}, b_{01}, b_{10}, and b_{11} are the coordinate vectors of the four control points. We assume that these four control points form the vertices of a convex quadrangle. We may understand the planar surface patch as an image of the parameter square in the uv-plane.

Fig. 13.17
A planar deformation of a square region may be performed with the aid of a Bézier map of degree (1,1) . This bilinear map is guided with the aid of four control points.

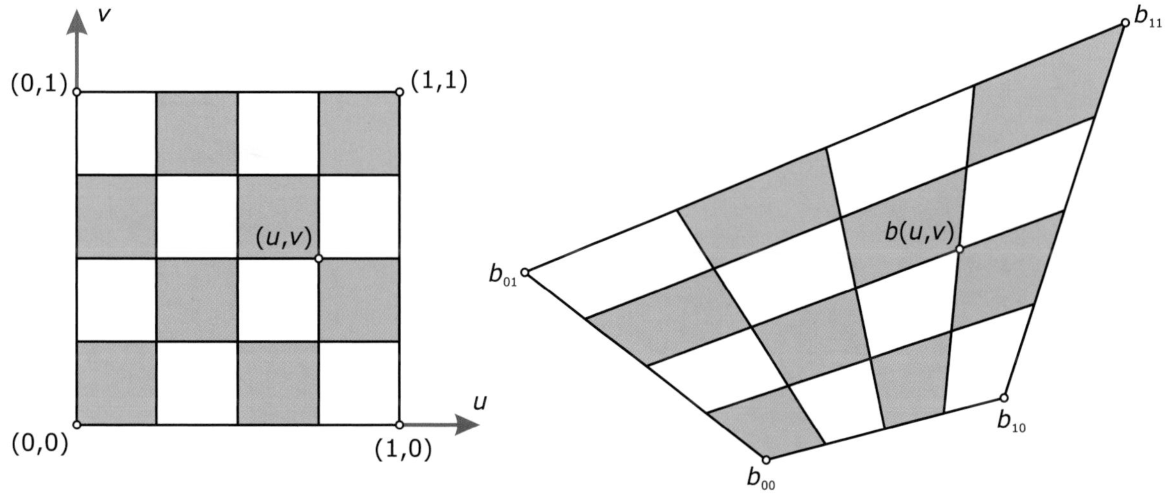

Recall that both parameters u and v are in the interval $[0,1]$ and therefore any pair of admissible parameters (u,v) describes a point in the parameter square. Hence, we have a deformation of the square into a region bounded by a quadrangle. To obtain a representation that looks more similar to those used previously, we may write (x,y) instead of (u,v) and write (x_1,y_1) instead of $b(u,v)$. It is more convenient to summarize the two equations for the coordinates into a single vector equation:

$$(x_1,y_1) = (1-x)(1-y)b_{00} + (1-x)yb_{01} + x(1-y)b_{10} + xyb_{11}.$$

We call this mapping *bilinear* because both x and y appear only linearly. However, because we have products $x{\cdot}y$ the mapping is not linear. In fact, it is quadratic. Straight lines are in general mapped to parabolas, exceptions being x-parallel or y-parallel lines whose images are straight lines as well (Figure 13.18). For a proof of this claim, one simply need note that a straight line l has a linear parameterization in t that results in a quadratic parameterization of the image curve l_1.

We have chosen a simple case of a Bézier surface to illustrate its use for planar deformations. It is rather straightforward to extend the idea to higher degrees. This is examined in the following in regard to three-dimensional maps.

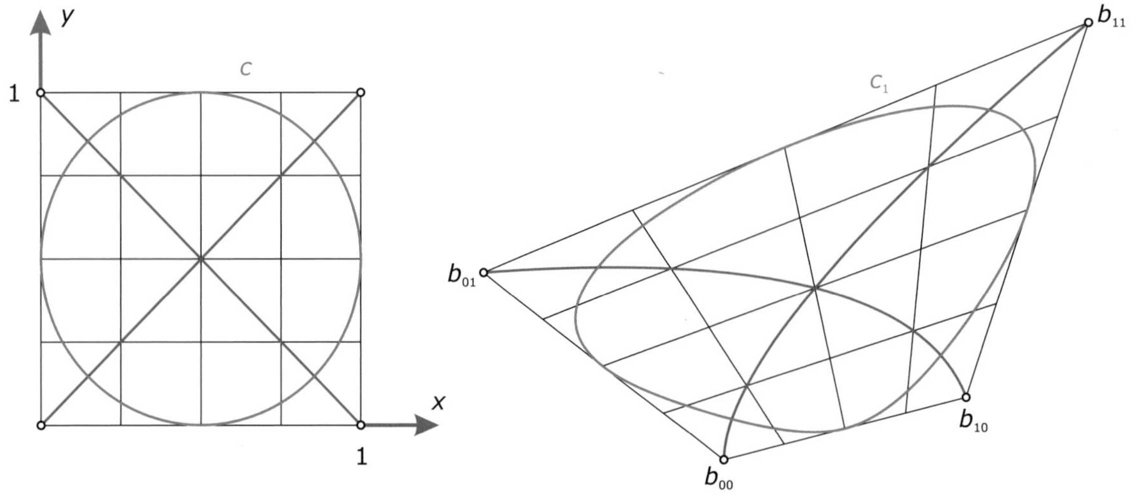

Fig. 13.18
A planar Bézier deformation of degree (1,1) is a bilinear map. Lines parallel to the x and y axes are mapped to straight lines. The images of general lines are parabolas. The figure also shows a circle c and its image curve c_1, which is not a circle (also not a conic).

Bézier deformations of degree (1,1,1). In a totally analogous way to the two-dimensional case, we can study Bézier deformations in three dimensions. Again, we start with the simplest case; namely, degree (1,1,1)—illustrated in Figure 13.19. As in the familiar two-dimensional case, we have an algorithm of de Casteljau for the construction of the image point p_1 of a given point p in the parameter domain. The parameter domain is usually assumed to be a cube.

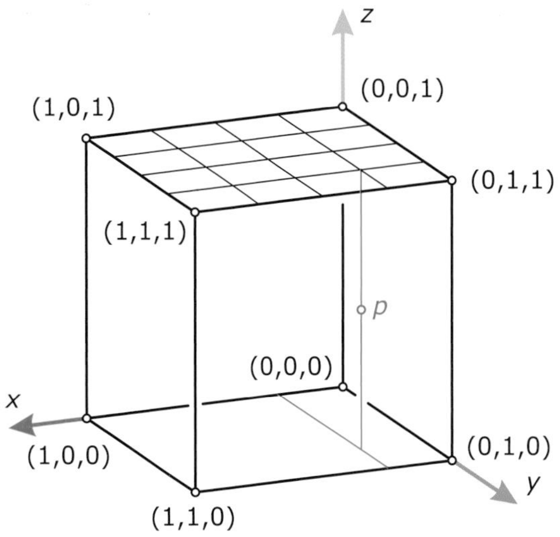

Fig. 13.19
A Bézier deformation of degree (1,1,1) deforms a cube S into a solid S_1 bounded by Bézier surfaces of degree (1,1); that is, hyperbolic paraboloids (or planes). Lines parallel to the edges of S are mapped to straight lines and ratios of points are preserved on them. This enables us to construct the image point p_1 of a given point p via a transfer of ratios (extension of the algorithm of de Casteljau).

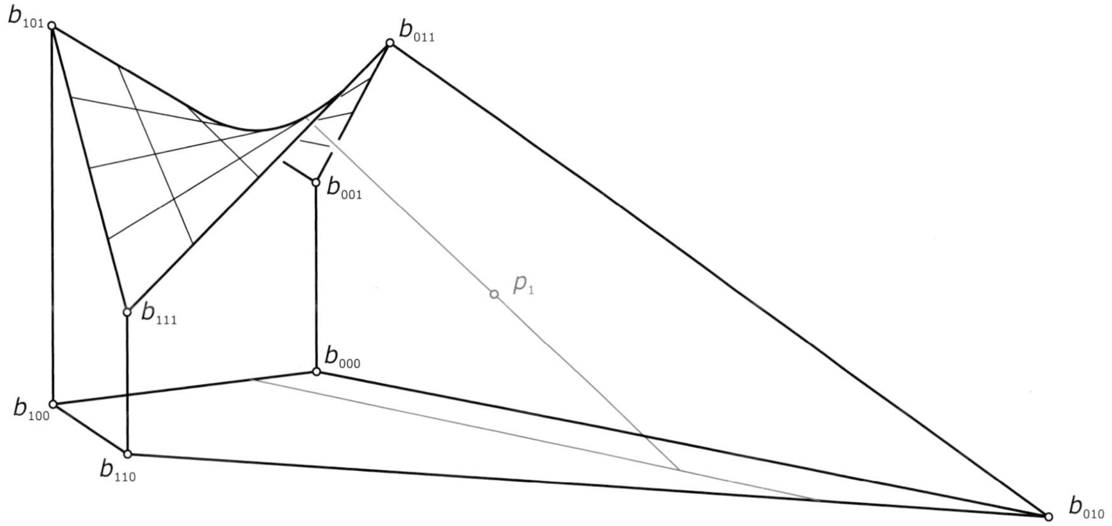

Math:

A mathematical description is based on the algorithm of de Casteljau and is totally analogous to the surface case discussed in Chapter 11. Using triple indices for the eight control points $b_{000},\dots,b_{111}$, we obtain the following representation of the mapping.

$$(x_1,y_1,z_1) = (1-x)(1-y)(1-z)b_{000} + (1-x)(1-y)zb_{001} + (1-x)y(1-z)b_{010} + (1-x)yzb_{011} + x(1-y)(1-z)b_{100} + x(1-y)zb_{101} + xy(1-z)b_{110} + xyzb_{111}$$

This is easy to remember because a factor $(1-x)$ implies a first index 0 of the corresponding control point and a factor x implies first index 1. Likewise, $(1-y)$ and y yield a second index 0 and 1, respectively. Finally, $(1-z)$ and z belong to third index 0 and 1, respectively.

The mapping is called trilinear because all variables x,y,z appear linearly but we also have the products $x\cdot y$, $x\cdot z$, $y\cdot z$, and $x\cdot y\cdot z$.

Fig. 13.20
The image of a straight line g under a Bézier map of degree (1,1,1) is in general a cubic curve g_1. A straight line h parallel to a coordinate plane but not parallel to a coordinate axis is mapped to a parabola. The figure also shows the image surface P_1 of a general plane P and the image surface S_1 of a sphere S.

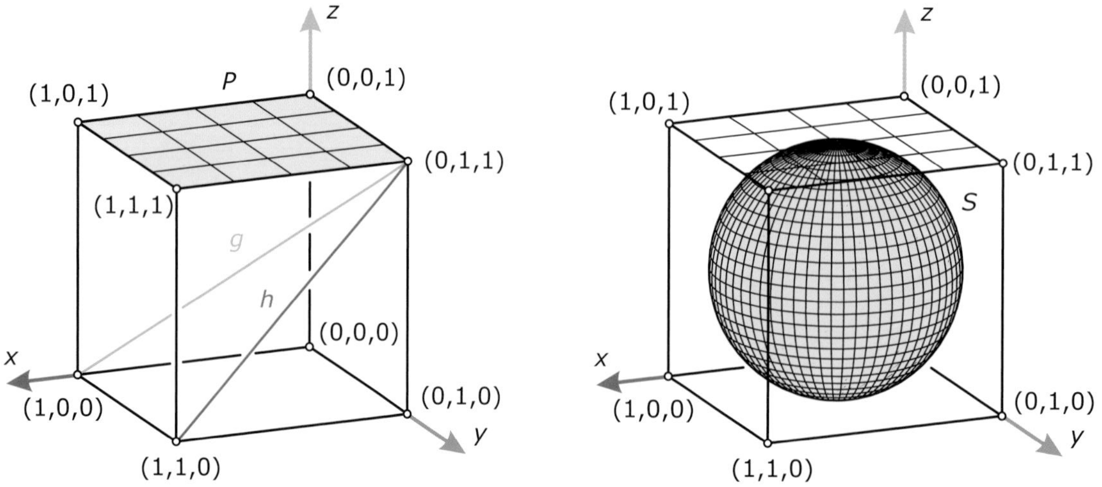

Properties of these trilinear maps follow easily from their analytic representation. Straight lines parallel to a coordinate direction are mapped to straight lines. Planes parallel to a coordinate plane (e.g., the faces of the parameter cube) are mapped in a bilinear way [i.e., their image is in general a hyperbolic paraboloid (Figure 13.19)]. In accordance, straight lines parallel to only one coordinate plane are mapped to parabolas. General straight lines g are mapped to cubic curves g_1 (Figure 13.20).

This is proved by taking a parameterization $(x,y,z) = (a_1 + a_2t, b_1 + b_2t, c_1 + c_2t)$ of g and inserting it into the representation of the trilinear map. Obviously, the resulting parameterization (x_1,y_1,z_1) of the image curve g_1 is cubic in t—which means that the highest-order terms in t are t^3 terms.

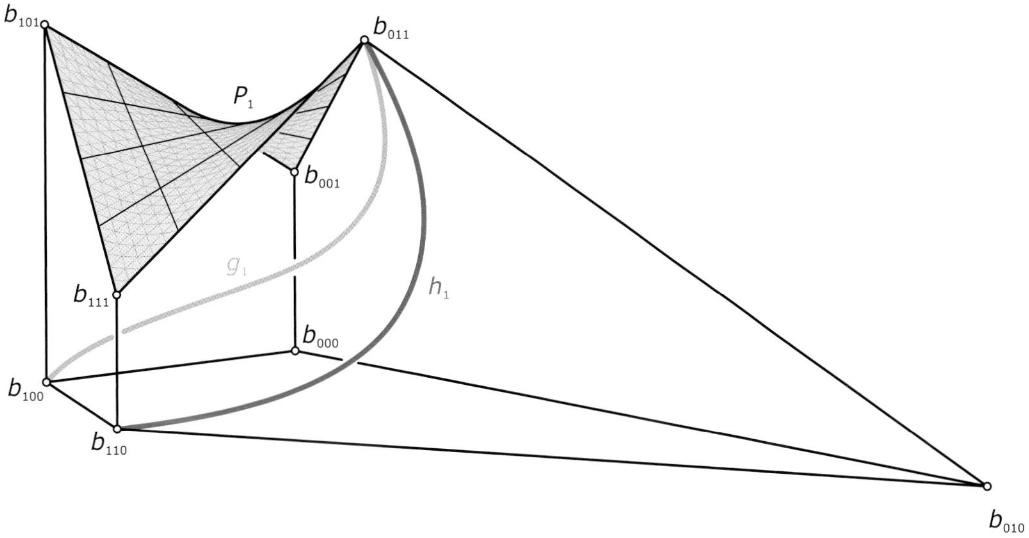

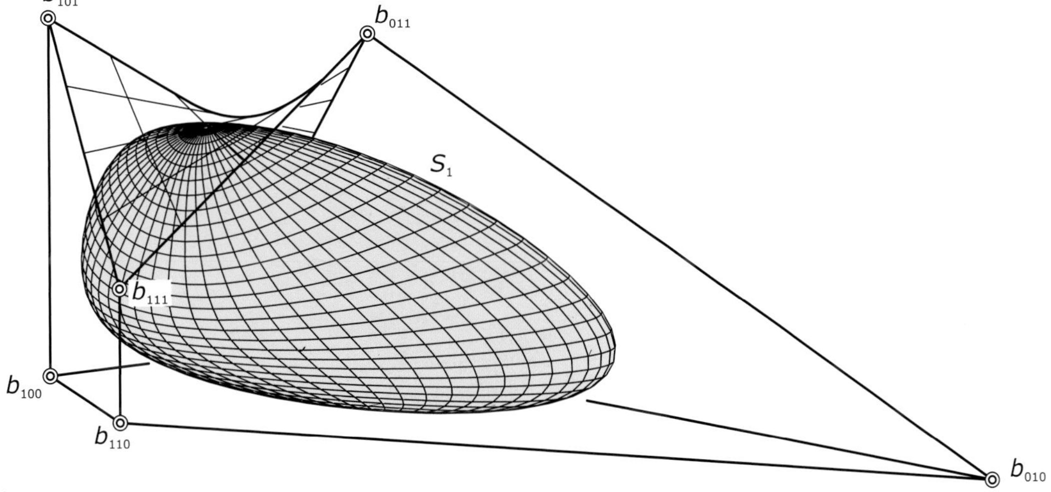

We can also use Bézier deformations of higher degree. Note that we can prescribe three degrees, corresponding to the x, y, and z directions. If these degrees are p, q, and r, respectively, we have to prescribe $(p+1)\cdot(q+1)\cdot(r+1)$ control points. Examples are shown in Figure 13.21.

Sometimes, one uses a parameter cuboid instead of a cube and represents this cuboid with the aid of regularly arranged control points (according to the degree). The new positions of the control points may then more easily be associated with the desired changes of the geometry (Figure 13.21). One may also use B-spline representations for freeform deformations.

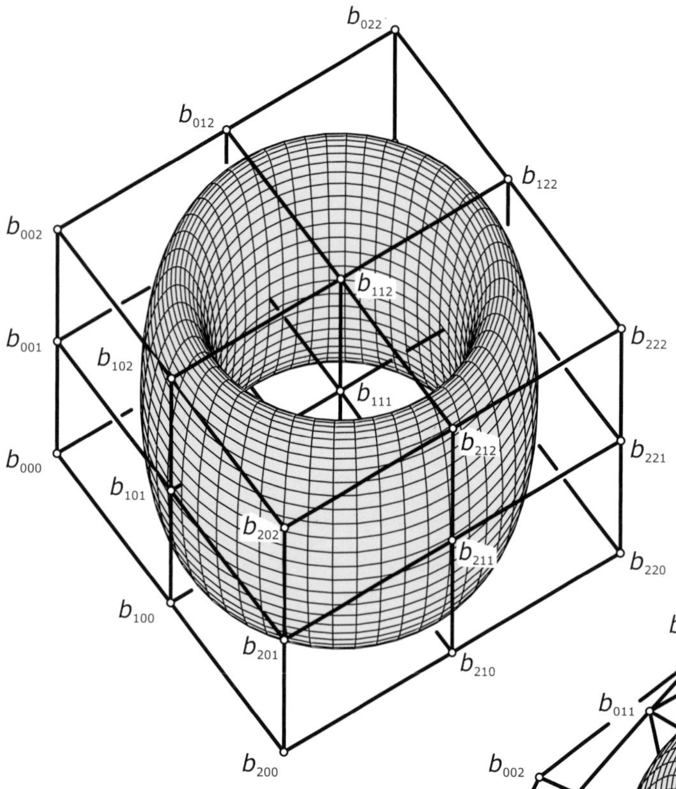

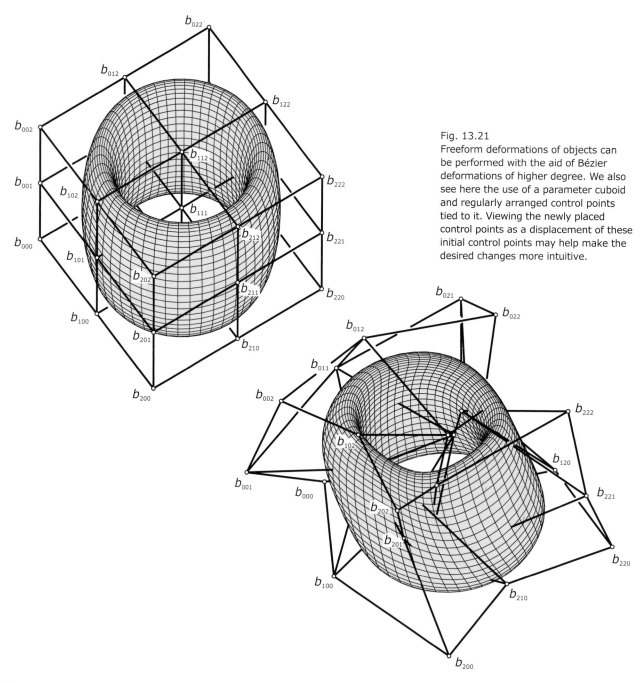

Fig. 13.21
Freeform deformations of objects can be performed with the aid of Bézier deformations of higher degree. We also see here the use of a parameter cuboid and regularly arranged control points tied to it. Viewing the newly placed control points as a displacement of these initial control points may help make the desired changes more intuitive.

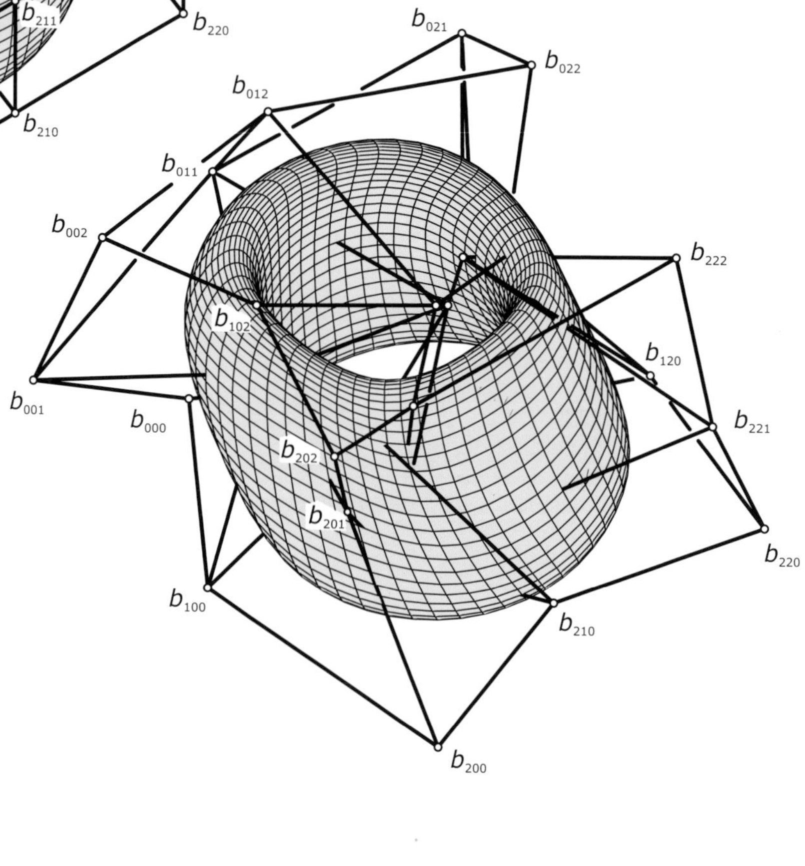

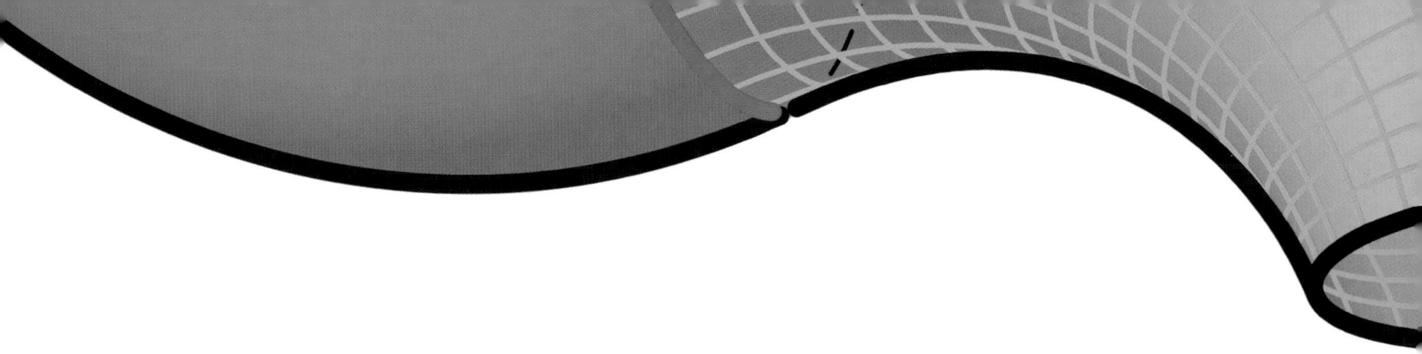

Inversions

In Chapter 5 we encountered the inversion at a circle with center o and radius r. A point p is mapped to a point p_1 on the line op such that the product of distances op and op_1 equals r^2. Using the same definition in three dimensions, we obtain the *inversion with respect to a sphere* S. Selecting the sphere center as the origin of a Cartesian coordinate system, the inversion has the representation

$$x_1 = r^2 \cdot x/(x^2 + y^2 + z^2),$$

$$y_1 = r^2 \cdot y/(x^2 + y^2 + z^2),$$

$$z_1 = r^2 \cdot z/(x^2 + y^2 + z^2).$$

As a control of this equation, we note that the distance of $p = (x,y,z)$ from the origin equals $\sqrt{x^2+y^2+z^2}$. The origin distance of $p_1 = (x_1,y_1,z_1)$ is equal to $\sqrt{x_1^2+y_1^2+z_1^2} = r^2/\sqrt{x^2+y^2+z^2}$, and thus the product of the two distances is r^2. Moreover, the vector p_1 is a multiple of p and therefore the two points p and p_1 lie on a line through o. Note that applying an inversion twice results in the original.

This is the same as for a reflection, and thus one also calls the inversion a *reflection at a sphere*. Many properties of inversions in three dimensions can be deduced from properties of the inversion in two dimensions. This follows from the fact that a spatial inversion acts in each plane through the center o like an inversion in this plane. Therefore, the image of a general straight line is a circle (Figure 13.22)—whereas any straight line through o is of course mapped onto itself.

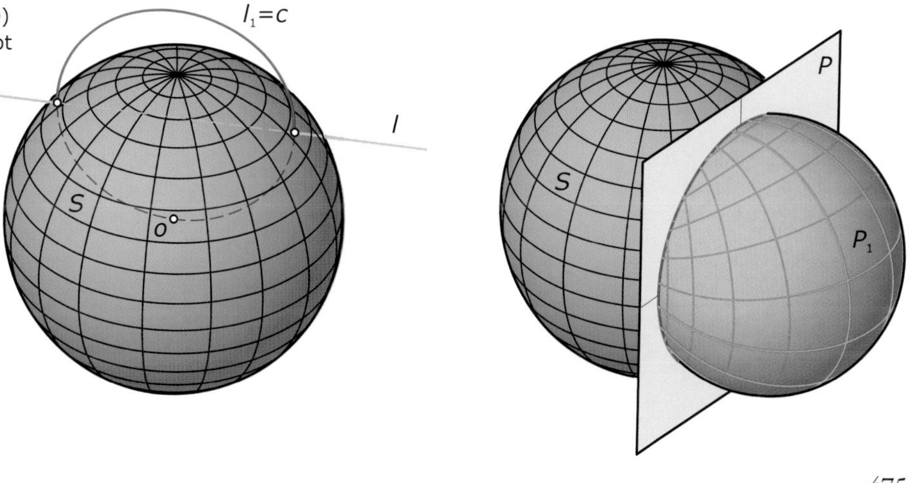

Fig. 13.22
The inversion with respect to a sphere maps
(a) straight lines to circles through the center o and
(b) planes P to spheres P_1 through o. Spheres (which do not pass through o) are mapped to spheres and circles (not through o) are mapped to circles.

The image of a plane (not through o) is a sphere through o. Applying the inversion again, we see that spheres through o are mapped to planes. Other spheres are transformed to spheres. A general circle c can be defined as the intersection curve of two spheres A, B. Therefore, the image c_1 is also the intersection of two spheres A_1, B_1 and is thus a circle.

Inversions are *conformal mappings*. This means that they preserve the intersection angles between curves and surfaces, respectively. As a first example, we consider the basic sphere S and another sphere A that intersects S along a circle c at a right angle. The inversion fixes S and c and maps A to a sphere that intersects S at a right angle. There is only one sphere that intersects S along c at a right angle and this is A. Hence, spheres that intersect the base sphere S at a right angle are mapped onto themselves. However, points outside S are mapped to points inside S, and vice versa (Figure 13.23). A further example of the angle-preserving property of the inversion is shown in Figure 13.24. In particular, Figure 13.25 illustrates that the *stereographic projection* may be obtained by restricting an inversion to a sphere through the inversion center o. Since the inversion preserves angles, the same holds for the stereographic projection.

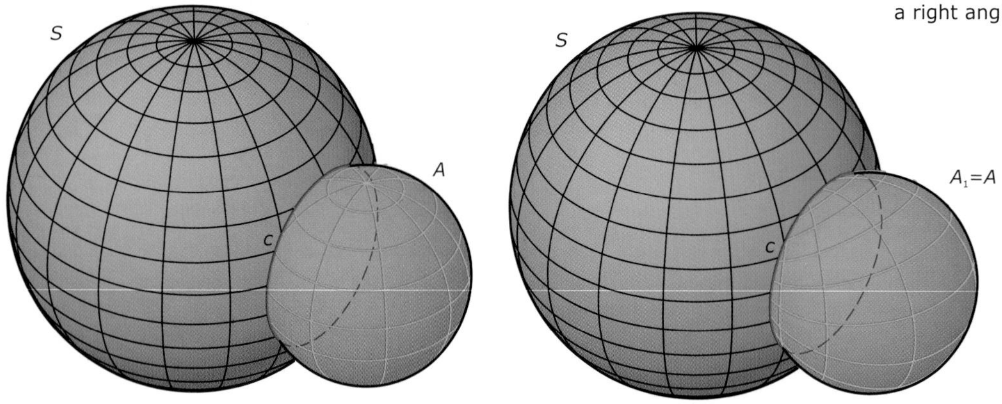

Fig. 13.23
An inversion with respect to a sphere S maps any sphere A that intersects S at a right angle onto itself.

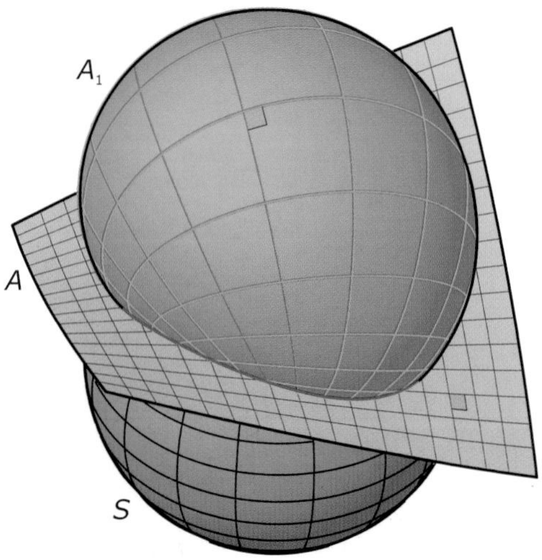

Fig. 13.24
Inversions do not change intersection angles between curves or surfaces. For example, an orthogonal curve network on a surface A is mapped to an orthogonal curve network on a surface A_1.

Any (differentiable) function $f(z)$ of one complex variable $z = x + iy$ defines a conformal (angle-preserving) mapping of the plane (see Chapter 5). In space, there are far fewer conformal mappings. The French mathematician Joseph Liouville (1809–1882) proved that a conformal mapping in three-dimensional space must be a Möbius transformation, which is either a similarity or the composition of a similarity and an inversion.

As a further example of the use of inversions, we apply an inversion to a torus—in this case, a ring torus T (Figure 13.26). The image surface is called a *Dupin cyclide* T_1. Some important properties of the Dupin cyclide follow easily from properties of the torus and inversions. A ring torus is the envelope of two families of spheres. One family of spheres is centered on the axis and has variable radius. The other family of inscribed spheres is centered on a circle and has constant radius. The inversion does not keep the constancy of the radius and does not map the center of a sphere to the center of the image sphere. However, spheres are mapped to spheres and thus the Dupin cyclide T_1 is the envelope of two families of spheres.

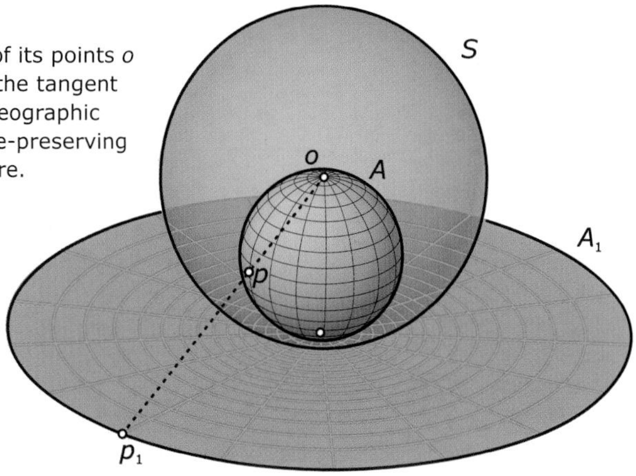

Fig. 13.25
An important example for the angle-preserving property of the inversion is obtained by its restriction to a sphere through o. This results in the *stereographic projection*, a projection of a sphere A from one of its points o to a plane A_1 parallel to the tangent plane of A at o. The stereographic projection provides angle-preserving planar maps of the sphere.

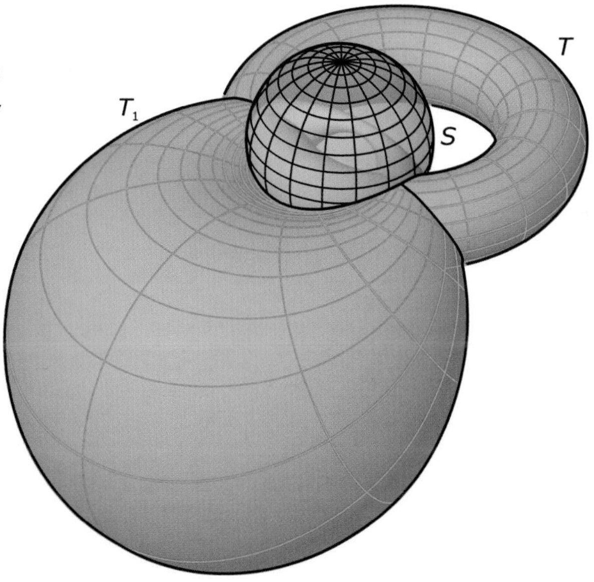

Fig. 13.26
An inversion maps a ring torus T to a Dupin cyclide T_1. Like the ring torus, the Dupin cyclide carries two families of circles. Along each of these circles, T_1 is tangent to a sphere. Therefore, T_1 is also a *double canal surface* (the envelope of two families of spheres).

Remarks on envelopes of spheres. As we have seen, a Dupin cyclide can be generated in two ways as the envelope of a family of spheres. Let's examine those surfaces C that can be defined as envelopes of a family of spheres. These surfaces are called *canal surfaces*. We consider the family of spheres $S(t)$ depending on some parameter t, which may be viewed as time. The sphere $S(t)$ to some time instance t has a center $m(t)$ and radius $r(t)$.

The locus of sphere midpoints $m(t)$ is called the *spine curve m* of the canal surface C. The radius $r(t)$ can vary with time t. If we take two spheres $S(t)$ and $S(t + h)$ to two close time instances t and $t + h$, they intersect in a circle k^* (see Figure 13.27). The rotational axis of k^* is the connecting line of the sphere centers $m(t)$ and $m(t + h)$. If we let h tend toward zero, the sphere $S(t + h)$ tends toward $S(t)$. The intersection circle k^* of the two spheres tends toward a circle $k(t)$, along which $S(t)$ touches the canal surface C.

The axis of k^* (a chord of the spine curve m) converges toward the tangent of m at $m(t)$. Thus, the axis $A(t)$ of $k(t)$ is the tangent of the spine curve at $m(t)$ (see Figure 13.27). In general, $k(t)$ is not a great circle of $S(t)$ and thus the centers of $k(t)$ and $S(t)$ are different.

If, however, the radius r is constant we obtain a *pipe surface C* as an envelope (see Chapter 9). Then, each inscribed sphere $S(t)$ is tangent to the pipe surface C along a great circle $k(t)$ of $S(t)$. Its axis is tangent to the spine curve at $m(t)$. This means that $k(t)$ lies in the normal plane of the spine curve at $m(t)$ (see Chapter 10). Another special type of canal surfaces are those with a straight line as spine curve m. These surfaces are obviously rotational surfaces with rotational axis m.

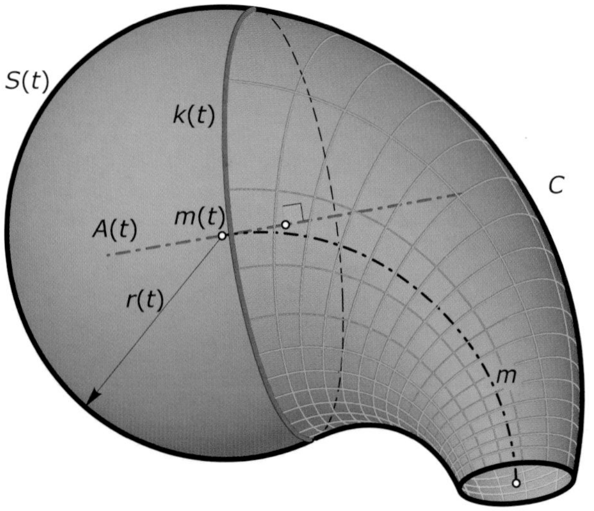

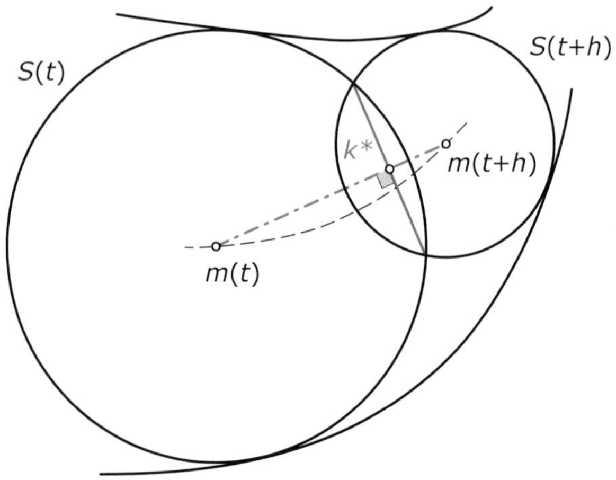

Fig. 13.27
A canal surface C is the envelope of a family of spheres. The locus of the midpoints of the spheres is a curve m. The radius r of the spheres is in general not constant. Each of these spheres $S(t)$ touches the surface along a circle $k(t)$, which is in general a small circle on S. The rotational axis $A(t)$ of the circle $k(t)$ is the tangent of the curve m at the center $m(t)$ of $S(t)$.

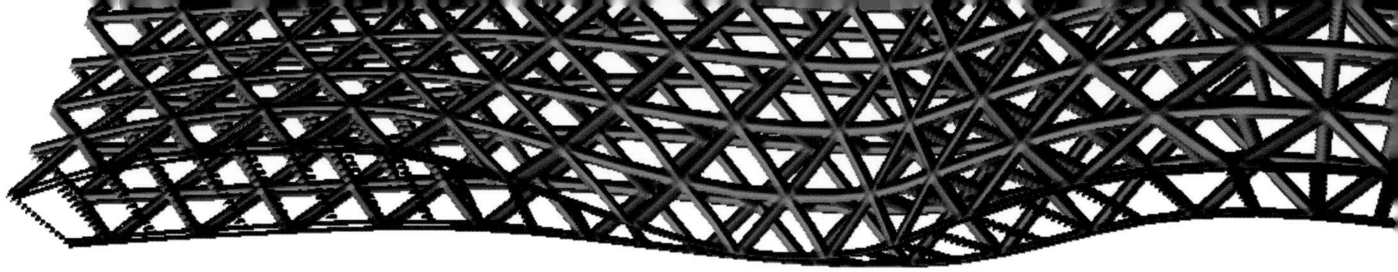

Three-Dimensional Textures

The generation of three-dimensional textures is closely related to certain deformations and thus it seems appropriate to briefly discuss them here. A familiar technique for the mapping of three-dimensional textures onto a smooth surface works as follows (see Figure 13.28). One views a three-dimensional texture as a topographic surface [i.e., the graph surface of a height field, which associates to each point p_1 of a surface S_1 a height $h(p_1)$ of the texture].

This height is measured along the surface normal at p_1. For the definition of the shape of the three-dimensional texture, we may use a height field defined over a plane S. Its shape is provided by the user. Then, the program (perhaps supported by some user input) defines an appropriate mapping of the plane S to the surface S_1 and carries over the heights. For a point p in the plane, we know its height $h(p)$ and use the same height as height $h(p_1)$ of the image point p_1 on the surface S_1.

Fig. 13.28
A three-dimensional texture may be added to a surface S_1 with the aid of a mapping between a plane S and S_1. Given the texture over the plane, the mapping is used for a transfer of the three-dimensional texture from S to S_1 via equal distances (heights h) above the base surfaces S and S_1, respectively.

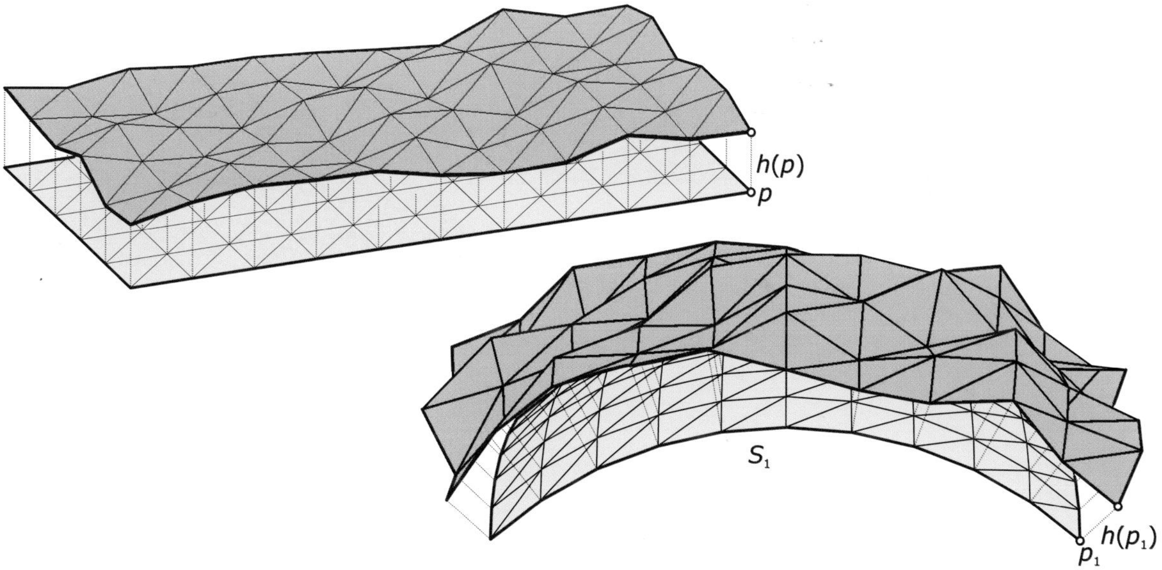

It is not really necessary that the original texture be a height field above the plane. We may use the normal-based mapping to define a *deformation* of a layer around the plane to a layer around the surface S_1. This deformation is then used to map a texture associated with S to a texture added to S_1. Figure 13.29 shows examples of three-dimensional textures created by an algorithm based on this principle.

Remark. A normal-based deformation maps a plane parallel to S (say, at distance d to S) to an offset surface of S_1 at distance d. We know already from Chapter 10 that offsets may have self-intersections. They arise from a *self-collision* of the normal-based deformation. It is clear that similar effects may occur for three-dimensional texture generation, especially if the texture goes too far away from the underlying surface S. Figure 13.30 illustrates this phenomenon—for the purposes of clarity and simplicity in regard to a two-dimensional equivalent.

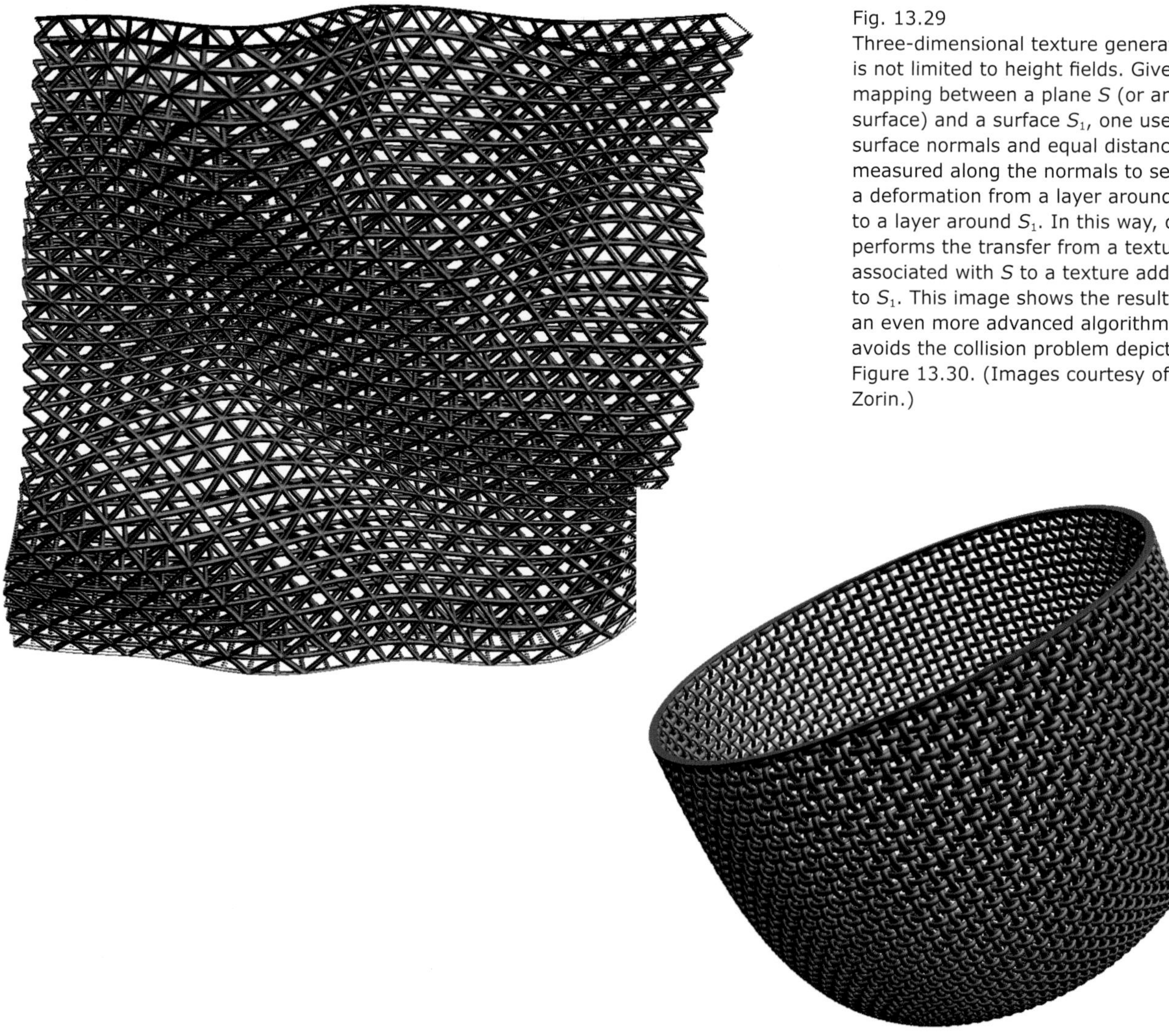

Fig. 13.29
Three-dimensional texture generation is not limited to height fields. Given a mapping between a plane S (or another surface) and a surface S_1, one uses the surface normals and equal distances measured along the normals to set up a deformation from a layer around S to a layer around S_1. In this way, one performs the transfer from a texture associated with S to a texture added to S_1. This image shows the result of an even more advanced algorithm that avoids the collision problem depicted in Figure 13.30. (Images courtesy of D. Zorin.)

Fig. 13.30
Normal-based three-dimensional texture mapping may create undesirable self-intersections of the texture to be added. This results from a self-collision of the normal-based deformation, which is illustrated here for the two-dimensional case. Such self-collisions may also happen for many of the three-dimensional deformations discussed.

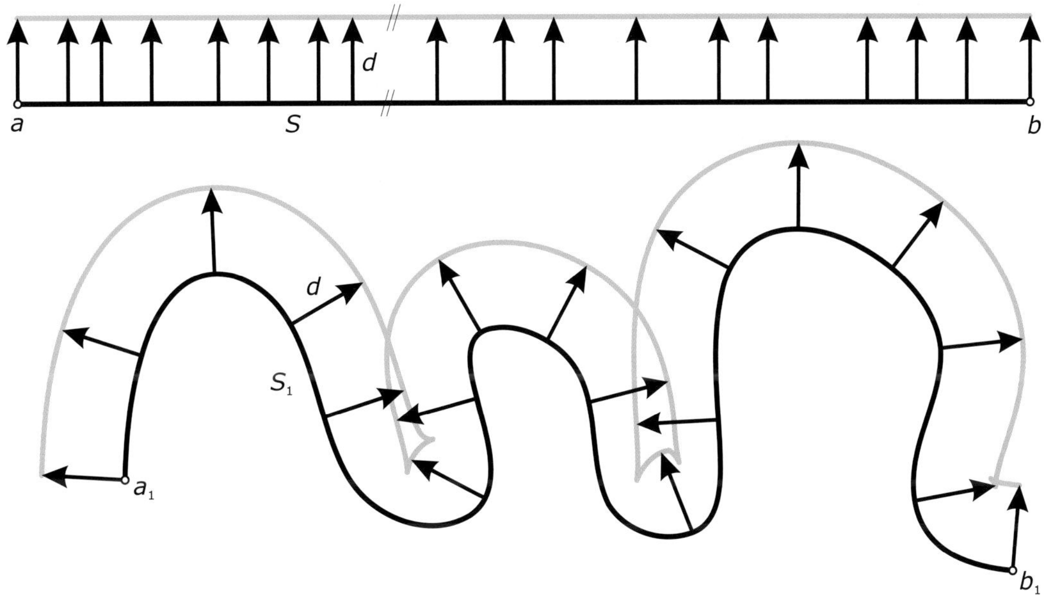

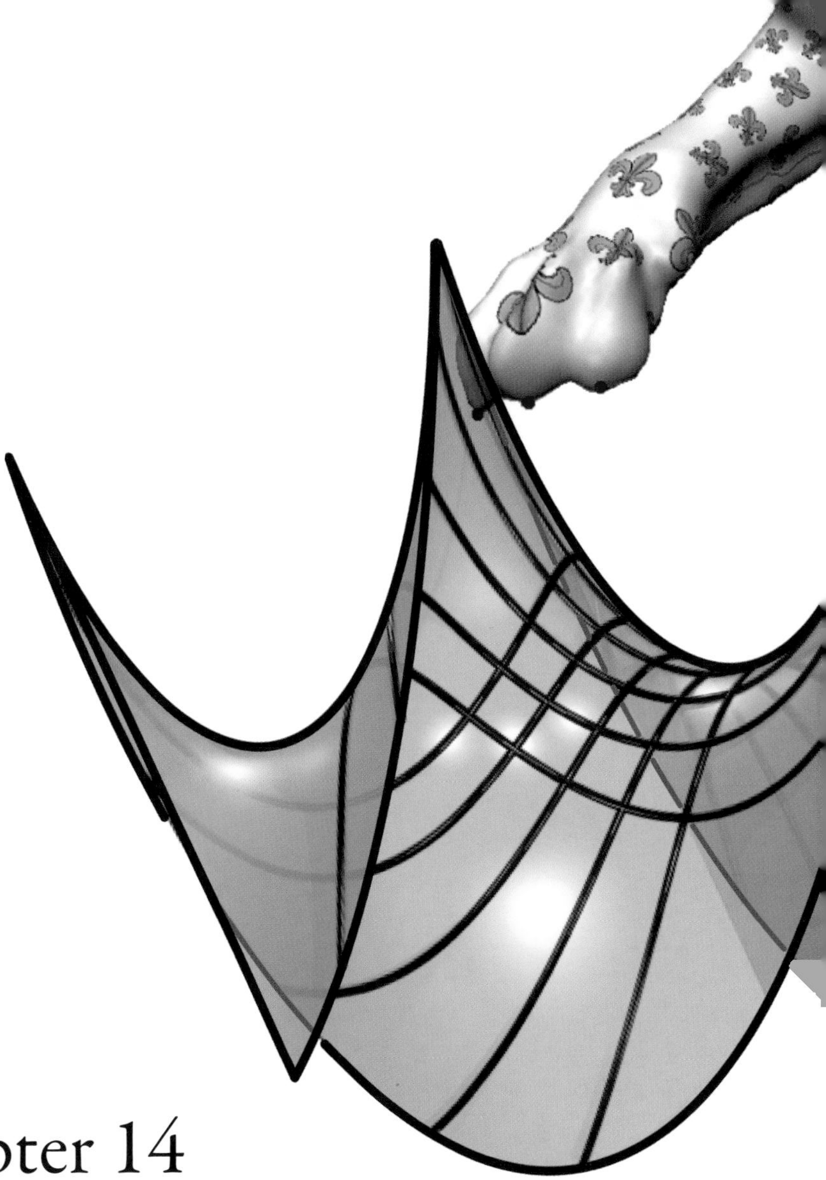

Chapter 14
Visualization and Analysis of Shapes

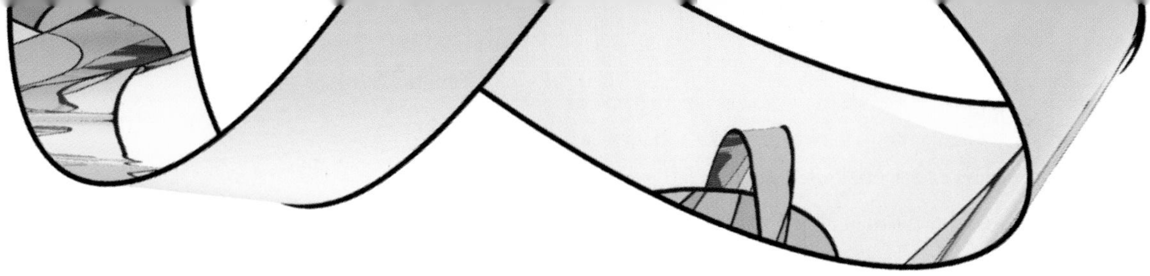

Visualization and Analysis of Shapes

Before producing a shape, one should analyze its suitability to the desired application. A deeper analysis should go beyond matters of realistic rendering. For example, certain undesirable effects (such as small bumps) may only be seen from a particular perspective under special lighting conditions. Here, *curvature of surfaces* comes into play. A more thorough analysis of a smooth surface may be based on curvatures. In fact, the judgment of a shape as visually pleasing depends largely on the way in which curvature varies along the surface. We try to keep the discussion of curvatures of surfaces as simple as possible, but there is no way around a little bit of mathematics. Knowing more about curvature will also let us better understand unexpected effects in reflections on a shiny surface (See Figure 14.1). Moreover, it is crucial to distortions under texture mapping, paper models, unfoldings, and shape optimization, among other issues.

Fig. 14.1
Smooth surface with reflections. The *Cloud Gate* (1999-2005) in the Chicago Millennium Park by artist Anish Kapoor (images courtesy of Steve McGinnis, RadioSpike photography).

To achieve a realistic look in a designed shape, we show how to map *texture* onto shapes. This is related to properties of mappings between a plane and a surface or between surfaces, and curvature plays an essential role here as well.

With the recent availability of three-dimensional digital data of terrain elevation and existing buildings, it is possible to build a complete three-dimensional model of the entire scene containing the new building. Therefore, we also discuss some basics on *digital elevation models*.

The final topic in this chapter is *topology*. We have encountered it at several places already. So now is the time to study it in more detail. Geometry and topology are the two main tools used to describe shapes. Starting with Euler's formula for polyhedra, we provide a crash course on a few basic topological properties. Non-orientable surfaces (including the famous Möbius strip and the Klein bottle) are discussed, as well as some basics on knots. (See Figure 14.2.)

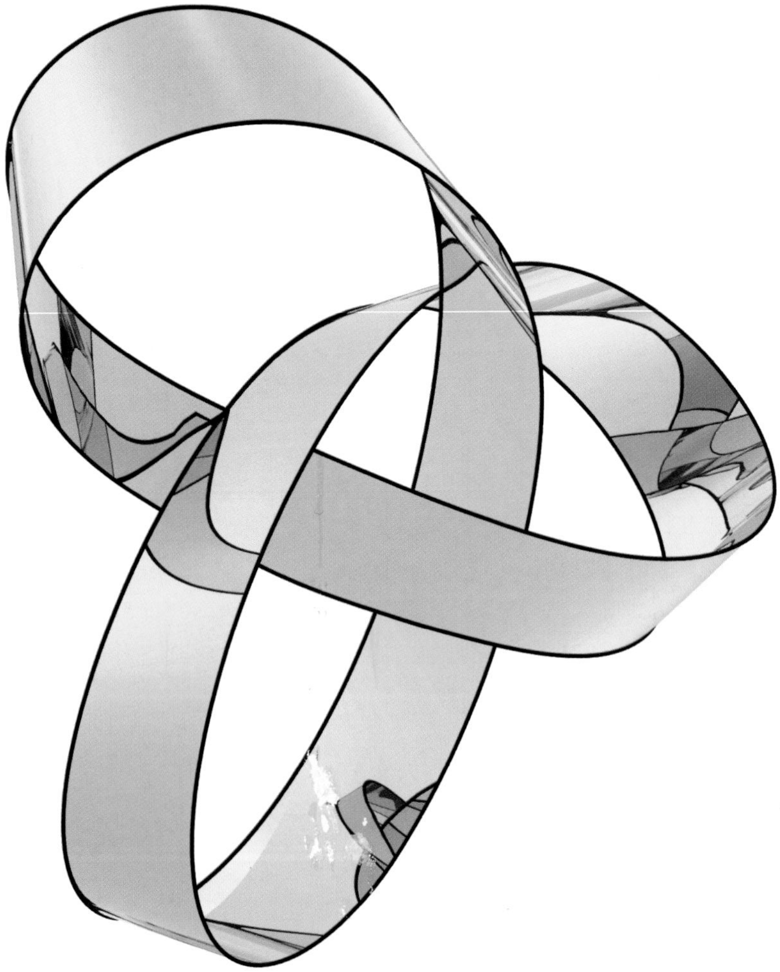

Fig. 14.2
There are several challenges in a good geometric understanding of this shape, all of them related to topics in this section.
(a) It is a strip of paper and therefore a developable surface, which is characterized by Gaussian curvature zero.
(b) We see smooth reflections, indicating that its curvature (not only Gaussian curvature) has no sudden changes.
(c) The surface is closed and one-sided, a so-called Möbius band.
(d) The band is an instance of a trefoil knot.

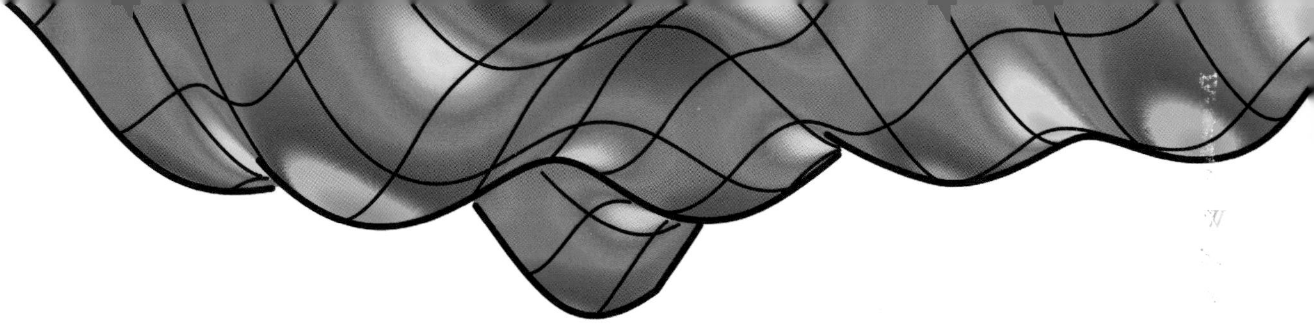

Curvature of Surfaces

Curves revisited. To compute the tangent of a curve, we need a first derivative of its mathematical representation. Recall from Chapter 7 what we have said about curvature and the osculating circle of a planar curve c. The computation of these entities requires derivatives up to second order, but not higher than that. This implies the following fact: There are many curves d that touch the given curve c at a chosen point p and have the same curvature k and osculating circle there.

We say that any of these curves *d osculates c at p*. Of course, the osculating circle itself is one example, but there are infinitely many osculating curves. An easy way to obtain an osculating parabola is based on Taylor's theorem (Figure 14.3). Let the curve c be given as the graph of a function $f(x)$; that is, the curve has the form $y = f(x)$. To pick a point on this curve, we choose an x value (e.g., $x = a$) and obtain the curve point $p = (a, f(a))$. We also compute the first and second derivative of f evaluated at $x = a$ and denote these values $f'(a)$ and $f''(a)$, respectively. We then consider the following function

$$g(x) = f(a) + f'(a)(x - a) + \tfrac{1}{2} f''(a)(x - a)^2. \quad (14.1)$$

If we insert $x = a$, we obtain $g(a) = f(a)$. This says that the curve d given by $y = g(x)$ passes through the point $p = (a, f(a))$. To compute the first derivative of g, we note that $a, f(a), f'(a)$, and $f''(a)$ are constants (do not depend on x). Thus,

$$g'(x) = f'(a) + f''(a)(x - a).$$

We see that $g'(a) = f'(a)$, which means that the curve d and our original curve c have the same tangent at p. The equation of the tangent is $y = f(a) + f'(a)(x - a)$. Curves c and d even have the same curvature at p! To prove this, we differentiate again as

$$g''(x) = f''(a).$$

Thus, the second derivative of g is constant and is the same as the second derivative of f at $x = a$. Because functions f and g agree at $x = a$ in all derivatives up to second order, their graph curves c and d osculate at p. The function g is a quadratic function of x and is called the second-order Taylor approximation of f at $x = a$. As the graph of a quadratic function, the curve d is a *parabola*. It is important to note that the second derivative $f''(a)$ is in general *not* the curvature at p. However, the following is a special case: If $f''(a) = 0$, the point p is an inflection point and the curve d is just the tangent of c at p.

Fig. 14.3
Taylor's theorem allows us to easily compute an osculating parabola of a curve given as graph of the function $y = f(x)$.

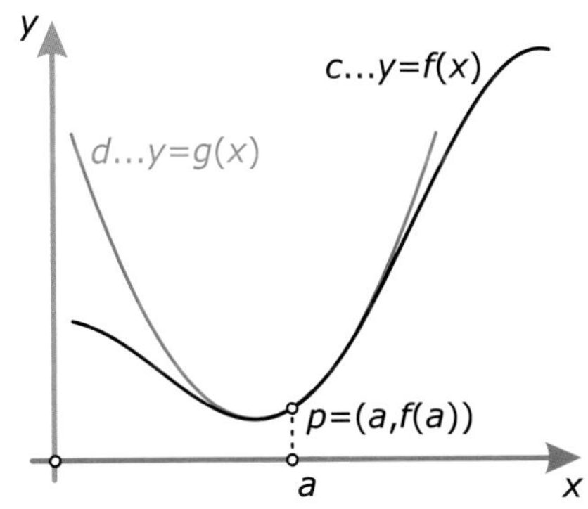

Example:

Curvatures of a sine curve. We let $f(x) = \sin x$; that is, we study the graph curve c of the sine function (Figure 14.4). Note that $f'(x) = \cos x$, $f''(x) = -\sin x$.

- Let's start with $a = 0$. Here, we have $f(0) = 0$, $f'(0) = 1$, $f''(0) = 0$. Inserting this into the second-order Taylor expansion g from Equation 14.1, we see that the osculating parabola $y = g(x)$ has the equation $y = 0 + 1 \cdot x + \frac{1}{2} \cdot 0 \cdot x^2$; that is, it agrees with the tangent $y = x$ in accordance with the fact that the point (0,0) is an inflection point of the sine curve. Inflection points also occur for $a = \pi$, $2\pi, \ldots, -\pi, -2\pi, \ldots$
- Next, we set $a = \pi/2$ and note $f(\pi/2) = 1$, $f'(\pi/2) = 0$, $f''(\pi/2) = -1$. This yields $g(x) = 1 + 0 \cdot (x - \pi/2) - \frac{1}{2} \cdot 1 \cdot (x - \pi/2)^2$, and thus we obtain the osculating parabola $y = 1 - \frac{1}{2} \cdot (x - \pi/2)^2$. Its vertex is the considered curve point $(\pi/2, 1)$, and its curvature at this point is -1 (see discussion following).
- Finally, we consider $a = -\pi/4$, which leads to $f(-\pi/4) = -\sqrt{2}/2$, $f'(-\pi/4) = \sqrt{2}/2$, $f''(-\pi/4) = \sqrt{2}/2$. This yields $y = (\sqrt{2}/2) \cdot [-1 + x + \pi/4 + \frac{1}{2} \cdot (x + \pi/4)^2]$ as the equation of the osculating parabola.

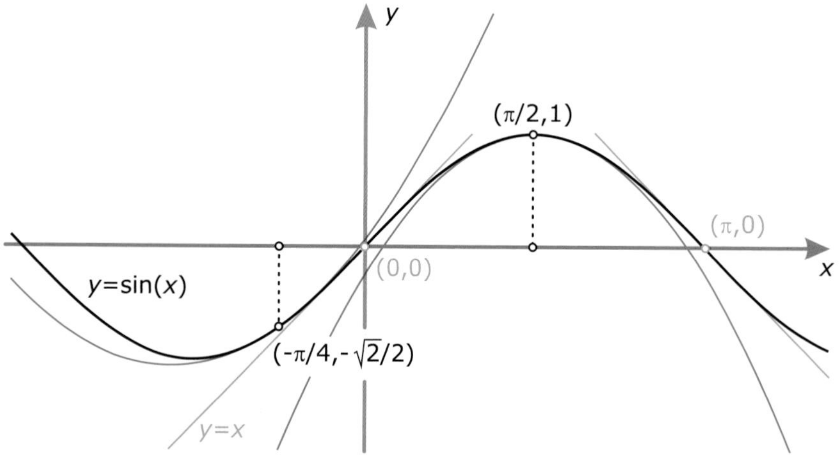

Fig. 14.4
Osculating parabolas for the curve $y = \sin x$. We focus on a few points of this curve: $(x,y) = (\pi/2, 1)$ describes a point p with vanishing first derivative (and there p is the vertex of the parabola); $(-\pi/4, -\sqrt{2}/2)$ is a "general" point; and (0,0) and $(\pi,0)$ are inflection points where the osculating parabola degenerates to the tangent.

We may take a special parabola, $y = \frac{1}{2}x^2$, and use the formula of Chapter 7 to compute its curvature k at the origin $(x,y) = (0,0)$, which is the vertex of this parabola (Figure 14.5). We find $k = 1$; that is, the radius r of the osculating circle at the vertex is also $r = 1$. This is in agreement with the fact that the radius of the osculating circle at the parabola's vertex equals twice the distance of the focal point to the vertex and this focal distance is ½.

In an analogous way, the curvature of the parabola $y = (k/2)x^2$ for some constant value k at the origin is equal to k. Note that k is also the second derivative of the function $g(x) = (k/2)x^2$. Therefore, in this special case the second derivative gives us the right value of the curvature at the origin. The reason behind this is the vanishing first derivative at the origin.

The osculating paraboloid. Now we are well prepared for a discussion of the curvature behavior of smooth surfaces. Inspired by the results on curves, we will use Taylor's theorem—but now for two variables, x and y. We do not even quote its general form, but just outline the considerations that lead to a simple result upon which the further discussion can be based.

The goal is to obtain a counterpart of an osculating parabola, but already in a special position, analogous with Figure 14.5. Hence, we select a point p of the surface S (where we want to study the curvature) and let p be the origin of the coordinate system. Moreover, we place our coordinate system such that the xy-plane (equation $z = 0$) is the tangent plane of S at p. Our osculating surface P at p, which is called the *osculating paraboloid of S at p*, now has an equation of the form

$$z = ax^2 + bxy + cy^2.$$

The values of a,b,c are certain second-order derivatives, but are not needed right now. This surface P is in general a paraboloid. In special cases, it is a parabolic cylinder. Alternatively, if $a = b = c = 0$, it is just the plane $z = 0$. Because all of these surfaces have two orthogonal planes of symmetry, we may further adapt our coordinate system and make sure that the xz-plane and the yz-plane are the symmetry planes. This removes the term bxy in the previous equation. We denote the resulting coefficients of x^2 and y^2 as $k_1/2$ and $k_2/2$, respectively. Thus, our surface P (which has the same curvature behavior as S at p) has the simple equation

$$z = (k_1/2)x^2 + (k_2/2)y^2. \qquad (14.2)$$

A complete derivation of this result would require more mathematics. For our purposes, it is sufficient to know that this equation contains the curvature behavior of a general smooth surface S where smoothness means that S has a twice-differentiable mathematical representation.

Note the relations of Equation 14.2 to the curve case. In the xz-plane (equation $y = 0$) we have the parabola p_1: $z = (k_1/2)x^2$ with curvature k_1 at the origin p. The intersection curve of P with the yz-plane (equation $x = 0$) is the parabola p_2: $z = (k_2/2)y^2$ with curvature k_2 at p. These curvatures k_1 and k_2 are called *principal curvatures* of P and S at p. The x- and y-axes, which we have chosen based on geometric considerations, are called *principal directions* at p.

Fig. 14.5
The curvature of the parabola $y = (1/2)x^2$ at its vertex (origin) is 1. More generally, the curvature of the parabola $y = (k/2)x^2$ at its vertex (0,0) is k. This is the constant value of the second derivative of the function $g(x) = (k/2)x^2$.

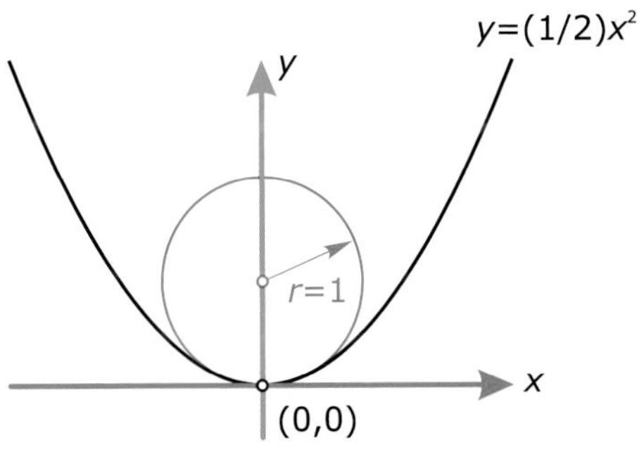

Normal curvatures. Normal curvatures of a surface S at a point p are obtained as follows. We intersect S with a plane R through the normal n of S at p and measure the curvature k_n of the resulting intersection curve at the point p. There are infinitely many normal curvatures, depending on which plane R we have chosen. We know from the previous discussion that we may use the osculating paraboloid P from Equation 14.2 instead of S.

The surface point p is then the origin and the normal at p is the z-axis. The plane R can be defined by its angle α against the x-axis (first principal direction). Introducing a coordinate system (u,z) in the plane R as shown in Figure 14.6, we have the following relations between the u coordinate of points in R and their x and y coordinates:

$$x = u \cdot \cos\alpha, y = u \cdot \sin\alpha.$$

We can insert this into Equation 14.2 and obtain for the intersection curve between P and R the equation

$$z = (1/2)[k_1(\cos\alpha)^2 + k_2(\sin\alpha)^2]u^2.$$

This is a parabola $p(\alpha)$, whose curvature at the origin is the desired normal curvature $k_n(\alpha)$ to direction angle α. Because the coefficient $(1/2)[k_1(\cos\alpha)^2 + k_2(\sin\alpha)^2]$ of u^2 equals $k_n/2$, we have the following result,

$$k_n(\alpha) = k_1(\cos\alpha)^2 + k_2(\sin\alpha)^2. \qquad (14.3)$$

Hence, knowing the principal curvatures k_1 and k_2 we can compute the normal curvature $k_n(\alpha)$ to any given direction angle α. The tangent of $p(\alpha)$ at p (u-axis in Figure 14.6; intersection line of the plane R and the tangent plane at point p) is also called the *direction* with which the normal curvature $k_n(\alpha)$ is associated.

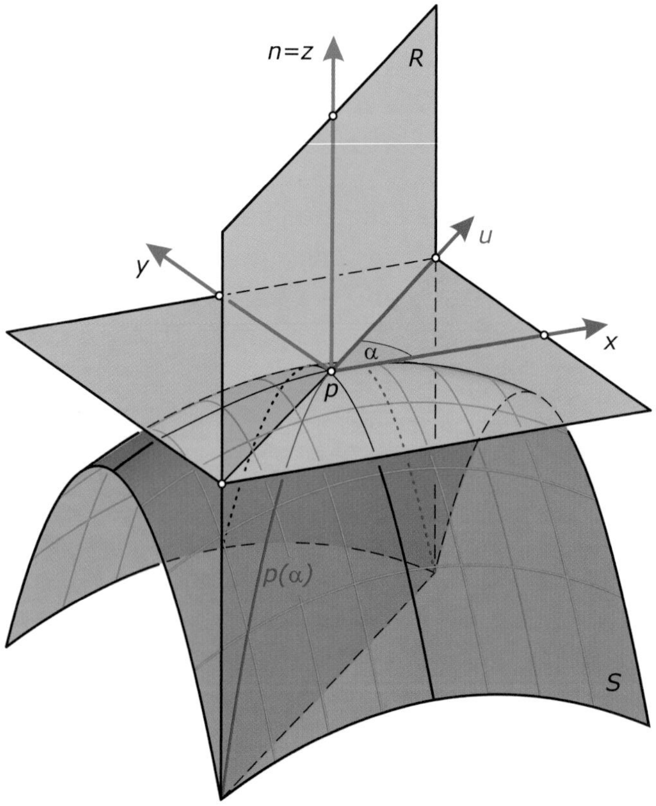

Fig. 14.6
Normal curvatures of a surface S at a point p are the curvatures of the intersection curves with planes R through the surface normal n. Using the paraboloid P from Equation 14.2, we can introduce a (u,z)-coordinate system in R and in this way obtain Euler's formula (Equation 14.3)—which relates the normal curvature to direction angle α with the two principal curvatures.

Classification of surface points. Surface points can be classified according to the type of the osculating paraboloid.

- **Elliptic surface point.** Here, the osculating paraboloid P is an *elliptic paraboloid* (Figure 14.7). Mathematically, in this case the principal curvatures k_1 and k_2 are of the same sign and different from zero. Geometrically, this implies that the parabolas p_1 and p_2 are open toward the same side. The paraboloid P and the underlying surface S lie locally on one side of the tangent plane T at the considered surface point p. A visualization via planar intersection curves is shown in Figure 14.8.
- **Hyperbolic surface point.** In this case, the osculating paraboloid P is a *hyperbolic paraboloid* (Figure 14.9). The principal curvatures k_1 and k_2 have different signs and thus the parabolas p_1 and p_2 are open toward different sides. P and the underlying surface S lie locally on both sides of the tangent plane T at p (Figure 14.10). T intersects the surface S along a curve, which has a double point at p. The tangents of this curve at the double point p are the so-called *asymptotic directions* along which the normal curvature vanishes. They are also the intersection lines between the osculating paraboloid P and T. Euler's formula (Equation 14.3) can be used to compute the angles α between principal directions and the asymptotic directions. We simply have to solve $k_n(\alpha) = 0$. Note that due to the different sign of k_1 and k_2 this equation has a solution. It does not have a solution at an elliptic point where k_1 and k_2 have the same sign.

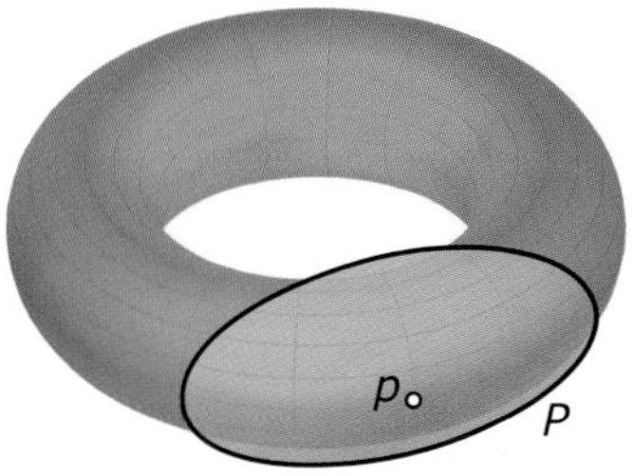

Fig. 14.7
At an elliptic surface point p, the osculating paraboloid P is an elliptic paraboloid.

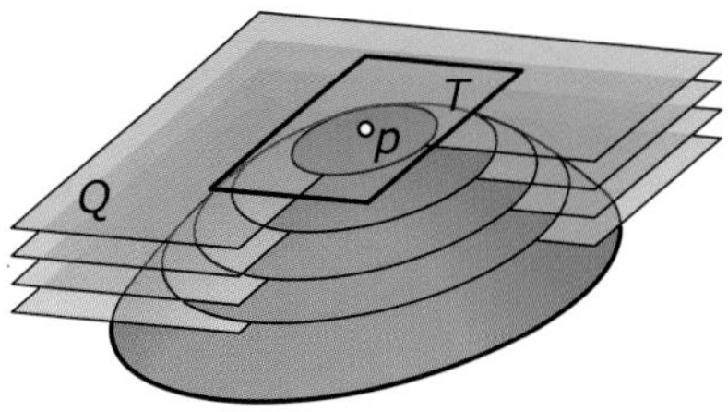

Fig. 14.8
At an elliptic surface point p, the surface S lies locally on the same side of the tangent plane T. Intersection with a plane Q that lies on this side and is parallel to T gives a closed curve whose shape approaches that of an ellipse as Q gets closer and closer to T.

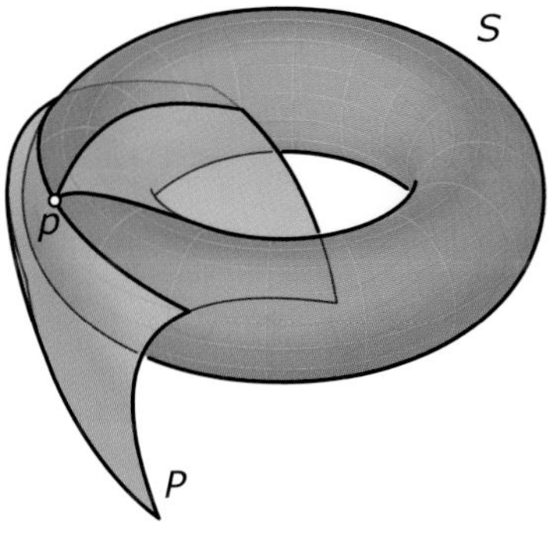

Fig. 14.9
At a hyperbolic surface point p of a surface S, the osculating paraboloid P is a hyperbolic paraboloid. Thus, the surface has locally a saddle-like shape.

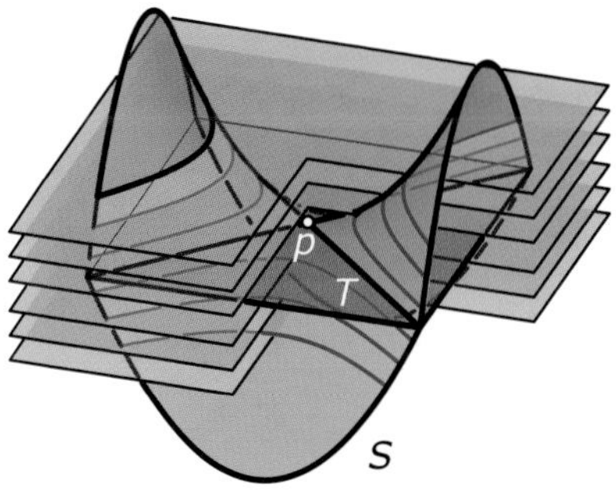

Fig. 14.10
At a hyperbolic surface point p, the surface S lies locally on both sides of the tangent plane T. The intersection curve between T and S passes through p and has a double point there. The figure also shows some intersection curves with planes parallel to T.

- **Parabolic surface point.** Here, the osculating paraboloid P is a *parabolic cylinder* (Figure 14.11). One principal curvature vanishes, and we may assume that $k_2 = 0$. The corresponding direction is the only direction with vanishing normal curvature. The local behavior with respect to the tangent plane is more complicated to explain. Some essential cases are shown in Figure 14.12. In general, parabolic points occur along curves that separate regions of elliptic points from regions with hyperbolic points.
- **Flat point.** In this case, both principal curvatures vanish and therefore all normal curvatures are zero. The osculating surface P degenerates to the tangent plane (Figure 14.13).

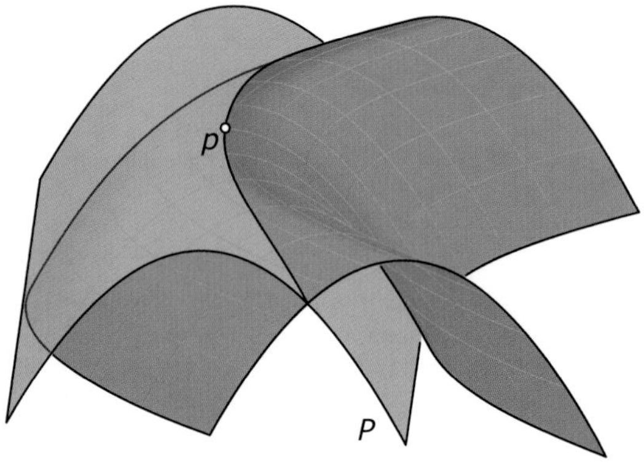

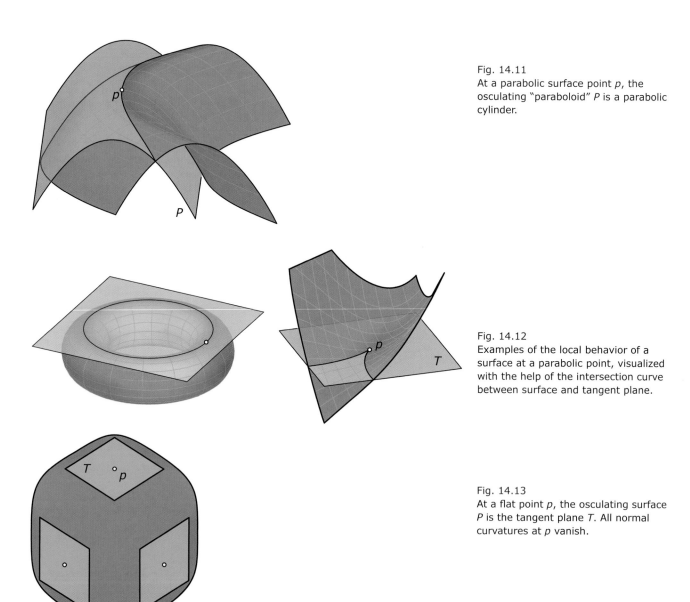

Fig. 14.11
At a parabolic surface point p, the osculating "paraboloid" P is a parabolic cylinder.

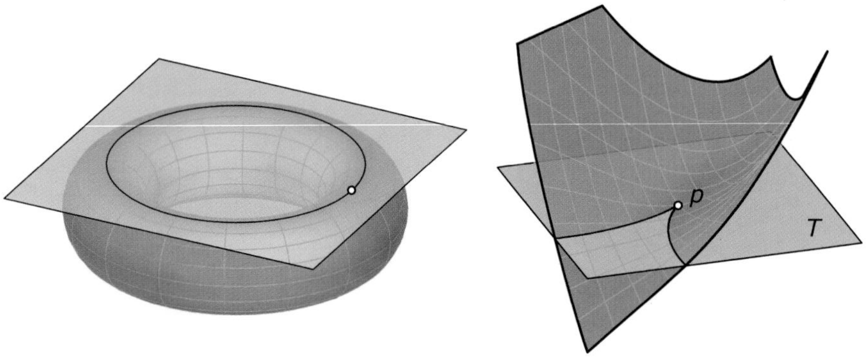

Fig. 14.12
Examples of the local behavior of a surface at a parabolic point, visualized with the help of the intersection curve between surface and tangent plane.

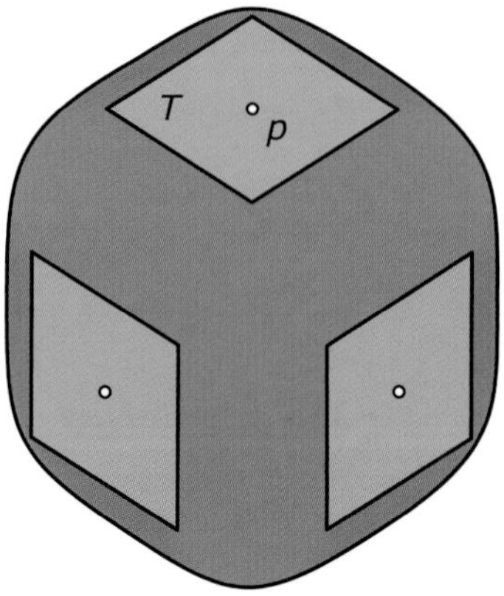

Fig. 14.13
At a flat point p, the osculating surface P is the tangent plane T. All normal curvatures at p vanish.

Example:

Surfaces of revolution. We illustrate the classification of surface points of a ring torus S (Figure 14.14). There are two planes orthogonal to the axis, each of which touches the torus along a circle. These circles contain the parabolic points. Obviously, the outer ring has only elliptic points because there the torus lies locally on the same side of the tangent plane.

Analogously, the remaining part is the one that has only hyperbolic points, where the torus lies locally on both sides of the tangent plane. At each point, the principal directions are the tangent to the circular profile and the tangent to the parallel circle (rotational path). Analogously, we can discuss the distribution of elliptic and hyperbolic points along other types of rotational surfaces. There, it is important to note that an inflection point of the profile gives rise to a parabolic surface point (Figure 14.15).

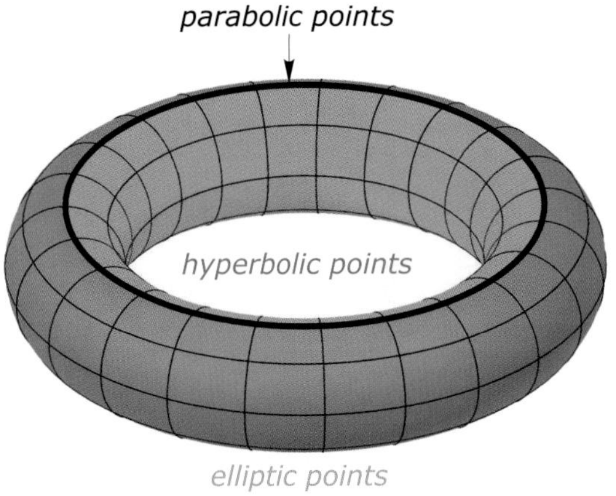

Fig. 14.14
Two circles segment a ring torus into a region with elliptic points and a region with hyperbolic points (saddle-like points). The two circles contain only parabolic surface points.

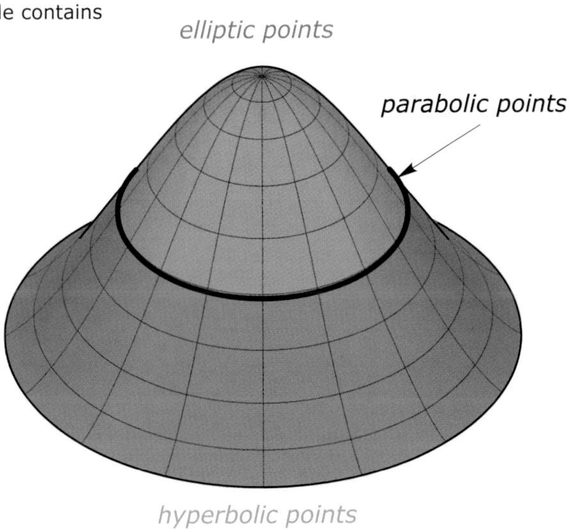

Fig. 14.15
A surface of revolution, classified into regions of elliptic and hyperbolic points. The separating circle contains the parabolic points.

Example:

Freeform surfaces. Segmentation of a surface into regions with elliptic and hyperbolic points can be done with modeling programs that have a tool for visualizing *Gaussian curvature* $K = k_1 \cdot k_2$, the product of principal curvatures. Gaussian curvature is further discussed in material following (Figure 14.16). Here, we can already note that Gaussian curvature zero characterizes a parabolic point or flat point. At an elliptic point, both principal curvatures have the same sign and thus we have a positive Gaussian curvature. Likewise, a hyperbolic point has principal curvatures of different sign and therefore it is also characterized by negative Gaussian curvature.

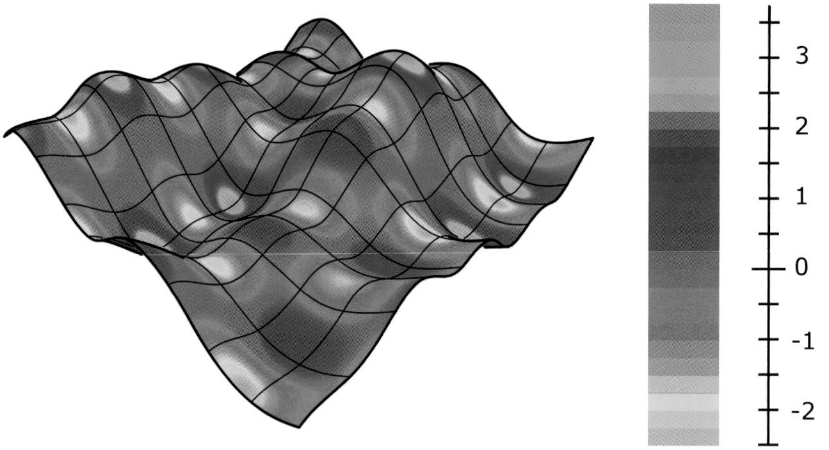

Fig. 14.16
A freeform surface with a color-based visualization of Gaussian curvature K. Positive K characterizes an elliptic point, negative K belongs to a hyperbolic point, and $K = 0$ holds at parabolic points.

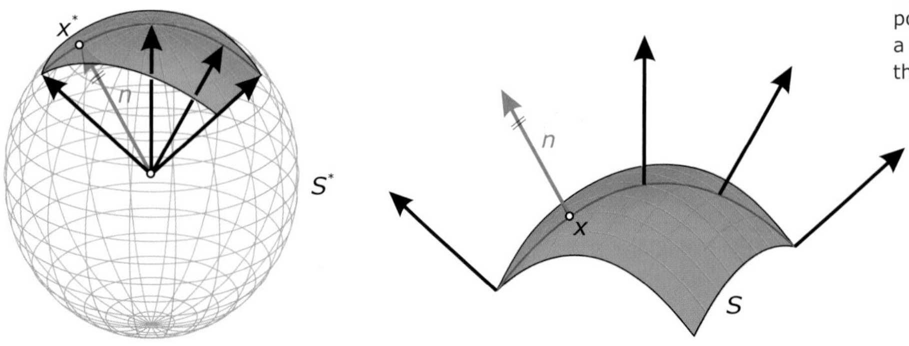

Fig. 14.17
The Gaussian spherical mapping views the outward unit normal vector at any point x of the considered surface S as a coordinate vector of a point x^* on the unit sphere S^*.

Gaussian curvature. The product $K = k_1 \cdot k_2$ of principal curvatures is called *Gaussian curvature*. Before we discuss some of the properties of Gaussian curvature, we briefly illustrate the approach taken by Carl Friedrich Gauss (1777–1855) to define this measure of surface curvature. It uses the following mapping from a surface S onto the *unit sphere* S^* (= sphere of radius 1 whose center is the origin of the underlying Cartesian coordinate system): In the neighborhood of the considered point p on S, we use a consistent orientation of the surface normals. This means that we distinguish between two sides of the surface, and call them the outer and inner side. In this way, each point x in a neighborhood of p has an outward unit normal vector (called n) that points to the outer side. This vector has length 1, and seen as coordinate vector of a point thus represents a point on the unit sphere S^*. Summarizing, we have to do the following (Figure 14.17): For a point x of S, we take the outward unit normal vector n and view it as coordinate vector of a point x^* on the unit sphere S^*. The mapping $x \rightarrow x^*$ is called *Gaussian spherical mapping*. The image of a surface S under this mapping is called its Gaussian image.

Let's consider some examples.

- If S is a *plane*, all normals are parallel and therefore any point of the plane is mapped to the same point of the Gaussian sphere. The entire Gaussian image of the plane S is this single point.
- Let S be a *sphere* of radius R (Figure 14.18). On S, we consider a disk D with spherical center p. The Gaussian mapping maps the disk D to another disk D^* on the Gaussian sphere S^*. Connecting the boundary circle k of D with the center of the sphere S, we obtain a cone of revolution N—which is also formed by the normals of S along k. The corresponding cone N^*, which connects the boundary circle k^* of D^* with the center of S^*, is congruent to N. Therefore, D results from D^* by applying a uniform scaling with factor R and a translation. Hence, the surface area A^* of D^* and the area A of D possess the ratio $A^*/A = 1/R^2$. Because the normal curvatures of the sphere R at any of its points equal $k_1 = k_2 = 1/R$, the Gaussian curvature $K = k_1 \cdot k_2$ of the sphere equals $K = 1/R^2$ and thus K agrees with the ratio A^*/A.

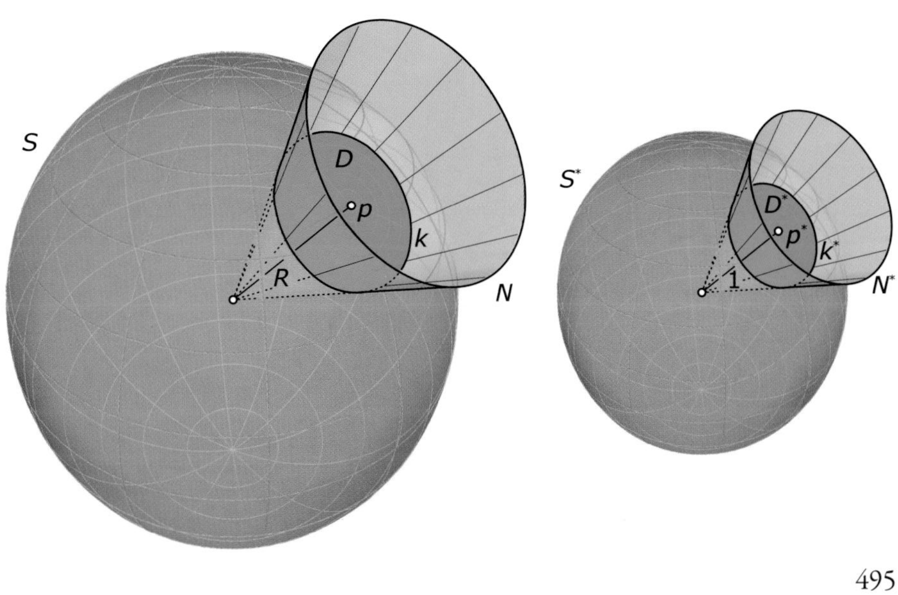

Fig. 14.18
The Gaussian spherical mapping applied to a spherical disk D. The normals at the boundary of D form a cone of revolution N, which is congruent to the corresponding cone N^* formed by the normals along the boundary circle k^* of D^*.

Let S now be an arbitrary surface, and let p be a point on it. We consider a local neighborhood D of p on S. With the Gaussian mapping, it is mapped onto a neighborhood D^* of p^* on the sphere S^* (see Figure 14.19). Obviously, if the variation of surface normals over D is strong the domain D^* will be larger than for a weak normal variation (see the examples considered previously). In other words, the ratio A^*/A of the area A^* of D^* and the area A of D will measure the variation of normals—which is clearly a measure of curvature.

Now one considers the limit of the area ratio A^*/A when D shrinks to a point p. Of course, also D^* shrinks to a point p^* and thus both areas are zero. This is no problem, because the limit of the ratio A^*/A exists (if the representation of the surface S is twice differentiable). *The limit of the ratio A^*/A is the Gaussian curvature K at p.* We have verified this previously for the very special example of a sphere, but it is true for general surfaces. We may therefore say that the *Gaussian curvature measures the local area distortion under the Gaussian spherical mapping.*

Isometric mappings and cartography. Cartography is concerned with the generation of planar maps of the earth's surface. If one approximates the surface of the earth by a sphere S, the problem is to find an appropriate mapping of a part D of S onto a planar domain D_1. Ideally, one would like to have a mapping that preserves the length of any path (river, street, and so on) on the earth—of course, up to an appropriate scaling factor that applies to all distances.

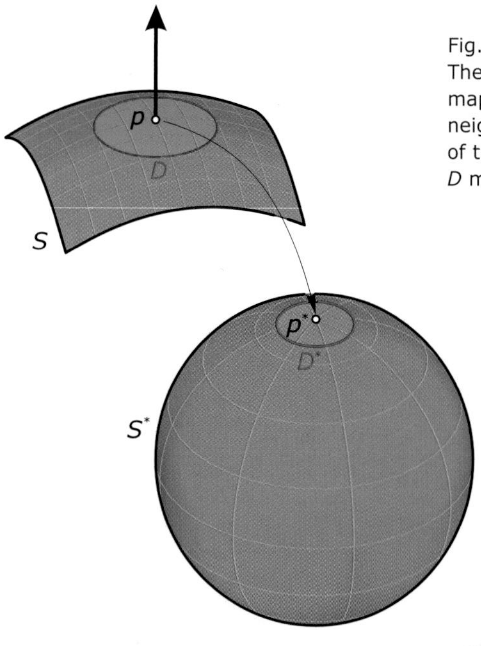

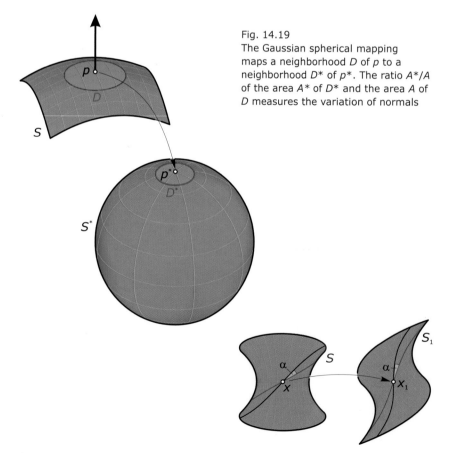

Fig. 14.19
The Gaussian spherical mapping maps a neighborhood D of p to a neighborhood D^* of p^*. The ratio A^*/A of the area A^* of D^* and the area A of D measures the variation of normals on D. This is an "averaged" measure of curvature on the domain D. The Gaussian curvature K is the limit of A^*/A when D shrinks to the point p.

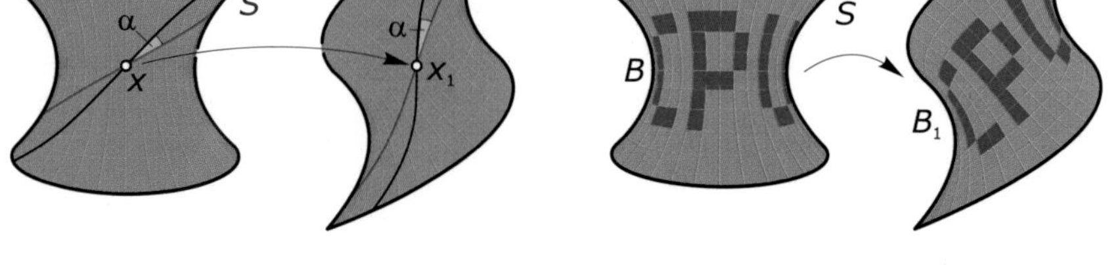

Fig. 14.20
An isometric mapping between two surfaces preserves the lengths of curves and the intersection angles between curves. The Gaussian curvature at corresponding points x and x_1 are equal. Moreover, the surface area of any domain B and its image domain B_1 are the same.

In this way, one would have the ideal impression of the distances between different places. However, such a mapping does not exist! A simple proof can be based on the fact that a circle c (spherical radius r) on S needed to be mapped onto a circle c_1 of radius r in the plane, but these circles have different length. Another proof follows from a much more general result by C. F. Gauss, which concerns so-called *isometric mappings* between two surfaces S and S_1 (see Figure 14.20).

Such a mapping maps any point x of S to a point x_1 of S_1. A curve c on S is mapped to a curve c_1 on S_1 such that c and c_1 have the same length. Hence, distances measured along curves are preserved. C. F. Gauss proved that *Gaussian curvature is preserved under isometric mappings*. If S has Gaussian curvature K at point x, S_1 must have the same Gaussian curvature K at the image point x_1 of x. Because the sphere has Gaussian curvature $1/R^2$ and the plane has Gaussian curvature zero, there is no way to find an isometric mapping between the sphere and the plane. Hence, *there is no distortion-free map of the earth*.

One can show that an isometric mapping $S \rightarrow S_1$ also *preserves* the intersection *angles* between curves (see Figure 14.20). Moreover, it *preserves surface areas*: a domain B in S and its corresponding domain B_1 in S_1 have the same surface area.

However, an angle-preserving mapping (also called *conformal mapping*) need not be an isometric one. In fact, there are many angle-preserving maps between any pair of surfaces. Let's compare this result with our discussion of the inversion in Chapter 13. If an inversion maps a surface S to a surface S_1, the mapping between the two surfaces S and S_1 generated in this way is conformal.

However, there are other ways of obtaining a conformal mapping between two surfaces S and S_1—ways that are actually related to the fact that there are many conformal mappings of the plane onto itself (see Chapter 5). Requiring angle preservation for a mapping of three-dimensional space onto itself (not just between two surfaces) is much more restrictive and only leads to similarities, inversions, and their combinations (see Chapter 13).

Likewise, there are many area-preserving mappings. Frequently used mappings of the earth are either angle preserving or area preserving (see Figure 14.21). However, they cannot have both properties because preservation of both angles and areas implies an isometric mapping.

Fig. 14.21
Examples of mappings used in cartography.
(a) The angle-preserving stereographic projection (see Chapter 2)
(b) An area-preserving mapping attributed to K. B. Mollweide (1805).

(a)

(b)

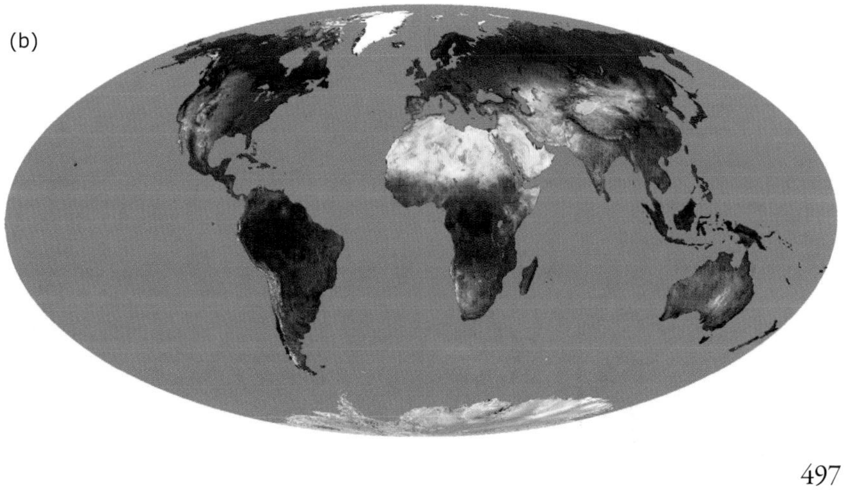

Developable surfaces. A surface S that can be mapped into the plane by an isometric mapping is called a *developable surface*, and the isometric planar image is called its *development*. Due to the preservation of Gaussian curvature under isometric mappings, a developable surface must have *vanishing Gaussian curvature* $K = 0$ at all of its points. Thus, these surfaces are also called *single curved surfaces* (in contrast to double curved surfaces with K different from zero; see Figure 14.22). We will study these surfaces in Chapter 15. Here, we only give two examples: cylinder surfaces and cones are developable surfaces.

Mean curvature. Another important measure of surface curvature is *mean curvature* $H = (k_1 + k_2)/2$, the arithmetic mean of the principal curvatures. Surfaces with vanishing mean curvature are *minimal surfaces*, which appear (for example) as shapes of soap films through a closed wire (Figure 14.23). These and related equilibrium shapes of surfaces are discussed in Chapter 18 in connection with shape optimization problems.

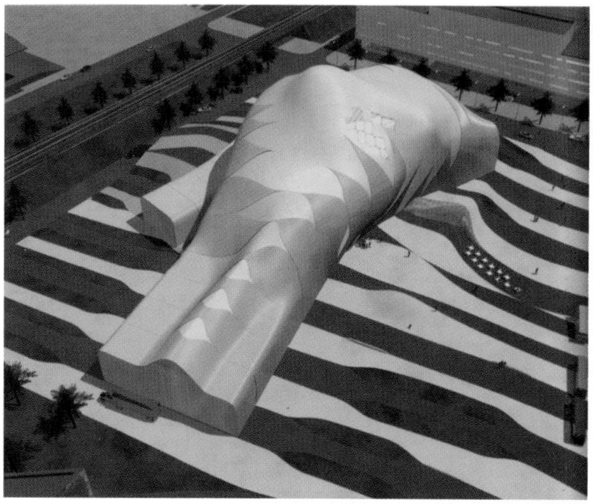

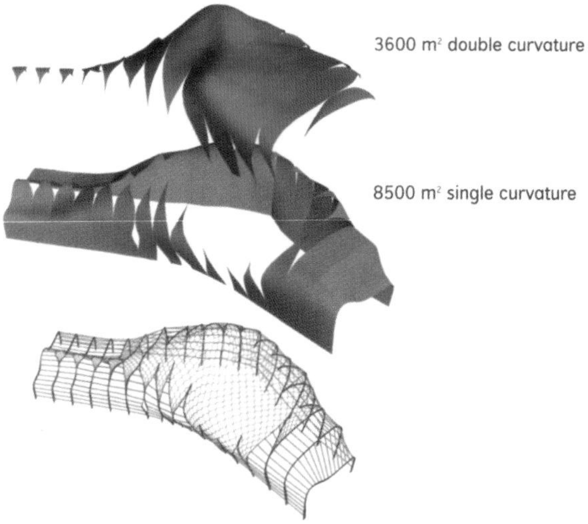

Fig. 14.22
An application of Gaussian curvature in architecture: Pompidou Two by NOX, invited competition for the City of Metz, France. The designed shape has been segmented into single curved areas and double curved parts. This segmentation is also reflected in the construction methodology.

Fig. 14.23
Minimal surfaces in form of soap films (images courtesy of K. Rittenschober). Minimal surfaces are characterized by vanishing mean curvature.

Visualization of the curvature behavior. The curvature behavior of a surface is difficult to convey by a shaded image. One means of visualizing such behavior employs color-coded images. The values of a given curvature measure—for example, Gaussian curvature K or mean curvature H (or another function of the principal curvatures)—are encoded according to color (Figure 14.24). In this way, minute imperfections of a surface can be made visible (see also Figure 14.16). The frequently used subdivision surfaces (Doo-Sabin, Catmull-Clark, Loop) possess a complicated and sometimes undesirable curvature behavior near irregular vertices of the base mesh; this can be visualized by curvature diagrams (Figure 14.25).

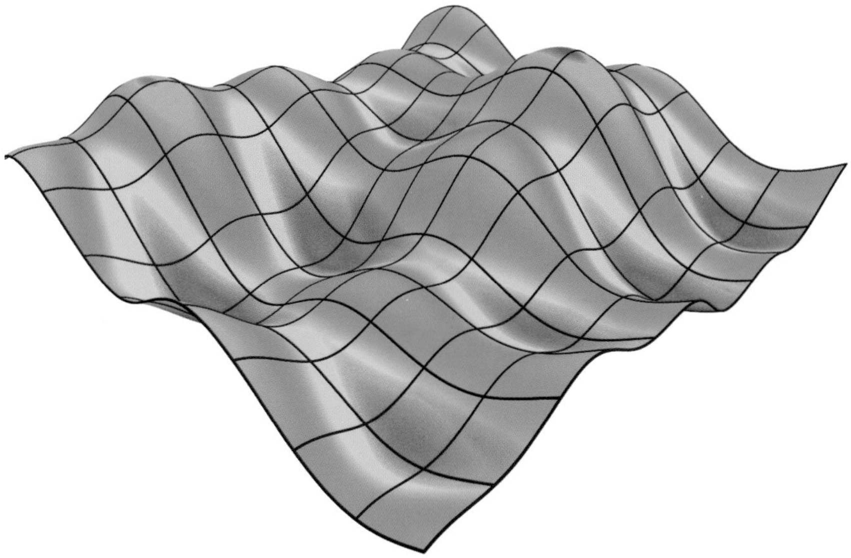

Fig. 14.24
Curvatures, here mean curvature, in a color-coded visualization are frequently used tools for surface analysis.

Fig. 14.25
The curvature behavior of a subdivision surface near an irregular vertex can be complicated and undesirable for certain applications.

This figure (courtesy of I. Ginkel and G. Umlauf) illustrates the problem for a Loop subdivision surface (left) via a color-coded Gaussian curvature diagram (right).

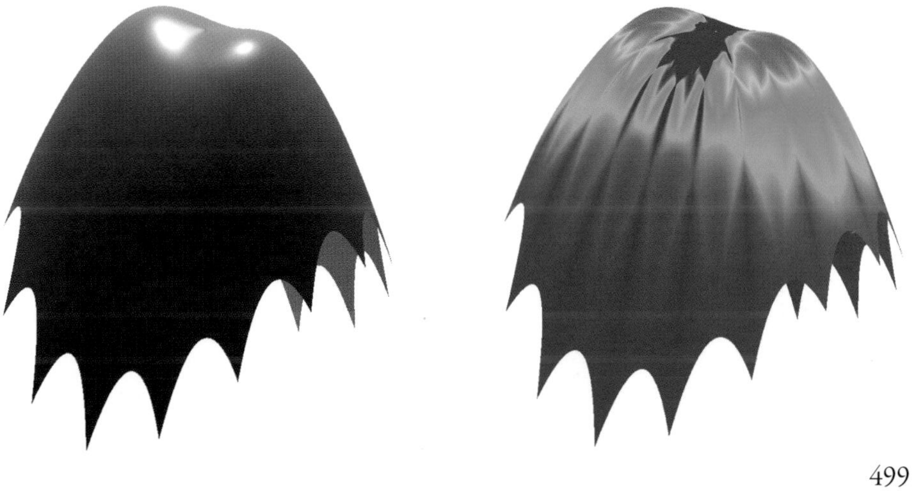

Principal curvature lines. To obtain an overview of the principal directions, one can use *principal curvature lines*. A principal curvature line is a curve on a surface whose tangents are in principal direction. Thus, through each general point of a surface there are two principal curvature lines that intersect at a right angle and touch the principal directions.

Some examples are shown in Figure 14.26. Principal curvature lines or related networks of curves are sometimes used for the generation of surface illustrations that aim at results that are similar to drawings made by artists. This is an instance of a *non-photorealistic rendering* technique (see Figure 14.27).

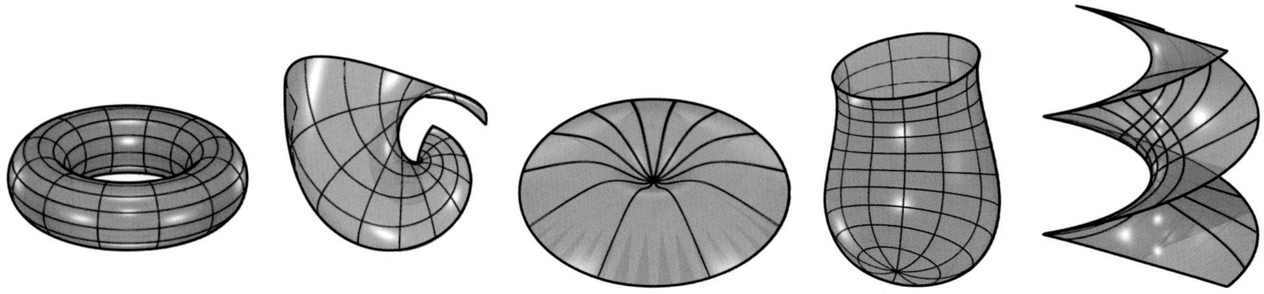

Fig. 14.26
The network of principal curvature lines of a surface represents fundamental shape characteristics.

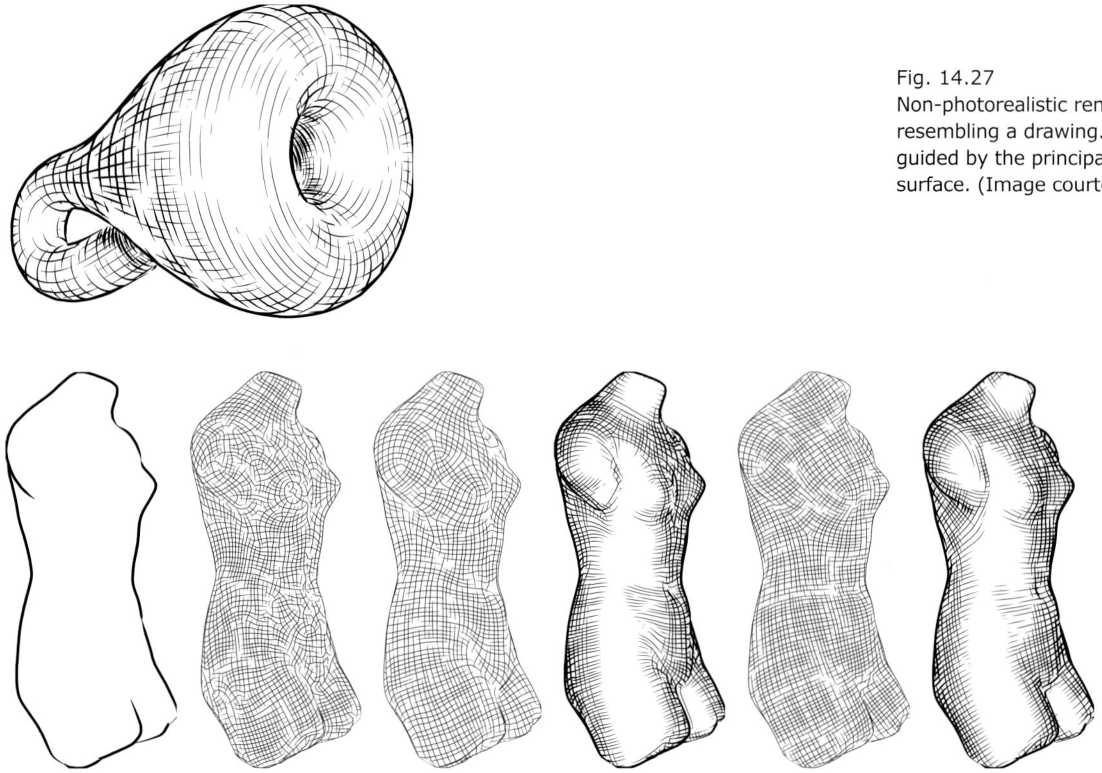

Fig. 14.27
Non-photorealistic rendering of a surface resembling a drawing. Hatching is guided by the principal directions on the surface. (Image courtesy of D. Zorin.)

Remark (umbilics). The principal directions are uniquely defined only if k_1 and k_2 are different. For $k_1 = k_2$, we have a special surface point called an *umbilic*. There, the osculating paraboloid P is a paraboloid of revolution or a plane ($k_1 = k_2 = 0$).
A sphere S (radius R) has only umbilics. The intersection curve with any plane through a surface normal is a great circle (radius R) and thus all normal curvatures equal $1/R$. At an umbilic, we have the same curvature behavior as for a sphere or a plane; in the latter case we also speak of a flat point (Figure 14.13). At an umbilic the network of principal curvature lines has a singularity (Figures 14.26 and 14.28).

Fig. 14.28
Principal curvature lines form the basis for the layout of freeform structures with planar quadrilateral glass panels. Here we only show such a structure. The geometric discussion for its generation is found in Chapter 19. The singular vertices in the mesh (valence 6) correspond to the umbilics (flat points) on an underlying smooth surface.

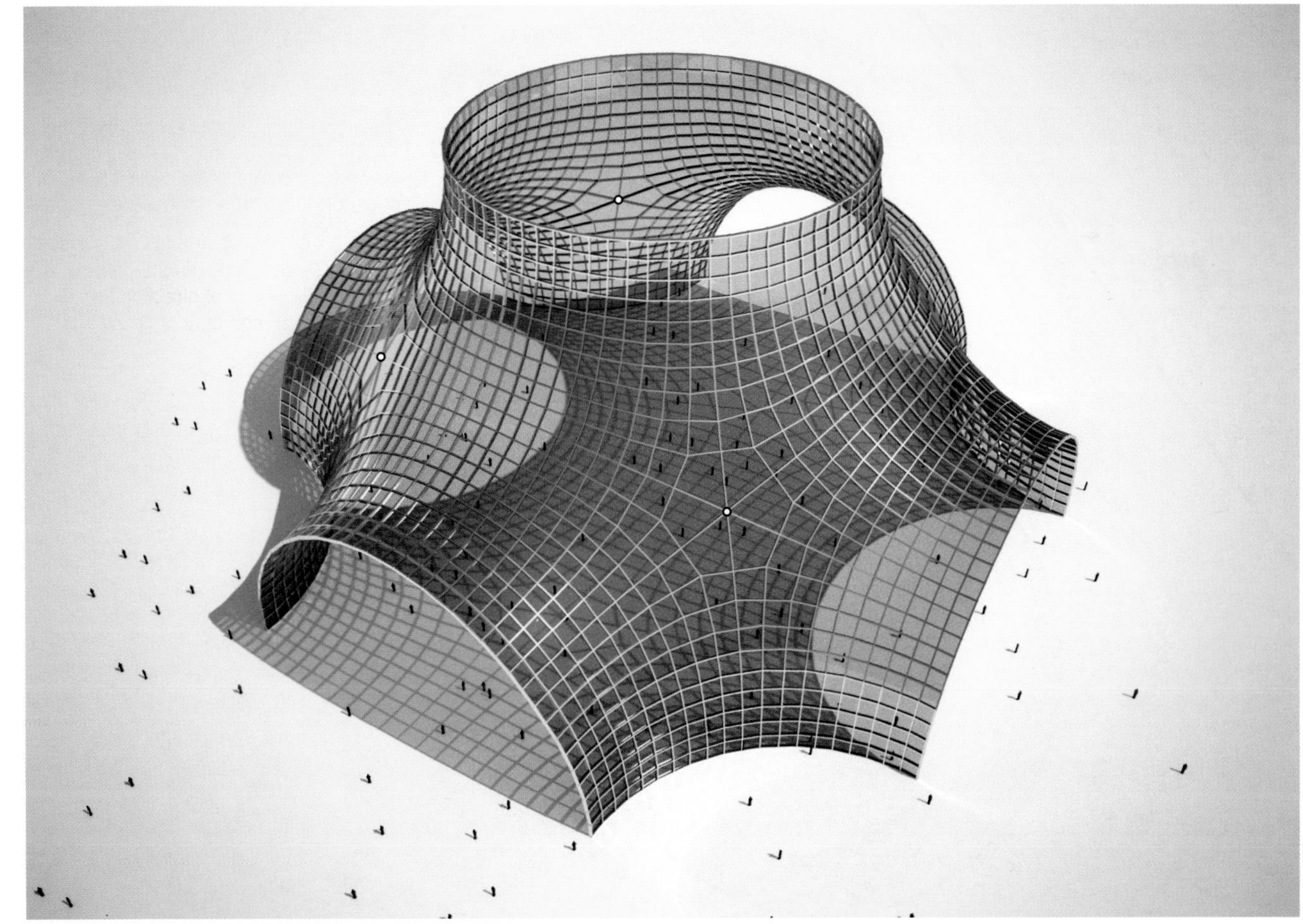

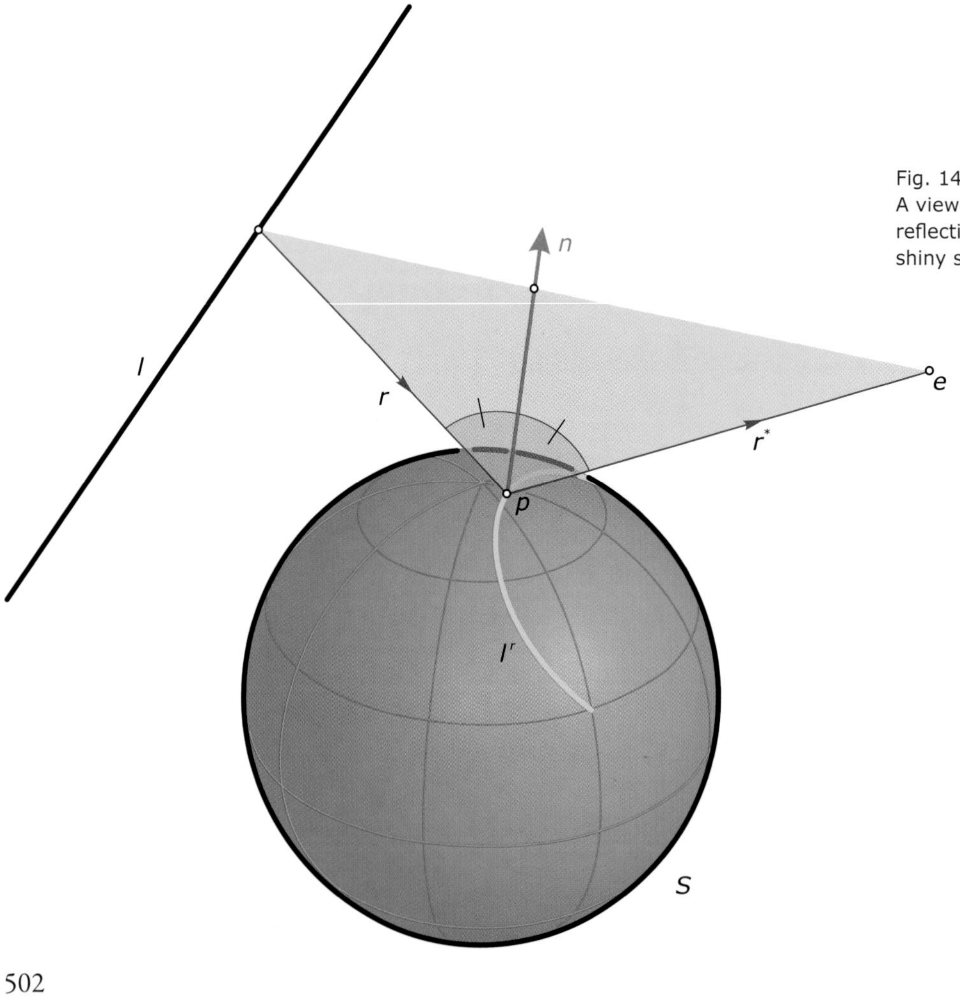

Fig. 14.29
A viewer with eye point e sees a reflection line l^r of a light source l on a shiny surface S.

Optical Lines for Quality Control

If a surface S is built from a shiny material, the surrounding scene will be reflected in it as in a mirror. These reflections are not simple projections. The way in which we see such mirror images also depends on the surface normals. Therefore, we observe some unexpected behavior. For example, even if the surface S has a well-defined tangent plane everywhere the mirror image of a smooth curve may have tangent discontinuities. To understand this effect and similar ones, we have to thoroughly examine the geometric situation.

Generation of a reflection line. Assume that we are given a shiny surface S (which we also call the mirror surface) and a straight line l, which we may assume to be a light source. Then, a viewer whose eye is placed at point e will see a reflected image l^r of l on S (Figure 14.29). For the geometric generation of l^r, we first recall the *law of reflection*: The incoming ray r and the reflected ray r^* lie in a plane through the surface normal n at the point p of reflection; moreover, the angle $\angle rn$ equals the angle $\angle nr^*$.

A point p is a point of the reflection line l^r if there is a ray r emanating from a point on the source l such that the reflected ray r^* passes through the eye point e. To test whether a point p of the surface S belongs to the reflection line, one reflects the ray $r^* = pe$ to obtain the ray r and checks whether this ray r intersects the source l. The light source need not be straight. We can take any curve l as a light source.

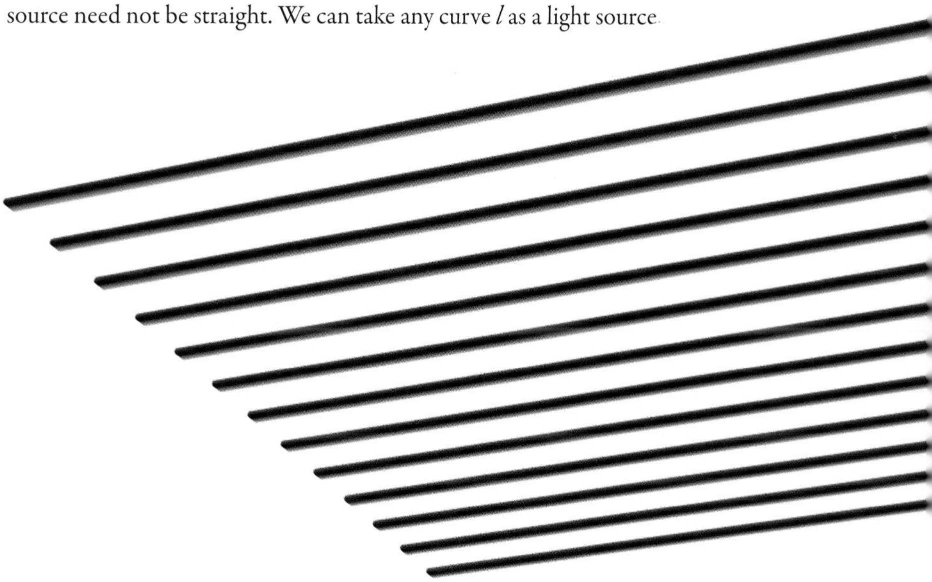

Math:

Let's sketch an analytic description of a reflection line. Assume that the surface is given in parametric form $p(u,v) = (x(u,v),y(u,v),z(u,v))$. We want to find the parameter values (u,v) of surface points $p(u,v)$, which belong to the reflection line. One has to connect $p(u,v)$ and e and reflect at the surface. To do so, we need the surface normal at p—which requires differentiation with respect to u and v (i.e., the partial derivative vectors p_u and p_v of $p(u,v)$ with respect to u and v). Thus, the reflected image r of the ray $r^* = pe$ contains in its mathematical representation functions of p, p_u, and p_v. Finally, the intersection condition between r and l is an equation of the form

$$F(p(u,v),p_u(u,v),p_v(u,v)) = 0.$$

One may view this as a definition of a curve in the (u,v) parameter domain that corresponds to the reflection line l^r. Because first-order derivatives of $p(u,v)$ are involved, we loose one order of differentiability. For example, a surface $p(u,v)$ with continuous first derivatives leads to a reflection line that has continuous positions but may have tangent discontinuities (sharp corners; see Figure 14.30). These effects are discussed in more detail in material following. Their origin is this loss of one order of differentiability, which in turn results from the fact that normals are involved in the definition of a reflection line.

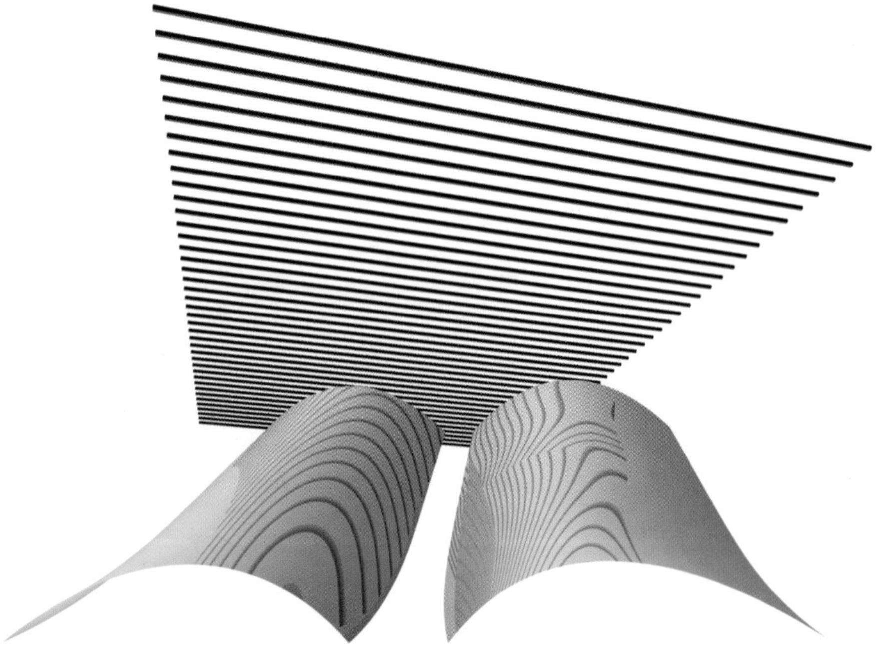

Fig. 14.30
If two patches are connected along a curve c such that the tangent planes agree along c but the curvature is not continuous there, this "defect" in smoothness is clearly seen in reflection lines. Those have tangent discontinuities (corners) at curvature discontinuities of the surface.

Isophotes. Before proceeding with a discussion of the behavior of reflection lines, we mention another family of optical lines (which may actually be seen as a special case of reflection lines). These are *isophotes*, whose definition also depends on the surface normals. One takes a fixed direction—determined, for example, by a vector v. Then, a curve c on S along which the surface normals form a constant angle α with v is called an *isophote* (Figure 14.31). In a simple shading model, these curves are isocurves of intensity. They have also been used in descriptive geometry for the enhancement of the realistic appearance of a drawing (Figure 14.32).

Contour generators. Consider a special isophote c on S along which the angle α between the normals and the viewing direction v is a right angle (Figure 14.33). At each point p of c, there is a line r parallel to v and normal to the surface normal (i.e., r is tangent to the surface). We may view r as a projection ray of a parallel projection parallel to v or as a light ray. Then, c has to be considered as contour generator or shadow contour.

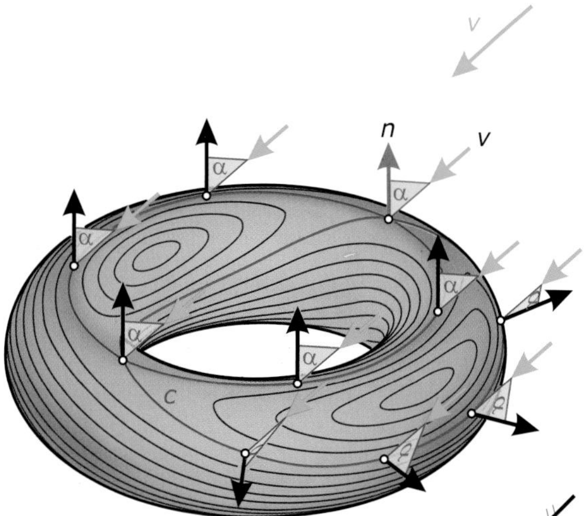

Fig. 14.31
Along an isophote c of a surface with respect to a direction v, all surface normals form a constant angle with v.

Fig. 14.32
Before the advent of computer graphics, the production of realistic images of objects was a time-consuming and tedious process. Constructions of isophotes served to enhance the realistic appearance of a drawing.

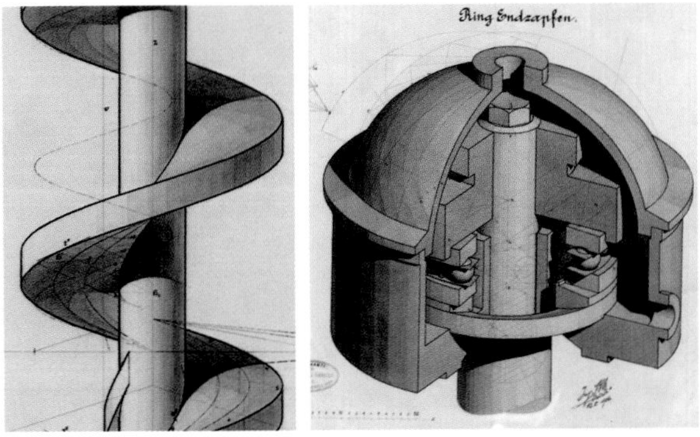

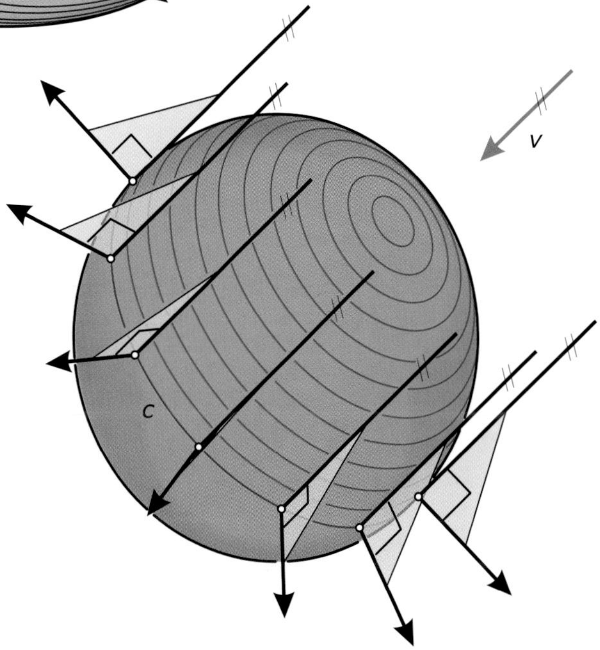

Fig. 14.33
A contour generator c is a special isophote. Along c, the surface normal is orthogonal to v (i.e., at each point of c there is a surface tangent r parallel to v).

Example:

Contour generator of simple objects. To support our claim that optical lines are less smooth than the original surface, we consider two very simple examples (Figure 14.34). The first is the union of a coaxial cone and a cylinder of revolution. For the shown viewing direction v, the contour generator consists of straight line segments (rulings of cone and cylinder) that are not connected at the common circle k. This follows from the fact that cylinder and cone have different tangent planes along k. Thus, although the object has a continuous surface the contour generator is not continuous.

The second object is even tangent continuous and has a hemisphere on top of a cylinder. There, the contour generator for the shown direction v consists of a half great circle (on the spherical part) and two straight line segments (on the cylindrical part). The contour generator as a whole is not smooth. There is a sharp corner at the common circle k of sphere and cylinder. Thus, the contour generator is not tangent continuous—whereas the surface has a well-defined tangent plane at every point.

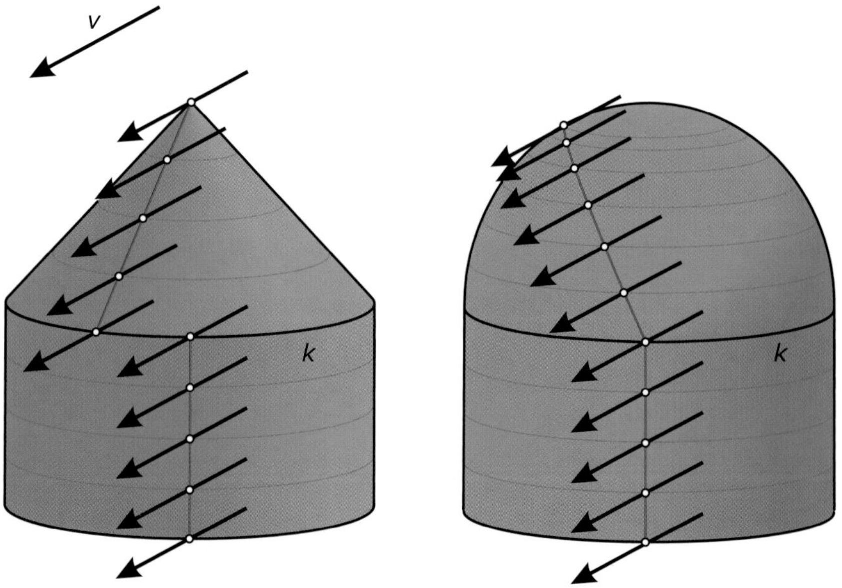

Fig. 14.34
Contour generators for objects consisting of a cone or a sphere on top of a right circular cylinder. The contour generator is discontinuous for the left-hand object and has tangent discontinuities for the tangent continuous object on the right side.

Optical lines for shape analysis. Optical lines (i.e., reflection lines or isophotes) are frequently used tools for quality control of surfaces. This is due to the following.

- An optical line c on a surface S in general has a discontinuity at a tangent discontinuity of S (Figure 14.35a).
- An optical line has a corner point (tangent discontinuity) at a curvature discontinuity of the underlying surface S (Figure 14.35b).
- For a curvature-continuous surface [e.g., a B-spline surface with degree greater or equal to three (and single knots)], all optical lines are smooth (Figure 14.35c).
- Optical lines are sensitive to small imperfections such as bumps (Figure 14.35d).

The proof of these facts follows from the mathematical formulation given previously.

Example:
Subdivision surface. Surfaces constructed with the subdivison algorithms of Doo-Sabin, Catmull-Clark or Loop are not curvature continuous at irregular vertices of the input mesh. Reflection lines clearly exhibit this defect of smoothness (Figure 14.36).

Fig. 14.35
(a) Optical lines are useful in detecting tangent discontinuities or
(b) curvature discontinuities on a surface.
(c) A smooth pattern of reflection lines is considered an indicator of a fair surface because
(d) small imperfections such as bumps are clearly seen in the reflection lines.

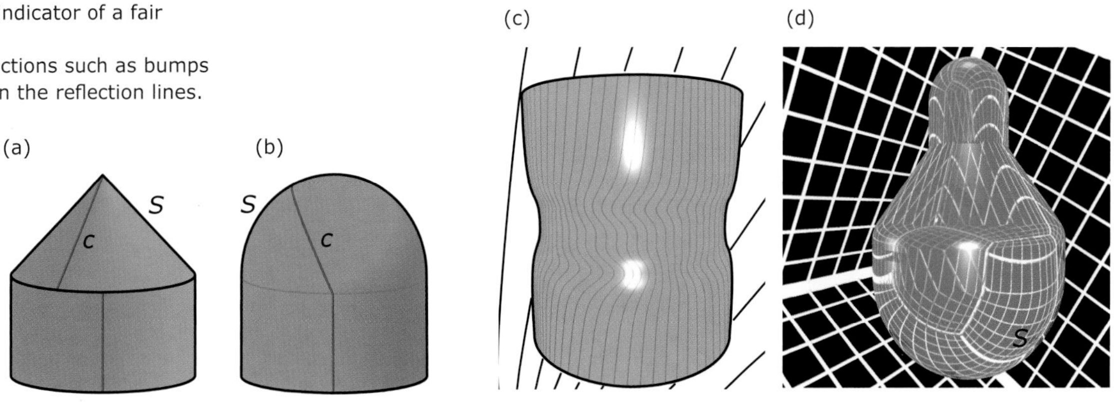

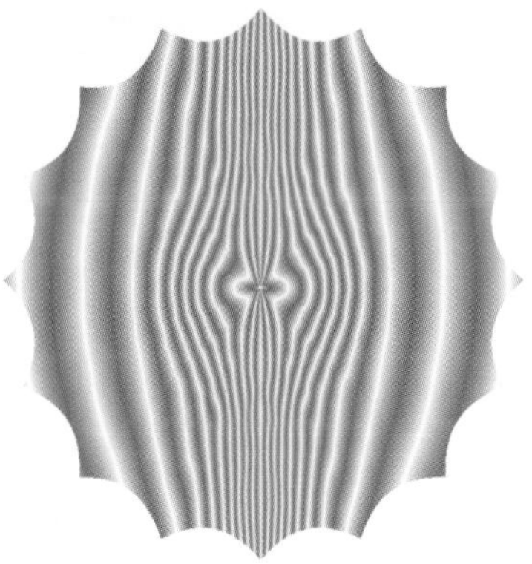

Fig. 14.36
The pattern of reflection lines reveals an undesirable curvature behavior of a Loop subdivision surface (cf. Figure 14.25) caused by an irregular vertex of the control mesh (image courtesy of I. Ginkel and G. Umlauf).

Implications on aesthetic design. If the curved surface will generate reflections, the quality of the surface is important (Figure 14.37). It can be tested with help of optical curves. There are also algorithms that allow us to modify a surface so that the pattern of reflection lines becomes more pleasing. In any case, we have to note that if we want to have smooth mirror images of smooth curves the mirror surface S must be curvature continuous. For a B-spline surface, this is achieved by using degree 3 or higher in both parameter directions.

Fig. 14.37
Reflections of a building in a car hood from different viewpoints.

Texture Mapping

We have seen in Chapter 1 that there are a number of possibilities for mapping texture onto an object in order to enhance its realistic appearance or to make it more attractive. An object can be represented in boundary or solid form. Likewise, we can map texture just to the boundary surface of the object or we can assign texture to the solid itself.

In the latter case, we will see the texture on all cuts of the object. Associated with the three basic coordinate systems (Cartesian, cylindrical, spherical), the embedding space may be textured. The object is then assigned this texture (Figure 14.38). Thus, this depends on the relative position between the underlying coordinate system and the object. In this way, one can handle both surface textures and solid textures.

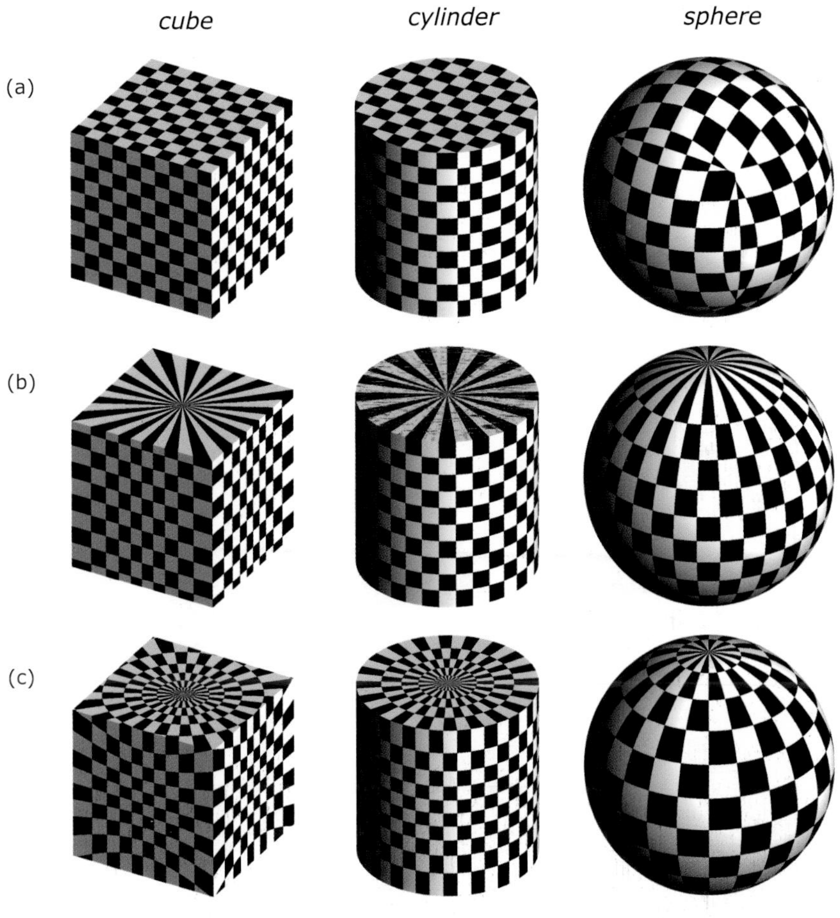

Fig. 14.38
A simple way of mapping texture onto a surface (or solid) is to take it from a spatial texture associated with the underlying coordinate system.
(a) We show here a Cartesian system,
(b) a cylindrical system, and
(c) a spherical system.

Under the application of a deformation, one may be able to deform the texture as well. Hence, if we model a more complicated object from a simpler one via a deformation it depends on the application and the desired effects whether we apply the texture before or after the deformation. Figure 14.39 illustrates the difference.

If a surface S is represented by a parameterization $(x(u,v), y(u,v), z(u,v))$, it is the image of a mapping from the uv-parameter domain to three-dimensional space. S may be seen as the image of a deformation of the parameter domain, and thus the method outlined previously can be applied. We can assign a texture to the uv-parameter domain and map it via the parametric representation onto the surface.

As we have seen previously, there are many different parameter representations that describe the same surface as a set of points. However, in connection with textures the points are assigned a color (texture value) and therefore the value has an influence on which parameterization one uses in regard to the final appearance of the texture. Figure 14.40 shows a simple grid texture mapped onto the same surface, but using two different parameterizations.

Many modeling systems will provide automatic solutions, based on the standard internal parameterization. However, there is also a large amount of research on texture mapping that is based on optimal parameterizations of the surface.

Unfortunately, unless a surface S is developable there are no isometric mappings from the parameter domain to S and thus the problem becomes difficult. Figure 14.41 shows a state-of-the-art result of texture mapping, which is based on an optimized parameterization. Its explanation would be far beyond the scope of this book.

Fig. 14.39
If an object S_1 results from an object S by a deformation, we have two different options for assigning a texture.
(left) We can map a basic texture to S and then deform toward S_1,
(right) or we can apply the texture to S_1 after the deformation.

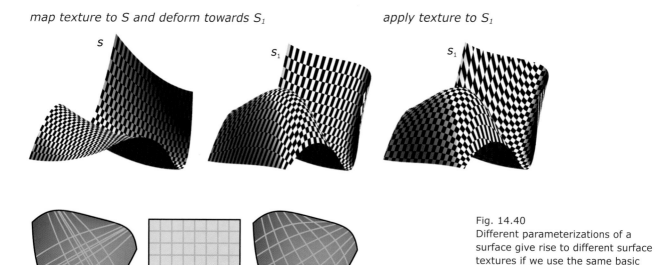

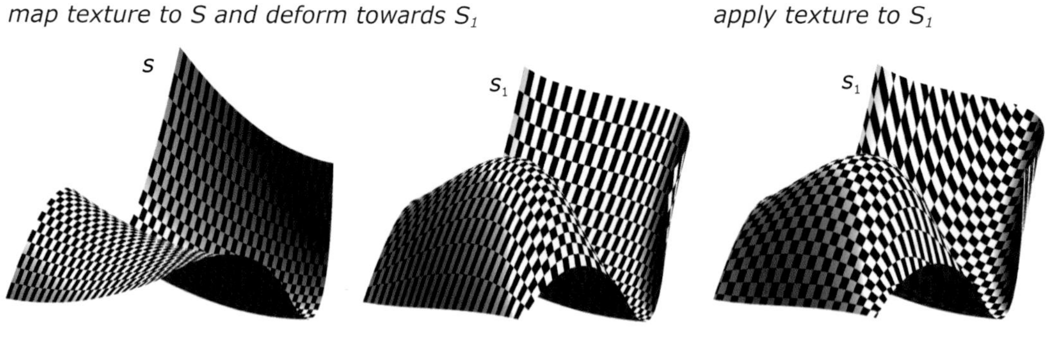

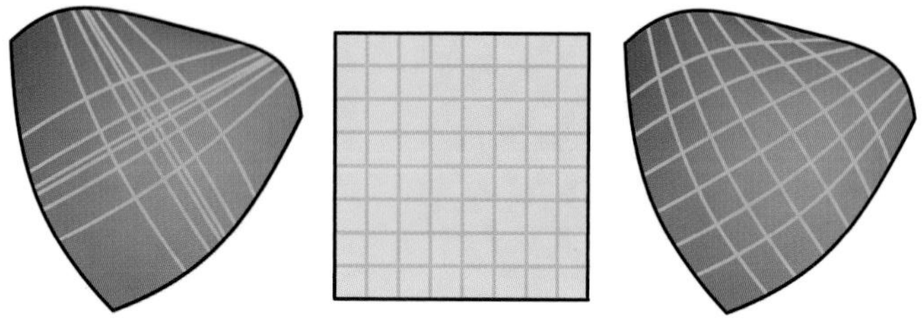

Fig. 14.40
Different parameterizations of a surface give rise to different surface textures if we use the same basic texture in the parameter domain.

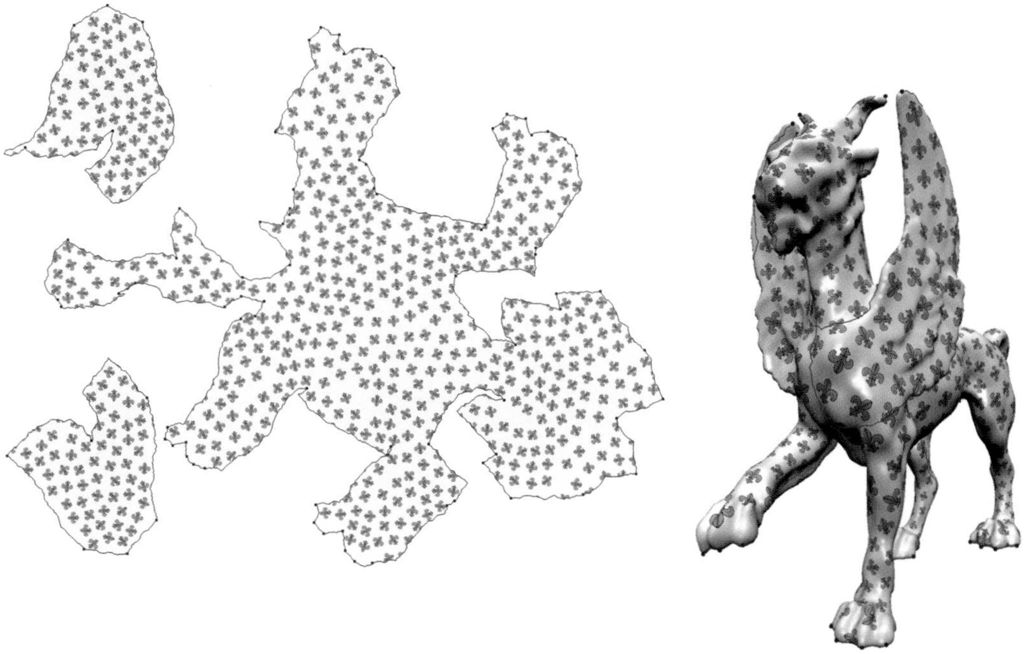

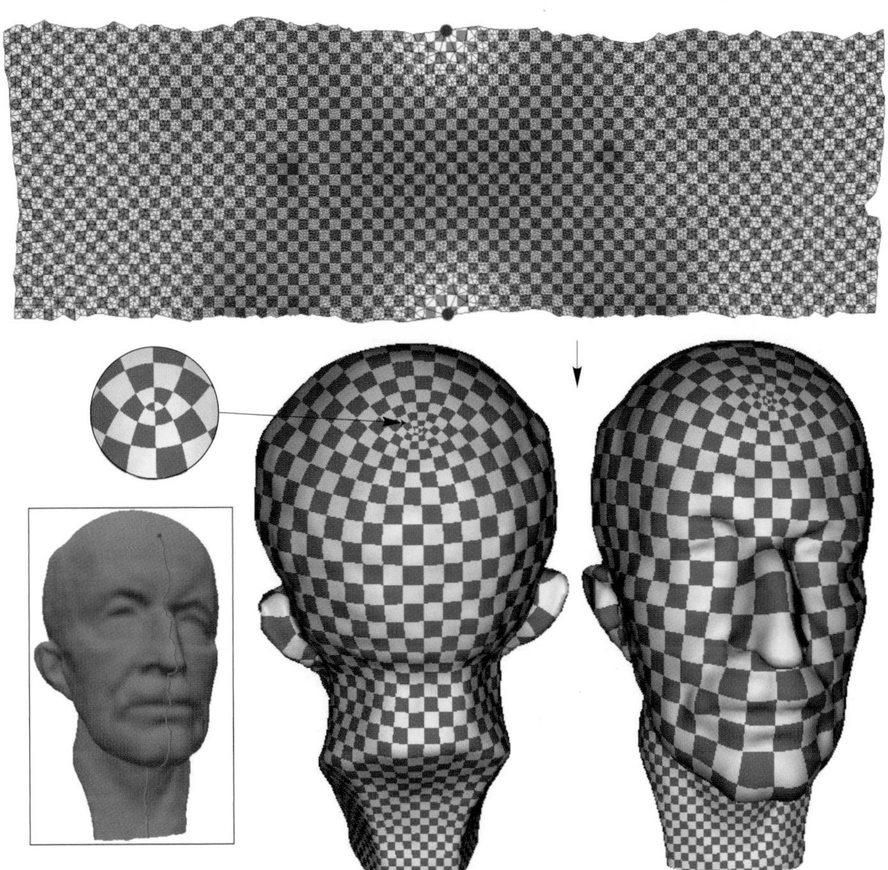

Fig. 14.41
High-quality texture mapping onto a complex surface such as the one shown here requires advanced mathematical methods, which are still an active topic of research. (Images courtesy of P. Schröder.)

Example:

Texturing a cone. The Tacoma Museum of Glass by Arthur Erickson (Figure 14.42) incorporates as its most striking feature a tilted cone covered by diamond-shaped stainless steel plates. Designing the pattern of the tiles may be seen as a problem of texture mapping. Although the cone is developable, we cannot just cut it along a generator line g and unfold it into the plane. Applying a planar texture to the developed cone may result in a clearly visible seam along g after mapping back to space.

To obtain a similar design, but one with tiles of constant vertex angles, we may proceed in another way. We start with a curve c_1 on the cone that intersects all rulings under a constant angle (spiral curve; see Chapter 7). Then we assemble N copies of it on the cone by successively rotating c_1 about the cone axis by an angle of $360/N$ degrees into new positions c_2, $c_3, \ldots, c_N = c_1$. (See Figure 14.43.)
Finally, this rotational system of curves is reflected at a plane through the cone axis, resulting in the desired tile pattern.

Further variants of this example may be obtained by mapping the cone pattern to another cone, which is no longer rotational. If this mapping is isometric, the pattern has again the constant intersection angle property. This example shows that texture mapping may also employ mappings between surfaces and not just plane-to-surface mappings.

Fig. 14.42
Museum of Glass (1998-2002) in Tacoma by Arthur Erickson.

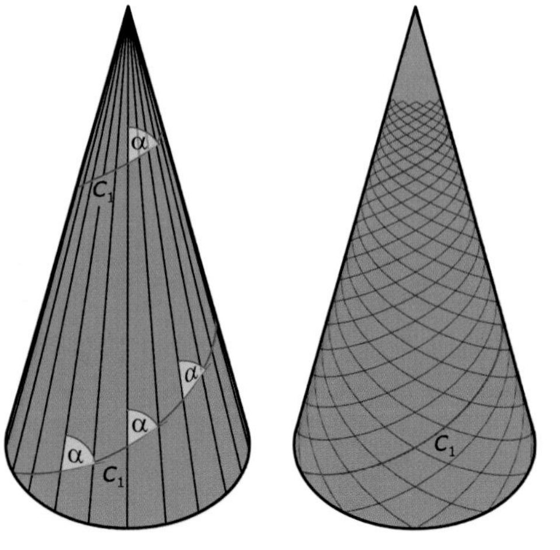

Fig. 14.43
In this design of a pattern on a cone, we start with a spiral curve on the cone. It intersects the cone rulings under a constant angle of 60 degrees. Rotated and reflected copies of c_1 finally give a pattern with diamond-shaped tiles. These tiles form a constant angle at each vertex.

Digital Elevation Models

Placing an architectural design within its environmental context is useful and interesting for purposes of visualization and presentation, and can be essential for the actual construction—especially if the local topography is more complicated or if one wants to use shapes of the surrounding landscape in the design (Figure 14.44). Thus, we briefly address a few aspects of computer representations and the geometry of topographic surfaces.

Fig. 14.44
Architecture in harmony with its environment. The Liaunig Museum (2004, project) by Odile Decq.

Data acquisition and main representations. Providing precise and sufficiently many measurements of the earth's topography has been a tedious and time-consuming task for surveyors. Today, the data acquisition process is greatly simplified by modern technologies such as airborne laser scanning. It results in millions of data points on the topographic surface.

After some processing (such as noise removal or filtering of measurement points, which are actually on the vegetation and not on the ground), one obtains a *digital elevation model.* Figure 14.45 shows two frequently used representations of topographic surfaces in digital elevation models: a grid-based approach and a triangulation.

A grid-based representation basically assigns heights to data points in a regular grid. Simple interpolation techniques are used to derive a surface from this data. Triangulations (polyhedral surfaces with triangular faces) are not restricted to a grid-like arrangement of vertices. Therefore, they have advantages in the representation of important features such as sharp ridges or peaks.

Topographic surfaces. Topographic surfaces are much less regular or smooth than the surfaces discussed so far. This complicated behavior implies that one actually needs to define a *resolution*; that is, a *level of detail* to which one wants to represent the surface. We all know this from topographic maps which come in different scales. At a larger scale, certain simplifications have to be made. Because this is not a topic of architecture, we will not discuss it further.

For the integration of architecture or other man-made constructions into the existing environment, and for presentations and simulations, it may be useful to know a few basic concepts of topographic surfaces. They stem from the fact that for a topographic surface the vertical direction (direction of gravity) plays a special role.

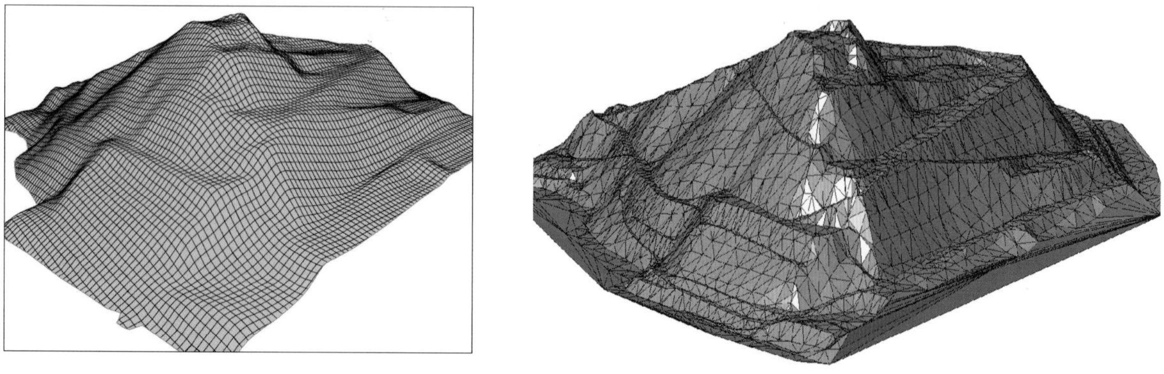

Fig. 14.45
The two main representations of topographic surfaces in digital elevation models are (left) the arrangement of data points over a regular grid in the plane and (right) a triangulation. (Image courtesy of G. Mandlburger.)

The intersection curves of a topographic surface S with a surface L of constant height above sea level (on a sufficiently small part of the earth, this surface L can be taken as a plane) is called a *contour line*. It is a level set of the height function (see Chapter 13). We may say that the contour lines on S are the horizontal curves that possess no ascent or descent.

Orthogonal to the contour lines are the *curves of steepest descent*, along which the water would flow down (if the surface were sufficiently smooth). In an orthogonal projection onto a plane of constant sea level we see the right angle between contour lines and curves of steepest descent (Figure 14.46).

Fig. 14.46
(a) Contour lines (curves of constant height above sea level) and
(b) curves of steepest descent (flow lines of water) form an orthogonal curve network on a topographic surface (image courtesy of T. Steiner).

(c, d) The right angles in this network are also seen in an orthogonal projection onto a plane of constant height.

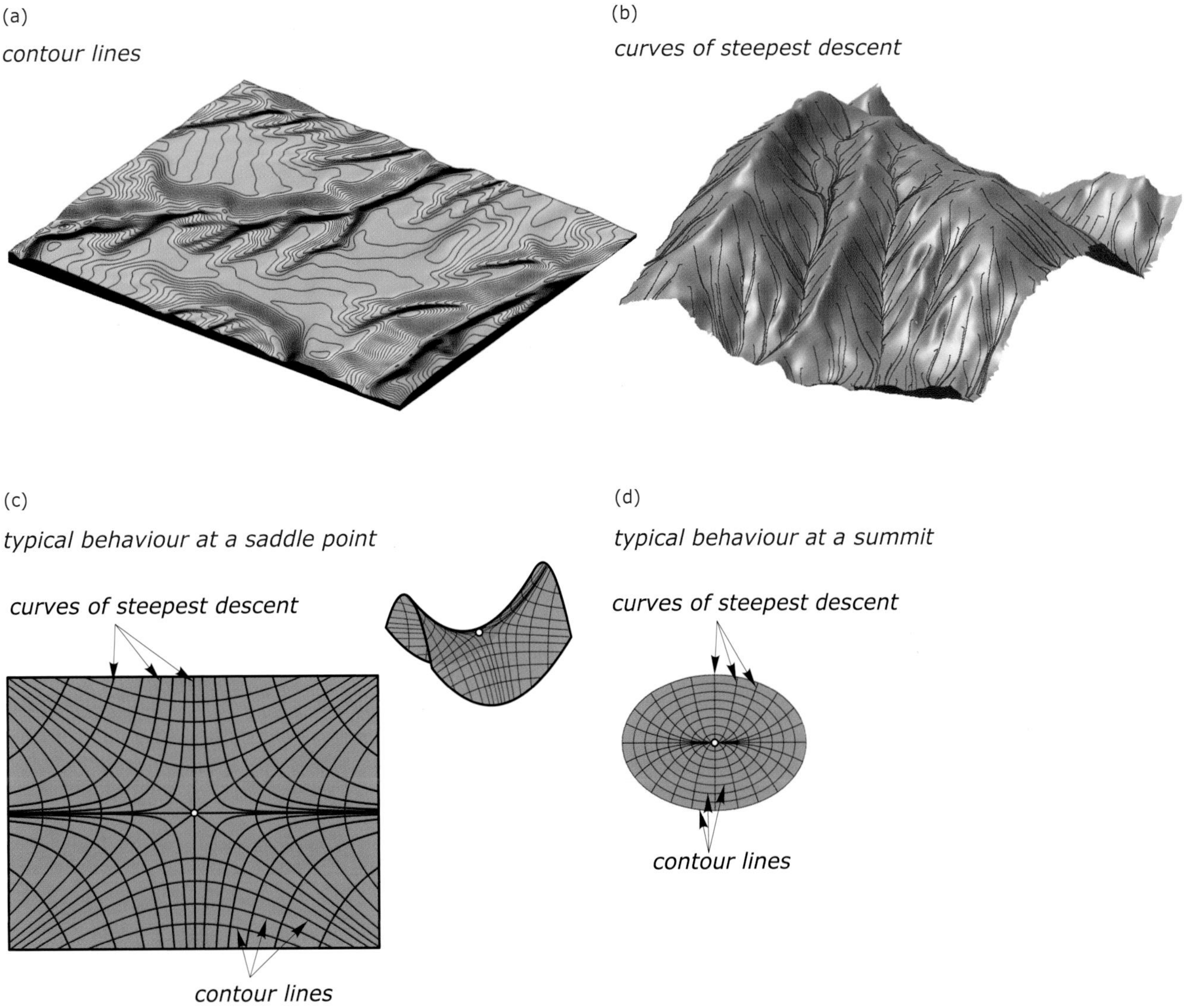

Assuming a smooth surface, the orthogonal network of level curves and curves of steepest descent is singular at *critical points*. These are defined as points with a horizontal tangent plane (see Figure 14.47). Some of them (like certain summits or even saddle points) may be important locations in the landscape. We will encounter critical points again in the following section on topology.

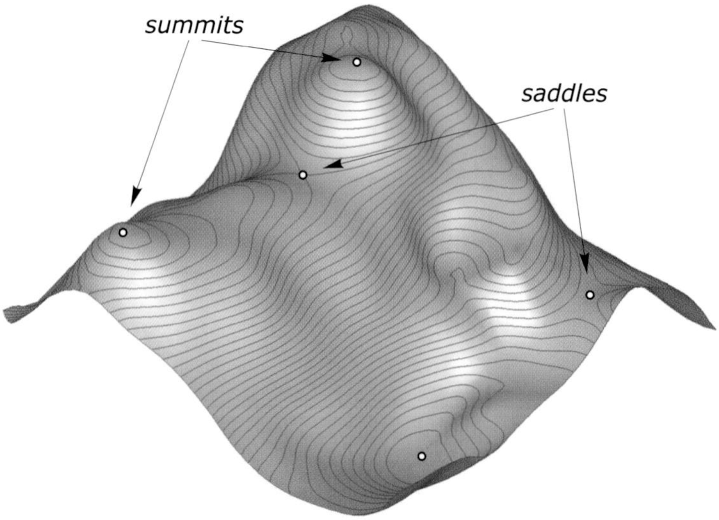

Fig. 14.47
Critical points of a topographic surface possess a horizontal tangent plane. They are locally highest points (summits), locally deepest points (e.g., at the bottom of a lake), or saddle points. In this figure, we also see the behavior of the level curves.

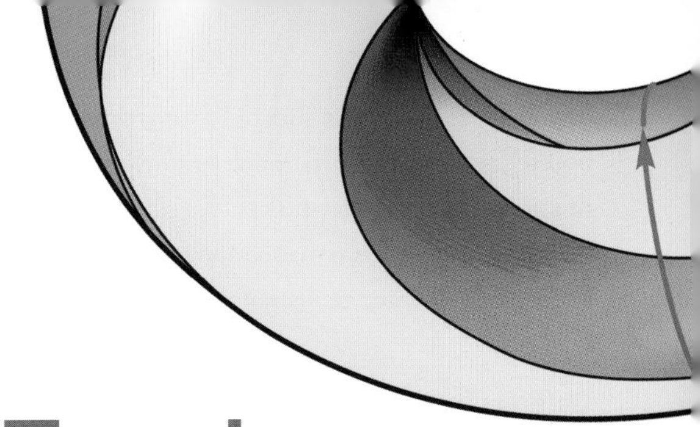

Geometric Topology and Knots

Open versus closed surfaces. Very roughly speaking, topology deals with a description of the way geometric objects are connected. The actual shape is not important. Nor does topology distinguish between smoothness and non-smoothness. For example, a rectangular surface patch bounded by four straight line segments, a spherical patch bounded by three circular arcs, and a circular disk are topologically equivalent objects. They are *open surfaces* because they have a boundary. Even more special, the surfaces in Figure 14.48 are confined by a single boundary curve. Of course, this single boundary curve (perhaps better termed a *boundary loop*) is not smooth for the first two examples.

The examples in Figure 14.48 are *simply connected*. They have a single boundary curve and no holes. More formally, a surface S is simply connected if any closed curve in S can be shrunk to a single point such that each intermediate position is in S. Figure 14.49 illustrates this property of a simply connected patch S and shows how it fails for some patches that are not simply connected.

Fig. 14.48
From the perspective of topology, all of these geometric objects are equivalent. They can be mapped into each other by a deformation, which does not change the way in which the objects are connected. In particular, such a topology-preserving deformation keeps boundaries but may change their smoothness.

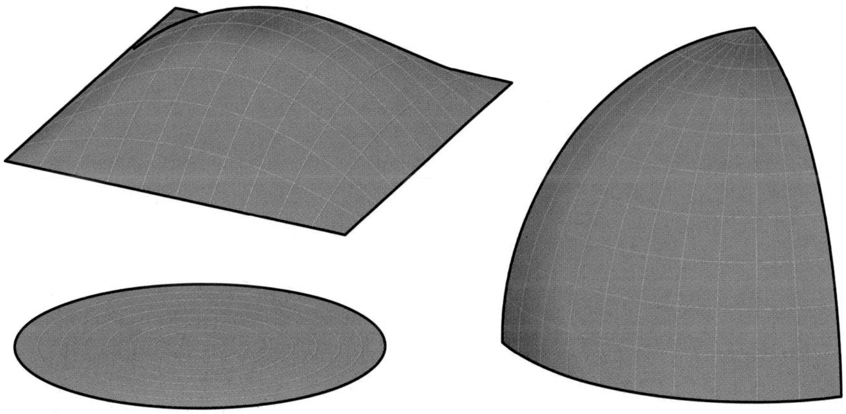

The cylindrical piece in Figure 14.49 (right) is also an open surface because it has boundary curves. A surface that has no boundary curves is called a *closed surface*. All of its points are interior points. We can walk from any point on the surface in any direction and always remain on the surface. Examples of closed surfaces are a torus or a sphere, or deformed images of these.

Deformations that do not change topology. When dealing with topology, it is important not to focus on special geometric properties but only have in mind how objects are connected. Let's look at an example. All surfaces in Figure 14.50 are topologically equivalent to a sphere. This is so because deformations that do not create new connections or holes can be found that map each of the surfaces into a sphere.

Imagine the objects made of thin rubber, with air blown into them as into a balloon. They will more and more obtain the shape of a sphere. Figure 14.51 shows an example of such a morphing into a sphere. Closed surfaces that are topologically equivalent to a sphere are said to have *topological genus zero*. Note that we cannot map a torus into a sphere, but obviously we can morph it into a sphere with a single handle—or into a cuboid with a hole (Figure 14.52).

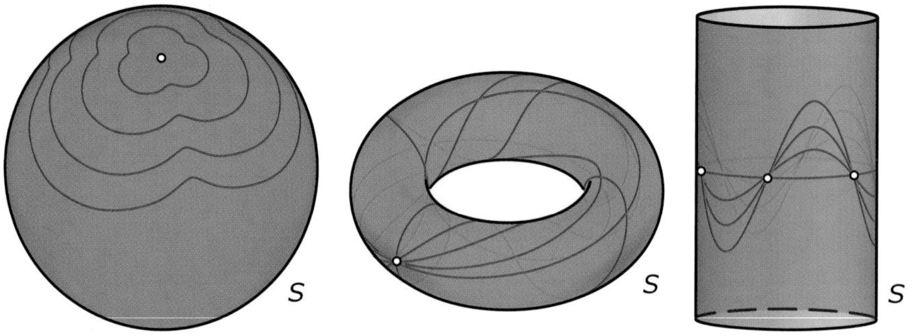

Fig. 14.49
On a simply connected surface S, each closed curve can be shrunk to a single point such that each intermediate position is in S. On a surface with holes (middle) or for the cylindrical piece on the right-hand side, this is not possible.

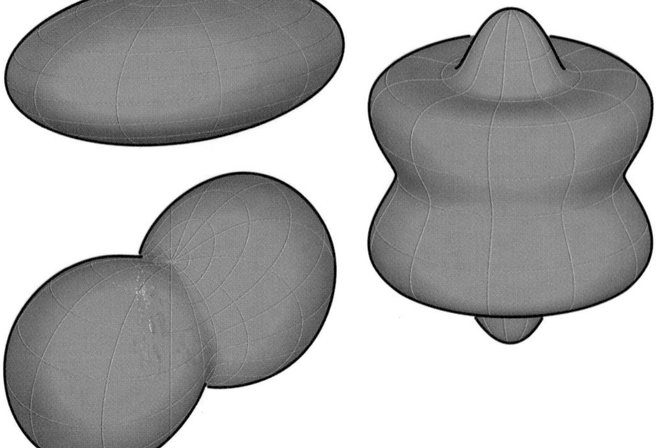

Fig. 14.50
All of these surfaces are topologically equivalent to a sphere.

Fig. 14.51
A surface of topological genus zero can be morphed into a sphere (images courtesy of Martin Kilian).

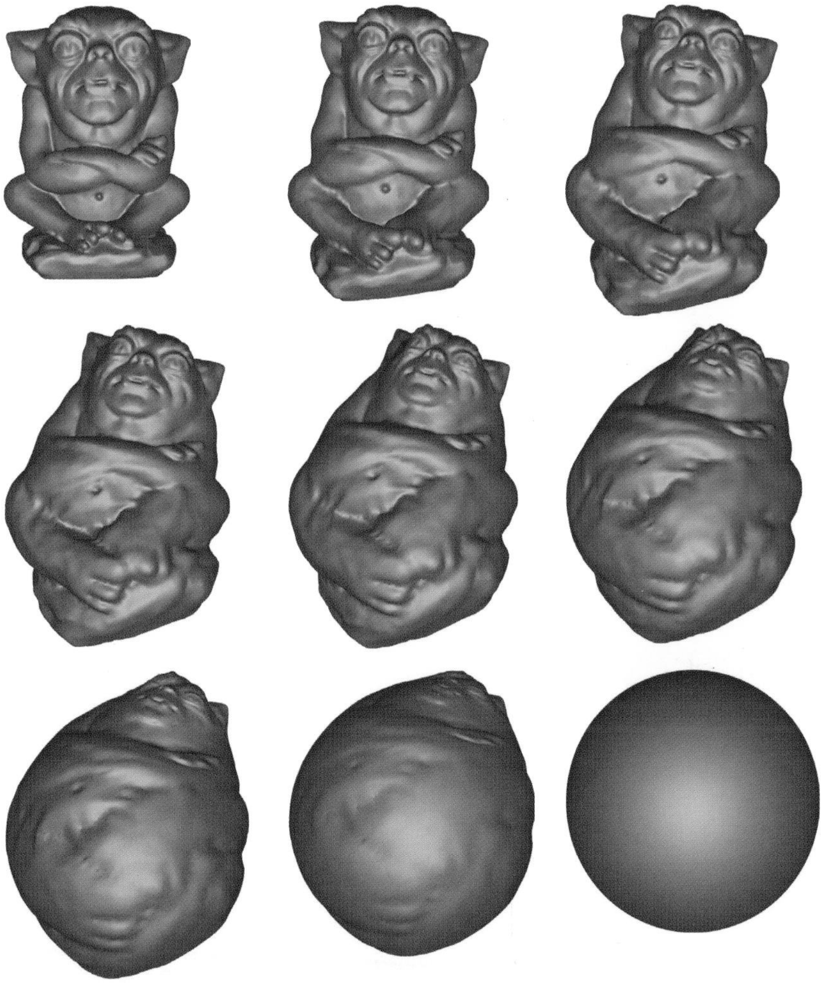

Fig. 14.52
Surfaces topologically equivalent to a torus.

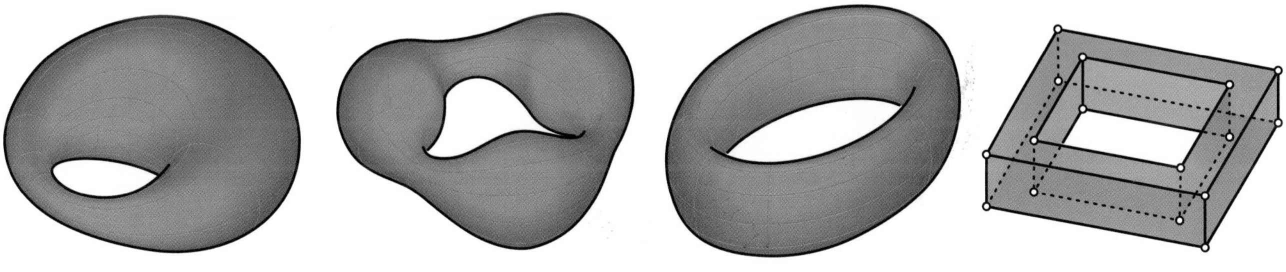

Orientable versus non-orientable surfaces. All surfaces we have studied in the previous examples are *orientable*; that is, they have two sides. We can paint these two sides in different colors. For example, the inner side of a sphere or a torus can be assigned a color different from the outer side. This is not always the case. For example, the Möbius band encountered in Chapters 9 and 12 does not have this property.

The Klein bottle shown in Figure 14.53 is another example of a non-orientable surface. Unlike the Möbius band, it has a self-intersection (but it is closed). The one-sided property of the Möbius band has fascinated artists and architects. We have seen Escher's version in Chapter 12. Figure 14.54 shows an architectural project that has been inspired by the Möbius band.

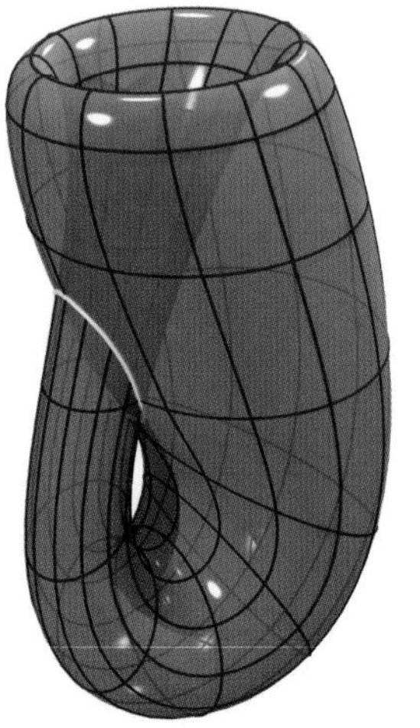

Fig. 14.53
A Klein bottle is an example of a non-orientable surface.

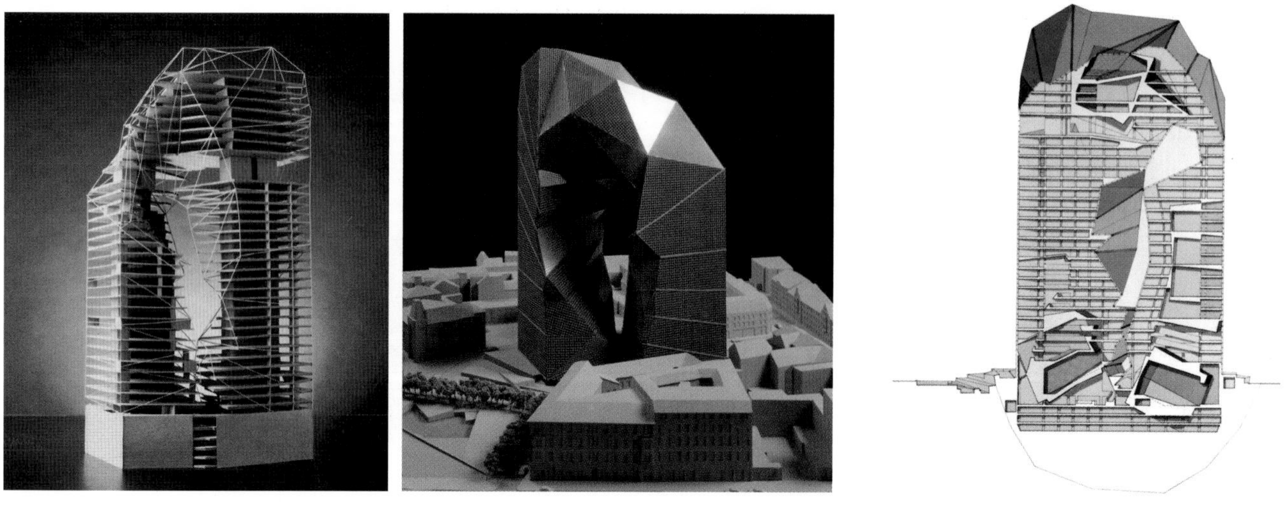

Fig. 14.54
The Max Reinhardt House project (1992) by Peter Eisenman has been inspired by the Möbius band, an example of a non-orientable surface (images courtesy of Eisenman Architects).

Euler's formula. In our study of polyhedra in Chapter 3, we encountered a remarkable relation among the number v of vertices, the number e of edges, and the number f of faces. If the polyhedron is topologically equivalent to a sphere, Euler's formula holds:

$$v - e + f = 2. \qquad (14.4)$$

This formula is much more widely applicable as follows. Given a closed surface, we decompose it into simply connected patches (cells, faces). In such a *cell decomposition*, vertices are points where at least two faces meet and edges are face boundaries connecting two vertices. (Essential vertices are only those where at least three faces meet, but keeping further ones does not cause problems.) In other words, we may draw a curve network on a surface that decomposes it into simply connected faces (see Figure 14.55).

To prove Euler's formula, we may think of these networks. Any network on a surface that is topologically equivalent to a sphere can be obtained as follows. We start from a very simple network, as shown in Figure 14.56a. It has one vertex, one (closed) edge, and two faces, and thus we have $v - e + f = 1 - 1 + 2 = 2$.

Fig. 14.55
Euler's formula $v - e + f = 2$ may also be applied to a curve network (cell decomposition) on a closed surface S that is topologically equivalent to a sphere. f is the number of (simply connected) cells (faces), v is the number of vertices, and e is the number of curve segments—each of which joins two vertices and separates two faces. In this case, we have $v = 12$, $e = 22$, and $f = 12$.

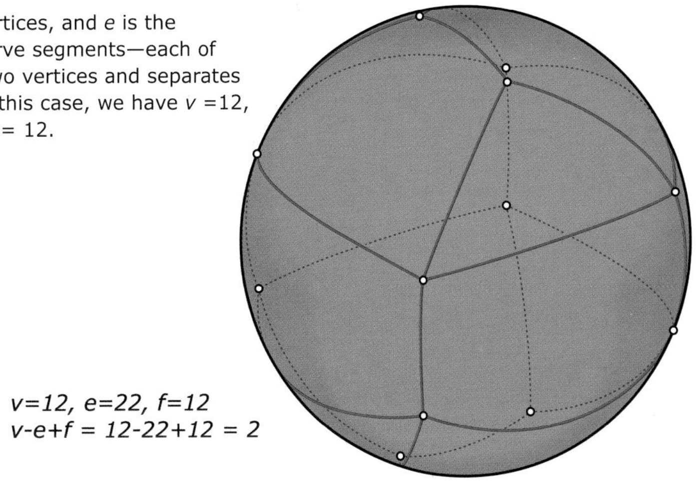

Fig. 14.56
A proof of Euler's formula $v - e + f = 2$ verifies it for the basic cell decomposition shown in (a) and (b) then observes that vertex insertion and (c) edge insertion do not change the value of $v - e + f$. By applying these operations one may obtain any cell decomposition.

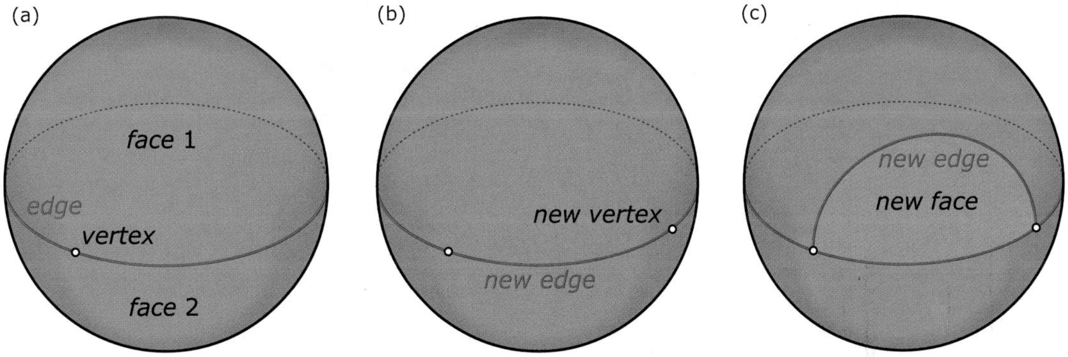

A more complicated network may be obtained from such a simple one by iterative application of two basic operations; namely, insertion of an additional vertex on an existing edge and joining two vertices by a new edge (which splits an existing face into two faces). Let's see why $v - e + f$ does not change its value under these operations.

- If we insert a new vertex, we increase v by one. However, the new vertex will split an existing edge into two pieces and will thus also increase the number of edges by one. The number of faces remains unchanged. If a prime indicates the numbers after the vertex insertion, we have $v' - e' + f' = v + 1 - (e + 1) + f = v - e + f$.
- Likewise, joining two vertices by a new edge (which splits an existing face into two faces) increases the numbers of edges and faces by one but does not change the number of vertices: $v' - e' + f' = v - (e + 1) + f + 1 = v - e + f$.

This is a proof of the formula, where admittedly we did not further argue why any network (cell decomposition) can be reached in the way outlined previously.

Euler's formula for other topological types. The value of $v - e + f$ can be computed for any cell decomposition of a surface S or any polyhedron S. It only depends on the topology of S, but not on the special decomposition one has chosen. One calls this number $\chi = v - e + f$ the *Euler characteristic* of S.

Example:

Torus. As a first simple example of a closed surface S that is not topologically equivalent to a sphere, we take a (topological) torus. The elementary network used in the previous proof is not sufficient here because it does not decompose the torus into simply connected domains. However, we may use the network shown in Figure 14.57 (left). It forms the boundary of a simply connected patch covering the torus. This special network has one vertex, two edges, and one face and thus $\chi = v - e + f = 0$. The insertion of new vertices and edges results in more general networks (cell decompositions) for which the same formula must hold. We may not obtain all networks in this way. However, it can be shown that the formula is valid for any cell decomposition and thus the Euler characteristic for a surface topologically equivalent to a torus is zero:

$$v - e + f = 0. \qquad (14.5)$$

Let's examine why simply connected cells are necessary. Joining two vertices on the boundary of a not simply connected face may not split the face into two, but it might still be just one face and this would change the value of $v - e + f$. If we determine $\chi = v - e + f$ for a polyhedron, we may have to introduce further edges to make sure that all faces are simply connected (Figure 14.57, right).

Example:

Möbius band. The Euler characteristic also makes sense for surfaces with boundaries. You may verify easily that $\chi = v - e + f = 1$ for a Möbius band. In fact, you can use the generation of this band via appropriate gluing of a rectangle to obtain a proof.

Example:

Planar domain with holes. Take a planar domain D with an outer boundary curve c and with h holes (see Figure 14.58). Each cut joins a point of c with a point on a hole's boundary. For this basic network—composed of $v = 2h$ vertices (the end points of the cuts), $e = 3h$ edges (h edges on c, the h boundaries of the holes, and the h cuts), and the resulting single face $f = 1$—we have $\chi = v - e + f = 2h - 3h + 1 = 1 - h$. For any other decomposition into simply connected cells, we obtain the same value for the Euler characteristic; namely, $\chi = v - e + f = 1 - h$.

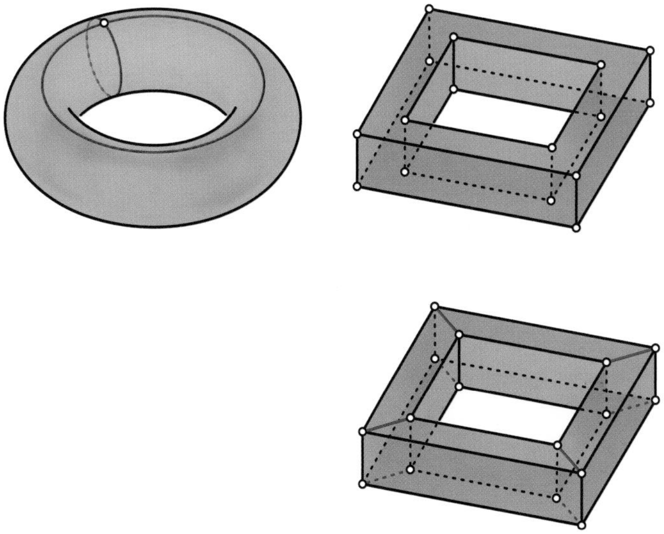

Fig. 14.57
(Left) Two cuts through a point on the torus can be made so that they form the boundary of a single simply connected patch.
(Right) The rule $v - e + f = 0$ for an object of the topology of a torus is only valid if all faces are simply connected. To determine the value of $v - e + f$ correctly, we may have to introduce further edges to make sure that all faces are simply connected.

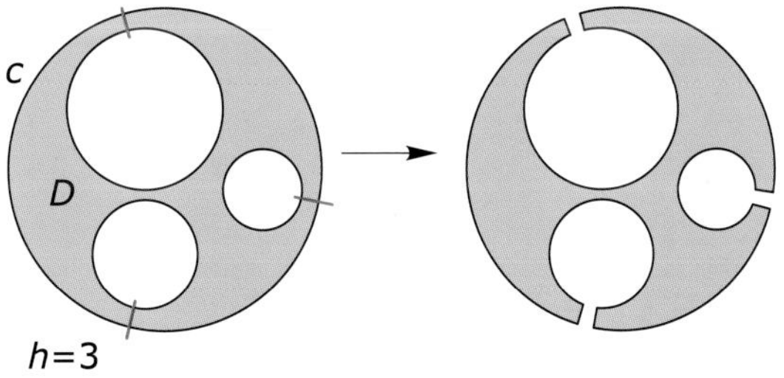

Fig. 14.58
With h cuts, a planar domain D with h holes can be cut into a simply connected domain. The result has been eroded near the cuts to better visualize the fact that we have a simply connected domain after the cutting operation.

Classification of closed orientable surfaces. A torus is equivalent to a sphere with one handle. It can be shown that any closed orientable surface S is equivalent to a sphere with a certain number g of handles. This number is called the *topological genus* of S. A sphere has genus $g = 0$, and a torus has genus $g = 1$. The Euler characteristic χ of a surface with genus g equals

$$\chi = v - e + f = 2 - 2g. \qquad (14.6)$$

It may be hard to visually determine the number g of handles for surfaces of higher genus, as for those shown in Figures 14.59 and 14.60. In addition, the use of a cell decomposition for computing the genus from Equation 14.6 may be difficult. To determine the genus in complicated cases, the following procedure can be used. We consider a height function on the surface. For example, we may just take the z coordinate of each point as the height value. Let's view the z-axis as vertical.

This function then has critical points at places where the tangent plane is horizontal. There are three types of critical points (see the section on topographic surfaces): local minima, local maxima, and saddle points. To a local minimum or maximum (elliptic surface point) we assign the value +1, and to a saddle point (hyperbolic surface point) we assign the value −1. It can then be shown that the Euler characteristic $\chi = 2 - 2g$ of the surface is the sum of all of these values (excluding certain degenerate cases of maxima, minima, or saddles whose explanation would require more math). Examples are shown in Figure 14.61.

Fig. 14.59
Higher-genus surfaces designed with an algorithm developed by Ergun Akleman (images courtesy of Jotero GbR)

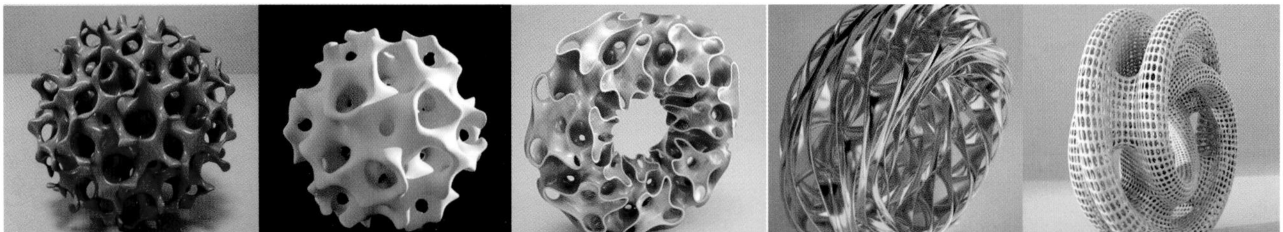

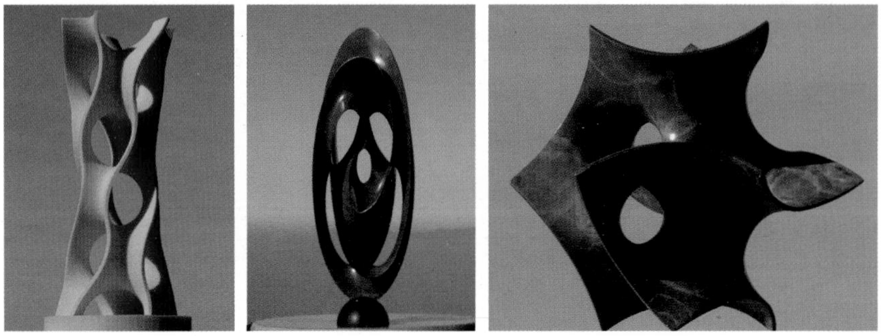

Fig. 14.60
As an exercise, the reader may determine the topological genus of the surfaces depicted in these sculptures by Carlo Sequin (images courtesy of Carlo Sequin). For this task, we consider the closed surface that confines the solid sculpture, though some of these objects may have been constructed from a thin solid layer around an open surface.

Other topological invariants. So far we have encountered several topological invariants, such as the number of boundary loops, the number of sides (orientable or non-orientable), the Euler characteristic, and the closely related genus. We mention here two further topological concepts that have a very intuitive explanation.

The first is the *maximal number of cuts* (closed cuts or cuts from boundary to boundary) one can make before a surface falls into two parts. For a sphere, this number is zero—and for a torus it is 2 (see Figure 14.57). Let's see how many cuts we can make until a Möbius band falls into two parts (see Figure 14.62). Making the first cut "in the middle" of the band, following roughly the direction of the boundary and making sure it is closed, the band does not fall apart. It becomes another closed band. One might think that the same trick works again. However, we obtain two closed bands that are linked (see Figure 14.62). Thus, we need to make another cut from boundary to boundary to obtain a simply connected domain. This illustrates (but does not prove) that the maximal number of cuts is two.

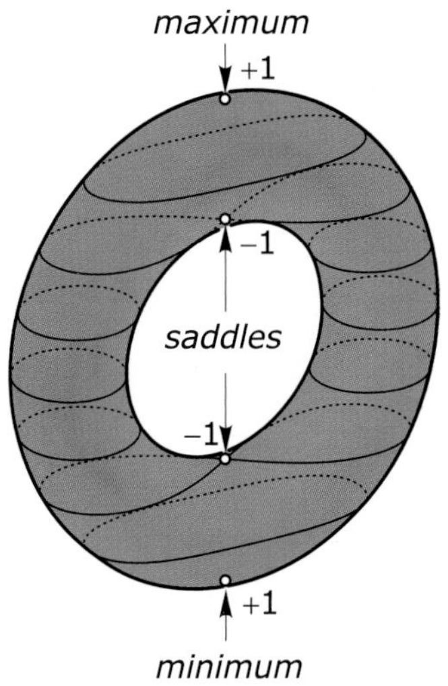

$\chi = 2 - 2 = 0$
$g = 1$

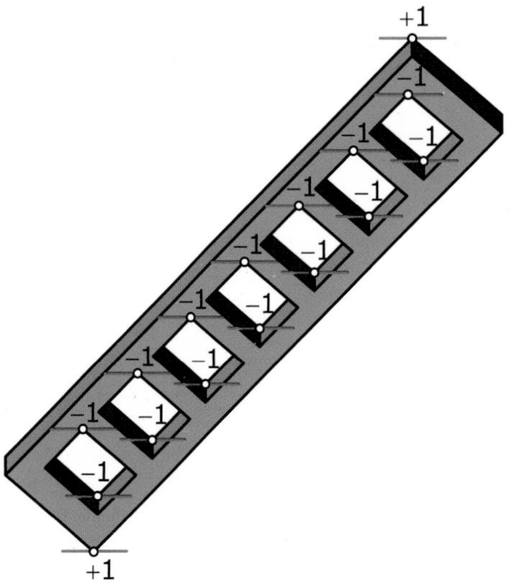

$\chi = 2 - 14 = -12$ $(= 2 - 2g)$
$g = 7$

Fig. 14.61
The genus g of a closed orientable surface can be determined with help of the critical points in a height function. One assigns the value +1 to local minima or maxima and the value −1 to saddles. Then, the Euler characteristic $\chi = 2 - 2g$ equals the sum of these values attached to critical points.

Fig. 14.62
We may make a closed cut in a Möbius band and obtain another closed band. Applying the procedure again, we obtain two linked bands.

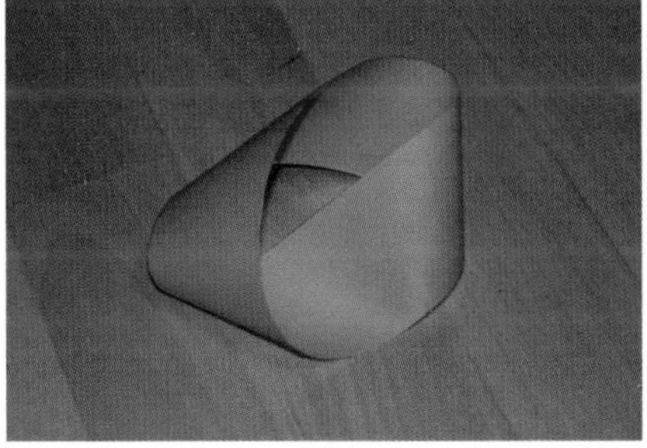

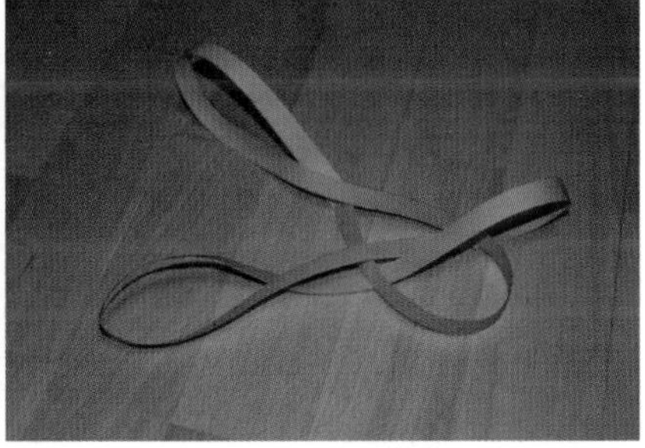

A further topological quantity is the *chromatic number*. It is the minimal number of colors we need to color code any possible map drawn on the surface such that (for example) adjacent countries have different colors along a common border. For the earth (a sphere), this number is four. A proof of that could not be given for a long time, but finally in 1977 one succeeded—but only with computer support. For a torus, the chromatic number turns out to be seven (see Figure 14.63).

Knots from the mathematical perspective. In mathematics, a *knot* is simply a *closed space curve without self-intersections*. For visualization, we may use a surface around this curve (for example, a pipe surface; Figure 14.64). The use of closed curves instead of "knotted" parts of an open curve has its origin in the much simpler formulation of admissible operations that do not change the type of knot.

One of these operations is shortening part of a knot (without introducing intersections). Shortening an open curve from an end may eventually remove any visually knotted parts, and finally the curve may totally vanish. Hence, we need to close our knots to avoid this type of problem.

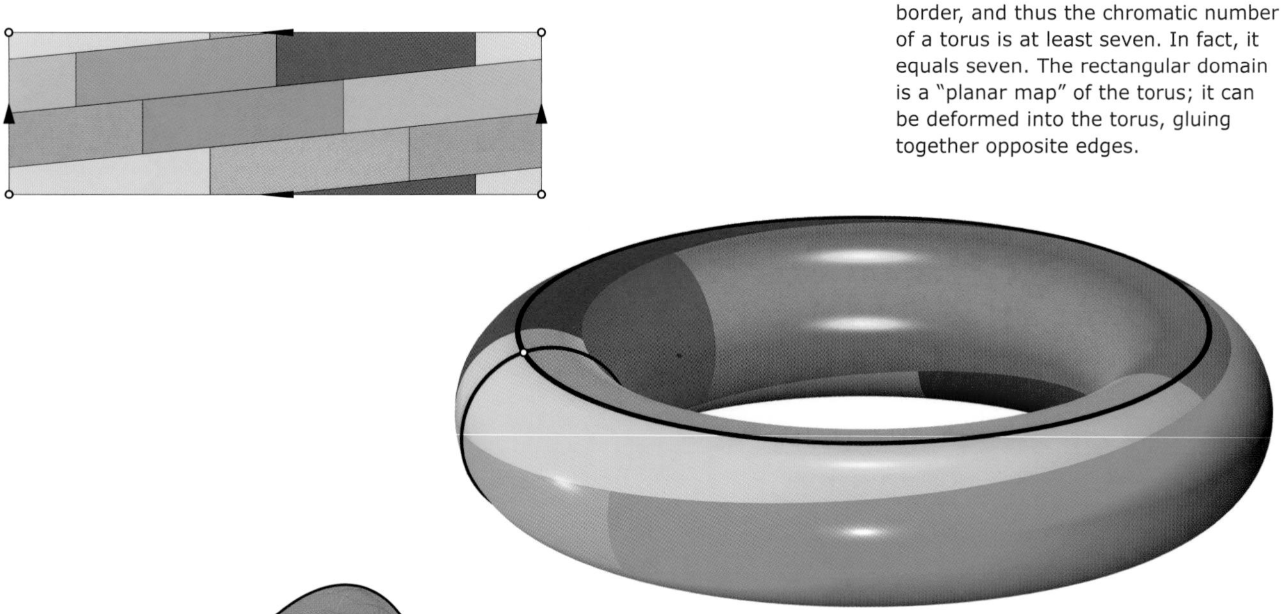

Fig. 14.63
The number of colors needed to color any possible map on a surface such that different countries exhibit a different color along a common border is a topological quantity. The number is four in the case of the sphere. One can distribute seven countries on a torus such that any two have a common border, and thus the chromatic number of a torus is at least seven. In fact, it equals seven. The rectangular domain is a "planar map" of the torus; it can be deformed into the torus, gluing together opposite edges.

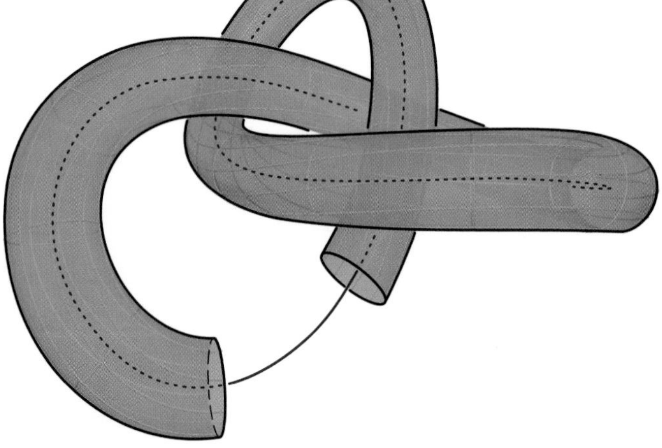

Fig. 14.64
A knot is a closed space curve without self-intersections. Its visualization may be enhanced with the help of a pipe surface wrapped around it.

One topic in knot theory is *knot equivalence*. It is exactly what one might attribute to equivalence in the presence of a closed knotted string. Figure 14.66 illustrates basic admissible operations that do not change the type of knot but may let it appear in a simpler way. Shortening of a part may not be possible with a given knotted string, but this is also admitted here because clearly the length of the string should not enter the discussion of types of knots.

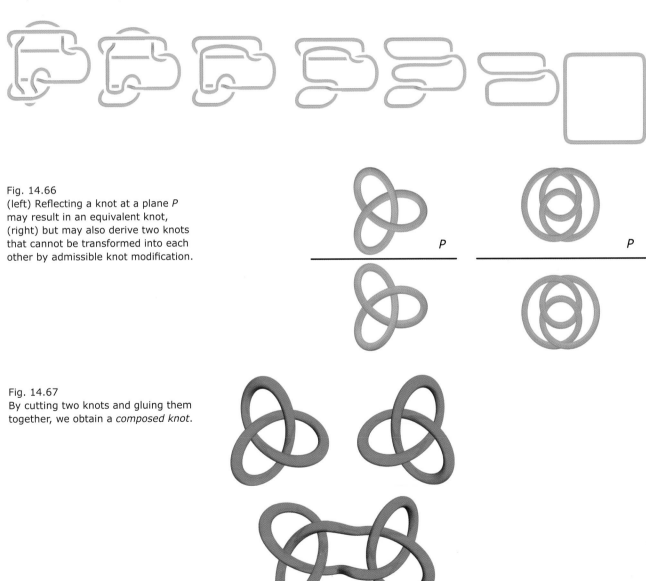

Fig. 14.65
Admissible modifications of a knot may reveal it as the *un-knot* (i.e., the knot is equivalent to a circle).

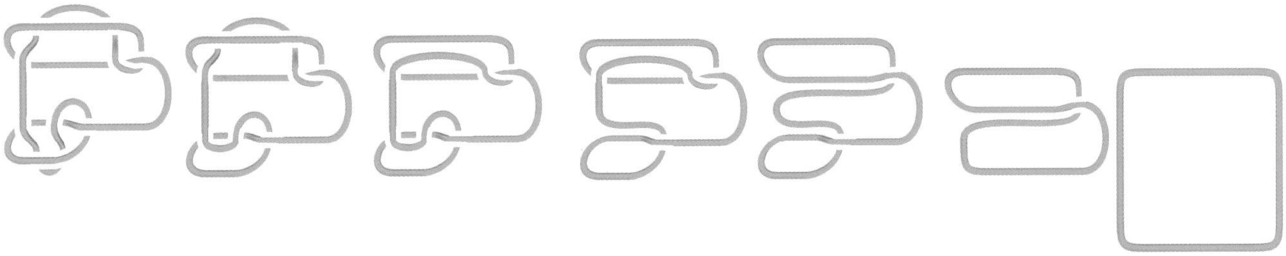

Fig. 14.66
(left) Reflecting a knot at a plane P may result in an equivalent knot, (right) but may also derive two knots that cannot be transformed into each other by admissible knot modification.

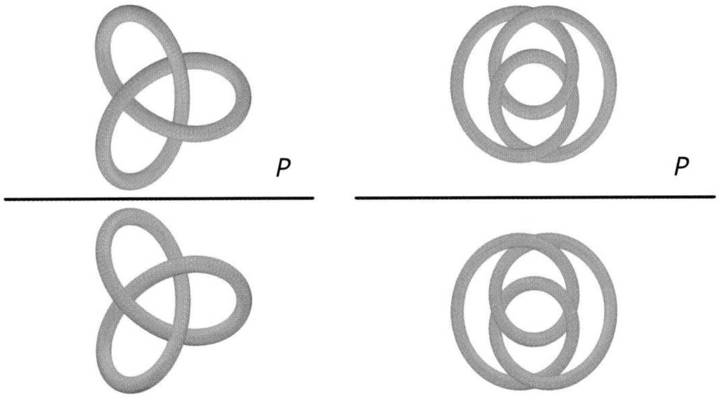

Fig. 14.67
By cutting two knots and gluing them together, we obtain a *composed knot*.

Reflected knots may or may not be equivalent. This is illustrated in Figure 14.67. From two knots, we can form a new *composed knot* by cutting each of them and gluing them together (as shown in Figure 14.68). The *classification of knots* is based on the *crossing number*, defined as the *minimum number of crossing points in a projection* (see Figure 14.69). There are some types of knots that appear in a systematic way and then have the same index in the labeling of types (e.g., 3_1, 5_1, 7_1, and so on).

Otherwise, the indices in the classification table are more of a historic than mathematical nature. Not listed are those knots obtained by composing simpler ones (in the sense of Figure 14.68). Reflected knots that are not identical to each other still have the same label (e.g., 3_1, 5_1). Recall that we have encountered the *trefoil knot* 3_1 in Figure 14.2.

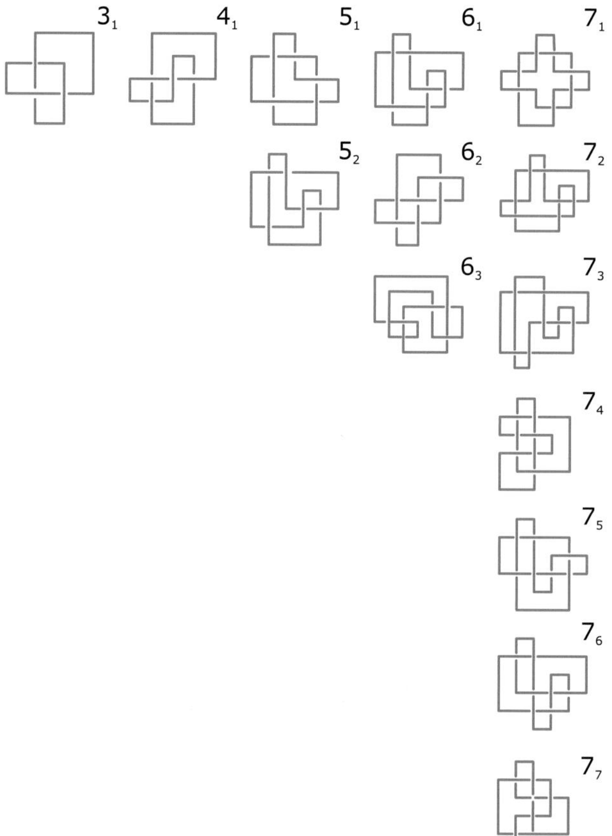

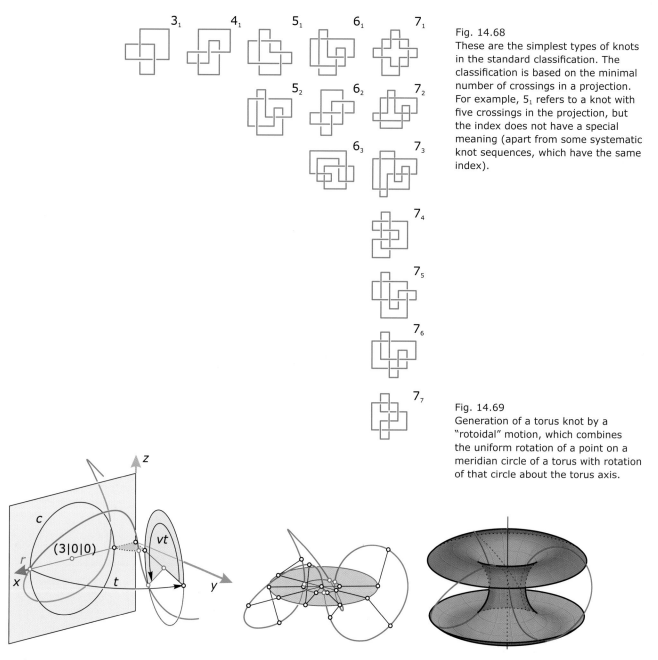

Fig. 14.68
These are the simplest types of knots in the standard classification. The classification is based on the minimal number of crossings in a projection. For example, 5_1 refers to a knot with five crossings in the projection, but the index does not have a special meaning (apart from some systematic knot sequences, which have the same index).

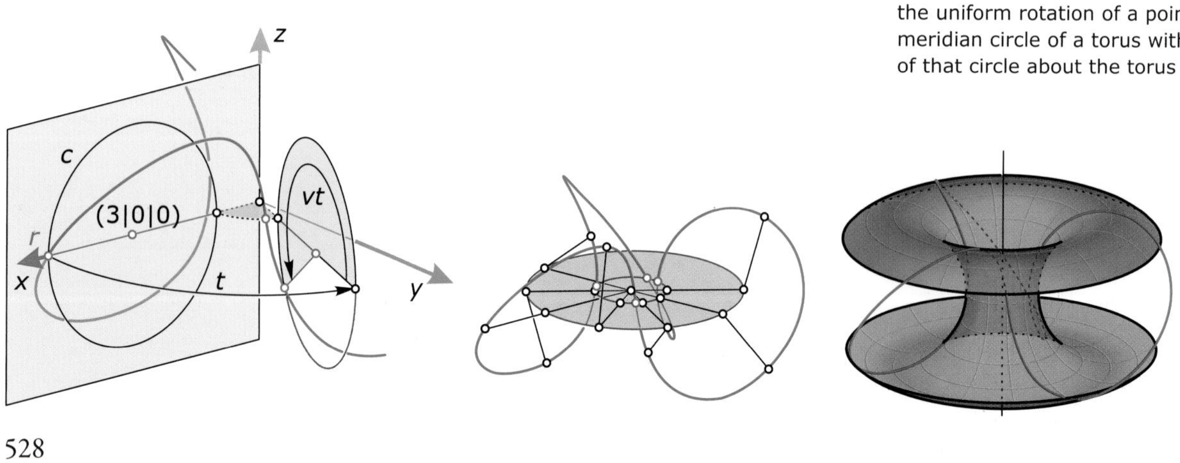

Fig. 14.69
Generation of a torus knot by a "rotoidal" motion, which combines the uniform rotation of a point on a meridian circle of a torus with rotation of that circle about the torus axis.

Example:

Torus knots. As an example of simple spatial motions, in Chapter 12 we discussed the superposition of two uniform rotations about orthogonal non-intersecting axes. Special trajectories of such motions can be used to create a sequence of knots (*torus knots*) as follows (Figure 14.69). We consider a circle c in the xz-plane, with radius 2 and midpoint (3,0,0). On this circle, a point r is rotating with angular velocity $v = q/p$—where p and q are integers without a common divisor. In time t, the rotation angle is $v{\cdot}t$ (and thus the motion of r) can be described as

$x = 3 + 2{\cdot}\cos(v{\cdot}t), y = 0, z = 2{\cdot}\sin(v{\cdot}t)$.

This rotation is combined with a rotation about the z-axis with angular velocity one. Under this rotation, c generates a ring torus and the rotating point r traces a *(p,q)-torus knot* whose parametric representation is given by

$x = [3 + 2{\cdot}\cos(v{\cdot}t)]{\cdot}\cos t,\ y = [3 + 2{\cdot}\cos(v{\cdot}t)]{\cdot}\sin t,\ z = 2{\cdot}\sin(v{\cdot}t)$.

The simplest torus knot—shown in Figure 14.70 (left)—is the (2,3)-torus knot, also known as the *trefoil knot* 3_1. The (2,5)-torus knot—depicted in Figure 14.70 (right)—is also called *Solomon's seal knot* and is listed in the classification as knot 5_1. The (2,7)-torus knot is the knot 7_1, and so on. There are of course further torus knots that do not belong to this sequence of the classification, such as the (3,8)-torus knot (Figure 14.71).

The crossing number of a (p,q)-torus knot is the minimum of the two numbers $(p - 1){\cdot}q$ and $(q - 1){\cdot}p$. Thus, the crossing number of the (2,3)-torus knot is the minimum of 1·3 and 2·2—which is 3, in accordance with the classification 3_1. The crossing number of the (3,8)-torus knot is 16; namely, the minimum of 2·8 and 3·7.

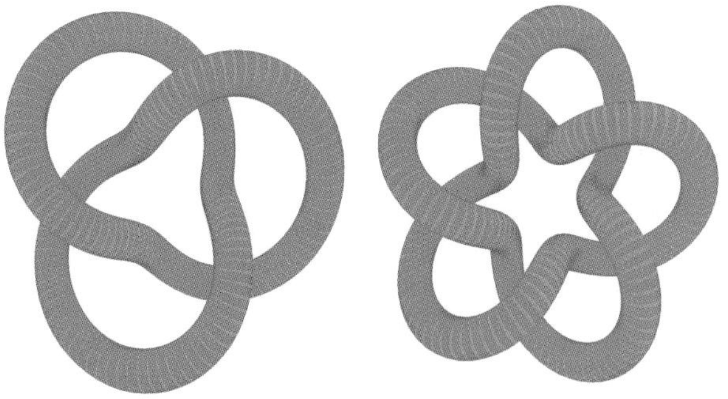

Fig. 14.70
The simplest torus knots are the (2,3)-torus knot (trefoil knot, left) and the (2,5)-torus knot (Solomon's seal knot, right).

Fig. 14.71
The (3,8)-torus knot (two views) has crossing number 16.

Chapter 15
Developable Surfaces and Unfoldings

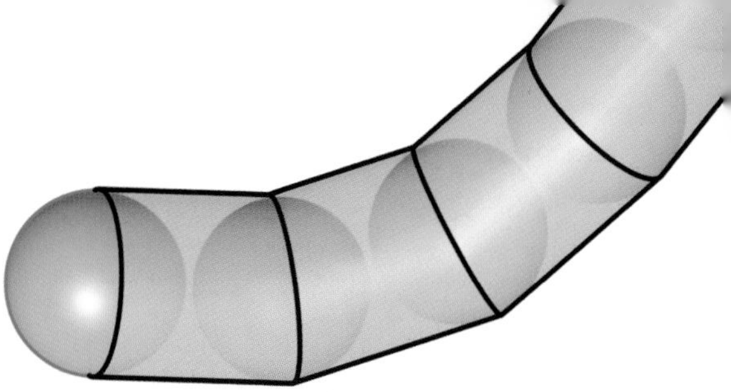

Developable Surfaces and Unfoldings

Physical three-dimensional models are an important medium in the architectural design process. One classical technique uses paper or cardboard to build geometric models. For that purpose, one generates a planar unfolding of the model on paper that can be cut out and glued together. It is relatively straightforward to unfold a polyhedral shape that consists of planar faces only. Here, the challenge is in the generation of a non-overlapping planar representation that consists of a small number of connected pieces.

For most curved surfaces, such as the freeform surfaces studied previously, an unfolding does not exist. However, there is a special class of surfaces (called *developable surfaces*) that behave just like paper if we bend or twist them without tearing or stretching. In this chapter, we study these special surfaces and show how to unfold them so that we can build paper models. Clearly, our ultimate goal is not these models.

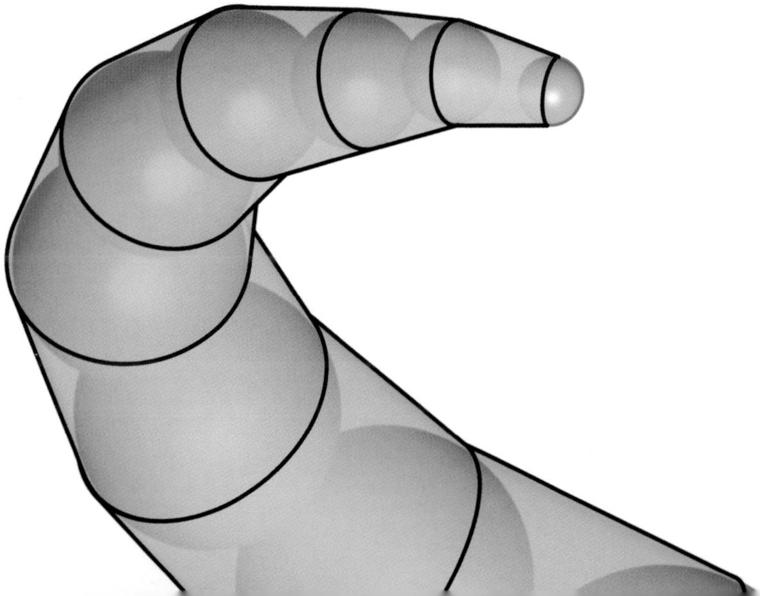

Developable surfaces have the great advantage that they can be easily covered with sheet metal. In fact, one only needs to roll out the sheet metal bands on such a surface. Moreover, these surfaces carry a family of straight lines—which also simplifies their construction. All of these properties are very attractive for the actual construction, and thus it is not surprising that one can find developable surfaces in a number of important architectural projects. Frank O. Gehry in particular has been using these surfaces quite extensively (Figure 15.1; see [Shelden 2002]).

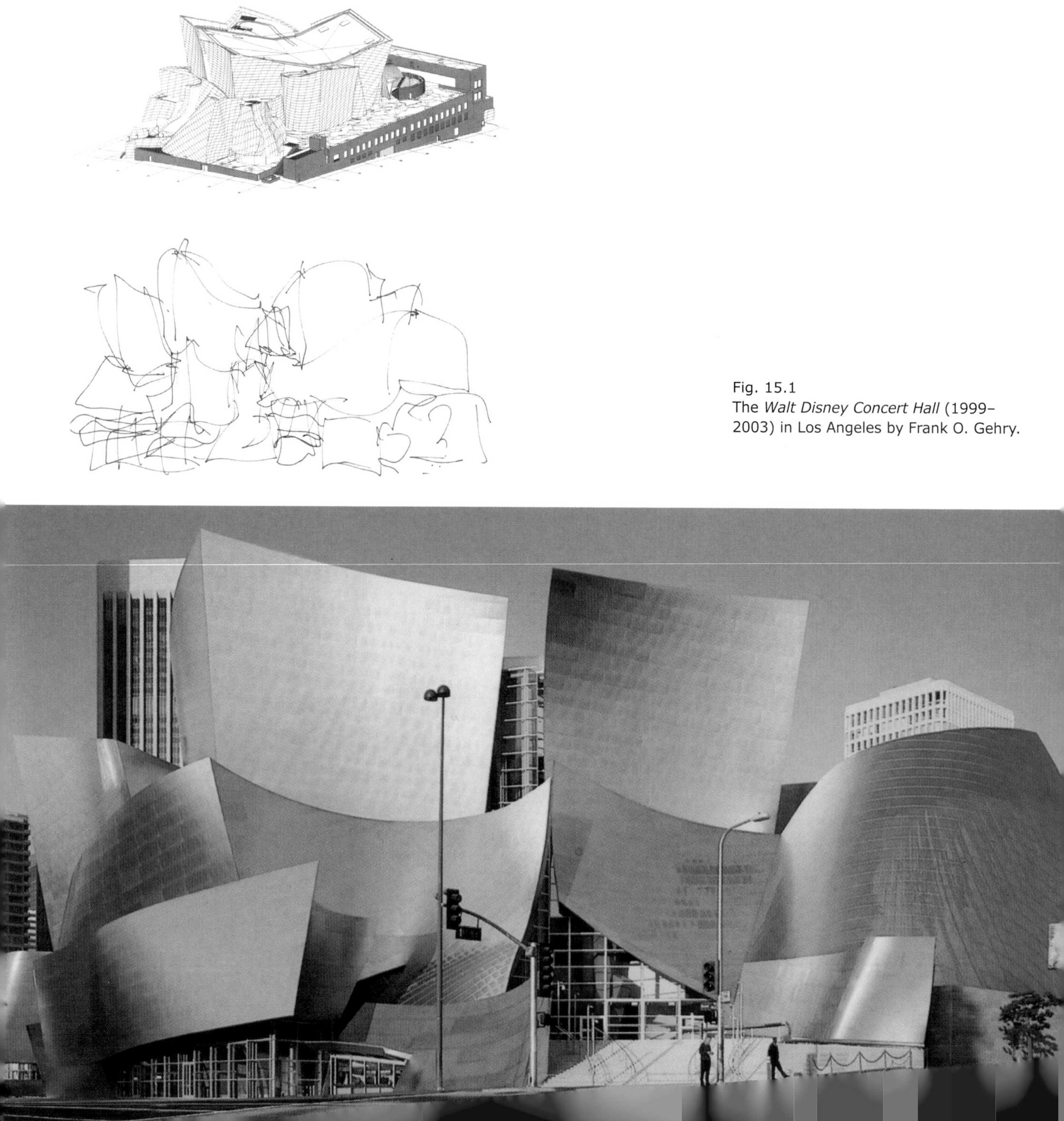

Fig. 15.1
The *Walt Disney Concert Hall* (1999–2003) in Los Angeles by Frank O. Gehry.

Surfaces That Can Be Built from Paper

Before studying this chapter, recall the basic facts on *ruled surfaces* discussed in Chapter 9. Moreover, one should bear in mind the curvature theory of surfaces as outlined in Chapter 14. We have also discussed isometric mappings (i.e., mappings between surfaces that preserve the length of any curve). *Developable surfaces* S *are characterized by the property that they can be mapped isometrically into the plane.*

The planar isometric image S^d is the planar unfolding of the surface. It is also called the *development of* S. Because isometric mappings preserve Gaussian curvature, a developable surface has the same Gaussian curvature as the plane (i.e., it has *vanishing Gaussian curvature*). Based on this fact, one can show that there are just three basic types of developable surfaces. All of them are ruled surfaces (Figure 15.2).

Moreover, any ruling of such a developable ruled surface must be a *torsal ruling* R. This means that the surface S has the same tangent plane at all points of the same ruling R (Chapter 9). Before stating more general results, we will study the three basic types: *cylinders*, *cones*, and *tangent surfaces of space curves*.

Fig. 15.2
Developable surfaces are special ruled surfaces. For each ruling there is a plane tangent to the surface along the entire ruling. More general developable surfaces are compositions of such developable ruled surfaces.

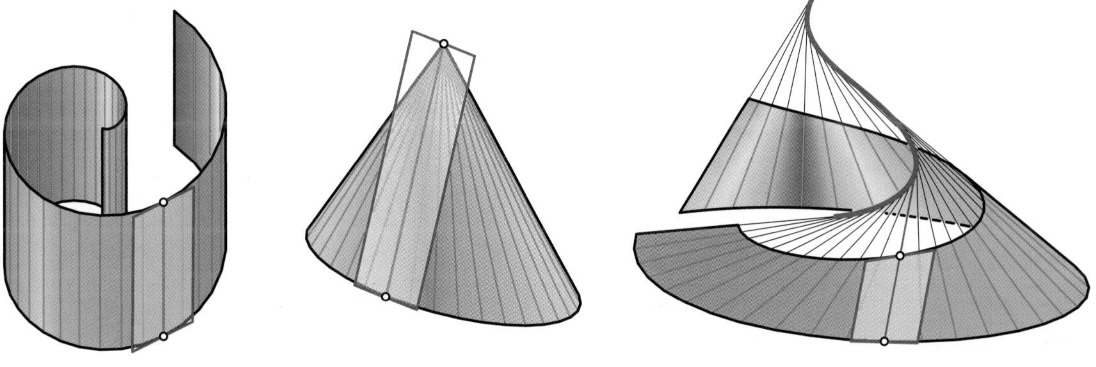

Cylinders. A cylinder surface S is formed by a family of parallel lines. To model a cylinder surface, we may prescribe a profile curve p and extrude it in some direction r by a *parallel extrusion*. If the profile curve p lies in a plane normal to r, we call p a *normal section*. The lines on the surface are all parallel to r and are called its *rulings*. To find the isometric mapping into the plane, we first consider a discrete model of a cylinder surface; namely, a *prismatic surface* (prism). We obtain it if we select a polygon p as a normal section (Figure 15.3).

If we refine the normal section polygon p of a prism toward a smooth curve, we obtain a smooth cylinder surface with p as normal section curve. The unfolding of the prism becomes in the limit the development of the cylinder surface. The development p^d of the profile curve p is a straight line segment. All rulings of S are parallel. They also appear as parallel lines in the development. Clearly, the right angle between normal section and rulings is also seen in the development (Figure 15.4).

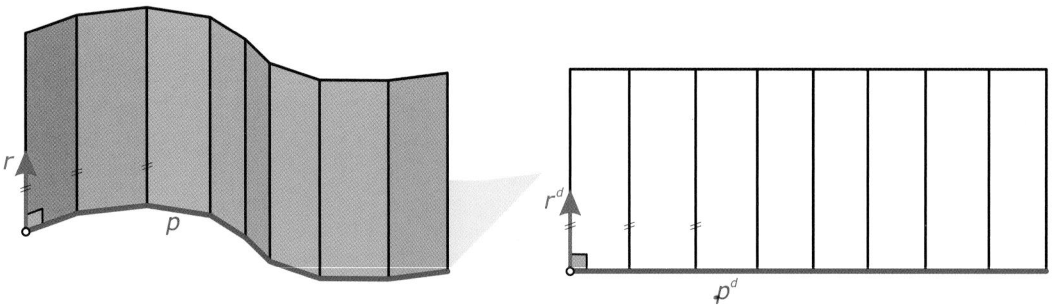

Fig. 15.3
Prismatic surface and its unfolding into the plane. A normal section of the prism is mapped into a straight line segment. Parallel edges of the prism are mapped to parallel lines of its unfolded version.

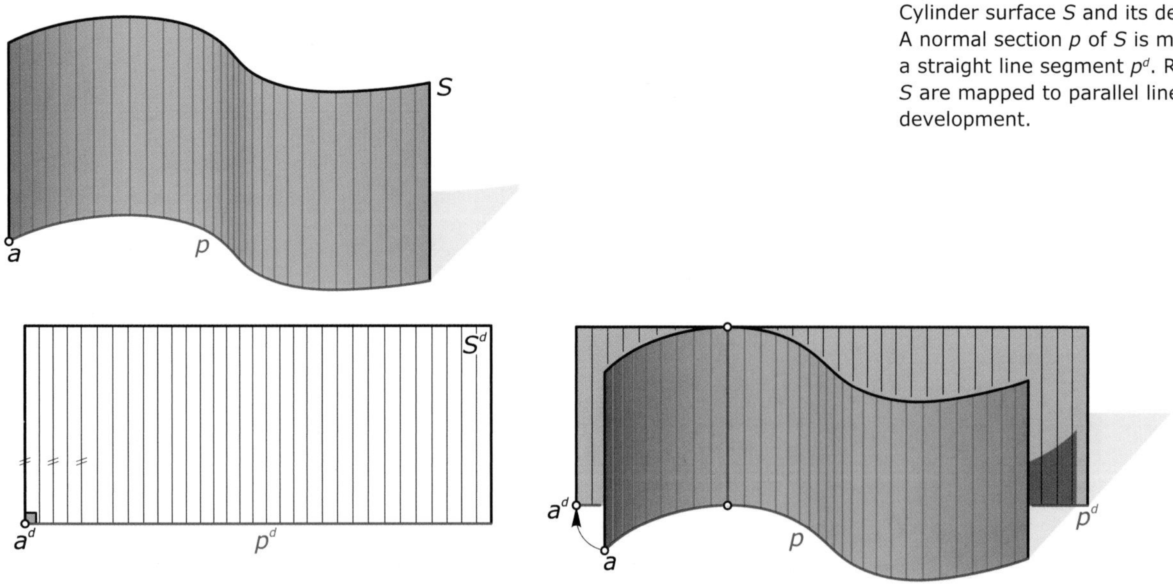

Fig. 15.4
Cylinder surface S and its development. A normal section p of S is mapped into a straight line segment p^d. Rulings of S are mapped to parallel lines in the development.

Example:

Cylinder of revolution and helixes. Figure 15.5 shows the development of a cylinder S of revolution. The base circle p of the cylinder has radius R and thus has length $L = 2\pi R$. Its development p^d is therefore a straight line segment of length L. Note that the cylinder is closed. Thus, we have to cut it along a ruling and then unfold it.

In the development, we consider a straight line l^d whose angle against p^d is denoted by α. We establish that α shall be different from zero and from a right angle. We want to study the reverse development (i.e., the original curve l on the cylinder S). The straight line l^d intersects the first and last ruling of the development (which belongs to the same ruling of S) in points a^d and b^d. a^d has some distance d from the base line p^d, and b^d is at height $d + h$ above p^d.

On S, points a and b lie on the same ruling—and their distance is h. Now we consider the midpoint m^d of a^d and b^d. Its height is $d + h/2$, which is also the height of m above the base circle p. m arises from a by rotation around the cylinder axis about an angle of 180 degrees and by a translation parallel to the axis of distance $h/2$.

Analogously, if we rotate a by a fraction $360/N$ of the full angle, we obtain a point x at height $d + h/N$, which also lies on l (and a corresponding point x^d on l^d). This shows that the curve l is a *helix*. Its properties follow easily from the development: l^d forms a constant angle $90 - \alpha$ with the developed rulings and because the development preserves intersection angles the helix l also intersects the rulings of the cylinder S at constant angle $90 - \alpha$. Thus, the tangents of the helix form a constant angle α with the plane of the base circle.

We may say that all tangents of the helix have a fixed inclination angle or a fixed slope. Therefore, one calls the helix a *curve of constant slope*. Shortest paths (*geodesics*) on the cylinder S correspond to shortest paths in the plane. Because the latter are straight lines, general geodesics on a cylinder of revolution are (segments of) helixes (circles or rulings in special cases).

Fig. 15.5
Development of a cylinder S of revolution. Straight lines l^d in the development that are not parallel or normal to the developed rulings belong to helixes l on S. Conversely, each helix on the cylinder has a straight image in the development. Thus, the helixes, circles, and rulings on S are the geodesics (shortest paths) on S.

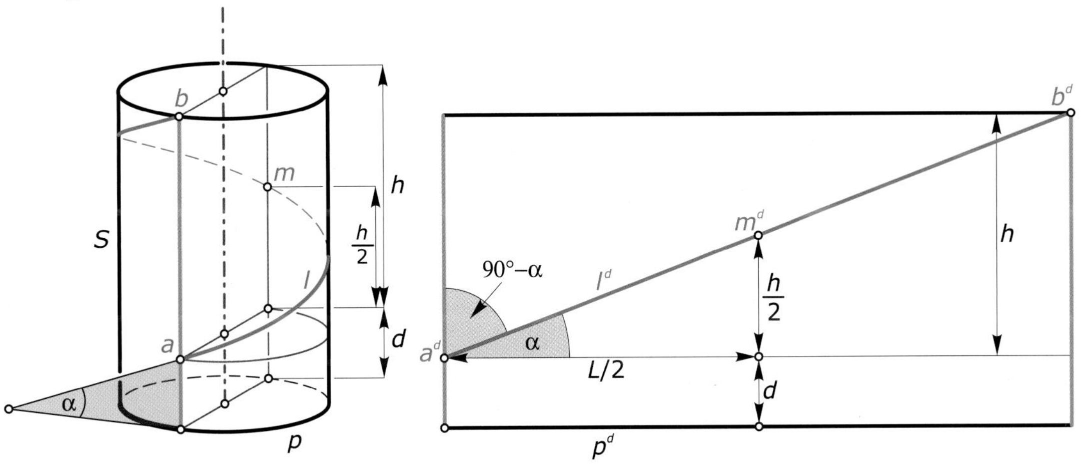

Figure 15.6 depicts the development e^d of an ellipse e on a cylinder of revolution S. The curve e^d is not an ellipse! Note the variation of the intersection angle between the ellipse and the rulings of the cylinder. Because angles are preserved, we have the same variation in the development. The inflection points may also be explained in this way. In Figure 15.6, the object contains a piece of a cylinder and two planar faces (one bounded by the ellipse and the other by the base circle). In an unfolding, we also obtain undistorted images of these planar faces.

Example:

Development of an oblique circular cylinder. Consider a cylinder surface S with a base circle p, where the rulings of S are *not* orthogonal to the plane of p. We call S an *oblique circular cylinder*. Now the base circle is not mapped to a straight line segment of the development because p is not a normal section of the cylinder. We can easily observe the variation of the intersection angle between p and the rulings.

This variation becomes visible in the development (Figure 15.7). The normal sections of S are ellipses. These ellipses are mapped to straight line segments in the development. Again, we note the following: those points c, d of p where the plane of p is orthogonal to the tangent plane of S are mapped to inflection points c^d and d^d of the development p^d.

Figure 15.7 shows the development of an approximation of a cylinder by a prism obtained via an approximation of the base circle by a polygon. Such a development of a polyhedron can easily be performed with any computer-aided design (CAD) system using the *unfold operation*.

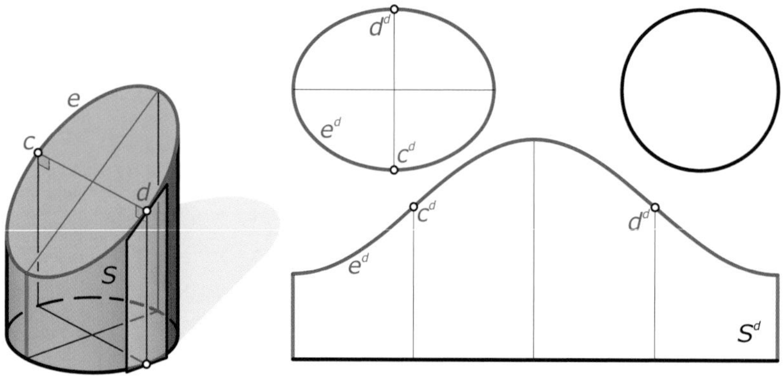

Fig. 15.6
Ellipses e on the cylinder do not correspond to ellipses in the development of the cylinder. The development e^d of an ellipse e is a sine curve with inflection points c^d, d^d arising from those points c and d on e where the plane of the ellipse e is orthogonal to the tangent plane of the cylinder S.

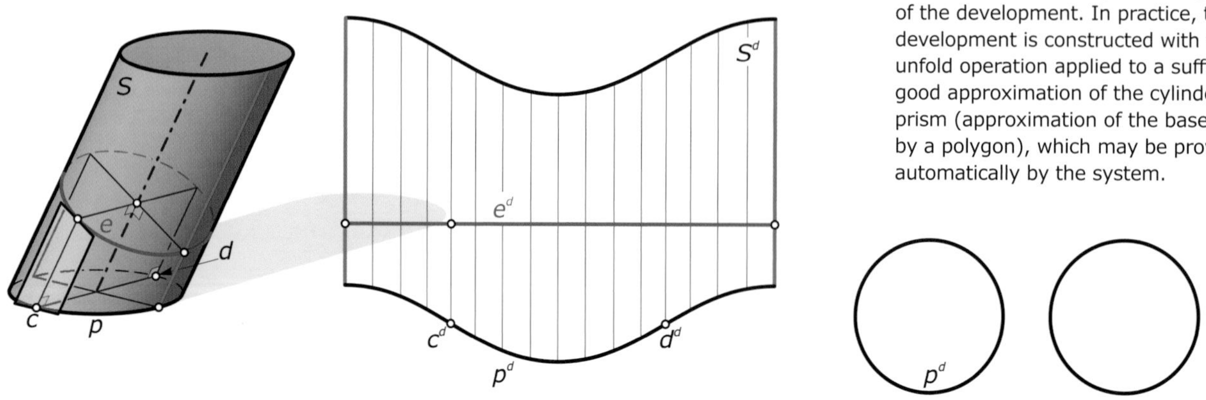

Fig. 15.7
Development of an oblique circular cylinder. The base circle p is mapped to a curve p^d in the development. Any normal section of the cylinder (ellipse) corresponds to a straight line segment of the development. In practice, the development is constructed with the unfold operation applied to a sufficiently good approximation of the cylinder by a prism (approximation of the base circle by a polygon), which may be provided automatically by the system.

Cones. Recall the definition of a general cone: Given a profile curve p and a vertex point v, the cone consists of all lines connecting v with points of p. We may also generate the surface by a *central extrusion*. Taking a polygon p as a profile, we obtain a *pyramid surface*. Pyramids may be seen as discrete counterparts of smooth cones, just as prisms are seen as discrete counterparts of cylinders.

We learn a lot about the development of a cone if we first study the unfolding of a pyramid (Figure 15.8). The simplest reference polygons q on a pyramid in connection with the development are those whose vertices lie at constant distance R from the vertex v. They are the counterparts of the normal sections of a prism. Clearly, their unfoldings q^d have vertices on the circle with center v^d and radius R.

Now we perform the transition to the case of smooth cones. We imagine that the profile polygon p is refined and becomes a smooth curve p in the limit (Figure 15.9). The smooth limit of the pyramid is a cone S. The polygon q at constant distance R from v becomes in the limit the intersection curve of S and a sphere with midpoint v and radius R. The development of that curve is a circular arc with center v^d and radius R. Of course, the total lengths of q and q^d are the same.

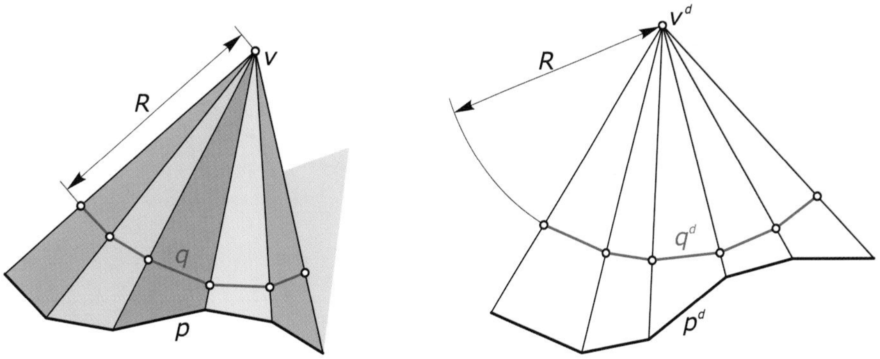

Fig. 15.8
Pyramid surface and its unfolding into the plane. A polygon q on the pyramid whose vertices lie at constant distance R from the vertex v corresponds to a polygon q^d whose vertices lie on the circle with center v^d and radius R.

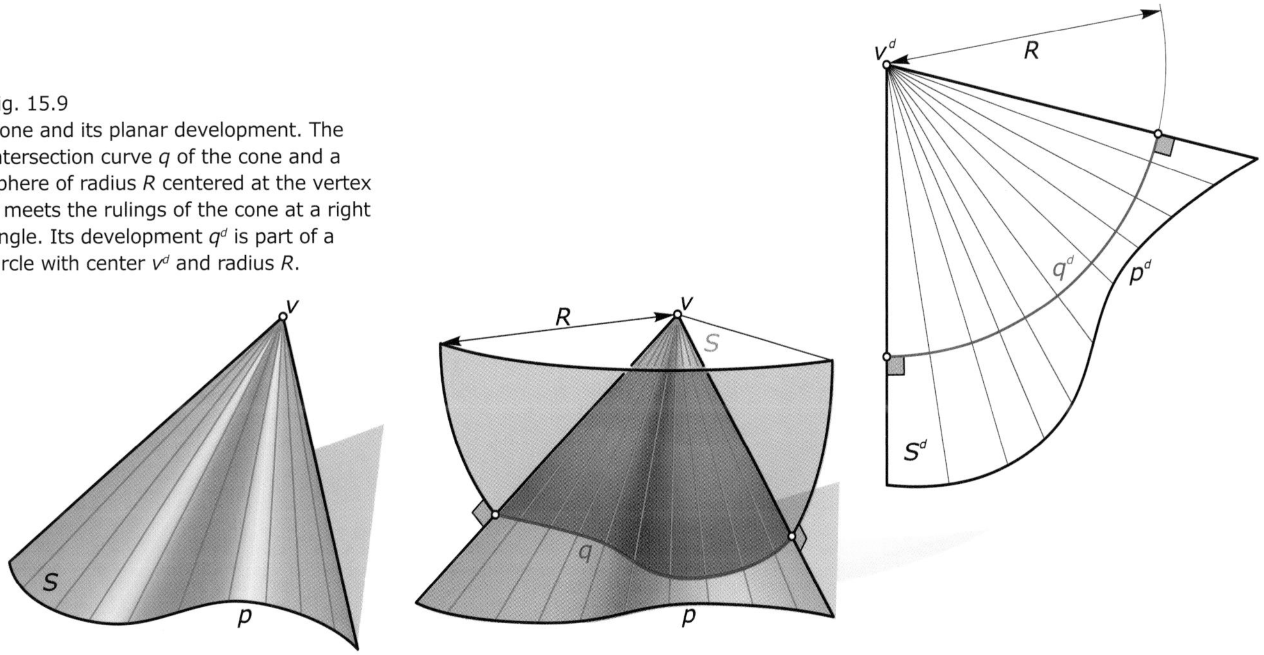

Fig. 15.9
Cone and its planar development. The intersection curve q of the cone and a sphere of radius R centered at the vertex v meets the rulings of the cone at a right angle. Its development q^d is part of a circle with center v^d and radius R.

Some examples of cones and their development are shown in Figures 15.10 and 15.11. As for cylinders, we construct them with the unfolding command in a modeling system. We only make a remark on the oblique circular cone: the intersection curve q with a sphere centered at v is not an ellipse but a curve of order 4 (Figure 15.11a).

We also note that such a cone carries two families of circles. Given one base circle in a plane P, clearly all intersections with planes parallel to P are also circles. The second family of circles may be found as follows (Figure 15.11). Pass a sphere through a circle k of the first family and intersect it with the cone S. The complete intersection curve consists of the circle k and another circle l, which defines the second family.

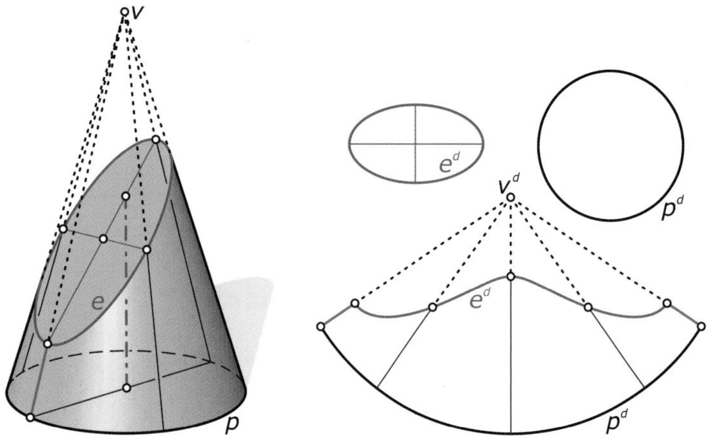

Fig. 15.10
Right circular cone bounded by a circle and an ellipse, and the development of this object.

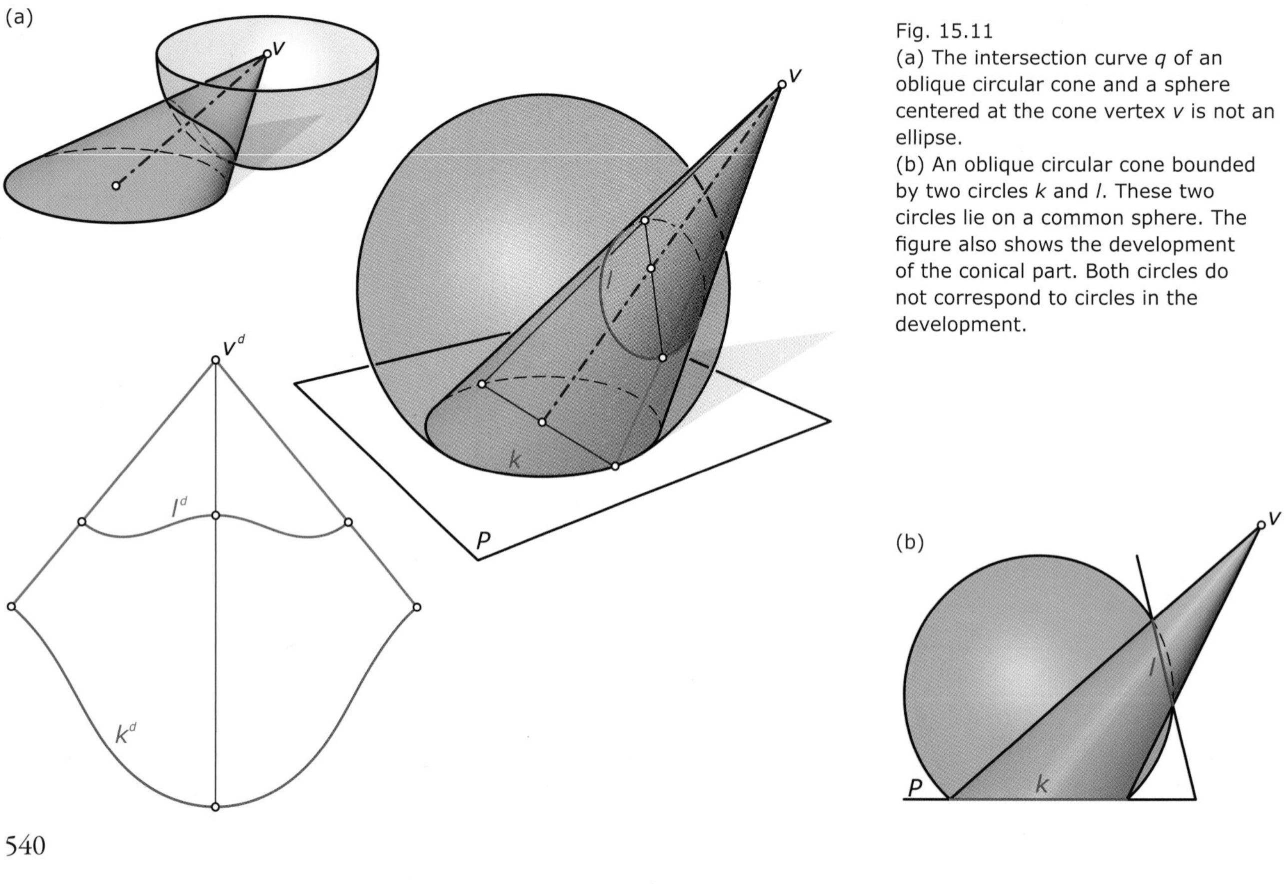

Fig. 15.11
(a) The intersection curve q of an oblique circular cone and a sphere centered at the cone vertex v is not an ellipse.
(b) An oblique circular cone bounded by two circles k and l. These two circles lie on a common sphere. The figure also shows the development of the conical part. Both circles do not correspond to circles in the development.

Strips formed by planar quadrilaterals. Approximations of the objects in Figures 15.10 and 15.11 by pyramids are actually compositions of planar quadrilateral faces pieced together to form a strip of planar quadrilaterals. However, the quads in these strips are very special because the edges along which they are joined all pass through a vertex v.

Looking at the foregoing prisms, the common edges of the faces are parallel. Now we want to investigate the general case of a *strip of planar quadrilaterals*, which we also call a *planar quad strip* or just a *PQ strip* (Figure 15.12). The two bounding polygons of the strip model shall be $p_1, p_2, \ldots$ and q_1, q_2, and so on. As edges of the model, we refer to the straight line segments p_1q_1, p_2q_2, and so on along which the quads are joined.

Consecutive edges are co-planar and therefore intersect at points r_1, r_2, and so on. These points form the vertices of a polygon, which is referred to as a *singular polygon* of the strip model. We may view the singular polygon as a discrete model of a space curve. The edges of this polygon are the discrete counterparts of the tangents of a space curve. Thus, we can say that our model is a discrete version of the set of tangents of a space curve (*tangent surface of a space curve*).

We need to be slightly more careful, however. Our quad strip does not correspond to the entire discrete tangent surface but just to a part of it bounded by the polygons p and q. Therefore, if we refine the model (see Figure 15.13) we obtain in the limit a patch on the tangent surface of a space curve.

PQ strips with a singular polygon are the general form of PQ strips. Strips arising from a pyramid have only one singular point (the vertex of the pyramid), and a prism has no singular point (it is at infinity). This observation indicates that tangent surfaces of space curves will be the most general form of developable surfaces and thus we need to discuss them in more detail. Fortunately, the discussion can nicely be based on the strip model.

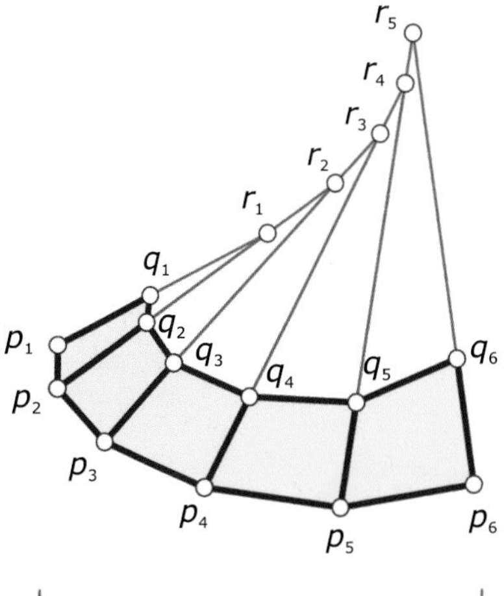

Fig. 15.12
Strip of planar quadrilaterals (PQ strip) as a discrete model of a developable surface. The quads are joined along a sequence of edges. Consecutive edges are co-planar and therefore intersect at points r_1, r_2, and so on. These points form the vertices of the so-called singular polygon of the strip model.

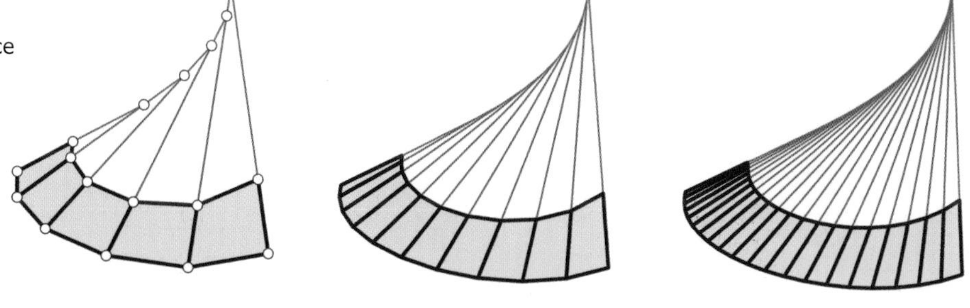

Fig. 15.13
Refinement of a PQ strip toward a patch on the tangent surface of a space curve.

Refinement of a PQ strip with perturbed subdivision. It is easy to consider the refinement of a PQ strip in theory. In practice, this is not as easy to achieve. Note that it is important that the strip retain its property of being formed by *planar* quads. This is the subtle part! Liu et al. [2006] have proposed an algorithm that works as follows. Given a PQ strip, subdivide it via a familiar algorithm such as Chaikin or Lane-Riesenfeld (Chapter 8). Subdividing the strip means application of the rule to both bounding polygons and joining of corresponding points. Unfortunately, one round of subdivision will destroy the planarity of some faces. Thus, after subdivision, the algorithm minimally perturbs the vertices of the bounding polygons to achieve planarity of the quads. Then one subdivides again, planarizes, subdivides, and so on. This amounts to a quite useful modeling tool for developable surfaces (see results in Figures 15.14 through 15.16).

Developable surfaces may appear in various stages of the architectural design process. Some architects use strips of paper in the form-finding process (Figure 15.17). Others prefer developable shapes in the final design (Figure 15.1).

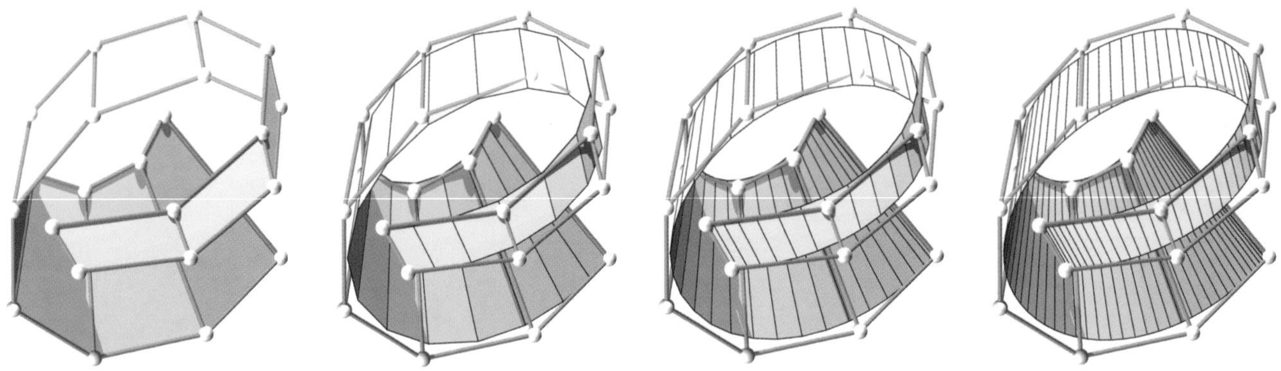

Fig. 15.14
Refinement of a PQ strip (upper left) with the cubic Lane-Riesenfeld subdivision algorithm, where each subdivision step is followed by a planarization step. This is necessary because pure subdivision would destroy planarity of some quads. The results after one, two, and three rounds of subdivision are shown.

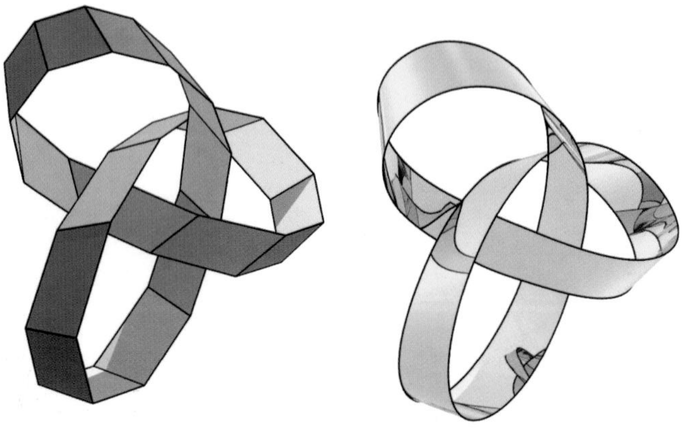

Fig. 15.15
Developable Möbius band in the shape of a trefoil knot, constructed with the combination of subdivision and planarization explained in Figure 15.14.

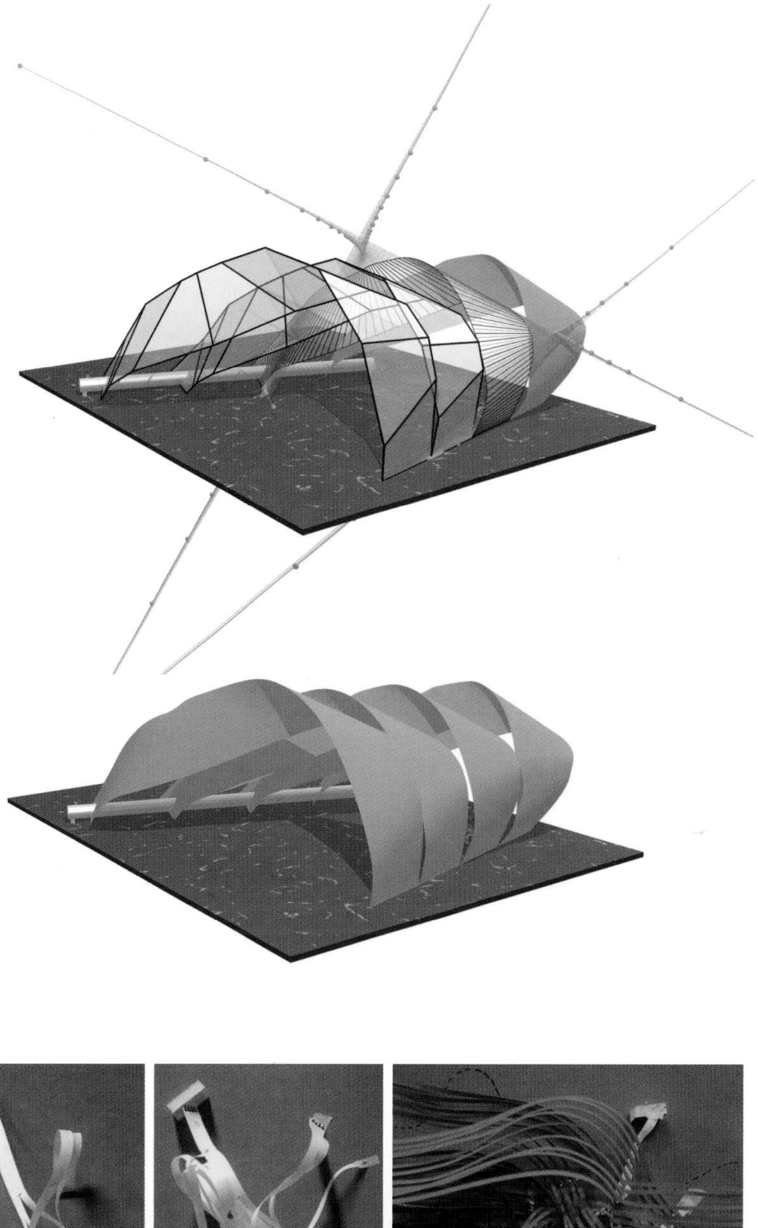

Fig. 15.16
Design studies with developable surfaces, generated with the perturbed subdivision method from Figure 15.14. The top part shows the original PQ strips for two of the four strips. It also shows the result of subdivision and the singular curves for the other two strips. The planarization step in the algorithm involves a technique that pushes the singular polygon away from the designed strip.

Fig. 15.17
Strips of paper employed by NOX (Rotterdam) in the form-finding process.

Tangent surfaces of space curves. Let P_r be a polygon with vertices r_1, r_2, r_3, and so on (Figure 15.18). From this polygon, we obtain a "discrete" (polyhedral) model M_r of a developable surface (as described previously). Any two consecutive vertices determine the edges r_1r_2, r_2r_3, and so on of the model—and any three consecutive vertices define a face plane $r_1r_2r_3$, $r_2r_3r_4$, and so on of the model.

If we take the complete edge lines and if we use from the face planes exactly the double-wedged part between the two edge lines in it, we obtain a polyhedral model that contains the polygon P_r as a singular polygon in the following sense: Intersecting the surface with a general plane Q, we obtain a polygon that has a sharp turning point at the intersection point of P_r and Q.

If P_r is refined and in the limit becomes a smooth curve r, the edges r_1r_2, r_2r_3, and so on of the model M_r become the tangents of r and thus the model itself in the limit becomes the tangent surface T_r of r (Figure 15.19). The face planes of M_r become in the limit the tangent planes of T_r. As limits of the connecting planes of three consecutive polygon vertices, these tangent planes are the osculating planes of r. We see that the tangent surface T_r is a special ruled surface because each tangent plane is tangent to the surface along an entire ruling and not just in a single point.

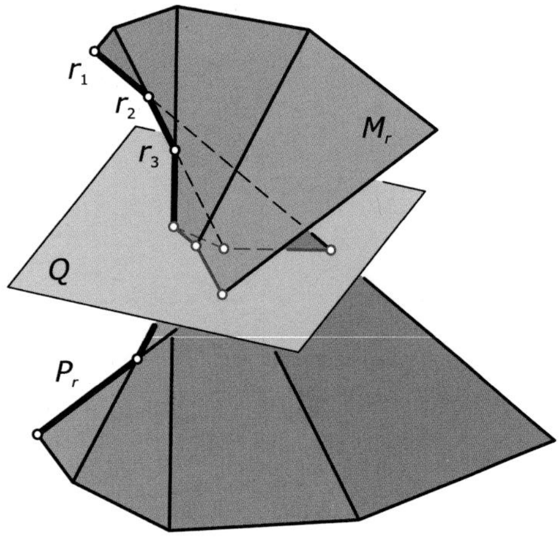

Fig. 15.18
Discrete model M_r of a developable surface, defined by a polygon P_r. A general plane Q intersects this polyhedral surface M_r in a polygon, which exhibits a sharp turning point (like a cusp) at the intersection point of P_r and Q. Thus, we call P_r the singular polygon on M_r.

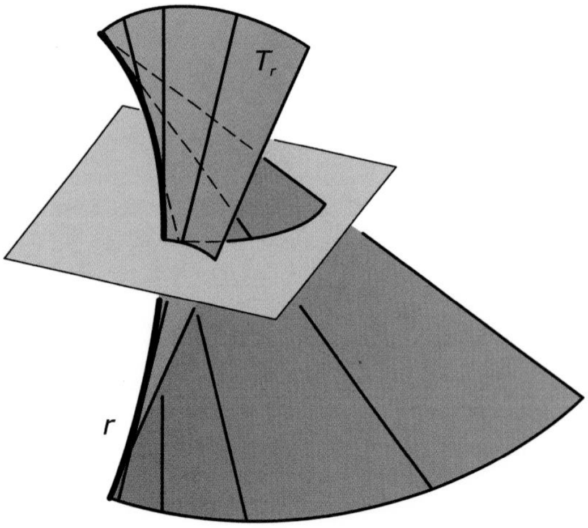

Fig. 15.19
Refinement of a polyhedral model M_r (as in Figure 15.18) yields in the limit the tangent surface T_r of a space curve r. Tangent surfaces of space curves are developable ruled surfaces. Each ruling R of the surface T_r is a tangent of r at some point p. In each point of a ruling R, the surface has the same tangent plane. This plane is the osculating plane of r at p. The curve r is a singular curve on the surface, also called its edge of regression or regression curve. This is visualized with a planar cut, which exhibits a cusp at the intersection point with r.

The fact that T_r is a developable surface follows from the obvious development of the model polyhedron M_r. We can also conclude it from the Gaussian spherical image of the surface (Figure 15.20). It is just a curve because all points of the same ruling of T_r have the same tangent plane. Thus, they have parallel normals and therefore the same Gaussian image point. Because the Gaussian spherical mapping shrinks every region on T_r to a curve segment on the unit sphere (which has area zero), the Gaussian curvature of the tangent surface of a space curve is zero.

Fig. 15.20
(a) The Gaussian spherical image of a developable surface *S* is a curve, and thus the Gaussian curvature of *S* is zero. This implies that such a surface can be mapped (unfolded) into the plane without distortions.

(b) A developable surface composed of several pieces of developable ruled surfaces has as Gaussian image a network of curves (bottom right images courtesy of A. Sheffer).

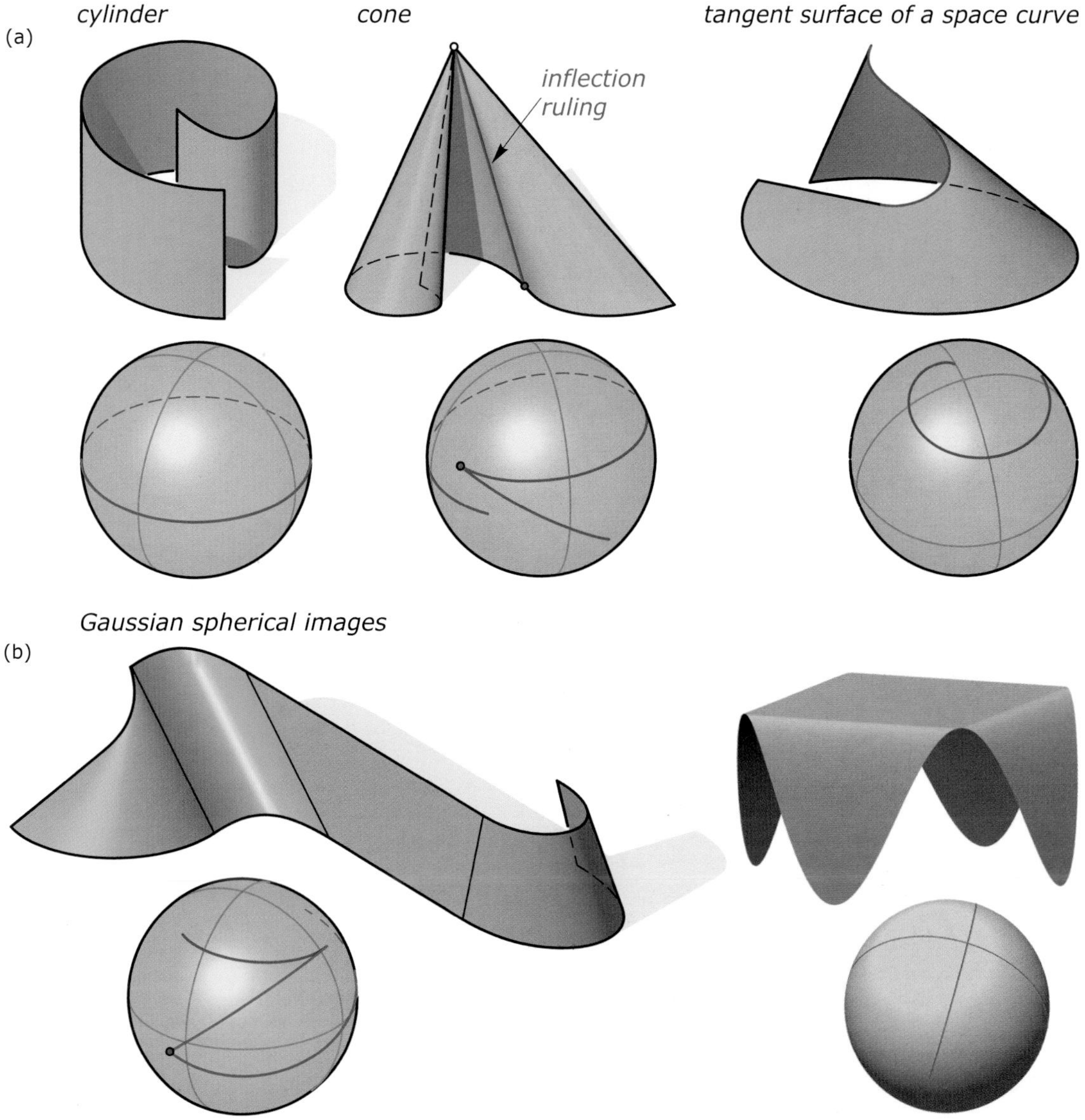

These are all developable surfaces. All three elementary types of developable surfaces addressed previously (cylinders, cones, tangent surfaces of space curves) have the following common properties: They are special ruled surfaces because a tangent plane is always tangent to the surface along an entire ruling and not just in a single point. We call such surfaces *developable ruled surfaces.*

Moreover, the surfaces have *vanishing Gaussian curvature* because their spherical Gaussian image is just a curve. Therefore, a developable surface contains only parabolic surface points or flat points. It can be shown that the three basic types of developable surfaces are all developable surfaces in the following sense: Any developable surface is a composition of such developable ruled surfaces (Figure 15.20b). Note that planar surfaces are included in any of these three types: as cylinders or cones with a straight profile and as tangent surfaces of planar curves.

Offsets are also developable. Because all points x on a ruling R of a developable surface S have the same tangent plane T (and thus parallel normals), the corresponding points x_d of an offset surface S_d at distance d lie on a straight line R_d at distance d to R (Figure 15.21). The tangent plane T_d of the offset surface is parallel to T and lies at distance d to T.

Thus, the offset surface S_d is also a developable surface. Its rulings and tangent planes are at distance d to the corresponding rulings and tangent planes of S. However, singular points of corresponding rulings R and R_d are not at constant distance d. We do not discuss this in more detail, but just point to the example of a right circular cone whose offset is also a right circular cone but for which the distance between the vertices depends on the opening angle of the cone.

It should be noted that *the offset surfaces of a cone are in general not cones*! Only cones of revolution (right circular cones) have cones as offsets. The proof of this fact follows by noting that the tangent planes of the offset surface S_d of a cone S with vertex v must touch a sphere with center v and radius d. Thus, if the offset shall be a cone as well it must be tangent to that sphere and therefore S_d and S must be cones of revolution.

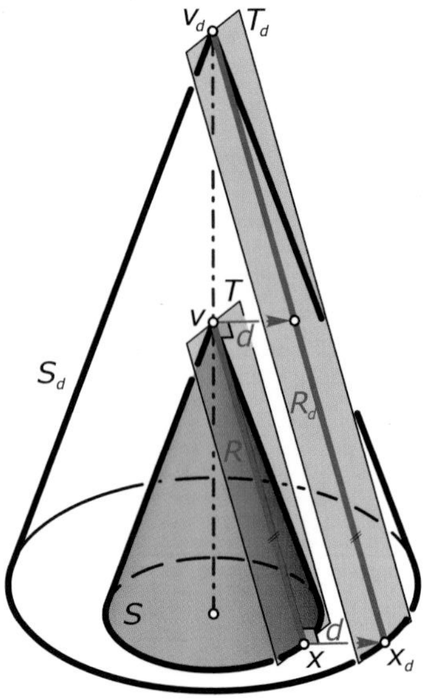

Fig. 15.21
The offset surfaces of a developable surface are also developable surfaces. Corresponding rulings and tangent planes lie at constant offset distance.

Surfaces of constant slope. We encountered surfaces of constant slope in Chapter 12 (on kinematics), but we want to address them here as well because they are developable surfaces. Let's start by asking the following question: What does a surface S look like if all of its tangent planes have a constant inclination angle α (different from zero and a right angle) with a fixed (e.g., vertical) direction?

Immediately, we find a simple example; namely, a cone of revolution with vertical axis. But there are many other surfaces with this property. Let's first have a look at their Gaussian spherical image. Because all surface normals of S must have a constant inclination angle, their parallels through the origin lie on a cone of revolution with vertical axis. Hence, the Gaussian spherical image S^* of S is a (small) circle (see Figure 15.22). Having a curve as Gaussian image, S is a developable surface.

To study these surfaces S, we assume that the intersection curve c with a horizontal plane H (e.g., the xy-plane of a Cartesian system) as well as the inclination angle α are given. Assume that c is a circle with center m. Then, S must be a cone of revolution whose vertex v lies "above" m [i.e., the top view of v is m (Figure 15.23)]. The cone can be found as an envelope of all planes with inclination angle α that touch the base circle c.

There are actually two such cones symmetric with respect to H. One cone has its vertex above H and the other below H. The following obvious facts are important for the generalizations discussed in material following. In each tangent plane of the cone S, the ruling is a line of steepest descent. The rulings of S are its curves of steepest descent and the circles on S are its curves of constant height (intersections with horizontal planes). Lines and circles intersect at right angles.

Fig. 15.22
The Gaussian spherical image of a surface of constant slope lies in a circle.

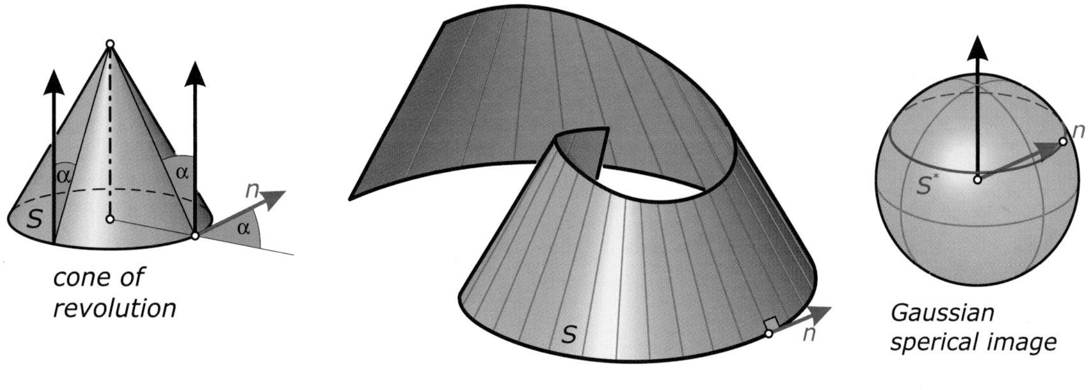

Fig. 15.23
The simplest surfaces of constant slope are cones of revolution. Their rulings are curves of steepest descent. The circles are the curves of constant height (i.e., the intersections with horizontal planes).

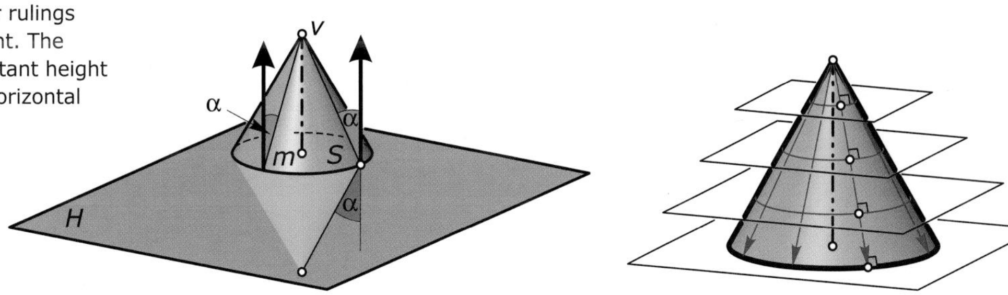

Let's now consider a general smooth curve c in H. Through each point p of H we can pass two planes of inclination angle α, which touch c at p. To make a consistent unique choice, we impose an orientation on c and take that plane $T(p)$ whose part above H has a top view to the left of the oriented tangent of c at p (see Figure 15.24).

If p varies along c, we obtain a family of planes $T(p)$ whose envelope is the desired surface S. Results about S can be deduced from the case of a cone as follows. We consider the osculating circle $k(p)$ of c at p. Because this circle approximates c very well in a neighborhood of p (mathematically speaking, it approximates c up to second order), we can expect that the same holds for the corresponding surfaces of constant slope. The surface of constant slope through the circle $k(p)$ is a cone. Its vertex $r(p)$ lies above the center of $k(p)$. Its ruling $R(p)$ through p is a line of steepest descent in the tangent plane $T(p)$ (Figure 15.24b). Thus, it also has constant inclination angle.

Because the cone describes the local behavior of S (up to second order), one can find the following results. The rulings of the surface S have a constant inclination angle α and form the curves of steepest descent on S. These rulings are the tangents of a curve r of constant slope. The intersection curves of S with horizontal planes intersect the rulings at a right angle.

Let's now look at the situation in the top view (Figure 15.24a). The top views of the rulings are the normals of c. The top views of two curves of constant height are a pair of offset curves because they have a common family of normals (top views of the rulings R of S). Thus, the top views of the curves of constant height form a family of offset curves. Their common evolute (Chapters 7 and 10) is the top view of the singular curve r of S.

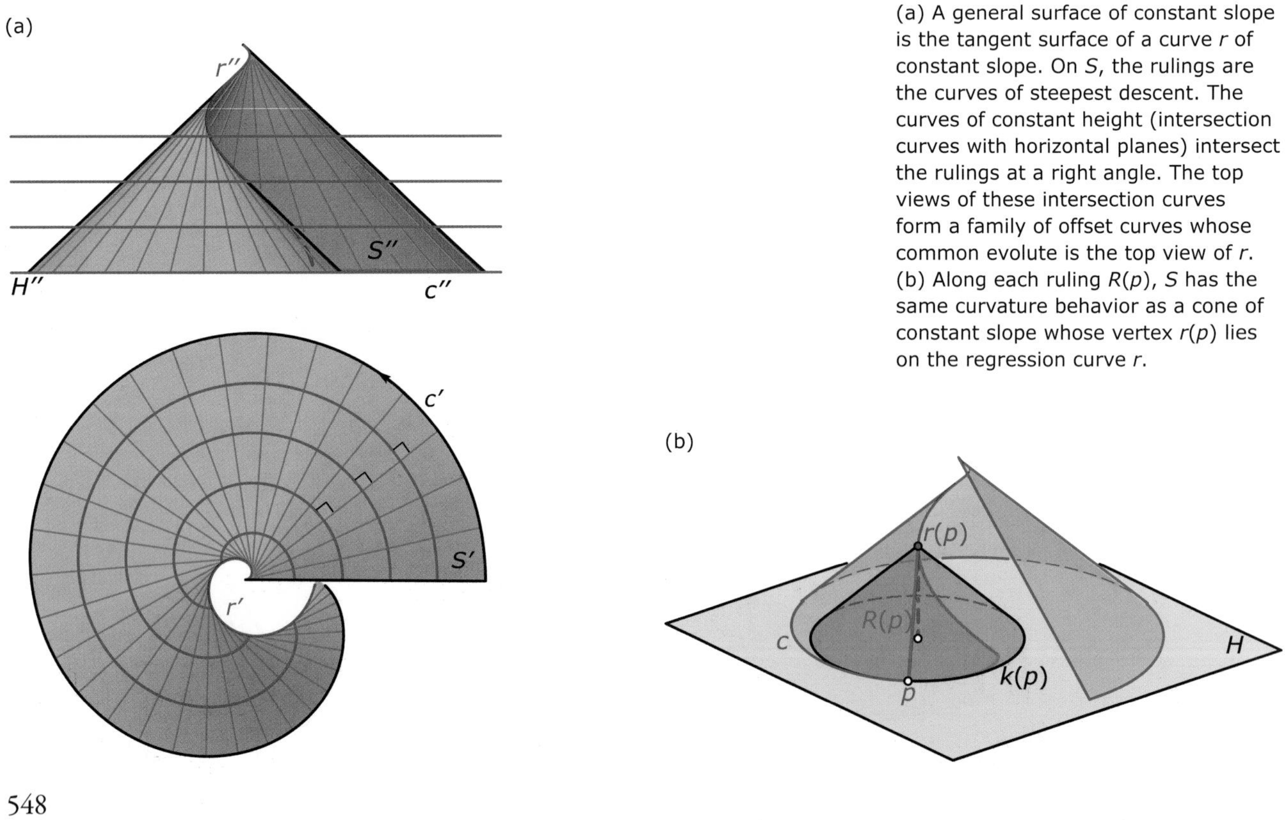

Fig. 15.24
(a) A general surface of constant slope is the tangent surface of a curve r of constant slope. On S, the rulings are the curves of steepest descent. The curves of constant height (intersection curves with horizontal planes) intersect the rulings at a right angle. The top views of these intersection curves form a family of offset curves whose common evolute is the top view of r.
(b) Along each ruling $R(p)$, S has the same curvature behavior as a cone of constant slope whose vertex $r(p)$ lies on the regression curve r.

We can easily derive the kinematic construction of these surfaces of constant slope as follows (see Chapter 12 and the previous discussion on the development of cylinders). The singular curve r is a curve of constant slope on some vertical cylinder E. It is a geodesic curve (shortest path) on E. Under the development of E, the curve r is mapped to a straight line.

To construct the curve r on E, we may roll a tangent plane T along E. During this rolling motion, a straight line L in T will generate the tangents of r (i.e., the rulings of S). (See Figures 12.23 and 12.24 and recall the applications of surfaces of constant slope as shapes of roofs or dams illustrated in Figure 12.25.)

Example:

Construction of a roof. Figure 15.25 shows a roof of constant inclination angle that passes through an ellipse c in a horizontal plane H. It has been constructed as a surface of constant slope, as discussed previously. The surface has a self-intersection (which is also part of an ellipse). Figure 15.25 also shows the extension of the surface beyond this self-intersection until the singular curve r is reached. The singular curve has four cusps corresponding to the vertices of c. They lie directly above the curvature centers of c's vertices.

Fig. 15.25
Roof of constant slope, constructed through an ellipse c in a horizontal plane. The figure shows two versions: the usual solution, trimmed at the self-intersection (part of an ellipse) of the surface, and the extension of the surface until the singular curve r is reached.

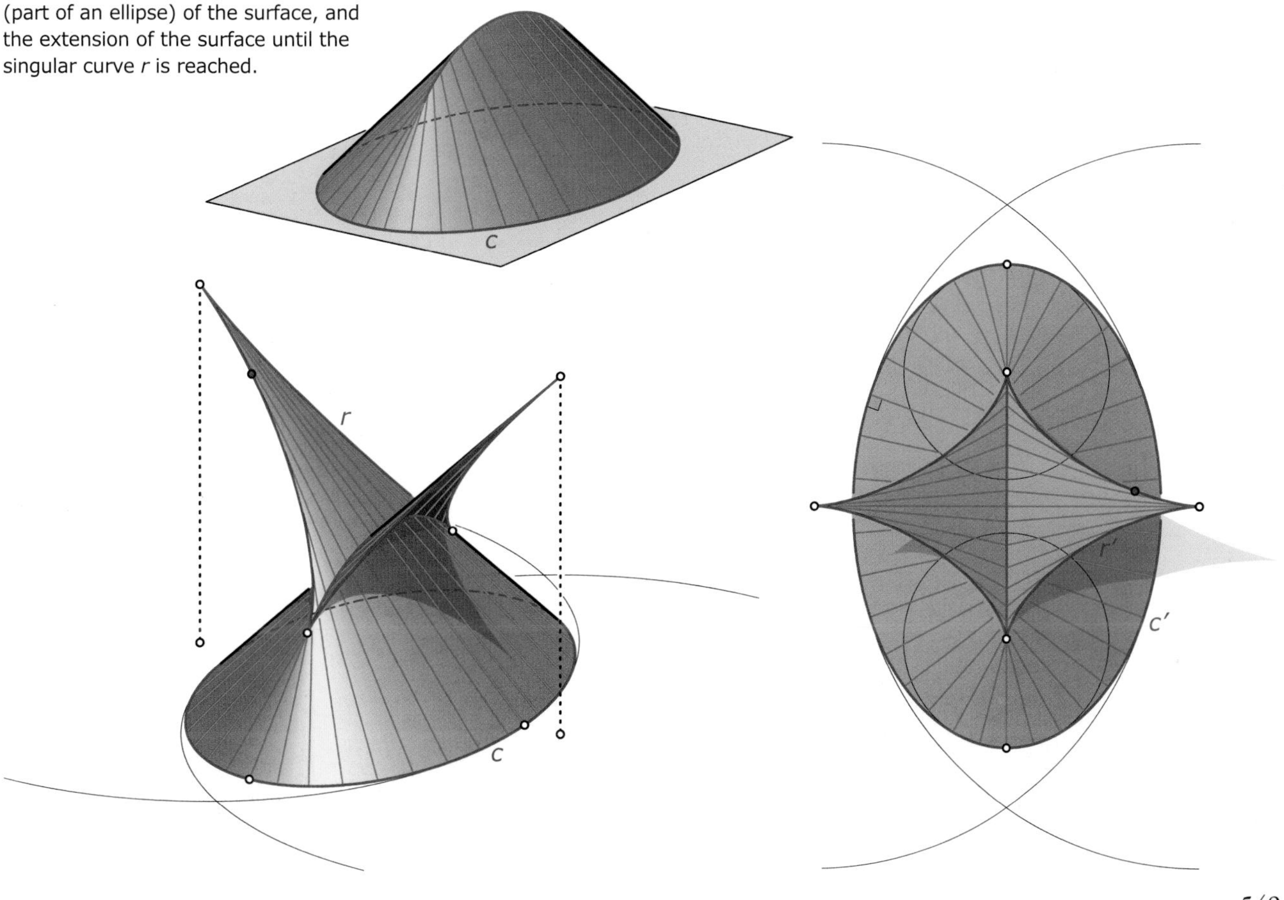

Example:

Helical developable surface. A developable surface that is also a helical surface must be a helical ruled surface. Because it also has to be a tangent surface, it is the tangent surface of a helix. Figure 15.26 shows different parts of such a surface.

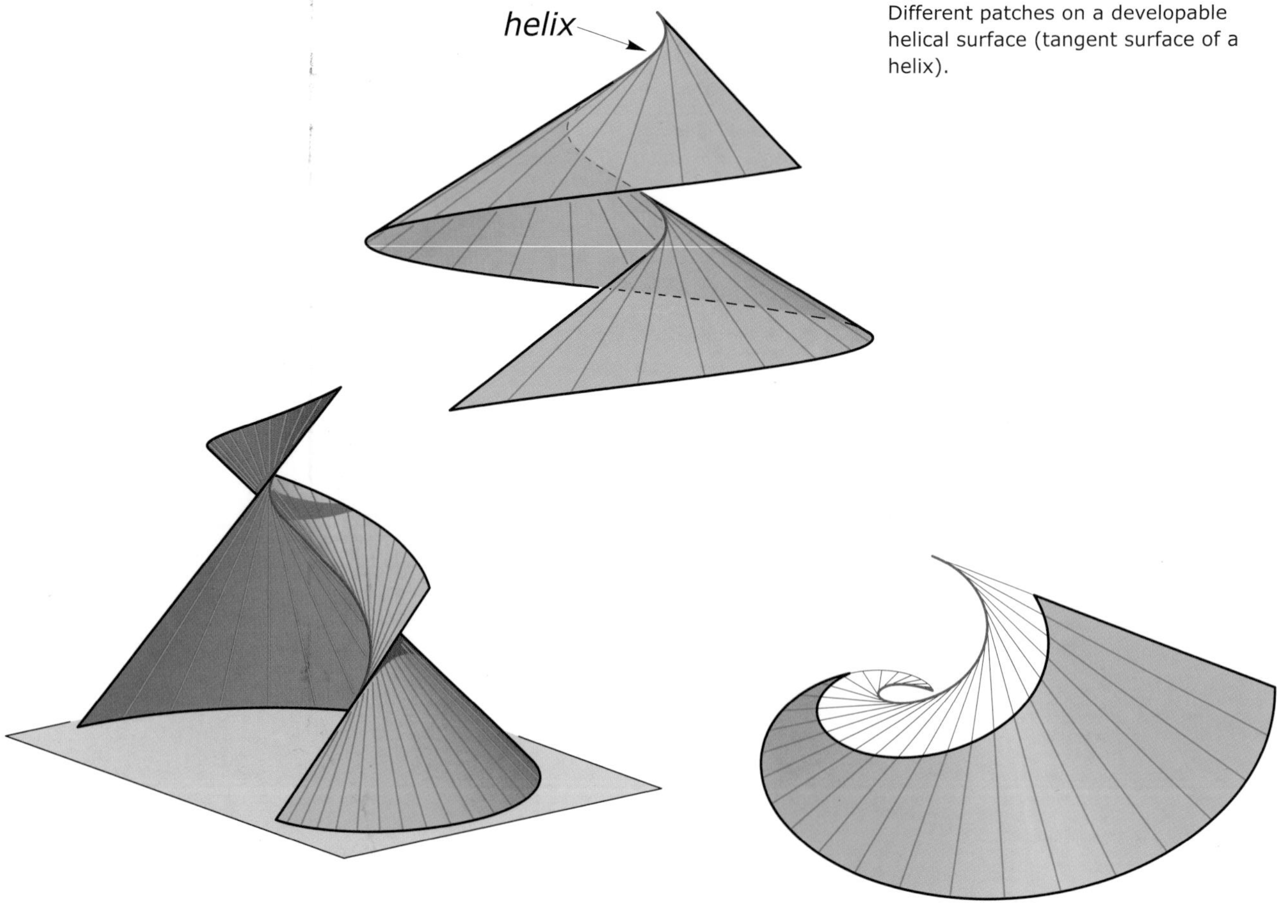

Fig. 15.26
Different patches on a developable helical surface (tangent surface of a helix).

Developable surfaces through curves. To connect two curves *c* and *d* by a developable surface, one has to note that the tangent planes of the surface must be tangent to both curves *c* and *d*. Moreover, the straight lines connecting the points of tangency are the rulings of *S*. Figure 15.27 shows a few solutions to special input curves. If one curve is a polygon, the solution surface contains planar segments.

The construction of developable surfaces through curves is not as simple as it may seem. There may be many solutions, only one or a few of which will be desirable solutions. Rose et al. [2007] developed an algorithm for computing those developable surfaces through boundary curves which are optimal in the sense of user-specified criteria; some results are depicted in Figure 15.27b.

Fig. 15.27
(a) To construct a developable surface *S* that joins two input curves *c* and *d*, we have to note that the tangent planes of *S* have to touch both curves and that the connecting lines of the points of tangency are the rulings of *S*.

(b) These objects have been modeled with an algorithm by Rose et al. [2007] that computes developable surfaces through given boundary curves. (Images courtesy of A. Sheffer.)

(a)

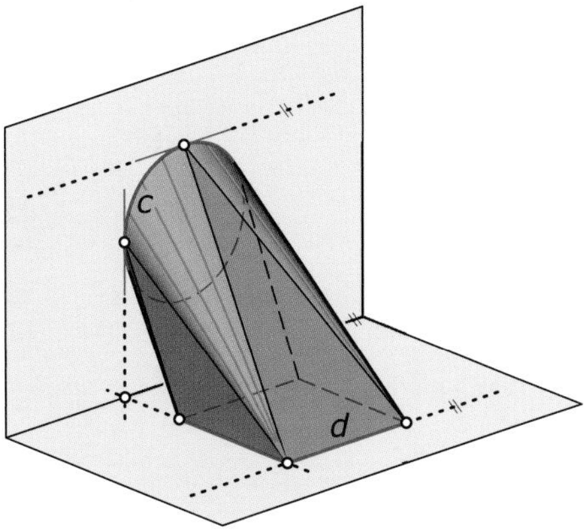

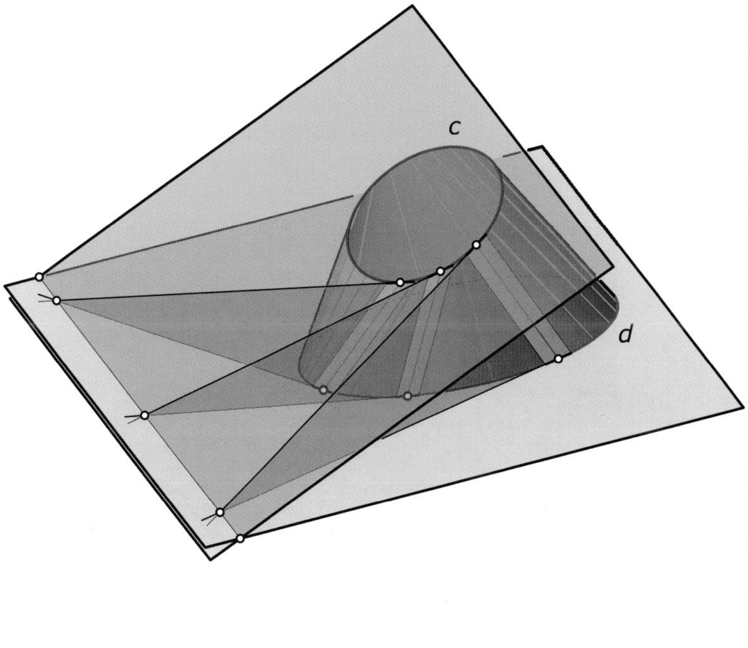

(b)

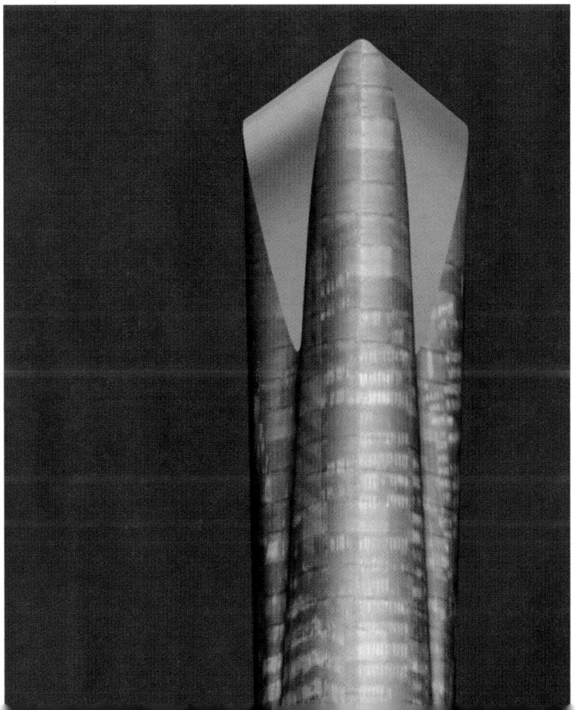

Example:

D-forms. A remarkable example of modeling with developable surfaces has been proposed by the British designer Tony Wills. He takes two planar sheets of unstretchable material (such as paper) bounded by convex curves c_1, c_2 of the same total length. Then he attaches these two sheets to each other, starting at an arbitrary point p_1 on c_1 and p_2 on c_2. Finally, the two sheets are glued together along their common boundaries. Computing these shapes is not easy and involves some nonlinear optimization (Figure 15.28). Some designs by Tony Wills are shown in Figure 15.29.

The development and the inverse operation. Any developable surface can be mapped into the plane without stretching or tearing (i.e., by an isometric mapping). This distortion-free mapping into the plane is called *development*. It is constructed in a CAD system with the unfold operation. We have previously discussed the following properties of the development.

- Corresponding curves c and c^d on S and the development S^d, respectively, have the same length.
- Corresponding regions R, R^d have the same surface area.
- The intersection angle between two curves c,d on S is the same as the intersection angle of the curves c^d and d^d in the development.

Figure 15.30 shows the development of a part of a helical developable surface S. The surface S is the tangent surface of a helix r. Its development is the tangent surface of a planar curve r^d. Because one can show that the curvature in corresponding points of r and r^d is the same and because the helix r has constant curvature, r^d also has constant curvature. Thus, r^d is a circle.

One can imagine to perform the development in a kinematic way by rolling S over a plane P. We may imagine S being covered with fresh paint. Then the rolling surface will color the plane P exactly at the development S^d. This is shown for a cylinder in Figure 15.31.

Fig. 15.28
D-forms are constructed by attaching two planar sheets to each other. The boundary curves of the planar sheets are of the same total length. This figure shows a few steps in an algorithm by M. Kilian that computes a D-form from the planar sheets.

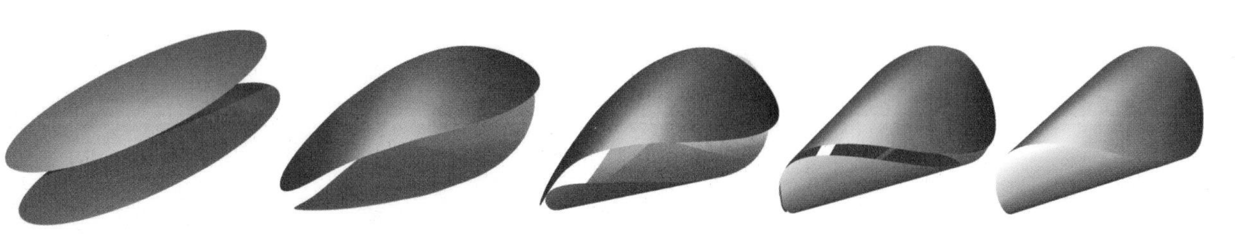

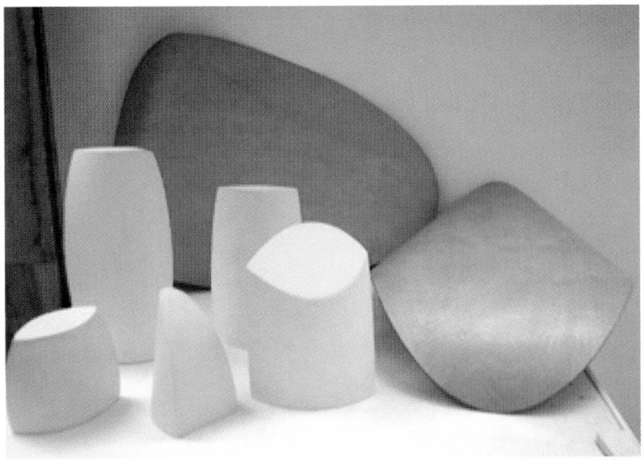

Fig. 15.29
D-forms designed by Tony Wills. (Images courtesy of T. Wills.)

Fig. 15.30
Helical developable surface S and its development. The development r^d of the curve of regression r (helix) of S turns out to be a circle r^d.

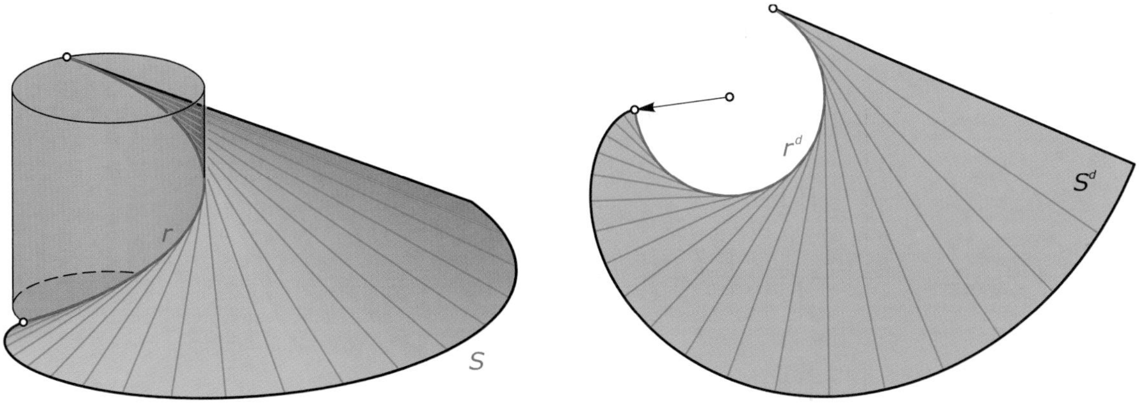

Fig. 15.31
The development of a developable surface (in the present case, a cylinder) can be obtained by rolling S over a plane (rolling projection).

Having computed the development, the mapping back to the surface S may also be of importance. For example, one may cover S^d by a texture and map the texture back to the surface without distortion (Figure 15.32). Especially, we may cover the development with parallel lines at constant distance w. Mapping them back to the surface, we obtain the curves along which we can roll out sheet metal bands to cover the surface. A discussion of geometric strategies for cladding architectural freeform designs can be found in Shelden [2002].

(a)

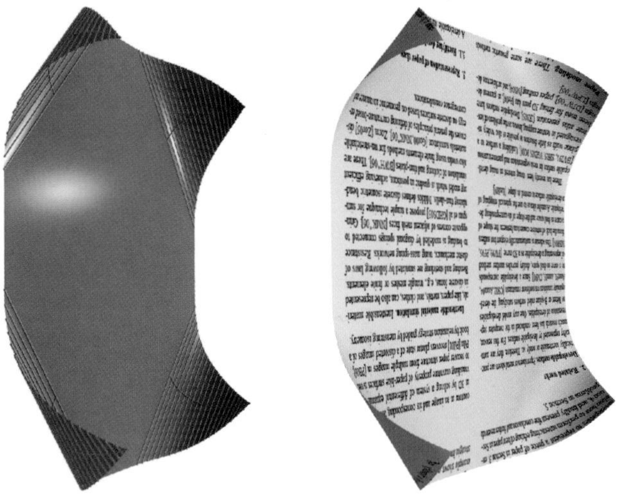

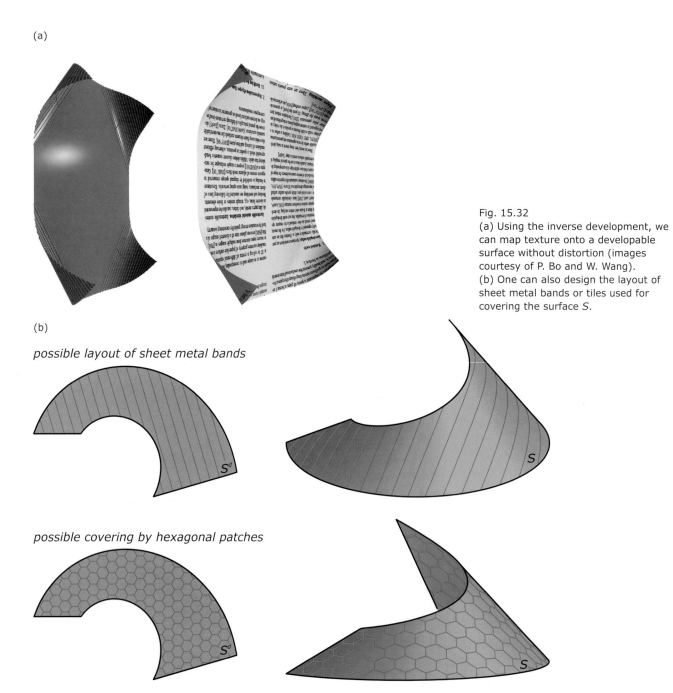

Fig. 15.32
(a) Using the inverse development, we can map texture onto a developable surface without distortion (images courtesy of P. Bo and W. Wang).
(b) One can also design the layout of sheet metal bands or tiles used for covering the surface S.

(b)

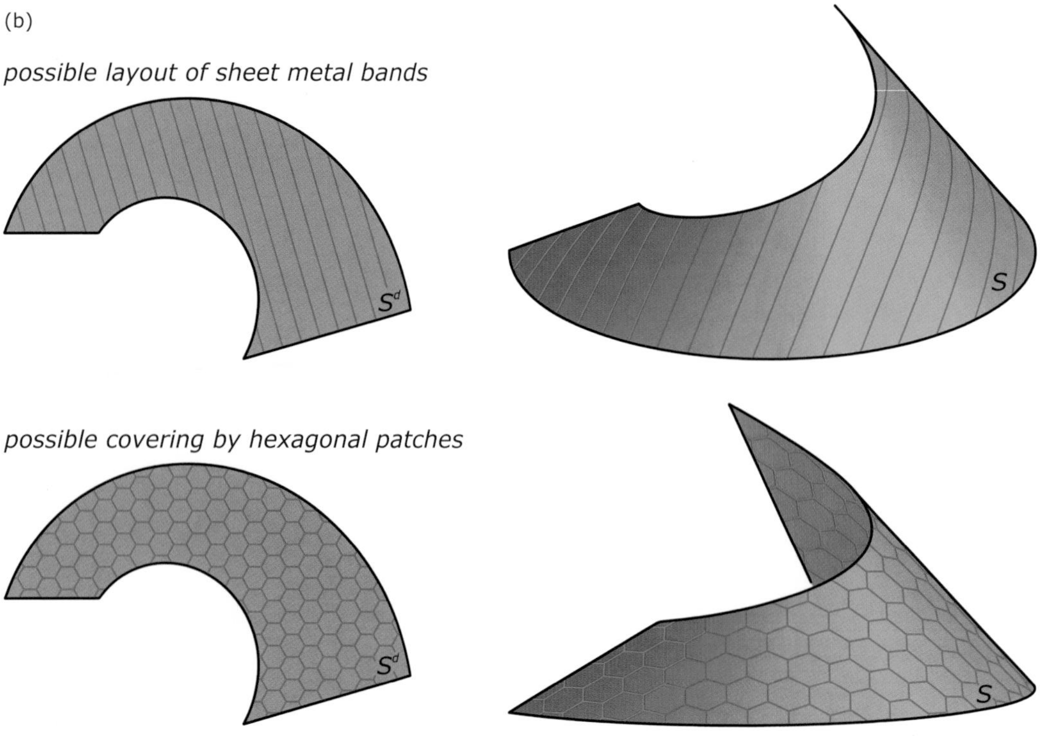

Developable surfaces related to principal curvature lines. Consider any surface *S* and a curve *c* on it. The surface normals along *c* form a ruled surface *N* (called the normal surface along *c*). It can be shown that *the ruled surface* N *is developable if (and only if)* c *is a principal curvature line of* S (Figure 15.33). This means that any tangent of *c* is in principal curvature direction.

Instead of proving this result, we look at a few special cases. Let *S* be a surface of revolution. Then, the circles and meridian curves (intersections with planes through the axis) are the principal curvature lines on it. In fact, the normal surface along a circle of *S* is a right circular cone (i.e., developable) and the normal surface along a meridian curve is contained in a plane (i.e., developable).

We also see that *the rulings of a developable surface* S *are principal curvature lines* because the normals along a ruling are parallel and thus lie in a plane. The second family of principal curvature lines on a developable surface *S* is the curves that intersect the rulings at a right angle. For a developable surface *S* of constant slope this second family is given by the curves at constant height.

The congruent profiles of a moulding surface *S* are principal curvature lines. This follows from the fact that all surface normals at points of a profile curve lie in the profile's plane because the surface intersects that plane at a right angle. The second family of principal curvature lines is the trajectories of the profile's motion.

Any curve *c* on a sphere *S* may be considered a principal curvature line. In fact, the normal surface along *c* is a cone with vertex at the midpoint of the sphere. Hence, if a sphere *S* touches a surface *F* along a curve *c* it follows that *F* and the sphere have the same normals along *c* and therefore *c* is a principal curvature line on *F*. For example, the circles along which a canal surface is tangent to its generating spheres are principal curvature lines.

Given a curve *c* on a surface *S*, we may consider the envelope surface of all tangent planes of *S* at points of *c*. This circumscribed developable surface *D* has a family of rulings. If *c* is a principal curvature line, the rulings of *D* are orthogonal to *c* (Figure 15.34). It is a useful exercise to consider the examples addressed previously and verify this property in regard to them.

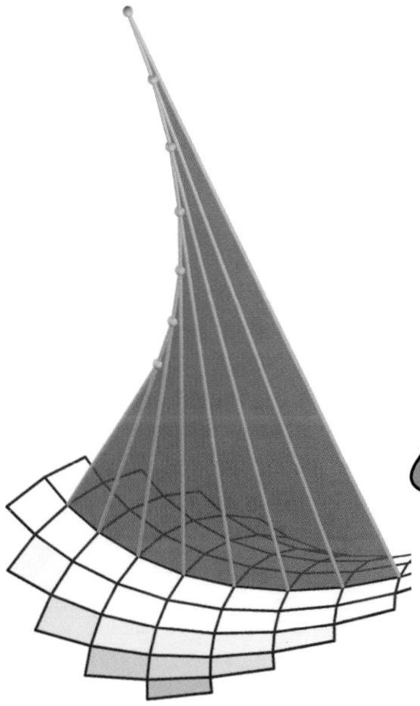

Fig. 15.33
The ruled surface formed by the normals of a surface *S* along a curve *c* is developable if and only if *c* is a principal curvature line of *S*.

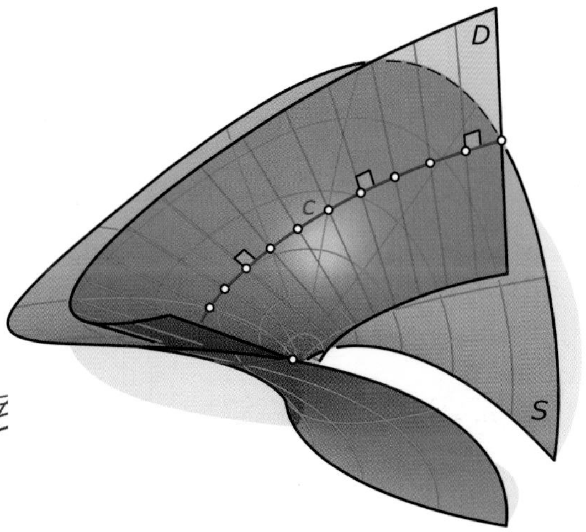

Fig. 15.34
The developable surface *D* tangent to a given surface *S* along a curve *c* has rulings orthogonal to *c* if and only if *c* is a principal curvature line of *S*.

Strip models of doubly curved surfaces. Because developable surfaces have a number of properties that are attractive for architecture, one may think about the approximation of a surface by a union of developable strips. This is not as easy as it sounds. One may try to prescribe a few curves on a given surface F and connect them by developable surfaces. But by doing so one may easily end up in situations in which the connecting surface is no longer smooth.

We therefore propose to use a few curves on F that are close to principal curvature lines. Then, the chance of becoming trapped in singular situations is reduced because rulings of these strips should be approximately orthogonal to their boundary curves (Figure 15.34). This follows from the previous discussion because the strips then approximate a tangent developable surface D. (See Figure 15.35.)

A simple special case where this becomes obvious is that of a rotational surface F. Its principal curvature lines are its circles and meridian curves. Strips bounded by circles lie on cones of revolution. Strips bounded by meridian curves lie on cylinder surfaces (Figure 15.36).

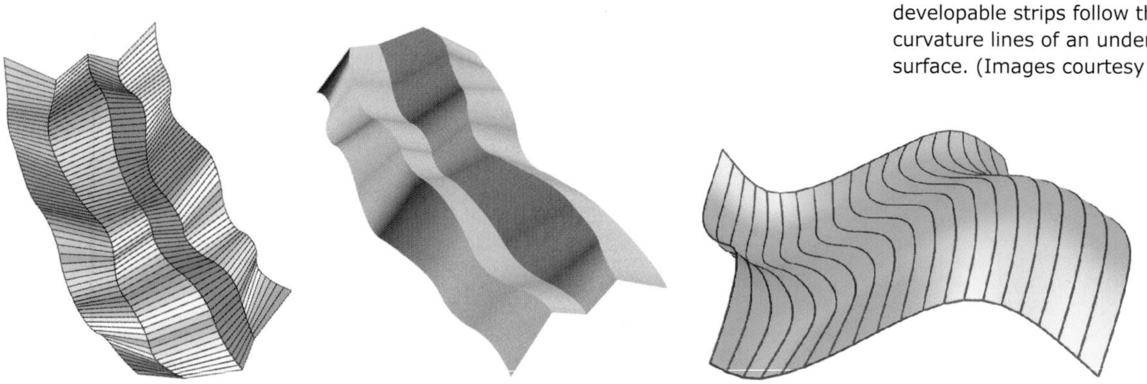

Fig. 15.35
Approximation of a surface F by a union of developable strips.
(a) A zigzag model and
(b) a model that approximates a smooth surface very well. Here, the developable strips follow the principal curvature lines of an underlying smooth surface. (Images courtesy of Yang Liu.)

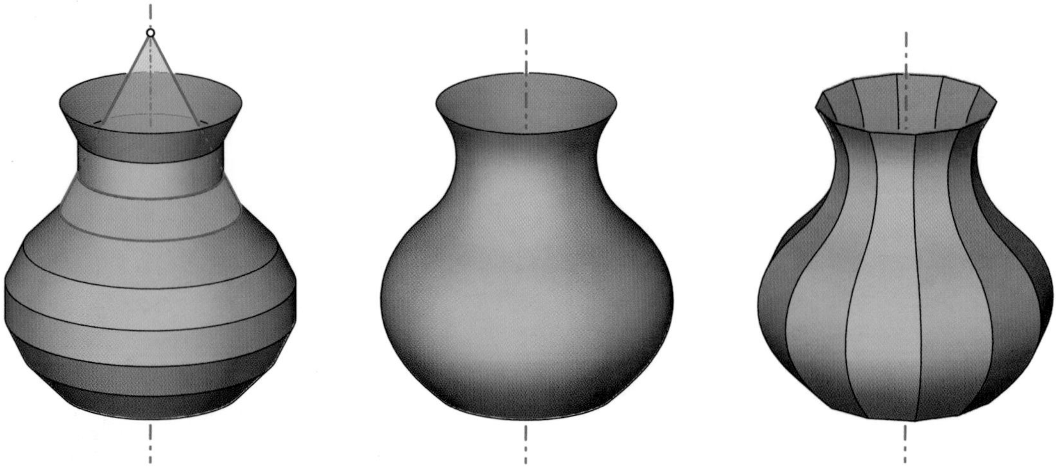

Fig. 15.36
Two very simple strip models of a rotational surface F with
(left) strips of right circular cones and
(right) strips of cylinder surfaces.

In Figure 15.37, we have put together some strip models of other traditional surface classes. A strip model of *a translational surface* can be generated by joining a sequence of profiles. Consecutive profile curves are related by a translation, and actually the translation vectors define the connecting strip on a cylinder surface. Thus, we obtain a model formed by cylinder surface strips.

Let's consider a sequence of congruent spheres. We circumscribe a tangent cylinder to consecutive spheres. Then, consecutive cylinders intersect in an ellipse (actually two ellipses, but only one is needed) and in this way we obtain a strip model of a pipe surface (Figure 15.37 b) formed by cylindrical strips.

We can proceed in an analogous way to obtain a model of a canal surface (Figure 15.37c), but there we start with spheres of different radii and use circumscribed rotational cones. Consecutive cones intersect in an ellipse. This is not obvious but is a special case of a result regarding degenerate intersections of quadrics (Chapter 7).

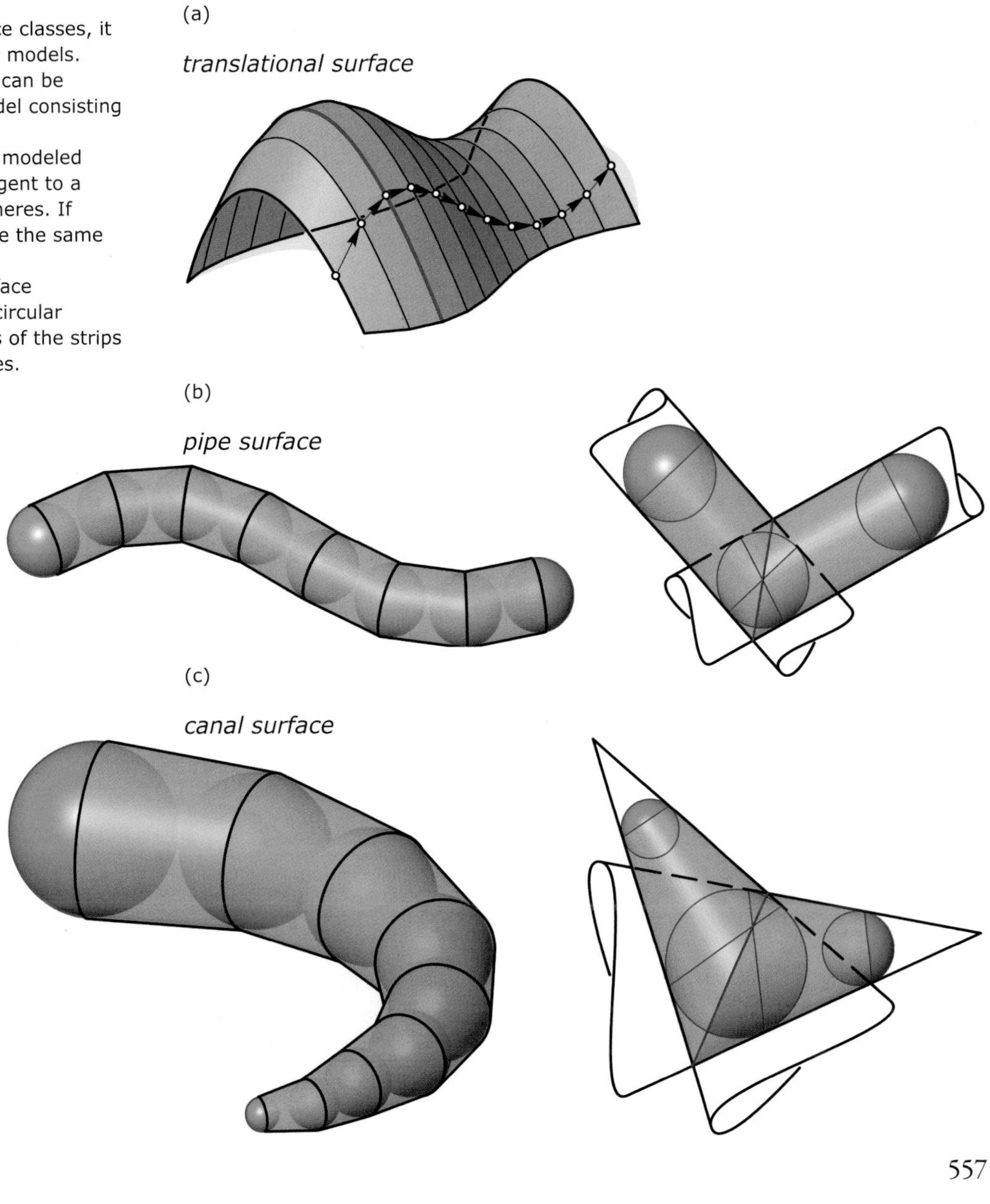

Fig. 15.37
For some traditional surface classes, it is very easy to derive strip models.
(a) A translational surface can be represented by a strip model consisting of cylinder strips.
(b) A pipe surface may be modeled by rotational cylinders tangent to a sequence of congruent spheres. If theses spheres do not have the same radius, we obtain
(c) a model of a canal surface formed by pieces of right circular cones. The junction curves of the strips in cases b and c are ellipses.

Strips of paper. Given a planar rectangular strip of paper, we can make a developable surface strip S from it. These strips are special in the sense that the development of the boundary curves c_1, c_2 are (parallel) straight lines c_1^d and c_2^d (Figure 15.38). In addition, the middle curve m is mapped to a line m^d; namely, the equidistant line of c_1^d and c_2^d. Hence, the curves c_1, c_2, and m are shortest paths on the strip surface. If two points a and b on m are given, the shortest path on S that joins a and b follows along m. As stated previously, we call such shortest paths on a surface its *geodesics*.

If the central curve m of a strip of paper is given (Figure 15.39), the strip lies on the *rectifying developable surface* R. It is formed by the rectifying planes of m. The rectifying plane of a curve m at a point p passes through the tangent of m at p and is normal to the osculating plane of m at p. We could also formulate the result as follows: The osculating planes of m are normal to the surface R. A system for modeling developable surfaces as rectifying developable surfaces of curves has been developed by Bo and Wang [2007].

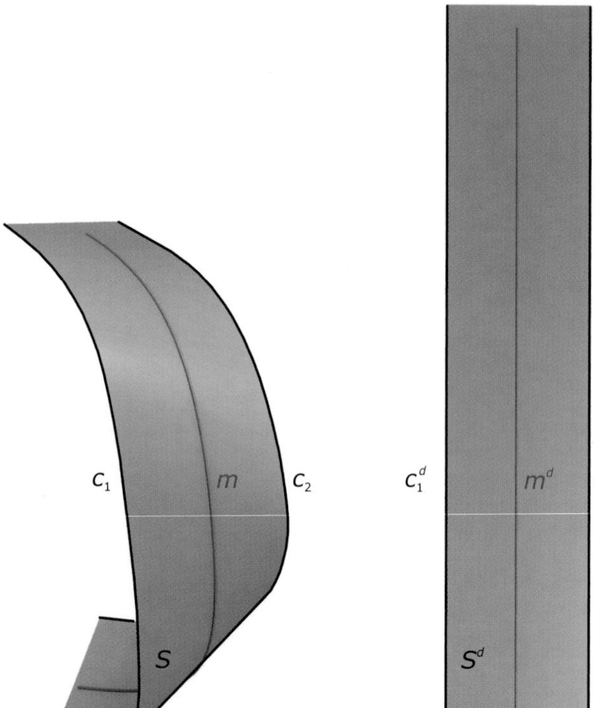

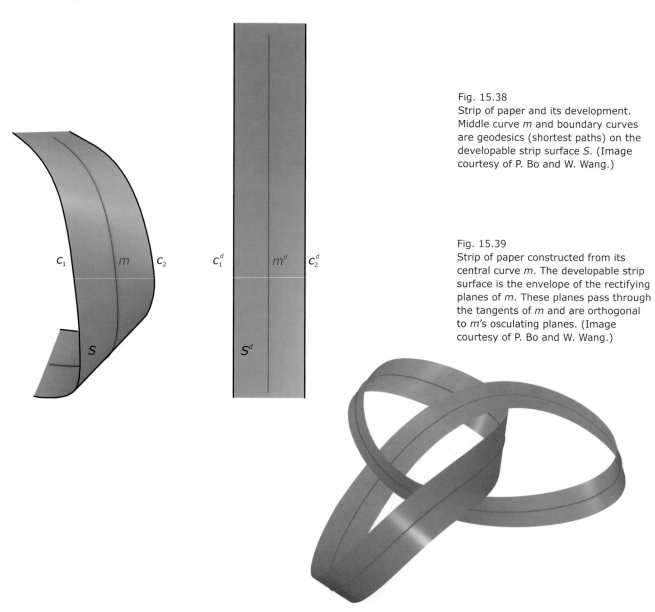

Fig. 15.38
Strip of paper and its development. Middle curve m and boundary curves are geodesics (shortest paths) on the developable strip surface S. (Image courtesy of P. Bo and W. Wang.)

Fig. 15.39
Strip of paper constructed from its central curve m. The developable strip surface is the envelope of the rectifying planes of m. These planes pass through the tangents of m and are orthogonal to m's osculating planes. (Image courtesy of P. Bo and W. Wang.)

Shortest paths on polyhedra and on smooth surfaces. Let's look at a shortest path on a polyhedron. Clearly, the path is a polygon because it must be straight on each face. We now investigate the crossing of an edge of the polyhedron. To understand this, we use an unfolding into the plane. In view of the straight unfolding, the shortest path crosses the edge of the polyhedron at equal intersection angles (see Figure 15.40a).

This fact can be used to construct shortest paths on polyhedra. A more careful investigation of the geometry at the crossing point x and refinement of the polyhedron to a smooth surface S yields the following property of a geodesic (shortest path) g on a surface S: *At each point of a geodesic* g, *the osculating plane of* g *is normal to* S (i.e., the osculating plane contains the surface normal). (See Figure 15.40b).

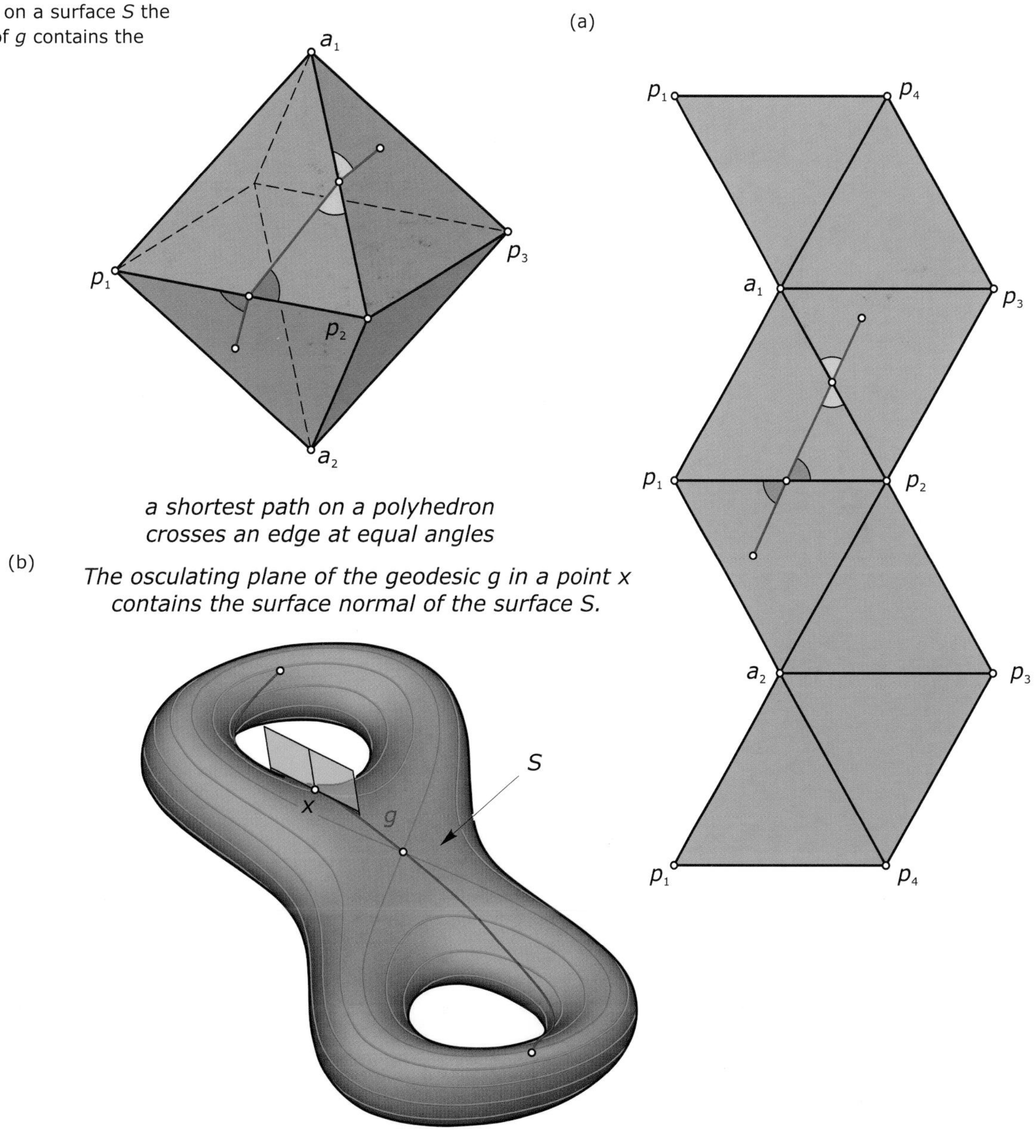

(a)
a_1
p_1
p_2
p_3
a_2
p_4
a shortest path on a polyhedron crosses an edge at equal angles
(b)
The osculating plane of the geodesic g in a point x contains the surface normal of the surface S.
S
x
g

Fig. 15.40
(a) A shortest path on a polyhedron crosses an edge at equal angles.
(b) At each point x of a shortest path g (geodesic) on a surface S the osculating plane of g contains the surface normal.

Geodesics may serve for a natural segmentation of surfaces into patches. A straight strip of paper laid over a smooth surface will follow a geodesic on the surface (Figure 15.41), which has implications on strategies for cladding and panelization of surfaces (see Spuybroek [2004]). J. Natterer used geodesics on surfaces for the beam layout in his wooden "polydome" constructions (see Figure 15.42 and Herzog et al. [2004]).

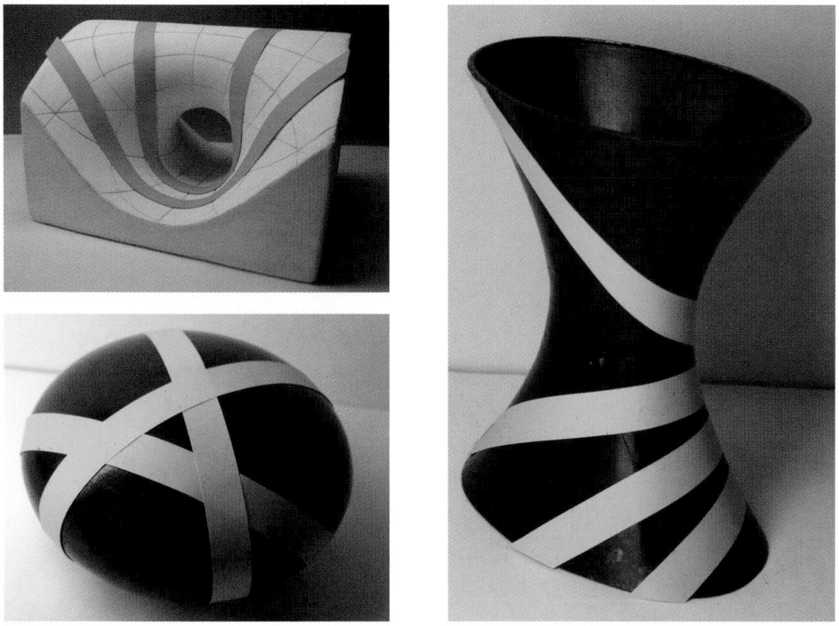

Fig. 15.41
Strips of paper glued onto a surface follow the shape of geodesics on the surface. This technique is useful for the layout of panels on a double-curved surface.

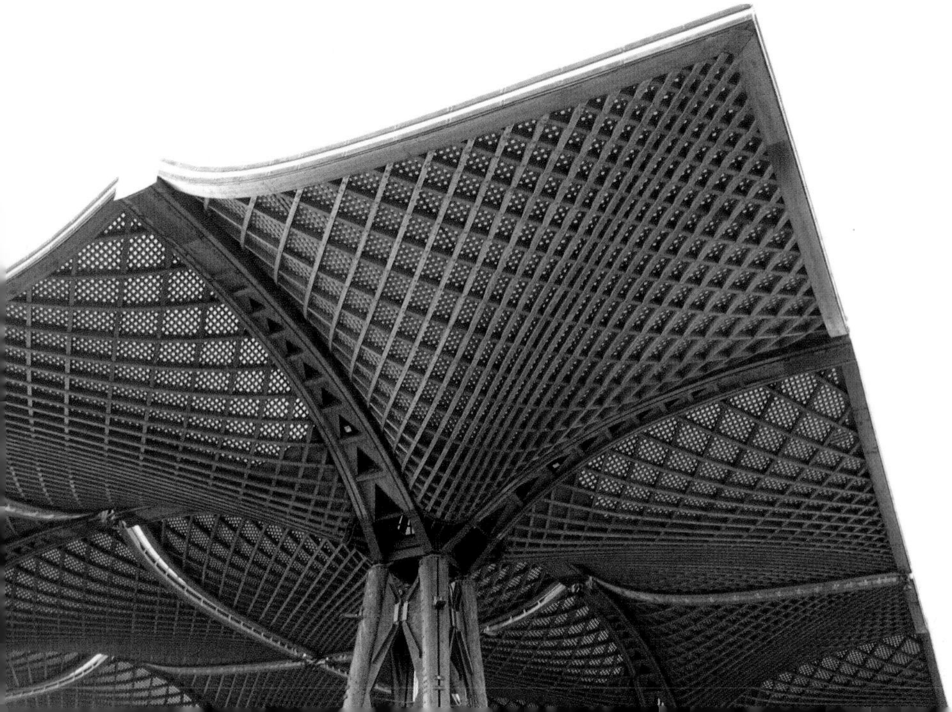

Fig. 15.42
Polydome by J. Natterer. The wooden beams follow geodesics on a smooth underlying surface (image courtesy of Jan Debertshäuser).

Unfolding a Polyhedron

Any surface may be approximated well (in fact, up to any desired accuracy) by a polyhedron (i.e., a surface with planar faces). CAD systems support this approximation to some extent. They also allow us to unfold a polyhedron. In an unfolding, the planar faces are shown in their actual size and shape. Any face of the unfolding is congruent to a face of the polyhedron.

So why is it then not possible to unfold an arbitrary surface in this way? The answer is obtained by looking at an example, as shown in Figure 15.43. The unfolding of a polyhedron yields a planar domain with numerous *gaps*. The more we refine the polyhedron the more gaps we introduce in the unfolding. Therefore, to unfold an approximating polyhedron of a surface is not a proper solution for the construction of a development.

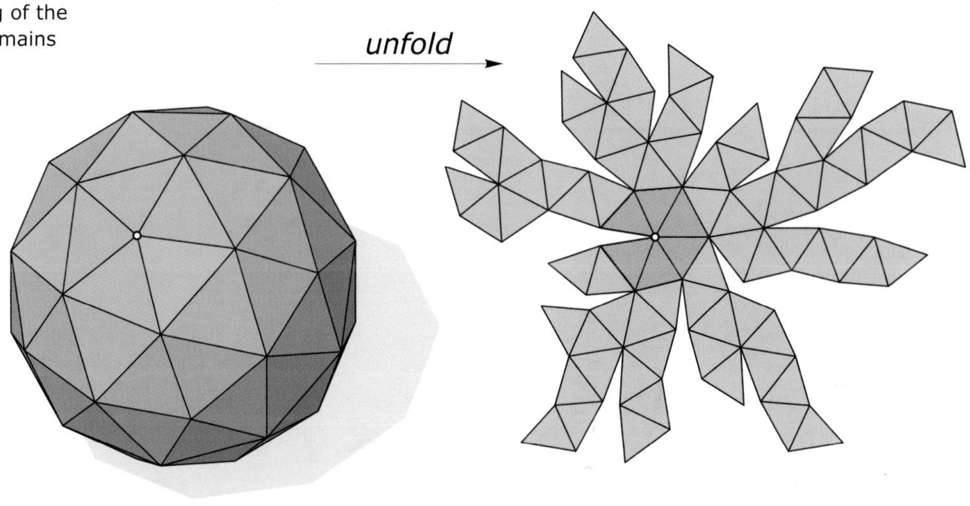

Fig. 15.43
Unfolding a polyhedron introduces a gap at each elliptic vertex. Because the sum of angles at such a vertex is less than 360 degrees, the unfolding of the star around an elliptic vertex remains connected.

In a development, we do not want to have these gaps! Note that the special polyhedral models of developable surfaces discussed previously do not create such gaps.

It is good to carefully think about the unfolding of a polyhedron; namely, about our chances of obtaining a connected unfolding. These chances may be quite limited, as the following discussion shows. Assume we have an *elliptic vertex* of a polyhedron (Figure 15.43). Recall from Chapter 3 that this is a vertex *v* where the sum of angles between consecutive edges (when we march around the vertex) is less than a full angle (360 degrees). To unfold the "star" of faces around *v*, we need to introduce at least one cut. This yields a gap in the development.

The situation is much worse if the vertex *v* is *hyperbolic* (i.e., if the sum of angles exceeds 360 degrees). If we would like to have an unfolding without overlaps, we need to introduce at least two cuts. This yields a separation of the development of the star around *v* into two pieces.

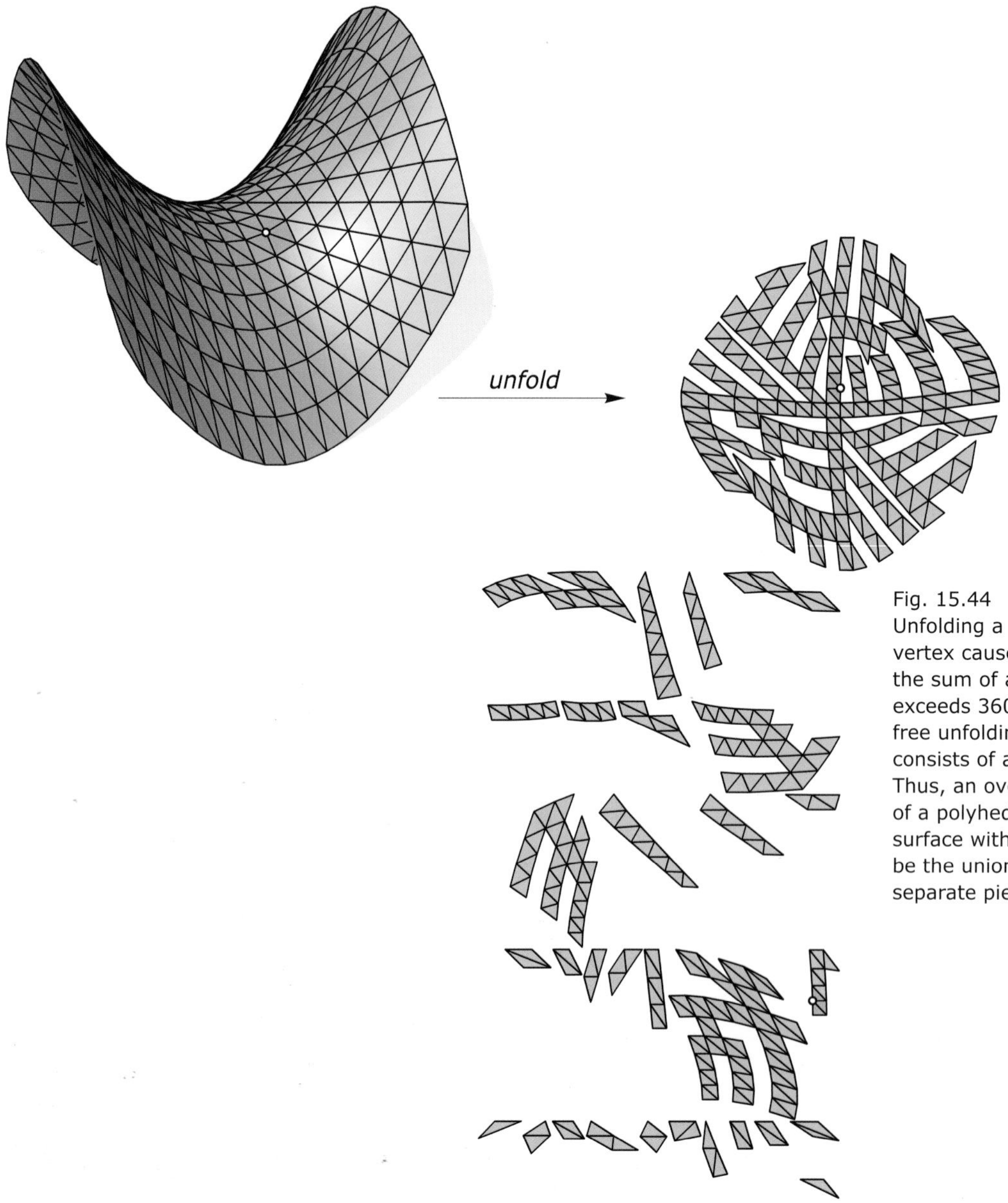

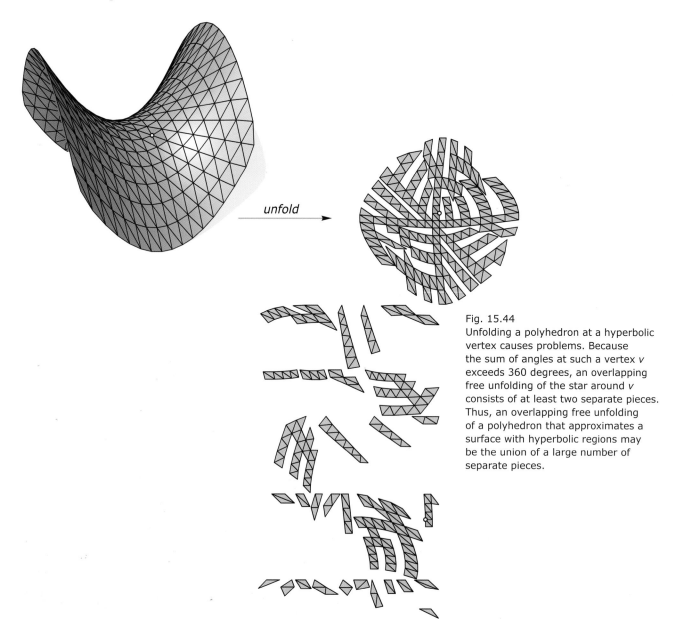

Fig. 15.44
Unfolding a polyhedron at a hyperbolic vertex causes problems. Because the sum of angles at such a vertex *v* exceeds 360 degrees, an overlapping free unfolding of the star around *v* consists of at least two separate pieces. Thus, an overlapping free unfolding of a polyhedron that approximates a surface with hyperbolic regions may be the union of a large number of separate pieces.

Elliptic and hyperbolic vertices of a polyhedron are counterparts of elliptic and hyperbolic points of a smooth surface. Therefore, if a polyhedron is a good approximation of a smooth surface that contains hyperbolic regions (regions with negative Gaussian curvature) there is no chance to obtain a connected unfolding without overlaps.

Avoiding overlaps will cause a decomposition of the unfolding into a potentially large number of pieces (see Figure 15.44). Aesthetically more pleasing models than those arising through a straightforward use of unfolding operations in CAD systems may be obtained after a careful geometric study of the shapes (Figure 15.45).

Whereas special surfaces may nicely be represented by strip models or unfoldings of polyhedral approximations, we have also encountered some limits and difficulties in the use of these model building techniques. Fortunately, modern technology provides further solutions to this problem—such as rapid prototyping and CNC machining. This is discussed in the following chapter.

Fig. 15.45
The fabrication of paper models of double-curved surfaces poses great challenges to the designer. These examples are student projects from model building classes at TU Wien. (Images courtesy of A. Aigner.)

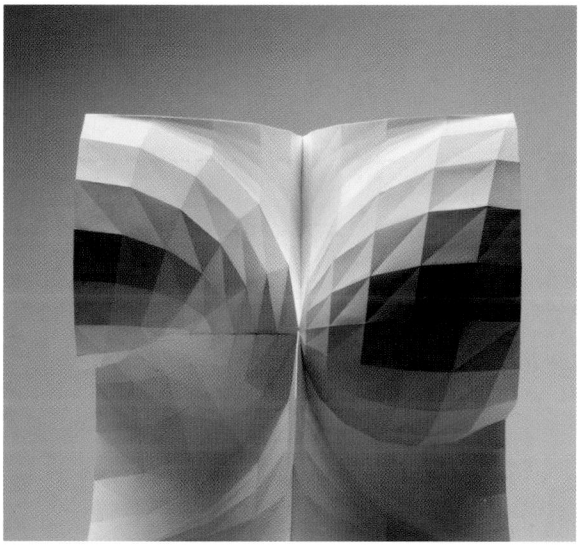

References and Further Reading

Aumann G. A simple algorithm for designing developable Bezier surfaces. Computer Aided Geometric Design 2003;20:601–19.

Bo P-B, Wang W. Geodesic-controlled developable surfaces for modeling paper bending. Computer Graphics Forum 2007;26 (in press).

Frey WH. Modeling buckled developable surfaces by triangulation. Computer-Aided Design 2004;36:299–313.

Herzog T, Natterer J, Schweitzer R. *Wood Construction Manual.* Basel: Birkhäuser 2004.

Liu Y, Pottmann H, Wallner J, Yang Y, Wang W. Geometric modeling with conical meshes and developable surfaces. ACM Transactions on Graphics 2006;25:681–89.

Rose K, Sheffer A, Wither J, Cani M-P, Thibert B. Developable surfaces from arbitrary sketched boundaries. *Proceedings of the Symposium on Geometry Processing 2007* (in press).

Shelden D. Digital surface representation and the constructibility of Gehry's architecture. PhD thesis, MIT, 2002.

Spuybroek L. *NOX: Machining Architecture.* London: Thames & Hudson 2004.

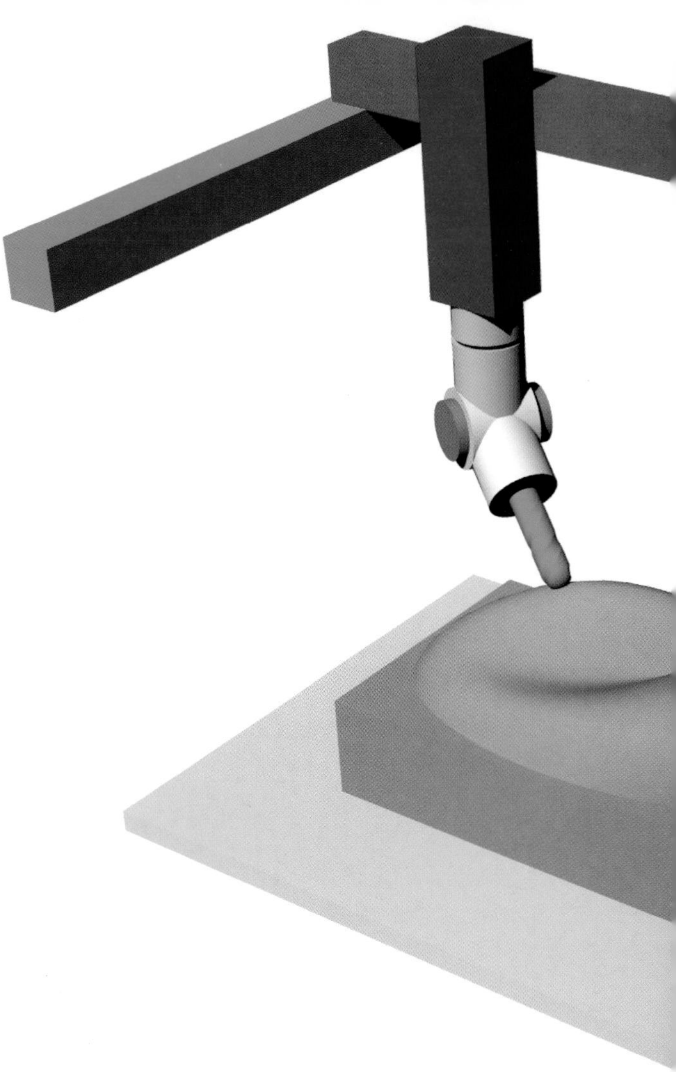

Chapter 16
Digital Prototyping and Fabrication

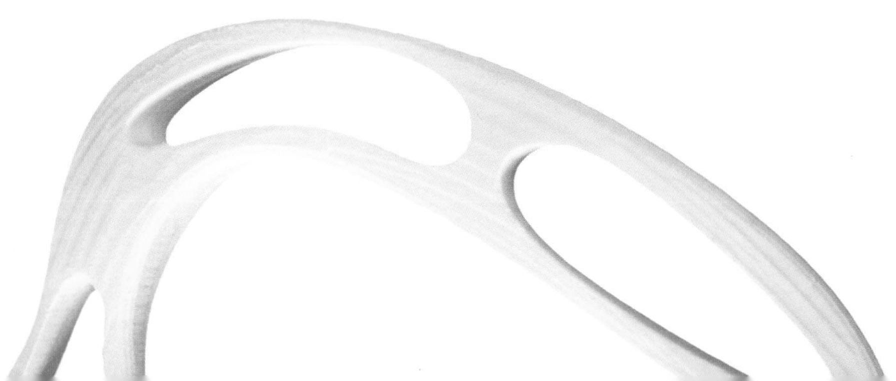

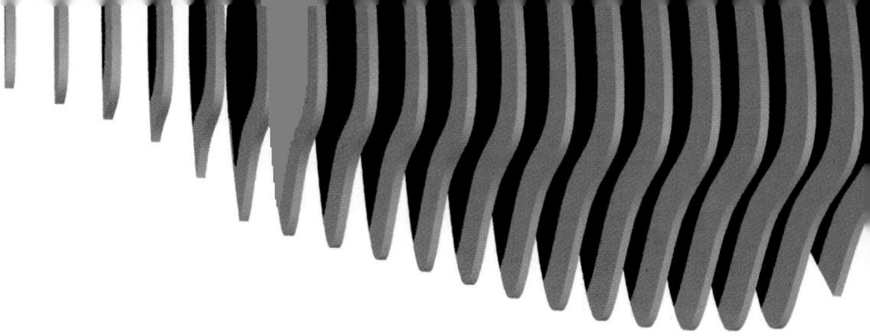

Model Making and Architecture

An architectural model is an integral part of most architectural design developments. Models play a role both in the development of a design and in the representation of the final design at different scales. Digital fabrication is used in close relationship with digital modeling. In this chapter, we assume we are working with digital data to produce a physical model. In the next chapter we study the inverse.

With freeform geometry, digital fabrication and rapid prototyping become especially important because producing a precise physical artifact from the digital data is much more difficult than with rectangular geometries. This has to do with the use of tools and ways of registering and measuring parts. Registering a quadrangular planar surface in space requires only four points, whereas a freeform surface may need hundreds of sample points to recreate it precisely.

For a manual process, this is not feasible in a reasonable amount of time and reproducible manner. In general, one distinguishes between rapid prototyping (in which digital techniques are used for quickly creating functioning prototypes of an idea) and digital fabrication and digital manufacturing (in which digital techniques are used to manufacture the final product at full scale).

The digitally supported techniques can be divided into computer numerically controlled (CNC) machining (in which material is removed from a block of material with tools to achieve the desired result) and the additive techniques—such as fuse deposition modeling (FDM)—which rely on adding material to build up the target geometry. When discussing model making, one also has to discuss scale.

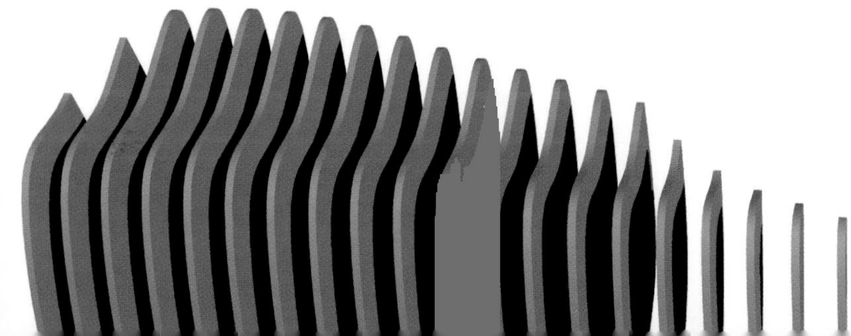

In the Renaissance, Michelangelo had an enormous 5 meter high wooden section model built of the new design for St. Peter's dome during the design phase as a way of studying the design and testing the construction geometries. With a model of such size, it was assembled of many parts—all crafted individually by hand and assembled (Figure 16.1). The scale of a model is the main driver for the level of abstraction of a model all the way to a 1:1 implementation. The same design geometry can support the development of mockups at all scales (Figure 16.2).

History:

The roots of digital fabrication go back to the 1950s, when the invention of numerically controlled machines created the demand for more sophisticated ways of driving these machines than manual punching in of numbers. The first attempts at translating form into numerical output for such machines was based on tracing physical drawings to digitize the information. It quickly became clear that a mathematical way of describing geometry was needed to make any real progress. The invention of mathematical freeform curves and surfaces (e.g., Bezier curves), discussed in earlier chapters, made it possible to make more efficient use of the numerically controlled machines for both model building and fabrication. It still took the past decades for those processes to make it into the mainstream of architecture. Model building is beginning to be dominated by digitally produced componentry (with prices of machines and output declining gradually), and full-scale architecture increasingly relies on digital fabrication for complex geometries.

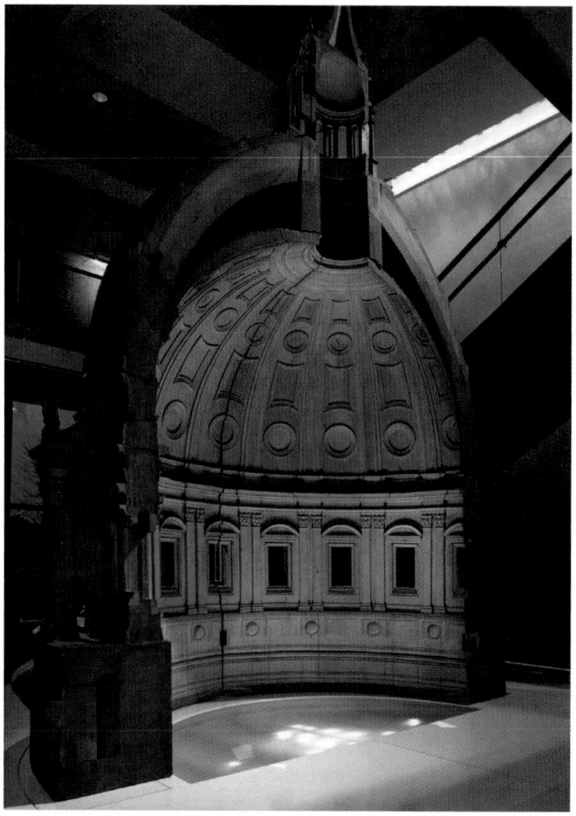

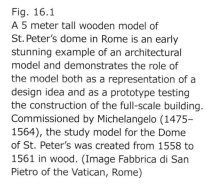

Fig. 16.1
A 5 meter tall wooden model of St. Peter's dome in Rome is an early stunning example of an architectural model and demonstrates the role of the model both as a representation of a design idea and as a prototype testing the construction of the full-scale building. Commissioned by Michelangelo (1475–1564), the study model for the Dome of St. Peter's was created from 1558 to 1561 in wood. (Image Fabbrica di San Pietro of the Vatican, Rome)

With digital fabrication processes, the boundary between model making and full-scale building blurs even further, as the same information used in model making may be used for fabricating the final building. In most cases, architectural parts at full scale far exceed the part envelope of any fabrication equipment—which makes subdivision of geometry for fabrication and the subsequent assembly of the parts a key step of the process (Figure 16.2e). This is adding additional geometric and procedural challenges of decomposition and assembly. In this chapter, we will discuss the benefits and drawbacks of the various techniques and methods mentioned.

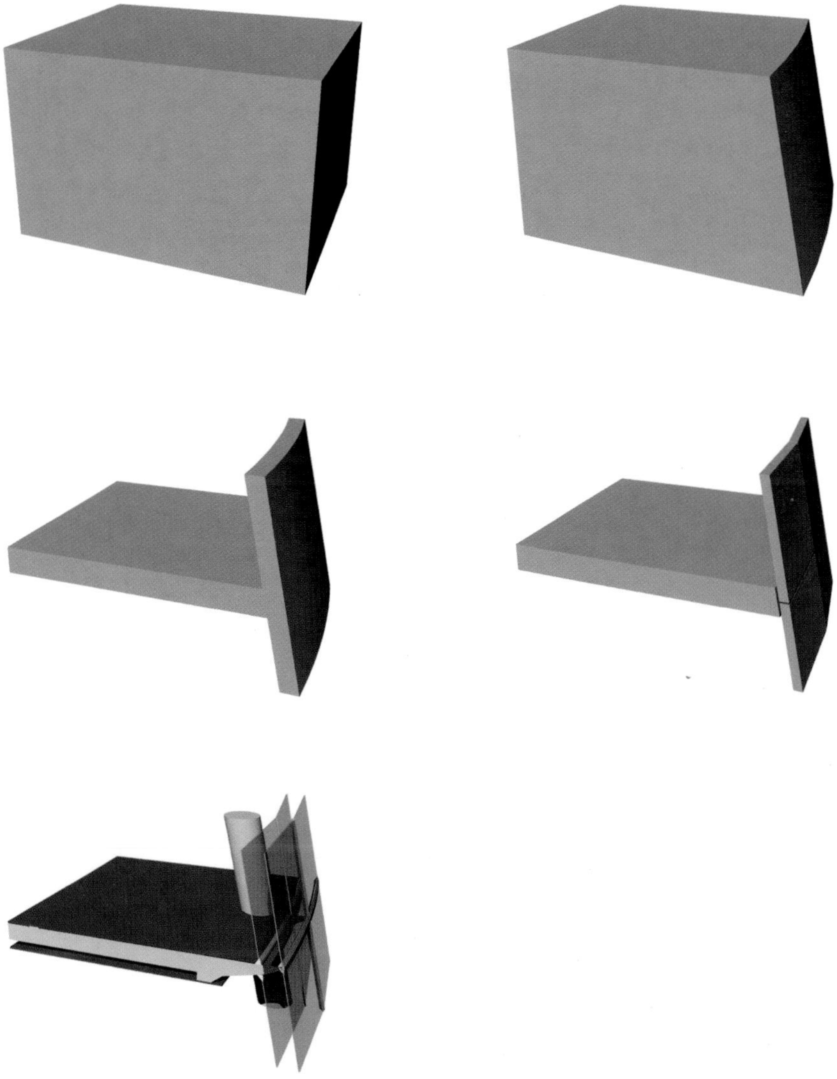

Fig. 16.2
The relationship between scale and geometry in architectural models is defined by the chosen level of abstraction. There are different forms of abstractions in design. A schematic example shows different levels of abstraction of a design geometry. The same underlying geometry can be used to generate different levels of detail from a massing model (a), shape model (b), floor model (c), panelization model (d), and a full scale detailed facade model (e).

From an architectural design point of view, the fabrication technique and the choice of material play a crucial role in the design process and in the aesthetics of the final product. The choice of a fabrication technique can lead to a particular aesthetic due to the geometric translation necessary to produce its parts. The geometric translation can have a big influence on design development (Figure 16.3). The translation of a design idea into fabrication processes can be a complex process.

The choice of a fabrication approach also affects the representation of the design, and each approach requires a slightly different process of abstraction of the core design idea. It poses particular challenges to the understanding of geometry, as the solutions must be valid for the production of a rendered image and robust enough to derive fabrication information from it that allows the geometry to be built using CNC machines.

We can distinguish three cases: representation models that abstract the design geometrically based on the scale of the model, mockups that are built to test physical implementation of parts of the overall design using actual material at full or close to full scale, and digital fabrication in which an entire building is manufactured using CNC techniques at full scale. All share similar geometric techniques and machinery but aim at different goals and are evaluated differently.

(a)

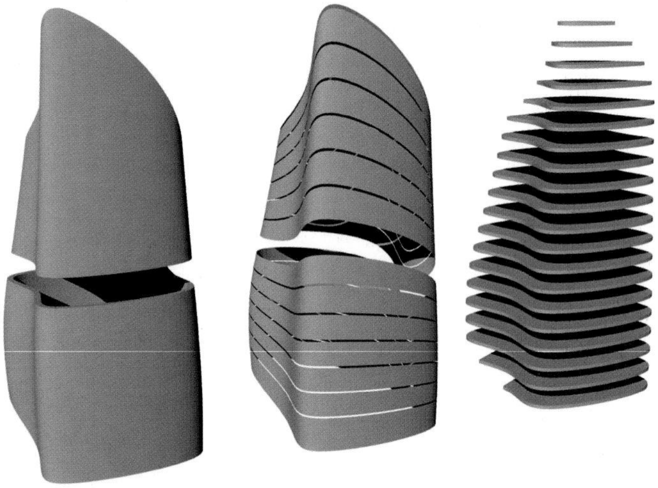

(b)

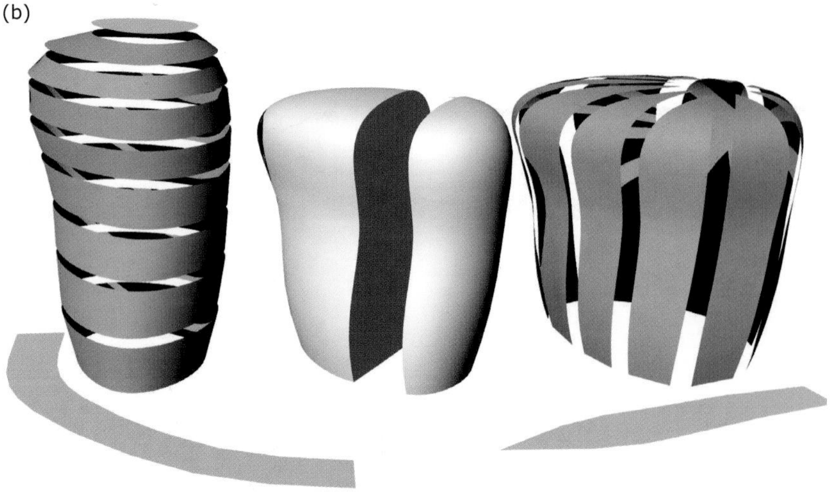

Fig. 16.3
(a) The design geometry of a model can be interpreted differently using its geometric properties. A thin-shell solid model of a surface creates a very different reading compared to an isocurve-based strip model or from a horizontal planar slice model. Each geometric abstraction emphasizes different features of the generating geometry.
(b) The orientation of the geometric features emphasizes different aspects of shape. In this case, a double curved surface is approximated with single-curvature developable strips following the U and V isocurves.

A special case of models not discussed in detail here is the process sketch model, often employed at the beginning of the design process to help formulate the initial ideas. In the following sections we present these three main categories (presentation models, papid prototyping models, and digital fabrication and assembly of parts) as they relate to architecture.

Representation models. Architecture has a long history of model building for representation purposes. The scaled models emphasize representing an idea of a project, as well as the project's proportions and overall context at different scales. Models have also traditionally served as test beds for building complex buildings and as references for all participants in the process of building. Due to the large size of architecture, representation models are usually built at small scales. This reduces the amount of detail that can be shown.

Abstraction of detail and material therefore play a major role in architectural model building. The choice of abstraction is informed by the most important aspect to be represented in the model. Geometric properties of materials can be more important in the context of geometric model building than realistic appearance. For instance, cardboard is frequently used for modeling developable surfaces in scale models due to its ease of use and suitability in modeling developable surfaces.

Materials used in models may also be chosen more for what they represent conceptually than as a representation of the final material choice. Three-dimensional printers offer the precision and intricacy of detail useful for depicting architectural representation models (Figure 16.4). Interestingly, for a small-scale model to be printable the geometry has to be changed and thickened to fit the machine printing constraints.

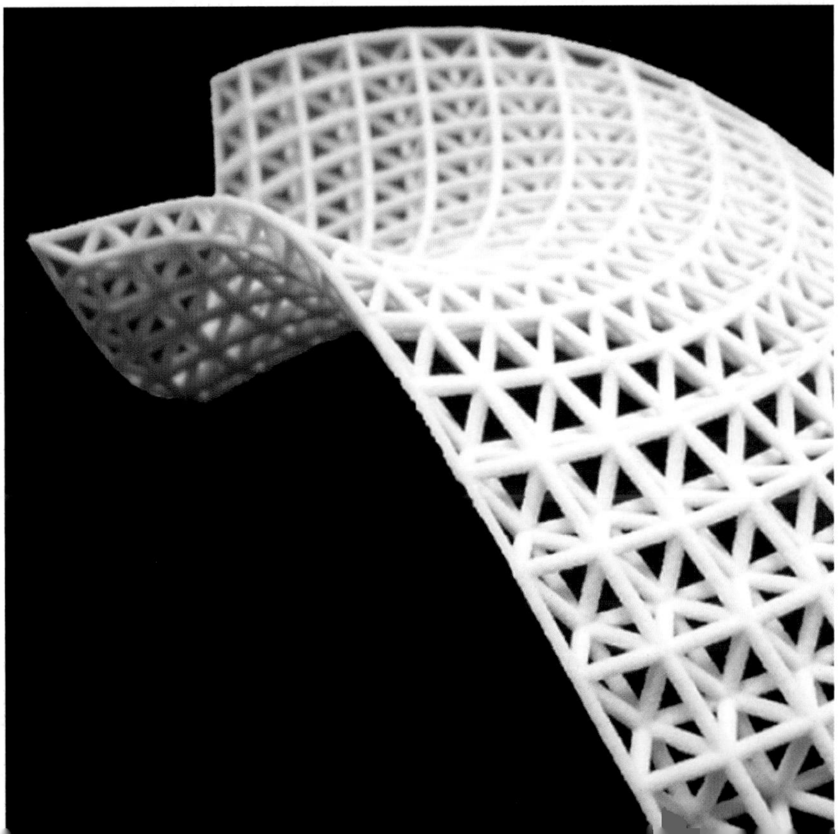

Fig. 16.4
Three-dimensional printers can create spatially complex small-scale models from one monolithic block of material. Most such models are representational, but with proper treatment they can be more durable prototypes. As purely representational models they help little in understanding the construction processes. (Image Axel Kilian, script generated space truss).

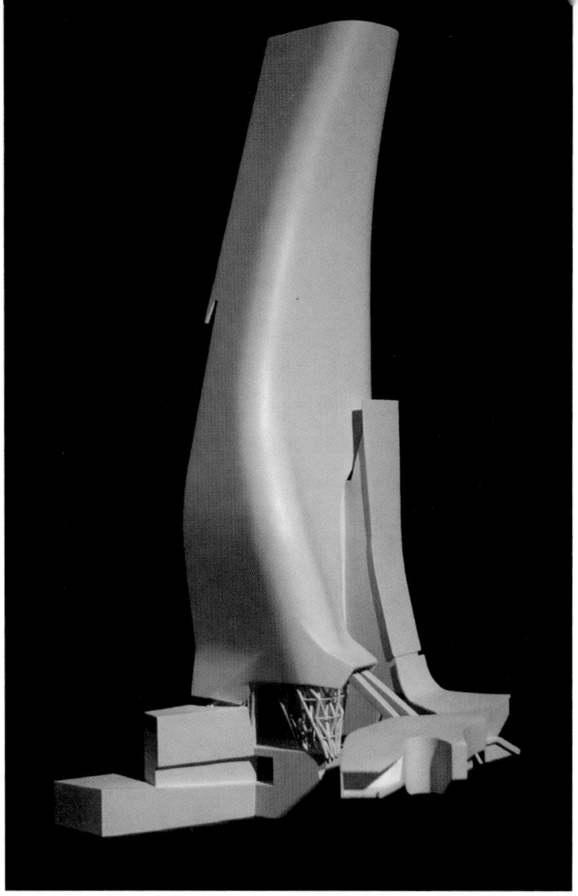

(b)

(c)

(a)

Fig. 16.5
The architecture office Morphosis makes extensive use of three-dimensional printing in the design process both for representational models and for design development.
(a) The Phare tower project in la defense (Paris) (Image Unibail-Morphosis)
(b) a 1:500 model of the Phare tower with much less detail then
(c) a large-scale 1:200 representation model (1:500 model photo John Carpenter, 1:200 model photo Nicolas Buisson, Morphosis)

Therefore, even a technique that is not limited by the types of geometries it can produce requires substantial scale-dependent adjustments of the geometry. The architectural practice Morphosis in Los Angeles has extensive experience in using three-dimensional printing at all steps in the design process and work with adapting models to different scales for design development and printing (Figure 16.5). Other much larger practices, such as Foster and Partner, also have adopted the technique more recently on an office-wide scale.

Rapid prototyping. The term *rapid prototyping* represents the next level of using CNC machines. Here, the models have to fulfill higher standards of physical robustness and tolerances. A rapid prototype is a partially or fully functional prototype at full scale produced using CNC machines. It is largely used in mechanical engineering and product design to evaluate and visualize complicated geometries. In architecture, these techniques are used for detail design of such things as facade joints. But increasingly these techniques also make it into the production of full scale component production such as in the case of ZipShape by the designtoproduction GmbH (Figure 16.6).

Fig. 16.6
The projects by designtoproduction show the power of an intelligent approach to fabrication that is design coherent. ZIP-Shape is a product that creates single-curvature curved sheets from two zipper like interlocking, custom milled sheets. (Image: designtoproduction, Concept: designtoproduction GmbH, CNC-Production: Bach Heiden AG, patent pending)

Rapid manufacturing is an extension of rapid prototyping in which the parts produced with CNC tools are directly usable as fully functional parts that obviate the need for mass production. There are only very few examples of rapid manufacturing, as digital fabrication techniques are still too limited in part size, production speed, and cost. Architecture is a special case because most buildings are a one-of-a-kind structure.

One could claim that each built structure is its own prototype compared to other industries. With freeform geometries, this gets even more challenging because even the parts of the building are non repetitive and require custom manufacturing. This becomes more common in architecture with many examples of CNC machined nodes for freeform facades with each part produced directly from CAD data. An experimental example of machined structure is the Swissbau Pavillion developed by the caad.designtoproduction team at the ETH Zurich (Figure 16.7), and the futurepolis installation by Studio Daniel Libeskind at the university St.Gallen (Figure 16.8).

Fig. 16.7
The firm designtoproduction has been involved in a number of projects using algorithmically generated and managed designs directly used to generate fabrication information for CNC machines. The Swissbau Pavilion sphere is an algorithmically generated geometry with a web of beams generated in response to opening constraints (as well as the cutting geometry) and directly output to a five-axis mill. (Image Contec AG, Geometry Consulting and Engineering: ETH Zürich, caad.designtoproduction, CNC-Production: Bach Heiden AG)

Fig. 16.8
Libeskind's Futuropolis is a complex sculpture for the University of St. Gallen (HSG), designed by Studio Daniel Libeskind and made up of thousands of parts that interlock precisely using a detail developed for use with five-axis mills. (Image: caad.designtoproduction, Geometry Consulting and Engineering: ETH Zürich, caad.designtoproduction, CNC-Production: Bach Heiden AG)

Digital fabrication and assembly. Fabrication of the parts is only one step of production. In architecture, due to the size of buildings the assembly of manufactured parts plays a major role. In comparison to car manufacturing, which makes use of controlled environments for assembly, architecture is largely constructed on site and is subject to weather and other unpredictable conditions. Laser range finders aid the precise positioning of parts with regard to a digital model, even in adverse conditions and within the scope of large tolerances.

The Stata Center by Frank Gehry is a good example of the combination of digital fabrication of parts. In this case, the freeform facade panels were produced in the Zahner factory in Kansas City and then trucked to the site. The assembly onsite was guided by site coordinate points measured using laser range finders with a locally established coordinate system.

Using adjustable fixtures, it was possible to achieve a high degree of precision in the placement of the prefabricated panel system even though the concrete structure was relatively inaccurate. Both the data for the digital fabrication of the panel systems and the positioning data onsite were derived from one central CATIA master model provided by the architects (Figure 16.9).

Fig. 16.9
Digitally assisted assembly of prefabricated facade elements onsite using three-dimensional data points directly from a digital master model. This way, the differences between offsite and onsite constructs caused by construction tolerances can be accommodated. (Image courtesy of Peter Schmitt)

More experimental is the use of robots in the assembly of parts. For instance, bricks were placed into exactly predefined positions by a robotic arm in a project by Fabio Gramazio and Matthias Kohler at the ETH, Zürich (Figure 16.10). To shift the CNC control from the production of parts to the assembly offers interesting new usage scenarios for traditional materials. Contour crafting by Dr. Behrokh Khoshnevis is an example of the combination of concrete and CNC techniques. Concrete is placed in viscous form layer by layer to build up concrete walls without the use of form work (Figure 16.11).

Fig. 16.10
Robotic assembly of standard parts. Gramazio & Kohler from the ETH (Zurich, Switzerland) developed the use of a robotic arm for algorithmically generated brick assemblies at 1:1 scale. The beauty of the approach is within the generation of a novel programmed brick pattern from standard parts using algorithmic processes. (Image courtesy of Gramazio & Kohler, Architecture and Digital Fabrication, ETH, Zurich)

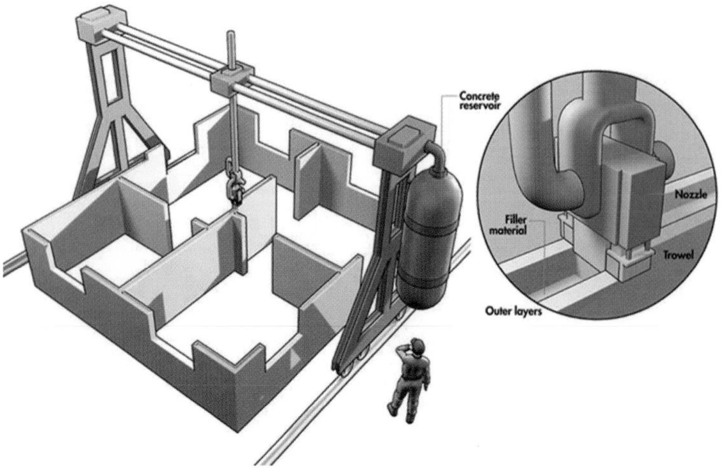

Fig. 16.11
Contour crafting is a technique using concrete in combination with digitally guided deposition nozzles to build three-dimensional concrete structures at full scale without additional scaffolding. Contour crafting was developed by Dr. Behrokh Khoshnevis of the University of Southern California.

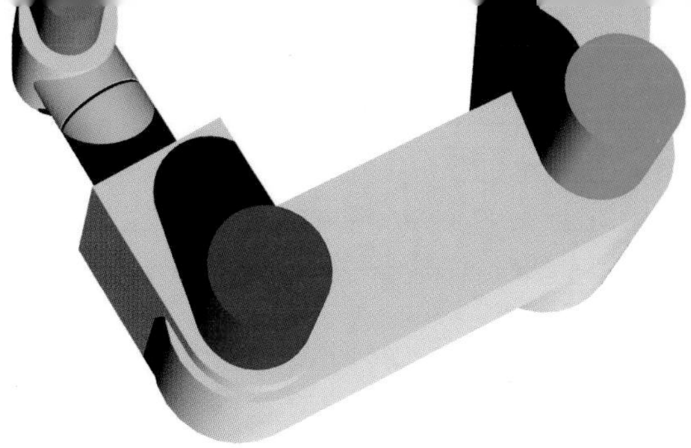

Fabrication Techniques

Overview. There are a number of fabrication techniques used in digital fabrication today. They can be grouped roughly by the governing principles of processes used. In part, the processes are based on the form of the material being worked on (e.g., flat sheet materials versus volumetric blocks). Another criterion is whether material is added to or subtracted from shape the design.

From the perspective of geometry, another aspect is of interest. There are processes in which the model geometry is pixelated into volumetric units and then assembled from scratch. Other processes are based on geometric features of the design being turned into spatial paths that are followed by arms with high degrees of freedom. These different approaches all affect the aesthetics and quality of the products, as well as the time it takes to produce them. For full-scale buildings, there are only very few experimental holistic fabrication approaches.

Most fabrication processes in architecture rely on assembly of parts that are fabricated separately. The machines used for CNC fabrication can be defined by the number of degrees of freedom. A degree of freedom (DOF) is a geometric definition of freedom of movement either along an axis in space or rotation about an axis in space. In three-dimensional space, there are six degrees of freedom: three degrees for movement in the x, y, and z directions and three degrees for rotation about the x, y, and z axes. Therefore, we would need a machine with only three degrees of freedom to reach any coordinate point in space. However, we would need a machine with six degrees of freedom to also orient a tool in any direction at any point in space.

Most CNC machines have far less DOF, as the higher the numbers the higher the cost and complexity of control. In addition, tolerances of moving parts accumulate—leading to lower-precision machining if parts of the same quality are to be used. The simplest machine in terms of DOF is a drill press with one axis of movement in the z axis. Although tremendously useful, one axis gives us too little flexibility to describe geometry in space.

The use of two DOF cutters is common—with laser cutters, waterjet cutters, and routers all using movement in the *x* and *y* axes to move the tool head in space. Refer to the diagrams shown in Figure 16.12 for a more complete set of machining approaches and their respective geometries and DOF. Each implementation has its limitations due to the physical constraints of a mechanical solution. The area reachable with the full set of degrees of freedom is referred to in motion studies and robotics as the *reach envelope*.

In model building, however, there are additional constraints. For instance, a three-axis three-dimensional powder-based printer can create any form using an additive process—even nested fully enclosed shapes. A much more complex six-DOF robotic milling arm would not be able to do so due to collisions with the model itself if it were to remove material from the innermost part. Therefore, the DOF is not the only criterion determining the power of a fabrication approach. It is a combination of fabrication technique and geometric DOF that enables us to build abstract geometry in physical form. In the following section we look at different techniques in fabrication and their geometric implications.

Fig. 16.12
Overview diagrams of the relationship of the degrees of freedom (DOF) and different fabrication machines. The different colors depict the various axes either as axes of movement or rotational degrees of freedom.

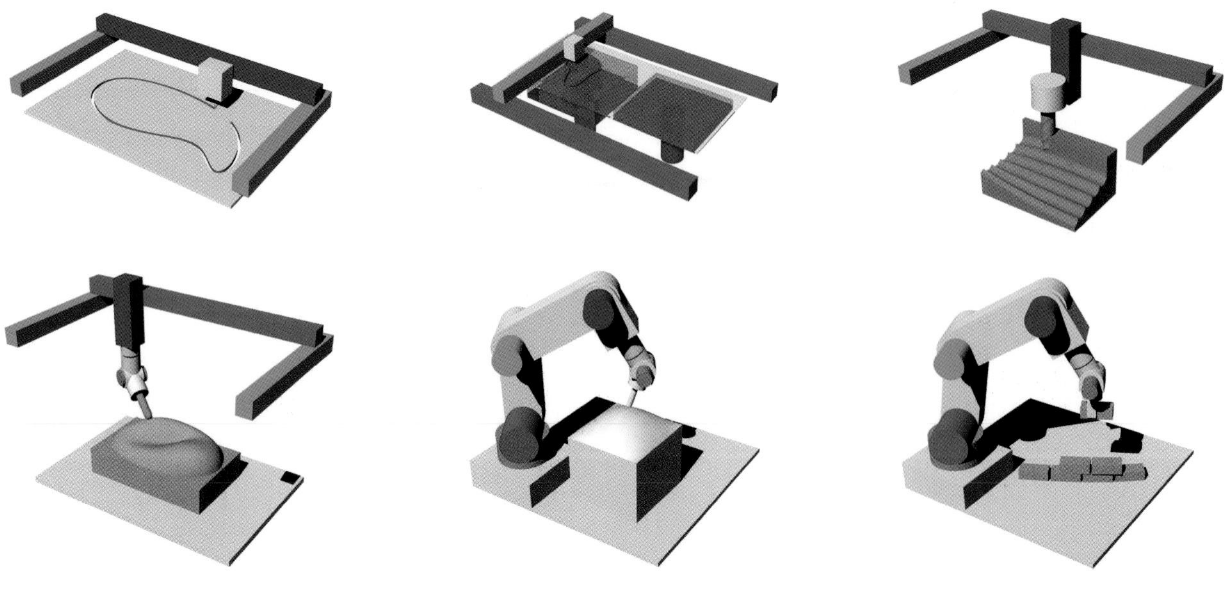

Cutting-Based Processes

Sheet-based cutting techniques. Sheet-based two-dimensional cutting processes are among the simplest CNC fabrication processes other than drilling holes. Simple models can be built by stacking sections panels to build up the model (Figure 16.13 a). They are fast and reliable and use material that is cheap and available in large quantities. Sheet-based processes also match the nature of many geometric surface-based representations.

Faceted models can be built using triangles or flat polygonal shapes cut from sheets (Figure 16.13 b), and even single-curvature developable forms can be build using parts produced with sheet cutting techniques (Figure 16.13 f). Especially for full-scale fabrication of buildings, the economy of a process and material cost play an important role. Working with sheet based materials is relatively standard practice. Also designers are familiar with faceting processes and can integrate them easier into existing workflows. This is changing slowly in favor of three-dimensional printing, but for now sheet-based techniques still play a major role in the creation of representational models.

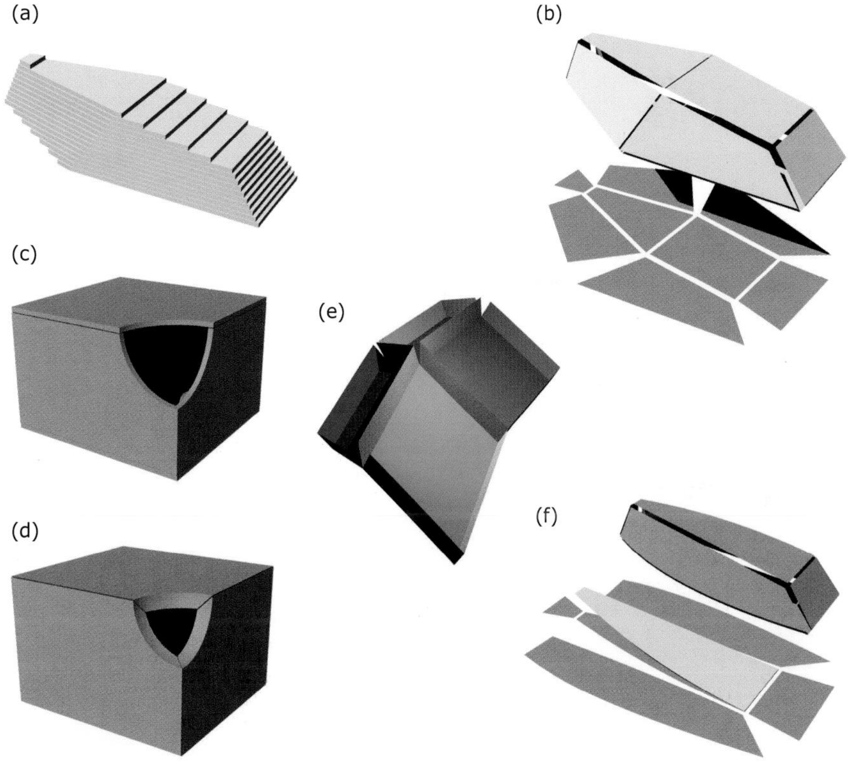

Fig. 16.13
(a) A simple diagram of using planar sheet cut to fit the sections to build up a freeform geometry. Depending on the sheet thickness and the alignment of the sheets to the geometry, the resolution of the model varies.
(b) faceting a shape is another standard option
(c) thickening the panels requires an offset strategy
(d) or miters joints
(e) Giving a freeform panel based geometry material thickness creates a geometric challenges because the topology of the offset mesh is not guaranteed to be the same as the original mesh. In the case shown, the equal offset of all panels creates an H-type intersection instead of the X type of the original mesh. This is caused by the different angles of the facets to one other causing their surfaces to no longer coincide in a single point (visible in the red wedge in the center).
(f) Using single-curvature developable sheets instead of planar facets allows for a closer match with curved design geometries while using planar cutting geometries.

Laser cutters and plasma cutters. Laser cutters are among the most widespread rapid prototyping machines. They are based on the usual *x,y* axis movement of a cutting head equipped with a set of mirrors that directs a laser beam from the back section of the machine vertically down onto the cutting material. The heat of the beam burns the material, leaving a cutting path or scoring mark in the sheet material varying by the thickness of the material and the power of the beam.

Like cutting, some limited relief is possible using subsequent passes on top of each other to remove layers of material. But the depth is limited due to the focus range of the lens bundling the laser beam. Similar machines exist in the steel industry with higher-powered lasers to cut metals. For plate steel, the laser is replaced with a plasma cutter that can cut through several inches of steel. Low-cost plasma cutters make this a relatively affordable fabrication technique.

Waterjet cutter. Waterjet cutters work with ballistic machining using a high-pressure water stream ejected through a very small nozzle and added abrasive material to blast through virtually any material—including several inches of steel, wood, plastic, or glass. The cutting happens with the part submerged under water to prevent excessive spray. The process is relatively expensive due to the abrasive material needed for cutting and the heavy machinery used. OMAX is one of the manufacturers of waterjet cutters (Figure 16.14).

Sheet cutter. The simplest cutting technique is using cutting blades on paper or thin foils. This technique is largely used for signage or simple paper cuts. Experimental use includes the cutting of flexible circuits out of thin copper sheets. Some large-format plotters have paper cutters integrated.

Fig. 16.14
(a) Cutting process using a waterjet cutter. The ballistic machining principle removes material by shooting a high-pressure waterjet together with abrasive sand onto the cutting material. Waterjet cutters require additional geometric processing of the cutting path to calculate path offsets to compensate for loss of material and to accommodate entry and exit points to pierce the material initially. These processes are automated in most driver software.
(b) A design prototyped in Aluminum using a waterjet cutter (Image and design Axel Kilian, Concept car design with Smart Cities Group, MIT Media Lab)

Additive Processes: Layered Fabrication

The layered manufacturing techniques offer a wide range of materials and processes. They are in principle similar to traditional craft lay-up processes (e.g., in pottery making). A shape is built up by successive stacking of layers of material, with each layer resting on the previous one. This stacking principle highlights one of the main challenges of the layer-based techniques.

Because each layer's weight has to be supported by the previous layer and share at least a part of the same footprint in order to transfer this load from one layer to the next, not all freeform shapes can be fabricated this way without additional processes in place. There are several techniques that involve support material. Others print within a volume of material or liquid (which is removed upon completion).

One major limitation of layer-based techniques is the lack of flexibility in adjusting the layering resolution direction locally with respect to the geometry of the part. Most techniques have some degree of stratification along the built-up layers, which can affect the strength and appearance of the parts.

Fuse deposition modeling (FDM). In FDM, strands of abs plastic are heated to just above melting temperature and passed through a nozzle and deposited in rings following the section of the part onto a previously placed strand. Due to the heat, a successive strand bonds with the strand from the previous pass (Figure 16.15). The mechanical head is moved in the *x* and *y* axes during the building of a layer, and the support platform is moved in the *z* axis to advance to the next layer—giving the machine three DOF.

Abs plastic printers use support material to get around the problem of protruding parts. Support material is dispensable material (usually of lesser quality) added to the main structure—in parallel with the build material—in support of protruding parts that occur in subsequent phase fo the building process. This way, the protruding part can be built resting on the support material column and is not subject to deformation or failure.

The support material is usually created in a less solid, brittle nature to facilitate later removal without damage to the main model. Other techniques are based on soluble material that can be removed in a water bath using ultrasonic sound to aid the process. The process is generally robust, offers a relatively affordable way of producing abs plastic-based models that reach about 80% of the strength of injection-molded parts, and can be used for functional prototypes with mechanical properties. The biggest setback is the high cost of the machines and the long printing time.

Fig. 16.15
(a) Additive processes such as fuse deposition modeling (FDM) create ABS-strength plastic constructs built directly from digital geometric data in a layered process using plastic string material. To build the forms shown here, support material (later removed) is required to hold the overhanging pieces.
(b) A sculptural piece by Carlo H. Séquin showing the use of FDM to build intricate nested geometries generated by a mathematical expression. Such structures would otherwise be very difficult to build (Image Carlo H. Séquin)

Powder-based processes. Other processes use plaster-like powders, such as Zcorp (Figure 16.16). The powder allows for a more homogenous, reduced texture finish compared to the plastic strand ripples from the FDM process. The fine powder is solidified using a liquid binder to wet the areas of the powder that are to become solid, leaving the remaining powder as support. The use of inkjet printer heads for the binder fluid allows for colored prints as well.

The process uses two parallel powder columns, with a piston in each adjusting the depth of the powder. One compartment contains the powder to be used, and the other the finished model embedded in the excess powder. At the beginning, the piston supporting the model is moved to the top and the model compartment is empty. With each move of the print head a rake scoops some powder from the top of the powder compartment and drags it over the model compartment, depositing a thin layer of powder on it.

This layer is the print layer. On the way back the print head prints the cross section of the model at this height into the powder and then returns to the powder compartment to start over again. With each cycle of the print head, the powder piston moves up to provide the next level of powder and the model piston moves down a bit to make room for the next model layer.

Fig. 16.16
(a) A ZCorp three dimensional printer with automated powder loading and recycling.(Image courtesy of Zcorp)
(b) Powder-based additive processes work with a plaster-like substance to build up the model. This makes the use of additional support material unnecessary because the piece is embedded and supported by the unused powder surrounding it. Similar geometries are possible, but a wider range of surface treatments is available to give the finished piece different properties. Another computationally generated sculpture by Carlo H. Séquin, printed using a powder-based process. (Image Carlos H. Séquin)

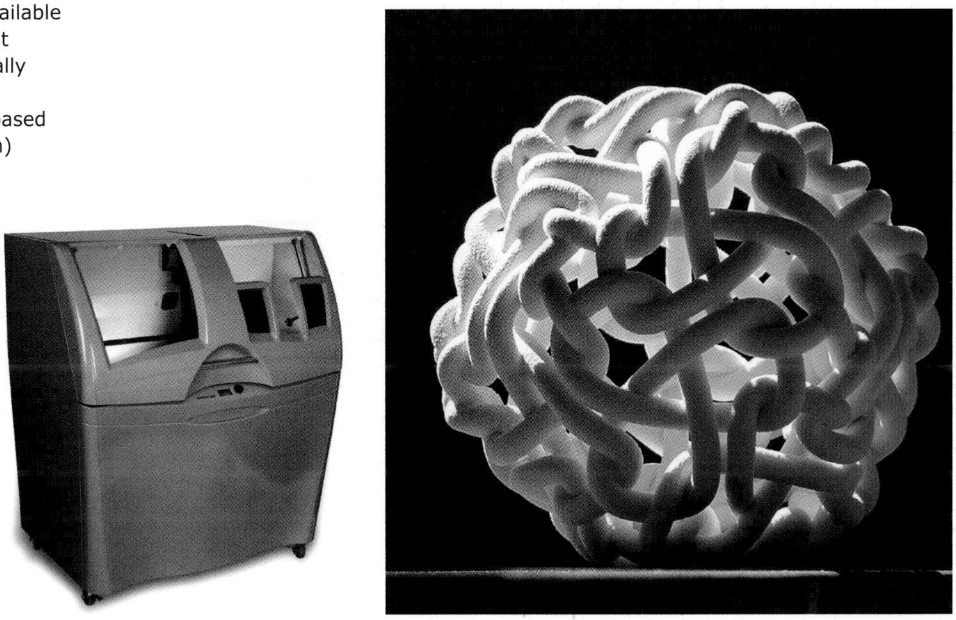

At the end of the process, the model is embedded in powder in the model compartment. It is removed and excess powder is dusted off, revealing the final model. Plaster-based models are fragile and require post-processing in the form of wax or epoxy infusion to harden the outer layer of the material for strength.

Stereolithography. Some of the earliest three-dimensional printing is the sintering-based Stereolithography (Figure 16.17). Here, a bath of material in liquid form is selectively cured using a laser beam inscribing the cross section onto the surface of the liquid. A submerged platform supports the cured part and with each step retracts further below the surface, keeping the growing model always just below the surface for the next layer to be added. This process produces some of the most detailed and highest-resolution models but it is also very slow and expensive.

Fig. 16.17
Stereolithography is one of the earliest three-dimensional printing processes. It uses a bath of a liquid material. A laser hardens the liquid section by section. The emerging piece is supported by a platform that is lowered into the liquid with each pass. This process produces very detailed models. (Image 3D system printer)

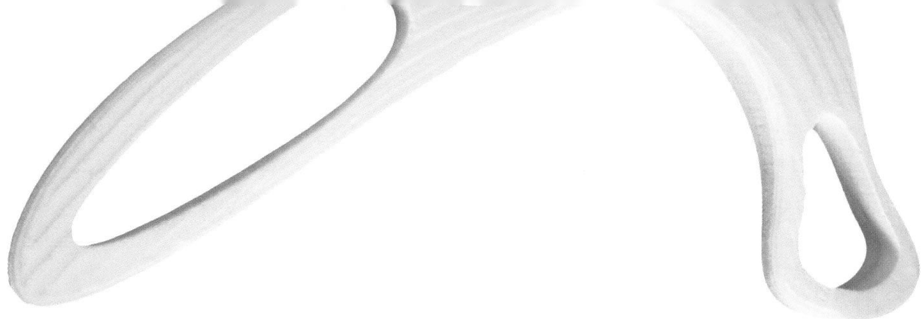

Subtractive Techniques

Machining models. Subtractive techniques create geometric models by removing material from a solid block or sheet. Layers of material are removed until the target surface is reached. This technique has the advantage that a large range of machinable materials (such as wood or stone) can be used in their natural forms. Machined parts have usually higher strength due to the material choices compared to the parts from additive processes. However, machining parts from blocks poses its own challenges.

The forces required to guide the tool can be very high, requiring stronger and more expensive machines. The tools need to follow the geometric features very closely and orient the cutting direction along the target surface. This requires at least five axes of movement or five DOF. For a complete-reach envelope, six DOF is ideal. The combination of high forces and high DOF makes such machines very bulky and requires high precision and expensive parts.

Most likely a model will not be machined out of a single block of material if it is large or is made up of complex geometry. In such cases, the decomposition of a model into machinable parts is a crucial step and is performed in parallel with machine and tool selection. Even in small models, some interior surfaces are simply not reachable without collision of the tool with the outer lying parts.

With 2.5-axis mills, undercuts are not possible and therefore the model has to be divided into surfaces that can be reached from above without model interference and surfaces that have to be milled from the opposite side. Even with mills with five axes, not all surfaces may be accessible due to the need to hold the stock. When flipping a part, a negative of the model may be milled to provide a fixture for the already-milled surface to rest on.

Mills and routers. There is a wide range of milling-based machines ranging in sizes and number of axes. The most simple mills and routers use 2.5 axes for moving the tool head. Machines with low axis count use cutting beds as the support to hold the cutting stock and are largely used with sheet material or material of moderate thickness (a few inches). The tool head is loaded with a fast-spinning router tool used for carving material when moved laterally (Figure 16.18).

Mill end bits are used when cutting parts in more than two dimensions. Mills with more than 2.5 axes become very complicated mechanically, and the degrees of freedom increase the complexity of tool path generation. Moving the tool tip along the target surface is only part of the problem. It is also necessary to reach the target position without passing through the stock or the machine itself. In addition, larger forces and strong vibration are generated during milling of hard material—especially aluminum and steel.

These forces have to be dealt with by securing the part, which further limits the accessible areas of the stock. Five-axis (or even a higher number) mills exist, but these are expensive due to demands on the hardware. Very large-scale mills exist for use in the automotive industry for milling full-size foam mockups for concept cars. These mills use soft milling foams that require less force compared to steel-based machining centers. Such mills can therefore be scaled up more easily.

Fig. 16.18
(a) Subtractive processes remove material from a solid block of stock material such as foam, wood, or metal. (b) The tool paths create a distinctive pattern at low resolution that can be used to reinforce the reading of the geometry.

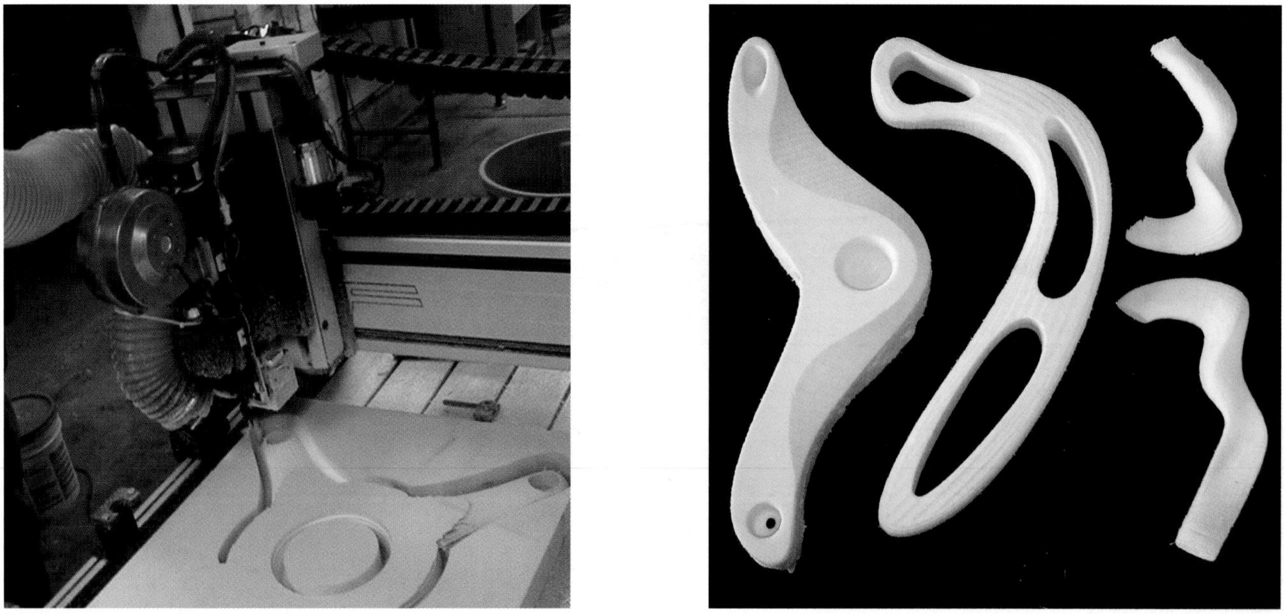

Foam cutters. Foam cutters use heated wires to slice through extruded polystyrene foams and are very fast. Machines with multiple axes of movement exist that allow the cutting of three-dimensional foam parts. The linear cutting wire limits the range of possible shapes and cutting geometries. The use of bend cutting wires is possible but requires retooling and limits possible forms to the extrusion and swept cross-section variety.

Robotic machining. A new trend is the combination of robotics and machining. As in other cases, the automotive industry has pioneered this approach for some time in post-processing steps such as degrading of injection mold pieces.

Robotic machining is interesting because it can take advantage of the highly developed hardware of robotic arms for automotive welding with six DOF and more. The robotic arms offer a larger-reach envelop than their own size, therefore overcoming one of the biggest limitations with other fabrication machines (Figure 16.19). Usually, the part size is equal to or smaller than the machine used in the process because the machine has to enclose the part to reach all points.

Robotic machining departs from the envelope idea and uses a high-degree-of-freedom articulated robotic arm. Such robotic arms have a large range of motion and due to the many DOF a high degree of flexibility in their reach envelope. Equipped with a router or mill bit as its tool, such arms can be used for foam milling of parts that can be larger than the machine itself if a simple track for lateral movement is added.

Fig. 16.19
Milling using robotic arms with a high number of degrees of freedom allows for much better surface finishes with fewer cuts. With higher degrees of freedom of the tool head, surface geometries such as overhangs can be cut that are not possible with three-axis processes.
(a) A robotic arm used for milling at the TU, Vienna.
(b) A milled surface produced with the robotic arm.

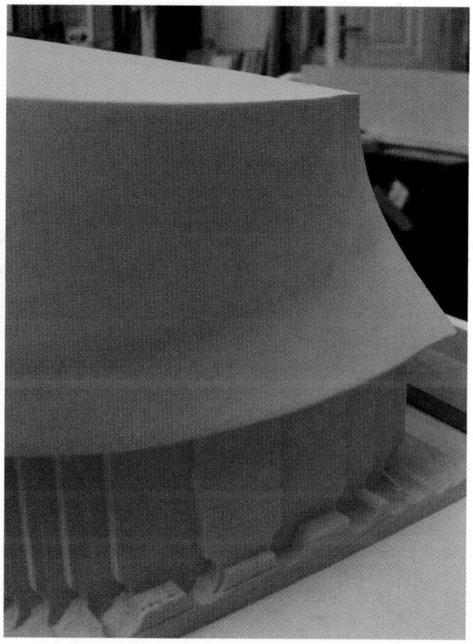

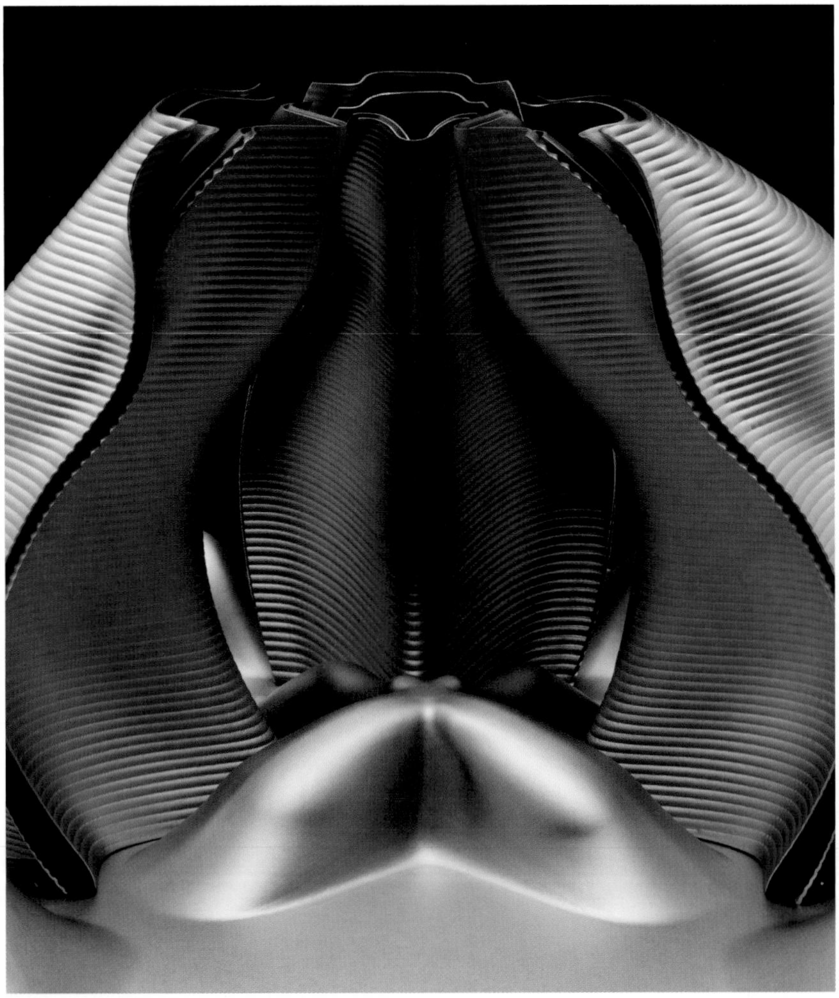

Fig. 16.20
Architects such as Greg Lynn have used the surface effect of milling as an aesthetic expression in their design. The geometry of the surface is emphasized by the cutting paths, which also link the product to its production process. Shown here is the Alessi Coffee and Tea Towers series designed by Greg Lynn FORM. Each coffee pot is uniquely shaped using a custom milled foam plug. The traces of the milling process are deliberately kept. (Image Carlo Lavatori)

Geometric Challenges Related to Machining and Rapid Prototyping

Challenges related to machining and rapid prototyping are numerous. CNC machines rely on data extracted from digital models to control movement in producing parts. The constraints of the machines constrain the possible operations. This may be a tool path following the edge of a part or a milling tool path in three dimensions following the surface of an object.

To adjust the tool in space with respect to the geometry to be cut is more complex because more degrees of freedom are involved. There are further problems with collision detection between parts to be machined and the tool and the machine itself. As the machining progresses, the situation constantly changes due to the removal of material. Tool orientation influences the possible surface qualities and cutting times.

The scale of the parts for most machines is determined by the maximum envelope of the machining bed, which is usually smaller than the overall size of the machine. Mobile robotic arms allow for bigger build envelopes, but this also affects precision and speed. Ultimately, some sort of assembly is required in most cases of architecture. Assembly of multiple machined parts for large-scale components is difficult in the uncontrolled environments of construction sites.

One challenge is the breaking apart of the initial geometry into meaningful components and ensuring that these parts can be fabricated with the given machinery. Another difficult geometric problem is the nesting of complex cutting geometries on planar cutting sheets to reduce material usage. Three dimensional nesting of printing geometry in the build envelope of a three-dimensional printer is yet another difficulty.

Aesthetics of fabrication and geometric implications. In architecture, the wider use of rapid prototyping techniques made designers more aware of the aesthetic choices involved with CNC fabrication. For instance, Greg Lynn kept the cutting marks on foam plugs used for forming the titanium sheet metal of his Coffee and Tea Towers series for Alessi as an aesthetic aspect of the creation process (Figure 16.20). The roughness of the cut emphasizes the custom shape of each pod because each pot has its own molding tool machined based on a set of unique parameters.

Fig. 16.21
Relationship between geometric properties of developable surfaces designed and refined using digital and physical model building and the final architecture. Gehry's Walt Disney Concert Hall shows the direction of curvature in the edge pattern of the metal facade sheets.

This mold is lost in the forming of the sheet metal using an explosive charge. To cut down on machine time, and as an aesthetic choice, the surface finish is deliberately left unfinished. There are multiple ways of generating tool paths for a given geometry. Similar to texture mapping in rendering, a tool path creates a physical tangible texture that can be used to emphasize geometric features in an object. Higher-axis machines in particular offer a degree of flexibility.

Similarly, the lines of ruling for developable surfaces are used to structure large freeform surfaces. Frank Gehry's Walt Disney concert hall masterly displays the geometric perfection of controlling fabrication and design geometry for an overall sculptural appearance (Figure 16.21). An integral part is the scale of the used components and the reflectiveness of the material. The sheet pattern aids in the reading of the geometry and breaks the large facades down into more perceivable units.

Choosing materials based on geometric properties. As discussed in previous chapters, the use of developable surfaces offers a fast way of building paper-based models with single-curvature surfaces. Some architecture offices (e.g., Gehry and Partners) use this approach extensively in developing designs and in testing and adjusting digital geometries in physical form as well as developing physical forms as starting points for a digital design. The use of paper also acts as a test of constructability using sheet-based materials in the full-scale building.

Additional material constraints are associated with wood, where the grain direction needs to be considered with respect to the direction of curvature. For double-curvature surfaces, either the material itself can be milled from a solid block or the material can be formed starting from a flat sheet. Glass sheets can be slumped over a curved form by applying heat. Metal plates can be stamped using solid steel tools milled into a positive and a negative form.

In shipbuilding, steel plates are rolled for single-curvature surfaces and partially heated for double-curvature surfaces. Most processes at a building scale still require substantial manual handling because machines do not exist for universal shaping of steel or glass. However, digital information is also of use in all of these hybrid cases. Tools for stamping are digitally calculated and CNC milled, and even manual processes rely on digital data as a guide and as a check of the results.

Implications for standardization. With the use of digital fabrication, the concept of standardization shifts from the notion of standards as a dimensional agreement that streamlined manufacturing following the industrial revolution to that of the agreement between parts. Because each part can be fabricated on demand, dimensions and geometries can be adjusted to the context of use.

This allows the departure of the dimensional standards based on measurements and replacement with standardization for the rules of matching parts (Figure 16.22). As long as each part fits its neighbors, the dimensions can be free to be adjusted to other factors such as forces, material properties, and geometric context.

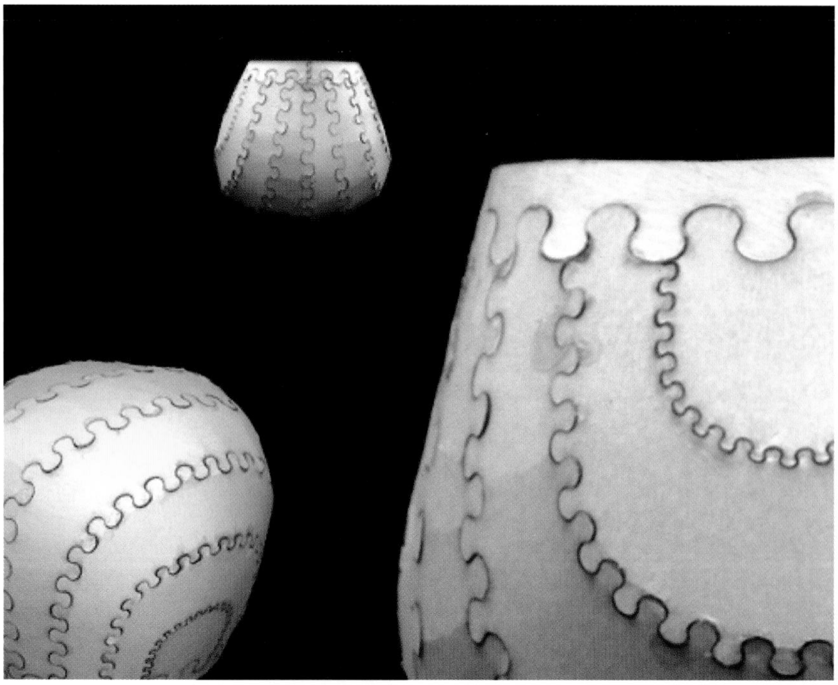

Fig. 16.22
Generating connection details dependent on the geometric context for laser-cut cardboard strips. (Project by Axel Kilian, 1999, programmed in AutoLisp and Laser cut using cardboard)

Assembly

Fastener-based assemblies. The use of fasteners for assemblies of parts has a long tradition with the use of wood and metal nails as well as screws in more recent times. Although the standardization of fasteners and precision machining contributed to the rationalization and predictability of assemblies for performance under loads, it also led to a simplification of many details.

Digital fabrication increases the precision of assemblies and often no adjustments are necessary. This is true for steel assemblies, and more recently for wood. Both part geometries and holes for fasteners can be machined precisely directly from CAD data. With the use of freeform geometries, there is an opportunity to revisit traditional joining techniques using spatial interlocking parts from carpentry (as discussed in the next section).

Geometry-based assemblies. The use of geometric assemblies without fasteners has an even longer tradition. It ranges from techniques of weaving to that of carpentry joints and stone masonry in which matching geometries of pieces keeps them in place. In the long run, geometry-based assemblies seem to have a greater life span than assemblies that make use of secondary fasteners or fillers.

Carpentry joint examples are found in Japanese and Chinese temples, and some Inca built and custom fit stone walls that withstood centuries of earthquakes (Figure 16.23). The standardization of parts, starting with the Industrial Revolution, has contributed to the simplification of construction part geometries in favor of inexpensive repetitive parts over sophisticated individually crafted components. In freeform geometries, this advantage is to an extent lost.

Because standardized parts require substantial customization as well, the gap to a fully customized part is closing—with faster and more effective machines becoming available (Figure 16.6). In parallel, skills necessary for complex assemblies need to be taught. This is not a plea for the return to a traditionalist craft but rather for the appreciation of the experience embedded within many of the traditional joinery techniques (e.g., Japanese carpentry).

Designs respond to many constraints, including longevity, aesthetics, and strength. With the introduction of sophisticated digital fabrication techniques, some of these techniques may return in adapted versions with manual skilled labor being translated into skilled fabrication (Figure 16.24).

Fig. 16.23
Complex geometries have long played a role in building, such as for stone walls built by the Incas. Adapting irregularly shaped rocks only minimally to fit together with their neighbors creates a stronger overall wall capable that withstood earthquakes and the elements for centuries.

Robotic assembly. As mentioned previously, a recent project by Fabio Gramazio and Matthias Kohler at the ETH, Zürich, explored the use of robotics to place standard parts in digitally generated patterns (Figure 16.10.) . This is an interesting combination of low and high technology. A customized appearance is achieved with zero machining but through precise placement of parts.

More variations on the use of robotics in creative ways may be created over time. Previous efforts focused on automating the standard process of building to increase cost efficiency. Now the goal is to use the technology in creative ways to create architectural designs not possible previously. Although currently the emphasis is on formal aspects, the performative side of architecture will become increasingly important and geometry can be of tremendous help here as well.

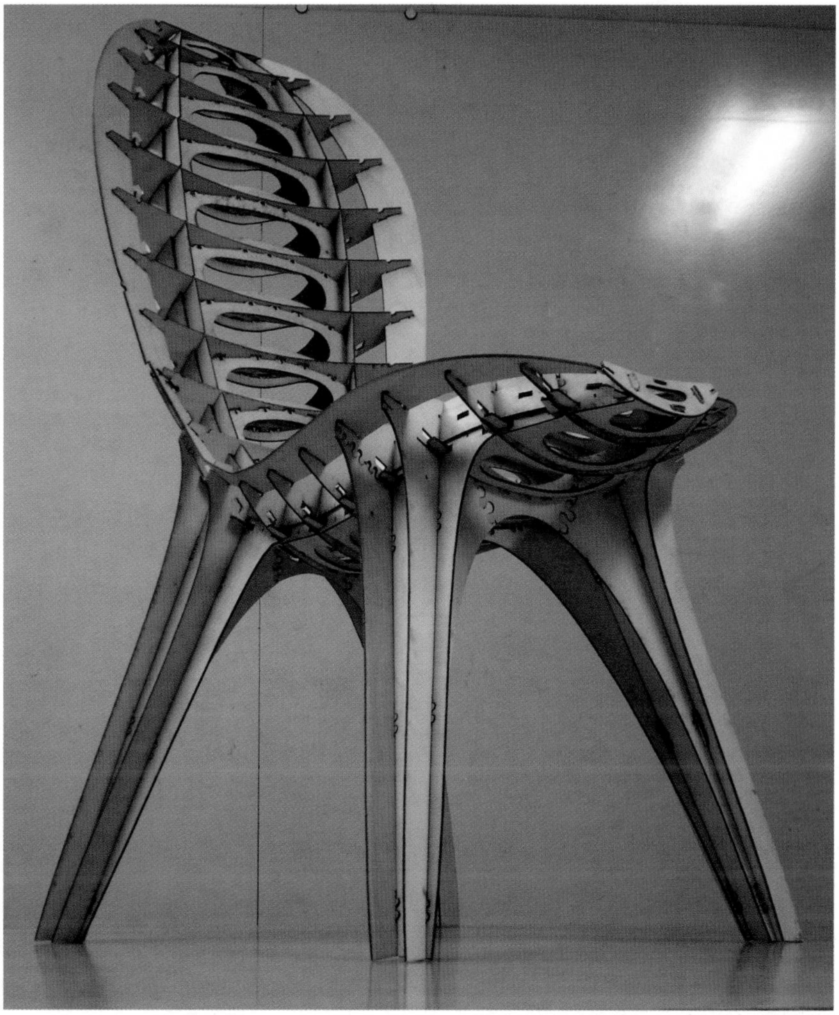

Fig. 16.24
A chair assembled from about 150 flat plywood sheet parts without adhesives relying only on interlocking geometries for structural stability and form. All pieces are forced into curvature in the assembly process, helping the overall stiffness and creating a continuous appearance that only works together with the resistance of the material. (Image Axel Kilian courtesy of the FRAC Center. Design Chair experiment by Axel Kilian)

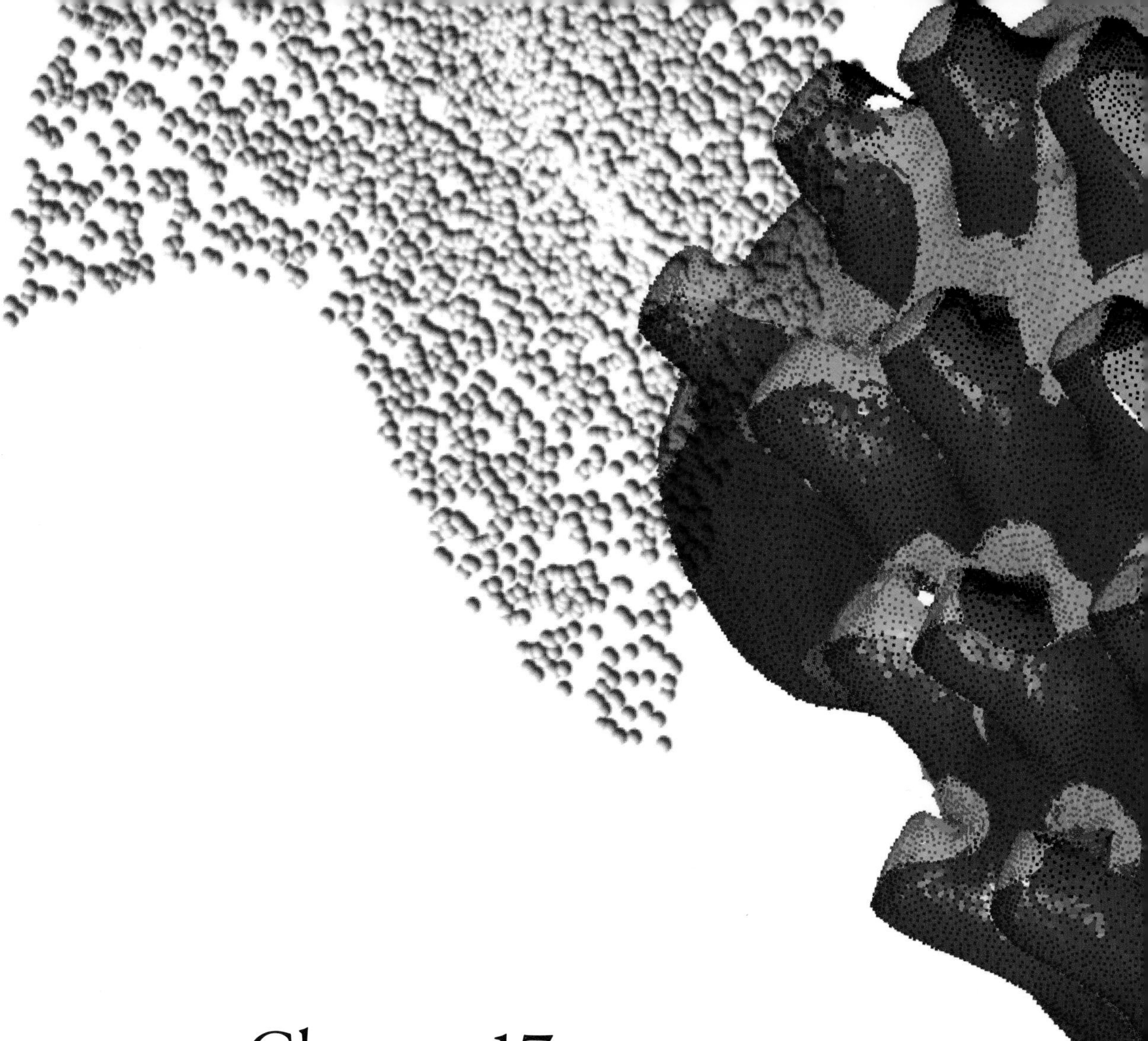

Chapter 17

Geometry for Digital Reconstruction

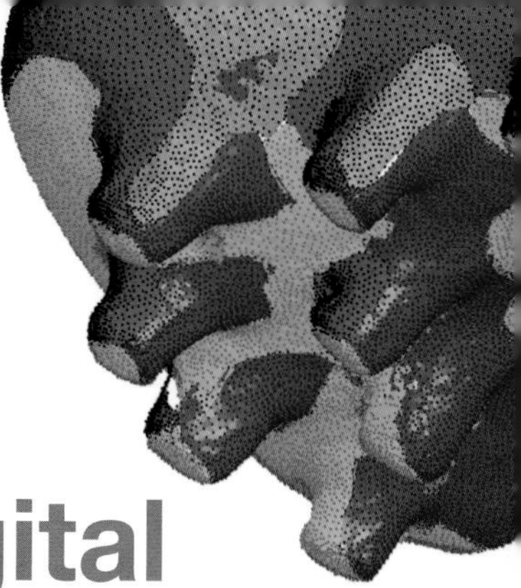

Geometry for Digital Reconstruction

At various stages of the design process, one may want to *change the medium*—from a virtual to a physical model, and vice versa. Often physically based design processes are advantageous over digital ones in the early stages of a project due to their open and collaborative nature. In addition, physical materials give important tangible feedback to the designer for purposes of hand/eye coordination. (See Figure 17.1.)

Here we are dealing with the *digital reconstruction problem*, i.e., the steps which are necessary to convert a physical model into a computer model. We discuss the entire pipeline, focusing particularly on requirements arising in architecture. Although there is powerful software to support us here, good geometric knowledge and a solid understanding of the procedure are necessary to get excellent results.

First, we need to think about what we perceive as relevant data to be captured. There are many aspects of an object: its surface geometry, its appearance, its materiality, and its geometric features. Directing our acquisition process is important because the data that can be gathered is finite and processing the data for meaningful results can be very time intensive. The digital reconstruction pipeline is well understood for applications in computer graphics [Bernardini and Rushmeier 2002] and in computer-aided design/computer-aided manufacturing (CAD/CAM) [Varady and Martin 2002]. However, architecture and design pose new challenges. The choice of the features to be digitized is crucial here. Just as a portrait of a person is less about the surfaces than about the distinct features defining nose and eye, a sculptural object might be best captured with a sparse set of key edges in space rather than with an undifferentiated point cloud from a three-dimensional scanner.

Fig. 17.1
The digital reconstruction of physical models is a valuable tool in the architectural design process. This image shows a model of a project by Frank O. Gehry.

The translation process is always a process of evaluation and adjustment, never a literal mapping. This is an especially powerful process in design exploration. Moreover, design and manufacturing requirements such as functionality, materials, statics, and cost lead to limitations and complications more so than in other application areas of digital reconstruction.

There are two general approaches to capturing physical form. One is the use of a tracking arm, especially suitable for capturing strings of point data from selected feature curves. The other method uses a laser range scanner and results in a large number of more or less regularly distributed measurement points from the surface of the given physical model.

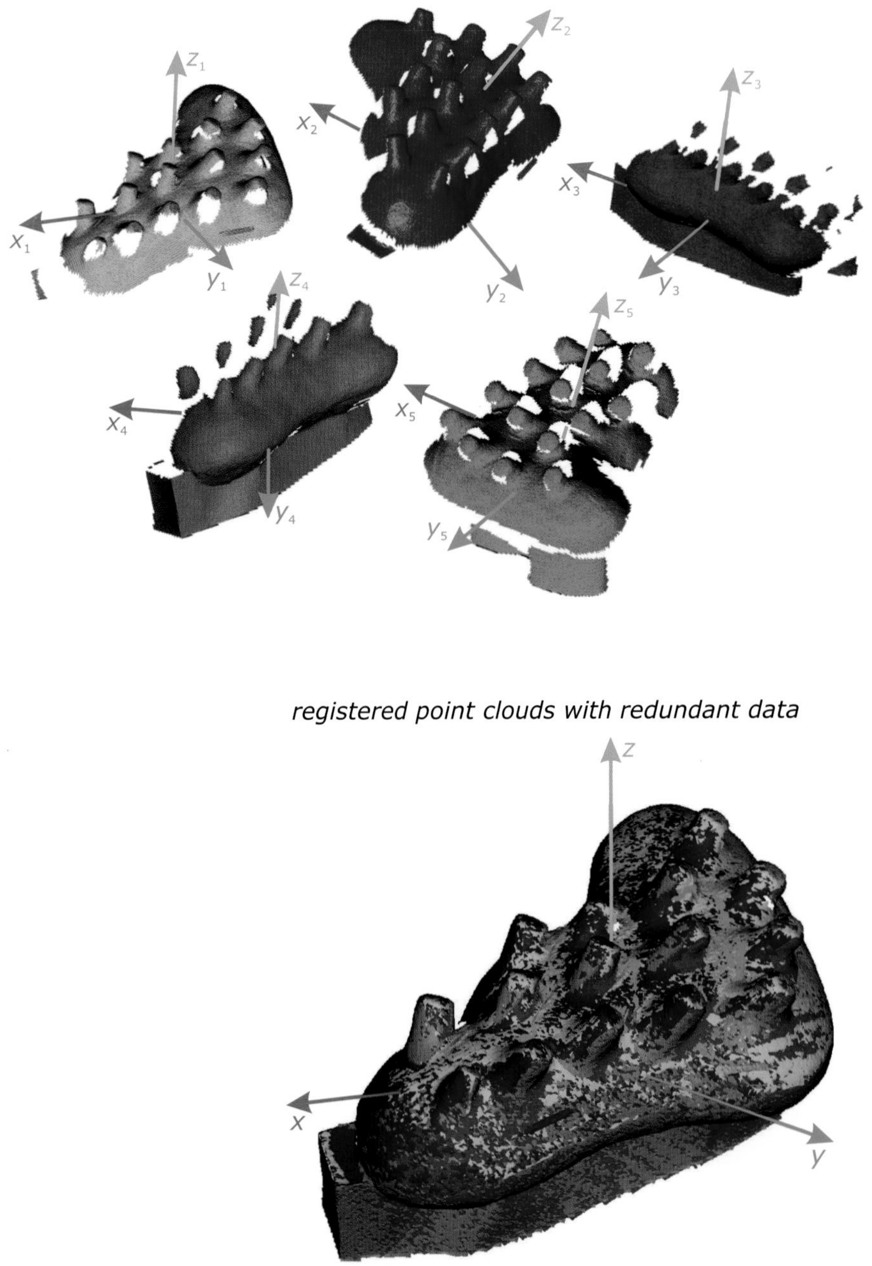

Fig. 17.2
Data acquisition and registration. Using a three-dimensional scanner, we obtain measurement points (coordinates) from the surface of an existing object. In general, one has to make several scans—which provide data in different coordinate systems. Supported by appropriate algorithms, these scans have to be merged (registered) into a single data point cloud represented in the same coordinate system.

An overview of the digital reconstruction pipeline. The procedure starts with *data acquisition*. Three-dimensional scanning devices are used to produce measurement data from a real three-dimensional object. We are talking here only about those scanners that measure points on the surface *S* of the object.

Volumetric imaging systems such as CT scanners even deliver information about the interior of an object. This is fundamental in applications such as medicine, but seems to be of less importance in architecture if surface capturing is the objective.

The measurement data consists of a large number of points, which is referred to as a *point cloud*. Ideally, these data points should be precise locations (coordinates) of points on the surface *S*, but in real applications there will be measurement errors we have to deal with. Only the regions of the surface *S* of the real object directly visible from the vantage point of the scanner will be captured, and thus a single scan usually contains only measurement data for a part of *S*.

Depending on the complexity of the surface, including such entities as undercuts and folds, we may have to produce a number of scans from different vantage points. This number can go into the hundreds if great detail is desired. In general, each scan produces a point cloud with its own coordinate system (Figure 17.2). Finally, all of these point clouds have to be merged into a single combined point cloud represented in the same coordinate system. This procedure is called *registration*.

In the merged point cloud, there may be redundant data—such as data points very close to one another. These redundancies will be removed. Moreover, we will have some noise (measurement errors) in the data that should be filtered by the digital reconstruction software. This completes the *point phase* of the process (Figure 17.3).

Fig. 17.3
Removal of redundant data points and filtering of noise (measurement errors) is advisable before leaving the "point phase" in the process. (Three-dimensional model courtesy of Florian Doblhammer.)

In the subsequent *polygon phase*, a triangle mesh is computed that approximates the given data within the desired accuracy (Figure 17.4). This procedure is not as simple as it might seem. Some key details are discussed in the material following.

The final *shape phase* may not be necessary for pure visualization tasks in graphics applications, but it will be crucial for architecture. We have to convert the triangle mesh into a CAD representation of an object that is appropriate for further processing, simulation, and manufacturing. Issues related to this phase include edge and feature line detection and decomposition into parts of different nature and geometry (e.g., planar parts, cylindrical patches, freeform patches). This process is also called *segmentation* (Figure 17.5). It requires a good geometric understanding and user interaction. Moreover, one has to approximate the data regions by the surface types identified in the segmentation step (Figure 17.6). This process is also known as *surface fitting*.

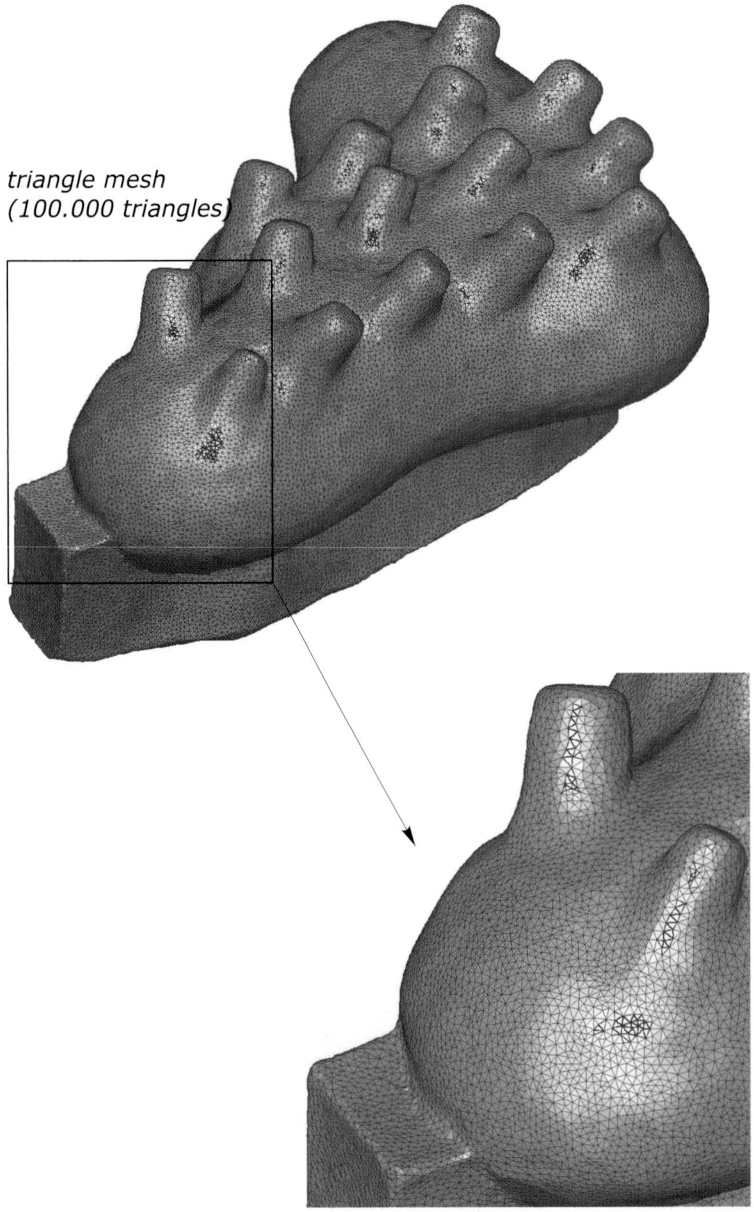

Fig. 17.4
In the "polygon phase," a triangle mesh is wrapped over the data point cloud and thus we obtain a first surface representation of the object.

Architecture then poses additional requirements tied to construction technology, structural analysis, and aesthetics. These are not part of the standard digital reconstruction pipeline and are largely unsupported by currently available software. We will address some of these issues in the last part of this chapter, hoping that it will stimulate further research and development.

Fig. 17.5
Segmentation splits the entire data set into regions of similar geometric behavior. For example, it will identify simple regions (such as planes and cylinders) and decompose the object into patches according to manufacturing constraints and aesthetic considerations. Especially for applications in architecture, this process is not fully automatic and the result greatly benefits from a good geometric understanding of the user. This example shows two different segmentation results.

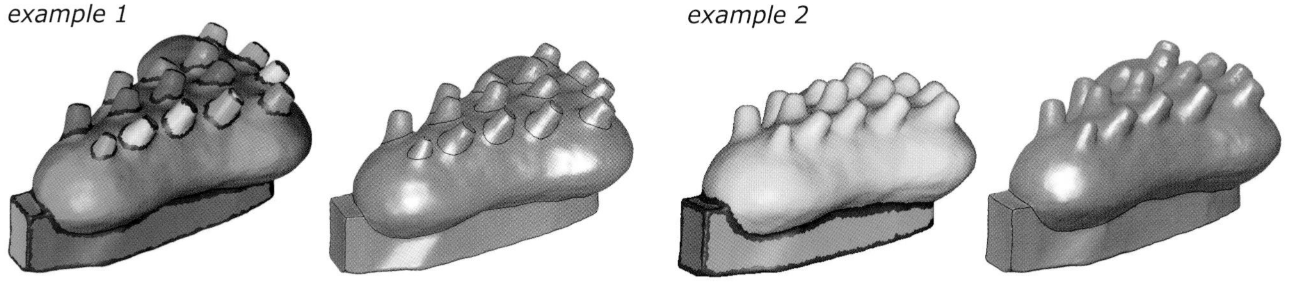

Fig. 17.6
Surface-fitting algorithms are used to approximate regions using surfaces of the correct type (here, plane and cylinder) according to the outcome of the segmentation phase. A standard digital reconstruction process may stop here, but architecture poses additional requirements (discussed at the end of this chapter).

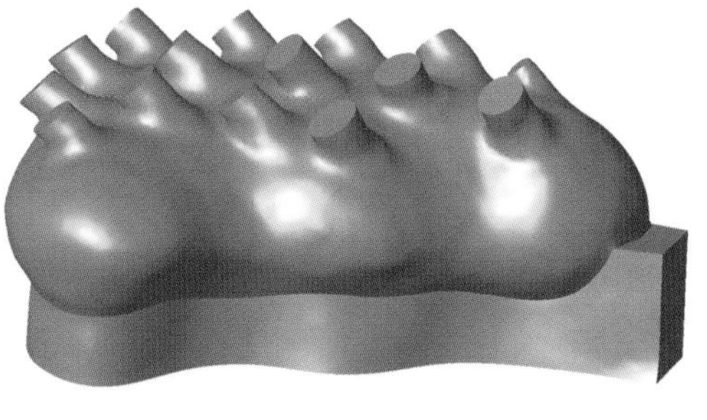

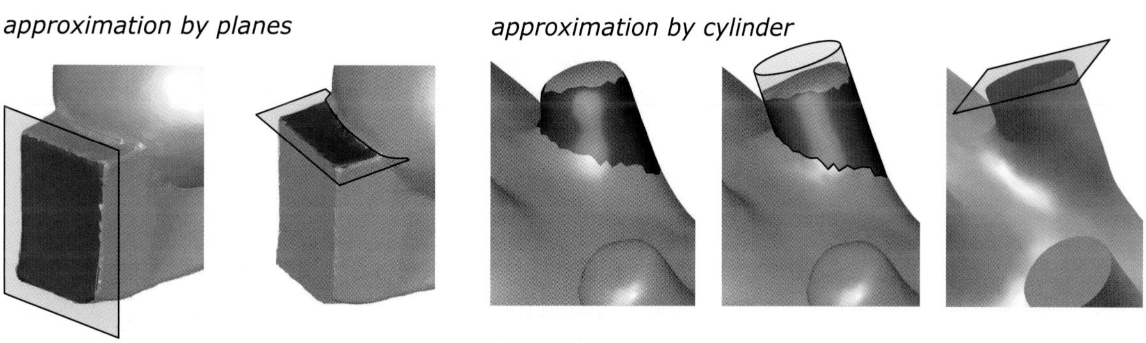

Fig. 17.7
Use of a digitizer arm at Coop Himmelb(l)au.

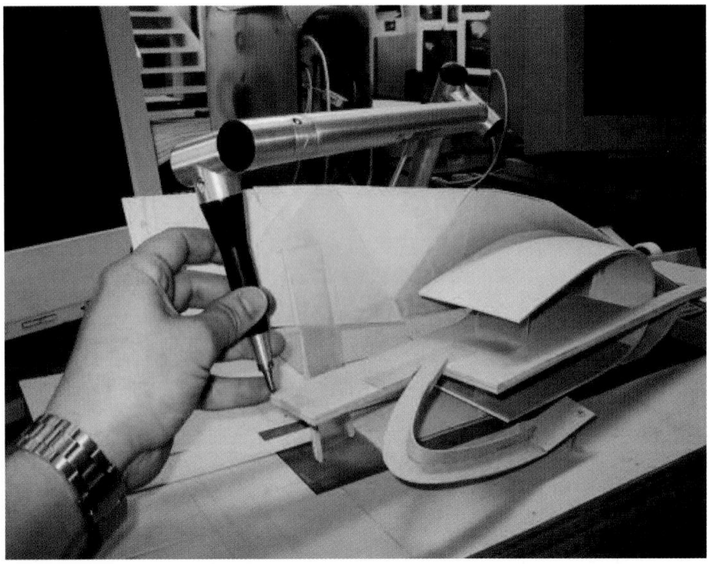

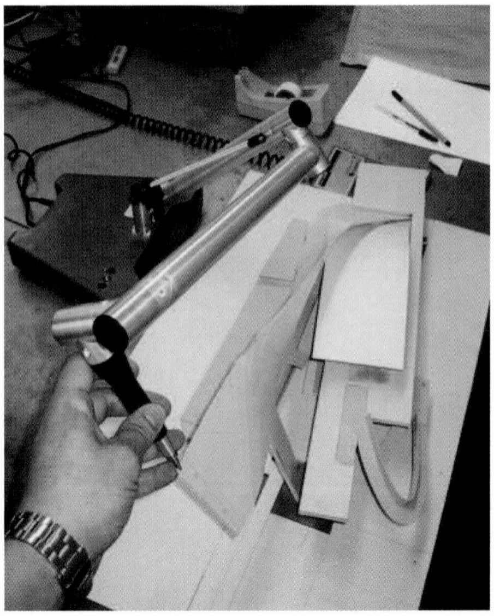

Data Acquisition and Registration

Digitizer arms. One approach to capturing a physical model is the use of a tracking arm with several degrees of freedom (Figure 17.7). Each joint is equipped with a sensor measuring the angle. From this data, the spatial point of the arm tip can be calculated. A designer can trace a physical object by running the tip along an edge to capture a string of point data. This results in a very sparse sampling, but has the advantage of being user driven and very selective. The method is very well suited to capturing particular selected features of a model.

Optical scanning devices. Modern three-dimensional scanning devices are largely based on optical technologies. *Near-range scanners*, which measure objects of a size less than a few meters, are typically used with a combination of laser projection and detection of the projected stripes or patterns with one or more cameras. The scanner shown in Figure 17.8a emits laser beams in a planar stripe P. The laser highlights on the object a curve c, namely the intersection curve of P and the object surface S.

The image c^* of c is detected in the digital photo produced by the camera. Each point p^* (pixel) of c^* may be connected with the optical center O of the camera to a projection ray, which intersects the plane P in that point p of c whose projection p^* has been detected in the digital photo (Figure 17.8b). The computation of the intersection is possible because camera and laser are calibrated (i.e., one knows their positions in the same coordinate system). In this way, we obtain for one position of the laser plane a series of points on the resulting curve c on the object.

The laser plane P is then rotated into new positions and thus the object is measured by a family of curve-like point sequences (see Figure 17.8c). The union of these points is referred to as a *point cloud*. There are various sources of errors. Just think about the detection error made for a point p^* in the digital image. The larger the ratio of distances $Op{:}Op^*$ (i.e., the larger the distance between object point p and scanner) the more the detection error of p^* is magnified into the measurement error of p. It is obvious that dark objects on which the laser stripe c can barely be detected will lead to low measurement quality. The same holds for shiny objects with a high level of total reflection.

Fig. 17.8
(a) A near-range scanner may combine laser projection and detection of the resulting light stripe by a camera. The accuracy of this scanner is about 0.1 mm.

(b) Acquisition of a data point p requires intersection of a projection ray Op^* with the laser plane P.
(c) This point cloud has been obtained with the scanner shown in *a*.

(a)

(b)

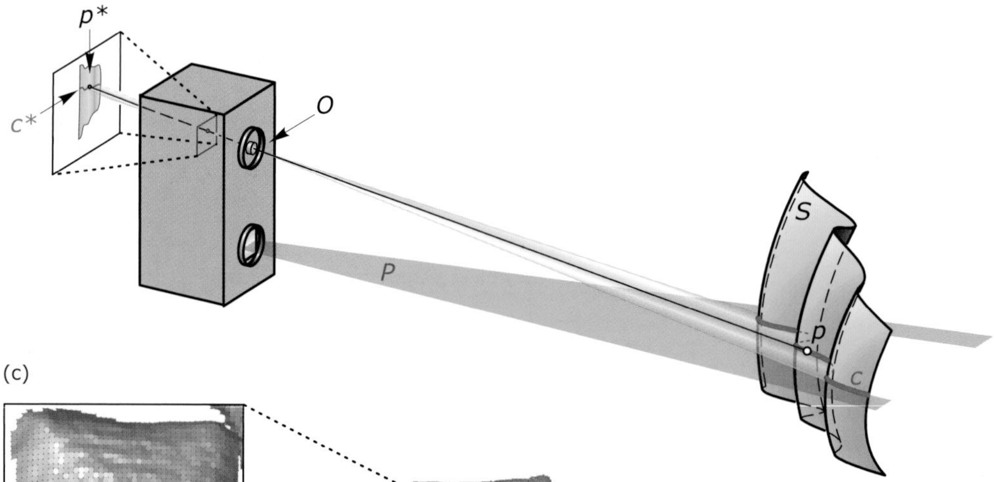

(c)

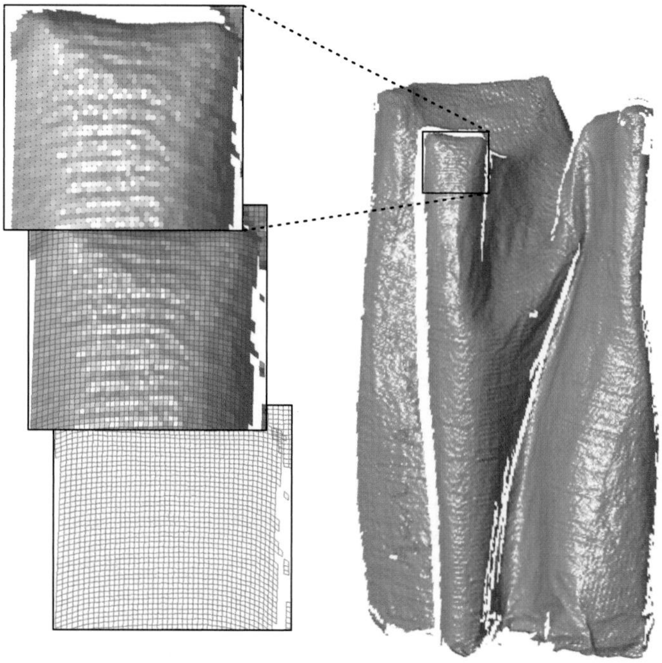

As soon as larger objects have to be scanned and the distance between scanner and object exceeds 2 meters, another technology is used. *Medium- and long-range scanners* emit a pulsed laser beam and measure the light returned by diffuse reflection on the object. From the time span between light emission and detection of the reflected light one computes the distance of the object point p to the measurement device on the corresponding laser ray and thus obtains the coordinates of p.

This has to be done for a large number of rays. Depending on the application, the measurement system will be placed on the ground (see Figure 17.9) or on an airplane. The latter technology is used to digitize three-dimensional topography and entire cities. This is an important input for applications such as geographic information systems or virtual reality models of cities. Figure 17.10 depicts an example that uses several data sources.

Fig. 17.9
Data captured by a midrange scanner.

Fig. 17.10
The inner city of Graz, Austria, was reconstructed by converting 2.5-dimensional data (top views plus heights) from a geographic information system into a simple block model. Image-based modeling was used to construct more detail for the facades based on photos taken from a truck-based mobile platform, and more roof detail based on aerial images of the region. (Courtesy of VRVIS, Vienna.)

Outlier removal and noise reduction. Measurement errors can be roughly put into two categories: outliers and noise (Figure 17.11). *Outliers* are significant measurement errors due to bad scanning conditions at specific places. They are visually easy to see as expressed by measurement points clearly too far away from the dense point cloud representing the object. Outliers may be detected by an algorithm, but there are also tools for removing them interactively.

The resolution of the hardware, the limitations in measurement accuracy and similar effects result in other type of errors that occur almost randomly and are known collectively as *noise*. Knowing the accuracy of the measurement device, noise can be reduced automatically with appropriate algorithms. Noise reduction may have undesirable smoothing effects at sharp edges. It may be performed in connection with smoothing techniques of the polygon phase.

Fig. 17.11
Outliers and parts not belonging to the desired object (red) in a data set can easily be removed with digital reconstruction software. The same holds for noise reduction.

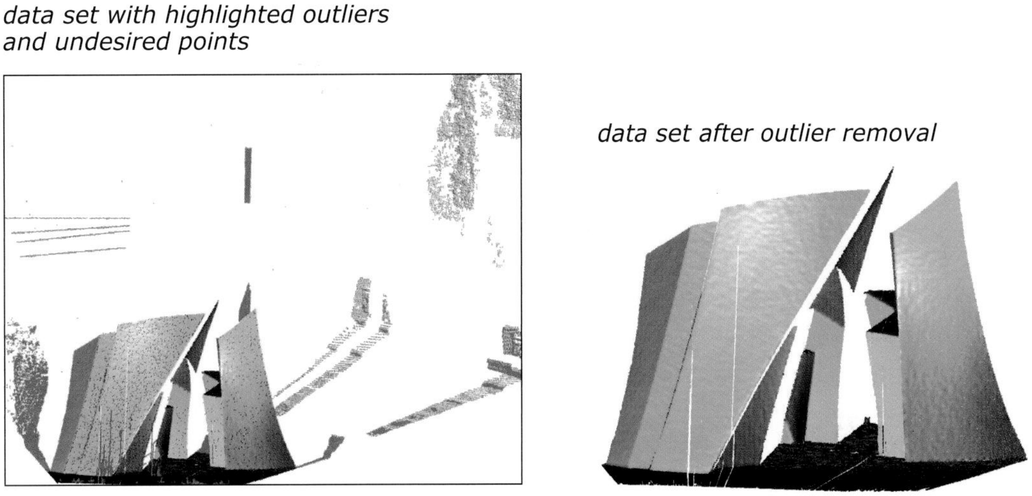

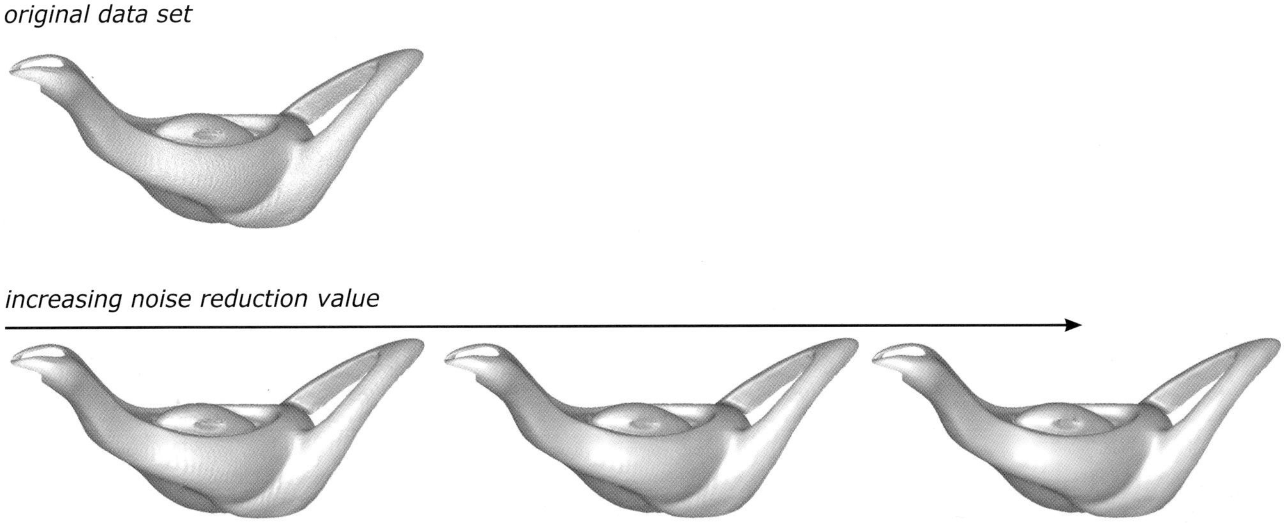

Registration. As previously mentioned, a single scan will only contain measurement points of those regions on the surface S of the real object that are visible for the scanner. Therefore, we have to make several scans. Their number depends on the complexity of the object. Unless one can use special hardware (such as a turntable or a scanner mounted on a robotic device), the individual scans will be given in different coordinate systems (Figure 17.2). For further processing, they have to be merged into a single combined point cloud represented in the same coordinate system—a procedure called *registration*. Most commercial systems contain registration algorithms according to the following workflow (Figure 17.12).

- First, the user specifies for each pair of overlapping scans (e.g., S_1, S_2) a few pairs of corresponding points (p_1, p_2), (q_1, q_2),..., on S_1 and S_2, respectively. These corresponding points shall (at least approximately) be the measurements of the same object point p, q,... of the real object surface S.

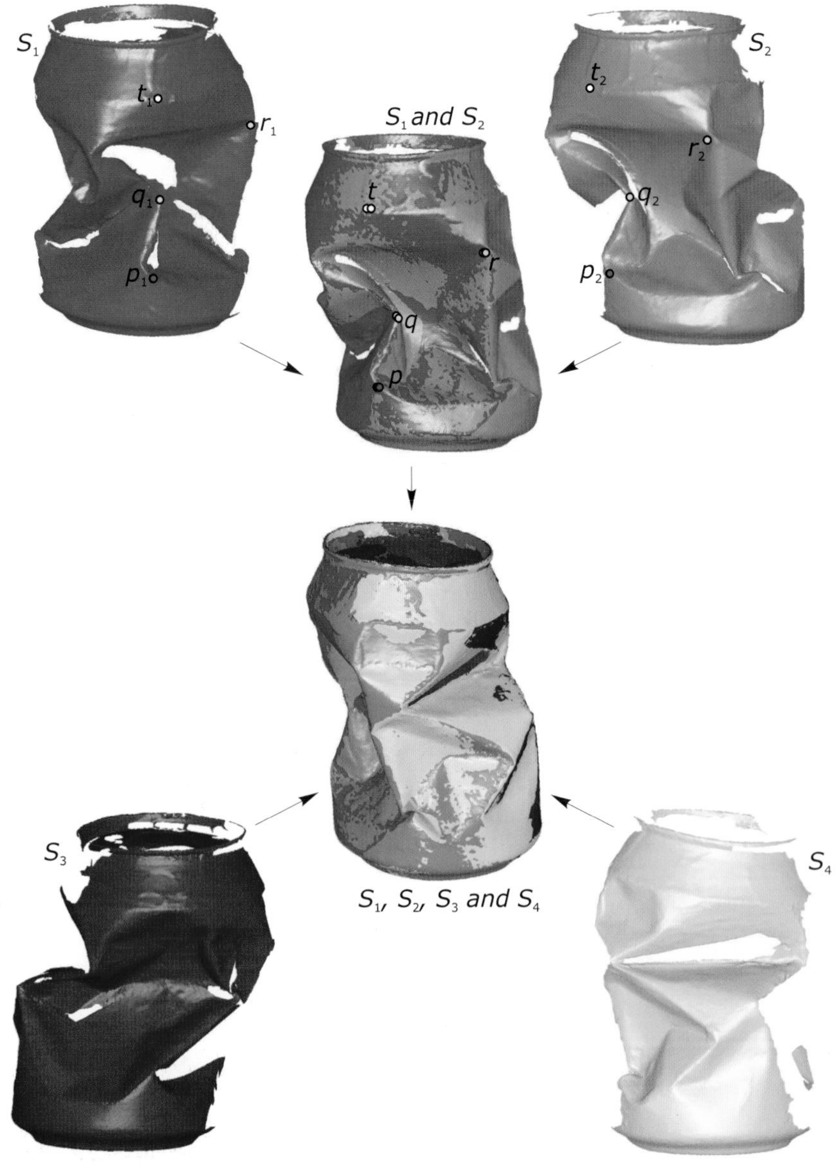

Fig. 17.12
Illustration of a registration workflow.

If there are clear features on the surface, this is a reasonable approach. The correspondences need not be precise. They simply facilitate *global registration*, which means roughly aligning the scans within the same coordinate system.

- The alignment is done by an algorithm. It moves one scan (e.g., S_2) into a new position S_2^* such that the new locations p_2^*, q_2^*,... of points p_2, q_2,... are as close as possible to their corresponding points p_1, q_1,... in scan S_1. Of course, this alignment has to be done for other pairs of scans as well, so that one finally obtains a prealignment of all scans in the same system.
- Global registration is followed by *local registration*, which is a fully automatic procedure. Describing the underlying optimization algorithms is beyond the scope of this text. However, we want to warn the reader that numerical optimization will always work in an "optimal" way. Apart from differences in the speed of various registration algorithms, they may not reach the desired optimal solution. This is largely due to inappropriate results of the global registration procedure. To visualize the phenomenon, we look at the much simpler problem of finding the minimizer x^* of a function $f(x)$ of one variable x. The value x^* is the x value with the minimal function value. Figure 17.13 illustrates that the algorithms being used iteratively improve an initial guess. Depending how good this initial guess has been, one ends up in the desired global minimizer or just in a local minimizer. The same holds for registration, which is a higher dimensional problem [the dimension equals $6(N - 1)$ if N is the number of scans]. After local registration, one usually removes redundant data points in the resulting point cloud. This may be followed by or combined with noise removal.

Fig. 17.13
The numerical computation of a minimizer of a function $f(x)$ of one variable x starts from an initial guess x_0 and improves it [e.g., by a descent strategy toward a value x^* with vanishing first derivative (tangent of the graph is parallel to the x-axis)]. Such a numerical optimization algorithm will end in a local minimizer x^*, not necessarily in the desired global minimizer. One has to start in the basin of attraction of the global minimizer (for the chosen algorithm). This task is not easy, especially if one has to find the global minimizer of a function which depends on many variables and possesses several local minimizers near the global minimizer.

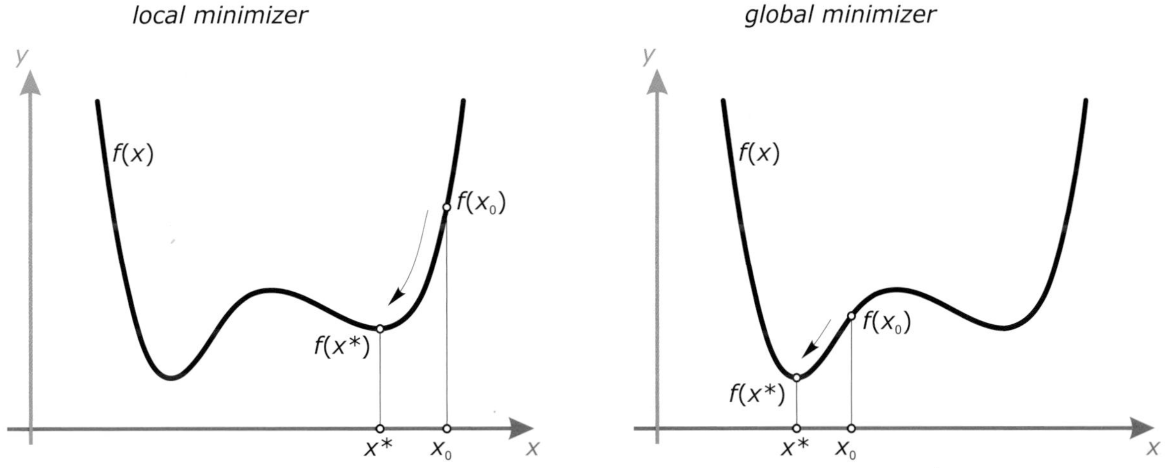

Fully automatic registration and surface matching. Current research is close to reaching fully automatic registration. This is particularly important if the interactive approach to global registration is too slow or even impossible due to a lack of clear features. One such application (namely, digital reconstruction of archaeological artifacts) is illustrated in Figure 17.14 (see Hofer et al. [2006]). Global registration algorithms are based on the identification of nearly congruent surface regions in large data sets. Therefore, they can be extended to algorithms for the automatic reassembly of three-dimensional objects from scanned fragments [Huang et al. 2006] (see Figure 17.15).

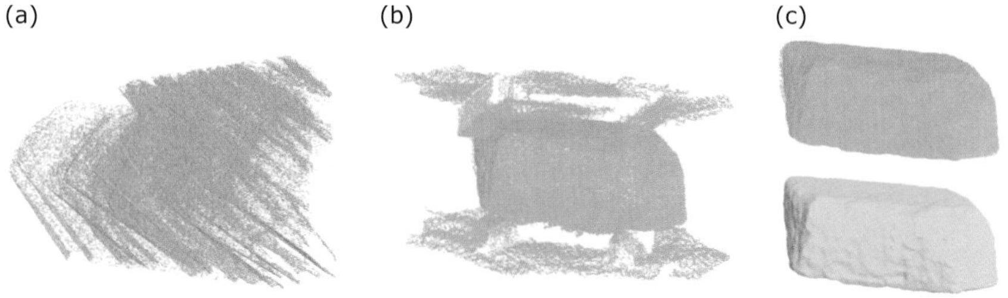

Fig. 17.14
(a) The original scanning data
(b) is aligned, including background information,
(c, top) which is removed after automatic registration.
(c, bottom) From this final point cloud, a mesh is generated.

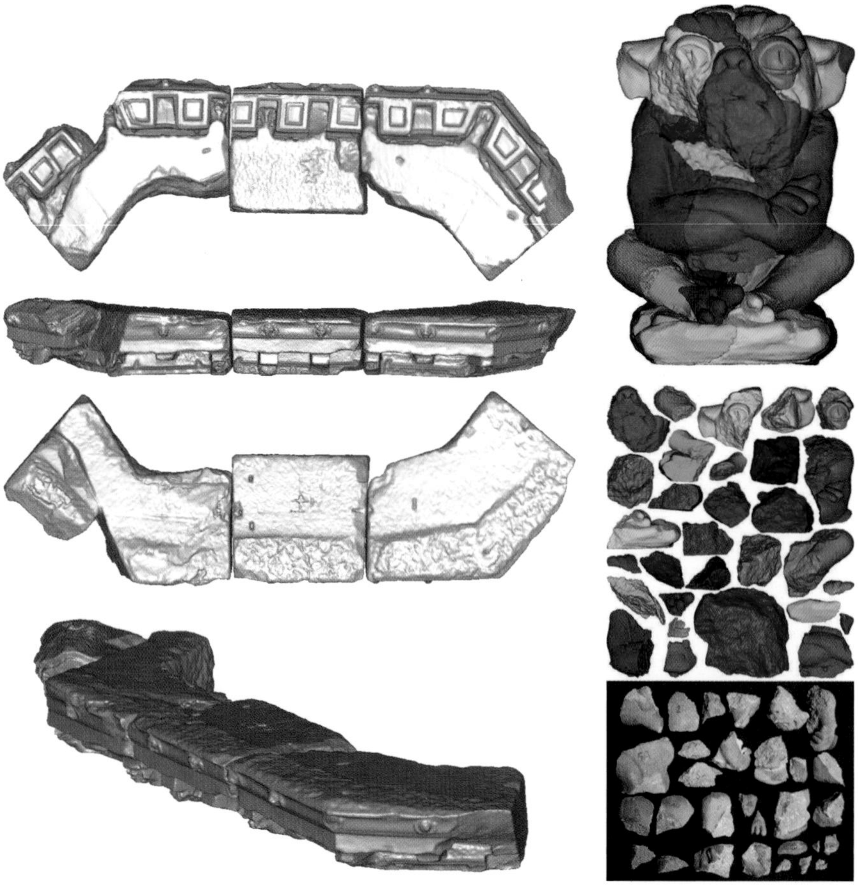

Fig. 17.15
Results of an algorithm for the automatic reassembly of a fractured object.
For the model on the right hand side, we also show images of the fragments and their digital versions.

The Polygon Phase

Triangulation. In the polygon phase, a triangle mesh that approximates the given point cloud has to be computed. In an initial step, one may use only data points as vertices of triangles—perhaps even all data points. However, there are many triangulations that have this property. To more easily convey this concept, it is better to first explore triangulations in two dimensions and then move into three dimensions.

Voronoi diagrams in the plane. Given a set of N points $p_1, p_2, \ldots, p_N$ in the plane, we want to compute a triangulation of (a part of) the plane that contains the given data points as vertices. It turns out that it is better to first discuss a *decomposition of the plane into nearest neighbor regions* $C(p_1), C(p_2), \ldots, C(p_N)$ of the given points $p_1, p_2, \ldots, p_N$. This is known as a *Voronoi diagram* of the point set and defined according to Figure 17.16. The Voronoi cell $C(p_i)$ of a point p_i contains all points of the plane that are closer to p_i than to any other input point. Simple properties of this structure are depicted in Figure 17.16.

Fig. 17.16
The Voronoi diagram of a point set $p_1, p_2, \ldots, p_N$ decomposes the plane into nearest-neighbor regions, called Voronoi cells $C(p_1), C(p_2), \ldots, C(p_N)$. The Voronoi cell $C(p_i)$ of a point p_i contains all points of the plane that are closer to p_i than to any other input point. Voronoi cells are convex.

A common edge of two neighboring cells [e.g., $C(p_1)$, $C(p_2)$] lies on the bisector of their defining points (p_1 and p_2). A common vertex of three cells [e.g., $C(p_1)$, $C(p_2)$, $C(p_3)$] is at equal distance to the defining points p_1, p_2, p_3 and hence the center of the circumcircle of the triangle $p_1p_2p_3$.

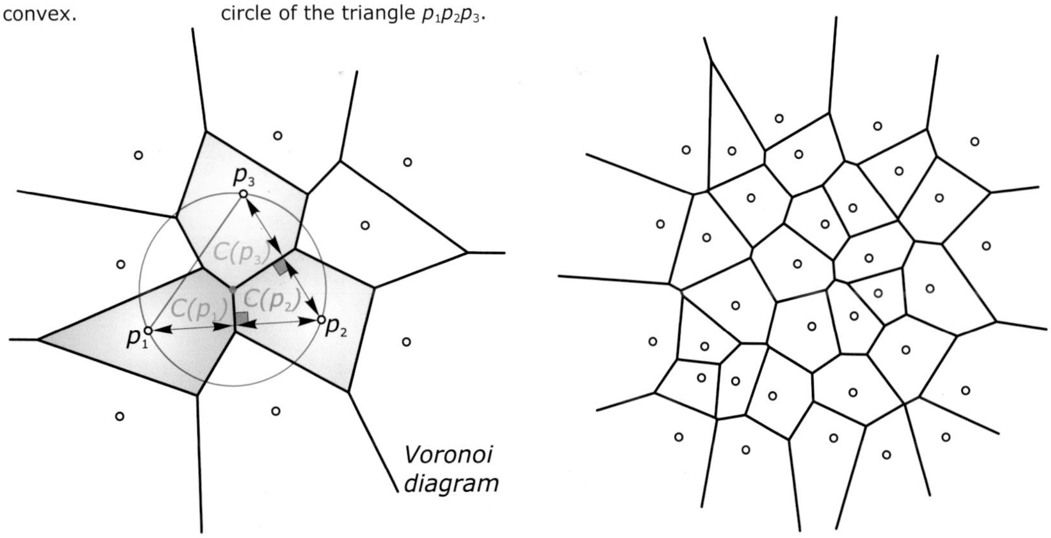

In addition, Figure 17.17 points out that the input points with an unbounded Voronoi cell form the boundary polygon of the convex hull of $p_1, p_2, ..., p_N$ (recall Chapter 8). Within the research area of *computational geometry*, efficient algorithms for the computation of Voronoi diagrams have been developed [CGAL]. Sometimes, one may observe structures similar to Voronoi diagrams in nature (Figure 17.18). The geometric beauty of Voronoi diagrams has recently received interest from architects. It may lead to a number of remarkable applications in architecture and design, other than the relation to triangulations discussed in material following.

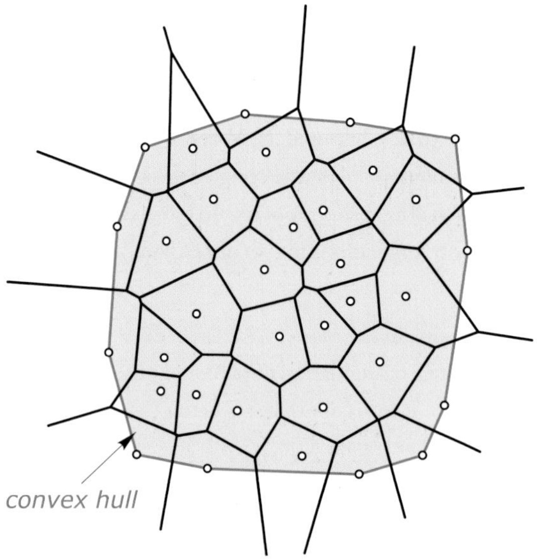

Fig. 17.17
Points with unbounded Voronoi cells lie on the boundary of the convex hull of the input set p_1, p_2, and so on.

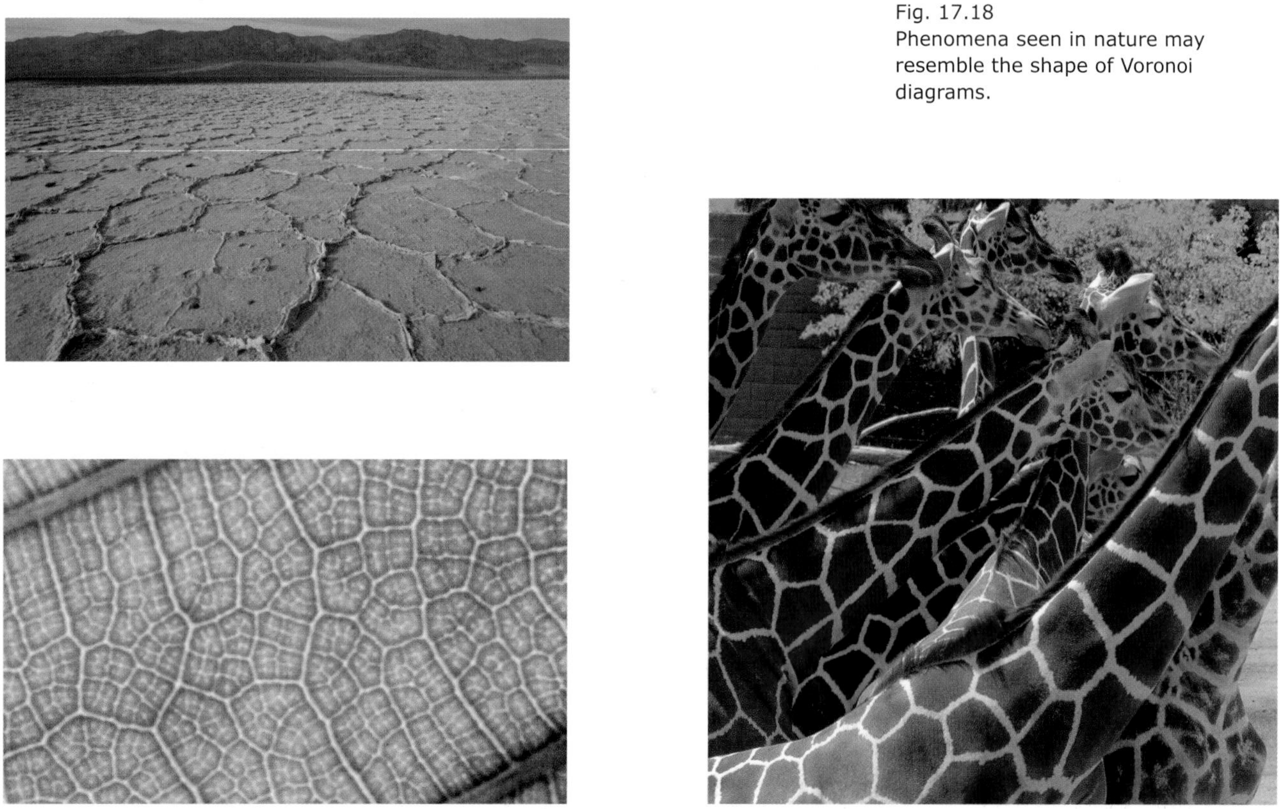

Fig. 17.18
Phenomena seen in nature may resemble the shape of Voronoi diagrams.

Two-dimensional Delaunay triangulation. In a triangulation of a set of points $p_1, p_2, \ldots, p_N$ in the plane, these points have to be the vertices of the triangles. It is no restriction to demand that the union of the triangles shall be the convex hull H of the input points. Recall that a convex domain D has the property that it contains the connecting straight line segment of any two points of D. Therefore, a triangulation cannot go beyond the convex hull H unless one inserts additional vertices.

Apart from the boundary edges of H, it is not yet clear which edges to join for a triangulation. There are many triangulations, and some may exhibit very thin triangles (i.e., triangles with at least one very small angle; Figure 17.19a).

Thin triangles are undesirable for a number of applications (e.g., numerical simulations with the finite element method). Thus, one may ask for a triangulation in which the smallest occurring angle is as large as possible. This triangulation is the *Delaunay triangulation*, whose relation to the Voronoi diagram is surprisingly simple (Figure 17.19b,c). *The Delaunay triangulation joins exactly those points from the input set $p_1, p_2, \ldots, p_N$ by an edge whose Voronoi cells share a common edge.* This is closely related to the "empty circle property" illustrated in Figure 17.19b. The Delaunay triangulation is unique, unless there are empty circum-circles of more than three input points. This happens if more than three Voronoi cells meet at a common vertex (Figure 17.20).

Fig. 17.19
(a) Whereas an arbitrary triangulation of a point set $p_1, p_2, \ldots, p_N$ may exhibit triangles with very small angles, (b,c) this phenomenon is avoided best with a Delaunay triangulation. The latter is obtained by joining those input points by an edge whose Voronoi cells are adjacent (have a common edge). This triangulation fulfills the *empty circle property*. The circum-circle of any triangle in the triangulation does not enclose any vertex of the triangulation.

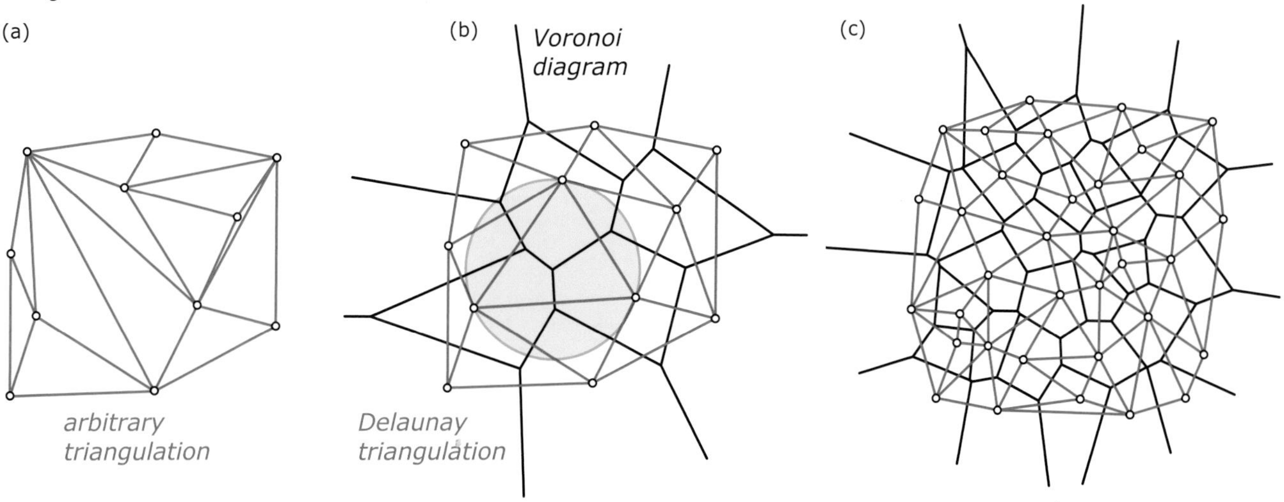

Fig. 17.20
In the case of an empty circum-circle of more than three input points (such as p_1, p_2, p_3, p_4 in this figure), there is an ambiguity in the construction of the Delaunay triangulation. In this case, more than three Voronoi cells meet at a vertex. Up to such special cases, the Delaunay triangulation is uniquely determined.

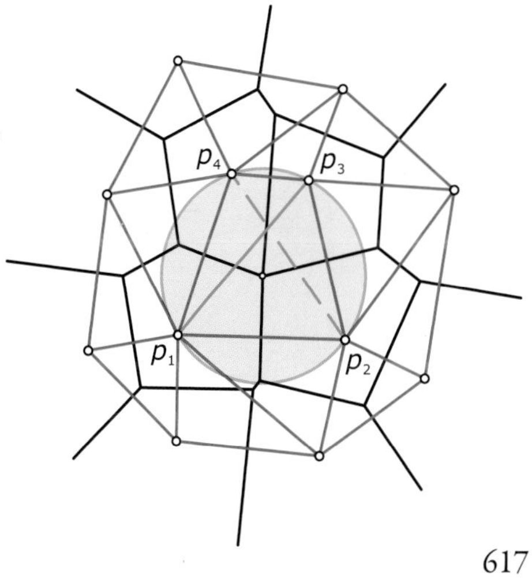

There is a remarkable procedure that may fix some input points and changes the remaining ones so that they are closer to the barycenter of their corresponding Voronoi regions. The resulting *centralized Voronoi diagrams* (Figure 17.21) also produce very nicely shaped triangles in the associated Delaunay triangulation. For details on this algorithm and an extension to the approximation of a smooth surface by polyhedral surfaces, see Cohen-Steiner et al. [2004].

It is a good preparation for understanding surface triangulations to look at the Voronoi diagram and Delaunay triangulation of a set of points sampled from a smooth curve (Figure 17.22). We observe elongated cells roughly orthogonal to the curve and see that the Delaunay triangulation contains a polygon that approximates the curve well.

Fig. 17.21
(a) To regularize a set of points, one may use an iterative procedure. In any step, it computes the Voronoi diagram and moves each point toward the barycenter of its Voronoi cell. Steps of this algorithm.

(b) Initial and final position of another example, together with the trajectories of the barycenters. (Courtesy of Pierre Alliez.)

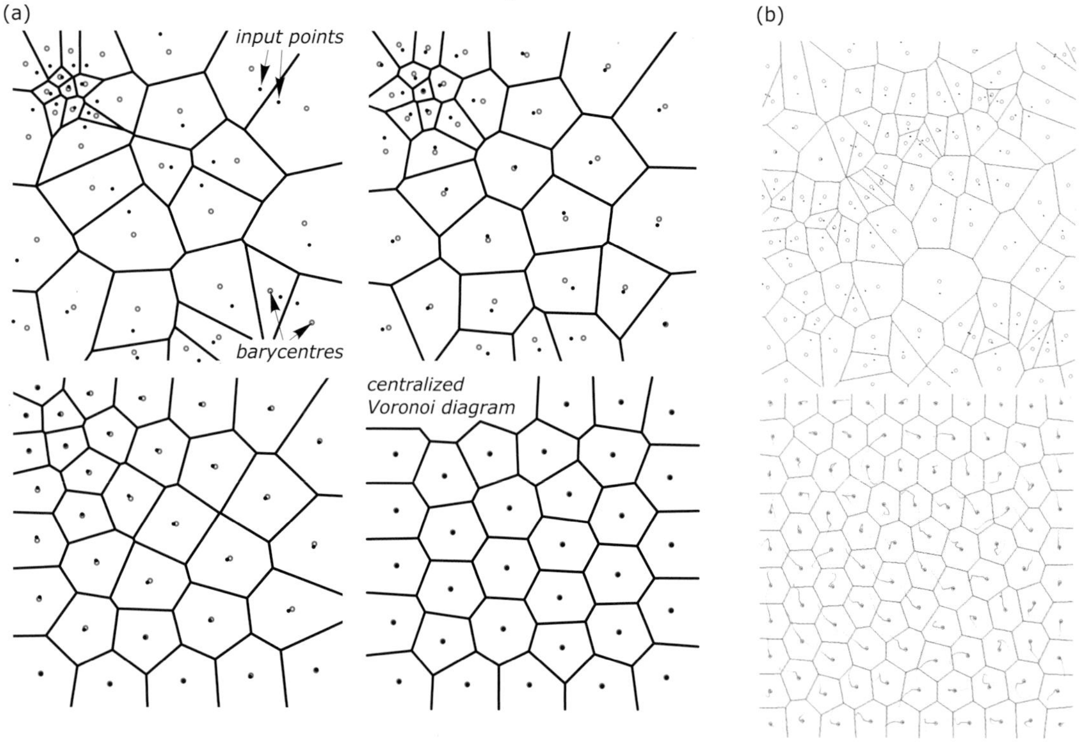

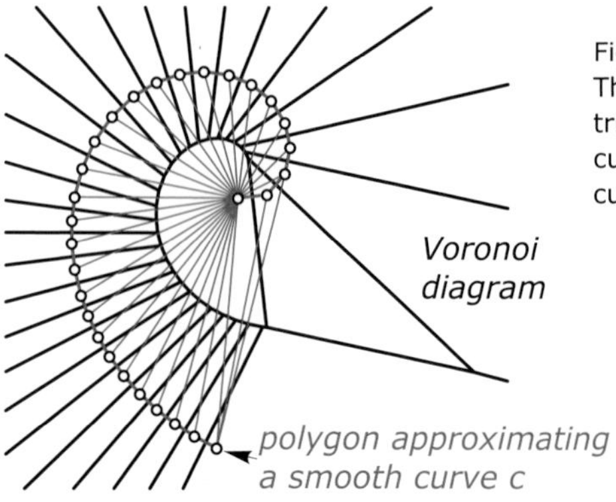

Fig. 17.22
The Voronoi diagram and Delaunay triangulation of points from a smooth curve c provide information about the curve even if c is not known.

Voronoi cells are elongated in direction orthogonal to c, and the Delaunay triangulation contains a polygon that approximates c well.

Voronoi diagrams in three dimensions. The definition of a Voronoi diagram in the plane also works in three dimensions. Voronoi cells are the *nearest neighbor regions* $C(p_1), C(p_2), ..., C(p_N)$ *of the given points* $p_1, p_2, ..., p_N$. Of course, the input points are now arbitrarily located in space. The Voronoi cells are convex. Their faces are bisecting planes of input points. Edges are intersections of (in general) three bisecting planes (axis of a circum-circle of three input points), and at the vertices four (or more) bisecting planes meet. Of course, the vertices are centers of spheres through four (in special cases, more) input points (Figure 17.23).

Three-dimensional Voronoi diagrams may comprise aesthetic arrangements of polyhedra—a fact that explains the interest in Voronoi diagrams by the architectural community (see Figure 17.24).

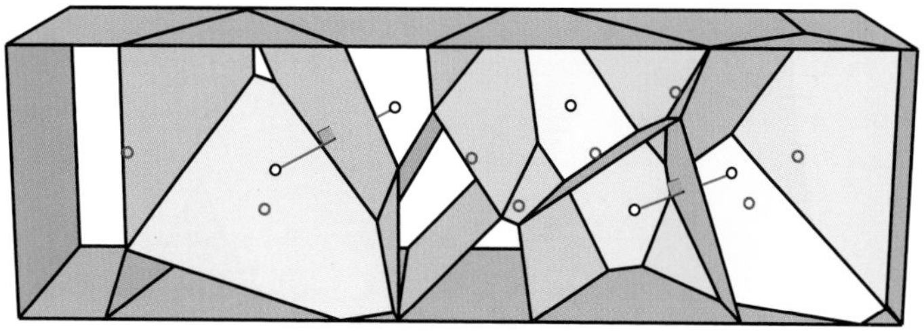

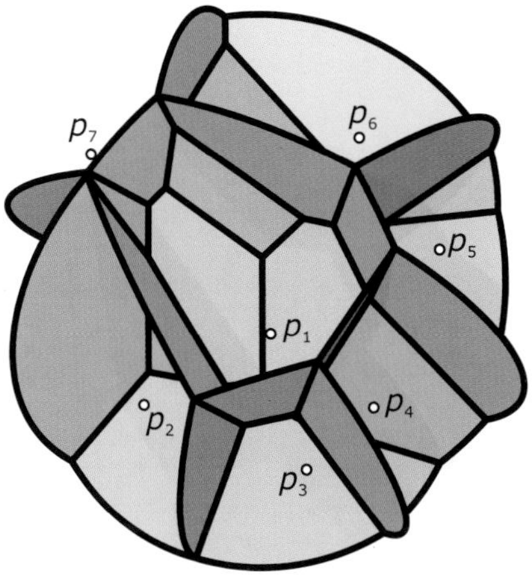

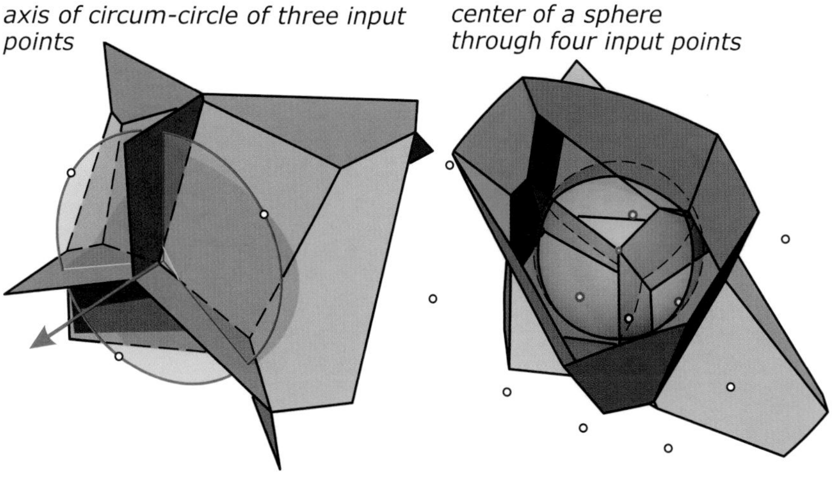

Fig. 17.23
Voronoi diagrams can also be constructed in space. Their properties are very similar to those of two-dimensional Voronoi diagrams.

Fig. 17.24
The design of the Watercube of the National Swimming Center, Beijing, is based on a three-dimensional Voronoi diagram.

Surface triangulations. Connecting those points by an edge, whose Voronoi cells share a common face, we obtain the edges in a *three-dimensional Delaunay triangulation*. We have to be careful here. We actually obtain a decomposition of the convex hull into a union of tetrahedra whose vertices are the input points. However, we are not really interested in the full three-dimensional Delaunay triangulation but only in a subset of it. Recall that our actual goal is the triangulation of a set of points from a surface S. There, the Voronoi diagram has a special behavior (Figure 17.25) analogous to the two-dimensional curve case shown in Figure 17.22.

For a sufficiently dense set of points on S, the Voronoi cells are elongated in a direction normal to the surface. We connect two points (e.g., p_1 and p_2) by an edge if their Voronoi cells $C(p_1)$, $C(p_2)$ share a common face and if this face intersects S. Because S is not explicitly given, this is not as simple as it sounds. However, it can be realized. It would go beyond our scope to proceed here with further details or to discuss the many suggested alternatives to the Delaunay approach. The point here is to realize that surface triangulation is not a simple task.

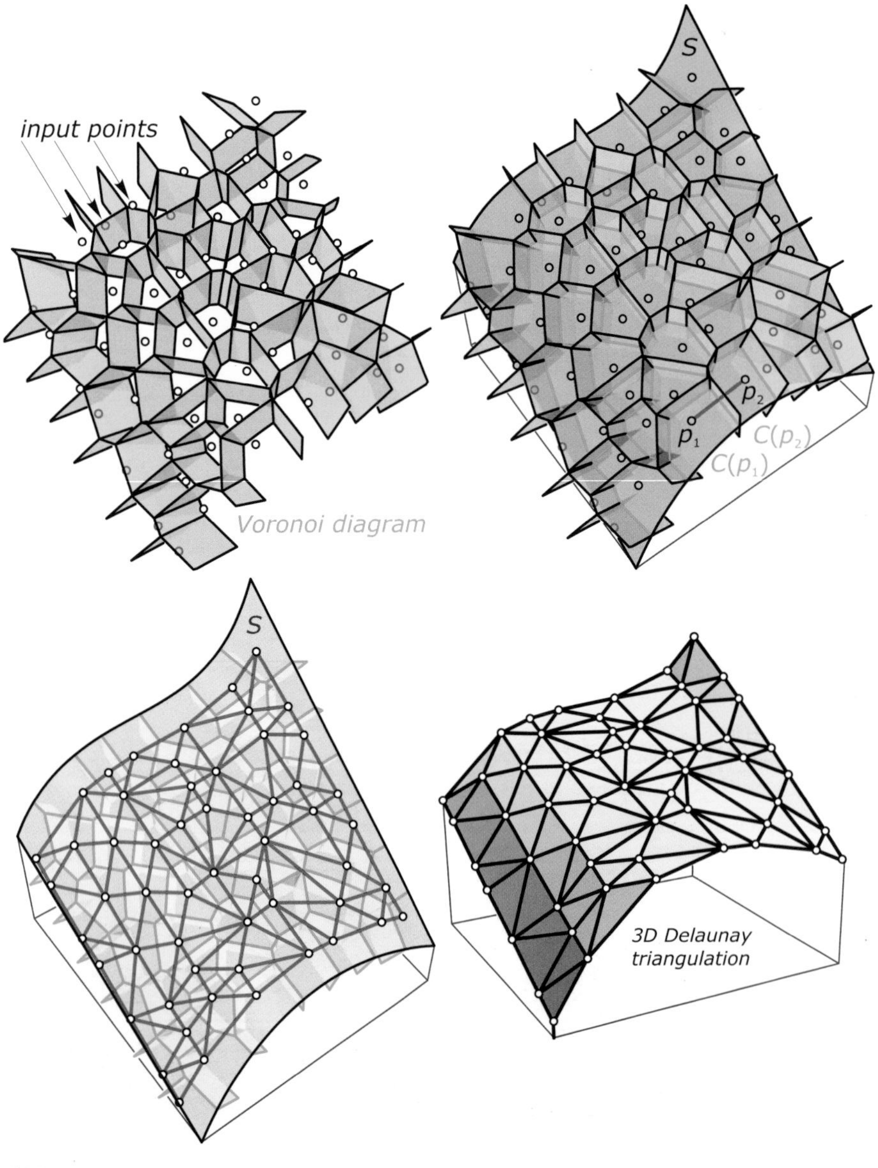

Fig. 17.25
Voronoi cells of measurement points from a smooth surface tend to be elongated in a direction normal to the surface. This helps to extract a surface triangulation from the three-dimensional Delaunay triangulation of the input points (see also the two-dimensional counterpart in Figure 17.22).

Interactive improvements. Especially under bad input conditions, such as large measurement errors or holes in the data set, the output of a triangulation program may not be satisfactory. It will require the application of some interactive tools (Figure 17.26). *Hole filling* requires the specification of part of the triangulation around the detected hole. Then the program computes a triangulated filling surface, which can result from an energy-minimizing principle. This means that the surface is as simple and as smooth as possible. There is also the possibility of specifying regions to be smoothed, a tool sometimes referred to as *sandpaper*.

Fig. 17.26
(a) Tools for interactive improvement of triangulations include hole filling and (b) local smoothing.

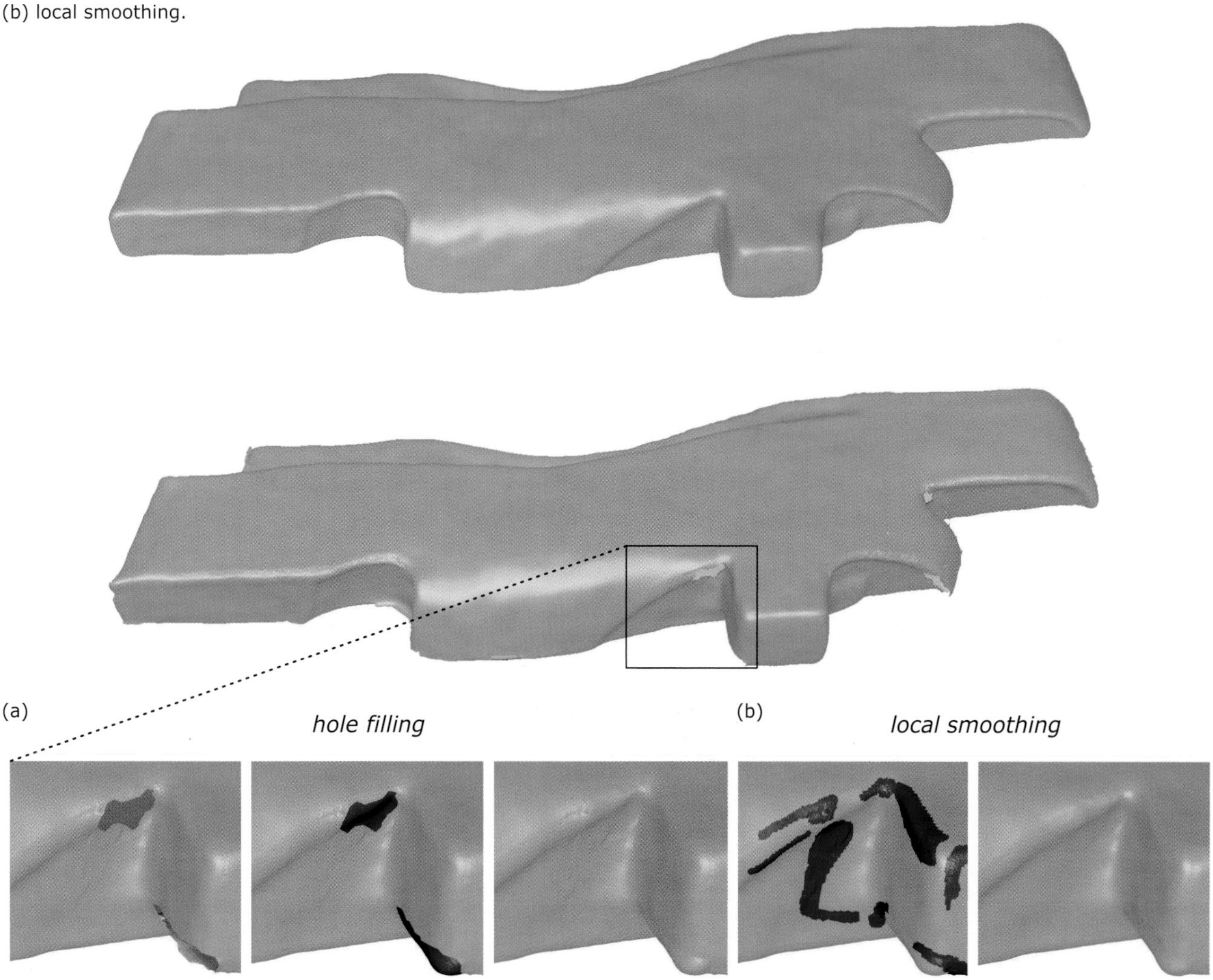

Relaxation and smoothing. Relaxation means to admit changes of the vertex positions in a mesh in order to obtain a "better" mesh that approximates the same underlying surface or a smoothed version of it (Figure 17.27). The quality measure depends on the application. For example, one may look for nearly equilateral triangles. We encountered this method in Chapter 11. Relaxation will also remove noise. However, too high a threshold for noise removal may result in too much smoothing of features and even have a shrinking effect on the entire model.

Mesh decimation. *Mesh decimation* is a *data reduction strategy*. It aims at removing triangles that are not necessary in capturing the shape at the chosen level of detail (resolution). Note that the scanning process produces a roughly constant data density, whereas the shape will not require constant density. It may exhibit simple regions, such as planar ones, where only a few triangles are necessary. At the same time, there may be highly complicated parts with many features that should be captured well. Thus, we need many triangles at these places.

Fig. 17.27
(a) Relaxation changes the vertex positions of triangles in order to optimize given criteria. It should result in a visually more pleasing triangulation.

(b) Admitting large displacements may smooth the model too much. Features become less prominent or even get removed.

(a)

a mesh before and after relaxation

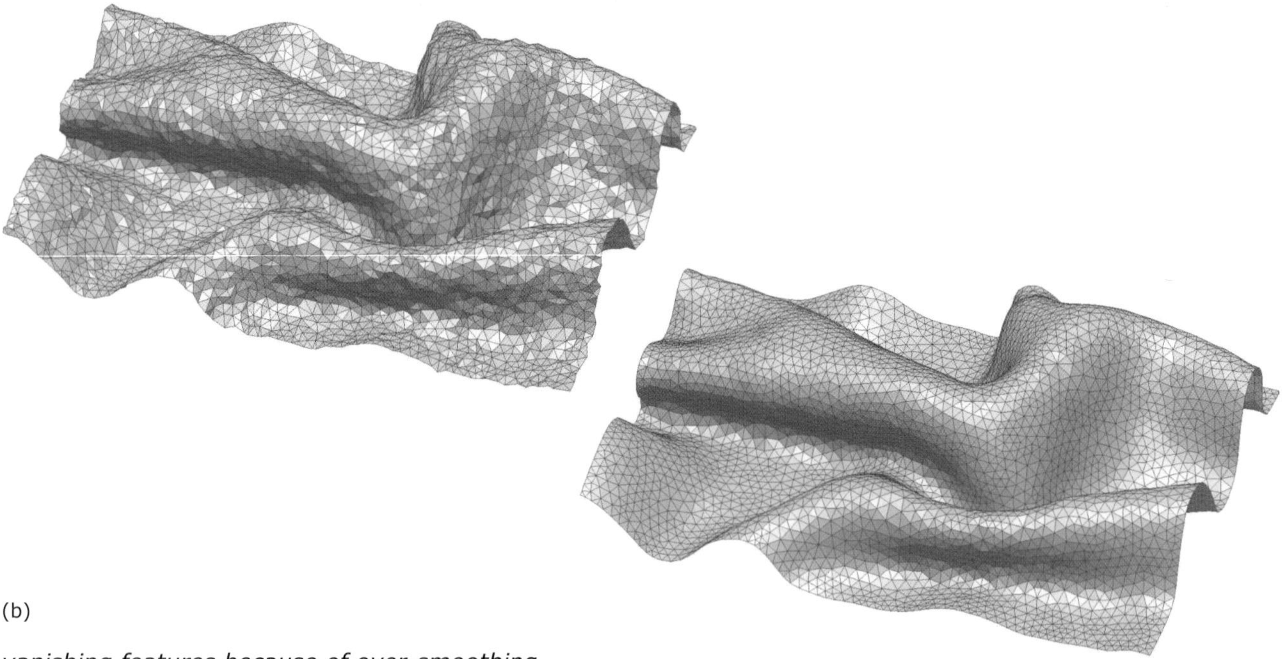

(b)

vanishing features because of over-smoothing

There are many variants of mesh decimation. One method works by *edge contraction*. An edge evaluated as "least important" in a ranking of edges (priority queue) is shrunk to a single point (Figure 17.28). The ranking of edges is often done with a local approximation of the neighborhood and by checking the effect edge contraction will have on it. Think of a nearly planar region. We may prefer large triangles there, and thus its edges will appear high in the priority queue for contraction.

If an edge is contracted to a point, the point's location is computed as an optimal one. Then, the new edges have to be checked and put into the appropriate place of the priority queue. Now the contraction process is continued until the queue is empty (i.e., there is no edge that can be contracted on the chosen level of detail). Mesh decimation has the nice effect that one obtains a hierarchic sequence of meshes at decreasing resolution. Computer graphics frequently uses this hierarchic approach because obviously it does not make sense to render a model with thousands of triangles if the image has the size of a few pixels.

Fig. 17.28
(a) Mesh decimation can be based on successive edge contraction.
(b) The goal is data reduction while preserving the shape of the object at the required level of detail. Mesh decimation produces a sequence of meshes with decreasing resolution.

(a)

edge contraction

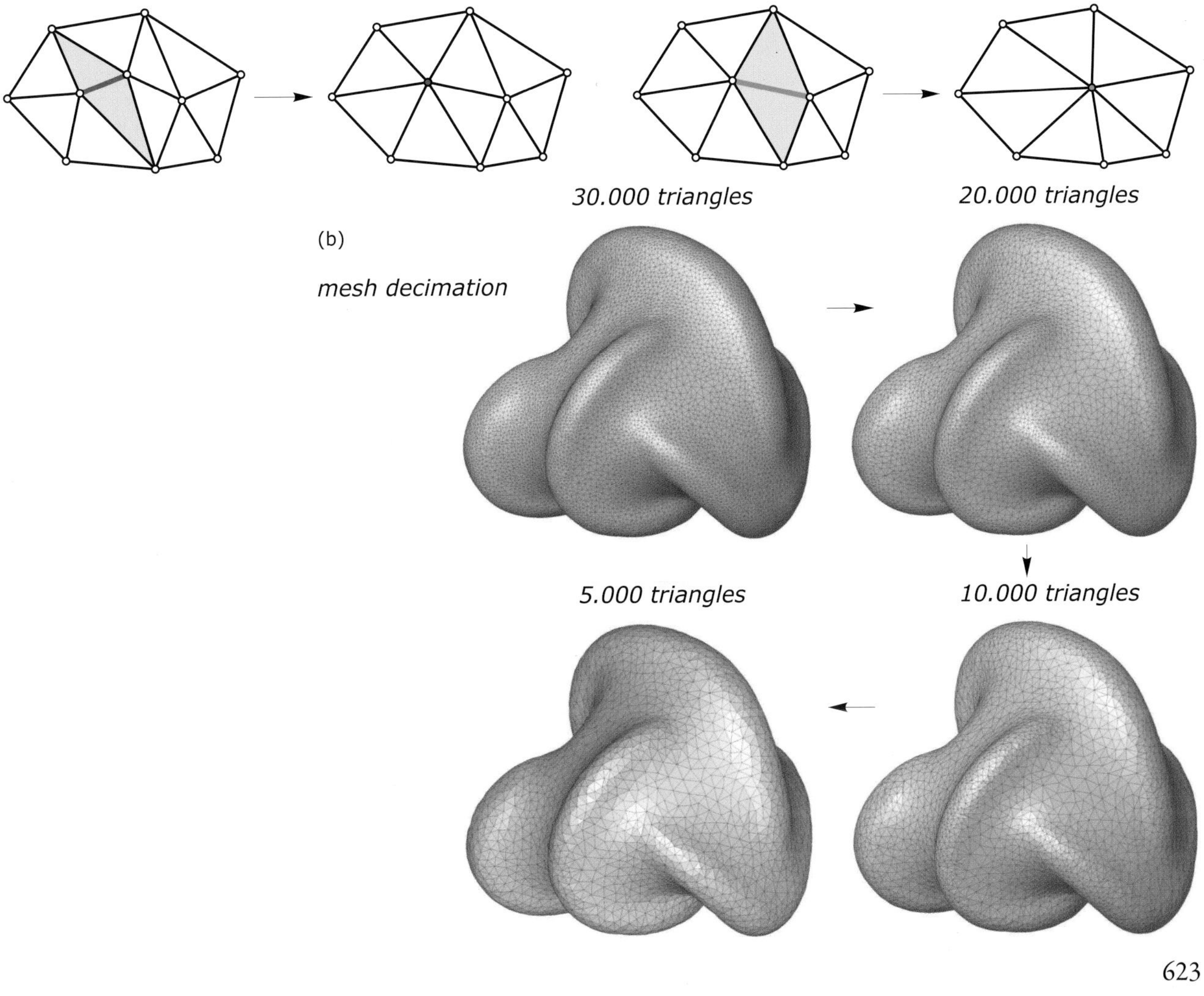

Fig. 17.29
Features on a geometric model can be detected according to the curvature behavior: small principal curvature in the direction of the feature, high principal curvature orthogonal to it. In this figure, the colors provide an automatic classification into ridges, valleys, and prongs. (Courtesy of Yukun Lai.)

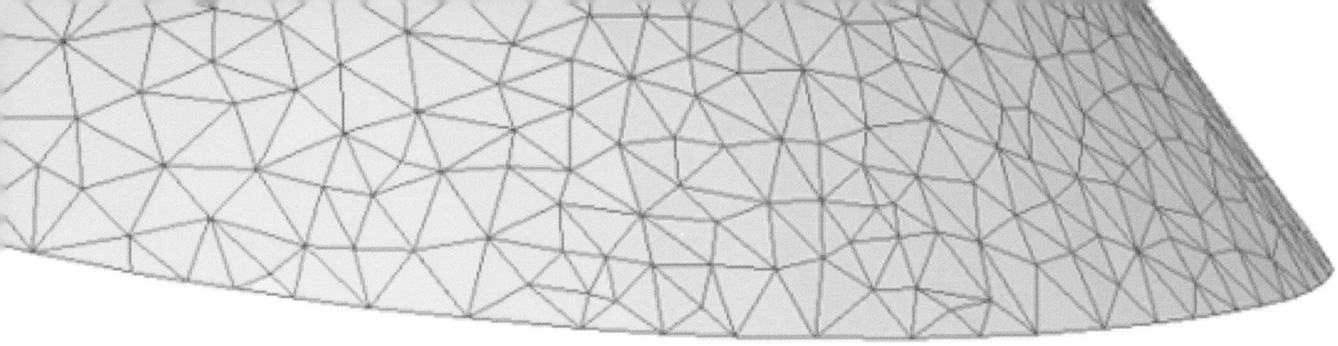

Segmentation

The following steps, often referred to as *segmentation*, are critical in an application such as architecture. One has to detect edges and features. The definition of a *sharp edge* on a surface composed of smooth patches is pretty clear: An edge e is a curve where smooth surfaces intersect (with different tangent planes on either side of the edge). However, *edge detection* on a triangulated model is not easy because the triangulation may not resolve the edges well. There are algorithms that can detect most parts of the sharp edges, but it is very likely that some user interaction will be necessary.

Feature detection is much more subtle. The problems start with a proper mathematical definition of *feature*. Often, a feature region is defined as one with a significant difference in the principal curvatures (i.e., with a small principal curvature in feature direction and a high one across the feature). This criterion has been used for feature detection in Figure 17.29. Architecture has simpler shapes than this figure, but at the same time the location of a curve representing the feature best is of much greater importance.

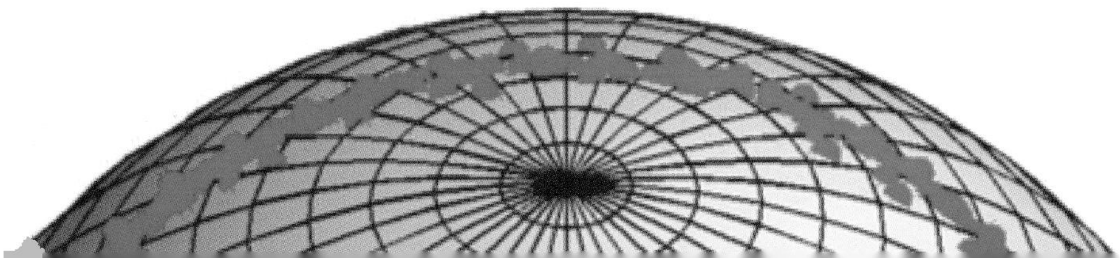

The detection of feature curves requires derivatives of principal curvatures and thus we will refrain from an explanation. Typical results achieved with state-of-the-art feature line detection algorithms (Ohtake et al. 2004,Hildebrandt et al. 2005) are shown in Figure 17.30. Obviously, architectural design will require interactive modifications and smoothing of feature lines if the latter are seen in the final coverage by panels or in the supporting beam structure.

Segmentation also includes the *detection of areas that belong to special surface classes* such as planes, spheres, cylinders, and cones. This can be done automatically. We sketch a method often used for the detection of planes, cylinders, and cones, but serves for detecting general developable surfaces as well (Figure 17.31).

From Chapters 14 and 15, recall the Gaussian spherical image formed by the unit normal vectors of a surface. If S is developable, the spherical image S^* is just a curve or a composition of several curve segments. This expresses the fact that a developable surface carries straight lines along which the tangent plane, and thus the unit normal vector is constant. A plane S has a single point S^* as a Gaussian image.

Fig. 17.30
(a) Feature curves on a geometric model computed at different levels of detail (courtesy of A. Belyaev)
(b) Feature curves on a technical object (courtesy of K. Polthier).

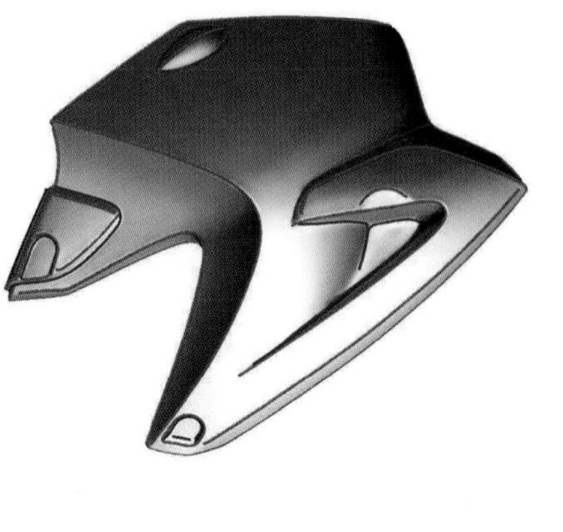

For a cylinder S, the spherical image S^* is a great circle. S^* is a small circle for a rotational cone S (but the same holds for a developable surface S of constant slope). Given a triangulated model S, we can compute S^* via the unit normal vectors of the triangular faces of S. If the model is almost planar, S^* consists of a cluster of points in a very small region of the unit sphere.

Likewise, if S approximates a cylinder or cone S^* is a point cluster close to a great circle or small circle, respectively. More general developable parts can be detected with this method because they give rise to curve-like point clusters on the unit sphere. It is beyond the scope of this book to discuss more advanced methods used to automatically recognize other types of surfaces.

Fig. 17.31
Detection of planes, cylinders, cones, and more general developable surfaces can be based on the Gaussian spherical image S^* defined by the unit normal vectors of the triangular faces.
(a) A planar part of S yields a point-like cluster of S^*,
(b) whereas a cylinder S is mapped to a point set S^* close to a great circle.
(c) A cone of revolution S possesses a Gaussian image S^* formed by data points close to a small circle on the unit sphere.
(d) More general developable surfaces are seen as general curve-like point sets S^*.

(a)

Gaussian spherical image of a planar part

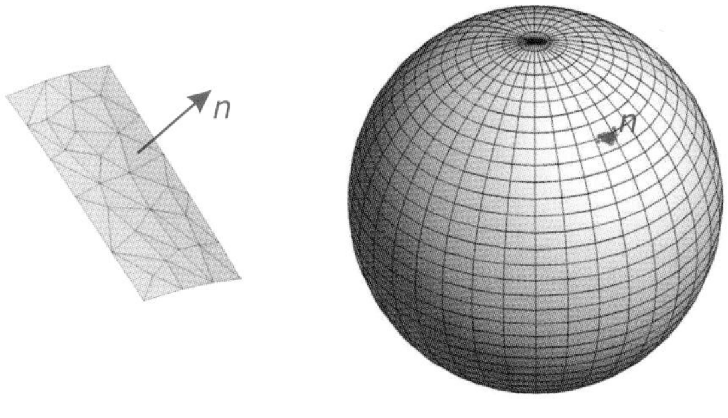

(b)

Gaussian spherical image of a cylinder

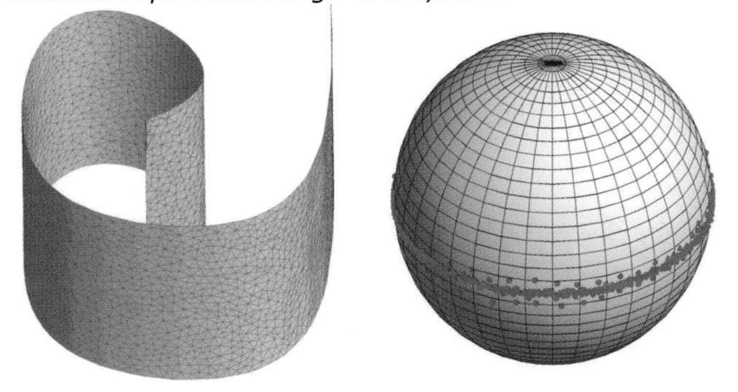

(c)

Gaussian spherical image of a cone

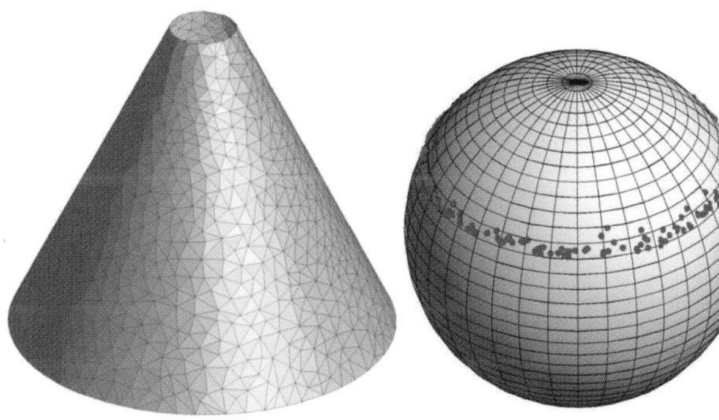

(d)

Gaussian spherical image of a more general developable surface

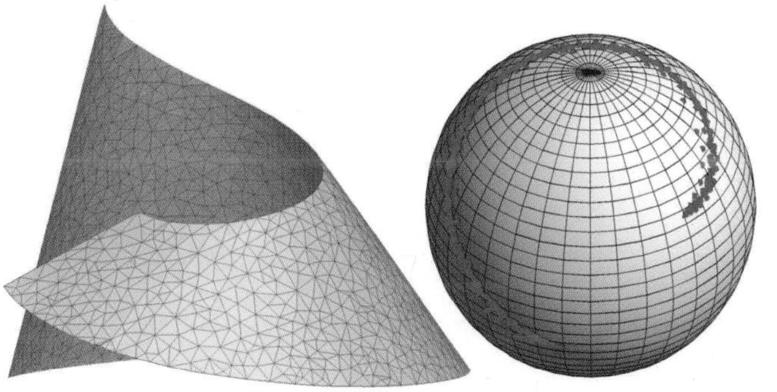

(a)

(b)

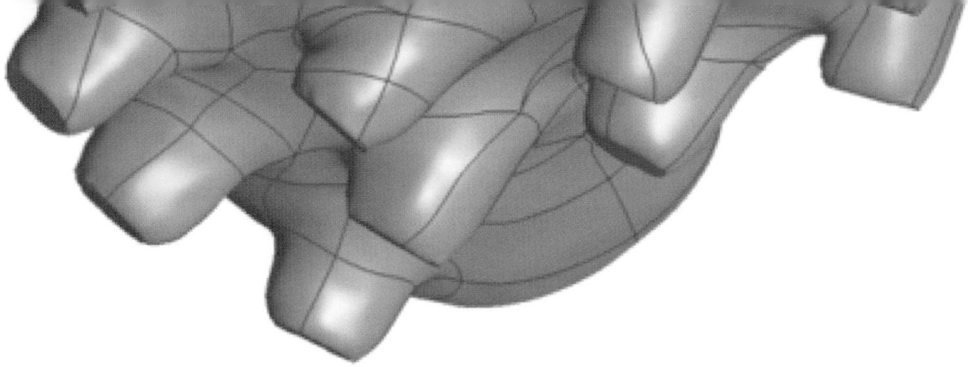

Surface Fitting

In regard to surface fitting we begin with an examination of technical objects (e.g., plane, sphere, cone, and cylinder) that exhibit only simple surfaces. These shapes are not only rather easy to detect automatically but approximations of them are not difficult to compute within the detected surface class (Figure 17.32). For example, a region identified as being planar in the segmentation phase will be approximated by part of a plane. Computing such an approximation plane (regression plane) is a simple task, especially if the noise level is low.

Similar statements hold for the other simple shapes. However, we may not yet have obtained the final result. Think of measuring a cube. Even if all faces have been nicely detected and approximated, the faces will in general not be exact squares (maybe not even rectangles). Thus, one has to impose certain constraints and run an appropriate approximation algorithm capable of maintaining the constraints. This is sometimes called *model beautification*.

Fig. 17.32
This technical object exhibits mainly simple surfaces and blending surfaces and has been obtained via digital reconstruction.
(a) Result of segmentation,
(b) shaded image of the reconstructed model and
(c) optical lines for quality control (images courtesy of Geomagic, Inc., Research Triangle Park, North Carolina).

(c)

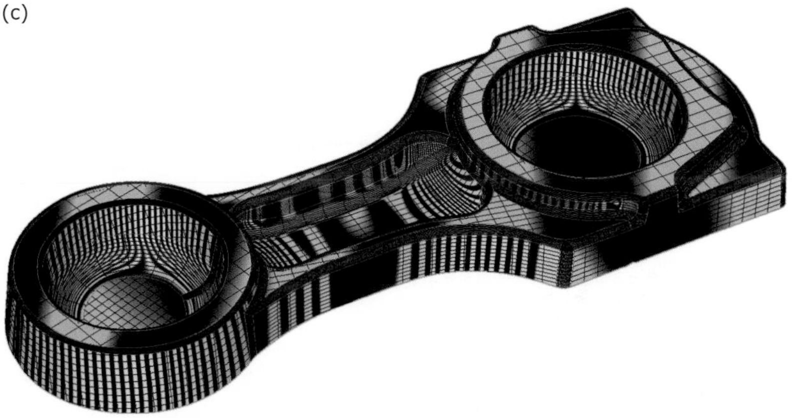

Symmetries. An important part of beautification concerns the achievement of the desired symmetries. This holds for all types of objects, not only those formed by simple surfaces, and includes more general symmetries than just reflective symmetry. Figure 17.33 shows an example of automatic *symmetry detection* [Mitra at al. 2006]. There are even algorithms for *symmetrization*, which makes nearly symmetric objects perfectly symmetric [Mitra et al. 2007]. This even holds for the mesh describing the shape, as shown in Figure 17.34.

Fig. 17.33
Results of an algorithm for symmetry detection by Mitra, Pauly, and Guibas. The six most significant modes of symmetry detected on a model of the Sydney Opera are shown. The algorithm detects symmetries with respect to planar reflection, translation, rotation, and uniform scaling.

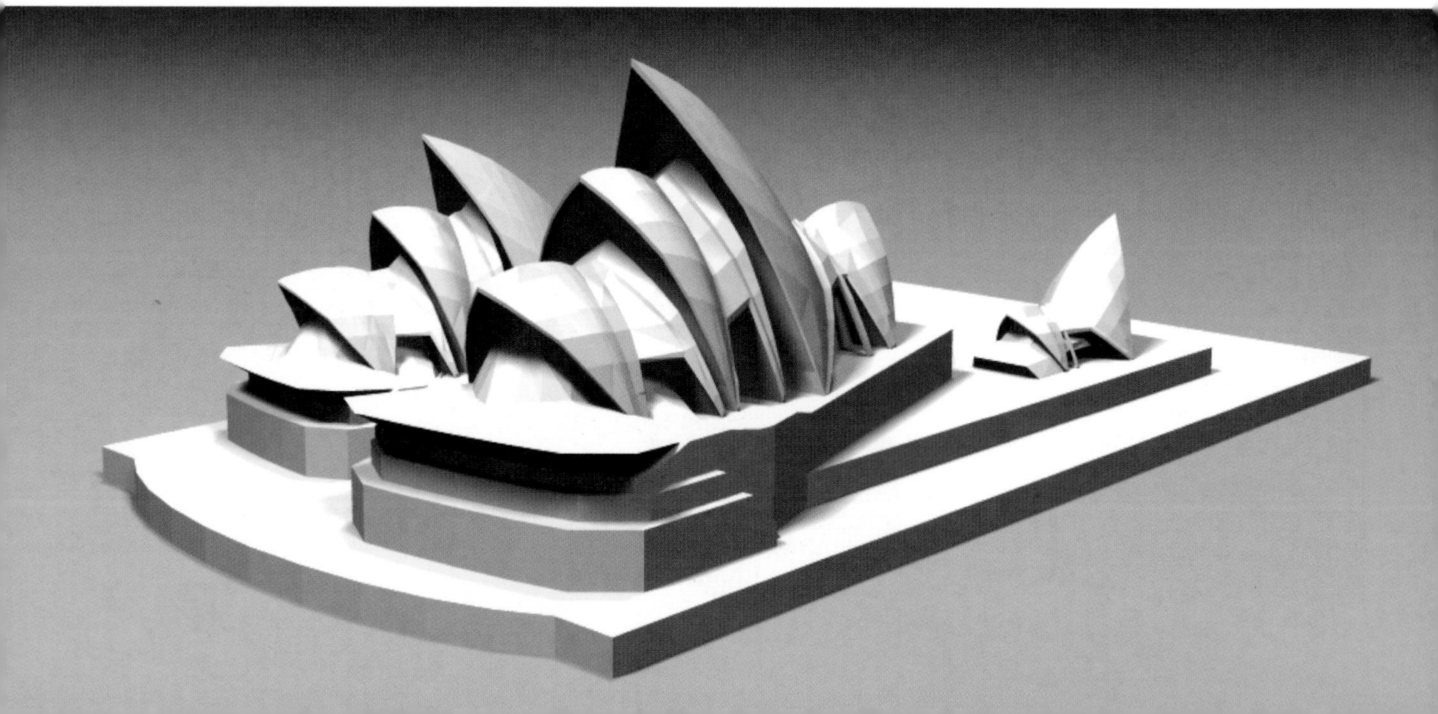

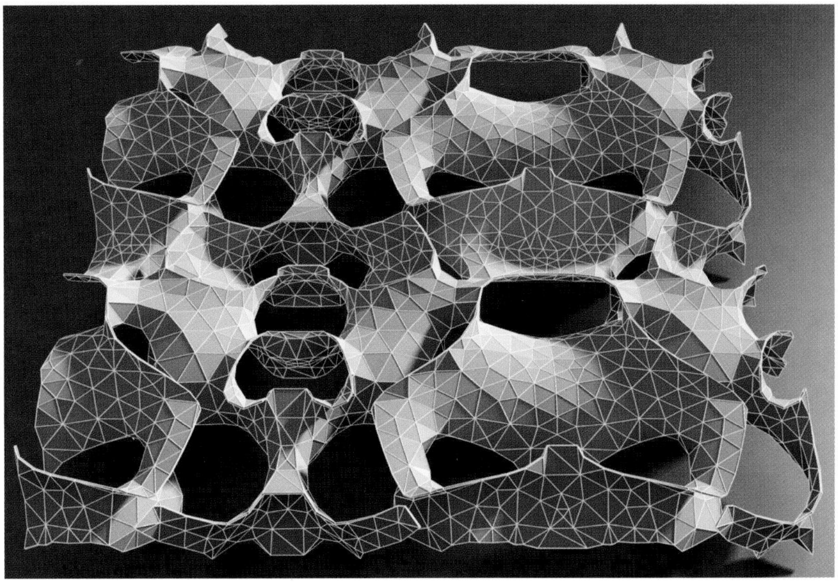

Fig. 17.34
Symmetrization applied to an architectural design study. The zooms in the middle row show how the meshing of the extracted symmetric element evolves during optimization. This element appears six times in different locations and orientations, as illustrated in the bottom row (images courtesy of N. Mitra).

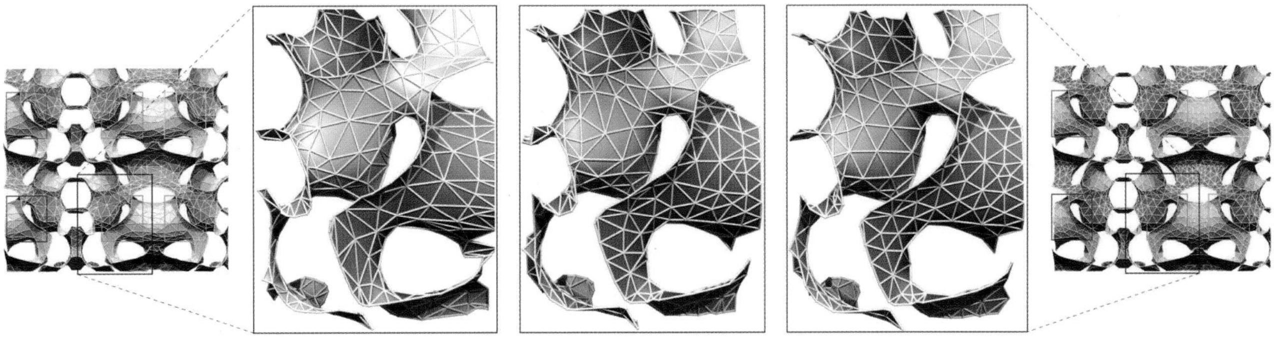

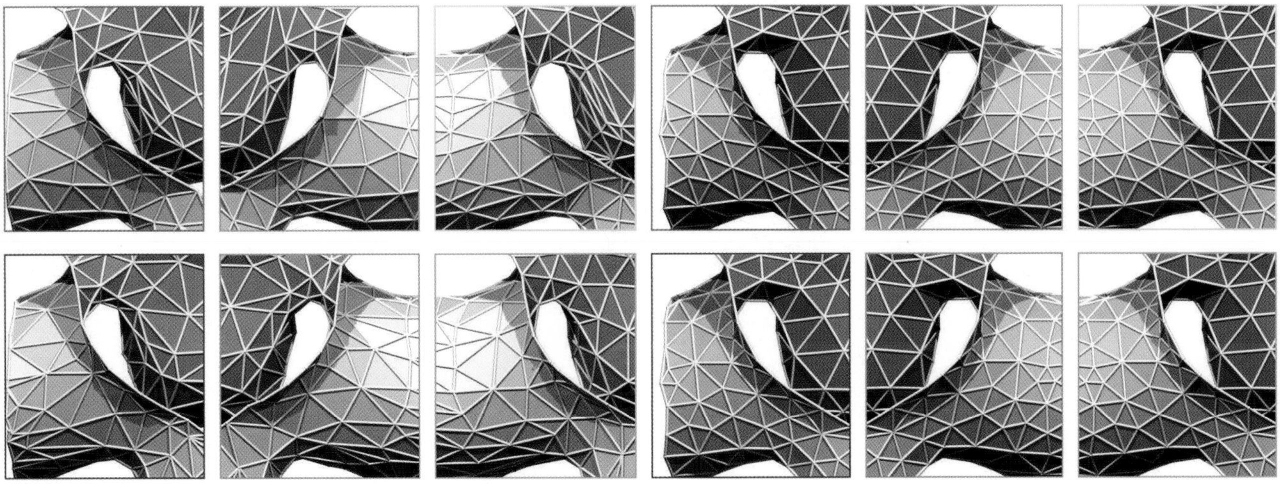

Freeform surface fitting. Neglecting for a moment the manufacturing constraints discussed in the following, one may regard all surfaces different from the simple ones as freeform geometry and approximate them with B-spline surfaces—a procedure also known as B-spline *surface fitting*. There are fully automatic algorithms for this purpose, but as a strategy these are not recommended (Figure 17.35).

The problem lies in the specification of patch boundaries. Ideally, and especially for architectural applications, these boundaries should follow features or other structure lines that are part of the design intent. A comparison of the automatic approach with the result of a careful patch boundary layout is illustrated by Figure 17.35.

Sometimes it is possible to decompose the model into *primary surfaces*, fit them individually, and construct the remaining parts via blending surfaces. Figure 17.35 depicts this in terms of a detail from a model resembling Kunsthaus Graz.

Fig. 17.35
The quality of a B-spline model significantly depends on the chosen patch layout. An automatic patch layout (example 1) will not likely lead to a meaningful segmentation into patches. For this data set, roughly resembling the shape of *Kunsthaus Graz*, a better result (example 2) is obtained by first approximating the main body, fitting the detail surfaces (here, cylinders; getting closer to the real object, one should use cones), and then computing smooth blending patches.

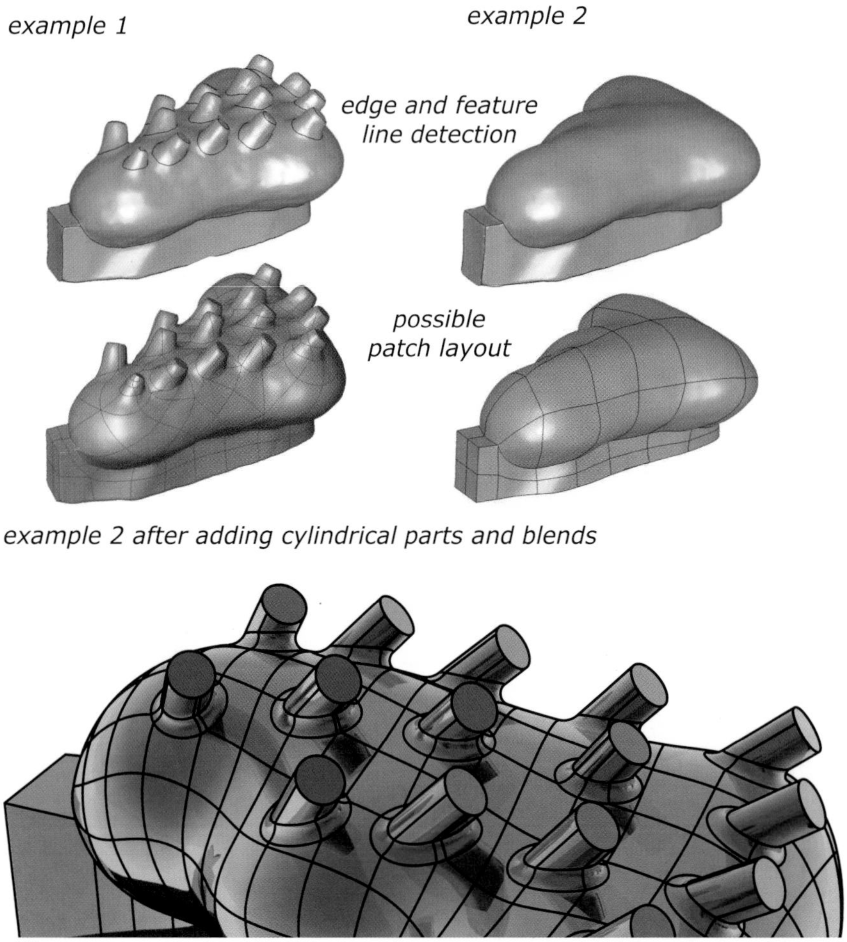

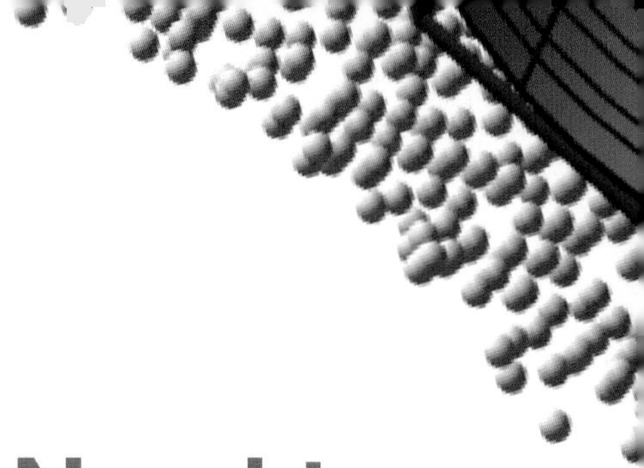

The Surfaces Need to Be Built

Standard digital reconstruction software will approximate freeform shapes by general B-spline surfaces. However, for applications in architecture it may be better to sacrifice some accuracy and try to approximate the measurement data by a union of surface patches that can "easily" be built. These surfaces include ruled surfaces, developable surfaces, and other kinematically generated surfaces.

A related challenge here is that we cannot simply minimize approximation errors or fairness functionals because the *panelization* itself is a crucial aspect of the design expression of a building. Looking, for example, at the experience music project by Gehry it is obvious that the orientation of the tiles was carefully designed. Unfortunately, there is not much research on the geometric facets of panelization. Some of it was described in Chapter 15, and we will address the problem again at the end of Chapter 19.

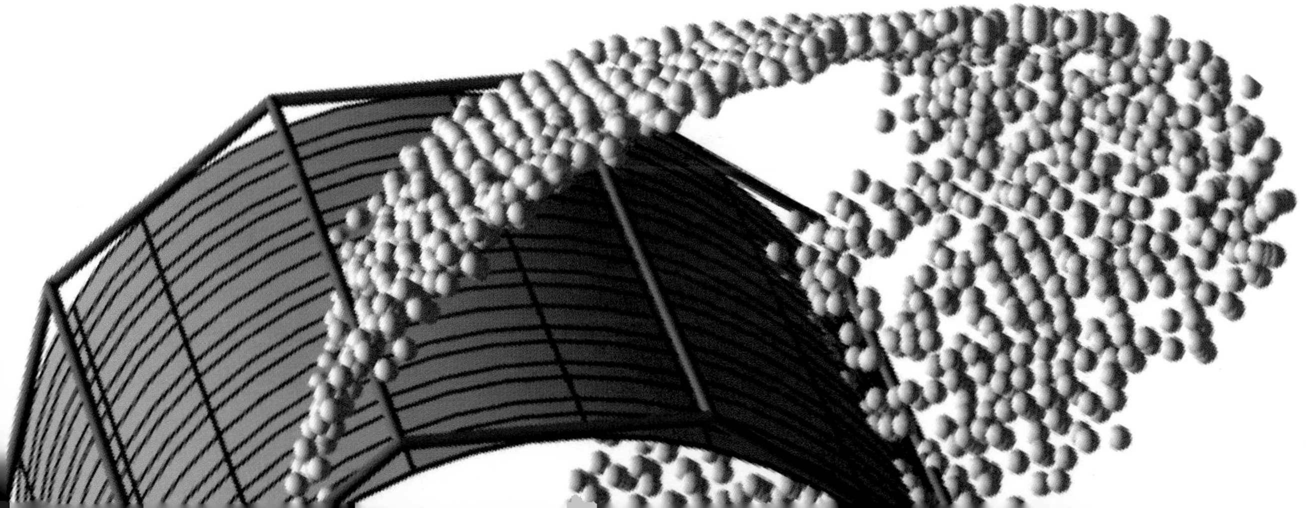

Approximation with ruled surfaces. Ruled surfaces have the great advantage of carrying a family of straight lines. This greatly simplifies the actual construction. Ruled surfaces are modeled by B-spline surfaces if we set one degree equal to 1 (see Chapter 11). However, standard fitting algorithms may not perform well. This is due to the mathematical formulation of the fitting procedure. An approach that can handle such a situation has been presented by Pottmann and Leopoldseder [2003]. A result of this algorithm is shown in Figure 17.36.

Developable surfaces. Developable surfaces are favorite shapes of some architects (see Chapter 15). However, fitting such surfaces to given models is not as simple as it may seem. Digital reconstruction software does not yet support this important surface class. Figure 17.37 shows results of an algorithm by Peternell [2004].

Fig. 17.36
Approximation by ruled surfaces is interesting for architecture because ruled surfaces can be more easily built than general freeform surfaces.
(left) Approximation algorithms evolve a simple ruled surface optimally toward the input data,
(right) which yields the final surface
(Images courtesy of Reinhard Gruber.)

point cloud and initial position of approximating surface

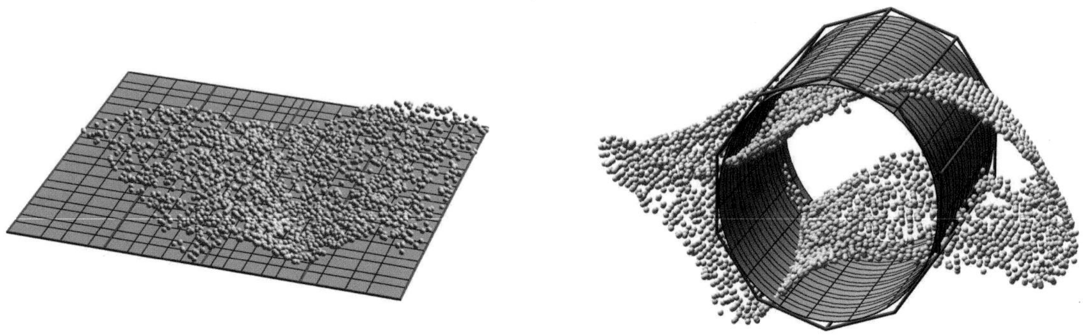

approximation of a point cloud by a ruled surface

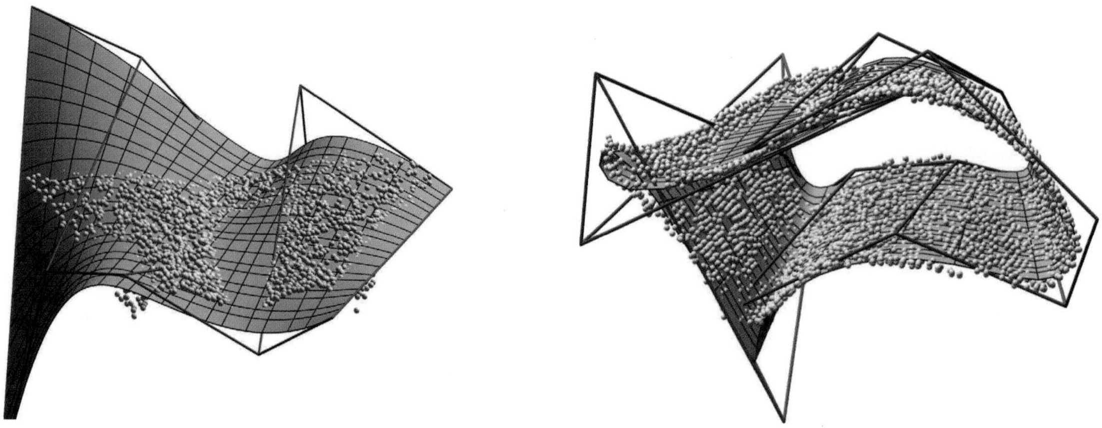

Fig. 17.37
Approximation by developable surfaces is more difficult than fitting arbitrary ruled surfaces to triangulated models. This figure shows results of an algorithm by M. Peternell that uses the Gaussian spherical image as an intermediate step.

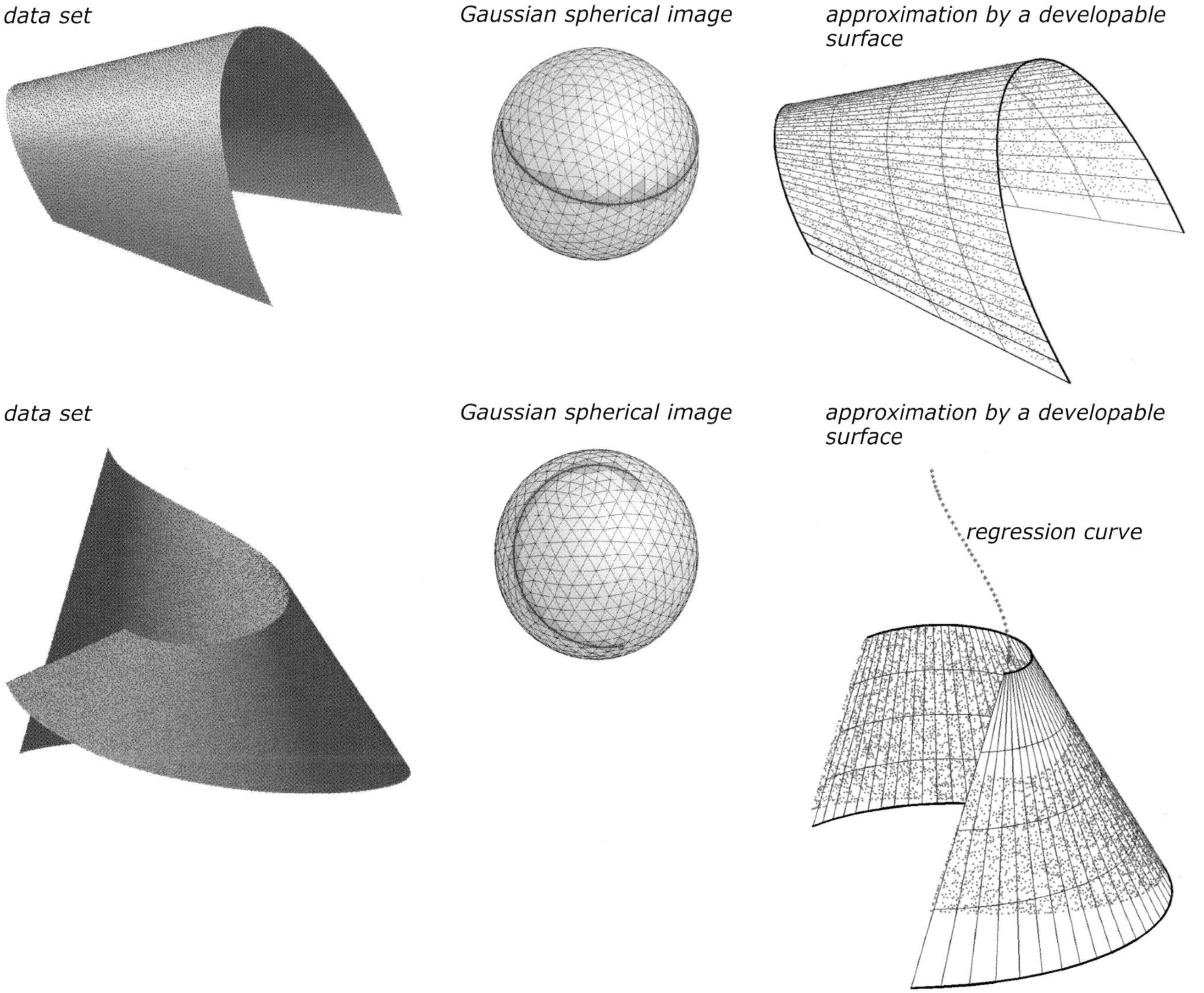

Translational surfaces and more general sweeping surfaces. From a computational perspective, fitting translational surfaces to a triangulated model is comparable to approximation by a ruled surface. Hence, the algorithm of Pottmann and Leopoldseder [2003] is also applicable in this case (Figure 17.38). Congruent profiles are also present on rotational surfaces, whose reconstruction is solved and supported by commercial software.

More general sweeping surfaces, which are obtained by moving a curve in space with a rigid body motion (Chapter 12), may be interesting candidates for digital reconstruction in architectural applications. However, we are not aware of an algorithm that would go beyond helical surfaces or moulding surfaces.

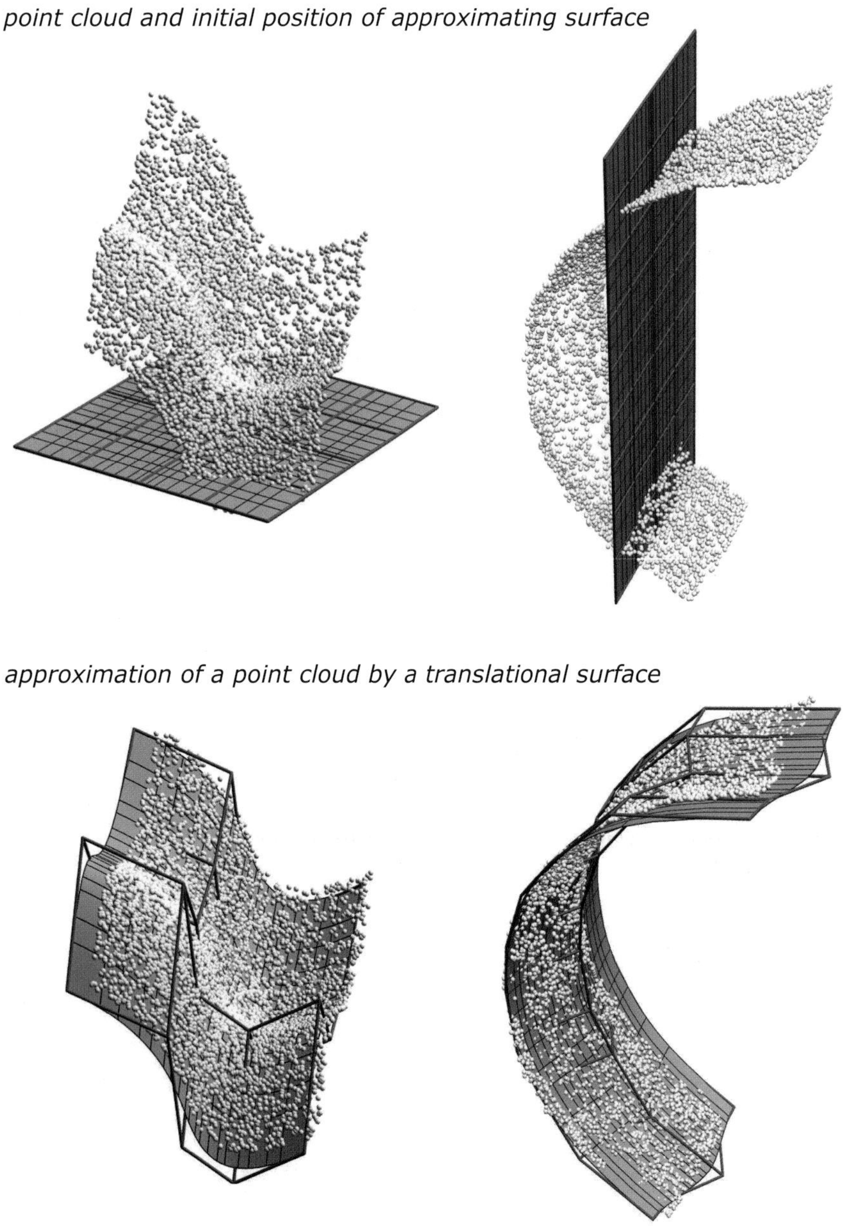

point cloud and initial position of approximating surface
approximation of a point cloud by a translational surface

Fig. 17.38
Approximation of data point clouds by translational surfaces (left, initial shape; right, result after optimization). (Images courtesy of Reinhard Gruber.)

References and Further Reading

Bernardini F, Rushmeier H. The 3D model acquisition pipeline. Computer Graphics Forum 2002;21:149–172.

CGAL (Computational Geometry Algorithms Library), *http://www.cgal.org/*.

Cohen-Steiner D, Alliez P, Desbrun M. Variational shape approximation. ACM Trans. Graphics 2004;23:905–914.

Hildebrandt K, Polthier K, Wardetzky M. Smooth feature lines on surface meshes. *Proceedings of the Eurographics Symposium on Geometry Processing* 2005:85–90.

Hofer M, Flöry S, Thuswaldner B, Huang Q-X, Thür H. 3D technology research challenges for the digital anastylosis of ancient monuments illustrated by means of the Octagon in Ephesos. Geometry Preprint 171, Vienna University of Technology, December 2006.

Huang Q-X, Flöry S, Gelfand N, Hofer M, Pottmann H. Reassembling fractured objects by geometric matching. ACM Trans. Graphics 2006;25:569–578.

Mitra N, Pauly M, Guibas L. Symmetrization. ACM Trans. Graphics 2007;26 (in press).

Mitra N, Guibas L, Pauly M. Partial and approximate symmetry detection for 3D geometry. ACM Trans. Graphics 2006;25:560–568.

Ohtake Y, Belyaev A, Seidel H-P. Ridge-valley lines on meshes via implicit surface fitting. ACM Trans.Graphics 2004;23: 609-612.

Okabe A, Boots B, Sugihara K, Chiu SN. *Spatial Tessellations: Concepts and Applications of Voronoi Diagrams, Second Edition*. Chichester: Wiley 2001.

Peternell M. Developable surface fitting to point clouds. Comp. Aided Geom. Design 2004; 21: 785–803

Pottmann H, Leopoldseder S. A concept for parametric surface fitting which avoids the parametrization problem. Comp. Aided Geom. Design 2003;20:343–362.

Varady T, Martin R. Reverse engineering. In G Farin, J Hoschek, M-S Kim (eds.), *Handbook of Computer Aided Geometric Design*. Amsterdam: North Holland 2002:651–681.

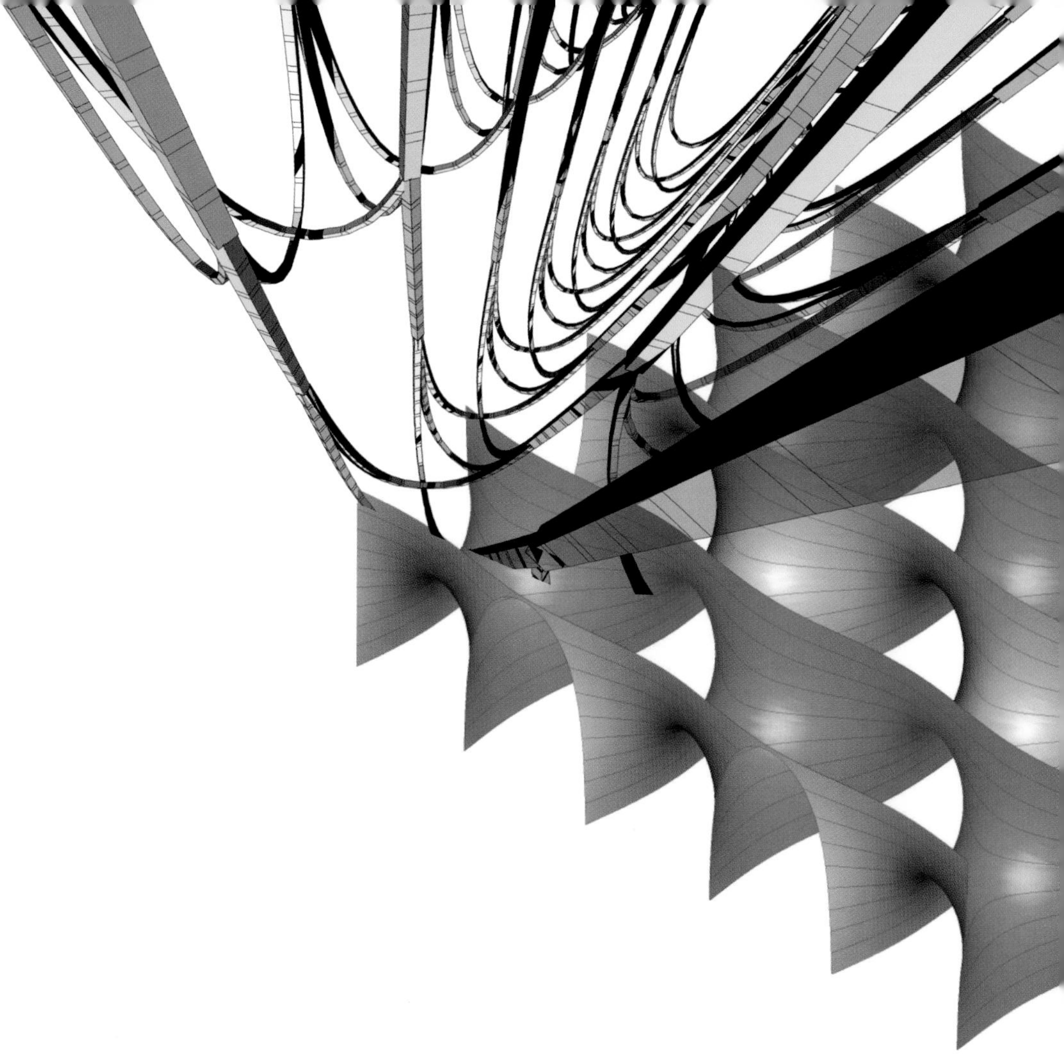

Chapter 18
Shape Optimization Problems

Shape Optimization Problems

The realization of a design idea in an optimal way, both from the aesthetic and functional perspective, is a difficult and complex problem area. The mathematical and algorithmic formulation of aesthetic shapes is also a complicated issue.

Adding functional requirements makes the overall problem even more difficult, especially in that functional optimization cannot be fully separated from shape optimization (see the example in Figures 18.1a and b). Because this book is focussing on geometry, we will only describe certain geometric optimization problems in detail and then briefly address a few functional optimization concepts closely related to geometric ways of thinking.

(a)

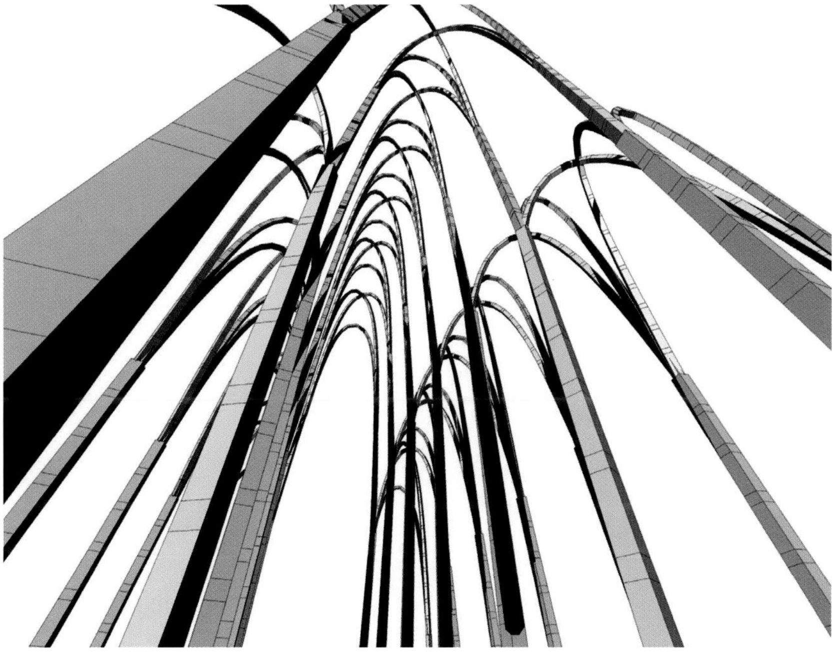

Fig. 18.1
A hanging chain application by Axel Kilian as an example of shape optimization driven by a functional goal.

(b)

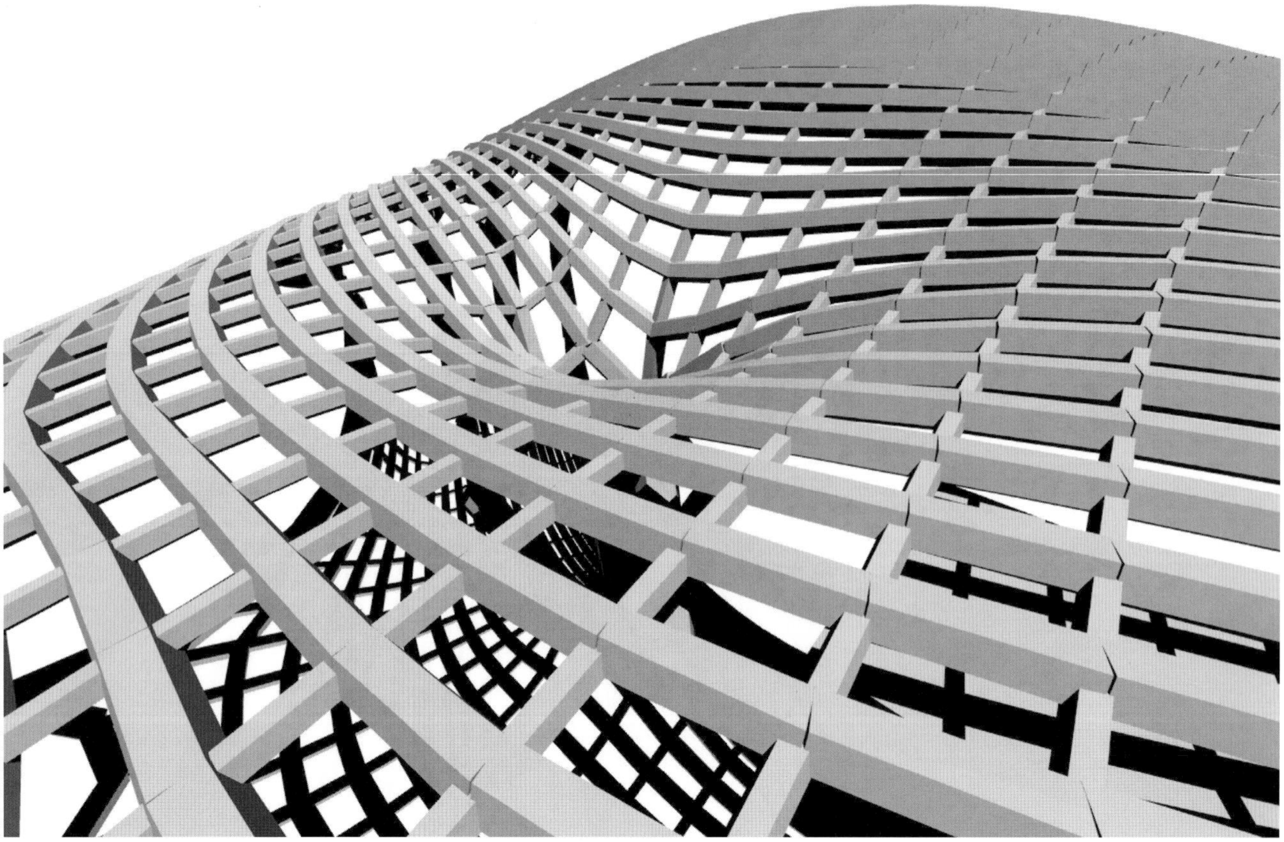

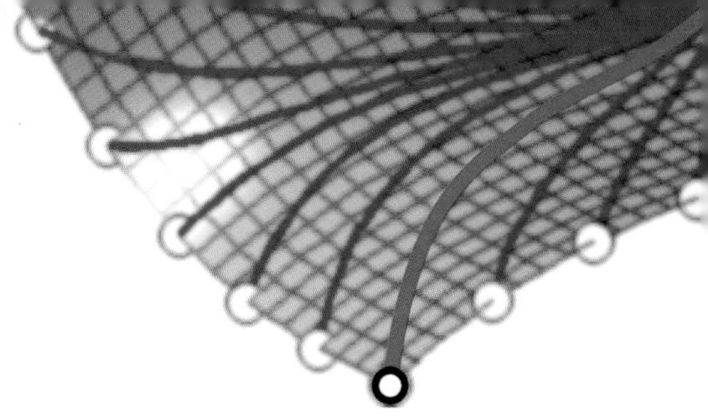

Remarks on Mathematical Optimization

To optimize a design, we need to define the problem in a quantifiable way—in the case of optimization using a function to describe the range of possible outcomes. It is already within this modeling of the problem that the optimization occurs. A badly defined model of the problem will never be made viable by even the best optimization approach. Thus, we offer the following postulate.

Any optimum is only an optimum within the conceptualization of the problem space and the boundary conditions applied.

If we can translate an aspect of a problem into a functional description, optimization can be a very powerful method. We have encountered optimization in the previous chapter. In regard to functions of one variable, we pointed out that numerical optimization techniques may not reach the desired "optimal result" if the initial guess is not within the basin of attraction. Here, we add further basic concepts and address functions of more than one variable.

We consider a function f (called *objective function*) that assigns to each point p of a domain D a real number $f(p)$. D may be in a high-dimensional space. Optimization deals with the computation of local or global minimizers of f. A *local minimizer* p^* is a point whose function value $f(p^*)$ is smaller than the function values of the points in a small neighborhood around p^*.

The function value $f(p^*)$ itself is called a *local minimum*. A global minimum on D is the smallest of all local minima and is attained at the *global minimizer*. Confining the search for minima to a domain D is actually a constraint, and minima may occur at the boundary of D. In the following, we will not address this boundary case. The reason one is only looking at minima is simple: A maximum of f is a minimum of the function $-f$ and thus it suffices to confine the discussion to minima.

To get an idea of optimization in the case where f depends on more than one variable, we address the case of two variables. This means that the objective function f shall be defined for points $p = (x,y)$ of the plane and thus we write it as $f(x,y)$.

Optimization needs the concept of differentiation. The *partial derivative* f_x of f with respect to x is computed like the derivative of a function of only one variable x. We simply treat the other variable y like a constant. The meaning of f_x can be visualized at hand of the graph surface $z = f(x,y)$ of f. It is the slope of the graph's tangent plane in the x direction. Analogous statements hold for the partial derivative f_y of f with respect to y.

Clearly, at a local minimizer the tangent plane T of the graph surface must be horizontal (parallel to the xy-plane). This means that its slope in any direction is zero, which is equivalent to requiring that both partial derivatives f_x and f_y be zero (Figure 18.2). Unfortunately, maxima or saddles with horizontal tangent plane exhibit vanishing first partial derivatives as well—and thus one also has to look at the second partial derivatives to confirm that one has a minimum. We omit the formulation of the resulting criteria.

Example (minimization of a quadratic function). We search for a minimizer of the quadratic function $f(x,y) = 3x^2 + y^2 - 6x - 4y + 8$. The partial derivatives are $f_x = 6x - 6$, $f_y = 2y - 4$, and setting them to zero yields as the only candidate for a minimizer the point $(x^*,y^*) = (1,2)$ with function value $f(1,2) = 1$. Looking at the function values at other points, it is easily seen that $(x^*,y^*) = (1,2)$ is really a minimizer of f. The graph surface $z = f(x,y)$ is an elliptic paraboloid with vertex $(1,2,1)$.

Admittedly, this example is extremely simple. However, it shows an important fact: The partial derivatives of a quadratic function f are linear functions and thus setting them to zero yields a system of linear equations. This holds for two variables as well as for an arbitrary number of variables.

The minimization of quadratic functions is a fundamental tool in optimization. Many numerical optimization techniques solve, in each iteration step, the minimization of a quadratic auxiliary function g—which approximates the function f in an appropriate way.

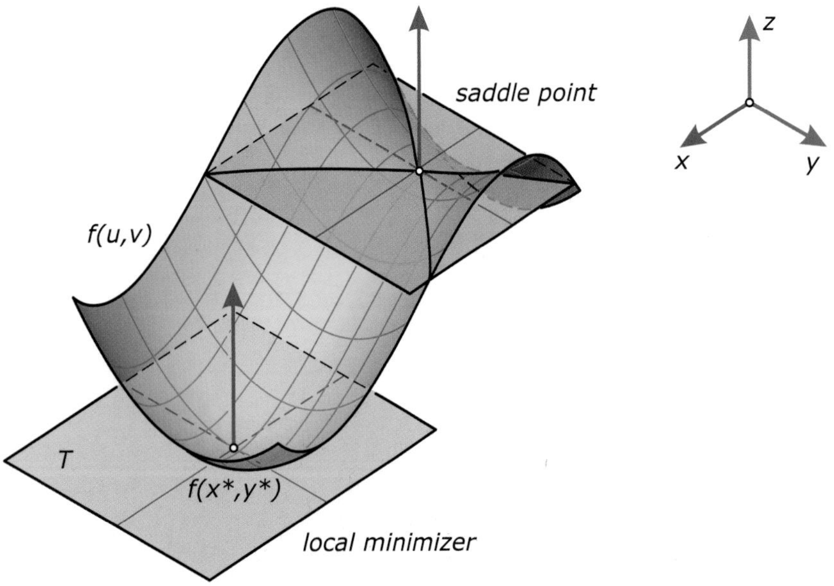

Fig. 18.2
At a local minimizer (x^*,y^*) of a function $f(x,y)$, the partial derivatives f_x and f_y of f are zero. This expresses the fact that the tangent plane T of the graph surface is parallel to the xy-plane. The same conditions hold at a maximum or at a saddle point with an xy-parallel tangent plane and thus the test for a minimum requires looking at the second derivatives as well.

Example

(roof design via least squares approximation). Assume that we want to span a roof in the shape of a hyperbolic paraboloid over a design. We have a number of points p_1, ..., p_N the roof shall pass through. However, they are numerous (more than six) to fulfill this requirement precisely.

To the rescue, we use *least squares approximation*. Among all hyperbolic paraboloids, we compute the one as close as possible to the N data points $p_1 = (x_1,y_1,z_1),\dots,p_N = (x_N,y_N,z_N)$. Due to structural reasons, we prefer a paraboloid P with vertical axis—which has in the underlying (x,y,z) coordinate system a representation of the form

$$P\colon z = ax^2 + 2bxy + cy^2 + dx + ey + f. \qquad \text{(P)}$$

For any choice of the coefficients a, b, c, d, e, f this is a paraboloid (for special choices, a parabolic cylinder or a plane). The condition for a hyperbolic paraboloid is $b^2 - ac > 0$. We do not include this inequality in our approximation because we assume that the best approximation to the input data will result in a hyperbolic paraboloid anyway. The (signed) distance of a data point, say p_1, to the paraboloid P (measured in the z direction) is computed as

$$d(p_1) = ax_1^2 + 2bx_1y_1 + cy_1^2 + dx_1 + ey_1 + f - z_1. \qquad \text{(D)}$$

Analogous expressions hold for the other data points. Least squares approximation now determines a,b,c,d,e,f such that the *sum of squared distances is minimized.* Thus, the objective function F is given by

$$F = d(p_1)^2 + d(p_2)^2 + \dots + d(p_N)^2.$$

Here, we have to insert expression D and similar ones for the occurring distances $d(p_i)$. The unknowns a,b,c,d,e,f occur linearly in the terms $d(p_i)$, and therefore quadratically in $d(p_i)^2$. Thus, F is a quadratic function of the six unknowns. According to the previous example, this eventually leads to the solution of a system of six linear equations. We do not provide the details of the system and just show a result in Figure 18.3.

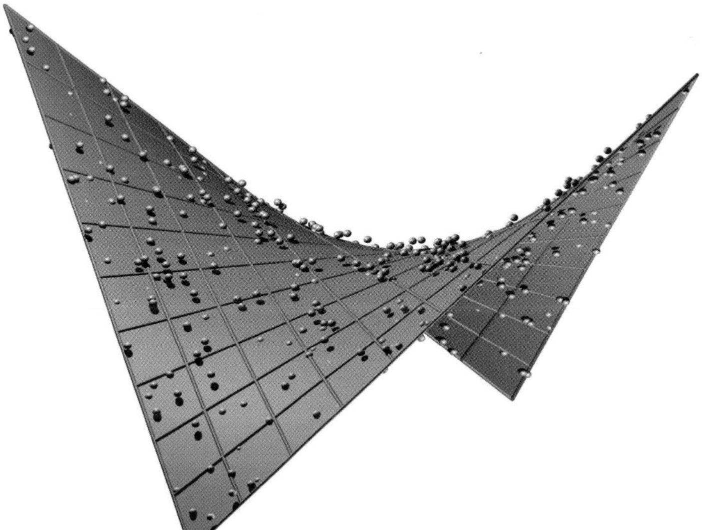

Fig. 18.3
The simple least squares approximation problem of optimally fitting a roof in the shape of a hyperbolic paraboloid to a number of points is an optimization problem in six dimensions.

We hope that the example shows why even simple problems end up in higher dimension. Note that we are *not* minimizing a function in x,y but a function in a,b,c,d,e,f (i.e., a function in six-dimensional space).

Gradient descent. Even at a point p that is not a minimizer, the partial derivatives are important. We form the *gradient* $\nabla f = (f_x, f_y)$, which is the vector whose coordinates are the partial derivatives of f with respect to x and y. The gradient is always pointing in the direction of steepest ascent and is thus orthogonal to the direction of no ascent [i.e., to the corresponding iso-line (level set) of f (recall Chapters 12 and 14 and see Figure 18.4)].

To move "downhill" toward a minimum one may always move in the direction of the negative gradient $-\nabla f$. This is the simplest numerical optimization algorithm, called *gradient descent*. At a local minimizer, the gradient vanishes and the descent algorithm stops there. This is exactly what one wants to achieve. There are much better gradient-based algorithms. Their idea is very similar to that which led us to pure gradient descent.

Shape optimization problems may be rather nasty from various perspectives. The objective function f may be very complicated and far away from a quadratic function. Moreover, the representation of a shape may depend on many variables. Just think of a surface represented as a triangle mesh.

Apart from a few mesh vertices, which may be fixed, the search for a surface that minimizes a certain objective function f has as unknowns the coordinates of the mesh vertices. For example, if the mesh is rather simple and only 100 vertices are subject to optimization the optimization problem has 300 variables.

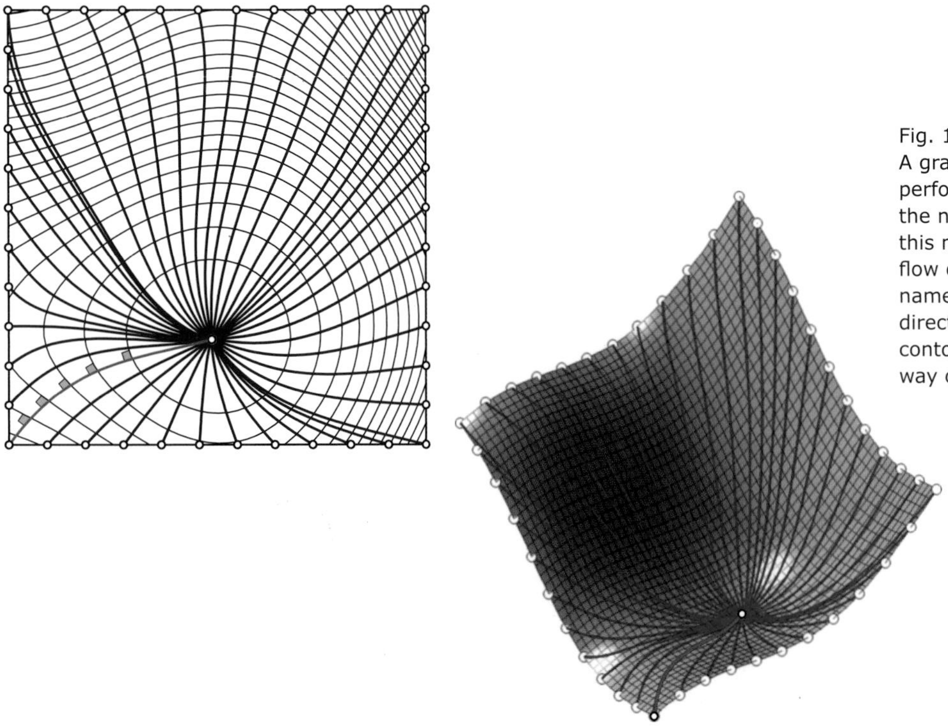

Fig. 18.4
A gradient descent algorithm iteratively performs small steps in the direction of the negative gradient. Geometrically, this means that one moves like the flow of water on the graph surface; namely, in the steepest descent direction (i.e., orthogonal to the contour lines). It is obvious that in this way one will reach a local minimizer.

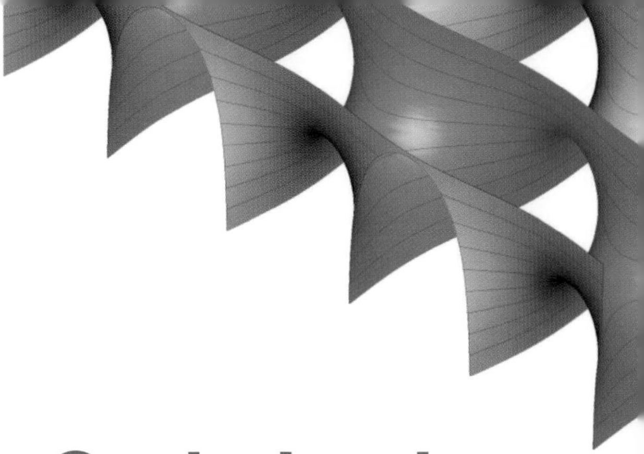

Geometric Optimization

We have previously encountered various geometric optimization problems such as registration, surface fitting, hole filling, and symmetrization. We will now focus on a few partially very famous types of curves, surfaces, and meshes that may be obtained as solutions of optimization problems and that merit attention from an architectural perspective.

Minimal surfaces. One of the oldest and most famous geometric optimization problems for surfaces is *Plateau's problem*, which was formulated by the French mathematician J. L. Lagrange (1769) but named after the Belgian physicist J. Plateau—who posed it in 1866 (Figure 18.5).

Given a smooth closed curve c without self-intersections, find the surface patch with boundary curve c that has the smallest surface area A.

The optimal surface S is called a *minimal surface*. We may observe a minimal surface as the shape of a soap membrane through a closed wire c. Neglecting gravity, surface tension implies that the soap membrane attains the shape of the surface with minimal surface area (recall Chapter 14). To obtain an interesting surface S, one requires c to be nonplanar because otherwise the solution S would be a planar patch.

The present problem is dependent on more than a finite number of variables, and in this sense it is more complicated than the optimization problems addressed previously. There is an infinite dimensional set of surface patches with a given boundary curve c, and among those one has to find the optimal solution (i.e., the one with the smallest surface area). Such a problem is called a *variational problem*.

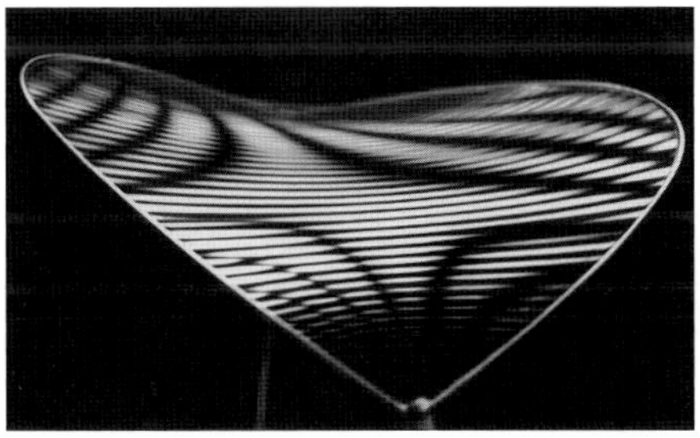

Fig. 18.5
Plateau's problem requires one to pass a surface with minimal surface area through a closed spatial curve c. Such surfaces can be observed at soap films. Frei Otto used soap films as "analogue computers" for form-finding purposes [Otto and Rasch 1995].
(left) Soap-film form-finding model with projected grid lines.
(right) Architectural realization at a church (1982–1983) in Bremen-Grolland by architect C. Schröck, consultant Frei Otto, and execution manager F. K. Schleyer and Company.

The variational equivalent to setting the gradient to zero yields a condition known as the Euler-Lagrange equation of the variational problem. Applying this method to the Plateau problem, one obtains an equation that expresses the following fundamental property: *A minimal surface has vanishing mean curvature in each of its points.*

Recall from Chapter 14 that mean curvature H is the mean value of the principal curvatures, $H = (k_1 + k_2)/2$. $H = 0$ is equivalent to $k_1 = -k_2$. Unless we have a flat point ($k_1 = k_2 = 0$), the two principal curvatures have different signs. Therefore, a generic surface point p of a minimal surface must be a *hyperbolic point* (saddle-like). At p, there is a locally approximating paraboloid (see equation (14.2), which is valid in an adapted coordinate system with origin at p, and x-axis and y-axis in principal curvature direction):

$$z = (k_1/2)(x^2 - y^2) = (k_1/2)(x + y)(x - y).$$

This is a hyperbolic paraboloid whose rulings in the plane $z = 0$ are the two orthogonal straight lines $x + y = 0$ and $x - y = 0$. These straight lines are the asymptotic directions (directions of vanishing normal curvature). We see that in each point of a minimal surface the asymptotic directions are orthogonal. In other words, the bisecting lines of the (always orthogonal) principal directions are the asymptotic directions.

A curve on a surface S in each point tangent to the corresponding asymptotic direction of S is called an *asymptotic curve*. Hence, on a minimal surface the asymptotic curves form an orthogonal curve network. It is the bisecting curve network of the network of principal curvature lines (Figure 18.6). The asymptotic curve network and the network of principal curvature lines can form the basis for realizations of minimal surfaces as frameworks of rigid straight rods with flexible connections. Applying appropriate forces at the boundary vertices, such frameworks may be brought into static equilibrium.

Fig. 18.6
A generic point of a minimal surface is a hyperbolic surface point with orthogonal asymptotic directions. The asymptotic curves, which always follow the asymptotic direction, form an orthogonal curve network that "bisects" the network of principal curvature lines.

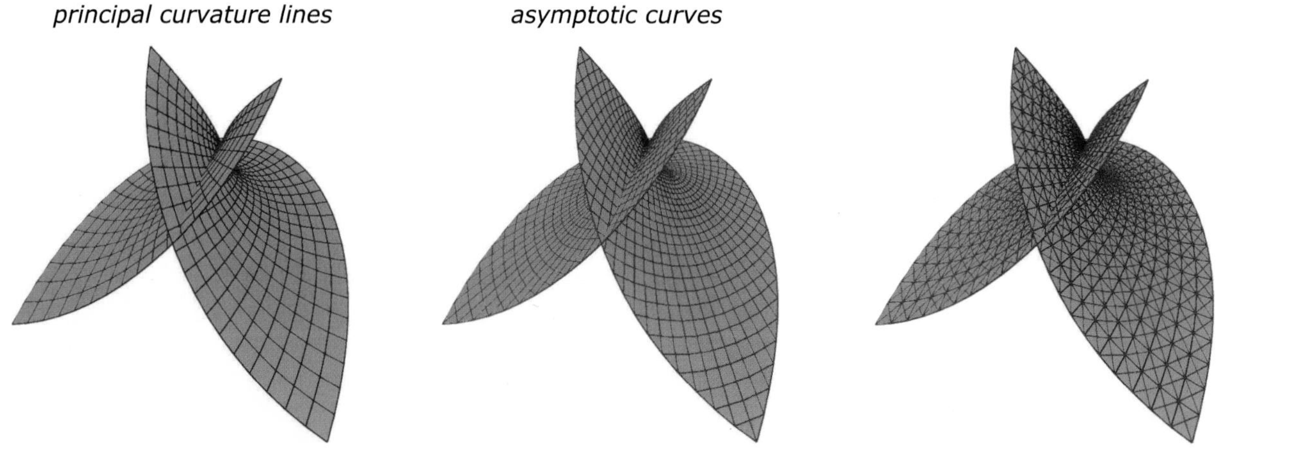

Minimal surfaces are also special with regard to the *Gaussian spherical mapping* G. Recall from Chapter 14 that G maps a surface point p onto that point p^* of the unit sphere S^*, which is described by the unit normal vector $n(p)$ of S at p. A curve c on S is mapped to a curve c^* on the sphere S^*.

For any (non-developable) surface S, the network of principal curvature lines on S is mapped onto an orthogonal curve network on S^*. For a minimal surface, the asymptotic curve network is also mapped to an orthogonal curve network of S^* (Figure 18.7). This is a result of the remarkable property that the *Gaussian spherical mapping of a minimal surface* S *to the unit sphere* S* *is conformal* (angle preserving).

In our study of nonlinear planar transformations (Chapter 5), we have mentioned that angle-preserving mappings of the plane are obtained via *complex functions*. It turns out that a minimal surface S can also be nicely represented with the help of a differentiable complex function—a fact related to the conformal Gaussian spherical mapping.

Let $t = u + iv$ be a complex variable (u and v are real) and $f(t)$ a complex function of t [i.e., the function values $f(t)$ are also complex]. Of course, i is the imaginary unit satisfying $i^2 = -1$. We call $R[t] = u$ the *real part* of a complex number $t = u + iv$, and $I[t] = v$ its *imaginary part*. Then, a representation of a minimal surface is given by

$$\begin{aligned} x &= I[(t^2 - 1)f''(t) - 2tf'(t) + 2f(t)], \\ y &= R[-(1 + t^2)f''(t) + 2tf'(t) - 2f(t)], \qquad \text{(M)} \\ z &= 2\,I[-tf''(t) + f'(t)]. \end{aligned}$$

Here, f' and f'' are the first and second derivatives, respectively. It is not allowed to insert a function f with vanishing third derivative, but otherwise one always obtains a minimal surface. Equations (M) may be seen as a parametric representation of a minimal surface in terms of u (real part of t) and v (imaginary part of t). The mapping from the uv-plane to S is always conformal. To illustrate the power of equations (M) for the generation of minimal surfaces, we give an example.

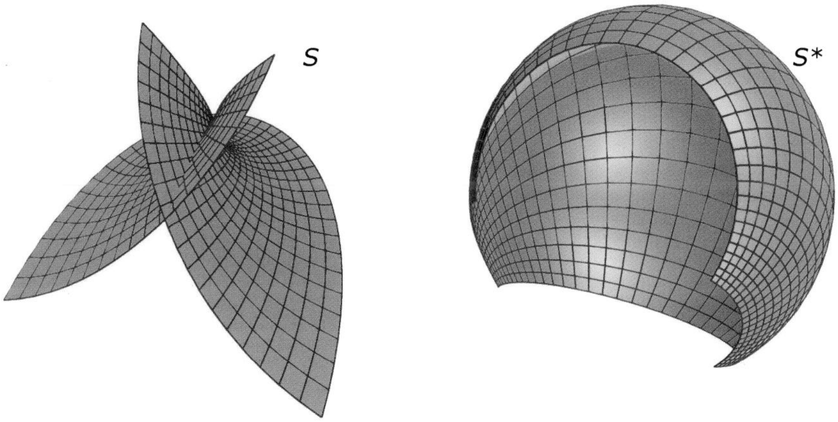

Fig. 18.7
The Gaussian spherical mapping of a minimal surface to the unit sphere preserves intersection angles of curves. This figure shows the orthogonal network of principal curvature lines on *S* and the corresponding orthogonal curve network on the unit sphere *S**.

Example:

Enneper surface. We set $f(t) = t^3$ in the representation (M). With $f'(t) = 3t^2$ and $f'(t) = 6t$ we obtain
$x = I[2t^3 - 6t), y = -R[2t^3 + 6t], z = 2I[-3t^2]$.

To return to real parameters u,v, we insert $t = u + iv$ and arrive at the parametric representation
$x = 6u^2v - 2v^3 - 6v, y = -2u^3 + 6uv^2 - 6u, z = -12\,uv$.

This simple polynomial minimal surface S is known as Enneper's minimal surface (Figure 18.8). The iso-parameter lines u = const and v = const are the asymptotic curves on S. The straight lines $u + v$ = const and $u - v$ = const of the uv parameter plane correspond to the principal curvature lines on S.

Both the asymptotic curves and the principal curvature lines are cubic curves. The principal curvature lines are even planar.

All minimal surfaces may be obtained from (M). We give a few further examples, but omit the derivation from equations (M).

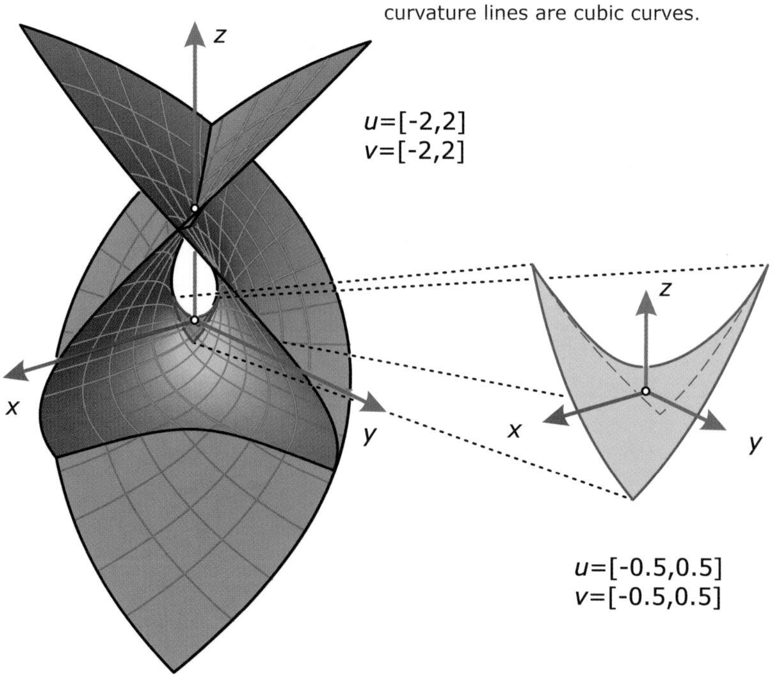

Fig. 18.8
Enneper's minimal surface is a polynomial minimal surface all of whose asymptotic curves and principal curvature lines are cubic curves.

Example:

Helicoid. We have already studied a minimal surface in Chapter 9; namely, the *helicoid*. Take a straight line G (e.g., the x-axis), which intersects an axis A (e.g., the z-axis) at a right angle. Then any helical motion about the axis A moves G along a helicoid. Helicoids are the only ruled surfaces among the minimal surfaces. Clearly, the rulings are one family of asymptotic curves. The other family of asymptotic curves constitute the helical paths (Figure 18.9).

Enneper's minimal surface: parameter lines

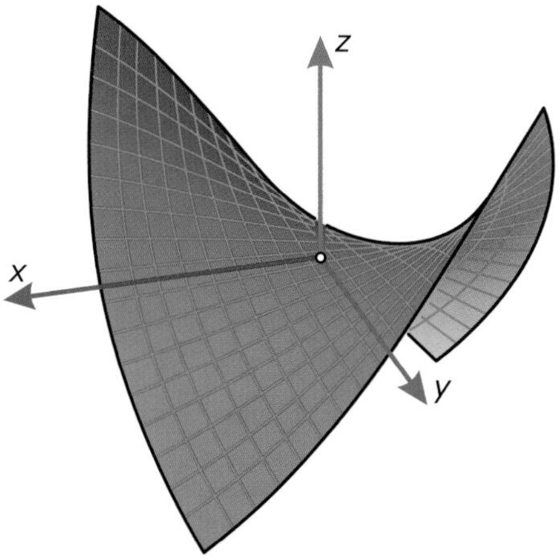

Enneper's minimal surface: principal curvature lines

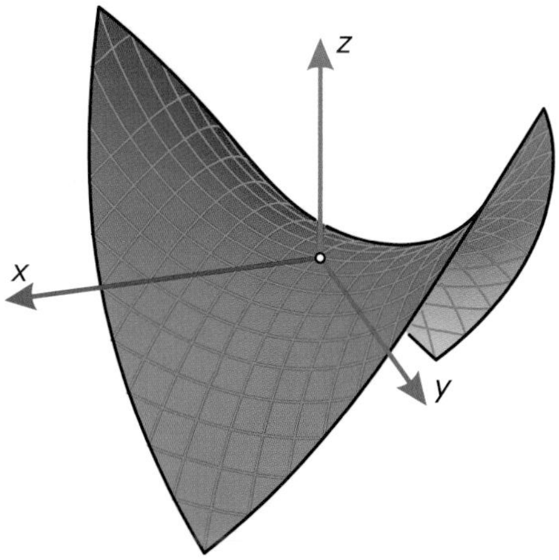

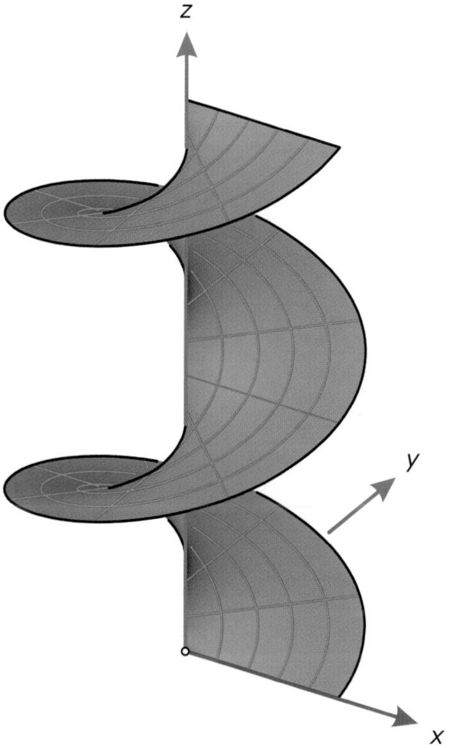

Fig. 18.9
Helicoids are the only ruled surfaces among the minimal surfaces (apart from the plane, which is minimal and ruled in an obvious way).

Example:

Rotational and helical minimal surfaces. Prior to the description of those minimal surfaces, which can be generated as rotational or helical surfaces, it is good to look at a remarkable planar curve—the *catenary* (Figure 18.10). It is the equilibrium shape attained by an idealized rope (homogeneous, completely flexible, and not extensible) under the influence of gravity.

An interesting property of the catenary is that the same curve appears as an equilibrium shape in multiple ways. Any two points of a catenary c can be used as support points, and one obtains the same curve c as equilibrium shape. The catenary (now gravity direction being inverted) is the ideal shape of an arc, and extensions of this idea are the frequently used hanging models (addressed later in this chapter). A mathematical representation of a catenary uses hyperbolic functions. These functions $\cosh(x)$ and $\sinh(x)$ are defined via the exponential function e^x as

$\cosh(x) = (e^x + e^{-x})/2$, $\sinh(x) = (e^x - e^x)/2$.

The catenary is basically the graph of the function $\cosh(x)$ and has the equation

$y = a\cosh(x/a)$.

Here, a is a constant that defines its point $(0, a)$ on the y-axis. Rotating the catenary about the x-axis, one obtains the *catenoid*—the only minimal surface of revolution.

To obtain all *helical surfaces among the minimal surfaces*, we consider $x = a \cdot \cosh(z/a)$ as an equation in an (x,y,z) system. It is a cylinder C with y-parallel rulings and a catenary as a base curve in the xz-plane. The envelope of this catenary cylinder C under any helical motion about the z-axis is a helical minimal surface.

Figure 18.11 shows some surfaces from a continuous sequence of helical minimal surfaces. These surfaces are isometric to each other [i.e., they can be bent into each other without stretching or tearing (the length of any curve on the surface remains unchanged)]. At the two ends of this bending sequence, we have the

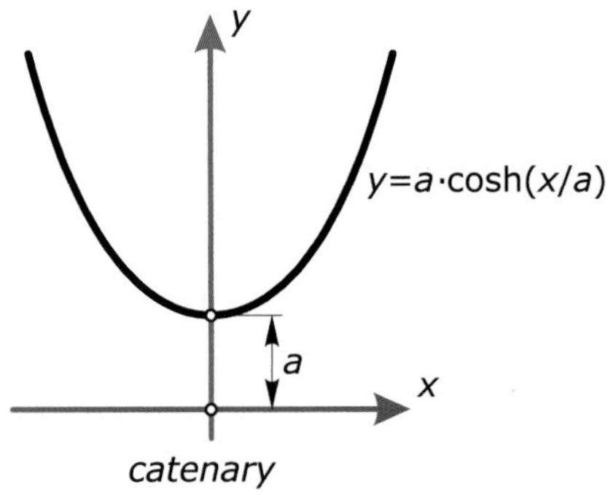

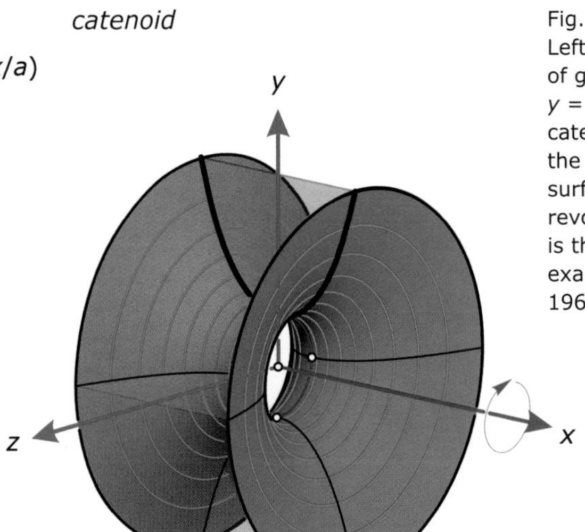

Fig. 18.10
Left: A rope attains under the influence of gravity the shape of the catenary $y = a\cosh(x/a)$. Right: Rotating the catenary about the x-axis, one obtains the catenoid. Up to similarities, this surface is the only minimal surface of revolution. Right page: The catenary is the ideal shape of an arc as for example in the Gateway Arch (1963–1965) in St. Louis by Eero Saarinen.

catenoid and the helicoid. To aid the reader in the implementation of this remarkable surface sequence, we add a parametric representation of helical minimal surfaces:

$x = a\cos(u)\cosh(v) + p\sin(u)\sinh(v),$

$y = a\sin(u)\cosh(v) - p\cos(u)\sinh(v),$

$z = av + pu.$

Here, u is the rotational angle about the z-axis and p is the pitch of the helical motion. With $p = 0$, one obtains the catenoid—whereas $a = 0$ yields a helicoid. To obtain the aforementioned bending sequence, we can select a and p according to $a = c{\cdot}\cos(\alpha)$, $p = c{\cdot}\sin(\alpha)$ and vary α in the interval $[0,\pi/2]$.

Fig. 18.11
After cutting the catenoid along a catenary, one can bend it (without changing the lengths of curves) into a part of a helicoid such that all intermediate positions are helical minimal surfaces.

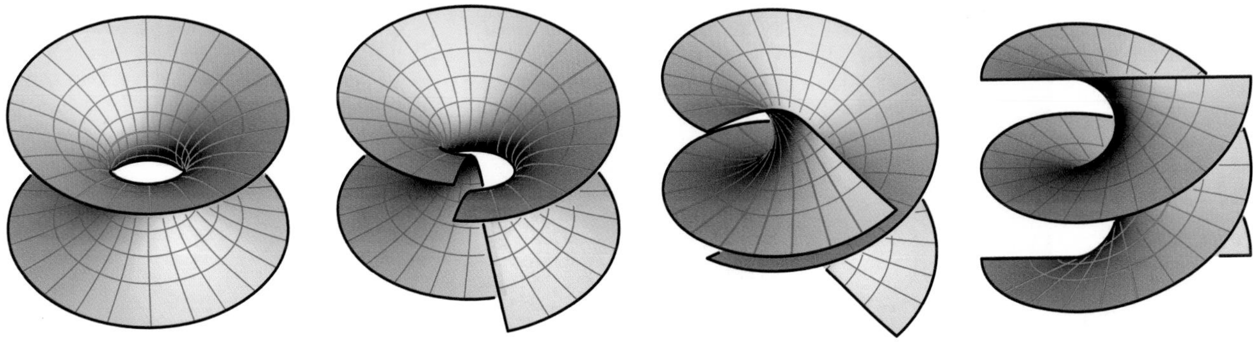

Example:

Scherk's minimal surface. A remarkable minimal surface was discovered by H. F. Scherk in 1834. Its explicit representation

$z = \ln(\cos y) - \ln(\cos x)$

shows that this surface is a translational surface. We may translate the planar curve $p_1 : x = 0, z = \ln(\cos y)$ along the planar profile curve $p_2 : y = 0, z = -\ln(\cos x)$ to obtain this surface (Figure 18.12). It is surprising that the Scherk surface can be generated as a translational surface in infinitely many ways. The complete Scherk surface has a periodic structure. Because we may write its equation as $z = \ln[\cos(y) / \cos(x)]$ and the logarithm is only defined for positive numbers, we can compute surface points only for those pairs (x,y) whose cosines $\cos x$, $\cos y$ have the same sign. This yields a regular pattern of squares in the xy-plane over which the surface is defined. The surface carries a few straight lines that fit well into this pattern (Figure 18.12).

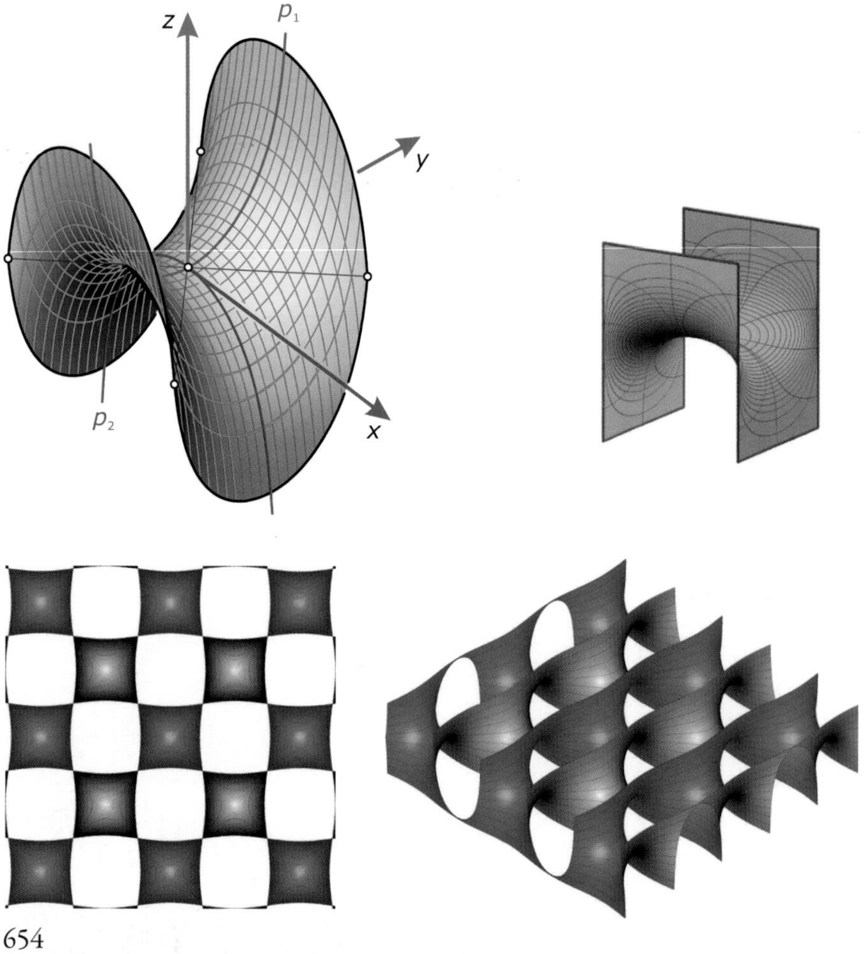

Fig. 18.12
Scherk's minimal surface can be generated by translation of a planar profile p_1 along another planar profile curve p_2.
(right) The Scherk surface carries straight lines and
(bottom) has a periodic structure.

Numerical solution of the Plateau problem. Although equations (M) (p.649) are capable of producing all possible minimal surfaces, they cannot be used to solve Plateau's problem for a given closed curve c. The solution of the Plateau problem is achieved with a numerical optimization algorithm. It approximates the given closed curve c with a polygon and the minimal surface with a mesh, typically a triangle mesh.

Usually, the connectivity of the mesh is specified in advance and only the geometry is found via optimization. Among all meshes of the given connectivity and with the given boundary vertices on c, the algorithm computes the mesh with the minimal surface area. This is an optimization problem with $3N$ unknowns, where N is the number of vertices in the mesh that are not on c (i.e., whose position has to be found by the algorithm).

Figure 18.13 shows examples that have been computed in such a way. A frequently used tool used to compute minimal surfaces and related optimal surfaces is K. Brakke's *surface evolver* [Brakke 1992].

(a)

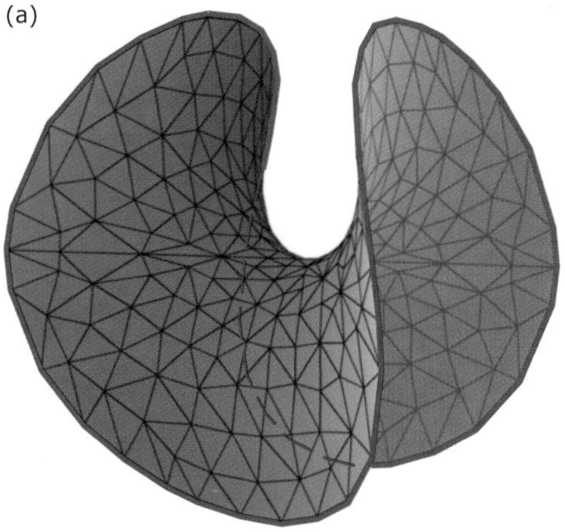

(b)

Fig. 18.13
(a) The Plateau problem can be solved via numerical optimization algorithms that approximate the surface to be constructed by a triangle mesh.
(b) The Costa minimal surface as shown in the movie "Touching Soap Films" (Image courtesy of A. Arnez, K. Polthier, M. Steffens, and C. Teitzel).

Surfaces with constant mean curvature. Minimal surfaces have constant mean curvature zero. Those surfaces whose mean curvature H has a constant value different from zero possess remarkable geometric properties. In fact, these *constant mean curvature* (CMC) *surfaces* occur in a generalization of Plateau's problem; namely, when looking for an area-minimizing surface under a volume constraint.

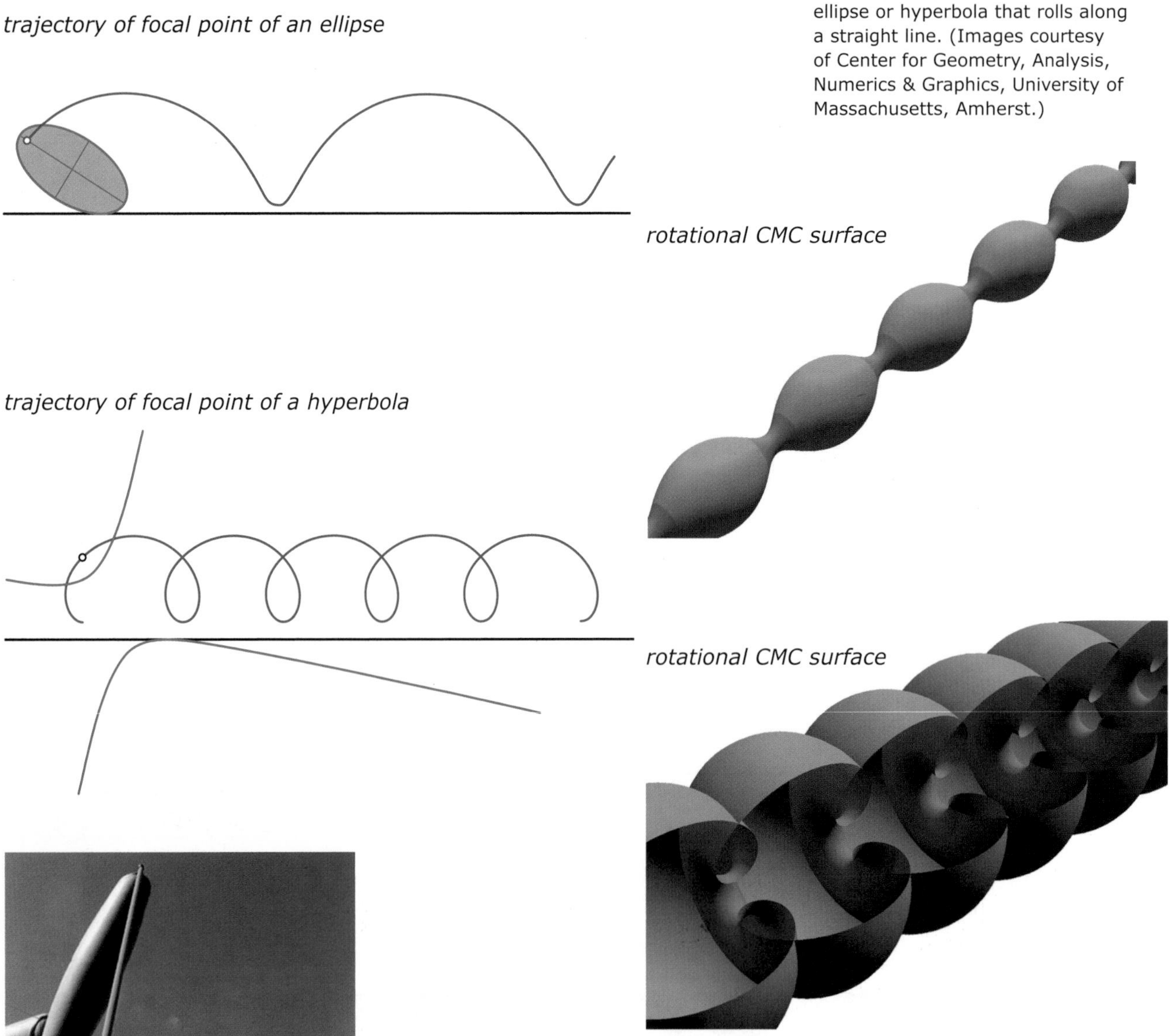

Fig. 18.15
The Delaunay surface is a surface of revolution with constant mean curvature. Its profile can be generated as a trajectory of the focal point of an ellipse or hyperbola that rolls along a straight line. (Images courtesy of Center for Geometry, Analysis, Numerics & Graphics, University of Massachusetts, Amherst.)

Fig. 18.14
Shapes closely related to surfaces of constant mean curvature occur in architecture at pneumatic constructions. Pneumatic Hall 'Airtecture' (1996) in Esslingen-Berkheim, Germany, constructed for Festo [Schock, 1997].

They arise as shapes of thin films in the presence of different pressure values on either side. One may see CMC surfaces at the boundaries of cells in foams. In architecture, approximate CMC surfaces occur at pneumatic constructions (Figure 18.14). The simplest CMC surface is of course a sphere. Figure 18.15 shows CMC surfaces of revolution. Their profile curves are trajectories of the focal point of an ellipse or hyperbola that rolls along a straight line. If the rolling conic is a parabola, the focus generates a catenary. The resulting catenoid (Figure 18.10) is a minimal surface and thus has constant mean curvature $H = 0$. Recent research in differential geometry has led to powerful software for the generation of minimal surfaces or CMC surfaces (see Figure 18.16).

Fig. 18.16
Some CMC surfaces generated with CMCLab, developed at the Center for Geometry, Analysis, Numerics & Graphics, University of Massachusetts, Amherst. (Images courtesy of F. Pedit.)

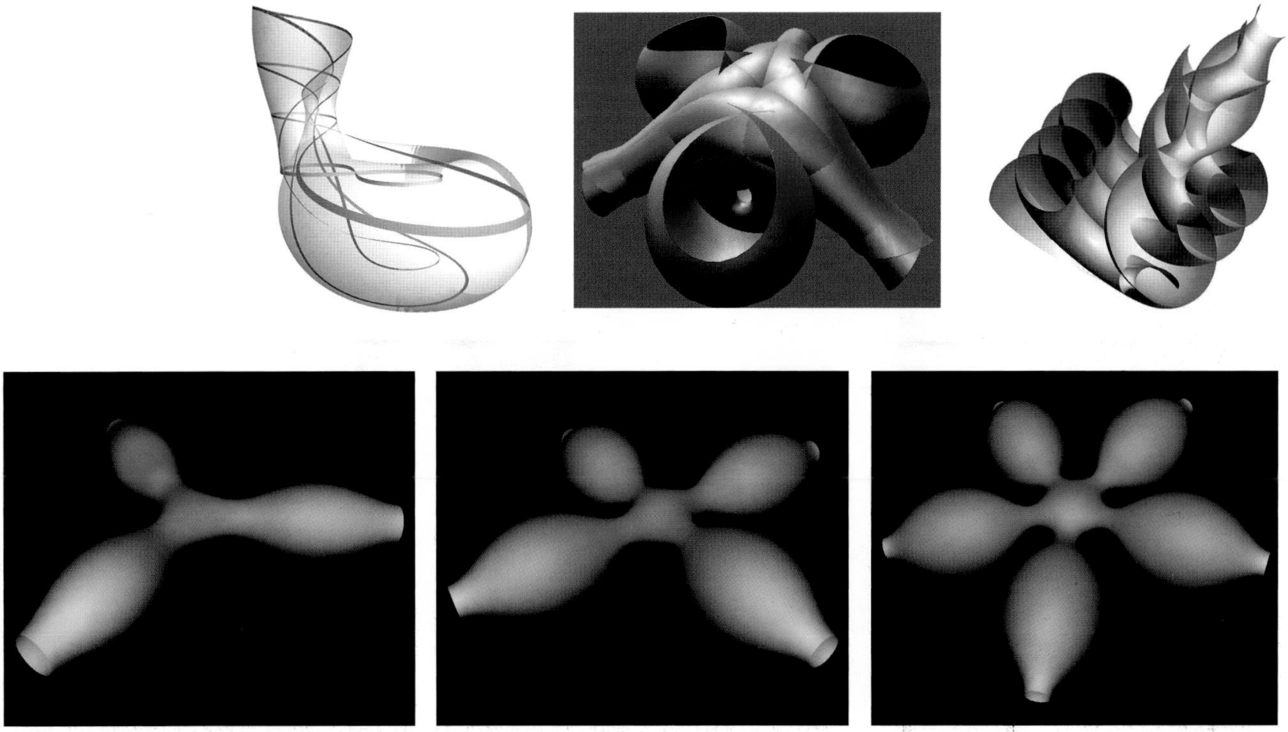

Willmore energy. The search for aesthetic shapes may be based on the minimization of objective functions that express a balanced distribution of curvature along the surface. Various ways of achieving this have been proposed in the literature (see, for example, Sequin [2005]). We address here one famous approach based on *Willmore energy* E_W:

Consider a surface S, form the squared difference $(k_1 - k_2)^2$ of principal curvatures at each point, and "sum up" these values. "Summing up" means integration over the surface S. With dA as surface area element, the surface area is the integral of the constant function 1 (i.e., $A = \int_S dA$). Willmore energy is the surface integral of the function $(k_1 - k_2)^2$:

$$E_W = \int_S (k_1 - k_2)^2 dA.$$

The surface integral is easily understood if we approximate the surface by a fine triangle mesh and assign a value $(k_1 - k_2)^2(T_j)$ to each triangle T_j. If A_j is the area of T_j, the integral is approximated by the sum of products $A_j \cdot (k_1 - k_2)^2(T_j)$ over all triangles.

Because $(k_1 - k_2)^2$ is never negative, E_W is never negative. The smallest possible value is obtained for a surface with $k_1 - k_2 = 0$ at all points (i.e., for a sphere). In some sense, we may say that the Willmore energy tries to make surfaces as spherical as possible. An important advantage of the Willmore energy is that one can prescribe a boundary strip (i.e., a boundary curve plus tangent planes along it) and compute an energy minimizer that interpolates these data.

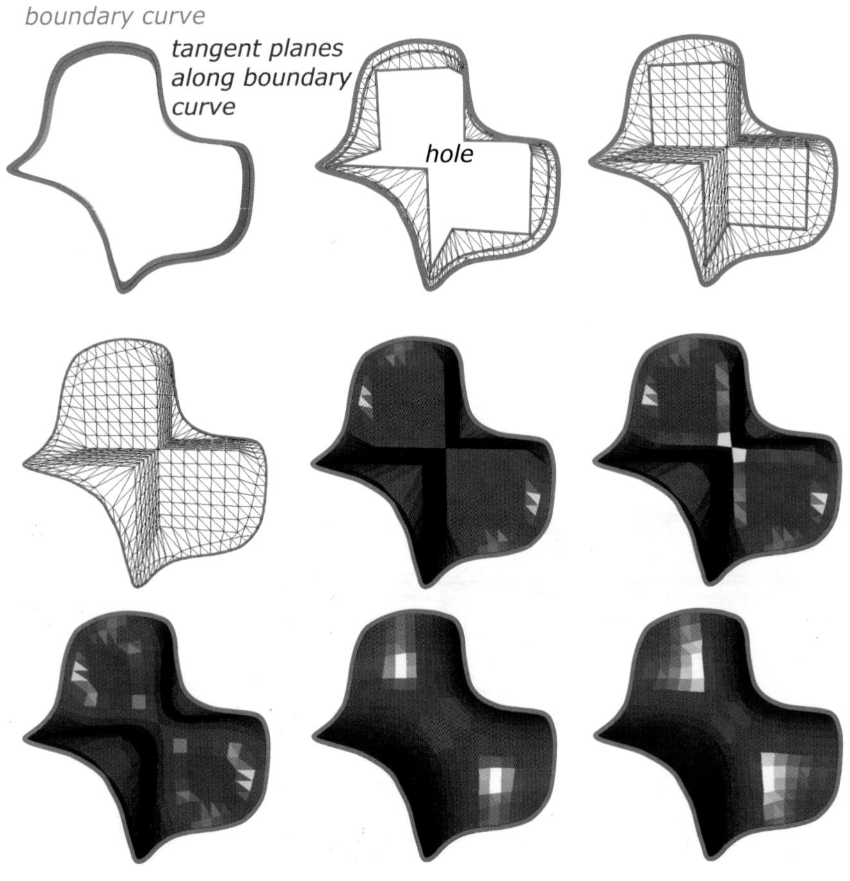

Fig. 18.17
For the minimization of Willmore energy, one may prescribe a boundary curve and tangent planes along it. Hence, one can use surfaces that minimize Willmore energy as smooth blending surfaces between given surfaces. A related application is to smoothly fill a hole of a surface. These images illustrate some steps of an optimization algorithm that iteratively reduces the Willmore energy. (Images courtesy of A. Bobenko and P. Schröder.)

Applications of this fact include the computation of smooth blending surfaces between given surfaces or smooth hole-filling techniques ([Bobenko and Schröder 2005], Figure 18.17). More complicated surfaces that are minimizers of the Willmore energy are shown in Figure 18.18. There is also a physical reason for studying Willmore energy. Thin flexible structures are governed by a surface energy (in which Willmore energy is involved) that reduces to the Willmore energy in a special case.

Fair curves and polygons. Let's now take a step back and discuss shape optimization for curves. We are doing this as preparation for the discussion of curve networks, which constitute a possible modeling tool for surfaces. The bending energy of an idealized thin elastic beam is proportional to the integral of the squared curvature, expressed as

$$E = \int_c k^2 \, ds.$$

The integral is taken over the curve, which may be understood as follows. We use a parameterization $c(s) = (x(s),y(s))$ of the curve (see Chapter 7), where the parameter s is the length of the curve segment from its initial point $c(0)$ to the point $c(s)$ under consideration. The parameter s runs from zero (initial point) to L, where L is the total length of the curve.

If $k(s)$ is the curvature of c at $c(s)$, the curve integral from the previous equation is an ordinary integral; that is, $E = \int (k(s))^2 ds$ extended from 0 to L. We may visualize the integral with a polygonal approximation of the curve. We form the sum $\sum k^2(e_j) \cdot L_j$. Here, the values k^2 are assigned to the edges e_j, and L_j are the corresponding edge lengths.

Fig. 18.18
Surfaces minimizing Willmore energy and computed by numerical optimization. (Images courtesy of F. Pedit.)

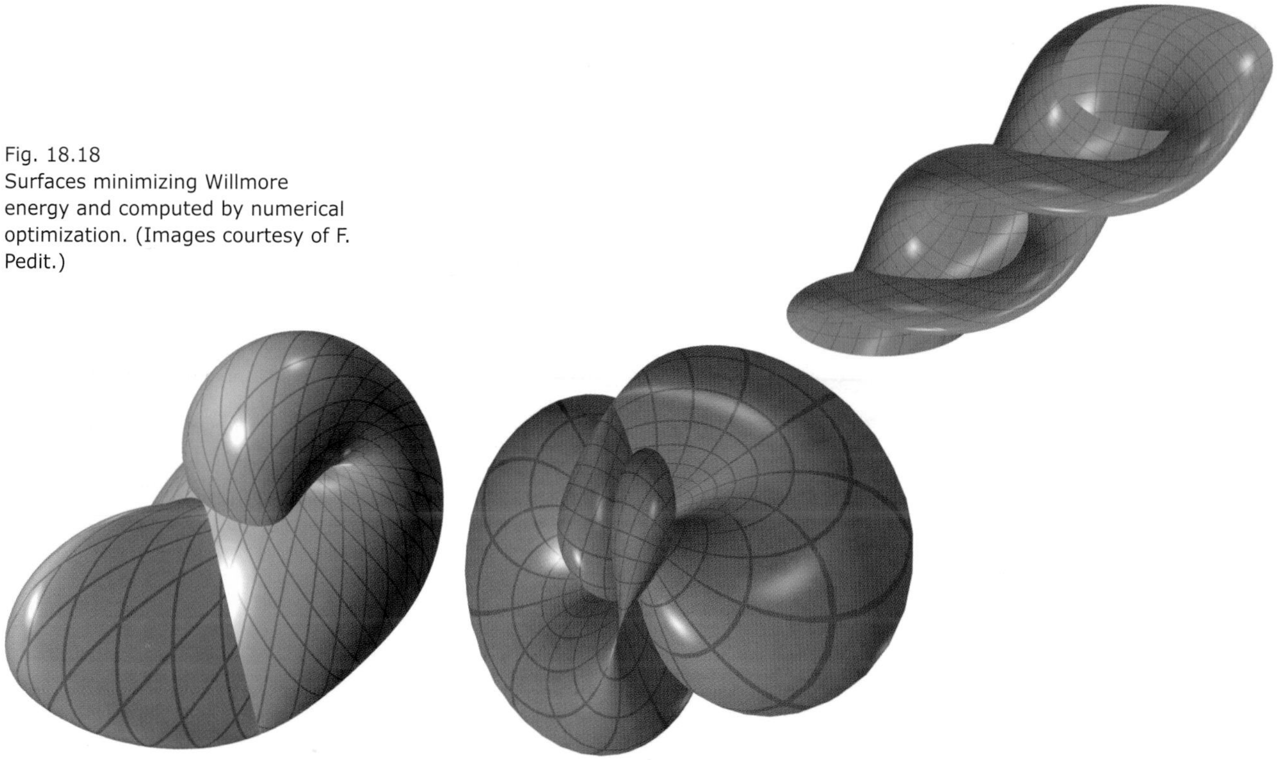

The minimization of E was studied by Leonhard Euler (1730), who coined the name *elastica* for the minimizers. More recently, Euler's elastica received interest in geometric computing (e.g., for the generation of aesthetic curves that pass through given points). In fact, the drawing tool of a spline (Chapter 8) produces shapes of least bending energy. Ordinary cubic spline interpolation is based on a simplification of the energy E. Instead of studying this simplification for smooth curves, we immediately proceed to the discrete version (which acts on polygons).

Consider a polygon, in the plane or in space, whose vertices are given by their coordinate vectors $v_1, v_2, ..., v_N$. We select a vertex (say v_2) and its neighboring vertices v_1 and v_3. Let $m_2 = (v_1 + v_3)/2$ be the midpoint of v_1v_3. We now compute the squared distance $d_2^2 = (v_2 - m_2)^2$ of points v_2 and m_2. Analogously, we can compute a squared distance value d_k^2 at any inner vertex v_k (Figure 18.19).

Assuming that the edge lengths of the polygon are not varying too much, the distance d_k is an appropriate discrete curvature measure at v_k. Hence, the sum E_s of these squared distances is a (rough) approximation of the bending energy E. Because $d_k^2 = (v_{k-1} + v_{k+1} - 2v_k)^2/4$ is a quadratic function of the coordinates of the involved vertices, the sum

$$E_s = (1/4) \sum (v_{k-1} + v_{k+1} - 2v_k)^2$$

is a quadratic function of the vertex coordinates. This makes the use of E_s simple. For example, if we want to interpolate some points we fix appropriate vertices and compute the remaining ones by minimization of E_s. Because it is a quadratic function in the unknown vertex coordinates, its minimization requires only the solution of a system of linear equations.

Because the resulting curves may exhibit undesirable undulations, one attaches some tension to it by adding a tension term $T = \sum (v_{k+1} - v_k)^2$ with some weight w. Minimization of the tension term alone would just give a straight line, but minimization of the combined objective function $E_t = E_s + w \cdot T$ is a useful tool for controlling the tension of the curve to be designed (see Figure 18.20).

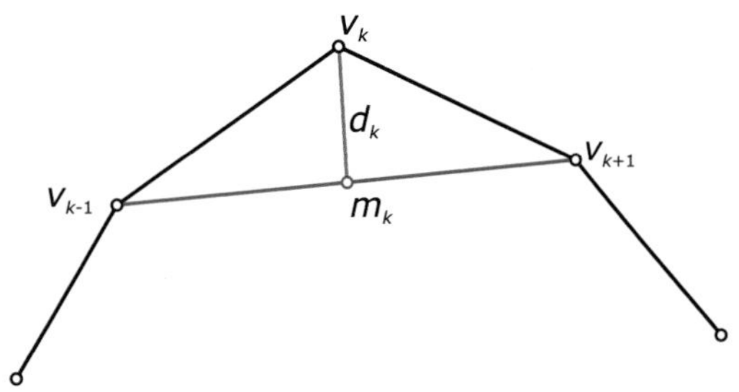

Fig. 18.19
The distance d_k between a vertex v_k of a polygon and the midpoint m_k of its left and right neighbor is a rough discrete curvature measure. The sum of the squared distances is a simple fairness measure for polygons. It is a quadratic function in the coordinates of the vertices and is therefore easy to minimize.

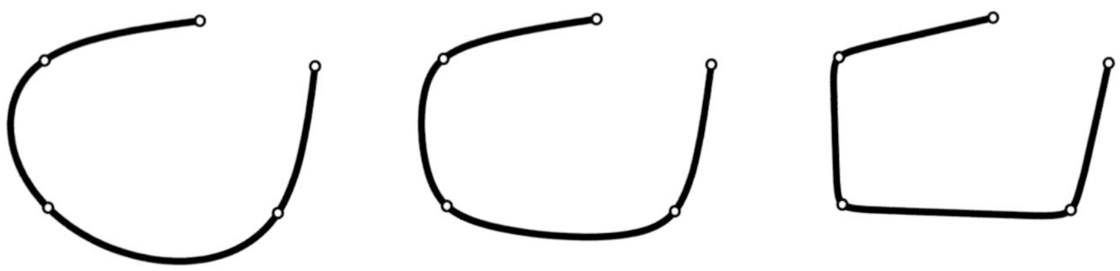

Fig. 18.20
(left) Minimization of the simplified discrete bending energy E_s
(middle and right) may lead to pleasing shapes, whose tension can be increased by adding a tension term with an appropriate weight w. The involved objective functions are quadratic and thus their minimization requires only the solution of a system of linear equations.

Fair curves on surfaces. Curve design based on minimization of E_s or E_t is so simple that extensions can also be handled well. Examples of such extensions include the design of smooth interpolating curves on surfaces (Figure 18.21), curves in the presence of obstacles (Figure 18.22), and even curves that follow features of surfaces (Figure 18.23) (see Hofer and Pottmann [2004]). Minimization of an energy consisting only of the tension term and restricting the curve to a surface yields a geodesic path (shortest path) on the surface (Figure 18.21, right; for geodesics, see Chapter 15).

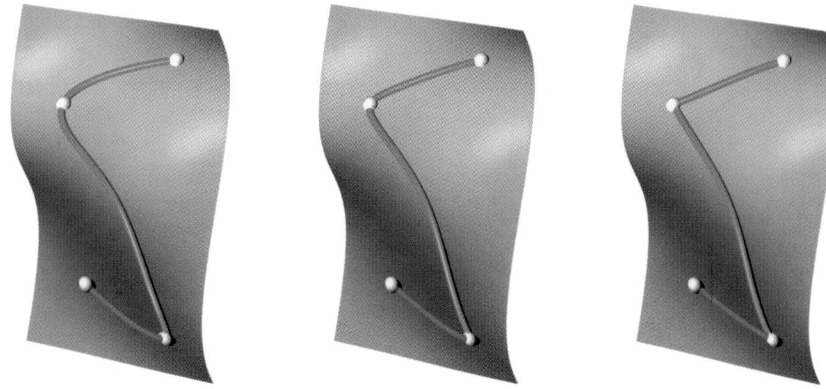

Fig. 18.21
(from left to right) Curve interpolation on surfaces with increasing tension can also be performed by minimization of the energies E_s or E_t. However, one has to make sure that the vertices of the polygonal approximations of these curves lie on the given surface. This is computationally more demanding.

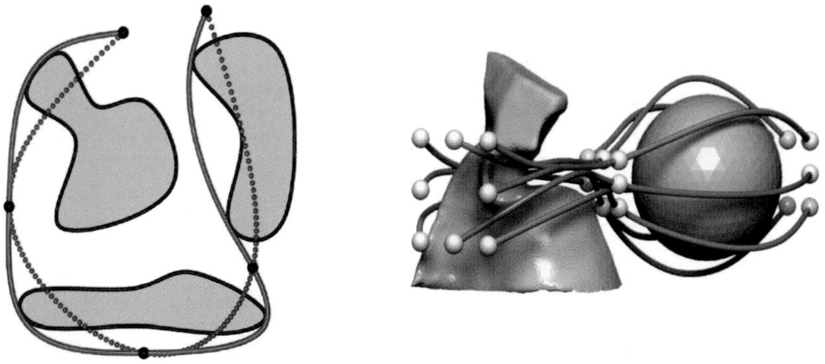

Fig. 18.22
Curve design based on discrete energy minimization is also nicely combinable with the avoidance of obstacles.

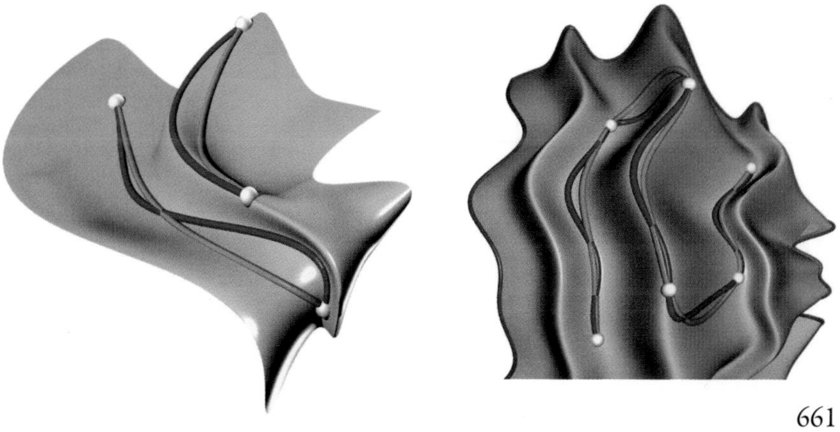

Fig. 18.23
There are algorithms that support the user in the design of curves following the features of the surface.

Fair webs and mesh beautification. A further extension of fair curves concerns *curve networks*. These networks may be free in space or be restricted to a given surface. The energy of the network is defined as the sum of energies of type E_s or E_t applied to each curve in the network. The resulting *fair webs* [Wallner et al. 2007] can be used for the generation of meshes that follow the design intent (Figure 18.24).

The aesthetic quality of meshes in architecture and other design applications where the meshes are actually materialized also depends on the behavior of the mesh polygons contained in the mesh. Therefore, a design tool that constructs such meshes by energy minimization of these polygons may be welcome. An attempt to use this in design is shown in Figure 18.24.

In connection with aesthetic meshes, we also have to recall relaxation (Chapter 11). The following form of relaxation is simple and easy to implement. Iteratively displace each vertex to the barycenter of its neighboring vertices. If one has to remain on a given surface S, one moves to the projection of the barycenter onto S. A result of relaxation for a real architectural data set is shown in Figure 18.25. In this example, we have constrained boundary vertices to boundary curves (not shown)—and the corner vertices have been fixed.

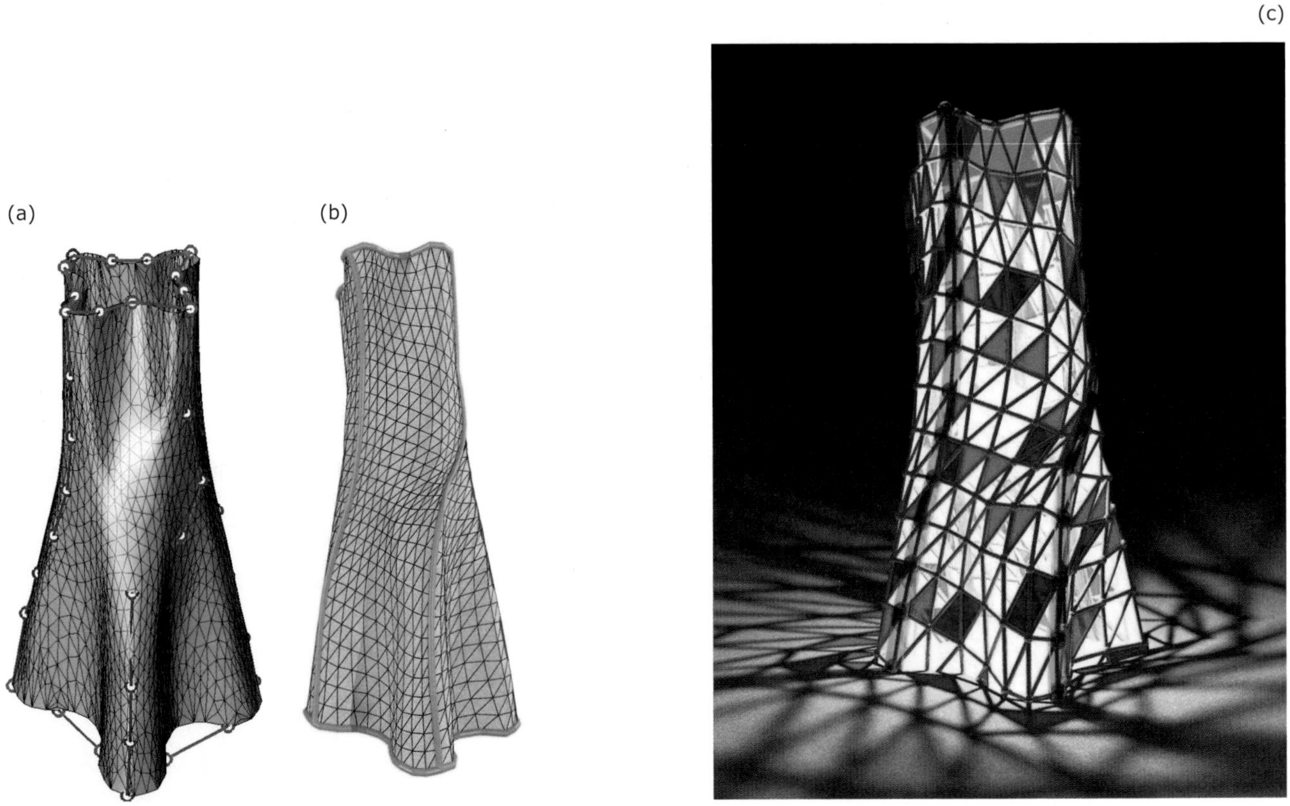

Fig. 18.24
Aesthetic remeshing of a triangulated model.
(a) User input on the original triangle mesh.
(b) Fair mesh interpolating the given input polygons.
(c) Design based on a coarser fair mesh interpolating the given input polygons.

Geometric constraints. In the previous discussion we encountered constraints at various places. These concern fixed boundaries, obstacles, curves or networks constrained to surfaces, curves close to features, and so on. Other constraints in geometric modeling for architectural applications may be constraints on enclosed volumes, maximal height, or avoiding local minima (for the flow of water).

The avoidance of local minima is always guaranteed for minimal surfaces because these have only saddle-like surface points. More precisely, they follow the *maximum principle* (i.e., the points with maximal and minimal height occur at the boundary curve of the considered surface patch). The inclusion of constraints is often not a simple task, but there are powerful optimization packages that can be used.

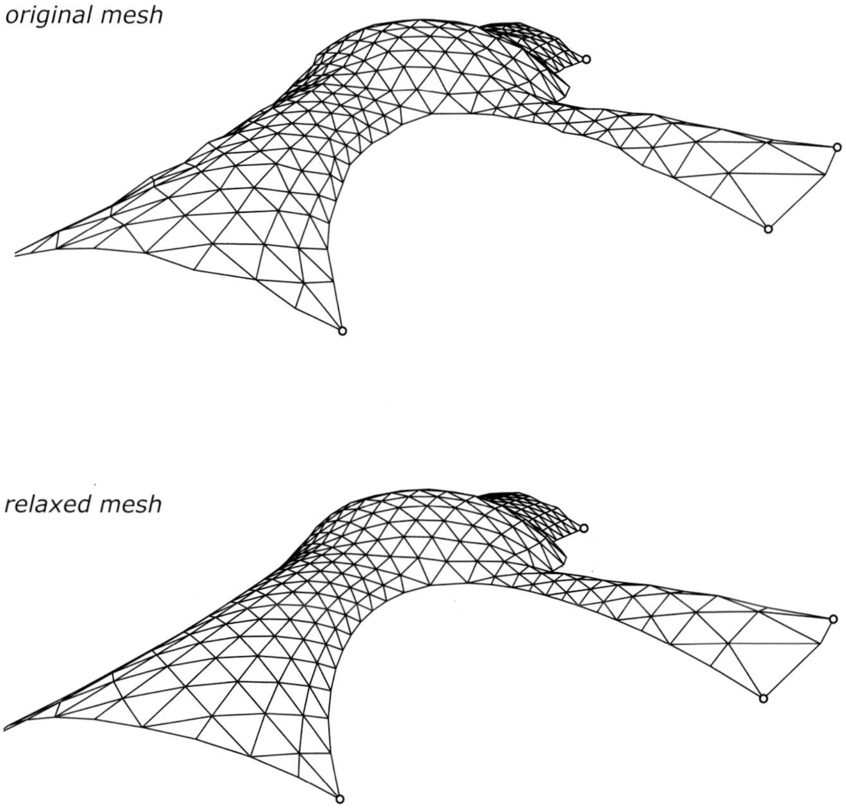

Fig. 18.25
An example of mesh relaxation (image courtesy of Simon Flöry).

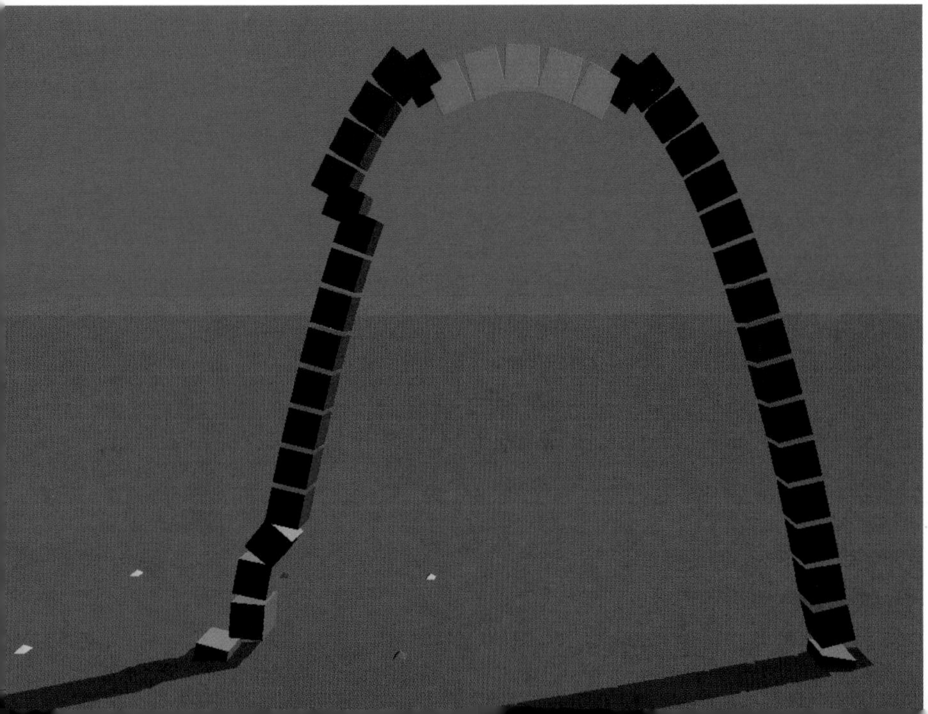

Fig. 18.26
Steering form example for a simple catenary chain of blocks. The blue and green sections have moment connections allowing for no catenary parts in the arc. (Image from research by Axel Kilian.)

Functional Optimization

Functional optimization goes beyond geometry and thus also beyond the objective of the present book. Therefore, only a few topics with a very geometric flavor are addressed.

Hanging models. The catenary curve can be easily computed by using the hyperbolic cosine function introduced previously. This simple case is applicable if a hanging line connects two fixed support points. But once three hanging lines—supported at different points—connect at a (non-fixed) point we cannot provide such a simple explicit solution. Of course in practice one uses much more complicated systems of hanging lines.

Here we have to adopt a solver-based approach to compute an equilibrium solution. The model we can choose is one of point masses (referred to as particles) and weightless springs, which generate a force when displaced from their rest length proportional to their spring constant. This model is called a particle spring model and is a general force-solving model that can be used to approximate the hanging model case.

The solver sums all forces present and moves each node in the system by a small step toward an equilibrium state that is reevaluated at each solver step based on the previous changes to the model. Recently, these solvers were greatly improved in stability and speed—mainly in an effort to make cloth simulation in animation more interactive and robust for design use [Baraff and Witkin 1998].

The particle spring model gives a good approximation of the catenary curve but is not perfect because the springs need to stretch in order for the solver to function. Therefore, the catenary chain is subject to small deformation. A further extension of optimization in design is the experimental use of optimization selectively to steer a form toward a desired form, allowing some suboptimal regions to occur. Most pure optimal hanging forms are rather limited in their formal language, and working with a mixture of optimal and suboptimal forms increases the vocabulary of forms (Figure 18.26).

Membranes. There is a long tradition of textile building in architecture, in particular around Frei Otto at the institute for Lightweight Structures in Stuttgart (see *http://www.uni-stuttgart.de/ilek/* and Otto and Rasch [1995]). Membranes are related to minimal surfaces, with the exception that they have a finite amount of material and therefore a finite resistance to stretching.

Nevertheless, when calculating a surface a pattern can be created that approximates the desired surface and finds its form under tension. In the physical application, the direction of fabric plays a crucial role in the membrane behavior because the stretch factor can vary dramatically depending on the thread direction.

Figure 18.27 shows applications of membrane structures. We refer here also to *Formfinder*, a software tool developed by R. Wehdorn-Roithmayr to assist architects in the preliminary design of form-active structures [Wehdorn-Roithmayr 2003].

A recent beautiful example of a membrane structure was the installation by Anish Kapoor at the Tate Modern in London. The membrane was carefully optimized by a group at Arup, London, under the lead of Cecil Balmond (Figure 18.28).

Fig. 18.27
Examples of membrane structures in architecture (images courtesy of Robert Wehdorn-Roithmayr).

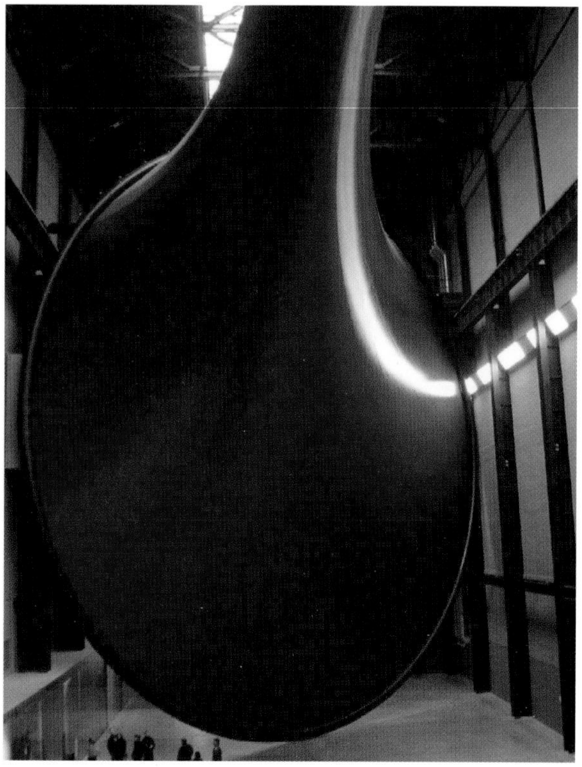

Fig. 18.28
Anish Kapoor's membrane installation at the Tate Modern in London.

References and Further Reading

Baraff D, Witkin A. Large steps in cloth simulation. Computer Graphics 1998;32:43–54.

Bobenko A, Schröder P. Discrete Willmore flow. *Proceedings of the Eurographics Symposium on Geometry Processing, 2005.* 2005:101–110.

Brakke K. The surface evolver. Experimental Math 1992;1:141–165. (*Surface Evolver Manual*: *http://www.susqu.edu/facstaff/b/brakke/evolver.*)

Hofer M, Pottmann H. Energy minimizing splines in manifolds. ACM Transactions on Graphics 2004;23:284–293.

Isler H. New shapes for shells. Bulletin of the IASS 1960;8.

Frei O, Rasch B. *Finding Form*. Stuttgart: Edition Axel Menges 1995.

Pinkall U, Polthier K. Computing discrete minimal surfaces and their conjugates. Experimental Math 1993;2:15–36.

Sequin C. CAD tools for aesthetic engineering. Computer Aided Design 2005;37:737–50.

Schock, H-J. *Soft Shells*. Birkhäuser 1997.

Tomlow J (with contributions by Graefe, R). Das Modell. Karl Krämer Verlag, 1989.

Wallner J, Pottmann H, Hofer M. Fair webs. Visual Computer 2007;23:83–94.

Wehdorn-Roithmayr R, Formfinder. PhD thesis, TU Vienna, 2003.

Chapter 19

Discrete Freeform Structures

Discrete Freeform Structures

The realization of freeform shapes in architecture poses great challenges to engineering and design. The complete design and construction process involves many aspects, including form finding, feasible segmentation into panels, functionality, materials, statics, and cost. Geometry alone is not able to provide solutions for the entire process, but a solid geometric understanding is an important step toward a successful realization of such a project. In particular, it is essential to know about the available degrees of freedom for shape optimization.

There is a current trend toward architectural freeform shapes based on *discrete surfaces*, largely realized as steel/glass structures (see Figure 19.1). The most basic, convenient, and structurally stable way of representing a smooth shape in a discrete way is via the use of *triangle meshes*. We will discuss them briefly, but then proceed toward attractive alternatives; namely, *quadrilateral meshes with planar faces* (*PQ meshes*).

The latter tend to have less weight and can be constructed with geometrically optimized nodes in the supporting beam layout. We will see that the geometry of such PQ meshes is more difficult than that of triangle meshes. Especially challenging are the aesthetic layout of edges, planarity of faces, and optimization of nodes in the underlying supporting beam structure.

Fig. 19.1
Zlote Tarasy in Warsaw at various stages of the construction (Images courtesy of Waagner-Biro Stahlbau AG).

Discrete surfaces may be present in freeform architecture in various ways. The discrete representation may not be visible and may simply be used to support the final skin (see Figure 19.2). On the other hand, in steel/glass or similar structures (such as those shown in Figure 19.1) the mesh directly determines the aesthetics of the entire building and thus the mesh must be optimized to very high quality. This high aesthetical mesh quality has hardly been touched so far by the research communities in geometric modeling or geometry processing.

Only very recently researchers became interested in the challenging problems that arise in connection with discrete surfaces in architecture. We have been involved in this research and we believe there is still a lot of room for future research. Thus, we would like to conclude our book with this topic—which is situated at the cutting edge of research in architectural geometry.

Fig. 19.2
The *Kunsthaus* (2000–2003) in Graz by P. Cook and C. Fournier.
(bottom) The fluid body of the outer skin.
(right) An interior view during construction, showing the triangulated and flat physical layers of the inner skin. (Images courtesy of S. Brell-Cokcan and M. Hofer.)

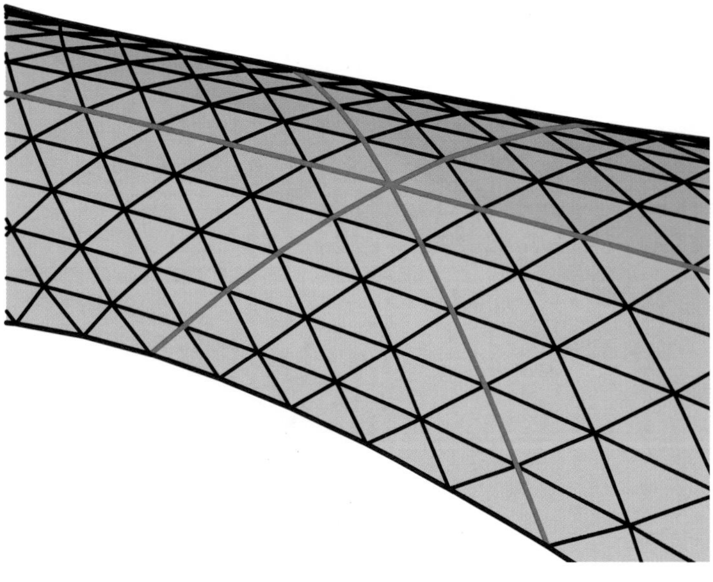

Fig. 19.3
Triangle meshes that can be arranged into three families of fair polygons tend to be visually pleasing.

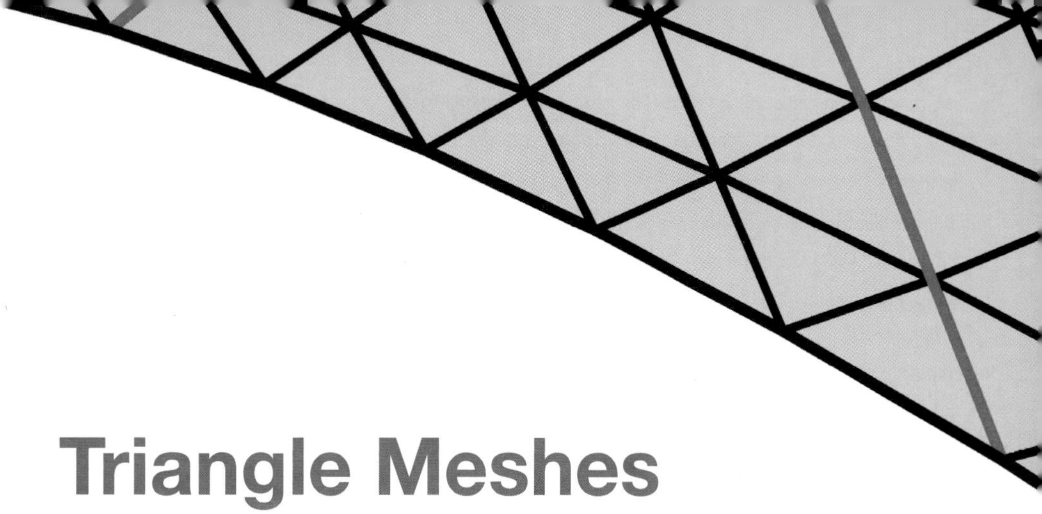

Triangle Meshes

Most of the basic tasks related to geometric computing with triangle meshes were addressed in Chapter 11. We would like to add here a few considerations specific to the applications we have in mind. These concern the layout of triangle meshes M on a given freeform surface S. It is not important in which way S is represented: S could be any surface designed with a 3D modeling system. It might even be just a fine triangle mesh.

The triangle mesh M we are looking for should approximate S well (i.e., stay within a user-specified tolerance region around the given design surface S). Aesthetics is greatly enhanced if the mesh can be decomposed into three families of fair polygons (structure lines), as shown in Figure 19.3. This means that the mesh should largely consist of vertices of valence 6 (i.e., six edges meeting at an inner vertex).

Let's add a further design requirement. To manufacture the mesh at the best possible cost, it may be necessary to meet rather tight constraints on the edge lengths and the angles in the triangular faces. We have been involved in a project for which the initial mesh M exhibited edge lengths that were too short (Figure 19.4), resulting in a too heavy and expensive construction. Redesigning this mesh with larger faces retains the

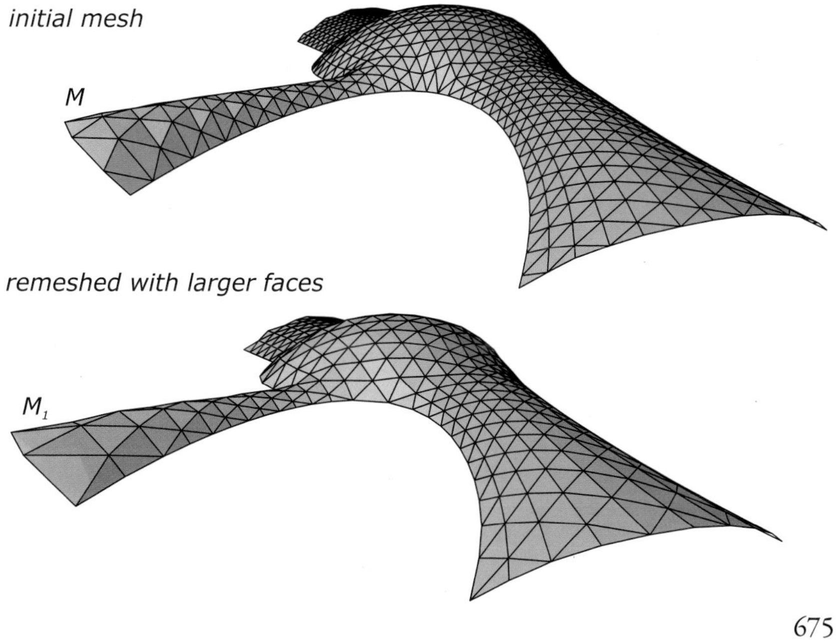

Fig. 19.4
The average edge length in the initial mesh M for the present design has been too small, resulting in high weight and cost. A remeshing scheme based on a mapping into a planar domain has been used to coarsen the mesh M toward a mesh M_1 that can be built at a lower cost. (Data courtesy of Waagner-Biro Stahlbau AG, Vienna.)

aesthetics and reduces the cost. The basic idea of our remeshing scheme is a mapping onto a planar domain (recall Chapter 13). First, remeshing is done in the planar domain—and then the resulting coarser mesh is mapped back to surface S.

A core problem is to find a mapping into the plane that handles the boundaries in the desired way. This *parameterization problem* has been widely studied in computer graphics [Floater and Hormann 2005], but the application in architecture may benefit from further work that gives the designer intuitive design handles for optimized triangle mesh layout on freeform geometries. Also recall the work on *fair webs*, addressed in the previous chapter. It aims at the generation of meshes that satisfy the aesthetic requirements in artistic design.

Triangle meshes are easy to deal with from the perspective of representing a given surface S with the desired accuracy. Even the aesthetic constraints are not really difficult to achieve. Moreover, statics is simpler if we stay with triangle meshes. However, there are the following issues—which make other solutions, in particular quadrilateral meshes with planar faces, attractive.

- In a steel/glass or other construction based on a triangle mesh, typically six beams meet in a node. This means a significantly higher node complexity compared to other types of meshes.
- Experience shows that the per-area cost of triangular glass panels is higher than that of quadrilateral panels. This is mainly due to the fact that quadrilaterals fill their smallest rectangular bounding boxes better than triangles do.
- Generally, one aims at less steel, more glass, and less weight, which also points to non-triangular faces.
- For the actual construction, optimized (torsion-free) nodes are preferred (see discussion following). The geometric theory, however, tells us that for triangle meshes in general torsion-free nodes do not exist.
- Apart from very simple cases, triangle meshes do not possess offsets at constant face-face or edge-edge distance. Neither is it possible to use triangle meshes as the basis of a multilayer freeform construction in which only the basic requirement of parallelism of layers is imposed.

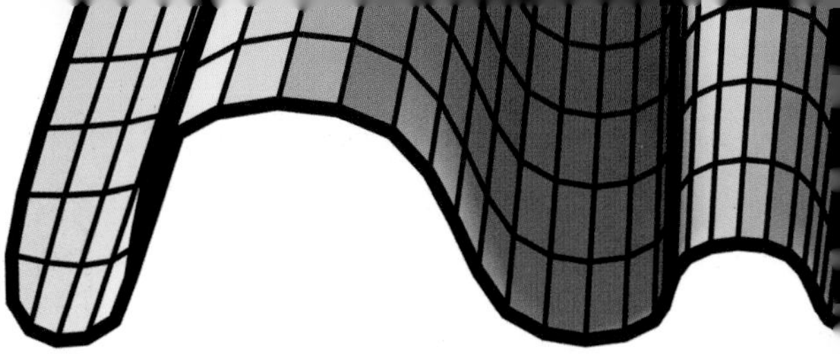

Quadrilateral Meshes with Planar Faces

Planar quad meshes of simple geometry. We have encountered meshes formed by planar quadrilaterals [called *planar quad (PQ) meshes* hereafter] in several previous chapters (see also Figure 19.5). For example, translational surfaces can easily be represented as PQ meshes by translating a polygon against another polygon. In a similarly simple way, we can obtain discrete rotational surfaces (Figure 19.6) or certain generalizations (sometimes referred to as cross-skinning surfaces; Figure 19.5 and Glymph et al. [2002]).

Slightly more advanced examples, including their representation via PQ meshes, have been discussed in Chapter 12; namely, moulding surfaces and generalized moulding surfaces. We would like to add here one simple fact: If we have designed a PQ mesh M, any affine transformation (e.g., obtained by scaling with different factors in x, y, and z directions) maps M onto another PQ mesh M_1 (Figure 19.5). This follows from the property that an affine map preserves planarity. The same holds for projective maps, but the latter will in general imply higher distortions to the face sizes and thus may be less suitable to the present application. For a detailed discussion of PQ meshes with simple geometry, see Glymph et al. [2002].

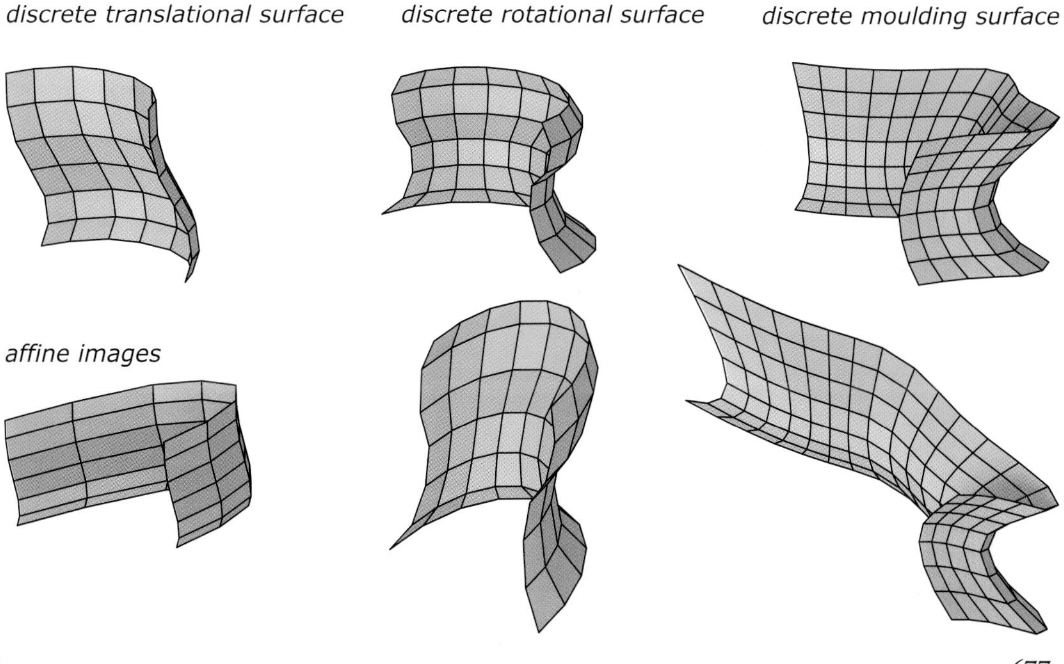

Fig. 19.5
PQ meshes can easily be designed for certain surfaces of simple geometry.

Example:

Rotational PQ mesh. To understand the geometric constraints on PQ meshes, we first look at a very simple example: a rotational surface represented by a PQ mesh M (Figure 19.6). This quad mesh can be decomposed into two families of mesh polygons: a family A of polygons representing rotational circles (also called *parallel circles*) and a family B of polygons representing the profiles in planes through the axis (these profile curves are also called *meridian curves*). Two adjacent polygons A_1 and A_2 of family A form a very simple PQ mesh called a *PQ strip*, which is a discrete version of a piece of a cone of revolution. Likewise, two adjacent polygons of family B form a *PQ strip*; namely, a discrete version of a general cylinder surface. Recall from Chapter 15 that PQ strips define discrete models of developable surfaces.

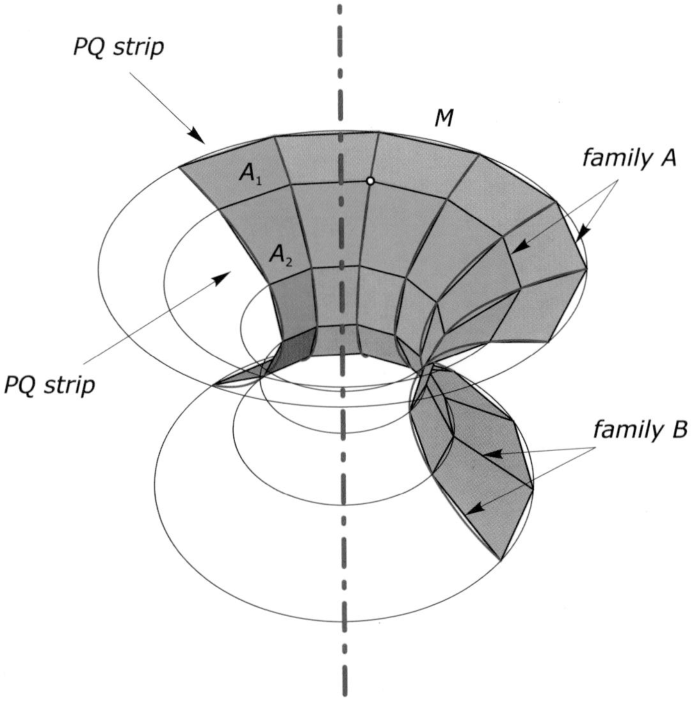

Fig. 19.6
Rotational PQ mesh M. The mesh polygons are aligned along parallel circles and meridian curves, respectively. Adjacent mesh polygons of the same family form PQ strips, which can be seen as discrete versions of developable surfaces tangent to a rotational surface S along the rotational circles and meridian curves (respectively). The network of parallel circles and meridian curves is an instance of a *conjugate curve network*, and the PQ mesh M can be seen as a discrete version of it.

If we refine our mesh toward a smooth rotational surface (Figure 19.7), the *PQ strips converge to developable surfaces* in the following sense: The edges of a strip (i.e., the line segments along which successive quads of a strip are connected; e.g., the connections of corresponding points in polygons A_1 and A_2 of Figure 19.6, seen as discrete rulings of a discrete developable surface) tend toward rulings of a smooth developable surface.

This developable surface is a cone of revolution if the strip comes from family A, and is a cylinder through a meridian curve if the strip arises from family B. Note that the edges of a strip from A are edges of polygons in family B and thus tend toward tangents of profile curves. This results in the obvious property that the tangents to the meridian curves taken at points of the same rotational circle lie in a cone of revolution (in special cases, we obtain a cylinder or a plane).

Likewise, the tangents of the rotational circles taken at the points of the same meridian curve form a cylinder surface. This property of the two families of rotational circles and meridian curves can be extended to the concept of *conjugate curve networks*, which plays a crucial role in the design of PQ meshes.

Fig. 19.7
The network of parallel circles and meridian curves on a rotational surface is an instance of a *conjugate curve network*. The tangents to the curves of one family at points of a single curve of the other family form a developable surface; namely, a cone of revolution or a general cylinder.

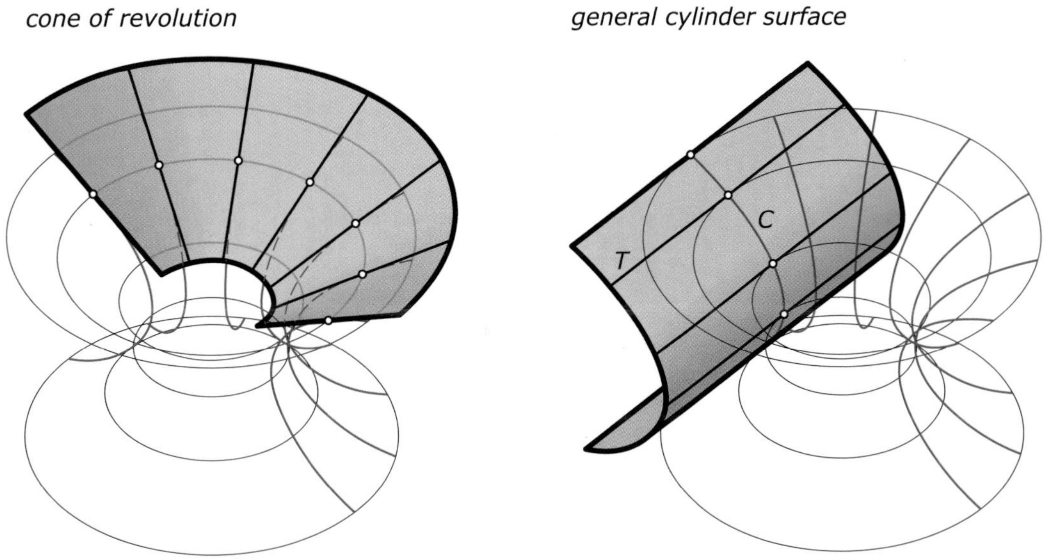

Conjugate curve networks. Assume that we are given two families of curves, denoted A and B, on a smooth surface S. These two families are said to form a *conjugate curve network* if the following property holds (Figure 19.8): *Pick a curve* c *in the network and compute in each of its points the tangent to the curve from the other family. Then, these tangents must form a developable ruled surface.* It is obvious that this developable surface touches S along c. Thus, it is the envelope of the tangent planes of S at the points of c. We simply speak of the *tangent developable surface along* c.

The rotational network from Figure 19.7 obviously has this property. The tangents to the meridian curves at points of a rotational circle form a cone (in special cases a cylinder or a pencil of lines in a plane, but it any case a developable surface). The tangents to the parallel circles at points of a fixed meridian curve form a cylinder.

A network of curves resulting by translation is another simple example of a conjugate curve network. Along each curve in the translational network, the tangents to the other network curve form a cylinder—which is a developable surface. For a generalized moulding surface (Chapter 12), we find cylinders as developable surfaces along the profiles—whereas the developable surfaces along the motion trajectories are already more general.

These examples are simple and hopefully illustrative, but they may be misleading. A surface S does not contain just a single conjugate curve network. It carries *infinitely many conjugate curve networks*! To realize this, we prescribe one arbitrary family A of curves (e.g., the intersections of S with a sequence of surfaces). We can then compute the conjugate family B as follows. Along each curve c of family A, we determine the tangent developable surface and consider its rulings. Thus, in each point of c we obtain such a ruling (called the conjugate direction to the tangent of c).

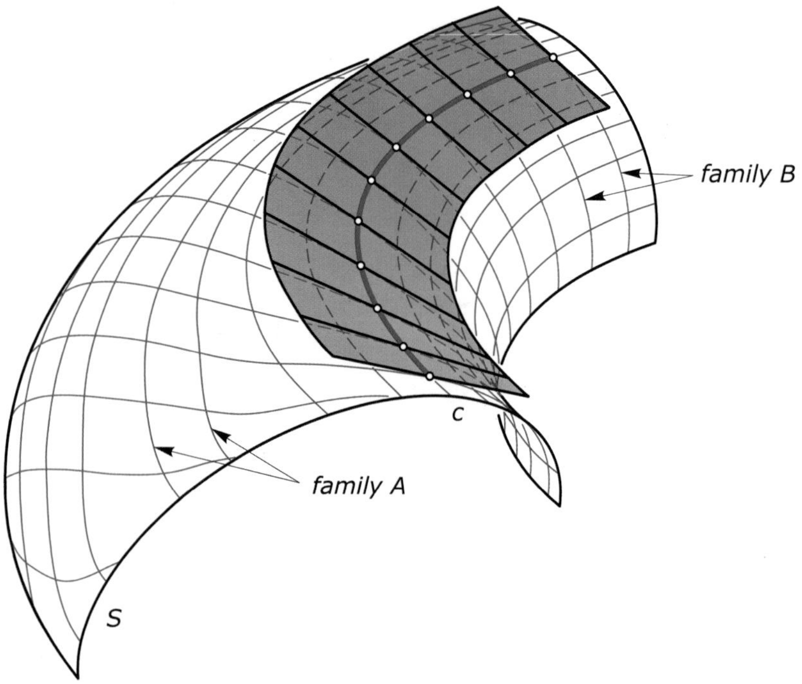

Fig. 19.8
Geometry of a conjugate curve network. The tangents to the curves of one family, taken at the points of a curve in the other family, form a developable ruled surface.

We then do this for all curves c in A. Finally, we have at each point of S a ruling (the surface tangent that defines the conjugate direction to the tangent of the curve in family A). It is known in mathematics that this system of conjugate directions can be "integrated" (i.e., one can compute a family B of curves whose tangents are exactly these given lines). In this way we have found the conjugate family B and have thus determined a conjugate network on S.

Although this procedure is in principle possible, the resulting network may not be suitable for our purpose. That is, it might not serve as a basis for the layout of a PQ mesh. To understand the problem, we look at a simple example.

Example:

Hyperbolic paraboloid. Figure 19.9 shows several conjugate curve networks on a hyperbolic paraboloid S. It does not exhibit a network that contains a family of rulings. This has a very simple reason. Along each ruling R, the tangent planes contain R and thus the tangent developable surface degenerates to R itself. We can say that the rulings are *self-conjugate* and thus cannot serve as the basis of a PQ mesh. The latter claim is obvious: two rulings of the same family are skew and thus one cannot form a strip of planar quads from them. The surface S, however, contains some very nice conjugate networks. One is translational and is formed by parabolas. Another is the network of principal curvature lines (see discussion following).

Negatively curved areas cause problems. The problem with the rulings in a skew ruled surface such as the hyperbolic paraboloid is a special case of a more general phenomenon: It turns out that the relation of conjugate tangent directions at a surface point depends on the curvature behaviour.

In a hyperbolic point of a surface (point of negative Gaussian curvature), we have two tangent directions with vanishing normal curvature (the rulings of the locally approximating hyperbolic paraboloid discussed in Chapter 14). These *asymptotic directions* are self-conjugate and thus cause problems with the layout of conjugate networks and the layout of PQ meshes (discussed in material following).

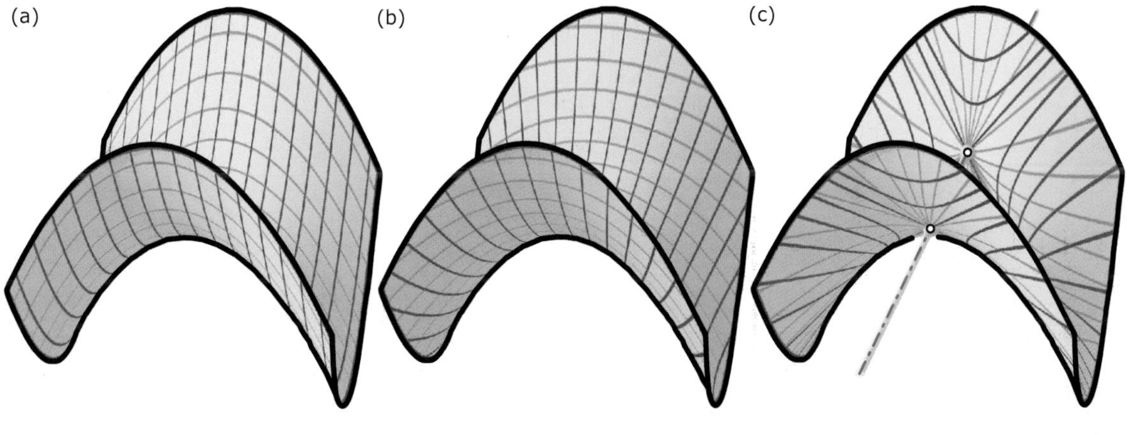

Fig. 19.9
Several conjugate curve networks on a hyperbolic paraboloid.
(a) Translational network formed by parabolas.
(b) Principal curvature lines.
(c) Intersection curves (red) with planes through an axis and their conjugate curves (black). In this case, the black curves also lie in planes through an axis.

Principal curvature lines. Ideally, one may want to have a conjugate curve network such as the rotational network discussed previously. In this network, called an *orthogonal curve network*, curves of different families intersect at right angles. We may therefore ask whether any surface S contains a curve network that is *conjugate and orthogonal*. The answer is affirmative: a surface S carries in general one such network; namely, the *network of principal curvature lines* (see Chapter 14; this network is not uniquely determined for a sphere or a plane S only).

The layout of PQ meshes with the help of principal curvature lines is a promising approach because principal curvature lines also nicely reflect basic shape properties and thus may be very suitable from an aesthetic perspective. The fact that this network is unique and thus does not give us design flexibility is of course a disadvantage of design principles relying on principal curvature lines.

Planar quad meshes are discrete versions of conjugate curve networks. The reader may wonder why we spent so much effort on conjugate curve networks. However, the answer has already been suggested by the example on rotational PQ meshes. It can be stated as follows: *PQ meshes* M *are discrete versions of conjugate curve networks*. The proof follows from the observation that any PQ strip formed by mesh polygons of family A is a model of a developable surface, and its edges may be seen as discrete tangents of polygons in family B (Figure 19.10).

There are special PQ meshes that are discrete versions of the network of principal curvature lines in a very precise way. These *principal meshes* are discussed in material to follow in connection with offsets. Here, we only mention one type of principal meshes, the *circular meshes*. A quad mesh is called circular if each of its quads possesses a circum-circle (Figure 19.11). The rotational meshes shown previously are circular meshes due to symmetry.

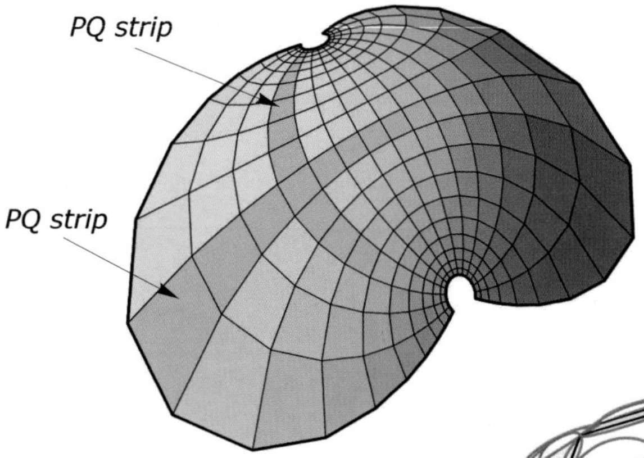

Fig. 19.10
A PQ strip in a PQ mesh is a discrete model of a tangent developable surface. The alignment of its edges with the polygons in the mesh shows that PQ meshes are discrete versions of conjugate curve networks. This has an important practical consequence. Only quad meshes roughly aligned along the curves of a conjugate network may serve as the basis of mesh optimization toward a PQ mesh.

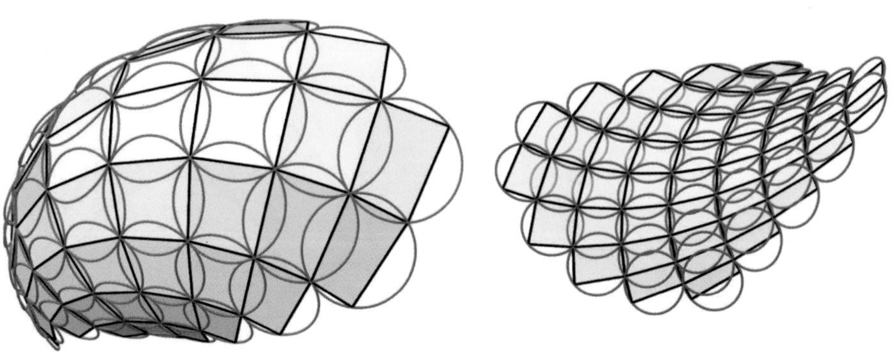

Fig. 19.11
A PQ mesh whose quads possess a circum-circle (circular mesh) can be seen as a discrete version of the network of principal curvature lines. Its quads being aligned with principal curvature directions, such a mesh is capable of representing fundamental shape characteristics.

A planarization algorithm. It is a natural idea to ask for an algorithm that takes as input a quad mesh whose quads are not planar and delivers as output a mesh that approximates the same smooth surface but exhibits only planar quads. Planarity of faces has to be provided at least within some tolerance so that one can use planar glass panels. Such an algorithm has been developed recently [Liu et al. 2006]. It is based on a rather sophisticated optimization strategy.

For the details, we refer you to the literature. Here, we focus on the practical use of such an algorithm. First, we cannot provide as input any quad mesh and hope that the algorithm will make quads planar while retaining aesthetic requirements and proximity to the underlying surface. However, if the *input mesh has been extracted from a conjugate curve network* chances are high that the optimization will not get stuck in an undesirable solution and thus may yield a practically useful result (Figure 19.12).

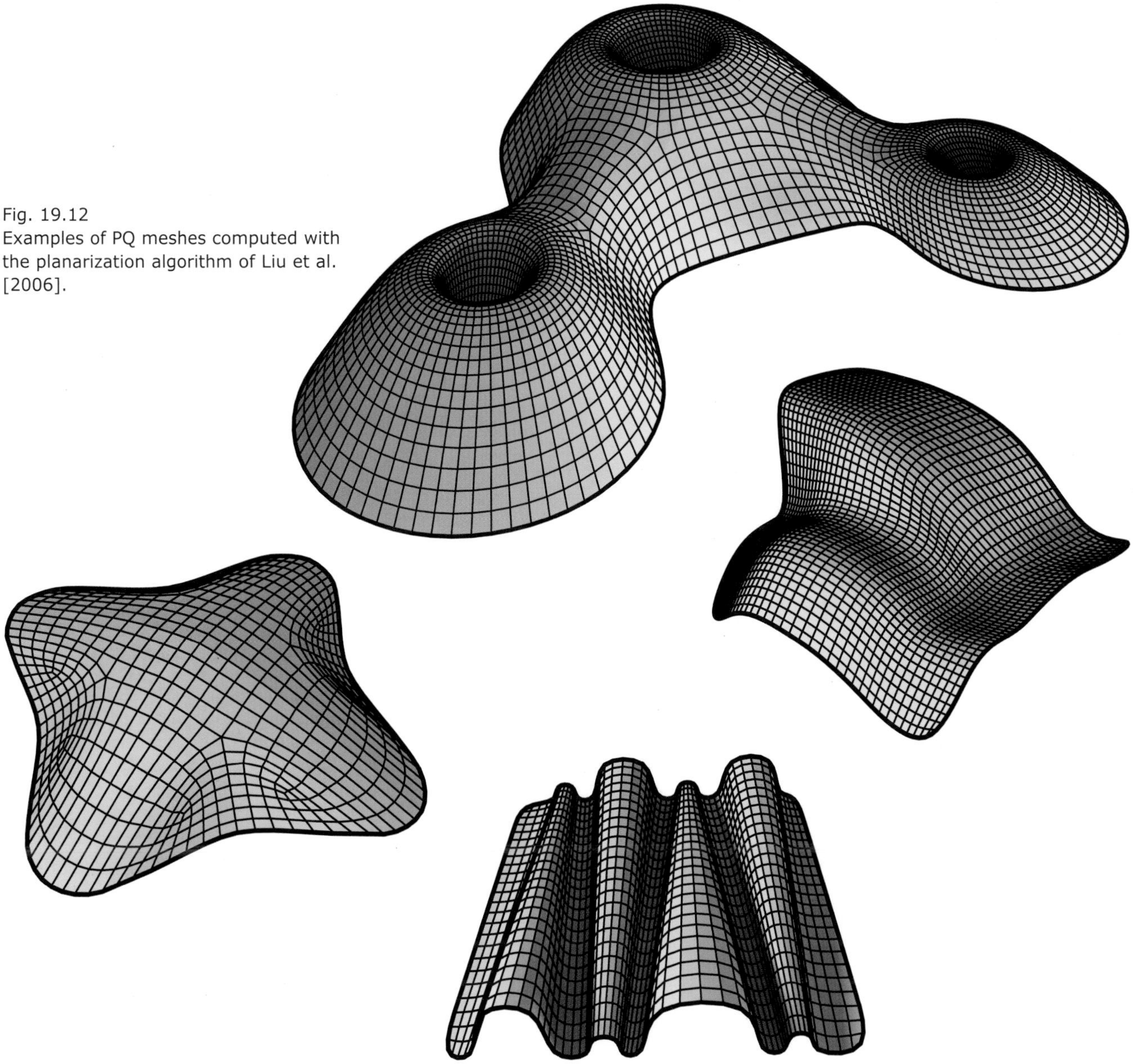

Fig. 19.12
Examples of PQ meshes computed with the planarization algorithm of Liu et al. [2006].

Limitations on meshing. The design of a PQ mesh that satisfies all of the high requirements of aesthetics and that is sufficiently close to a provided input surface is an unsolved research problem. We will be able to compute a solution if the network of principal curvature lines can be used as a basis of a mesh that is then improved via optimization. However, singularities as well as large variations in cell sizes caused by the flow of principal curvature lines may make this approach unfeasible (Figure 19.13).

Combination of subdivision and planarization as a design tool. Aiming at a mesh with planar quads already in the form-finding process greatly raises the chance of success in realizing even a complicated freeform shape with a PQ mesh. A strategy that has proved to be very effective is to combine quad-based subdivision algorithms and the planarization algorithm of Liu et al. [2006] (recall Chapters 11 and 15). This means that one applies planarization after each subdivision step. Subdivision alone, unfortunately, destroys planarity of faces. Meshes that have been designed with this strategy are depicted in Figure 19.14.

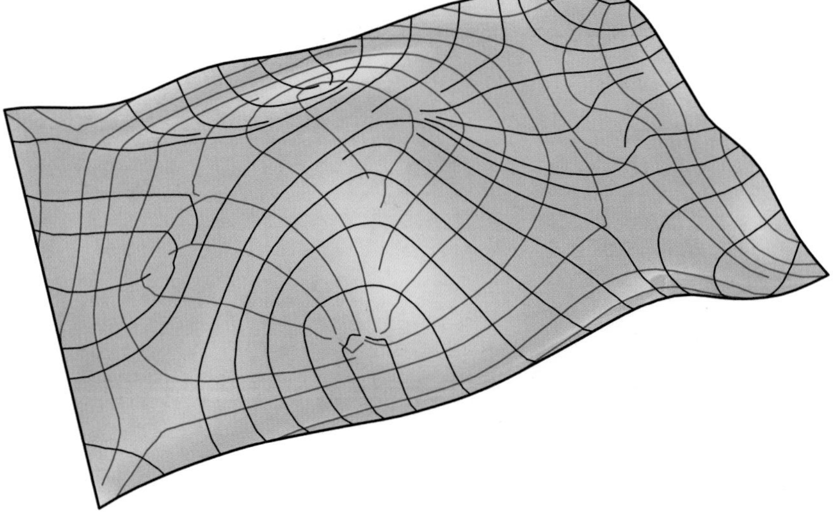

Fig. 19.13
An architectural design surface whose principal curvature lines are not suitable as the basis for the layout of a PQ mesh.

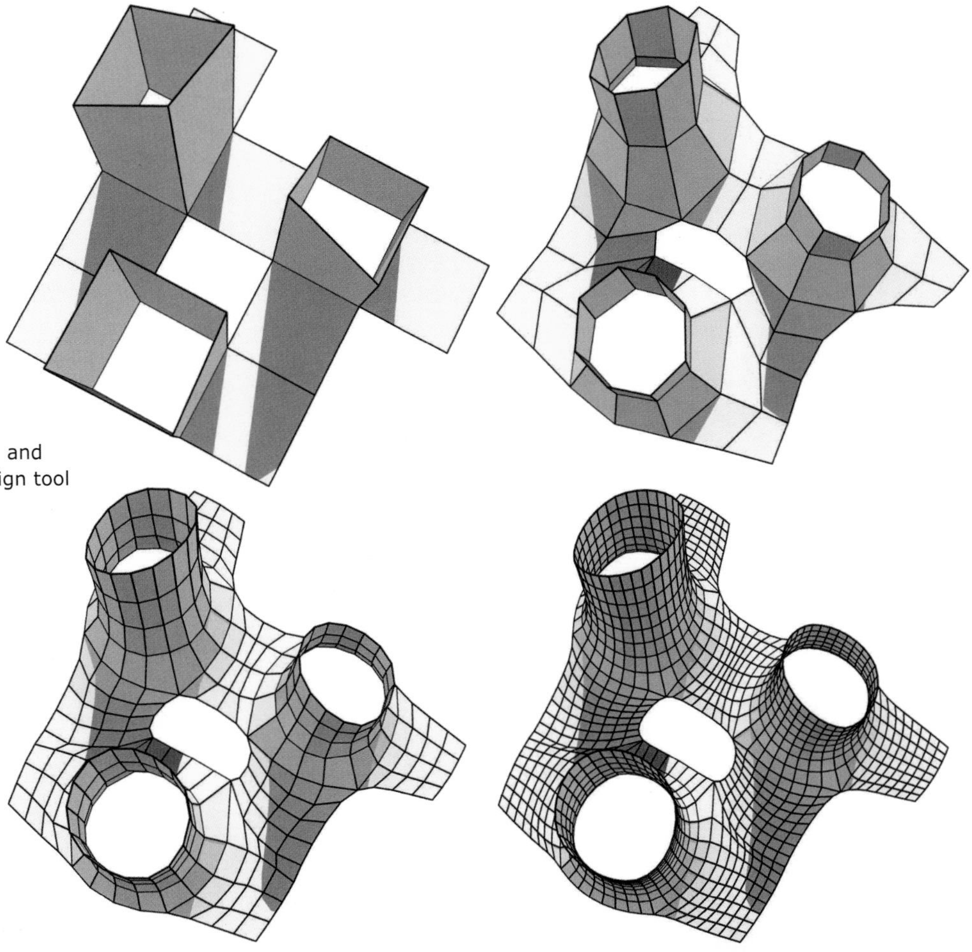

Fig. 19.14
Alternating between subdivision and planarization is an effective design tool for PQ meshes.

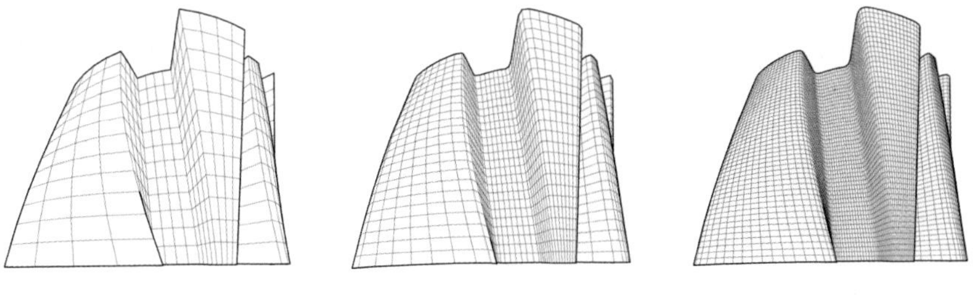

One reason for the success of this method is that the required changes are made by optimization at different levels of detail, at first at the coarsest level and then proceeding toward finer levels. Another reason is that one can include further requirements on the final mesh into the optimization part. For example, the meshes shown in Figure 19.15 have been optimized to be circular.

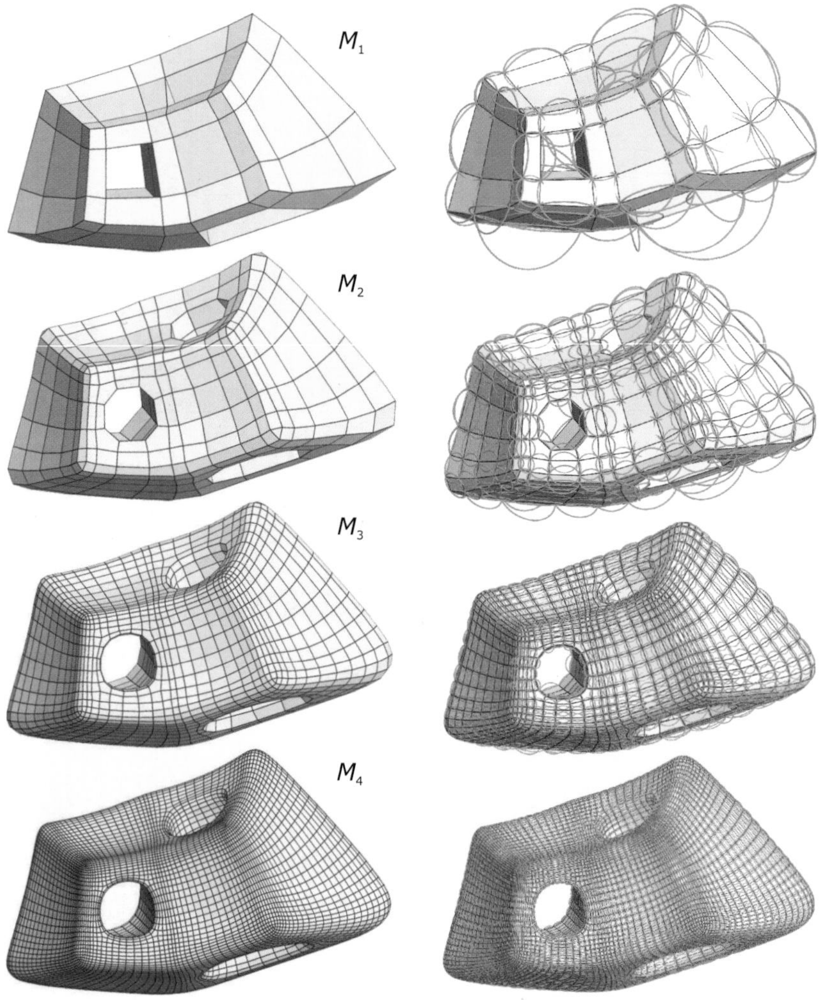

Fig. 19.15
Alternation between subdivision and optimization (extended version of planarization) allows for inclusion of further requirements into the optimization part. In this example, the sequence of meshes M_1, M_2, and so on has been optimized so that these meshes are even circular.

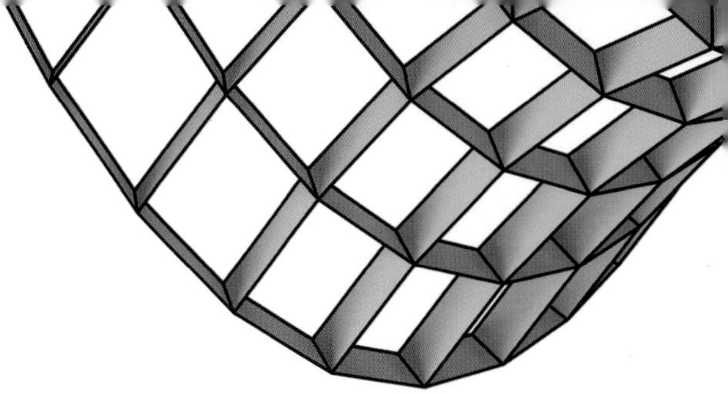

Parallel Meshes, Offsets, and Supporting Beam Layout

Parallel meshes and multilayer constructions. A steel/glass construction based on a mesh can be viewed as a physical realization of the vertices, edges, and faces of that mesh. Conversely, the mesh is a mathematical abstraction of such a construction. However, the passage from the concrete construction to the abstract mesh is not unique. Structures such as those shown in Figure 19.16 yield several meshes, corresponding to the different layers of the construction. It is natural to demand that meshes that correspond to different layers be "parallel."

Fig. 19.16
Sketches of multilayer constructions based on two parallel meshes M, M^* at approximately constant distance. On the bottom, the lower layer of the glass roof is suspended from the upper layer—which has a structural function. The right-hand image shows a rudimentary construction of a glass facade for which the closed space between layers has an insulating function.

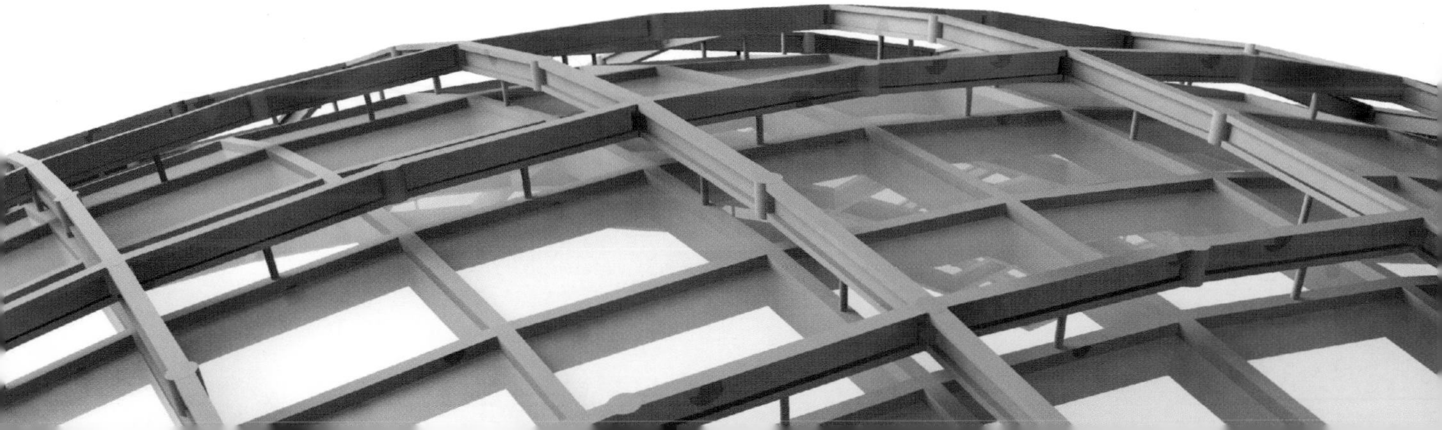

We call two meshes M, M parallel if there is a one-to-one correspondence among their vertices, edges, and faces* (such meshes are called combinatorially equivalent) *and if corresponding edges are parallel* (Figure 19.17). We use this definition only if the faces of M (and hence of M^*) are planar. They need not be quadrilaterals, but in most of the discussion following they are quads. Because corresponding edges of parallel meshes are parallel and their faces planar, corresponding faces lie in parallel planes. Hence, any mesh parallel to a PQ mesh is also a PQ mesh.

Beams and nodes. In the actual realization of a mesh M as a steel/glass roof, planar glass panels are held by prismatic *beams* following the edges of M (Figure 19.18). A beam is symmetric with respect to its *central plane*, which passes through the edge corresponding to the beam. A *node* corresponds to a vertex of M and connects incoming beams in a way that supports the force flow imposed by the overall statics of the structure.

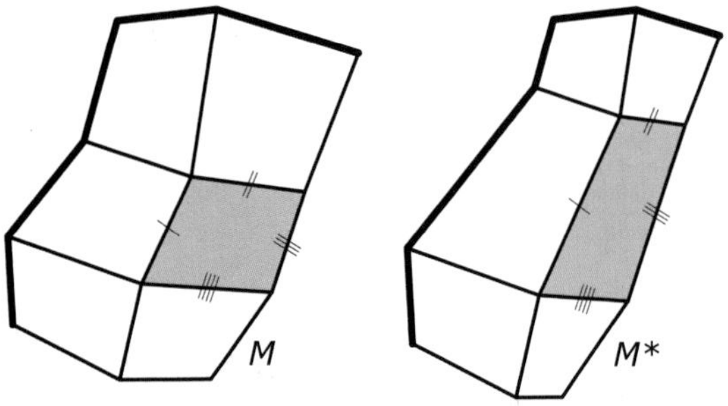

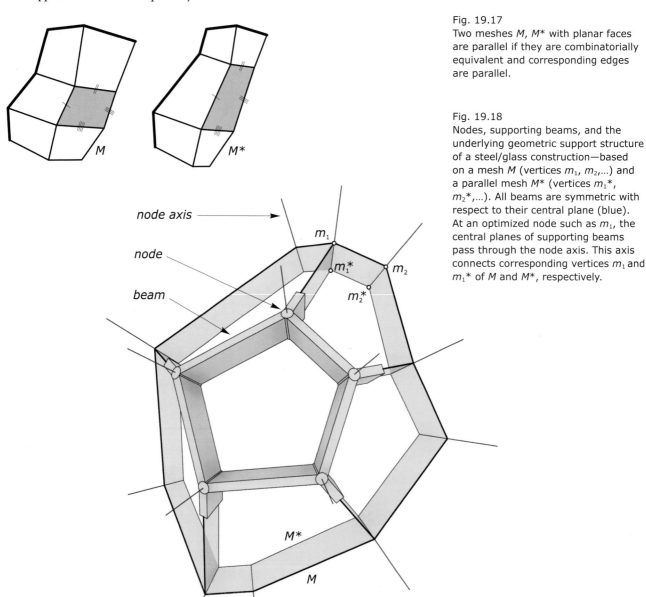

Fig. 19.17
Two meshes M, M^* with planar faces are parallel if they are combinatorially equivalent and corresponding edges are parallel.

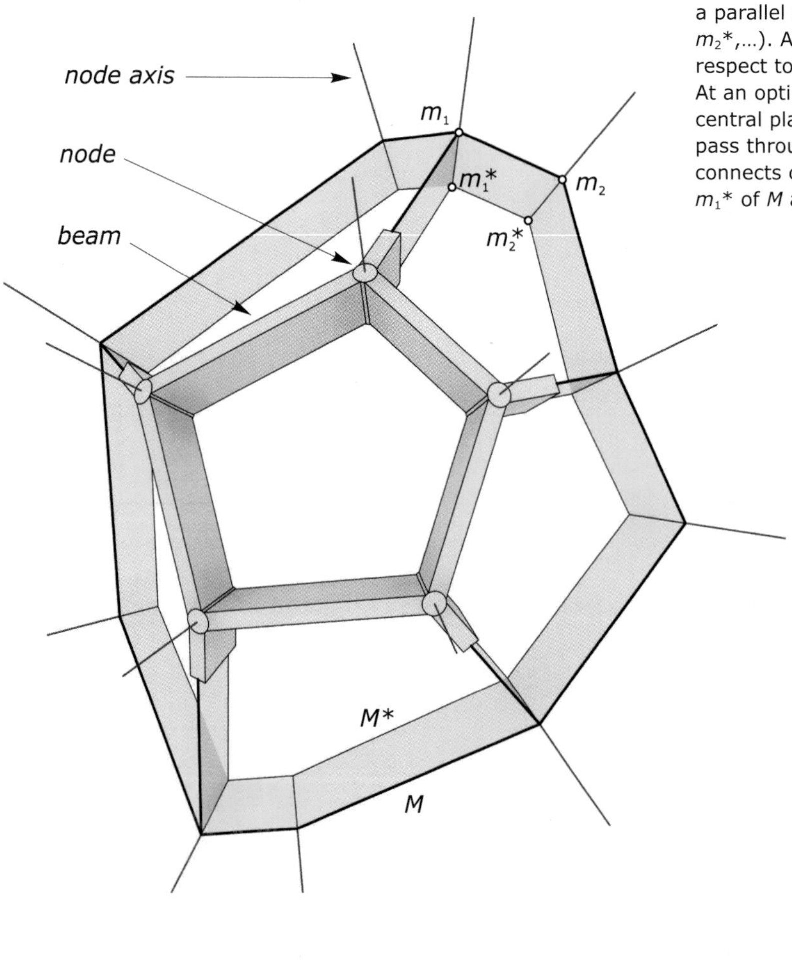

Fig. 19.18
Nodes, supporting beams, and the underlying geometric support structure of a steel/glass construction—based on a mesh M (vertices m_1, m_2,...) and a parallel mesh M^* (vertices m_1^*, m_2^*,...). All beams are symmetric with respect to their central plane (blue). At an optimized node such as m_1, the central planes of supporting beams pass through the node axis. This axis connects corresponding vertices m_1 and m_1^* of M and M^*, respectively.

Node construction and manufacturing are greatly simplified if there is a *node axis A*, which is contained in the central planes of incoming beams (Figure 19.18). Figure 19.19 shows a case of a welded node that does not have a node axis. Obviously, the handling and manufacturing of such *nodes with torsion* is more complicated than the case of a node with an axis (such a node is also called a *torsion-free node*).

Geometrically, straight lines $A_1, A_2,$... passing through the vertices $m_1, m_2,$ ... of a given mesh M are a suitable collection of node axes if and only if adjacent axes (i.e., the axes at the end points of any edge in the mesh) lie in a common plane. This plane is then used as the central plane of a supporting beam. To avoid pathologic cases, we forbid that node axes lie in edges.

The following simple but fundamental result relates node axes to an auxiliary mesh M^* parallel to the given mesh M (see Figures 19.18 and 19.20, and Brell-Cokcan and Pottmann [2006] and Pottmann et al. [2007]). If the meshes M (with vertices $m_1, m_2,$...) and M^* (with vertices $m_1^*, m_2^*,$ ...) are parallel, the connecting lines $A_1 = m_1m_1^*$, $A_2 = m_2m_2^*$, ... of corresponding vertices can serve as node axes for the mesh M.

Conversely, assume that a (simply connected) mesh M is equipped with node axes $A_1, A_2,$ ... passing through its vertices. Then there exists a mesh M^* parallel to M such that the node axes are connecting lines of corresponding vertices in M and M^*.

Thus, we see that suitable node axes of M are obtained via a parallel mesh M^*. There are infinitely many parallel meshes, and most of them are not ideal for the actual supporting beam layout. In practice, one wants to have node axes that are roughly orthogonal to M (as shown in Figure 19.20). One obtains them with a parallel mesh M^* lying at approximately constant distance to M, and thus M^* can be seen as an offset of M.

Before we enter the interesting geometry of offset meshes, we define the concept of a *geometric support structure*, which essentially simplifies the geometry of supporting beam layout by looking only into their central planes. A geometric support structure is a *collection of planar quads which connect corresponding parallel edges of two parallel meshes M, M** which are used for the definition of node axes (see Figure 19.20).

Fig. 19.19
A node without an axis (i.e., a node with geometric torsion). (Image courtesy of Waagner-Biro Stahlbau AG.)

Fig. 19.20
Any collection of node axes is obtained by connecting corresponding vertices of two parallel meshes M and M^*. The connecting planar quads of corresponding parallel edges form a *geometric support structure*.

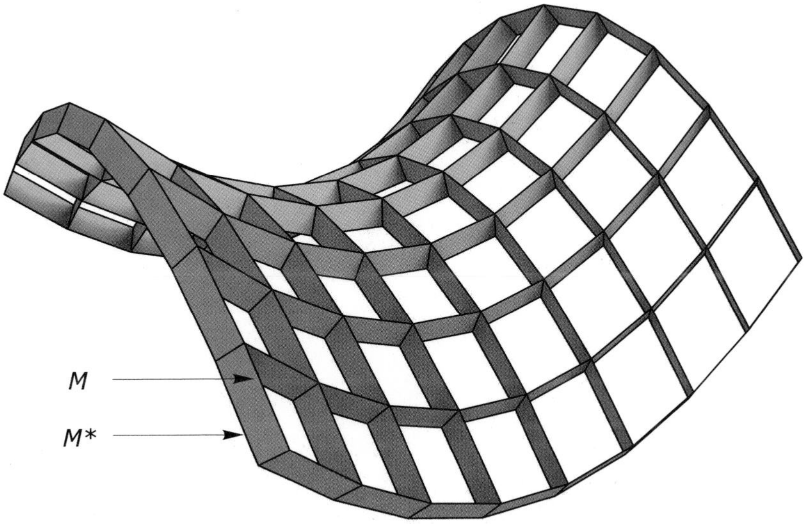

If all quads in the geometric support structure have the same height (i.e., if corresponding edges of M and M^* are not only parallel but even at constant distance), we call M^* an *edge offset* of M. Then, beams of constant height are perfectly aligned on both the upper (outer) and lower (inner) side of the construction (Figure 19.21). In general, M and M^* will not be edge offsets. In this case, perfect alignment of beams of the same height can only be achieved on one side (Figure 19.22).

Triangle meshes. For triangle meshes, the concept of parallel meshes is less interesting. Two triangles with parallel edges are related by a similarity transformation. Hence, a parallel mesh M^* of a triangle mesh M is just a *scaled version of* M. This has an important implication to the construction of support structures.

A geometric support structure of a connected triangle mesh M with torsion-free nodes can only be very simple. Either all node axes must be parallel or must pass through a single point. Requiring that the node axes be roughly orthogonal to the underlying design surface implies that the mesh M has planar or spherical shape. For a general freeform triangle mesh M, there is no chance to construct a practically useful support structure with torsion-free nodes.

Fig. 19.21
Beams of constant height are perfectly aligned on both sides of the construction if the underlying parallel meshes M and M^* are *edge offsets* of each other (corresponding edges in M and M^* lie at constant distance).

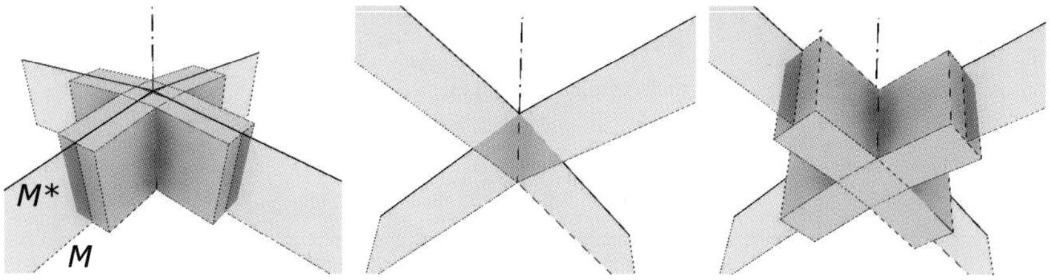

Fig. 19.22
This geometric support structure is defined by two parallel meshes that are not of constant edge-edge distance. We nevertheless employ beams of constant height to physically realize this support structure.

(left) The resulting misalignment is not visible from the outside,
(middle) hardly visible from the beams' mid sections lying in the respective central planes,
(right) but it is clearly visible from the inside.
Still, this node has no torsion and central planes of beams intersect in the node axis.

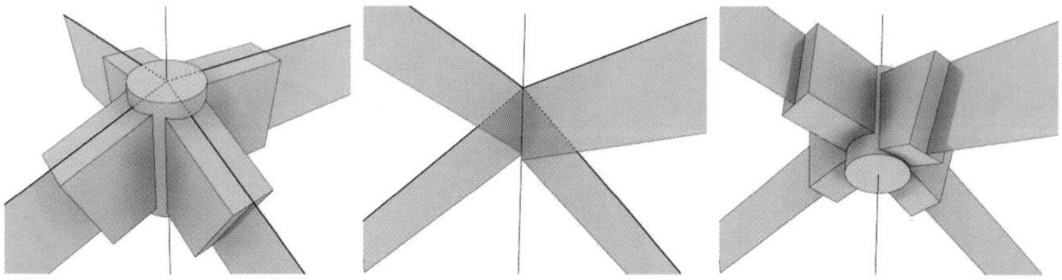

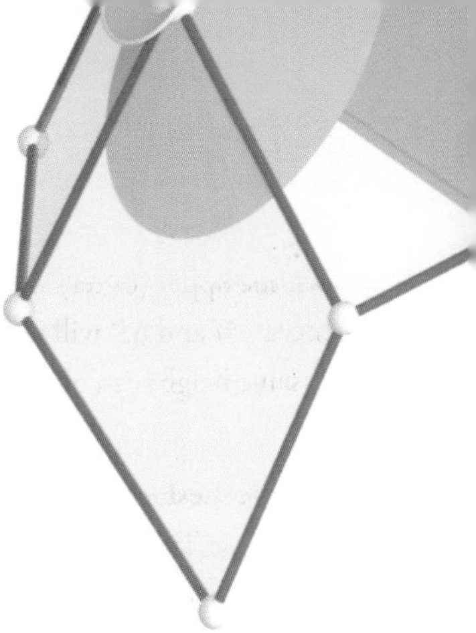

Offset Meshes

Offset surfaces revisited. An offset surface F^d of a smooth surface F lies at constant normal distance d to F (see Chapter 10). Let $\boldsymbol{x}(u,v)$ be a parametric representation of the surface F, and let $\boldsymbol{n}(u,v)$ denote the normal vectors of F (normalized to length 1 and pointing to a chosen side of the surface). The unit normal vectors $\boldsymbol{n}(u,v)$ describe a part of the unit sphere S^* (sphere of radius 1 with center at the origin o) known as the Gaussian spherical image of F (see Chapter 14).

Then, the offset surface F^d at distance d has the representation $\boldsymbol{x}^d(u,v) = \boldsymbol{x}(u,v) + d \cdot \boldsymbol{n}(u,v)$. Note that the normals of F are normals of F^d as well, and hence F is also an offset of F^d. The tangent planes at corresponding points of F and F^d are parallel and at constant distance d. If we know the representations $\boldsymbol{x}(u,v)$ and $\boldsymbol{x}^d(u,v)$ of the two surfaces F and F^d, respectively, we can compute the Gaussian spherical image as scaled difference surface $\boldsymbol{n}(u,v) = [\boldsymbol{x}^d(u,v) - \boldsymbol{x}(u,v)]/d$. This equation encodes a basic relation that will help us study offset meshes in a simple geometric way.

PQ meshes with exact offsets. The definition of the offsets of a smooth surface F uses its normals and requires constant distance along the normals. It is not straightforward to extend the definition to meshes with planar faces. In fact, we will see that there are several meaningful definitions of an offset in the case of meshes. Most of the definitions and investigations given in the material following are valid for general meshes with planar faces and generically more than three edges per face. However, we will confine the discussion to PQ meshes M.

Having the parallelism of tangent planes in a pair of smooth offset surfaces in mind, it is natural to use the following definition: *An offset mesh* M^d *of a PQ mesh* M *is parallel to* M *and lies at constant distance* d *to* M. Of course, this definition is not yet complete because we have to say how the constant distance d shall be measured. There are three precise ways of doing this. They are not equivalent and thus have to be studied separately.

- *Vertex offsets*: The distance of corresponding vertices of M and M^d has a constant value d, which does not depend on the vertex.
- *Edge offsets*: The distance of corresponding parallel edges of M and M^d (actually, lines that carry these edges) does not depend on the edge and equals d.
- *Face offsets*: The distance of corresponding faces of M and M^d (actually, the parallel planes of corresponding faces) is independent of the face and equals d.

Before proceeding with the study of offset meshes, we want to point to a fundamental difference in relation to the smooth case: we cannot prescribe an arbitrary PQ mesh M and then construct a vertex offset, an edge offset, or a face offset. We will see in material following that the existence of vertex offsets characterizes special PQ meshes M (circular meshes). Likewise, face offsets can only be constructed for another type of special PQ mesh—and it is even more difficult to construct meshes M that possess edge offsets.

Discrete Gaussian image and characterization of meshes with precise offsets. An offset pair of smooth surfaces with parametric representations $\boldsymbol{x}(u,v)$ and $\boldsymbol{x}^d(u,v)$ defines the Gaussian image via the difference surface, scaled with factor $1/d$: $\boldsymbol{n}(u,v) = [\boldsymbol{x}^d(u,v) - \boldsymbol{x}(u,v)]/d$. Given a pair of offset meshes M and M^d, we therefore define the *discrete Gaussian image* (*Gaussian image mesh*) as the scaled difference mesh $S = (M^d - M)/d$ of the two (parallel) meshes M and M^d.

S is computed as follows. If $\boldsymbol{m}_1, \boldsymbol{m}_2, \ldots$ and $\boldsymbol{m}_1^d, \boldsymbol{m}_2^d, \ldots$ are the coordinate vectors of corresponding vertices in M and M^d, one forms the scaled difference vectors $\boldsymbol{s}_1 = (\boldsymbol{m}_1^d - \boldsymbol{m}_1)/d$, $\boldsymbol{s}_2 = (\boldsymbol{m}_2^d - \boldsymbol{m}_2)/d, \ldots$ and uses them as coordinate vectors of the vertices $s_1, s_2, \ldots$ of the mesh S. Note that the vectors $\boldsymbol{s}_1, \boldsymbol{s}_2, \ldots$ are connecting corresponding vertices of M and M^d and thus are also direction vectors of node axes. Figure 19.23 illustrates the fact that *the Gaussian image mesh* S *is parallel to* M *and* M^d and that *distance properties between* M *and* M^d *are also reflected in distances between* S *and the origin.*

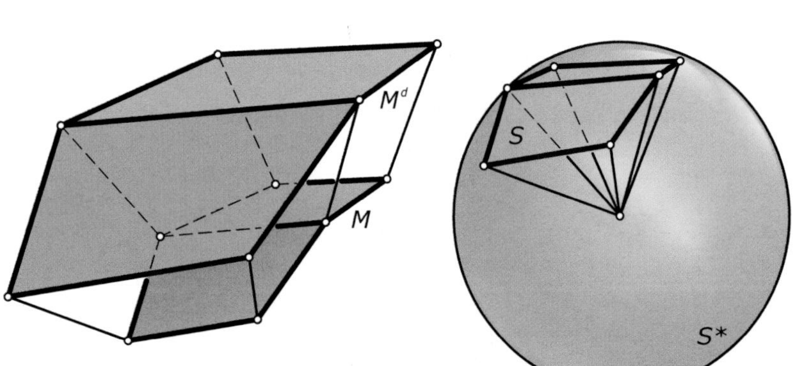

Fig. 19.23
The scaled difference mesh $S = (M^d - M)/d$ of two parallel meshes M and M^d is parallel to M and M^d.

M and M^d shall exhibit constant distance d in an appropriate sense. Hence, the Gaussian image S must have distance 1 to the origin in the same sense (i.e., S approximates the unit sphere S^*). This can be specified as follows (the main derivation is provided in the following; see also Pottmann et al. [2007]).

Consider a PQ mesh M, its offset mesh M^d at distance d, and the Gaussian image mesh $S = (M^d - M)/d$. Then the specific offset properties are encoded in the Gaussian image mesh S as follows.

- M^d is a vertex offset of M if and only if the vertices of the Gaussian image mesh S are contained in the unit sphere S^* (Figure 19.24). In this case, M and M^d are *circular meshes* (i.e., each face has a circum-circle).
- M^d is an edge offset of M exactly if the edges of the Gaussian image mesh S are tangent to the unit sphere S^*.
- M^d is a face offset of M if and only if the faces of the Gaussian image mesh S are tangent to the unit sphere S^*. In this case, M and M^d are *conical meshes* (see material following).

Fig. 19.24
A circular mesh M has circular offset meshes M^d at constant vertex-vertex distance d and a Gaussian image mesh S whose vertices lie in the unit sphere S^*.

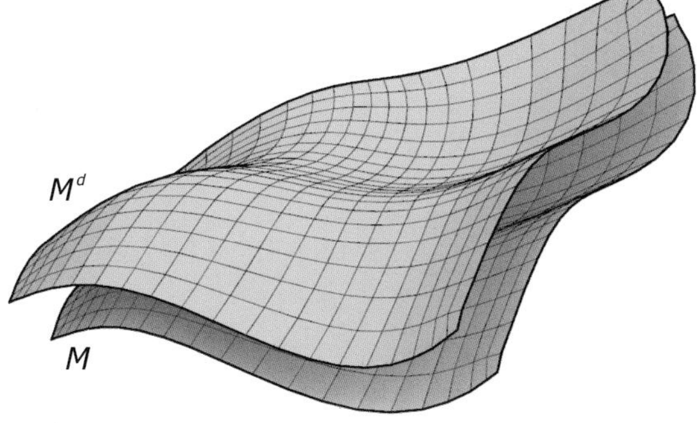

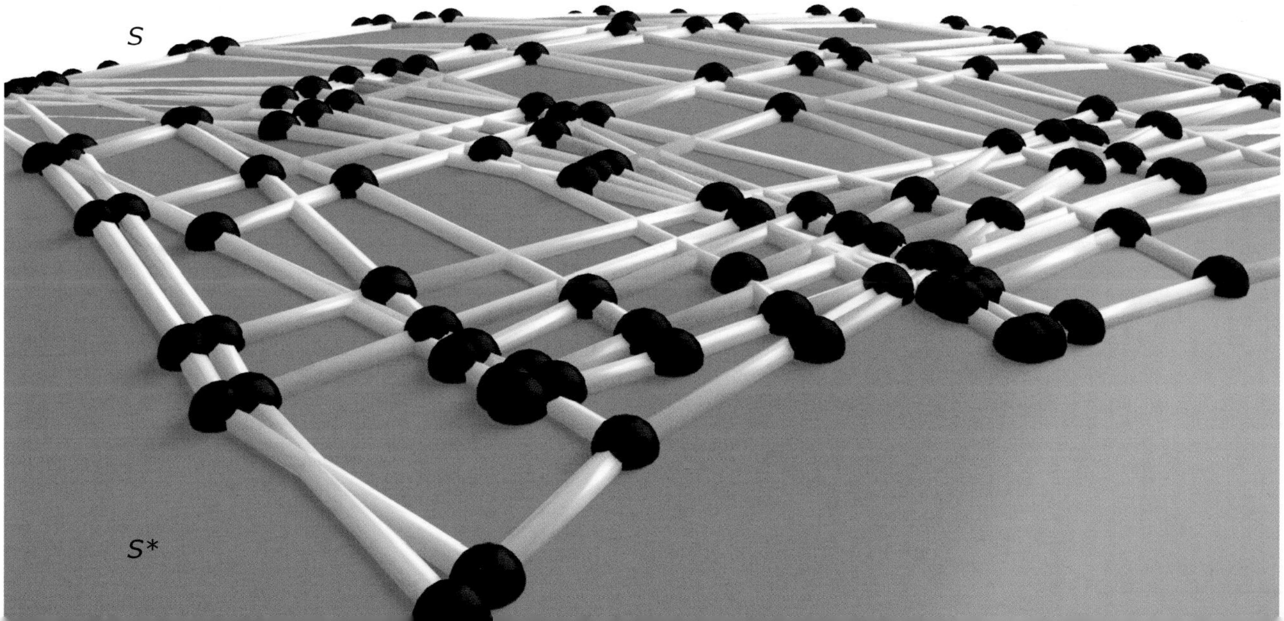

Vertex offsets: circular meshes. Due to the constant distance d between corresponding vertices of M and M^d, the coordinate vectors $\boldsymbol{s}_1 = (\boldsymbol{m}_1^d - \boldsymbol{m}_1)/d$, $\boldsymbol{s}_2 = (\boldsymbol{m}_2^d - \boldsymbol{m}_2)/d$, ... of the Gaussian image mesh S have length 1 and thus describe points on the unit sphere S^*. Thus, S has its vertices on the unit sphere S^*. Each face of S is planar and the plane of that face intersects S in a circle. Hence, each face of S has a circum-circle and therefore S is a circular mesh. M and M^d are parallel to S.

To show that M and M^d are also circular meshes, it is sufficient to prove the following property (Figure 19.25): If a planar quad 1234 has a circum-circle, any parallel quad 1*2*3*4* also has a circum-circle. A circular mesh M with Gaussian image S and vertex offset M^d are shown in Figure 19.24. We will not further discuss circular meshes and their vertex offsets, but instead refer you to the literature.

Face offsets: conical meshes. The existence of face offsets leads to a class of meshes that is particularly interesting for architecture [Liu et al. 2006]. Due to the constant distance between the parallel planes of corresponding faces in a face offset pair M, M^d, the Gaussian image mesh S has face planes that lie at constant distance 1 to the origin o. This means that the face planes of S are tangent to the unit sphere S^* (Figure 19.26).

We say S is circumscribed to S^*. Consider a vertex; for example, s_1 of S. The four face planes that meet at s_1 are tangent to S^*. Because all tangent planes of S^* that pass through that vertex s_1 envelope a cone of revolution C_1^* (with axis passing through the center o of S^*), the planes of faces meeting at s_1 are also tangent to the cone C_1^*.

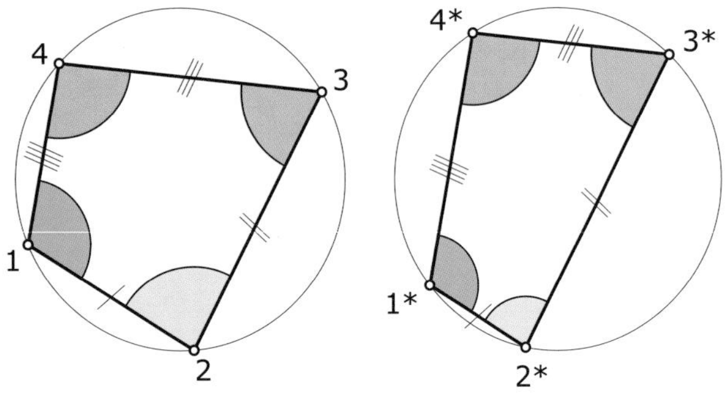

Fig. 19.25
For a quad 1234 with a circum-circle, the sum of opposite angles equals 180 degrees. Any quad 1*2*3*4* parallel to 1234 has the same angles and thus also has a circum-circle.

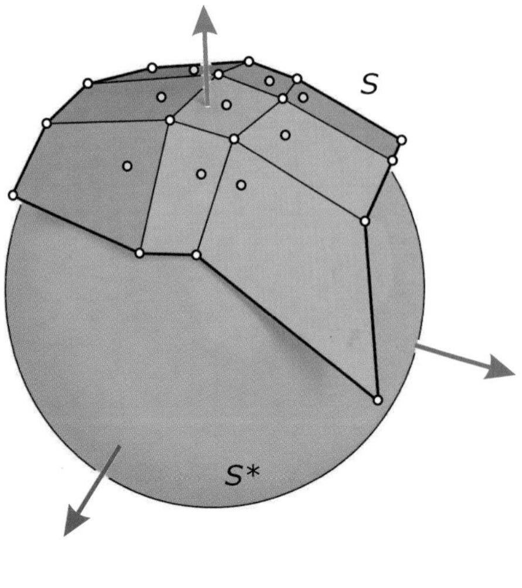

Fig. 19.26
The Gaussian image mesh of a conical mesh is a PQ mesh whose faces are tangent to the unit sphere.

Consider now the vertex m_1 of our mesh M (parallel to S), which corresponds to s_1. Because corresponding face planes in parallel meshes are parallel, the face planes meeting at m_1 are tangent to a cone of revolution C_1. We just have to translate the cone C_1^* so that its vertex s_1 moves to m_1. This translation moves face planes of S into corresponding face planes of M and thus moves C_1^* to a cone C_1 tangent to all face planes meeting at m_1. Because this holds for any other vertex as well, the mesh M has the property that *the face planes meeting at any vertex are tangent to a cone of revolution* associated with this vertex (Figure 19.27). Such a mesh M is therefore called a *conical mesh*.

A precise description requires the use of *oriented face planes* (e.g., oriented toward the outer side of the building). Various reasons this is more precise and has advantages in the study of conical meshes are given in the literature [Liu et al. 2006].

According to the previous general results, the node axis A_1 at a vertex m_1 of M contains the corresponding vertex m_1^d of the offset mesh M^d and thus A_1 is parallel to the line os_1, which connects the origin o (center of the unit sphere S^*) with the corresponding vertex s_1 of S. Because the line os_1 is the axis of the cone C_1^*, the node axis A_1 at m_1 must be the rotational axis of the cone C_1.

This can also be verified as follows. If we pass from M to a face offset M^d at distance d, we have to offset all face planes around a vertex m_1 by distance d. Thus, the translated planes will be tangent to the offset cone C_1^d of C_1, which has the same axis A_1. Hence, the corresponding vertex m_1^d lies on the cone axis A_1 and thus the *cone axis is seen as a discrete surface normal* at m_1. As we know, the collection of node axes (i.e., cone axes) defines a geometric support structure.

Even without the general theory, we see that neighboring cone axes lie in the same plane (Figure 19.28). The cones C_1, C_2 attached to the end points m_1, m_2 of an edge are tangent to the planes T_1, T_2 of the two faces meeting at that edge. Given two tangent planes T_1, T_2 of a cone of revolution, the axis of the cone must lie in their bisecting plane (here it is useful to have oriented planes T_1, T_2).

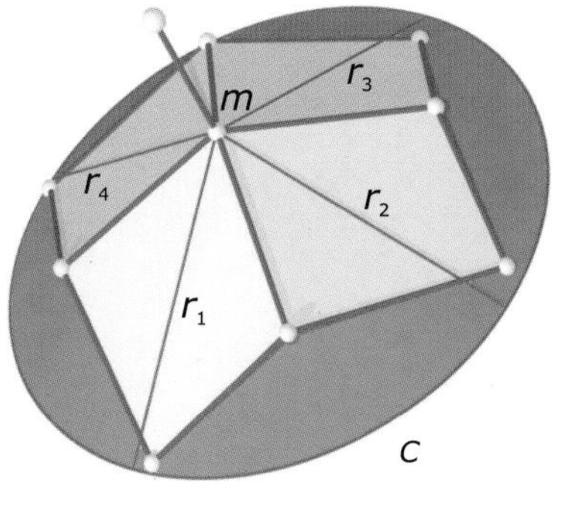

Fig. 19.27
In a conical mesh M, the planes of faces meeting at a vertex m are tangent to a cone of revolution C. This figure also shows the rulings $r_1, \ldots, r_4$ along which the face planes are tangent to the cone.

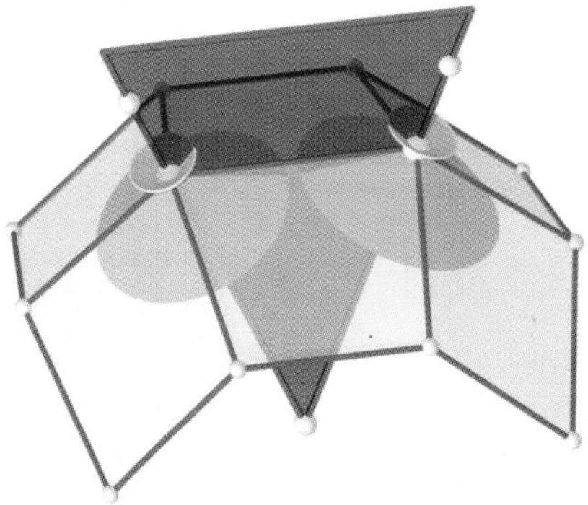

Fig. 19.28
In a conical mesh M, the node axes are the axes of the vertex cones. Node axes at the end points of any edge are co-planar because they lie in a bisecting plane of the two face planes meeting at that edge. Hence, the cone axes are suitable for the definition of a geometric support structure.

We can define a unique bisecting plane as the set of all points that have equal signed distance to T_1 and T_2 and lie on the same side (outer or inner side) of both planes. Hence, the axes A_1, A_2 of the two adjacent cones lie in the bisecting plane of the two face planes T_1, T_2. Thus, we again see that the cone axes are suitable for the definition of node axes and a geometric support structure.

It turns out that the *cone condition* at a vertex can also be formulated in terms of angles (see Figure 19.29a). The sum of opposite edge angles must be equal:

$$\omega_1 + \omega_3 = \omega_2 + \omega_4.$$

The proof of this relation is easily derived for a convex vertex (as for the one in Figure 19.29b), but there are other cases (Figure 19.29c,d) that are more difficult to understand and for which the proof requires more work.

The angle condition is very useful for optimization procedures aimed at changing a mesh toward a conical mesh. This angle balance condition may also be seen as a *discrete condition for orthogonality of the two mesh polygons passing through a vertex.* Because conical meshes are orthogonal and conjugate in a discrete sense, *conical meshes are a discrete version of the network of principal curvature lines on a smooth surface.*

This is important for practical design as well. The layout of a conical mesh on a given surface can be based on an optimization algorithm whose input mesh has been derived from the network of principal curvature lines. Figure 19.30 depicts conical meshes designed with the strategy of alternating between subdivision and mesh optimization (see Liu et al. [2006]).

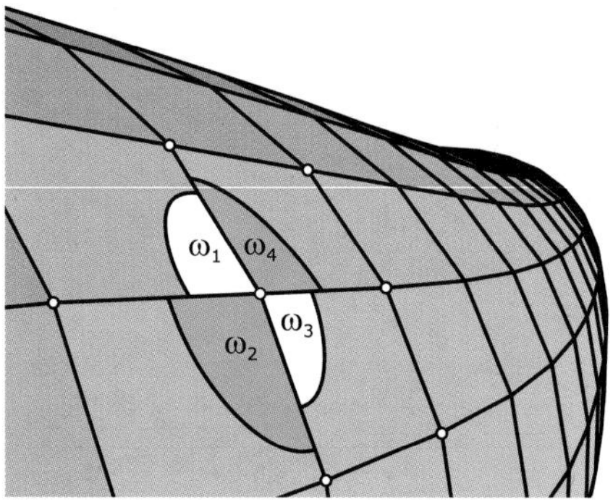

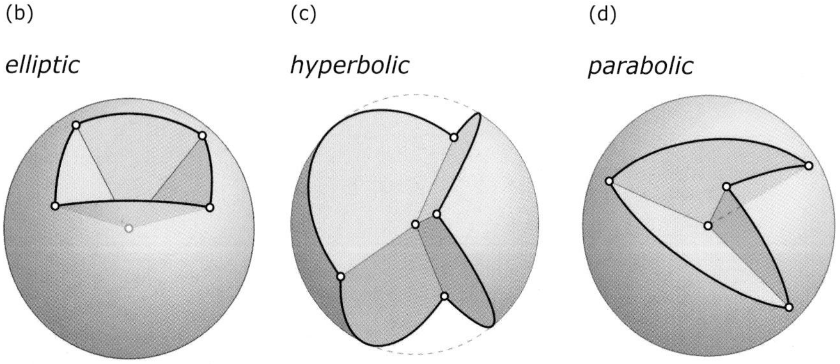

Fig. 19.29
(a) At a vertex of a conical mesh, the sum of opposite edge angles is equal: $\omega_1 + \omega_3 = \omega_2 + \omega_4$.
(b)Although this is easy to prove for a convex vertex,
(c,d) other types of vertices require a more detailed analysis.

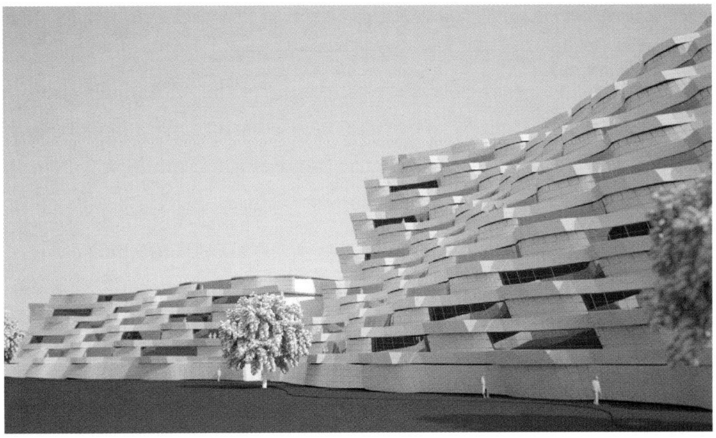

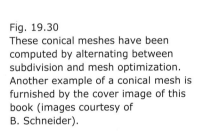

Fig. 19.30
These conical meshes have been computed by alternating between subdivision and mesh optimization. Another example of a conical mesh is furnished by the cover image of this book (images courtesy of B. Schneider).

Meshes with edge offsets. The construction of PQ meshes with *edge offsets* is more difficult than the cases of vertex offsets or face offsets. Thus, we will keep the discussion short and refer you to the literature [Pottmann et al. 2007] for a thorough discussion. A pair of meshes M and M^d at constant edge-edge distance d has as Gaussian image mesh S a PQ mesh whose edges are tangent to the unit sphere S^*. Such a mesh, known as a *Koebe mesh*, has an interesting geometry (Figure 19.31).

The face planes of S intersect S^* in circles, which are the inscribed circles of the faces. In this way, we obtain a (special) circle packing on the sphere S^*. Computing such circle arrangements is possible, even on-line [Sechelmann 2006], but the underlying mathematics is beyond the scope of this book. Therefore, we simply assume that we have computed a Koebe mesh S with one of the available tools. Then, any mesh M parallel to S has the edge offset property. The offsets M^d are the meshes $M + d \cdot S$ (understood in the same sense as the scaled difference mesh).

Since four edges emanating from a vertex s_1 of S are tangent to S^*, they are rulings of a right circular cone with vertex s_1 circumscribed to S^*. The axis os_1 of the cone forms equal angles with all rulings, and hence forms equal angles with all edges of S meeting in s_1. By parallelism of corresponding edges in M and S, the same holds for M.

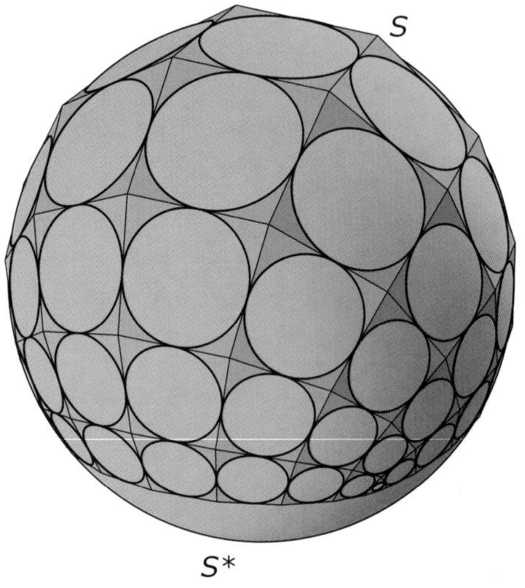

Fig. 19.31
A mesh M with edge offsets is parallel to a Koebe mesh S. The mesh S has planar faces, and its edges are tangent to the unit sphere S^*. The inscribed circles of the faces of S form a circle packing on the sphere.

Fig. 19.32
A practically useful geometric support structure can be assigned to a given mesh M with the help of a parallel mesh S approximating the unit sphere S^*.

Here, S has an over-folding due to a change in the sign of Gaussian curvature in M and is contained in the layer between radii 0.98 and 1.04.

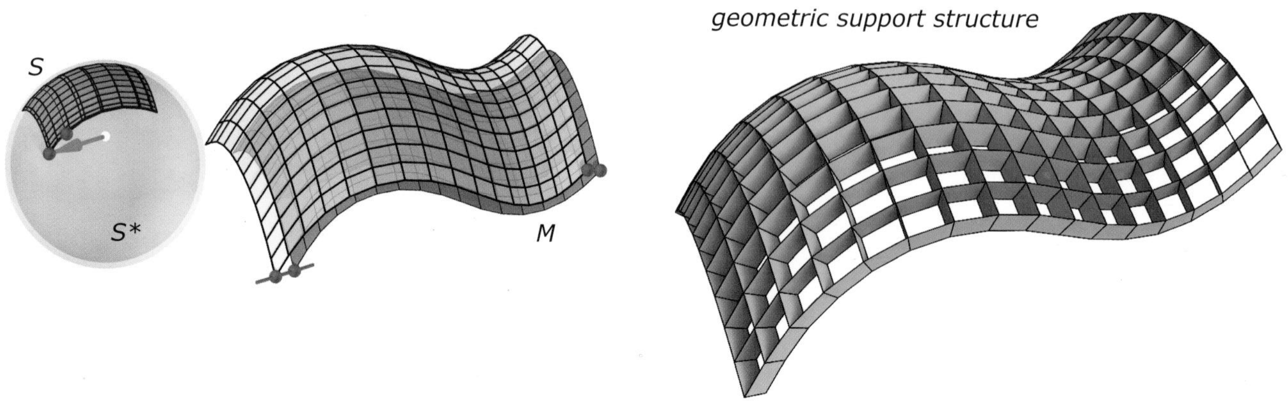

The edges meeting at a vertex m_1 lie in a cone of revolution whose axis A_1 is the node axis. Thus, its incoming edges form the same angle with the node axis. This is in accordance with the fact that beams of constant height meet at the node in a perfect way (Figure 19.21). Unfortunately, quad meshes with edge offsets are not capable of approximating arbitrary shapes and thus we do not further discuss them.

Approximate offsets: computing a support structure for a PQ mesh. Assume that we have constructed a PQ mesh M, but the mesh M does not have precise offsets. To compute a geometric support structure for M, we have to find a suitable parallel mesh M^*—ideally at constant edge-edge distance d to M. If corresponding edges of M and M^* lie at approximately constant edge-edge distance d, the edges of the scaled difference mesh $S = (M^* - M)/d$ must have approximately distance 1 to the origin.

This means that the edges of S should be nearly tangent to the unit sphere S^*. In practice, only M is given. To compute a support structure for M, one first computes the parallel mesh S that best approximates the unit sphere S^*. This problem turns out to be a rather simple optimization problem in the (linear) space of all meshes parallel to M. The vertices of S determine the node axes, the parallel mesh $M^* = M + dS$, and thus the geometric support structure. Examples are provided by Figures 19.32 and 19.33. For details on the optimization, see Pottmann et al. [2007].

Fig. 19.33
These support structures have been computed with the method outlined in Figure 19.32. The auxiliary mesh S employed in the construction of the support structure for the mesh M is of extremely low aesthetic quality but still serves very well for the purpose of supporting beam layout. The mesh S also shows that a mesh parallel to a fair mesh such as M need not be fair as well.

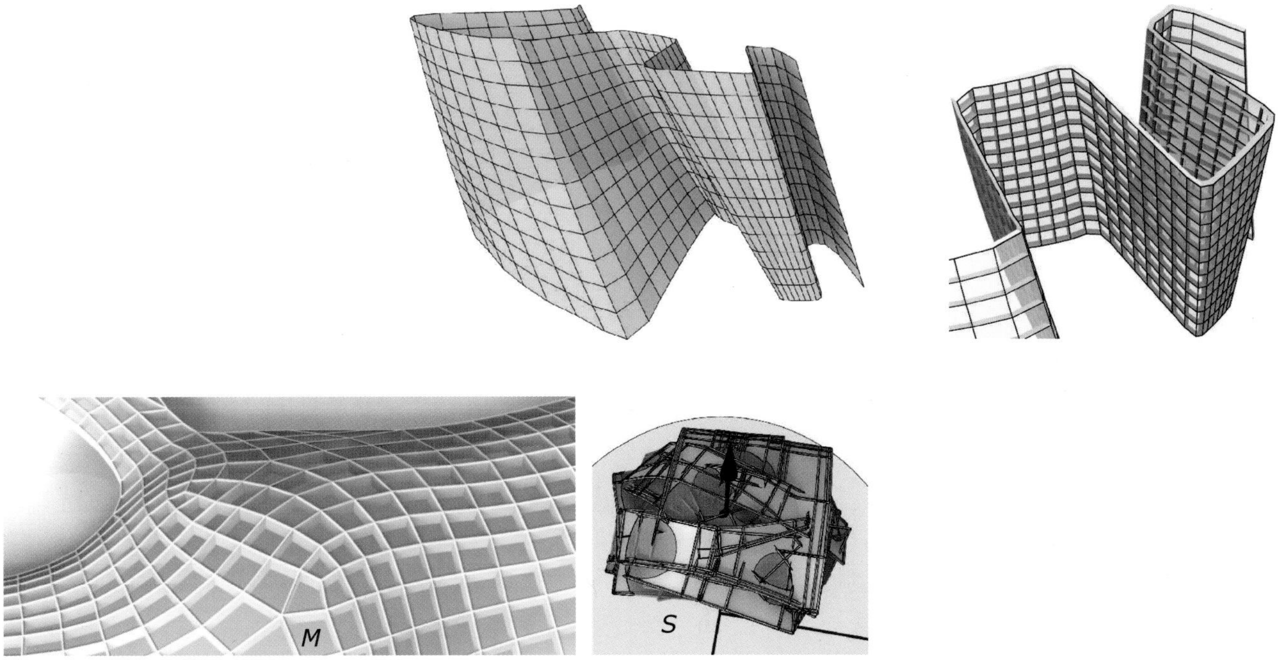

Fig. 19.34
(a) A quad Q^* in a Koebe mesh S and the corresponding parallel quad Q in the mesh M that represents a discrete minimal surface have reverse orientation and parallel diagonals (13 parallel 2*4*, 24 parallel 1*3*).
(b) Discrete minimal surface M (catenoid; see Chapter 18) obtained from a Koebe mesh S with rotational symmetry.

(a)

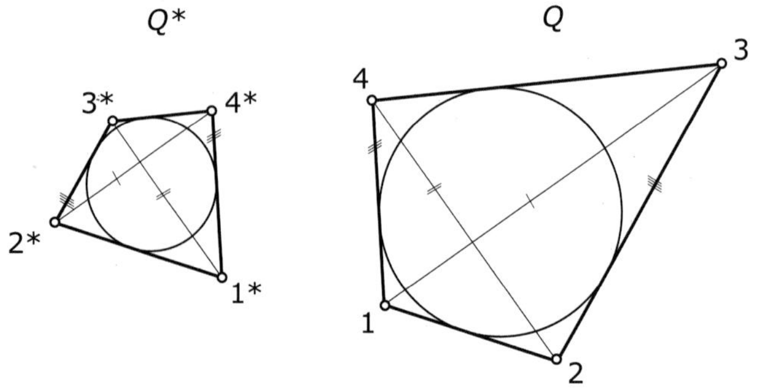

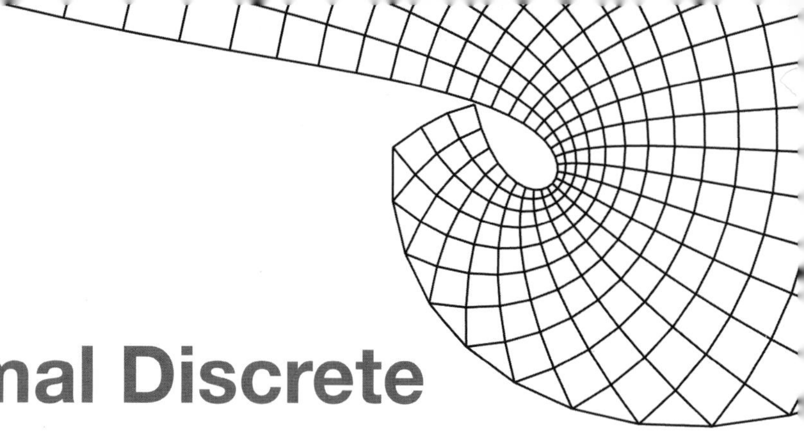

Optimal Discrete Surfaces

We conclude our study of discrete surfaces for architecture with a few discrete analogues to surfaces that result from optimization problems. Mainly, we examine minimal surfaces and surfaces closely related to them. These considerations will also lead us to meshes in static equilibrium.

Discrete minimal surfaces. The Koebe meshes S introduced in connection with edge offsets (Figure 19.32) are the basis of an elegant construction of discrete minimal surfaces [Bobenko et al. 2006]. The construction starts with a Koebe mesh S and transforms it into a discrete minimal surface M. The mesh M is parallel to S, and its faces are constructed as illustrated in Figure 19.34. Let $Q^* = 1^*2^*3^*4^*$ be a quadrilateral face of S,. The corresponding quad $Q = 1234$ of M then has parallel edges, reversed orientation, and parallel diagonals as follows.

$$13 \text{ parallel } 2^*4^*, \; 24 \text{ parallel } 1^*3^*$$

(b)

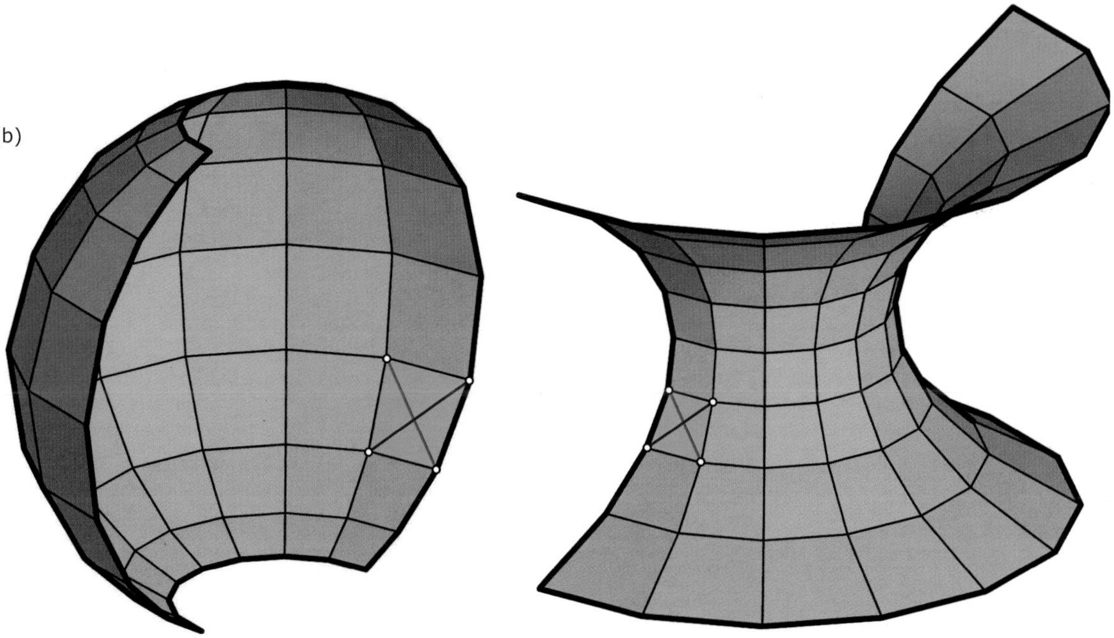

We start the entire construction of M with any face Q^* of S. For Q, we still have the choice of one vertex position and one edge length. Now we continue with adjacent faces and will observe that there are no contradictions in the construction. Four faces meeting in a vertex of S will lead to four faces meeting in the corresponding vertex of M. An interesting result is illustrated in Figure 19.35 (for details on this discrete Schwarz minimal surface, see [Bobenko et al. 2006]).

The minimal meshes M possess edge offsets because they are parallel to Koebe meshes. It is remarkable that the existence of an inscribed circle of the face Q^* in the Koebe mesh implies that the corresponding face Q of M has an inscribed circle (Figure 19.34a). Thus, these discrete minimal surfaces M are also formed by a collection of circles.

There are various reasons the meshes M can be considered discrete counterparts of minimal surfaces. One is that one can develop an appropriate curvature theory and then see that M has vanishing discrete mean curvature [Pottmann et al. 2007]. Another reason is that the relation between M and S can be viewed as a discrete conformal (i.e., angle-preserving) mapping. A variety of further beautiful analogues to results on smooth minimal surfaces are found in Bobenko et al. [2006].

The Christoffel dual: static equilibrium of diagonal meshes. Applying the construction of Figure 19.34 to a Koebe mesh S will yield the mesh M in a consistent way. We call M the *Christoffel dual* of S. Applying the construction to M, we return to S. Christoffel duality is a symmetric relation. As mentioned previously, the consistency of the construction is not obvious. Starting with an arbitrary PQ mesh S and applying the construction, one will fail to obtain a mesh M. This is easily seen as follows. Assume that we have used the construction to obtain three quads Q_1, Q_2, and Q_3 of M, meeting at a vertex m. The fourth quad Q_4 follows from parallelism of its edges to the corresponding edges in S, and thus the parallel diagonal property cannot be guaranteed for Q_4 and Q_4^*.

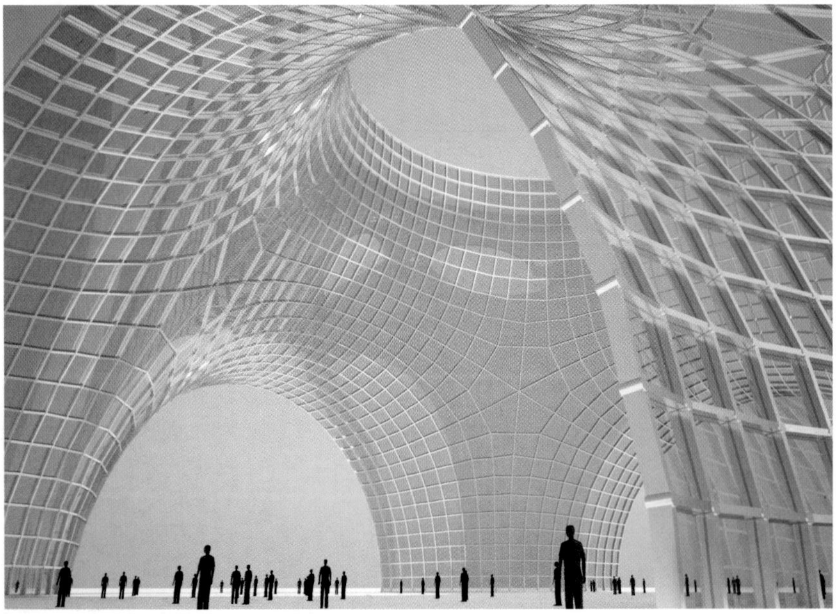

Fig. 19.35
This discrete minimal surface (Schwarz surface) is computed from Koebe meshes via the face-wise construction illustrated in Figure 19.34 (mesh courtesy of S. Sechelmann).

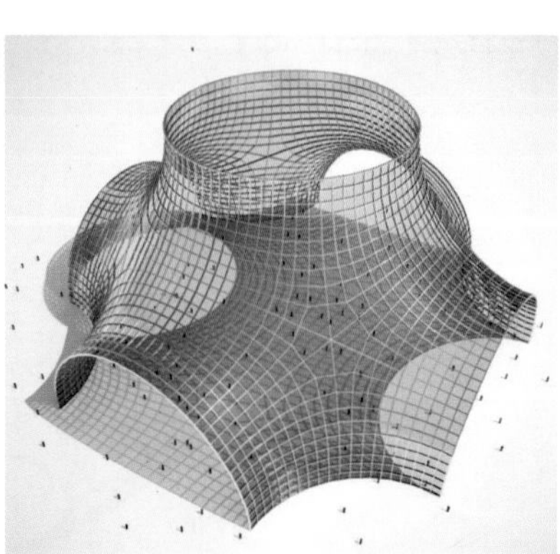

In other words, a mesh S to which the construction can be applied needs to satisfy certain criteria. These criteria are understood if we look at the meshes formed by the diagonals of S and M. In fact, S has two *diagonal meshes* D_1^* and D_2^*, and M has two diagonal meshes D_1 and D_2. These are quadrilateral meshes (in general, with nonplanar faces). Due to the parallel diagonal property of Figure 19.34, we can use a notation such that corresponding edges in D_1 and D_1* are parallel (likewise, corresponding edges in D_2 and D_2^* are parallel).

Edges of a face in D_1^* correspond to edges emanating from a vertex in D_1, and vice versa (Figure 19.36). Such meshes are called *reciprocal parallel* and arise *as reciprocal force diagrams in graphical statics*. Let's view D_1 as a framework of rods connected with spherical joints. We assume that in some vertices external forces are applied. A system of internal forces is an assignment of a pair of opposite forces to each edge, one for either end. Such a system of forces is in equilibrium if for each vertex the sum of forces equals zero.

Then the existence of the reciprocal mesh D_1^* implies that there is an assignment of forces such that the resulting system is in static equilibrium (the external forces to be applied at the boundary follow from the reciprocal diagram). Omitting a more thorough discussion, we can state that a mesh S can be transformed by the Christoffel dual construction if its diagonal meshes can be brought into static equilibrium (if one diagonal mesh can be brought into equilibrium, the same holds for the other diagonal mesh). Note that the diagonal meshes may be materialized to stiffen a quad mesh with planar faces (see Figure 19.37).

It is known that the existence of static equilibrium is preserved when affine or even projective transformations are applied. Hence, we may apply the Christoffel dual to any mesh resulting from a Koebe mesh by a projective transform.

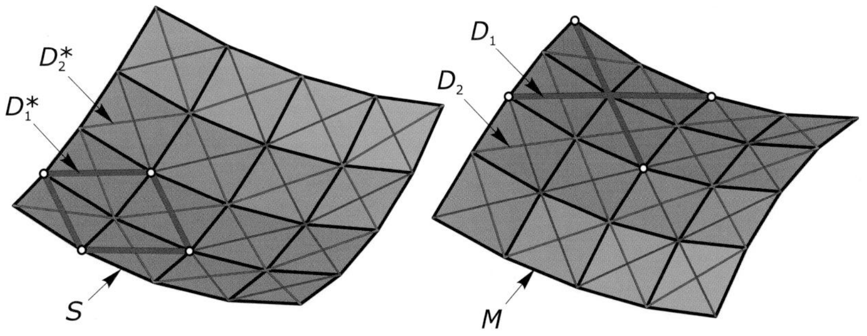

Fig. 19.36
Diagonals in a pair of meshes *S*, *M* that are related by the Christoffel dual construction of Figure 19.34 can be arranged into reciprocal parallel meshes. Hence, these diagonal meshes can be brought into static equilibrium. Only meshes whose diagonal meshes are in equilibrium possess a Christoffel dual.

Fig. 19.37
Diagonal meshes may be used as stiffening elements in a steel/glass construction based on a PQ mesh. (image courtesy of Schlaich Bergermann and Partners.)

The mesh in Figure 19.38 has been constructed in this way. A Koebe mesh has been transformed such that the sphere S^* is mapped to a paraboloid of revolution with vertical axis, and then the Christoffel dual has been computed (for geometric properties of such meshes, see Pottmann and Liu [2007]). Christoffel duality also plays a central role in the computation of discrete counterparts to surfaces with constant mean curvature and may be extended to meshes with planar hexagonal faces.

Beyond quad meshes. Most of what we have said about offsets of PQ meshes can be extended to meshes formed by planar N-gons, with N greater than 4. Pentagonal and hexagonal meshes that possess edge offsets and a certain type of shape optimality are shown in Figures 19.39 and 19.40. They have been computed with recently developed methods from discrete differential geometry [Pottmann et al. 2007]. Note that these meshes possess non-convex faces in negatively curved areas. Structural considerations will lead to the insertion of additional stiffening diagonals, which are missing in the figures.

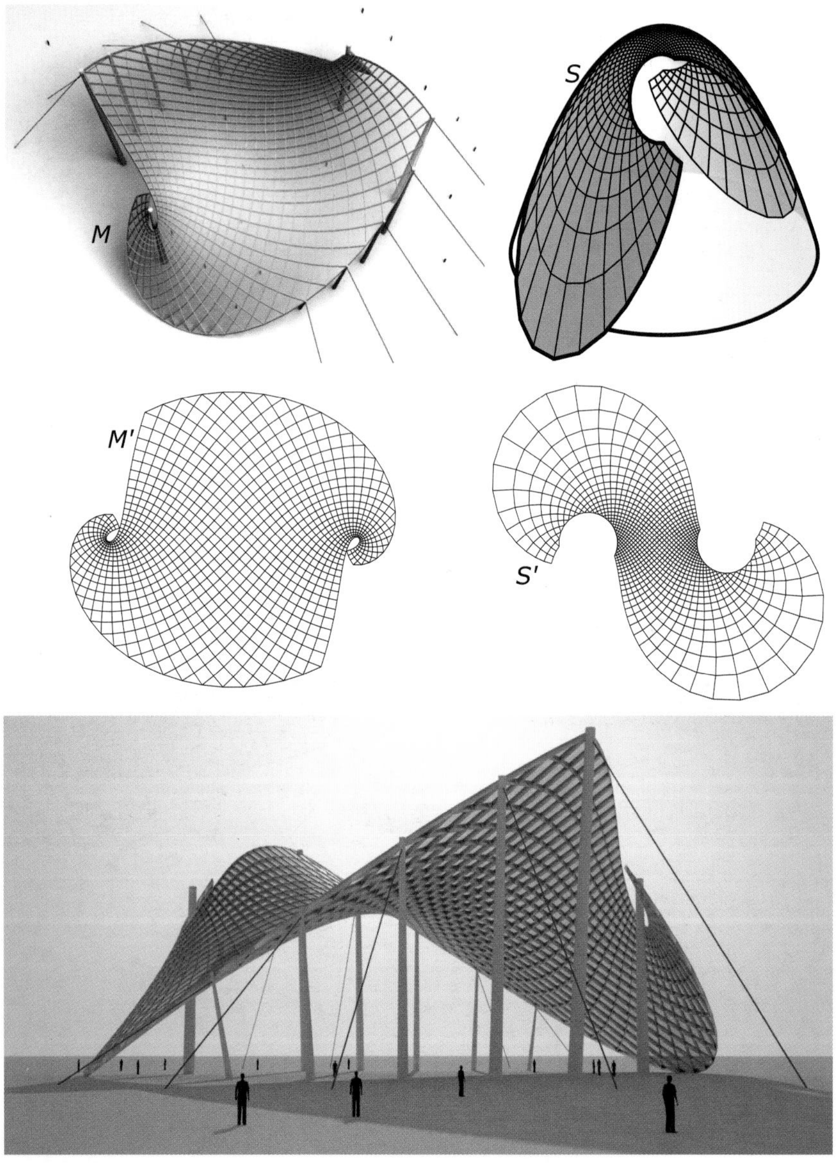

Fig. 19.38
This PQ mesh M has been computed via Christoffel duality from a mesh S whose edges are tangent to a paraboloid of revolution with vertical axis. It can be shown that the top views M' and S' of M and S, respectively, are discrete versions of orthogonal curve networks.

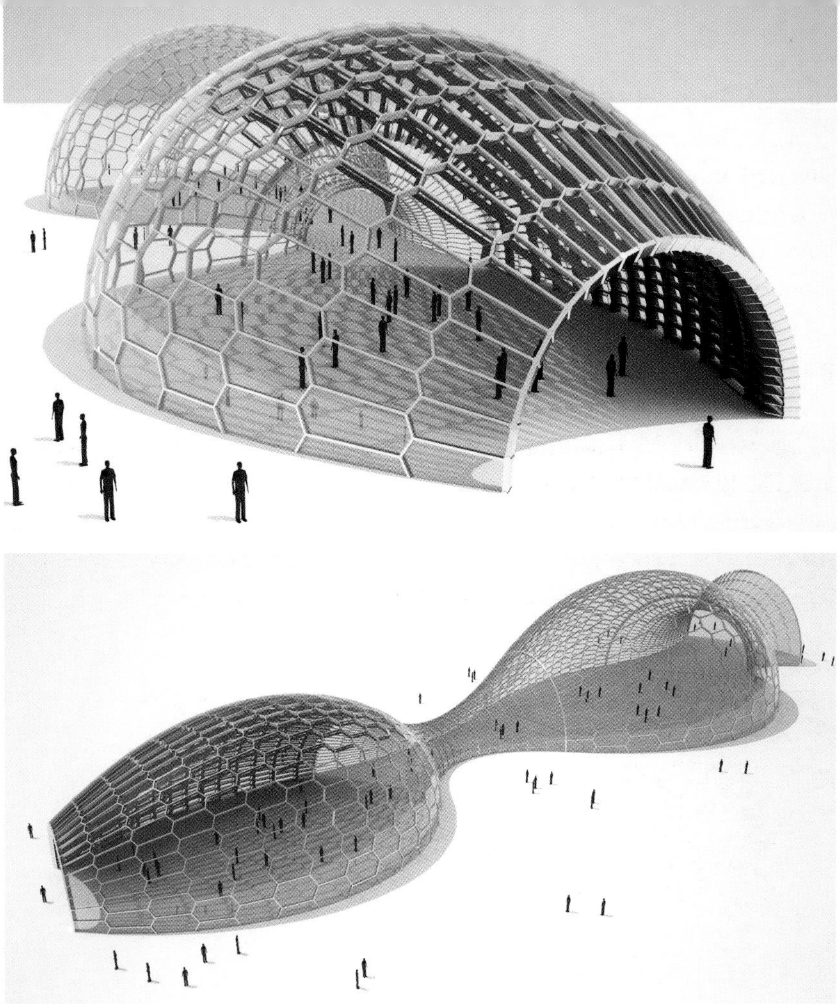

(b)

(a)

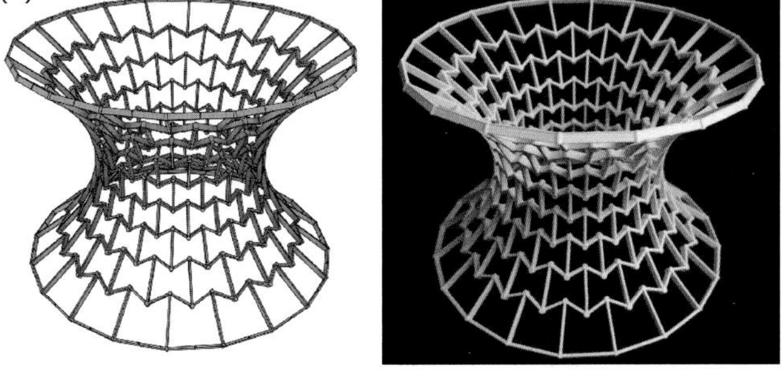

Fig. 19.39
Two hexagonal edge offset meshes.
(a) This mesh, also shown as a model obtained by rapid prototyping, is a discrete version of a catenoid (rotational minimal surface).
(b) This mesh is related to a surface with constant mean curvature (via a Laguerre transformation). The planar hexagons are convex in areas with positive Gaussian curvature and non-convex in the negatively curved parts.

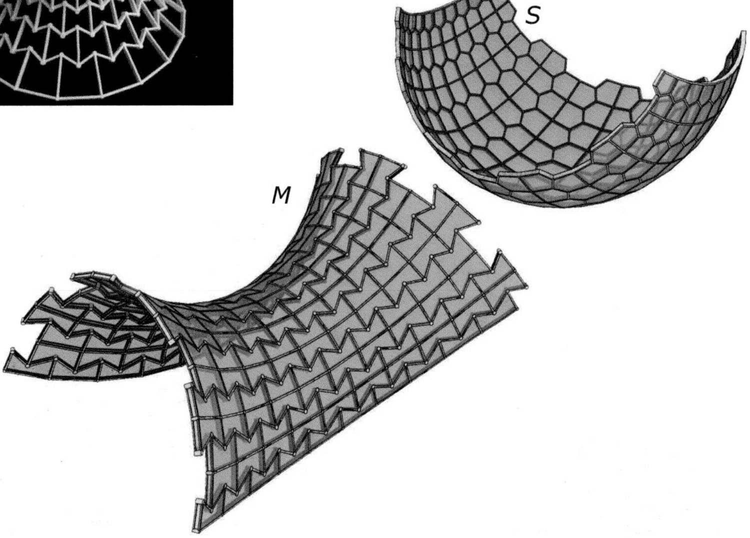

Fig. 19.40
The pentagonal edge offset mesh *M* has been constructed from the parallel Koebe mesh *S* by a change of face orientations and by an optimization procedure that aims at fairness of *M*. In negatively curved areas, planarity of faces can only be achieved by the use of non-convex pentagons.

Future Research

We have reached here the current frontier of research in architectural geometry. There is quite a lot of work ahead of us. We would like to address a few important directions for future research, especially in order to stimulate more work at the interesting border between architectural design and geometry processing.

- We need new and intuitive tools for the design of PQ meshes. Because PQ meshes are discrete versions of conjugate curve networks, a possible approach would be an interactive method for the design of conjugate curve networks in which the network curves "automatically" avoid asymptotic directions and consequently intersect transversely. These curve networks can then be used to construct quad meshes capable of optimization.
- In architectural design, the aesthetic value of meshes is of great importance. It is natural to employ geometric objective functions and consider their minimizers. Minimal surfaces are an example, but more work is needed in this area.
- Optimization should not neglect statics and structural considerations.
- The climate within glass structures demands separate attention. Geometric questions that occur here have to do with light and shade, the possibility of shading systems tied to support structures, and even a layout of supporting beams with regard to shading (for an initial result, see Figure 19.39b). In addition, the aesthetic component is present here at all times.
- A challenge is to devise a geometric optimization strategy of freeform surfaces that supports the architectural design process.
- The "right" choice of an overall segmentation of a multilayered building skin with a good planar mesh is an important problem.
- We have confined our discussion so far to planar panels. Depending on the chosen manufacturing technology, other panel shapes (such as cylinders or developable surfaces) are very well suited [Shelden 2002]. This topic requires a lot of future research. We conclude by quoting Lars Spuybroek: "The panellization of complex double curved surfaces is a hugely important issue, aesthetically and methodologically. ... The least interesting method is triangulation,... The most interesting techniques are based on variability, which is a 'textile' way of thinking, where flexible bands precede the hardened ceramic tile." [Spuybroek 2004].

References and Further Reading

Bobenko A, Hoffmann T, Springborn B. Minimal surfaces from circle patterns: Geometry from combinatorics. Annals of Math 2006;164:231–364.

Brell-Cokcan S, Pottmann H. Supporting structure for feeform surfaces in buildings. Patent No. A1049/2006.

Floater M, Hormann K. Surface parameterization: a tutorial and survey. In N A Dodgson et al. (eds.), *Advances in Multiresolution for Geometric Modeling.* Springer 2005:157–186.

Glymph J, Shelden D, Ceccato C, Mussel J, Schober H. A parametric strategy for freeform glass structures using quadrilateral planar facets. In *Acadia*, ACM 2002:303–321.

Liu Y, Pottmann H, Wallner J, Yang Y, Wang W. Geometric modeling with conical meshes and developable surfaces. ACM Transactions on Graphics 2006;25:681–689.

Pottmann H, Liu Y. Discrete surfaces in isotropic geometry. Mathematics of Surfaces 2007; Lecture Notes in Computer Science Vol. 4647:341–363.

Pottmann H, Brell-Cokcan S, Wallner J. Discrete surfaces for architectural design. In P Chenin, T Lyche, L Schumaker (eds.), *Curves and Surfaces: Avignon 2006.* Nashboro Press 2007.

Pottmann H, Liu Y, Wallner J, Bobenko A, Wang W. Geometry of multi-layer freeform structures for architecture. ACM Transactions on Graphics 2007;26 (in press).

Schober H. Freeform glass structures. In *Proceedings of Glass Processing Days 2003.* Tampere (Finland): 46–50.

Shelden D. Digital surface representation and the constructibility of Gehry's architecture. Ph.D. thesis, MIT, 2002.

Spuybroek L. *NOX: Machining Architecture*. New York: Thames & Hudson 2004.

Appendix A – Geometry Primer

In this appendix we provide short descriptions of a few basic geometric concepts, as well as some comments on our notation.

Nomenclature

We label *points*, *straight lines*, and *curves* with lowercase characters in *italic font*. In most cases, we use the first letter of the name of the corresponding point or line to denote them. For example, a general point is denoted p, whereas a general line is labeled l, and a tangent with t. As a consequence, an axis should be labeled with the small letter a. But this could be confusing in some text passages. Thus, for the sake of readability we use the capital letter A to label an axis.

In three-dimensional space, we also have *planes* (which can be considered flat surfaces). Planes and *surfaces* are labeled with uppercase characters in *italic font*. For example, a plane might be labeled P and a cylinder (surface) C.

In Chapter 7 (on curves and surfaces), the letter t is reserved for describing the parameter. Thus, to avoid misunderstandings in that chapter we label a tangent with the capital letter T.

To label a set of points corresponding to one geometric object, it is often convenient to use the same label p together with a counting number i, which we add as an *index* to the name of each point. Instead of giving different points of the same object different labels p, q, r, and so forth we denote them with p_0, p_1, p_2, and so forth. In the notation p_i the letter p indicates "point" and the small subscript i indicates the "index."

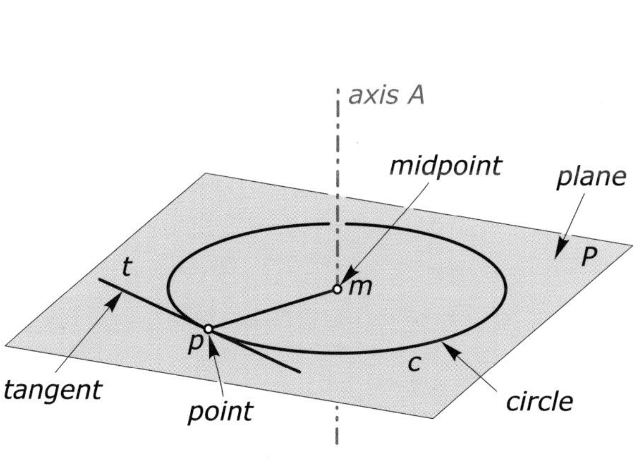

Basic Operations on Vectors

The *addition* of two **vectors**↑ **a** and **b** results in a vector **c** = **a** + **b**, which is constructed by appending one of the two vectors at the terminal point of the other (parallelogram rule). If the coordinates of the input vectors are **a** = (a_1,a_2,a_3) and **b** = (b_1,b_2,b_3), the sum of the two vectors is **c** = $(a_1 + b_1, a_2 + b_2, a_3 + b_3)$.

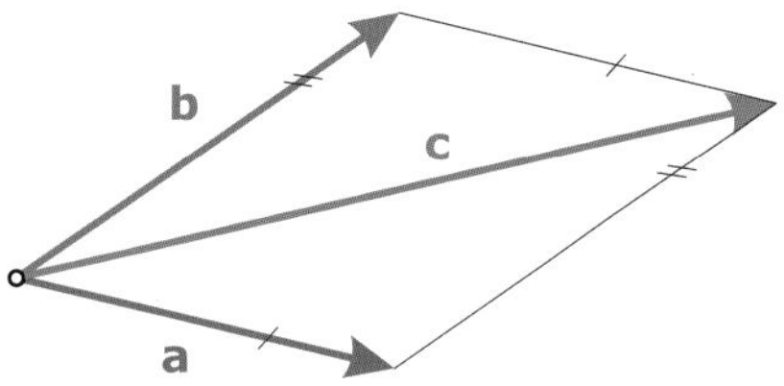

Multiplication of a vector **a** = (a_1,a_2,a_3) with a real number t yields the vector = $(t{\cdot}a_1,\ t{\cdot}a_2,\ t{\cdot}a_3)$. This scales the vector with factor t. Multiplication by a negative number t reverses the orientation. Because addition and multiplication by a number correspond to the ordinary addition and multiplication in each coordinate, familiar rules such as $t{\cdot}(\mathbf{a} + \mathbf{b}) = t{\cdot}\mathbf{a} + t{\cdot}\mathbf{b}$ and $(s + t){\cdot}\mathbf{a} = s{\cdot}\mathbf{a} + t{\cdot}\mathbf{a}$ hold.

Complex Numbers

A complex number is an expression of the form $a + b{\cdot}i$. Here, i is the imaginary unit satisfying the rule $i^2 = -1$. a and b are real numbers. We call a the real part and b the imaginary part of the complex number. Complex numbers whose complex part is equal to zero are real numbers. One can add and multiply complex numbers like ordinary terms, but we have to obey the rule $i^2 = -1$. For example, $(3 + 2i){\cdot}(1 - i) = 3 + 2i - 3i - 2i^2 = 3 + 2i - 3i - 2{\cdot}(-1) = 5 - i$.

Complex numbers can be viewed as **position vectors**↑ of points in the plane (called *Gaussian plane*), where the x-axis denotes the real part and the y-axis denotes the complex part. The *absolute value* of a complex number z is defined as the length of the position vector. It is calculated with the help of the **Pythagorean theorem**↑ as $|z| = \sqrt{a^2+b^2}$

The *argument* of z = atan (b/a) is the angle between the oriented x-axis and the position vector. The *complex conjugate* of a complex number $z = a + b{\cdot}i$ is defined as $\bar{z} = a - b{\cdot}i$. The two points z and $\bar{z}$ are symmetric with respect to the real axis.

Example: The complex number $z_1 = 3 + 4i$ has the real part 3 and the complex part 4. The absolute value is calculated with $5 = \sqrt{3^2+4^2}$, whereas the argument is atan(4/3) which is approximately 53,13°.

The complex conjugate of z_1 is $\bar{z}_1 = 3 - 4i$.

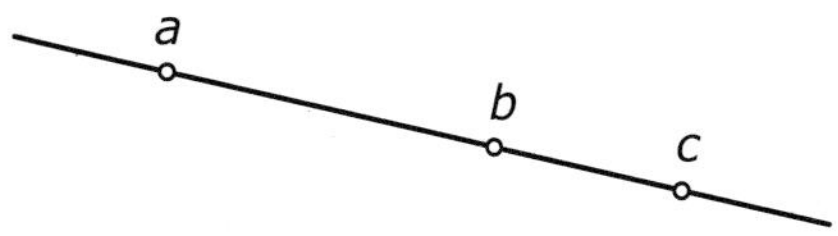

Collinear

Points are called *collinear* if they are contained in the same straight line.

Coordinates of a Vector

A **vector**↑ **a** viewed as a position vector emanates from the origin and has a terminal point with certain coordinates (a_1,a_2,a_3). These are the coordinates of the vector **a**. A direction vector may be translated to any initial point. To determine its coordinates, we translate it such that its initial point lies at the origin. Then the coordinates are those of the terminal point (as for a position vector). Clearly, in two dimensions we have only two coordinates.

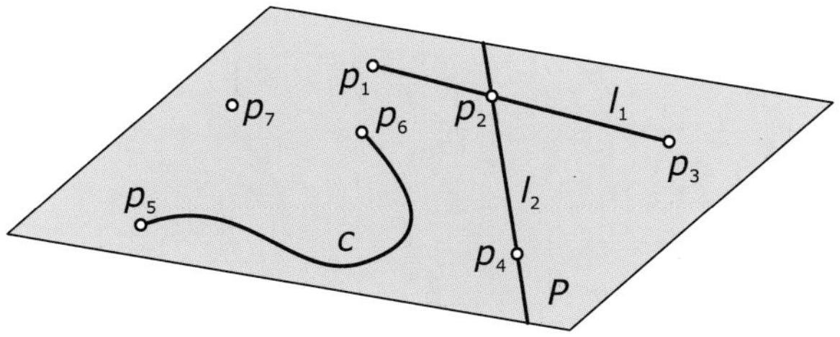

Co-planar

Geometric objects such as points, lines, and curves are called *co-planar* if they are contained in the same plane.

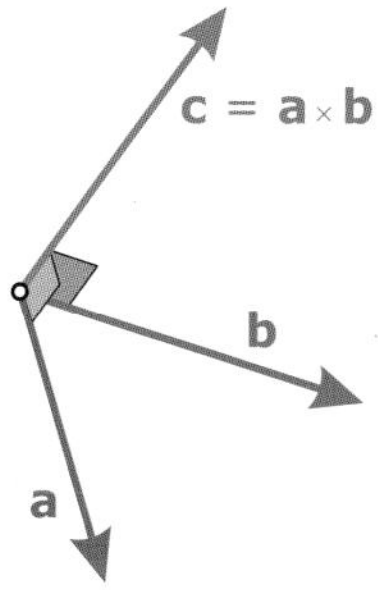

Cross Product of Vectors

In three-dimensional space, the cross product of two **vectors**↑ **a** and **b** results in a vector $\mathbf{c} = \mathbf{a} \times \mathbf{b}$ that is orthogonal two both vectors **a** and **b**. The cross product of $\mathbf{a} = (a_1,a_2,a_3)$ and $\mathbf{b} = (b_1,b_2,b_3)$ can be calculated by

$$\begin{aligned}\mathbf{c} &= (c_1,c_2,c_3)\\ &= (a_2{\cdot}b_3 - a_3{\cdot}b_2,\, a_3{\cdot}b_1 - a_1{\cdot}b_3,\, a_1{\cdot}b_2 - a_2{\cdot}b_1).\end{aligned}$$

Note that the cross product of two vectors results in a vector, whereas the **dot product**↑ results in a real number.

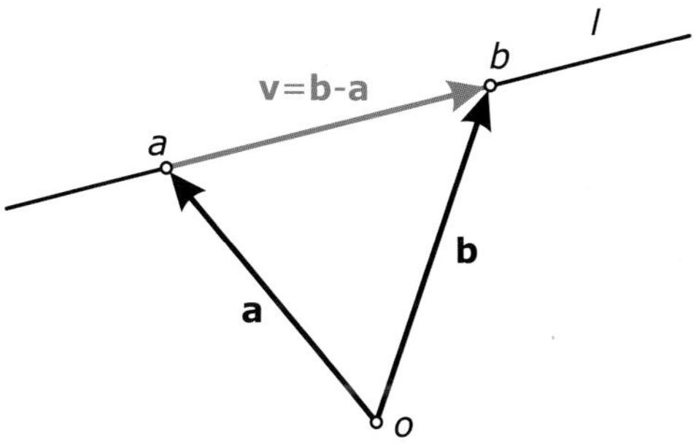

Direction Vector

A direction vector may be visualized as an arrow that can be translated to other positions (parallel arrows). Its initial point can be any point. It will always be clear from the context whether a vector has to be seen as a **position vector**↑ (of a point) or direction vector (of a straight line). The direction vector **v** joining two points with position vectors $\mathbf{a} = (a_1,a_2,a_3)$ and $\mathbf{b} = (b_1,b_2,b_3)$ is the vector $\mathbf{v} = \mathbf{b} - \mathbf{a} = (b_1 - a_1,\, b_2 - a_2,\, b_3 - a_3)$.

Dot Product of Vectors

The dot product (inner product, scalar product) of two **vectors**↑ $\mathbf{a} = (a_1,a_2,a_3)$ and $\mathbf{b} = (b_1,b_2,b_3)$ is a number computed as

$$\mathbf{a}\cdot\mathbf{b} = a_1 \cdot b_1 + a_2 \cdot b_2 + a_3 \cdot b_3.$$

If the two vectors have length $||\mathbf{a}||$ and $||\mathbf{b}||$ and if they enclose the angle α, the dot product satisfies

$$\mathbf{a}\cdot\mathbf{b} = ||\mathbf{a}|| \cdot ||\mathbf{b}|| \cdot \cos(\alpha).$$

Orthogonal vectors **a** and **b** belong to $\alpha = 90°$, and hence $\cos(\alpha) = 0$, and thus their dot product is equal to zero.

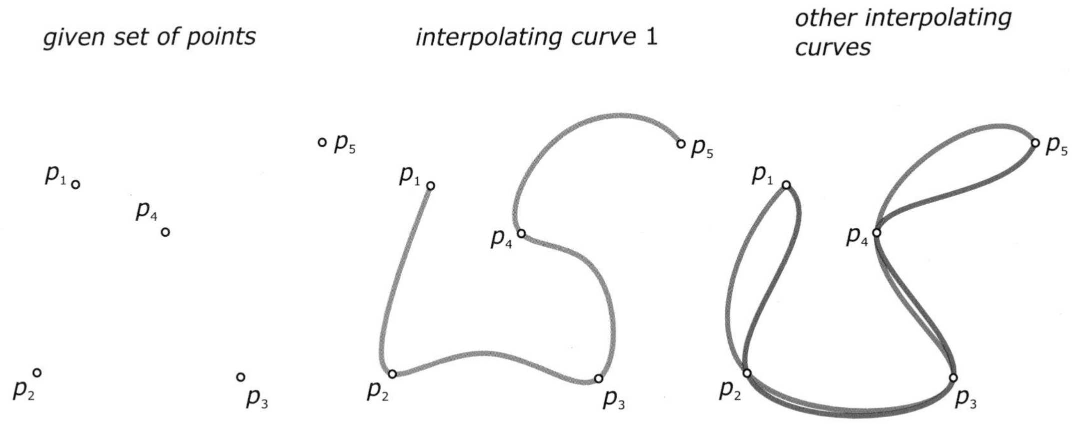

Interpolation

Given is a set of points. The aim of interpolation is to find a curve that exactly passes through the given points. In general, there are many different solutions to the problem and one needs to select an appropriate one. A special case of interpolation is **linear interpolation**↑, which joins two points by a straight line.

Length (Norm) of a Vector

If we view a vector as an arrow, the length of this arrow is the length (or norm) of the vector. A vector $\mathbf{a} = (a_1,a_2,a_3)$ has length $||\mathbf{a}|| = \sqrt{a_1^2+a_2^2+a_3^2}$.

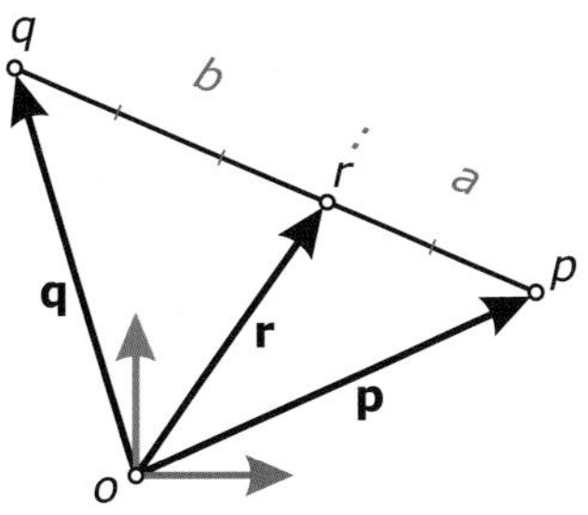

Linear Interpolation

Given are two points p and q. We want to find a point r that interpolates p and q such that it divides the straight line segment pq in a certain given **ratio**↑ $\text{dist}(p,r):\text{dist}(r,q) = a:b$. Noting $\text{dist}(p,r):\text{dist}(p,q) = a:(a+b)$, we find for the position vectors **p**,**q**, and **r** of the involved points

$$\mathbf{r} = \mathbf{p} + a/(a+b)\cdot(\mathbf{q} - \mathbf{p})$$
$$= (1 - a/(a+b))\cdot\mathbf{p} + a/(a+b)\cdot\mathbf{q}.$$

If we denote the fraction $a/(a+b)$ by t, we can rewrite the previous equation as

$$\mathbf{r} = (1-t)\cdot\mathbf{p} + t\cdot\mathbf{q}.$$

To indicate that the point r depends on the parameter t we often write $r(t)$ instead of r. Thus,

$$\mathbf{r}(t) = (1-t)\cdot\mathbf{p} + t\cdot\mathbf{q}. \qquad (1)$$

If the parameter t takes on all real numbers, the point $r(t)$ describes the entire straight line connecting the two points p and q. Equation (1) only involves linear functions of t and thus one speaks of linear interpolation. Note that if the parameter t assumes only values in the interval $[0,1]$ we obtain exactly the line segment between p $(t = 0)$ and q $(t = 1)$.

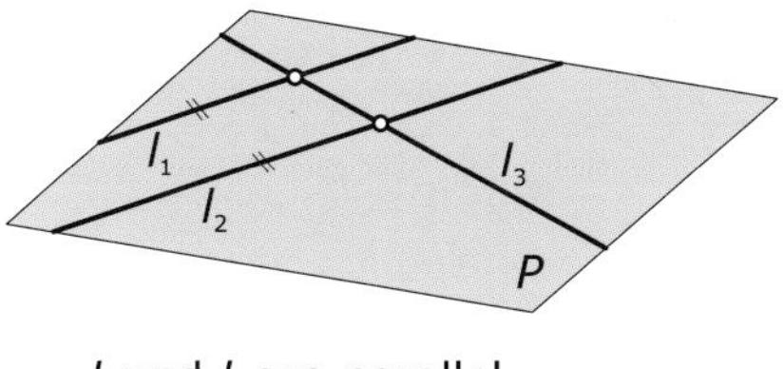

l_1 and l_2 are parallel
l_1 intersects l_2 and l_3

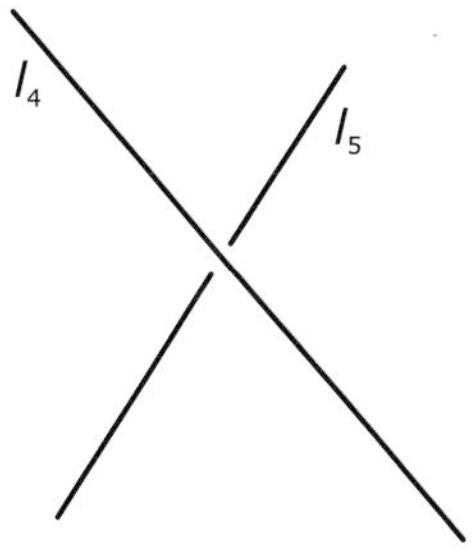

Mutual Positions of Lines

In two dimensions, lines are either *parallel* or *intersect*. In three dimensions, two lines either lie in a plane (they intersect or are parallel) or they are *skew*. In the latter (generic) case, they do not lie in a common plane and thus form a truly spatial configuration.

Normal to a Plane

A normal to a plane P (or a planar polygonal face) is a line perpendicular to all lines contained in the plane P. The direction of the normal can be computed with the help of the **cross product**↑ of two vectors parallel to P.

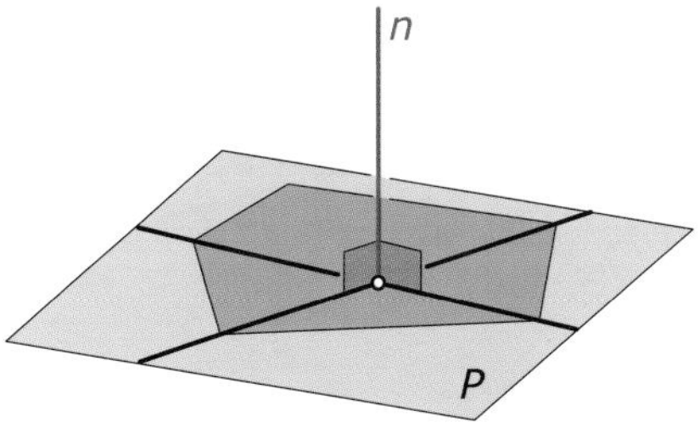

Parallelogram

A parallelogram is a planar quadrilateral with opposite sides parallel. Thus, opposite sides are of equal length and opposite angles are also equal.

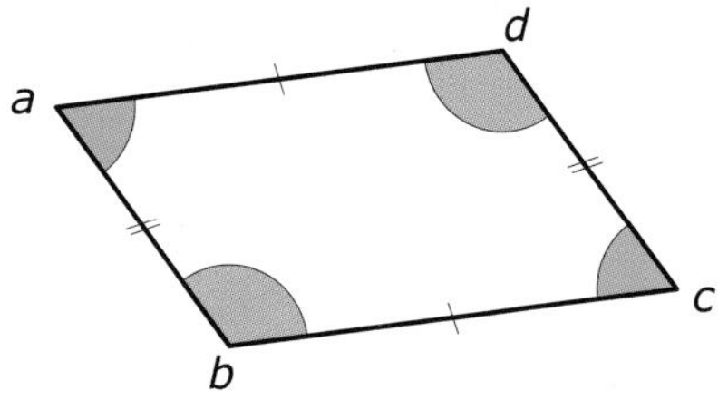

Planes

The analytical representation of planes in three dimensions bears some similarity with that of straight lines and thus we recommend studying them together. A plane P can be spanned by three points p,q,r that form a triangle. Then, we introduce the direction vectors $\mathbf{a} = \mathbf{q} - \mathbf{p}$ and $\mathbf{b} = \mathbf{r} - \mathbf{p}$. Multiples of these vectors, $u{\cdot}\mathbf{a}$ and $v{\cdot}\mathbf{b}$, are parallel to the plane and thus $\mathbf{x} = \mathbf{p} + u{\cdot}\mathbf{a} + v{\cdot}\mathbf{b}$ is the position vector of a point in the plane. This is called the *parametric representation* of the plane. The parameters u and v are real numbers that may be chosen arbitrarily. Different choices lead to different points of the plane.

A vector $\mathbf{n}$ normal to the plane can be computed as the cross product of $\mathbf{a}$ and $\mathbf{b}$ as $\mathbf{n} = \mathbf{a} \times \mathbf{b}$. Now the position vector $\mathbf{x}$ describes a point of the plane P exactly if the vector $\mathbf{x} - \mathbf{p}$ is normal to $\mathbf{n}$ [i.e., the dot product of these two vectors is zero, $\mathbf{n}{\cdot}(\mathbf{x} - \mathbf{p}) = 0$]. This is the *implicit equation* of a plane. For example, the plane with normal vector $\mathbf{n} = (2,-1,3)$ that passes through the point $\mathbf{p} = (1,2,0)$ has the equation $(2,-1,3){\cdot}(x - 1,y - 2,z) = 0$ (i.e., $2x - y + 3z = 0$. All points whose coordinates (x,y,z) satisfy this equation lie in the plane [obviously the origin (0,0,0) is among these].

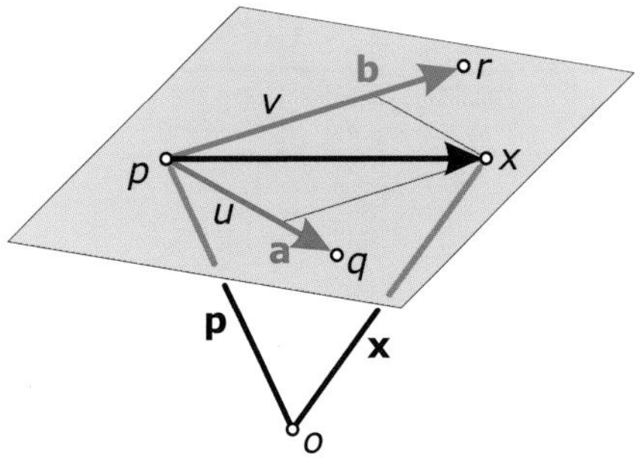

$\mathbf{x}=\mathbf{p}+u{\cdot}\mathbf{a}+v{\cdot}\mathbf{b}$

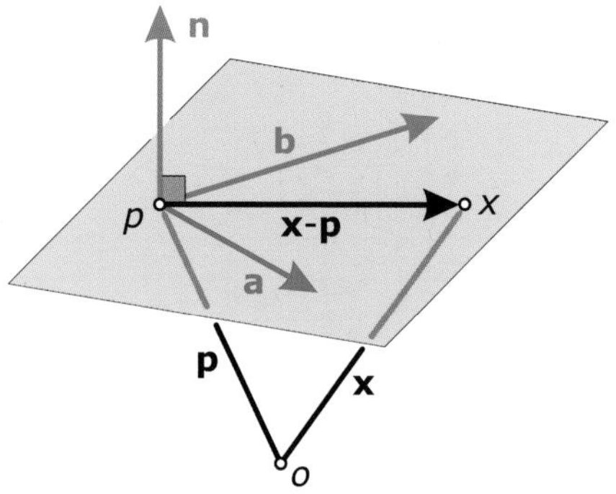

$\mathbf{n}{\cdot}(\mathbf{x}-\mathbf{p})=0$

Polygon and Polyline

A *polygon* (or *polyline*) is a figure that consists of a sequence of straight line segments called *edges*. Adjacent edges meet in points called *vertices*. We mainly use the term *polygon* for a closed figure, and *polyline* otherwise. However, we could not strictly follow this rule because a *control polygon* (which is standard terminology in geometric design) need not be closed.

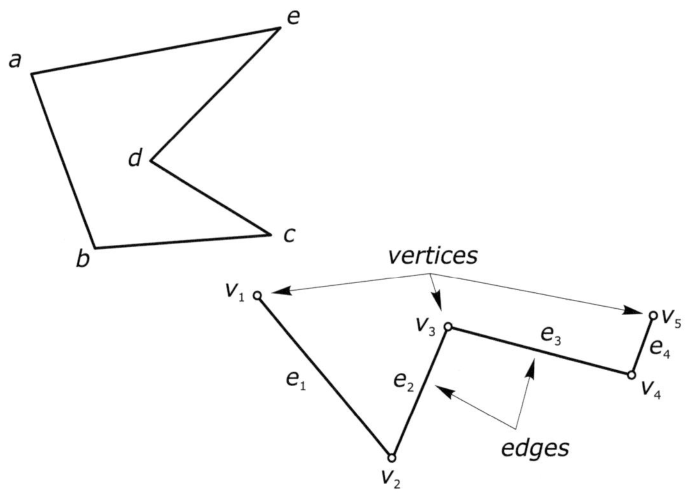

Position Vector

A position vector **p** is a **vector**↑ that describes the position of a point p relative to the origin. Its initial point is the origin, and its terminal point is the point p. The coordinates of the vector **p** are identical to those of the point p.

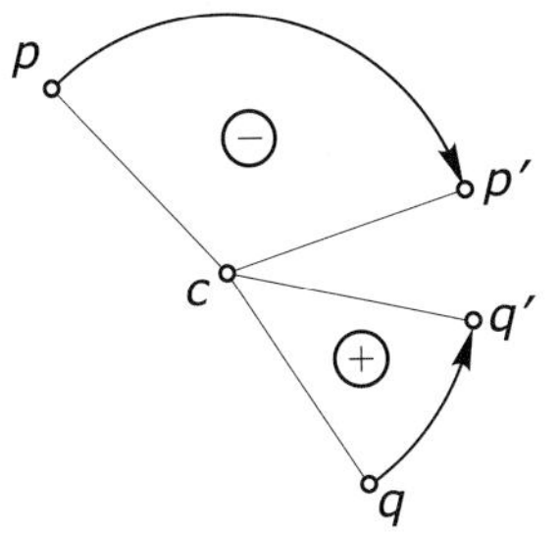

Positive and Negative Rotation

In two dimensions, a *mathematically positive* rotation is a counterclockwise rotation—whereas a clockwise rotation is called *mathematically negative*.

Radian Measure

A frequently used measure for an angle formed by two straight line segments meeting at a common point p is obtained as follows. We consider the circle c with center p and an arbitrary radius r. The angle determines an arc on the circle whose length shall be called s. Then, the ratio $\alpha = s{:}r$ is used as a measure (the *radian measure*) of the angle. Note that this ratio does not depend on the radius of the circle. Noting that a circle of radius r has length $2\pi r$, we see that an angle of 360 degrees has radian measure 2π, 90 degrees corresponds to radian measure $\pi/2$, and so on. The formula relating the radian measure α of an angle with its value $\alpha°$ in degrees is $\alpha = \pi \cdot (\alpha°/180)$. If one works with oriented angles, the radian measure has the sign as explained for a positive and negative rotation.

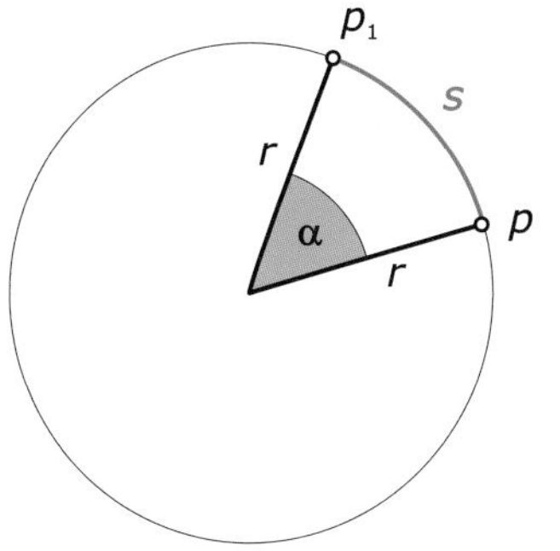

Ratio

In this book, the term *ratio* is used for the ratio of two distances formed with the aid of three points on a straight line. Often it is used to describe the exact position of a point r on a straight line segment pq. In the Figure, r divides pq in the ratio $\text{dist}(p,r){:}\text{dist}(r,q) = 2{:}3$.

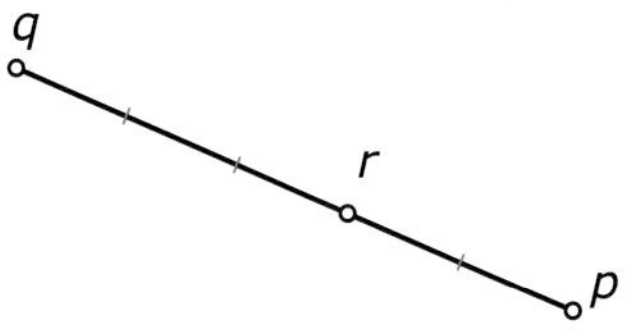

Regular Polygon

A closed polygon is regular (i.e., is a regular n-gon) if all n vertices lie on a circle and consecutive vertices are seen from the center of the circle under an angle of $360/n$ degrees. Thus, all n edges have the same length. The *inner angle* of a regular n-gon has $180 \cdot (n-2)/n$ degrees.

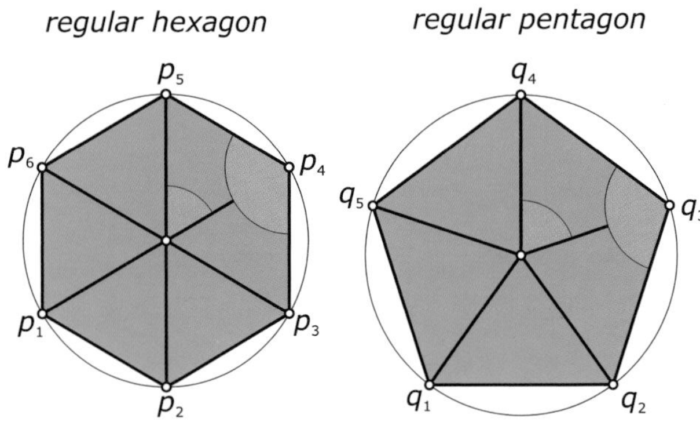

Straight Lines

A straight line l can be defined by two points p and q. Let $\mathbf{p}$ and $\mathbf{q}$ be their position vectors. Then, a direction vector of the line is given by $\mathbf{v} = \mathbf{q} - \mathbf{p}$. Adding any multiple $t \cdot (\mathbf{q} - \mathbf{p})$ of it to $\mathbf{p}$, we always arrive at a position vector $\mathbf{x}$ of a point on l: $\mathbf{x} = \mathbf{p} + t \cdot (\mathbf{q} - \mathbf{p})$. We call $\mathbf{x} = \mathbf{p} + t \cdot (\mathbf{q} - \mathbf{p})$ or $\mathbf{x} = \mathbf{p} + t \cdot \mathbf{v}$ a *parametric representation* of the line l. Here, t is a parameter. Different values of t yield different points of the straight line. If t ranges in the entire set of real numbers, we obtain the entire straight line. Note the close relation to **linear interpolation**↑ in that $\mathbf{x} = \mathbf{p} + t \cdot (\mathbf{q} - \mathbf{p}) = (1 - t) \cdot \mathbf{p} + t \cdot \mathbf{q}$. This representation works in two dimensions and in three dimensions.

In two dimensions, there is another method of representing a straight line. Let $\mathbf{n} = (n_1, n_2)$ be a vector normal to the direction vector $\mathbf{v} = (v_1, v_2)$. A simple choice for $\mathbf{n}$ is $\mathbf{n} = (-v_2, v_1)$. Now $\mathbf{x}$ represents a point on the line if the vector $\mathbf{x} - \mathbf{p}$ is a direction vector of l (i.e., if it is normal to $\mathbf{n}$). The latter property is expressed via the dot product $\mathbf{n} \cdot (\mathbf{x} - \mathbf{p}) = 0$.

This is the *implicit equation* of a straight line. For example, let $\mathbf{x} = (x,y)$, $\mathbf{p} = (1,2)$, and $\mathbf{n} = (3,-1)$. Then the equation reads $(3,-1) \cdot (x-1, y-2) = 0$, which is the same as $3 \cdot (x-1) + (-1) \cdot (y-2) = 0$ and can be simplified to $3x - y - 1 = 0$. Recall its meaning: the line l is the set of all points (x,y) that satisfy this equation.

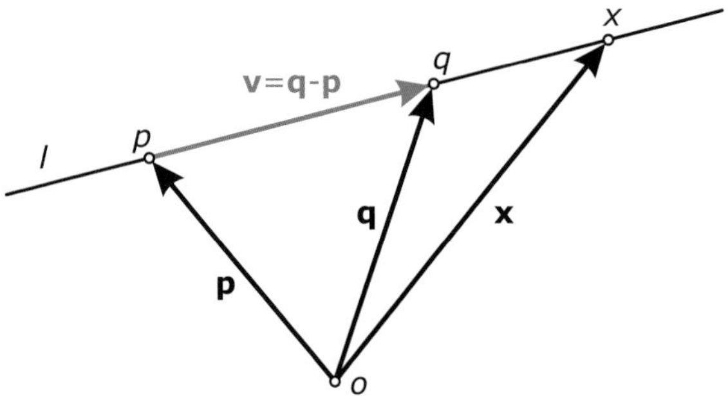

$\mathbf{x} = \mathbf{p} + t \cdot (\mathbf{q} - \mathbf{p})$

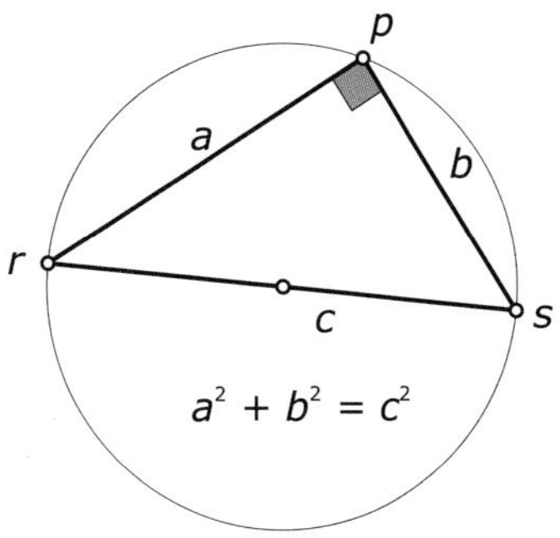

Theorem of Pythagoras

The Pythagorean theorem relates the lengths of the three sides of a right-angled triangle. Let c be the length of the longest side (hypotenuse; opposite the right angle) and a and b the lengths of the two other sides (adjacent to the right angle). Then these lengths are related by
$a^2 + b^2 = c^2$.

Theorem of Thales

Connecting the endpoints r and s of a circle's diameter with any further point p of the circle, we obtain two orthogonal straight lines. Likewise, the locus of all points p whose connecting lines with two fixed points r and s are orthogonal is a circle. Its center is the midpoint of the line segment rs.

Vector

We visualize a vector as an arrow emanating from an initial point and ending at a terminal point. If the initial point is the origin of the underlying coordinate system, the vector may used to describe the terminal point p. We speak of a position vector **p** (see also **coordinates of a vector**↑ and **direction vector**↑). From Chapter 1 to Chapter 10, vectors are emphasized by boldface font.

Zero Vector

The *zero vector* is the unique vector whose coordinates are 0 (initial point and terminal point agree). The zero vector in three dimensions is $\mathbf{o} = (0,0,0)$. As a **position vector**↑, it represents the origin o.

List of Symbols

$\in$	Element of
$\notin$	Not an element of
$\cap$	Intersection
$\cup$	Union
$\backslash$	Difference of sets: $A \backslash B$ contains all elements of A that are not in B
$<$	Less than
$>$	Greater than
$\leq$	Less than or equal to
$\geq$	Greater than or equal to
∞	Infinity
$[a,b]$	Closed interval: set of all real numbers x between a and b, including a and b
(a,b)	Open interval: set of all real numbers x between a and b, excluding a and b
$[a,b)$	Half-open interval: set of all real numbers x satisfying $a \leq x < b$
$\|x\|$	Absolute value of a real number x (cuts off a possible negative sign)
$\sqrt{\ }$	Square root
$\mathbf{a} \times \mathbf{b}$	Cross product of two vectors **a** and **b**
$\|\|\mathbf{v}\|\|$	Length of a vector **v**
f', f''	First and second derivatives of a function f
$\int$	Integral

Index

Photo Credits

Page 3-4 / Figure 1.1 - courtesy of Gehry Partners, LLP; **Page 5 / Figure 1.3** - courtesy of Michael Hofer; **Page 19 / Figure 1.22** - courtesy of Google Earth™ Mapping Service**; Page 20 / Figure 1.25** - courtesy of Tamara Weikel/Life as Art; **Page 21 / Figure 1.26a** - courtesy of Marcus Tschaut; **Page 21 / Figure 1.26b** - courtesy of Jens Shaumann; **Page 21 / Figure 1.26c** - courtesy of Sebastian Schubanz; **Page 25 / Figure 2.1** - courtesy of The Trustees of the British Museum; **Page 28 / Figure 2.5** - courtesy of Chia-yao Tsao; **Page 29 / Figure 2.6** - M.C. Escher's "Ascending and Descending" © 2007 The M.C. Escher Company-Holland. All Rights Reserved. www.mcescher.com; **Page 30 / Figure 2.9 left** - courtesy of Gustav Peichl; **Page 30 / Figure 2.9 right** - courtesy of Max Risselada and Dick van Gameren, originally published in "Raumplan Versus Plan Libre" by Delft University Press, 1988; **Page 34 / Figure 2.14 top** - courtesy of Paul Moody; **Page 34 / Figure 2.14 bottom** - courtesy of Matthew Buckley; **Page 44 / Figure 2.24a** - courtesy of Graeme Parker www.digi-studio.co.uk; **Page 45 / Figure 2.24b** - courtesy of Michael Hofer; **Page 45 / Figure 2.24c** - courtesy of Lars Kristensen; **Page 56 / Figure 2.37** - courtesy of Alexander Wilkie and Andreas Wieland; **Page 60 / Figure 2.43** - courtesy of Michael Hofer; **Page 62 / Figure 2.46** - courtesy of Daniel von Charmier; **Page 64 / Figure 2.48** - courtesy of Daniel von Charmier; **Page 69 / Figure 2.54** - courtesy of FotoStudio Ulrich Ghezzi, Oberalm © 2007 Residenzgalerie Salzburg; **Page 69 / Figure 2.54b** - courtesy of Georg Glaeser, Vienna; **Page 73 / Figure 3.1 left** - courtesy of Bart van den Berg; **Page 73 / Figure 3.1 right** - courtesy of Waagner-Biro Stahlbau AG; **Page 74 / Figure 3.2c** - courtesy of Bruno Klomfar; **Page 74 / Figure 3.2d** - courtesy of Jeroen Musch; **Page 77 / Figure 3.5a** - courtesy of Samuel Tamayo; **Page 77 / Figure 3.5b** - courtesy of Sheila Thomson; **Page 77 / Figure 3.5c** - courtesy of Stefan Reiss; **Page 77 / Figure 3.5d** - courtesy of Calvin Kuo; **Page 78 / Figure 3.6a** - courtesy of Alberto Bizzini; **Page 78 / Figure 3.6b** - courtesy of Gunter Schneider; **Page 83 / Figure 3.11** - courtesy of Pierre Alliez; **Page 88 / Figure 3.16** - courtesy of Ciro Miguel; **Page 90 / Figure 3.19a** - courtesy of Dr. Jano van Hemert; **Page 90 / Figure 3.19b** - courtesy of Nanao Wagatsuma; **Page 96 / Figure 3.25a** - courtesy of Colin Murtaugh; **Page 96 / Figure 3.25b** - courtesy of Ian McHugh; **Page 96 / Figure 3.25c** - courtesy of Asten Rathburn; **Page 101 / Figure 3.32** - courtesy of Martin Reis; **Page 102 / Figure 3.33 top left** - courtesy of Xia Ming; **Page 102 / Figure 3.33 top right, and bottom three** - courtesy of PTW Architects/arup/cscec; **Page 102 / Figure 3.34** - courtesy of Benjamin Schneider; **Page 103 / Figure 3.35c** - courtesy of Lyndon Maher; **Page 104 / Figure 3.36a** - courtesy of EU2005.lu/ccrn/Menn_Bodson; **Page 106 / Figure 3.37** - courtesy of

Waagner-Biro Stahlbau AG; **Page 107 / Figure 3.38** - courtesy of Pierre Alliez; **Page 124 / Figure 4.12d** - courtesy of Luke M. van Grieken; **Page 124 / Figure 4.12e** - courtesy of Jan Bitter; **Page 132 / Figure 4.17a** - courtesy of Martin Reis; **Page 133 / Figure 4.17b** - courtesy of Martin Reis; **Page 133 / Figure 4.17c** - courtesy of Michael Hofer; **Page 133 / Figure 4.17d** - courtesy of Hiepler Brunier; **Page 140 / Figure 5.1b** - courtesy of Martin Reis; **Page 140 / Figure 5.1c** - courtesy of Delta G Photo, wwwdeltagphoto.com; **Page 140 / Figure 5.1d** - courtesy of Kevan Davis; **Page 151 / Figure 5.16a** - courtesy of Lenora Genovese; **Page 151 / Figure 5.16b** - courtesy of Monica Shaw; **Page 151 / Figure 5.16c** - courtesy of Robin Kimball; **Page 151 / Figure 5.16d** - courtesy of Martin Reis; **Page 155 / Figure 5.21** - M.C. Escher's "Symmetry Drawing E21" © 2007 The M.C. Escher Company-Holland. All Rights Reserved. www.mcescher.com; **Page 156 / Figure 5.22** - M.C. Escher's "Symmetry Drawing E73" © 2007 The M.C. Escher Company-Holland. All Rights Reserved. www.mcescher.com; **Page 156 / Figure 5.23** - M.C. Escher's "Symmetry Drawing E70" © 2007 The M.C. Escher Company-Holland. All Rights Reserved. www.mcescher.com; **Page 157 / Figure 5.24a** - M.C. Escher's "Symmetry Drawing E41" © 2007 The M.C. Escher Company-Holland. All Rights Reserved. www.mcescher.com; **Page 157 / Figure 5.24b** - M.C. Escher's "Symmetry Drawing E35" © 2007 The M.C. Escher Company-Holland. All Rights Reserved. www.mcescher.com; **Page 158 / Figure 5.24c** - M.C. Escher's "Symmetry Drawing E25" © 2007 The M.C. Escher Company-Holland. All Rights Reserved. www.mcescher.com; **Page 176 / Figure 6.8a** - courtesy of Artur Images; **Page 176 / Figure 6.8b** - courtesy of Artur Images; **Page 177 / Figure 6.8c** - courtesy of Godefroy Le Guisquet; **Page 186 / Figure 6.16a** - courtesy of Mevr. J. Zweistra; **Page 187 / Figure 6.16b** - courtesy of Ricky Rew, www.easyrew.com; **Page 187 / Figure 6.16c** - courtesy of Andreas Tille; **Page 194 / Figure 6.24** - courtesy of Red Rover Studios; **Page 197 / Figure 6.27c** - courtesy of Charlotte Claeson; **Page 197 / Figure 6.27d** - courtesy of Keith Stenhouse, www.flickr.com/photos/ksten; **Page 198 / Figure 6.29** - courtesy of Ramon Duran; **Page 200 / Figure 6.31a** - courtesy of Hauskapelle in Texing; **Page 200 / Figure 6.31b** - courtesy of Phil Palmer kcmo; **Page 204 / Figure 6.33** - courtesy of Institute of Photogrammetry and Remote Sensing, Technical University, Vienna; **Page 205 / Figure 6.34** - courtesy of H. Cornelius, D. Martinec, and T. Pajdla; **Page 213 / Figure 7.1a** - courtesy of Richard Mayer; **Page 214 / Figure 7.1b** - courtesy of Unto This Last; **Page 214 / Figure 7.1c** - courtesy of Andy Stagg/VIEW; **Page 214 / Figure 7.1d** - courtesy of Dennis Gilbert/VIEW (ECA-DG); **Page 217 / Figure 7.3a** - courtesy of Bildarchiv Monheim; **Page 217 / Figure 7.3b** - courtesy of Bildarchiv Monheim; **Page 233 / Figure 7.27a** - courtesy of Waagner-Biro Stahlbau AG; **Page 233 / Figure 7.27b** - courtesy of Nils Jakob Darger; **Page 234 / Figure 7.29a** - courtesy of Walter Obermayer; **Page 234 / Figure 7.29b** - courtesy of Walter Obermayer; **Page 234 / Figure 7.29c** - courtesy of Peter Kaminsky; **Page 237 / Figure 7.33b** - courtesy of Erich Leissing/Art Resource, NY; **Page 239 / Figure 7.34** - courtesy of Ernst Mrazek; **Page 241 / Figure 7.40** - courtesy of Oliver Labs; **Page 247 / Figure 7.48a** - courtesy of Jost Schilgen/AKG London; **Page 247 / Figure 7.48b** - courtesy of Martin Reis; **Page 256 / Figure 8.2** - courtesy of H. Nowaki; **Page 256 / Figure 8.2a** - courtesy of Edson International, New Bedford, MA USA; **Page 289 / Figure 9.3a** - courtesy of Montse Gerones Lucea, Barcelona, Spain; **Page 290 / Figure 9.3b** - courtesy of John-Paul Rowe; **Page 290 / Figure 9.3c** - courtesy of Waagner-Biro Stahlbau AG; **Page 290 / Figure 9.3d** - courtesy of Federico Dosil; **Page 294 / Figure 9.9b** - courtesy of RFR; **Page 294 / Figure 9.9c** - courtesy of Dominique Poncin; **Page 298 / Figure 9.14a** - courtesy of Wikipedia.Org; **Page 298 / Figure 9.14b** - courtesy of Craig Tanner; **Page 298 / Figure 9.14c** - courtesy of Stephen D Harper Photography; **Page 298 / Figure 9.14d** - courtesy of Tetsuya Kawamura, k13a.com; **Page 298 / Figure 9.14e** - courtesy of Marcus Trimble; **Page 302 / Figure 9.19a** - courtesy of Waagner-Biro Stahlbau AG; **Page 302 / Figure 9.19b** - courtesy of Mark Kirchner; **Page 306 / Figure 9.26a** - courtesy of Roland Halbe/Artur/VIEW; **Page 306 / Figure 9.26b** - courtesy of Roland Halbe/Artur/VIEW; **Page 307 / Figure 9.27b** - courtesy of Schlaich Bergermann & Partner; **Page**

311 / Figure 9.33a - courtesy of Dirk Heuer, Verden; **Page 311 / Figure 9.33b** - courtesy of Hofrichter-Ritter Architekten; **Page 312 / Figure 9.35b** - courtesy of Roland Halbe/Artur/VIEW; **Page 313 / Figure 9.35c** - courtesy of Ronan McCann; **Page 316 / Figure 9.42a** - courtesy of Ullrich Welling; **Page 316 / Figure 9.42b** - courtesy of Andrew Schile; **Page 325 / Figure 9.55** - courtesy of Michael Hofer; **Page 329 / Figure 9.63** - courtesy of Andrew Maher, sculpture by Cat Macleod and Michael Bellemo; **Page 333 / Figure 10.1** - courtesy of Mike Gregory; **Page 343 / Figure 10.10a** - courtesy of Alan Karchmer/ESTO; **Page 343 / Figure 10.10b** - courtesy of Hufton+Crow/VIEW; **Page 344 / Figure 10.11b** - courtesy of Christian Richters; **Page 344 / Figure 10.11c** - courtesy of Toshiharu Kitajima; **Page 344 / Figure 10.11d** - courtesy of Raf Makda/VIEW; **Page 353 / Figure 10.24** - courtesy of Winchester Mystery House, San Jose California; **Page 362 / Figure 11.2a** - courtesy of Javier Novo Rodriguez; **Page 362 / Figure 11.2b** - courtesy of Pawel Jagiello; **Page 362 / Figure 11.3c** - courtesy of Astrophysikalisches Institut Potsdam; **Page 363 / Figure 11.4a** - courtesy of D. Reynolds/A.Ganz/Typeoff.de; **Page 363 / Figure 11.4b** - courtesy of Ian A. Duncan; **Page 363 / Figure 11.5** - courtesy of Bjarte Sorensen; **Page 364 / Figure 11.6a** - courtesy of Hug Sargatal; **Page 364 / Figure 11.6b** - courtesy of Laurent Massoptier, www.loloieg.free.fr; **Page 383 / Figure 11.28a** - courtesy of Wikipedia.org; **Page 382 / Figure 11.28b** - courtesy of Chung-Chi Lo, www.flickr.com/photos/linolo/; **Page 383 / Figure 11.28c** - courtesy of Schlaich Bergermann & Partner; **Page 383 / Figure 11.28e** - courtesy of Marlene Monschein; **Page 383 / Figure 11.28f** - courtesy of Stefani Diego; **Page 389 / Figure 11.38** - courtesy of Doreen G. Denton; **Page 395 / Figure 11.46** - courtesy of Chris Williams; **Page 397 / Figure 11.48 Left** - courtesy of Deborah Coleman/Pixar; **Page 397 / Figure 11.48 Middle Left** - courtesy of Malcolm Sabin; **Page 397 / Figure 11.48 Middle Right** - courtesy of Deborah Coleman/Pixar; **Page 397 / Figure 11.48 Right** - courtesy of Charles Loop; **Page 398 / Figure 11.48 opposite page Left** - © 2003 Disney Enterprises, Inc. and Pixar; **Page 398 / Figure 11.48 opposite page Right** - © 2006 Disney Enterprises, Inc. and Pixar; **Page 414 / Figure 12.2a** - courtesy of Jeff Millies, Hedrich Blessing, LTD; **Page 414 / Figure 12.2b** - courtesy of Timothy Hursley; **Page 421 / Figure 12.11** - courtesy of Georg Glaeser, Vienna; **Page 426 / Figure 12.20** - courtesy of Neil M. Denari Architects, Inc.; **Page 429 / Figure 12.25 top** - courtesy of Marlene Hofer; **Page 429 / Figure 12.25 bottom** - courtesy of Martin Reis; **Page 429 / Figure 12.25 right** - courtesy of Nils Gore; **Page 430 / Figure 12.27 right** - M.C. Escher's "Moebius Strip II" © 2007 The M.C. Escher Company-Holland. All Rights Reserved. www.mcescher.com; **Page 430 / Figure 12.27 left** - courtesy of Gershon Elber; **Page 435 / Figure 12.33** - courtesy of Michael Hofer; **Page 435 / Figure 12.34 left** - courtesy of Masaki Endoh; **Page 435 / Figure 12.34 right** - courtesy of Hiro Sakaguchi; **Page 438 / Figure 12.36 top** - courtesy of Klaus Frick; **Page 440 / Figure 12.39** - courtesy of Benjamin Schneider; **Page 446 / Figure 12.46** - courtesy of Benjamin Schneider; **Page 447 / Figure 12.47** - courtesy of Fritz Busam; **Page 457 / Figure 13.6a right** - courtesy of Sean Kisby www.flickr.com/photos/seankisby/; **Page 457 / Figure 13.6a left** - courtesy of Paul Richter; **Page 457 / Figure 13.6b left** - courtesy of Thorsten M. Heisig, Thorsten@heisin.info; **Page 457 / Figure 13.6b right** - courtesy of Andreas Nicht, Dresden; **Page 462 / Figure 13.10b** - courtesy of Martin Reis; **Page 466 / Figure 13.14b** - courtesy of Christian Selchow; **Page 485 / Figure 14.1** - courtesy of RadioSpike Photography, www.radiospike.com; **Page 497 / Figure 14.21a** - courtesy of Georg Glaeser, Vienna; **Page 498 / Figure 14.22** - courtesy of NOX; **Page 498 / Figure 14.23** - courtesy of Katharina Rittenschober; **Page 499 / Figure 14.25** - courtesy of Georg Umlauf; **Page 500 / Figure 14.27** - courtesy of Denis Zorin; **Page 508 / Figure 14.37** - courtesy of Michael Hofer; **Page 511 / Figure 14.41** - courtesy of Peter Schroder; **Page 512 / Figure 14.42** - courtesy of Nic Lehoux; **Page 513 / Figure 14.44** - courtesy of Odile Decq, Benoit Cornette Architects; **Page 514 / Figure 14.45** - courtesy of Gottfried Mandelburger; **Page 519 / Figure 14.51** - courtesy of Martin Kilian; **Page 520 / Figure 14.54** - courtesy of Cyndia Davidson at Eisenman Architects; **Page 524 / Figure 14.59** - courtesy of Torolf Sauermann; **Page 524 / Figure 14.60** -

courtesy of Carlos Sequin; **Page 525 / Figure 14.62** - courtesy of Michael Hofer; **Page 534 / Figure 15.1** - courtesy of Christian Richters; **Page 543 / Figure 15.17** - courtesy of NOX; **Page 551 / Figure 15.27b** - courtesy of Alla Sheffer; **Page 553 / Figure 15.29** - courtesy of Tony Wills; **Page 553 / Figure 15.31** - courtesy of Markus Forstner; **Page 554 / Figure 15.32** - courtesy of P. Bo and W. Wang; **Page 556 / Figure 15.35** - courtesy of Yang Liu; **Page 558 / Figure 15.38** - courtesy of P. Bo and W. Wang; **Page 558 / Figure 15.39** - courtesy of P. Bo and W. Wang; **Page 560 / Figure 15.41** - courtesy of Markus Forstner; **Page 560 / Figure 15.42** - courtesy of Jan Debertshaeuser, www.debertshaeuser.com; **Page 563 / Figure 15.45** - courtesy of Anita Aigner; **Page 570 / Figure 16.1** - courtesy of Scala/Art Resource, NY and Archivio Fotografico; **Page 573 / Figure 16.4** - courtesy of Axel Kilian; **Page 573 / Figure 16.5a** - courtesy of Morphosis; **Page 573 / Figure 16.5b** - courtesy of Morphosis; **Page 573 / Figure 16.5c** - courtesy of Morphosis; **Page 575 / Figure 16.6** - courtesy of Design to Production; **Page 576 / Figure 16.7** - courtesy of Design to Production; **Page 576 / Figure 16.8** - courtesy of Design to Production; **Page 577 / Figure 16.9** - courtesy of Peter Schmitt; **Page 578 / Figure 16.10** - courtesy of Gramazio & Kohler, Zurich; **Page 578 / Figure 16.11** - courtesy of Dr. Behrokh Khoshnevis; **Page 582 / Figure 16.14b** - courtesy of Axel Kilian; **Page 584 / Figure 16.15b** - courtesy of Carlos Sequin; **Page 585 / Figure 16.16a** - courtesy of ZCorp; **Page 585 / Figure 16.16b** - courtesy of Carlos Sequin; **Page 586 / Figure 16.17** - courtesy of 3D Systems Corporation; **Page 589 / Figure 16.19** - courtesy of Axel Kilian; **Page 590 / Figure 16.20** - courtesy of Greg Lynn/FORM, Photo by Carlo Lavatori; **Page 594 / Figure 16.22** - courtesy of Axel Kilian; **Page 596 / Figure 16.23** - courtesy of Tom Coulson; **Page 597 / Figure 16.24** - courtesy of Axel Kilian; **Page 601 / Figure 17.1** - courtesy of Thomas Mayer Archive; **Page 606 / Figure 17.7** - courtesy of Stefan Laub; **Page 608 / Figure 17.8a** - courtesy of Markus Forstner; **Page 609 / Figure 17.9** - courtesy of Michael Hofer; **Page 610 / Figure 17.10** - courtesy of VRVis; **Page 616 / Figure 17.18 top left** - courtesy of Jeff Thomas ©; **Page 616 / Figure 17.18 bottom left** - courtesy of Stephen Morris, Nonlinear Physics, University of Toronto; **Page 616 / Figure 17.18 right** - courtesy of Rick Hebenstreit; **Page 619 / Figure 17.24** - courtesy of Vector Foiltec; **Page 624 / Figure 17.29** - courtesy of Yukun Lai; **Page 626 / Figure 17.30a** - courtesy of A. Belyaev; **Page 626 / Figure 17.30b** - courtesy of Konrad Polthier; **Page 629 / Figure 17.32** - courtesy of Tamas Varady; **Page 630 / Figure 17.33** - courtesy of Niloy Mitra; **Page 631 / Figure 17.34** - courtesy of Niloy Mitra; **Page 634 / Figure 17.36** - courtesy of Reinhard Gruber; **Page 636 / Figure 17.38** - courtesy of Reinhard Gruber; **Page 647 / Figure 18.5** - courtesy of ILEK; **Page 653 / Figure 18.10** - courtesy of Karen M Bushey; **Page 655 / Figure 18.13b** - courtesy of Konrad Polthier; **Page 656 / Figure 18.15** - courtesy of GANG; **Page 657 / Figure 18.16** - courtesy of GANG; **Page 658 / Figure 18.17** - courtesy of A. Bobenko; **Page 659 / Figure 18.18** - courtesy of F. Pedit; **Page 663 / Figure 18.25** - courtesy of Simon Flory; **Page 666 / Figure 18.27** - courtesy of Robert Wehdorn-Roithmayr; **Page 671-672 / Figure 19.1** - courtesy of Waagner-Biro Stahlbau AG; **Page 673 / Figure 19.2 top** - courtesy of Sigrid Brell-Cokcan; **Page 673 / Figure 19.2 bottom** - courtesy of Markus Hofer; **Page 675 / Figure 19.4** - courtesy of Waagner-Biro Stahlbau AG; **Page 689 / Figure 19.19** - courtesy of Waagner-Biro Stahlbau AG; **Page 702 / Figure 19.35** - courtesy of S. Sechelmann (mesh courtesy); **Page 703 / Figure 19.37** - courtesy of Schlaich Bergermann & Partner; **Page 705 / Figure 19.39b** - courtesy of Michael Hofer

All remaining figures are courtesy of the authors. If any credit has been made incorrectly, please contact the Bentley Institute Press at 685 Stockton Drive; Exton, PA 19341